W9-BVZ-831

Home **ORTHO**®
Gardener's
Problem
Solver

Meredith® Books
Des Moines, Iowa

Ortho Home Gardener's Problem Solver
Editor: Denny Schrock
Contributing Writer: L. Patricia Kite
Senior Associate Design Director: Tom Wegner
Assistant Editor: Harijs Priekulis
Copy Chief: Terri Fredrickson
Copy and Production Editor: Victoria Forlini
Editorial Operations Manager: Karen Schirm
Managers, Book Production: Pam Kvitne,
    Marjorie J. Schenkelberg, Rick von Holdt, Mark Weaver
Contributing Proofreaders: Jane Carlson, Fran Gardner, Sara
    Henderson, Nancy Humes, Terri Krueger, Barb Stokes
Contributing Map Illustrator: Jana Fothergill
Additional Contributors: Spectrum Communication
    Services, Inc., Janet Anderson, Beth Ann Edwards
Indexer: Ellen Davenport
Editorial and Design Assistants: Kathleen Stevens,
    Karen McFadden

This book is based on *The Ortho Problem Solver,*
Sixth Edition
Editor: Michael D. Smith
Contributing Writers: Clare A. Binko, Rick Bond, Gene
    Joyner, Wayne S. Moore, Robert D. Raabe, Deni Stein,
    Bernadine Strik, Lauren B. Swezey
Contributing Illustrators: Deborah Cowder, Ellen Blonder

Meredith® Books
Editor in Chief: Linda Raglan Cunningham
Design Director: Matt Strelecki
Executive Editor, Gardening and Home Improvement:
    Benjamin W. Allen
Executive Editor, Gardening: Michael McKinley

Publisher: James D. Blume
Executive Director, Marketing: Jeffrey Myers
Executive Director, New Business Development:
    Todd M. Davis
Executive Director, Sales: Ken Zagor
Director, Operations: George A. Susral
Director, Production: Douglas M. Johnston
Business Director: Jim Leonard

Vice President and General Manager: Douglas J. Guendel

Meredith Publishing Group
President, Publishing Group: Stephen M. Lacy
Vice President-Publishing Director: Bob Mate

Meredith Corporation
Chairman and Chief Executive Officer: William T. Kerr

Chairman of the Executive Committee: E. T. Meredith III

Meredith® Books gratefully acknowledges the following
authorities for their expertise and assistance in expanding
the problem range maps to include Canada:

Dr. Alain Asselin, Agronomist and Professor,
Faculty of Agronomical and Food Sciences,
Université Laval, Quebec, Canada

Adam Brown, Biologist,
Department of Biology,
Université Laval, Quebec, Canada

Louise Dumouchel, Entomologist,
Canadian Food Inspection Agency,
Plant Health Risk Assessment,
Agriculture Canada, Nepean, Ontario, Canada

Larry Hodgson, Project Coordinator,
Horticom Inc.,
Sainte-Foy, Quebec, Canada

Dr. Jeremy McNeil, Entomologist and
Professor,
Department of Biology,
Université Laval, Quebec, Canada

Susanne Roy, Assistant Project Coordinator,
Horticom Inc.,
Sainte-Foy, Quebec, Canada

All of us at Meredith® Books are dedicated to providing
you with the information and ideas you need to enhance
your home and garden. We welcome your comments and
suggestions about this book. Write to us at:
    Meredith Corporation
    Meredith Gardening Books
    1716 Locust St.
    Des Moines, IA 50309–3023

If you would like to purchase any of our gardening, home
improvement, cooking, crafts, or home decorating and
design books, check wherever quality books are sold. Or visit
us at: meredithbooks.com

If you would like more information on other Ortho
products, call 800/225-2883 or visit us at: www.ortho.com

Note to the Readers: Due to differing conditions, tools,
and individual skills, Meredith Corporation assumes no
responsibility for any damages, injuries suffered, or losses
incurred as a result of following the information published
in this book. Before beginning any project, review the
instructions carefully, and if any doubts or questions remain,
consult local experts or authorities. Because codes and
regulations vary greatly, always check with authorities
to ensure that your project complies with all applicable
local codes and regulations. Read and observe all of the
safety precautions provided by manufacturers of any
tools, equipment, or supplies, and follow all accepted
safety procedures.

Contents

Consultants

This has been a vast project, and we have received help from hundreds of people—members of County Extension offices, horticulturalists, nursery professionals, and knowledgeable amateur gardeners. The following names are those of major consultants—people who spent many hours checking manuscripts for accuracy and patiently answering our questions about fine points of obscure garden problems. The accuracy and validity of this book are due to the careful work of these people.

Jan Abernathie, Ph.D.
Plant Pathologist
Chesapeake, Virginia

J. Ole Becker, Ph.D.
R & D Consultant, Plant Pathology
Riverside, California

James Beutel, Ph.D.
Extension Pomologist
University of California, Davis

Darrel R. Bienz, Ph.D.
Professor of Horticulture
Washington State University

Eugene Brady, Ph.D.
Professor of Entomology
University of Georgia

Jerome Brezner, Ph.D.
Department of Environmental
    and Forest Biology
State University of New York, Syracuse

Bartow H. Bridges Jr.
Landscape Architect and Horticulturalist
Virginia Beach, Virginia

Jack Butler, Ph.D.
Department of Horticulture
Colorado State University

Ralph S. Byther, Ph.D.
Extension Plant Pathologist
Washington State University

Robert Carrow, Ph.D.
Agronomy Department
University of Georgia Experimental Station
Griffin, Georgia

William E. Chaney
Cooperative Extension
Gilroy, California

Eric Clough
Landscape Architect
Winlaw, British Columbia, Canada

Sharon J. Collman
County Extension Agent
Seattle, Washington

Samuel D. Cotner, Ph.D.
Extension Horticulturalist
Texas A & M University

G. Douglas Crater, Ph.D.
Extension Horticulturalist, Floriculture
University of Georgia

T. E. Crocker, Ph.D.
Professor of Fruit Crops
University of Florida

J. A. Crozier, Ph.D.
Plant Pathologist
Novato, California

R. Michael Davis, Ph.D.
Cooperative Extension Specialist,
    Plant Pathology
University of California, Davis

Spencer H. Davis Jr. Ph.D.
Horticultural Consultant
North Brunswick, New Jersey

Eric R. Day
Manager, Insect Identification Lab
Virginia Polytechnic Institute
    and State University

August A. De Hertogh, Ph.D.
Professor of Horticultural Science
North Carolina State University

James F. Dill, Ph.D.
Extension Professor of Entomology
University of Maine, Orono

Clyde Elmore, Ph.D.
Extension Weed Scientist
University of California, Davis

Thomas E. Eltzroth, Ph.D.
California Polytechnic University
San Luis Obispo, California

Barbara H. Emerson
Senior Product Specialist, Union Carbide
    Agriculture Products Company
Research Triangle Park, North Carolina

James R. Feucht, Ph.D.
Extension Professor, Department
    of Horticulture
Colorado State University

Ralph Garren Jr., Ph.D.
Small Fruit Specialist, Cooperative
    Extension
Oregon State University

Greg Giusti
Cooperative Extension
Kelseyville, California

Cathy Haas
Instructor, Ornamental Horticulture
Monterey Peninsula College, California

Frank A. Hale, Ph.D.
Associate Professor, Entomology
    and Plant Pathology
University of Tennessee

Mary Ann Hansen
Instructor and Plant Clinic Manager
Virginia Tech

Ali Harvandi, Ph.D.
Turfgrass Scientist
Oakland, California

Duane Hatch
Cooperative Extension
Utah State University

Sammy Helmers, Ph.D.
Area Extension Horticulturalist
Stevenville, Texas

Kermit Hildahl
Cooperative Extension
University of Missouri

Larry Hodgson
Horticultural Consultant
Quebec City, Quebec, Canada

Gerald J. Holmes
Assistant Professor of Plant Pathology
North Carolina State University

Everett E. Janne
Landscape Horticulturalist,
    Texas Agricultural Extension Service
College Station, Texas

Alan L. Jones, Ph.D.
Professor of Plant Pathology
Michigan State University

Ron Jones, Ph.D.
Department of Plant Pathology
North Carolina State University

Gene Joyner
Palm Beach County Extension
West Palm Beach, Florida

L. Patricia Kite
Entomology Writer
Newark, California

Caroline Klass
Senior Extension Associate,
    Department of Entomology
Cornell University

Steven T. Koike
Plant Pathologist
Salinas, California

Tony Koski, Ph.D.
Associate Professor, Horticulture,
    Extension Turfgrass Specialist
Colorado State University

Charles A. McClurg
Extension Vegetable Specialist
University of Maryland

Frederick McGourty
Mary Ann McGourty
Hillside Gardens
Norfolk, Connecticut

S. Mansour
Extension
Oregon State University

Charles Marr, Ph.D.
Extension Horticulturalist
Kansas City University

Bernard Moore
Extension Plant Diagnostician (Retired)
Oregon State University

Stephen T. Nameth, Ph.D.
Associate Professor of Plant Pathology
Ohio State University

Lester P. Nichols
Professor Emeritus of Plant Pathology
Pennsylvania State University

Norman F. Oebker, Ph.D.
Vegetables Specialist, Cooperative
  Extension
University of Arizona

Howard Ohr, Ph.D.
Plant Pathologist, Cooperative Extension
University of California, Riverside

Albert O. Paulus, Ph.D.
Plant Pathologist
University of California, Riverside

Jay W. Pscheidt
Extension Plant Pathology Specialist
Oregon State University

Robert D. Raabe, Ph.D.
Extension Plant Pathologist
University of California, Berkeley

David Robson
Extension Educator, Horticulture
University of Illinois

Charles Sacamano, Ph.D.
Professor of Horticulture
University of Arizona

Donald L. Schuder, Ph.D.
Professor Emeritus, Department
  of Entomology
Purdue University

Arden Sherf, Ph.D.
Professor, Department of Plant Pathology
Cornell University

David J. Shetlar, Ph.D.
Associate Professor of Landscape
  Entomology
Ohio State University

Gary Simone, Ph.D.
Extension Plant Pathologist
University of Florida

Arthur Slater
Environmental Health and Safety
University of California, Berkeley

Kenneth Sorensen, Ph.D.
Extension Entomologist
North Carolina State University

Walter Stevenson, Ph.D.
Associate Professor of Plant Pathology
University of Wisconsin

Steven Still, Ph.D.
Department of Horticulture
Ohio State University

Bernadine Strik, Ph.D.
Professor of Horticulture, Extension Berry
  Crops Specialist
Oregon State University

O. Clifton Taylor, Ph.D.
Statewide Air Pollution Research Center
University of California, Riverside

William Titus
County Coordinator, Cooperative
  Extension
Plainview, New York

John Tomkins, Ph.D.
Associate Professor of Pomology
Cornell University

Carl A. Totemeier
Director, Old Westbury Gardens
Old Westbury, New York

Marian Van Atta
Editor, *Living Off the Land*
Melbourne, Florida

John White
County Extension Agent, Horticulture
El Paso, Texas

Gayle Worf, Ph.D.
Extension Plant Pathologist
University of Wisconsin

SPECIAL CONSULTANTS

Many other gardening professionals and gifted amateurs have shared their experience and wisdom with us. The people on the following list are specialists for particular problems. They have often been able to supply answers when nobody else could, and we are deeply indebted to them for their contributions.

Maynard Cummings, Ph.D.
Extension Wildlife Specialist
University of California, Davis

Don Egger
President, Cebeco Lilies
Aurora, Oregon

Harold E. Greer
President, Greer Gardens Nursery
Eugene, Oregon

Phil Horne
Mosley Nurseries
Lake Worth, Florida

Lloyd A. Lider, Ph.D.
Professor of Viticulture
University of California, Davis

Wayne S. Moore, Ph.D.
Entomologist
Berkeley, California

Joseph R. Onwinski
Turfgrass Consultant
Lake Worth, Florida

John Pehrson
Extension Agent
Parlier, California

Warren G. Roberts
Arboretum Superintendent
University of California, Davis

Donald Rosedale
Cooperative Extension Service
University of California, Riverside

Terrel P. Salmon, Ph.D.
Extension Wildlife Specialist
University of California, Davis

Ross R. Sanborn
University of California Farm Adviser
Contra Costa County, California

Joseph Savaage
Entomologist, Cooperative Extension
  Service
Cornell University

Arthur Slater
Senior Environmental Health and
  Safety Technologist
University of California, Berkeley

Richard Tassan
Staff Research Associate
University of California, Berkeley

5

Ortho's Home Gardener's Problem Solver is designed to help you diagnose a problem with a plant and provide potential solutions.

Diagnosing plant problems requires careful observation of plants and their environments. The key to accurate diagnosis is knowing how to look for clues to a problem and what types of clues to look for. The checklist on pages 8 and 9 gives a step-by-step procedure for gathering clues and diagnosing a problem. It will help you develop a case history, eliminate unlikely explanations for sources of the problem, and find the real cause.

HOW TO OBSERVE

Begin your observations by examining the plant from a distance. Note its general condition. Is the entire plant affected or only a few stems, branches, or leaves? If the entire plant shows symptoms, the cause will probably be found on the trunk, on the roots, or in the soil.

Look for patterns and relationships with other plants. Is the problem confined to the sunny side? Is only the new growth affected? Are many sick plants in one spot?

Locate a part of the plant that shows symptoms and take a closer look. Mottled or discolored leaves may indicate an insect or disease problem. A 5- to 15-power hand lens will allow you to see insects or symptoms not easily visible to the naked eye.

If the initial inspection does not reveal any obvious reason for the symptoms, developing a case history for the plant may lead you to a less conspicuous cause of the problem. How has the weather been recently? Have temperatures fluctuated drastically? What kind of winter was it? An unusually dry, cold winter can cause dieback that may not become apparent until new growth begins on trees and shrubs in the spring.

Study the recent care of the plant. Has the plant been watered or fertilized regularly? All plants require fertilizer; without regular feeding, their leaves turn yellow, and growth is poor.

When observing the area around the plant, be aware of changes in the environment. Construction around established plants can damage them, although symptoms of decline may not appear for several years. Drastic changes in light may cause problems that appear many days later, as when a houseplant is moved

from a sunny window to a dark corner or when a fruit tree is heavily pruned, exposing new parts to the sun.

You may have to dig into the plant or the soil to find the cause of a problem. If a stem has a hole in it, cut into it. Or slice a piece of bark off a wilting branch to determine whether the wood is discolored or healthy.

The only way to learn about the roots of a sick plant is to dig up a small plant or to carefully dig a hole to examine the roots of a large plant. The key to a root problem may be in the soil. Investigate the drainage, probe the soil with an auger to determine the soil depth and type, or test the pH of the soil with a pH kit. Look at all sides of the question, and explore each clue.

Particular types of plants are susceptible to typical problems at certain times of the year. For instance, cherries are usually plagued with fruit flies in the spring when the fruit is ripening, and snapdragons are likely to be infected with rust in the spring and summer when temperatures are warm and moisture is present.

PUTTING IT ALL TOGETHER

After studying the ailing plant or plants, read the introduction to the pertinent chapter in this book. The introduction may contain information that relates directly to your problem or gives you a tip about where to look next. Then look through the general problem headings at the tops of the pages in the problem-solution sections. Find the

heading that applies to your problem, then look for your specific plant and see if its problem is listed. If you know the name of your plant, the problem it has, or the insect that is bothering it, you can look up the name in the index at the back of the book. For uncommon problems, you may want to refer to The Ortho Problem Solver— a professional edition found at many nurseries and in garden and home-improvement centers—but these pages will discuss most of the problems you will encounter.

When you're reading about a plant problem in Ortho's Home Gardener's Problem Solver, read carefully. Every word and phrase is important for understanding the nature of the problem. "May" means that the symptom develops only sometimes. And certain phrases offer you clues about the problem, such as the time of year to expect it ("in spring to midsummer…") and where to look for the symptom ("…on the undersides of leaves").

Unfortunately, plants frequently develop more than one problem at a time. Plants have natural defenses against diseases and insects. But when one problem weakens a plant, and lowers its defenses, other problems are able to infect it. For instance, borers are often responsible for a tree's decline, but borers are seldom a serious problem on healthy trees. A borer problem may indicate another problem, such as a recent severe winter or root rot.

How to Use This Book

All gardeners have problems with pests or diseases from time to time. *Ortho's Home Gardener's Problem Solver* was created to help you solve these problems.

In a straightforward way, it will help you discover what kind of problem you have and what's causing it, and it will tell you more about the problem—such as how serious it can get if you don't do anything. Then it will offer solutions to the problem.

The photographs at the top of the pages are arranged so that similar symptoms are grouped together. Select the picture that looks most like your problem. The small map under the photograph shows how likely the problem is to be present in your part of the country. If your region is colored red, the problem is commonplace or severe. If it is colored yellow, the problem is occasional or moderate. If it is neither color, the problem is nonexistent or minor.

A word of explanation is needed about the solutions we offer. The solution section of each problem assumes that you have seen the problem at the time when the symptoms first become obvious. Each solution begins by telling you what you can do immediately to alleviate the problem. Then it tells you what changes you can make in the environment or in your gardening practices to prevent the problem from recurring. In many cases, a chemical spray is recommended as an immediate solution and a cultural change or the planting of a resistant variety as a long-range solution.

We offer several solutions for most of the problems in this book. We tell you, for example, that you can protect your sycamore tree from anthracnose by spraying it with a fungicide in the spring. If your sycamore is 7 feet high, you might choose to spray it the following spring. If the tree is 40 feet high, however, you will find that hiring an arborist to spray it will be expensive. From our description of the problem, you know that anthracnose seldom does permanent harm to the tree, so you may choose to do nothing.

When Ortho has products to treat a problem, we identify them by name. If Ortho does not make a product to solve a particular problem, we recommend chemical solutions by their generic names—the common name of the active ingredients. For example, we might suggest that you apply a product "containing" a particular active ingredient. This wording alerts you to the fact that you may not find a product by that name but must study the active ingredients

listed on product labels. Ask your retailer to help you select an appropriate product, or see pages 528 and 529.

When we recommend an Ortho product, we know that it will do the job for which we recommend it and that it will not harm your plant if you use it according to label directions. But when choosing products by a generic name—even if these are Ortho products—read the labels carefully. Although all *malathion* is the same, all products containing it are not. Even though we know *malathion* will solve a particular problem and tell you so, some products that contain *malathion* may be manufactured for a different purpose and may injure your plant. Be sure that the plant you wish to spray is listed on the product label. Always read pesticide labels carefully and follow label directions to the letter.

This book is based in large part on research done for *The Ortho Problem Solver,* a professional reference tool for solving plant problems. We have drawn on that research to create this book to help you, as a home gardener, solve the problems you are most likely to encounter. The pages of both this book and *The Ortho Problem Solver* present the experience of many experts, most of them members of cooperative extension services of various states. These men and women have shared the most current and practical information available. If you follow their advice in terms of immediate solutions and long-term prevention, you will approach the realization of every gardener's dream: to garden in such a way that you reduce problems, leaving you free to enjoy the full beauty and bounty of your garden.

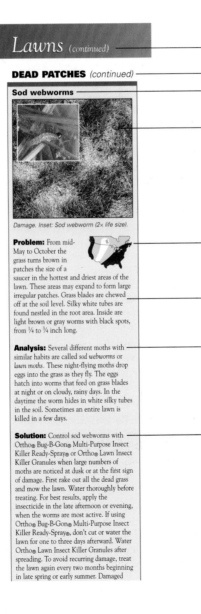

Lawns *(continued)*

DEAD PATCHES *(continued)* —————— Group of similar symptoms

Sod webworms ——————— The problem name

Damage. Inset: Sod webworm (2× life size).

Problem: From mid-May to October the grass turns brown in patches the size of a saucer in the hottest and driest areas of the lawn. These areas may expand to form large irregular patches. Grass blades are chewed off at the soil level. Silky white tubes are found nestled in the root zone. Inside are light brown or gray worms with black spots, from ¼ to ¾ inch long.

Analysis: Several different moths with similar habits are called *sod webworms* or *lawn moths.* These night-flying moths drop eggs into the grass as they fly. The eggs hatch into worms that feed on grass blades at night or on cloudy, rainy days. In the daytime the worm hides in white silky tubes in the soil. Sometimes an entire lawn is killed in a few days.

Solution: Control sod webworms with Ortho® Bug-B-Gon® Multi-Purpose Insect Killer Ready-Spray® or Ortho® Lawn Insect Killer Granules when large numbers of moths are noticed at dusk or at the first sign of damage. First rake out all the dead grass and mow the lawn. Water thoroughly before treating. For best results, apply the insecticide in the late afternoon or evening, when the worms are most active. If using Ortho® Bug-B-Gon® Multi-Purpose Insect Killer Ready-Spray®, don't cut or water the lawn for one to three days afterward. Water Ortho® Lawn Insect Killer Granules after spreading. To avoid recurring damage, treat the lawn again every two months beginning in late spring or early summer. Damaged

Chapters are usually divided into two sections: "Problems Common to Many" and "Problems of Individual Plants."

A photograph (sometimes with an inset) depicting a typical symptom or organism

A range map of the United States and southern Canada accompanies each problem. In areas that are red, the problem is severe or commonplace. In areas that are yellow, the problem is secondary or occasional. In areas that are white, the problem is rare or nonexistent.

The problem section describes the symptom or symptoms.

The analysis section describes the organisms or cultural conditions causing the problem, including life cycles, natural processes, typical progress of the problem and its seriousness.

The solution section provides short-term and long-term techniques to mitigate or cure the problem.

Checklist for Diagnosis

Use this checklist to develop a case history for the problem and to identify symptoms that will lead to an accurate diagnosis. Answer each question that pertains to your plant carefully and thoroughly. When looking for symptoms and answering questions about the condition of the plant, begin with the leaves, flowers, or fruit (unless it is apparent that the problem is elsewhere), because they are the easiest to examine. Once you've eliminated these possibilities, move down the plant to the stems or branches and trunk. Inspect the roots after rejecting all other possibilities.

WHAT TO LOOK FOR

Kind of plant
- ☐ What type of plant is it?
- ☐ Does it prefer moist or dry conditions?
- ☐ Can it tolerate cold, or does it grow best in a warm climate?
- ☐ Does the plant grow best in acid or alkaline soil?

Age
- ☐ Is the plant young and tender, or is it old and in a state of decline?

Size
- ☐ Is the plant abnormally small?
- ☐ How much has the plant grown in the last few years?
- ☐ Is the size of the trunk or stem in proportion to the number of branches?

Time at present site
- ☐ Was the plant recently transplanted?
- ☐ Has it had time to become established, or are its roots still in the original root ball?
- ☐ Is the plant much older than the housing development or nearby buildings?

Symptom development
- ☐ When were the symptoms first noticed?
- ☐ Have symptoms been developing for a long time, or did they appear suddenly?

Condition of plant
- ☐ Is the entire plant affected, or is the problem found only on one side of the plant?
- ☐ What parts of the plant are affected?
- ☐ Are all the leaves affected, or only those on a few branches?
- ☐ Are the leaves abnormal in size, color, shape, or texture?
- ☐ Do the flowers and fruit show symptoms?
- ☐ Is there abnormal growth, discoloration, or injuries on the branches, stems, or trunk?
- ☐ Is there anything wrapped around and girdling the plant or nailed into the wood?
- ☐ Does the trunk have a normal flare at the base, or is it constricted and straight like a pole at ground level?
- ☐ If the entire plant is affected, what do the roots look like? Are they white and healthy, or are they discolored? Use a trowel to dig around the roots of large plants; pull up small, sick plants and look at the roots; and examine roots of container plants by removing the container. Is the bark brown and decayed?
- ☐ Have the roots remained in the root ball, or have they grown into the surrounding soil?
- ☐ Are insects on the plant, or is there evidence of insects, such as holes, droppings, sap, or sawdustlike material?
- ☐ Has the problem appeared in past years?

Location of property
- ☐ Is the property near a large body of freshwater or saltwater?
- ☐ Is the property located downwind from a factory, or is it in a large polluted urban area?
- ☐ Is the property part of a new housing development that was built on landfill?

Location of plant
- ☐ Is the plant growing next to a building? If so, is the location sunny or shady? Is the wall of the building light in color? How intense is the reflected light?
- ☐ Has there been any construction, trenching, or grade change nearby within the past several years?
- ☐ Have there been any natural disturbances?
- ☐ How close is the plant to a road? Is salt used to deice the road in the winter?
- ☐ Is the plant growing on top of or near a gas, water, or sewer line or next to power lines?
- ☐ Is the ground sloping, or is it level?

Relationship to other plants

☐ Are there large shade trees overhead?
☐ Is the plant growing in a lawn or ground cover?
☐ Are nearby plants also affected? Do the same species show similar symptoms? Are unrelated plants affected? How close are other affected plants?

Weather

☐ Have weather conditions been unusual (cold, hot, dry, wet, windy, snowy, and so on) recently or during the past few years?

Microclimates

☐ What are the weather conditions in the immediate vicinity of the plant?
☐ Is the plant growing under something that blocks rainfall or sprinkler water?
☐ How windy is the location?
☐ How much light does the plant receive? Is it the optimum amount for the type of plant?

Soil conditions

☐ In what kind of soil is the plant growing? Is it predominantly clay, sand, or loam?
☐ How deep is the soil? Is a layer of rock or hardpan beneath the topsoil?
☐ What is the pH of the soil?
☐ Does the soil drain well, or does the water remain on the surface after a heavy rain or watering? Does the soil have a sour smell?
☐ Is the soil hard and compacted?
☐ Has the soil eroded from the roots?

Soil coverings

☐ Does asphalt, concrete, or another solid surface cover the soil around the plant? How close is it to the base of the plant? How long has it been there?
☐ Has the soil surface been mulched or covered with crushed rock?
☐ Was the mulch obtained from a reputable dealer?
☐ Are weeds or grass growing around the base of the plant? How thickly?

Recent care

☐ Has the plant or surrounding plants been fertilized or watered recently?

☐ If fertilizer was used, was it applied according to label directions?
☐ Has the plant or the area been treated with fungicide or insecticide?
☐ Was the treatment for this problem or another one?
☐ Was the pesticide registered for use on the plant? (Is the plant listed on the product label?)
☐ Was the pesticide applied according to label directions?
☐ Did rain wash off the spray immediately after it was applied?
☐ Did you repeat the spray if the label suggested it?
☐ Have weed killers or lawn weed-and-feed fertilizers been used in the area in the past year? How close?
☐ Did you spray on a windy day?
☐ Has the plant been pruned heavily, exposing previously shaded areas to sun?
☐ Were stumps left after pruning, or was the bark damaged during pruning?

How a Plant Works

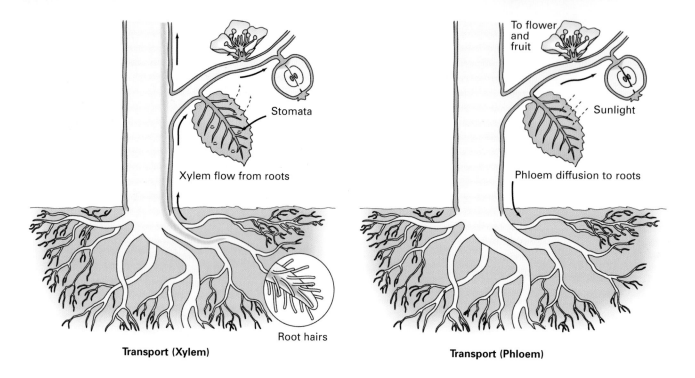

Transport (Xylem)

Transport (Phloem)

TRANSPORT

A plant's transport system serves the same function as a human's circulatory system does, but it is different because it does not move in a circle, as the human bloodstream does. Plants have two transport systems: one carrying water and dissolved minerals from the roots to the top of the plant, and the other carrying sugars and other manufactured material from the leaves to all other parts of the plant.

Xylem flow: The part of a plant's transport system that carries water upward flows through a system of microscopic tubes called the *xylem* (pronounced ZYE-lem). In woody plants, the xylem is the outermost layer of wood. This wood, which is just under the bark, contains the xylem tubes. These tubes extend into the leaf, its veins and into all its parts. The xylem tubes end in the leaf tissue. Water leaves the xylem in the leaf tissue and evaporates through microscopic pores called *stomata* in the leaf surface.

Transpiration: Evaporation from the stomata is called *transpiration*, which not only provides the power that moves water and nutrients into the top of the plant, but also cools the leaf, just as evaporation of sweat cools a human. Although the principles are different, you can think of transpiration as pulling water from the roots to the leaves just as liquid is sucked through a drinking straw. Because plants can transport only nutrients that are dissolved in water, insoluble material is not available to them.

Three main factors reduce xylem flow: dry soil, a sick root system, and a plugged or cut xylem system. If the xylem flow is reduced by a certain point, the leaves receive fewer nutrients than they need to

sustain good health and begin to show symptoms of nutrient deficiencies, usually by turning pale green or yellow, with the veins remaining green. If the xylem flow is reduced when the water demand is high—during hot weather—the leaves may wilt or scorch. This happens because the leaves lose water faster than it can be replaced through the transport system.

Stomata control: A plant controls transpiration by opening and closing its stomata. The stomata close at night and open in the morning, but may shut partially if the light is dim. Stomata also close if a leaf runs out of water. This usually happens before any sign of wilting appears. If the weather is hot when the leaf runs out of water and if the leaf is in the sun, the leaf is likely to overheat and burn. This is called *sunburn* or *scorch*, depending on the pattern of the burning.

Phloem flow: The part of the transport system that carries sugars and other manufactured material from the leaves to other parts of the plant is called the *phloem* (FLO-em). This system of tubes lies inside the bark. If you peel off some bark in the spring, the phloem is visible as the white part of the bark. Flow in the phloem is by diffusion and is much slower than xylem flow. Sugars and other material manufactured in the leaves diffuse through the phloem to growing shoots, flowers, fruit, and roots. Most of the phloem flow in the trunk of a tree is downward to nourish the large root system.

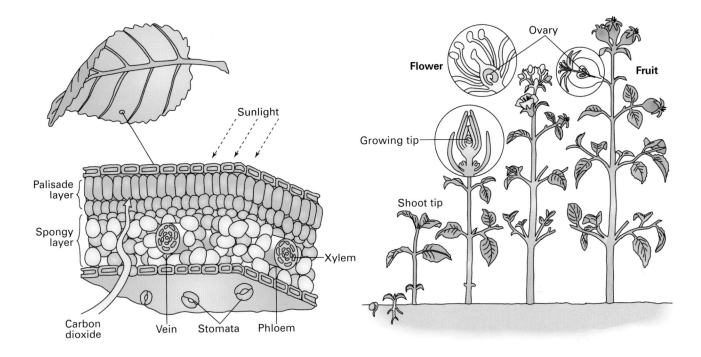

Flower · Ovary · **Fruit**

Sunlight

Palisade layer

Spongy layer

Xylem

Growing tip

Shoot tip

Carbon dioxide · Vein · Stomata · Phloem

PHOTOSYNTHESIS

Photosynthesis is a chemical reaction that uses the sun's rays to form a chemical that supports plant life. This reaction takes carbon dioxide from the air and combines it with water from the soil to make sugars. Photosynthesis takes place in the green parts of plants. The green pigment is called *chlorophyll*. A plant's chlorophyll collects and focuses the energy in light to make sugar. Most photosynthesis takes place in leaves in a layer of cells, called the *palisade layer*, near the upper surface of the leaf. Carbon dioxide enters the leaf through the stomata in the lower surface and enters the palisade cells, where it combines with water to make sugar. As a byproduct of this reaction, oxygen is released into the air. The sugars are then transported through the phloem to all parts of the plant, where they are used by the plant as energy. All animals and humans depend on both the sugars and the oxygen produced by plants, so all life on earth depends on photosynthesis.

Light: Light is necessary to combine with carbon dioxide and water to make sugar. The more light a plant receives, the more sugar it makes, the faster it grows, and the more flowers and fruit it produces. In dim light, a plant makes barely enough sugar to maintain its life, but in bright light, it makes a surplus that it uses for growth and reproduction.

Water stress: Carbon dioxide enters the leaves through the stomata. Because most plants can't store carbon dioxide, photosynthesis can take place only when the stomata are open. If a plant does not have enough water, it closes its stomata to avoid losing water it needs to survive. When the stomata are closed, however, photosynthesis stops. One of the first effects of water stress is that photosynthesis—and growth—stops.

TOP GROWTH

Unlike human growth, which takes place in all parts of the body, plant growth occurs only in the *growing points*. The growing points in a plant are in the tips of the roots and shoots and, in woody plants, just under the bark.

Tip growth: The growing points in the tips of shoots and roots are composed of tiny bunches of cells that divide repeatedly, building the organs of the plant, but the new growth is only in these areas. The new plant parts are tiny while they are in the growing point, but they are complete, with all the cells they'll ever have. As the growing point moves beyond them, the new parts fill with water and swell until they reach their full size. No new cell division takes place as they expand, however.

Buds: The growing point moves ahead, but a bud is left at the base of each leaf. A bud is a growing point that is, for the moment, dormant. On some plants, such as tomatoes, these axillary buds begin growing as soon as they are formed. On others, such as apple trees, the buds remain dormant until the following spring. Then they all begin growing at once. Some buds never open by themselves, but pinching off the growing point at the end of the branch they are on makes them open and begin to grow.

Stem growth: The other place a woody plant grows is under the bark. A sheet of cells, called the *cambium*, lies between the wood and the bark. These cells divide repeatedly just as those in the shoot and root tips do. As they divide, they produce xylem cells toward the center of the stem and phloem cells toward the outside. When growth is fastest, in the spring, new xylem cells are large; as growth slows in the summer, smaller cells are made. The difference in the size of these cells makes up the annual rings visible in most wood.

Flowers and fruit: Flowers are produced by the growing point just as the leaves and stems are. Flowers begin as buds, which open immediately in some plants and not until the following spring in others. At the base of each flower is an ovary, an organ that will contain the seed and, in some plants, become the fruit.

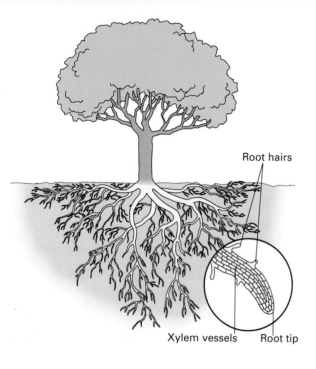

Root hairs

Xylem vessels   Root tip

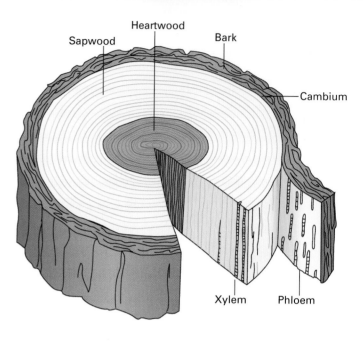

Sapwood   Heartwood   Bark

Cambium

Xylem   Phloem

ROOT GROWTH

Plants live in two distinctly different environments: the air and the soil. The root system of a plant "mines" the soil for water and nutrients, the raw materials used by the plant. These raw materials are transported through the stems to the leaves, where they are combined with carbon dioxide to make sugars and complex chemicals. These processed chemicals are then transported through the stems back to the roots, where they are used for growth.

Root tips: As the growing points at the end of the root move through the soil, they leave behind soft, white, threadlike root tips. Downy root hairs grow from the tips. Most water and nutrient absorption is through these root tips. As a root ages, it becomes yellow and then brown, and the root hairs disintegrate. By the time the root turns brown, it no longer absorbs much water from the soil.

Root system: Roots need three things for vigorous growth: oxygen, water, and nutrients. Of these three, oxygen is most frequently in short supply. Because plants can't transport oxygen, each part of the plant must absorb it directly from the air. Oxygen diffuses through the spaces between soil particles to reach the roots. When roots find an abundance of these three necessities in their environment, they proliferate.

The root system of a plant is often thought of as extending through the soil about as far as the top growth does above the ground. But plants vary greatly in the extent of their root systems. Trees may have roots that extend dozens or even hundreds of feet beyond their top growth, especially if the soil is dry. Also, the root system is not symmetrical but is dense on the side that receives the most food or water.

Although some plants have deep root systems, garden plants absorb most of their nutrients from the top foot of soil. For this reason, plants are sensitive to the condition of the soil surface. If the soil is paved over or becomes compacted, the roots near the surface receive less oxygen and water, and the plant may die.

TRUNK GROWTH

Growth of tree trunks and expansion of the stems of woody plants take place in the cambium, a layer of dividing cells just under the bark. As each cell in the cambium divides, one of the two new cells becomes either a xylem cell or a phloem cell, and the other remains a cambium cell and divides again.

Wood: As the newest xylem cells expand, they push the cambium layer a little farther from the center of the tree. Each new cell lives for only a year or two; then it becomes plugged with detritus and ceases to function. By this time, the cell is deep in the wood of the tree and is heavily packed with a material called *lignin*, the material that gives stiffness and rigidity to wood.

Bark: The phloem cells that form in the cambium are pushed to the outside layer of the tree by their expansion and the expansion of the new xylem cells. Like the xylem cells, phloem cells transport nutrients for a couple of years. Then they die and dry out to become the bark of the tree. The green bark on a young stem is composed of a living layer of cells called the *epidermis*. As the twig ages and expands, dead phloem cells replace this living bark.

Girdling: If the phloem and xylem are cut through in a ring around the trunk of a tree, the flow of water to the top of the tree is stopped, the leaves wilt, and the top of the plant dies. The roots may die, or the stem may resprout and grow a new top. If only the bark is cut through—by root weevils, for instance—water can still reach the top of the tree, and wilting does not occur. But the flow of sugars and nutrients from the leaves to the roots has been stopped, and the roots slowly starve. As they cease functioning, the top also starves, and inevitably the tree dies.

Bark wounds: Any wound in the bark of a tree trunk interrupts the flow of water and nutrients through the tree. If a spot is repeatedly wounded, as frequently happens when a tree is hit by a lawn mower, the growth of the plant is slowed and stunted.

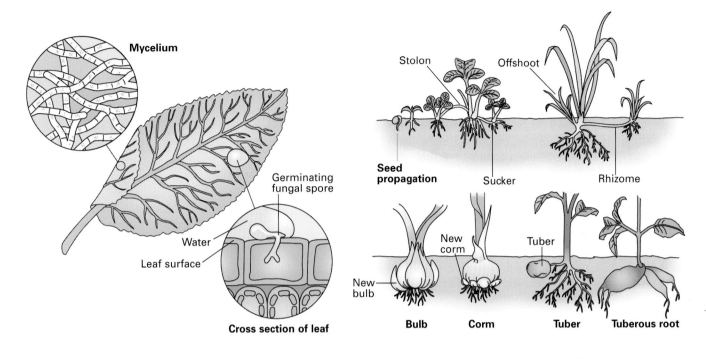

Mycelium

Germinating fungal spore

Water

Leaf surface

Cross section of leaf

Stolon

Offshoot

Seed propagation

Sucker

Rhizome

New bulb

New corm

Tuber

Bulb

Corm

Tuber

Tuberous root

FUNGI

Fungi are primitive plants that don't contain chlorophyll, so they can't make their own sugars as green plants do. Their structure is simple; most fungi are composed of a network of threads, which are sometimes bundled into cords. These threads and cords are called the *mycelium* (my-SEE-lee-um) and make up the body of the fungus. They are most easily seen as the fragile white threads that form under rotting leaves. Most fungi decompose dead plant matter into simpler chemicals. They are responsible for most of the decay of plant material in nature. But some fungi cause plant disease by invading living plants. Fungus diseases spread in several ways, but most commonly through the soil, by splashing water, or by the wind.

Soil-spread fungi: Fungi that live in the soil and attack plant roots are most commonly spread when soil or infected plants are moved from one place to another. Soil-borne fungi are often brought to the garden on the roots of a transplant, then spread from one end of the garden to the other by irrigation water or cultivation.

Water-spread fungi: Other fungi depend on splashing water to spread their spores. Many of the fungi that cause leaf spots on trees and shrubs spend the winter as spores on the bark or on fallen leaves and are then washed to new leaves in the spring by splashing rain water.

Wind-spread fungi: The third common way fungi spread is by dustlike spores that are carried by the wind to other plants. Many of these spores live for only a few hours or days after they are released into the air, so they must soon find suitable conditions for germination. For most such fungi, a "suitable condition" is a drop of water on a leaf surface. A fungus spore takes four to eight hours to germinate and penetrate a leaf. If the drop of water in which it is growing dries out during this time, the spore dies. One notable exception, powdery mildew, does not need a drop of water to germinate; its spores can germinate on a dry leaf, but this mildew is more active in wet conditions.

HOW PLANTS SPREAD

Plants have two ways of propagating: from seed and from new plants grown from parts of old ones.

Seed propagation: Most plants make seeds, and some make thousands of them. Annual plants (those that live only one growing season) depend on seeds to continue their species. They often put all their energy into ripening a crop of seeds. Annual weeds, such as crabgrass, usually make thousands of seeds per plant. It is important to kill these weeds before they produce seeds, or the same job will need to be repeated the following year.

Offshoot: All other methods of propagation involve some form of growing new plants from parts of old ones. Offshoots are new plants that arise from the base of the old one and, if allowed to continue, will eventually lead to a dense bunch of plants. Offshoots can usually be broken or cut off and planted to make new plants.

Rhizome and stolon: These horizontal stems form new plants at a distance from the mother plant. Rhizomes travel underground and make new plants where they near the surface. Stolons travel aboveground and form new plants where they come in contact with the ground.

Sucker: The word *sucker* has two different but similar meanings. It refers to a stem that grows from the base of the trunk. It also refers to a plant that arises from the roots of the parent plant, often at some distance from the trunk. Plants that sucker freely, if left to their own devices, will form a thicket in a couple of years. The type of sucker that arises from a root is a whole plant and can be removed and planted elsewhere.

Bulb: Plants form a wide variety of underground food storage organs. Most of these organs remain dormant for part of the year and then, because of the large amount of food stored in them, burst into vigorous growth. If the storage organ is formed from fleshy leaves, it is called a *bulb*. If it is formed from a vertical stem, it is called a *corm*. If it is formed from a rhizome, it is called a *tuber*. If it is formed from a root, it is called a *tuberous root*. When dormant, these organs can be moved to new locations, or they can be stored before being replanted.

Abscission: A natural dropping of leaves, flowers, and other plant parts.

Acaricide: A chemical that kills spider mites and other types of mites. *See also* Miticide.

Acclimate: To adjust to a change in the environment.

Acid reaction: A property of fertilizer that makes soil more acid. This reaction may be slow and apparent only after continued fertilizer use. The strength of the acid reaction is expressed on the fertilizer label in a phrase such as "Potential acidity 400 lb calcium carbonate equivalent per ton." This means that 400 pounds of lime (calcium carbonate) would be necessary to neutralize the acidity produced by a ton of the fertilizer.

Acid soil: Soil with a pH below 7.0. Acid soil can cause problems when its pH is below 5.5.

Adventitious: Forming in unusual locations—for example, roots growing from leaves or aboveground stems.

Aerate: To increase the amount of air space in the soil by tilling or otherwise loosening the soil.

Algae: Simple plants without visible structure that grow in wet locations. Some types of algae form a slippery black or green scum on wet soils, plants, walkways, and other surfaces.

Alkaline soil: Soil with a pH above 7.0. Alkaline soil slows the growth of many plants when its pH is above 8.0.

Annual plant: A plant that grows, flowers, produces seeds or fruit, and dies in one year or less. Many herbaceous flowers and vegetables are annual plants.

Antidesiccant: A chemical that slows transpiration from leaves, used when roots have been damaged by transplanting or when water is not available for other reasons. Some antidesiccants coat the leaf with a thin plastic film; others chemically close the stomata. Also called an antitranspirant.

Axil: The location on a stem between the upper surface of a leaf or leafstalk and the stem from which it is growing.

Axillary bud: A bud that forms in a leaf axil, between the petiole and stem.

Bactericide: A chemical agent that can kill bacteria.

Balled-and-burlapped plant: A tree or shrub that is dug out of the ground with the intact soil ball surrounding the roots; the soil ball is then wrapped in burlap or plastic.

Bare-root plant: A tree or shrub that is dug out of the ground and sold with its roots bare of soil. Roses and fruit trees are commonly sold in this manner. Bare-root plants are available in the winter.

Biennial plant: A plant that grows, flowers, produces seeds or fruit, and dies in two years. Some herbaceous flowers and vegetables are biennial. Most biennial plants produce foliage the first year and bloom the second year.

Bolting: The rapid development of flowers and seed heads in vegetables. Hot weather, drought, or lack of nutrients may stimulate premature bolting.

Bract: A modified leaf that is sometimes brightly colored, resembling a petal.

Bud: A condensed shoot consisting mainly of undeveloped tissue. Buds are often covered with scales. They develop into leaves, flowers, or both.

Burl: A mass of bud tissue that grows from the side of a tree. Burls are healthy wood and are natural. *See also* Gall.

Callus: A mass of cells, often barklike in appearance, that forms over wounded plant tissue.

Cambium: A thin ring of tissue within the stem, branch, and trunk; continually forms nutrient- and water-conducting vessels.

Canker: A discolored lesion that forms in a stem, branch, or trunk as a result of infection. Cankers are often sunken and may exude a thick sap.

Castings, worm: Soil that has passed through an earthworm. The earthworm's digestive tract breaks down organic matter into simpler forms that are more readily taken up by plants.

Chilling requirement: The need of some plants to have several weeks below a certain temperature (usually around 45°F) in order for their flower buds to open. Bulbs, trees, and perennial flowers native to cold-winter regions often have chilling requirements. *See also* Vernalization.

Chlorophyll: The green plant pigment that is necessary for photosynthesis.

Chlorosis: The yellowing of foliage due to a loss or breakdown of chlorophyll. Chlorosis may result from disease or infestation, poor growing conditions, or lack of nutrients. *See also* Yellowing.

Cold frame: A protective structure for plants that uses the sun's energy to provide heat. Plants may be grown in cold frames early in the spring before all danger of freezing is past.

Complete fertilizer: A fertilizer containing nitrogen, phosphorus, and potassium; the three nutrients most commonly deficient in plants.

Compost: Partially decomposed organic matter used to amend soil. Compost is often made from household organic waste, grass clippings and leaves.

Conifer: A woody tree or shrub that produces cones. Common conifers are pines, firs, spruces, junipers, redwoods, and hemlocks.

Conk: A mushroomlike fruiting body of any of several different kinds of tree-decaying fungi. Conks are platelike growths from the trunk of the tree.

Corm: A short, solid, enlarged underground stem from which roots grow. Corms are food-storage organs, similar to bulbs and tubers. They contain one bud that will produce a new plant.

Crown: (1) The part of a plant where the stem or trunk enters the ground, or the base of a grass plant. (2) The top or leafy portion of a tree.

Cultivar: Short for "CULTIvated VARiety." A plant variety bred by humans and not found in nature.

Deadhead: The removal of old blossoms to encourage continued bloom or to improve the appearance of a plant.

Deciduous: Shedding all leaves annually, usually in the fall.

Defoliation: Leaf drop that often results from infection, insect infestation, or adverse environmental conditions.

Desiccation: Dehydration or loss of water.

Dormancy: A state of rest and reduced metabolic activity in which plant tissues remain alive but do not grow.

Dormant oil: Oil sprayed on deciduous trees or shrubs while they are dormant. Dormant oils are used to kill overwintering insects or insect eggs on plant bark. For plants with green leaves, summer oil should be used instead. *See also* Horticultural oil.

Edema: Watery blisters or swellings that form on many herbaceous plants. These swellings may burst, forming rust-colored lesions on leaves or stems.

Espalier: To train a plant (usually a tree or vine) along a wall railing, or trellis so that the branches grow flat against the support.

Evergreen: A plant that retains all or most of its foliage throughout the year.

Fasciation: An abnormal fusion of stems, leaves, or flowers, or the production of distorted growth.

Fertilizer: A substance that contains plant nutrients. Fertilizer may be liquid or dry and may be formulated in many different ways.

Flag: A tuft of dead foliage in an otherwise-healthy tree. Flags are visible from a distance and are used to determine the presence of several insects and diseases.

Force: To cause a plant to bloom outside its normal flowering season by manipulating periods of light and dark. Blooming mums bought any season except fall are forced.

Formulation: The form in which a compound may be produced. For example, a pesticide may be powdered, liquid, or granular, or it may be in an oil solution.

Frass: Sawdustlike insect excrement.

Frond: The large, flat leaf of a fern or palm.

Fruiting body: A fungal structure that produces spores.

Fungicide: A chemical that kills fungi or prevents them from infecting healthy plant tissue.

Gall: An abnormal growth that forms on a plant root, shoot, or leaf. A gall often results from infection or insect infestation.

Germination: The sprouting of seeds.

Girdle: To encircle plant roots, stems, trunks, or branches, constricting the plant part or reducing water and nutrient flow through the affected plant part.

Graft: To unite a stem or bud of one plant with a stem or root of another plant.

Grub: A thick, soft insect larva (usually of a beetle).

Gummosis: The oozing of plant sap, often from a plant wound or canker. Gummosis may occur as a result of infection or insect infestation.

Hardening off: The process of plant adjustment to cold temperatures.

Hardiness: The ability of a plant to withstand cold temperatures.

Hardpan: A layer of rocklike soil that sometimes forms a foot or two under the surface. Hardpan is most common in arid regions and is formed by deposits of chemicals that cement soil particles together.

Heartwood: The inner core inside a woody stem or trunk.

Herbaceous: Being mainly soft and succulent, with little or no woody tissue.

Herbicide: A chemical that kills or retards plant growth. Herbicides may kill the entire plant, or they may kill only the aboveground plant parts, leaving the roots alive. *See also* Weed killer.

Honeydew: A syrupy substance secreted by many insects of the aphid order. Much of the sugar in the sap the insects drink passes through their bodies undigested and coats leaves and objects under them.

Horticultural oil: Petroleum oil formulated to be mixed with water and sprayed on plants to kill insects. Because the oil kills by smothering, rather than by poisoning, insects do not develop resistance to it. A less-refined version called dormant oil is used only on dormant trees and shrubs. A more highly refined version called summer oil or superior oil can be sprayed on green leaves. *See also* Dormant oil, Summer oil.

Host: An organism that is parasitized by another organism, such as a plant that is infected by a fungus or infested by an insect.

Humidity: The amount of water vapor (moisture) in the air.

Humus: The relatively stable end product of the decomposition of organic matter in soil. Humus is a complex mixture of chemicals that supplies plant nutrients to and improves the structure of soil.

Hybrid: The offspring of two distinct plant species; a plant obtained by crossing two or more species, subspecies, or varieties of plants. Hybrids often produce a plant that has the best qualities of each parent.

Immature: An early growth phase of a plant differentiated from later growth by distinctly different leaf shapes, habits of growth, or other characteristics. *See also* Juvenile.

Immune: Not susceptible to a disease or insect infestation.

Infiltration, soil: The process by which water moves into the soil.

Inflorescence: The flowering part of a plant, often referring to groups of flowers.

Insect growth regulator: An insecticide that has a hormonelike effect on insects, usually interfering with molting.

Insecticide: A chemical that kills insects.

Insoluble: Not easily dissolved. *See also* Solubility.

Instar: A stage in the life of insects and mites. Each instar ends with the molting of the insect.

Internode: The section of stem between two nodes.

Interveinal: The area between the leaf veins. Interveinal yellowing, or chlorosis, refers to a discoloration occurring between the leaf veins.

Juvenile: An early growth phase of a plant differentiated from later growth by distinctly different leaf shapes, habits of growth, and other characteristics. *See also* Immature.

Larva: An immature stage through which some types of insects must pass before developing into adults. Caterpillars are the larvae of moths and butterflies, and grubs are the larvae of beetles. Larvae are typically wormlike in appearance.

Lateral bud: A bud formed along the side of a stem or branch rather than at the end.

Leach: To remove salts and soluble minerals from the soil by flushing the soil with water.

Leader: The main stems or trunk of a tree or shrub from which side stems or branches are produced.

Leaf margins: The edges of a leaf. Variations in the shapes of leaf margins are used to help identify many plants and differentiate among them.

Leaf scar: A tiny mark left on a twig or stem after a leaf or petiole drops off.

Leafstalk: The part that attaches a leaf to a stem. *See also* Petiole.

Leggy: Having leaves spaced too far apart along the stem.

Lesion: A wound, discoloration, or scar caused by disease or injury.

Loam: Medium-textured garden soil containing a balance of sandy and clay soils and organic matter.

Macronutrient: A nutrient required in large quantities by plants for normal growth. nitrogen, phosphorus, and potassium are the primary macronutrients.

Maggot: A legless grub; the larva of a member of the fly family.

Metamorphosis: The changes in body shape undergone by many insects as they develop from eggs into adults.

Microclimate: The environment immediately surrounding a plant; very localized climate conditions. Many different microclimates may occur at the same time in different areas of a garden.

Micronutrient: A minor nutrient required by plants for normal growth. Most plants need micronutrients such as iron, zinc, and manganese in small quantities.

Mite: A tiny animal related to spiders. Many mites feed on plants.

Miticide: A chemical agent that kills spider mites and other types of mites. *See also* Acaricide.

Mulch: A layer of organic or inorganic material on the soil surface. Mulches help to moderate the temperature of the soil surface, reduce loss of moisture from the soil, suppress weed growth, and reduce runoff.

Mycelia: Microscopic fungal strands that form the major part of a fungal growth.

Nematode: A microscopic worm that lives in the soil and feeds on plant roots. Some nematodes feed on plant stems and leaves.

Node: The part of a stem where leaves and buds are attached.

Nodule: A small knob on a plant root. Nematodes, nitrogen-fixing bacteria, and other organisms may cause nodules.

Nonsystemic: Not spread throughout. *See also* Systemic.

Nymph: An immature stage through which some types of insects must pass before developing into adults. Nymphs usually resemble the adult form, but they lack wings and can't reproduce.

Organic matter: A substance derived from plant or animal material.

Overfertilized: Fertilized too much. *See also* Fertilizer.

Overwinter: To survive the winter season. An "overwintering form" of an insect is the stage of growth, such as an egg, in which the insect spends the winter.

Ovipositor: An insect's egg-laying organ. In many insects, it is a drill-like or knifelike organ that can deposit eggs within a leaf or even deep under the bark of a tree.

Ozone: A common air pollutant that may cause plant injury.

Palisade cells: Columnar cells located in a layer just beneath the upper surface of a leaf.

PAN (peroxyacetyl nitrate): A common air pollutant that may cause foliar injury to plants.

Panicle: A complex compound inflorescence. The flowers are often drooping.

Parasite: An organism that obtains its food from another living organism. A parasite lives on or in its host.

Pathogen: An organism (such as a fungus, bacterium, mycoplasma, or virus) capable of causing a disease.

Peat: Partially degraded vegetable matter found in marshy areas. Peat is commonly used as a soil amendment.

Perennial plant: A plant that lives for more than two years, often for many years. Most woody plants and many herbaceous plants are perennials.

Permanent wilting point: The point of soil dryness at which plants can no longer obtain water from the soil. Once plants have reached the permanent wilting point, they do not recover even if supplied with water.

Pesticide: A chemical used to kill an organism considered a pest.

Petiole: A stalk that attaches a leaf to a stem. *See also* Leafstalk.

pH: A measure of the acidity or alkalinity of a substance; a measure of the relative concentration of hydrogen ions and hydroxyl ions in solution.

Phloem: The nutrient-conducting vessels found throughout a plant. Phloem tubes transport nutrients produced in the foliage down through the stems, branches, and trunk to the roots.

Photosynthesis: The process by which plants use the sun's light to produce food (carbohydrates).

Phylum: The largest grouping of the animal kingdom. Mollusks, mammals, and birds are all phyla.

Plant disease: Any condition that impairs the normal functioning and metabolism of a plant. A plant disease may be caused by a fungus, bacterium, or virus or by an environmental factor such as sunburn or lack of nutrients.

Predaceous: Living by preying on others.

Propagation: The means of reproducing plants, such as by seeds, cuttings, budding, and grafting.

Protectant: A chemical that protects a plant from infection or insect infestation.

Pupa: An immature resting stage through which some types of insects must pass before becoming adults.

Pustule: A colored bump or blister caused by a disease organism.

Resistance, chemical: The ability of insects or pathogens to tolerate chemicals meant to control them; acquired through mutation and selection as a result of frequent exposure to the poison.

Resistance, plant: Not likely to be damaged by a particular problem. For example, a drought-resistant plant withstands more dryness than other plants. When discussing plant diseases, a resistant plant is one that has defenses against the pathogen, so is not infected. *See also* Tolerant.

Resting structure: A dormant phase of a fungus in which it is able to survive for months or years until conditions for growth are again present.

Rhizome: An underground stem from which roots grow. Rhizomes function as storage organs and may be divided to produce new plants. *See also* Rootstock.

Root zone: The volume of soil that contains the roots of a plant.

Rootstock: (1) The roots and crown or the roots, crown, and trunk of a plant upon which another plant is grafted. (2) The crown and roots of some types of perennial herbaceous plants. *See also* Rhizomes.

Rosette: A plant growth pattern in which the leaves form a flat, crowded ring close to the ground.

Runner: Aboveground trailing stem that forms roots at its nodes when it makes contact with moist soil. *See also* Stolon.

Sapwood: The outer cylinder of wood in a trunk, between the heartwood and the bark.

Saturated soil: Soil that is so wet that all the air pores in it are filled with water.

Scalp: To mow a lawn close to the ground. This damages the grass and may kill it. Scalping usually happens when the ground surface is uneven or when a mower bounces in dense turf.

Sclerotia: A compact mass of fungal strands (mycelia) that functions as a resting stage for a fungus. Sclerotia are usually brown or black, about the size of a pea, and can withstand adverse environmental conditions. A genus of fungi is called *Sclerotium* after the sclerotia it produces.

Seed piece: A small tuber or section of a tuber planted to grow more plants.

Semidormant: Partially dormant; partially inactive in growth. *See also* Dormant.

Semiparasitic: Partially parasitic. *See also* Parasite.

Shot hole: Small round holes in leaves that look as if they were made by shotgun pellets; often caused by leafspot disease, in which the diseased tissue drops out.

Slow-release fertilizer: A fertilizer that releases its nutrients into the soil slowly and evenly over a long period of time.

Soil heaving: The expansion and contraction of soil during periods of freezing and thawing. Plant roots may be sheared, or plants may be lifted out of the ground during this soil movement.

Soil penetrant: A substance that changes the surface tension of water or another liquid, causing it to cut through a repellent surface more thoroughly. Dish soap is an effective soil penetrant.

Solubility: The degree to which a compound will dissolve in water. Compounds with high solubility dissolve in water more readily than compounds with low solubility. *See also* Insoluble.

Soluble fertilizer: A fertilizer that dissolves easily in water and is immediately available for plant use. *See also* Fertilizer.

Spike: A flower stalk with flowers directly attached to the stalk, without stems.

Spikelet: (1) A small, single spike of flowers that forms part of a compound inflorescence. (2) The flower of grasses.

Spore: A microscopic structure produced by fungi, mosses, and ferns that can germinate to form a new plant or a different life stage of the same plant.

Spreader-sticker: Spray additive with two functions. It weakens the surface tension of water, keeping it from beading on waxy or fuzzy plant surfaces, and also glues the active ingredient to the leaf, making it more resistant to washing off.

Spur: A compressed lateral branch bearing buds that will develop into flowers and then form fruit.

Stolon: A horizontal plant stem above the soil surface that gives rise to new plants. *See also* Runner.

Stomata: Tiny pores located mainly on the underside of leaves. Oxygen, carbon dioxide, water vapor, and other gases move in and out of the leaf through these pores.

Stone fruit: A tree fruit that contains a large single seed, such as an apricot, cherry, peach, or plum.

Succulent: Full of water. A plant that stores water in its tissues, such as a cactus.

Sucker: A shoot or stem that grows from an underground plant part.

Summer oil: Highly refined petroleum oil mixed with an emulsifier to be applied in water. Used to kill soft-bodied insects and smother eggs on actively growing plants. Also called superior oil. *See also* Horticultural oil.

Sunscald: Damage to leaves, bark, or fruit caused by the heat of the sun.

Surfactant: A substance added to a spray to increase its wetting and spreading properties. *See also* Soil penetrant and Wetting agent.

Systemic: Taken into the plant and spread throughout it. A systemic plant disease, such as a virus, spreads through the plant rather than remaining localized. A systemic pesticide or herbicide is transported throughout the plant.

Taproot: An undivided main root that penetrates deeply into the ground.

Tender plant: A plant that cannot tolerate freezing temperatures.

Terminal bud: A bud at the tip or end of a stem or branch.

Thatch: A layer of dead grass stems on top of the soil. Thatch more than ½ inch deep can be harmful to the lawn.

Tilth: The structure of soil, especially regarding its suitability for plant growth. Soil in good tilth has a soft, loose structure.

Tolerant: A plant that, when infected by a disease, shows few symptoms. A plant tolerant of a disease is infected but not damaged severely, but can transmit the disease to other plants. A plant resistant to a disease does not acquire the disease, so does not transmit it to other plants. *See also* Resistance, plant.

Toxin: A poisonous substance produced by a plant or an animal.

Translocation: The movement of a compound from one part of a plant to another.

Transpiration: The evaporation of water from plant tissue. Transpiration occurs mainly through the stomata in the leaves.

Tuber: An underground storage and reproductive organ derived from stem tissue; bears dormant buds called "eyes."

Underfertilized: Not fertilized enough. *See also* Fertilizer.

Vascular system: The system of tissues (phloem and xylem) that conducts nutrients and water throughout the plant.

Vein clearing: A lightening or total loss of color in leaf veins. This often results from infection or nutrient deficiency.

Vernalization: A cooling period required by many plants in order to germinate, grow, or flower properly. *See also* Chilling requirement.

Vigor: The health of a plant. A vigorous plant grows rapidly and produces healthy, normal amounts of foliage and flowers. A nonvigorous plant grows slowly, if at all, and produces stunted, sparse growth.

Weed killer: A chemical that kills or retards plant growth. Weed killers may kill the entire plant, or they may kill only the aboveground plant parts, leaving the roots alive. *See also* Herbicide.

Wetting agent: A substance that changes the surface tension of water or another liquid, causing the liquid to penetrate a repellent surface more thoroughly. Wetting agents are often used with pesticides sprayed on waxy or fuzzy foliage to improve pesticide coverage. *See also* Soil penetrant and Surfactant.

Wing pad: An incompletely developed wing, often present on immature stages (instars) of winged insects.

Witches'-broom: A dense cluster of twigs that looks like a witch's broom. Any of several different insects and diseases may cause witches'-broom.

Xylem: The water-conducting vessels found throughout a plant. Xylem tubes transport water and minerals from the roots upward through the plant.

Yellowing: The yellowing of foliage from a loss or breakdown of chlorophyll. Yellowing may result from disease or insect infestation, poor growing conditions, or lack of nutrients. *See also* Chlorosis.

Houseplants

Houseplants are an appealing and inexpensive decor for any room. **From left to right:** *heartleaf philodendron, spathiphyllum, cyclamen, African violet, spotted dumb cane, and English ivy topiary.*

When a houseplant stops blooming or drops its leaves, the home gardener may be tempted to discard the plant rather than seek out the problem. Bud failure or leaf drop may be caused by low temperatures, poor soil, drafts, lack of fertilizer, too much or too little water, or too much or too little light. All these problems may be corrected. Saving the plant is entirely possible.

PURCHASING HOUSEPLANTS

When you go to a nursery or garden center to buy a houseplant, you want a specimen that is appropriate for the conditions you can provide. And, of course, you want a healthy plant that is pest-free.

Appropriate plants: The most important factor in choosing a species of plant is the amount of light it will receive in your home. To learn how to evaluate indoor lighting, read the section called Providing Light, on page 20. Note whether the proposed growing area receives bright, medium, or low light. Take a houseplant reference book with you when you shop, or ask if the nursery has references available on-site. Look up your intended purchase to see whether your home has the light the plant needs. Flowering plants and cacti need the most sunlight. Pothos, cast-iron plants, and some ivies grow slowly but well in indirect light. Prima donnas, such as orchids, have specific light requirements in order to bloom; make sure your site can meet their needs before selecting them.

Healthy plants: How can you tell if a plant is healthy? The leaves of a healthy plant are green unless they are naturally variegated or multicolored, as are some pothos, Chinese evergreens, zebra plants, and others. Unhealthy leaves may have tips or edges that look burned, brown spots, or a yellowish cast. Or they may appear crumpled or tend to droop. Readily apparent leaf problems can be a result of powdery mildew, aphids, whiteflies, spider mites, or other insects. Inspect leaf undersides and leaf-to-stem junctions for signs of disease or insects. Of the plants that appear healthy, select the most compact and fully leafed.

When buying a flowering plant for indoor use, look for a specimen with ample buds as well as flowers. Minimal buds on a plant usually mean it has passed the peak of blooming; it may be another year before it blooms copiously again. A plant with many buds will be colorful throughout the current season. If you find a sturdy, well-budded plant with some flowers, give it a gentle shake. If many flowers drop off, the plant has been subjected to severe stress. Select a healthier specimen.

After bringing your purchase home, set it off by itself for about a week. Even though you did not see any insect pests, the plant may harbor microscopic insect eggs. Check the plant carefully after the quarantine period. If you see even a few insects, treat the new plant with insecticide before placing it near any other plant.

PURCHASING THE PERFECT POT

Among the many choices available for indoor-plant potting are unglazed clay, plastic, and glazed ceramic in designs to match every decor.

A clay pot is especially appropriate on a porch or in a rustic atmosphere. Since moisture evaporates quickly through clay, use clay pots as containers for plants which tolerate dryness. If you place other types of plants in clay pots, they will need more moisture than normal. Since water tends to seep through clay-pot bottoms, place a nonporous saucer underneath to prevent water stains on rugs or counters.

Plastic pots are lightweight and often used for hanging plants. Plastic pots hold water longer than clay pots, so be careful not to overwater. Many plastic pots are sold with removable saucers.

Glazed ceramic pots are as effective in water control as plastic pots. Many ceramic pots do not have drainage holes, however, a deficiency that can result in overwatering. Place a plastic pot with drainage saucer inside the glazed pot.

PROVIDING SOIL

In nature, plant roots spread to seek nutrients. In a pot, what's there is what the plant gets. If vitamins and minerals are lacking, the plant fails to thrive. Nutrients are as important to the plant as adequate light and sufficient moisture.

Most houseplants can thrive in all-purpose potting soil. Fussier plants, such as African violets, may grow better in a commercial potting soil formulated especially for the species. Other types of commercial soils are formulated for specific situations—for example, terrariums. Soilless growing mediums are also available.

You can make your own potting mix, using varying proportions of pasteurized garden soil, sand, peat moss, vermiculite, and leaf mold. The gardener who uses homemade potting mix, however, runs the

A sunny kitchen window with a waterproof, tiled surface is an ideal spot for houseplants.

Houseplant potting soil that has been allowed to dry out completely can be difficult to rewet. Submerge the entire pot in a pan of tepid water for a half hour, then drain.

risk of bringing in insect pests and disease organisms. Commercial potting soil is inexpensive, convenient, and free of pests and disease.

PROVIDING WATER

Water causes more plant problems than any other single factor. These problems include overwatering, underwatering, and using tainted water or practicing inappropriate watering techniques.

Too much water: A water overdose without adequate drainage rots roots slowly but steadily, causing plant death. One sign of overwatering is green moss that grows on the surface of the soil. Plant symptoms include lower-leaf wilting, faded leaf colors, and poor growth. The lower portion of the plant's main stem, right above the soil line, may darken. Roots are brown and mushy.

If damage has not destroyed the roots, rescue attempts can include removing standing water, trimming brown roots, and repotting the plant in well-draining soil. An alternative is to take cuttings from healthy stems and start over.

Too little water: Many gardeners worry so much about overwatering that they under water. A water-stressed plant conserves moisture by slowing or stopping new growth. Without adequate water, green leaves turn dull green or yellow. Drooping occurs.

If buds are present, they may fall off.

When to water? Poke your finger about ½ inch into the potting soil. It should feel moist but not wet. If it feels dry or barely moist, water immediately and thoroughly. Ensure adequate drainage or the standing water will turn the underwatering problem into a case of overwatering.

Watering techniques and tainted water: Water most houseplants from the top. Within an hour, pour off excess water from the saucer underneath the pot.

Most drinkable tap water is adequate for plants. Use it at room temperature. The sodium in some types of artificially softened water can prove a problem, however, if used consistently over a long period. Some tap water may also contain salts, which accumulate quickly in plant containers. Salt damage is evidenced by brown leaftips or edges. Damage occurs on older leaves first, and affected leaves eventually die. The plant may also be stunted, with brittle leaves that curl downward. An accumulation or overdose of fertilizer salts causes similar damage. If you see symptoms of salt accumulation, flush the plant thoroughly with water. (For instructions, see page 22). If salts are built up on the rim or at the soil line in the pot, repot the plant in fresh soil to dilute salt levels.

Some gardeners collect rainwater for indoor plant use. Rainwater may carry pollutants, depending on where you live.

In a pot, pollutants may accumulate quickly and deter plant growth.

PROVIDING LIGHT

The secret to providing appropriate light is to match the plant to a location.

Site evaluation: During prime light time, place a sheet of white paper on the table or sill where a plant will reside. Hold your hand about 12 inches above the paper. If a clearly defined dark shadow results, the site receives bright light. If a muted but clearly definable shadow results, the light is medium. If your hand shadow is barely visible, the amount of light is low. Make sure any plants you purchase can prosper in the lighting conditions you can provide.

Symptoms of inappropriate light: Inadequate light produces a leggy, weak plant that may suddenly drop its leaves. Growth slows. The lower leaves turn a lighter green, and the plant does not flower. Plants lean toward the light source; rotating plants regularly encourages even growth.

An African violet that does not bloom is probably not receiving adequate light. These plants require about 12 hours of bright light every day.

Although most complaints are about insufficient light, some rooms are too sunny. Dry patches on leaves may be symptoms of sunburn. If the site gets hot enough, buds

Supplemental lighting fixtures are fairly basic. The main difference is in the type of bulbs they use. Make a choice according to your plants' needs and your budget.

and flowers drop and the entire plant may wilt. To prevent further damage, try moving the plant away from the window, shading the window with filmy curtains, or replacing the plant with a heat-tolerant species, such as a cactus.

Cacti are the plants of choice for sunny locations. Watering them once a week or less will do, except when you want them to flower. Do not allow cacti to dry out totally during the flowering season.

Artificial light: In sites that receive little sun, artificial light may be the only answer. Fluorescent bulbs and incandescent bulbs provide different types of light. Cool-white fluorescent bulbs give off little heat. They do not bake the moisture out of plants, even if placed 4 inches from the foliage. With adequate fluorescent lighting, you need no outdoor light; you could grow plants in a closet if you provided a fan for air circulation.

To help support plant growth with incandescent light, you must use a bulb of at least 100 watts. Such a bulb produces a lot of heat; keep incandescent light at least 2 feet above plant tops to keep from burning the foliage and baking the soil.

PROVIDING FERTILIZER

Outdoors, soil is constantly improved with leaf mold, earthworm castings, decaying plants, and animal droppings.

Indoors, once a plant has used up the nutrients in the pot, there's nowhere for it to get more unless the gardener adds some type of fertilizer.

Symptoms of nutrient shortage: Plants quickly reflect a nutrient shortage. A nitrogen shortage shows up as yellowing leaves and poor growth. If a plant has leaves a darker green than normal, poor growth, and leaf stems with a purplish tinge, a shortage of phosphorus is probably the cause. A potassium shortage appears as yellowing leaves with brown tips and edges. A lack of iron appears as the yellowing of older leaves, on the bottom portions of stems. This yellowing starts at leaf edges and progresses inward.

Fertilizer selection and application: Many types of indoor plant fertilizer are available. The numbers on the container describe the relative proportions of nitrogen (N), phosphorus (P), and potassium (K). The designation 20-20-20 means the fertilizer contains equal portions of each element. A 5-10-5 mixture is higher in phosphorus than in nitrogen or potassium.

Nitrogen helps make healthy green leaves. Phosphorus encourages a strong root system as well as luxuriant flowers. Potassium aids in disease resistance, promotes plant vigor, increases bloom, and strengthens stems. In addition, plants need trace elements, such as iron, which is essential in minute amounts for chlorophyll production and enzyme functioning. Plants grown in soilless mediums, such as sand or vermiculite, need a dose of one-third-strength fertilizer with each watering, because they contain no soil nutrients.

A little bit of fertilizer may be fine, but a lot of fertilizer is almost always too much. Extra fertilizer accumulates in soil, causing tip burn or browning. Too much nitrogen causes rapid growth at the expense of plant vigor. The plant becomes large and spindly, does not set flowers, and is prone to insect infestation.

If you have applied too much fertilizer, take action quickly. Repot the plant in fresh soil or rinse and drain the current soil to wash out fertilizer residue. When applying fertilizer, always follow label instructions.

GROWING OUTDOOR PLANTS INDOORS

Outdoor potted plants purchased for indoor bloom—such as chrysanthemums, freesias, hydrangeas, hyacinths, and narcissus—may be subject to rapid bud withering if kept in areas with constant hot, dry air. Avoid placing these plants in extremely sunny kitchen windows or near microwaves, ovens, and heating vents.

Given appropriate light, sufficient water, and ample air circulation, outdoor plants will bloom indoors for several weeks. If the soil is allowed to become dry during blooming time, future flowers may not form, even though foliage may recuperate.

When bulbs and other outdoor plants cease flowering, they probably will not bloom again indoors. Plant them outdoors in appropriate surroundings, however, and they

Easter cactus

may blossom normally after recovery from the low-light conditions indoors.

Holiday plants, such as poinsettias and Christmas cacti, are grown under controlled conditions to produce blooming during specific seasons. Gardeners often expect them to bloom again next year at the same time. This will probably not happen unless light is strictly regulated.

Extended periods of light encourage foliage rather than flowers. For poinsettias and Christmas cacti to reflower, you must provide total uninterrupted darkness during evening and night hours. After poinsettias bloom the first time, cut back stems to 8 inches and repot the plants in fresh houseplant soil. Beginning in October, cover both poinsettias and Christmas cacti with a large carton from sunset to sunrise. Remove the carton every morning. Do this until flowers appear.

Gift plants, such as azaleas, may lose their flowers quickly indoors if placed in direct sun. Do not let them dry out. Place them away from drafts, and keep them moist and cool. Getting azaleas to bloom indoors a second time is extremely difficult. After the plants bloom the first time, some gardeners place them outdoors in appropriate surroundings, where the azaleas may do well. Others keep azaleas as foliage plants indoors.

Other gift plants that generally do not bloom again indoors are cineraria and cyclamen. Try placing them outdoors in good soil and growing conditions, and after the first or second spring they may surprise you with flowers.

Too little water

Dry poinsettia.

Problem: Leaves are small, and plants fail to grow well and may be stunted. Plant parts or whole plants wilt; leaves may yellow and drop. Margins of leaves or the tips of leaves of narrow-leaf plants may dry and become brittle but still retain a dull green color. Bleached areas may occur between the veins. Such tissues may die and remain bleached or may turn tan or brown. Plants may die.

Analysis: Plants need water to grow. Besides making up most of the plant tissue, water is also the medium that carries nutrients into the plant, so a plant that is frequently short of water is also short of nutrients. Water also cools the leaves as it evaporates off them. If a leaf has no water to evaporate, it may overheat in the sun and burn. If plants wilt and then are given water, sometimes the margins or tips of the leaves will have completely wilted and will not recover. If this occurs, the margins or tips die and become dry and brittle but retain a dull green color.

Solution: Water plants immediately and thoroughly. If the soil is completely dry, soak the entire pot in a tub of water for a couple of hours. For normal watering of container plants, apply enough water so that some water drains from the bottom and collects in a saucer under the pot. After watering, empty the water from the saucer. Water again when the soil just below the surface is barely moist. Plants in containers without drainage holes are difficult to water properly. Water accumulates in the bottom of the container, causing root rot. If the soil is allowed to become too dry, it may be difficult to rewet.

Too much water or poor drainage

Overwatering damage to schefflera.

Problem: Plants fail to grow and may wilt. Leaves lose their glossiness and may become light green or yellow. The roots are brown and soft and lack white tips. The soil in the bottom of the pot may be very wet and have a foul odor. Plants may die. Root balls can be inspected without harming the plant. The plant must be established in the container, however or much of the root ball will fall apart when the plant is removed from the pot. If your plant is small enough to hold in one hand, put your hand on the soil surface with the plant stem between your fingers. Invert the container and gently knock the rim on the edge of a table or other firm surface. Roots will be visible on the outside of the root ball. Healthy roots have many white or tan threadlike tips.

Analysis: Although plants need water to live, the roots also need air. If the soil is kept too wet, the air spaces are filled with water, and the roots are weakened and may die. Weakened plants are more susceptible to root-rot fungi, which wet soils favor. Plants with diseased roots do not absorb as much water as they did when they were healthy, so the soil remains wet. If roots are damaged or diseased, they can't pick up water and nutrients needed for plant growth.

Solution: Discard severely wilted plants and those without white root tips. Repot into a smaller pot until roots regrow. Clean the pot before reuse. Don't water less-severely affected plants until the soil is barely moist. Then follow the instructions on watering given at left. Prevent the problem by using a light soil with good drainage.

Salt damage

Salt damage to a spathiphyllum.

Problem: The leaf margins of plants with broad leaves or the leaf tips of plants with long, narrow leaves turn dark brown and die. This browning occurs on the older leaves first, but when the condition is severe, new leaves may also be affected. Plants may be stunted, with brittle leaves curling downward. On some plants, the older leaves may yellow and die.

Analysis: Salt damage is a common problem with container-grown plants. The roots pick up soluble salts, which accumulate in the margins and tips of the leaves. When concentrations become high enough, the tissues are killed. Salts can accumulate from water or from the use of fertilizers, or they may be present in the soil used in potting. Salts accumulate faster and do more harm if plants are not watered thoroughly. Water that is high in lime does not cause as much salt damage as water that is high in salts.

Solution: Leach excess salts from the soil by flushing with water. Water thoroughly at least three times in a row, letting the water drain from the pot each time. This is most easily done if the pot is placed in the bathtub or sink, or outside in the shade to drain. If a saucer is used to catch the water, empty the saucer 30 minutes after each watering. If the plant is too large to lift, empty the saucer with a turkey baster. Never let a plant stand in drainage water. To prevent further salt accumulation, follow the watering instructions at left.

Sunburn

Sunburn on dieffenbachia.

Problem: Dead tan or brown patches may develop on leaves that are exposed to direct sunlight, or leaf tissue may lighten or turn gray. In some cases, the plant remains green but growth is stunted. Damage is most severe when the plant soil dries out.

Analysis: Sunburn or bleaching occurs when a plant is exposed to more intense sunlight than it can endure. Plants vary widely in their ability to tolerate direct sunlight. Some plants can tolerate full sunlight; others burn or bleach if exposed to any direct sun. Bleaching occurs when light and heat break down chlorophyll, causing the damaged leaf tissue to lighten or gray. On more sensitive plants or when light and heat increase in intensity, damage is more severe and plant tissues die. Sometimes tissue inside the leaf is damaged but outer symptoms do not develop. Instead, growth is stunted. Plants are more susceptible to bleaching and sunburn when they are allowed to dry out, because the normal cooling effect of water evaporating from leaves is reduced. Plants grown in low-light conditions can burn easily if suddenly moved to a sunny location.

Solution: Move plants damaged by direct sunlight to a shady spot, or cut down light intensity by closing the curtains when a plant is exposed to direct sun. Prune badly damaged leaves or trim damaged leaf areas to improve plants' appearance. Keep plants well watered. (For information on watering, see page 22.)

Insufficient light

Leaf drop on zebra plant.

Problem: Plants fail to grow well. Leaves may be lighter green and smaller than normal. Lobes and splits that are normal in leaves may fail to develop. Lower leaves may yellow and drop. On some plants, leaves at first are abnormally large and thinner than normal, then are smaller than normal. Stems and leafstalks may elongate and be spindly and weak. Plants lean toward a light source. Flowering plants fail to produce buds, and plants with colorful foliage become pale. Variegated plants may lose their stripes and become green.

Analysis: Plants use light as a source of energy and grow slowly in light that is too dim for their needs. If most available light comes from one direction, stems and leaves bend in that direction. If the light is much too dim, plants grow poorly. Although foliage plants generally need less light than plants grown for their flowers or fruit, plants with colorful foliage need abundant light.

Solution: Move the plants gradually to a brighter location. The brightest spots in most homes are the sills of windows that face east, west, or south or locations as close to these windows as possible. To avoid sunburn on sensitive plants, close lightweight curtains when the sun shines directly on the plants. If enough light is not available, supply extra light. Move plants from one location to another until you find a place where they grow well.

Nitrogen deficiency

Nitrogen-deficient Swedish ivy plant.

Problem: The oldest leaves—usually the lower leaves—turn yellow and may drop. Yellowing starts at the leaf margins and progresses inward without producing a distinct pattern. The yellowing may progress upward until only the newest leaves remain green. Growth is slow, new leaves are small, and the whole plant may be stunted.

Analysis: Plants use the nutrient nitrogen in many ways, including for the production of chlorophyll. Nitrogen is used in large amounts. When there is not enough of the nutrient for an entire plant, nitrogen is taken from older leaves for use in new growth. Nitrogen is easily leached from soil during regular watering. Of all the plant nutrients, it is the one most likely to be lacking in soil.

Solution: Fertilize houseplants with Miracle-Gro® Water Soluble All-Purpose Plant Food. Add the fertilizer at regular intervals, as recommended on the product label.

Spider mites

Spider mite damage to prayer plant.

Problem: Leaves are stippled, yellowing, and dirty. Leaves may dry out and drop. There may be webbing covering flower buds, between leaves, on the growing points of shoots, or on the undersides of leaves. To determine if a plant is infested with mites, examine the bottoms of the leaves with a hand lens. Or hold a sheet of white paper underneath a suspect leaf and tap the leaf sharply. Minute specks the size of pepper grains will drop to the paper and begin to crawl. The pests are easily seen against the white background.

Analysis: Spider mites, related to spiders, are major pests of many houseplants. They cause damage by sucking sap from the undersides of leaves. As a result of their feeding, chlorophyll disappears, producing the stippled appearance. Spider mite webbing traps cast-off skins and debris, making the plant dirty. Under warm, dry conditions, mites can build up to tremendous numbers. (For more information on spider mites, see page 457.)

Solution: Isolate infested plants from others. Take plants outside or into a shower and wash the mites off the leaves using a strong spray of water. Spray infested plants with Ortho® Rose & Flower Insect Killer, or take them outside and spray with Ortho® Systemic Insect Killer. Keep air humid to help prevent infestation and proliferation. Avoid bringing mites into the house. (For information on preventing houseplant problems, see page 414.)

Scales

Immature scale (100× life size).

Problem: Nodes, stems, and leaves are covered with white, cottony, cushionlike masses; brown, crusty bumps; or clusters of somewhat flattened reddish, gray, or brown scaly bumps. The bumps can be scraped or picked off easily. They don't move when touched. Leaves turn yellow and may drop. A shiny or sticky material may cover the leaves. Mold fungi may be growing on the sticky substance.

Analysis: Several different types of scale insects attack houseplants. Some types can infest many different plants. Scales hatch from eggs. The young, called *crawlers*, are small (about 1/10 inch) soft-bodied, and move around on the plant and to other plants. After a short time, they insert their mouthparts into the plant, withdrawing the sap. Some develop a soft covering over their bodies, others a hard covering. Some species of scales are unable to digest all the sugar in the plant sap, and they excrete the excess in a sticky fluid called *honeydew*, which may cover the leaves or drop onto surfaces below. (For more information on scales, see page 444 to 447.)

Solution: Isolate infested plants as soon as scales are discovered. Remove as many scales as possible with a cloth or toothbrush dipped in soapy water. Spray plants with Ortho® Rose & Flower Insect Killer or a horticultural oil labeled for use indoors, or take the plants outside and spray with Ortho® Systemic Insect Killer. To kill newly hatched insects, repeat the treatment weekly for three weeks. Inspect new plants to avoid bringing scale crawlers into the house. (For information on preventing houseplant problems, see page 414.)

Aphids

Aphids on oleander (life size).

Problem: Leaves are curling, discolored, and reduced in size. A shiny or sticky substance may coat the leaves. Leaves may become littered with cast-off insect skins. Tiny (1/8-inch) nonwinged, yellow or green soft-bodied insects cluster on buds, young stems, and leaves. Winged insects are occasionally seen at the beginning of the aphid infestation.

Analysis: Aphids do little damage in small numbers. They are extremely prolific, however, and populations can rapidly build up to damaging numbers on houseplants. Damage occurs when the aphids suck the juices from the leaves. Aphids are unable to digest all the sugar in the plant sap, and they excrete the excess in a sticky fluid called *honeydew*, which often drops onto the leaves below. Any furniture below the plant may become coated with honeydew.

Solution: Spray plants with Ortho® Rose & Flower Insect Killer, or take the plants outside and spray with Ortho® Systemic Insect Killer. Inspect new plants and keep them isolated if there are any signs of infestation. Avoid working in the outdoor garden and then on indoor plants without washing up and changing your clothing first.

Mealybugs

Citrus mealybugs on coleus (2× life size).

Long-tailed mealybugs (4× life size).

Problem: White cottony or waxy insects are on the undersides of leaves, on stems, and particularly in crotches or where leaves are attached. The insects tend to congregate, giving a cottony appearance. Cottony masses that contain eggs of the insects may also be present. A sticky substance may cover the leaves or drop onto surfaces below the plant. Sooty mold can result from the sticky substance. Infested plants are unsightly, do not grow well, and may die if severely infested.

Analysis: Mealybugs are among the more serious problems of houseplants. There are many different types of mealybugs, and these insects attack virtually all houseplants. Male mealybugs, rarely seen, are winged and can fly. Female mealybugs have soft bodies that appear to have segments and are covered with waxy secretions, giving them a cottony appearance. The female produce live young or deposit hundreds of yellow to orange eggs in white, cottony egg sacs. The young insects, called *nymphs*, crawl on the same plant or to nearby plants. Males do no damage because they don't feed and are short-lived. Female mealybugs feed by sucking sap from the plant. They take in more than they can use and excrete the excess in a sugary fluid called *honeydew*, which coats the leaves and may drop to surfaces below the plant. This fluid may mar finished furniture. (For more information on mealybugs, see page 444.)

Solution: Separate infested plants from healthy. If only a few mealybugs are present, wipe them off with cotton swabs dipped in rubbing alcohol or with a damp cloth. Spray infested plants with Ortho® Rose & Flower Insect Killer, or take them outside and spray with Ortho® Systemic Insect Killer. Repeat applications at intervals of two weeks and continue for a little while after mealybugs appear to be under control. The waxy coverings on the insects and egg sacs, and the tendency of the insects to group together, protect them from insecticides. Carefully check all parts of the plant to make sure all insects have been removed. Search for egg sacs under the rims or bottoms of pots, in cracks or on the undersides of shelves, and on brackets or hangers. Wipe off any sacs; they are a constant source of new insects. Discard severely infested plants and avoid taking cuttings from such plants. Thoroughly clean the growing area with soapy water before starting new plants. Be on a constant vigil for mealybugs and start control measures immediately if the bugs appear. Inspect new plants thoroughly before allowing them in the house.

Whiteflies

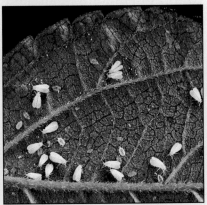

Greenhouse whiteflies (2× life size).

Problem: Tiny white-winged insects feed mainly on the undersides of leaves. Nonflying, scalelike larvae covered with white, waxy powder may also be present on the undersides of leaves. When the plant is touched, insects flutter rapidly around it. Leaves may be mottled and yellowing.

Analysis: Whitefly (*Trialeurodes vaporariorum*) is a common pest of many houseplants. The four-winged adult lays eggs on the undersides of leaves. The larvae are the size of a pinhead, flat, oval, and semitransparent. They feed for about a month before changing to the adult form. Both larval and adult forms suck sap from the leaves. The larvae are more damaging because they feed more heavily. Feeding often transmits viral diseases from plant to plant. Adults and larvae can't completely digest all the sugar in the sap, and they excrete the excess in a fluid called *honeydew*, which coats the leaves and may drop from the plant. Black, brown, or white fungal mold may grow on the honeydew. (For more information on whiteflies, see page 448.)

Solution: Remove heavily infested leaves. Vacuum plants to pick up adults. Spray plants with Ortho® Rose & Flower Insect Killer or take the plants outside and spray with Ortho® Systemic Insect Killer. Spray the foliage thoroughly, being sure to cover the upper and lower surfaces of leaves. Treat plants at night when insects are not flying. Spray weekly as long as the problem continues. Whiteflies may also be partially controlled with yellow sticky traps. Inspect new plants before putting them in the house or near other plants.

AGLAONEMA (Chinese evergreen)

Fungus gnats

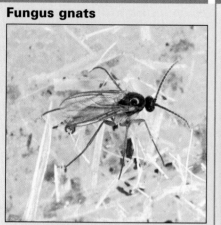

Fungus gnat.

Problem: Small (up to ⅛ inch), slender, dark insects fly slowly around when plants are disturbed. They frequently run across the foliage and soil and may also be found on windows. Grublike larvae with black heads may be seen on the soil surface near the stem of the plant. Roots may be damaged, and seedlings may die.

Analysis: Fungus gnats are small flies that do little damage but are unpleasant if present in large numbers. They lay their eggs in soil that contains organic material. After a week, the eggs hatch and the larvae crawl through the upper layer of the soil. The larvae are white, about ¼ inch long, and have black heads. They feed on fungi that grow on organic matter. The larvae usually do not damage plants but, when present in large numbers, may feed on the roots of some plants, killing seedlings. The larvae feed for about two weeks before maturing into adults. Many generations may occur per year.

Solution: Apply Ortho® Rose & Flower Insect Killer or the bacterial insecticide *Bacillus thuringiensis israelensis* according to label directions. Place yellow sticky traps in pots to catch the adults. Keep doors and windows closed to keep fungus gnats out. Water plants less often, and drain the saucer under the plant pot.

Root and stem rot

Root rot.

Problem: Plants fail to grow, and the lower leaves may turn yellow, wilt, and die. An area of dead tissue may be found on the main stem just at the soil line. Many of the roots are brown, mushy, and easily detached. (For information on inspecting roots, see page 22.) Roots and potting mix may smell of rot. Infected plants may die.

Analysis: Root and stem rot is caused by any of several soil-dwelling fungi, as well as by *water molds* (For more information on water molds, see page 419.) *Rhizoctonia solani* may attack portions of the main stem and form brown, sunken areas. The fungus may girdle the stem, causing the portion above to die. *Rhizoctonia* and *Pythium* species may attack the roots, turning them brown and mushy with dark tips. If the roots are severely damaged or killed, they can't supply the plant with adequate moisture and essential nutrients.

Solution: Drench the soil with a fungicide containing *metalaxyl*. If the plant is only mildly affected, let the soil dry out between waterings. (For more information on this technique, see page 419.) If the soil mix is heavy or the container does not drain well, transplant the plant into a container that drains freely. Trim any rotted roots. Use a soil mix that drains well. Discard severely infected plants and the soil in which they grew. Wash and disinfect the pots with a ten percent (1 part bleach to 9 parts water) chlorine bleach solution before reuse.

Mealybugs

Mealybugs.

Problem: White, oval, insects up to ¼ inch long form white, cottony masses on leaves, on stems, and in the crotches where leaves are attached. A sticky material may coat the leaves. Sooty mold may result from the sticky substance. Leaves may be spotted or deformed. When the condition is severe, leaves and plants may die.

Analysis: Several species of this common insect feed on Chinese evergreen. The immature mealybugs, called *nymphs*, crawl on the plant and onto nearby plants. Soon after they begin to feed on the plant's sap, they produce white, waxy filaments that cover their bodies, giving them a cottony appearance. As they mature, they become less mobile. Mealybugs can't digest all the sugar in the sap, and they excrete the excess in a fluid called *honeydew*, which coats the leaves and may drop onto surfaces below the plant. (For more information on mealybugs, see page 444.)

Solution: Separate infested plants from healthy ones. If only a few mealybugs are present, wipe them off with a damp cloth or with cotton swabs dipped in rubbing alcohol. Spray infested plants with Ortho® Rose & Flower Insect Killer or take them outside and spray with Ortho® Systemic Insect Killer. Repeat applications at intervals of two weeks. Inspect new plants before putting them in the house. (For information on preventing houseplant problems, see page 414.) For more information on mealybugs, see page 444.)

ARAUCARIA
(Norfolk Island pine)

Mealybugs

Mealybugs (4× life size).

Problem: White, oval insects up to ¼ inch long form white, cottony masses on needles, on stems, and in the crotches where branches are attached. A sticky material may coat the needles. Sooty mold may develop on the sticky substance. Growth may be deformed. When the condition is severe, plants may die.

Analysis: Several species of this common insect feed on Norfolk Island pine. Mealybugs damage plants by sucking sap, causing leaf distortion and death. The adult female mealybug may produce young or lay eggs in a white, fluffy mass of wax. The immature mealybugs, called *nymphs*, crawl on the plant and onto nearby plants. Soon after they begin to feed, they produce white, waxy filaments that cover their bodies, giving them a cottony appearance. As they mature, they become less mobile. Mealybugs can't digest all the sugar in the plant sap and excrete the excess in a fluid called *honeydew*, which coats the plant and may drop onto surfaces below. (For more information on mealybugs, see page 444.)

Solution: Separate infested plants from healthy ones. If only a few mealybugs are present, wipe them off with a damp cloth or cotton swabs dipped in rubbing alcohol. Spray infested plants with Ortho® Rose & Flower Insect Killer or take them outside and spray with Ortho® Systemic Insect Killer. Repeat applications at intervals of two weeks. Inspect new plants thoroughly before putting them in the house. (For information on preventing houseplant problems, see page 414.)

ASPARAGUS
(Asparagus fern)

Insufficient light

Weak stems.

Problem: Plant leaves (which are needlelike) turn pale green or yellow, beginning with the older leaves and progressing toward the tip of the stem. Yellow leaves may drop. Stems may be elongated and weak; sometimes they bend toward the light. Stems in the center of the plant may die and turn tan or brown.

Analysis: Plants use light as a source of energy and grow slowly in light that is too dim for their needs. If most available light comes from one direction, stems and leaves bend distinctly in that direction. If the light is much too dim, the plant has little energy and grows poorly. Although foliage plants generally need less light than plants grown for flowers or fruit, asparagus fern needs relatively long exposure to bright light.

Solution: Move the plants gradually to a brighter location. Asparagus fern will tolerate direct sun if it is kept well watered. If it is allowed to become dry while in direct sunlight, however, it will sunburn. (For more information on sunburn, see page 23.) If a brighter location is not available, provide supplemental lighting. If you wish to grow a houseplant in a dim location, select a plant that tolerates low light. (See the list on page 541 in the appendix.)

BEGONIA

Powdery mildew

Powdery mildew.

Problem: Powdery, white often circular patches appear on the leaves, stems, and flowers. Leaves may be covered with the powdery growth. This material usually appears first on older leaves and on the upper surfaces of leaves. Tissue under the powdery growth may turn yellow or brown. Sometimes such leaves drop from the plant.

Analysis: Powdery mildew on begonia is caused by a fungus (*Erysiphe cichoracearum*). The powdery patches on begonia are composed of fungus strands and spores. Air currents carry these spores, which are capable of infecting leaves, stems, and flowers of the same or nearby plants. The disease flourishes in dim light and during warm days with cool nights. Older leaves are more susceptible than new leaves, as are plants in dry soil. Severe infections cause yellowing, browning, and leaf drop.

Solution: Take the plant outside and spray with Ortho® RosePride® Rose & Shrub Disease Control. Remove infected leaves. Move plants to locations with more light. Keep plants out of cool drafts and in rooms with temperatures as even as possible. Do not crowd plants together.

BEGONIA (continued)

Spider mites

Spider mites.

Problem: Leaves are stippled, yellow, and dirty; they may dry out and drop. There may be webbing over flower buds, between leaves, or on the undersides of leaves. To determine if a plant is infested with mites, examine the bottoms of the leaves with a hand lens. Or hold a sheet of white paper underneath an affected plant and tap the leaves sharply. Minute specks the size of pepper grains will drop to the paper and begin to crawl. The pests are easily seen against the white background.

Analysis: Spider mites, related to spiders, are major pests of many houseplants, including begonias. They cause damage by sucking sap from the undersides of leaves. As a result of this feeding, chlorophyll disappears, causing the stippled appearance. Spider mite webbing traps cast-off skins and debris, making the plant dirty. Under warm, dry conditions, mites can build up to tremendous numbers. (For more information on spider mites, see page 457.)

Solution: Isolate infested plants from others. Take plants outside or into a shower and wash the mites off the leaves using a strong spray of water. Spray infested plants with Ortho® Rose & Flower Insect Killer or take them outside and spray with Ortho® Systemic Insect Killer. Keep air humid to help prevent infestation and proliferation. Avoid bringing mites into the house. (For information on preventing houseplant problems, see page 414.)

Whiteflies

Whiteflies (10× life size).

Problem: Tiny white-winged insects feed mainly on the undersides of leaves. Nonflying, scalelike larvae covered with white, waxy powder may also be present on the undersides of leaves. When the plant is touched, insects flutter rapidly around it. Leaves may be mottled and yellowing.

Analysis: Whitefly is a common pest of begonia. The four-winged adults lay eggs on the undersides of leaves. The larvae are the size of a pinhead, flat, oval, immobile, and semitransparent, with white, waxy filaments radiating from their bodies. They feed for about a month before changing to the adult form. The larvae are more damaging because they suck more sap from the plants than do the adults. They cannot digest all the sugar in the sap they remove, and they excrete the excess in a sugary material called *honeydew*, which coats the leaves and may drop from the plant.

Solution: Remove heavily infested leaves. Vacuum plants to pick up adults. Spray plants with Ortho® Rose & Flower Insect Killer or take the plant outside and spray with Ortho® Systemic Insect Killer. Spray the foliage thoroughly, being sure to cover the upper and lower surfaces of leaves. Treat plants at night when insects are not flying. Spray weekly as long as the problem continues. Whiteflies may also be partially controlled with yellow sticky traps. Inspect new plants before taking them into the house. (For information on preventing houseplant problems, see page 414.)

Scales

Scales (3× life size).

Problem: Stems and leaves are covered with white, cottony, cushionlike masses or brown, crusty bumps. The cottony masses do not move when touched. The bumps can be scraped or picked off easily. Leaves turn yellow and may drop. A shiny or sticky material may cover the leaves and stems.

Analysis: Several different types of scale insects attack begonias. Some types can infest many different plants. Scales hatch from eggs. The young, called *crawlers*, are small (about $\frac{1}{10}$ inch), soft-bodied, and move around on the plant and onto other plants. After moving for a short time, they insert their mouthparts into the plant, feeding on the sap. The legs disappear, and the scales remain in the same place for the rest of their lives. Some develop a soft covering, others a hard covering. Some species of scales are unable to digest all the sugar in the plant sap, and they excrete the excess in a fluid called *honeydew*, which may cover the leaves or drop onto surfaces below. (For more information on scales, see page 444 to 447.)

Solution: Isolate infested plants as soon as scales are discovered. Remove as many scales as possible with a cloth or toothbrush dipped in soapy water. Spray plants with Ortho® Rose & Flower Insect Killer or a horticultural oil labeled for use indoors, or take the plants outside and spray with Ortho® Systemic Insect Killer. Some varieties of begonia are sensitive; test the spray on a small area before spraying the entire plant. To kill newly hatched eggs, repeat weekly for four weeks. Avoid bringing scale crawlers into the house.

BRASSAIA (Schefflera)

Root and stem rot

Root rot.

Problem: Plants fail to grow. Lower leaves may turn yellow and drop. The roots are brown, soft, and mushy. Potting mix may smell of rot. When the condition is severe, no roots are found on the outside of the root ball, and plants may wilt and die. (For information on examining the root ball, see page 22.)

Analysis: Root and stem rot is caused by any of several soil-dwelling fungi (*Pythium* species) that are also known as *water molds*. (For more information on water molds, see page 419.) The fungi attack the roots, turning them brown and mushy with dark tips. The disease is usually an indication that the plant has been watered too frequently or that the soil mix is too heavy and does not drain well. The fungi are common in garden soils, but pasteurized soil or soilless potting mixes are free of them unless they are introduced on a plant or dirty pot or transferred from another pot on dirty fingers. Root rot spreads quickly through a root system if the soil remains wet for extended periods.

Solution: If the plant is only mildly affected, let the soil dry out between waterings. (For more information on this technique, see page 419.) If the soil mix is heavy or the container does not drain well, transplant the plant into a container that drains freely. Trim any rotten roots. Use a soil mix that drains well. Discard severely infected plants and the soil in which they grew. Wash and disinfect the pots before reuse.

Spider mites

Spider mite damage and webbing.

Problem: Leaves are stippled, yellow, and dirty; they may dry out and drop. There may be webbing between leaves or on the undersides of leaves. To determine if a plant is infested with mites, examine the bottoms of the leaves with a hand lens. Or hold a sheet of white paper underneath an affected plant and tap the leaves sharply. Minute specks the size of pepper grains will drop to the paper and begin to crawl. The pests are easily seen against the white background.

Analysis: Spider mites, related to spiders, are major pests of many houseplants, including schefflera. They cause damage by sucking sap from the undersides of leaves. As a result of their feeding, chlorophyll disappears, causing the stippled appearance. Spider mite webbing traps cast-off skins and debris, making the plant dirty. Under warm, dry conditions, mites can build up to tremendous numbers. (For more information on spider mites, see page 457.)

Solution: Isolate infested plants from others. Take plants outside or into a shower and wash the mites off the leaves using a strong spray of water. Spray infested plants with Ortho® Rose & Flower Insect Killer or take them outside and spray with Ortho® Systemic Insect Killer. Keep air humid to help prevent infestation and proliferation. Avoid bringing mites into the house. (For information on preventing houseplant problems, see page 414.)

BROMELIADS

Heavy soil

Overwatering damage.

Problem: Plants fail to grow. Root development is poor, and roots may rot. The whole plant can be lifted easily from the soil. The plant may die.

Analysis: Most bromeliads grown as houseplants are epiphytes (plants that grow on other plants instead of in the ground). Because of this, their roots are usually exposed to the air and can't tolerate wet conditions for very long. If bromeliads are planted in heavy soil or in soil that is too wet, water fills the spaces between the soil particles so that the roots can't get enough air, which could cause the plant to die.

Solution: Grow most bromeliads only in a planting mix that has exceptional drainage—such as coarse bark, lava rock, or osmunda fiber—or in a mix designed for orchids and epiphytic plants. Prune out rotted roots and repot damaged plants into a smaller pot until roots regrow. Water the plants lightly every day until the roots are established. After that, water one or two times per week.

BROMELIADS *(continued)*

CACTUS

Dieback

Bromeliad dieback.

Problem: Growth on main plant ceases after the plant flowers, although new shoots (pups) sprout from the base. The flower stalk may remain green for up to several months, but eventually it dries up. Bottom leaves begin to turn brown and shrivel, starting at the tips. Eventually the center leaves of the rosette also turn brown until the plant is entirely dead. Pups continue to grow while the main stalk dies back. This entire process can take a year or more.

Analysis: Bromeliads die after blooming. Most stay in apparent good health for several months to more than a year, until pups appear. As pups become big enough to survive on their own, the mother plant slowly dies. Dieback is part of the normal growth cycle.

Solution: Once a bromeliad has flowered, nothing can prevent dieback. After the pups have attained about one-third the size of the mother plant, they can be cut away and potted up on their own. Once they have reached adult size (depending on the species, this can take from nine months to several years), they in turn bloom, and the cycle begins anew. If a mother plant still shows some green growth when the first generation of pups is removed, it may produce another series before dying.

Bacterial soft rot

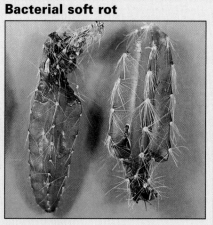

Bacterial soft rot.

Problem: Soft, mushy, circular areas appear on the stems. As these areas enlarge, they become sunken and the tissues die. These cavities are frequently surrounded by tissue that appears to be water-soaked. Rotted tissue may develop an unpleasant odor. The whole stem may rot, and the plant may die.

Analysis: Bacterial soft rot is caused by any of several bacteria species (*Erwinia*) that enter the cactus through a wound under wet conditions. Once established, the bacteria produce materials that dissolve the layers between the cells. As the cells die, liquids are released from them, producing a soft, mushy rot. At high temperatures, the bacteria move through the tissue rapidly. The dead tissue dries, producing sunken cavities. The bacteria may invade the whole stem and kill the plant.

Solution: Cut out the diseased area with a knife. Remove at least ½ inch of healthy-looking tissue around the diseased spot. Disinfect pruning tools between cuts. The operation disfigures the plant, but the cactus may live and produce new portions that can be used to propagate more plants. Avoid getting the plants wet. Keep them separated enough for good air circulation to keep them dry. If only the upper portion of the plant remains healthy, it may be possible to graft or reroot the plant.

Scab

Scab.

Problem: Irregular brown, corky, or leathery areas develop on the stems, usually at the base. These areas may continue to enlarge until much of the plant is covered. When these areas develop on younger tissue, they may cause sunken areas and deformities on the stem.

Analysis: The cause of scab on cacti is generally unknown, although the disease sometimes results from spider mite damage. It seems to be most prevalent on plants subjected to high humidity and low light. It sometimes appears to spread, however, which suggests that it may be infectious.

Solution: Grow cacti under conditions that are as close to ideal as possible, with adequate light and dry air and soil. Discard severely affected plants, and do not propagate from them. Isolate mildly affected plants. (For more information on spider mites see page 457.)

CHLOROPHYTUM (Spider plant)

Dead leaf tips

Tip burn.

Salt damage.

Problem: The tips of leaves turn brown or tan. The damaged area develops slowly along the leaf. Older leaves are most severely affected.

Analysis: Spider plant leaf tips die for several reasons. Frequently the problem has a combination of causes.

Solution: Remove dead tips by trimming the leaves to a point with a pair of scissors. The numbered solutions below correspond to the numbered items in the analysis.

1. Salt damage: Salts from irrigation water or from fertilizer accumulate in the soil. Excess salts are carried to the leaves and deposited in the tips of pointed leaves such as those on spider plants. When enough salts accumulate there, the leaf tip dies. Salts are taken into the plant more rapidly when the soil is dry.

1. Leach excess salts from the soil by flushing with water. Water the plant at least three times, letting the water drain through each time. This is done most easily in a bathtub, laundry sink, or outside. Always water spider plants from the top of the pot. Add enough water each time so that some drains through the pot. Empty the saucer under the pot after the water has drained. If the plant is too large to handle easily, use a turkey baster to remove the drainage water. (For more information on watering, see page 22.) Do not overfertilize. Repot into fresh soil mix if salts have accumulated on the pot.

2. Plant too dry: The leaf tip, being farthest from the roots, is the first part of the leaf to die when the plant does not get enough water.

2. Water the plant regularly. (For information on watering, see page 22.)

3. Toxic salts: Some chemicals, usually in the form of soluble salts, are damaging in very small amounts. They accumulate in leaf tips as other salts do, killing the tissue there. The most common of these chemicals are fluoride, chloride, and borate.

3. You can't do much about traces of toxic chemicals in the water, except to find another source of water. Distilled or deionized water is always free of chemicals.

CISSUS (Grape ivy)

Salt damage

Salt damage.

Problem: Margins of older leaves die and turn brown and brittle. In severe cases, all leaves may have dead margins. Tissues adjacent to the dead margins of older leaves may turn yellow. New leaves may be distorted. White to yellowish mineral salts may accumulate on pot edges and on the lower part of plant stems.

Analysis: Grape ivy and kangaroo ivy are sensitive to excess salts. Soluble salts are picked up by the roots and accumulate in the leaf margins, where concentrations may become high enough to kill the tissues. Salts can accumulate from water or from the use of fertilizers, or they may be present in the soils used in potting. Salts accumulate more rapidly and do more harm if the plant is not watered thoroughly and is allowed to become excessively dry between waterings.

Solution: Leach excess salts from the soil by flushing with water. Water the plant at least three times, letting the water drain each time. This is done most easily in a bathtub, laundry sink, or outside. It is usually best to water grape ivy and kangaroo ivy from the top of the pot. Enough water should be added at each watering so that some drains through the pot. Empty the saucer under the pot after the water has drained. If the plant is too large to handle easily, use a turkey baster to remove the drainage water. (For information on watering, see page 22.) Do not overfertilize. If salts have accumulated on the pot, repot into fresh soil mix.

CITRUS

Scales

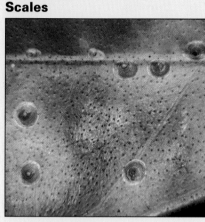

Scales (3× life size).

Yellowing leaves

Yellowing caused by nitrogen deficiency.

Iron-deficient leaves.

Problem: Stems and leaves are covered with white, cottony, cushionlike masses or brown, crusty bumps. The cottony masses do not move when touched. The bumps can be scraped or picked off easily. Leaves turn yellow and drop. A shiny or sticky material may cover the leaves and stems. Sooty mold may develop on the sticky substance.

Analysis: Several different types of scale insects attack citrus plants. Some types can infest many different plants. Scales hatch from eggs. The young, called *crawlers*, are small (about ⅒ inch), soft-bodied, and move about on the plant and onto other plants. After moving around for a short time, they insert their mouthparts into the plant, feeding on the sap. The legs disappear, and the scales remain in the same place for the rest of their lives. Some develop a soft covering, others a hard covering. Some species of scales are unable to digest all the sugar in the plant sap, and they excrete the excess in a fluid called *honeydew*, which may cover the leaves or drop onto surfaces below. (For more information on scales, see pages 444 to 447.)

Solution: Isolate infested plants as soon as scales are discovered. Remove as many scales as possible with a cloth or toothbrush dipped in soapy water. Spray plants with Ortho® Rose & Flower Insect Killer or a horticultural oil labeled for use indoors, or take the plant outside and spray with Ortho® Systemic Insect Killer. To kill newly hatched eggs, repeat the treatment weekly for four weeks. Check plants for scales before bringing them into the house. (For information on houseplant problems, see page 414.)

Problem: Older (lower) leaves start turning yellow at the margins; yellowing progresses inward on the leaves and upward on the plant. Older leaves may drop, and the plant may wilt. Or yellowing may start on new growth, with the leaf margins losing their green color first and the areas surrounding the veins losing their color last.

Analysis: Yellow leaves on citrus may be caused by any of several factors.

Solution: The numbered solutions below correspond to the numbered items in the analysis.

1. If the older leaves turn yellow but the new leaves remain green, the problem is probably nitrogen deficiency. Nitrogen is an essential plant nutrient. If it is deficient, the plant will withdraw nitrogen from the old leaves for the sake of the new growth. (For more information on nitrogen deficiency, see page 23.)

1. For a quick response, spray the leaves with a chelated iron fertilizer. Feed citrus plants regularly with a balanced fertilizer.

2. Yellowing of older leaves may be associated with root rot, a plant disease caused by any of several fungi, some of which are known as *water molds*. Examine the root system as explained on page 22. If the roots are brown, dead, and soft, without white tips, root rot is the problem. Rotted roots are unable to absorb nutrients and water needed by the plant. (For more information on water molds, see page 419.)

2. Avoid excess watering of soil in which citrus is growing. (For information on watering, see page 22.) Plant citrus in soil mix that drains well.

3. If only the new leaves are yellow, the plant is probably deficient in iron. This condition is caused by alkaline soil. In alkaline soil, iron is less available to the plant, and some plants cannot absorb all the iron they need. (For more information on acid and alkaline soils, see page 407.)

3. Fertilize citrus with a chelated iron fertilizer. Treat the soil with ferrous sulfate to increase acidity. In the future, fertilize with Miracid Plant Food to maintain soil acidity.

CODIAEUM (Croton)

Mealybugs

Mealybugs.

Problem: White, oval insects up to ¼ inch long form white, cottony masses on leaves, stems, and in the crotches where branches or leaves are attached. A sticky material may coat the leaves. Mold may grow on the sticky material. Leaves may be spotted or deformed. The plant may weaken and die.

Analysis: Several species of this common insect feed on croton. Mealybugs damage plants by sucking sap, causing leaf distortion and death. The adult female mealybug may produce young or lay eggs in a white, fluffy mass of wax. The immature mealybugs, called *nymphs*, crawl on the plant and onto nearby plants. Soon after they begin to feed, they produce white, waxy filaments that cover their bodies, giving them a cottony appearance. As they mature, they become less mobile. Mealybugs can't digest all the sugar in the sap, and they excrete the excess in a fluid called *honeydew*, which coats the leaves and may drop onto surfaces below the plant. (For more information on mealybugs, see page 25.)

Solution: Separate infested plants from healthy ones. If only a few mealybugs are present, wipe them off with a damp cloth or with cotton swabs dipped in rubbing alcohol. Spray infested plants with Ortho® Rose & Flower Insect Killer or take them outside and spray with Ortho® Systemic Insect Killer. Repeat applications at intervals of two weeks. Inspect new plants thoroughly before putting them in the house. (For information on preventing houseplant problems, see page 414.)

Mite damage

Mite damage.

Problem: Leaves are stippled, yellow, and dirty. Leaves may dry out and drop. There may be webbing between leaves or on the undersides of leaves. To determine if a plant is infested with mites, examine the bottoms of the leaves with a hand lens. Or hold a sheet of white paper underneath an affected leaf and tap the leaf sharply. Minute specks the size of pepper grains will drop to the paper and begin to crawl. The pests are easily seen against the white background.

Analysis: Spider mites, related to spiders, are major pests of many houseplants, including croton. They cause damage by sucking sap from the undersides of leaves. As a result of their feeding, chlorophyll disappears, producing the stippled appearance. Spider mite webbing traps cast-off skins and debris, making the plant dirty. Under warm, dry conditions, mites can build up to tremendous numbers. (For more information on spider mites, see page 457.)

Solution: Isolate infested plants from others. Take plants outside or into a shower and wash the mites off the leaves using a strong spray of water. Spray infested plants with Ortho® Rose & Flower Insect Killer or take them outside and spray with Ortho® Systemic Insect Killer. Keep air humid to help prevent infestation and proliferation. Avoid bringing mites into the house. (For information on preventing houseplant problems, see page 414.)

Insufficient light

New green leaves.

Problem: New leaves are green instead of brightly colored. Stems may be thin and bend toward a light source. Lower leaves may drop.

Analysis: Plants use light as a source of energy and grow slowly in light that is too dim for their needs. If most available light comes from one direction, stems and leaves are bent in that direction. Leaves remain green, without bright colors.

Solution: Move the plants gradually to a brighter location. A lightly curtained, sunny window is ideal. If a brighter location is not available, provide supplemental lighting. Crotons may be grown outside in the summer. When moving them outdoors, place the plants in light shade for at least a week before putting them in full sun. If you wish to grow a houseplant in a dim location, select a plant that tolerates low light from the list on page 541.

CORDYLINE (Ti)

Salt damage

Salt damage.

Problem: Tips of older leaves die and turn brown and brittle. This condition progresses down the margins of the leaves. In severe cases, all leaves may have dead tips and margins. Tissues adjacent to the dead margins may turn yellow. White to yellowish mineral salts may accumulate on pot edges and on the lower part of plant stems.

Analysis: Cordylines are very sensitive to excess salts. Soluble salts are picked up by the roots and accumulate in the leaf tips, where concentrations may become high enough to kill the tissues. Salts can accumulate from water or from the use of fertilizers, or they may be present in the soil used in potting. Salts accumulate more rapidly and do more harm if the plant is not watered thoroughly.

Solution: Leach excess salts from the soil by flushing with water. Water the plant at least three times, letting the water drain through each time. This is done most easily in a bathtub, laundry sink, or outside. Enough water should be added at each watering so that some drains through the pot. Empty the saucer under the pot after the water drains. If the plant is too large to handle easily, use a turkey baster to remove the drainage water. (For information on watering, see page 22.) If salts have accumulated on the pot, replant into fresh soil mix. Do not overfertilize.

CRASSULA (Jade)

Root rot

Root rot.

Problem: The leaves and stems darken and turn soft and mushy, beginning with the lower leaves and stems. Leaves drop from the plant. Potting mix may smell of rot. Examination of the root ball reveals roots that appear brown and mushy. When the disease is severe, all the roots are rotted and the plant can be lifted easily from the soil. (For information on inspecting roots, see page 22.)

Analysis: Any of several fungi species (*Pythium*) favored by wet soil cause this plant disease. These fungi decay plant roots. If the roots are severely damaged or killed, they cannot supply the plant with moisture and nutrients. The disease is an indication that the plant has been watered too frequently or that the soil mix is too heavy and does not drain well.

Solution: Remove the plant from the pot and shake most of the soil from the roots. Let the plant dry for one or two days or until the mushy leaves and stems have dried. When repotting, trim rotted roots. Repot the plant in a light soil mix that drains well. Don't water until the soil is almost dry.

CYCLAMEN

High temperatures

Damage from high temperatures.

Problem: Outer leaves turn yellow. Leaves may die and turn brown, and their stems become soft. Plants stop flowering, eventually lose their leaves, and go dormant.

Analysis: Although cyclamen are cool-weather plants, they tolerate warm days as long as they have cool nights (below 55°F). Cool temperatures initiate flower buds. Constant high temperatures inhibit flower buds, and plants stop flowering. Warm temperatures also prevent the plant from growing well, causing leaves to lose their green color and die. Most cyclamens naturally go dormant during the summer months.

Solution: Grow cyclamen plants in a cool room with as much light as possible. If a cool room is not available, put them near a window at night. If temperatures are not below freezing, put the plants outside at night. Under alternating temperatures, they will flower for long periods. Keep plants adequately watered and fertilized. If cyclamen do go dormant, keep them dry and store them in darkness until cool fall temperatures return, then water lightly until growth begins.

Cyclamen mite

Cyclamen mite damage.

Problem: Leaves become curled, wrinkled, and cupped in scattered areas. New leaves may be more severely affected, remain very small, have a bronze discoloration, and be misshapen. Flower buds are distorted and may drop or fail to open.

Analysis: Cyclamen mite (*Steneotarsonemus pallidus*), related to spiders, are too small to be seen with the naked eye. These mites attack several houseplants and can be very damaging on cyclamen. Their feeding injures the plant tissues, causing the leaves and flower buds to be malformed and stunted. Cyclamen mites infest new growth most heavily but will crawl to other parts of the plant or to other plants. They reproduce rapidly.

Solution: Spray plants with Ortho® Rose & Flower Insect Killer or a miticide containing *hexakis* that is labeled for use indoors, or take plants outside and spray with Ortho® Systemic Insect Killer. Repeat every two weeks until new growth is no longer affected. Discard severely infested plants. Houseplants showing cyclamen mite damage should be isolated from other plants until the mites are under control. Nearby plants should be observed closely so that they can be sprayed if symptoms appear. Avoid touching leaves of infested plants and then other plants. Don't work in the garden and then on indoor plants without washing up and changing clothes in between.

Insufficient light

Spindly growth.

Problem: Lower leaves turn yellow, starting at the margins. These leaves may wilt, die, and turn light brown. Dead leaves hang down and remain attached to the stem. This condition may progress up the stem until only a few green leaves are left at the top of the plant. Plants may become weak, and the remaining leaves may face toward the light.

Analysis: Plants use light as a source of energy and grow slowly in light that is too dim for their needs. If most available light comes from one direction, the stems and leaves are bent in that direction. If the light is much too dim, the plant has little energy and grows poorly. Foliage plants generally need less light than plants grown for their flowers or fruit. Dieffenbachia is adaptable to varying amounts of light from relatively bright to relatively dim.

Solution: Move the plants gradually to a brighter location. If it is allowed to become dry while in direct sunlight, it will sunburn. (For information on sunburn, see page 23.) If a brighter location is not available, provide supplemental lighting. If you wish to grow a houseplant in a dim location, select a plant that tolerates low light from the list on page 541. If your dieffenbachia has lost most of its lower leaves, reroot the top, cutting the stem back to two nodes. The stem will resprout.

Sunburn

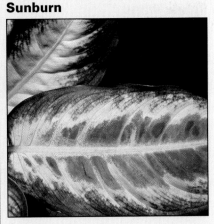

Sunburn.

Problem: Areas between the veins near the margins of older leaves turn yellow and then tan or light brown. Very light green or white tissues of variegated varieties turn brown between the veins. The plant has recently been in a bright location.

Analysis: Leaf tissue deficient in chlorophyll is very susceptible to sunburn, so if variegated dieffenbachias are grown in direct sunlight or in very bright light, they may sunburn. Leaves on plants that dry out are also susceptible to sunburn. Older leaves are the first to be affected by sunburn when a plant dries out.

Solution: Grow variegated dieffenbachias that have white areas in filtered light. Try not to let dieffenbachias dry out. (For information on watering, see page 22.) Avoid moving plants directly from very dim light to very bright light.

35

DIEFFENBACHIA (Dumb cane) *(continued)*

Spider mites

Spider mite damage.

Problem: Leaves are stippled, yellow, and dirty; they may dry out and drop. There may be webbing between leaves or on the undersides of leaves. To determine if a plant is infested with mites, examine the bottoms of the leaves with a hand lens. Or hold a sheet of white paper underneath an affected plant and tap the leaves sharply. Minute specks the size of pepper grains will drop to the paper and begin to crawl. Mites are easily seen against the white background.

Analysis: Spider mites, related to spiders, are major pests of many houseplants, including dieffenbachia. They cause damage by sucking sap from the undersides of leaves. As a result of their feeding, chlorophyll disappears, causing the stippled appearance. Spider mite webbing traps cast-off skins and debris, making the plant dirty. Under warm, dry conditions, mites can build up to tremendous numbers. (For more information on spider mites, see page 457.)

Solution: Isolate infested plants from others. Take plants outside or into a shower and wash the mites off the leaves using a strong spray of water. Spray infested plants with Ortho® Rose & Flower Insect Killer or take them outside and spray with Ortho® Systemic Insect Killer. Keep air humid to help prevent infestation and proliferation. Avoid bringing mites into the house. (For information on preventing houseplant problems, see page 414.)

Bacterial leaf spot

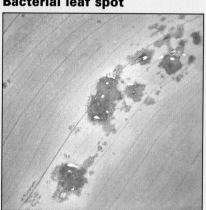

Bacterial leaf spot.

Problem: Small yellow spots with translucent centers appear on the leaves. The spots may enlarge to ¼ inch in diameter and may become orange with clear centers. Under humid conditions, glistening mounds of bacteria may appear, first on the undersides and then on the upper sides of the spots. The spots may merge and cover large areas. The spots are sometimes angular, because they are bounded by the veins. If the spots are numerous, leaves have a speckled appearance. Infected leaves may turn yellow, wilt, and die.

Analysis: Bacterial leaf spot is caused by a bacterium (*Xanthomonas dieffenbachiae*). Under humid conditions, the bacteria gain entrance through wounds or natural openings in the leaves of dieffenbachia. Inside the leaf, the bacteria rot the tissue, causing the spots. Under very humid conditions, so many bacteria may be produced that they ooze out of the tissue in a mass. If numerous infections occur, the leaf dies.

Solution: Once leaves are infected, the spots already formed can't be controlled. Prevent spread of the disease to other portions of the leaf or to other plants by keeping the leaves dry. Do not mist the plants. Keep the plants in a room where condensation does not form on the leaves. Remove and destroy severely infected leaves. Avoid purchasing plants that show any of these symptoms.

Salt damage

Salt damage.

Problem: Tips of older leaves turn brown and brittle and die. Brownish spots and streaks may appear in both young and old leaves. White to yellowish mineral salts may accumulate on pot edges and on the lower part of plant stems.

Analysis: Dieffenbachia is sensitive to excess salts. Soluble salts that are absorbed by the roots accumulate in the leaves, where concentrations become high enough to kill the tissues. Salts can accumulate from the use of fertilizers, or they may be present in the soil used in potting. In some cases, chloride and other damaging salts may be present in tap water. An acidic soil mix (below pH 5.5) will increase the amount of spotting caused by some of these salts. Salts accumulate more rapidly and do more harm if the plant is not watered thoroughly.

Solution: Leach excess salts from the soil by flushing with water. Do this at least three times in a row, letting the water drain through each time. This is done most easily in a bathtub, laundry sink, or outside. As part of normal care, it is usually best to water dieffenbachia from the top of the pot. Enough water should be added at each watering so that some drains through the pot. Empty the saucer under the pot after the water drains. If the plant is too large to handle easily, use a turkey baster to remove the drainage water. Check the soil pH, and if the soil is too acidic, raise the pH to 6.0 to 7.0 by adding a mixture of ground dolomitic limestone in lukewarm water (about 2 table-spoons per quart) to the potting soil. Water thoroughly afterward. Recheck the pH after two to three weeks.

DRACAENA

Fusarium

Fusarium leaf spot.

Problem: Circular, reddish brown spots appear on the leaves. The spots are surrounded by a yellow margin. Several spots may join to form blotches. Badly spotted leaves may turn yellow and die.

Analysis: Fusarium leaf spot is caused by a fungus (*Fusarium moniliforme*). Fungal spores are spread from plant to plant by splashing water. The spores germinate on a wet leaf surface within a matter of hours, causing a new spot. In most cases, spotting is unsightly but not harmful. If spotting is severe, however, the leaf may weaken and die.

Solution: Clip off badly spotted leaves. Keep the foliage dry to prevent spread of the fungus. If spotting continues, spray the plants with Ortho® Garden Disease Control. Select resistant varieties.

Spider mites

Spider mite damage.

Problem: Leaves are stippled, yellow, and dirty; they may dry out and drop. There may be webbing between leaves or on the undersides of leaves. To determine if a plant is infested with mites, examine the bottoms of the leaves with a hand lens. Or hold a sheet of white paper underneath an affected plant and tap the leaves sharply. Minute specks the size of pepper grains will drop to the paper and begin to crawl. Mites are easily seen against the white background.

Analysis: Spider mites, related to spiders, are major pests of many houseplants, including dracaena. They cause damage by sucking sap from the undersides of leaves. As a result of their feeding, chlorophyll disappears, causing the stippled appearance. Spider mite webbing traps cast-off skins and debris, making the plant dirty. Under warm, dry conditions, mites can build up to tremendous numbers. (For more information on spider mites, see page 457.)

Solution: Isolate infested plants from others. Take plants outside or into a shower and wash the mites off the leaves using a strong spray of water. Spray infested plants with Ortho® Rose & Flower Insect Killer or take them outside and spray with Ortho® Systemic Insect Killer. Keep air humid to help prevent infestation and proliferation. Avoid bringing mites into the house. (For information on preventing houseplant problems, see page 414.)

Salt damage

Salt damage.

Problem: Tips of older leaves die and turn brown and brittle. In severe cases, tips of new leaves may be dead and brown. Tissues adjacent to the dead tips on older leaves may be yellow. White to yellowish mineral salts may accumulate on pot edges and on the lower part of plant stems.

Analysis: Dracaena is very sensitive to excess salts. Soluble salts are picked up by the roots and accumulate in the leaf tips, where concentrations become high enough to kill the tissues. Salts can accumulate from water or from the use of fertilizers, or they may be present in the soil used in potting. Salts accumulate more rapidly and do more harm if the plant is not watered thoroughly.

Solution: Leach excess salts from the soil by flushing with water. Water the plant at least three times, letting the water drain each time. This is done most easily in a bathtub, laundry sink, or outside. It is usually best to water dracaena from the top of the pot. Enough water should be added at each watering so that some drains through the pot. Empty the saucer under the pot after the water drains. If the plant is too large to handle easily, use a turkey baster to remove the drainage water. If salts have accumulated on the pot, replant into fresh potting mix. (For information on watering, see page 22.) Trim dead tips to a point with a pair of scissors. Do not overfertilize.

EUPHORBIA (Poinsettia)

Leaf drop

Leaf drop.

Problem: Lower leaves turn yellow and drop. The leaf dropping may progress up the stem until only the colored bracts are left on the plant.

Analysis: Leaf drop on poinsettias may be caused by any of several factors.
1. Root rot. When root rot kills the roots, the top of the plant may not get water.
2. Inadequate or irregular watering.
3. Too much water. Even in the absence of disease-producing organisms, too much water results in lack of air to the roots, causing leaf drop.
4. Insufficient light.

Solution: The numbered solutions below correspond to the numbered items in the analysis.
1. Root rot caused by overwatering is discussed on page 22.
2. and **3.** Keep plants adequately watered, as discussed on page 22.
4. Give poinsettia plants as much light as possible. Grow them in a sunny window. Supplemental light may be desirable.

Failure to bloom

Failure to bloom.

Problem: Plants continue to produce new leaves but fail to produce flower heads.

Analysis: Poinsettias form flower buds in the fall when the days are less than 12 hours long. For flower buds to be produced, the plants need to be kept in total darkness for at least 13 hours per day for seven weeks. If this does not occur, the plants will continue to grow and produce new leaves but no flower heads.

Solution: In the fall, place poinsettias in a sunny window in a room that is not lit at night. If no such room is available, place the poinsettias in a dark closet at night. Leave them in the closet overnight for at least 13 hours. Make sure that the plants are not exposed to any light during that time. During the day, place plants where they will receive direct sunlight. If you want flowers by Christmas, this process is best begun by September 15 and must begin no later than October 1. During the summer, you can grow poinsettias outside. To prevent sunburn, place them in partial shade for at least two days before moving them into direct sun. If poinsettia stems are weak and long, prune them back in July or August.

FERN

Low humidity

Dieback caused by low humidity.

Problem: Leaves turn yellow and eventually die. Fronds may die from the tips down. The center, tender parts of the plant are more likely to be severely affected than are the outer portions.

Analysis: Most ferns need higher humidity than homes provide. The ferns used as houseplants are adapted to forest floors and creeksides, where the air is usually moist. In the winter, when homes are heated, the air can become especially dry, particularly near heater vents or radiators. The problem is made more severe if the soil in which the fern is growing is allowed to dry out.

Solution: Move the fern to a more humid location, such as a well-lighted bathroom. Place several plants together, and keep them away from drafts. Misting does not help relieve stress on the fern; it dampens the fronds for only a few minutes at a time. Placing the plant in a tray of gravel in which some water is kept raises the humidity around the plant only if the damp air is not allowed to escape. If air moves freely around the plant, the practice is of little value. A portable humidifier raises the humidity in the immediate vicinity. Plant ferns in a potting mix that drains quickly and contains a high proportion of organic material, such as peat moss or ground bark. Never allow the potting mix to dry out.

Salt damage

Salt damage.

Problem: Margins of older leaves die and turn brown, beginning at the base of the fronds and progressing outward. In severe cases, all fronds may have dead margins. Tissues adjacent to the dead margins of older fronds may turn yellow. White to yellowish mineral salts may accumulate on pot edges and on the lower part of plant stems.

Analysis: Ferns are sensitive to excess salts. Soluble salts are picked up by the roots and accumulate in the leaf margins, where concentrations may become high enough to kill the tissues. Salts accumulate from water or from the use of fertilizers, or they may be present in the soil used in potting. Salts accumulate more rapidly and do more harm if the plant is not watered thoroughly.

Solution: Leach excess salts from the soil by flushing with water. Water the plant at least three times, letting the water drain each time. This is done most easily in a bathtub, in a laundry sink, or outside. It is usually best to water ferns from the top of the pot. Enough water should be added at each watering so that some drains through the pot. Empty the saucer under the pot after the water drains. If the plant is too large to handle easily, use a turkey baster to remove the drainage water. (For information on watering, see page 22.) If salts have accumulated in the pot, replant into fresh soil mix. Do not overfertilize.

Insufficient light

Insufficient light.

Problem: The plant grows slowly or stops growing entirely. More fronds grow from the side of the pot nearest the light source. Some of the fronds may turn yellow or brown and die, beginning with the older leaflets and progressing toward the tip of the frond. Fronds may be weak and spindly.

Analysis: Ferns use light as a source of energy and grow slowly in dim light. If most available light comes from one direction, the fronds grow mainly from that side. If the light is much too dim, the plant cannot support healthy, vigorous growth. Although foliage plants generally need less light than plants grown for their flowers or fruit, many ferns need relatively long exposure to bright light for best growth.

Solution: Move the plants gradually to a brighter location, such as a lightly curtained sunny window. If a bright location is not available, provide supplemental lighting. If you wish to grow a houseplant in a low location, select a plant that tolerates dim light from the list on page 541.

Scales

Florida wax scale (2× life size).

Problem: Stems and leaves are covered with white, cottony, cushionlike masses or brown, crusty bumps. The bumps can be scraped or picked off easily. Leaves turn yellow and may drop. A shiny or sticky material may cover the leaves and stems. Black sooty mold may develop on the sticky substance.

Analysis: Several types of scale insects attack ficus. Some types can infest many different plants. Scales hatch from eggs. The young, called *crawlers*, are small (about $\frac{1}{10}$ inch), soft-bodied, and move around on the plant and onto other plants. After moving about for a short time, they insert their mouthparts into the plant, feeding on the sap. The legs disappear, and the scales remain in the same place for the rest of their lives. Some develop a soft covering, others a hard covering. Some species of scales are unable to digest fully all the sugar in the plant sap, and they excrete the excess in a fluid called *honeydew*, which may cover the leaves or drop onto surfaces below. For more information on scales, see pages 444–447.

Solution: Isolate infested plants as soon as scales are discovered. Remove as many scales as possible with a cloth or toothbrush dipped in soapy water. Spray plants with Ortho® Rose & Flower Insect Killer or a horticultural oil labeled for use indoors, or take the plants outside and spray with Ortho® Systemic Insect Killer. To kill newly hatched eggs, repeat the treatment weekly for four weeks. Inspect new plants to avoid bringing scale crawlers into the house. (For information on preventing houseplant problems, see page 414.)

FICUS (Ornamental fig) *(continued)*

Leaf drop

Leaf drop.

Yellow leaves.

Problem: Leaves of weeping fig drop. This may cause defoliation of many branches or, in severe cases, the entire plant. Dropping leaves may be green and healthy looking or yellow and discolored.

Analysis: Weeping ornamental figs may drop their leaves in response to any of the following conditions.

1. Overwatering: When plants are watered too frequently or soil drainage is poor, the roots are susceptible to root-rotting fungi. Weak and decaying roots can't provide enough water and nutrients for proper plant growth.

2. Underwatering: Ornamental figs need constantly moist soil. If plants are not watered frequently enough or if the soil is not thoroughly soaked at each irrigation, the plants respond by dropping their leaves.

3. Insufficient light: The plants need bright indirect light or direct sunlight for best growth. They may drop their leaves even in locations that are bright enough for most other foliage plants.

4. Transplant shock: Transplanting always results in some disturbance to the root ball. Plants are likely to drop some leaves even when the disturbance to roots is minimal.

5. Changes in environment: Drafts and extreme fluctuations in temperature, light levels, and watering patterns are likely to cause leaf drop. When a greenhouse-grown plant is brought into a drier, darker, cooler home environment, it often responds to the change by dropping many of its leaves.

Solution: Solutions below correspond to the numbered items in the analysis.

1. Allow the plant to dry out slightly between waterings. The soil just beneath the surface should be moist but not wet when you water. Empty the saucer under the pot after the water drains. If the pot does not drain well, transplant to a pot with a good drainage hole, and use a light soil mix that drains well.

2. Check the soil periodically. Water when the soil just below the surface is still moist but is no longer wet.

3. Move plants to a location in direct sunlight or bright indirect light. If the plants have been growing in a dark area, first move them for two weeks to a location that receives bright indirect light or only one to two hours of morning sun; then place them in direct sunlight.

4. Transplant carefully, to avoid disturbing the root ball. Some leaf drop after transplanting is normal. The plant will stop dropping leaves after a few weeks if given proper care.

5. Avoid drafty areas and sudden environmental changes. Place new plants where conditions are as similar as possible to those from which they came. Some leaf drop is normal for a few weeks until the plant becomes acclimated.

HEDERA (Ivy)

Sunburn

Sunburn.

Problem: Pale green to yellow blotches appear between the leaf veins. These blotches may become bleached white or tan as the tissue between the veins dies. Whole sections between veins may be affected. Spots may merge, affecting larger areas.

Analysis: Excessive sunlight causes chlorophyll to disappear in ivy leaves. This happens most often when the plant has dried out. Once the tissues have lost their chlorophyll, the sunlight kills the tissues between the veins. The underlying color of different ivy species determines the color of the dead tissues. Plants moved from inside to direct sunlight sunburn severely.

Solution: Keep ivy plants moist and don't allow them to dry out, particularly if they are in direct sunlight. If you are moving plants from inside to outside, place them in the shade for several days before putting them in direct sunlight.

Edema

Edema.

Problem: Small (³⁄₁₆-inch) yellow or red to black spots appear on the upper surfaces of leaves. On the undersides of these spots are raised corky areas that first appear light green and water-soaked. Eventually they become dark brown or black. In severe cases, leaves may become yellow.

Analysis: Edema is a condition found on many plants. It is not infectious but, instead, results from unfavorable environmental factors. Excessive watering during periods of high humidity is believed to cause edema, but it occasionally occurs with low humidity and on plants that have been kept dry. (For more information on edema, see page 430.)

Solution: Grow ivy with adequate moisture and fertilizer. Keep plants in a well-lit site. Avoid keeping soil too wet or too dry. (For information on watering, see page 22.) Avoid overcrowding plants.

MONSTERA (Split-leaf philodendron)

Insufficient light

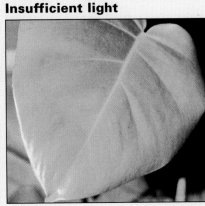

Failure to split.

Problem: New leaves do not grow as large as older leaves, are darker green, and have fewer or no splits in them. The stem is elongated, with more space between the new leaves. Leaves turn toward the light. Older leaves may turn yellow.

Analysis: Split-leaf philodendrons need a lot of light to grow correctly. The large split leaves for which they are known are the mature form of the plant. In dim locations, the plant reverts to an immature form, which has smaller leaves that do not split.

Solution: Provide enough light so that normal splitting of the leaves occurs. If leaves do not split, move the plant gradually to a brighter area. Although the plant will tolerate reduced levels of light, split-leaf philodendrons grow best in a curtained window that faces south, east, or west.

ORCHIDS

Insufficient light

Failure to bloom.

Problem: Plants do not bloom. Leaves are a deep green.

Analysis: Plants use light as a source of energy and will not bloom unless they have more than enough light to fulfill their needs for growth. Although orchids are adapted to blooming in shaded locations, they still need relatively bright light to blossom compared with houseplants grown for their foliage.

Solution: Move the plants gradually to a brighter location, but do not put them in direct sun. If the light is too bright, the leaves will turn yellow and burn. A lightly curtained window that receives more than four hours of sun per day is an ideal location for orchids. If a suitable location is not available, provide supplementary lighting or select a plant that will tolerate dim light from a list on page 541.

ORCHIDS *(continued)*

PALMS

Viruses

Virus.

Salt damage

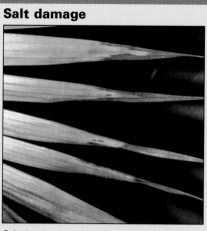

Salt damage.

Spider mites

Spider mites (life size), webs, and damage.

Problem: Leaves are mottled with yellow blotches, or they have yellow streaks or flecks that later turn dark brown or black. Leaves may have partial, complete, or concentric rings of dark-colored tissue. New leaves may be stunted and cupped. Flowers may be mottled and the colors broken. They are moderately or severely distorted and may have brown flecks or streaks in them. Affected flowers do not last long.

Analysis: Several viruses infect orchids. Some infect many different types of orchids, and others infect only a few. Viruses cause a plant to manufacture new viruses from its protein. In the process, the metabolism of the plant is upset. Different symptoms appear, depending upon the orchid and the virus present. Viruses are easily transmitted on tools used in cutting orchid plants.

Solution: Observe the effects of viruses on the plants. If flowers are badly malformed or discolored, discard the plants. Keep plants that are virus free separate from those showing viral symptoms, because the viruses are easily transmitted. Disinfect cutting tools when moving from one plant to another. Do not purchase plants that show symptoms.

Problem: Tips of older leaves die and turn brown, progressing toward the base of the fronds. In severe cases, all fronds may have dead margins. Tissues adjacent to the dead margins of older fronds may turn yellow. White to yellowish mineral salts may accumulate on pot edges and on the lower part of plant stems.

Analysis: Palms are sensitive to excess salts. Soluble salts are picked up by the roots and accumulate in the leaf margins, where concentrations may become high enough to kill the tissues. Salts can accumulate from water or from the use of fertilizers, or they may be present in the soil used in potting. Salts accumulate more rapidly and do more harm if the plant is not watered thoroughly.

Solution: Leach excess salts from the soil by flushing with water. Water the plant at least three times, letting the water drain each time. This is done most easily in a bathtub, laundry sink, or outside. It is usually best to water palms from the top of the pot. Enough water should be added at each watering so that some drains through the pot. Empty the saucer under the pot after the water drains. If the plant is too large to handle easily, use a turkey baster to remove the drainage water. (For information on watering, see page 22.) If salts have accumulated in the pot, replant into a fresh pot with fresh soil mix. Do not overfertilize, and do not fertilize in the winter or when the plant is not growing. Move the plant to a brightly lit location. If practical, use scissors to trim damaged leaf tips to a point.

Problem: Fronds or leaflets are stippled, yellow, and dirty; they may dry out and drop. There may be webbing between leaflets or on the undersides of leaflets. To determine if a plant is infested with mites, examine the bottoms of the leaflets with a hand lens. Or hold a sheet of white paper underneath an affected plant and tap the frond sharply. Minute specks the size of pepper grains will drop to the paper and begin to crawl. The pests are easily seen against the white background.

Analysis: Spider mites, related to spiders, are major pests of many houseplants, including palms. They cause damage by sucking sap from the undersides of leaflets. As a result of their feeding, chlorophyll disappears, causing the stippled appearance. Spider mite webbing traps cast-off skins and debris, making the plant dirty. Under warm, dry conditions, mites can build up to tremendous numbers. (For more information on spider mites, see page 457.)

Solution: Isolate infested plants from others. Take plants outside or into a shower and wash the mites off the leaves using a strong spray of water. Spray infested plants with Ortho® Rose & Flower Insect Killer or take them outside and spray with Ortho® Systemic Insect Killer. Keep air humid to help prevent infestation and proliferation. Avoid bringing mites into the house. (For information on preventing houseplant problems, see page 414.)

Mealybugs

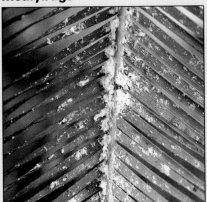

Mealybugs (½ life size).

Problem: White, oval insects up to ¼ inch long form white, cottony masses on fronds, leaflets, or stems and in the crotches where fronds are attached. A sticky material, called *honeydew*, may coat the leaflets. Sooty mold may develop on the sticky substance. Leaflets may be spotted or deformed. When the condition is severe, leaves and plants may die.

Analysis: Several species of this common insect feed on palms. Mealybugs damage plants by sucking sap, causing leaf distortion and death. The adult female mealybug may produce young or lay eggs in a white, fluffy mass of wax. The immature mealybugs, called *nymphs*, crawl on the plant and onto nearby plants. Soon after they begin to feed, they produce white, waxy filaments that cover their bodies, giving them a cottony appearance. As they mature, they become less mobile. Mealybugs can't digest all the sugar in the sap, and they excrete the excess in a fluid called *honeydew*, which coats the leaflets and may drop onto surfaces below the plant. (For additional information on mealybugs, see page 25.)

Solution: Separate infested plants from those not affected. If only a few mealybugs are present, wipe them off with a damp cloth or with cotton swabs dipped in rubbing alcohol. Spray infested plants with Ortho® Rose & Flower Insect Killer or take them outside and spray with Ortho® Systemic Insect Killer. Repeat applications at intervals of two weeks. Inspect new plants thoroughly before putting them in the house. (For information on preventing houseplant problems, see page 414.)

Root and stem rot

Root and stem rot.

Problem: Plants fail to grow and are stunted. Roots are brown and soft, without white tips. (For information on examining roots, see page 22.) The stem may have brown, sunken areas at or below the soil line. Leaves may die and turn black. Potting mix may have a musty smell. Plants may wilt and die.

Analysis: Root and stem rot is caused by any of several fungi, including those known as *water molds* (For more information on water molds, see page 419). These soil-dwelling fungi (*Pythium, Phytophthora parasitica,* and *Rhizoctonia solani*) infect the roots of many plants. They invade the small roots and spread through the root system, killing it. The fungi are favored by wet soil. *Phytophthora* and *Rhizoctonia* can also infect the crown and lower stem, causing the tissues to collapse.

Solution: Drench the soil with a fungicide containing *metalaxyl* or *azoxystrobin*. If the plant is only mildly affected, let the soil dry out between waterings. (For more information on this technique, see page 419.) If the soil mix is heavy or the container does not drain well, transplant the plant into a container that drains freely. Trim rotted roots, dipping cutting tools into bleach solution between cuts. Use a soil mix that drains well. If root rot or stem rot occurs but the top of the plant is still vigorous, cut off the plant above the diseased area and root it. Discard severely infected plants and the soil in which they grew. Wash and disinfect the pots before reuse.

Mealybugs

Mealybugs (life size).

Problem: White, oval insects up to ¼ inch long form white, cottony masses on leaves, on stems, and in the crotches where leaves are attached. A sticky material may coat the leaves. Sooty mold may develop on the sticky substance. Leaves may be spotted or deformed. When the condition is severe, leaves and plants may die.

Analysis: Several species of this common insect feed on peperomia. Mealybugs damage plants by sucking sap, causing leaf distortion and death. The adult female mealybug may produce young or lay eggs in a white, fluffy mass of wax. The immature mealybugs, called *nymphs*, crawl on the plant and onto nearby plants. Soon after they begin to feed, they produce white, waxy filaments that cover their bodies, giving them a cottony appearance. As they mature, they become less mobile. Mealybugs can't digest all the sugar in the sap, and they excrete the excess in a fluid called *honeydew*, which coats the leaves and may drop onto surfaces below the plant. (For more information on mealybugs, see page 25.)

Solution: Separate infested plants from healthy ones. If only a few mealybugs are present, wipe them off with a damp cloth or with cotton swabs dipped in rubbing alcohol. Spray infested plants with Ortho® Rose & Flower Insect Killer or take them outside and spray with Ortho® Systemic Insect Killer. Repeat applications at intervals of two weeks. Inspect new plants thoroughly before putting them in the house. (For information on preventing houseplant problems, see page 414.)

PHILODENDRON

Salt damage

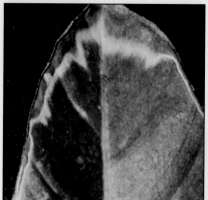

Salt damage.

Root rot

Root rot.

Bacterial leaf spot

Bacterial leaf spot.

Problem: Margins of older leaves die and turn brown and brittle. In severe cases, all leaves may have dead margins. Tissues adjacent to the dead margins of older leaves may turn yellow. White to yellowish mineral salts may accumulate on pot edges and on the lower part of plant stems.

Analysis: Philodendrons are sensitive to excess salts. Soluble salts are picked up by the roots and accumulate in the leaf margins, where concentrations may become high enough to kill the tissues. Salts can accumulate from water or from the use of fertilizers, or they may be present in the soil used in potting. Salts accumulate more rapidly and do more harm if the plant is not watered thoroughly.

Solution: Leach excess salts from the soil by flushing with water. Water the plants at least three times, letting the water drain each time. This is done most easily in a bathtub, in a laundry sink, or outside. It is usually best to water philodendrons from the top of the pot. Enough water should be added at each watering so that some drains through the pot. Empty the saucer under the pot after the water drains. If the plant is too large to handle easily, use a turkey baster to remove the drainage water. (For information on watering, see page 22.) If salts have accumulated on the pot, replant into fresh potting mix. Do not overfertilize.

Problem: The lower leaves turn yellow. Leaves may drop from the plant. Plants may be stunted. Potting mix may have a musty smell. Roots may be soft and brown, with no white tips. (For information on examining roots, see page 22.)

Analysis: Any of several fungi, including those known as *water molds*, cause this plant disease. (For information on water molds, see page 419.) These fungi (*Pythium* and *Rhizoctonia* species) are favored by wet soil. The disease is usually an indication that the plant has been watered too frequently or that the soil mix is too heavy and does not drain well. The fungi are common in garden soils, but pasteurized soil or soilless potting mixes are free of them unless they are introduced on a plant or a dirty pot or are transferred from another pot on dirty fingers. Root rot spreads quickly through a root system if the soil remains wet.

Solution: Drench the soil with a fungicide containing *metalaxyl*. If the plant is only mildly affected, let the soil dry out between waterings. (For more information on this technique, see page 419.) If the soil mix is heavy or the container does not drain well, transplant the plant into a container that drains freely. Trim rotted roots and use a soil mix that drains well. If stem or root rot occurs but the top of the plant is still vigorous, cut off the plant above the diseased area and root it. Discard severely infected plants and the soil in which they grew. Wash and disinfect the pots with a ten percent chlorine bleach solution (1 part bleach to 9 parts water) before reuse.

Problem: Small, water-soaked spots appear on the leaves. These spots enlarge to irregular blotches, surrounded by yellow margins. Infected tissue turns brown or black. Severely infected leaves turn yellow, die, and drop from the plant.

Analysis: Bacterial leaf spot is caused by bacteria that also attack dieffenbachia and other foliage plants. Under humid conditions, the bacteria gain entrance through wounds or natural openings in the leaves. Inside the leaf, the bacteria rot the tissue, causing the spots. Under very humid conditions, large numbers of bacteria may be produced and may ooze out of the tissues in a mass. If infection is severe, so much wilting results that the leaf dies.

Solution: Once leaves are infected, no measures will control the spots already formed. To keep the disease from spreading to other plants, keep the leaves dry. Don't mist the plants. Keep plants in rooms where condensation does not form on the leaves. Remove and destroy infected leaves. Avoid touching diseased leaves and then uninfected leaves.

SAINTPAULIA (African violet)

Insufficient light

Failure to bloom.

Problem: Although the plant seems healthy, it does not bloom.

Analysis: Violets, like other flowering plants, won't bloom unless they are properly fed and watered. If the plant is a good green color and is growing well but not blooming, it is probably not receiving enough light. Plants use light as a source of energy and will not bloom unless they can afford the energy to do so. African violets bloom at lower levels of light than most other plants, but they do require a fairly bright location to bloom well.

Solution: Move the plants gradually to a brighter location. The ideal light level for African violets is as bright as possible but not direct sun. If the light is coming through a window exposed to the sun, draw a curtain so that the sunlight is not quite bright enough to make shadows. If the light is too bright, the leaves will lose their bright green color and become pale with an orange or yellow cast. If the light is both bright and hot, the leaves will burn. If you don't have a bright enough location in your house, give the plants supplemental light. Use fluorescent fixtures, and place them as close to the top of the plants as possible.

Water spots

Water spots.

Problem: White to light yellow blotches in various patterns, including circles, occur on the older leaves. Small islands of green may be separated by the discolored areas. Brown spots sometimes appear in the colored areas.

Analysis: Members of the African violet family are very sensitive to rapid temperature changes. Water spots occur most commonly when cold water is splashed on the leaves while the plant is being watered. If this happens in light, chlorophyll is destroyed. In this plant family, all of the chlorophyll in the leaves is found in a single layer of cells near the upper surface. If the chlorophyll in that layer is broken down, the green color disappears, and the color of the underlying leaf tissue is exposed.

Solution: Avoid getting cold water on African violet leaves when watering. Or use water at room temperature, which will not cause spotting if it touches the leaves. Spotted leaves will not recover. Pick them off if they are unsightly.

Powdery mildew

Powdery mildew.

Problem: Powdery white or gray patches appear on the leaves, stems, buds, and flowers. Leaves and flowers may be covered with the powdery growth. This material usually appears first on the upper surfaces of the older leaves. The affected plant parts may turn yellow or brown and shrivel up and die.

Analysis: Powdery mildew on African violets is caused by a fungus species (*Oidium*). The powdery patches consist of fungal strands and spores. Air currents carry the spores to healthy leaves and flowers of the same plant and to other African violets. The fungus robs the plant of its nutrients, causing yellowing or browning of the tissues. Dim light, warm days, and cool nights encourage the growth of powdery mildew.

Solution: Spray with a fungicide containing *triforine* or *thiophanate-methyl*. Remove infected flowers, buds and badly infected leaves. Keep plants in bright, indirect light away from cold drafts.

SYNGONIUM (Nephthytis)

Bacterial leaf spot

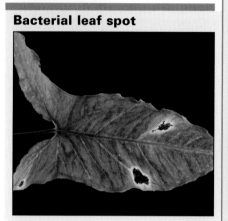

Bacterial leaf spot.

Problem: Irregular, oblong spots appear scattered on the leaves. New spots are very small but rapidly enlarge so that they may cover much of the leaf. Spots at first may be dark green but eventually become dark brown or black as the tissue dies. Tissues around the dead areas look water-soaked and have a yellow margin. Shiny drops may be found on the undersides of the spots. As these dry, they may become white or dark brown. Leaves may die.

Analysis: Bacterial leaf spot is caused by either of two bacteria (*Erwinia chrysanthemi* or *Xanthomonas vitians*). The bacteria may be carried internally in the stems of syngonium, or they may be on leaf surfaces. High temperatures and high humidity favor infection and disease development. When conditions are favorable, the bacteria rapidly invade leaf tissues, killing them as they progress through the leaf.

Solution: Break off and discard infected leaves. Avoid getting water on the foliage. Space plants so that air can circulate around the leaves to keep them dry. Discard severely infected plants. Before using the pot again, wash it, and then soak it for 30 minutes in a solution of 1 part household bleach to 9 parts water.

TOLMIEA (Piggyback plant)

Viruses

Virus.

Problem: All leaves have blotches of various shades of yellow and green. Plants showing color blotches fail to grow as rapidly as green plants of the same type. Infected plants are of a variegated variety.

Analysis: Several viruses have been found in variegated piggyback plants. The most common is the cucumber mosaic virus. Viruses disrupt the normal functioning of the cells and, as a result, not as much chlorophyll is produced. This causes different shades of green and yellow to appear in the leaves. Aphids and other insects transmit the virus from one plant to another. (For more information on aphids, see page 24.)

Solution: Keep variegated piggyback plants isolated from other plants, because aphids can transmit the viruses to other susceptible plants. Control aphids as described on page 24.

Iron deficiency

Iron deficiency.

Problem: The newest leaves turn yellow at the margins. The veins usually remain green. In severe cases, the entire leaf is yellow and small. The plant may be stunted.

Analysis: Iron deficiency is a common problem with acid-loving plants such as the piggyback, which grow best in soil with a pH between 5.5 and 6.5. (For more information on soil acidity, see page 407.) The leaf yellowing is caused by a deficiency of iron and other minor nutrients in the plant. Plants use iron in the formation of chlorophyll in the leaves. The soil is seldom deficient in iron, but iron is often found in an insoluble form that is not available to piggyback plants, especially when the soil pH is too high. The problem worsens if the plant is in dim light or is allowed to dry out excessively between waterings.

Solution: To correct the iron deficiency, spray the foliage with a chelated iron fertilizer and apply fertilizer to the soil in the pot. Add Miracid® ProSelect™ Water Soluble Plant Food to keep the soil acid. When potting or transplanting piggybacks, use an acid soil mix that contains about 50 percent peat moss. Avoid lime or dolomite in the soil mix.

TRADESCANTIA (Wandering Jew)

Dieback

Dieback.

Problem: Tips of older leaves turn yellow, then die and turn brown. This condition occurs more frequently on long stems than on short stems. The longer the stem, the more tip burn is found.

Analysis: The cause of dieback is unknown. It looks like salt damage (see page 22) but often occurs without an accumulation of salts in the soil. As wandering Jew stems grow long, the plant does not support the old leaves, and they turn yellow and die starting at the tips.

Solution: Remove dead leaves as they appear. Keep pinching the tips of the stems so they do not become too long. This will force new buds to grow farther back on the stems. New leaves will not show this problem. Plants may occasionally need to be cut back severely to only several inches on each stem. After cutting back, reduce the amount of water and fertilizer until the plant resumes active growth.

ZYGOCACTUS (Christmas cactus)

Bud drop

Bud drop.

Problem: Flower buds form at the tips of branches and begin to develop normally but fall off before opening. Fallen buds appear normal. The situation worsens if the plant is moved after it is in bud. Bud drop can be partial or total.

Analysis: Zygocactus (*Schlumbergera*) flowers are sensitive to excess heat, exposure to ethylene gas, and lack of light. In response to one or more of these conditions, buds drop off rather than drying up, as they would on some other stressed flowering plants. Damage may also occur shortly after the zygocactus is moved.

Solution: Avoid exposing zygocactus to excessive warmth when the plant is about to bloom. A nighttime temperature range from 40° to 70°F is appropriate; daytime temperatures should be from 60° to 80°F. If daytime temperatures do not reach 60°F, flowering will be delayed. Ethylene gas is a result of incomplete combustion, so keep zygocactus away from fireplaces, gas heaters and heating vents, and other possible sources of ethylene-contaminated air. These sources also include fruit, especially apples, which give off ethylene gas as they ripen. Insufficient light can also cause bud drop. Bright light with at least some morning sun is usually necessary to prevent loss of buds. Moving the plant after flower buds have formed also seems to cause bud drop. The cause may be physiological damage or a drastic change in environment. Spraying with a silver nitrate solution can help prevent bud drop.

Root and stem rot

Stem rot.

Problem: Stems wilt and turn lighter green and dull. Plants stop flowering, are stunted, and may die. Large brown, circular, sunken areas may appear on the stem at or just below the soil line. Potting mix may have a musty smell.

Analysis: Root and stem rot is caused by any of several fungi, including those known as *water molds* (For information on water molds, see page 419). These soil-inhabiting fungi (*Phythium* and *Phytophthora*) spread through the root system. Stems of plants weakened by these root-rotting fungi are susceptible to attack by the stem-rotting fungus *Fusarium oxysporum*. The fungus causes large brown sunken areas on the main stems near the soil line. If it girdles the stem, the plant will die.

Solution: Drench the soil with a fungicide containing *metalaxyl*. If the plant is only mildly affected, let the soil dry out between waterings. If the soil mix is heavy or the container does not drain well, transplant the plant into a container with a soil mix that drains well. Trim rotted roots, dipping cutting tools into a bleach solution between cuts. If the top of the plant is still vigorous, cut it off above the diseased area and root it. Discard severely infected plants and the soil in which they grew. Wash and disinfect the pots before reuse.

No other ground cover is as inviting for foot traffic as luxurient turfgrass. When installing pavers in a lawn, set them flush with the soil surface to allow for easy mowing with no need for edging.

Replanting the lawn is often the first phase of landscaping at a newly purchased home. Putting in a new lawn involves removing the old one, preparing the soil, then planting seed or installing sod.

A new lawn placed over a still-viable old lawn results in holdover weeds rapidly taking the place of delicate seedlings. Before sodding or seeding, spray with a glyphosate compound to kill any growing vegetation and avoid much hand weeding later.

Soil pH: Before seeding or laying sod, test the soil in the lawn area to determine the pH level. The pH scale ranges from 0 to 14, with neutral at 7.0. The ideal pH for most grass is between 6.5 and 6.8. The pH determines the rate at which nutrients are released from the soil, if these nutrients are already present.

Acidic soil: In soil that is acidic (with a pH of 5.5 or lower), magnesium, phosphorus, and calcium are less available for plant use than in neutral soil. Nitrogen is only partially released in acidic soil because the soil organisms that free it are less active. When soil has a pH of 5.0 or lower, soil organisms cease working altogether and no nitrogen is released. Acidic soil is also called sour soil.

Lawns in overly acidic soil may grow slowly. Leaves may be pale and root development may be poor. Overly acidic soil promotes disease mechanisms. Applying fertilizer may not help because the low pH stops or slows nutrient release. Neutralize acidic soil by applying finely ground dolomitic limestone, working it into the soil.

Alkaline soil: Sometimes called sweet soil, alkaline soil has a pH above 8.0. When the pH exceeds 8.0, iron and manganese are no longer available to the grass. The lawn becomes pale or yellow. To correct alkaline soil, spade in iron and sulfate compounds.

Testing for pH: In general, acidic soils are high in organic material and occur in areas with annual rainfall of 30 inches or more. Alkaline soils are high in calcium and are common in areas where rainfall is minimal.

To measure pH precisely, take soil samples to a professional testing service. In some states, soil testing is offered by university extension services. To find a soil-testing service, look under "Soil" in the local telephone directory or ask the local county extension agent for advice.

Take samples from about 15 areas within a prospective lawn site. A soil-sampling tube, available at your local nursery, works best, but the hollow shaft of an old curtain rod will do. Insert the tube in the soil to a depth of 6 inches. If your home is on an established property, mix the various samples together in a freshly cleaned nonmetal container. You should now have about 2 cups of soil. Remove stones, roots, or debris. If your home is on land subject to recent construction activities, keep the samples separate. This allows identification of areas that need special work. Label all containers, cover them, and keep them dry. In an accompanying letter, tell the extension service about land slope and other pertinent details.

Alternatively, you can use a home soil-testing kit you may purchase at a nursery. Though this is not as accurate as a professional analysis, it is inexpensive, easy, and usually adequate. When you know the pH of the lawn area, you can correct it, if necessary, when you add organic additives.

Organic amendments: Although some grasses do well enough in poor soil, none is at its best. Seedlings may fail to thrive or even emerge. Mature grass remains straggly, bare spots form, and insect pests can attack the weakened blades.

For the lawn to thrive, you must improve poor soil. Topsoil should be used only when you must raise the land grading. Knowing the origin of topsoil is difficult. The soil may be poor; contain weed seeds, disease organisms, nematodes, or insect pests in larval or egg form; or have a high chemical content. Purchase topsoil carefully.

Organic amendments actually do improve poor soil. Adding ample organic material to clay soil can lessen the problems of runoff and compaction. This causes particles to be crumbly rather than sticky stiff. Ample organic matter mixed into sandy soil helps hold moisture and nutrients in the root zone. Five organic amendments most often used are peat moss, compost, manure, ground bark, and sawdust.

■ **Peat moss:** Peat moss is best reserved for acid-loving plants such as azaleas. Few lawn grasses do well in soil heavily fortified with peat moss, although it can be used sparingly. By itself, peat moss has an acidic pH of 3.5 to 4.5. If acidic soil is fortified with peat moss, the highly acidic result may not release valuable plant nutrients. Also, peat moss sheds water if allowed to dry out, so a soil high in peat moss may be harmful to drought-sensitive seedlings. If your lawn has a high peat moss component, add a wetting agent to the water. Wetting agents are available at most nurseries.

■ **Compost:** Whether from a compost pile or purchased by the bag or truckload at a nursery, compost is any organic material that has begun to decompose. By decomposing, dead plant parts release their nutrients. In addition, compost makes clay or compacted soil crumblier. When soil particles have air spaces between them, water penetrates better, nutrients reach root zones, and drainage is improved. In sandy soil, compost acts like a sponge, holding moisture and nutrients in the root zone. These benefits bode well for delicate grass seedlings, which need all the help they can get.

■ **Manure:** Cow and horse manure, if treated to remove insect eggs and weed seeds, is an effective soil conditioner. It is used by itself or with compost. The amount of nutrients in the manure varies with what the animals have been eating. Manure may have a high salt content, which can prevent seedling germination. Avoid cow or horse manure if the soil is already high in salt or is alkaline. Fresh manure can't be used safely on or around a new or established lawn. Gases given off by the ammonia in fresh manure may severely damage grass and grass roots. If obtained directly from a farm or stable, manure must first be composted to destroy undesirable organisms. Other forms of manure—such as chicken, sheep, or swine—are sometimes available; as with cow or horse manure, compost them first.

■ **Ground bark and sawdust:** Although less expensive than compost or soil mixes, ground bark and sawdust are wood by-products that add few nutrients. In the soil, sawdust decomposes with the aid of bacteria that use nitrogen, taking nitrogen away from growing grass. Add a 10-10-10 general-purpose plant food while working wood by-products into the soil.

■ **Amendment application:** Regardless of which organic amendment you choose, a sprinkling of it will not solve your soil problems. You must add an amendment layer 1 to 4 inches deep to effect a change in soil structure. Work the new material in thoroughly with a tiller, spade, or rake.

Rocks or large dirt clods can cause problems by altering water flow. Rake them

When overseeding an existing lawn, prepare the old lawn by mowing it as closely as possible, raking up the clippings, then scratching the soil vigorously with a metal rake. You'll need to sow seed at two to three times the amount recommended on the package.

out of the top 2 inches of soil. Make sure the ground is level. Water the soil, then go over it with a garden roller; do this several times to see how the soil settles. Make corrections as needed to avoid puddling and runoff.

SEEDING LAWNS

Successful seed sowing is a matter of seed quality, timing, effective distribution, and proper care.

■ **Seed quality:** Always check the date on the seed container before purchasing grass seed. Buy only seed that is produced for sale in the current year. If the box is a holdover from the previous year, some seeds may have sprouted in the container. After planting, the others may sprout poorly or not at all.

■ **Sowing time:** Planting at the right time helps prevent seedling death. Fall and spring planting give the best results. Fall sowing is preferred by many experienced gardeners. It reduces the problem of heat damage to seedlings. Allow six weeks of growing time before the weather turns cold. Seed sown later may not germinate. Fall seeding is usually done no later than mid-September. Estimates are that for every day after this, 10 percent of the seeds are lost, except in areas of continual warm weather.

The benefits of spring lawn planting include ample sunlight. Combined with ample water, the result may be a deep cushiony lawn. Weed growth is quite active, however, in spring. Even the most dense mature grass can't crowd out weeds while the grass is in the seedling stage.

Summer heat is also hard on seedlings.

Most grasses do best between 50°F and 70°F. A successful springtime planting requires careful watering. Make sure the sprinkler system irrigates the entire planted area. Water it for 20 minutes in the morning; 20 minutes in the evening, and, if the air temperature rises above 80°F, an additional 20 minutes in the afternoon. If you must use a hose to water, provide a fine spray or mist to avoid washing seeds away. In dry weather, keep seedlings moist by covering them with a ¼- to ½-inch-deep mulch sawdust or straw. Do not use peat moss, which promotes water runoff when dry.

■ **Seed distribution:** Use a drop or broadcast spreader to sow seeds. Hand-distribution tends to be irregular, resulting in both bare and overly seeded areas. As soon as seeds are distributed, rake the planted area lightly. Then roll the earth with a light roller. This avoids wind drift by pressing the seeds firmly into the soil. Seeds should be no more than ½ inch deep. Improper planting depth may slow or stop seed germination. Seeds spread on top of thatch or left on top of soil instead of being pressed into the soil may dry out without sprouting.

■ **Care of newly planted areas:** Keep foot and animal traffic off a newly seeded lawn to avoid uncovering or disturbing germinating seeds. Insert small brightly colored flags to warn pedestrians. To keep animals off, put up a temporary barrier.

Improper watering is a common cause of seed failure. Once a seed has germinated and the protective seed coat is broken, adequate moisture is a must. If the soil around the seedling dries out, so does the seedling.

Overly wet soil with a high nitrogen component, however, encourages the proliferation of fungi that cause damping-off. These fungi are a major cause of seed failure to thrive. The infection may attack seeds before germination. If seeds do germinate, the fungi infect the growing tips of the grass and kill the seedlings before they emerge from the soil. Even after seedling emergence, the fungi remain a problem because they may attack stems and roots at or just below soil level. The lawn seedlings lie on the ground instead of standing upright. Surviving seedlings may have stunted roots, lessening their nutrient retention. If damping-off causes lawn-seed failure, improve drainage before reseeding. Do not add nitrogen fertilizer until seedlings have fully sprouted.

Sod lawns: Gardeners who do not have time to plant seed and monitor seedlings or who want an immediate lawn thick enough to forestall wind-carried weed seeds often prefer to lay sod.

■ **What to install:** Sod comes in strips from 6 to 9 feet long. It should be uniformly green, moist, and ¾ to 1 inch thick. Overly thick sod roots slowly. Overly thin sod dries out too fast, depriving leaves and roots of necessary water. If sod falls apart when handled, reject it. Do not put down sod that is wet, dry, spotted with brown, or yellowing. Sod with any of these characteristics has not been grown under healthy conditions, is old, has been stored improperly, or has been injured in transit.

■ **When to install:** Lay cool-season sod, such as bluegrass or bentgrass, in early spring or in late summer to early fall. Lay warm-season grass sod, such as bermudagrass, bahiagrass, centipedegrass, or St. Augustine-grass, in late spring or early summer.

■ **How to install:** Healthy sod can be expensive and must be carefully handled to avoid ruining it. Prepare the soil before sod installation to avoid problems from incorrect pH, holdover weeds, uneven ground, insects, nematodes, and disease. Install the sod as soon as possible after it has been cut.

Unroll one strip of sod at a time. Lay the strips so that the seams are staggered from row to row, as the mortar lines between bricks in a walkway are staggered. The sod strips should fit snugly against each other, but be careful not to stretch them. Sod tends to shrink, and stretching increases that tendency and results in yellow stripes that run through the lawn. For two weeks, you may have to water daily to keep the soil moist but not wet at all times. Pay special attention to pathway and driveway borders; these are the first to dry out and the last to knit with the soil. Test for sod rooting by tugging gently at the corner of a strip. If it resists, the sod has taken hold. A sod lawn can be functional in as little as two weeks, although heavy foot traffic should be routed elsewhere initially.

■ **Warning signals:** Symptoms of sod failure include newly laid areas turning yellow, then brown. Instead of meshing with the underlying soil, failing sod rolls up easily, like a carpet. When you roll it, no roots are visible on the bottom of the sod. If your sod exhibits these symptoms, it may have been subjected to heat or water stress either in the field or in storage; sod may be damaged within two days of digging and initial rolling if the weather is hot. To try to save failing installed sod, water it diligently. Damaged sod can recover partially with good care.

Sod failure can also occur if the soil dries out, either because water is lacking or because sod is placed directly on thatch. If sod is placed on compacted soil, the roots can't penetrate well. Soil preparation prevents these problems.

Once the sod is well-established, the next issue is when to begin mowing it.

MOWING LAWNS

In new lawns, begin mowing when grass is at least 3 inches high. Before that, seedlings are not well rooted and you may pull out young plants. After the initial mowing, mow to the height recommended for your grass variety.

In mature lawns, you may be blaming yellow lawn patches on insects or fungus when your mower or mowing technique may be the culprit. Like most chores, mowing can be done correctly or incorrectly.

Mower types: To mow correctly, you must use good-quality equipment appropriate for the job.

■ **Reel mowers:** These mowers work with a scissorslike motion. They are precise and recommended for grass that must be short and well tended—golf course–type grass. If you have zoysiagrass or hybrid bermudagrass or bentgrass, you should use a reel mower.

The disadvantage of reel mowers is that their cutting does not follow the lay of the land. The results may be slightly longer grass

One of the best ways to reduce your mowing time is to use the largest mower that's practical for your lawn. Mowing a one-acre lawn with a 24-inch mower will take about an hour less than mowing the same lawn with an 18-inch-wide mower.

in a sunken area and slightly shorter grass on a rise. Reel mowers are not as effective as rotary mowers in lawns that contain high weeds, high grass, or rough ground. To avoid problems with a reel mower, have it serviced three times during the growing season. Signs of dull reel blades are an overly "striped" effect after mowing, untouched grass blades, and lawn areas that appear rough.

■ **Rotary mowers:** These power mowers are easier to maintain than reel mowers. Also, the rotary models are lighter and easier to handle. They are effective on high grass, plant stalks, and tall weeds. Rotary mowers can trim close to trees, walls, fences, and other standing objects. In addition, they chop up lawn leaves effectively. Rotaries work well if you cannot mow your lawn on a precision timetable; however, do not expect that precision look. Rotary mowers give a knifelike cut, fraying and bruising leaf tips more than reel mowers do. This is particularly true if you neglect to have the blades sharpened often enough.

Dull mower blades shred grass tips, and the result is a lawn with a sickly brown or gray tinge. This is most noticeable in dry weather. Also, shredded tips act as entry points for lawn diseases. Sharpen blades of a rotary mower after every six to eight mowings.

■ **Push mowers:** Small hand-powered push mowers are time-effective for lawns less than 2,000 square feet. You don't have to hunt for fuel, check the parts, and so on; you just have to oil the bearings and get the mower sharpened once a year to keep it in top form. But hand-powered mowers do

require more muscle to operate than the power varieties.

■ **Electric mowers:** Those with large lawns often consider electric mowers. The major disadvantage of an electric mower is that it remains anchored to a power outlet. This creates a maneuvering problem when you are cutting around trees, for example. Electrics are quiet, however, and easy to start. Never use a corded electric mower or edger on wet grass.

Frequency of mowing: Cutting a lawn too often, particularly with the blade set low, exposes the lower portions of grass leaves to bright sun, burning them. If this happens repeatedly, grass reacts by developing shallow roots. Shallow-rooted lawns are particularly prone to disease and weed problems. In addition, poor rooting does not provide enough nutrients to the grass leaves. A lawn with shallow roots may eventually die out.

Mowing infrequently often means taking off too much grass at one time. There is a direct relationship between root depth and lawn height. Long roots are to the lawn's advantage. They not only reach out for more lawn nutrients, but they also help the grass resist drought. If you let grass grow too long and then lop off more than half of it, the roots go into shock. Eventually the lawn may develop a thin, spotty, or burned look. For best results, never remove more than one-third of the height of the grass.

The table on page 52 lists recommended grass heights according to grass type. If your lawn is a mixture of types, cut to the length recommended for the dominant one. Mow

Bentgrass is the lowest growing and has the finest blades and highest maintenance of all the cool-season turfgrasses. It requires frequent mowing, watering, and fertilizing.

whenever grass is one-third to one-half higher than the height mentioned.

CHOOSING A LAWN TYPE

Given all available lawn grasses, you can choose from more than 40 varieties. There are also grass substitutes, such as dichondra, to consider. Basically, grass is categorized as a hardy, or cool-season, variety for cold-winter areas or as a subtropical, or warm-season, variety for areas where frost is rare. Whether you are installing a new lawn or caring for the lawn you already have, knowing the needs of the grass is important. If you are installing a lawn, you must choose a type that is appropriate for the climate and has maintenance requirements you can satisfy. Knowing the variety of an existing lawn helps you provide the care it needs and diagnose problems.

Most lawns are a blend of grasses, which makes them more resistant to disease and infestation than lawns of a single type. The problems that afflict one grass may not affect another variety.

Bahiagrass: Warm season. Makes a coarse, open lawn. So tall and fast growing that in finer lawns it is thought of as a weed. Spreads by runners. Most varieties are grown for hay; Pensacola and Argentine are lawn varieties. Easy to maintain, drought-resistant, shade tolerant, and needs little fertilizer. Problems are chlorosis (yellowing), dollar spot (see page 66), and mole cricket invasion (see page 71).

RECOMMENDED MOWING HEIGHTS

Type of grass	Mowing height (inches)
Bahiagrass	2–3
Bentgrass	⅜–¾
Bermudagrass	½–1½
Bluegrass	2–3
Centipedegrass	1–2
Dichondra	½–1½
Fescue	
Chewings	1–2
Red	2–3
Tall	3–4
Ryegrass	
Annual	1½–2
Perennial	1–2½
St. Augustinegrass	1–2½
Zoysiagrass	½–1½

Bentgrass: Cool season. Leaves are small, well textured, fine, fairly flat, and upright. Color may be bluish green, medium green, or apple green. Several varieties are available. Spreads by rooting at the joints. If well cared for, bentgrass presents an exceptionally uniform appearance. Often used on golf courses and putting greens. Offers some shade tolerance. Problems arise when bentgrass is not mowed often enough or cut short enough, and it builds a heavy thatch layer quickly. A few varieties require mowing three times per week. Bentgrass is fussy. It suffers under drought and requires regular, heavy applications of fertilizer. In hot, muggy weather or cool, damp conditions, it is susceptible to fungal diseases. Bentgrass is not recommended for most home lawns.

Bentgrass becomes a weed when it is accidentally introduced into lawns of other types that do not require such frequent mowing. In bluegrass, fescue, and lawns, bentgrass looks matted. In areas between the other grasses, bentgrass may appear dead with long straggly stems. In the spring, it remains brown much longer than the surrounding grasses. It may also take over the lawn, because it grows quickly.

If you do not want the high maintenance of a predominantly bentgrass lawn or do not like its appearance in your chosen lawn type, use a systemic herbicide containing *glyphosate*. The treatment does not affect roots of surrounding trees or shrubs. Bentgrass areas die out within four weeks of treatment, and you can sow selected lawn seed within seven days.

Bermudagrass: Warm season. Regional names include devilgrass, manienie, and wiregrass. Color differs with variety; bermudagrass may be grayish green, bright deep green, deep blue-green, light green, yellow-green, or dark green. Leaf blades range from ⅛ to ¼ inch wide. Common bermudagrass has bronze seed spikes. Stolons, or stems, creep along the soil surface. Stolons range from 6 to 18 inches long. Bermudagrass requires sun. It roots deeply and is drought-tolerant. In general, bermudagrass lawns are dense. New varieties have a medium to fine texture.

Bermudagrass is usually pest- and disease-free if well tended. When thick, it resists weed sprouting. Because it provides rapid coverage and withstands a lot of foot traffic, it is used for play areas and athletic fields. In winter, expect bermudagrass to turn brown or straw-colored. Help it stay green longer by applying fertilizer in late fall and removing thatch, which blocks sunlight. Some gardeners dye dormant bermudagrass green in winter. Once bermudagrass is fully dormant (without naturally green stems or leaves) in winter, use contact weed killer to kill a wide range of grassy weeds and broadleaf weeds in the lawn.

Before extensive hybridization, early varieties of bermudagrass were considered a worse lawn pest than crabgrass. Even modern "common" varieties can occasionally become a lawn problem. Bermudagrass spreads rapidly by surface and underground runners. If it gets in lawns of other grasses or flower beds, its deep root system may make it difficult to eradicate. Bermudagrass is sometimes confused with quackgrass (see page 79), a weed, because both spread in the same stolen-creeping manner. (For information on control in lawns, see page 59). Control invasive bermudagrass in ground cover or shrubs with the selective herbicide Ortho® Grass-B-Gon® Grass Killer for Landscapes which kills grassy weeds but does not affect most broadleaf plants.

Kentucky bluegrass: Cool season. Despite its name, Kentucky bluegrass is not a Kentucky native; English settlers brought it to the state in packing hay. There is "common" Kentucky bluegrass and "improved" Kentucky bluegrass. Both spread by rhizomes. Bluegrass is generally dark green and has fine texture. Density is moderate to thick. It is considered the best of all lawn grasses in appearance. The improved version, usually sold as a blend of varieties, has deeper color, higher density, and better heat resistance. Improved Kentucky bluegrass is also more resistant to diseases such as leaf spot (see page 75), fusarium blight (see page 65), and stripe smut.

When considering bluegrass for your lawn, select varieties carefully to avoid problems. Delta, Kenblue, Newport, and Park are susceptible to leaf spot. Delta and Park have problems with chlorosis (yellowing) in alkaline soils. Newport, Fylking, and Park seem susceptible to fusarium blight. Merion does not do well in shade and is prone to mildew, stripe smut, and rust. All bluegrass requires ample water; the grass goes dormant and turns brown in even short drought periods, but it does recover if watered well. Bluegrass needs regular applications of a medium to large amount of fertilizer. The grass does not prosper if mowed severely.

Do not confuse perennial Kentucky bluegrass with its pest relative, annual bluegrass (see page 78), which is also called annual speargrass, dwarf speargrass, and walkgrass. Annual bluegrass, which is generally considered a weed, is pale green. In mid- to late spring, white seed heads appear.

Centipedegrass: Warm season. Medium green with a tendency toward yellowing from chlorosis. Needs iron supplements. Centipedegrass has a coarse texture and will grow in some shade. Adaptable to poor soil, it does well in acidic conditions and is aggressive enough to crowd out weeds. Spreads by runners. Centipedegrass needs little general maintenance, though its shallow root system makes it drought-sensitive. With sufficient watering, however, a centipedegrass lawn recovers quickly. This hardy grass is resistant to chinchbug attack and brown patch disease. If centipedegrass gets into ornamental plant areas, control it with Ortho® Grass-B-Gon® Grass Killer for Landscapes.

Dichondra: Warm season. Dichondra is not a grass, but, instead, is a ground-hugging broad-leafed plant that can make a bright green carpet. It spreads by reseeding and from underground runners, and it stays green throughout the year. Because it needs little mowing, it is used instead of grass for many small to medium-size areas that are not subject to foot traffic. The plant thrives in heat but tolerates some shade. It needs much water and fertilizer. Weeds are hard to control in dense dichondra.

Dichondra is susceptible to a few diseases, including brown patch and alternaria leaf spot. Dichondra is also susceptible to cutworms, snails, slugs, red spider mites, gnats, flea beetles, and nematodes. To rid dichondra of nematodes (see page 73), you may have to remove the entire lawn, cultivate deeply, and then replant. Because nematodes can be brought in with flats of dichondra, treat new plants with a soil fumigant before installing them.

Fescue: Cool season. Types of fescue include chewing fescue, red fescue, and tall fescue. Most fine fescue spreads slowly, but tall fescue can spread rapidly. Fescue tends to present a rather stiff and windswept appearance. It remains medium to dark green all year and makes a rugged lawn. Tall fescue is used for play areas. Fescue can survive in city conditions, including smog. It adapts to dry growing conditions and poor soil, and it needs little fertilizer. Tall fescue produces bunchy clumps that may be considered a lawn nuisance. Occasionally it does so well

St. Augustinegrass is a robust, fast-growing, warm-season perennial with broad, dark blue-green blades. It is among the most shade-tolerant of warm-season grasses.

53

Because it exhibits the best wear tolerance of any cool-season grass, perennial ryegrass has received a lot of attention from turf breeders. The result has been turf-type perennial ryegrass varieties that are fine-bladed, rich green, and resistant to pests and diseases.

it becomes a weed. Red fescue tolerates acidic soil, dry areas, and some shade. In moist fertile soil and in hot climates, it is prone to summer diseases such as red thread. This disease, also called pink patch, affects ryegrass, bluegrass, and bentgrass as well as fescue. Infected grass turns light tan to pink in areas ranging from 2 inches to 3 feet in diameter. Pink webs, almost resembling tangled sewing thread, bind the leaves together. Though seldom fatal, red thread does affect lawn appearance. Try adding nitrogen to the soil as a control.

Ryegrass (annual): Cool season. Also called Italian ryegrass and common ryegrass, the annual type of this grass is coarse, with leaves far apart. It does not make a tightly knit lawn. Annual ryegrass is often used for quick lawn cover. It needs a lot of water but tolerates some shade. Annual ryegrass does not survive cold winters or extremely hot summers. It must be replanted each year.

Ryegrass (perennial): Cool season. This grass is somewhat coarse with a waxy shine on the leaves, which grow far apart. Perennial ryegrass tolerates some shade and needs only moderate applications of fertilizer and water. Traditionally, its bunchy growth habit did not create the lush lawn look, but selective breeding has developed ryegrass

with a fine leaf resembling bluegrass. This improved ryegrass creates a beautiful lawn that is tough enough to plant in play areas. And it is an easy grass to grow, though it can be hard to mow in summer.

St. Augustinegrass: Warm season. A dark blue-green coarse grass with hard, flat stems and flat broad leaves. Grows quickly and tolerates salty soil and shade. St. Augustinegrass is not always durable under heavy traffic, and it turns brown in winter. Its coarse texture makes cutting with a power mower a necessity. This type of lawn needs much iron. It tends to creep into flower beds; fortunately, it is shallow-rooted and easily removed by hand. Unfortunately, chinch bugs (see page 69) find this grass a favorite food.

Zoysiagrass: Warm season. The several varieties of this grass have wiry blades that may be broad at the base and taper to a point at the tips. Zoysiagrass is dark green and easy to maintain. It requires a moderate amount of water and fertilizer. This grass tolerates heavy foot traffic and is drought- and weed-resistant. Few pests trouble it. This grass is moderately winter-hardy. Winter dormancy turns it straw-colored except in mild-winter areas. Zoysiagrass does not turn green again until warm weather. Lawns of this grass are slow to

establish. Without regular rotary mowing it becomes difficult to cut. Zoysiagrass tends to build up a thatch layer.

USING GRASS CLIPPINGS

Some say grass clippings are good for a lawn; some say they prevent sunlight from reaching the lawn; and others say they foul the mower. There's truth in all three views. If you mow regularly and the clippings are less than 1 inch long, you can leave them on the lawn without causing a problem. When grass is mowed properly, the clippings take about a day to disappear. They are 90 percent water and dry up to almost nothing; they can't pile up or entangle with thatch and impede the mower. As much as one-third of a lawn's nitrogen requirements may be supplied by decomposing lawn clippings. This is welcome news because many communities now ban yard wastes and grass clippings from normal trash collection, in an effort to slow down the rapid filling of available landfills.

In dry-summer areas or with infrequent mowing, clippings do not decay quickly enough. The clippings can mound, entangling in thatch and making mowing difficult. Excess clippings are not only unsightly, but they also shade growing grass underneath. They provide an excellent source of nutrition and humidity for disease fungi, which may soon attack living grass underneath the matting. Some of the new composting rotary mowers effectively chop clippings small and scatter them so they do not build up into a problem.

Clipping disposal is not difficult if you have an active compost pile. Gather up the clippings, scatter them in the pile with other garden leaves and waste material, and turn the pile regularly to promote air circulation. An alternative is to spread clippings no more than 1 inch thick as a mulch in dahlia, rose, or shrubbery beds.

Clippings can create a problem if you pile them up, however—especially if the pile is near the house. Grass has a high water content. In a pile, there's no room for air movement or water evaporation. Smell-producing bacteria thrive, turning the grass into yellow-brown slime. The pile becomes a breeding place for houseflies, false stable flies, and soldier flies. Turning over just one small section of decaying, piled grass may expose as many as 3,000 fly maggots.

WATERING MATURE LAWNS

Even the most drought-tolerant lawns—such as bermudagrass, zoysiagrass, and fescue—can't live with prolonged lack of water (see page 72). Other grasses suffer from even brief water deprivation. The first sign of a drought problem is the dark bluish-green tinge caused partly by leaf folding. The lawn loses its springiness, and footprints remain evident following any foot traffic. Most lawns go dormant about three days after drought-caused wilting begins.

Many factors determine a proper watering program. These include turf type, soil, climate, temperature, wind velocity, humidity, rain, and maintenance practices. If only the top few inches of soil are regularly watered, roots do not seek water any deeper. Shallow roots force you to water more often to maintain a green lawn. But frequent watering keeps soil constantly wet, encouraging weeds and disease. Water should regularly penetrate 6 to 8 inches to encourage deep lawn rooting. This enables lawns to go longer between waterings, cutting down on disease potential.

Sprinkler efficiency: Inefficient sprinkler placement results in overwatering in some areas, underwatering in others. Test the sprinkler by setting shallow containers of the same size at regular intervals throughout the lawn area. Put some close to the sprinkler and some at the farthest reach of the water. Make a diagram of your container layout, then record the amount of water in each container after a normal sprinkling. Over its entire surface, a lawn needs 1 to 2 inches of water per week. Adjust sprinkler heads accordingly.

Soil type: The type of soil in your lawn affects how much water the grass actually receives. Two soil extremes cause watering problems: clay soil and sandy soil.

■ **Clay soil:** This type of soil is composed of individual mineral particles of less than $\frac{1}{125,000}$ inch. Because of their extremely small size, clay particles tend to pack together and become dense, slowing water penetration and absorption.

Water clay soil slowly to avoid runoff. Clay soils may require several shorter periods of watering rather than one longer irrigation to adequately wet the rooting zone of turf. Many gardeners believe they are giving

Oscillating-arm sprinklers are designed to apply water over large areas, and they are highly adjustible. Individual sprinklers differ; test yours to be certain of its watering pattern.

ample water to lawns growing in clay soils, while runoff is causing a water shortage that results in brown or yellow grass. Soil packing and subsequent runoff become even worse if the grass is walked on when wet.

Once wet, clay subsoil holds water for quite a while. This is true even if the topsoil looks dry and cracks. Waterlogged soil decreases air penetration and may lead to many fungal diseases. Because the topsoil is dry, you may mistakenly believe the grass needs watering.

■ **Sandy soil:** This type of soil provides quick drainage and effective air circulation, but it does not retain moisture well. You may be watering enough, yet still see lawn yellowing or browning. Water moves rapidly through sand particles, which range in size from $\frac{1}{500}$ inch for fine sand to $\frac{1}{12}$ inch for coarse sand.

Type determination: To determine the type of soil in your lawn, fill a quart jar about two-thirds full of water. Fill the jar with soil until it is almost full. Add a bit of commercial dispersing agent, such as Calgon, to get best results. Replace the top tightly. Shake the jar vigorously. Now let the soil settle. A sand layer becomes visible in a short time, the heaviest sand settling out first. Clay and silt take hours to settle; fine clay may remain suspended indefinitely. Many soils are a mixture of types, but one type usually predominates.

Effectiveness tests: If your watering schedule is not producing desired results, purchase a soil-moisture tester, or coring tube. The coring tube takes up a long earth plug that shows you the deep-down moisture level. A simple test, but not as diagnostic, is poking a long screwdriver into the ground. If it pokes through 6 inches of soil easily, the lawn is usually wet enough. Test soil moisture 12 hours after watering. Soil should be moist 6 to 8 inches down.

Changes in water availability: Since lawn browning can occur quickly, the response must be prompt. When water availability becomes restricted, do not apply fertilizer except during the fall rainy season. Fertilizer promotes growth that is not supported by adequate moisture. Remove all weeds, which compete for water. Don't cut grass as short, and mow less often, but don't let it grow higher than one third over the recommended mowing height. Less-frequent mowing may require clipping removal.

With restricted watering, a lawn does not look lush. It may develop a spotty, thin appearance. Some gardeners under mandatory water rationing prefer to let a lawn die out altogether. If drought is recurrent, replant with drought-tolerant turf or drought-resistant ground cover.

If a lawn suddenly becomes spongy, the cause may be thatch buildup. Some gardeners confuse thatch with loose grass clippings. Clippings can be raked out.

PREVENTING WEEDS

Weeds produce huge numbers of seeds. The seeds are lightweight and often have built-in travel mechanisms that allow them to stick to fur or be wafted by the wind. In addition, weed seeds travel by means of transported soil, soil amendments, and garden seeds that are not weed-free; birds and other animals; rain; equipment; and the gardener who unknowingly has weed seeds clinging to clothing. Some planted grasses become weeds when they invade nonlawn areas or lawns of different types.

In general, lawn weeds are a sign that growing conditions are not optimal for grass. In nature, the strongest vegetation usually survives in an area for which it is best suited. The correct lawn grass for the area, put in properly and given prime care, can usually preclude newly arriving weeds. Conversely, weeds thrive in an area where planting preparation has been poor, soil unimproved, water minimal, and fertilizer scarce.

In the ongoing lawn weed battle, your primary strategy in its control is to create optimal growth conditions for planted grass, that will crowd out weeds. To grow the healthiest grass possible, consider the questions that follow.

■ Is soil acidity slowing grass growth?
■ Is drainage adequate?
■ Is soil compaction inhibiting roots?
■ Are the grass types planted best suited to the climate?
■ Is fertilizer application timed to coincide with the needs of the lawn throughout its seasonal life cycle?
■ Is mowing technique and frequency appropriate for the type of grass?
■ Is watering deep enough?
■ Is intermittent overwatering creating soggy soil?
■ Are trees and shrubs blocking sunlight necessary for adequate growth?
■ Have pest insects, nematodes, or disease weakened the grass?
■ Does foot traffic create soil compaction that prevents the grass from thriving?

If your analysis shows that growing conditions are hindering the grass, correct the conditions by following the suggestions in the appropriate sections of this book. Time spent encouraging grass will be time saved from pulling weeds.

In addition, reduce the opportunity for weed seeds to take hold by purchasing weed-free seed and treating the soil with a preventative before planting. During prime lawn-growing season, consider spraying emerging weeds before they send out roots or runners or create seeds. Control measures to prevent weed seed formation, keep new seeds from finding a place to set roots, and quickly eliminate any seedlings that do take hold, form an effective prevention trio of methods.

Weed seeds are extremely durable. Some seeds may germinate quickly upon finding a satisfactory site; others may lie dormant for a year or more before germinating. Repeat weed-control measures each season. If you are thorough, weeds will not invade your lawn or your free time.

IDENTIFYING WEEDS

Correctly identifying lawn weeds allows you to plan effective control measures. Knowing whether your weeds reproduce from roots, rhizomes, stolons, seeds, or a combination allows you to take appropriate action. For example, the dandelion multiplies not only from seeds, but also from its long root system. If you leave even a small portion of root in the ground, the dandelion will reemerge.

In general, weeds are categorized as annuals or perennials and as warm-season or cool-season plants.

Warm-season annuals: About 80 percent of lawn weeds are annuals. Summer, or warm-season, annual weeds peak at midsummer, when heat slows the growth of competing cool-season grass. The seeds of these plants germinate as soon as soil temperature reaches 60° to 65°F. These seeds are not shade-tolerant, so if perennial lawn grasses are present and growing strongly, warm-season annual weeds have problems germinating because of lack of light. Even tree shade slows germination. But where lawn is thinning, weed seedlings establish rapidly and aggressively crowd out grass.

In warm climates, applying fertilizer early in the season gives lawn grass a growth spurt before annual summer weeds germinate. Letting the lawn grow a little taller before cutting, particularly in spring and summer months, provides shade that slows annual weed seedlings. Water carefully. Light, frequent watering helps weeds and discourages grass growth. Water deeply and only when needed.

In cool climates, apply fertilizer and mechanically improve the growing area at the end of summer. Follow this with an application of fertilizer early the next spring. Common warm-season annual weeds include foxtail, goosegrass, and sandbur.

■ **Foxtail:** Annual foxtail is found throughout the United States and in parts of Canada. Its leaves are 2 to 6 inches long,

When applying lawn weed killer with a hose-end sprayer, avoid spraying on windy days and follow all label directions carefully.

flat, and ¼ to ½ inch wide; they sometimes appear twisted. Topsides of green foxtail leaves are hairy. Yellow foxtail leaves are smooth. Both thrive in sunny, bare spots. Both types of foxtail grow best in damp, well-fertilized soil.

If a lawn is frequently mowed, foxtail forms a low mat. If unmowed, hairy flower spikes resembling bristles appear between June and September. Each bristle may be 2 to 4 inches long and resemble a fox's tail. Foxtail is often confused with crabgrass, because both grow in clumps. However, foxtail clumps are not as wide as crabgrass clumps. Since foxtail reproduces only from seeds, rather than from reproductive stems or runners, it can be removed with a trowel or by hand. Keep it under control by removing lawn clippings that contain seed heads. Chemical controls include Ortho® Weed-B-Gon® Crabgrass Killer for Lawns, Ortho® Grass-B-Gon® Grass Killer for Landscapes, or Roundup® Weed & Grass Killer.

■ **Goosegrass:** This warm-season annual resembles crabgrass but is darker green with a silver center. Its smooth, flat stems form a rosette. Leaf blades are 2 to 10 inches long and ⅓ inch wide. Goosegrass germinates when soil temperatures are between 60° and 65°F, several weeks after crabgrass. It multiplies from seeds, expands by spreading, and has an extensive root system. It does not root at stem joints. Seeds are produced on stalks 2 to 6 inches high that appear from July to October. Mature plants die with first frost. Seeds are dormant over winter. It prefers compacted soils that have poor drainage and light, frequent watering. To control, treat with Ortho® Grass-B-Gon® Grass Killer for Landscapes. Prevent goosegrass with a preemergent herbicide containing *trifluralin* or *pendimethalin*.

■ **Sandbur:** Also called burgrass, this annual grassy weed has yellow-green leaf blades that are 2 to 5 inches long and ¼ inch wide. The topsides of weeds may be rough. In mowed lawns, sandbur tends to form low mats. In unmowed lawns, it may reach 2 feet tall. Spiked straw-colored seed burrs ½ inch long appear from July to September. Sandbur grows best in sandy dry soil. Begin control by improving soil with organic matter and encouraging strong lawn growth. If weeds persist, spot-treat with Ortho® Weed-B-Gon® Crabgrass Killer For Lawns, Ortho® Grass-B-Gon® Grass Killer for Landscapes, or Roundup® Weed & Grass Killer.

Cool-season annuals: Cool-season annual weeds generally start growth from seeds in late summer or fall. They grow rapidly until the first solid frost, then go into a partial resting phase. With spring, they grow rapidly again, this time setting seeds. They die out in early summer.

Cool-season weeds have the advantage of growing when most grasses are partially or entirely dormant. They thrive in early spring, when desired grasses are just getting started, and in fall, when desired grasses are slowing down for winter. Unrestricted, cool-season annual weeds may ruin a lawn before it gets into full spring growth.

If your lawn has just a few cool-season weeds, eliminate them completely before any flowers or seeds appear. In southern states, plant a winter grass in fall that crowds weeds out. In northern states, leave the grass slightly higher in spring and fall to shade out weed seedlings. Rake up grass clippings if weed seeds are present. Chemical controls are effective when cool-season grasses don't respond to manual measures.

■ **Shepherd's purse:** Also called shepherd's-bag and lady's-purse, this annual weed may appear throughout the year in warm-winter areas. Its arrow-shaped leaves are toothed or lobed and form a rosette. Tiny white flower clusters appear on stems that can reach up to 18 inches high. Seeds are in triangular pods resembling small purses. Seeds can remain dormant for several years before germinating in spring. In warm-weather areas, seeds may germinate in fall. Shepherd's purse is not fussy about soil, but it will not grow in shade. Mechanical control consists of hand-pulling. Chemical control consists of a treatment with Ortho® Weed-B-Gon® Weed Killer for Lawns. Treat when plants are actively growing.

■ **Downy brome:** Downy brome is a slender, upright annual weed that grows throughout the United States except some southeastern areas. It grows to 2 feet tall. Light green coarse, hairy leaves are 2 to 6 inches long. Drooping purple flower clusters appear in spring. Seeds can remain viable in soil for more than two years. Germination is in fall or early spring. Downy brome weeds turn purplish when mature. They prosper in poor sandy or gravelly soil and cool growing conditions. Remove by hand-pulling. Chemical control includes Ortho® Grass-B-Gon® Grass Killer for Landscapes. To keep downy brome from returning, apply *trifluralin* or *pendimethalin*.

Top: Goosegrass
Bottom: Shepherd's purse

■ **Prostrate knotweed:** Prostrate knotweed grows quite low to the ground and has smooth blue-green oval leaves, each about 1 inch long and ¼ inch wide. The leaves attach to wiry stems at visible joints. The stems range from 4 to 24 inches long. Knotweed is an annual that forms mats that can reach 2 feet wide, crowding out lawn grasses. It grows throughout the United States and southern Canada. The weed is usually found in compacted soil. The fastest growth period for prostrate knotweed is from early spring to early fall. Tiny green-white flowers bloom in clusters at the leaf and stem joints from June to November. Knotweed reproduces from seeds, which are plentiful. Though knotweed can't get started in healthy, dense turf, it is common in areas of heavy foot traffic. Aeration helps control prostrate knotweed. Pull out young plants. There is no preemergent control. If necessary, treat the lawn with Ortho® Weed-B-Gon® Weed Killer for Lawns or Scotts® GreenSweep® Weed & Feed in early spring.

■ **Black medic:** Other names for black medic include yellow trefoil and black clover. It is sometimes confused with clover. Black medic has three-leaflet cloverlike leaves that are slightly toothed at the tips. Its low-growing stems are slightly hairy. Black medic is common in lawns throughout the United States from May through September.

Ground ivy.

Broadleaf plantain.

It forms thick mats that crowd out desirable lawn grasses. Small bright yellow flowers bloom in late spring and early summer. In warm-weather areas, black medic can bloom until December. Blooms are followed by black kidney-shape seed pods. Black medic is an annual that multiplies only from seeds. It is prevalent in nitrogen-deficient lawns. To eliminate small black medic patches, try hand-pulling. Increase lawn nitrogen with fertilizer where appropriate. Treat the lawn with Scotts® GreenSweep® Weed & Feed or Ortho® Weed-B-Gon® Weed Killer for Lawns.

■ **Common groundsel:** This weed grows 6 inches to 1½ feet tall, with 4-inch-long toothed leaves of medium green. Yellow flowers 1 inch long appear from April to October. It reproduces by seeds and by stems that may take root at the lower joints. The plant grows best in moist, rich soil. Hand-pull groundsel before it produces seeds. Spot-treat with Roundup® Weed & Grass Killer.

Warm-season grassy perennials: These weeds are more difficult to control than annual weeds. Since they are a different color and texture than lawn grasses, they stand out, possibly ruining a lawn's appearance. If grassy perennial weeds take over, it may be necessary to pull out the present lawn and replace it.

■ **Dallisgrass:** A clumpy rosette-type weed, dallisgrass has coarse-textured leaves. Each leaf is 4 to 10 inches long and ½ inch wide. Stems 2 to 6 inches long emerge from the plant center in a starlike pattern. Dallisgrass reproduces from seeds and underground stems. This perennial has extremely deep roots. It has a tendency to turn brown in the center. Although it is primarily a summer weed in cool areas, it grows all year in mild climates. Growth begins quite early in spring. Dallisgrass grows best in warm weather; low, wet ground; and high-cut lawns. Once established, however,

it spreads rapidly in low-cut lawns. This weed is a severe problem in the southern United States. There is no preemergent control. Try draining soil to eliminate dallisgrass. If the weed persists, treat it in early spring or summer with Ortho® Grass-B-Gon® Grass Killer for Landscapes, Ortho® Weed-B-Gon® Crabgrass Killer for Lawns, or Roundup® Weed & Grass Killer.

■ **Nimblewill:** Also termed nimbleweed and dropseed, nimblewill has smooth, flat, light green or bluish green leaves up to 2 inches long on wiry stems up to 10 inches tall. In spring nimblewill turns green after other grasses. The result is brown patches in infested lawns. Nimblewill stems root at lower nodes as the plants reach outward. It thrives in hot, dry areas and in thin turf during drought. For small infestations, dig out patches of the weed. Eliminate it in lawns with Ortho® Grass-B-Gon® Grass Killer for Landscapes. Begin control in early spring.

■ **Nutsedge:** Other names for nutsedge are nutgrass, cocosedge, and cocograss. The most common nutsedge forms are yellow or purple. There are annual varieties as well as perennial. Nutsedge has greenish yellow leaves emerging from triangular stems. In flower, nutsedge has umbrellalike clusters topping its stems. Seed heads are yellow-brown. In summer, nutsedge grows more rapidly than lawn grass, is easily seen, and disfigures lawns. It can be extremely difficult to eliminate, because it multiplies from tubers, seeds, and underground stems. The tuber stores nutrients. If any tuber is left in the ground after the rest of the plant is removed, nutsedge can regrow. This weed prefers overly watered soil. Control includes changing lawn-watering techniques or increasing soil drainage. To treat nutsedge chemically, use Ortho® Weed-B-Gon® Crabgrass Killer for Lawns. Begin spraying in early spring and repeat the treatment according to label instructions.

Cool-season perennial broadleaf weeds: The leaves of these weeds can be lance-shape, arrow-shape, scalloped, or oval. Basically, they are not grasslike. All make a ragged appearance in lawns. This category includes broadleaf plantain, dandelion (see page 83), mouse-ear chickweed, ground ivy, speedwell, and clover (see page 81).

■ **Broadleaf plantain:** Also called common plantain, broadleaf plantain has thick, egg-shape, wavy-edged leaves growing in a ground-hugging rosette. It grows throughout the United States and southern Canada. The gray-green leaves of broadleaf plantain range from 2 to 10 inches long. From May to September seed heads appear in a long cluster from a central upright stem. Plantain multiplies from seeds and from resprouting roots. The weed germinates best in rich, moist, compacted soil. As broadleaf plantains grow, they suffocate surrounding lawn grass. To mechanically control plantain, dig out roots with a trowel. Do not let flowers or seeds form. Aerate the lawn. There is no preemergent control. Spray the lawn with Ortho® Weed-B-Gon® Weed Killer for Lawns, or Roundup® Weed & Grass Killer in the spring or fall.

■ **Mouse-ear chickweed:** This plant can appear in the finest of well-kept lawns. Not directly related to the annual common chickweed, this broadleaf perennial multiplies rapidly and can crowd out desired grasses. Mouse-ear chickweed has a different color and texture than grass.

The ½-inch-long leaves of the weed are both fleshy and fuzzy. Stems are low and spreading. Small white flowers appear from April through June. The period of fastest growth is in early spring. Mouse-ear chickweed multiplies from seeds and runners, which root easily at the nodes. This prevalent weed thrives in moist, poorly drained soil in sun or shade. Mechanical control consists of keeping runners and stems off the ground so they can't take root. Mouse-ear chickweed is extremely difficult to eliminate by hand-pulling, since it can resprout from pieces left in the soil. To discourage mouse-ear chickweed, cut the lawn short. Remove clippings containing runners and discard them. There is no preemergent control. Treat the lawn with Ortho® Weed-B-Gon® Weed Killer for Lawns in early spring or late fall.

■ **Ground ivy:** This plant is also called creeping ivy and gill-over-the-ground. It is a cool-season, perennial weed that grows 3 to 6 inches tall. Bright green leaves are scalloped, round, and about 1 inch wide. Tiny light blue to purple flowers appear from spring through summer. Reproduction is from seeds and creeping stems that root upon soil contact. Ground ivy does well in sun or shade as long as soil is damp. Plants form a dense mat that can completely crowd out lawn grass. There is no preemergent control. Cut grass short and rake to keep runners from touching the ground. Hand-pulling must be thorough because pieces left in the ground can resprout. Treat the lawn with Ortho® Weed-B-Gon® Weed Killer for Lawns or Scotts® GreenSweep® Weed & Feed in the the spring or fall.

■ **Speedwell:** Also called creeping veronica, in a few years this perennial weed can cover an entire lawn. It has bright green, roundish, scallop-edged leaves ½ inch long. Each plant is about 4 inches high. Tiny bluish-white flowers bloom on stalks that grow somewhat above leaves. Heart-shaped seedpods form on stems below flowers. Speedwell reproduces from creeping stems that root easily upon touching ground. It is not usually found in well-drained sunny areas that receive fertilizer regularly. It grows best in moist, shady lawn and acidic soil, but it can grow in sunlight if soil remains moist. To discourage speedwell, cut grass short and remove all clippings to avoid stem rooting. Spray with Ortho® Weed-B-Gon® Weed Killer for Lawns when the plant is flowering or actively growing.

Cool-season perennial grassy or grasslike weeds:

■ **Bermudagrass:** This plant can be a valued warm-season turfgrass or a nasty weed in cool season lawns. It is often confused with quackgrass, because both spread in the same creeping fashion and form mats. Bermudagrass blades are about ⅛ inch wide. Stems are gray-green, hairy, and 6 to 18 inches long. This grass reproduces from seeds, aboveground stems, and underground stems. Roots may grow several feet deep. Seeds are formed on 3-inch-wide fingerlike segments that grow slightly above stems. From three to seven of these segments grow on each plant. Bermudagrass is a fast-growing perennial that turns brown when temperatures drop below 50°F. It is slow to turn green in spring, creating brown patches throughout the lawn.

Though drought- and heat-tolerant, this annual does not grow vigorously in shade. In sunny areas, however, bermudagrass may quickly crowd out desirable lawn. Mechanically control bermudagrass by hand-pulling. Remove all roots—any piece of root left can resprout. The best time to begin chemical control is in spring, when shoots are just appearing; use Ortho® Grass-B-Gon® Grass Killer for Landscapes according to label instructions. Six weeks later, re-treat any new green stems and leaves. Bermudagrass can be spot-treated with Ortho® Grass-B-Gon® Grass Killer for Landscapes any time grass is actively growing. After one week, mow as close as possible and reseed the area. Multiple treatments may be needed. There is no preemergent treatment. To prevent bermudagrass invasion in cool-season areas, apply a heavy dose of fertilizer in fall. Give the lawn adequate water during the summer.

■ **Zoysiagrass:** Like bermudagrass, zoysiagrass is a valued lawn grass in warm-weather areas but a weed in other regions. In cold areas, this perennial becomes dormant with the first fall frost and remains so until late spring. The result is that small to large irregular patches of brown suddenly develop amid cool-weather grasses that stay green, such as bluegrass, fescue, and bentgrass. The browning is often attributed to insect invasion, but the zoysiagrass is still perfectly healthy. Its tops have died back, but its roots are merely resting. Though it grows slowly, zoysiagrass is hardy. It often takes hold in a lawn in areas of heavy traffic, then invades the surrounding area. Mechanical control consists of digging up clumps and reseeding. If zoysiagrass is a continuing problem, some gardeners let it take over lawns growing in full sun, then spray it with green dye in winter. Chemical control consists of spot treatment with Roundup® Weed & Grass Killer. Treat while zoysiagrass is still green; once it turns brown, anything but digging is ineffective.

■ **Wild garlic and wild onion:** Wild garlic is often mistaken for wild onion and vice versa. Though they are similar in habits, they are not the same. Both are often the first growth seen in spring. They resemble grasses, but are not. Both grow from small underground bulbs and have a garlicky or oniony odor. Leaves are slender, hollow, and round, joining together near the plant base. Greenish purple or white flowers appear at leaf height. Germination occurs in spring

and fall. Bulblets may appear at leaf tips. The bulblets fall to the ground and sprout. Wild garlic and onion spread rapidly from spring to midsummer. They thrive in heavy, wet soil. They are drought and cold hardy. There is no preemergent control. Mowing when wild garlic and wild onion first appear can lessen infestation, but bulbs must be totally removed for full control. Postemergent control is most effective in late fall, when wild garlic or onion is still small and vulnerable. Once these perennials take hold, they can be extremely difficult to eliminate. Treat the lawn with Ortho® Weed-B-Gon® Weed Killer for Lawns or an herbicide containing *dicamba* as the leaves emerge in the spring. Repeat the application in two weeks. Repeat treatments for two or three years.

■ **Timothygrass:** This blue-green bunching grass thrives in thin, poorly fertilized lawns. Its leaves are broad and pointed. Timothygrass grows best in spring and fall. To control it, dig up all clumps.

■ **Velvetgrass:** This perennial can grow to 4 feet tall in unmowed areas. In mowed areas, the bright green velvety leaves stay flat. The plants root wherever joints touch the soil. Seed heads 2 to 4 inches long appear from July to August. Seeds remain dormant over winter and germinate in spring. Perennial velvetgrass thrives in damp areas with good soil, but it tolerates partial shade. To eliminate velvetgrass, use Roundup® Weed & Grass Killer Ready-to-Use at any time, but spraying before seed heads mature will be most effective.

Hand-pulling weeds is easier on the back with long-handle weeders, but dandelions will regenerate if even a tiny piece of root is left in the soil.

USING CHEMICAL CONTROLS

Herbicides are powerful formulations that must be used on the appropriate plants at the proper time. The time of application defines into which of two major categories a chemical fits. These categories are *preemergent herbicides* and *postemergent herbicides.*

A preemergent control stops sprouting at an early stage. It is most effective when placed in or on soil before weed seedlings poke out of the ground. If applied properly, few, if any, of the targeted weeds emerge. A postemergent control is effective after the weeds have emerged and begun to grow.

Many modern preemergent and postemergent controls are quite specific as to what weeds they eliminate. Used improperly, these herbicides can create more problems than the weeds themselves. Desired grass and surrounding plants can be temporarily or permanently harmed.

Read the herbicide label before purchasing the product. Make sure the chemical is appropriate for the plant you want to treat, and see if using the product requires special precautions. Use all controls at the appropriate time. Postemergent controls are not effective during the weed's dormant season. Use them on lawn grasses when soil is moist and weeds are growing strongly. Avoid spraying or dusting on windy days. Wind can waft weed killer to nearby

Most mushrooms do not damage a lawn, but some gardeners find them unsightly. The easiest solution, although it is only temporary, is to break the mushrooms with a rake or mower.

plants. If they are susceptible to the control, they may soon brown or die. Apply chemical controls early in the morning or at dusk, when the air is generally calm. If the herbicide label lists a nearby plant as particularly sensitive to the control, protect the plant with a cardboard or wood barrier.

Lack of patience may result in control overdose. A treatment can take from 3 to 10 days to produce visible results. Do not reapply the product if weed browning does not occur a day or two after spraying or dusting. Herbicide overdoses are dangerous to surrounding grasses.

Weed killers do not gain effectiveness if mixed at a concentration stronger than the instructions recommend. Using too strong a mixture can damage or kill desirable plants.

Don't use a weed killer on newly seeded lawns, even if the control is not supposed to affect grass of the type that is planted. Any type of weed control used around seedling grasses can kill them. Seedlings are far more sensitive to control ingredients than mature plants. If you want to use a postemergent control, do so far in advance of reseeding the grass; this will give the control ingredients time to weaken in the soil. The time required differs for different controls. Read the label of the product you buy to determine a safe time for treatment.

Sometimes desirable plants brown long after the application of a weed control but soon after the application of an insecticide. If the same applicator was used for both, the cause could be herbicide contamination. If even a little bit of an herbicide remains in the applicator, it can affect plants. Wash all applicators thoroughly with water and detergent to remove traces of herbicide. Better yet, use separate applicators for herbicides and insecticides.

SOLVING TREE-RELATED LAWN PROBLEMS

When trees and grass grow in the same area, two problems often develop: surface roots, and excess shade from tree canopies and fallen foliage.

Surface roots: Because of their marked natural tendency to develop surface roots, some trees are best left out of lawn areas. These include acacia, ailanthus, silver maple, alder, Pacific dogwood, fig, evergreen ash, honey locust, mulberry, sycamore, poplar, elm, sumac, black locust, and willow. If you

move into a home where the lawn has severe surface root problems, consider removing the trees and replacing them with appropriate species. Those include maple, silk tree, smoke tree, hawthorn, Modesto ash, golden rain tree, crape myrtle, magnolia, and flowering cherry, peach, and plum.

Surface rooting is caused by external factors as well as natural tendencies. One of the most common is lawn watering. Tree roots need regular watering that penetrates from 6 inches to 3 feet into the soil—the depth necessary depends on the tree species. Sprinkler systems tend to water shallowly. Tree roots, suffering from drought in deeper, unirrigated soil, move upward, instead of downward, to get moisture.

Excess standing water around lawn trees is another cause of surface rooting. Water fills the air spaces in the soil. As a result, the only readily available oxygen is near the surface, so the tree roots move upward. If a natural or created basin surrounds the tree, you might want to dig a drainage area. Irrigate less often near the tree base so soil dries out between waterings. When you do irrigate the tree, water it deeply, perhaps using a root irrigator.

Compacted soil can also cause tree roots to move upward, seeking oxygen. To allow deeper oxygen penetration, loosen soil around tree roots. Try not to harm the roots themselves. Severe root injury can permit disease and insect attack.

Fertilizer application practices can also encourage surface rooting. If nutrients remain at the surface, the roots do, too. To prompt downward growth, place fertilizer in 12-inch-deep holes. Space holes evenly under the full expanse of the leaf canopy.

If surface rooting remains a problem after watering, drainage, soil compaction, and fertilizer application has been adjusted, root pruning may be necessary. Some root pruning can be done without harming the tree. If you prize the tree, consider hiring a professional to do the job.

If surface roots are allowed to remain, you may have to adjust your mowing practices. If you do not want to leave the root area bare, consider placing a ring of bark mulch around the tree or planting a hardy ground cover.

Regardless of tree type and maintenance practices, some lawn upheaval may occur near old or large trees. Their big roots, even at a depth, displace ground. Adding good weed-free soil as a yearly topdressing can improve appearance.

Tree shade: The fact that your lawn is shaded by trees does not necessarily mean the grass gets too much shade. Trees with naturally sparse canopies, such as birch, can allow enough filtered light to permit shade-tolerant grass to grow. If the lawn thins and turns dark green, however, or if moss and algae take hold, corrective action is needed.

To increase the amount of sun under trees, try trimming back or cutting off all limbs that extend below or grow less than 6 feet from the ground. Thinning a dense tree crown can also help. If the lawn does not improve after the pruning, you may have to replant the area.

In an area that receives less than two hours of direct sunlight each day, consider planting a shade-tolerant nongrass species such as vinca, wild ginger, sweet woodruff, mondo grass, winter creeper, ajuga, Japanese spurge, or even ivy, if it can be controlled.

If the area receives at least two hours of direct sun daily, a shade-tolerant grass can probably survive. Under deciduous trees in cool-winter areas, put in shade-tolerant lawns in late summer or early fall. This gives the grass time to establish during the tree's leafless period.

Under nondeciduous trees in cool climates, reseed or resod in early spring. Consider creeping, red, or chewing fescue. Some of the bluegrass varieties also tolerate part shade. Where warm-season grasses can grow, replant just after the grass-growing season begins in early spring. Among the shade-tolerant, warm-season choices are zoysiagrass, centipedegrass, St. Augustine-grass, and carpetgrass. Since tree roots interfere with soil preparation, care will be needed to make a healthy seedbed.

Always remove fallen leaves under deciduous trees planted in lawn areas. Fallen foliage shades grass even when light is available. When removing leaves from newly seeded areas, take care not to damage the seedlings or seedbed.

Shady areas call for care in mowing as well. When light is scarce, grass grows a bit taller in its reach for the sun. Close mowing of shaded grass can be harmful since it reduces the productive leaf blade area. Adjust your lawn mower accordingly when moving from turf in sun to turf in tree shade; let the shaded grass grow a little taller than the grass in the sun.

In lawn areas that have been overplanted with trees, regardless of tree type, shading will eventually become a problem. Over-planting is fairly common in new-home areas where owners want, in a short time, to create the leafy look of an old neighborhood. In addition to creating too much shade, overplanting impedes air flow. Lack of air circulation discourages grass growth and encourages lawn diseases. If the planting is extremely thick, pruning is not enough; trees must be removed to alleviate the shading problem.

CONTROLLING LAWN PESTS

Gardeners usually think of lawn pests in two categories: insects and larger animals.

Lawn insects: Insect pests do an ample share of lawn destruction. At varying times of the year, chiggers (see page 511), chinch bugs (see page 69), billbugs (see page 71), armyworms, cutworms, European crane flies, grubs (see page 67), sod webworms (see page 67), flea beetles, fiery skipper butterfly larvae, fleas (see page 512), fire ants, fruit flies, grasshoppers, greenbugs, leafhoppers, mites, scales, wireworms, and mole crickets (see page 71) can invade in small or large numbers. Healthy lawns can tolerate more insect damage than poorly maintained lawns. Some perennial ryegrasses are not attractive to pests such as armyworms, billbugs, cutworms, and sod webworms. Large populations of any pest insect species usually call for intervention by the gardener. Predators—such as birds, parasitic wasps, *Bacillus thuringiensis* (Bt), ladybugs, and green lacewing larvae—can help the gardener control insect pests without chemicals.

■ **Armyworms:** These pests chew grass blades and stems, causing circular bare patches in lawns. In large numbers, armyworms can chew a lawn to the ground in three days. Found throughout the United States except in the coldest areas, the fall armyworm is one of the worst southern lawn pests. These worms move from lawn to garden, then may return to do more damage. Newly hatched worms are white with black heads. Mature worms are green, tan, or brown with dark or orange back and side stripes. Adult size is 1½ inches long. Parents are 1-inch-wide tan or mottled gray moths. Like the adults, armyworms are most active at night and on overcast days. In daylight, they hide in the soil around grass roots. The first generation, which appears in spring, causes the most damage.

Bacillus thuringiensis is partially effective as a natural control of larvae.

■ **Cutworms:** The larvae of moths, cutworms feed on grass stems and leaf blades. Cutworms are brown, gray, or nearly gray; there are spotted and striped varieties. A full-size larva can be up to 2 inches long. Cutworms curl up when touched. Adults are dark 2-inch-wide night-flying moths. Often called miller moths, they are common at night around outdoor lights. Cutworms feed at night. During the day, they hide in the upper soil layers. Some types never emerge, feeding only on grass roots. Their feeding causes 2-inch-wide bare spots in the lawn. A closer look shows grass sheared off at or below ground level. Birds often seek out cutworms as food. *Bacillus thuringiensis* sprays and parasitic wasps help destroy cutworms. Apply chemical controls in late afternoon or early evening; Controls include Scotts® GrubEx® Season-Long Grub Control.

■ **European crane fly larvae:** These larvae eat grass roots, causing yellow-brown patches in summer dry seasons. Damage often begins at the lawn periphery and moves inward. The brownish wormlike maggots develop a tough skin and are sometimes called leatherjackets. A larva is about 1 inch long. Crane flies are found throughout the United States. Adults look like long-legged mosquitoes. An adult's body size, not including the legs, is about 1 inch long. Crane flies do not sting or do other harm. To ascertain whether damage is caused by crane fly larvae, water damaged areas thoroughly, then cover them overnight with black plastic. If crane fly larvae are present, they will be lying on the soil surface under the plastic the next morning. Crane fly feeding stops naturally in mid-May. Treatment is most effective in early April; use Ortho® Bug-B-Gon® Multi-Purpose Insect Killer Ready-Spray® or Scotts® GrubEx® Season-Long Grub Control.

■ **Fiery skipper butterfly larvae:** By destroying grass blades, these insects create isolated brown spots in lawns. Initially these dead areas are 1 inch wide, but they can expand to cover larger lawn areas. The adult butterfly is orange, brown, or both. It is usually seen during warm weather, flying over lawns in midday. The larvae are small brownish yellow worms that may be found within grass blades. White cottony masses may appear in the lawn—these are the cocoons of a butterfly parasite. The parasites can sometimes control an infestation.

■ **Fire ants:** Infestations are becoming increasingly serious as fire ants move their territory from southern states to other warm-winter areas. Their tunnels and mounds can obstruct mowers, and tunneling can eliminate a lawn. Their bites are painful and, if numerous, can severely injure animals and people. Fire ants are more of a problem in sunny, clay soils than other areas. Control fire ants by using Ortho® Orthene® Fire Ant Killer, Ortho® Fire Ant Killer Broadcast Granules, or various baits.

■ **Fruit fly larvae:** These pests live in young grass stems. They eat and gradually destroy the central shoots. Grass then sends out side shoots. Parents are tiny black flies. The females lay eggs on the grass blades. As many as 10 larvae can live inside a single blade. Control is difficult because larvae are well-protected by the stems.

■ **Grasshoppers:** These insects can become lawn problems in areas near farmland; they migrate to yards when crop sustenance is insufficient. Dry, windy weather encourages grasshopper populations. In large numbers, grasshoppers can eat grass to the base. If the number is small, hand-picking can be effective. This job is easier early in the morning, when grasshoppers move slowly. If grasshopper lawn invasions occur repeatedly, slow down the next infestation with a bran bait containing *Nosema locustae*, a grasshopper disease organism. This may take several years to achieve full effect. Seasonal controls include Ortho® Systemic Insect Killer applied with a lawn sprayer over the entire lawn.

■ **Greenbugs:** Small light green aphids that feed on plant sap, greenbugs usually infest Kentucky bluegrass lawns. Their damage appears as rusty-looking lawn areas. These areas expand as greenbug populations increase. Greenbugs do not do much damage in lawns with enough sun; in shaded areas, they can become pests. To control greenbugs, use Ortho® Systemic Insect Killer or an insecticidal soap.

■ **Leafhoppers:** These ⅛-inch wedge-shaped yellow, green, or gray insects live on most lawns. They hop and fly easily from one leaf blade to another and suck out leaf sap. As a result, individual leaves develop white spots. With large infestations, leafhopper damage is demonstrated by lawn fading. Severe infestations can eradicate an emerging lawn. Leafhoppers are most abundant in warm weather. The appearance of damaged seedlings may mimic drought injury. However, if leafhoppers are present, they are almost surely doing the damage.

Small infestations are usually not bothersome to plants, but their presence may annoy gardeners. Use Ortho® Systemic Insect Killer, Ortho® Bug-B-Gon® Multi-Purpose Insect Killer Ready-Spray® or Scotts® GrubEx® Season-Long Grub Control.

■ **Mites:** Grass turns straw-colored as mites suck sap from the blades. The lawn then becomes brown and sparse. Some gardeners working in areas where mites are present may experience skin irritation. Three types of mites generally infest lawns: bermudagrass mites, which prey on bermudagrass only; clover mites; and winter grain mites, which attack bluegrass, fescue, and bentgrass. Most mites are too small to be seen without a microscope. Under magnification, these 1/30-inch pests vary in color, depending on species. They have eight legs and are insect relatives rather than insects. Bermudagrass mites may be seen by shaking an infested plant over a sheet of dark paper. The mites are visible as creamy specks that begin crawling. Mites thrive in hot, dry weather. Adequate watering keeps populations down. Controls include insecticidal soap, Ortho® Bug-B-Gon® Multi-Purpose Insect Killer Ready-Spray®, or Scotts® GrubEx® Season-Long Grub Control.

■ **Scales:** Infestations of scales on lawns are difficult to control. Scales are legless insects with hard shells. They are extremely small and look like bumps on leaves or roots. Pearl scales attack the roots of bermudagrass, St. Augustinegrass, and centipedegrass. Bermudagrass scale feeds on bermudagrass stems, giving the plant a moldy appearance. Rhodesgrass scales attack grass crowns, causing blades to wither and die.

■ **Wireworms:** These brown hard-shelled larvae are the offspring of click beetles. A full-size larva is 1½ inches long. Wireworms feed in groups on grass roots, causing irregular areas of wilted grass. The larvae are most prevalent in soggy soil. Create an organic control by digging several 3-inch-wide by 3-inch-deep holes in the lawn. Bury a potato in each hole and mark each one by inserting a stake or some other device in the ground. In a few days the potatoes will be filled with feeding wireworms. Remove and destroy the potatoes; do not compost them.

Other lawn pests: Moles, rabbits, and gophers top the list of lawn-destroying animals, although in certain areas armadillos, skunks, crayfish, birds, voles (meadow mice), and field mice can cause significant damage.

■ **Moles:** In digging tunnels that serve as feeding pathways, moles create raised ridges that may eventually crisscross a lawn. Ridges range from 3 to 5 inches wide. Because mole tunneling destroys grass roots, ridge areas brown quickly. Moles build new feeding tunnels constantly and may not use the same one twice. If you look carefully, you may find the entry and exit mounds. These are round, conical, fan-shape, or irregular in shape. The hole usually has dirt in it but is still visible. The mounds are connected to main runways, which moles use repeatedly. These are 12 to 18 inches underground and not usually visible aboveground.

Moles are 4 to 6 inches long with gray to black velvety fur. They have slender, hairless snouts and small eyes and ears. Moles' front feet are large with long claws. Despite many tunnels, one lawn is usually home to only one mole. Except for breeding season, in early spring, moles tend to live solitary lives. Moles eat insects and earthworms. Controls include trapping, bait, repellents, and fumigation. Bait and repellents are not as effective as other controls. Aboveground and below-ground mole traps are available. Move tunnel traps daily if a mole is not caught.

■ **Gophers:** These rodents are occasionally seen poking their heads out of newly constructed dirt mounds early in the morning. Gophers are brown, have small eyes and ears, and have conspicuous pouches on both sides of their mouths. Gophers protect their territories. The number of mounds in your lawn may seem to indicate the presence of a gopher colony, however, each lawn usually contains just one gopher. The mounds consist of finely pulverized soil that is quite visible in a green lawn. Each mound may contain a visible hole, or an earth clump may camouflage the hole. Tunnels 6 to 8 inches below the lawn surface connect the mounds. Gophers don't create lawn ridges. The rodents eat roots of grass and other plants, pulling them down into underground burrows. Traps are the most efficient form of control. Both wire traps and box traps are sold at many hardware stores and plant nurseries. Dig down to an active horizontal tunnel, and place two traps in it. Follow instructions that accompany the trap.

■ **Rabbits:** When hungry, rabbits eat almost every type of green plant, including lawn grass. They can be minor pests or major ones, depending on the supply of food in the area. The most effective control is keeping rabbits out. Owning a cat or dog that annoys animal pests is sometimes a solution. Another control is a fence made of 1-inch-wide wire mesh. This should be 2 feet high and extend 6 inches underground to avoid rabbit jumping and tunneling. Keeping jackrabbits out requires an even higher fence. Rabbit repellents are sometimes effective. They repel rabbits by making grass taste unpleasant. Repellents must be reapplied as grass grows or is mowed.

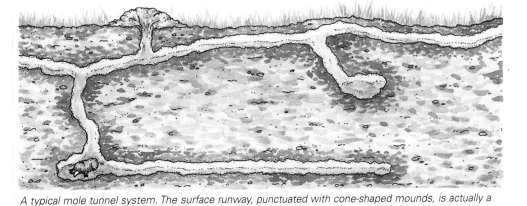

A typical mole tunnel system. The surface runway, punctuated with cone-shaped mounds, is actually a feeding tunnel that may only be used once. The burrow, or main tunnel system that serves as the animal's living quarters, is usually 12 to 18 inches deep.

■ **Field mice and voles:** These rodents sometimes take up residence in abandoned gopher and mole burrows or create their own burrows. If they make a lawn their winter residence, they may work under snow cover. Lawn runways become visible when snow disappears. Voles feed on grass during the winter and can cause extensive damage. A cat that annoys these rapidly multiplying pests can be an effective control. Other controls include mousetraps, rattraps, and box traps. If children or pets are in the area, do not use poison bait in the open.

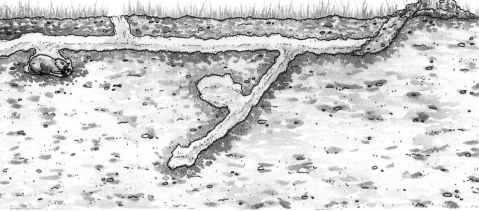

A typical pocket gopher tunnel system. Unlike those of moles, the feeding runways of gophers are not visible from the surface. The large mounds created through excavation are crescent-shaped with an obviously visible plug of earth. In addition to the mounds, each burrow may have several smaller feeding-tunnel openings that give the animal access to plants aboveground.

■ **Skunks and armadillos:** In residential areas adjacent to woodland or farmland, skunks and armadillos can cause lawn damage as they dig up grass to feed on insects, particularly grubs. Lawn grubs from an infestation of pest beetles, such as Japanese beetles or June beetles, attract them. Removing their food supply usually causes skunks and armadillos to go elsewhere. If the problem becomes serious, apply a beetle pest control.

■ **Birds:** Lawns containing earthworms, chinch bugs, sod webworms, cutworms, and caterpillars are a valuable food source for birds. Birds do not cause many problems in high-cut lawns; the insects they eliminate would do much more damage. In low-cut lawns, however, mass feeding may create an abundance of pecking holes that detract from appearance. Since bug pests are a prime attraction, using Ortho® Bug-B-Gon® Multi-Purpose Insect Killer Ready-Spray® or Ortho® Lawn Insect Killer Granules usually causes the birds to turn elsewhere. Be certain to treat lawns in late afternoon so insecticides are dry by the following day when birds return—freshly applied insecticide may be harmful to birds.

■ **Crayfish:** Also called crawfish and crawdads, crayfish are water-loving creatures that resemble miniature lobsters. Crayfish become a lawn problem only if a lawn is constantly soggy. This can be due to watering practices, poor drainage, or a high water table. Crayfish construct soil mounds around a hole about 1 inch wide. In severe infestations, these mounds must be leveled out to permit mowing. Control consists of correcting drainage problems or easing up on watering. Without hospitable surroundings, crayfish usually go elsewhere. If the growing site is not fully correctable, consider using crayfish bait. Spring treatment is most effective, particularly after a rain.

■ **Snails and slugs:** The silvery trails of snails and slugs wind across lawns and are visible in the morning and on overcast days. These familiar lawn pests hide under ground cover or leaves during the day to avoid sunlight. Both mollusks eat grass. Control snails and slugs by using Ortho® Bug-Geta® Snail & Slug Killer. Place the bait in the same areas each time, near the creatures' hiding places as well as in a band around the areas you wish to protect.

DEAD PATCHES

Dog urine injury

Dog urine spots.

Problem: Circular spots, straw brown in color and 8 to 10 inches in diameter, appear in the lawn. A ring of deep green grass may surround each patch. Other patches may be dark green in color, without any dead areas in them. No spots or webbing appear on the grass blades, and the grass does not mat. Dogs have been in the area.

Analysis: Dog urine burns grass. The salts in the urine cause varying stages of damage, from slight discoloration to outright death. The nitrogen in the urine may encourage immediately surrounding grass to grow rapidly, resulting in a dark green, vigorously growing ring. Lawns suffer the most damage in hot, dry weather.

Solution: Water the affected areas thoroughly to wash away the urine. This reduces but does not eradicate the brown discoloration. Surrounding grass eventually fills in the affected areas. For quick repair, spot-sod. If possible, keep dogs off the lawn.

Chemical or fertilizer burn

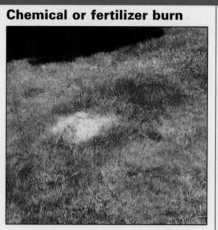

Burn caused by a fertilizer spill.

Problem: Grass dies and turns yellow in irregular patches or in definite, regular stripes or curves. Grass bordering the areas is a healthy green color. Yellow areas do not spread or enlarge. They appear within two to five days after fertilization or after a chemical has been spilled on the lawn.

Analysis: Chemicals such as pesticides, fertilizers, gasoline, and hydrated lime may burn the grass if applied improperly or if accidentally spilled on turf. When excessive amounts of these materials contact grass plants, they cause the blades to dessicate and die.

Solution: Prevent or minimize damage by picking up the spilled material, then washing the chemical from the soil immediately. If the substance is water soluble, water the area thoroughly— three to five times longer than usual. If the substance is not soluble in water, such as gasoline or weed oil, flood the area with a solution of dish soap diluted to about the same strength as used for washing dishes. Then water as indicated above. Some substances, such as preemergent herbicides, can't be washed from the soil. In such a case, replace the top foot of soil in the spill area. Prevent further damage by filling gas tanks, spreaders, and sprayers on an unplanted surface, such as a driveway. Apply chemicals according to the label instructions. Apply fertilizers when the grass blades are dry and the soil is moist. Water thoroughly afterward to dilute the fertilizer and wash it into the soil. Keep drop spreaders closed when stopped or turning.

Summer patch

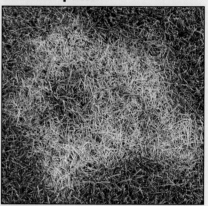

Summer patch.

Problem: Scattered patches of dead turf 1 to 2 feet in diameter appear during hot summer weather. Usually the dead grass forms a ring around a patch of healthy grass, creating a frog's-eye pattern. If hot weather persists, the center of the patch also dies. Patches are usually circular or crescent shaped, although serpentine patterns sometimes occur.

Analysis: Summer patch usually occurs from June through September, when hot, dry weather follows a wet period. The disease is caused by a fungus (*Magnaporthe poae*) that infects the roots during cool weather (60° to 65°F), usually in late spring. When hot weather arrives, the roots can't provide enough water, and the top dies. Summer patch is most prevalent in compacted soils and lawns with excessive thatch buildup, especially on exposed sites and steep slopes. It is worsened by infrequent watering and excessive nitrogen applications. It can affect many types of lawn grasses, including bentgrass, Kentucky and annual bluegrass, and fescue—especially when cultivars are unsuitable for local conditions. The symptoms of necrotic ring spot (see page 65) are so similar to those of summer patch that the two diseases can't readily be distinguished outside the lab.

Solution: Dethatching and regular aeration help prevent summer patch, as do frequent, light waterings and regular but light applications of nitrogen. Apply Ortho® Lawn Disease Control or Scotts® Lawn Fungus Control to infected areas. Reseed seriously affected areas with appropriate cultivars.

Fusarium patch

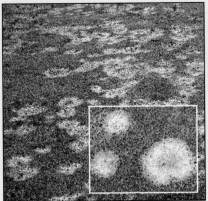

Fusarium patch. Inset: Close-up.

Problem: Yellow-green spots a few inches in diameter form, usually when the snow melts but possibly any time during cool weather from late fall to early spring even if no snow is present. Spots grow and become pinkish white. Affected leaves become matted and turn light tan while patches grow outward from a rusty pink border. A patch can grow up to 1 foot in diameter. Circular patches can join, displaying extensive damage.

Analysis: A plant disease that primarily affects cold-season grasses, fusarium patch (also known as *pink snow mold*) is caused by the fungus *Microdochium nivale*. Active only at cold temperatures (32° to 60°F) when moisture is abundant, fusarium patch is most likely to occur after snow has been on the ground for several months. Prolonged cold weather worsens symptoms; turf quickly recovers if warm weather follows the melting of snow. Prolonged rainy periods in winter also promote this disease. Serious infection leads to crown and root rot.

Solution: Reduce shade in infected areas. Do not apply excessive nitrogen-rich fertilizer in the fall. Overly tall grass is susceptible to fusarium patch, so mow lawns in autumn before snowfall. Reduce thatch buildup. Lightly infected turf usually recovers on its own. For seriously affected areas, apply Ortho® Lawn Disease Control according to label directions.

Necrotic ring spot

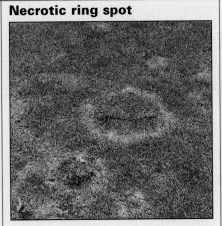

Necrotic ring spot.

Problem: Circular patches of straw-colored or red blades appear. The patches may be from 6 inches to several feet in diameter and usually form a ring around a patch of healthy grass. The result is a doughnut-shape depression. Eventually the dead part of the ring fades to tan. When several patches are present, the area takes on a pockmarked look. Patches spread outward, eventually joining together to form a large blighted area.

Analysis: Caused by the fungus *Leptosphaeria korrae*, this disease occurs from March through November. It appears most frequently in spring and fall when hot, dry conditions follow cool weather. Dense turf with excessive thatch buildup is especially susceptible. Necrotic ring spot is most prevalent in compacted soils and heavily thatched lawns, especially on exposed sites and steep slopes. It can affect most types of lawn grasses, including bermudagrass, Kentucky bluegrass, fescues, ryegrass, and zoysiagrass.

Solution: Dethatching and regular aeration help prevent necrotic ring spot. Avoid drought stress and apply the required amounts of fertilizer. During hot summer months, leave grass a little longer than in cool periods. This helps keep the soil cool, a condition detrimental to the spread of the fungus. Apply Scotts® Lawn Fungus Control or a fungicide containing *azoxystrobin* or *fenarimol*. Fertilize regularly with Scotts Turf Builder to encourage lawn to fill in. Reseed seriously affected areas.

Brown patch

Brown patch.

Problem: Circular patches of dead grass a few inches to a few feet in diameter appear in the lawn during periods of high humidity and warm temperatures (75° to 85°F). Dark purplish smoky rings sometimes surround brown areas. Filmy white to tan tufts may cover grass in the early morning if the dew is heavy. After two to three weeks, the center brown grass may recover and turn green, and brown areas form a doughnut shape.

Analysis: Brown patch is caused by a fungus (*Rhizoctonia solani*). It is one of the most prevalent diseases in warm, humid areas, attacking all types of turfgrass. Lush, tender growth from excessive nitrogen fertilization is the most susceptible to attack. Sometimes only the blades are affected, and the grass recovers in two to three weeks. When the infection is severe and warm weather continues, the disease attacks plant crowns and kills the grass.

Solution: Control brown patch with Ortho® Lawn Disease Control or Scotts® Lawn Fungus Control. Spray when the disease is first noticed and at least three more times at 14-day intervals. Repeat the treatments as long as warm, humid weather continues. Keep grass as dry as possible to slow down disease spread. Water only in the morning, one or two times per week. To reduce recurring infections, follow the cultural practices for mowing and watering described on pages 51 and 55.

DEAD PATCHES *(continued)*

Dollar spot

Dollar spot damage. Inset: Close-up.

Problem: The grass turns light brown to straw colored in circular areas from the size of a silver dollar to 6 inches in diameter during the warm, wet weather of May to June and September to October. The small dead areas may merge to form large irregular patches. Small, light brown blotches with reddish brown borders appear on the leaf blades. These spots extend across the entire width of the blade. In the early morning before the dew dries, a white cobwebby growth may cover the infected grass blades.

Analysis: Dollar spot, also called *small brown patch*, is caused by a fungus (*Sclerotinia homoeocarpa*). It is most active during mild (60° to 80°F), moist days and cool nights. It attacks many kinds of lawn grasses but is most severe on bentgrass, bermudagrass, and Kentucky bluegrass. Lawns troubled by dollar spot are usually under stress from lack of moisture and nitrogen. An infection seldom causes permanent damage, although the lawn takes several weeks or months to recover. Shoes, hoses, mowers, and other equipment spread the fungus organisms.

Solution: Control dollar spot with Ortho® Lawn Disease Control or Scotts® Lawn Fungus Control. Make applications as needed, 28 days apart, beginning when the disease is first evident. The grass recovers quickly if treated promptly. Keep grass as dry as possible. Water only in the morning, one or two times per week. It is important to maintain proper nutrient levels; applying nitrogen will help the lawn to recover if it has a nitrogen deficiency.

Fusarium blight

Fusarium blight.

Problem: During hot weather, dead patches form in bluegrass lawns in enlarging rings that may grow up to a foot in diameter. Weeds invade the center of a dead spot, creating a frog's-eye appearance. Patches may merge to form large dead areas. Each patch begins as a circular grayish green area about 2 inches in diameter. The grass in these patches grows slowly, wilts easily, and dies to a yellow-brown color in hot weather. Eventually weeds invade the entire dead circle.

Analysis: Fusarium blight is caused by a soil-borne fungus (*Fusarium*), often in combination with one or more other pathogenic fungi. It primarily attacks Kentucky bluegrass and annual bluegrass. The disease begins as a small spot, then grows. As it kills the grass, the dead spot fills in with resistant plants, usually weeds, causing the frog's-eye look. This is a hot-weather disease, being favored by hot, dry, windy conditions.

Solution: Once symptoms are well-developed, it's too late to spray for the current season. Irrigate regularly to keep the thatch and soil evenly moist. Avoid heavy nitrogen fertilization. The following spring, treat with Scotts® Lawn Fungus Control or a fungicide containing *mancozeb* or *triadimefon* before or as soon as symptoms appear. When replanting, select a resistant variety of bluegrass, or choose ryegrass or fine fescue, or plant a mix of 20 percent (by weight) perennial ryegrass and 80 percent Kentucky bluegrass, which is more resistant to fusarium blight than pure bluegrass.

Spring dead spot

Spring dead spot.

Problem: Circular dead spots develop in bermudagrass lawns when the lawn begins growth in the spring. Spots vary from a few inches to several feet in diameter. The dead grass is sunken and straw-colored, and the stolons and roots are blackened and decayed. Weeds may invade the affected areas. Bermudagrass sometimes slowly fills in by the end of summer, but the grass is shorter than the surrounding healthy grass. Grass may grow back only in the center of the spot, creating a frog's-eye or island pattern. In bermudagrass lawns that have been overseeded with a cool-season grass, affected areas appear as light green spots.

Analysis: Spring dead spot is caused by fungi (*Leptosphaeria korrae, Ophiosphaerella herpotricha*, and *Gaeumannomyces graminis* var. *graminis*) that affect bermudagrass, causing stolon and root rot. Spring dead spot is common in areas where temperatures drop low enough to promote winter dormancy of bermudagrass. It is most likely to develop in lawns with excess thatch and in lawns that are overfertilized or fertilized late in the growing season.

Solution: Avoid overfertilization and late-season fertilization. Keep thatch to a thickness of no more than ¾ inch. Keep the lawn healthy and vigorous to encourage bermudagrass regrowth into dead areas. Replace the sod and soil of badly diseased areas. Apply a fungicide containing *azoxystrobin, myclobutanil* or *fenarimol* in late summer or early fall.

Sod webworms

Damage. Inset: Sod webworm (2× life size).

Problem: From mid-May to October the grass turns brown in patches the size of a saucer in the hottest and driest areas of the lawn. These areas may expand to form large irregular patches. Grass blades are chewed off at the soil level. Silky white tubes are found nestled in the root area. Inside are light brown or gray worms with black spots, from ¼ to ¾ inch long.

Analysis: Several different moths with similar habits are called *sod webworms* or *lawn moths*. These night-flying moths drop eggs into the grass as they fly. The eggs hatch into worms that feed on grass blades at night or on cloudy, rainy days. In the daytime the worm hides in white silky tubes in the soil. Sometimes an entire lawn is killed in a few days.

Solution: Control sod webworms with Ortho® Bug-B-Gon® Multi-Purpose Insect Killer Ready-Spray® or Ortho® Lawn Insect Killer Granules when large numbers of moths are noticed at dusk or at the first sign of damage. First rake out all the dead grass and mow the lawn. Water thoroughly before treating. For best results, apply the insecticide in the late afternoon or evening, when the worms are most active. If using Ortho® Bug-B-Gon® Multi-Purpose Insect Killer Ready-Spray®, don't cut or water the lawn for one to three days afterward. Water Ortho® Lawn Insect Killer Granules after spreading. To avoid recurring damage, treat the lawn again every two months beginning in late spring or early summer. Damaged lawns may recover rapidly if the insects are controlled early.

Improper mowing

Scalped spot in lawn.

Problem: Grass has yellow patches or strips after mowing. A few days later, patches may turn brown and die.

Analysis: Grass becomes damaged when too much is removed during mowing. This can happen in two ways.
1. Scalping: Mowing near the soil level, or scalping, occurs when the mower cuts too low in some areas. If the lawn is bumpy, high spots may get scalped. Where the grass has been cut too short, the lower parts of the grass blades are exposed to and burned by sunlight. If scalping damages the base of the grass plant, the grass may die. Otherwise, it will probably recover in a week or so.
2. Insufficient mowings: If the mower is cutting at the proper height but the grass has grown too long between mowings, the lower parts of the grass blades are exposed and burned. Waiting too long to mow seldom kills the grass, but the lawn remains unsightly for a week or two.

Solution: Damaged spots need no special care. To prevent further damage:
1. If the lawn surface is uneven, level the high spots. If the lawn is spongy from an accumulation of thatch, follow the procedure described on page 72. Raise the mower blade to the suggested height.
2. Mow frequently enough so that you don't remove more than half the length of grass blades. If the grass is very tall when you mow, raise the mower blade to half the grass height and lower it gradually over the next several mowings.

Grubs

Damaged lawn. Inset: White grub (2× life size).

Problem: From August through October the grass appears to wilt and turns brown in large, irregular patches. Brown areas of grass roll up easily like a carpet. Milky white grubs from ⅛ to 1 inch long, with brown heads and three pairs of legs, lie curled in the soil. Birds and animals may be digging in the lawn.

Analysis: Grubs are the larvae of different kinds of beetles, including May and June beetles (also called *white grubs*) and Asiatic, Japanese, and masked chafer beetles. The grubs feed on turf roots and may kill the entire lawn. Some birds and animals dig up the lawn to feed on the grubs. Adult beetles don't damage the lawn, but they lay eggs in the soil. May and June beetles lay eggs in the spring and summer. Asiatic, Japanese, and masked chafer beetles lay eggs in mid- to late summer. Eggs hatch and grubs feed on roots 1 to 3 inches deep in the soil. In late fall they move deep into the soil to overwinter; they resume feeding in spring.

Solution: Apply Ortho® Bug-B-Gon® Multi-Purpose Insect Killer Granules when you first notice damage and grubs. Water thoroughly after application. Repeat in 7 to 14 days if necessary. Or apply Scotts® GrubEx® Season-Long Grub Control from spring through summer to prevent young grubs from damaging your lawn. Water well after applying. To save areas just beginning to fade, keep the soil moist but not wet.

DEAD PATCHES *(continued)*

Pythium blight

Pythium blight on seedlings.

Seeds fail to grow

Bare spots in newly seeded lawn.

Poor seed germination.

Problem: In hot, humid weather from April to October, the grass wilts, shrivels, and turns light brown in irregular spots ½ to 4 inches in diameter. Spots enlarge rapidly, forming streaks 1 foot wide or wider or patches 1 to 10 feet in diameter. Infected grass blades mat together when walked on. Blades are often meshed together by white threads in the early morning before the dew dries. Grass sometimes dies within 24 hours.

Analysis: Pythium blight, also called *grease spot* or *cottony blight*, is caused by a fungus (*Pythium*). It attacks lawns under stress from heat (85° to 95°F), poorly drained soil, and excessive moisture. Dense, lush grass is the most susceptible. All turfgrasses are affected, ryegrasses the most severely. The fungus spores spread easily in free-flowing water, on lawn mower wheels, and on the soles of shoes. The disease is difficult to control because it spreads so rapidly. Pythium blight is common in the fall on top-seeded ryegrass.

Solution: Treat the lawn with a fungicide containing *azoxystrobin, metalaxyl, chloroneb,* or *ethazole* as soon as the disease is noticed. Repeat treatments every 5 to 10 days either until the disease stops or until cooler weather resumes. Keep traffic off the diseased area to avoid spreading spores. Don't overwater in hot, humid weather. Severely infected areas often do not recover, so reseed or resod to reestablish the lawn. Treat the new lawn during hot, humid weather. Wait until cool weather to overseed ryegrass.

Problem: Seeds in newly planted lawns sprout slowly or not at all, or seedlings rot and fall over at the soil line.

Analysis: Lawn seeds may not grow for several reasons.

1. Lack of water: Once the seed germinates, the soil must stay evenly moist. If the soil around the seedling dries out, the seedling will die; however, excessive water may rot seeds and seedlings.

2. Temperature: Seeds planted at the wrong time of year, when the temperature does not promote healthiest growth, take longer or fail to sprout. If planted at the proper time, seeds should sprout within four weeks of planting.

3. Old seeds: Seeds left over from the previous year will sprout if they've been stored in a cool, dry place. Seeds older than one year and seeds that have not been stored properly sprout poorly if at all.

4. Seeds planted too deep: Seeds planted deeper than ¼ to ½ inch usually don't sprout.

5. Unprepared soil: Seeds must be in direct contact with the soil to sprout. Seeds that sprout in thatch or directly on top of the soil may dry out.

6. Damping-off: This plant disease is caused by fungi (*Pythium* and *Rhizoctonia*). If the soil is too wet and is rich in nitrogen, damping-off is likely. It kills seedlings either before or after their emergence.

Solution: Solutions below correspond to the numbered items in the analysis.

1. Water a newly planted lawn frequently enough that only the surface is allowed to dry out. To conserve moisture, mulch the seedbed lightly with a ¼-inch layer of straw or sawdust.

2. Plant warm-season grasses (bermudagrass, centipedegrass, and bahiagrass) in late spring or early summer as the weather warms. Plant cool-season grasses (rye, fescue, bentgrass, and bluegrass) in early to midfall or as early as practical in spring.

3. Use seed produced for sale in the current year. Check the seed testing date on the box before purchasing.

4. After sowing the seed, gently rake the soil to mix the seed into the top ¼ inch.

5. To ensure good soil contact, till or rake the soil surface before planting; don't throw seed on top of thatch or unprepared soil.

6. When reseeding blank spots, spray the seed bed with a fungicide containing *metalaxyl* or *captan*. Fill in any low spots where water may puddle. Water less often; let the soil surface dry slightly between waterings until the seedlings are 1 inch high.

Chinch bugs

Damage. Inset: Chinch bug (6× life size).

Problem: In April through October the grass wilts, turns yellowish brown, dries out, and dies in sunny areas and along sidewalks and driveways. To check for chinch bugs, select a sunny spot on the edge of an affected area where yellow grass borders healthy green grass. Cut out both ends of a tin can. Push one end of the can 2 to 3 inches into the soil. Keep it filled with water for 10 minutes. Black to brown insects with white wings ⅛ to ¼ inch long, float to the surface. Pink to brick-red nymphs with a white stripe around the body may also be numerous in the lawn.

Analysis: Chinch bugs (*Blissus* species) feed on many kinds of lawn grasses, but St. Augustinegrass and zoysiagrass are favorites. Both the adults and the nymphs suck the juices out of the grass blades. At the same time, they inject a poison that causes the blades to turn brown and die. Heavy infestations may completely kill the lawn. These sun- and heat-loving insects seldom attack shady lawns. They can move across an entire lawn in several days.

Solution: Control chinch bugs with Ortho® Bug-B-Gon® Multi-Purpose Insect Killer Ready-Spray® or Ortho® Lawn Insect Killer Granules as soon as you see damage. Mow and water the lawn before spraying, applying ½ to 1 inch of water to bring the insects to the surface. To prevent recurring damage from newly hatched nymphs, treat every two months until frost. In southern Florida, repeat the applications year-round.

Sod fails to establish

Sod not rooted.

Dying patches of sod.

Problem: Newly sodded areas turn yellow, then brown. Sod rolls up easily like a carpet. No roots are visible on the bottoms of the sod pieces.

Analysis: Sod should establish in two to three weeks. Test by gently tugging a corner. If the sod resists tugging, then the roots have grown into the soil. Sod can fail to establish for several reasons.

1. Sod dried out: Until the roots grow into the soil, sod is very susceptible to drying out.

2. Unprepared soil: If the sod is laid directly on thatch, it dries out quickly. If it is laid on hard soil, the roots have difficulty growing into the soil.

3. Old sod: Old sod has many yellow grass blades among the green blades. It may be weak from water or heat stress and will establish poorly or not at all. Sod may be damaged by remaining rolled for two days or fewer in hot weather. In cool weather it can remain rolled for a week without damage.

4. Time of year: Sod can be installed almost any time of the year, but it will establish slowly if it is laid when the grass is not actively growing.

Solution: The numbered solutions below correspond to the numbered items in the analysis at left. (For information on sod, see page 50.)

1. Water frequently enough to keep the sod and the soil under it moist.

2. Before laying sod, till or thoroughly rake the soil. Remove all dead grass and debris, and level the grade.

3. Choose uniformly green sod that is not turning yellow or pale green. Lay the sod as soon as possible. Don't leave it rolled and stacked for more than a day in hot weather. It can be stored rolled for two to three days in a shady area, however. Keep the soil on the outer pieces moist.

4. Lay cool-season grass sod (bluegrass or bentgrass) in late summer to early fall or early spring. Avoid midsummer. Lay warm-season grass sod (bermudagrass, bahiagrass, St. Augustinegrass, or centipedegrass) in the late spring and early summer.

69

DEAD PATCHES *(continued)*

Warm-weather grasses becoming dormant

Dormant bermudagrass.

Annual bluegrass dying

Annual bluegrass dying.

Crabgrass dying

Crabgrass dying.

Problem: Brown patches of irregular shape and size develop with the first fall frost. The leaf and stem structure looks different on the dead grass than on the living grass. No signs of insect or disease damage appear.

Analysis: Warm-weather perennial grasses become dormant with the onset of cold weather. The tops die back, but the perennial roots live over the winter and resprout in the spring. Two of the most common invading warm-weather grasses are zoysiagrass and bermudagrass. They turn brown in the fall, while cool-weather grasses (bluegrass, fescue, and bentgrass) remain green through the winter. (For information on bermudagrass, see page 79.)

Solution: Eradicating these grasses from the lawn is very difficult. Once the grass turns brown, it is too late to treat. The following year, spot-treat the undesirable grasses with Ortho® Grass-B-Gon® Grass Killer for Landscapes. If new plants emerge in the spring, spot-treat with the same herbicide.

Problem: Areas of grass that were once lush and green die and turn straw brown. Grass appears whitish in late spring, and with the onset of hot summer weather, these places become irregular dead patches.

Analysis: Annual bluegrass (*Poa annua*) is one of the most troublesome but least noticed weeds in the lawn. This member of the bluegrass family is lighter green, more shallow rooted, and less drought tolerant than Kentucky bluegrass. As its name suggests, annual bluegrass usually lives only for one year, although some strains are perennial. The seed germinates in cool weather from late summer to late fall. Annual bluegrass grows rapidly in the spring, especially if the lawn is fertilized then. Seed heads appear in mid- to late spring at the same height that the grass is cut. The seed heads give the lawn a whitish appearance. When hot, dry weather arrives, the plants turn pale green and die. The seeds fall to the soil and wait for cooler weather to germinate. Annual bluegrass is most serious where the soil is compacted.

Solution: When dead patches appear in hot weather, the annual bluegrass is dead. The lawn is laced with its seeds, however, which will germinate with cooler fall weather. Patch the dead spots. When the weather begins to cool in the fall, treat the lawn with Scotts® Halts® Crabgrass Preventer to kill the seeds as they germinate. Don't cut the lawn too short. Lawns more than 2½ inches tall have very little annual bluegrass. Aerate the lawn in compacted areas (see page 405).

Problem: Brown patches develop in the lawn with the first fall frost. Close examination of the dead spots reveals, not dead lawn grass but, a weed.

Analysis: Crabgrass (*Digitaria* species) is an annual grassy weed. It forms large, flat clumps, smothering lawn grass as it spreads. Crabgrass dies with the first killing frost in the fall or with the onset of cold weather, leaving dead patches in the lawn. Crabgrass sprouts from seeds in early spring.

Solution: In early spring, two weeks before the last expected frost, treat the lawn with Scotts® Halts® Crabgrass Preventer. This preemergent weed killer kills the seed as it germinates. Kill actively growing crabgrass with Ortho® Weed-B-Gon® Crabgrass Killer for Lawns. Maturing plants are harder to kill. Repeat treatments two more times at four to seven day intervals if necessary. Prevent crabgrass by keeping the lawn at least 2½ inches deep. A deep, thick lawn seldom contains much crabgrass. (For information on crabgrass, see page 79.)

Billbugs

Billbug damage. Inset: Larvae (life size).

Problem: The grass turns brown and dies in expanding patches from mid-June to late August. When pulled, the grass lifts easily. Lying in the soil are fat, humpbacked white grubs with brown heads and no legs, and from ¼ to ½ inch long. Adults—black, slow-moving, snouted weevils ¼ to ½ inch long—occasionally walk on sidewalks and driveways in May and October.

Analysis: The larvae of billbugs (*Sphenophorus* species) damage lawns by hollowing out the grass stems and chewing off the roots. They can destroy an entire lawn. In May, the adults lay eggs in holes they chew in grass stems. The newly hatched larvae feed inside the stems, hollowing out the stem and crown and leaving fine sandlike excrement. Large larvae feed on roots.

Solution: Control billbugs with Ortho® Lawn Insect Killer Granules. Repeated treatments are not usually necessary unless the billbugs are migrating from neighboring yards. Small damaged areas usually recover if the larvae are killed. Water and fertilize the lawn to stimulate new growth. Reseed or resod large areas. Maintain proper soil moisture and turfgrass fertility programs.

Salt damage

Dead patch from salt accumulation.

Problem: Grass slowly dies, especially in the lowest areas of the lawn. A white or dark crust may be present on the soil.

Analysis: Salt damage occurs when salt accumulates in the soil to damaging levels. This can happen in either of two ways: (1) the lawn does not receive enough water from rainfall or irrigation to wash the salts from the soil, or (2) the drainage is so poor that water does not pass through the soil. In either case, as water evaporates from the soil and grass blades, salts that were dissolved in the water accumulate near the surface of the soil. In some cases, a white or dark brown crust of salts forms on the soil surface. Salts can originate in the soil, in irrigation water, or in applied fertilizers.

Solution: The only way to eliminate salt problems is to wash the salts through the soil with water. If the damage is only at a low spot in the lawn, fill in the spot to level the lawn. If the entire lawn drains poorly, improve drainage by aerating according to the directions on page 405, or improve the soil as described on page 406. If the soil drains well, increase the amount of water applied at each watering by 50 percent or more, so that excess water will leach salts below the root zone of the grass. Fertilize according to the instructions in the nitrogen deficiency section on page 74.

Mole crickets

Damaged lawn. Inset: Mole cricket (¾ life size).

Problem: Small mounds of soil are scattered on the soil surface. The lawn feels spongy underfoot. Large areas of grass turn brown and die. To determine if the lawn is infested with mole crickets, make a solution of 1 ounce of liquid dishwashing detergent to 2 gallons of water. Drench 4 square feet of turf with the mixture. Mole crickets—greenish-gray to brown insects, 1½ inches long, with shovel-like feet—will come to the surface within three minutes.

Analysis: Several species of mole crickets (*Scapteriscus* and *Gryllotalpa* species) attack lawns. They prefer bahiagrass and bermudagrass but also feed on St. Augustinegrass, zoysia, and centipedegrass. They damage lawns by tunneling through the top 1 to 2 inches of soil, loosening it and uprooting plants so that the plants dry out. Mole crickets also feed on grass roots, weakening the plants. They feed at night and may tunnel as many as 10 to 20 feet per night. In the daytime, they return to their underground burrows. Adults migrate to new areas twice a year, from March to July and again from November to December.

Solution: In June or July, after the eggs hatch and before the young nymphs cause much damage, treat the lawn with Ortho® Bug-B-Gon® Multi-Purpose Insect Killer Ready-Spray®. Mole crickets are not active in dry soil, so mow and water thoroughly before applying. Or treat the lawn with Ortho® Lawn Insect Killer Granules. Water after application. If damage continues, treat again in late summer to early fall. Keep the lawn watered to encourage new root growth.

DEAD PATCHES
(continued)

Black turfgrass ataenius beetle

Black turfgrass ataenius beetles (4× life size).

Problem: Turf on fairways, tees, and greens (rarely home lawns) wilts despite abundant moisture. Damage begins in late spring and becomes worse with hot, dry weather. Small irregular dead patches converge to form large dead sections. Weakened and dead turf is easily removed, revealing numerous pupae and grubs of various sizes. Grubs are similar to young European chafer and Japanese beetle grubs but are much smaller (1/8 to 1/4 inch long). Adults are reddish brown to shiny black beetles, also 1/8 to 1/4 inch long.

Analysis: The black turfgrass ataenius beetle (*Ataenius spretulus*) prefers closely mowed annual and Kentucky bluegrasses and bentgrasses. Only one generation occurs per year in the North; two or three generations occur from the middle latitudes south. Adults overwinter in nearby wooded areas, among leaf litter and mulch, and return to turf in early spring. The grubs cause damage by feeding on roots where soil and thatch meet. Damage is heaviest just before larvae pupate in early summer.

Solution: Control with Scotts® GrubEx as soon as damage is apparent. One application is sufficient. To prevent damage next year, apply GrubEx in late April. Control annual bluegrass weeds to make the lawn less attractive to females.

GRASS THIN

Drought

Lawn damaged by drought.

Problem: Footprints in the lawn make a long-lasting imprint instead of bouncing right back. The grass blades turn a dull bluish-green or slate-gray color and wilt. In the cool evening, the grass recovers until the sun and heat of the following day make it darken and wilt. Areas begin to thin out. After a few days the lawn begins to look and feel like straw and dies.

Analysis: A lawn suffers from drought damage when water evaporates from the lawn faster than the roots absorb it. Drought damage occurs first in the hottest and driest areas of the lawn where sun is reflected—along sidewalks, driveways, south- or west-facing slopes, south sides of buildings, and areas with sandy soil. Grass blades don't wilt as broadleaf plants do. They don't droop but, instead, roll or fold up lengthwise.

Solution: Water the lawn immediately, following the guidelines on page 55. If the grass has turned yellow, the affected areas will require several weeks to recover. If you aren't conscientious about watering, plant a drought-tolerant turfgrass.

Thatch

Thatch.

Problem: Grass thins out in sunny or shady areas of the lawn. Weeds invade the sparse areas. Grass may suddenly die in large patches during summer heat and drought. Cut and lift several plugs of grass 2 to 3 inches deep. Look to see if the stringy, feltlike material between the grass and soil surface is thicker than 1/2 inch.

Analysis: Thatch is a tightly intermingled layer of partially decomposed stems and roots of grass that develops between the actively growing grass and the soil surface. Thatch slows grass growth by restricting the movement of water, air, and nutrients in the soil. Thatch is normal in a lawn, but when it is thicker than 1/2 inch, the lawn begins to suffer. As the layer accumulates, the grass roots grow into the thatch instead of down into the soil. Thatch is encouraged by overly vigorous grass growth caused by excessive fertilizing and frequent watering.

Solution: To reduce the thatch and increase the lawn's vigor, power rake or dethatch the lawn. Dethatch cool-season grasses in the fall and warm-season grasses in late spring or early summer. Avoid dethatching while new growth is turning green. The machines for the job can be rented, or hire a contractor. Dethatchers, also called *verticutters*, have vertical rotating blades that slice through the turf, cutting out thatch. Mow the lawn as short as possible. Go over it one to three times with the dethatcher. Remove the debris, fertilize, and water to hasten the lawn's recovery.

72

Surface roots

Surface roots.

Problem: Tree and shrub roots are exposed or are making bumps by growing just beneath the turf. Exposed roots may be lumpy and malformed. (For more information on surface roots, see page 60.)

Analysis: Several factors can cause large surface roots to develop in lawns.
1. Waterlogged soil: Waterlogged soil has very little oxygen available for root growth. The oxygen that is available is near the soil surface, so the roots develop there.
2. Compacted or heavy soil: Such soils contain very little oxygen, so root growth is restricted to near the surface.
3. Light irrigation: If plants growing in or near lawns aren't deeply watered, they often develop surface roots.
4. Natural tendency: Some trees and shrubs are more likely to develop surface roots than others.

Solution: Solutions below correspond to the numbered items in the analysis.
1. If the soil is waterlogged, cut back on watering.
2. Loosen the soil around tree roots. Aerate the lawn area to improve soil compaction (see page 405).
3. Water trees and shrubs deeply. Apply enough water to wet the soil to a depth of 6 inches to 3 feet, depending on the species. Look up your plant in the section beginning on page 204 to determine the correct depth and frequency of irrigation.
4. For a list of plants likely to develop surface roots, see page 548. If practical, replace them with plants adapted to growing in a lawn (see page 548).

Leaf spot

Lawn with leaf spot. Inset: Spotted blades.

Problem: The grass turns brown to reddish brown and thins out in irregular patches 2 or more feet in diameter from spring until fall. Both the green and the brown grass blades have small oval spots with straw-colored centers and dark maroon borders.

Analysis: Several fungi (*Bipolaris, Drechslera,* and *Exserohilum* species) can cause leaf spot. Many were formerly called *helminthosporia* leaf spots. *Melting out* is a common one and very destructive to Kentucky bluegrass. In cool spring and fall weather, leaf spot occurs on grass blades but don't kill them. In warm summer weather the fungi can kill the grass blades, spread to the base of the plant, and kill entire plants. Lawns that are excessively lush from high nitrogen fertilizing or under stress from short mowing, thick thatch, and frequent watering are the most susceptible to fungal leaf spot attack.

Solution: Spray the lawn with Ortho® Multi-Purpose Fungicide Daconil 2787® Plant Disease Control when leaf spotting is first noticed. Make at least three more applications, 7 to 10 days apart. Keep your lawn healthy and vigorous by following the guidelines for lawn care on pages 48 to 63. Be particularly careful to use a balanced lawn fertilizer, reduce the thatch layer, and water thoroughly and infrequently. To keep the grass dry at night, avoid watering in early evening or late afternoon.

Nematodes

Nematode damage.

Problem: The grass grows slowly, thins out, and turns pale green to yellow. In hot weather the turf may wilt in irregular patterns. Main roots are short with few side roots, or many roots may grow from one point.

Analysis: Nematodes are microscopic worms that live in the soil. They are not related to earthworms. Nematodes feed on grass roots, damaging and stunting them. The damaged roots can't supply sufficient water and nutrients to the grass blades, and the grass is stunted or slowly dies. Nematodes are found throughout the country but are most severe in the South. They prefer moist, sandy loam soils. They can move only a few inches each year on their own, but they may be carried long distances by soil, water, tools, or infested plants. Testing roots and soil is the only positive method for confirming the presence of nematodes. Contact your local County Extension office (see page 527) for sampling instructions and addresses of testing laboratories. Soil and root problems such as poor soil structure, drought stress, nutrient deficiency, and root rot also can produce symptoms of decline similar to those caused by nematodes. Eliminate these problems as causes before sending soil and root samples for testing. (For information on soil problems and root rots, see page 419.)

Solution: No chemicals available to homeowners kill nematodes in planted soil. Soil fumigation or solarization, however, can be used to control nematodes before a new lawn is planted.

PALE OR YELLOW LAWN

Iron deficiency

Iron deficiency.

Problem: Irregular patches of grass are yellow. Individual blades are yellow between the veins; the veins remain green. If the condition persists, the leaves may become almost white and die back from the tips. In severe cases, the grass is stunted.

Analysis: Iron deficiency is a common problem in many plants and is usually caused by alkaline soil conditions. In alkaline soil, much of the iron forms insoluble compounds that are unavailable to grass plants. Lack of iron may also be caused by an iron deficiency, excess phosphorus, a poor root system, overwatering, or the use of water that contains large amounts of bicarbonate salts. Plants use iron in the formation of chlorophyll in the leaves. When iron is lacking, new growth is yellow. Many turfgrass species—including Kentucky bluegrass, perennial ryegrass, fine fescue, creeping bentgrass, and bermudagrass— are susceptible to iron deficiency.

Solution: For a quick green-up, spray the lawn with Scotts® GreenSweep® Lawn Food Plus Iron. In the future, fertilize with Miracle-Gro® Water Soluble Lawn Food, which contains iron. Lower the alkalinity of the soil by adding ferrous sulfate or ferrous ammonium sulfate. Water the lawn thoroughly after applying one of these amendments. Never add lime to soil in which iron deficiency is a problem. Some turfgrass varieties are resistant to iron deficiency; when replanting, ask for one of these at your nursery.

Nitrogen deficiency

Unfertilized lawn with green clover.

Problem: Grass is pale green to yellow and grows more slowly than usual. If the condition persists, the grass becomes sparse and weeds invade the lawn.

Analysis: Nitrogen is a key element in maintaining a healthy lawn with few insect and disease problems. Clover stays green because it obtains nitrogen from the air, but grasses can't. It is best to maintain a level of nitrogen in the soil that (1) does not stimulate excessive leaf growth, which would increase the frequency of mowing; (2) does not encourage shoot growth at the expense of root growth; and (3) varies according to the cultural and environmental conditions present. Because heavy rains and watering leach nitrogen from the soil, periodic feedings are necessary throughout the growing season. Acid soil may cause nitrogen to be unavailable to the grass.

Solution: Apply Scotts Turf Builder fertilizer according to the instructions on the label. Properly fertilized lawns are dense and have a nice green color without excessive growth. To prevent burning and to move nutrients into the soil, water thoroughly after application. Grass begins using the nitrogen in the fertilizer within 15 to 24 hours. Recycle the nitrogen by leaving grass clippings on the lawn if they are not extremely long. (For information on fertilizing, see page 409.) If the soil is acid (below pH 5.5), liming is necessary for effective nitrogen utilization. (For information on pH and liming, see pages 406 to 407.)

Dull lawn mower

Grass blades damaged by a dull lawn mower.

Problem: When viewed from a distance, the lawn has a white or gray cast. Leaf ends are ragged and dead at the tips. White hairs may protrude from the cut tips.

Analysis: If a reel or rotary lawn mower is dull, it tears the tips off the grass blades rather than cutting cleanly. This can occur on any grass but especially on perennial ryegrass and tall fescues, which have tough fibers running the length of the blade. If the blade tips are torn, these fibers usually remain protruding from the torn ends. It is particularly important to keep the mower sharp when cutting these grasses.

Solution: Sharpen reel mowers two or three times during the growing season. Sharpen rotary mowers after every few mowings. Reel mowers may be sharpened at a hardware store that offers this service. Rotary mower blades can be removed and sharpened with a file.

Septoria leaf spot

Septoria leaf spot.

Problem: In the spring and fall, the lawn has a gray cast. The tips of the grass blades are pale yellow to gray with red or yellow margins. Pale areas may be ⅛ to 1 inch long. Tiny black dots are scattered in the diseased spots on blades. From a distance, damage may resemble dull-mower injury.

Analysis: Septoria leaf spot, also called *tip burn*, is a lawn disease caused by a fungus (*Septoria* species) that infects most northern grass species and bermudagrass. It is most prevalent in the cool, wet weather of early spring and fall. Lawns that have not been fertilized are most susceptible. The disease usually attacks in the spring, declines during the hot summer months, and returns in the fall. Because the disease infects leaf tips first, frequent mowing removes much of the diseased part of the blades.

Solution: Treat the infected lawn with a fungicide containing *mancozeb* or *myclobutanil* as soon as discoloration appears. Repeat the treatment three more times, 7 to 10 days apart, or as long as weather favorable to the disease continues. Keep the lawn healthy and vigorous by following the guidelines for good lawn care on pages 48 to 63. Mow the lawn regularly. Because no variety is completely resistant, plant a blend of two or three disease-tolerant varieties.

Rust

Rust.

Problem: Grass turns orange-yellow or reddish brown and begins to thin out. An orange powder that looks like rust coats the grass blades and rubs off on fingers, shoes, and clothing. Reddish-brown lesions under the powder do not rub off.

Analysis: Rust is a lawn disease caused by a fungus (*Puccinia* species) that occurs most frequently on Kentucky bluegrass, ryegrass, tall fescue, and zoysiagrass. It is most active during moist, warm weather (70° to 75°F) but can be active all winter in mild winter areas. Heavy dew helps its development. Grasses under stress from nitrogen deficiency and lack of moisture are most susceptible to attack. Rust is also more severe in the shade. The orange powder is composed of millions of microscopic spores that spread easily in the wind. Lawns attacked severely by rust are more likely to suffer winter damage.

Solution: Rust develops slowly, often more slowly than the grass grows. Apply a high-nitrogen fertilizer to maintain rapid growth. Mow frequently, removing the clippings. If the disease is severe, treat with Ortho® Lawn Disease Control or a fungicide containing *triadimefon*. Repeat the application every 14 to 28 days as needed.

Powdery mildew

Powdery mildew.

Problem: Whitish-gray mold develops on the upper surfaces of grass blades during cool rainy weather. The lawn looks as if it has been dusted with flour. Leaf tissue under the mold turns yellow and then tan or brown. Severely infected plants wither and die.

Analysis: Powdery mildew is a lawn disease caused by a fungus (*Erysiphe graminis*) and occurs when the nights are cool (65° to 70°F) and damp, and the days warm and humid. It is most severe on Kentucky bluegrass but also attacks fescues and bermudagrass. Lawns growing in the shade are the most affected. Powdery mildew slows the growth of leaves, roots, and underground stems, causing gradual weakening of the grass and making the grass more susceptible to other problems. Lawns growing rapidly because of excessive nitrogen fertilizing are very susceptible to attack from this fungus. The fine white mildew on the blades develops into powdery spores that spread easily in the wind.

Solution: Treat the lawn with Ortho® Lawn Disease Control when the mildew is first seen. Repeat every 14 to 28 days as needed. Reduce the shade and improve air circulation by pruning surrounding trees and shrubs. Follow the guidelines on pages 48–63 for a healthy, vigorous lawn.

POWDERY MATERIAL ON GRASS *(continued)*

DARK GREEN AREAS

Slime mold

Slime mold.

Problem: Bluish-gray, black, or yellow pinhead-size balls cover grass blades in the spring, summer, and fall following heavy rains or watering. Balls feel powdery when rubbed between the fingers. Affected areas range in size from a few inches to several feet in width.

Analysis: Slime molds are fungi that feed on decaying organic matter in the soil. They don't feed on green plants. When the powdery covering is heavy, it may damage the grass by shading the blades from sunlight, causing them to turn yellow. Slime molds occur on dichondra, all turfgrasses, and some weeds. While slime molds are feeding on decaying organic matter in the soil, they are white, gray, or yellow slimy masses on the soil. When they are ready to reproduce, they extend up onto grass blades and form powdery balls containing spores. This phase of the life cycle is more noticeable than the slimy mass phase.

Solution: In most cases control is not necessary. Although slime molds are unsightly, they do not permanently damage the lawn. Remove the molds from the grass by spraying with a strong stream of water or by sweeping with a broom.

Fairy ring

Fairy ring.

Problem: Circles or arcs of dark green grass occur in the lawn. The circles may be as small as 1 foot or as large as hundreds of feet in diameter. The grass just inside the darker area may be lighter green than the rest of the lawn. Mushrooms may grow in the dark green area.

Analysis: Fairy ring condition is caused by one of several fungi that grow on organic matter in the soil. Neither fungus harms the grass directly but may inhibit water flow into the soil. The ring of darker green grass is caused by nutrients released as the fungus breaks down organic matter. If the lawn is low in nutrients, the darker area will be more pronounced in contrast to the paler grass around it. The fungus begins growth at a central point and grows outward at a rate of 1 to 2 feet per year, forming the circle. Mushrooms, which are the fruiting bodies of the fungus, appear when weather conditions are right for them.

Solution: Fairy ring is not a turfgrass disease and does not harm the lawn. It is very difficult to control, but its effects can be masked by fertilizing the lawn outside the ring well and using less fertilizer within the fairy ring so that all the grass will be dark green. If there is a region of pale green or yellow grass within the ring, aerate the lawn and water thoroughly so that water penetrates the soil surface. (For information on aerating, see page 405. For information on watering, see pages 55 and 407.) If chemical control is desired, apply a fungicide containing *azoxystrobin*.

Fertilizing

Uneven fertilization.

Fertilizers supply the nutrients a lawn needs to grow well and remain healthy. Follow these guidelines for proper fertilizing:

■ Use a fertilizer that supplies all three major nutrients: nitrogen, phosphate, and potash. For a discussion of plant nutrients, see pages 409 to 410.

■ Too much nitrogen fertilizer during periods of stress causes lawn diseases. Avoid heavy fertilizing during stress periods. Warm-season grasses are under stress during the cool part of the year; cool-season grasses are under stress during hot weather.

■ Spread the fertilizer evenly over the lawn with a drop spreader or a broadcast spreader.

■ Water thoroughly immediately after fertilizer application. This dilutes the dissolved fertilizer and prevents it from burning the lawn.

■ Some general guidelines for feeding grasses: If you live in Zone A (see map on page 542), feed in midspring, early fall, and late fall. If you live in Zone C, fertilize when the grass begins growing in the spring and repeat every six weeks until cool weather. If you live in Zone B and your lawn turns brown every winter, follow the directions for Zone C. If the lawn remains green during the winter, feed in early spring, late spring, early fall, and late fall.

ANIMAL DAMAGE

Birds

Bird damage.

Problem: Many birds are pecking the lawn.

Analysis: Pecking birds indicate an insect problem in the lawn. Starlings, crows, sparrows, grackles, and robins are commonly found feeding on grubs, chinch bugs, and sod webworms. When cutworms or armyworms are active, birds will feed on them. If left untended, the insects will probably do more damage than the birds, which disturb the lawn's root system only slightly by tearing and pulling the roots while searching for insects.

Solution: The best way to keep birds from digging in your lawn is to rid it of insects. (For information on controlling grubs and sod webworms see page 67, for chinch bugs see page 69). Treat lawns in late afternoon so insecticides are dry by the next day when birds return; otherwise, some may be injured by contacting freshly applied insecticides.

Moles

Ridges in lawn caused by mole tunnels.

Problem: Raised ridges, 3 to 5 inches wide, irregularly crisscross the lawn. These ridges sometimes turn brown.

Analysis: Moles are small rodents that live underground. They feed on grubs, earthworms, and other insects. Moles are four to six inches long, with velvety fur and small hidden eyes. They use their strong forelegs, with long trowel-like claws, to dig and push as they move through the soil. As they make tunnels, they sever the grass roots and raise the sod. These raised and loosened areas dry out quickly. Moles are also objectionable because their ridges give the lawn an uneven surface that can result in scalping when mowed. (For more information on moles, see pages 62 and 496.)

Solution: Moles are often attracted to a lawn by grubs. If grubs are present, treat the lawn for grubs. (For information on grubs, see page 67.) If moles are a problem when there are no grubs, they are probably feeding on earthworms. Traps are the most effective way to control them. Set the traps on active tunnels. To determine which tunnels are active, roll or tamp down the ridges in the early morning. Those that are raised by the afternoon are still active. Several kinds of mole traps are available in hardware and rental stores. Poison baits are not always effective and should be used with caution around children and pets.

Miscellaneous

Damage from skunk digging.

Problem: Holes appear in the lawn. Ragged sections of turf have been torn out in patches 3 inches in diameter or larger. Bare soil is exposed underneath, often in a cone-shape hole.

Analysis: Several wild animals dig in lawns to feed on grubs or other insects. Skunks are the usual culprits, but raccoons, rodents, and even armadillos may occasionally dig in lawns. Skunks are primarily insectivores, relishing a meal of grubs. They are nocturnal, so they are seldom seen except in the light from windows. They may revisit the lawn regularly, causing fresh damage each time.

Solution: The easiest way to stop skunk damage is to eliminate the grubs. (For information on getting rid of grubs in lawns, see page 67.) Replace loosened turf before it dries out. Fill holes with soil, and patch them with pieces of sod. Keep the replaced pieces and patches moist until roots reestablish, within about two weeks.

DIGGING IN LAWN *(continued)*

GRASSLIKE WEEDS

Earthworms

Earthworm on putting green.

Problem: Small mounds or clumps of granular soil appear scattered throughout the lawn. Earthworms are frequently seen at night or after a heavy rain.

Analysis: Earthworms feed on dead roots and stems and are usually an indication of fertile soil. They prefer moist, medium- to fine-texture soil that is high in organic matter. They are seldom found in dry, sandy soil. Although castings—earthworm excretions that look like small piles of soil—may mar the appearance of the lawn, and earthworms may damage new seedlings, their activity improves the soil in several ways. Their movement from the surface to underlying soil helps mix the organic matter on the top with the soil below and reduces thatch accumulation. Their channels in the soil improve air and water movement through the soil. The castings also help improve the soil structure.

Solution: Earthworms are beneficial to the soil, so control measures are not required. Break up the mounds of soil with a rake or a vertical mower, or treat with a light power rake to even the soil surface.

Ants

Ant hill.

Problem: Small mounds or hills of soil occur in the lawn. Each mound has a hole in the center. Ants scurry about.

Analysis: Ants live underground in hot, dry areas of the lawn. They do not feed on grass, but when numerous, they may damage the plants in several ways. The mounds of soil in their hills smother and kill grass plants. As the ants tunnel among grass roots, the soil may dry out, also killing the plants. Ants feed on newly planted grass seeds and sometimes store the seeds in their nests. Some ants, especially fire ants and harvester ants, bite people and animals. Most become a nuisance when they travel from their mounds and invade homes. (For more information on ants, see pages 61 and 459.)

Solution: Treat ant hills with Ortho® Bug-B-Gon® Multi-Purpose Insect Killer Ready-Spray® or Ortho® Lawn Insect Killer Granules. Repeat the application as new mounds appear and for as long as the ants are active. Once the ants have disappeared, reseed any bare or dead spots.

Annual bluegrass

Seed heads. Inset: Annual bluegrass.

Problem: In midspring, abundant seed heads give the grass a whitish appearance. Pale green grassy weeds grow among desirable grasses. They turn yellow and die with the onset of hot weather.

Analysis: Annual bluegrass (*Poa annua*) is one of the most troublesome but least noticed weeds in the lawn. This member of the bluegrass family is lighter green, more shallow rooted, and less drought tolerant than Kentucky bluegrass. As its name suggests, annual bluegrass usually lives for only one year, although some strains are perennial. The seed germinates in cool weather from late summer to late fall and grows rapidly in the spring. Whitish seed heads appear in mid- to late spring at the same height that the grass is cut. When hot, dry weather arrives, the plants turn pale green and die. The seeds fall to the soil and wait for cooler weather to germinate. Annual bluegrass is most serious where the soil is compacted or overwatered and where drainage is poor.

Solution: Weed killers are only partially effective in controlling annual bluegrass. Prevent seeds from germinating by applying Scotts® Halts® Crabgrass Preventer as a preemergent treatment in late summer to early fall. Don't use if you plan to reseed the lawn in the fall. Replace the dead areas in the summer with sod. Do not cut the lawn too short. Lawns more than 2½ inches tall have very little annual bluegrass. Aerate the lawn in compacted areas (see page 405). Space waterings far enough apart that the surface of the ground has time to dry.

Bermudagrass

Bermudagrass.

Problem: In southern areas of the United States, patches of fine- to coarse-texture grass grow in the lawn. The slightly hairy gray-green stems, or stolons, creep along the soil surface and are 6 to 18 inches long. Leaf blades are 1/8 to 1/4 inch wide. This grass turns brown in the winter if subjected to temperatures below 50°F.

Analysis: Bermudagrass (*Cynodon dactylon*) is one of the most widely used lawn grasses in the South. It has a very deep root system and is drought and heat tolerant. The leaves are not cold tolerant and turn brown when the temperature approaches freezing. Its vigorous, creeping growth habit makes it a weed that invades other types of lawns and flower beds.

Solution: Spot-treat the bermudagrass with Ortho® Grass-B-Gon® Grass Killer for Landscapes anytime the grass is actively growing, up to two to four weeks before the first killing frost. After one week, mow the treated grass as close as possible, and reseed. The grass will still be green when it is mowed, but roots will die in three to four weeks and will not resprout. If regrowth occurs in the spring, spot-treat with the same herbicide. To prevent bermudagrass from invading your lawn from other lawns, mow higher than 1½ inches, spot-treat as needed each summer, and water the lawn adequately during the summer. Avoid spreading creeping stems to new areas with lawn mowers. Fertilize more heavily in the fall than at any other time of year if you have a cool-season grass.

Quackgrass

Quackgrass.

Problem: A grassy weed with hollow stems grows in a newly seeded lawn. Wheatlike spikes grow at the tips of the stems. The narrow leaf blades are bluish green and rough on the upper surface. A pair of "claws" occurs at the junction of the blade and the stem. Rings of root hairs grow every 3/4 to 1 inch along the underground stems.

Analysis: Quackgrass (*Elytrigia repens*), a cool-season perennial, also called *couchgrass* or *witchgrass*, spreads extensively through the lawn by long, white underground stems. It reproduces by seeds and these underground stems. The seeds may lie dormant in the soil for up to two years. Quackgrass is found most frequently in fertile, newly seeded lawns. It grows much more rapidly than grass seedlings, often crowding them out. (For more information on quackgrass, see page 466.)

Solution: Quackgrass is difficult to control in lawns. If the entire lawn is infested with it, the lawn will need to be killed and another planted. If isolated areas are infested only, kill them and replant these spots. The quackgrass must be actively growing before it is sprayed. Let it grow to 4 to 6 inches high, then spray with Ortho® Grass-B-Gon® Grass Killer for Landscapes. If regrowth occurs, repeat the treatment.

Crabgrass

Crabgrass seed head.

Problem: A grassy weed forms broad, flat clumps in thin areas of the lawn. It grows rapidly through the summer, rooting at the stem joints. The pale green blades of crabgrass are 2 to 5 inches long and 1/3 inch wide. Seed heads 2 to 6 inches tall grow from the center of the plant.

Analysis: Crabgrass (*Digitaria* species) sprouts from seeds in the early spring, growing rapidly and producing seeds all summer until the first killing frost in the fall. Then the plants turn brown and die. The seeds lie dormant over the winter and sprout in the spring. Crabgrass is one of the most common lawn weeds in its area of adaptation. When a lawn begins to thin out from insects, disease, or poor maintenance, crabgrass is one of the first weeds to invade the area.

Solution: Kill actively growing crabgrass with Ortho® Weed-B-Gon® Crabgrass Killer for Lawns. Older plants are harder to kill; repeat the treatment two more times at four- to seven-day intervals. To kill crabgrass seeds as they germinate, apply Scotts® Halts® Crabgrass Preventer in late winter or early spring, two weeks before the last expected frost (about the time forsythia and dogwood bloom). Follow the guidelines on pages 48 to 63 for a healthy, vigorous lawn; crabgrass is not usually a serious problem in lawns with thick, healthy growth.

Lawns *(continued)*

GRASSLIKE WEEDS *(continued)*

Tall fescue

Tall fescue.

Problem: Clumps of very coarse, tough grass invade thin areas of the lawn. The medium-dark green blades, each ½ inch wide, are ribbed on the top surface and smooth on the bottom. In the spring and fall, the lower parts of the stems turn reddish purple. The blades tend to shred when mowed.

Analysis: Tall fescue (*Festuca arundinacea*), a cool-season, perennial, bunch-type grass, is very durable. It is commonly used on athletic fields because it holds up well under hard wear. Tall fescue makes an attractive turf when grown by itself. When it is seeded with, or invades, bluegrass, bermudagrass, or ryegrass lawns, however, it is considered a weed. It becomes very clumpy and makes an uneven turf. When insects and diseases attack the desirable grasses in the lawn, the tall fescue is usually not affected. It resists diseases and grubs, and sod webworms attack it only if they've eaten everything else. It is also somewhat heat tolerant, and its deep roots help it survive periods of heavy moisture and drought.

Solution: Kill clumps of tall fescue with Ortho® Grass-B-Gon® Grass Killer for Landscapes while it is actively growing from early summer to early fall. Omit a regular mowing before treating to allow for enough leaf tissue to absorb the chemical. This type of herbicide will also kill any desirable grasses it contacts. One week after spraying, mow the tall fescue and reseed the area.

Barnyardgrass

Barnyardgrass.

Problem: In summer and fall, a low-growing grassy weed with reddish-purple stems 1 to 3 feet long grows in the lawn. The smooth leaves of barnyardgrass are ¼ to ½ inch wide, with a prominent midrib.

Analysis: Barnyardgrass (*Echinochloa crus-galli*) also called *watergrass,* is a warm-season annual weed that is usually found in poorly managed lawns of low fertility. It reproduces by seeds and develops into a plant with a shallow root system. Although the natural growth habit of barnyardgrass is upright, when mowed regularly it forms ground-hugging mats.

Solution: Kill mats of actively growing barnyardgrass with Ortho® Weed-B-Gon® Crabgrass Killer for Lawns. Improve soil fertility and maintain a dense, healthy lawn by following the guidelines on pages 48 to 63. To kill barnyardgrass seedlings as they sprout, apply Scotts® Halts® Crabgrass Preventer in the early spring, two weeks before the last expected frost.

Nutsedge

Nutsedge. Inset: Underground stems and tubers.

Problem: In the summer, this weed grows more rapidly than the grass and stands above the turf. The erect, single, triangular stem has narrow, grasslike, yellow-green leaves arranged in threes from the base of the plant. Seed heads are yellow-brown.

Analysis: Nutsedge (*Cyperus* species), also called *nutgrass,* is a hard-to-kill perennial weed. Both yellow and purple nutsedge are common weeds. Nutsedge reproduces by underground stems, seeds, and tubers. The tubers, the size of popcorn kernels, sprout in late spring and early summer. The plant tops die back in the fall, leaving new tubers in the soil to repeat the cycle the following year. The tubers and underground stems are firmly anchored in the ground. When a plant is pulled up, some of the tubers and underground stems are left behind to resprout into new plants. (For more information on nutsedge, see page 470.)

Solution: Nutsedge is difficult to control. Treat with Ortho® Weed-B-Gon® Crabgrass Killer for Lawns when the plants first become active in the spring. Repeat two or three more times 10 to 14 days apart. If you miss a treatment, the weeds recover and take longer to control. Treat again the following spring to kill any persistent tubers. These herbicides may temporarily (for two to four weeks) discolor desirable grasses. On centipedegrass and St. Augustinegrass lawns, use Scotts® Bonus® S Weed And Feed in January, February, or March, before the weeds germinate.

BROADLEAF WEEDS

Clover

Clover.

Problem: A weed with leaves composed of three round leaflets at the top of a hairy leafstalk, 2 to 4 inches tall, grows in the lawn. The leafstalks sprout from the base of the plant. White or pink-tinged flowers, ½ inch in size, bloom from June to September. They often attract bees.

Analysis: Clover (*Trifolium* species) is a common perennial weed in lawns throughout the United States. Although some people like it in a lawn, others consider it messy, or they don't like the bees attracted to the flowers. Clover reproduces by seeds and aboveground rooting stems. The seeds can live in the soil for 20 years or more. The plant, which has a creeping, prostrate habit, suffocates lawn grasses, resulting in large patches of clover. When buying a box of grass seed, be sure to read the label carefully. Clover seeds are sometimes contained in seed mixtures. Because clover produces its own nitrogen, it thrives in lawns that are underfertilized.

Solution: Treat the lawn with Ortho® Weed-B-Gon® Weed Killer for Lawns, Ortho® Weed-B-Gon® Chickweed, Clover and Oxalis Killer for Lawns, or Scotts® GreenSweep® Weed & Feed in the spring and early fall. Repeated treatments are often necessary for adequate control.

Oxalis

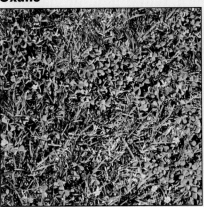

Oxalis.

Problem: A weed with pale green leaves divided into three heart-shaped leaflets invades thin areas of the lawn. The leaves are ¼ to ¾ inch wide and similar to clover. The stems root at the lower joints and are often thinly covered with fine hairs. Small, bright yellow flowers are ½ inch long with five petals. Cucumber-shaped, light green seedpods develop from the fading flowers. Plants may be 4 to 12 inches high with a prostrate-to-erect growth habit.

Analysis: Oxalis (*Oxalis stricta* and *O. corniculata*), also called *yellow woodsorrel* or *creeping woodsorrel*, is a perennial plant that thrives in dry, open places but may also be a problem in moist, well-fertilized lawns. It often invades lawns that are beginning to thin from insect, disease, or maintenance problems. Oxalis reproduces from the seeds formed in the seedpods. When the pods dry, a light touch causes them to explode, shooting their seeds several feet in all directions. Oxalis leaves contain oxalic acid, which makes them sour. (For more information on oxalis, see page 477.)

Solution: Control oxalis with Ortho® Weed-B-Gon® Weed Killer for Lawns or Ortho® Weed-B-Gon® Chickweed, Clover and Oxalis Killer for Lawns. The most effective time to spray is when the weeds are actively growing, in the spring or late summer to fall. Oxalis is not easy to kill; several treatments are usually needed. Check the soil pH level (see page 406), and follow the guidelines on pages 48 to 63 for a healthy, vigorous lawn. A healthy lawn helps smother the oxalis.

Spotted spurge

Spotted spurge.

Problem: A low-growing weed with oval pale to dark green leaves ¼ to ¾ inch long appears in the lawn. Each leaf may have a purple spot. Stems ooze milky white sap when broken. The leaves are slightly hairy on the underside and smooth on top. Tiny pinkish white flowers bloom in midsummer. The many pale green stems fan out on the soil surface and over the top of the grass, forming mats up to 2 feet in diameter.

Analysis: Spotted spurge (*Euphorbia maculata*), also called *milk purslane* or *prostrate spurge*, invades thin areas of the lawn, smothering the grass. Spurge sprouts from seeds in the spring and dies with the first frost. This weed commonly invades lawns that are dry and infertile, but it can also be found in well-maintained lawns. (For more information on spotted spurge, see page 476.)

Solution: In the late spring or early summer, treat the lawn with Scotts® GreenSweep® Weed & Feed or Ortho® Weed-B-Gon® Weed Killer for Lawns. Keep the lawn well watered (see page 55) to discourage spurge from invading dry areas.

BROADLEAF WEEDS *(continued)*

Common chickweed

Common chickweed.

Problem: A weed with small (½-inch-long) teardrop-shape leaves and starlike white flowers grows in thin spaces in the lawn. A single row of white hairs appears on one side of the stem. The stems root easily at their joints. Common chickweed is most often found in shady or moist areas.

Analysis: Common chickweed (*Stellaria media*) grows from seeds that sprout in the fall; the plants live for less than a year. Common chickweed grows primarily in damp, shady areas under trees and shrubs and on the north side of buildings, but it can also occur in dormant warm-season grasses. Common chickweed invades home lawns when they begin to thin out from insects, disease, mechanical damage, or shade. It reproduces by seeds and by the creeping stems that root at their joints wherever they touch the soil. It has a low prostrate growing habit, forming a dense mat that crowds out the grass. (For more information on common chickweed, see page 475.)

Solution: Treat the lawn with Ortho® Weed-B-Gon® Weed Killer for Lawns or Ortho® Weed-B-Gon® Chickweed, Clover and Oxalis Killer for Lawns when it is growing actively in the early spring or late fall. Repeated applications may be necessary. Do not water for two days after applying.

Henbit

Henbit.

Problem: A weed with rounded, toothed leaves, ¾ inch wide, grows in the lawn. The lower leaves are attached to the square (four-sided) upright stems by short leafstalks; upper leaves attach directly to the stems. Stems root easily at lower joints. Lavender, ½-inch flowers appear from March to June and again in September.

Analysis: Henbit (*Lamium amplexicaule*), a weed also known as *dead nettle* or *bee nettle*, is found in lawns and flower and vegetable gardens across the country. It is a winter annual that sprouts from seeds in late summer and grows rapidly in the fall and the following spring, producing conspicuous purple flowers early in the spring. Henbit also reproduces by stems that root easily wherever the stem joints touch the soil. Henbit most frequently invades thin areas in lawns with rich soil. (For more information on henbit, see page 488.)

Solution: Treat the lawn with Scotts® GreenSweep® Weed & Feed or Ortho® Weed-B-Gon® Weed Killer for Lawns in early spring when henbit is growing most rapidly. Do not water for 24 hours after treating. An infestation of a few small plants can be hand-pulled.

Purslane

Purslane.

Problem: A low-growing weed with reddish-brown, thick, succulent stems is found in thin areas or newly seeded lawns. The leaves are thick, fleshy, and wedge-shape. Small yellow flowers sometimes bloom in the leaf and stem joints. Stems root where they touch the soil.

Analysis: Purslane (*Portulaca oleracea*), a summer annual weed that thrives in hot, dry weather, is seldom found in the spring when the lawn is being treated for other weeds. Purslane grows vigorously, forming a thick mat. The small yellow flowers open only in the full sunlight. Purslane primarily invades bare spots in lawns or thin lawns that have not been watered properly. Purslane stores water in its thick, fleshy stems and leaves and therefore it survives longer than grass during dry weather. (For more information on purslane, see page 476.)

Solution: Spray the lawn with Ortho® Weed-B-Gon® Weed Killer for Lawns when the weed is actively growing. If the lawn has just been reseeded, do not treat until the seedlings have grwon enough to require mowing three times. Wait three to four weeks before seeding bare areas.

Ground ivy

Ground ivy.

Problem: A low-growing, creeping weed with rounded, scalloped leaves grows in shady areas of the lawn. The nickel- to quarter-size leaves grow at the end of a long leafstalk. The stalks are paired opposite each other along the square (four-sided) stem. Light blue to purple flowers, ½ to ¾ inch long, bloom from April to July.

Analysis: Ground ivy (*Glechoma hederacea*), also called *creeping ivy*, is a perennial that was originally planted in some areas as a ground cover. It has now become a major weed in the North. Ground ivy reproduces by seeds and creeping stems that root wherever they touch the soil. This plant has shallow roots and forms a dense mat throughout the lawn, crowding out grasses. Although it is found primarily in shaded areas, ground ivy also survives in sunlight. (For more information on ground ivy, see page 478.)

Solution: Treat the lawn with Ortho® Weed-B-Gon® Weed Killer for Lawns or Ortho® Weed-B-Gon® Chickweed, Clover & Oxalis Killer for Lawns in the spring or fall when the plants are growing actively. A spring treatment gives the best result by killing the plants before the leaves mature. Where the ground ivy has formed a dense mat, it may be necessary to apply the herbicide for several years in a row. Hand-pulling is not a good way to control ground ivy because the roots readily resprout into new plants. Ground ivy may indicate that the area is too shady for a lawn to grow.

Dandelion

Dandelion.

Problem: From spring to fall, a weed with bright yellow flowers blooms in the lawn. In southern states it may bloom all winter. Flower stems grow 2 to 10 inches above the plants. The medium-green leaves, 3 to 10 inches long, are deeply lobed along the sides. The plant has a deep, fleshy taproot.

Analysis: Dandelion (*Taraxacum officinale*) is the most common and easily identified perennial weed in the United States. It reproduces by seeds and from shoots that grow from the fleshy taproot. This taproot grows 2 to 3 feet deep into the soil, surviving even the severest of winters. They are most numerous in full sunlight. In the early spring, new sprouts emerge from the taproot. As the yellow flowers mature and ripen, they form white "puff balls" containing seeds. The wind carries the seeds for miles to other lawns. The tops die back in late fall, and the taproot overwinters to start the cycle again in the spring. Dandelions prefer wet soil and are often a sign of overwatering. (For more information on dandelion, see page 483.)

Solution: Treat the lawn with Ortho® Weed-B-Gon® Weed Killer for Lawns or Scotts® GreenSweep® Weed & Feed. For best results, make two applications, first in the early summer and again in the early fall. Do not water or mow for two days afterward. Feed the grass adequately to keep it dense. Mow frequently enough to keep the flowers from becoming seed heads. Hand-digging and removal is impractical, because pieces of root broken off and left in the soil will sprout into new plants.

Sheep sorrel

Sheep sorrel.

Problem: Arrow-shaped leaves, 1 to 3 inches long, with two lobes at the base of each leaf, form a dense rosette. Erect, upright stems grow 4 to 14 inches tall. Two types of flowers appear in midspring; one is reddish green, the other yellowish green.

Analysis: Sheep sorrel (*Rumex acetosella*), a cool-season perennial, is also called *red sorrel* or *sourgrass* because of its sour taste and reddish coloration. It grows in dry, sterile, sandy or gravelly soil and is usually an indication of acid soil or low nitrogen fertility. Sheep sorrel reproduces by seeds and red underground root stalks. The root system is shallow but extensive and is not easily removed. (For more information on sheep sorrel, see page 483.)

Solution: In spring or fall, treat with Ortho® Weed-B-Gon® Weed Killer for Lawns. Do not mow for five days before or two days after treating. Sheep sorrel is difficult to control, so several treatments may be necessary. To discourage sheep sorrel, test the soil pH as outlined on page 406 and correct to between 6.0 and 7.0 if necessary. Improve the soil fertility by following the fertilizing guidelines on page 409.

BROADLEAF WEEDS (continued)

Mallow

Mallow.

Problem: A weed with hairy stems, 4 to 12 inches long, spreads over the lawn. The stem tips turn upward. Round, heart-shaped, hairy leaves ½ to 3 inches wide and slightly lobed along the edges are attached to the stems by a long leafstalk. White to lilac flowers, 2½ inches in diameter with five petals, bloom singly or in clusters at the leaf and stem junction. Mallow is often mistaken for ground ivy, but the spreading branches do not root when they contact soil as the branches of ground ivy do.

Analysis: Mallow (*Malva* species), also called *cheeseweed*, is found throughout North America in lawns, fields, and along roadways. It is an annual or sometimes a biennial and reproduces by seeds. It has a straight, nearly white taproot that is difficult to pull from the soil. Mallow is most commonly found in poorly managed lawns and in soils high in manure content. (For more information on mallow, see page 480.)

Solution: Treat the lawn with Ortho® Weed-B-Gon® Weed Killer for Lawns from midspring to early summer. Maintain a thick, healthy lawn by following the guidelines on pages 48 to 63.

Field bindweed

Field bindweed.

Problem: A plant with long twining stems grows across the lawn. The leaves are arrowhead-shape and up to two inches long. White to pink funnel-shaped flowers, about 1 inch across, appear from spring to fall.

Analysis: Field bindweed (*Convolvulus arvensis*) a deep-rooted perennial weed also known as wild morning glory, is found throughout most of the United States in lawns, gardens, and fields and along roadways. It is one of the most troublesome and difficult weeds to eliminate because of its extensive root system. The roots may grow 15 to 20 feet deep. Roots or pieces of roots left behind from hand-pulling or spading easily resprout. Field bindweed, which reproduces by seeds and roots, twines and climbs over shrubs and fences and up into trees. It prefers rich, sandy, or gravelly soil but will grow in almost any garden soil. (For more information on field bindweed, see page 487.)

Solution: Treat plants from late spring through early summer or from early to late fall with Ortho® Weed-B-Gon® Weed Killer for Lawns. Because of the deep roots, repeated treatments may be necessary. Treat again whenever new growth appears.

Plantain

Buckhorn plantain. Inset: Broadleaf plantain.

Problem: A weed forming a rosette with long, narrow, hairy leaves 4 to 12 inches long and held off the ground grows in the lawn. The leaves have three to five nearly parallel, prominent veins. Erect white flower spikes, 4 to 12 inches tall, appear from spring into fall. A similar weed has broad, egg-shape leaves attached to 1-inch leafstalks that are, in turn, attached to the center of a rosette. These leaves are 2 to 10 inches long, with five to seven prominent veins, and lie flat on the soil. Erect greenish-white flower spikes, 2 to 10 inches tall, bloom from spring to fall.

Analysis: Both buckhorn plantain (*Plantago lanceolata*), with long, narrow leaves, and broadleaf plantain (*P. major*), with egg-shape leaves, are common perennial weeds that resprout from their roots each year. They reproduce from seeds formed on the flower spikes and from new shoots from the roots. As thin areas develop in the lawn from insect, disease or maintenance problems, either or both of these weeds can move in. As the plants grow larger and lie flat on the soil, they crowd out the surrounding grass. (For more information on plantain, see page 481.)

Solution: Spray the lawn with Ortho® Weed-B-Gon® Weed Killer for Lawns in the spring or fall when the plants are actively growing. Repeated applications are often necessary. An application in early fall gives the best results by reducing infestation the following year. Do not mow five days before or two days after spraying.

MISCELLANEOUS

Mushrooms

Mushrooms.

Problem: Mushrooms sprout up in the lawn after wet weather. They may be growing in circles of dark green grass. When the weather gets colder or the soil dries out, they disappear.

Analysis: Mushrooms, also called *toadstools* or *puffballs*, live on organic matter buried in the soil. The mushroom is the aboveground fruiting or reproductive structure of a fungus that lives on and helps to decay the organic matter. The organic matter may include buried logs, lumber, roots, or stumps. Most mushrooms do not damage the lawn but are objectionable because they are unsightly. Mushrooms growing in circles of dark green grass, called *fairy rings*, may make the soil impervious to water and injure the grass.

Solution: There is no practical or permanent way to eliminate mushrooms. When buried wood is completely decayed, the mushrooms will disappear. The easiest and most practical solution, although it is only temporary, is to break the mushrooms with a rake or lawn mower.

Algae

Algae.

Problem: A green to black slimy scum covers bare soil and crowns of grass plants. When dry, it becomes crusty, cracks, and peels easily.

Analysis: Algae (*Symploca* and *Oscillatoria* species) are freshwater plants that invade shady, wet areas of the lawn. They injure grass by smothering or shading it as they grow over the crowns of the plants. Invaded areas become slippery. Algae live in compacted soil and soil that is high in nitrogen and organic matter. They need constantly or frequently wet conditions to survive. Organic fertilizers encourage algae, especially in the cool seasons. Algae may be carried from place to place by animals, equipment, people, and birds. Water taken from ponds, lakes, and streams and used for irrigation usually contains algae.

Solution: Patches of algae may be sprayed with a fungicide containing *mancozeb* or wettable sulfur two times, one month apart, in early spring. This is only a temporary solution. Algae will soon return if the conditions are not corrected. Reduce soil compaction (see on page 405). Improve drainage (see on page 406), and prune nearby trees to reduce shading. Avoid high-nitrogen fertilizers in late fall and winter. Maintain a healthy, vigorous lawn according to the lawn maintenance guidelines on pages 48 to 63.

Moss

Moss.

Problem: Green, velvety, low-growing plants cover bare soil in shady areas of the lawn.

Analysis: Moss invades thin or bare areas of the lawn. It does not grow in a vigorous lawn. Moss is encouraged by poor fertility, poor drainage, compacted soil, shade, and high acidity. Moss plants sprout from spores and fill in bare or thin areas.

Solution: Shortly after mowing, apply Scotts® Moss Control Granules for Lawns or Ortho® Moss-B-Gon® Granules for Lawns while grass is moist. Moss may also be removed by hand or power raking. Reduce shade by pruning nearby trees. Correct soil compaction (see page 405), and improve drainage (see page 406.) Test the soil pH, and correct it if necessary. Follow the lawn maintenance guidelines on pages 48 to 63 to promote a healthy, vigorous lawn.

A healthy ajuga ground cover under a Japanese aralia. Ajuga looks best in the shade.

Ground covers shade out weeds and add both texture and color to small or large areas. They can be remarkably drought-resistant. But ground covers, like other lawn and garden plants, require nurturing to stay lush.

CONSIDERING THE SOIL

The first step in establishing ground cover is to ensure that the soil can provide plants with the aeration, nutrients, and pH they need for proper growth.

Dense soil: Some soils, such as clay, tend to be naturally dense. Clay soil cracks and becomes quite hard when dry. Water may run off rather than sink in, creating droughtlike conditions.

To tell if you have dense soil, dig a hole 2 feet deep. Fill the hole with water. If the water level drops less than 1/10 inch per hour, your soil is dense and has a drainage problem that should be corrected.

Correcting dense soil is hard work but necessary. The most permanent solution is to dig the entire planting area to a depth of 6 inches and work in such soil amendments as gypsum and organic matter. This is also a good time to correct soil pH (see "Inappropriate pH", at right).

Compacted soil: Some soils are naturally compact. Others are compacted by construction work or foot traffic. Whatever the cause, the result can be hardpan and struggling ground cover unless the gardener corrects the situation.

Hardpan: A planting hole in hardpan, even when filled with organic amendments, collects water, creating a basin where roots rot. If your ground cover site contains hardpan, you must correct the soil before planting. In mild cases, correction consists of using a soil auger to bore deep holes in the soil. The holes allow air and water to flow downward and ease the way for growing roots. If the planting area is small but the soil is quite compact, use a hand-operated aerating tool to make 3-inch-deep holes about 3 inches apart. The practical approach to breaking up hardpan in large areas is deep plowing—you may have to hire a contractor to do the job. Talk to a knowledgeable nursery professional or a landscape gardener about the best approach to your situation.

If you have an area subject to constant foot traffic, consider installing paving stones or building a paved pathway. Plant shrubbery to prevent pedestrians from taking shortcuts.

Nutrient shortage: Slow growth is often a sign of a nutrient shortage. Other symptoms are yellowing or pale green leaves that remain small. To correct the soil, apply a general-purpose fertilizer regularly according to label instructions. If leaves turn pale but leaf veins remain normal, supplemental iron may be needed.

In some cases, the soil contains sufficient nutrients but its pH keeps plants from absorbing them. Read the next section to determine if your planting site is too acidic or alkaline.

Inappropriate pH: Kits for testing soil pH are available at nurseries. The kits are easy to use and supply valuable information.

■ **Acidic soil:** Plants unsuited to acidic soil grow slowly. Their leaves turn yellow or pale green. To improve acidic soils, apply a ground dolomitic limestone additive formulated especially for gardens. (For more information on acidic soil, see page 92.)

■ **Alkaline soil:** Plants grown in overly alkaline soil develop yellow areas between the veins on new leaves. This yellowing may be due to the lack of iron and manganese, which alkaline soil keeps plants from absorbing. To remedy the problem, make soils more acidic by applying aluminum sulfate, ferrous sulfate, or other sulfur. Use a fertilizer that creates an acidic reaction, such as a fertilizer formulated for azaleas.

Amend ground cover beds with organic matter and fertilizer before planting.

When planting many ground cover plants over a large area, lay out the bed in a staggered, or triangular, pattern.

Supplementary soil: If you decide to add topsoil to your planting site, make sure the new soil is free of weeds and weed seeds. Soil delivered by the truckload from construction sites is particularly suspect. Buy supplementary topsoil from a reputable nursery, and make sure you specify a weed-free and herbicide-free product. If it saves you from weed control, clean topsoil is worth the extra cost.

CONSIDERING GROUND COVERS

In selecting a ground cover, consider its growth habit, its ability to crowd out weeds, and its requirements for sun or shade and water as well as its ornamental value.

Invasive ground covers: A ground cover is often selected for its rapid growth habit. But this can turn the ground cover into a nuisance that moves into areas reserved for other plants. Any ground cover marked "Rapid growth, and very hardy" might be invasive given the right environment. Included in the possibly invasive list are Aaron's beard, dwarf bamboo, crown vetch, gill ivy, goutweed, honeysuckle, some mints, Indian mock strawberry, and sweet woodruff. If a ground cover becomes too energetic and regular cutting does not deter it, treat it as a weed and kill it by applying a systemic herbicide.

Weed-shading ground covers: Some ground covers eventually grow thick enough to shade the ground beneath them. This decreases weed germination. Given the best environment, essentially weed-free ground covers include ajuga, chamomile, Irish moss, snow-in-summer, wild strawberry, cinquefoil, lamb's ears, and vinca.

Sun and shade requirements: A shade-loving ground cover, such as Irish moss, will not grow well where sunlight plays on it most of the day. A sun-loving ground cover, such as chamomile, may die out in shady areas.

Study the planting area before rushing out to buy plants. You must know what the environment can support. If you live in or near an established area, one way to find out what will grow is to walk past thriving gardens in your neighborhood. If a neighbor's planting area faces the same direction yours does, given the same care, the same ground cover will probably do well for you. Don't limit yourself, however, by choosing a ground cover that is already established nearby. If you see a thriving ground cover, research its growing requirements. Then find other plants that thrive in similar conditions.

Signs of inadequate sunlight include poor growth, leggy growth, leaf drop, unusually dark green leaves, and insect attack.

Increase the sunlight the ground cover receives by trimming adjacent shrubbery or tree limbs. If providing more sunlight is not possible, carefully transfer the affected plants to a more suitable area. Replant with a shade-tolerant species.

Signs of too much sun include faded leaves. In severe situations, leaves may turn yellowish white. Growth slows. Too much sun breaks down plant tissue. Chlorophyll (green leaf pigment), which is necessary for leaf functioning, disappears. Wind and drought make the problem more severe. Place affected plants in a shadier location with sufficient water. Replace them with a more sun-tolerant species.

Resilient ground covers: If your planting site is subject to heavy foot traffic, choose a ground cover that can tolerate it. The list of such plants includes dichondra, chamomile, Irish moss, lippia, and mazus.

Drought- and moisture-tolerant ground covers: If you live in a drought area, consider using a drought-tolerant ground cover.

The selection includes low-growing California buckwheat, ground cover ceanothus, coyotebrush, lippia, and woolly yarrow.

Quite a few ground covers can prosper in damp soil, as long as you provide adequate drainage. These include ajuga, bunchberry, wild ginger, mint, and pachysandra.

PREVENTING WEEDS

Unfortunately, prime conditions for ground cover also encourage weeds. Hand-picking weeds from ground cover is difficult; getting a firm grip on a weed usually means tearing out some ground cover, too. Practical solutions include plastic or fabric sheets that block weeds, weed blocks, and herbicides.

Weed blocks: If it is thick enough to block sunlight, a black plastic sheet spread over the planting area can effectively prevent weeds. Holes cut in the plastic allow the ground cover to grow. In addition to preventing weeds, weed blocks conserve soil moisture. Weed block fabric, a fairly new innovation, is better than black plastic because it allows water, air, and nutrients to pass into the soil but does not readily allow weed growth.

Weed blocks present a few disadvantages, however. Plastic cracks with age and needs to be replaced. Weeds may sprout through cracked plastic or through the holes intended for ground cover. Though a weed block is an excellent defense against weeds, you may need to use herbicides as well.

Herbicides: One way herbicides are classified is according to the time they are applied.

■ **Preemergent herbicides:** Weed killers of this type are applied before weeds sprout; these herbicides prevent weed germination while allowing desirable plants to grow normally. Preemergent herbicides, which are usually applied in granular form, permeate the top inch or so of soil. When applied under a weed block, these products contribute to highly effective weed control. Check the label to ensure that the product is safe for your ground cover.

Preemergent herbicides do not kill existing weeds, which must be treated separately. The products lose some of their effectiveness if the soil is used as a path or disturbed by feeding birds, digging animals, or cultivation.

■ **Postemergent herbicides:** If weeds emerge, consider postemergent herbicides. Some are systemic, which means they work throughout the plant (including the root). Some can be applied without injury to specific ground covers. Others must be applied only to weeds; they will kill your desirable plants as well as weeds.

Before selecting a postemergent herbicide, read the label instructions carefully. Find out if your ground cover is susceptible to the product and how you need to apply it to protect garden plants. In lush ground cover you may have to use a narrow paintbrush to treat weeds. Use postemergent herbicides only on windless days, when chemicals can't drift on the breeze. Shield susceptible ground cover to protect it from inadvertent exposure.

WATERING GROUND COVERS

Soil that is too dry or soggy may be due to factors other than too little or too much rain. Soil permeability, soil type, and irrigation systems affect the amount of water plants actually absorb.

Drought conditions: During droughts, plants begin to yellow. Leaf edges may turn brown. Bare spots may appear. If you have been watering adequately, drought can still

occur because compacted soil is prohibiting water penetration. Rapid watering causes runoff rather than slow absorption. Hand-watering is often the culprit—which is not to say that sprinkler systems are perfect. Sprinkler heads may fall out of adjustment and leave some areas dry. To test the coverage, put a few small cans throughout the watering area. All areas should get an equal amount to catch the sprinkler water,

appropriate to the type of ground cover. If the cans contain different amounts, correct the system.

Overwatered ground covers:
Too much water causes root rot. Ground cover may die in spots or fail to thrive. Lower leaves turn yellow, then upper leaves. If too much rain is the cause—not excess watering—install drain tile.

By its third season of growth, the bed of pachysandra shown being planted on page 88 has completely filled in to become a lush, solid bed of green.

BARE SPOTS

Insufficient light

Irish moss in a dark location.

Problem: The planting is thin, with bare spots. Plants are spindly and leggy, with leaves that are darker green than usual. Leaves may drop, beginning with the lowest leaves and progressing upward.

Analysis: Plants use light to manufacture the food they need to survive. Without enough light, they become weak, stunted, and susceptible to attack from insects and disease. The plants that suffer most in low-light areas are those that require full sun. Shade-loving plants will tolerate varying degrees of shade.

Solution: If a tree shades the planting, consider pruning some of the branches to let more light pass through to the ground cover. If there is a group of trees, consider removing one or more of the trees. Consider using deciduous trees with open canopies so that the ground cover can recover during the cool months. Or plant a ground cover that tolerates shade.

Compacted soil

Compacted area in vinca.

Problem: Leaves turn yellow and do not grow as large as usual. Plants are stunted and die in some areas, leaving bare spots. No signs of insect or disease damage appear. The soil is dense and compacted.

Analysis: Soil compacts easily in areas where foot or vehicular traffic is heavy. This is especially a problem where a ground cover has been planted in an area that used to be lawn or a path. Compaction prevents air and water from penetrating into the soil and to the roots. Air in the soil is necessary for healthy root growth. Plants growing in compacted soil are more subject to disease, primarily root and crown rots, because the soil doesn't drain properly. Water often puddles on top of compacted soil.

Solution: If the soil is dry, use a soil penetrant to increase the wetting capacity of the soil. A lawn aerator that removes plugs of compacted soil can be used in low-growing ground covers, such as dichondra and creeping thyme. Poke holes around the plants with a lawn aerator to allow air and water to penetrate the soil. The holes must be at least 3 inches deep and no more than 3 inches apart. Cultivate the bare spots, add organic matter, and replant.

Drought

Polygonum dying from lack of water.

Problem: Bare spots appear in the ground cover. Plants are pale green and grow slowly. The edges of the leaves turn brown and crisp. The soil is frequently dry. Drought-tolerant weeds easily invade the area.

Analysis: The plants are not receiving enough water. This may be caused by one of several problems.
1. Not enough water is applied at each watering. This frequently happens with hand-watering. Although the ground is moist after watering, the water may not have penetrated to the plant roots.
2. Water is applied too infrequently. If rainfall is not supplemented by irrigation during drought periods or if watering is too infrequent, plants use up all the water in the soil and suffer stress before more water is applied.
3. Water runs off on the surface instead of entering the soil. This occurs when the soil is dense or compacted or when water is applied faster than the soil can absorb it.

Solution: Follow these guidelines to prevent drought damage.
1. Apply at least 1 inch of water at each watering. Set containers within the sprinkler area, and water until 1 inch of water has accumulated in each.
2. Water whenever the soil feels just barely moist 1 inch or so deep.
3. If water is running off the ground cover, irrigate with a sprinkler head that applies water more slowly. Or water until runoff begins, stop for a half hour to let the soil absorb the water, then continue until 1 inch has been applied. Aerate compacted soil.

Excess water

Bare spots from excess water.

Problem: Leaves turn yellow, starting with the older, lower leaves and progressing to the younger leaves. Plants grow very little. The roots are shallow and may be rotted. The soil is very moist.

Analysis: Excess moisture in the soil can result from watering too frequently or from too much rainfall. Roots need oxygen to grow and develop. Waterlogged soil has little oxygen available for root growth because the soil pores are filled with water. The only available oxygen is near the soil surface, so roots grow only in the upper layer of soil. These shallow-rooted plants are smaller than usual and more susceptible to drought. Many root- and crown-rotting fungi thrive in wet soil, killing plants. Ground covers growing in wet soil seldom spread to fill in the planted area.

Solution: Allow the soil to dry out partially between waterings. The soil 1 inch or so beneath the surface should be just barely moist before you water again. If you replant the area, improve drainage (see page 406) before replanting. If soil drains quickly, excess water seldom damages plants.

Lack of nutrients

Underfertilized ajuga.

Problem: Leaves are smaller than usual and turn pale green to yellow. Plants grow very slowly or very little.

Analysis: Fertilizer supplies the nutrients plants need to stay vigorous and healthy; adequate fertilizing may result in fewer insect and disease problems. The three essential nutrients that plants require in the largest amounts are nitrogen (N), phosphorus (P), and potassium (K). *Nitrogen* gives the leaves their green color and encourages rapid growth. Without nitrogen, plants turn pale green to yellow. *Phosphorus* encourages flowering and fruiting and helps build a strong root system. *Potassium* increases the plant's resistance to disease and aids in overall growth. Most garden fertilizers contain all three nutrients. On the bag are three numbers, called the N–P–K ratio or fertilizer grade, which state the nutrient content. For example, a fertilizer bag reading 5–10–10 has, by weight, 5 percent nitrogen, 10 percent phosphate (phosphorus), and 10 percent potash (potassium). Many fertilizers also supply trace, or minor, nutrients that plants need in minute amounts, which may be lacking in the soil. (For more information on fertilizing, see page 409.)

Solution: Fertilize your ground cover at regular intervals with Scotts® Water Soluble All Purpose Plant Food. Follow label instructions for amounts and timing of fertilizing. Water well after fertilizing to dilute the fertilizer and wash it into the soil.

Iron deficiency

Iron deficiency in pachysandra.

Problem: Leaves turn pale green or yellow. The newest leaves (those at the tips of the stems) are most severely affected. Except in extreme cases, the veins of affected leaves remain green. In extreme cases, the newest leaves are small and all-white or yellow. Older leaves may remain green.

Analysis: Plants frequently suffer from deficiencies of iron and other minor nutrients such as manganese and zinc, elements essential to normal plant growth and development. Deficiencies can occur when one or more of these elements are depleted in the soil. Often minor nutrients are present in the soil, but alkaline (pH of higher than 7.0) or wet soil conditions cause them to form compounds that the plant can't use. An alkaline condition can result from overliming or from lime leached from cement or brick. Regions where soil is derived from limestone or where rainfall is low usually have alkaline soils.

Solution: Spray the foliage with a chelated iron fertilizer, and apply the fertilizer to the soil around the plants to correct the deficiency of minor nutrients. Check the soil pH. Correct the pH of the soil by treating it with ferrous sulfate or elemental sulfur and watering it in well. Maintain an acid pH by fertilizing with Miracid® Plant Food.

DISCOLORED LEAVES *(continued)*

Acidic soil	Scorch	Powdery mildew

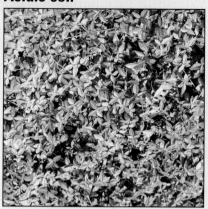

Leaf yellowing on vinca caused by acidic soil.

Winter burn on ivy.

Powdery mildew on euonymus.

Problem: Plants grow slowly, and leaves turn pale green to yellow. Plants don't improve much when fertilized. A soil test shows a pH of below 6.0.

Analysis: Soils with a pH of less than 6.0 are common in areas of heavy rainfall. Heavy rains leach lime from the soil, making it more acidic. The amounts and types of nutrients available to plants are limited in acidic soils. Below a pH of 5.5, the availability of nitrogen, phosphorus, potassium, calcium, magnesium, and other nutrients decreases. These nutrients are essential for healthy plants. Plants vary in their tolerance for acidic soils. Most plants grow best with a soil pH between 6.0 and 7.5. (For more information on soil pH, see page 406.)

Solution: Test your soil pH with an inexpensive test kit available at garden centers. Many county extension offices also test soil pH. To make a soil less acidic, apply lime. See page 531 for instructions, or follow the directions given with the soil testing kit. Soil acidity corrections are only temporary. Add lime to your soil every one to two years if you live in an acid-soil area.

Problem: Leaf tips and edges are brown and dead. Leaves may fall.

Analysis: Leaf scorch may be caused by any of several conditions.
1. Heat scorch: In hot weather, water evaporates rapidly from the leaves. If the roots can't absorb and convey water fast enough to replenish this loss, the leaves turn brown and wither. This condition often occurs when shade-loving plants receive too much sun.
2. Winter burn occurs on plants growing in full sun. On a clear winter day, the sun heats the leaf surface, increasing the need for water. If the ground is frozen or if it has been a dry fall and winter, the roots can't get enough water.
3. Salt injury results from excess salts in the soil. These salts can come from irrigation water, salts used to melt snow and ice, or fertilizers. This condition is worse in poorly drained soils, where salts can't easily be leached.

Solution: Follow these guidelines to prevent scorching.
1. Keep ground covers well watered during hot weather. For a list of sun- and shade-tolerant ground covers, see page 544.
2. To prevent winter burn be sure the soil is moist before the ground freezes. Provide shade during clear, cold weather.
3. Leach the salts from the soil with very heavy waterings. If your irrigation water is salty, leach regularly to keep salt from accumulating in the soil. When you fertilize, apply only the amounts recommended on the label, and water thoroughly afterward.

Problem: Powdery grayish-white patches partially or entirely cover leaves and stems, primarily the upper surfaces of leaves. Leaves die and may drop off.

Analysis: Powdery mildew, a common plant disease, is caused by several fungi that thrive in both humid and dry weather. The powdery patches consist of fungal strands and spores. The spores are spread by the wind to healthy plants. The fungus saps plant nutrients, causing yellowing and sometimes death of the leaf. A severe infection may kill the plant. Because powdery mildew attacks many different kinds of plants, the fungus from a diseased plant may infect other types of plants in the garden. See page 537 for a list of powdery mildews and the plants they attack. During favorable conditions, powdery mildew can spread through a ground cover in a matter of days or weeks.

Solution: Spray with Ortho® RosePride® Rose & Shrub Disease Control. Make sure that your plant is listed on the product label. These fungicides don't kill the fungus on leaves that are already diseased. They do, however, protect healthy leaves by killing the mildew spores as they germinate. Spray when weather conditions favor disease development. Follow label directions regarding frequency of application. Remove infected leaves and debris from the garden.

INSECTS

Greenhouse whiteflies

Greenhouse whiteflies (20× life size).

Problem: Tiny, white, winged insects ¹⁄₁₆ inch long feed mainly on the undersides of leaves. Nonflying, scalelike larvae covered with white, waxy powder may also be present on the undersides of leaves. When the plant is touched, insects flutter rapidly around it. Leaves may be mottled and yellow. The plant may grow poorly.

Analysis: The greenhouse whitefly (*Trialeurodes vaporariorum*) is a common insect pest of many garden and greenhouse plants. The adult lays eggs on the undersides of leaves. The larvae are the size of a pinhead and look quite different from the adult. The larvae feed for about a month before changing into adults. Both larval and adult forms suck sap from the leaves. The larvae are more damaging because they feed more heavily. Adults and larvae can't digest all the sugar in the plant sap, and they excrete the excess in a fluid called *honeydew*. Sooty mold, a black moldy fungus, grows on the honeydew. In warm-winter areas, the insect can be active year-round. Whiteflies are unable to live through freezing winters. Spring reinfestations in freezing-winter areas come from migrating whiteflies from more southerly areas and infested plants placed in the garden.

Solution: Control whiteflies by spraying with Ortho® Systemic Insect Killer. Make sure that your plant is listed on the product label. Treat every 7 to 10 days as necessary. Spray the foliage thoroughly, covering both the upper and lower surfaces of the leaves. Whiteflies may also be partially controlled with yellow sticky traps.

Spider mites

Spider mites (50× life size).

Problem: Leaves are stippled, yellowing, and dirty. Leaves may dry out and drop. There may be webbing over flower buds, between leaves, or on the lower surfaces of leaves. To determine if a plant is infested with mites, examine the undersides of the leaves with a hand lens. Or hold a sheet of white paper underneath an affected branch and tap the branch sharply. Minute specks the size of pepper grains will drop to the paper and begin to crawl. The pests are easily seen against the white background.

Analysis: Spider mites, are major pests of many garden and greenhouse plants. They cause damage by sucking sap from the undersides of leaves. As a result of their feeding, the plant's chlorophyll disappears, producing the stippled appearance. Spider mite webbing traps cast-off skins and debris, making the plant dirty. Some spider mites are active throughout the growing season, but most are favored by hot, dry weather (70°F and higher). By midsummer, they have built up to tremendous numbers. Other mites are most prolific in cooler weather. They feed and reproduce primarily during spring and, in some cases, fall. By the onset of hot weather (70°F and higher), these mites have caused their maximum damage.

Solution: Treat infested plants with Ortho® Systemic Insect Killer or Ortho® Bug-B-Gon® Multi-Purpose Insect Killer Ready-Spray® when mites first appear. Make sure that your plant is listed on the product label. Repeat the treatment two more times 7 to 10 days apart. Continue treatments if mites reappear.

Aphids

Aphids on ivy leaf (2× life size).

Problem: Leaves are curled, distorted, and yellow. A shiny, sticky substance may coat the leaves. Tiny (¹⁄₈-inch) pale green to black soft-bodied insects cluster under leaves and stems. Ants may be present. If infestation continues, plants may become stunted.

Analysis: Aphids do little damage in small numbers. They are extremely prolific, however, and populations can rapidly build up to damaging numbers during the growing season. Damage occurs when the aphid sucks the juices from the leaves of the ground cover. The aphid is unable to digest all the sugar in the plant sap, and it excretes the excess in a fluid called *honeydew*. Ants feed on honeydew and are often present where there is aphid infestation. (For more information on aphids, see page 443.)

Solution: Spray with Ortho® Bug-B-Gon® Multi-Purpose Insect Killer Ready-Spray®, Ortho® Systemic Insect Killer, or an insecticidal soap as soon as the insects appear. Repeat the spray if the plant becomes reinfested. Make sure that the plant is listed on the product label.

INSECTS *(continued)*

Snails and slugs

Snail and slug damage to ivy.

Problem: Stems and leaves may be sheared off and eaten. Silvery trails wind around on the plants and soil nearby. Snails or slugs may be seen moving around or feeding on the plants, especially at night. Inspect the garden for them at night by flashlight.

Analysis: Snails and slugs are mollusks and are related to clams, oysters, and other shellfish. They feed on a wide variety of garden plants. Like other mollusks, snails and slugs need to be moist all the time. For this reason, they avoid direct sun and dry spots and hide during the day in damp places, such as under flowerpots or in thick ground cover. They emerge at night or on cloudy days to feed. Snails and slugs are similar, except that the snail has a hard shell into which it withdraws when disturbed. Slugs lay white eggs encased in a slimy mass in protected places. Snails bury their eggs in the soil, also in a slimy mass. The young look like miniature versions of their parents.

Solution: Scatter Ortho® Bug-Geta® Snail & Slug Killer in bands around the areas you wish to protect. Also scatter the bait in areas where snails or slugs might be hiding, such as in dense ground cover, weedy areas, compost piles, or pot-storage areas. Before spreading the bait, wet down the areas to be treated to encourage snail and slug activity that night. Repeat the application every two weeks for as long as snails and slugs are active. Remove scrap lumber and other debris near the ground cover that create cool, damp breeding places.

AJUGA

Crown rot

Crown rot.

Problem: Lower leaves turn yellow. White cobwebby strands may cover crown and stems and spread over the soil surface. Large patches suddenly wilt and die during warm, humid weather. Plants pull up easily, with most of the roots and crown rotted away. Tiny, hard, yellow-brown to white pellets are found on the cobwebby strands.

Analysis: Crown rot is a disease caused by a fungus (*Sclerotium* species) that occurs mostly in wet, poorly drained soil. The fungus can be a serious problem on other herbaceous perennials besides ajuga. The fungus enters the plant through the roots and crown. It spreads into the stem, rotting it and causing the plant to wilt and die. In mild infections, new growth sometimes sprouts from buds that have not been killed. The tiny fungal pellets found in the soil survive winters and other unfavorable conditions to infect other plants. The fungus most frequently enters the garden in infested soil or plants and lives for years in the soil.

Solution: Remove and destroy all infected plants and discard the soil around them. Do not replant in the area until the fungus-infested soil has been removed. The fungicide *flutolanil* is registered for control of southern blight on ornamentals, but is available only to licensed pest control operators. To prevent crown rot, plant ajuga in well-drained soil.

DICHONDRA

Flea beetles

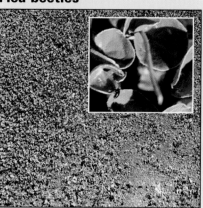

Flea beetle damage. Inset: Flea beetle (life size).

Problem: From May to October, dichondra leaves turn brown, first along the edges of the lawn, then progressing toward the center. Small round holes like shot holes are chewed in the upper surfaces of the leaves. To determine if this is an insect problem, spread a white handkerchief on the border between a damaged area and a healthy area. Black insects, about ⅟₂₅ inch long, hop onto the white cloth and are easily seen.

Analysis: The adult flea beetle is the most damaging pest of dichondra but does not feed on grass lawns. Although it hops like a flea, it is a true beetle. The adult spends the winter in garden trash and weeds, emerging with the warm spring weather to begin feeding and laying eggs. Damage is spotty at first because the beetles are so small. In a short time, however, they can destroy a lawn.

Solution: Treat infested dichondra with Ortho® Bug-B-Gon Multi-Purpose Insect Killer Concentrate, Ortho® Bug-B-Gon® Multi-Purpose Insect Killer Granules, or Ortho® Lawn Insect Killer Granules at the first sign of damage. Water the area first; then apply the insecticide according to the directions on the label. Repeat once a month throughout the growing season. A healthy planting of dichondra is more resistant to attack from flea beetles than an unhealthy one and recovers more quickly if it does become infested. Fertilize with Miracle-Gro Plant Food once a month from March to September.

Annual bluegrass

Annual bluegrass.

Problem: Clumps of pale green grass with whitish seed heads grow in the dichondra.

Analysis: Annual bluegrass (*Poa annua*) is one of the most troublesome and difficult weeds to control in dichondra. This member of the bluegrass family is lighter green, more shallow-rooted, and less drought tolerant than the bluegrass used for lawns. As its name suggests, annual bluegrass lives only one year. The seeds germinate in cool weather from late summer to late fall. Annual bluegrass grows rapidly in the spring, especially if the dichondra is fertilized then. In mid- to late spring, seed heads give the grass a whitish appearance. When hot weather arrives, the annual bluegrass dies.

Solution: Pull out minor infestations. Apply Ortho® Grass-B-Gon® Grass Killer for Landscapes to remove grassy weeds in dichondra. Prevent seeds from germinating by applying an herbicide containing *bensulide* in late summer. Keep children and pets off the lawn until the herbicide has been washed into the soil and the leaves have dried. Keep your dichondra lawn healthy to help it resist invasion by annual bluegrass.

Bermudagrass

Bermudagrass.

Problem: Patches of a fine-textured grass grow horizontally in dichondra lawns. The slightly hairy, gray green stems creep along the soil. The erect shoots are 6 to 8 inches tall, and leaf blades are ⅛ inch wide. This grass turns brown in the winter if temperatures drop below 50°F.

Analysis: Bermudagrass (*Cynodon dactylon*), also called *devilgrass* or *wiregrass*, is widely used as a lawn grass in the southern and western United States. Its deep root system makes it very drought tolerant, but its vigorous creeping habit makes it a weed in dichondra lawns, gardens, and other planted areas. This grass reproduces from seeds, roots, and stem segments.

Solution: Pull out minor infestations using a slender digging tool to help remove the roots. Control bermudagrass in dichondra lawns with Ortho® Grass-B-Gon® Grass Killer for Landscapes. If the dichondra has not been recently fertilized, fertilize five to seven days before treating with the weed killer. Water thoroughly one to two days before the treatment. Use the weed killer according to the directions. Don't water after applying the weed killer until the dichondra shows signs of drought stress. Control of bermudagrass is slow; retreatment will probably be necessary. Any adjacent bermudagrass lawn should be edged so it won't spread into the dichondra. Keep dichondra lawns thick and healthy by fertilizing with Miracle-Gro® Plant Food once per month from March to September.

FRAGARIA
(Wild strawberry)

Leaf spot

Leaf spot.

Problem: Spots and blotches appear on the leaves. The spots may be yellow, red, tan, gray, or brown and range in size from barely visible to ¼ inch in diameter. Several spots may join to form blotches. Leaves often turn yellow, die, and fall off. Leaf spotting is most severe in warm, humid weather. In damp conditions, a fine gray mold sometimes covers the infected leaf tissue.

Analysis: Several different fungi cause leaf spot on wild strawberry. Some of these eventually kill the plant. Others merely spot the leaves and are unsightly but not harmful. The fungi are spread from plant to plant by splashing water, wind, and contaminated tools. They survive the winter on diseased plant debris left in the garden. Most of the leaf spot fungi do their greatest damage in humid conditions and mild weather (temperatures between 50° and 85°F).

Solution: Spray the infected planting with a fungicide containing *mancozeb* every 3 to 10 days. Because leaf spot fungi are most active during warm, humid weather, spray more frequently during these weather conditions. The fungicide protects the new, healthy foliage but doesn't kill the fungus on leaves that are already infected. Avoid overhead watering, particularly late in the day.

HEDERA (Ivy)

Scorch

Sun scorch.

Problem: Dead brown spots appear on the leaves. The spots are always on the part of the leaf exposed most directly to the sun. Plants grow in direct sun.

Analysis: Ivy can suffer from two kinds of scorch: sun scorch and winter burn. Leaf scorch is caused by excessive evaporation from the leaves. In hot weather, water evaporates rapidly from the leaves. If the roots can't absorb and convey water fast enough to replenish this loss, leaf tissue is killed. Scorch particularly affects ivy growing on a sunny wall because the wall reflects the sun's heat onto the plants. Winter injury occurs on plants growing in the full sun of a southern or western exposure. On a very sunny, clear winter day, the sun heats leaf surfaces, increasing the plants' water requirement. If the ground is frozen or if the fall and winter have been dry, ivy roots can't absorb the needed water. The leaves then turn brown and dry out.

Solution: Keep ivy amply watered during hot weather. Fertilize heavily to encourage quick regrowth. In areas with hot summers, ivy does best in shady locations. To reduce the chance of winter burn, be sure the soil is moist before the ground freezes. Mow affected plantings in spring to remove damaged leaves and to invigorate the plants.

Fungal leaf spots

Fungal leaf spot.

Problem: Large tan to brown spots appear on the leaves. These oval or circular areas occur on both the upper and lower surfaces of the leaves. Spots often enlarge to cover most of the leaf surface. Small black specks may be seen scattered over the surface of the spots. Leaves may turn brownish red, die, and fall.

Analysis: Several different fungi cause leaf spotting on ivy. Some of these fungi may kill tender stems. Others merely spot the leaves and are unsightly. The fungi are spread from plant to plant by wind, splashing water, insects, and contaminated tools. They spend the winter on diseased plant debris left in the garden. Leaf spot affects a wide variety of plants, including flowers, vegetables, and ground covers. Most leaf spot fungi do their greatest damage in temperatures between 50° and 85°F.

Solution: Spray the infected planting every 3 to 10 days with a fungicide containing *mancozeb*. Because leaf spot fungi are most active during warm, humid weather, be sure to spray more frequently during those weather conditions. *Mancozeb* protects the new, healthy foliage but does not remove the spots on leaves that are already infected. Remove and throw away leaves that are spotted over more than half their surface to reduce the spread of infection to less severely affected plants. Avoid working in the diseased plants when the leaves are wet, because this helps spread the fungi. Water early in the day to allow the leaves to dry before nightfall.

Bacterial leaf spot and stem canker

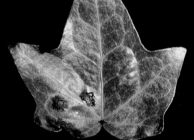

Bacterial leaf spot.

Problem: Pale green, greasy-looking angular areas spot the leaves. As the spots enlarge, they turn brown and black with red margins. They eventually dry out and crack. Leaf stems turn black and shrivel. A black decay begins on the stems and spreads to the older wood. Brown-black lesions form on the stems. During warm, humid weather, an ooze flows from the infected stems.

Analysis: Bacterial leaf spot and stem canker, a disease caused by a bacterium (*Xanthomonas campestris* pv. *hederae*); occurs frequently on English ivy growing in humid areas. Leaves kept constantly moist are particularly susceptible to invasion by these bacteria. The bacteria spread from plant to plant in splashing rain, on insects such as ants, bees, and flies, and on contaminated equipment. People also spread the bacteria when they work around wet, infected plants. Other organisms often enter the dying tissue and stem lesions, causing further decay.

Solution: When the foliage is dry, remove and destroy infected leaves and plants. As long as the disease is present, spray the entire planting once a week with a bactericide containing a copper-based fungicide. Avoid planting English ivy in hot, humid areas. Water early in the day to allow the foliage to dry quickly.

Scales

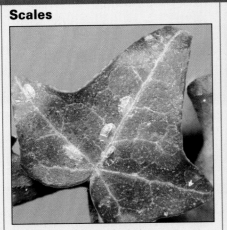

Brown soft scale (2× life size).

Problem: Raised tan to reddish-black crusty or waxy bumps cover the stems or the undersides of leaves. The bumps can be picked off; the undersides are usually soft. Leaves may turn yellow and fall off. In some cases, a sticky substance coats the leaves. A black, sooty mold often grows on the sticky material. Ants may be present.

Analysis: Scales are insects that spend the winter on the trunk and twigs of the plants. They lay eggs in spring and in early summer (late spring in the South); the young scales, called *crawlers*, settle on leaves and twigs. The small (1/10-inch), soft-bodied young feed by inserting their mouthparts and sucking sap from the plant. The legs usually atrophy, and a hard crusty or waxy shell develops over the body. Mature female scales lay their eggs underneath their shell. Some species of scales that infest English ivy are unable to digest all the sugar in the plant sap, and they excrete the excess in a fluid called *honeydew*. A black, sooty mold fungus may develop on the honeydew. Ants feed on the sticky substance and are often present where scales cluster. An uncontrolled infestation of scales may kill the vines after one or two seasons. (For more information on scales, see pages 444 to 447.)

Solution: Spray with Ortho® Systemic Insect Killer in early summer (late spring in the South) when the young are active. Early the following spring, before new growth begins, spray the vines with a dormant horticultural oil to control overwintering insects.

Sooty mold

Sooty mold.

Problem: A black, sooty mold grows on leaves and stems. It can easily be wiped off the plant parts.

Analysis: This common black mold is one of several species of fungi. These fungi grow on the sugary material left on plants by aphids, mealybugs, scales, whiteflies, and other insects that suck sap from the plant. The insects are unable to digest all the sugar in the sap, and they excrete the excess in a fluid called *honeydew*, which coats the leaves. The honeydew may also drip from infested overhanging trees and shrubs onto ivy growing beneath them. Sooty mold is unsightly but is fairly harmless because it does not infect the leaf tissue. Extremely heavy infestations prevent light from reaching the leaf and may cause the leaf to turn yellow. The presence of sooty mold indicates that the ivy or another plant above it is infested with insects.

Solution: Rain will eventually wash off sooty mold. Plants can also be rinsed with a solution of soapy water, using a mild soap. If only a few leaves are infested, it may be practical to wipe off the mold with a wet rag. Prevent more sooty mold from growing by controlling the insect that is producing the honeydew. Inspect the leaves and stems of the ivy and plants growing in the area to determine what type of insect is present. (For more information, see the following pages: for aphids, page 443; for mealybugs, page 444; for scales, pages 444 to 447; for whiteflies, page 448.)

Root rot

Root rot. Inset: Close-up.

Problem: Leaves turn yellow, starting with the older, lower leaves and progressing to the younger ones. Plants grow very little. When they are pulled up, the roots appear black, soft, and rotted. The soil is very moist.

Analysis: Root rot is a plant disease caused by several different fungi that are present in moist soils. These fungi normally do little damage, but they can cause root rot in waterlogged soils. Waterlogged soil may result from overwatering or from poor soil drainage. Infection causes the roots to decay, resulting in wilting, yellowing leaves and the death of the plant. (For more information on root rot, see page 419.)

Solution: Ice plant is drought tolerant and needs very little watering. Allow the soil around the plants to dry out between waterings. (For more information on watering, see page 408.) Remove and discard severely infected plants. Avoid future root rot problems by planting in well-drained soil. (For information on soil drainage, see page 406.)

PACHYSANDRA (Japanese spurge)

Scorch

Scorch.

Problem: Irregular blotches, light to dark brown, spot the leaves. Leaves are crisp, shrivel up, and sometimes fall off. Plants may be growing in the full sun.

Analysis: Pachysandra can suffer from two kinds of scorch: sun scorch and winter burn. Scorch is caused by excessive evaporation of moisture from the leaves. In hot weather, water evaporates rapidly from the leaves. If the roots can't absorb and convey water fast enough to replenish this loss, the leaves turn brown and wither. In very hot weather, scorch may occur even though the soil is moist. Winter injury occurs on plants growing in the full sun of a southern or western exposure. Although pachysandra may be in the shade of a tree during the spring and summer, the plants are in full sun during the winter after the sheltering tree has dropped its leaves. On a clear winter day, the sun heats the leaf surface, increasing the plants' water requirements. If the ground is frozen or if it has been a dry fall and winter, the pachysandra roots can't absorb the needed water.

Solution: Keep the soil moist. Too much moisture, however, is apt to induce root rot. If scorch persists, consider a ground cover more resistant to drought. Keep the soil moist until the ground is frozen.

Leaf and stem blight

Leaf and stem blight.

Problem: Irregular brown and black blotches appear and spread to cover most of the leaf. Plant leaves are soft and water-soaked. Areas on the stems turn black, soft, and sunken. In wet weather, pinkish spore masses may appear along the stem and on the leaf spots.

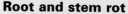

Analysis: Leaf and stem blight is a disease caused by a fungus (*Volutella pachysandrae*). Plants are more susceptible to attack from this fungus if they are weak from spider mites or winter injury, crowded, planted in full sun or waterlogged soil, or if the area stays too moist from tree leaves falling into the bed. The fungus is most active in rainy, cool spring weather and spreads from plant to plant in splashing water and on contaminated tools. The spores survive the winter on infected stems and leaves left in the garden. If not controlled, this blight can kill an entire planting of pachysandra in one or two seasons.

Solution: Pull out and discard all diseased plants. Although this may seem like an endless job, doing so will give you much better control of this stubborn plant disease. Then spray the cleaned bed with Ortho® Garden Disease Control at intervals of one week, beginning when the disease is discovered or when new growth starts in the spring. Thin and shear the beds periodically to improve air circulation. Rake out leaves in the fall to reduce the chance of the disease occurring in the spring. Keep pachysandra healthy by controlling scales and reducing winter burn. Do not overwater.

VINCA (Periwinkle)

Root and stem rot

Root and stem rot.

Problem: Shoot tips wilt and die. There are no black specks on the affected stems. Plants pull up easily, with most of the roots and lower stem soft and rotted away. Individual plants are affected first, and within several weeks, entire clumps wilt and die.

Analysis: Root and stem rot is a plant disease caused by a fungus (*Pellicularia filamentosa*). It is the most serious disease affecting periwinkle. It occurs mostly in heavy, poorly drained soil and during periods of wet weather. It can be found throughout the growing season in most periwinkle plantings. The fungus enters the plant through the roots and crown, and it rots the cells, causing the plant to wilt and die. The fungus persists indefinitely in the soil and spreads from plant to plant on contaminated tools and in splashing water.

Solution: Remove and destroy badly infected plants. Allow the soil to dry between waterings (see page 408) until the spread of the disease is halted. If the area is replanted, improve the drainage (see page 406). To prevent recurrence of the disease, allow the soil to dry between waterings until it is barely moist.

Gray mold

Gray mold.

Problem: Brown or black spots appear on the edges of the leaves and spread inward, sometimes covering the entire leaf. Flowers may be discolored or spotted. As the disease progresses, a fuzzy brown or grayish mold forms on the infected tissue especially during cool, wet weather.

Analysis: Gray mold is a widespread plant disease caused by a fungus (*Botrytis cinerea*) that is found on most dead plant tissue. The fungus initially attacks foliage and flowers that are weak or dead, causing spotting and a fuzzy mold. Once gray mold has become established on plant debris and weak or dying leaves and flowers, it can invade healthy plant tissue. The fungus is spread by splashing water or by infected pieces of plant tissue contacting healthy tissue. Cool temperatures and high humidity promote gray mold growth. Rain and overhead watering enhance the spread of the fungus. Infection is more of a problem in spring and fall, when temperatures are lower. In mild-winter areas where freezing is rare, gray mold can be a year-round problem. (For more information on gray mold, see page 418.)

Solution: Remove and discard all fading flowers and diseased leaves. Treat plants with a fungicide containing *azoxystrobin* or *captan*. For best control, add a spreader-sticker to the spray.

Canker and dieback

Dieback.

Problem: Shoot tips wilt, turn brown, and die. The infection progresses down the stem to the soil surface, killing the plant. Affected stems turn black. Tiny black specks are often seen on the diseased stems. Dark brown spots sometimes develop on leaves, which then die and fall off. Individual plants are affected first, but within several weeks entire clumps wilt and die.

Analysis: Canker and dieback is a disease caused by two fungi (*Phomopsis livella* and *Phoma exigua*) that attack periwinkle in the spring soon after the new growth begins. This disease is most prevalent during very rainy seasons. The fungal spores spread from plant to plant on splashing water and contaminated tools. This disease can be devastating, killing an entire planting in a few weeks.

Solution: Spray infected plants every seven days with a fungicide containing copper or *mancozeb*. Remove badly infected plants. Avoid overhead watering. To reduce the chances of new infections, water early in the day, rather than late afternoon, so the leaves have time to dry before nightfall.

Scorch

Scorch.

Problem: Yellow or brown blotches appear on the leaves directly exposed to the sun. Severely affected leaves may die and fall off.

Analysis: Periwinkle can suffer from two kinds of scorch: heat scorch and winter burn. Scorch is caused by excessive evaporation from the leaves. In hot weather, water evaporates rapidly from the leaves. If the roots can't absorb and convey water fast enough to replenish this loss, leaf tissue is killed. Winter injury occurs on plants growing in the full sun of a southern or western exposure. On a sunny, clear winter day, the sun heats the leaf surface, increasing the plants' water requirements. If the ground is frozen or dry, periwinkle roots can't absorb the needed water. Leaves then turn yellow or brown and dry out.

Solution: Keep periwinkle amply watered during hot weather. Fertilize the plants with a nitrogen-rich fertilizer to encourage quick regrowth. In areas with hot summers, periwinkle does best in shady locations. To reduce the chance of winter burn, be sure the soil is moist before the ground freezes. Mulch plants or cover them with tree boughs during cold, sunny weather.

Lush flower borders are easy to grow when you choose plants appropriate to your site. In this sunny northeastern garden, daisies, daylilies, Asiatic lilies, delphiniums, feverfew, and baby's breath transform a modest house into a lavish wonderland.

Flowers can turn a drab yard into a showplace. Indoors, a bouquet of cut flowers—whether a formal arrangement in a porcelain vase or a bunch of black-eyed Susans in a jar—seems to bring sunlight and a touch of elegance into the house. Home gardeners turn to annuals, perennials, biennials, and bulbs to provide a supply of blooms. Each type of plant requires a different approach in terms of planning, planting, and care.

PICKING PLANTS TO SUIT THE JOB

Buying plants calls for research. Which species grow in your climate? What are the sunlight, drainage, or fertilizer requirements? (Before purchasing plants and fertilizer, read the section "Assessing and Improving Soil," which appears later in this chapter.) Buying plants that flower takes special attention in terms of learning the blooming patterns and life cycle of each species.

Climate: Passion flowers are from South America, a climate that is warm most of the year. Logically, a warm climate is what this showy vine needs to grow at its best. Peonies originated in China and range into northern Siberia; hot climates do not always promote their flowering. Agapanthus and pelargoniums came from South Africa, so while they will take some drought, they are also accustomed to warmth. Though a plant may be available for purchase in your area, it may not be well suited to grow there.

Research growing conditions carefully, keeping your microclimate in mind.

Time of purchase: Outdoor plants are seasonal. Each may flower for a week, or a month, but then enter a foliage-only phase, or may die back altogether. If you buy a plant in full bloom, it may be at the close of its blooming season. Buy flowering plants at the beginning of their blooming season.

Time of flowering: Plan ahead for color areas by checking the full flowering period of each plant in your growing zone. Go beyond learning whether the species you are considering is an annual, perennial, or biennial; learn about the habits of this particular variety.

Some plant species, such as pinks and bellflowers, have biennial, perennial, and annual varieties. And labels don't always identify the plant type. If you unknowingly buy an annual variety, assuming it's perennial, you may think you have a plant problem when the plant dies after a single blooming period. To prevent such surprises, bring a reference book with you to the nursery or garden center, or consult one there. Make sure the habits of the variety you choose suit the plans you have for your garden.

If you are buying through a catalog, be aware that the catalog description may not agree with what will happen in your neighborhood. A catalog may state clearly that a certain plant is a perennial, but in your climate it may grow as an annual. Blooming time stated in the catalog is usually based on weather where the catalog originates, and it may be far from what you experience in your part of the country. Bacteria and viruses found in local conditions can markedly change flower color, so the red tulips you bought may come up streaked. Talk with your neighbors and gardening professionals to learn how specific plants behave in your area.

Container camouflage: If you have a highly visible site that is homely unless kept camouflaged by colorful plants, select flowering plants in containers. Chrysanthemums, daylilies, and many other vivid plants thrive this way. The containers can be hidden with a natural mulch or redwood chips, or you can use large decorative pots. When the plants finish blooming, move the containers elsewhere and replace them with another set of full-flowered container plants.

Buying seeds: Packets of seeds can provide an ample rainbow of beauty for a small amount of money. Patient gardeners may find planting seeds more satisfying than installing transplants, and seed packets often offer a greater variety of plant species than local nurseries. Take care when purchasing seeds, however. Buy only from a reputable dealer, and always check the package date to be sure the seeds are fresh. Stale seeds don't germinate as well as fresh ones. In addition, the information on the packet is often sparse and fairly generic. Read up on the varieties you have chosen to determine appropriate sowing and transplanting times, and proper garden conditions.

PLANTING AND GROWING ANNUALS

Annual plants—such as pansies, marigolds, impatiens, and zinnias—live and die in a year or less. If annuals get through this period, grow, flower, and produce seeds, their disappearance is a natural phenomenon, not a problem. You have wisely satisfied their requirements for amount of sunlight, ample water, effective drainage, and soil of at least average quality.

If you want flowers in your garden on a continual basis throughout the season, plant annuals. Healthy annuals may bloom for several months, one flower following another, from the moment of first bud to the first severe cold spell. Gardeners living in an area with no frost or occasional frost can plant a series of annuals to provide flowers almost all year long.

Annuals do have their disadvantages. You might not have abundant flower production unless you prepare soil beforehand, preferably a month in advance. This gives added ingredients—such as compost, manure, or fertilizers—a chance to blend and nurture the soil. The roots of most annuals tend not to reach out as much as other plants, so they generally must draw on the nutrients they find where they are placed. If required nutrients and minerals aren't present, an annual might continue

Impatiens is North America's most popular annual for shade.

Many long-lived and easy-care perennials make effective landscape plants. Top: 'Goldsturm' black-eyed Susan, Siberian iris, 'Autumn Joy' sedum, and garden phlox make a dramatic statement when massed in generous numbers. Above: two ornamental grasses (Pennisetum alopecuroides *and* Miscanthus sinensis)*, variegated yucca, and asters provide a late-season backbone for annuals and vegetables next to a deck.*

by marking perennial plant sites with small labeled stakes. Or, if you live in a warm area, buy perennials that stay green the entire year for a leafy backdrop in winter.

You may see the phrase "Perennial treated as an annual" on plant labels or in books. The phrase refers to perennials, such as wax begonia, snapdragon, and coleus, which may not survive cold winters. Gardeners who live in areas where winters are harsh should treat these plants as an annual and plan to replace it each year.

Division: Some perennials, such as chrysanthemums, require division every few years, when the plant grows into a crowded unattractive clump. Other signs that you need to divide perennials include extra-tall growth, weak stems, and few blooms. Divide perennials in the spring. Expose the root ball and divide its segments to create separate plants. Transplant the newly formed perennials to a site where they do not have to compete for light and nutrients. To increase the number of flowers, pinch plants back after transplanting. Do this every few weeks until the plants become bushy and full of new shoots.

Transplant shock: To ease transplant shock in divided or new perennials, work when the weather is cool, in early mornings or evenings. Try not to damage roots. Each root is valuable in water acquisition. After transplanting, nip back about one-third of the old growth. Water well, using a diluted solution of liquid plant food. Despite the best of care, you may still see some symptoms of transplant shock, including leaf drop, flower drop, and wilting.

blooming for a time after purchase, drawing on nutrients already within the leaves. Flowers will become smaller and smaller, however, and finally cease altogether. As a result of their relatively limited root systems, annuals are susceptible to transplant shock.

If you are planning on bouquets of summer annuals, do not wait for summer weather to put in the plants. Summer may seem prime for planting, but it is often too hot for newly transplanted annuals. The summer sun encourages top growth that the annuals' meager root systems can't support. The result may be stunted plants and minimal flowering. Solve the problem by planting summer-flowering annuals when spring weather is still a bit on the cool side but not cold enough to risk frost damage.

PLANTING AND GROWING PERENNIALS

Perennials—such as daylilies, herbaceous peonies, irises, and asters—bloom for a limited time per year, but they make up for it by having a longer life. Unlike shrubs, which are woody plants, perennials are nonwoody, or soft-stemmed, plants.

Perennials usually bloom once a season. This can be for a week or a month. Some perennials completely die back and disappear after flowering, then emerge the following year. Resting perennials often get chopped up when enthusiastic gardeners think they have empty space and begin planting something new. Avoid this problem

PLANTING AND GROWING BIENNIALS

Biennial plants have two-year lives. They start their life cycle one year, go dormant in winter, then bloom and complete their lives the following year. Many gardeners think something is wrong with plants like foxgloves, hollyhocks, and Canterbury bells because the first year they grow but do not flower. Waiting for these plants to flower takes patience. If you want blooming biennials on a continual basis, plant some new ones each year to flower the following year, being careful not to disturb those planted previously.

PLANTING AND GROWING BULBS

Bulbs should be as easy to grow as annuals, biennials, and perennials, but some gardeners seem to have no luck with them. The most frequent problems are caused by unhealthy bulbs, poor drainage, animal pests, and improper care.

Bulb selection: Some problems are inherent in the price of the bulb. With bulbs, you tend to get what you pay for. In many cases, bargain bulbs are "bargains" for a reason. They may be undersized, diseased, poorly stored, inaccurately labeled, improperly matured, or of inferior stock.

Examine bulbs carefully before purchase. Do a light squeeze test. Healthy bulbs, regardless of type, are quite firm and feel heavy for their size. They are free of deep, dark areas; cuts; or soft spots. No mold grows on the outside covering.

Bulb diseases: The bulb holds nutrients much as a storage tank does. The nutrients enable the plant to send up flowers in spring or early summer. Viruses and fungi can interfere with this process.

■ **Viruses:** If soil- or insect-borne viruses enter the bulb, they move quickly through the entire plant, affecting every stage of growth. The many types of viruses can be seen only with an electron microscope. Effects of virus damage are highly visible, however, and account for much plant damage and loss.

■ **Fungi:** Root and stem rots are common causes of a plant's failure to thrive. They are caused by fungi, which thrive in standing water. Plant fungi invade and plug the nutrient channels. The infection remains long after standing water has finally disappeared. Sometimes plant descriptions can help you avoid bulb infection. Be wary of bulbs with labels reading "Needs well-drained soil," "Keep on dry side," or "Requires good aeration." Standing water suffocates plant roots of all kinds by filling necessary air spaces in the soil with water. Roots can't absorb water and nutrients unless oxygen is present. A plant top can wilt from drought while its roots are standing in water.

Do not confuse standing water with ample water. If soil is permeable to air and water, the danger of overwatering is slight. Standing water, however, offers an open invitation to fungi.

Bulbs in containers need excellent drainage; use a fast-draining potting mix, and be sure pots have adequate drainage holes. In cold-winter areas, plant bulbs in containers in the fall. Keep the pots moist over winter in a cool place protected from freezing (such as an attached garage). In mild-winter areas, purchase prechilled bulbs or prechill them yourself in the vegetable bin of a refrigerator for 10 weeks prior to planting in pots. After planting, place the pots in the coolest part of your garden until shoots emerge in spring.

Hole preparation: In poorly drained areas, improve drainage and minimize the chance of disease by digging planting holes at least 1½ to 2 feet deep. Slant the excavation so that it drains water away from the site. If you are placing a great number of bulbs in the same poorly drained area, install drain tiles to keep excess water from accumulating in the planting hole.

Proper soil preparation encourages bulb longevity and reproduction. If you have clay or some other heavy soil, dig planting holes 12 inches deep. Place the bulbs in the holes, then fill them with commercial potting soil. Or consider growing bulbs in raised beds.

Bulb foliage: The health of the bulb through the dormant season is related to the longevity of the foliage. Do not cut back the leaves of a bulb plant until after the foliage dies back naturally. Cutting leaves before they wither or cutting off many leaves when you cut flowers can impede the storage of nutrients and cause bulbs to decline.

SOIL TEXTURE

Good soil texture that provides roots with aeration as well as retention of water and nutrients is important for healthy plants. As a rough check on your garden soil, try to squeeze a moist handful into a ball. Soil high in sand (large, irregularly shaped soil particles) will crumble and not hold its shape well. Sandy soil offers roots lots of air but little water and nutrient retention. Soil high in clay (extremely small, platelike particles that adhere closely together) will form a solid, sticky mass that doesn't easily break apart. Clay soil retains water and nutrients, but little air. Good garden loam, such as the soil shown above, is roughly even in its percentage of silt (medium-size soil particles), clay, and sand. It will hold together when squeezed, yet break apart easily when prodded with the fingers. Especially when high in organic matter, good garden loam retains water and nutrients well, yet also allows the air to penetrate the soil that roots need to thrive.

More precise than the "squeeze test" is the "settling test," shown at right. Take enough samples from the top 6 inches of soil at different garden locations to add up to about 3 cups. Let the samples dry, then pulverize them with a rolling pin. Fill a quart jar two-thirds full of water, stir in 1 teaspoon of low-suds dishwasher detergent or a water softener, add the soil, cover, and shake vigorously. After two minutes, the sand will have settled to the bottom of the jar. After several hours, the silt will have settled into a layer on top of the sand. After a week, most of the clay will have settled into a layer on top of the silt. Measure the three levels to determine the relative proportions of sand, silt, and clay in your soil.

ASSESSING AND IMPROVING SOIL

In terms of soil, annuals, perennials, biennials, and bulbs need a growing site that provides an appropriate pH and essential mineral nutrients.

Soil pH: The pH of soil reflects the concentration of hydrogen ions in it; this determines how acidic or alkaline the soil is. pH is measured on a scale from 0.0 to 14.0. A soil that measures pH 7.0 is neutral; it is neither acidic nor alkaline.

In terms of plant growth, acidity or alkalinity is important because it determines how quickly the soil can release nutrients—or whether the nutrients can be released from the soil at all. For example, in acidic soil with a pH of 5.2, magnesium, phosphorus, and calcium are less available for plant use than they would be in neutral soil. Nitrogen is released only partially because soil organisms that create it are less active in acidic soil. When soil has a pH of 5.0 or lower, these organisms often cease working altogether so that no nitrogen is released. Conversely, at a pH below 5.0, manganese and aluminum may become available in harmful amounts.

How do you know the pH of the soil you have? Generally, acidic soils are found in areas of high rainfall; alkaline soils are found in desert areas or areas of low rainfall. Every region contains microclimates, however, so the general principle may not provide an accurate assessment. To get a precise pH reading, take soil samples to a professional testing service. The local county extension office can tell you about such services in your area. Or try looking under "soil" in the telephone directory. The testing service will give instructions about taking the samples. Most services ask you to take samples from different garden areas by digging to a depth of 6 inches and taking a thin soil slice from the edge of each hole. Then you mix the samples together in a clean nonmetal container. You should now have about 2 cups of soil. Remove any stones, roots, or debris. Cover the container, and keep it dry until analysis.

An alternative to professional testing is using a home soil-testing kit, which you can buy at a nursery or garden center. A home test is not as accurate as a professional analysis, but a kit is inexpensive, easy to use, and usually adequate.

■ **Acidic soil:** Plants placed in acidic soil often grow slowly and have pale green or yellow leaves. Roots are few and small. Overly acidic soil promotes disease. Adding fertilizer does not help the plants, because low pH slows nutrient release.

To correct acidic soil, apply finely ground dolomitic limestone. This not only raises soil pH, but also supplies needed calcium and magnesium. The heavier the soil, the more limestone you need. Liming to increase alkalinity is especially helpful for clay soils, making them more friable, or crumbly. Liming is not permanent. You will have to recheck pH every two years and reapply limestone as necessary.

If you have acidic soil and are unable to correct it, consider planting rhododendrons, azaleas, camellias, and other acid-loving plants. These plants don't have to depend on soil organisms to release nitrogen from soil. A beneficial fungus on the plants' roots can convert soil nitrate into usable nitrate. If you put acid-loving plants in nonacidic soil, sufficient iron may not be released for their needs. Yellow areas may appear between the veins of new leaves, affecting plant appearance. Leaves weakened in this way can't support normal flowering.

■ **Alkaline soil:** Soil with a pH more than 7.0 is alkaline. Some plants thrive at this level. When pH reaches 8.0, however, the soil does not release certain nutrients. Iron and manganese are no longer available to plants. Older leaves remain green, but new leaves have yellow areas between their veins. Flowering plants do not generally tolerate alkaline soil. If you live in a highly alkaline region and want to put in annuals, perennials, or bulbs, consider using raised beds or containers in the garden. Fill these with a commercial soil mix.

To correct mildly alkaline soil, apply acidic peat or an acidic mulch made of pine needles. Use a fertilizer for acid-loving plants, which will create reactions that lower soil pH. Ordinary powdered sulfur corrects alkalinity, but you must strictly regulate the rate of application according to soil needs. Use ferrous sulfate instead of powdered sulfur; the combination product is less prone to application error. For the first treatment, use 2 pounds of ferrous sulfate per 100 square feet. Applying lime-sulfur spray is also helpful.

Soil nutrients and fertilizers:

Applying the wrong type of fertilizer may cause as many flowering-plant problems as overfertilizing. The "big three" fertilizer elements are nitrogen, phosphorus, and potassium. Other elements, present in trace amounts, are also important to plant growth.

■ **Nitrogen:** This element is a vital component of plant protein. Symptoms of nitrogen shortage include slow growth and yellowing leaves. Too much nitrogen forces lush foliage but not strong stems. The plant becomes vulnerable to weather variables, attacks by insects, and diseases.

■ **Phosphorus:** Only phosphorus can promotes stem growth to hold leaves and flowers up to sunlight and pollination. A shortage of phosphorus slows root growth, flowering, and seed production. Leaves turn purplish or become dark gray-green. Symptoms appear in older leaves first. With severe phosphorus deficiencies, plant flowering is minimal.

■ **Potassium:** In North American soils potassium tends to be plentiful but in a form difficult for plants to use. Potassium is necessary for photosynthesis; without photosynthesis, plants starve. In addition, potassium is essential for strong stems on flowering plants and for the formation of bulbs and tubers. Symptoms of potassium

Annuals, perennials, ornamental grasses, and flowering shrubs combine in a mixed border for abundant, long-lasting color.

shortage include mottled yellow or pale green mature leaves with scorched edges. Flower yield is minimal.

■ **Other soil nutrients:** Fertilizer labels often list elements in addition to nitrogen, phosphorus, and potassium. These include iron, calcium, magnesium, zinc, manganese, and sulfur. Though plants use them in minuscule amounts, these trace elements have significant growth effects. Of the secondary nutrients, iron is the one usually in shortest natural supply. Iron deficiency causes yellowing plant leaves, though leaf veins generally remain green. The newest leaves are the most severely affected. Applying fertilizer containing iron to the soil corrects yellowing. If necessary, also spray foliage and soil with an iron solution.

■ **Fertilizer selection:** To correct nitrogen, phosphorus, or potassium imbalance, purchase a fertilizer that meets your immediate and long-term needs. Fertilizer labels look more complex than they really are. The numbers on the container tell you, in relative terms, how much of each of the three major elements is present. Nitrogen (N) is always listed first, followed by phosphorus (P), and potassium (K). If the label says "20-20-20," the fertilizer contains equal portions of nitrogen, phosphorus in the form of phosphate, and potassium in the form of potash. A 5-10-5 mixture is higher in phosphorus than in nitrogen or potassium.

PREVENTING AND SOLVING PROBLEMS

Cultural techniques such as disbudding, pinching back, and staking can prevent many growth problems. When growth is healthy, plants are in the best position to fend off external threats, such as frost, diseases, and insects.

Cultural techniques for problem prevention: Plants—like people—have a finite energy supply. By using cultural techniques to direct a plant's energy toward healthy growth, you can save the energy you would otherwise expend on treating disease or replacing damaged plants.

■ **Deadheading:** Make certain poor flowering isn't caused by old flowers left on the stems. In many plants, especially roses, flower production slows when older blossoms use energy to create seed. To encourage continual flowering, cut off, or deadhead, flowers past their prime.

■ **Disbudding:** If your plants produce many flowers but the flowers are not large enough to be attractive in cut displays, try disbudding. This technique involves removing some flower buds while they

are about the size of a bean. With fewer buds to develop, the plant has more energy to use in creating larger blooms from the remaining buds. Disbudding is a common practice on peonies, dahlias, carnations, chrysanthe-mums, and roses.

■ **Pinching back:** Snapdragons, chrysanthemums, dahlias, fuchsias, blood leaf, salvias, and garden geraniums tend toward ranginess, though the problem can strike just about any plant. To encourage sturdy, bushy growth, pinch back the stems by using your thumb and forefinger to nip them off just above a leaf bud. Pinching back does delay blooming, but the long-term result is a stronger, more attractive plant. Snapdragons do well with just one pinching. Chrysanthemums may need up to four.

■ **Stem support:** Long-stemmed flowering plants may fall over because of stem or blossom weight. Grabbing a handful of stems and tying them to a pole is not the answer to this problem. If the plants have just a few slim stems, such as delphiniums or carnations, loosely tie each stem to a slender stake. If the plants are bushy, provide support by surrounding them with metal hoops that are made for the purpose. Be sure to anchor the hoops securely into the ground. Whether using hoops or stakes, always maintain the natural growth habit of plants.

Problems in the environment:
Encroaching shade, burning sun, sudden frosts, and hungry insects threaten flowering plants. With a little help from you, your flowers can survive, thrive, and reward you with an array of blossoms.

■ **Insufficient sunlight:** Flowering plants need plenty of sun. Though they may continue to grow in less than optimum light conditions, they may not flower or flowering may be sparse. In some cases, just enlarging the open space around the plants may give them the boost of sunlight they need to prosper. Sometimes the remedy is to cut back overhanging branches that shade the garden. (Before cutting, make sure the limbs are not critical to the survival

of the tree or shrub. Practice correct pruning techniques to prevent damage or consult an arborist.) In other cases, the only course is to move the struggling plants to a sunnier spot. Though transplanting is always a risk, continuing shade could mean certain failure.

■ **Sunburn:** Though plenty of sunlight encourages flowering plants, too much sunlight can damage them. Symptoms of sunburn include faded and bleached leaves or leaves that turn pale and yellowish. Foliage may become brittle. To prevent sunburn, temporarily shade the plants with some sort of loose cover. Make sure they get all the water they need during periods of sunburn danger.

■ **Frost:** Whenever it occurs, frost is a danger to plants. Symptoms of frost damage include blackened leaf parts and failure of the plant to thrive.

Some perennials and biennials must survive frost during the dormant season. Protect them with a covering of mulch. Mulch vulnerable plants before the first hard frost; the layer of mulch insulates them from low temperatures. Mulch hardy perennials and biennials after the ground freezes. Because the plants are hardy, they are likely to begin spring growth after the first significant thaw. The first thaw is often a false spring, and the frost that follows may damage or kill delicate shoots. By mulching hardy perennials after the ground freezes, you protect them from weather fluctuations. In this case, the mulch keeps the plants cold until sprouting is safe.

Evergreen branches, wood chips, straw, pine needles, and corn stalks are effective mulches, because they allow air circulation. Avoid using fallen leaves as mulch unless the leaves are well-composted or shredded. Uncomposted whole leaves tend to form a thick, soggy mass that compacts and smothers most plants.

A 3-inch layer of mulch usually provides the needed protection. The layer should be loose so air can penetrate to the soil. Through the winter, some of the mulch decomposes. By spring, the soil is clear enough for plants to sprout but still sufficiently covered for protection from drying and weed encroachment.

■ **Pests:** Among the hungry horde of insects that plague flowering plants are ants, aphids, bulb flies, a number of caterpillars, cutworms, leafhoppers, leafminers, mealybugs, spittlebugs, and thrips. Correct diagnosis is 90 percent of cure. Consult the

Cosmos respond to deadheading, or the removal of spent flowers, by producing more abundant blooms. Many other flowers respond well to deadheading, including blanket flower, coreopsis, geranium, carnation, marigold, petunia, pot marigold, sage, Shasta daisy, snapdragon, Stokes' aster, yarrow, and zinnia.

problem-solving section of this book for photographs and a detailed discussion of insect pests.

Some problems are easily recognizable. Look closely and you can see budworms of varying ages hiding in your decimated petunia blossoms. Cut the stem of a dying hollyhock or aster and 1-inch-long yellow or pale pink corn borers are suddenly out in the open. The 1½-inch-long green cabbageworm can eliminate your entire nasturtium bed and then move over to your alyssum, carnations, and geraniums. Hungry caterpillars can defoliate and deflower an entire flower bed. Woolly bears like cannas, dahlias, violets, petunias, hollyhocks, and verbena, among many other perennials and annuals. Caterpillar parents are moths and pretty butterflies. The sight of parents flying about each spring and summer should make you alert to potential caterpillar problems in the flower garden.

Earwigs are familiar to gardeners in all but the coldest parts of the country. Normally they are beneficial scavengers, eating waste materials such as decaying fruit and plant litter. But sometimes they multiply and become pests, feeding on flowers and seedlings. Because earwigs like to hide in dark, damp places, try trapping them in rolled-up newspapers and overturned flowerpots. Each morning shake the catch out into a pail of soapy water. Continue trapping until no new earwigs appear. If that does not work, spray with Ortho® Home Defense® Perimeter & Indoor Insect Killer Pull 'N Spray.

Grasshoppers emerge only during certain weather conditions, but their appearance can signify disaster to flowering plants. They often move into planted areas from nearby fields in dry weather. Seedlings disappear first. Then grasshoppers begin chewing large holes around leaf edges. They often begin work in areas near weed patches. Begin your control program as soon as you see grasshoppers, because the first few act as scouts for the rest. Treat with Ortho® Bug-Geta® Plus Snail, Slug & Insect Killer Ready-Spray®, Ortho® Bug-B-Gon® Multi-Purpose Insect Killer, Ortho® Rose & Flower Insect Killer or spray with an insecticide containing *malathion*. Repeat weekly if plants become reinfested.

Like insect pests, animal pests can endanger the flower garden. Bulbs sometimes seem particularly vulnerable to attack by animal pests.

Mice use mole runs to get at bulbs underground. Tulip, lily, and crocus bulbs are particular favorites. Bulbs wilt rapidly after being gnawed, and they may be completely destroyed. Adding a liberal load of stone chips or pebbles to the soil when planting discourages mice. Another solution is to encircle the entire bulb bed with 12-inch-high fine-mesh netting. Bury this vertically so that only about 3 inches extend above the surface. Do not mulch the bulb bed in winter until the ground is frozen. If drainage continues, plant bulbs that mice do not like as well, such as narcissus.

Deer often seek out spring bulbs. Since keeping high-jumping deer out of a garden is extremely difficult, one solution is to plant more than you need so you have enough to share. Keep deer favorites close to the house, where the wild animals may be more reluctant to venture. Place nylon stockings with human hair or small sacks of blood meal near plants you want to protect. On yard perimeters, plant narcissus. Deer normally will not touch this bulb, and you can choose from many beautiful varieties.

Rabbits can be a garden menace. They eat almost any growing thing they can reach. Rabbits devour all parts of crocus plants and can finish a tulip bed off while it is still in bud form. For emergency protection, apply a thick layer of blood meal around bulb plants. Cover early spring bulbs with evergreen limbs from your Christmas tree—a good recycling project. Leave the green covering over crocus bulbs until the spring sprouts leaf out. Keep tulips covered until stems are 12 inches high. Though dogs and cats can cause other garden problems, they do help keep rabbits away.

Behind every successful flower garden lie regular watering, fertilizing, weeding, and pest control. This well-tended border of daylilies, sage, Asiatic lilies, loosestrife, Shasta daisy, baby's breath, coreopsis, astilbe, feverfew, and black-eyed Susan shows what is possible.

POOR FLOWERING

Transplant shock

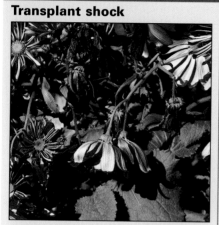

Transplant shock on cineraria.

Poor flowering

Poor flowering on gazanias.

Small petunia blossoms.

Problem: Recently transplanted flowers drop their flower buds before they open. Often, blossoms and leaves also drop prematurely. The plant may wilt during the hot part of the day even if the soil is moist.

Analysis: Even under ideal conditions, many plants drop some of their buds, flowers, and leaves when transplanted. Bud and leaf drop result from root damage that occurs during transplanting. Tiny hairlike rootlets that grow at the periphery of the root system absorb most of the water the plant uses. When these rootlets are damaged during transplanting, the amount of water that can be supplied to the foliage and flowers is decreased. Flower buds, flowers, and leaves fall off, and the plant wilts. The more the roots are damaged during transplanting, the greater will be the leaf and bud drop. Also, because plants lose water rapidly during hot, dry, windy periods, transplanting at these times will cause plants to undergo greater shock. They will not recover as quickly. As the root system regrows, new flower buds will form.

Solution: Transplant when the weather is cool, in the early morning, in the late afternoon, and on cloudy days. Whenever possible, transplant small plants rather than large ones. When transplanting, disturb the soil around the roots as little as possible. Preserve as much of the root system as possible. If the roots have been disturbed or if the plant is large or old, pinch off about one-third of the growth to reduce the amount of foliage needing water.

Problem: There are few blooms, and the flowers may be small.

Analysis: Lack of flowers can result from any of several causes.

Solution: The numbered solutions below correspond to the numbered items in the analysis section at left.

1. Insufficient light: Many plants require full- or part-day sun to flower properly. Even plants that flower well in filtered light will not produce many blossoms when planted in deep shade. Plants receiving inadequate light are often leggy or spindly.

1. Check the light requirements of your plants by looking in the alphabetical section beginning on page 122. If plants are not receiving enough light, move them to a sunnier location.

2. Diseased plants: Plants that have been attacked by disease or insect pests rarely flower well. Mottled, discolored, or dying foliage or chewed leaves usually indicate the presence of a disease organism or plant pest.

2. Look up your plant in the alphabetical section beginning on page 122 to find what diseases may affect it, and treat accordingly.

3. Old flowers left on plant: Many plants slow down their flower production when the older blossoms are allowed to fade and form seeds. The plant diverts its energy into producing seeds rather than flowers.

3. Remove flowers as they start to fade.

4. Overcrowding: Plants that are overcrowded must compete for light, nutrients, and water. When supplies of nutrients are inadequate, overall plant growth, including flowering, decreases.

4. Thin overcrowded plantings.

5. Too much nitrogen: Plants require a balanced diet of nutrients (nitrogen, phosphorus, and potassium) to grow and bloom properly. Excessive nitrogen from high-nitrogen fertilizers throws off the balance of nutrients and encourages lush, green leaf growth at the expense of flower production.

5. Fertilize your plants with Miracle-Gro® Bloom Booster. The extra phosphate in the fertilizer helps to promote flowering.

Thrips

Thrips damage to gladiolus.

Problem: Flower buds turn brown and die before they open. Silvery white streaks are often on the leaves. Flowers that have opened are often streaked and distorted. If the flower buds are peeled open, tiny (1/20-inch) insects resembling brown or straw-colored wood slivers can be seen moving around at the base of the petals.

Analysis: Several species of this common insect pest attack garden flowers. Thrips are found in protected parts of the plant, such as the insides of flower buds, where they feed by rasping the soft plant tissue, then sucking the released plant sap. The injured tissue dies and turns white or brown, causing the characteristic streaking of the leaves and flowers. Because thrips migrate long distances on wind currents, they can quickly infest widespread areas. In cold climates, thrips feed and reproduce from spring until fall. With the onset of freezing weather, they find sheltered areas and hibernate through the winter. In warm-weather climates, thrips feed and reproduce all year. These pests reach their population peak in late spring to midsummer. They are especially troublesome during prolonged dry spells.

Solution: Thrips can't be eliminated completely, but they can be kept under control. Spray infested plants with Ortho® Rose & Flower Insect Killer or Ortho® Systemic Insect Killer. Spray two or three times at intervals of 10 days as soon as damage is noticed. Make sure that your plant is listed on the product label. Repeat the spray if reinfestation occurs. Pick off and destroy old, infested flowers.

Many small flowers

Chrysanthemums that have not been disbudded.

Problem: The plant produces many small flowers rather than a few large, showy flowers. The leaves are healthy.

Analysis: Large, showy flowers will not be produced on certain plants, such as chrysanthemums, dahlias, and carnations, unless most of the flower buds are removed. Generally, these plants produce long stems with a terminal flower bud at the end and secondary flower buds at the base of each leaf. The plant has only a limited amount of nutrients with which to nourish each bud. If the plant has many buds, each bud will receive only a small amount of nutrients and will develop into a small flower.

Solution: Pinch off the side flower buds as soon as they are large enough to be handled. The earlier they are removed, the larger the terminal flowers will be.

Insufficient light

Geraniums in low light.

Problem: The plant grows slowly or not at all and is located in a shaded area. Growth is weak and leggy, and flowering is poor. The leaves may be dark green and larger than normal. The oldest leaves may drop off. There are no signs of disease or insect pests.

Analysis: Plants contain chlorophyll, which uses sunlight to produce energy. This energy is used to make food for plant growth and development. Plants differ in the amount of light they need to grow properly. Some plants need many hours of direct sunlight daily, while others thrive in shaded locations. Any plant that receives less light than it requires can't produce as much food as it needs. It grows slowly and is weak and leggy.

Solution: Look up your plant in the alphabetical section that begins on page 122 to determine the light requirement of your flower. If your plant is not receiving enough light, transplant it to a sunnier location.

SLOW GROWTH *(continued)*

Poor growth

Zinnias planted too late.

Phosphorus-deficient columbine.

Problem: The plant fails to grow, or it grows very slowly. No signs of insects or diseases are present.

Analysis: A plant might grow slowly for many reasons.

Solution: Solutions below correspond to the numbered items in the analysis.

1. Improper planting time: Many plants require warm temperatures and long hours of sunlight to grow well. If transplants that need warm weather are set out too early in the spring or too late in the fall, when temperatures are cool, they will not grow.

1. Check page 545 for a list of common flowers and their growing seasons. As the weather warms up, the plants will start to grow.

2. Unseasonable cool spell: If the weather is unseasonably cool or cloudy, most plants—even those adapted to cool temperatures—will slow down their growth rate.

2. Plants will start to grow again when unseasonable cool spells have passed. If the weather is especially cloudy and moist, check for signs of disease. Fungal and bacterial infections are especially troublesome during periods of moist weather. (For information on plant diseases, see the section beginning on page 417.)

3. Natural dormancy: Many perennials and bulbs undergo a period of no growth, soon after they have flowered. Although the plant may seem to be inactive, it is actually developing roots, bulbs, or rhizomes for the following year's growth. The foliage of many perennials and bulbs eventually dies back completely, and the plant becomes dormant.

3. Check the list of common flowers on page 545 to see if your plant is a bulb or a perennial with a natural dormancy period.

4. Phosphorus deficiency: Phosphorus is a plant nutrient essential to normal plant growth and development. Many garden soils are deficient in phosphorus. When plants do not receive enough phosphorus, they usually grow very slowly or stop growing altogether. Sometimes their foliage also turns dark green, or it may redden slightly.

4. For a quick response, spray the leaves with Miracle-Gro® Bloom Booster. Fertilize the plants with the same fertilizer, which is high in phosphate.

WILTING

Root problems

Wilting snapdragons.

Problem: The plant is wilting. The leaves are discolored to yellow or brown and may be dying. The soil may be moist or dry.

Analysis: These symptoms are caused by one of several root problems.

1. Stem and root rot: Many fungi and bacteria decay plant roots and stems. In addition to leaf wilting and discoloration, spots and lesions frequently form on the leaves and stems. The infected tissue may be soft and rotted, and the plant pulls out of the ground easily. Most of the disease-causing organisms thrive in wet soil.

2. Fertilizer burn: Excessive fertilizer causes leaves to wilt and become dull and brown. Later they become dark brown or black and dry. When too much fertilizer is applied, a concentrated solution of fertilizer salts is formed in the soil. This solution makes it difficult for plants to absorb the water they need and may even draw water out of the plant. A high concentration can cause roots to die and can lead to the death of the entire plant.

3. Nematodes: These microscopic worms live in the soil and feed on plant roots. While feeding, they inject a toxin into the roots. The result is that roots can't supply adequate water and nutrients to the aboveground plant parts, so the plant slowly dies. Infested plants are weak, are slow growing, often turn bronze or yellowish, and wilt on hot, dry days, even when the soil is wet. If you pull the plant up, you see stunted roots that are often dark and stubby and may have nodules on them.

Wilting pincushion flowers.

Heat or acute root damage

Transplant shock on begonias.

Poor drainage on impatiens.

Problem: The plant is wilting, but the foliage looks healthy. No signs of disease or insects are present. The soil is moist.

Solution: Solutions below correspond to the numbered items in the analysis.

1. Look up your plant in the alphabetical section beginning on page 122 to determine which stem and root rot diseases may affect it. Treat accordingly. (See page 419 for more information on root rot.)

2. Dilute the fertilizer in the soil and leach it below the root zone by watering the soil heavily. Soak the affected area thoroughly with plain water, let it drain, then soak again. Repeat three or four times. Cut off dead plant parts. Follow directions carefully when fertilizing.

3. If you have a chronic problem with wilting, yellowing plants that slowly die and if you've eliminated other possibilities, test for nematodes. Testing roots and soil is the only positive method for confirming the presence of these pests. Contact your local county extension office for sampling instructions, addresses of testing laboratories, and control procedures for your area.

Analysis: If a plant wilts in moist soil but the leaves look healthy, one of the following situations has probably occurred recently.

1. Intense heat or wind: During hot, windy periods, plants may wilt even though the soil is wet. Wind and heat cause water to evaporate quickly from the leaves. The roots can't take in water as fast as it is lost.

2. Transplant shock: Plants frequently wilt soon after being transplanted as a result of injured roots. Roots are usually broken or injured to some degree during transplanting. Damaged roots are unable to supply the plant with enough water, even when the soil is wet. As the root system restores itself, its water-absorbing capacity increases. Unless they are severely injured, plants will soon recover.

3. Rodents: The roots, underground stems, and bulbs of many plants are often fed upon by pocket gophers and field mice. Root, bulb, and stem damage can result in rapid wilting and sometimes in death of the plant.

4. Mechanical injury: Cultivating, digging, hoeing, thinning, weeding, and any other kind of activity that damages plant roots can cause wilting.

Solution: Solutions below correspond to the numbered items in the analysis.

1. As long as the soil is kept moist during periods of intense heat and wind, the plants will probably recover without harm when the temperature drops or the wind dies. Shading the plants and sprinkling them with water to cool off the foliage and reduce the rate of water evaporation from the leaves may hasten recovery.

2. Preserve the root system as much as possible when transplanting. Keep as much of the soil around the roots as possible. Transplant when the weather is cool, in the early morning, or late afternoon, or on cloudy days. If the roots have been disturbed, or if the plant is large and old, prune about one-third of the growth. If possible, transplant when the plant is dormant.

3. Rodents may be trapped or baited. (For details about rodent control, see page 494 to 496.)

4. Prevent mechanical injury to plants by working very carefully around them. Cultivate as shallowly as possible.

WILTING *(continued)*

DISCOLORED OR SPOTTED LEAVES

Lack of water

Leaf-edge damage caused by wilting.

Problem: The plant wilts often, and the soil is frequently or always dry. The leaves turn brown, shrivel, and may be crisp.

Analysis: The most common cause of plant wilting is dry soil. Plant roots transport water up into the stems and leaves, and it evaporates into the air through microscopic breathing pores in the surface of the leaves. Water pressure in the plant cells keeps the cell walls rigid and prevents the plant from collapsing. When the soil is dry, the roots are unable to furnish the leaves and stems with water, the water pressure in the cells drops, and the plant wilts. Most plants will recover if they have not wilted severely. Frequent or severe wilting, however, will curb a plant's growth and eventually kill it.

Solution: Water the plant thoroughly, applying enough water to wet the soil to the bottom of the root zone. If the soil is crusted or compacted, cultivate the soil around the plant before watering. To help conserve soil moisture, apply a mulch around the plant, or incorporate peat moss or other organic matter into the soil. (For information on watering, see page 407.) Do not allow the plant to wilt between waterings. Look up your plant in the alphabetical section beginning on page 122 to determine its moisture requirements.

Overwatering

Overwatering damage on primrose.

Problem: Leaves turn light green or yellow. Leaf edges may turn brown, and some of the leaves may die. In many cases the plant is stunted. Flowering is poor. If the plant is pulled out of the ground, the roots are found to be soft and rotted. The soil is frequently or constantly wet.

Analysis: Overwatering is a serious and common problem that often results in the decay and death of plant roots. Roots require oxygen to function normally. Oxygen is contained in tiny air spaces (*pores*) in the soil. When water is applied to the soil, the air is pushed out of the soil pores and replaced with water. If this water can't drain properly or is constantly reapplied, the soil pores remain filled with water. The roots can't absorb the oxygen they need in such saturated conditions, and they begin to decay. As the roots continue to rot, they are less able to supply the plant with nutrients and water, resulting in the decline and eventual death of the plant.

Solution: Allow the soil to dry out slightly between waterings. If the soil is poorly drained, it is critical to improve the soil drainage. (For information on drainage, see page 406.) Use plants that will grow in wet soil (see page 533).

Lack of nitrogen

Nitrogen-deficient impatiens.

Problem: Leaves turn pale green, then yellow, beginning with the older leaves. Growth is slowed. Older leaves may drop. New leaves are small. Severely affected plants may die.

Analysis: Garden soils are frequently deficient in nitrogen, the most important nutrient for plant growth. Nitrogen is essential in the formation of plant protein, chlorophyll (green leaf pigment), and many other compounds. When a plant becomes deficient in nitrogen, it breaks down proteins and chlorophyll in the oldest leaves to recover nitrogen to be recycled for new growth. This loss of chlorophyll causes the older leaves to turn yellow. A continuing shortage of nitrogen results in overall yellowing. Because nitrogen is leached from the soil more readily than other plant nutrients, and because it is needed in larger quantities than other nutrients, it must be added to most garden soils and for all flowers. Nitrogen leaches from sandy soil more readily than from clay soil, and it leaches more quickly when rainfall or irrigation is heavy.

Solution: Fertilize with Miracle-Gro® Plant Food. Repeat applications according to directions. Fertilize more frequently in sandy soils or where rainfall is heavy. Check that plants aren't suffering from saturated soil and even possibly root rot, as these conditions may cause plants to exhibit symptoms of nitrogen deficiency.

Leaves are discolored

Iris leaves discolored by lack of water.

Dried-out crocus.

Iron deficiency

Iron-deficient chrysanthemum.

Problem: Leaves turn pale green to yellow. The plant may be stunted. In many cases, leaf edges turn brown and crisp, and some leaves shrivel and die. No signs of disease or pests are present. Leaves do not discolor from the base of the plant upward as they do with nitrogen deficiency. (For information on nitrogen deficiency, see page 112.)

Analysis: Leaves discolor for several reasons.

Solution: The numbered solutions below correspond to the numbered items in the analysis.

1. Frequent water stress: Plants require at least a minimal supply of water to remain healthy and grow properly. When they are allowed to dry out once or twice, they usually survive. Plants that suffer from frequent drought stress, however, undergo changes in their metabolism that result in leaf discoloration, stunting, and lack of growth. If the soil is allowed to dry out completely, the plant will die.

1. Don't let plants wilt between waterings. Consult the alphabetical section beginning on page 122 for the moisture needs of your plant. Provide plants with adequate water. (For information on watering, see page 407.)

2. Salt buildup in the soil: Leaf discoloration and browning occur when excess salts dissolved in the soil water are taken into the plant and accumulate in the leaf tissue. Soil salts build up to damaging levels in soils that are not occasionally flushed. Salt buildup commonly occurs in arid regions of the country.

2. Flush out soil salts periodically by watering deeply and thoroughly.

3. Sunburn: Shade-loving plants placed in a sunny location will develop discolored leaves. Sunburned leaves often develop a whitish or yellow bleached appearance. Leaves not directly exposed to the sun usually remain green and uninjured.

3. Check to see whether your plant is adapted to sun or shade. Consult the alphabetical section beginning on page 122 for the light needs of your plant. Transplant shade-loving plants to a shady location.

Problem: Leaves turn pale green or yellow. The newest leaves (those at the tips of the stems) are most severely affected. Except in extreme cases, the veins of affected leaves remain green. In extreme cases, the newest leaves are small and all-white or yellow. Older leaves may remain green.

Analysis: Plants frequently suffer from deficiencies of iron and other minor nutrients such as manganese and zinc, elements essential to normal plant growth and development. Deficiencies can occur when one or more of these elements are depleted in the soil. Often these minor nutrients are present in the soil, but alkaline soils with a pH of 7.5 or higher or wet soil conditions cause them to form compounds that can't be used by the plant. An alkaline condition can result from overliming or from lime leached from cement or brick.

Solution: Spray the foliage with a chelated iron fertilizer, and apply the fertilizer to the soil around the plants to correct the deficiency of minor nutrients. Correct the pH of the soil before planting by using ferrous sulfate or soil sulfur (see page 407). Maintain an acid-to-neutral pH by fertilizing with Miracid® Plant Food.

113

DISCOLORED OR SPOTTED LEAVES *(continued)*

Leaf and flower spots

Fungal leaf spot on impatiens.

Leaf spot.

Problem: Spots and blotches appear on the leaves and flowers.

Analysis: Several factors contribute to spotting and blotching of leaves and flowers.

1. Fungal leaf spots: Spots caused by fungi are usually small and circular and may be found on all of the leaves. The spots range in size from barely visible to an inch in diameter. They may be yellow, red, tan, gray, brown, or black. Often the leaves are yellow and dying. Infection is usually most severe during moist, mild weather (50° to 85°F).

2. Bacterial leaf spots: Spots caused by bacteria are usually tiny and angular in shape. They are usually dark and are accompanied by rotting and oozing from infected areas. Bacterial spots may be found on all parts of the plant and are most often promoted by warm, moist conditions.

3. Sunburn: Shade-loving plants placed in a sunny location will develop spots and blotches. Sun-loving plants may also develop sunburn symptoms if they are allowed to dry out. Initially, sunburned leaves develop a whitish or yellowish bleached appearance. Large, dark blotches form on damaged tissue.

4. Spray damage: Spotting of foliage and flowers may also be caused by insecticide, fungicide, or herbicide spray damage. Sprays may drift in from other areas.

Solution: Solutions below correspond to the numbered items in the analysis.

1. Picking off diseased leaves may give adequate control. Clean up plant debris. If plants are severely infected, spray them with Ortho® Garden Disease Control or a fungicide containing *mancozeb*. Make sure that your plant is listed on the fungicide label before spraying. These sprays are protectants, not controls. Old leaves will remain diseased. Water early in the day so that the foliage can dry thoroughly.

2. If practical, pick off and destroy spotted leaves. If the plant is severely infected, discard it. Clean up plant debris. Avoid overhead watering. Clean contaminated tools with rubbing alcohol.

3. Pick off the injured leaves and plant parts. Check to see whether your plant is adapted to sun or shade. Transplant shade-loving plants to a shaded location, or provide shade. Water plants adequately, especially during hot, sunny, or windy days.

4. Once damage has occurred, you can't reverse. Read and follow directions carefully when spraying. Avoid spraying on windy days when the spray can drift. If spray drifts onto the wrong plant, rinse the leaves immediately with water.

Powdery mildew

Powdery mildew.

Problem: Powdery grayish-white spots and patches cover the leaves and stems, often primarily the upper surfaces of leaves. Infected leaves eventually turn yellow.

Analysis: Powdery mildew, a common plant disease, is caused by several closely related fungi that thrive in both humid and dry weather. The powdery patches consist of fungal strands and spores. The spores are spread by the wind to healthy plants. The fungus saps plant nutrients, causing the leaves to turn yellow and sometimes to die. A severe infection may kill the plant. Since some powdery mildews attack many different kinds of plants, the fungus from a diseased plant may infect other types of plants. Under certain conditions, powdery mildew can spread through a closely spaced planting in a matter of days. In the late summer and fall, the fungus forms small, black, spore-producing bodies, which are dormant during the winter but which can infect more plants the following spring. Powdery mildew is generally most severe in the late summer and under humid conditions.

Solution: Look up your plant in the alphabetical listing beginning on page 122 to determine which of the different fungicides should be used. Spray at regular intervals of 10 to 12 days or as often as necessary to protect new growth. Remove and destroy severely infected plants. Where practical, pick off diseased leaves. Clean up and destroy plant debris. Plant in sites that have good air movement and receive early morning sun.

Rust

Pelargonium rust.

Problem: Yellow or orange spots appear on the upper surfaces of leaves. Yellowish-orange pustules of spores develop on the undersides of leaves. Infected leaves usually dry up and die. The plant may be stunted.

Analysis: The plant disease rust is caused by any of several related fungi. Most rust fungi spend the winter as spores on living plant tissue and, in some cases, in plant debris. Some rust fungi also infect various weeds and woody trees and shrubs during part of their life cycle. Flower infection usually starts in the early spring as soon as conditions are favorable for plant growth. Splashing water and wind spread the spores to healthy plants. Some rust fungi can't infect the flower host unless the foliage is wet for six to eight hours. Rust is favored by moist weather, cool nights, and warm days.

Solution: Several different fungicides are used to control rust. Look up your specific plant in the alphabetical listing beginning on page 122 to determine which fungicide to use. Spray plants thoroughly at the first sign of disease, covering both the upper and lower surfaces of the leaves. Some plants are so susceptible to rust that you may need to spray at weekly intervals throughout the summer. Fungicides will protect only uninfected tissues; they will not cure diseased leaves. To allow wet foliage to dry out more quickly, water in the morning rather than in the late afternoon or evening. Remove and destroy all infected plants in the fall to prevent them from infecting new plantings. Plant rust-resistant varieties (see page 546).

Air pollution

Nasturtiums damaged by ozone.

Problem: The upper surfaces of leaves may be bleached, with white flecks or reddish-brown spots. Sometimes the leaves are distorted. Older leaves are affected more than new ones.

Analysis: Some gases released into the atmosphere from cars and factories damage plants. The most common type of pollution is *smog*. Air pollution damage is most commonly a problem in urban areas, but it also occurs in rural areas where gardens are located downwind from factories. Some plants are severely affected and may even die. Flower production is reduced on pollution-damaged plants. (For information on the three most common pollutants—ozone, PAN (peroxyacetyl nitrate), and sulfur dioxide—see page 424.) Many different environmental factors affect a plant's susceptibility to air pollution, including temperature, air movement, light intensity, and soil and air moisture.

Solution: Air pollution injury is usually a localized problem. Check with your neighbors to see if the same plants in their gardens have been affected similarly. Because injury from air pollutants is similar in appearance to injury from nutrient deficiencies, insects, diseases, and mites, these problems should be eliminated as causes before the damage is attributed to air pollution. Nothing can be done about effects of air pollutants.

Viruses

Virus-damaged gladiolus.

Problem: Leaves may be mottled yellow-green or may be uniformly yellowing. In some cases, the foliage develops yellow rings, or the veins may turn yellow. Flowers and leaves may be smaller than normal and distorted. The plant is usually stunted, and flowering is generally poor.

Analysis: Several different plant viruses infect flowering plants. These viruses include mosaics, yellows, and ring spots. The severity of viral infections depends on the plant and on the strain of virus. In some cases, symptoms of infection may not show up unless several viruses are present in the plant at the same time. Viral infections do not generally kill the plant but may greatly reduce its overall vigor and beauty. Many viruses are spread by aphids, which feed on diseased plants and transfer the virus to healthy plants. If diseased plants are touched or pruned, some viruses can be transferred to healthy plants on hands and equipment contaminated by plant sap. Viruses usually persist in the plant indefinitely.

Solution: No chemicals control or eliminate plant viral diseases. Remove and destroy weak, infected, and stunted plants. Wash your hands thoroughly, and disinfect pruning shears after working on infected plants. Purchase only healthy plants. Keep the aphid population under control, and remove nearby weeds that may attract and harbor aphids.

DISCOLORED OR SPOTTED LEAVES *(continued)*

INSECTS

Spider mites

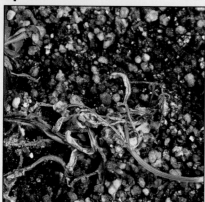

Spider mite damage to columbine.

Problem: Leaves are stippled, yellowish, bronze, or reddish and often dirty. There may be webbing over flower buds, between leaves, or on the lower surfaces of leaves. To determine if a plant is infested with mites, examine the undersides of the leaves with a hand lens. Or hold a sheet of white paper underneath an affected leaf and tap the leaf sharply. Minute specks the size of pepper grains will drop to the paper and begin to crawl. These pests are easily seen against the white background.

Analysis: Spider mites, common pests of many garden and greenhouse plants, are related to spiders. They cause damage by sucking sap from the undersides of leaves. As a result of their feeding, the plant's chlorophyll disappears, producing the stippled, discolored appearance. Spider mites are active throughout the growing season but favor hot, dry weather (70°F and higher). By midsummer, they have built up to tremen-dous numbers. During cold weather, spider mites hibernate in the soil, on weeds and plants retaining foliage, and on tree bark.

Solution: Spray infested plants with Ortho® Systemic Insect Killer or Ortho® Rose & Flower Insect Killer. Make sure that your plant is listed on the product label. Spray plants thoroughly, being sure to cover both the upper and lower surfaces of the leaves. Repeat the spray at least two more times at intervals of five to seven days. If the plant can tolerate heavy watering, spraying the foliage can also help to reduce the number of spider mites.

Leafminers

Leafminer damage to dahlia.

Problem: Light-colored irregular trails wind through the leaves. Blotches may eventually appear on infested leaves. Some of the trails and blotches are filled with black matter. Severely infested leaves may dry up and die.

Analysis: Most insects that cause this type of damage belong to the family of leafmining flies. The tiny adult flies lay their eggs on the undersides of leaves. The maggots that hatch from these eggs penetrate the leaf and live between the upper and lower surfaces. They feed on the inner leaf tissue, creating winding trails and blotches. Their dark excrement may dot or partially fill sections of the trails. Generally, the larvae emerge from the leaves to pupate. Leafminers are present from spring until fall. The last generation of maggots pupates in the soil or plant debris through the winter and emerges as adult flies the following spring. (For more information on leafminers, see page 455.)

Solution: Spray infested plants with Ortho® Rose & Flower Insect Killer or Ortho® Systemic Insect Killer. Pick off and destroy infested leaves. Remove and destroy all plant remains in the fall.

Aphids

Aphids on ornamental peppers (4× life size).

Problem: Leaves are curled, distorted, and yellowing. Often the flowers are malformed. Tiny (⅛-inch) yellow, green, or dark-colored soft-bodied insects are clustered on leaves, stems, and flowers. A shiny, sticky substance may coat the leaves. Ants may be present.

Analysis: These common insects do little damage in small numbers. They are extremely prolific, however, and populations can rapidly build to damaging numbers during the growing season. Damage occurs when the aphid sucks the sap from the leaves and buds. The aphid is unable to digest all the sugar in the sap, and it excretes the excess in a fluid called *honeydew,* which often drops onto the leaves below. A sooty mold fungus may develop on the honeydew, causing the leaves to appear black and dirty. Ants feed on this sticky substance and are often present where there is an aphid infestation. In warm areas, aphids are active year-round. In cooler climates, where winter temperatures drop below freezing, the adults can't survive. Eggs the aphids lay in the fall on tree bark, old leaves, and plant debris, however, can survive the winter and cause reinfestation in the spring. Aphids transmit viral plant diseases such as mosaics.

Solution: Spray with Ortho® Rose & Flower Insect Killer or Ortho® Bug-B-Gon® Multi-Purpose Insect Killer Ready-Spray®. Make sure that your plant is listed on the product label. Clean up plant debris in the fall. (For more information on disease-carrying insects, see page 449.)

Ants

Ants on euphorbia (½ life size).

Problem: Ants crawl on the plants and soil. In many cases, these plants are infested with aphids, scales, mealybugs, or whiteflies.

Analysis: Ants, the insects familiar to gardeners throughout the country, do not directly damage plants. Ants may be present for any of several reasons. Many ants feed on *honeydew*, a sweet, sticky substance excreted by several species of insects, including aphids, scales, mealybugs, and whiteflies. Ants are attracted to plants infested with these pests. In order to ensure an ample supply of honeydew, ants may actually carry aphids to healthy plants. Aphid infestations are frequently spread in this manner. Ants may also feed on flower seeds and nectar. Although they do not feed on healthy plants, they may eat decayed or rotted plant tissue. Ants generally live in underground colonies or nests. Certain species may form colonies in trees or in building foundations. (For more information on ants, see page 459.)

Solution: Control ants by spreading Ortho® Bug-B-Gon® Multi-Purpose Insect Killer Granules or Ortho® Bug-Geta® Plus Snail, Slug & Insect Killer throughout the flower bed. Control aphids, scales, mealybugs, and whiteflies by spraying the plants with Ortho® Systemic Insect Killer. Make sure that your plant is listed on the product label. Avoid spraying when flowers and bees are present. Ants can be kept off individual plants with sticky barriers that trap the ants as they crawl of the barrier.

Spittlebugs

Spittlebug froth.

Problem: Masses of white, frothy foam are clustered between the leaves and stems. If the froth is removed, small, green, soft-bodied insects can be seen feeding on the plant tissue. The plant may be stunted.

Analysis: Spittlebugs, insects also known as *froghoppers*, appear in the spring. Spittlebug eggs, laid in the fall, survive the winter to hatch when the weather warms in the spring. The young spittlebugs, called *nymphs*, produce a foamy froth that protects them from sun and predators. This froth envelops the nymphs completely while they suck sap from the tender stems and leaves. Adult spittlebugs are not as damaging as the nymphs. The adults are ¼ inch long, pale yellow to dark brown, and winged. They hop or fly away quickly when disturbed. Spittlebugs seldom harm plants, but if infestation is very heavy, plant growth may be stunted. The presence of spittlebugs on plants is usually objectionable only for cosmetic reasons.

Solution: Wash spittlebugs from plants with a garden hose. If plants are heavily infested, spray with Ortho® Bug-B-Gon® Multi-Purpose Insect Killer Concentrate according to label directions. Make sure that the plant is listed on the product label. Repeated treatments are rarely necessary.

Greenhouse whiteflies

Whiteflies on fuchsia (2× life size).

Problem: Tiny, white, winged insects ¹⁄₁₆ inch long feed mainly on the undersides of leaves. Nonflying, scalelike larvae covered with white waxy powder may also be present on the undersides of leaves. When the plant is touched, insects flutter rapidly around it. Leaves may be mottled and yellow. In warm-winter areas, black mold may cover the leaves. The plant may grow poorly.

Analysis: The greenhouse whitefly (*Trialeurodes vaporariorum*) is a common insect pest of many garden and greenhouse plants. The four-winged adult lays eggs on the undersides of leaves. The larvae feed for about a month before changing to the adult form. Both larval and adult forms suck sap from the leaves. The larvae are more damaging because they feed more heavily. Adults and larvae can't fully digest all the sugar in the plant sap, and they excrete the excess in a fluid called *honeydew*, which often drops onto the leaves below. A sooty mold fungus may develop on the honeydew. In warm-winter areas, whiteflies can be active year-round, but they are unable to live through freezing winters. Spring reinfestations in freezing-winter areas come from migrating whiteflies and from infested greenhouse-grown plants.

Solution: Spray infested plants with Ortho® Rose & Flower Insect Killer, Ortho® Systemic Insect Killer, or Ortho® Bug-B-Gon® Multi-Purpose Insect Killer Ready-Spray®. When spraying, cover both the upper and lower surfaces of the leaves. Whiteflies may also be partially controlled with yellow sticky traps.

INSECTS (continued)

LEAVES, FLOWERS CHEWED

Aster leafhoppers

Aster leafhopper (4× life size).

Beetles

Cucumber beetle feeding on zinnia (½ life size).

Japanese beetles

Damaged zinnias. Inset: Japanese beetle (life size).

Problem: Spotted, pale green insects up to ⅛ inch long hop or fly away quickly when the plant is touched; nymphs crawl away sideways like crabs. The leaves are stippled and may be yellowing.

Analysis: The aster leafhopper (*Macrosteles fascifrons*), an insect also known as the *six-spotted leafhopper*, feeds on many vegetable and ornamental plants. It generally feeds on the undersides of leaves, sucking the sap, which causes stippling. This leafhopper transmits aster yellows, a plant disease that can be quite damaging. (For information on aster yellows, see page 423.) Leafhoppers at all stages of maturity are active during the growing season. They hatch in the spring from eggs laid on perennial weeds and ornamental plants. Even areas where winters are so cold that the eggs can't survive are not free from infestation, because leafhoppers migrate from warmer regions on wind currents in the spring.

Solution: Spray plants with Ortho® Systemic Insect Killer, Ortho® Malathion Plus® Insect Spray Concentrate, or Ortho® Bug-B-Gon® Multi-Purpose Insect Killer Ready-Spray®. Check to make sure that your plant is listed on the product label. Avoid spraying when flowers and bees are present. Eradicate nearby weeds—especially thistles, plantains, and dandelions—that may harbor leafhopper eggs and aster yellows. (For more information on controlling disease-carrying insects, see page 449.)

Problem: Insects chewing holes in the leaves and flowers have hard wing covers folded across their backs, meeting in a straight line down the center. They are frequently shiny and brightly colored.

Analysis: Many different species of beetles infest flowers. In the spring or summer, beetles fly to garden plants and feed on flowers, buds, and leaves. Punctured flower buds usually fail to open, and fully open flowers are often eaten. Because many beetles feed at night, only their damage may be noticed, not the insects. Female beetles lay their eggs in the soil or in flowers in late summer or fall. Emerging larvae crawl down into the soil to spend the winter, or they mature and pass the winter in plant debris. The larvae of some beetles feed on plant roots before maturing in the fall or spring.

Solution: Spray infested plants with Ortho® Systemic Insect Killer, Ortho® Malathion Plus® Insect Spray Concentrate, or Ortho® Bug-B-Gon® Multi-Purpose Insect Killer Ready-Spray®. Make sure that your plant is listed on the product label.

Problem: Leaf tissue has been eaten between the veins, making the leaves appear lacy. Flowers are eaten. Metallic green-and-bronze, winged beetles, ½ inch long, feed in clusters on the flowers and foliage.

Analysis: As its name suggests, the Japanese beetle (*Popillia japonica*) is native to Japan. It was first seen in New Jersey in 1916 and has since become a major pest in the eastern United States. It feeds on hundreds of different species of plants. The adult beetles are present from June to October. They feed only in the daytime and are most active on warm, sunny days. The female beetles live for 30 to 45 days. Just before they die, they lay their eggs directly under the soil surface in lawns. The grayish-white grubs that hatch from these eggs feed on grass roots. As the weather turns cold in the late fall, the grubs burrow 8 to 10 inches into the soil, where they hibernate. When the soil warms up in the spring, the grubs migrate back to the surface and resume feeding. They pupate and, in late May or June, reemerge as adult beetles.

Solution: Spray infested plants with Ortho® Rose & Flower Insect Killer, Ortho® Bug-B-Gon® Multi-Purpose Insect Killer, or Ortho® Systemic Insect Killer. Make sure that your plant is listed on the product label.

Caterpillars

Caterpillar (life size).

Problem: Holes appear in the leaves and buds. Leaves, buds, and flowers may be entirely sheared off. Caterpillars are feeding on flowers and foliage.

Analysis: Many species of these moth or butterfly larvae feed on garden plants. Usually the adult moths or butterflies begin laying eggs on garden plants with the onset of warm spring weather. The larvae that emerge from these eggs feed on the leaves, flowers, and buds for two to six weeks, depending on weather conditions and species. Mature caterpillars pupate in cocoons either buried in the soil or attached to leaves, tree bark, or buildings. Some caterpillar species have only one generation per year. With these species, all the caterpillars hatch, grow, and pupate at the same time. Other species have numerous generations, so caterpillars of various sizes may be present throughout the growing season. The last generation of caterpillars in the fall survives the winter as pupae. The adult moths and butterflies emerge the following spring. Many caterpillars feed only at night and are not obvious during the day. Look at night with a flashlight.

Solution: Spray infested plants with Ortho® Rose & Flower Insect Killer, Ortho® Malathion Plus® Insect Spray Concentrate, Ortho® Systemic Insect Killer, or with the bacterial insecticide *Bacillus thuringiensis* (Bt). Make sure that your plant is listed on the product label. Avoid spraying when bees are present. Small numbers of caterpillars may be removed by hand.

Nocturnal insects

Cineraria damaged by nocturnal insects.

Problem: Holes appear in the leaves and flowers. Some of the leaves, stems, and flowers may be sheared off. No insects are seen feeding on the plants during the day. When affected plants are inspected at night with a flashlight, insects may be seen feeding on the foliage and flowers.

Analysis: Several kinds of insects feed on plants only at night, including some beetles, weevils, and caterpillars and all earwigs and cutworms. Beetles are hard-bodied insects with tough, leathery wing covers. The wing covers meet in the middle of the back, forming a straight line. Weevils are a type of beetle with a long snout. Earwigs are reddish brown, flat, elongated insects up to 1 inch long with pincers projecting from the rear of the body. Caterpillars and cutworms are smooth or hairy, soft-bodied worms. These insects usually hide in the soil, in debris, or in other protected locations during the day.

Solution: Control these insects by spraying with insecticides. (For more information on nocturnal insects, see beetles on page 434; caterpillars on page 439; cutworms on page 440; earwigs on page 460; and weevils on page 435.)

Snails and slugs

Snails feeding on hosta (¼ life size).

Problem: Holes are chewed in the leaves or entire leaves may be sheared from the stems. Flowers are partially eaten. Silvery trails wind around on the plants and soil nearby. Snails or slugs may be seen moving around or feeding on the plants, especially at night. Check for them by inspecting the garden at night by flashlight.

Analysis: Snails and slugs are mollusks and are related to clams, oysters, and other shellfish. They feed on a wide variety of garden plants. Like other mollusks, snails and slugs need to be moist all the time. For this reason, they avoid direct sun and dry places and hide during the day in damp places, such as under flowerpots or in thick ground covers. They emerge at night or on cloudy days to feed. Snails and slugs are similar in appearance except that the snail has a hard shell into which it withdraws when disturbed. Slugs lay white eggs encased in a slimy mass in protected places. Snails bury their eggs in the soil, also in a slimy mass. The young look like miniature versions of their parents.

Solution: Scatter Ortho® Bug-Geta® Snail & Slug Killer in bands around the areas you wish to protect. Also scatter the bait in areas where snails or slugs might be hiding, such as in dense ground covers, weedy areas, compost piles, and flower pot storage areas. Before spreading the bait, wet down the treated areas to encourage snail and slug activity at night. Repeat the application every two weeks for as long as snails and slugs are active.

SEEDLINGS DIE

Wilted seedlings

Damping-off of marigold seedlings.

Germination problems

Damping-off of petunia.

Damping-off of snapdragon.

Problem: Seedlings die soon after emerging from the soil and are found lying on the ground.

Analysis: Seedlings may wilt and die from lack of water or from disease.

1. Dehydration: Seedlings are succulent and have shallow roots. If the soil dries out even an inch or so below the surface, seedlings may die.

2. Damping-off: Young seedlings are very susceptible to damping-off, a plant disease caused by fungi. Damping-off is more frequent in wet soil with a high nitrogen level. Damping-off can be a problem when the weather remains either cold or cloudy and wet while seeds are germinating or if seedlings are too heavily shaded.

Solution: The numbered solutions below correspond to the numbered items in the analysis.

1. Do not allow the soil to dry out completely. Water when the soil surface starts to dry slightly. During warm or windy weather, you may need to water several times a day.

2. Allow the soil surface to dry slightly between waterings. Start seeds in Scotts® Starter Fertilizer. Add Miracle-Gro® Plant Food after the seedlings have produced their first true leaves. Protect seeds during germination by coating them with a fungicide containing *captan* or *thiram*. Add a pinch of fungicide to a packet of seeds (or ½ teaspoon per pound), and shake well to coat the seeds with the fungicide. (For more information on damping-off, see page 420.)

Problem: Seedlings fail to emerge.

Analysis:

1. Dehydration: Once the seeds have started to grow, even before they have emerged from the soil, they will die easily if allowed to dry out.

2. Damping-off: Germinating seedlings are very susceptible to damping-off, a plant disease caused by fungi. These fungi inhabit most soils, decaying the young seedlings as they emerge from the seed. Damping-off is favored by wet, cool soil.

3. Slow germination: Seeds of different kinds of plants vary considerably in the amount of time they require to germinate.

4. Poor seed viability: Seeds that are old, diseased, or of inferior quality may fail to germinate.

5. Wrong planting depth: Seeds vary in their planting depth requirements. If planted too deeply or shallowly, the seeds may fail to germinate.

6. Seeds washed away: If a seedbed is watered with a forceful spray or heavy rain, seeds may wash away.

7. Cold weather: Cold weather may delay seed germination considerably or prevent germination entirely.

Solution:

1. Do not allow the soil to dry out completely. Check the seedbed and seed flats at least once a day. Water when the soil surface starts to dry slightly.

2. Allow the soil surface to dry slightly between waterings. Start seeds in Scotts® Starter Fertilizer. Add Miracle-Gro® Plant Food after the seedlings have produced their first true leaves. Delay planting in spring until the soil warms. Use seed treated with a registered fungicide.

3. Check the list of flower germination periods on page 545 to see if your seeds germinate slowly.

4. Purchase seeds from a reputable nursery or seed company. Plant seeds packed for the current year.

5. Plant seeds at the proper depth. Follow the instructions on the commercial seed packet or consult a reputable nursery.

6. Water seedbeds gently. Don't allow the water to puddle and run off. Use a watering can or nozzle that delivers a gentle spray.

7. Even though germination may be delayed, many of the seeds will probably sprout when the weather warms up. The following year, plant seeds later in the season, after the soil has warmed.

Snails and slugs

Seedlings sheared off by snails.

Problem: Seedlings are sheared off and eaten, with only the stems emerging from the ground. Silvery trails wind around on the plants and soil nearby. Snails or slugs may be seen moving around or feeding on the plants, especially at night. Confirm their presence by inspecting the garden after dark with a flashlight.

Analysis: Snails and slugs are mollusks and are related to clams, oysters, and other shellfish. They feed on a wide variety of garden plants. Like other mollusks, snails and slugs need to be moist all the time. For this reason, they avoid direct sun and dry places and hide during the day in damp places, such as under flowerpots or in thick ground covers. They emerge at night or on cloudy days to feed. Snails and slugs are similar in appearance, except that the snail has a hard shell into which it withdraws when disturbed. Slugs lay white eggs encased in a slimy mass in protected places. Snails bury their eggs in the soil, also in a slimy mass. The young look like miniature versions of their parents.

Solution: Apply Ortho® Bug-Geta® Snail & Slug Killer in bands around the areas you wish to protect. Use the bait in areas where snails or slugs might be hiding, such as in dense ground covers, weedy areas, compost piles, or flowerpot storage areas. Before applying the bait, wet down the treated areas to encourage snail and slug activity that night. Repeat the application every two weeks for as long as snails and slugs are active.

Cutworms

Cutworm damage to petunia seedlings.

Problem: Seedlings are chewed or cut off near the ground. Gray, brown, or black worms, 1½ to 2 inches long, may be found about 2 inches deep in the soil near the base of the damaged plants. The worms curl up into a C-shape coil when disturbed.

Analysis: Several species of cutworms attack plants in the flower garden. The most likely pests of seedlings planted early in the season are the surface-feeding cutworms. A single surface-feeding cutworm can sever the stems of many young plants in one night. Cutworms hide in the soil during the day and feed only at night. Adult cutworms are dark, night-flying moths with bands or stripes on their forewings. In the South, cutworms may also attack fall-planted seedlings. (For more information on cutworms, see page 440.)

Solution: Apply Ortho® Bug-Geta® Plus Snail, Slug & Insect Killer around the base of undamaged plants when stem cutting is observed. Because cutworms are difficult to control, applications may need to be repeated at weekly intervals. Before transplanting in the same area, apply a preventive treatment of the above product and work it into the soil. Cultivate the soil thoroughly in late summer and fall to expose and destroy eggs, larvae, and pupae. Work Ortho® Bug-B-Gon® Multi-Purpose Insect Killer Granules into the soil before planting. Further reduce damage with cutworm collars around the stem of each plant. (For information on cutworm collars, see page 414.)

Animal pests

Celery seedlings eaten by mice.

Problem: Plants and seedlings may be partially or entirely eaten. Mounds of soil, ridges, or tunnels may be clustered in the yard. There may be tiny holes in the soil and small, dry, rectangular brown pellets on the ground near the damaged plants. Various birds and animals may be seen feeding in the garden, or their tracks may be around the damaged plants.

Analysis: Several different animals feed on flowers. Pocket gophers (found primarily in the West), field mice, rabbits, and deer cause major damage by eating seedlings or mature plants. Certain species of birds feed on seedlings. Moles, squirrels, woodchucks, and raccoons are generally less damaging but may also feed on flower roots, bulbs, and seeds. Even if animals are not directly observed, their presence is evidenced by their burrows, droppings, and tracks.

Solution: Fences, cages or screens, traps, repellents, or baits will protect most garden plants from animal damage or at least greatly reduce the damage. (For information on specific animal pests and their control, see the section beginning on page 492.)

AGERATUM (Floss flower)

Gray mold

Gray mold.

Problem: Brown spots and blotches appear on the leaves and possibly on the stems. As the disease progresses, a fuzzy brown or grayish mold forms on the infected tissue. Gray mold and spots may appear on the flowers, especially during periods of cool, wet weather. The leaves and stems may be soft and rotted.

Analysis: Gray mold, a widespread plant disease, is caused by a fungus (*Botrytis cinerea*). The fungus initially attacks foliage and flowers that are weak or dead, causing spotting and mold. The fuzzy mold that develops is composed of millions of microscopic spores. Once gray mold has become established on plant debris and weak or dying leaves and flowers, it can invade healthy plant tissue. The fungus is spread by splashing water and by bits of infected plant debris that land on the leaves. Crowded plantings, rain, and overhead watering enhance the spread of the disease. Cool temperatures, moisture, and high humidity promote gray mold growth. (For more information on gray mold, also called botrytis blight, see page 418.)

Solution: Spray infected plants with a fungicide containing *chlorothalonil*, repeating according to label directions as long as mold is visible or the weather remains favorable for the disease. Remove old flowers and dying or infected leaves and stems. Clean up and destroy plant debris. Avoid wetting the foliage.

Greenhouse whiteflies

Whiteflies (½ life size).

Problem: Tiny, white, winged insects ¹⁄₁₆ inch long feed mainly on the undersides of leaves. Nonflying, scalelike larvae covered with white waxy powder may also be present on the undersides of leaves. When the plant is touched, insects flutter rapidly around it. Leaves may be mottled and yellow. In warm-winter areas, black mold may cover the leaves. The plant may grow poorly.

Analysis: The greenhouse whitefly (*Trialeurodes vaporariorum*) is a common insect pest of many garden and greenhouse plants. The four-winged adult lays eggs on the undersides of leaves. The larvae remain attached to the undersides of leaves for about a month before changing to the adult form. Both larval and adult forms suck sap from the leaves. The larvae are more damaging because they feed more heavily. In warm-winter areas, the insect can be active year-round, with eggs, larvae, and adults present at the same time. The whitefly is unable to live through freezing winters. Spring reinfestations in freezing-winter areas come from migrating whiteflies and from infested plants placed in the garden.

Solution: Control whiteflies by spraying with Ortho® Rose & Flower Insect Killer, Ortho® Systemic Insect Killer, or Ortho® Malathion Plus® Insect Spray Concentrate every 7 to 10 days as necessary, being careful to cover both the upper and lower surfaces of the leaves. Whiteflies may also be partially controlled with yellow sticky traps. Eliminating weed hosts in and around the garden will help reduce whitefly populations.

Tobacco budworms and corn earworms

Corn earworms (⅛ life size).

Problem: Striped green, brown, or yellow caterpillars are chewing holes in leaves and buds. The caterpillars range in size from ¼ to 2 inches long.

Analysis: The closely related caterpillars, tobacco budworm and corn earworm (*Heliothis* species), are the larval stages of night-flying moths. In addition to feeding on many different ornamental plants, the caterpillars of both moths are major agricultural pests. The corn earworm especially is considered one of the most destructive pests of corn in the country. The moths survive the winter as pupae in the soil, emerging in the spring to lay their light yellow eggs singly on the undersides of leaves. The caterpillars hatch in two to eight days and feed for several weeks on leaves and buds, then crawl into the soil and pupate. The new adults emerge one to three weeks later to begin the cycle again, laying eggs in the evenings and on warm, overcast days. In cooler areas of the country, the caterpillars are present from early spring to the first frost. In warmer areas, the feeding caterpillars are present year-round.

Solution: Control corn earworms and tobacco budworms with Ortho® Systemic Insect Killer or Ortho® Rose & Flower Insect Killer. Apply when the caterpillars first appear. Repeat every 10 to 14 days as needed. Deep cultivating in the fall and winter will help destroy some of the overwintering pupae.

ALCEA (Hollyhock)

Rust

Rust.

Problem: Yellow or orange spots appear on the upper surfaces of leaves in the early spring. Grayish-brown pustules develop on the undersides of leaves. These pustules may turn dark brown to black as the growing season progresses. Severely infected leaves shrivel, turn gray or tan, and hang down.

Analysis: A fungus (*Puccinia malvacearum*) causes rust, the most serious and widespread disease on hollyhocks. The fungus spends the winter as spores on living plant tissue and plant debris. Infection starts in the early spring as soon as conditions are favorable for plant growth. Splashing water and air currents spread the spores to healthy plants. Several weeds known as cheeseweeds or mallows (*Malva* species) are frequently infected with rust and are a source of spores. Rust favors wet conditions.

Solution: Spray with Ortho® Garden Disease Control or with a fungicide containing *triadimefon* in the spring as soon as the first signs of infection are noticed. Spray the foliage thoroughly, being sure to cover both the upper and lower surfaces of the leaves. The fungicide protects the new, healthy foliage but will not eradicate the fungus on diseased leaves. Spray once every 7 to 10 days or as often as necessary to protect new growth until the end of the growing season. Remove and destroy all infected foliage and any nearby cheeseweeds in the fall when the plant has stopped growing and again in early spring. Pick off and destroy infected plant parts during the growing season. Water early in the day so that foliage will dry thoroughly.

ALLIUM (Ornamental onion)

Two-spotted spider mites

Spider mites and webbing.

Problem: Leaves are stippled, yellowing, and dirty. Leaves may dry out and drop. There may be fine webbing over flower buds, between leaves, or on the lower surfaces of leaves. Plants lose vigor. Discoloration is most severe during hot, dry weather. To determine if a plant is infested with twospotted spider mites, hold a sheet of white paper underneath an affected leaf and tap the leaf sharply. Minute specks the size of pepper grains will drop to the paper and begin to crawl. These pests are easily seen against the white background. Mites can also be seen with a 10× hand lens.

Analysis: Two-spotted spider mites (*Tetranychus urticae*), related to spiders, are major pests of many garden and greenhouse plants. They cause damage by sucking sap from the undersides of leaves. As a result of their feeding, the chlorophyll disappears, producing the stippled appearance. Spider mite webbing traps cast-off skins and debris, making the plant dirty. Mites are active throughout the growing season but favor hot, dry weather (70°F and higher). (For more information on spider mites, see page 457.)

Solution: Spray with Ortho® Systemic Insect Killer or Ortho® Rose & Flower Insect Killer when damage is first noticed. Spray the foliage thoroughly, covering both the upper and lower surfaces of the leaves. Repeat the spraying two more times at 7- to 10-day intervals.

Thrips

Thrips feeding damage.

Problem: Silvery white streaks appear on the leaves, and the leaf tips may be brown and distorted. The leaves may eventually wither and die. If affected leaves are peeled away from the stem, tiny (1/25-inch) insects resembling brown or straw-colored wood slivers can be seen moving around.

Analysis: Several species of this common insect pest, including onion thrips (*Thrips tabaci*), attack allium. Thrips are usually found in the protected area between the base of the leaves and the stem, where they feed by rasping the soft plant tissue, then sucking the released sap. In cold climates, thrips feed and reproduce from spring until fall. With the onset of freezing weather, they find sheltered areas, such as grass clumps, and hibernate through the winter. In warm-winter climates, thrips feed and reproduce all year. These pests reach their population peak in late spring to midsummer. They are especially troublesome during prolonged warm, dry spells.

Solution: Thrips can be kept under control but not eliminated entirely. Spray plants with Ortho® Rose & Flower Insect Killer or Ortho® Systemic Insect Killer Concentrate two or three times at weekly intervals. Repeat the spray if reinfestation occurs. Remove and destroy infested leaves.

ANTIRRHINUM (Snapdragon)

Rust

Rust.

Problem: Pale yellow spots appear on the upper surfaces of leaves. Reddish-brown pustules of spores develop on the undersides of leaves. Often these pustules form concentric circles. Spore masses may be on the stems. Severely infected leaves dry up. The plant is stunted and may die prematurely.

Analysis: Rust is a common disease of snapdragons caused by a fungus (*Puccinia antirrhini*). Wind and splashing water spread the fungal spores. Rust can survive only on living plant tissue and as spores on seed. It does not persist on dead plant parts. Plants must be wet for six to eight hours before the fungus can infect the leaf surface. The disease favors moist conditions, cool nights (50° to 55°F), and warm days (70° to 75°F). Temperatures in the 90°F range and higher kill the spores.

Solution: Spray infected plants with Ortho® Lawn Disease Control or with a fungicide containing *mancozeb* at intervals of five to eight days. Avoid wetting the foliage. To give foliage a chance to dry out, water in the morning rather than in the late afternoon or evening. Pick off and destroy infected plant parts during the growing season. Remove all snapdragon plants at the end of the growing season to prevent infected plants from infecting new plantings. Space plants far enough apart to allow good air circulation. Plant resistant varieties.

Root and stem rot

Root and stem rot.

Problem: The plant may suddenly wilt and die, or it may die slowly from the top down. The leaves turn yellow, and overall growth is stunted. There may be lesions on the stems. The roots are decayed.

Analysis: Root and stem rot is a disease caused by several different fungi that live in the soil. These fungi thrive in waterlogged, heavy soils. They can attack the plant stems and roots directly or enter them through wounds. Infection causes stems and roots to decay, resulting in wilting, yellowing leaves and plant death. These fungi are generally spread by infested soil and transplants, contaminated equipment, and moving water. Many of these organisms also cause *damping-off* of seedlings (see page 420).

Solution: Let the soil dry out between watering. (For more information on this technique, see page 419.) Improve soil drainage. (For information on drainage, see page 406.)

AQUILEGIA (Columbine)

Columbine leafminers

Leafminer damage.

Problem: White or gray winding trails appear in the leaves. Some of the trails contain scattered black matter. Infested leaves may be almost covered by white trails. Leaves may die.

Analysis: The columbine leafminer (*Phytomyza aquilegivora*) is an insect that belongs to the family of leafmining flies. The pale brown adult fly lays its eggs on the undersides of leaves. The eggs hatch, and the larvae that emerge penetrate the leaf and live between the upper and lower surfaces of the leaf. They feed on the inner leaf tissue, creating winding trails. Dark excrement may dot or partially fill sections of the trails. The larvae may be present continually from spring through fall.

Solution: Spray with Ortho® Rose & Flower Insect Killer or Ortho® Systemic Insect Killer. Respray at the first sign of further infestation. Pick off and destroy infested leaves. Remove and destroy all plant remains in the fall.

Crown rot or wilt

Crown rot.

Problem: Leaves and stems are wilting. The diseased branches slowly dry out and finally die. White fungal strands may grow on the stems of severely infected plants. When sliced open, an infected stem may be filled with white fungal threads and small black fungal pellets. The soil around the plant may be filled with white fungal strands and brown spherical pellets the size of a pinhead.

Analysis: Crown rot or wilt is a disease caused by a fungus (*Sclerotinia sclerotiorum*) that lives in the soil. The fungus survives the winter as fungal strands and dormant pellets in plant debris or in the soil. It favors high humidity and moist soils and attacks plant roots or stem tissue at the soil line. *Sclerotinia* produces windblown spores in the spring and summer that may also infect the foliage. As the fungus spreads within the plant, wilting and eventual death occur. *Sclerotinia* can persist in the soil for three years or more. It is spread by infested soil and transplants.

Solution: Remove and destroy diseased plants and discard the soil immediately around them. The fungicide *flutolanil* is registered for control of southern blight on ornamentals, but is available only to licensed pest control operators. Let the soil dry out between waterings. (For information on watering, see page 419.) Cultivate the soil around the crown of the plant to help it dry out more quickly.

Aphids

Aphid (10× life size).

Problem: Young leaves are curled, distorted, and yellowing. Flowers may be malformed. A sticky or shiny substance may coat the leaves. Tiny (⅛-inch) pale green to black, soft-bodied insects are clustered on the leaves and stems. Ants may be present.

Analysis: Aphids do little damage in small numbers. They are extremely prolific, however, and populations can rapidly build to damaging numbers during the growing season. Damage occurs when the aphids suck the juices from the leaves and flower buds. The aphids are unable to digest all the sugar in the plant sap and excretes the excess in a fluid called *honeydew*. The honeydew often drops onto the leaves below. Ants feed on this sticky substance and are often present where there is an aphid infestation. (For more information on aphids, see page 443.)

Solution: Spray with Ortho® Systemic Insect Killer or Ortho® Bug-B-Gon® Multi-Purpose Insect Killer Ready-To-Use as soon as the insects appear. Repeat the spray if the plant is reinfested. Avoid spraying when bees are present.

Root nematodes

Root nematode damage.

Problem: The plant is stunted and growing poorly. Leaves may be curled and yellowed. The plant pulls out of the ground easily. Roots are sparse, short, and dark. Small knots (¹⁄₁₆ inch) may be visible on roots.

Analysis: Root nematodes are microscopic worms that live in the soil. They feed on plant roots, damaging and stunting them or causing them to become enlarged. The damaged roots can't supply sufficient water and nutrients to the above-ground plant parts, and the plant becomes stunted or slowly dies. Nematodes are found throughout the United States, especially in areas with moist, sandy loam soil. They can move only a few inches per year on their own, but they may be carried long distances by soil, water, tools, or infested plants. Laboratory testing of roots and soil is the only positive method for confirming the presence of nematodes. Contact your local county extension office for sampling instructions and addresses of testing laboratories. Problems such as poor soil structure, drought stress, overwatering, nutrient deficiency, and root rots can produce symptoms of decline similar to those caused by nematodes. Root weevils, such as the black vine weevil, may also cause similar symptoms. Eliminate these problems as causes before sending soil and root samples for testing.

Solution: No chemicals available to homeowners kill nematodes in planted soil. Nematodes can be controlled before planting, however, by soil fumigation or solarization techniques.

BEGONIA

Gray mold

Gray mold.

Problem: Brown spots and blotches appear on leaves and possibly on the stems. As the disease progresses, a fuzzy brown or grayish mold forms on the infected tissue. Gray mold and spots often appear on the flowers, especially during periods of cool, wet weather. The leaves and stems may be soft and rotted.

Analysis: Gray mold is a widespread plant disease caused by a fungus (*Botrytis cinerea*) that is found on most dead plant tissue. The fungus initially attacks foliage and flowers that are weak or dead, causing spotting and mold. The fuzzy mold that develops is composed of millions of microscopic dark spores. Once gray mold has become established on plant debris and weak or dying leaves and flowers, it can invade healthy plant tissue. The fungus is spread by splashing water and by bits of infected plant debris that land on the leaves. Cool temperatures, moisture, and high humidity favor the growth of gray mold. Crowded plantings, rain, and overhead watering also promote the spread of the disease. Infection is a greater problem in spring and fall, when temperatures are lower. In warm-winter areas where freezing is rare, gray mold can be a year-round problem. (For more information on gray mold, see page 418.)

Solution: Control gray mold with a fungicide containing *chlorothalonil* or *mancozeb*. Spray every one to two weeks for as long as the mold is visible. Clean up plant debris, and remove dying or infected leaves, stems, and flowers. Provide enough space between plants to allow good air circulation. Avoid wetting the foliage when watering.

Leaf spot

Leaf spot.

Problem: Spots and blotches appear on the leaves. The spots may be yellow, red, tan, gray, or brown. They range in size from barely visible to ¼ inch in diameter. Several spots may join to form blotches. Leaves may be yellowing and dying. Leaf spotting is most severe in warm, humid weather.

Analysis: Begonias are susceptible to several fungi that cause leaf spot. Some of these fungi may eventually kill the plant or weaken it so that it becomes susceptible to attack by other organisms. Others merely cause spotting that is unsightly but not harmful. These fungi are spread by splashing water, wind, insects, tools, and infected transplants and seed. They survive the winter in diseased plant debris. Some leaf spot organisms affect a large number of plants. Most of these fungi do their greatest damage during mild weather (50° to 85°F). Infection is promoted by moist conditions.

Solution: Spray with a fungicide containing *chlorothalonil* or *mancozeb* every 7 to 10 days. Because leaf spots thrive in warm, humid conditions, it is important to spray frequently during these periods. This fungicide protects the new, healthy foliage. It will not eradicate the fungus on leaves that are already infected, however. Clean up and destroy infected leaves and debris. Water early in the day to allow the leaves to dry by nightfall.

Bacterial leaf spot

Bacterial leaf spot.

Problem: Small, blisterlike spots appear on the leaves. The spots are translucent and turn brown with yellow margins. Spots enlarge and run together, giving the leaf a blotchy appearance. Sometimes a slimy substance oozes from the infected areas, turning light brown as it dries. Infected leaves often die prematurely. If the stems become infected, the entire plant may collapse.

Analysis: Bacterial leaf spot is a disease caused by bacteria (*Xanthomonas campestris* pv. *begoniae*) that infect tuberous and fibrous begonias. The slimy substance that oozes from infected lesions is composed of bacterial cells that can live for three months or more. The bacteria are spread by splashing water, contaminated equipment, and infected transplants. Infection is promoted by high humidity. Localized leaf infection causes early leaf drop. If the plant's water-conducting tissue is infected, the whole plant softens and collapses.

Solution: Spray with a copper-based compound at intervals of 7 to 10 days to prevent the spread of the disease. Infected tissue will not recover, but new growth and healthy leaves will be protected. Cut off and discard infected plant parts. Disinfect tools after working with diseased plants. Remove and destroy severely infected plants and the soil immediately surrounding them. Avoid wetting or splashing water on the leaves. Space plants far enough apart to allow good air circulation.

Leaf nematode

Leaf nematode damage.

Problem: Angular brown leaf blotches develop first on the lower leaves, then on the upper. The blotches enlarge, and eventually the leaves curl up, wither, and drop off. The plant is stunted, and new leaf buds may not develop.

Analysis: This plant condition is caused by leaf nematodes (*Aphelenchoides olesistus*)—microscopic worms that live and feed inside the leaf tissue. Infestation occurs when the foliage is wet. Nematodes migrate in the thin film of water on the outside of the leaf to infect healthy tissue. They are spread from plant to plant by splashing water and are most severe in warm, humid areas. Leaf nematodes can survive for three years or more in plant debris and in the soil.

Solution: Remove and destroy severely infested plants. Pick off and destroy all infested leaves and the two leaves directly above them. Nematodes can be killed with heat. Soak infested plants in hot water (130° to 140°F) for 15 minutes. As much as possible, avoid wetting the foliage. Inspect new plants carefully to be sure they are not diseased, and do not plant in infested soil.

Mealybugs

Mealybugs (½ life size).

Problem: White, oval insects up to ¼ inch long form white, cottony masses on stems and leaves. Leaves may be deformed and withered. Infested leaves may be shiny and sticky or covered with a sooty mold.

Analysis: Several species of this common insect feed on begonias. Mealybugs damage plants by sucking sap, causing leaf distortion and death. The adult female mealybug may produce young or deposit her eggs in white, fluffy masses of wax. The immature mealybugs, called *nymphs*, are very active and crawl on the plants. Soon after the nymphs begin to feed, they exude filaments of white wax that cover their bodies, giving them a cottony appearance. As they mature, their mobility decreases. Mealybugs can't digest all the sugar in the sap, and they excrete the excess in a fluid called *honeydew*. Mealybugs can be spread when they are brushed onto uninfested plants or when young, active nymphs crawl to nearby plants. They may also be spread by the wind, which can blow egg masses and nymphs from plant to plant. Mealybug eggs and some adults can survive through the winter in warm climates. Spring reinfestations in colder areas come from infested new plants placed in the garden.

Solution: Spray infested plants with Ortho® Rose & Flower Insect Killer or Ortho® Systemic Insect Killer. Spray at intervals of 7 to 10 days until the mealybugs are gone. Spray water on plants to wash off honeydew. Remove and destroy severely infested leaves and plants.

Cabbage loopers

Cabbage loopers (⅓ life size).

Problem: Foliage and flower buds are chewed. Leaves have ragged edges and irregular or round holes. Green caterpillars up to 1½ inches long with faint white stripes feed on the leaves.

Analysis: Cabbage loopers (*Trichoplusia ni*) are destructive caterpillars that feed on many garden ornamentals and vegetables. With the warm weather of spring, the brownish adult moth lays its tiny, pale green eggs at night on the upper surfaces of leaves. The eggs hatch into active green larvae, which feed extensively on buds and foliage for two to four weeks. Looper damage can occur from early spring through late fall. The caterpillars spend the winter as pupae attached to plant leaves.

Solution: Spray with Ortho® Systemic Insect Killer or Ortho® Bug-B-Gon® Multi-Purpose Insect Killer Ready-To-Use when the caterpillars first appear. Repeat 10 to 14 days later if reinfestation occurs. In the fall, remove plant debris and weeds that may harbor pupae. The bacterial insecticide *Bacillus thuringiensis* (Bt) is effective when sprayed on young loopers.

CALLISTEPHUS (China aster)

Aster yellows

Aster yellows.

Problem: Leaf veins pale and may lose all their color. Part or all of the foliage yellows. The flowers are distorted and may turn green. The plant may grow many thin stems bearing pale, spindly leaves. The plant is usually dwarfed.

Analysis: Aster yellows is a plant disease caused by phytoplasmas, microscopic organisms similar to bacteria. The phytoplasmas are transmitted from plant to plant by leafhoppers. (For information on leafhoppers, see page 448.) The symptoms of aster yellows are more severe and appear more quickly in warm weather. Although the disease may be present in the plant, aster yellows may not manifest its symptoms in temperatures of 55°F or lower. Aster yellows infects many ornamental plants, vegetables, and weeds. (For a list of plants susceptible to aster yellows, see page 546.)

Solution: Aster yellows can't be eliminated entirely, but it can be controlled. Remove and destroy infected China asters and other ornamentals showing aster yellows infection. To remove sources of infection, eradicate nearby weeds that may harbor aster yellows and leafhopper eggs. Spray leafhopper-infested plants with Ortho® Systemic Insect Killer or Ortho® Rose & Flower Insect Killer. Repeat the spray whenever leafhoppers are seen.

CAMPANULA (Bellflower)

Leaf spot

Leaf spot.

Problem: Spots and blotches appear on the leaves. The spots may be yellow, red, tan, gray, or brown. They range in size from barely visible to ¼ inch in diameter. Several spots may join to form blotches. Leaves may be yellow and dying. Leaf spotting is most severe in warm, humid weather. In damp conditions, a fine gray mold sometimes covers the infected leaf tissue.

Analysis: Several different fungi cause leaf spot. These fungi usually cause spotting that is unsightly but not harmful. They are spread by splashing water, wind, insects, and tools. They generally survive the winter in diseased plant debris. Most of the leaf spot organisms do their greatest damage in mild weather (50° to 85°F).

Solution: Spray the diseased plants with a fungicide containing basic copper sulfate at intervals of 5 to 10 days. Pick off severely infected leaves. Because leaf spot thrives in warm, humid conditions, it is important to spray frequently during these periods. Basic copper sulfate protects the new, healthy foliage but will not eradicate the fungus on infected leaves.

CANNA

Bud rot

Bud rot.

Problem: The newly opened young leaves may be partially or entirely black, or they may be covered with tiny white spots. The older leaves may be distorted and are often covered with yellow or brown spots and streaks. In many cases, the flower buds turn black and die before they open. Entire stalks are often decayed. A sticky substance may coat infected leaf tissue.

Analysis: Bud rot is a plant disease caused by bacteria (*Xanthomonas* species) that usually attack the young canna leaves and flowers while they are still curled in the buds. The bacteria can spread from the leaves and flowers into the stems, causing plant death. Some of the infected tissue may exude a sticky ooze filled with bacteria. The bacteria are spread by splashing water and rain and by direct contact with equipment, hands, and insects. Wet conditions enhance the spread of the disease. Bud rot survives through the winter in diseased rhizomes, contaminated soil, and infected plant debris.

Solution: There are no effective chemical controls for this disease. To control bud rot, it is important to reduce excess moisture around the plants. Water in the morning so the foliage will dry out during the day. Avoid wetting the foliage. Space plants far enough apart to allow good air circulation. Pick off infected leaves and flowers. Remove severely diseased plants and the soil immediately surrounding them. Clean up plant debris. Plant only healthy plants and rhizomes. (For information on choosing healthy plants, see page 415.)

CATHARANTHUS

Phytophthora blight

Phytophthera blight.

Problem: Leaves shrivel and turn brownish green, then brown or black. Eventually the entire plant collapses. The roots are healthy.

Analysis: Phytophthora blight is a plant disease caused by a soil-borne fungus (*Phytophthora parasitica*) that infects a wide variety of garden plants. It is the most serious disease of periwinkle, capable of killing a plant in two weeks. Although the fungus is found in the soil, it doesn't attack the roots; it attacks only the stems and leaves of periwinkle. It can be distinguished from root rot diseases by the healthy roots. The spores are splashed by rain or watering drops onto the plant tops. This fungus, one of a group called *water molds*, is promoted by waterlogged soil and humid or wet weather. (For more information on water molds, see page 419.) During hot, wet conditions, it can destroy whole beds in a short time.

Solution: Infected plants can't be cured. To avoid future problems, mulch the bed to avoid splashing spores onto the plants. Space plants far enough apart to allow good air circulation. Use drip irrigation if possible. If you use overhead watering, do it early enough in the day that the plants will dry quickly. In the future, select tolerant flowers.

CENTAUREA

Root and stem rot

Root and stem rot on dusty miller.

Problem: Leaves turn yellow, wilt, and eventually die. The roots and lower part of the stems may be soft and rotten. There may be white fungal strands on infected stems and around the base of the plant.

Analysis: Root and stem rot is a disease caused by any of several different fungi, also known as *water molds*, that persist indefinitely in the soil. These fungi thrive in waterlogged, heavy soil. Some of them attack the plant stems at the soil level, while others attack the roots. Infection causes the roots and stems to decay. This results in wilting, then yellowing leaves, and eventually the death of the plant. These fungi are generally spread by infested soil and transplants, contaminated equipment, and splashing or running water. Many of these organisms also cause damping-off of seedlings. (For more information on damping-off, see page 420.)

Solution: Allow the soil around the plant to dry out. (For more information on this technique, see page 419.) Remove and discard severely infected plants. Avoid future root rot problems by planting in well-drained soil.

CHRYSANTHEMUM

Leggy growth

Weak, leggy growth.

Problem: Plants are leggy, and many of the stems are thin and spindly. Some plants topple and may need to be tied.

Analysis: Leggy growth in mums can be caused by two things.
1. Natural growth pattern: Most mum varieties grow tall and leggy.
2. Too much shade: Mums are sun-loving plants. When planted in a shaded area the plants produce thin, leggy growth even when pinched back. Under shady conditions, the plants may not flower well.

Solution: The numbered solutions below correspond to the numbered items in the analysis. To prevent leggy growth, follow these guidelines:
1. Plants that are leggy may be pinched back to encourage bushier growth as long as they have not yet formed flower buds. The following year, when new plants are 6 to 8 inches tall, carefully pinch or nip off the young growing tips just above a leaf. The tiny side bud located between this leaf and the stem will grow into a new branch. Every two weeks, pinch back all the new growing points that have formed as a result of the previous pinching. Stop pinching the plant by August to let flower buds develop. Purchase low-growing mum varieties.
2. Move or transplant chrysanthemums to a location that receives at least four or five hours of direct sun daily.

CHRYSANTHEMUM *(continued)*

Powdery mildew

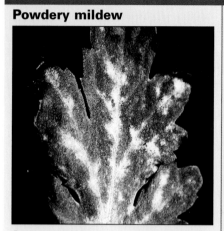

Powdery mildew.

Problem: Powdery grayish-white powdery spots and patches cover the leaves and stems, primarily the upper surfaces of leaves. The leaves eventually yellow and wither.

Analysis: Powdery mildew is a common plant disease caused by a fungus (*Erysiphe cichoracearum*) that thrives in both humid and dry weather. The powdery patches consist of fungal strands and spores. The spores are spread by the wind to healthy plants. The fungus saps plant nutrients, causing leaf yellowing and sometimes death of the leaf. Since this powdery mildew attacks many different kinds of plants, the fungus from a diseased plant may infect other types of plants in the garden. (For a list of plants susceptible to powdery mildew, see page 537.) Under favorable conditions, powdery mildew can spread rapidly through a closely spaced planting.

Solution: Spray infected plants with Ortho® Garden Disease Control to stop the spread of the disease. The fungicide protects the new, healthy foliage but will not eradicate the fungus on leaves that are already infected. Spray at regular intervals of 7 to 10 days or as often as necessary to protect new growth. Space plants far enough apart to allow good air circulation. Plant in a site with good aeration and early morning sun. Clean up and destroy infected leaves and debris.

Rust

Rust.

Problem: Pale spots appear on the upper surfaces of leaves. Chocolate-brown pustules of spores form on the undersides of leaves and on the stems. Infected leaves may wither and fall prematurely. The plant is stunted and may die.

Analysis: Rust is a common disease of chrysanthemums caused by a fungus (*Puccinia tanaceti*). Wind and splashing water spread the fungal spores. Rust can survive only on living plant tissue and as spores on seed; it does not persist on dead plant parts. Plants must remain wet for six to eight hours before the fungus can infect the leaf surface. The disease is favored by moist conditions, cool nights, and warm days. Temperatures of 90°F and higher, if maintained for 24 hours, kill the spores.

Solution: Spray infected plants with Ortho® Garden Disease Control at weekly intervals as soon as the disease is noticed; continue spraying throughout the growing season when weather conditions are favorable for disease. To allow wet foliage to dry out more quickly, water in the morning rather than in the late afternoon or evening. Pick off and destroy infected plant parts during the growing season. Space plants far enough apart to allow good air circulation. Remove and destroy all infected plants in the fall to keep them from reinfecting new plantings. The following year, grow only rust-resistant varieties. Rust can survive the winter on old infected plant parts. (For mums resistant to rust, see page 546.)

Leaf nematodes

Leaf nematode damage.

Problem: Fan-shaped or angular yellow-brown to gray leaf blotches develop progressively upward from the lower leaves. The blotches join together, and the leaf turns brown or black. The leaf then withers, dies, and hangs along the stem. The plant is stunted, and new leaf buds don't develop. In the spring, young, succulent, leafy growth becomes thickened, distorted, and brittle.

Analysis: The cause of this damage is a microscopic worm called a leaf nematode (*Aphelenchoides ritzema-bosi*) that lives and feeds inside the leaf tissue. The nematode is restricted in its movement by larger leaf veins. This confined feeding range creates the angular shape of the blotch. When the foliage is wet, the nematode migrates in the thin film of water on the outside of the leaf to infect healthy tissue. This pest is spread from plant to plant by splashing water. It penetrates the plant tissue by entering through small breathing pores on the underside of the leaf. Leaf nematodes are most damaging in warm, wet-summer regions of the country. They can survive for three years or more in plant debris and in soil.

Solution: Remove and destroy severely infested plants. Pick off and destroy all infested leaves and the two leaves directly above them. Avoid wetting the foliage as much as possible. Check new plants carefully to be sure they aren't diseased, and don't replant them in infested soil.

Leaf spot

Leaf spot.

Problem: Spots and blotches appear on the leaves. The spots may be yellow, tan, brown, or black. They range in size from barely visible to more than 1 inch in diameter. Several spots may join to form blotches. Leaves may turn yellow and drop, or they may wither and hang along the stem.

Analysis: Several different fungi cause leaf spot on chrysanthemums. Some of these may eventually kill the plant or weaken it so that it becomes susceptible to attack by other organisms. Others merely cause spotting that is unsightly but not harmful. These fungi are spread by splashing water or by wind. They generally survive the winter in diseased plant debris. Most of these fungi do their greatest damage in moist, mild weather (50° to 85°F).

Solution: Where practical, pick off and destroy infected leaves. Spray the plants weekly throughout the growing season with a fungicide containing *chlorothalonil*.

Thrips

Thrips damage.

Problem: Silvery white streaks and flecks appear on the leaves and flowers. Damaged leaves may become papery and distorted, dropping prematurely. Many shiny black specks are scattered on leaf surfaces. The leaves and flowers may be distorted and brown. Damage may appear in one location, then slowly spread over the plant. Shake a blossom or tap a leaf over a sheet of paper. Tiny (1/20-inch) insects resembling brown or straw-colored wood slivers can be seen. When disturbed, they hop or fly.

Analysis: Several species of this common insect attack chrysanthemums. Thrips are generally found in protected locations such as the insides of the leaf and flower buds, where they feed by rasping the soft plant tissue, then sucking the released plant sap. The injured tissue dies and turns white, causing the characteristic streaking of the leaves and flowers. In cold climates, thrips feed and reproduce from spring until fall, then hibernate through the winter. In warm-winter climates, thrips feed and reproduce all year. These pests reach their peak in late spring to midsummer. They are especially troublesome during prolonged dry spells.

Solution: Thrips can be kept under control but not eliminated entirely. Spray plants before they bloom with Ortho® Systemic Insect Killer, Ortho® Rose & Flower Insect Killer, or Ortho® Orthenex® Garden Insect & Disease Control Aerosol two or three times at weekly intervals. Repeat the spray if reinfestation occurs. Pick off and destroy old infested leaves and flowers. Keep beds and borders free of weeds.

Verticillium wilt

Verticillium wilt.

Problem: Leaves yellow, wilt, and die, starting with the lower leaves and progressing up the plant. Older plants may be stunted. Leaf wilting and death often affect only one side of the plant. Flowering is poor. Dark brown areas may be on the infected stems. When the stem is sliced open near the base of the plant, dark streaks and discoloration of the water-conducting inner stem tissue are revealed.

Analysis: Verticillium wilt disease affects many ornamental plants. It is caused by a soil-inhabiting fungus (*Verticillium* species) that persists indefinitely on plant debris or in the soil. The disease is spread by contaminated seeds, plants, soil, equipment, and groundwater. The fungus enters the plant through the roots and spreads up into the stems and leaves through the water-conducting vessels in the stems. These vessels become discolored and plugged. This plugging cuts off the flow of water to the leaves, causing leaf yellowing and wilting. (For more information on verticillium wilt, see page 420.)

Solution: No chemical control is available. It is best to destroy infected plants. *Verticillium* can be removed from the soil only by fumigation or solarization techniques. The best solution is to plant flowers that are resistant to *Verticillium*.

Annuals, Perennials, and Bulbs *(continued)*

CHRYSANTHEMUM *(continued)*

Mosaic virus

Mosaic virus.

Problem: Leaves are mottled, and the leaf veins may turn pale. Plants may be dwarfed and bushy. Flowers are small and may have brown streaks. Leaves, stems, and flowers may be deformed.

Analysis: Mosaic virus is a plant disease caused by several different viruses. Mosaic is primarily transmitted from plant to plant by aphids. The symptoms of mosaic virus can vary considerably in their severity depending on the type of virus and variety of chrysanthemum. Viruses can be transmitted to chrysanthemums from many weeds and ornamental plants. Some plants may be infected with mosaic virus without showing the typical symptoms.

Solution: Infected plants can't be cured. They should be immediately removed and destroyed. Spray aphid-infested plants in the area with Ortho® Systemic Insect Killer or Ortho® Malathion Plus® Insect Spray Concentrate. Repeat the spray at intervals of seven days as often as necessary to keep the aphids under control. For spot-treatment of a few plants use Ortho® Rose & Flower Insect Killer according to label directions. To reduce the numbers of plants that may harbor viruses, keep your garden free of weeds.

Aster yellows

Aster yellows.

Problem: Leaf veins pale and may lose all their color. Part or all of the foliage turns yellow. Leaf edges may turn brown. The flowers are dwarfed and distorted and may turn green. The plant may grow many thin stems bearing pale, spindly leaves. The plant is generally stunted.

Analysis: Aster yellows is a plant disease caused by phytoplasmas, microscopic organisms similar to bacteria. The phytoplasmas are transmitted from plant to plant primarily by leafhoppers. (For information on leafhoppers, see page 448.) The symptoms of aster yellows are more severe and appear more quickly in warm weather. Although the disease may be present in the plant, aster yellows may not manifest its symptoms in temperatures of 55°F or lower. The disease infects many ornamental plants, vegetables, and weeds. (For a list of plants susceptible to aster yellows, see page 546.)

Solution: Aster yellows can't be eliminated entirely, but it can be controlled. Remove and destroy infected ornamental plants. To remove sources of infection, eradicate nearby weeds that may harbor aster yellows and leafhopper eggs. Spray leafhopper-infested plants with Ortho® Systemic Insect Killer or Ortho® Bug-B-Gon® Multi-Purpose Insect Killer Ready-To-Use. Repeat the spray whenever leafhoppers are seen. (For more information on disease-carrying insect control, see page 449.)

Leafminers

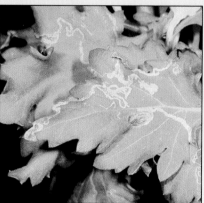

Leafminer trails in chrysanthemum leaf.

Problem: Light-colored, irregular, winding trails or tunnels appear in the leaves. Some of the trails are filled with black matter. Severely infested leaves dry up and hang along the stems or drop off.

Analysis: The chrysanthemum leafminer (*Phytomyza syngenesiae*) is an insect that belongs to the family of leafmining flies. The minute adult fly lays its eggs in punctures it makes in young leaves. The larvae that emerge tunnel just below the upper leaf surface. They feed on the inner leaf tissue, creating winding trails. Their dark excrement may dot or partially fill sections of the trails. The larvae are present from spring through fall.

Solution: Spray with Ortho® Rose & Flower Insect Killer or Ortho® Systemic Insect Killer. Respray at the first sign of further infestation. Pick off and destroy infected leaves. Remove and destroy all plant remains in the fall.

Aphids

Aphids (life size).

Problem: Young leaves are curled, stunted, and yellowing. Flowers may be malformed. A sticky or shiny substance may coat the leaves. Tiny (⅛-inch) soft-bodied insects that range in color from pale green to dark brown or black are clustered on the leaves and stems. Ants may be present.

Analysis: Aphids do little damage in small numbers. They are extremely prolific, however, and populations can rapidly build to damaging numbers during the growing season. Damage occurs when aphids suck the juices from the chrysanthemum leaves and flower buds. Aphids are unable to digest all the sugar in the plant sap and excretes the excess in a fluid called *honeydew*. The honeydew often drops onto the leaves below. Ants feed on this sticky substance and are often present where there is an aphid infestation. Aphids can also be responsible for spreading viral diseases. (For more information on aphids, see page 443.)

Solution: Spray with Ortho® Systemic Insect Killer, Ortho® Rose & Flower Insect Killer, or Ortho® Malathion Plus® Insect Spray Concentrate as soon as the insects appear. Repeat the spray if the plant is reinfested. For spot treatment of a few plants, use Ortho® Rose & Flower Insect Killer according to label directions.

Whiteflies

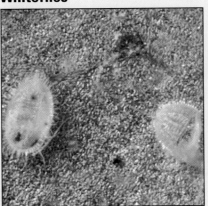

Greenhouse whitefly larvae (10× life size).

Problem: Tiny, white, winged insects, ¹⁄₁₆ inch long, feed mainly on the undersides of leaves. Nonflying, scalelike larvae covered with white, waxy powder may also be present on the undersides of leaves. When the plant is touched, insects flutter rapidly around it. Leaves may be mottled and yellow. The plant may grow poorly.

Analysis: The greenhouse whitefly (*Trialeurodes vaporariorum*) is a common insect pest of many garden and greenhouse plants. The four-winged adult lays eggs on the undersides of leaves. The larvae remain attached to the leaves for about a month before changing to the adult form. Both larval and adult forms suck sap from the leaves. The larvae are more damaging because they feed more heavily. Whiteflies excrete a fluid called *honeydew*, which coats the leaves. A sooty mold fungus may develop on the honeydew, causing leaves to appear black and dirty. In warm-winter areas, insects can be active year-round. The whitefly is unable to live through freezing winters. Spring reinfestations in freezing-winter areas come from migrating whiteflies and from infested greenhouse-grown plants.

Solution: Control whiteflies by spraying with Ortho® Bug-B-Gon® Multi-Purpose Insect Killer Ready-Spray®, Ortho® Systemic Insect Killer, or Ortho® Malathion Plus® Insect Spray Concentrate every 7 to 10 days as necessary. Spray the foliage thoroughly, being sure to cover both the upper and lower surfaces of the leaves. Whiteflies may also be partially controlled with yellow sticky traps.

Mealybugs

Mealybugs (5× life size).

Problem: White, oval insects up to ¼ inch long form white, cottony masses on the stems and leaves. Leaves may be deformed and withered. The infested leaves are often shiny and sticky. Ants may be present.

Analysis: Several species of this common insect feed on coleus. Mealybugs damage plants by sucking sap, causing leaf distortion and death. The adult female mealybug may produce young or deposit her eggs in white, fluffy masses of wax. The immature mealybugs, called *nymphs*, are very active and crawl on the plant. Soon after the nymphs begin to feed, they exude filaments of white wax that cover their bodies, giving them a cottony appearance. As they mature, their mobility decreases. Mealybugs can't digest all the sugar in the sap, and they excrete the excess in a fluid called *honeydew*, which coats the leaves. Ants may feed on the honeydew. Mealybugs are spread by the wind, which may blow egg masses and nymphs from plant to plant. Ants may also move them, or nymphs may crawl to nearby plants. Mealybug eggs and some adults can survive the winter in warm climates. Spring reinfestations in colder areas come from infested new plants placed in the garden.

Solution: Spray infested plants with Ortho® Rose & Flower Insect Killer or Ortho® Systemic Insect Killer. Spray at intervals of 7 to 10 days until the mealybugs are gone. Gently hose down plants to knock off mealybugs and wash off honeydew. Remove and destroy severely infested leaves and plants.

COREOPSIS

CYMBIDIUM

Spotted cucumber beetles

Spotted cucumber beetles.

Problem: Yellow-green, winged beetles, ¼ inch long with black spots, are chewing small holes in the leaves and flower petals.

Analysis: Several closely related spotted cucumber beetles (*Diabrotica* species, one of which is also known as the *southern corn rootworm*) feed on many vegetable and ornamental plants. The adult beetle hibernates in weeds and perennials. When temperatures reach 70°F in the spring, the adult resumes feeding on leaves and flowers. The female beetle lays eggs in or on the soil around the base of the plants. The wormlike, yellowish-white larvae feed on the plant roots and are very damaging to many vegetable crops, such as corn, cucumbers, melons, and squash. The larvae pupate in midsummer and emerge as adult beetles, which feed exclusively on foliage and flowers. The beetles are especially attracted to light-colored, late-summer flowers such as coreopsis and sunflowers.

Solution: Spray plants with Ortho® Bug-B-Gon® Multi-Purpose Insect Killer Concentrate or Ortho® Malathion Plus® Insect Spray Concentrate. Repeat the spray when plants are reinfested, allowing at least seven days between applications. Avoid spraying when bees are present because bees are also sensitive to the spray. To kill the larvae, thoroughly cultivate the soil as soon as temperatures reach 70°F in the spring. Reduce the number of hibernating beetles by cleaning up weeds in the fall.

Aster leafhoppers

Aster leafhopper damage.

Problem: Pale green, winged insects, up to ⅛ inch long, usually feed on the undersides of leaves. They hop away quickly when the plant is touched. Leaves may be stippled.

Analysis: The aster leafhopper (*Macrosteles fascifrons*), also known as the *six-spotted leafhopper,* is an insect that feeds on many ornamental and vegetable plants. It generally feeds on the undersides of leaves, sucking the plant sap, which causes the stippling. This leafhopper can infect plants with the disease aster yellows (see page 423). Leafhoppers at all stages of maturity are active throughout the growing season. Adult leafhoppers can't overwinter where temperatures approach freezing. The eggs they lay in the fall survive on perennial weeds and ornamental plants, however. The eggs hatch and the emerging insects reinfest plants when the weather warms up in the spring. Even areas that have winters so cold that the eggs can't survive are not free from infestation, because leafhoppers can migrate in the spring from warmer regions.

Solution: Spray plants with Ortho® Systemic Insect Killer or Ortho® Bug-B-Gon® Multi-Purpose Insect Killer Ready-To-Use, being sure to cover the undersides of leaves. Repeat the spray as necessary to keep the insects under control, allowing at least 10 days to pass between applications. Avoid spraying when bees are present. Eradicate nearby weeds that may harbor leafhopper eggs and aster yellows. (For more information on controlling disease-carrying insects, see page 449.)

Mosaic virus

Mosaic virus.

Problem: Leaves are mottled or streaked. Pale rings may develop on the foliage. As the leaves grow older, black or brown stripes develop along the leaf veins, and irregular, sunken blotches may form. The flowers may be marred with dark green or light-colored rings or streaks.

Analysis: Mosaic virus is a plant disease caused by several closely related viruses. The symptoms of mosaic infections vary in their severity, depending on the strain of virus and the cymbidium variety. Viral infections generally don't kill the plant but may greatly reduce its overall vigor and beauty. Mosaic persists in the plant indefinitely. Cuttings or divisions made from the diseased plant will also be infected. If diseased plants are touched or pruned, the virus can be transferred to healthy plants on contaminated hands, knives, and other gardening tools. Aphids and other insects may also transmit these viruses.

Solution: No chemicals control or eliminate viral diseases. Discard all infected plants. Wash your hands and dip pruning shears into rubbing alcohol after working on infected plants. Purchase only healthy plants. (For information on selecting healthy plants, see page 415.) Keep aphids under control. (For more information on disease-carrying aphids and their control, see page 449.)

DAHLIA

Tuber rot

Tuber rot.

Problem: Tuberous roots in storage develop dark brown, sunken areas that are usually dry and firm but are sometimes soft and mushy. Tufts of pink and yellow mold may cover part or all of the roots. Tuberous roots that have been planted may not produce any foliage. If they do, the foliage turns yellow and wilts. When dug up, the roots are rotted and moldy.

Analysis: Tuber rot is a plant disease caused primarily by two common soil-inhabiting fungi (*Fusarium* and *Botrytis* species). The fungi generally don't infect the tuberous roots unless the roots are wounded. If the roots are damaged when they are dug out of the ground, the fungi will penetrate the wounds and rot the tissue. The roots rot rapidly when they are stored in warm, humid conditions. If tuberous roots suffer frost damage while they are in storage, they will also be susceptible to fungal invasion. Sometimes tuberous roots in storage are contaminated, but the fungal decay has not progressed far enough to be noticed. When they are planted the following spring, they may not produce foliage. If they do produce foliage, the fungus causes wilting, yellowing, and eventually death of the plant. (For more information on fusarium wilt, see page 420.)

Solution: Infected roots can't be saved. To prevent tuber rot the following year, dig up the roots carefully after they have matured. Discard any roots that show decay. Handle them carefully to prevent injuries. Store the roots in peat moss in a cool, dark place that is safe from frost.

Wilt disease

Wilt disease.

Problem: The lower leaves turn yellow, wilt, and die; or all of the foliage may turn yellow and then wither. Older plants may be stunted. Yellowing and wilting often affect only one side of the plant. Flower heads droop. There may be dark brown areas on the infected stem. When the stem is split open near the base of the plant, dark streaks and discoloration are seen on the inner water-conducting stem tissue. The root system may be partially or entirely decayed.

Analysis: Wilt disease affects many ornamental plants. It is caused by either of two soil-inhabiting fungi (*Verticillium dahliae* or *Fusarium* species) that persist indefinitely on plant debris or in the soil. The disease is spread by contaminated seeds, plants, soil, and equipment. The fungus enters the plant through the roots and spreads into the stems through the water-conducting vessels in the stems. The vessels become discolored and plugged. This plugging cuts off the flow of water to the leaves, causing leaf yellowing and wilting. (For more information on wilt disease, see page 420.)

Solution: No chemical control is available. It is best to destroy infected plants. *Verticillium* and *Fusarium* can be removed from the soil only by fumigation or solarization techniques. The best solution is to use plants that are resistant to verticillium and fusarium wilt diseases.

Mosaic virus

Mosaic virus.

Problem: Leaf veins and leaf tissue next to the veins turn pale green, or the leaves may be mildly to severely mottled. The leaves are often distorted or yellowing. The plant may be stunted and bushy.

Analysis: Mosaic virus is a plant disease caused by a virus that is transmitted from plant to plant by aphids. The symptoms of mosaic virus vary considerably in their severity, depending on the plant variety. Severely affected plants will not die from mosaic, but their overall vigor and beauty are greatly reduced. In contrast, some plants infected with mosaic don't show any symptoms at all. The virus survives the winter in the roots of perennial ornamental plants and weeds.

Solution: Once infected, the plants can't be cured. Control mosaic virus by eliminating the virus-carrying aphids. Spray aphid-infested plants with Ortho® Systemic Insect Killer, Ortho® Rose & Flower Insect Killer or Ortho® Bug-B-Gon® Multi-Purpose Insect Killer Concentrate. For spot-treatment of a few plants, use Ortho® Rose & Flower Insect Killer according to label directions. Remove and destroy infected plants and nearby weeds that may harbor the virus. (For more information on controlling disease-carrying aphids, see page 449.)

DELPHINIUM

Snails and slugs

Snail and slug damage.

Problem: Holes are chewed in the leaves, or entire leaves may be sheared from the stems. Silvery trails wind around on the plants and soil nearby. Snails or slugs may be seen moving around or feeding on the plants, especially at night. Check for them by inspecting the garden at night by flashlight.

Analysis: Snails and slugs are mollusks and are related to clams, oysters, and other shellfish. They feed on a wide variety of garden plants. Like other mollusks, snails and slugs need to be moist all the time. For this reason, they avoid direct sun and dry places and hide during the day in damp places, such as under flowerpots or in thick ground covers. They emerge at night or on cloudy days to feed. Snails and slugs are similar in appearance, except that the snail has a hard shell into which it withdraws when disturbed. Slugs lay white eggs encased in a slimy mass in protected places. Snails bury their eggs in the soil, also in a slimy mass. The young look like miniature versions of their parents.

Solution: Apply Ortho® Bug-Geta® Snail & Slug Killer in bands around the areas you wish to protect. Also use the bait in areas where snails or slugs might be hiding, such as in dense ground covers, weedy areas, compost piles, or flowerpot-storage areas. Before applying the bait, wet down the treated areas to encourage snail and slug activity that night. Repeat the application every two weeks for as long as snails and slugs are actively feeding.

Leaf spot

Leaf spot.

Problem: Spots and blotches appear on the leaves. The spots may be yellow, red, tan, gray, or brown. They range in size from barely visible to ¼ inch. Several spots may join to form blotches. Leaves may be yellow and dying. Leaf spotting is most severe in warm, humid weather. In damp conditions, a fine gray mold sometimes covers the infected leaf tissue.

Analysis: Several different fungi cause leaf spot. Some of these may eventually kill the plant or weaken it so that it becomes susceptible to attack by other organisms. Others merely cause spotting that is unsightly but not harmful. These fungi are spread by splashing water, wind, insects, and tools. They generally survive the winter in diseased plant debris. Most of the leaf spot organisms do their greatest damage in moist, mild weather (50° to 85°F).

Solution: Spray with a fungicide containing *chlorothalonil* or *mancozeb* at intervals of 7 to 10 days. Because leaf spot favors warm, humid conditions, it is important to spray frequently during these periods. These fungicides protect the new, healthy foliage but won't eradicate the fungus on leaves that are already infected. These leaves may be picked off. Clean up plant debris during the growing season and in the fall.

Cyclamen mites

Cyclamen mite damage.

Problem: Flower buds are deformed and blackened. They may not open, or the flowers may be distorted and shriveled. The leaves are curled, cuplike, wrinkled, thickened, and brittle and may have a purplish discoloration. The plant may be stunted to only a quarter of its normal size.

Analysis: Cyclamen mites (*Steneotarso-nemus pallidus*) are microscopic pests. These members of the spider family are ¹/₁₀₀ of an inch long and can be seen only with a hand lens. Although the mites are not visible to the unaided eye, their damage is distinctive. Mites generally live and feed in leaf and flower buds and rarely venture onto exposed plant surfaces. These pests crawl from one overlapping leaf to another. They are also spread on contaminated tools, clothing, and hands of gardeners. Cyclamen mites are seldom active during the hot summer months. They are most injurious from early spring until June and again in late summer, with the greatest damage occurring in periods of high humidity.

Solution: Spray infested plants with Ortho® Systemic Insect Killer or Ortho® Rose & Flower Insect Killer; respray two more times at intervals of 7 to 10 days. Spray the foliage thoroughly, covering both the upper and lower surfaces of the leaves. Space plants far enough apart so that their foliage doesn't overlap. This discourages the mites from spreading. Wash your hands and tools after working on an infested plant to prevent spreading mites to healthy plants.

DIANTHUS (Carnation, pink)

Fusarium wilt

Fusarium wilt.

Problem: Leaves and stems turn gray-green, then pale yellow, and then wilt. Yellowing and wilting often affect only one side of the plant. Plant shoots may be curled and distorted. Stems are soft and can easily be crushed. When a stem is split open, dark streaks and discoloration of the inner water-conducting stem tissue are revealed. The roots generally appear healthy.

Analysis: Fusarium wilt disease affects many ornamental plants. It is caused by a soil-inhabiting fungus (*Fusarium oxysporum* var. *dianthi*) that persists indefinitely on plant debris or in the soil. The disease is spread by contaminated seeds, plants, soil, and equipment. The fungus enters the plant through the roots and spreads up into the stems and leaves through water-conducting vessels in the stems. The vessels become discolored and plugged. This plugging cuts off the flow of water to the leaves, causing leaf yellowing and wilting. (For more information on fusarium wilt, see page 420.)

Solution: No chemical control is available. It is best to destroy infected plants. *Fusarium* can be removed from the soil only by fumigation or solarization techniques. The best solution is to use plants that are resistant to fusarium.

Gray mold

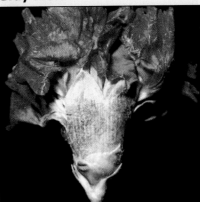

Gray mold.

Problem: Brown spots and blotches appear on leaves and possibly on stems. As the disease progresses, a fuzzy brown or grayish mold forms on the infected tissue. Gray mold and spots often appear on the flowers, especially during periods of cool, wet weather. The leaves and stems may be soft and rotted.

Analysis: Gray mold is a widespread plant disease caused by a fungus (*Botrytis cinerea*) that is found on most dead plant tissue. The fungus initially attacks foliage and flowers that are weak or dead, causing spotting and mold. The fuzzy mold that develops is composed of millions of microscopic spores. Once gray mold has become established on plant debris and weak or dying leaves and flowers, it can invade healthy plant tissue. The fungus is spread by wind or splashing water or by infected pieces of plant tissue contacting healthy tissue. Cool temperatures and high humidity promote gray mold growth. Crowded plantings, rain, and overhead watering also enhance the spread of the disease. Infection is more likely in spring and fall, when temperatures are lower. In warm-winter areas, gray mold can be a year-round problem. (For more information on gray mold, see page 418.)

Solution: Spray infected plants with Ortho® Garden Disease Control or a fungicide containing *mancozeb* at regular intervals of 10 to 14 days for as long as mold is visible. Remove dying or infected leaves, stems, and flowers. Clean up and destroy plant debris. Provide enough space between plants to allow good air circulation. Try to avoid wetting the foliage when watering.

Bacterial wilt

Bacterial wilt.

Problem: Stems and sometimes entire plants wilt. Leaves dry, turn yellow, and die. Roots are often rotted. Cracks may appear around the base of the stem, with yellow streaks extending up the length of the stem. When the stems are split open, yellowish to brownish discolorations of the stem tissue are revealed. The infected interior portions of the stem are sticky.

Analysis: Bacterial wilt is a disease of carnations and pinks caused by a bacterium (*Pseudomonas caryophylli*) that lives in the soil. Bacteria penetrate the plant stems through wounds or cuts in the roots or the base of the stem. Once inside, the organisms multiply and clog the water-conducting stem tissue, causing the plant to wilt and die. The bacteria can also move down into the root system, causing decay. A sticky fluid, which coats infected stems and roots, contains millions of bacteria. The bacteria are spread to other plants by water, handling, contaminated soil, plant debris, and contaminated equipment. Bacterial wilt damage increases as the temperature grows warmer.

Solution: Once a plant is infected, it can't be cured. It is best to remove and destroy all infected plants. Clean up plant debris. If you've been handling infected plants, wash your hands thoroughly with soap and hot water, and disinfect any contaminated tools. Don't replant healthy carnations or pinks in contaminated soil. Avoid damage to plants when cultivating.

DIANTHUS (Carnation, pink) *(continued)*

Stem rot

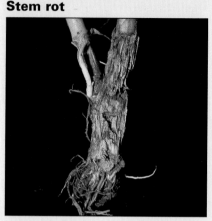

Rhizoctonia stem rot.

Problem: The leaves turn pale and wilt, sometimes suddenly. The lower leaves are rotted. The stem is slimy and decayed. Minute black pellets may be just barely visible around the base of the plant.

Analysis: Stem rot is a plant disease caused by a fungus (*Rhizoctonia solani*) found in most soils. It penetrates the plant at or just below the soil level, rotting through the outer stem bark into the inner stem tissue. Unlike the soft, outer stem rot, the inner stem tissue becomes dry and corky when infected. As the rot progresses up the stem, the lower leaves rot, the foliage pales and withers, and the plant may die. *Rhizoctonia* thrives in warm, moist conditions.

Solution: If all the foliage is wilted, it is best to replace the plant. Plants not so severely affected can sometimes be saved but will often worsen and die. An effective cultural method to help control the disease is to let the soil dry out between waterings. (For information on this technique, see page 419.) Before planting the following year, spray or dust the soil with a fungicide containing *PCNB* (see page 529).

Viruses

Virus.

Problem: The leaves are mottled or have yellow to reddish spots, rings, or streaks parallel to the leaf veins. The lower leaves may turn yellow. Sometimes blotches are on the leaves. The flowers may be streaked or blotched with light or dark colors, or coloring may be uneven.

Analysis: Several different viruses infect carnations. Viral infections are not generally very harmful to the plant. In fact, symptoms of infection may not show up unless several viruses are present in the plant at the same time. In severe infections, however, viruses can cause the lower leaves to turn yellow by suppressing the development of chlorophyll in the leaf tissue. As a result, the leaves produce less food, causing the plant to be weakened. Certain viruses are spread by aphids, which feed on diseased plants and transfer the virus to healthy plants. Other viruses can be spread when diseased plants are pruned or handled and the virus is transferred to healthy plants on contaminated hands or equipment.

Solution: Once a plant is infected, no chemical will control the virus. Remove weak and stunted plants. Wash your hands thoroughly and disinfect pruning shears after working on infected plants. Keep the aphid population under control by spraying infested plants with Ortho® Systemic Insect Killer Concentrate or Ortho® Bug-B-Gon® Multi-Purpose Insect Killer Concentrate. Purchase only healthy plants.

Alternaria leaf spot

Alternaria leaf spot.

Problem: Dark purple spots surrounded by yellow-green margins appear on the leaves and stems. Sunken, grayish-brown dead areas develop in the center of the spots. Individual spots enlarge and merge to form blotches. Infected leaves turn yellow, blacken, and then die. Lesions develop on stems, especially at the bases. Flowers may be spotted. The leaves at the tips of infected stems may become mottled, turn yellow, and wilt. The entire plant may wilt and die.

Analysis: Alternaria leaf spot is a plant disease caused by a fungus (*Alternaria saponariae*) that infects carnations, pinks, and sweet William. Infection is most severe in wet, humid conditions. Spores are spread by wind and splashing water. Infection occurs when spores germinate on wet leaves, stems, or petals. The fungus survives as spores on plant debris.

Solution: Pick off and destroy infected plant parts and clean up and destroy plant debris. Spray with Ortho® Garden Disease Control or a fungicide containing *azoxystrobin* according to label directions. Water in the morning so the foliage will have a chance to dry out. Avoid wetting the foliage when watering. Thin out dense plantings to allow air circulation. Fertilize with Scotts® All Purpose Plant Food or Miracle-Gro® Water Soluble All Purpose Plant Food according to label directions.

Rust

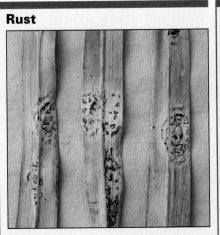

Rust.

Problem: Chocolate-brown pustules of spores appear on the leaves, stems, and flower buds. Infected plants are often stunted. Leaves curl up and may wither and drop.

Analysis: Rust (*Uromyces dianthi*) causes a common and easily recognizable disease of carnations and pinks. Infection starts in the early spring as soon as conditions are favorable for plant growth. Wind and splashing water spread rust spores from plant to plant. The plant must be wet for six to eight hours before the fungus can infect it. Rust survives only on living plant tissue and as spores on seeds. It does not remain infectious on dead plant parts or in the soil. The disease spreads easiest in moist conditions, cool nights, and warm days. Temperatures above 90°F kill the spores.

Solution: Spray infected plants with Ortho® RosePride® Rose & Shrub Disease Control or Ortho® Orthenex® Garden Insect & Disease Control at intervals of 7 to 10 days throughout the growing season. Spray thoroughly, making sure to cover both the upper and lower surfaces of the leaves. The fungicides in these products protect the new, healthy foliage by killing the rust spores as they germinate on the leaves. They will not eradicate the fungus on diseased leaves. These leaves may be picked off. To allow foliage to dry, water in the morning rather than in the late afternoon or evening. Space plants far enough apart to allow good air circulation. Remove and destroy all infected plants in the fall to prevent them from surviving the winter and reinfecting new plantings.

Foxglove anthracnose

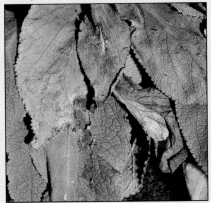

Foxglove anthracnose.

Problem: Light or purplish-brown spots up to ⅛ inch appear on the leaves. The spots are circular or angular and have purplish margins. Often black, rough areas develop in the centers of the leaf spots. Sunken lesions may occur on the leaf veins and stems, and severely infected leaves turn yellow, wither, and drop off. Often plants are stunted and die, especially during periods of warm, moist weather. Seedlings may wilt and die.

Analysis: Foxglove anthracnose is a plant disease caused by a fungus (*Colletotrichum fuscum*) that infects only foxgloves. The fungal spores are spread from plant to plant by splashing water or rain, insects, animals, and contaminated tools. If the leaves are wet, the spores germinate and infect the leaf tissue, creating spots and lesions. Anthracnose is favored by warm temperatures and moist conditions. The fungus survives the winter in diseased plant debris and infected seed. This fungus also causes damping-off of foxglove seedlings. (For information on damping-off, see page 420.)

Solution: If practical, pick off infected leaves. Treat with a fungicide containing *azoxystrobin*. Repeat at 7- to 14-day intervals as long as conditions are favorable for the disease. Water in the morning so the foliage will have a chance to dry out. Avoid wetting the foliage when watering. Remove and destroy plant debris at the end of the growing season. The following year, plant foxglove in a different bed, with plants spaced far enough apart to allow good air circulation.

Wilt disease

Wilt.

Problem: The lower leaves turn yellow, then wilt and die; or all of the foliage may turn yellow and then wither. Flower heads may droop. Often, the plant is affected only on one side. When the stem is split open near the base of the plant, dark streaks and discoloration of the inner water-conducting stem tissue are revealed. The root system may be partially or entirely rotted.

Analysis: Wilt disease affects many ornamental plants. It is caused by either of two soil-inhabiting fungi (*Verticillium albo-atrum* or *Fusarium* species) that persist indefinitely on plant debris or in the soil. The disease is spread by contaminated seeds, plants, soil, and equipment. The fungus enters the plant through the roots and spreads up into the stems and leaves through the water-conducting vessels in the stems. The vessels become discolored and plugged. This plugging cuts off the flow of water to the leaves, causing leaf yellowing and wilting (see page 420).

Solution: No chemical control is available. It is best to destroy infected plants. *Verticillium* and *Fusarium* can be removed from the soil only by fumigation or solarization techniques.

GERBERA (Transvaal daisy)

Root rot

Root rot.

Problem: Leaves wilt, turn reddish, and eventually die. The crown (where the stems meet the roots) and roots are soft, water-soaked, and blackish brown.

Analysis: Root rot is a plant disease caused by a soil-dwelling fungus (*Phytophthora* species) that penetrates the crown of the plant, then moves down into the roots. Infection causes the crown and roots to decay, resulting in wilting, reddened leaves and eventually in the death of the plant. Root rot is most severe in heavy, poorly drained soil and generally moist conditions. The fungus is spread by contaminated soil, transplants, tools, and moving water. (For information on stem and root rot, see page 419.)

Solution: Destroy all severely infected plants; they rarely recover. Allow the soil around the plants to dry out. (For information on the drying-out technique, see page 419.) Don't replant gerbera in infested soil for several years. Plant in well-drained soil. (For information on drainage, see page 406.)

Aphids

Aphid damage.

Problem: Leaves may be curled, distorted, and yellowing. Flowers are often malformed. Tiny (⅛-inch) yellow to pale green soft-bodied insects cluster on the leaves, stems, and flowers. A shiny, sticky substance may coat the leaves. Ants are sometimes present.

Analysis: Aphids do little damage in small numbers. They are extremely prolific, however, and populations can rapidly build to damaging numbers during the growing season. Damage occurs when the aphids suck the sap from gerbera leaves and flower buds. The aphids are unable to digest all the sugar in the plant sap and excrete the excess in a fluid called *honeydew*. The honeydew often drops onto the leaves below. Ants feed on this sticky substance and are often present where there is an aphid infestation. (For more information on aphids, see page 443.)

Solution: Spray with Ortho® Systemic Insect Killer or Ortho® Rose & Flower Insect Killer as soon as the insects appear. Repeat the spray if the plant becomes reinfested with aphids.

GLADIOLUS

Gladiolus thrips

Gladiolus thrips damage.

Problem: Silvery white streaks appear on flowers and foliage. The leaves turn brown and die. Flowers may be deformed and discolored. In early morning, late afternoon, or on overcast days, blackish brown, slender, winged insects 1/16 inch long can be seen on foliage and flower petals. On warm, sunny days these insects hide between leaves and in flower buds. They can be detected by pulling apart a flower bud or two overlapping leaves.

Analysis: Gladiolus thrips (*Taeniothrips simplex*), is one of the most common insect pests of gladiolus plants. Both the immature and adult thrips feed on plant sap by rasping the plant tissue. The injured tissue turns white, causing the characteristic streaking and silvering of the leaves and flowers. The adult female thrips inserts her eggs into growing plant tissue; the emerging young mature within two to four weeks. Thrips actively feed and reproduce from spring until the first frost of fall. They can't survive freezing temperatures. In warm-winter climates, adult thrips hibernate in the soil until spring. In cold-winter climates, they overwinter by hibernating on gladiolus corms (bulbs) in storage. Corms infested by thrips turn brown and corky and may fail to grow, or they may produce only stunted, poor-quality flowers and foliage.

Solution: Spray infested plants with Ortho® Systemic Insect Killer. Repeat the spray at intervals of no less than seven days if reinfestation occurs. Treat corms with Ortho® Malathion Plus® Insect Spray Concentrate before storing. Discard brown, corky corms.

Viruses

Virus streaking.

Problem: Leaves and flowers are streaked, spotted, or mottled. The leaves may also be yellowing, stiff, or thickened. Often the plant blooms prematurely, and the flowers open only partially and then fade rapidly. The entire plant may be dwarfed, although sometimes only the flower spike is stunted.

Analysis: Several different plant viruses infect gladiolus plants. Depending on weather conditions and plant variety, the symptoms of infection can vary from barely noticeable to quite severe. Viral infections rarely cause a plant to die but can weaken it seriously. The virus increases in the corms (the "bulbs" of the gladiolus plant) year after year. Successive plantings from diseased corms provide flowers of poor quality. Viruses are spread by aphids and leafhoppers. These insects feed on diseased plants and transfer the virus to healthy plants at subsequent feedings.

Solution: Once a plant is infected, no chemical will control the virus. To prevent spread of the disease to healthy plants, remove and destroy infected plants. Infected corms can't be reused even if the stem growth is removed. Keep the aphid population under control by spraying plants with Ortho® Systemic Insect Killer. Because two of the viruses that infect gladiolus are common on vegetables in the bean and cucumber families, where practical, avoid planting gladiolus near beans, clover, cucumbers, squash, melons, and tomatoes. (For more information on controlling disease-carrying insects, see page 449.)

Fusarium yellows

Fusarium yellows.

Problem: Foliage and flower spikes are stunted, and flowers may be small and faded. Yellowing starts on the leaf tips and spreads through the entire plant, which finally dies. When the dying plant is pulled out of the ground, the roots are found to be rotted and the corm (the "bulb" of the gladiolus plant) is spotted with circular, firm, brown or black lesions. In some cases, the corm appears normal. When it is split open, however, brown, discolored inner tissue is revealed.

Analysis: Fusarium yellows is a very common and widespread disease of gladiolus plants and corms caused by a soil-inhabiting fungus (*Fusarium oxysporum* f. *gladioli*). The fungus may penetrate and rot the corms in storage or in the ground. Wet soils and warm temperatures (70°F and higher) promote the rapid development of this disease. Corms in storage are sometimes contaminated, but the fungal decay may not have progressed far enough to be noticed. When these corms are planted the following spring, they may not produce foliage if severely infected. If they do produce feeble growth, it soon turns yellow and dies. The fungus survives in diseased corms and soil for many years. Corms that have been removed from the soil prematurely are especially susceptible to infection.

Solution: Destroy all plants and corms that show signs of infection. Dig them up only when they have fully matured. Don't replant healthy corms in soil in which diseased plants have grown. Store corms in a dry, cool (40° to 50°F) place.

Scab

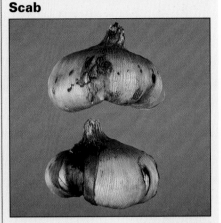

Scab.

Problem: Sunken brown to black lesions on the corm (the "bulb" of the gladiolus plant) are covered with a shiny, varnishlike material and are encircled by raised, brittle rims. Later in the season, after the corms have been planted, many tiny, raised, reddish brown specks develop on the bases of the emerging leaves. These specks become soft, elongated dead spots. In wet weather these spots may be covered with and surrounded by a shiny, oozing material. The leaves usually fall over.

Analysis: Scab, a disease caused by bacteria (*Pseudomonas marginata*), earns its name from the scablike lesions it produces on the gladiolus corms. The bacteria penetrate the corm tissue, usually where the corm has been injured by soil insects or bulb mites, and then move up into the stem base, producing a soft, watery rot. This decay causes the leaves to fall over. The shiny, varnishlike spots that form on the leaves and corms contain millions of bacteria. Wet, heavy soil and warm temperatures favor the rapid development of this disease. The bacteria can live for several years in infected corms and plant debris. The bacteria are usually spread by insects, but they may also be spread by splashing water and by contaminated corms, soil, and tools. Severely infected plants may die.

Solution: No chemical controls this disease. Destroy infected corms. Remove and destroy infected plants. Plant healthy corms in well-drained soil where diseased gladiolus haven't previously grown. Control soil insects.

141

GLADIOLUS *(continued)*

HELIANTHUS (Sunflower)

Neck rot

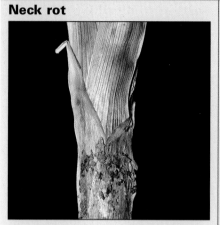

Neck rot.

Penicillium corm rot

Penicillium corm rot.

Verticillium wilt

Verticillium wilt.

Problem: Foliage turns yellow and dies prematurely. Leaf bases are rotted and may be shredded. Black fungal pellets the size of pepper grains may cover the decayed leaf bases and husks of the corms (the "bulbs" of the gladiolus plant). Dark brown to black sunken lesions occur on the corms. Lesions are dry and corky. They may enlarge and join, destroying the entire corm.

Analysis: Neck rot is a plant disease caused by a fungus (*Stromatinia gladioli*) that attacks corms either in storage or in the ground. After the initial infection, the decay spreads up into the leaf bases, killing the leaves prematurely. Corms that are planted in cold, wet soil or stored in moist conditions are most susceptible to neck rot. The fungus is spread by contaminated soil and corms. The tiny black fungal pellets that form on infected tissue can survive for 10 years or more in the soil.

Solution: Discard infected corms and plants. Plant in well-drained soil. Dig corms before the onset of cold, wet weather, and store them in a cool, dry place. If you wish to replant in areas where infected corms have been growing, fumigate or solarize the soil in the planting bed.

Problem: Corky, reddish-brown, sunken lesions, ½ inch or larger, appear on the corm (the "bulb" of the gladiolus plant). In cool, moist conditions, the rotted areas of the corm become covered with a blue-green mold. Infected corms that have been planted may not produce any foliage. Foliage that is produced turns yellow and wilts. The corms are rotted and moldy.

Analysis: Penicillium corm rot is a disease caused by a fungus (*Penicillium gladioli*) that infects the corm through wounds that occur when the corm is dug out of the ground to be put into storage. The problem rarely occurs when corms are properly cured after harvest. After the initial infection, the rot spreads throughout the corm and up into the stem tissue. The corms rot rapidly when they are stored in warm, humid conditions. The fungus forms masses of blue-green spores and tiny brown fungal pellets that can survive dry conditions and extremes of temperatures to invade healthy corms. If mildly infected corms are planted, they may or may not produce foliage, depending upon the severity of the infection.

Solution: Dig corms carefully only after gladiolus leaves have turned entirely yellow in the fall. Destroy all corms showing decay. Handle healthy-looking corms carefully to prevent injuries. Dry and cure corms for a week at 85° to 90°F immediately after digging. Dip them in a fungicide solution containing *captan* before storing and again before planting. Store cured corms in a dry, cool (40° to 45°F) location.

Problem: Mottling, yellowing, and wilting start on the lower leaves and progress slowly upward. Diseased leaves soon wither. Dark brown areas may appear on the infected stems. When a stem is sliced open near the base of the plant, dark streaks and discoloration of the inner water-conducting stem tissue are revealed. Sunflowers often do not show symptoms until they flower.

Analysis: Verticillium wilt disease affects many ornamental plants. It is caused by a soil-inhabiting fungus (*Verticillium* species). The plant disease is spread by contaminated seeds, plants, soil, and equipment. The fungus enters the plant through the roots and spreads up into the stems and leaves through the water-conducting vessels in the stems. The vessels become discolored and plugged. This plugging cuts off the flow of water to the leaves, causing leaf yellowing and wilting. (For more information on verticillium wilt, see page 420.)

Solution: No chemical control is available. It is best to destroy infected plants. *Verticillium* can be removed from the soil only by fumigation or solarization techniques. The best solution is to use plants that are resistant to verticillium. (For a list of plants resistant to verticillium wilt, see page 540.)

Powdery mildew

Powdery mildew.

Problem: Powdery grayish-white patches partially or entirely cover the leaves and stems, primarily the upper surfaces of leaves. The leaves may be yellowing and dying.

Analysis: Powdery mildew is a common plant disease caused by a fungus (*Erysiphe cichoracearum*) that thrives in both humid and dry weather. The powdery patches consist of fungal strands and spores. The spores are spread by the wind to healthy plants. The fungus saps plant nutrients, causing yellowing and sometimes death of the leaf. Since this mildew attacks many different kinds of plants, the fungus from a diseased plant may infect other types of plants in the garden. Under favorable conditions, powdery mildew can spread rapidly through a closely spaced planting.

Solution: Treat infected plants with Ortho® Orthenex® Garden Insect & Disease Control or wettable sulfur. Repeat every 7 to 10 days or as often as necessary to protect new growth. Space plants far enough apart to allow good air circulation. Clean up infected leaves and debris.

Black spot

Black spot.

Problem: Large, round or elliptical black spots develop on both sides of the leaves. Spots also form on the stems, flower stalks, and sometimes petals. Concentric rings may form within the spots. Infected stems shrivel and topple, and flower buds and leaves growing on infected stems wilt and die. Foliage yellows and dies prematurely, and overall growth is weak and sparse.

Analysis: Black spot is a plant disease caused by a fungus (*Coniothyrium hellebori*) that infects only hellebores. The fungal spores are spread from plant to plant by wind and splashing water. If the foliage is wet, the spores germinate and infect leaf, stem, and petal tissue. Black spot thrives in moist conditions. In wet, humid weather, black spot can spread through an entire planting in several days. The fungus survives the winter in infected plant debris.

Solution: Remove dying plants and plant debris. Cut off and destroy all diseased plant parts. Spray with a fungicide containing *captan* at intervals of 10 to 14 days until the spotting no longer occurs. Resume spraying during wet weather.

Leaf spot

Leaf spot.

Problem: Spots and blotches ranging in size from barely visible to ¼ inch appear on the leaves. Several spots may join to form blotches. Leaves may be yellow and dying. Leaf spotting is most severe in warm, humid weather.

Analysis: Several different fungi cause leaf spot. Some of these may eventually kill the plant or weaken it so that it becomes susceptible to attack by other organisms. Others merely cause spotting that is unsightly but not harmful. These fungi are spread by splashing water, wind, insects, and contaminated tools. They generally survive the winter in diseased plant debris. Most of these fungi do their greatest damage in mild weather (50° to 85°F).

Solution: Spray at weekly intervals with a fungicide containing basic copper sulfate. Because leaf spot is worse in warm, humid conditions, it is important to spray conscientiously during these periods. These fungicides protect the new, healthy foliage but will not eradicate the fungus on leaves that are already infected. Pick off and destroy severely infected leaves.

HEMEROCALLIS
(continued)

Aphids

Aphids (¼ life size).

Problem: Tiny (⅛-inch) pale green to brown soft-bodied insects are clustered on the leaves. Leaves may be curled, distorted, and yellowing. Flowers may be malformed. A sticky, shiny substance may coat the leaves. Ants are often present.

Analysis: Aphids do little damage in small numbers. They are extremely prolific, however, and populations can rapidly build to damaging numbers during the growing season. Damage occurs when the aphid sucks the sap from daylily leaves. The aphid is unable to digest all the sugar in the plant sap, and it excretes the excess in a fluid called *honeydew*, which often drops onto the leaves below. Ants feed on this sticky substance and are often present where there is an aphid infestation. (For more information on aphids, see page 443.)

Solution: Spray infested plants with Ortho® Systemic Insect Killer or Ortho® Rose & Flower Insect Killer. Repeat the spray if the plant becomes reinfested.

HEUCHERA (Coral bells)

Leaf spot

Leaf spot.

Problem: Spots and blotches appear on the leaves. The spots may be yellow or brown. They range in size from barely visible to ¼ inch. Several spots may join to form blotches. Leaves may be yellow and dying. Leaf spotting is most severe in warm, moist weather. In damp conditions, a fine gray mold sometimes covers the infected leaf.

Analysis: Several different fungi cause leaf spot. Some of these may eventually kill the plant or weaken it so that it becomes susceptible to attack by other organisms. Others merely cause spotting that is unsightly but not harmful. These fungi are spread by splashing water, wind, insects, and contaminated tools. They generally survive the winter in diseased plant debris. Most of the leaf spot organisms do their greatest damage in mild weather (50° to 85°F).

Solution: Where practical, pick off the diseased leaves. Spray with a fungicide containing *iprodione* every 7 to 10 days or frequently enough to protect the new foliage as it grows. This fungicide protects the healthy foliage but will not eradicate the fungus on leaves that are already infected. Because leaf spot thrives in humid conditions, it is important to spray frequently during these periods.

HOSTA

Snails and slugs

Snail damage.

Problem: Irregularly shaped holes with smooth edges are chewed in the leaves. Leaves and stems may be chewed off entirely. Silvery trails wind around on the plants and nearby soil. Snails and slugs may be seen moving on the ground or feeding on the plants, especially at night. Check for them in the garden at night by flashlight.

Analysis: Snails and slugs are mollusks and are related to clams, oysters, and other shellfish. They feed on a wide variety of garden plants. Like other mollusks, snails and slugs need to be moist all the time. For this reason, they avoid direct sun and dry places and hide during the day in damp places, such as under flowerpots or in thick ground covers. They emerge to feed at night or on cloudy days. The young look like miniature versions of their parents.

Solution: Apply Ortho® Bug-Geta® Snail & Slug Killer around the areas you wish to protect. Also use the bait in areas where snails or slugs might be hiding, such as in dense ground covers, weedy areas, compost piles, or flowerpot-storage areas. Before applying the bait, wet down the treated areas to encourage snail and slug activity that night. Repeat the application every two weeks if snails and slugs are active.

HYACINTHUS (Hyacinth)

Short stems

Short stems.

Problem: Flower stalks are very short, and flowers may be smaller than normal. Sometimes only the tip of the flower stalk emerges and blooms at ground level. No signs of insects or disease are present, and the foliage appears healthy.

Analysis: Short stems are the result of inadequate chilling. Hyacinth bulbs contain embryonic flowers and stems. A minimum of 6 weeks of exposure to cool temperatures (45° to 50°F) during the winter stimulates the stem cells to elongate, causing the bud to emerge from the ground. During cool spring weather (50° to 55°F), the stems continue to elongate to their full length, at which point the flowers mature and open. In warm-winter areas, hyacinth stems often fail to elongate properly because of inadequate chilling. During unseasonable spring hot spells (when air temperature reaches 70°F or higher), hyacinth flowers are stimulated by heat to mature and open before the stems have entirely emerged from the ground.

Solution: You can't do anything to increase the length of the hyacinth stem once the flower has matured. If warm spring temperatures are common in your area, plant hyacinths in locations where they will receive direct sun in the morning or late afternoon or only filtered light. The lower air and soil temperatures in such areas should help to increase stem lengths.

Bacterial soft rot

Diseased bulb on left.

Problem: Bulbs that have been planted may not produce any foliage, or, if foliage is produced, the flower stalk may not form. Sometimes the flower stalk develops but the flowers open irregularly and rot off. The entire stalk may rot at the base and fall over. If pulled gently, the leaves and flower stalk may lift off the bulb, which is soft, rotted, and filled with a white, thick, foul-smelling ooze.

Analysis: Bacterial soft rot is a plant disease caused by bacteria (*Erwinia carotovora*) that infect hyacinth bulbs both in storage and when planted in the ground. The bacteria initially penetrate and decay the upper portion of the bulb. The disease then progresses upward into the leaves and flower stalks and down through the bulb and roots. The thick ooze that accompanies the decay is filled with millions of bacteria. Bulbs that are infected before they are planted produce little, if any, growth. Even well-established, healthy plants may decay quite rapidly after they are infected, sometimes within three to five days. The bacteria survive in infected plant debris and bulbs, and they are spread by contaminated insects and tools and by diseased bulbs and plants. Soft rot thrives in moist conditions. If bulbs freeze while they are in storage, they are especially susceptible to infection.

Solution: No cure exists for this disease. Remove and destroy all bulbs and plants showing signs of decay. Store bulbs in a dry, cool (40° to 45°F) location. Plant only healthy bulbs in well-drained soil. Do not overwater. (For information on watering, see pages 407 to 408.)

Rodents

Rodent damage.

Problem: Hyacinths don't emerge in the spring. Hyacinth stems and leaves may be chewed off. The entire plant sometimes disappears. When bulbs are dug for storage, the ripened foliage may pull up unattached to the bulb, which has often been partly devoured. Crescent-shape mounds of soil may be clustered in the yard, or tiny holes appear in the soil and small, dry, rectangular brown pellets are on the ground.

Analysis: Pocket gophers and field mice are two types of rodents that feed on hyacinth bulbs. Pocket gophers, found in the West, are tan, furry, 6-inch-long rodents that live primarily underground. They form clustered mounds of dirt that indicate their presence. Field mice live both above ground in protective vegetation and below ground in shallow tunnels and burrows. Signs of field mice include clusters of tiny droppings and small holes in the soil that are entrances to the underground tunnels. Both gophers and mice feed on bulbs throughout the year.

Solution: Prevent gopher damage by lining the inside of the planting bed with ½-inch mesh chicken wire along the bottom and up the sides. To prevent mouse damage, lay hardware cloth on the top of the planted area, burying the edges. Remove hardware cloth before shoots emerge in the spring.

IMPATIENS (Balsam)

Leaf spot

Leaf spot.

Problem: The leaves are spotted or blotched with brown spots that may range in size from barely visible to ¼ inch. Several spots may join to form blotches. The leaves may turn yellow and die. Leaf spotting is most severe in wet weather.

Analysis: Several different fungi cause leaf spot. Some of these will eventually kill the plant, while others merely cause spotting that is unsightly but not harmful. These fungi are spread by splashing water, wind, insects, and contaminated tools. Fungal strands or spores survive the winter in plant debris. Most of the leaf spot organisms do their greatest damage in moist conditions and temperatures of 50° to 85°F.

Solution: Spray infected plants with a fungicide containing *captan* at intervals of 7 to 10 days. Make sure that your plant is listed on the product label. Because leaf spot thrives in warm, wet conditions, it is important to spray conscientiously during these periods. Pick off diseased leaves, and clean up and destroy plant debris.

IRIS

Leaf spot

Leaf spot.

Problem: Tiny brown spots from ⅛ to ¼ inch appear on the leaves. Spots have distinct reddish borders and may be surrounded by water-soaked margins that later turn yellow. After the plant has flowered, spots may join to form blotches. Spotting is most severe in wet weather. Leaves die prematurely.

Analysis: Leaf spot is a disease caused by a fungus (*Mycosphaerella macrospora*) that infects only irises and a few other closely related plants. This fungus attacks leaves, flower stalks and buds, but not iris roots, bulbs, or rhizomes. Infection occurs early in the season, but spots don't appear until flowering. Although the fungus doesn't directly kill the plant, repeated infection resulting in premature leaf death each summer greatly reduces rhizome and bulb vigor. When the leaves are wet, or during periods of high humidity, the fungal spots produce spores that are spread to other plants by wind or splashing water. The fungus spends winters in old infected leaves and debris.

Solution: Spray plants with Ortho® Garden Disease Control or with a fungicide containing *azoxystrobin* or *mancozeb*. Repeat the spray every 7 to 10 days until the foliage starts to die back. Clean up and destroy plant debris and clip off diseased foliage in the fall. Spray in the spring as soon as new growth appears, and repeat four to six more times at intervals of 7 to 10 days. Use a spreader-sticker when spraying.

Rust

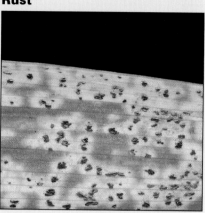

Rust.

Problem: Rust-colored, powdery pustules appear on both sides of the leaves. Later in the season, these pustules turn dark brown. Severely infected leaves may die prematurely, but the plant is seldom killed.

Analysis: Several closely related fungi (*Puccinia* species) cause this plant disease. The rust-colored pustules are composed of millions of microscopic spores. Some of the spores spend the winter on iris leaves that have not died back entirely, while others overwinter on other kinds of plants. Infection usually starts in the spring as soon as conditions are favorable for plant growth. Splashing water and wind spread the spores to healthy plants. Because iris varieties vary greatly in their susceptibility to rust, some leaves may be killed prematurely, while others may not be affected. Rust thrives in wet weather.

Solution: Spray infected plants with Ortho® Lawn Disease Control. Repeat the spray two or more times at intervals of 7 to 10 days. Remove and destroy old and dying iris leaves in the fall. Water in the morning to allow the foliage a chance to dry out before nightfall. Plant rust-resistant varieties, if available.

Crown rot

Crown rot.

Problem: Leaves of irises grown from rhizomes (elongated underground stems) die, starting with the leaf tips and progressing downward. Leaf bases and possibly the rhizomes are dry, brown, and rotted. Leaves of irises grown from bulbs are stunted, turn yellow, and die prematurely. Leaves and stems at the soil level are rotted, and bulbs are soft and crumbly. White matted fungal strands cover the crown (where the stem meets the roots) and soil, surrounding both rhizomatous and bulbous irises. Small tan to reddish-brown pellets the size of mustard seeds form on the infected plant tissue and soil.

Analysis: Crown rot is a disease caused by a fungus (*Sclerotium rolfsii*). It decays and kills leaf and stem bases, bulbs, and often part or all of the rhizomes. Crown rot is spread by moving water, diseased transplants, infested soil, and contaminated tools. Fungal pellets can survive for many years in dry soil and at extremes of temperature to reinfect healthy plants when conditions are suitable. Crown rot is most severe in overcrowded plantings with warm temperatures (70°F and up) and moist conditions.

Solution: Remove and destroy infected plants, bulbs, and rhizomes and the soil immediately surrounding them to 6 inches beyond the diseased area. The fungicide *flutolanil* is registered for control of southern blight on ornamentals, but is available only to licensed pest control operators. Plant in well-drained soil with roots covered and rhizomes showing through the top of the soil. Plant only healthy bulbs and rhizomes. Thin out overcrowded plantings.

Iris borers

Iris borer damage.

Problem: Dark streaks, water-soaked spots, and possibly slits develop in new leaves in the spring to early summer. Leaf edges may be chewed and ragged. By midsummer, the foliage is wilting and discolored. Leaf bases are loose and rotted. Rhizomes (elongated underground stems) are often filled with holes and may be soft and rotted. Pink caterpillars 1 to 2 inches long are feeding inside the rhizomes.

Analysis: Iris borer (*Macronoctua onusta*), the larva of a night-flying moth, is the most destructive insect pest of iris. In the fall, the adult moth lays 150 to 200 eggs in old leaf and flower stalks. The eggs hatch in late April or early May. Emerging larvae initially feed on the leaf surface, producing ragged leaf edges and watery feeding scars. They then bore into the inner leaf tissue and gradually mine their way down into the rhizome, on which they feed throughout the summer. The damaged rhizome is very susceptible to bacterial soft rot. The larvae leave the rhizome, pupate in the soil, and emerge as adult moths in the fall.

Solution: To kill the borers in lightly infested rhizomes, poke a wire into borer holes. In May and June, squeeze the leaves in the vicinity of feeding damage to kill feeding borers inside. Destroy heavily infested plants and rhizomes. Kill the larvae before they enter the leaves with an insecticide containing *malathion*. Spray weekly from the time growth first starts until the beginning of June. Clean up and destroy plant debris by April to eliminate overwintering borer eggs.

Bacterial soft rot

Bacterial soft rot.

Problem: Leaves turn yellow, wilt, and die. Dieback often starts at the leaf tips and progresses downward. The entire leaf cluster may be found lying on the ground. If pulled gently, the leaf cluster sometimes lifts off the rhizome. Leaf bases and rhizomes are often rotted and foul smelling.

Analysis: Bacterial soft rot is a plant disease caused by a bacterium (*Erwinia carotovora*). It is a serious and common disease of bearded and other rhizomatous irises. The bacteria enter the plant through wounds in the leaves and rhizomes, which are frequently made by iris borers. As infection develops, the plant tissue decays into a soft, foul-smelling mass. Finally, the plant dies and the inner rhizome tissue disintegrates. Infection and rapid decay are accelerated by moist, dark conditions. These bacteria live in the soil and in plant debris. They are spread by contaminated plants and rhizomes, soil, insects, and tools.

Solution: Remove and destroy all diseased plants; they can't be cured. Discard diseased rhizomes before planting. If only a small portion of the rhizome is infected, you may possibly save it by cutting off the diseased portion. Avoid wounding the rhizomes when digging them up. After dividing rhizomes, let the wounds heal for a few days before replanting. Plant irises in a sunny, well-drained location. Plant the rhizome shallowly, so the upper portion is exposed. Clean up plant debris in the fall. Control iris borers.

LANTANA

Greenhouse whiteflies

Greenhouse whiteflies (2× life size).

Problem: Tiny, white, winged insects, 1/16 inch long, feed mainly on the undersides of leaves. Nonflying, scalelike larvae covered with white, waxy powder may also be present on the undersides of leaves. When the plant is touched, insects flutter rapidly around it. Leaves may be mottled and yellow. In warm-winter areas, black mold may cover the leaves. The plant may grow poorly.

Analysis: The greenhouse whitefly (*Trialeurodes vaporariorum*) is a common insect pest of many garden ornamentals and greenhouse plants. The four-winged adult lays eggs on the undersides of leaves. The larvae are the size of a pinhead, flat, oval-shape, and semitransparent, with white, waxy filaments radiating from the body. They feed for about a month before changing to the adult form. Both larval and adults suck sap from the leaves. The larvae are more damaging because they feed more heavily. In warm-winter areas, the insect can be active year-round. The whitefly is unable to live through freezing winters. Spring reinfestations in such areas come from migrating whiteflies and from infested greenhouse-grown plants placed in the garden.

Solution: Control whiteflies by spraying with Ortho® Rose & Flower Insect Killer, Ortho® Systemic Insect Killer, or Ortho® Malathion Plus® Insect Spray Concentrate every 7 to 10 days as necessary. Spray both the upper and lower surfaces of the leaves. Whiteflies may also be partially controlled with yellow sticky traps.

LATHYRUS (Sweet pea)

Powdery mildew

Powdery mildew.

Problem: Powdery grayish-white spots and patches develop on the stems and on both surfaces of the leaves. Leaves eventually turn yellow and wither.

Analysis: Powdery mildew is a common plant disease caused by a fungus (*Erysiphe polygoni*) that can be severe on sweet peas. Powdery mildew thrives in both humid and dry weather. The powdery patches consist of fungal strands and spores. The spores are spread by the wind to healthy plants. The fungus saps plant nutrients, causing yellowing and sometimes death of the leaves, especially older leaves. A severe infection may occasionally kill the plant. Since this powdery mildew attacks many different kinds of plants, the fungus from a diseased plant may infect other types of plants in the garden. (For a list of plants susceptible to powdery mildew, see page 537.) Under favorable conditions, powdery mildew can spread rapidly through a closely spaced planting.

Solution: Spray infected plants with Ortho® RosePride® Rose & Shrub Disease Control or a fungicide containing *thiophanate-methyl* or *triadimefon*, or dust them with sulfur. Remove severely infected plants. Spray or dust at regular intervals of 7 to 10 days or as often as necessary to protect new growth. Clean up plant debris. Plant in a site with good air circulation and exposure to early morning sun.

LILIUM (Lily)

Root and bulb rot

Root and bulb rot. Diseased plant on right.

Problem: Plants are stunted and wilting, and the lower leaves turn yellow. The tips of the lower leaves may be dying and brown, and dead patches may appear along leaf edges. Flower buds may wither and fail to open. The bulbs and roots are rotted.

Analysis: Root and bulb rot are problems common with lilies. These plant diseases are caused by various fungi (*Rhizoctonia, Phytophthora, Pythium, Fusarium,* and *Cylindrocarpon* species). These fungi attack and decay the bulbs and roots, causing stunting, wilting, and eventually death of the foliage and flowers. These bulb and root rot organisms live in the soil and stored bulbs and are favored by wet soil. Sometimes bulbs in storage are lightly infected, but the fungal decay hasn't progressed far enough to be easily noticed. When planted, these bulbs may rot so quickly that they do not produce any foliage.

Solution: Remove and destroy infected plants. Drench the soil with a fungicide containing *metalaxyl*. Check all bulbs carefully, and discard any that are moldy, rotted, or dry and crumbly. Plant in well-drained soil. Store bulbs in a cool (35° to 40°F), dry location.

Viruses

Virus.

Problem: Leaves are mottled and streaked light and dark green. The plant may be stunted and dying. Leaves may be spotted with tiny yellow, brown, or gray flecks. Flecks are elongated and run parallel to the leaf veins. Plants with these flecks are often stunted and have small, streaked flowers that do not fully open. Leaves may be twisted or curled and frequently die, starting from the bottom of the plant.

Analysis: Several viral diseases of lilies cause mottling or flecking of the foliage. *Mosaic viruses* produce leaf mottling and discoloration. Depending on the species or variety, the symptoms of infection can be mild or severe. *Fleck* is produced if a plant is simultaneously infected by the *symptomless lily virus* and the *cucumber mosaic virus*, which may or may not produce mottling by itself. Leaf flecking is usually accompanied by stunting, and poor-quality flowers and foliage. The plant is generally disfigured. Viruses remain in infected bulbs year after year, so successive plantings of diseased bulbs will produce only poor-quality flowers and foliage. All of these viruses are spread by aphids, which pick up each virus while feeding on diseased plants and then transmit it to healthy plants at later feedings.

Solution: No chemical controls viruses. Remove and destroy infected plants. Control aphids by spraying infested plants with Ortho® Bug-B-Gon® Multi-Purpose Insect Killer Concentrate or an insecticide containing *malathion*. Respray if reinfestation occurs. Plant mosaic-resistant or immune lilies.

Aphids

Aphids (life size).

Problem: Leaves may be curled, distorted, and yellowing. Flowers are sometimes malformed. Tiny (⅛-inch) pale green to black soft-bodied insects are clustered on the leaves and stems. A sticky, shiny substance may coat the leaves. Ants are often present.

Analysis: Several different species of aphids, a common insect, feed on lilies. Aphids cause their damage by sucking plant sap; this feeding produces leaf curling, yellowing, and distortion. The aphid is unable to digest all the sugar in the plant sap, and it excretes the excess in a fluid called *honeydew*. The honeydew often drops onto the leaves below. Ants feed on this sticky substance and are often present where there is an aphid infestation. Aphids can also spread viral diseases. In the process of feeding, certain aphids can infect lilies with mosaic virus disease. (For more information on aphids, see page 443.)

Solution: Spray infested plants with Ortho® Systemic Insect Killer or Ortho® Rose & Flower Insect Killer. Repeat the spray if reinfestation occurs, allowing at least a week to pass between applications. In the fall, clean up plant debris that might harbor aphid eggs over winter.

Leaf scorch

Leaf scorch.

Problem: Brown semicircular or crescent-shaped areas develop along leaf margins. Leaf tips may be brown. Usually the lower leaves are affected first. When the soil pH is tested, it is found to be acidic.

Analysis: Leaf scorch is a condition that may develop in lilies when they are growing in acid soil with a pH lower than 6.5. Toxic amounts of aluminum and manganese salts become available and are absorbed by plant roots in acidic soils. Leaf scorch is most likely when the plant is not receiving adequate or balanced supplies of nutrients, such as nitrogen and calcium. During the rapid part of the growing season, significant changes in temperature also can cause leaf scorch.

Solution: Add ground dolomitic limestone to the soil to decrease its acidity. (For more information on decreasing soil acidity, see pages 406 to 407.) Fertilize with Scotts® Bulb Slow Release Plant Food according to label directions.

149

LOBULARIA (Sweet Allysum)

Root and stem rot

Root and stem rot.

Problem: Leaves and stems turn yellow, wilt, and die. The lower leaves and stems may be soft and rotted. White fungal strands may grow around the base of the plants.

Analysis: Root and stem rot is a disease caused by several different fungi that persist indefinitely in the soil. These fungi thrive in waterlogged, heavy soil. Some of them attack the plant stems at the soil level, while others attack the roots. Infection causes the roots and stems to decay. This results in wilting, then yellowing leaves, and eventually the death of the plant. These fungi are generally spread by infested soil and transplants, contaminated tools, and splashing or running water. Some of these organisms also cause damping-off of seedlings. (For information on damping-off, see page 420.)

Solution: Allow the soil around the plants to dry out. (For more information on this technique, see page 419.) Remove and discard severely infected plants. Avoid future root rot problems by planting in well-drained soil. (For information on drainage, see page 406.)

NARCISSUS (Daffodil, jonquil)

Failure to bloom

Failure to bloom.

No flowers due to weak growth.

Problem: Foliage is healthy but may be sparse. Few or no flowers are produced. Flowers that are produced may be smaller than normal.

Analysis:

1. Overcrowding: Bulbs multiply each year, producing larger clumps the following spring. If the bulbs are not divided every few years, they become overcrowded.

2. Too much shade: Daffodils planted in shade usually bloom well the first year, but they require a sunny location for continued flowering over a long period of time. Leaves use light to manufacture food, which is stored in the bulbs for the next year's growth and flowering. Inadequate light reduces the amount of stored food in the bulbs, resulting in few or no flowers.

3. Overheating: If bulbs are stored at warm temperatures (80°F and higher), the flower embryo inside the bulb is killed. Leaves grow in the spring, but flowers are not produced.

4. Undersized bulbs: If flower bulbs are smaller than normal, they may produce only foliage for the first one to two years. Undersized bulbs don't store enough food to produce leaves and blossoms, but bulbs will grow larger until they do produce flowers.

5. Foliage removed too soon: After a daffodil flowers, the remaining foliage continues to use the sun's rays to manufacture food for new bulbs and the next year's flowers. If the foliage is removed before it has a chance to die back naturally, the new bulbs may not have enough food stored to produce a flower.

Solution:

1. Divide bulbs when flower production drops off. As a general rule, divide bulbs every three to four years.

2. Grow daffodils in a location where they will receive four hours or more of full sun. Transplant daffodils from the shade to a sunny location any time after the flowering period. Try to keep the soil and roots immediately surrounding the bulb intact when transplanting.

3. Store bulbs at cool temperatures (55° to 60°F) and in a well-ventilated location.

4. Purchase only large, healthy bulbs. Fertilize with Scotts® Bulb Slow Release Plant Food in fall and when shoots emerge.

5. Let the foliage turn yellow before removing it.

Fusarium bulb rot

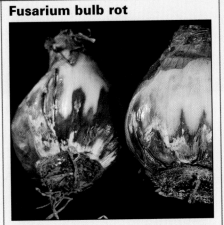

Fusarium bulb rot.

Problem: Leaves turn yellow, and the plant is stunted and dies prematurely. If the bulb is unearthed, few or no roots may be seen. Bulbs in storage develop a chocolate or purple-brown spongy decay that is especially noticeable when the outer fleshy bulb scales are pulled away. White to pink fungal strands may grow on the bulbs.

Analysis: Fusarium bulb rot is a disease caused by a fungus (*Fusarium oxysporum* var. *narcissi*) that attacks both growing plants and bulbs in storage. Growing plants are infected through their roots, while stored bulbs may be infected through wounds or abrasions in the bulb tissue. Infected bulbs that are planted continue to decay in the ground and produce few or no roots and stunted, yellowing foliage. The fungus can persist in the soil for many years and is spread by contaminated bulbs, soil, and tools. Generally, bulb rot is most destructive when soil temperatures reach 60° to 75°F. The disease is most common in warm climates where temperatures rarely drop below freezing and in daffodils that are forced for indoor winter use.

Solution: Discard all diseased plants and bulbs and the soil surrounding the bulb for 6 inches. Dig bulbs up carefully to prevent wounds. Store them in a cool (55° to 60°F), well-ventilated place. Do not replant healthy bulbs in an area where diseased plants have previously grown. In warmer climates, use fusarium-resistant cultivars. Harvest before soil warms in the spring. Avoid planting in warm soil.

Narcissus bulb flies

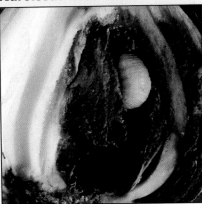

Narcissus bulb fly larva (life size).

Problem: Narcissus and daffodil bulbs feel soft and spongy and produce little or no growth after they are planted. Foliage that does emerge is yellow, stunted, and looks grassy. No flowers are produced. In the spring, when daffodils start to bloom, flying insects that resemble small bumblebees (½ to ¾ inch long) hover around the plants. These black, hairy insects have bands of yellow, buff, or orange around their bodies.

Analysis: Narcissus bulb fly (*Merodon equestris*) is a member of the fly family that occasionally attacks other flower bulbs. In the spring, the adult fly lays its eggs on the leaf bases and soil immediately surrounding the plant. The emerging larvae tunnel through the soil to the bulb and feed on the bulb tissue throughout the summer, making it soft and pulpy. The larvae spend the winter in the bulb as wrinkled, plump, grayish-white to yellow maggots ½ to ¾ inch long. In the spring, they either remain in the bulb or move out into the surrounding soil to pupate. After 1 to 2½ months, the adult bulb fly emerges and starts the egg-laying cycle again.

Solution: Check all bulbs carefully before planting. If they are soft or spongy, discard them. In May, drench the foliage and surrounding soil with an insecticide containing *trichlorfon* to kill the adults and emerging larvae. Make sure that daffodils are listed on the insecticide label.

Gray mold

Gray mold.

Problem: New shoots wilt and die. The bases of the wilted stems are brownish black and rotted. Young flower buds turn black and wither. Older buds and open flowers turn soft and brown and develop a gray or brown fuzzy covering in wet weather. This fuzzy growth, which may develop on all infected plant parts, is distinctive. Its presence helps distinguish this disease from phytophthora blight (see page 152), with which it is often confused. Irregular brown lesions or patches form on the leaves. In severe cases, the plant base and roots may decay.

Analysis: Gray mold is a common disease of peonies caused by a fungus (*Botrytis paeonia* or *B. cinerea*). Gray mold is most serious in the wet, cool conditions of early spring. Fungal growth on the stems, leaves, and flowers causes spotting, blackening, and decay. The fuzzy growth that forms on infected tissue is composed of millions of tiny spores. This fungus is spread by wind, splashing rain or water, contaminated plants, soil, or tools. The fungus forms small black pellets that survive in plant debris and in the soil for many years. (For more information on gray mold, see page 418.)

Solution: Remove and destroy all decayed or wilting plant parts. Clean up plant debris during the growing season and again in the fall. In the spring, spray emerging shoots with a fungicide containing *mancozeb*. Repeat the spray two more times at intervals of 5 to 10 days. Respray if weather favorable for the disease continues.

PAEONIA (Peony) *(continued)*

Failure to bloom

Failure to bloom.

Problem: Peonies fail to produce flower buds, or they produce buds that fail to develop fully.

Analysis: Peonies may fail to bloom for several reasons.

1. Crown (where the stems meet the roots) buried at wrong depth: Peonies planted too deep or too shallow often fail to develop blooms.

2. Immature transplants: Peony roots that have been divided and transplanted usually fail to flower for at least 2 years. If the divisions were extremely small, the plants may not flower for as long as 5 years.

3. Crowded plantings: Old, established peony clumps eventually become overcrowded and stop producing flowers.

4. Too much shade: Peonies stop blooming when they are heavily shaded by trees, tall shrubs, or buildings.

5. Lack of fertilization: Peonies that are not fed enough fail to bloom.

Solution: Numbered solutions correspond to the numbered items in the analysis.

1. Carefully dig up and reset the crown so that the eyes are 1½ to 2 inches below the soil surface.

2. With time, the young plants will mature and start flowering.

3. Peonies usually need to be divided after 6 to 10 years or anytime when flower production starts to drop off. Dig up and divide old clumps into divisions containing three to five eyes. These divisions may be replanted in the garden.

4. Transplant to a sunny location.

5. Apply Scotts® All Purpose Plant Food in early spring and work it in lightly around each plant.

Phytophthora blight

Peonies infected with phytophthora blight.

Problem: New shoots wilt and turn black. Flowers, buds, leaves, and stems shrivel and turn dark brown and leathery. Black lesions several inches long often appear on lower sections of the stem. The plant pulls up easily. Roots are black and rotted. The fuzzy growth characteristic of gray mold (see page 151) does not occur in this disease.

Analysis: Phytophthora blight is a disease of peonies and many other plants caused by a fungus (*Phytophthora cactorum*) that is common in most soils. Like gray mold, this fungus thrives in the cool, wet conditions of early spring. Its spores can survive in the soil and in plant debris for many years. Initially the fungus attacks either the roots or the developing shoots at the soil level, causing shoot wilting and a dark decay of the stem tissue. Wherever the fungus is splashed onto the plant, it may cause lesions, spots, and a typical brown, leathery decay. This disease is spread by splashing rain or water and by contaminated plants, soil, and tools. It is most serious in heavy, poorly drained soils.

Solution: Remove and destroy plants with decayed roots. Pick off and destroy infected plant parts. Clean up plant debris. Spray the foliage and drench the base of the plant with a fungicide containing *mancozeb*. Spray three times at intervals of 5 to 10 days. Reapply the spray if infection recurs. Thin out overcrowded plants. Plant peonies in well-drained soil.

Bud blast

Bud blast.

Problem: Flower buds begin to develop normally, but growth ceases when they reach the size of peas. Buds turn black or brown and eventually dry up.

Analysis: Bud blast is a disease that was previously blamed on gray mold (*Botrytis* fungus), but the cause is usually cultural. Any factor not conducive to healthy growth is a possible cause. These factors include dry spells, lack of potassium, low temperatures during early spring, overly deep planting, excessive root competition or shade, infertile soil, and root infestation by nematodes.

Solution: Supply ample sun and deep waterings, and improve general growing conditions as needed. If the peony was planted too deep (eyes should be set only 1½ inches into the soil), replant carefully, disturbing the roots as little as possible. Fertilize regularly with Scotts® All Purpose Plant Food or Miracle-Gro® Water Soluble All Purpose Plant Food according to label directions. Do not cut plants back until foliage naturally turns brown in the fall.

PELARGONIUM (Geranium)

Gray mold

Gray mold.

Problem: Brown spots and blotches form on leaves and stems. As the disease progresses, a fuzzy brown or grayish mold forms on the infected tissue. Gray mold and spots often appear on the flowers, especially during periods of cool, wet weather. The leaves and stems may be soft and rotted.

Analysis: Gray mold is a widespread plant disease caused by a fungus (*Botrytis cinerea*) that is found on most dead plant tissue. The fungus initially attacks foliage and flowers that are weak or dead, causing spotting and mold. Once gray mold has become established on plant debris and weak or dying leaves and flowers, it can invade healthy plant tissue. The fungus is spread by water or by bits of infected plant debris that land on the leaves. Cool temperatures and moisture promote gray mold growth. Crowded plantings, rain, and overhead watering aid the spread of the disease. Infection is more of a problem in spring and fall, when temperatures are lower. In warm-winter areas where freezing is rare, gray mold can be a year-round problem. (For more information on gray mold, see page 418.)

Solution: Remove dying or infected leaves, stems, and flowers. Clean up and destroy plant debris. Spray infected plants with Ortho® Garden Disease Control or with a fungicide containing *mancozeb* at regular intervals of 10 to 14 days for as long as the weather is favorable for the disease. Provide enough space between plants to allow good air circulation. Try to avoid wetting the foliage when watering.

Rust

Rust.

Problem: Yellow spots, up to ¼ inch, appear on the leaves and stems. Reddish-brown spore pustules develop within the spots on the undersides of leaves. These pustules may be arranged in concentric circles. Severely infected leaves may turn yellow and drop prematurely.

Analysis: Rust is a plant disease caused by a fungus (*Puccinia pelargonii-zonalis*). Wind and splashing water spread rust spores to healthy plants. After a leaf has been wet for five hours, the spores germinate, forming a spot and, several days later, a pustule. Rust generally does not kill the plant, but heavily infected plants may drop some leaves. The fungus survives only on living plant tissue and fresh plant debris. Wet conditions favor the development and spread of this disease.

Solution: Pick off and destroy infected leaves; then spray with Ortho® Garden Disease Control or with a fungicide containing *azoxystrobin*, *mancozeb*, or *triadimefon* at intervals of 10 days. Spray the foliage thoroughly, making sure to cover both the upper and lower surfaces of leaves. These fungicides protect the new, healthy foliage from infection but will not eradicate the fungus on diseased leaves. Clean up plant debris. If possible, avoid wetting the foliage. Water early in the day to allow foliage to dry out before evening.

Edema

Edema on ivy geranium.

Problem: Water-soaked spots appear on the leaves. Eventually, these spots turn brown and corky. Affected leaves may turn yellow and drop off. Corky ridges may form on the stems and leafstalks. In most cases, the soil is moist and the air is cool and humid.

Analysis: Edema is not caused by a pest but as the result of an accumulation of water in the plant. Edema often develops when the soil is moist or wet and the atmosphere is humid and cool. Under these conditions, water is absorbed rapidly from the soil and lost slowly from the leaves, resulting in an excess amount of water in the plant. This excess water causes cells to burst. The ruptured cells eventually form spots and ridges. Edema occurs most frequently in greenhouses and in late winter and early spring during cloudy weather. (For more information on edema, see page 430.)

Solution: Plant geraniums in soil that drains well, and avoid overwatering them. (For information on watering, see pages 407 to 408.)

PELARGONIUM (Geranium) (continued)

Alternaria leaf spot

Alternaria leaf spot.

Problem: Dark brown, irregularly shaped spots appear on the leaves. The spots range in size from barely visible to ⅓ inch. Larger spots may contain several dark concentric rings. Spots may be surrounded by a diffuse yellow halo. Spotting occurs mostly on the older leaves, although new growth may also be affected. Severely infected leaves shrivel, turn black, and fall off. Only the leaves are affected.

Analysis: Alternaria leaf spot is a disease of geraniums caused by a fungus (*Alternaria alternata*) that is favored by prolonged cool, moist conditions and low fertility. Infection rarely kills the plant but can weaken and disfigure it. The fungus forms spores on the diseased leaves; these spores are readily blown or splashed onto healthy leaves. If the leaf surface is wet, the spores will germinate and initiate new infections. The fungus survives on plant debris and is spread by the wind and splashing water.

Solution: Pick off and destroy infected leaves and clean up debris. Fertilize with Scotts® All Purpose Plant Food or Miracle-Gro® Water Soluble All Purpose Plant Food according to label directions. If infection is severe and persistent, spray the plants with Ortho® Garden Disease Control or a fungicide containing *azoxystrobin* or basic copper sulfate. Spray every 7 to 10 days until spotting has diminished.

Bacterial blight

Bacterial leaf blight.

Problem: Tan to brown circular, sunken spots up to ¼ inch or larger, and angular dead areas appear on leaves. Leaves wilt and die. They either fall off the plant immediately or hang along the stem for several weeks. Many stems shrivel and turn brown or black. The roots are black but not rotted. When an infected stem is sliced open, a thick yellow fluid may ooze from the cut surface. Older diseased plants may retain only a few tufts of leaves at the stem tips.

Analysis: Bacterial blight is a very common and widespread disease of geraniums caused by bacteria (*Xanthomonas campestris* pv. *pelargonii* or *Pseudomonas* species). The disease develops most rapidly when the plants are growing vigorously and during periods of warm, moist weather. The bacteria decay the leaf tissue, causing small spots and lesions, then may penetrate throughout the entire plant, causing wilting and rotting. The bacteria can live in plant debris and in the soil for three months or more. Plants are not always killed by this disease. They often remain weak, stunted, and disfigured. The bacteria can be present in plants that show no symptoms. Cuttings taken from such plants carry the disease. Plants may suddenly collapse when environmental conditions favor the disease.

Solution: Remove and destroy infected plants. Clean up plant debris. Avoid overhead watering. Disinfect contaminated tools. Wash your hands thoroughly after handling infected plants. Purchase only healthy plants. Don't make cuttings from plants that have shown symptoms.

Black stem rot

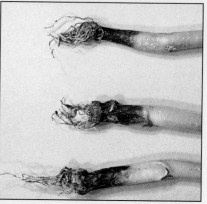

Black stem rot.

Problem: Dark lesions form at the base of the stems. These lesions enlarge and turn black and shiny. The blackening progresses up the stem. The leaves wilt and drop, and the plant may eventually die.

Analysis: Black stem rot is a common disease of geraniums caused by a fungus (*Pythium* species) that lives in the soil. It thrives in wet, poorly drained soil. The fungus attacks the stems at the soil level, then spreads upward. The stems decay and the foliage wilts, shrivels, and eventually dies. Black stem rot is spread by contaminated soil, transplants, and tools.

Solution: Remove and destroy infected plants. If they have been growing in containers, throw out the soil in which they grew. Wash and disinfect contaminated tools and pots. Plant healthy geraniums in well-drained soil and let them dry out between waterings. (For information on this technique, see page 419.)

Caterpillars

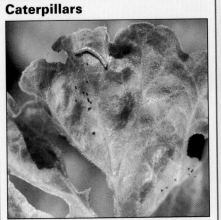

Geranium budworm (2× life size).

Problem: Irregular or round holes appear in the leaves and buds. Leaves, buds, and flowers may be entirely chewed off. Worms or caterpillars are feeding on the plants.

Analysis: Many species of moth or butterfly larvae feed on geraniums and other garden plants. Some common caterpillars include budworms, hornworms, and loopers. Usually, the adult moths or butterflies begin to lay their eggs on garden plants with the onset of warm spring weather. The larvae that emerge from these eggs feed on the leaves, flowers, and buds for two to six weeks, depending on weather conditions and species. Mature caterpillars pupate in cocoons attached to leaves or structures or buried in the soil. One generation or several overlapping generations may occur during the growing season. The last generation of caterpillars in the fall survives the winter as pupae. Adult moths and butterflies emerge the following spring.

Solution: Treat infested plants with Ortho® Rose & Flower Insect Killer, Ortho® Systemic Insect Killer, or the bacterial insecticide *Bacillus thuringiensis* (Bt). Repeat the spray if reinfestation occurs, allowing at least 7 to 10 days between applications of insecticide.

Gray mold

Gray mold.

Problem: Gray or brown spots appear on the flowers, especially during periods of wet weather. Brown spots and blotches may appear on the leaves and stems. As the disease progresses, a fuzzy brown or grayish mold may form on the infected tissue.

Analysis: Gray mold is a widespread plant disease caused by a fungus (*Botrytis* species) that is found on most dead plant tissue. The fungus initially attacks foliage and flowers that are weak or dead, causing spotting and sometimes mold. The fuzzy mold that may develop is composed of millions of microscopic spores. Once gray mold has become established on plant debris and weak or dying leaves and flowers, it can invade healthy plant tissue. The fungus is spread by the wind, splashing water, or infected pieces of plant tissue contacting healthy tissue. Cool temperatures and high humidity favor gray mold growth. Crowded plantings, rain, and overhead watering also enhance the spread of the disease. Infection is more of a problem in the spring and fall, when temperatures are lower. In warm-winter areas where freezing is rare, gray mold can be a year-round problem. (For more information on gray mold, see page 418.)

Solution: Spray infected plants with Ortho® Garden Disease Control at regular intervals of 10 to 14 days for as long as the weather is favorable for the disease. Remove infected flowers and leaves, and clean up plant debris. Avoid wetting the flowers when watering.

Caterpillars

Caterpillars.

Problem: Irregular or round holes appear in the leaves and buds. Leaves, buds, and flowers may be entirely chewed off. Smooth or hairy caterpillars up to 4 inches long are feeding on the plants.

Analysis: Numerous species of moth or butterfly larvae feed on petunias and many other garden plants. Some common caterpillars include armyworms, budworms, cutworms, hornworms, and loopers. As a rule, the adult moths or butterflies start to lay eggs on garden plants with the onset of warm weather in spring. The larvae that emerge feed on leaves, flowers, and buds for two to six weeks, depending on weather conditions and species. Mature caterpillars pupate in cocoons attached to leaves or structures or buried in the soil. One generation or several overlapping generations may occur during the growing season. The last generation of caterpillars in the fall survives the winter as pupae. Adult moths and butterflies emerge the following spring.

Solution: Spray infested plants with Ortho® Rose & Flower Insect Killer, Ortho® Systemic Insect Killer, or the bacterial insecticide *Bacillus thuringiensis* (Bt). Repeat the spray if reinfestation occurs, allowing at least 7 to 10 days between applications. Bt is most effective when caterpillars are young.

PETUNIA (continued)

Cutworms

Cutworm damage.

Problem: Young plants are chewed or cut off near the ground. Many leaves may be sheared from the stems. Gray, brown, or black worms 1½ to 2 inches long may be found about 2 inches deep in the soil near the base of the damaged plants. The worms coil when disturbed.

Analysis: Several species of cutworms attack petunias and many other flowers and vegetable plants. The most likely pests of young petunia plants set out early in the season are the surface-feeding cutworms and climbing cutworms. Climbing cutworms shear the leaves off of older plants. Cutworms hide in the soil during the day and feed only at night. Adult cutworms are dark, night-flying moths with bands or stripes on their forewings. (For more information on cutworms, see page 440.)

Solution: Treat plants with Ortho® Bug-B-Gon® Multi-Purpose Insect Killer Concentrate or Ortho® Bug-B-Gon® Multi-Purpose Garden Dust as soon as damage is observed. To prevent damage next year, apply Ortho® Bug-Geta® Plus Snail, Slug & Insect Killer around the base of plants when cutworm activity is expected. Because cutworms are difficult to control, treatments may need to be repeated at weekly intervals. Work Ortho® Bug-B-Gon® Multi-Purpose Insect Killer Granules into the soil before planting. Cultivate the soil thoroughly in late summer and fall to expose and destroy eggs, larvae, and pupae. Further reduce damage with a cutworm collar around the stem of each plant.

PHLOX

Powdery mildew

Powdery mildew.

Problem: Powdery grayish-white spots and patches cover the leaves and stems, primarily the upper surfaces of the older leaves. The leaves eventually turn yellow and wither.

Analysis: Powdery mildew is a common plant disease that can be caused by either of two closely related fungi (*Erysiphe cichoracearum* or *Sphaerotheca humuli*) that thrive in both humid and dry weather. The powdery patches consist of fungal strands and spores. The spores are spread by the wind to healthy plants. The fungus saps plant nutrients, causing yellowing and sometimes death of the leaves. A severe infection may kill the plant. Since these powdery mildews attack many different kinds of plants, the fungus from a diseased plant may infect other types of plants in the garden. (For a list of susceptible plants, see page 537.) Under favorable conditions, powdery mildew can spread through a planting in a matter of days or weeks.

Solution: Spray infected plants with Ortho® RosePride® Rose & Shrub Disease Control. These products protect new, healthy foliage but will not eradicate the fungus on leaves that are already infected. Damaged leaves may be picked off. Remove severely infected plants. Spray at regular intervals of 7 to 10 days or as often as necessary to protect new growth. Space plants far enough apart to allow good air circulation. Plant where they will be exposed to early morning sun. Clean up and destroy plant debris.

RANUNCULUS

Bird damage

Bird damage.

Problem: Tender young leaves are torn. Seedlings may be entirely eaten. Birds may be feeding in the garden, or their tracks may be around the damaged plants.

Analysis: Birds are fond of ranunculus and frequently eat the tender parts of the plants. Individual birds may develop the habit of feeding on ranunculus and visit the plants every day.

Solution: Protect emerging shoots and young transplants with cages or coverings made of 1-inch mesh chicken wire. Cages about 10×10×24 inches are self-supporting. Larger cages may need to be reinforced with heavy wire. Cheesecloth cages supported by stakes, wire, or string also may be used.

Mosaic virus

Mosaic virus.

Problem: Leaves are mottled yellow-green. Plants may be stunted, and flowers may be smaller than normal. In some cases, the petals are streaked.

Analysis: Ranunculus mosaic virus is a disease that infects ranunculus plants and tubers. The severity of infection varies from plant to plant. Mosaic does not kill ranunculus but it does greatly reduce overall vigor and beauty. The virus is spread by aphids that feed on diseased plants, then transmit the virus to healthy plants when they feed again. Mosaic persists in the plant indefinitely. Tubers obtained from diseased plants are also infected.

Solution: No chemicals control viral diseases. Discard infected plants. Prevent the spread of the virus by keeping the aphid population under control. (For more information on disease-carrying aphids, see page 449.)

RUDBECKIA
(Gloriosa daisy)

Verticillium wilt

Verticillium wilt.

Problem: Leaves yellow, wilt, and die, beginning with the lower leaves and progressing up the plant. Older plants may be stunted. Yellowing and wilting often affect only one side of the plant. Flowering is poor. Dark brown areas may be on the infected stems. When the stem is sliced open near the base of the plant, dark streaks and discoloration of the inner water-conducting tissue are seen.

Analysis: Verticillium wilt disease affects many ornamental plants. It is caused by a soil-inhabiting fungus (*Verticillium* species) that persists indefinitely on plant debris or in the soil. The disease is spread by contaminated seeds, plants, soil, and tools. The fungus enters the plant through the roots and spreads up into the stems and leaves through the water-conducting vessels in the stems. The vessels become discolored and plugged. This plugging cuts off the flow of water to the leaves, causing leaf yellowing and wilting. (For more information on verticillium wilt, see page 420.)

Solution: No chemical control is available. It is best to destroy infected plants. *Verticillium* can be removed from the soil only by fumigation or solarization techniques. The best solution is to use plants that are resistant to *Verticillium* wilt.

SALVIA (Sage)

Verticillium wilt

Verticillium wilt. Diseased plant on right.

Problem: Leaves yellow, wilt, and die, starting with the lower leaves and progressing up the plant. Older plants may be stunted. Yellowing and wilting often affect only one side of the plant. Flowering is poor. Dark brown areas may be on the infected stems. When the stem is sliced open near the base of the plant, dark streaks and discoloration of the inner water-conducting stem tissue are seen.

Analysis: Verticillium wilt disease is caused by a soil-inhabiting fungus (*Verticillium* species) that persists indefinitely on plant debris or in the soil. The disease is spread by contaminated seeds, plants, soil, and tools. The fungus enters the plant through the roots and spreads up into the stems and leaves through the water-conducting vessels in the stems. The vessels become discolored and plugged. This plugging cuts off the flow of water to the leaves, causing leaf yellowing and wilting. (For more information on verticillium wilt, see page 420.)

Solution: No chemical control is available. It is best to destroy infected plants. *Verticillium* can be removed from the soil only by fumigation or solarization techniques. The best solution is to use plants that are resistant to *Verticillium* wilt.

SEDUM

Stem and root rot

Stem and root rot.

Problem: Leaves and stems may be dark, soft, and rotted, or they may turn dull gray, then yellow. Finally, they shrivel and drop off. Sometimes the base of the plant and the lower stems are covered with matted white strands. These strands eventually develop small black or brown pellets.

Analysis: Stem and root rot is a disease caused by several different fungi (including *Sclerotium rolfsii*). These fungi may persist indefinitely in the soil. They thrive in waterlogged, heavy soil. Some of these fungi attack roots directly, while others penetrate either the roots or stems. Infection causes the roots and stems to decay, resulting in wilting, rotting leaves and finally in the death of the plant. These fungi are generally spread by infested soil and contaminated transplants, equipment, and moving water. Some of these fungi may survive the winter in the form of fungal pellets and strands in the soil and plant debris.

Solution: Let the soil dry out between waterings. (For information on this technique, see page 419.) Remove and destroy all infected plants and debris. Improve soil drainage by adding organic matter. (For information on drainage, see page 406.)

TAGETES (Marigold)

Spider mites

Spider mite damage.

Problem: Leaves are stippled, yellowing, and dirty. Leaves may dry out and drop. Webbing may be over flower buds, between leaves and stems, or on the lower surfaces of leaves. To determine if a plant is infested with spider mites, examine the bottoms of the leaves with a hand lens. Or hold a sheet of white paper underneath an affected leaf and tap the leaf sharply. Minute specks the size of pepper grains will drop to the paper and begin to crawl around. These pests are easily seen against the white background.

Analysis: Spider mites are related to spiders and are major pests of many garden and greenhouse plants. They cause damage by sucking sap from the undersides of leaves. As a result of their feeding, chlorophyll disappears, producing the stippled appearance. Mite webbing traps cast-off skins and debris, making the plant dirty. Mites are active throughout the growing season but more so in hot, dry weather (70°F and higher). By midsummer, they may have built up to tremendous numbers. (For more information on mites, see page 457.)

Solution: Spray with Ortho® Systemic Insect Killer or Ortho® Rose & Flower Insect Killer according to label directions when damage is first noticed. Spray the foliage thoroughly, being sure to cover both the upper and lower surfaces of the leaves. Repeated applications may be necessary.

Wilt and stem rot

Wilt and stem rot.

Problem: Leaves wilt and die. The lower stems have a dark, water-soaked appearance. They eventually shrivel and turn brown near the soil line. The plant pulls up easily to reveal rotted roots. The plant usually dies within one to three weeks.

Analysis: Wilt and stem rot is a disease caused by a widespread fungus (*Phytophthora cryptogea*) that persists indefinitely in the soil. The fungus attacks the roots, then spreads up into the stems. As the roots and stems decay, the leaves wilt and turn yellow, and the plant dies. The fungus thrives in cool, waterlogged soils. This disease is spread by contaminated soil, moving water, transplants, and equipment. African marigolds (*Tagetes erecta*) are susceptible, but French marigolds (*T. patula*) and other dwarf varieties are resistant to this fungus.

Solution: Discard infected plants and the soil immediately surrounding them. Let the soil dry out between waterings. (For information on this technique, see page 419.) Plant marigolds in well-drained soil. Drench infected flower beds with a fungicide containing *captan* to help reduce the severity or chances of return of the disease. Plant resistant French and dwarf marigolds.

Gray mold

Gray mold.

Problem: Gray mold and spots often appear on the flowers during periods of cool, wet weather. The petals may turn black. Brown spots and blotches appear on the leaves and possibly on the stems. Mold may appear on infected leaf and stem tissues. The leaves and stems may be soft and rotted.

Analysis: Gray mold is a widespread plant disease caused by a fungus (*Botrytis cinerea*) that is found on most dead plant tissue. The fungus initially attacks foliage and flowers that are weak or dead, causing spotting and mold. The fuzzy mold that develops is composed of millions of microscopic spores. Once gray mold has become established on plant debris and weak or dying leaves and flowers, it can invade healthy plant tissue. The fungus is spread by wind or splashing water or by infected pieces of plant tissue contacting healthy tissue. Cool temperatures, moisture, and high humidity favor gray mold growth. Crowded plantings, rain, and overhead watering also enhance the spread of the disease. Infection is more of a problem in spring and fall, when temperatures are lower. In warm-winter areas where freezing is rare, gray mold can be a year-round problem.

Solution: Spray infected plants once every 10 to 14 days with a fungicide containing *mancozeb*. Continue spraying for as long as the weather is favorable for the disease. Clean up plant debris, and remove dying or infected leaves, stems, and flowers. Provide enough space between plants to allow good air circulation. Avoid wetting the foliage and flowers when watering.

Cutworms

Cutworm (¼ life size).

Problem: Young plants are chewed or cut off near the ground. Many leaves may be sheared from their stems. Gray, brown, or black worms 1½ to 2 inches long may be found in the top 2 inches of soil near the base of the damaged plants. The worms coil when disturbed.

Analysis: Several species of cutworms attack marigolds and many other flowers and vegetable plants. The most likely pests of young marigold plants, early in the season, are surface-feeding and climbing cutworms. A single surface-feeding cutworm can sever the stems of many young plants in one night. Climbing cutworms may shear the leaves off older plants. Cutworms hide in the soil during the day and feed only at night. Adult cutworms are dark, night-flying moths with bands or stripes on their forewings.

Solution: Apply Ortho® Bug-B-Gon® Multi-Purpose Insect Killer Concentrate when cut stems are observed. Because cutworms are difficult to control, treatments may need to be repeated at weekly intervals. Before transplanting into the area, apply a preventive treatment of Ortho® Bug-B-Gon® Multi-Purpose Insect Killer Granules and work it into the soil. Cultivate the soil thoroughly in late summer and fall to expose and destroy eggs, larvae, and pupae. Further reduce damage with a cutworm collar around the stem of each plant.

TROPAEOLUM
(Nasturtium)

Leaf spot

Leaf spot.

Problem: Red, yellow, tan, gray, or black spots and blotches appear on the leaves. They range in size from barely visible to ¼ inch. Several spots may join to form blotches. Some of the leaves may be yellow and dying. Leaf spotting is most severe in warm, humid weather.

Analysis: Nasturtiums are susceptible to several fungi that cause leaf spot. Some of these fungi may eventually kill the plant or weaken it so that it becomes susceptible to attack by other organisms. Others merely cause spotting that is unsightly but not harmful. These fungi are spread by splashing water, wind, insects, contaminated tools, and infected transplants and seed. They survive the winter in diseased plant debris. Most of these fungi do their greatest damage during moist, mild weather (50° to 85°F).

Solution: Picking off the diseased leaves generally gives adequate control. If infection is severe, spray during wet periods with a copper-containing fungicide, such as one with basic copper sulfate, or with *mancozeb*. Clean up debris.

TULIPA (Tulip)

Short stems

Short stems.

Failure to bloom

Old planting.

Undersized bulbs.

Problem: Flower stems are very short, and the flowers may be smaller than normal. Sometimes the flowers bloom at ground level. The foliage appears healthy.

Analysis: Short stems are the result of warm spring temperatures, a lack of adequate winter cooling, or a combination of both. Tulip bulbs contain embryonic flowers and stems. A minimum of 15 weeks of cool temperatures (40° to 50°F) stimulates stem cells to elongate, causing the immature tulip to emerge from the ground. During cool spring weather (40° to 50°F), stems continue to elongate fully, and then the flowers mature and open. In warm-winter areas, stems often fail to elongate properly. During unseasonably warm spells in spring (temperatures of 60°F and higher), the tulip flower is stimulated by the heat to mature and open before the stems have grown to their full potential.

Solution: You can't do anything to increase the length of the tulip stem once the flower has matured. If warm spring temperatures and short winters are common in your area, plant tulips where they will receive direct sun only in the early morning or filtered light. Plant single-flowered, long-stemmed tulips such as Darwin hybrid, single late, and lily-flowered tulips. If you live in a warm-winter area, place tulip bulbs in paper bags in the fall and store them in the refrigerator for 15 weeks before planting; or buy precooled bulbs. In zones 9 and 10 (see page 530 for zone map), delay planting tulips until mid-December.

Problem: Tulip bulbs produce healthy foliage but fail to bloom.

Analysis:

1. Lack of cooling: To flower properly, tulip bulbs require a minimum exposure of 15 weeks to cool temperatures (40° to 50°F) in fall and winter. Cooling stimulates the embryonic flower stem within the bulb to elongate and emerge from the ground.

2. Foliage removed too soon: After a tulip flowers, the remaining foliage continues to manufacture food for new bulbs and flowers for the next year.

3. Lack of nutrients: When tulips are grown in infertile soil for more than one season, they form small, poor-quality bulbs. Such bulbs produce only sparse foliage and few, if any, flowers.

4. Undersized bulbs: Bulbs smaller than 2½ inches in circumference may not contain an embryonic flower. They will produce only foliage for 1 to 2 years, until they are large enough to produce a flower.

5. Old plantings: Tulip flowers are largest and most prolific the first spring after newly purchased bulbs have been planted. After flowering, the original bulb usually disintegrates, and several small "daughter bulbs" form. Often these daughter bulbs are too small to provide many flowers. A planting of tulips generally continues to flower only for two to four years. Tulips are especially short-lived in warm-winter areas (see page 530 for zone map).

Solution:

1. In warm-winter areas (Zones 9 and 10; see page 530 for zone map), precool bulbs before planting, or buy precooled bulbs. Postpone planting until mid-December.

2. Let foliage turn yellow before removing it.

3. Add Scotts® Bulb Slow Release Plant Food when planting, when the new leaves appear on the plants in the spring, and again after flowers bloom. (For details on fertilizing, see pages 409 to 410.)

4. Purchase only large, healthy bulbs from a reputable nursery or mail-order company.

5. Replace old tulips with fresh bulbs. Unless your soil and climate conditions are ideal for growing tulips, the bulbs and flowers will never be as large and prolific as they were the first year. You can prolong the flowering life of a tulip bed by planting the bulbs deeper than usual. Place them 12 inches deep in the soil rather than the usual 6 inches. The soil must be well-drained to prevent rot.

Failure to grow

Poor growth.

Diseased plants.

Rodent damage

Rodent damage.

Problem: Tulip bulbs don't produce much growth in the spring.

Problem: Tulips don't emerge in the spring. Bulbs have been partially or completely eaten. Tulip stems may be chewed off. The entire plant sometimes disappears. Crescent-shaped mounds of soil may be evident in the yard, or tiny holes may be dug in the soil. Small, dry, rectangular, brown pellets are on the ground.

Analysis:

1. Lack of cooling: Tulip bulbs require a period of cooling to develop properly. They need to spend at least 15 weeks below 50°F for proper development. If new bulbs are not precooled, or if soil temperatures remain at 55°F or above during the winter, root formation, flower emergence, and the production of new daughter bulbs for future flowering are inhibited.

2. Foliage removed too soon: After a tulip flowers, the remaining foliage uses the sun's rays to manufacture food for the developing bulbs and the following year's flowers. If the foliage is removed before it turns yellow naturally, the new bulbs are very small.

3. Lack of nutrients: After the first year, tulips don't perform well when planted in infertile soil. They form only weak, small bulbs and flowers. After several years, they stop producing growth.

4. Root rot: Infected tulip bulbs planted in heavy, poorly drained soil frequently decay.

5. Rodents: Mice, pocket gophers, and other rodents may feed on tulips. Dig where the bulbs were planted to check for underground tunnels and half-eaten bulbs. Both indicate rodent damage.

Solution:

1. In warm-winter areas (Zones 9 and 10; see page 530 for zone map), refrigerate newly purchased bulbs for 15 weeks.

2. Allow foliage to turn yellow before removing it.

3. Fertilize emerging tulips with Scotts® Bulb Slow Release Plant Food in the spring and once a month after the plants have flowered until the foliage dies back.

4. Before planting, discard discolored, spongy, or moldy bulbs. Plant in well-drained soil. (For information on drainage, see page 406.)

5. The most effective method of protecting tulips is to plant them in baskets made of ¼-inch wire mesh. Traps or baits may also be used. (For information on rodent control, see the "Gallery of Animal Pests," beginning on page 492, or the item at right.)

Analysis: Pocket gophers and field mice are rodents that feed extensively on tulip bulbs. Pocket gophers, found primarily in the West, are tan, furry rodents, 6 inches long, that live mostly underground. They form crescent-shaped mounds of dirt. Field mice live both above ground in protective vegetation and below ground in shallow tunnels and burrows. Signs of field mice include small holes in the soil, which are entrances to their underground tunnels, and clusters of tiny droppings. Both of these animals feed on bulbs throughout the year.

Solution: Prevent gopher damage by lining the inside of the planting bed with ½-inch mesh chicken wire along the bottom and up the sides. To prevent mouse damage, lay ¼-inch hardware cloth on top of the bulb planting area, burying the edges several inches under the soil surface. Remove the hardware cloth before shoots emerge in the spring.

161

TULIPA *(continued)*

Root and bulb rot

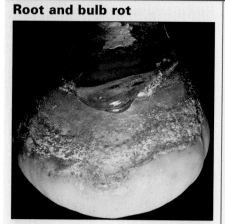

Bulb rot.

Botrytis blight

Botrytis blight. Inset: Infected bulbs.

Viruses

Virus color breaking.

Problem: Foliage is sparse and stunted. Often the leaves turn red, wilt, and die. When the plant is dug up, rotted bulbs are revealed. The bulbs may be mushy or firm and chalky. Usually they are covered with a white, pink, or gray mold. Reddish-brown to black pinhead-size pellets may be on the bulb husks and leaf bases and in the soil immediately surrounding the plant.

Analysis: Root and bulb rot is a disease of tulips caused by several different soil-inhabiting fungi that attack and decay the bulbs and roots. Some of these fungi form tiny pellets on the bulbs and in the soil. These pellets survive through dry conditions and extremes of temperature. Root and bulb rots thrive in wet, poorly drained soils. Bulbs injured during digging or storing are especially susceptible to infection. Sometimes bulbs in storage are lightly infected, but the fungal decay hasn't progressed far enough to be easily noticed. When planted, these bulbs may rot so quickly that they don't produce any foliage.

Solution: Remove and destroy infected plants and the soil immediately surrounding them. Check and discard infected bulbs before planting. Avoid wounding bulbs when cultivating around them or handling them. Plant in a well-drained location. Do not replant tulips in infested soil for at least three years.

Problem: Light to dark-colored spots appear on the leaves and flowers. Spots enlarge to form extensive gray blotches, which may cover the entire leaf and flower. During periods of cool, moist weather, a fuzzy brown or grayish mold forms on the infected tissue. Many of the leaves and stems are distorted, and they often rot off at the base. Dark, circular, sunken lesions appear on infected bulbs. Dark brown pinhead-size pellets form on the bulb husks.

Analysis: Botrytis blight is a common disease of tulips caused by a fungus (*Botrytis tulipae*). The fungus persists through the winter and hot, dry periods as tiny fungal pellets in the soil, plant debris, and bulbs. In the spring, these pellets produce spores that attack foliage and flowers, causing spotting, decay, and mold. Wounded, weak, and dead plant tissues are especially susceptible to infection. The fungus is spread by splashing water. Botrytis blight is most serious during periods of cool, moist weather. Tulip bulbs that are injured when dug up to be stored are especially vulnerable to infection.

Solution: Destroy diseased plants, leaves, flowers, and debris. Before planting tulip bulbs, check them for signs of infection, and discard diseased bulbs. Start spraying emerging plants when they are 4 inches tall with a fungicide containing *mancozeb*. Use a spreader-sticker when spraying. Spray plants every five to seven days until the flowers bloom. Remove tulip flowers just as they start to fade, and cut off the foliage at ground level when it turns yellow. Rotate plants to a new location the following year.

Problem: Flowers are streaked, spotted, or mottled in irregular patterns. The leaves may also be streaked or mottled with light green or white. The plant may be stunted and grow poorly.

Analysis: Several plant viruses commonly infect tulips, causing a characteristic streaking or mottling of the flowers and foliage. Stunted growth may accompany the infection. Viral infections rarely cause a plant to die but can weaken it seriously. The viruses increase in the bulbs year after year. Successive plantings from diseased bulbs yield infected flowers and foliage of poor quality. Some viruses are spread by aphids. These insects feed on diseased plants and transfer viruses to healthy plants at subsequent feedings.

Solution: Once a plant is infected, no chemical will control the virus. To prevent the spread of the virus to healthy tulips, remove and destroy infected plants and all the bulbs associated with those plants. Keep the aphid population under control by spraying with Ortho® Systemic Insect Killer. Because these viruses may also infect lilies, avoid planting tulips near lilies. (For more information on controlling disease-carrying insects, see page 449.) Parrot tulips may exhibit showy streaked patterns, but the streaking is genetic in origin and can't be transferred to other tulips.

Powdery mildew

Powdery mildew.

Problem: Powdery grayish-white spots and patches cover the leaves and stems, primarily the upper surfaces of leaves. Infected leaves eventually turn yellow and wither.

Analysis: Powdery mildew is a common plant disease caused by a fungus (*Erysiphe cichoracearum*) that thrives in both humid and dry weather. The powdery patches consist of fungal strands and spores. The spores are spread by the wind to healthy plants. The fungus saps plant nutrients, causing yellowing and sometimes death of the leaves. A severe infection may kill whole plants. Since this powdery mildew attacks many different kinds of plants, the fungus from a diseased plant may infect other types of plants in the garden.

Solution: Spray infected plants with Ortho® Orthenex® Garden Insect & Disease Control or a fungicide containing *thiophanate-methyl*. Spray at regular intervals of 10 to 12 days or as often as necessary to protect new growth. This fungicide protects the new, healthy foliage but won't eradicate the fungus on leaves that are already infected. Remove and destroy severely infected plants. Where practical, pick off diseased leaves. Clean up and destroy plant debris. Plant verbenas in a site having good air movement and exposure to early morning sun.

Gray mold

Gray mold.

Problem: Brown spots and blotches appear on the leaves and possibly on the stems. As the disease progresses, a fuzzy brown or grayish mold forms on the infected tissue. Gray mold and spots often appear on the flowers, especially during periods of cool, wet weather. The leaves and stems may be soft and rotted.

Analysis: Gray mold is a widespread plant disease caused by a fungus (*Botrytis* species) that is found on most dead plant tissue. The fungus initially attacks foliage and flowers that are weak or dead, causing spotting and mold. Once gray mold has become established on plant debris and weak or dying leaves and flowers, it can invade healthy plant tissue. The fungus is spread by splashing water or by bits of infected plant tissue contacting healthy tissue. Cool temperatures, moisture, and high humidity favor gray mold growth. Crowded plantings, rain, and overhead watering also encourage the spread of the disease. Infection is more of a problem in spring and fall, when temperatures are lower. In warm-winter areas where freezing is rare, gray mold can be a year-round problem. (For more information on gray mold, see page 418.)

Solution: Spray infected plants every 10 to 14 days with a fungicide containing *mancozeb*. Continue spraying for as long as the weather is favorable for the disease. Clean up plant debris, and remove dying or infected leaves, stems, and flowers. Provide enough space between plants to allow good air circulation. Try to avoid wetting the foliage when watering.

Two-spotted spider mites

Two-spotted spider mite damage.

Problem: Leaves are stippled, yellowing, and dirty. Leaves may dry out and drop. There may be fine webbing over flower buds, between leaves, or on the lower surfaces of leaves. Plants lose vigor. Discoloration is most severe during hot, dry weather. To determine if a plant is infested with two-spotted spider mites, hold a sheet of white paper underneath an affected leaf and tap the leaf sharply. Minute specks the size of pepper grains will drop to the paper and begin to crawl. These pests are easily seen against the white background. Mites can also be seen with a 10× hand lens.

Analysis: Two-spotted spider mites (*Tetranychus urticae*), related to spiders, are major pests of many garden and greenhouse plants. They cause damage by sucking sap from the undersides of leaves. As a result of their feeding, the plant's chlorophyll disappears, producing the stippled appearance. Spider mite webbing traps cast-off skins and debris, making the plant dirty. Mites are active throughout the growing season but prefer hot, dry weather (70°F and up). By midsummer, they have built up to tremendous numbers. (For more information on spider mites, see page 457.)

Solution: Spray infested plants with Ortho® Systemic Insect Killer or Ortho® Orthenex® Garden Insect & Disease Control. Repeat the spray two more times at 7- to 10-day intervals.

VIOLA (Pansy, violet)

Leaf spot

Leaf spot on viola.

Spindly growth and poor flowering

Spindly growth and poor flowering.

Root and stem rot

Root and stem rot.

Problem: Leaves and stems are spotted or blotched. The spots may be grayish white, yellow, tan, or brown and range in size from barely visible to ¼ inch. Sometimes these spots are bordered with black margins. Often they join to form blotches. The petals may be distorted and disfigured with brown lesions. The leaves may turn yellow and die. Sometimes elongated, sunken lesions also develop on the stems and flower stalks. Severely infected plants may die.

Analysis: Several different fungi cause leaf spot on pansies, violas, and violets. Some of these will eventually kill the plant, while others merely cause spotting that is unsightly but not harmful. These fungi are spread by splashing water and wind. Fungal strands or spores survive the winter in plant debris. Most of the leaf-spot organisms do their greatest damage during moist, mild weather (50° to 85°F).

Solution: Remove dying plants. Where practical, pick off infected leaves, and clean up plant debris. Spray plants with a fungicide containing *mancozeb* at weekly intervals. When spraying, use a spreader-sticker for more thorough coverage.

Problem: Leaves are small and thin, and stems are long and spindly. Flowering is poor, and flowers are small.

Analysis: Several cultural problems may contribute to spindly growth.
1. Failure to remove old flowers: If fading flowers remain on the plant, only a few small new flowers are produced. When the old flowers are allowed to remain, the plant uses its energy to develop seed instead of to produce new flowers.
2. Inadequate light: Pansies and violas grow lanky and flower poorly when planted in deep shade. They require at least strong filtered light to grow compactly, and they flower most profusely in full sun during mild weather.
3. Old age: Pansies and violas are perennials, but in cold-winter climates, freezing temperatures kill them. In warm-winter areas, they often produce lanky, unattractive growth after the first growing season.
Solution: The numbered solutions below correspond to the numbered items in the analysis.
1. Remove faded flowers.
2. Grow plants in full sun, part-day sun, or strong filtered light.
3. Treat pansies and violas as annuals. Plant them in the spring, or fall in zones 9 and 10 (see page 530 for zone map), and replace them when they start to decline. Pinch back one-third of the spindly stems to one-third of their height to rejuvenate rangy plants.

Problem: Leaves turn yellow, wilt, and die. The roots and lower stems are soft and rotten. There may be white fungal strands on infected stems and around the base of the plant.

Analysis: Root and stem rot is a disease caused by several fungi that persist indefinitely in the soil. These fungi thrive in waterlogged, heavy soils. Infection causes the stem and roots to decay, resulting in wilting, yellowing leaves, and the death of the plant. These fungi are generally spread by infested soil and transplants, contaminated equipment, and splashing or running water.

Solution: Remove dead and dying plants. It is important to allow the soil to dry between irrigations; root and stem rots are encouraged by wet conditions. Improve soil drainage. (For more information on drainage, see page 406.)

Powdery mildew

Powdery mildew.

Problem: Powdery grayish-white spots and patches cover the leaves and stems, primarily the upper surfaces of leaves. The leaves eventually turn yellow and wither.

Analysis: Powdery mildew is a common plant disease caused by a fungus (*Erysiphe cichoracearum*) that thrives in both humid and dry weather. The powdery patches consist of fungal strands and spores. The spores are spread by the wind to healthy plants. The fungus saps plant nutrients, causing yellowing and sometimes death of the leaf. A severe infection may kill the plant. Since this powdery mildew attacks many kinds of plants, the fungus from a diseased plant may infect other types of plants in the garden. Under favorable conditions, powdery mildew can spread rapidly through a closely spaced planting.

Solution: Spray infected plants with Ortho® RosePride® Rose & Shrub Disease Control or Ortho® Garden Disease Control. Spray at regular intervals of 7 to 10 days or as often as necessary to protect new growth. These products protect the new, healthy foliage but will not eradicate the fungus on leaves that are already infected. Pick off severely infected leaves. Space plants far enough apart to allow good air circulation. Clean up and destroy plant debris. Avoid planting in shady areas.

Alternaria blight

Alternaria blight.

Problem: Reddish-brown circular or irregular spots up to ½ inch appear on the leaves. The centers of the spots may turn grayish white. The blossoms are also often spotted. Severely infected leaves, stems, and flowers turn brown and die. Dark, sunken lesions may be at the base of the plant stems.

Analysis: Alternaria blight, a common and widespread disease of zinnias, is a leaf spot caused by a fungus (*Alternaria zinniae*). The disease is favored by moist conditions. The fungal spores are spread from plant to plant by wind and splashing water. The fungus survives on infected debris in the soil and on contaminated seed. This fungus also causes damping-off of seedlings. (For more information on damping-off, see page 420.)

Solution: Remove dying plants. Spray infected plants with Ortho® Lawn Disease Control or Ortho® Garden Disease Control. Pick off infected leaves and flowers. Clean up and destroy plant debris. Avoid overhead watering.

Gray mold

Gray mold.

Problem: Brown spots and blotches appear on the leaves and possibly on the stems. As the disease progresses, a fuzzy brown or grayish mold forms on the infected tissue. Gray mold and spots often appear on the flowers, especially during periods of cool, wet weather. The leaves and stems may be soft and rotted.

Analysis: Gray mold is a widespread plant disease caused by a fungus (*Botrytis cinerea*) that is found on most dead plant tissue. The fungus initially attacks foliage and flowers that are weak or dead, causing spotting and mold. Once gray mold has become established on plant debris and weak or dying leaves and flowers, it can invade healthy plant tissue. The fungus is spread by splashing water or by infected pieces of plant tissue contacting healthy tissue. Cool temperatures, moisture, and high humidity encourage gray mold growth. Crowded plantings, rain, and overhead watering also enhance the spread of the disease. Infection is more of a problem in spring and fall, when temperatures are lower. In warm-winter areas where freezing is rare, gray mold can be a year-round problem. (For more information on gray mold, see page 418.)

Solution: Spray infected plants with Ortho® Garden Disease Control every 10 to 14 days. Continue spraying for as long as the weather is favorable for the disease. Clean up plant debris, and remove dying or infected leaves, stems, and flowers. Provide enough space between plants to allow good air circulation. Avoid wetting the foliage when watering.

Sharing the planting of a tree ties generations together like few other acts.

Unless trees or shrubs start browning drastically or suddenly fall over, many gardeners tend to take them for granted. The shade, color, and serenity trees provide may not be as conspicuous as brilliantly flowering anemones or a startlingly large squash.

Given optimal surroundings, trees live hundreds or even thousands of years. But sometimes something goes wrong: Insect pests, virus and fungus infections, grading changes, too much or too little water, and pollution take their toll. Unlike flower problems, which can be seen merely by looking down, tree problems may begin at the towering top or be hidden among the branches. By the time you notice the damage, it may be severe. But, with knowledge and persistence, most trees and shrubs can be saved.

STAYING ALERT FOR SYMPTOMS

Part of effective shrub and tree management is maintaining an awareness of their health. Make a visual inspection each week as you go about your normal gardening chores. Distorted leaf growth is often the first eye-level symptom to develop. Leaves may be crinkled, rolled, or otherwise different from normal. Leaves may or may not change color. Some develop brown spots, others develop red highlights out of season. Since leaf distortion is an unmistakeable sign that something is bothering the tree, it is time to play gardener detective before the problem progresses.

REMEDYING GROUND POLLUTION

If the tree is receiving water but looks as if it is suffering from drought, ground pollution may be the problem. Road salt is one possible cause. Improper herbicide application is another. The wind may carry herbicide from nearby weeds, the intended targets, to garden plants. Damage may also result when spray equipment used to apply an herbicide is not cleaned thoroughly before being used to apply an insect control on trees or shrubs. Whatever the cause, this sort of damage usually appears several days after herbicide spraying.

Symptoms include puckered leaves or twisted needles. Leaves may seem off-color, yet still be green. If garden plants receive a significant dose of herbicide, distorted new growth may continue throughout the growing season.

To remedy ground-pollution effects, give soil around the tree several ample waterings to flush out chemicals. Prune twigs or branches with distorted leaves. If damage to the tree is not severe, apply fertilizer to prevent tree stress and aid recovery.

To prevent future problems, apply herbicide on a windless day and aim the sprayer carefully; follow label directions. Use one sprayer for herbicides and another for pesticides.

MITIGATING AIR POLLUTION

Air pollution is a worsening problem, and the average gardener can take little control. Because it begins so gradually, its initial effects on trees and shrubs are subtle. Yet pollution paves the way for a host of insect annoyances—including the seemingly ever-present bark beetles, which attack weak or injured trees.

Most air pollution falls into two categories: ozone and smog.

Ozone: This type of air pollution does considerable damage throughout the United States and is the prime cause of pollution damage on the East Coast. Though the ozone layer in the outer atmosphere is essential to our well-beings, ozone at lower elevations is a threat to plants and animals. Ozone forms when the gases produced by an industrialized society combine once they get into the air.

Ozone enters trees and shrubs through leaf pores. Once in foliage, it destroys cell membranes, causing them to collapse. Cell membrane death shows up as white to tan leaf markings. In pines, new needles are flecked with yellow. Older needles may be deep yellow and smaller than normal. Needles may drop. If just some leaves or needles are affected, tree and shrub growth slows. Blossoms may fall. If enough foliage is affected, as has happened in heavily polluted areas, trees die.

Smog: On the West Coast, smog is the type of air pollution that causes the most severe damage. The damage-causing component of smog is peroxyacetyl nitrate (PAN), which affects shrubs and smaller plants to a greater degree than it affects trees. Young, rapidly growing spring foliage is especially sensitive to smog.

Smog enters leaves through pores. The undersides of leaves turn silver as a result of

internal damage. In severe cases, damaged leaves turn light beige and die.

Pollution solutions: No magic can eliminate air pollution, but you can alleviate the damage it causes to your home landscape. If possible, plant American arborvitae, European white birch, gray dogwood, Norway maple, or winged euonymus—these species are more smog- and ozone-tolerant than others. Apply fertilizer regularly, and make certain that watering is sufficient to reach all tree roots. Avoid overwatering, because sitting in soggy soil makes some species prone to pollution damage, particularly in warm climates. Make certain that all or some of the damage is not attributable to insects, disease, or nutrient deficiences, which are problems you can counter directly.

PROVIDING FERTILIZER

Nutrient deficiencies tend to affect a rapidly growing young tree more than a mature one. For this reason, aid young growth by applying fertilizer in the spring. Providing nutrients early will make the most of growing time so, when winter comes, the new growth has sufficient strength to withstand the cold.

Treating a sapling and a mature specimen to the same fertilizer program is not always

Balled-and-burlapped trees, their trunks wrapped for protection, are a common sight at nurseries everywhere.

wise. A mature ornamental tree with healthy leaf color and a growth rate appropriate for the variety needs little fertilizer. Overfertilizing can increase leaf density to the point where interior leaves do not get enough sun to survive. Any plants under such a thick leafy umbrella may also fail. In addition, the ground under the canopy remains moist, opening up the door for a variety of fungal infections.

Assessing Foliage Drop

Leaf drop causes many gardeners to apply fertilizer too soon. Falling foliage may be a symptom of tree illness or damage that fertilizer will alleviate; or falling leaves may be a natural part of the life cycle. In autumn, for example, the level of green pigment (chlorophyll) in the leaves of deciduous trees changes in preparation for an annual foliage drop. Exquisite reds, golds, and oranges take the place of greens, then the leaves fall. Leaf drop in deciduous trees allows them to enter a resting, or dormant, state in which they can survive the winter.

Evergreens also shed leaves and needles as part of their life cycles. Usually the older needles are the ones that fall, leaving room for new growth. Pines shed needles the second year after they appear; junipers hold needles 10 years or more before they drop. Evergreen foliage may fall throughout the year or in batches during particular seasons. Many evergreen trees in dry climates routinely lose some older foliage at the beginning of summer. Holly leaves drop in late winter.

If you are worried about what appears to be abnormally heavy leaf shedding, inspect the tree carefully. The most common cause of excessive leaf drop is insufficient sunlight. Perhaps the tree once received enough sun, but changes in surrounding growth have altered the light pattern. Sometimes the shape of the tree blocks sunlight from reaching lower leaves. Pruning may restore the tree's vigor. Always look for signs of insect damage, another cause of abnormal foliage drop, and take control measures if needed. Some climatic conditions, such as drought or heavy rainfall, may cause changes in the amount of leaf fall. Changes in grading or runoff direction can also cause shedding. Reduce tree stress by watering or correcting drainage, and the amount of foliage drop may return to normal.

Solving Root Problems

If the full branch spread of a tree is 25 feet wide, the roots often reach out at least three times that far. The wide spread of tree roots often leads to problems.

Far-reaching roots: If the roots of your tree extend into your neighbor's yard and your neighbor does any construction, your tree may suffer damage over which you can't control. The practical way to avoid this problem is to research mature tree size before purchase, then pace off the eventual root zone to determine whether there will be encroachment on nearby lots. When in doubt, plant the smaller tree. Many exquisite shrubs, growing no more than 8 to 10 feet high, can be clipped or trained to look like trees.

Of course the opposite can happen: Roots from a neighbor's tree may invade your property and compete with your plants for nutrients. Some trees, such as willow and birch, can be aggressive in seeking water, and they can cause dry ground and mineral deprivation around neighboring plants by removing the water and nutrients they need for survival. You may not be able to grow anything in these areas.

Two antidotes for far-reaching roots are root pruning and root barriers.

Root pruning: If the amount of needed pruning is extensive, hire a professional arborist to do the work. If the job requires cutting only a few small roots, do the pruning yourself. After cutting, the tree growth may slow for a bit but the tree will be unaffected otherwise.

Root barriers: If root pruning is not feasible, consider installing a root barrier. Dig a trench at least 3 feet deep just outside the area affected by the invading tree roots. The deeper the trench, the more effective the barrier. Cut roots that cross the trench. Insert a thin wall of concrete, sheet metal, or rolled roofing material into the trench to inhibit tree roots from reaching into the planted area. Fill the trench. Even with the best barrier, you may have to remove persistent tree roots every five years or so.

If root competition is severe and uncontrollable, your only choice may be to install drought-tolerant plants. Compensate for nutrient loss caused by the invasive roots by applying fertilizer.

Roots in plumbing lines: Roots frequently clog plumbing lines. The problem tree may be quite a distance away, on your property or your neighbor's. Some trees are known for their invasive tendencies. Others become problems because the amount of water they get is inadequate for their needs, so they seek it elsewhere. The best way to prevent root-clogged lines is to thoroughly research any tree before planting it into curb strips, near house foundations, next to patios, in lawns, and near any plumbing line. If you are planning to install a new line, ask your supplier about pipe that is relatively rootproof.

If a drain is plugged with tree roots, a plumber needs specific equipment to clear it. Some firms specialize in sewer and drain-line clearing. To prevent further plugging, pour 1 pound of copper sulfate crystals into the lowest entry point to the sewer line (such as a toilet or basement drain) at a time when drains and sewer lines are not being used (such as just before you go to bed). Copper sulfate is highly poisonous; use it with the utmost care. Flush the toilet or wash the crystals into the pipe with a bucket of water. The copper sulfate collects in the root mass and kills the roots, which rot in a few weeks. It is not circulated through the tree, so the tree itself is not harmed. You may have to repeat the treatment from time to time, as long as the invasive tree remains.

Pruning Away Excess Shade

Trees are a wonderful addition to the garden, but sometimes they create more shade than you—or your neighbor—desire. It's always good to research a tree's ultimate growth pattern before you plant, but if you underestimated it, or if you inherit a large shade tree with newly purchased property, you may need to make some changes.

Jobs for professionals: Limbs and large branches—with their thousands of food, water, and sunlight-gathering leaves— are a vital part of a tree's survival system. Cutting limbs off without planning can result in severe shock that may injure or even kill a mature tree. Hire a licensed tree surgeon or arborist to prune limbs. Your garden center or nursery may be able to recommend a local professional. Before the surgeon starts pruning, discuss the specifics of the job to ensure that the final result suits your landscape plan and budget.

Prune-it-yourself jobs: Home gardeners with the proper equipment and technique can undertake limited branch pruning. The rewards will be immediate and long-lasting: In addition to removing undesirable shade, the pruning is likely to slow new growth so you won't have to prune again soon. To limit growth, don't prune in early spring, because the nutrients that would normally feed the removed area will be diverted into other branches, forcing them into a growth spurt. Prune later in the season, when growth has slowed.

In general, you can remove any branch that crosses another, dead branches, branches growing inward toward the trunk, and branches growing downward. Cut small sections off a large branch before you go after the whole. If a branch is really heavy with growth, its falling weight may tear bark all the way to the trunk.

Don't get so carried away with pruning that you eliminate the tree. More trees are ruined by incorrect pruning than by complete neglect. After you have cut the most obvious of the branches mentioned previously, stand back, take a rest, and perhaps finish the job another day, when you have a fresh supply of objectivity.

Overzealous pruners can do more than harm the tree; they can hurt themselves. Take the time for safety precautions. Pay attention to the cutting angle so the limb falls away from you. Prune only what allows you to keep both feet on the ground. Pruning shears and saws with extension handles let you reach up quite a distance.

In general, leave pruning cuts open to the air—sealing them may trap fungi inside the tree. If a wound does not appear to be healing well, however, apply a pruning sealer. Available as liquids or foams, sealers protect the tree from dehydration and prevent excess sap flow, which could be an invitation to insects. Apply sealer evenly over the entire cut.

TREATING BARK WOUNDS

Bark protects a tree by covering the xylem and phloem, the system that conveys water, minerals, sugar, and protein throughout the tree. If bark wounds do not heal quickly and properly, the xylem and phloem are exposed to sun and wind and will quickly dry out and die. This deprives the tree of vital nutrition.

Bark wounds can be caused by insects, animals, pruning, or mechanical injury.

Monitor bark wounds carefully. If the wound occurs during an infection from a serious disease such as oak wilt or fire blight, apply a pruning sealer.

TREATING CANKERS

A tree canker is a lesion caused by bacteria or fungi. The infected wood is discolored, sunken, and oozing. If cankers are widespread, consult an arborist for treatment. If cankers are few and isolated, try treating them yourself.

Remove cankered branches by pruning off the branch at the trunk or at least 6 inches below the canker. If the canker is on the main trunk or a main branch, use a chisel and a sharp knife to remove the lesion. Remove all discolored and oozing wood and bark. Sterilize equipment after each cut by dipping it in a solution— 1 part household bleach and 9 parts water— to avoid infecting other tree segments. If cankers are extensive and treatment is ineffective, the tree may have to be removed.

REMOVING TREES

A tree may grow too large for its allotted space, be too diseased to save, or may have to make way for new construction. Removing a large tree is a job for a licensed professional, who has the correct equipment for cutting and climbing.

Such a job takes a professional's knowledge as well as equipment. The tree's weight must be lessened by judicious pruning before it is felled. Limbs must be cut so that they fall without injury or damage.

After a tree has been removed, stump treatment is necessary.

TREATING AND REMOVING STUMPS

The aggressive growth that may have caused you to remove the tree may be evident in its regrowth. Within 30 minutes of tree removal, treat freshly cut stumps with Ortho® Brush-B-Gon® Poison Ivy, Poison Oak, and Brush Killer, which acts systemically. Before you begin, remove suckers from the sides of the stump. Then paint or daub the brush killer over the entire stump surface.

If some time has passed before stump treatment, use a hatchet to make multiple notches around the stump, angling downward into the bark. Cut through the bark without removing it. Pour brush killer into the notches, following label directions. If the herbicide tends to leak from the stump and desirable plants are nearby, cover the stump with a plastic bag secured at the stump base.

You may want to remove a stump altogether. This is best done when the stump, roots and all, is dead. A stump is dead if it fails to resprout the season after the tree has been cut. Digging out the stump is quite a job. If you undertake it, avoid back injury by lifting and prying the stump safely. A landscape contractor with proper equipment can remove a stump in a short time.

When you obtain an estimate for tree removal, ask if the price includes grinding the stump. Burying stumps can cause fungal problems later.

Securely wrapping a tree for the trip home from the nursery helps reduce the amount of dehydration the wind causes as well as protects the leaves from shredding or tattering.

PLANTING AND TRANSPLANTING TREES

Many trees fail due to root injury and lack of preparation during planting or transplanting. The tree begins to die back from the outer portions inward and from the top down. With care, however, the home gardener can move small trees successfully. A tree with a trunk up to 2 inches in diameter is in the plant-it-yourself category. The more mature the tree, the more difficult it is to move, though professional tree movers can transplant even large trees successfully.

Deciduous trees are best moved in spring, before leaves begin to appear, or in fall, after leaves drop. Evergreen trees are best planted in September.

Hole preparation: Prepare the receiving hole before moving the tree. The hole needs to be at least twice the width of the root system of the tree to be planted. Dig the hole deep enough to allow the tree to remain at its current level. You must provide good soil to allow root penetration to the full depth and width of eventual root growth. Healthy roots will ultimately spread to three to four times the branch spread of the full-grown tree. If soil is sandy or heavy clay, improve it with organic material.

If soil turns out to be hardpan, you have a problem. Sometimes referred to as shallow

soil or caliche, hardpan is formed by extensive compaction from construction, or it may be the natural soil formation in the region. Hardpan may feel like bedrock, but it's not. Bedrock is actually solid rock. If you encounter it, plant elsewhere or garden in containers or raised beds.

When you hit hardpan, your shovel feels like it has hit brick. Instead of moving easily through soil, you scrape dirt away a bit at a time. Eventually, if you scrape down far enough, you may get through the hardpan. But it can extend for quite a distance.

Even if you are able to complete the hole, the remaining hardpan can present a problem for the tree planted in it. Rain or irrigation water tends to remain in hardpan for hours or even days. Standing water blocks nutrient absorption and invites fungi and bacteria to form. To compensate, you should make the hole even larger than normal, difficult as that may be.

If you decide to finish the digging yourself, drill through soil with an auger or posthole digger. Break up the hardpan to a depth of 2 feet for trees, 1 foot for shrubs. A less strenuous option is to hire a contractor to plow the hardpan and complete the digging. Don't put hardpan back into the planting hole. Fill it with topsoil mixed with organic material.

Don't plant a tree in uncorrected hardpan. Not only will it not prosper, but also its roots will remain shallow, and a heavy windstorm could topple it.

If the work or expense of planting in hardpan does not coincide with your definition of recreational gardening, remember the option of planting the tree in a container. Drought-tolerant species that perform adequately in restricted growing places include dwarf mugo pines, redbuds, silk trees, and strawberry trees.

Tree preparation for transplanting: Avoid pruning the tree before digging it out. Pruning removes energy reserves stored in branches and twigs and further stresses the tree. However, do prune broken and crossing branches and branches that are too close to each other.

To excavate a tree 10 feet high, dig a trench around the tree at least 4 feet in diameter and about 18 inches deep. Generally, roots spread three times as far as branches. If thick roots obstruct the space, move farther away from the trunk and, with a digging fork, carefully remove anchoring

soil from around the exposed roots. Leave as much soil around the roots as possible. Sway the tree gently to loosen it's hold.

The move: With a ball of earth surrounding the roots, immediately move the tree into the receiving hole. Don't let the roots dry out. If the move will take some time, spray the trunk and branches with water to slow down water loss, or wrap exposed portions of the tree with moist burlap to cut down on evaporative moisture loss. Remove the burlap when transplanting is completed.

Continuing care: With careful transplanting, you have given the tree a boost toward a long healthy life in the new site. The transplant still needs your special attention, however.

Place a 4-inch-deep layer of mulch around the transplanted tree to further conserve moisture. To prevent fungal diseases encouraged by moisture buildup, keep mulch away from the trunk. Don't overwater or overfertilize—that may stimulate top growth that the traumatized roots can't handle.

■ **Sucker pruning:** Suckers may appear around the base of a transplanted tree. If this happens and no top growth is evident, the tree has sustained damage that may hinder its survival. In such a situation, suckers indicate root injury and failure to prune the treetop sufficiently before transplanting. Keeping suckers diligently pruned may help the tree to recover.

■ **Trunk support:** In heavy-wind areas, a transplanted trunk may need support. There are two widely used methods of wind staking. The first is to hammer a strong stake near the center of the hole, then set the tree close to the stake. Since this method presents the possibility of the trunk rubbing the stake, some gardeners prefer a two-stake method. This involves placing a stake at each side of the tree but not touching it. These stakes should be aligned at a right angle to the usual wind direction. Either rot-resistant wood stakes or metal ones serve the purpose.

In the past, experts thought using tall stakes was necessary to prevent any tree movement. Current studies indicate that some trunk movement encourages eventual sturdiness. Using short stakes might be an effective compromise. Allow some room for tree sway when installing the stakes, and

170

orient the tree so that the side with the most branches faces into the wind. Place the largest root in the direction of the wind for strongest support. Loosely connect each stake to the tree with a nonabrasive tape in a figure-eight pattern. Do not use rope or wire, which will cut into the tree.

Another option, often used for larger trees, is to hammer three or four pegs into the ground several feet from the tree. The tree is then secured to the pegs with shielded guy wires. A piece of old garden hose makes an excellent shield, or purchase shielded holding wires designed for trunk support. After the first year, if the tree is flourishing and seems well-established, remove the stakes of guy wires. Remove remaining restraints by the second year.

Trunk injury may occur when wires or other restraints are left on a growing tree. Sometimes the restraints become so embedded in the tree that they are almost invisible. Since the nutrient system for the tree is directly under the bark, such a restraint begins to choke off circulation. New leaves may be small and discolored, twigs and then larger branches may die, and tree growth may slow. The entire tree above the restraint can die. Removing an embedded restraint can be difficult. The deeper it gets, however, the more circulation it impedes. Use wire cutters at exposed sites. If you can't free the embedded material, consult an arborist.

PREVENTING ROOT PROBLEMS

Girdling is a common root malady that can take two forms: container girdling and girdling roots.

Container girdling: If the roots of a tree you are considering for purchase meander out of the container or wrap around the outside of the container, choose another plant. This root condition, called container girdling, is a visible sign of problems ahead. So are circling roots at the soil surface. To check for roots circling within the container, stick your finger in the top 2 or 3 inches near the trunk. Brush away a bit of topsoil. Roots that look or feel damaged, broken, or tightly compacted might be circling within the limited space of the container.

If you do buy a container-grown tree with a tight or circling rootball, the tree may still be salvageable. Remove any ties around the rootball. Carefully move the roots apart so they spread out normally in the planting hole. To accomplish this, you may have to cut and remove some of the circling roots. Removing one-quarter of the roots in the outer inch of the rootball should not damage the tree. Place the tree in the receiving hole. Add and firm soil around the roots gradually to get the best root contact.

Girdling roots: A girdling root is any root that wraps itself completely around the trunk, either above soil level or just below it. Girdling roots may occur if trees are grown in hardpan. They are also common when container-grown trees are placed in too small a hole or if the tree suffered from container girdling before it was planted.

As the trunk enlarges, the rootball tightens, effectively cutting off circulation. Tree leaves are small and discolored. They may drop out of season. Twigs, then larger branches, may die. If the girdling is below the soil surface, the problem may become severe before the cause is discovered. One clue to belowground girdling is a trunk that narrows where it enters the soil—a normal trunk exhibits a slight flare at that point. A severely constricted trunk may break in a heavy windstorm.

The girdling root must be completely or partially removed to open up tree circulation. Since you are removing part of the root system, which provides the tree with nutrients, compensate for the loss by pruning back weak, crowded, or excess branches. If constriction at the base is severe, stake the tree for a few years to prevent wind breakage. In serious cases that require professional attention, the tree surgeon can sometimes save a girdled tree by using a procedure called bridge grafting.

TREATING GALLS

Sometimes a tree or shrub develops an odd-looking bump or bumps. They can be small or very large. They may appear to be part of the tree or completely separate, almost like a piece of fruit. These strange plant growths are called galls (see page 181). They occur because a foreign substance has been injected into the tree. As a protective measure, the tree surrounds the foreign substance with firm tissue.

Gardeners often worry about gall formation. But aside from changing the appearance of a plant, most galls do no serious damage. Small plants may be stunted if the gall blocks the flow of nutrients, but if the plant is ill, something else is usually causing the problem. The exception is crown gall, which can grow so rapidly that nutrient flow is markedly decreased. A tree with crown gall will usually survive for years but will decline slowly and eventually die.

Each gall is specific to the tree type. In addition, each gall is specific to the insect, bacterium, or fungus causing it. Oaks can develop 805 different galls; rosebushes can develop 133; and maple trees can develop 48. Nematodes cause nodulelike cysts on plant roots. Mite infestation may cause bladder gall and spindle gall. Bacteria cause euonymus crown gall and wartlike galls on oleander. Fungi cause camellia leaf gall; the white, thick azalea leaf gall; and gall rust, the large, rough, round orange swellings on pine trunks and branches.

Insects cause most gall formations. Psyllids cause the cylindrical nipple-like growths of hackberry leaf gall. Aphids cause the green pineapple galls seen on spruce and the white cottony galls found on fir. Other gall-forming insects include gall midges, gall wasps, caterpillars, beetles, and thrips.

Galls caused by insects begin when an adult female places an egg in a plant bud. Plant cells begin to close around the egg. Some insects even inject a toxin that stimulates rapid and abnormal cell growth, hastening development of the gall. The egg

When purchasing container-grown trees or shrubs, ask the nursery or garden center salesperson if you can lift the rootball from the pot to inspect the roots. Healthy roots have good color and are not so dense as to be pot bound. Avoid plants with girdling roots near the trunk.

171

hatches, and the larva begins development. The plant cells, responding to the larva within, begin to enlarge, forming the gall. When the larva completes its growth, it chews its way out of the gall.

A tiny hole remains, and so does the gall. Some galls are home to just one larva, others to many.

Oak galls, or oak apples, are most commonly seen as round balls growing on twigs. However, oak galls can be round, spiny, star-shaped, flat, or long, and may be found on leaves and branches as well as twigs. Occasionally the leaf galls slow nutrient use by leaves, resulting in discoloration and premature drop. Some twig galls can cause twig dieback.

Nothing can cure a tree of galls. If they are causing a problem or if you simply do not like their appearance, prune away the affected growth. To help prevent recurrence, cut off the galls and destroy them before the adult insects emerge in spring. If galls are especially numerous or unsightly, controlling the insects or diseases causing them may be necessary. Identification of the insect or disease responsible can be difficult. Take samples to a garden center, or consult an arborist or cooperative extension agent.

CONTROLLING INSECT PESTS

The battle with insect pests seems as old as time. Modern research has provided a new strategy for the fight, however, and understanding the enemy will help protect your garden.

Integrated pest management:
Today, integrated pest management (IPM) is the buzzword for gardeners seeking healthy trees and shrubs, with an economy of labor and a concern for the environment. IPM calls for planting resistant species, using natural controls, supplying fertilizer and water for maximum plant strength, and using pesticides only where necessary and always according to label directions.

Beneficial insects such as ladybugs, lace wings, syrphids (also called flowerflies or hover flies), mantises, and parasitic wasps are part of any IPM program. Encourage their presence by providing thick shrubs. These provide not only shade, but also protection from predators such as birds. If you have several large shrubs on your property and want to nurture beneficial bugs, leave the bases of the shrubs

untrimmed. That slightly untidy area is a favorite trysting spot for helpful insects, and under its protection they climb up the shrub or tree, often to deposit eggs. Leafy branches then cover both eggs and larvae and keep them high enough off the ground to avoid many predators. (Be aware, however, that this also provides cover for unwanted pests such as rodents. If you are having problems with mice or rats, you may be forced to trim shrubs.)

Many garden centers offer a variety of beneficial insects for you to release in your garden. Once released, they are free to go where they please, but if you have provided appropriate living conditions, it is likely that they will remain to feed on pests.

Hopping insects: Trees are afflicted with their share of these common pests. Some, such as leafhoppers, are extremely small. Others are weirdly shaped, such as treehoppers. And some are large and noisy, such as cicadas.

Cicadas infest both shade and fruit trees. Most of the damage they do results from egg-laying, which damages twigs. The twigs then turn brown and drop. Nymphs chew tree roots, and their feeding may eliminate both flowers and fruit. Adults suck sap from limbs and twigs. Broods of the periodic cicada may be large and destructive or small and merely an annoyance. Cicadas usually appear where they have appeared before, because trees harbor eggs from previous generations. As many as 40,000 cicadas have been known to infest a single tree.

Each brood may spend 13 or 17 years underground, feeding on tree roots, before appearing in masses above ground. The species with the 13-year life cycle is found primarily in eastern states; the 17-year species is found primarily in southeastern states. Cicadas are wedge-shaped and black-bodied. They have red-orange eyes and red wing edges. An adult's full size is about 1½ inches long. Males make the annoying high-pitched droning that seems to go on forever. The females puncture twigs with knifelike egg-laying organs. Each female deposits up to 600 eggs within the twig.

Cicada young, or nymphs, resemble brown ants when young. They drop to the ground and enter soil. For the 13 or 17 years they take to complete development, nymphs feed on tree roots. In May or June of a breeding year, they crawl up from the ground on tree trunks or almost any other

available object. They change to adults and begin breeding.

Cicada control consists of monitoring cicada outbreaks. Where heavy populations are known to occur, avoid planting new trees while cicadas are visibly present. Prune damaged twigs where the females have laid eggs. To protect small trees, cover them with netting or cheesecloth during cicada outbreaks. *Carbaryl* sprays are effective against cicadas. Spray when the males first begin to drone, and respray after one week.

Plant bugs: Small shield-shaped insects, plant bugs often live with leafhoppers. These insects are extremely mobile—they both run and fly when disturbed. They feed by sucking sap, and several species inject toxins as they feed. The attacked tree parts wither and die.

The plant-bug category includes many species. The four-lined plant bug is greenish yellow with black stripes and is 1/16 inch long. It infests many ornamental trees and shrubs as well as crop plants. Leaves develop tan to reddish-brown spots. The spots may join to totally discolor the leaves. The yellowish sycamore plant bug, 1/8 inch long, is common on sycamore as well as ash, mulberry, and hickory trees. Feeding on leaves causes yellowish or reddish spots. Sometimes holes appear where dead leaf tissue has dropped out. The yucca-plant bug appears only on yucca, causing stippled leaves covered with black waste matter. The adult of the species is blue-black with reddish head and throat. Its nymphs are bright scarlet and may be plentiful on the spiney leaves.

Control plant bugs with Ortho® Malathion Plus® Insect Spray Concentrate when you first notice damage in spring. Make certain to cover both the upper and lower surfaces of leaves. Repeat as necessary.

Leaf-destroying insects: Leaves plagued by insects may look as if they are punctured with shotgun pellets, cut with scissors, the victims of a hole punch, or suddenly transformed into fine lace. Sometimes leaves disappear almost overnight. Leaf-destroying insects include alder flea beetles, bagworms (see page 177), cankerworms (see page 440), gypsy moth caterpillars (see page 176), holly leafminers (see page 232), Japanese beetles (see page 176), leaf beetles, leafcutter bees (see page 266), mimosa webworms (see page 230),

roseslugs (see page 267), slugs, snails (see page 184), stain moth caterpillars, tent caterpillars (see page 177), two-banded taxus weevils, and woolly bear caterpillars (see page 441).

Insect pests of pines: The increasing use of pines for reforestation, conservation, city areas, yard ornamentation, and holiday trees has caused an increase in pine-infesting insects. Many times the problem is a direct result of planting pines in clusters rather than mixing species in a natural way. Pine moths, pine sawflies, and other pests move quickly from one pine to another. Insect populations quickly build up to numbers natural predators can't control. In general, avoid planting new pines near areas that contain pest-infested trees. Do not use bluegrass in pine-planted areas. Bluegrass encourages field mice, known to girdle pine trees.

Regular inspection of pines is crucial. Trouble signs include off-color foliage, unusual leaf drop, distorted growth, and insect presence. If caught in time, problems can be eased or eliminated. If you remove damaged pine wood, destroy it—prunings are an invitation to bark beetle invasion.

Insects attacking pine or spruce include Eastern pine shoot borers, European pine sawflies, European pine shoot moths (see page 249), irregular pine scales, Nantucket pine tip moths, pales weevils, pine engraver beetles, pine needle miners, pine root collar weevils, pine tortoise scales, pine tube moths, pine webworms (see page 249), pitch-mass borers, redheaded pine sawflies, Saratoga spittlebugs (see page 248), southern pine beetles, white pine aphids (see page 248), white pine sawflies (see page 249), white pine weevils (see page 251), and Zimmerman pine moths (see page 250). Spider mites (see pages 247 and 457) and nematodes also attack pine.

In general, supply optimum water and fertilizer to make trees less appealing to these pests. Frequent inspection will help in early detection, which will allow you to solve the problem by pruning infested branches or spraying with appropriate chemicals before you lose the tree.

LEAF-DESTROYING INSECTS

Leafcutter bees (*Megachile* species) Stout-bodied, hairy. Can be black, green, purple, or metallic blue. Females cut precise circles or ovals from leaf edges. Valuable pollinators. Control not recommended.

Roseslugs (*Endelomyia aethiops*) About ½ inch long, greenish white to dark green, velvety or covered with bristles. Skeletonize topsides of leaves; leaves turn brown. Damage can be mistaken for rust. Control with *carbaryl* or *acephate* (Orthene) on foliage at first sign of feeding. Repeat sprays as necessary.

Cankerworms (*Alsophila pometaria* and *Paleacrita vernata*) Inch-long caterpillars, wingless moth adult females. Chew leaves and can defoliate entire trees. Tree banding with sticky substance such as Tanglefoot helps prevent caterpillars from crawling up trunk. Spray with Ortho® Systemic Insect Killer or *Bacillus thuringiensis* (Bt) in late April to early May. Respray as leaves expand if cankerworms are still present.

Woolly bear caterpillars (*Diacrisia virginica*) Black or yellow fuzzy 2-inch-long caterpillars. Black type feeds mainly on weeds, but yellow type is destructive to desirable plants. May skeletonize shrubs in fall. If numbers are small try hand-picking; otherwise, try *Bacillus thuringiensis* (Bt) or Ortho® Rose & Flower Insect Killer spray to control woolly bear caterpillars.

Taxus weevils (*Otiorhynchus sulcatus*) White larvae underground; ⅜-inch black adults with long snouts. Notch leaf edges as if trimmed with a hole punch. May also chew bark. Spray foliage and soil with Ortho® Systemic Insect Killer. Respray plants as necessary.

Holly leafminers (*Phytomyza ilicis*) Minute black flies. Multiple feeding punctures resemble pinpricks and distort leaves. Begin spraying with Ortho® Systemic Insect Killer as soon as you notice the adult flies.

PINE-DESTROYING INSECTS

Pine engraver beetles (*Ips* species) Brown or black beetles, ⅛ inch long. Create small circular holes in branches or trunk. White pine and spruce particularly susceptible. Serious problem in California. Needles turn yellow, then red, then die. Contact an arborist to protect your trees.

Liquidambar styraciflua, *sometimes called sweet gum, is native to riversides in the South. It is a beloved street tree throughout much of the United States, notable for its excellent fall color.*

No effective sprays are available to homeowners. If more than half of foliage has yellowed, remove the tree.

Zimmerman pine moths (*Dioryctria zimmermani*) Reddish gray adults, 1 inch long; white to reddish yellow larvae, ¾ inch long. Browning and wilting of new growth. Resin masses near whorls. Prune infested branches before August; destroy them. Spray foliage and bark with *chlorpyrifos* in mid-April and mid-August.

Pine webworms (*Tetralopha robustella*) Adults are 1 inch long and have purple-black forewings and smoky black hind wings; larvae are yellow-brown, ¾ inch long, and have stripes along their sides. Brown, globular nests of silk, old needles, and brown sawdustlike waste matter. Remove and destroy nests. Spray with *Bacillus thuringiensis* (Bt) or Ortho® Bug-B-Gon® Multi-Purpose Insect Killer before protective webbing appears on needles.

NO FLOWERS

Few or no flowers

Flowerless dogwood in dark location.

Flower buds pruned off crape myrtle.

Buds die or drop

Drought.

Problem: Plants fail to bloom, or they bloom only sparsely and sporadically.

Problem: Many or all of the buds or flowers die or drop off.

Analysis:

1. Juvenility: Plants, like people, must reach a certain age or size before they are able to reproduce. They will not develop flowers or fruit until this time.

2. Inadequate winter cooling: In order to produce flowers, many plants must undergo a period of cooling during the winter. A plant must be exposed for a certain number of hours to temperatures between 30° and 45°F. The number of hours needed varies for different plant species. If the cooling requirement is not satisfied, flowering will be delayed and reduced, and flower buds may drop off. This is a common problem when plants adapted to cold climates are grown in the South.

3. Improper pruning: If a plant is pruned improperly or too severely, flower and fruit production can be reduced or, in some cases, prevented. Drastic pruning, especially on young plants, stimulates a flush of green growth, which inhibits flowering. Flowering is also reduced if flower buds are pruned off.

4. Nutrient imbalance: Plants overfertilized with nitrogen produce a flush of green growth. Some plants don't make flowers while they are growing vigorously.

5. Shade: Flowering plants require a certain amount of light to produce flowers. If these plants are grown in inadequate light, they produce few or no flowers.

Solution:

1. Plants will eventually begin to flower if they are otherwise healthy and adapted to the area. The juvenile stage in some trees and vines may last 15 years.

2. Plant trees and shrubs adapted to your area. Consult your local garden center or your county extension office.

3. Prune lightly, at a time when no flower buds are present.

4. Don't overfertilize plants or make a heavy application of nitrogen before flowering. (For information on fertilizing, see page 409.)

5. Thin out shading trees, or move plants to a sunnier area. (For a list of shade-loving plants, see page 549.)

Analysis:

1. Transplant shock: Whenever a tree or shrub is transplanted, it goes through a period of shock. Dormant plants usually recover more quickly and are injured less than growing plants. Even when transplanted properly, however, dormant plants may still lose some of their buds. Plants that have begun growth or are in bloom often drop many of their flower buds or flowers shortly after transplanting. Some buds may remain on the plant but not open.

2. Cold or frost injury: Flower buds or flowers may be killed by cold or freezing temperatures. Many either fail to open or drop off. Cold injury occurs during winter when temperatures drop below the lowest point tolerated by buds of that particular plant species. Frost injury is caused by an unseasonal cold snap in fall or spring that damages buds, developing flowers, and tender shoots of growing plants.

3. Drought: Flowers or flower buds dry and drop off when there is a temporary lack of moisture. This may be caused by minor root injuries, dry soil, or anything that disrupts water movement to the top of the plant.

4. Insects: Certain insects, such as thrips and mites, feed on flower buds. When infestations are heavy, their feeding kills flower buds, causing them to dry and drop off. Some infested buds may open but be distorted.

Bud drop caused by cold injury.

Excess flowers and fruits

Messy fruit drop.

Beetles

Long-horned beetle (2× life size).

Solution:

1. Whenever possible, transplant trees and shrubs during the dormant season. Avoid wounding the roots when planting, and do not let the plant dry out. (For more information on watering, see page 408.) Apply an antidesiccant spray to plants a few days before transplanting.

2. Plant trees and shrubs adapted to your area. Consult your local garden center or your county extension office. Protect shrubs and small trees from early or late cold snaps by covering them with burlap or a plastic tent. Placing a light underneath the covering offers additional protection.

3. Water trees and shrubs regularly. Most plants recover from minor root injuries. Frequent shallow waterings and light fertilizing (see page 409) may speed the recovery process. Avoid wounding plants.

4. Control insects with various chemicals. (For information on thrips and mites and their controls, look under the specific plant in the index or on pages 456 to 457.)

Problem: Trees and shrubs drop flowers, seedpods, or fruit, creating unwanted litter.

Analysis: Most trees and shrubs produce flowers or flower structures that develop into seedpods or fruit. Some plants, such as juniper and boxwood, produce inconspicuous flowers and fruit. Others, such as ornamental crabapple, olive, sweet gum, horse chestnut, and glossy privet, produce many conspicuous flowers, seedpods, or fruits. The dropping flowers and fruits of such plants create litter that may detract from the beauty of the landscape and increase time spent in garden upkeep.

Solution: If available, select and plant male-flowering varieties, which produce no fruit. Prevent flower and fruit production by spraying with a compound containing the growth regulator NAA (*naphthalene acetic acid*) when flower buds are forming. Contact your local county extension office to determine this period for your particular plant. Make sure that your plant is listed on the product label, and follow directions carefully. If plants are small enough to be moved, transplant them to a location where their flower and fruit drop will not be a nuisance. If spraying is impractical, replace messy trees and shrubs with plants that do not produce litter.

Problem: Shiny or dull, hard-bodied insects with tough, leathery wing covers appear on the plant. The wing covers meet in the middle of the back, forming a straight line down the insect's body. Leaf tissue is chewed, notched, or eaten between the veins, making the leaves appear lacy. The bark may be chewed, or flowers may be eaten. Holes may be found in branches or in the trunk.

Analysis: Many different types of beetles feed on ornamental trees and shrubs. In most cases, both larvae (grubs) and adults feed on the plants, so damage is often severe. The insects spend the winter as grubs inside the plant or in the soil. Adults hide in bark crevices or in places on the ground. Adult beetles lay eggs on the plant or on the soil during the growing season. Depending on the species, the grubs may feed on foliage, mine inside the leaves, bore into stems or branches, or feed on roots. Beetle damage to leaves rarely kills the plant. Grubs feeding inside the wood or underground are much more damaging and often kill branches or the whole plant. (For more information on beetles, see page 434.)

Solution: Grubs feeding in the soil or inside the plant are difficult to detect and control. Control measures are often aimed at the adults. Several different insecticides may be used to control these pests. Make sure that your plant is listed on the label. Look under the specific plant in the alphabetical section beginning on page 204.

INSECTS *(continued)*

Gypsy moths

Gypsy moth larvae (2× life size).

Gypsy moth and egg masses (2× life size).

Japanese beetles

Japanese beetle (2× life size).

Problem: Leaves are chewed; the entire tree is often defoliated by late spring or early summer. Large (up to 2½ inches long), hairy, blackish caterpillars with rows of red and blue spots on their backs are feeding on the leaves, hiding under leaves or bark, or crawling on buildings, cars, or other objects outdoors. Some people are allergic to the hairs. Insect droppings accumulate underneath the infested tree. Trees defoliated for several consecutive years, especially weak ones, may be killed.

Analysis: The gypsy moth (*Lymantria dispar*) is a general feeder, devouring more than 450 species of plants. Gypsy moth populations fluctuate from year to year. When moths are low in number, they prefer oaks as their host. When their numbers increase, moths defoliate entire forests and spread to other trees and shrubs. Repeated, severe defoliation weakens trees and reduces plant growth. Defoliated deciduous trees are rarely killed unless already in a weakened condition. They are more susceptible, however, to attack by other insects and by plant diseases that may kill them. Gypsy moths are also an extreme nuisance in urban areas and in parks and campgrounds. Overwintering masses of eggs, covered with beige or yellow hairs, are attached to almost any object outdoors. Eggs hatch from mid- to late spring. Tiny larvae crawl to trees to feed. They drop on silken threads to be carried by the wind to other plants. As caterpillars mature, they feed at night and rest during the day. The larvae may completely cover sides of houses or other objects during these resting periods. When population levels are high, the insects feed continually on the tree, and large amounts of excrement accumulate beneath it. The larval hairs may cause allergies. The larvae pupate in sheltered places, and dark brown male or white female moths emerge in midsummer.

Solution: If the insects are bothersome or if trees are weak or unhealthy either from the previous year's gypsy moth feeding or from drought, mechanical damage, other insects, or plant diseases, treatment with an insecticide is required. Apply the insecticide from the beginning of hatching until the larvae are 1 inch long, about the blooming period of *Spiraea vanhouttei.* Cover the tree thoroughly. Contact a professional arborist for large trees. Spray smaller trees with the bacterial insecticide *Bacillus thuringiensis* (Bt), Ortho® Systemic Insect Killer, or Ortho® Bug-B-Gon® Multi-Purpose Insect Killer when tiny larvae are first noticed. Repeat the spray at weekly intervals if damage continues. Homeowners can reduce infestations by destroying egg masses during winter months. In the spring, when larvae are feeding, place burlap bands on trees, leaving the bottom edge unattached. Larvae will crawl under these flaps to hide during the day. Collect and destroy them daily. Keep trees healthy. Fertilize regularly, and water during periods of drought. When planting trees, choose species that are less appealing to the gypsy moth. (For a list of plants favored by the gypsy moth, see page 551.) Trees less favored by the insects are damaged only slightly by larval feeding. In addition, when interplanted with more favored hosts, they may reduce damage by preventing a large buildup of insects in the area. It is a federal offense to transport items that have eggs or larvae attached to them.

Problem: Leaf tissue is chewed between the veins, giving the leaves a lacy appearance. The entire plant may be defoliated. Metallic green-and-bronze winged beetles, ½ inch long, feed in clusters on the plant.

Analysis: As its name suggests, the Japanese beetle (*Popillia japonica*) is native to Japan. It was first seen in New Jersey in 1916 and has since become a major pest in the eastern United States. It feeds on hundreds of different species of plants. Adult beetles are present from June to October. They feed only in the daytime and are most active on warm, sunny days. The female beetles live for 30 to 40 days. Just before they die, they lay their eggs under the soil surface in lawns. Grayish-white grubs soon hatch and feed on grass roots. As the weather turns cold in the late fall, the grubs move 8 to 10 inches down into the soil, where they remain dormant for the winter. When the soil warms up in the spring, the grubs move back up near the soil surface and resume feeding on roots. They soon pupate, and in late May or June, they reemerge as adult Japanese beetles.

Solution: Control the adults with Ortho® Systemic Insect Killer, Ortho® Bug-B-Gon® Multi-Purpose Insect Killer Concentrate, or Ortho® Rose & Flower Insect Killer in late May or June. Make sure that your plant is listed on the product label. Repeat the spray 10 days later if damage continues. In the fall, apply milky spore disease to your lawn to control the grubs. The following year, begin spraying as the adults emerge.

Leaf-feeding caterpillars

Looper (2× life size).

Problem: Caterpillars are clustered or feeding singly on the leaves. The surface of the leaf is eaten, giving the remaining tissue a lacy appearance, or the whole leaf is chewed. Sometimes the leaves are covered with webs. The tree may be completely defoliated. Damage appears anytime between spring and fall.

Analysis: Many different species of caterpillars, such as loopers, feed on the leaves of trees and shrubs. Depending on the species, the moths lay their eggs from early spring to midsummer. The larvae that hatch from these eggs feed singly or in groups on buds, on one leaf surface (these are called *skeletonizers*), or on the entire leaf. Certain caterpillars web leaves together as they feed. In some years, damage is minimal because of unfavorable environmental conditions or control by predators or parasites. When conditions are favorable, however, entire plants may be defoliated. Defoliation weakens the plants because no leaves are left to produce food. When heavy infestations occur several years in a row, branches or entire plants may be killed.

Solution: Spray with Ortho® Systemic Insect Killer, Ortho® Bug-B-Gon® Multi-Purpose Insect Killer Concentrate, or the bacterial insecticide *Bacillus thuringiensis* (Bt) when damage is first noticed. Spray the leaves thoroughly. Repeat the spray if the plant becomes reinfested. Make sure that your plant is listed on the product label.

Tent caterpillars and fall webworms

Western tent caterpillars (¼ life size).

Problem: In the spring or summer, silk nests appear in the branch crotches or on the ends of branches. Leaves are chewed; branches or the entire tree may be defoliated. Groups of caterpillars are feeding in or around the nests.

Analysis: Tent caterpillars and fall webworms (*Malacosoma* species and *Hyphantria cunea*) feed on many ornamental trees. In the summer, tent caterpillars lay masses of eggs in a cementing substance around twigs. They hatch in early spring as the leaves unfold, and the young caterpillars construct their nests. On warm, sunny days, they emerge from the nests to devour the surrounding foliage. In mid- to late summer, brownish or reddish moths appear. The fall webworm lays many eggs on the undersides of leaves in the spring. In early summer, the young caterpillars make nests over the ends of branches, and feed them inside. As the leaves are devoured, the caterpillars extend the nests over more foliage. Eventually the entire branch may be enclosed with this unsightly webbing. The caterpillars drop to the soil to pupate. Up to four generations occur between June and September. Damage is most severe in the late summer.

Solution: Spray with Ortho® Systemic Insect Killer, Ortho® Bug-B-Gon® Multi-Purpose Insect Killer Concentrate, or the bacterial insecticide *Bacillus thuringiensis* (Bt). Make sure that your plant is listed on the product label. The bacterial insecticide is most effective against young caterpillars. Remove egg masses found in winter.

Bagworms

Bagworm case on honeylocust (life size).

Problem: Leaves are chewed; branches or the entire tree may be defoliated. Hanging from the branches are carrot-shaped cases, or "bags," from 1 to 3 inches long. The bags are constructed from interwoven bits of dead foliage, twigs, and silk. When a bag is cut open, a tan or blackish caterpillar or a yellowish grublike insect may be found inside. A heavy attack by bagworms may stunt deciduous trees or kill evergreens.

Analysis: Bagworms (*Thyridopteryx ephemeraeformis*) eat leaves of many trees and shrubs. Larvae hatch in late May or early June and immediately begin feeding. Each larva constructs a bag that covers its entire body; as the larva develops, it adds to the bag. The worm partially emerges from its bag to feed. When all leaves are eaten off a branch, the bagworm moves to the next one dragging its bag along. By late August, the larva spins silken bands around a twig, attaches a bag permanently, and pupates. In fall, the winged male moth emerges from his case, flies to a bag containing a female, mates, and dies. The female bagworm spends her entire life inside her bag. After mating, she lays 500 to 1,000 eggs and dies. Eggs spend the winter in the mother's bag.

Solution: Spray with Ortho® Systemic Insect Killer, Ortho® Bug-B-Gon® Multi-Purpose Insect Killer Ready-Spray, or *Bacillus thuringiensis* (Bt) between late May and mid-July to kill the young worms. Older bagworms are more difficult to control. Repeat the spray after 10 days if leaf damage is still occurring. Handpick and destroy bags in winter to reduce the number of eggs.

INSECTS (continued)

SCALES OR POWDER ON PLANT

Aphids

Aphids on hawthorn (life size).

Scales

Lecanium scales on redbud (life size).

Cottony cushion scales / mealybugs / woolly adelgids

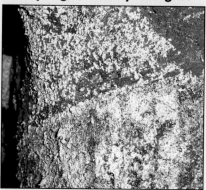

Pine bark adelgids on white pine (¼ life size).

Problem: Tiny (⅛-inch) green, yellow, black, brownish, or gray soft-bodied insects cluster on the bark, leaves, or buds. Some species are covered with white, fluffy wax. The insects may have wings. Leaves are discolored and may be curled and distorted. They sometimes drop off. A shiny or sticky substance may coat the leaves. Black, sooty mold often grows on the sticky substance. Plants may lack vigor, and branches sometimes die. Ants may be present.

Analysis: Many types of aphids infest ornamental trees and shrubs. They do little damage in small numbers. They are extremely prolific, however, during a cool growing season. Damage occurs when the aphids suck the sap from the plant. Sap removal often results in scorched, discolored, or curled leaves and reduced plant growth. A severe infestation of bark aphids may cause branches to die. Aphids are unable to digest all the sugar in the plant sap, and they excrete the excess in a fluid called *honeydew*, which contaminates anything beneath the tree or shrub. A sooty mold fungus may develop on the honeydew, causing the leaves to appear black and dirty. Ants feed on this sticky substance and are often present where there is an aphid infestation. (For more information on aphids, see page 443.)

Solution: Spray with Ortho® Systemic Insect Killer or Ortho® Malathion Plus® Insect Spray Concentrate when damage is first noticed. Make sure that your plant is listed on the product label. Repeat the spray if the plant becomes reinfested.

Problem: Crusty or waxy bumps or clusters of somewhat flattened scaly bumps cover the leaves, stems, branches, or trunk. Bumps can be scraped or picked off; the undersides are usually soft. Leaves turn yellow and may drop. In some cases, a shiny or sticky substance coats the leaves. Black, sooty mold often grows on the sticky substance.

Analysis: Many types of scales infest trees and shrubs. They lay their eggs on leaves or bark, and in spring to midsummer the young scales, called *crawlers*, settle on the leaves, branches, or trunk. The small (⅒-inch), soft-bodied young feed by sucking sap from the plant. The legs usually atrophy, and a hard crusty or waxy shell develops over the body. Female scales lay their eggs underneath their shell. Some species of scales are unable to digest all the sugar in the plant sap, and they excrete the excess in a fluid called *honeydew*. A sooty mold fungus may develop on the honeydew, causing the leaves to appear black and dirty. An uncontrolled infestation of scales may kill a plant after two or three seasons. (For more information on scales, see pages 444 to 447.)

Solution: Spray with Ortho® Systemic Insect Killer when the young are active. Early the following spring, before new growth begins, spray the trunk and branches with Ortho® Volck® Oil Spray to control overwintering insects. Use Volck® Oil Spray only when temperatures will remain above 40°F for 24 hours following the treatment.

Problem: Undersides of leaves and stems, or branch crotches are covered with white, cottony masses. Leaves may be curled, distorted, and yellowing. Knotlike galls may form on the stems or trunk. Sometimes a shiny or sticky substance coats the leaves. Black, sooty mold may grow on the sticky substance. Twigs and branches may die.

Analysis: Cottony cushion scales, mealybugs, pine bark adelgids, and woolly adelgids all produce white, waxy secretions that cover their bodies. This visual similarity makes separate identification difficult for the home gardener. Young insects are usually inconspicuous on the host plant. Their bodies range in color from yellowish green to brown, blending in with the leaves or bark. As the insects mature, they exude filaments of white wax, giving them a cottony appearance. Mealybugs and scales generally deposit their eggs beneath the waxy covering or among the white, fluffy masses. Damage is caused by the withdrawal of plant sap from the leaves, branches, or trunk. Because the insects are unable to digest all the sugar in the plant sap, they excrete the excess in a fluid called *honeydew*, which often drops onto the leaves or plants below. A sooty mold fungus may develop on the honeydew, causing the leaves and twigs to appear black and dirty.

Solution: Spray with Ortho® Systemic Insect Killer. The following spring, before growth starts, spray with Ortho® Volck® Oil Spray. Use Volck® Oil Spray only when temperatures will remain above 40°F for 24 hours following the treatment.

Powdery mildew

Powdery mildew on London plane tree.

Problem: Leaves, flowers, and young stems are covered with a thin layer or irregular patches of a grayish-white powder. Infected leaves may turn yellowish or reddish and drop. Some leaves or branches may be distorted. In late fall, tiny black dots (spore-producing bodies) that look like ground pepper are scattered over the white patches.

Analysis: Powdery mildew is a common plant disease caused by any of several fungi that thrive in both humid and dry weather. Some fungi attack only older leaves and plant parts; others attack only young tissue. Plants growing in shady areas are often severely infected. The powdery patches consist of fungal strands and spores. The spores are spread by the wind to healthy plants. The fungus saps plant nutrients, causing discoloration and sometimes the death of the leaf. Certain powdery mildews also cause leaf or branch distortion. Powdery mildews often attack many different kinds of plants in the garden.

Solution: Several fungicides—including those containing *triforine* (Ortho® RosePride® Rose & Shrub Disease Control), *chlorothalonil*, and *cycloheximide*—are used to control powdery mildew. (For control information, look up the specific plant in the alphabetical section beginning on page 204.)

Leaf and stem rust

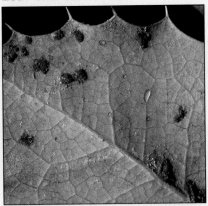

Rust on Oregon grapeholly.

Problem: Yellow, orange, red, or black powdery pustules appear on the upper or lower surfaces of leaves or occasionally on the bark. The powdery material can be scraped or rubbed off. Leaves are discolored or mottled yellow to brown. Leaves may become twisted and distorted and may dry and drop off. Infected stems may be swollen or blistered or may develop oblong or hornlike galls up to 2 inches long.

Analysis: Many species of leaf and stem rust fungi infect trees and shrubs. Some rusts produce spore pustules on leaves or stems; others produce galls or hornlike structures on various parts of the plant. Most rusts attack only one species or a few related species of plants. Some rusts require two different plant species to complete their life cycles. Part of the cycle is spent on the tree or shrub and part is spent on other plants. In most cases, the symptoms produced on the two hosts are different. Wind and splashing water spread rust spores to healthy plants. When conditions are favorable (moisture and temperatures 55° to 75°F), the spores germinate and infect the tissue.

Solution: Several fungicides, including those containing *triforine* (Ortho® RosePride® Rose & Shrub Disease Control), *chlorothalonil*, *ferbam*, *mancozeb*, and *cycloheximide*, may be used to control rust. Look under the entry for your plant in the alphabetical section beginning on page 204 to determine which fungicide is appropriate. Some rust fungi are fairly harmless to the plant and do not require control measures. Rake up and destroy leaves in the fall.

Sooty mold

Sooty mold on camellia.

Problem: A black, sooty mold grows on the leaves and twigs. It can be completely wiped off the surfaces. Cool, moist weather hastens the growth of the mold.

Analysis: These common black molds are found on a wide variety of plants in the garden. They are caused by any of several fungi that grow on sticky material left on plants by aphids, mealybugs, scales, whiteflies, and other insects that suck sap from the plant. The insects are unable to digest all the sugar in the sap, and they excrete the excess in a fluid called *honeydew*, which drops onto the leaves below. The honeydew may also drop out of infested trees and shrubs onto plants growing beneath them. The sooty mold fungi develop on the honeydew, causing the leaves to appear black and dirty. Sooty molds are unsightly but are fairly harmless because they do not attack the leaf directly. Extremely heavy infestations prevent light from reaching the leaf, so the leaf produces fewer nutrients and may turn yellow. The presence of sooty molds indicates that the plant is infested with insects.

Solution: Wipe sooty molds from the leaves with a wet rag, or rain will eventually wash them off. Prevent more sooty mold from growing by controlling the insect that is producing the honeydew. Inspect the leaves and twigs above the sooty mold to find out what type of insect is present. (For control information, see the following pages: aphids, page 443; mealybugs, page 444; scales, pages 444 to 447; whiteflies, page 448.)

179

SPOTS ON LEAVES

Spots on leaves

Entomosporium leaf spot on photinia.

Leaf spots on liquidambar.

Problem: Spots and blotches appear on the leaves and flowers.

Analysis:

1. Fungal leaf spot: Spots caused by fungi are often small and circular and may be found on all of the leaves. Sometimes only the older or younger leaves are affected. The spots range in size from barely visible to ¾ inch. They can be yellow, red, tan, gray, brown, or black and may have a definite margin. Spots sometimes join to form blotches. Often the leaves turn yellow and die. Infection is usually most severe during moist, mild weather (50° to 85°F).

2. Insects: Several different types of insects, including lace bugs, leafhoppers, mites, plant bugs, and thrips, cause spotting of leaves. Leaves may be spotted brownish, yellow, or white, or they may be completely discolored. Sometimes the insects are visible, feeding on the lower or upper surfaces of leaves. (For more information on these insects, look in the insect section starting on page 432.)

3. Sunburn: Shade-loving plants placed in a sunny location develop spots and blotches on the leaves most directly exposed to the sun. Sun-loving plants also develop sunburn symptoms if they are allowed to dry out. Initially, sunburned leaves develop a whitish or yellowish bleached appearance between the veins. Large, dark blotches form on the damaged tissue. Leaves not directly exposed to the sun remain green and uninjured.

Solution:

1. Spray plants with a fungicide containing *chlorothalonil, mancozeb,* or *zineb* when new growth begins. Repeat at intervals of 2 weeks for as long as the weather remains favorable for infection. Make sure that your plant is listed on the product label. Raking and destroying leaves in the fall may help control the fungus.

2. These insects can be controlled with various types of insecticides. (For effective chemicals, look under the entry for your plant in the alphabetical section beginning on page 204.)

3. Where practical, pick off the injured leaves and plant parts. Check to see whether your plant is adapted to sun or shade by looking it up in the alphabetical section beginning on page 204. Provide shade, or transplant shade-loving plants. (For a list of trees and shrubs for shady areas, see page 549.) Water plants regularly, especially on hot, sunny, or windy days. (For watering instructions, see pages 407 to 408.)

DISTORTED GROWTH

Leaves distorted or curled

Leaf distortion on ash caused by aphids.

Problem: Leaves are distorted or curled; new growth may also be deformed. Insects are sometimes found on distorted leaves, and affected leaves are often discolored.

Analysis: Leaves may be distorted by herbicides, insects, or cold.

1. Herbicide damage: Phenoxy herbicides, such as 2,4–D, cause new growth on trees or shrubs to be deformed. Leaves and stem tips may be distorted and gnarled. Leaves are often discolored but may remain green. Distorted new growth often continues to appear throughout the growing season. In severe cases, the plant is killed. Herbicide damage may be caused by misapplication of weed killers, spray drift from neighbors, or spray equipment that has been used for other purposes and not cleaned after an herbicide application.

2. Insects: Many types of insects cause leaf distortion and curling. Thrips, certain caterpillars, and sucking insects—including aphids, leafhoppers, mealybugs, mites, scales, and whiteflies—may cause leaf distortion or curling as a result of their feeding on plant tissue. These insects are usually found on the lower surfaces of leaves or inside curled leaves during spring or summer. Leaves are often discolored, and plant growth is slowed.

3. Frost injury: Leaves become distorted, crinkled, and discolored, and shoot tips on evergreens curl downward. The injury is caused by low temperatures after growth starts in the spring or by sudden cold periods, which damage young, tender tissue before plants are dormant in the fall. Buds and flowers may die, and bark may crack.

GALLS OR GROWTHS

Galls or growths on leaves branches or trunks

Herbicide damage on forsythia.

Galls on Virginia witch hazel.

Leaf galls on willow.

Problem: Swellings, thickenings, and growths develop on the leaves, shoots, branches, or trunk. Plants with numerous galls on branches or the trunk may be weak, and leaves may be yellowing. Branches may die.

Solution: Solutions below correspond to the numbered items in the analysis.

1. Damaged plants usually survive. Prune off injured parts and water the plant thoroughly. If a granular herbicide has been applied, flush the soil with water several times. To avoid future damage, don't spray on windy days. Wash herbicides from sprayers thoroughly before spraying desirable plants, or keep a second sprayer for herbicides.

2. Various insecticides control these insects. (For information on the insects and their controls, check under the specific plant in the alphabetical section beginning on page 204.)

3. Where practical, remove injured parts. If cold temperatures are expected in spring or fall when plants are growing, cover them with burlap. Don't apply fertilizer late in the growing season. This encourages tender new growth, which may be damaged. Plant trees and shrubs adapted to your area.

Analysis: These growths can be caused by any of three factors.

1. Fungal leaf or stem gall: Several different fungi, including rust fungi, cause enlargement and thickening of leaves and shoots. Affected plant parts are usually many times larger than normal and are often discolored and succulent. Some leaf or stem galls turn brown and hard with age. The galls are unsightly but rarely harmful to the plant. Fungal galls are most severe when spring weather is wet.

2. Bacterial crown gall: This plant disease is caused by a soil-inhabiting bacterium (*Agrobacterium tumefaciens*) that infects many ornamentals, fruits, and nuts in the garden. The bacteria enter the plant through wounds in the roots or the base of the trunk (the crown). The galls disrupt the flow of water and nutrients up the roots, stems, and trunk, weakening and stunting the top growth. Galls do not usually kill the plant. (For more information on crown gall, see page 422.)

3. Insect galls: Many insects cause galls by feeding on plant tissue or by injecting a toxin into the tissue during feeding. As a result of this irritation, blisters or growths of various shapes form on leaves, swellings develop on roots or stems, and buds and flowers grow abnormally. Most gall-forming insects cause minor damage to the plant, but the galls may be unsightly.

Solution: Solutions below correspond to the numbered items in the analysis.

1. Pick off and destroy affected parts as soon as they appear. If galls are a problem this year, spray next spring with a fungicide containing *ferbam* or *mancozeb* just before the buds open. Add a spreader-sticker to the spray. Repeat the spray two weeks later.

2. Infected plants can't be cured. They often survive for many years, however. To improve the appearance of shrubs with stem galls, prune out and destroy affected stems below the galled area. Disinfect pruning shears after each cut. Destroy severely infected shrubs. Consult a professional horticulturist to remove galls from valued trees. The bacteria will remain in the soil for at least two to three years. (For a list of plants resistant to crown gall, see page 548.)

3. Many gall-forming insects require no controls. If you feel the galls are unsightly, however, or if the galls cause dieback, control measures may be necessary. (For control measures, look under the entry for the plant in the alphabetical section beginning on page 204.)

181

GALLS OR GROWTHS (continued)

Mushroom and conk

Conk on the trunk of a bigleaf maple.

Problem: Mushrooms appear around the base of the tree. Or white, yellow, gray, or brownish growths protrude from the trunk. The plant may appear unhealthy.

Analysis: Mushrooms and conks (hard, woody growths that protrude from tree trunks) are the reproductive bodies of fungi. Most mushroom fungi live on decaying matter. When conditions are favorable, the fungi produce mushrooms and conks containing spores that are spread by the wind. Several different mushroom fungi decay the heartwood of living trees. Most of these grow only in older wood, which they enter through wounds. Mushrooms or conks usually appear annually in the dead portions of the trees. Some conks may remain attached to the wood for years. *Armillaria mellea*, a fungus that causes a disease called armillaria root rot, mushroom root rot, oak root fungus, or shoestring root rot, invades healthy roots. In the fall or winter, mushrooms appear around the base of the plant, growing on the infected roots.

Solution: By the time conks or mushrooms appear on the trunk, it is too late to do anything about the wood rot. Inspect the tree to determine the extent of decay (contact a professional arborist if necessary). Trees or branches with extensive decay are dangerous and should be removed. Keep plants vigorous by fertilizing and watering regularly. The spread of armillaria root rot may be inhibited if the rot is only in part of the roots.

Leafy mistletoe

Leafy mistletoe.

Problem: Leafy olive green plants up to 4 feet across are attached to the branches. The tufts are most noticeable during the winter on trees without their leaves. Affected branches are often swollen. Some may break from the weight of the plants. Branches beyond the growth occasionally die.

Analysis: Leafy mistletoes (*Phoradendron* species) are semiparasitic plants that manufacture their own food but depend on their host plants for water and minerals. The mistletoe produces sticky seeds that are spread by birds from one tree to another or by falling from higher to lower branches. The seeds germinate almost anywhere but penetrate only young, thin bark. The rootlike attachment organs of the plant penetrate the tree's water-conducting vessels, which they tap for mineral nutrients and water. At the point of attachment, the branch or trunk swells, sometimes to two or three times its normal size. Growth of mistletoe is slow at first, but after six or eight years, plants may be 3 feet across. Trees heavily infested with mistletoe may be weakened and sometimes die.

Solution: Prune limbs 18 inches below the point of mistletoe attachment. The rootlike attachment organs may spread through host tissue up to 1½ feet from the swollen area. They must be removed or the mistletoe will resprout. To prevent the spread of seeds, remove tufts before seeds form in the spring. If it is impractical to prune the tree limbs, remove the mistletoe and wrap the infected areas with black plastic to smother the resprouting mistletoe.

Dwarf mistletoe

Dwarf mistletoe. Inset: Seeds.

Problem: Twigs and small branches of conifers are swollen and have cankers (discolored lesions). Witches'-brooms (many small tufts of branches; see page 183) usually form on infested branches. As swellings or witches'-brooms increase in size, the tree loses vigor. Foliage becomes sparse and yellowish, and over a period of years the portion of the tree above the mistletoe may die. Short, succulent, leafless, yellow, brown, or olive-green shoots develop in the bark of affected branches.

Analysis: Dwarf mistletoe (*Arceuthobium* species) is a parasitic plant that infests many conifers. Dwarf mistletoe lacks a normal root system and true leaves. It relies on its host plant to supply most of its nutrients. It is different from leafy mistletoe, which depends on its host plant only for water and minerals. In midsummer, dwarf mistletoe spreads by sticky seeds that are explosively discharged for distances up to 50 feet. Seeds land on needles and slide down to the bark when needles are moistened. When seeds germinate, usually the following spring, rootlike structures penetrate the bark. The structures form a network in the branches, causing swellings and the formation of cankers. Dwarf mistletoe weakens the tree as it saps nutrients and water and distorts the growth of branches. Within one to three years after infestation, aerial shoots are produced that are from ½ to 4 inches long.

Solution: Remove heavily infested trees. Prune off branches of less severely infested trees, making the cuts at the trunk. Remove new infestations as they appear.

Algae, lichen, and moss

Lichen.

Problem: Brown, gray, green, or yellow crusty, soft, or leaflike growths develop on trees in moist forested areas. The growths are usually found on the lower or shaded parts of trunks and branches.

Analysis: Algae, lichens, and mosses are sometimes mistaken for plant diseases, especially if the tree to which they are attached appears unhealthy. They do not harm the plant, however. Most algae grow where moisture is abundant, on the lower, shaded side of the trunk. They appear only as a green shading that is not very noticeable on the bark. Lichens are a combination of green algae and fungi. They range in color from brown to green and appear crusty or leaflike. They are sensitive to air pollution and are found only in areas where the air is clean. True mosses are small green plants growing in a mat and having tiny leaves and stems. They are abundant in moist areas and are much more apparent than algae. Spanish moss is a flowering plant (in the pineapple family) that is very noticeable hanging from branches of trees in the Southern United States.

Solution: Algae, lichens, and mosses do not harm the plant, but they may be unsightly. Control them by pruning away surrounding vegetation to increase the amount of light and air flow, which will reduce the moisture in the soil and air around the plant.

Witches'-broom

Witches'-broom on hackberry.

Problem: A dense tuft of small, weak twigs develops on a branch. Leaves on the tuft may be smaller than normal and off-color. The branches are weak and unhealthy.

Analysis: A witches'-broom is a dense proliferation of twig growth, usually caused by an insect, a plant disease, or mistletoe (see page 182). The witches'-broom looks messy but does not harm the plant. The insect or disease that caused it, however, may be harmful.

Solution: If the witches'-broom affects the appearance of the plant, prune it off. It may be difficult for the home gardener to identify the cause of brooming. If witches'-broom continues to develop, contact a professional arborist or your local county extension office.

Leafrollers

Leafroller on linden.

Problem: Leaves are rolled, usually lengthwise, and tied together with webbing. Rolled leaves are chewed. When a rolled leaf is opened, a green caterpillar, ½ to ¾ inch long, may be found feeding inside. Flower buds may also be chewed.

Analysis: Several different leafrollers feed on the leaves and buds of woody ornamentals. Some species feed on only one plant. Others feed on many plants in the garden. Leafrollers are the larvae of small (up to ¾-inch) brownish moths. The insects spend the winter as eggs or larvae on the plant. In the spring the larvae feed on the young foliage, sometimes tunneling into and mining the leaf first. They roll one or more leaves around themselves, tying the leaves together with a silken webbing, then feed within the rolled leaves. This provides protection from weather, parasites, and chemical sprays. Some leafrollers mature in summer and have several generations each year. Other leafrollers have only one generation. In the fall, the larvae either mature into moths and lay overwintering eggs or spend the winter inside the rolled leaf.

Solution: Spray with Ortho® Systemic Insect Killer or the bacterial insecticide *Bacillus thuringiensis* (Bt) in the spring when leaf damage is first noticed. For insecticides to be most effective, they should be applied before larvae are protected inside the rolled leaves. Check the plant periodically in the spring for the first sign of infestation.

HOLES OR TRAILS IN LEAVES *(continued)*

Leafminers

Leafminer damage to holly.

Problem: Green or whitish translucent winding trails, blisters, or blotches develop on leaves. The trails, blisters, or blotches later turn brown. If an infested leaf is torn open, one to several small green, yellowish, or whitish insects may be found between the upper and lower surfaces of the leaves.

Analysis: Leafminers are the larvae of flies, moths, beetles, or sawflies. The larvae feed between the upper and lower surfaces of leaves. Adult female moths lay their eggs on or inside the leaves, usually in early to late spring. The emerging larvae feed between the leaf surfaces, producing blisters, blotches, or trails. The infested tissue stands out prominently against the normal green foliage as it turns whitish or light green to brown. The insects pupate inside the leaves or in the soil and emerge as adults. Some adults also feed on the leaves, chewing holes or notches in them. (For more information on leafminers, see page 455.)

Solution: Control of leafminers is difficult because they spend most of their lives protected inside the leaves. Insecticides are usually aimed at the adults. Once leafminers are noticed in the leaves, inspect the foliage periodically, or check with your local county extension office to determine when the adults emerge. Then spray with Ortho® Systemic Insect Killer. Make sure that your plant is listed on the product label.

Nocturnal insects

Weevil damage to rhododendron.

Problem: Holes or notches appear in leaves and flowers. Some of the leaves, stems, and flowers may be sheared off. Severely infested plants may be stripped of foliage. No insects are visible on the plants during the day. When the affected plants are inspected at night with a flashlight, insects may be seen feeding on the foliage and flowers.

Analysis: Several types of insects feed on plants only at night, including weevils, other beetles, and caterpillars. Weevils are a type of beetle with a long snout. Beetles are hard-bodied insects with tough, leathery wing covers. The wing covers meet in the middle of the back, forming a straight line. Caterpillars are smooth or hairy, soft-bodied worms. Nocturnal insects usually hide in the soil, debris, or other protected places during the day.

Solution: Control these insects with insecticides. (For more information on nocturnal insects and how to control them, see beetles and weevils, pages 434 to 435; and caterpillars, page 439.)

Snails and slugs

Slug damage on hosta.

Problem: Irregular holes with smooth edges are chewed in leaves. Leaves may be sheared off entirely. Silvery trails wind around the plants and soil nearby. Snails and slugs may be seen moving around or feeding on the leaves, especially at night. Check for them by inspecting the garden at night by flashlight.

Analysis: Snails and slugs are mollusks and are related to clams, oysters, and other shellfish. They feed on a wide variety of plants, including ornamentals and vegetables. Like other mollusks, snails and slugs need to be moist all the time. For this reason, they avoid direct sun and dry places and hide during the day in damp places, such as under flowerpots or in thick ground covers. They emerge at night or on rainy days to feed. Snails and slugs are similar, except that the snail has a hard shell it withdraws into when disturbed. Slugs lay white eggs encased in a slimy mass in protected places. Snails bury their eggs in the soil, also in a slimy mass. The young look like miniature versions of their parents.

Solution: Apply Ortho® Bug-Geta® Snail & Slug Killer around the trees and shrubs you wish to protect. Also apply the bait in areas where snails or slugs might be hiding, such as in dense ground covers, weedy areas, compost piles, or flowerpot-storage areas. Before spreading the bait, wet down the treated areas to encourage snail and slug activity that night. Repeat the application every two weeks for as long as snails and slugs are active.

WILTING

Lack of water

Wilting mockorange.

Problem: The plant wilts often, and the soil is frequently or always dry. The leaves or leaf edges may turn brown and shrivel.

Analysis: Water in the soil is taken up by plant roots. It moves up into the stems and leaves and evaporates into the air through microscopic breathing pores in the surfaces of the leaves. Water pressure within plant cells keeps the cell walls rigid and prevents the leaves and stems from collapsing. When the soil is dry, the roots are unable to furnish the leaves and stems with water, the water pressure in the cells drops, and the plant wilts. Most plants will recover if they have not wilted severely. Frequent or severe wilting, however, will curb a plant's growth and may eventually kill it.

Solution: Water the plant immediately. To prevent wilting, follow the instructions for your plant found in the alphabetical section beginning on page 204. (For information on watering, see pages 407 to 408.)

Damaged trunk or stem

Leaf drop on dogwood caused by borer infestation.

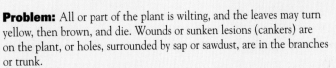

Wilting rhododendron.

Problem: All or part of the plant is wilting, and the leaves may turn yellow, then brown, and die. Wounds or sunken lesions (cankers) are on the plant, or holes, surrounded by sap or sawdust, are in the branches or trunk.

Analysis: Damage to the wood or bark disrupts water and nutrient movement through the plant, causing wilting.

Solution: Solutions below correspond to the numbered items in the analysis.

1. Wounds: Any kind of mechanical injury that breaks roots, stems, or bark causes the plant to wilt. A plant may be accidentally wounded by a motor vehicle, lawn mower, animal, or foot traffic; its roots may be damaged by soil disturbance, cultivation, compaction, or construction injuries. In severe cases, the plant dies.

1. Thin out some of the branches and keep the plant well watered. During hot weather, provide shade to reduce evaporation from leaves. Prevent mechanical injuries to plants by being careful when working around the roots and stems. If necessary, place barriers around plants to prevent damage from vehicles, animals, and foot traffic.

2. Cankers: Cankers are sunken, dark-colored lesions that develop as a result of infection by fungi or bacteria. Cankers on small or young plants often cause the portion of the plant above the canker to wilt. Branches or the entire plant may eventually die.

2. Prune dying branches below the canker. Avoid wounding plants.

3. Borers: Most borers are the larvae of beetles or moths. Many kinds of borers infest stems, branches, or trunks. The larvae feed by tunneling through the bark, sapwood, and heartwood, stopping the flow of nutrients and water in that area. Large trees and shrubs usually turn yellow and brown rather than wilt.

3. Prune out stems with borers. Keep the plant well watered. Feed regularly with Scotts® Evergreen, Flowering Tree & Shrub Slow Release Plant Food. (For more information on borers and their controls, see page 189.)

WILTING (continued)

Extreme heat or wind

Wilting dogwood.

Problem: The plant is wilting, but the foliage usually looks healthy. No signs of insects or disease are present, and the soil is moist. Wilting is most common on shrubs or plants with limited root systems.

Analysis: During hot, windy periods, small or young plants may wilt, even though the soil is wet. Wind and heat cause water to evaporate quickly from the leaves. If roots can't absorb and convey water fast enough to replenish this loss, leaves wilt.

Solution: Keep the plant well watered during hot spells, and sprinkle it with water to cool off the foliage. The plant will usually recover when the temperature drops or the wind dies. Provide shade during hot weather, and use temporary windbreaks to protect from wind. Plant shrubs adapted to your area.

Planted too shallow

Arborvitae planted too shallow.

Problem: A recently planted tree or shrub wilts frequently. Roots or the rootball may be exposed to air.

Analysis: Newly planted trees and shrubs may wilt frequently if they are planted too shallowly. Plants that have been set in the ground at a higher level than they were originally growing wilt because the exposed rootball dries out quickly. This may kill the surface roots, especially if the soil washes away, exposing them.

Solution: Remove the plant, along with its rootball, and replant it deeper. The plant should be set at the same level as when it was growing in the pot or the ground. Be careful not to plant too deep, because this can create an equally serious problem that may not show up for a few years. Water the plant thoroughly so the entire rootball is moist. Keep the plant well watered until it becomes established. In poor drainage areas, plants may be set slightly high with a small amount of soil covering the rootball, as long as the soil is covered by a generous portion of mulch.

Dry rootball

Dry rootball.

Problem: The entire plant is wilting. The soil surrounding the plant is moist, but the rootball is dry. The tree has been recently planted.

Analysis: Plants sold balled and burlapped at a nursery are grown in fields. When the plants reach a size suitable for selling, they are dug up with a ball of soil around their roots. Sometimes the soil in which they are grown is extremely heavy. When the heavy soil is balled and burlapped, it sometimes shrinks as it dries or is compacted, and the ball becomes impermeable to water. After the plant is replanted, water runs off the outside of the ball rather than moistening the soil inside, causing the roots to dry out. Rootballs of balled-and-burlapped plants or of container plants may also dry out if the soil in which the plant is set is much lighter or heavier than the soil in the rootball. Water runs into the lighter soil instead of moistening the soil around the roots; or the surrounding heavy clay soil draws out the water from the light soil in the rootball, causing the rootball to dry out.

Solution: To wet the rootball, build a basin around the plant the diameter of the rootball. Keep water in the basin for three hours. Add a wetting agent (which can be purchased at your local nursery) to the water initially. Continue watering in the basin for six weeks. Water whenever the rootball (not the surrounding soil) is moist but not wet 1 inch below the surface. Water or soak the rootball before planting. If the soil texture in the rootball is very different from that of the surrounding soil, provide a transition zone, using a mix of rootball and native soil.

Transplant shock

Transplant shock.

Problem: The plant wilts, but the foliage usually looks healthy. No signs of insects or disease are present, and the soil is moist. The plant has been recently transplanted.

Analysis: Plants frequently wilt or stop growing for a while after being transplanted. Transplant "shock" is the result of roots being cut or injured during transplanting. Wilting occurs when the roots are unable to supply the plant with enough water, even when the soil is wet.

Solution: To reduce the water requirement of the plant, prune off one-fourth to one-third of the branches. Water the plant well until it becomes established. (For information on watering, see pages 407 to 408.) If necessary, provide shade during hot weather. Transplant when plants are dormant, if possible, and when the weather is cool, in early morning, late afternoon, or on a cloudy day.

Slime flux

Slime flux on poplar.

Problem: Sour-smelling sap oozes from wounds, cracks, and branch crotches, mainly during the growing season. The sap drips down the bark and dries, causing unsightly gray streaks. Some wilting and leaf scorch may occur on affected branches. Insects are attracted to the sour-smelling ooze. Elms and poplars are commonly infected.

Analysis: Slime flux, also called *wetwood,* is caused by several different bacteria. The bacteria infect the heartwood, producing abnormally high sap pressure. This pressure is caused by bacterial fermentation and forces the fermented sap, or *flux,* out of wounds, cracks, or crotches in the tree. Flux is especially copious when the tree is growing rapidly. Large areas of the bark may be coated with the smelly, bacteria-laden sap, which dries to a grayish white color. Wounds do not heal, and the bark is unsightly. A tree with this problem is often under water stress, which may cause drought damage (wilting, scorched leaves, and dieback) to the branches. The problem may persist for years.

Solution: There are no controls for this condition. To diminish the unsightly stained bark, bore a slightly upward-slanting drainage hole into the water-soaked wood below each oozing wound. Insert a ½-inch-diameter plastic tube just until it stays firmly in place. (If the tube penetrates the water-soaked wood inside the tree, it will interfere with drainage.) The tube will carry the dripping sap away from the trunk, but it will not cure the disease. Disinfect tools after pruning infected trees.

Honeydew

Honeydew on maple.

Problem: A shiny or sticky substance coats the leaves and sometimes the twigs. Insects may be found on the leaves directly above; ants, flies, or bees may be present. A black, sooty mold often grows on the sticky substance.

Analysis: Honeydew is a sweet, sticky substance secreted by aphids, mealybugs, psyllids, scales, and whiteflies. These sucking insects can't digest all the sugar in the plant sap, and they excrete the excess in a fluid called *honeydew,* which drops onto the leaves directly below and adheres to anything beneath the tree or shrub. Lawn furniture or cars beneath infested plants may be stained. Ants and certain flies and bees feed on honeydew and may be found around the plant. A sooty mold fungus often develops on the sticky substance, causing the leaves and twigs to appear black and dirty. The fungus doesn't infect the leaves but instead, grows superficially on the honeydew. Extremely heavy fungus infestations may prevent light from reaching the leaves, reducing food production.

Solution: Wipe honeydew from the leaves with a wet rag, or hose it off. Eventually the rain will wash it off. Prevent more honeydew by controlling the insect that is producing it. Inspect the leaves and twigs above the honeydew to find out what type of insect is present. (For control information, see the following pages: aphids, page 443; mealybugs, page 444; psyllids, page 449; scales, pages 444 to 447; whiteflies, page 448.)

FLUID ON BARK OR LEAVES (continued)

Oozing sap

Oozing sap on cherry.

Oozing sap on Coulter pine.

Problem: Beads of amber-colored or whitish sticky sap appear on healthy bark. Or sap oozes from patches of bark, cankers, wounds, or pruning cuts.

Analysis:

1. Natural tendency: Certain species of plants have a tendency to ooze sap. Frequently, small beads of sap form on healthy bark of these plants.

2. Environmental stress: Plants that are stressed because they are growing in wet soil may produce large quantities of sap, even though they are not diseased. Many plants respond to changes in weather conditions or soil moisture by oozing profusely.

3. Mechanical injury: Most plants ooze sap when bark is wounded. This is especially noticeable on maple and birch. If these trees are injured during the fall, they ooze a large amount of sap the following spring.

4. Disease: Plants respond to certain fungal and bacterial infections by forming cankers—dark, sunken areas that gum profusely. Gummosis, or oozing sap, is one of the initial signs of infection.

5. Borer damage: Many different insects bore holes into bark. Sap oozes from these holes. The tunnels these insects bore in the wood often become infected by decay-causing organisms.

Solution:

1. As long as the bark appears healthy, there is nothing to worry about.

2. If your plant is growing in wet, poorly drained soil, allow the soil to dry out between waterings. Provide for drainage away from trunks and roots. If oozing sap occurs as a result of rapid changes in weather and soil moisture, reduce the effects of stress on the plant by keeping it healthy. Maintain health and vigor of the plant by fertilizing and watering regularly. (For information on watering and fertilizing, see pages 407 to 409.)

3. Avoid mechanical injuries to the plant. Stake, tie, and prune properly. (For information on pruning and treating wounds, see page 412.)

4. Remove badly infected branches and cut out cankers. Keep the plant vigorous by fertilizing and watering regularly.

5. Borers are difficult to control once they have burrowed into the wood. (For more information on borers and their controls, see page 189.)

HOLES OR CRACKS IN BARK

Sapsuckers

Sapsucker holes.

Problem: Rows of parallel holes, ¼ inch in diameter, appear on the trunk. Sap often oozes from the holes, and portions of the surrounding bark may fall off. When damage is severe, part or all of the tree is killed. Yellow-bellied or red-breasted birds may be seen pecking on the tree.

Analysis: Two species of sapsuckers, members of the woodpecker family, feed on tree bark and sap. The red-breasted sapsucker is found in the Pacific Northwest. The yellow-bellied sapsucker is common throughout much of the United States. Sapsuckers peck into many trees before finding a suitable one that has sap with a high sugar content. Once the birds find a favorite tree, they visit it many times per day and feed on it year after year. Portions of the bark often fall off after sapsuckers have pecked many holes. If the trunk is girdled, the tree above the damaged area dies. Sometimes disease organisms enter the holes and damage or kill the tree.

Solution: It is difficult to prevent sapsucker damage to trees. Wrapping the damaged trunk with burlap or smearing a sticky material (such as the latex used for ant control) above and below the holes may inhibit new pecking. (For a list of trees most commonly attacked by sapsuckers, see page 547.)

Bark-feeding animals

Rodent damage to crabapple.

Porcupine damage to elm.

Borers

Borer emergence holes.

Problem: Bark has been chewed or gnawed from the trunk and lower branches. In some cases, the trunk is entirely girdled. Deer, rabbits, mice, or squirrels may have been seen in the yard, or their tracks may be evident on the ground or snow. Damage is usually most severe during the winter, when other food sources are scarce.

Analysis: Several animals chew on tree bark.
1. Deer: These animals feed on leaves, shoots, buds, and bark. They feed by pulling and twisting the bark or twig tissue, leaving ragged or bent twig ends or patches of bark. Generally they feed on the lower branches and upper trunk. The males may also damage plants by rubbing their antlers on the trunk and branches.
2. Rabbits: These animals chew on the bark at the base of the trunk. They chew bark and twigs off cleanly, leaving a sharp break. The damaged trunk is often scarred with paired gouges left by the rabbit's front teeth. Rabbits generally feed no more than 2 feet above the ground or snow level. They damage small or young plants more severely.
3. Field mice or voles: These animals damage plants by chewing off the bark at the base of the trunk just at or slightly above or below ground or snow level. They may girdle the trunk, often killing the plant. Mice leave tiny scratches in the exposed wood. Some species of mice feed on plant roots, causing the slow decline and death of the plant.
4. Squirrels: These animals damage trees and shrubs by wounding the bark. Red squirrels feed on maple sap in the spring. The resulting bark wounds are V-shape. Canker disease fungi sometimes invade the wounds, weakening or killing the tree. Some squirrels feed on bark when food is scarce in the winter. Other squirrel species use bark and twigs for building nests.
5. Porcupines: During the winter, porcupines eat tree bark, sometimes stripping large patches of bark high above the ground. If the trunk is girdled, the top of the tree may die.

Solution: Various methods may be used to exclude or control deer, rabbits, mice, squirrels, and porcupines in the garden. These methods usually involve protecting the plants with fencing and tree guards or controlling the animals with traps. (For more information on the animals and their controls, see page 499 for deer; pages 496 to 497 for squirrels; page 497 for rabbits; page 494 for field mice; and page 498 for porcupines.) Trapping or killing these animals is illegal in some states. Contact your state's Department of Fish and Game to determine local regulations.

Problem: Foliage on a branch or at the top of the tree may be sparse; eventually the twigs and branches die. Holes or tunnels are apparent in the trunk or branches. Sap or sawdust usually surrounds or drips from the holes. Bark may die over the tunnels and slough off, or knotlike swellings may be on the trunk and limbs. Weakened branches break during storms. Weak, young, or newly transplanted trees may be killed.

Analysis: Borers are larvae of beetles or moths. Females lay their eggs in bark throughout the summer. Larvae feed by tunneling through bark, sapwood, and heartwood. This stops the flow of nutrients and water in that area by cutting the conducting vessels; branch and twig dieback result. Sap flow acts as a defense against borers if the plant is healthy. When the insect burrows into the wood, tree sap fills the hole and drowns the insect. Factors that weaken the tree—such as mechanical injuries, transplanting, damage by leaf-feeding insects, and poor growing conditions—make it more attractive to egg-laying females.

Solution: Cut out and destroy all dead and dying branches, and remove severely infested young plants. Spray or paint the trunk and branches with an insecticide containing *permethrin* or *bifenthrin*. Timing of spraying and pruning is critical. Contact your local county extension office for the best time to spray and prune trees in your area. Maintain plant health and vigor by watering and fertilizing regularly. Remove dead and dying trees promptly, and do not pile freshly cut firewood near desirable trees.

189

HOLES OR CRACKS IN BARK (continued)

Cankers

Canker on ceanothus.

Problem: Sunken, oval, or elongated dark-colored lesions (cankers) develop on the trunk or branches. The bark at the edge of the canker may thicken and roll inward. In some cases, sticky, amber-colored sap oozes from the canker. Foliage on infected plants may be stunted and yellowing. Some of the leaves may turn brown and drop off. Twigs and branches may gradually die, and the plant may eventually be killed.

Analysis: Many species of fungi and bacteria cause cankers and dieback. Infection usually occurs through injured or wounded tissue. Bark that has been damaged by sunscald, cold, pruning, or equipment is especially susceptible. Some decay organisms infect the leaves first, then spread down into healthy twigs. Cankers form as the decay progresses. Some plants produce a sticky sap that oozes from the cankers. The portion of the branch or stem above the canker may die from the clogging of the water and nutrient-conducting vessels in the branch. Cankers that form on the trunk are the most serious and may kill the tree. The plant may halt the development of a canker by producing callus tissue, a growth of barklike cells, to wall off the decay.

Solution: Remove badly infected branches and cut out cankers. Avoid wounding the plant. Keep the plant vigorous by fertilizing and watering regularly. (For more information on fertilizing and watering, see pages 407 to 409.)

Bark shedding

Bark shedding on madrone.

Problem: Bark is cracking or peeling, usually on the older branches and trunk.

Analysis: The shedding or cracking of bark is often noticeable, but it is a natural process. The outer bark changes over the lifetime of a tree. The bark of young trees is live tissue, usually smooth and relatively soft. As the trees mature, the bark dies and hardens, sometimes becoming rough. Trunks and branches increase in diameter with age. The increase in girth causes the outer bark of many plants to crack in a variety of patterns. With some tree species, such as white birch, cracking develops to such an extent that the bark peels and falls off. Newly exposed bark is often smooth and lighter in color than the bark that was shed. Some trees, such as sycamore and shagbark hickory, characteristically have loose outer bark. The bark is constantly in the process of peeling and shedding.

Solution: This process is normal. No controls are necessary.

Lightning damage

Lightning damage to tree.

Problem: Part or all of the tree suddenly turns brown and dies. No external signs of damage may appear, or a strip of bark may be burned or missing from the entire length of the trunk. In less severe cases, trees survive for several years or recover completely. Sometimes tops of trees or branches explode, leaving a jagged stub.

Analysis: Tall trees, trees growing in open locations, and trees growing in moist soil or along riverbanks are susceptible to damage by lightning. Lightning damage is variable. Some trees die suddenly from internal damage or burned roots without any external sign that lightning has struck. Other trees burst into flames or explode when hit. Sometimes only a strip of bark is burned or missing from the trunk and the tree recovers. Some species of trees are more resistant to lightning than others. (For a list of trees susceptible to lightning injury, see page 547.) Some scientists believe that trees high in starch, deep-rooted species, and decaying trees are more susceptible to damage than trees high in oils, shallow-rooted species, or healthy trees.

Solution: Remove all loose and injured bark. To reduce or prevent damage, water trees during dry spells. Remove severely damaged trees. Valuable old trees can be protected with lightning conductors. Contact a professional arborist.

Sunscald

Sunscald.

Sunscald on dogwood.

Frost cracks

Frost cracks.

Problem: Patches of bark die, crack, and later develop into cankers. The dead bark eventually sloughs off, exposing undamaged wood. The affected bark area is always on the southwest side of the tree. Trees with dark bark are likely to be more severely affected. The cracks and cankers develop in either summer or winter.

Analysis: When a tree growing in a deeply shady location is suddenly exposed to intense sunlight or when a tree is heavily pruned, the southwest side of newly exposed bark is injured by the rapid change in temperature. This may develop when a forested area is excessively thinned or when a tree is moved from a shady nursery to a more exposed area such as a lawn.

1. Summer sunscald: With intense summer heat, exposed bark is killed and a canker develops, usually revealing the undamaged wood beneath the bark. Within several seasons, the tree may break at the canker area and topple. Summer sunscald is most severe when the soil is dry.

2. Winter sunscald: Bark injury develops with rapid changes in bark temperature from cold nights to sunny winter days. Exposed bark becomes much warmer than the air during the day but cools rapidly after sunset. This rapid temperature change often results in bark cracking. Later, a canker forms. Trees with thin, dark bark such as apple, cherry, crabapple, maple, linden, and plum are most severely affected.

Solution: Once the bark is injured, you can't do anything about sunscald. Wrap the trunks of recently exposed or newly transplanted trees with tree-wrap paper, available at nurseries. White interior latex paint or whitewash is also effective. The wrap or paint should be left on for at least two winters. Remove the wrap for the spring and summer months to prevent it from harboring plant diseases and insects. Reapply the paint the second season if it has washed off. Trees will eventually adapt to increased exposure by producing thicker bark. Give trees, especially recently transplanted trees, adequate water in the summer and, if necessary, in the fall. Water transplants when the top 2 inches of the rootball are dry. Remove badly infected branches and cut out cankers. Avoid wounding the plant. Keep the plant vigorous by fertilizing and watering regularly. (For more information on fertilizing and watering, see pages 407 to 409.)

Problem: Vertical cracks develop on the trunk, usually on the south and southeast, and sometimes on the west, sides. The cracks generally close during the growing season.

Analysis: Frost cracks develop from the expansion and contraction of bark and wood during periods of wide temperature fluctuations. This causes internal mechanical stress, which causes already weakened or decayed areas of the bark and outer wood to split. The sudden break is often accompanied by a loud noise like a gunshot. Cracks usually heal during the growing season, but they may remain partially open after the weather warms or reopen during the following winter.

Solution: If a large crack fails to heal, a rod or bolt may be installed to hold it together. Consult a professional arborist. Plant trees adapted to your climate. Protect young trees by applying tree-wrap paper in late fall, or whitewash on the trunk.

TWIGS OR BRANCHES BREAK

Limb breakage

Limb breakage caused by weak fork.

Limb breakage caused by snow load.

Twig pruners and twig girdlers

Twig girdler (2× life size).

Problem: Healthy branches break and fall, usually during storms or high winds. Some may drop in the middle of the day during a hot spell.

Analysis: Several different environmental factors cause limb breakage.
1. Weak fork: The angle between a branch and the trunk, called a fork, is normally greater than 45 degrees in most species. If the angle is much less than this, bark is sometimes trapped between the branch and the trunk, preventing the wood from growing together at that point. This weakens the branch. As the branch and trunk increase in length, the additional weight causes the fork to split at the weak junction. A large portion of the tree may fall. Some trees that develop weak forks break more readily than others because of their growth habits and brittle wood.
2. Wind: Branches may fall during high winds, especially in areas where there are tornadoes, hurricanes, and other forms of extreme winds. Moderate winds often hasten the dropping of limbs weakened by injury, insects, or plant disease.
3. Sudden limb drop: Large limbs sometimes drop during the middle of the day for no apparent reason. This usually occurs on hot, calm days. The cause is not known.
4. Snow and ice: Plants heavily coated with snow or ice may lose large limbs because of the additional weight. Evergreen trees or deciduous trees with leaves still attached are most susceptible because of the greater surface to which the snow or ice can adhere, causing the extreme weight.

Solution: If the break is a split, or if at least one-third of the bark at the break is intact, the limb can be bolted back in place. If less than one-third of the bark is intact, or if the branch has fallen off the tree, prune the remaining branch stub. To prevent further damage, brace or cable trees, and knock off snow and ice constantly to prevent buildup. In areas with high winds, prune back some of the branches to reduce the wind load. In the future, don't plant trees with brittle wood that breaks easily. (For a list of trees with weak forks and brittle wood, see page 547.)

Problem: Small, cleanly cut twigs, ¼ to 2 inches in diameter, lie under the tree in the fall. The tree is often abnormally bushy. Small (up to 1-inch), whitish larvae may be found inside the fallen twigs.

Analysis: Several species of wood-boring beetles cause unsightly damage to trees by altering their natural form. In midsummer to fall, the wood-boring beetles lay their eggs in the wood of small twigs. The *twig pruner* larvae tunnel toward the base of the twigs, eating all but the outer bark. In the fall, they back into the hollowed-out twigs. High winds cause the nearly severed twigs containing the larvae to break and drop to the ground. Adult *twig girdlers* lay eggs in twigs, then chew a circle around the outside of the twigs. The girdled twigs die and break off. The eggs in the fallen twig are able to develop without being hindered by the flow of sap through the twig. Both twig pruner and twig girdler larvae mature in the twigs on the ground. The damage to the tree is the result of excessive pruning on the branch tips. Several new side shoots develop where the twigs break off, causing abnormal bushiness and an unnatural shape.

Solution: Chemical control isn't usually necessary or practical. Gather and destroy all severed twigs in the late fall, when the insects are inside them. Also gather severed twigs from nearby trees. This practice usually controls the pest. If necessary to protect small trees, spray with an insecticide containing *bifenthrin* in late summer to kill the adults before they lay eggs. Repeat twice at 30-day intervals.

Tree squirrels

Tree squirrel.

Problem: Many small twigs with healthy leaves attached are lying under the tree or shrub. Squirrels may be seen in the area.

Analysis: Tree squirrels may damage trees by shearing off small twigs, which they use for building nests. Twigs appear to have been cut with a dull knife or shears. The squirrels gather the twigs and carry them to their nests, but they usually leave many behind. They normally clip two or three times more twigs than they need. Trees heavily pruned by squirrels may be bushier than normal.

Solution: Squirrels usually don't harm the tree by clipping twigs. If they are altering the shape of the tree, however, protect the tree with tree guards wrapped around the trunk, or control the squirrels by using live traps. (For more information on tree squirrels, see page 496.)

Heart rot

Heart rot.

Problem: Branches break and fall, usually during storms. The wood in the area of breakage is discolored and often spongy. Mushroomlike growths may be found on the wood.

Analysis: Heart rot is caused mainly by fungi. Fungal decay organisms rot deadwood (such as fallen trees) as part of nature's recycling process. Several of them may also invade live trees through wounds. Healthy, vigorous trees may stop the spread of decay by producing cells that wall off the invaded area. Old trees with many wounds are rarely very resistant to microorganisms, and decay spreads through the wood. The decay doesn't usually kill the living tissue of the tree, so branches and leaves are kept alive. But internal decay reduces the strength of affected limbs. During a storm, weakened branches fall. Some of the decay organisms develop yellowish to brown, mushroomlike growths, called *conks*, on the outside wood in areas where decay is present. (For more information on mushrooms and conks, see page 182.)

Solution: Cut off the remaining branch stub flush against the larger branch or tree trunk. Inspect the rest of the tree to determine the extent of decay (you may need to contact a professional arborist). Branches or the entire plant should be removed if decay is extensive. As much as possible, avoid wounding plants. Keep them vigorous by fertilizing and watering regularly. (For information on watering and fertilizing, see pages 407 to 409.)

Salt burn

Salt burn on mockorange.

Problem: Tips and edges of older leaves turn dark brown or black and die. The rest of the leaf may be lighter green than normal. The browning or blackening can develop in both dry and wet soils, but it is more severe in dry soil. In the worst cases, leaf drop occurs.

Analysis: Salt burn is common along the seashore and in areas of low rainfall. It also occurs in soils with poor drainage, in areas where salt has been used to melt snow and ice, and in areas where too much fertilizer has been applied. Excess salts dissolved in the soil water accumulate in the leaf tips and edges, where they kill the tissue. These salts also interfere with water uptake by the plant. This problem is rare in areas of high rainfall, where the soluble salts are leached from most soils. Poorly drained soils also accumulate salts because they do not leach well; much of the applied water runs off instead of washing through the soil. Fertilizers, most of which are soluble salts, cause salt burn if too much is applied or if they are not diluted with a thorough watering after application. (For more information on salt burn, see page 426.)

Solution: In areas with low rainfall, leach accumulated salts from the soil with an occasional heavy watering (about once a month). Improve drainage around the plants. (For information on drainage, see page 406.) Follow package directions when using fertilizers; several light applications are better than one heavy application. Water thoroughly afterward. Avoid the use of bagged cow manure, which may contain large amounts of salts.

DISCOLORED LEAVES (continued)

Bacterial leaf scorch

Bacterial leaf scorch.

Leaf scorch

Leaf scorch on maple.

Leaf scorch on birch.

Problem: In mid- to late summer, leaf edges and the tissues between the veins turn tan or brown. The brown areas are surrounded by a narrow border of yellow. Older leaves are affected before younger ones. Infected leaves often remain attached until fall. As the disease progresses, the twigs die back. Trees decline over several years, eventually dying.

Analysis: Bacterial leaf scorch is a plant disease caused by a bacterium (*Xylella fastidiosa*) that infects a wide variety of plants. It causes no symptoms in many of the plants, but infected plants are a source of bacteria for other plants. The disease causes scorch symptoms in several shade trees, including elm, maple, mulberry, oak, plum, and sycamore. The bacterium was first identified in 1978 but seems to have been in this country at least since the 1950s and is common throughout the Southeast. The bacteria clog the water-conducting vessels in the leaves and twigs. The scorch symptoms in the leaves are caused by a lack of water. Bacteria are transferred from plant to plant by sharpshooter leafhoppers and spittlebugs as they feed. (For more information on leafhoppers and spittlebugs, see pages 448 and 449.)

Solution: No control is presently available for this plant disease. Prune out diseased branches. Remove severely infected trees, and replant with resistant species. Contact your local county extension office for scorch-resistant trees for your area. Avoid conditions that cause stress to trees.

Problem: Leaf edges and the tissues between the veins turn tan or brown. Leaves are scorched and have a dry appearance. Brown areas often increase in size until little green is left except around the center vein. Dead leaves may remain attached to the plant, or they may drop. Leaf scorch is most severe in the upper branches and when the soil is dry.

Analysis:
1. Extreme heat and wind: Excessive evaporation of moisture from the leaves can cause leaf scorch. In hot or windy weather, water evaporates rapidly from the leaves. If the roots can't absorb and convey water fast enough to replenish this loss, the leaves turn brown and wither. This usually occurs in dry soil, but leaves can also scorch when the soil is moist and temperatures are near 100°F for extended periods. Young plants with limited root systems are most susceptible.

2. Winter burn: Winter burn is similar to scorch from intense heat or wind except that it occurs during unusually warm, windy days in late winter. In colder climates, water can't be replaced by the roots because the soil is frozen, resulting in leaf desiccation. Conifers are most susceptible, especially those planted in exposed areas. Symptoms may not appear until spring.

3. Damaged roots: Trees and shrubs may develop scorched and yellow leaves, early fall color, and dieback after the roots have been injured.

4. Underwatering: Many plants survive even when regularly underwatered. They do not function normally, however, and the leaves frequently burn and wilt over the entire plant.

Solution:
1. To prevent further scorch, deep-water plants during periods of hot weather to wet down the entire root space. Because of their limited root systems, recently transplanted trees and shrubs should be watered more often than established plants. Water them when the rootball is dry 2 inches below the surface. If the leaves scorched when the soil was moist, provide shade during hot weather and screens for protection from wind—or transplant to a protected area.

2. Provide windbreaks and shelter for plants growing in cold, windy regions. Covering smaller plants with burlap helps prevent leaf drying. If necessary, water in late fall or winter to ensure adequate soil moisture. Mulch plants after they are dormant to reduce the depth of frost penetration into the soil.

3. For more information on damaged roots, see pages 200 and 201.

4. Don't let the soil dry out to the point where leaves scorch. Check the moisture needs of your plant. (For moisture needs, check for the plant in the alphabetical section beginning on page 204.)

Leaf rust

Cedar-apple rust on hawthorn.

Problem: Leaves are discolored or mottled yellow to brown. Yellow, orange, red, or blackish powdery pustules appear on the leaves. The powdery material can be scraped off. Leaves may become twisted and distorted and may dry and drop off. Twigs may also be infected. Plants are often stunted.

Analysis: Many different species of leaf rust fungi infect trees and shrubs. Some rusts require two different plant species to complete their life cycles. Part of the life cycle is spent on the tree or shrub and part on various weeds, flowers, or other woody trees or shrubs. Rust fungi survive the winter as spores on or in living plant tissue or in plant debris. Wind and splashing water spread the spores to healthy plants. When conditions are favorable (with moisture on the leaf in the form of rain, dew, or fog and with moderate temperatures, 54° to 74°F), the spores germinate and infect the tissue. Leaf discoloration and mottling develop as the fungus saps plant nutrients. Some rust fungi produce spores in spots or patches, while others develop hornlike structures.

Solution: Several fungicides, including those containing *triforine* (Funginex), *chlorothalonil, ferbam, zineb,* or *cycloheximide,* may be used to control rust. (For information on which fungicide is appropriate, look under the entry for the plant in the alphabetical section beginning on page 204.) Some rust fungi are fairly harmless to the plant and do not require control measures. Where practical, remove and destroy infected leaves as they appear. Rake up and destroy leaves in the fall.

Spider mites

Spider mite damage and webbing.

Problem: Leaves are stippled yellow, white, or bronze and are dirty. A silken webbing is sometimes on the leaves or stems. New growth may be distorted, and the plant may be weak and stunted. To determine if a plant is infested with spider mites, examine the bottoms of the leaves with a hand lens. Or hold a sheet of white paper underneath an affected leaf or branch and tap it sharply. Green, red, or yellow specks the size of pepper grains will drop to the paper and begin to crawl.

Analysis: Spider mites, related to spiders, are major pests of many plants. They cause damage by sucking sap from leaves and buds. As a result of their feeding, the plant's chlorophyll disappears, producing the stippled appearance. While they feed, many mites produce a fine web over the foliage that collects dust and dirt. Some mites are active throughout the growing season but are especially favored by dry weather with temperatures of 70°F and above. Other mites, especially those infesting conifers, are prolific in cooler weather. They are most active in the spring and sometimes fall and during warm periods in winter in mild climates. At the onset of hot weather, these mites have usually caused their maximum damage. (For more information on spider mites, see page 457.)

Solution: Spray with Ortho® Systemic Insect Killer or Ortho® Rose & Flower Insect Killer when damage is first noticed. Repeat the spray two more times at intervals of 7 to 10 days. Make sure that your plant is listed on the product label.

Leafhoppers

Leafhopper damage to dogwood.

Problem: Leaves are stippled white, yellow, or light green, and leaves and stems may be distorted. Sometimes the plant has a burned appearance. Infested leaves may drop prematurely. When infestations are severe, twigs and small branches sometimes die. Whitish or green wedge-shaped insects, up to ½ inch long, hop and fly away quickly when the plant is touched.

Analysis: Many species of leafhoppers infest ornamental trees and shrubs. Some leafhoppers cause only minor damage to the leaves, while other species severely retard plant growth. Leafhoppers usually spend the winter as eggs in slits in the bark made by the females, although some may overwinter in the South and migrate north in the spring. Injury to the bark from egg-laying may kill twigs. When the weather warms in the spring, young leafhoppers emerge and settle on the undersides of leaves, where they suck the plant sap, causing the stippling and distortion. Severely infested leaves often drop in midsummer. Some leafhoppers cause a condition known as *hopperburn*. Insect feeding causes distortion and gives the leaves a burned appearance. Several generations of leafhoppers may occur each year. (For more information on leafhoppers, see page 448.)

Solution: Spray with Ortho® Systemic Insect Killer or Ortho® Bug-B-Gon® Multi-Purpose Insect Killer when damage is first noticed. Cover the lower surfaces of the leaves thoroughly. Make sure that your plant is listed on the product label.

DISCOLORED LEAVES *(continued)*

Lace bugs

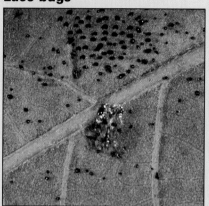

Lace bug and droppings (4× life size).

Problem: The upper surfaces of leaves are mottled or speckled yellow or gray, or white and green. The mottling is distinguished from other insect damage—such as that caused by spider mites or leafhoppers—by the shiny, hard, black droplets found on the undersides of damaged leaves. Small (⅛-inch), light or dark, spiny, wingless insects or brownish insects with clear lacy wings may be visible around the droplets. Plant growth is usually stunted. Damage occurs in spring and summer.

Analysis: Many species of lace bugs feed on trees and shrubs. Each species usually infests only a few related types of plants. Depending on species, lace bugs spend the winter as adults in protected areas on plants or as eggs in leaf veins or cemented to the lower surface of leaves in a crusty brown material. Both the spiny, wingless, immature insects and the lace-winged adults suck sap from the undersides of leaves. The chlorophyll disappears, resulting in the characteristic speckling or mottling. As lace bugs feed, droplets of black excrement accumulate around them. Damage is unsightly, and food production by the leaf is reduced, resulting in loss of plant vigor.

Solution: Spray with Ortho® Systemic Insect Killer when damage first appears in the spring. Cover the undersides of leaves thoroughly. Repeat the spray 7 to 10 days later. A third application may be necessary if the plant becomes reinfested in midsummer.

Thrips

Greenhouse thrips damage to coffee tree.

Problem: Young leaves are severely curled and distorted. Parts of the leaf may die and turn black, or the entire leaf may drop from the plant. Or leaves are flecked and appear bleached or silvery, often becoming papery and wilted. Shiny black spots may cover the surfaces. Flowers and buds also may be affected. They may have white streaks or be brown and distorted. Minute (½₅-inch) white or yellow spindle-shaped insects and black or brown winged insects are barely visible inside the distorted leaves and flowers or on undersides of leaves. Heavily infested plants may be stunted.

Analysis: Thrips are a common pest of many garden and greenhouse plants. Some species cause leaf or flower distortion; others cause a flecking of the leaves, producing a bleached appearance. Thrips feed by rasping the soft plant tissue, then sucking the released plant sap. Some leaf thrips leave unsightly, black, varnishlike spots of excrement around the areas where they feed. The black or brown adults have wings. They can spread rapidly by flying to new plants, or the wind may blow them long distances. They lay their eggs either on the plant or in surrounding weeds. The young are yellow or white and spindle-shaped. Some thrips can transmit diseases.

Solution: Spray the leaves or buds and flowers with Ortho® Systemic Insect Killer or Ortho® Malathion Plus® Insect Spray Concentrate. Make sure that your plant is listed on the product label. Remove and destroy infested buds and flowers to reduce thrips populations.

Overwatering or poor drainage

Overwatering damage to yew hedge.

Problem: Leaves turn light green to yellow and may drop. The edges of the leaves may be brown. In many cases, the plant grows very little. It may pull out of the ground easily, because the roots are soft and rotted. The soil is frequently or constantly wet.

Analysis: Overwatering and poor drainage are serious common problems that often kill plants. Roots require air to function normally. Air is contained in tiny pores in the soil. When the soil is watered, air is forced out of the soil pores and replaced with water. If water can't drain out of the soil, or if it is constantly reapplied, the soil pores remain filled with water. The roots can't absorb the oxygen they need in such saturated conditions, and they die. As the roots rot, the root system is less able to supply the plant with nutrients and water, resulting in starvation and eventually in the death of the plant.

Solution: Don't apply water so frequently that the soil is constantly wet. Depending on the particular requirements of your tree or shrub allow the soil to dry partially or completely between waterings. (For information on a specific plant, see the alphabetical section beginning on page 204. For information on watering, see pages 407 to 408.) If your soil drains poorly, improve drainage. (For information on drainage, see page 406.)

Lack of nitrogen

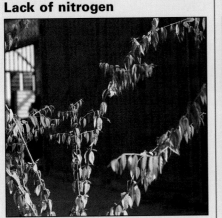

Nitrogen-deficient fuchsia.

Problem: Leaves turn yellow and may drop, beginning with the older leaves. New leaves are small, and growth is slow.

Analysis: Nitrogen, one of the most important nutrients for plant growth, is deficient in most soils. Nitrogen is essential in the formation of chlorophyll and many other compounds necessary for plant growth. When short on the nutrient, plants take nitrogen from their older leaves for new growth. Poorly drained, overwatered, compacted, and cold soils are often infertile. Plants growing in these soils often show symptoms of nitrogen deficiency. Various soil problems and other nutrient deficiencies also cause leaf discoloration.

Solution: For a quick response, spray the leaves and the soil beneath the plant with liquid or water-soluble fertilizer. Feed plants regularly with Scotts® Evergreen, Flowering Tree & Shrub Slow Release Plant Food. Add organic amendments to compacted soils and those low in organic matter, and improve drainage in poorly drained soils. Don't keep the soil constantly wet. (For more information on watering, see pages 407 to 408.)

Iron deficiency

Iron-deficient azalea.

Problem: New leaves are pale green or yellow. The veins may remain green, forming a Christmas-tree pattern on the leaf. Old leaves remain green. In extreme cases, new leaves are all-yellow and stunted.

Analysis: Plants frequently suffer from deficiencies of iron and other minor nutrients, such as manganese and zinc, elements essential to normal plant growth and development. Deficiencies can occur when one or more of these elements are depleted in the soil. Often these minor nutrients are present in the soil, but alkaline (pH of above 7.0) or wet soil conditions cause them to form compounds that can't be used by the plant. An alkaline condition can result from overliming or from lime leached from cement or brick. Regions where soil is derived from limestone or where rainfall is low usually have alkaline soil pH.

Solution: To correct the iron deficiency, spray the foliage with a chelated iron fertilizer, and put the fertilizer to the soil around the plant. Apply soil sulfur or ferrous sulfate to correct the pH. (For more information on pH, see page 406.) Maintain an acid pH by fertilizing with Osmocote® Azalea, Camellia, Rhododendron Slow Release Plant Food. When planting in an area with alkaline soil, add a handful of soil sulfur, or add enough peat moss to make up 50 percent of the amended soil, and mix well.

Fire blight

Fire blight on crabapple.

Problem: Blossoms and leaves of some twigs suddenly wilt and turn black as if scorched by fire. Leaves curl and hang downward. Tips of infected branches may hang down in a "shepherd's crook." The bark at the base of the blighted twig becomes water-soaked, then dark, sunken, and dry; cracks may develop at the edge of the sunken area (canker). In warm, moist spring weather, drops of brown ooze appear on the sunken bark.

Analysis: Fire blight is a disease caused by a bacterium (*Erwinia amylovora*) that is very destructive to many trees and shrubs. Bacteria spend the winter in the cankers on the branches. In the spring, the bacteria ooze out of the cankers on the branches and trunk and are carried by insects to the plant blossoms. The bacteria spread rapidly through the plant tissue in warm (65°F or higher), humid weather. Bees visiting infected blossoms spread the disease. Rain and tools may also spread the bacteria.

Solution: During spring and summer, prune infected branches 12 inches beyond any visible discoloration, and destroy them. Disinfect pruning tools after each cut. A protective spray of basic copper sulfate or *streptomycin* applied before bud-break in the spring helps prevent infection. Repeat at intervals of five to seven days until the end of bloom. Don't add too much nitrogen fertilizer in the spring and early summer. Nitrogen forces succulent growth, which is more susceptible to fire blight. In summer or fall, after the disease stops spreading, prune out any remaining infected branches.

BRANCHES DIE *(continued)*

Twig or branch dieback

Dog urine damage to boxwood.

Canker on sycamore.

Problem: Branches are dying. The leaves usually turn brown and may drop off. In some cases, wounds or sunken, dark-colored lesions are on the dead branches, or the branches may have holes in them surrounded by sawdust or sap.

Analysis: Dieback can result from any of several causes.

Solution: Solutions below correspond to the numbered items in the analysis.

1. Mechanical injury: Any type of injury that causes a wound may kill branches. Branches on shrubs or trees may be wounded by motor vehicles, lawn mowers, animals, wires, nails, or tools. If the wound girdles the branch, nutrients and water can't reach the leaves, and the branch dies. Wounds are also entrance points for many diseases and pests.

1. Dying limbs with large wounds that almost girdle the branch should be removed. Repair small wounds by removing ragged edges and dead bark. (For more information on bark wounds, see page 412.) Don't use bare wire on branches, and don't nail anything to trees. If necessary, place protective barriers around plants to prevent damage. Don't plant trees and shrubs in areas where they are likely to be hit by vehicles.

2. Cankers: Cankers are sunken, dark-colored lesions caused by fungi and bacteria. They kill living tissue underneath the bark. If a canker covers as much as half the circumference of a branch, the branch dies.

2. For more information on cankers and their controls, see page 190.

3. Borers: Borers are the larvae of beetles or moths. Larvae feed by tunneling through bark, sapwood, and heartwood. This cuts the flow of nutrients and water in that area, killing the branch beyond the tunneling.

3. For more information on borers and their controls, see page 189.

4. Dog urine: The leaves on branches near the ground turn brown and die when dogs urinate on them. The salts in the urine burn the leaves. Dogs repeat their visits to certain shrubs or hedges, eventually killing branches.

4. If a dog has recently urinated on a plant, wash urine off the leaves and soak the ground around the plant. Twigs and branches already damaged may recover. Prune any deadwood. Protect plants from new damage with a repellent containing *methyl nonyl ketone*; or erect barriers around the plants.

WEAK OR DYING PLANT

Lawn mower and string trimmer blight

Lawn mower blight on oak.

Problem: Leaves are small and discolored and often drop prematurely. Twigs may die. The plant is stunted and in a general state of decline. Bark at the base of the trunk is wounded. The tree is planted in a lawn.

Analysis: Trees growing in lawns may be severely injured by slight but repeated injuries to the bark from lawn mowers or string trimmers. Lawn mower blades and trimmer strings may also slice through the bark into the wood. Nutrients and water can't pass through the damaged part of the trunk to reach the top of the tree. In severe cases, young trees die. Wounds are often entry points for disease-producing organisms that may kill the tree. (For more information on bark wounds, see page 412.)

Solution: Prune dying twigs and branches, and fertilize with Scotts® Evergreen, Flowering Tree and Shrub Slow Release Plant Food. To prevent additional damage to the trunk, kill all grass around the base of the tree with an herbicide. Or install a tree guard to eliminate the need for edging and trimming around the trunk. (For more information on protecting trees, see page 412.)

Compacted soil

Stunted ash growing in compacted soil.

Problem: Leaves are small and discolored and often drop prematurely. Eventually twigs and then larger branches die. The plant is stunted and in a general state of decline. The soil under the tree is hard and dense, probably from heavy traffic.

Analysis: Constant vehicle or foot traffic in an area compacts soil. Compacted soil is too dense to admit air. Plant roots, which need air, stop growing or die. Water also enters the soil very slowly, so the tree or shrub suffers frequently from drought. Soil compaction is most common along roads or paths where traffic is heavy. Compacted soil is hard and difficult to probe when digging with a hand trowel or shovel.

Solution: Divert traffic from plants. If necessary, erect barriers to keep traffic out, using fences, walls, or dense or thorny shrubbery. Remove severely affected plants. Relieve compaction to a depth of 4 to 6 inches with a soil aerator. Prevent further compaction by planting ground covers with deep roots or by covering the compacted area with 2 to 4 inches of stone, crushed rock, or bark mulch. (For more information on compaction, see page 405.)

Girdling roots

Girdling roots.

Problem: Tree leaves are small, discolored and often drop prematurely. Eventually twigs and then larger branches die. The plant is stunted and in a general state of decline. A root is wrapped around the trunk, at or just below the surface of the soil. It completely encircles the trunk and is imbedded in it.

Analysis: A girdling root is a root that wraps itself around the main root system or the trunk. As the trunk enlarges, it is strangled by its own root, slowly reducing the flow of nutrients and water to the top of the tree. The girdling root may be visible above ground, or it may develop underground and remain undetected until the tree is in a severe state of decline. Trees with girdling roots often lack a normal flare where the trunk enters the soil but instead, plunge directly into the soil like a pole. The trunk may even be slightly constricted. Girdling roots usually develop when a container tree is planted or transplanted into too small a hole or twisted in the ground at planting. If the roots that normally circle the inside of a container are not trimmed, they may eventually girdle the tree. The trunk is weakened if it is severely constricted and may break in a high wind.

Solution: Remove the part of the root that is girdling the trunk. If the girdling root is large (more than one-quarter of the diameter of the trunk), prune the tree to compensate for the roots that were lost. If the trunk is severely constricted, guy or stake the tree for a few years to prevent breakage at the narrow point.

Injury to trunk

Ash trunk injured by wire.

Problem: Leaves are small and discolored, and they often drop prematurely. Eventually twigs and then larger branches die. The plant is stunted and in a general state of decline. A large patch of bark is damaged, or a wire circles the trunk and is deeply imbedded in it.

Analysis: Anything that slows the flow of water and nutrients through the trunk harms the tree. Since the nutrient and water-circulation system of the tree is immediately under the bark, damage to the bark usually interrupts circulation between the aboveground portion of the tree and its roots. Damage most commonly occurs from a large wound on the trunk. If the wound covers more than half the circumference of the trunk, it is major damage and threatens the life of the tree. Wires or cables wrapped around the trunk grow tighter as the trunk expands, cutting into the wood and slowly reducing circulation.

Solution: Remove loose, discolored bark splinters and wood from the wound. Remove any girdling wires and dead or dying branches. Water regularly, and feed with Scotts® Evergreen, Flowering Tree and Shrub Slow Release Plant Food according to label directions. Don't wrap wires around trees. Use rubber or plastic ties made for the purpose, and remove them after one year.

199

WEAK OR DYING PLANT (continued)

Bark beetles

Bark beetle damage.

Problem: Leaves are small and discolored and often drop prematurely. Eventually twigs and larger branches die. The plant is stunted and in a general state of decline. Many small holes are in the bark. Sap, pitch, or sawdust may be coming out of the holes.

Analysis: Bark beetles may seriously damage older, mature trees growing in the home garden. They usually infest only weakened trees, trees under stress from drought or disease, and recently pruned trees. Adult beetles make tunnels between the bark and the wood, where they mate and lay eggs. Whitish larvae hatch from these eggs and form tunnels that radiate through the bark and cut off the flow of nutrients and water through the trunk. The larvae mature and may emerge to produce a new generation of beetles. Some beetles also transmit plant diseases.

Solution: Once trees are infested, they are difficult to save. Prevent infestation by removing beetle breeding sites. Cut down dead trees and trees in which 50 percent of the foliage is yellowing. Do not leave infested wood in the area. Burn the wood immediately, or strip off and burn the bark before storing the stripped wood. Water trees during periods of drought, and fertilize weakened trees regularly with Scotts® Evergreen, Flowering Tree and Shrub Slow Release Plant Food. Ask your county extension office for the best time to prune susceptible trees.

Mechanical injuries to roots

Dieback caused by injury to roots.

Problem: Leaves turn yellow and then brown. Branches die. The tree declines, usually over a period of several years, and may die. Trenching or construction has occurred under the tree within the past two years.

Analysis: Roots may be severed during excavation for building, trenching for cables and pipes, when soil is tilled, or when any other type of activity around a tree disturbs its roots. Root injuries may be difficult to detect or diagnose. Check the area for overturned soil, patched lawn, or fresh patches of asphalt. If the tree is growing very near a recent construction site and shows decline symptoms, its roots were probably damaged and then covered with soil. Excavate the soil around the declining tree by hand to determine if the roots are injured and to what extent.

Solution: Remove the tree if it is in a severe state of decline. If it is only mildly affected, thin out the branches so the top of the tree is in proportion to the remaining roots. (If 20 percent of the roots are damaged, prune off 20 percent of the branches.) If the roots are uncovered, refill the hole as soon as possible. Water during dry periods. In the future, avoid excavating or trenching around plants. If it is unavoidable, cut as few roots as possible. Dig as far away from the trunk as possible. If the trench must pass near the tree, fewer roots will be damaged if you tunnel under the tree rather than trench near it.

Root nematodes

Root nematode damage.

Problem: Leaves are small and discolored and often drop prematurely. Eventually twigs and then larger branches die. The plant is stunted and in a general state of decline.

Analysis: Root nematodes are microscopic worms that live in the soil. They feed on plant roots, damaging and stunting them or causing them to become enlarged. The damaged roots can't supply sufficient water and nutrients to the aboveground plant parts, and the plant is stunted or slowly dies. Nematodes are found throughout the United States, especially in southern areas with moist, sandy loam soil. They can move only a few inches per year on their own, but they may be carried long distances by soil, water, tools, or infested plants. Laboratory testing of roots and soil is the only positive method for confirming the presence of nematodes. Contact your local county extension office for sampling instructions and addresses of testing laboratories. Soil and root problems—such as poor soil structure, drought stress, overwatering, nutrient deficiency, and root rots—can also produce symptoms of decline similar to those caused by nematodes. Eliminate these problems as causes before sending soil and root samples for testing.

Solution: No chemicals available to homeowners kill nematodes in planted soil. Nematodes can be controlled before planting, however, by soil fumigation or solarization. Mulch, water, and fertilize with Scotts® Evergreen, Flowering Tree & Shrub Slow Release Plant Food to minimize stress.

Paving over roots

Paving over roots.

Grade change

Tree death caused by grade change.

Tree decline due to construction and grade change.

Problem: Leaves turn yellow and then brown. Branches die back. The tree declines, usually over a period of several years, and may die. A large part of the soil under the tree has been recently paved.

Analysis: Impervious soil coverings, such as cement and asphalt, placed over the roots of an established tree may kill the tree. The greater the coverage of roots, the more likely the tree will die. The supply of water and air to the roots is blocked, stopping their growth and eventually killing them. Some species of trees are more resistant than others, and young trees are more resistant than established trees. In areas where the water table is high, some trees may survive. Soil sterilants, often used by paving companies to kill weeds, will increase the probability of the tree dying.

Solution: Remove the tree if it is in a severe state of decline. If the tree shows only mild symptoms and is a valuable specimen, it may be saved if the pavement is removed. Before laying pavement in the future, protect trees by installing a system of tile pipes in gravel under the paving, which allows for the passage of water and air. If it is necessary to kill weeds, use a weed killer rather than a soil sterilant.

Problem: Leaves turn yellow and may drop. Branches die. The tree declines, usually over a period of several years, and may die. The soil level under the tree was recently changed, either raised or lowered.

Analysis: Raising or lowering the level of the soil (the grade) around trees can be very damaging. If the grade has been raised, the tree emerges from the soil like a pole (no flare at the base of the trunk). If the grade has been lowered, roots are exposed.

1. Grade raised: A large quantity of soil dumped around a tree usually suffocates the roots by cutting off their supply of air and water. The extent of damage depends on the kind of tree, its age and condition, type and depth of fill, and how much of the root system is covered. Young, healthy trees are much more tolerant than old trees, and soil containing gravel or sand causes less severe injury than clay soil. If only a portion of the root system is covered, or if the fill is shallow (less than 3 inches of porous soil or less than 1 to 2 inches of clay soil), the tree will be weakened but usually won't die. Severe decline symptoms (progressive dieback from the top down) often don't occur for several years. Insects or diseases may kill the weakened plant sooner than it would have died otherwise.

2. Grade lowered: Many roots may be severed when soil is removed from around a tree, and exposed roots will dry out. The number and size of the roots severed determines the extent of damage. Cutting large roots close to the trunk is more likely to kill the tree than cutting the ends of roots. The plant is often unstable and may blow down in a strong wind.

Solution: Once symptoms of decline have developed, significant damage has already occurred. The numbered solutions below correspond to the numbered items in the analysis at left.

1. By the time symptoms caused by raising the grade are noticed, it is usually too late to do anything. If fill has been around the tree for less than one growing season and no symptoms have yet appeared, remove the fill if possible. If the tree is in severe decline, remove it. If decline symptoms are not severe, therapeutic treatments may save the tree. Remove all dead and dying branches and remove the soil from around the base of the trunk. Dig holes to the original soil level every few feet over the entire root area (under the branches) and place 6-inch bell tiles in the holes. In the future, protect valuable trees by installing tile pipes in a thick bed of gravel covered with a minimum amount of fill. For a list of trees that are severely, moderately, or rarely damaged by fill, see page 547.

2. If a tree is in a severe state of decline caused by lowering the grade, remove the tree. Cable unstable trees to a stable object, or remove them. For trees with symptoms, prune damaged roots and torn bark. Cut back the top growth so it is in balance with the remaining roots (if 20 percent of the roots are damaged, cut off 20 percent of the branches). Water trees during dry periods.

WEAK OR DYING PLANT (continued)

Overwatering

Tree decline caused by poor drainage.

Problem: Leaves are small and discolored and often drop prematurely. Eventually twigs and then larger branches die. The plant is stunted and in a general state of decline. Soil is constantly wet, either from frequent watering or because the soil drains slowly.

Analysis: Many trees and shrubs don't grow well in soil that is constantly wet. This condition is most common around lawns, especially when the soil drains slowly. Lawns need much more water than do most trees and shrubs. When the soil is constantly wet, the roots can't absorb the oxygen they need to function normally, they begin to decay, and the plant slowly declines. This problem is common in areas of low rainfall when lawns are planted around established plants or native trees that can't tolerate the increased soil moisture from frequent waterings.

Solution: Don't continually apply water, making the soil constantly wet. Depending on the requirements of your tree or shrub, allow the soil to dry partially or fully between waterings. (For information on a specific plant, see the alphabetical section beginning on page 204.) If possible, move the tree or shrub to a new location with better drainage. Replace it with a plant that tolerates poor drainage, or improve the drainage (see page 406). If the plant can't be moved, water it less frequently. Cover the area under the tree with a mulch or with a ground cover that requires little water.

Root weevil larvae

Root weevil damage to azalea.

Problem: Leaves are small and discolored and often drop prematurely. Eventually twigs and then larger branches die. The plant is stunted and in decline. If soil is removed from around the base of the plant, exposing some roots, bark on the roots or small rootlets are seen to be chewed. White grubs may be found in the soil around the roots.

Analysis: Root weevil larvae, called *grubs*, infest the roots of many ornamental plants. Damage caused by grubs is often so gradual that the insects are well-established before injury is apparent. If the grubs remain undetected, the plant may die abruptly with the onset of hot, dry weather. Females lay eggs at the soil line near plants during the summer months. The emerging grubs burrow into the soil. They feed on the roots in the fall and then spend the winter in the soil. Most root weevils cause their major damage in the spring. Their feeding girdles the roots and stems, disrupting the flow of nutrients and water through the plant and causing the roots and the top of the plant to die.

Solution: Discard dying plants. Because the grubs are in the soil, they are difficult to kill. To prevent the next generation of weevils from causing damage, eliminate the adults. Check periodically for notched leaves, or search for feeding adults in leaf litter around the plant. Disturbed adults often "play dead" for a few minutes before moving. You may also search for them on the plants with a flashlight after dark. Spray foliage and the ground under plants with Ortho® Systemic Insect Killer.

INVADING ROOTS

Surface roots

Roots cracking pavement.

Problem: Roots are exposed on the surface of the soil or make bumps by growing just beneath it. Or roots crack and raise the pavement. Exposed roots may be lumpy and misshapen.

Analysis:

1. Surface roots in lawns: If plants receive light irrigation on the soil surface, roots in this upper zone will expand, pushing above the surface. Plants growing in lightly irrigated lawns often have shallow roots.

2. Waterlogged soil: Roots need oxygen to grow and develop. Waterlogged soil has little oxygen available for root growth because the soil air pores are filled with water. The only available oxygen is near the soil surface, so the surface roots develop most.

3. Natural tendency: Some plant species are more likely than others to develop surface roots.

4. Compacted soil: Trees and shrubs growing in compacted soil develop exposed surface roots.

5. Confined roots: Plants growing in areas with limited root space often have roots growing on the soil surface.

6. Planting strips: Trees growing in planting strips adjacent to lawns frequently crack the sidewalks that separate them from the lawns. All of the available water and food is beyond the walk, in the lawns. The roots that extend under the walk into the lawn expand rapidly, cracking the walk.

Surface roots in a lawn.

Tree topples

Shallow roots.

Tree blown over by wind.

Problem: The entire tree falls over with part or all of the roots attached.

Solution:

1. In addition to watering the lawn, deep-water trees in lawns every two weeks, to a depth of 3 or 4 feet. Cover the roots by slowly raising the level of the lawn (1 inch per year) with soil topdressing.

2. If the soil is waterlogged from overwatering, cut back on watering. (For information on watering, see pages 407 and 408.) If necessary, improve drainage around the plant (see page 406). Cover the exposed roots with 2 to 4 inches of soil. Before planting new trees and shrubs, make sure drainage is adequate.

3. For a list of plants likely to develop surface roots, see page 548.

4. Loosen compacted soil with a crowbar. Before planting in compacted soil, loosen the soil (see page 405).

5. Plant shrubs or small trees adapted to growing in confined root areas. (See page 548 for a listing of adapted plants.)

6. Sever small roots that are pushing up pavement. If possible, avoid cutting large roots. In the future, plant large trees on the lawn side of the sidewalk and use shrubs in planting strips.

Analysis: Anything that drastically affects the size or strength of the roots may decrease the stability of the tree.

1. Root rot: Several different soil fungi and bacteria cause the roots to rot. When roots decay, they lose their ability to support the plant. The plant may fall when the foliage still appears healthy, or it may turn brown first. Only a few of the roots may be attached when the plant falls.

2. Severed roots: Roots may be severed during construction where trenching and earth-moving equipment is used. Size and number of roots severed determine the probability of the plant falling.

3. Wet soil: Plants growing in excessively wet soil may fall, especially after a long period of rain, when the soil no longer gives good support. A leaning tree, or one pushed by the wind, can pull loose. Plants with shallow root systems are most susceptible.

4. Shallow roots: Plants with shallow root systems may fall during strong winds. Those growing in compacted, shallow, or soggy soil, or where surface watering has been practiced, have shallow root systems.

5. Undeveloped root system: Young plants, or plants with girdled or balled roots, have root systems that may not support the rest of the plant. During a storm with high winds, the plant may blow over.

Solution: If the tree is leaning only slightly, saturate the soil and force the plant upright. Stake or wire it in place.

1. Once the tree has fallen, nothing can be done. In the future, avoid wounds to the roots, a common entrance point for root rot organisms. Don't overwater plants, and keep them in a vigorous growing condition. (For additional information on root rots, see page 419.)

2. Avoid severing roots, especially large supporting roots, during construction activities. If damaging many of the roots is unavoidable, either remove the plant or brace it.

3. Do not keep the soil constantly wet. If you live in an area that receives heavy rains, stake or brace the plant, or provide additional drainage. (For more information on improving soil drainage, see page 406.)

4. Reduce soil compaction, improve soil drainage, and water deeply to encourage deep rooting.

5. Stake young trees until roots are well-established. Prevent girdled and balled roots by using proper planting techniques.

TREE FALLS OVER
(continued)

ABIES (Fir)

Internal decay

Internal decay.

Spruce budworms

Spruce budworm (2× life size).

Balsam twig aphids

Balsam twig aphid damage.

Problem: The tree bends or the trunk breaks at or above the soil line.

Analysis: Internal decay is caused by fungi that enter the tree through wounds. Healthy and vigorous trees may stop the spread of decay by walling off the invaded area. Old trees with many wounds are rarely very resistant to microorganisms, and decay spreads through the wood. Enough healthy tissue is usually left to keep the branches and leaves alive. But when a storm occurs, or sometimes on a calm day, the entire tree may crack in the decayed area and fall over. This condition can also develop on individual branches.

Solution: If only part of the tree has fallen, inspect the rest of it to determine the extent of decay. It may be necessary to contact a professional arborist. Remove the entire tree if decay is extensive. Avoid wounding trees, and keep them in a vigorous growing condition by watering regularly and fertilizing with Scotts® Evergreen, Flowering Tree and Shrub Slow Release Plant Food. (For more information on watering and fertilizing, see pages 407 to 409.)

Problem: Needles on the ends of branches are chewed and webbed together. In mid-July, the branch ends often turn reddish brown. Branches or the entire tree may die after three to five years of defoliation. Green to reddish-brown caterpillars, 1¼ inches long with yellow or white raised spots, are feeding on the needles.

Analysis: Spruce budworms (*Choristoneura* species) are very destructive to ornamental spruce, fir, and Douglas fir and may infest pine, larch, and hemlock. The budworm is cyclical. It comes and goes in epidemics about every 30 years. The moths are small (½ inch long) and grayish, with bands and spots of brown. The females lay pale green eggs in clusters on the needles in late July and August. The larvae that hatch from these eggs crawl to hiding places in the bark or in lichen mats; or they are blown by the wind to other trees, where they hide. The tiny larvae spin a silken case and hibernate until spring. In May, when the weather warms, the caterpillars tunnel into needles. As they grow, they feed on opening buds; later they chew off needles and web them together. The larvae feed for about five weeks, pupate on twigs, and emerge as adults.

Solution: When buds have fully expanded in late May or early June, spray with Ortho® Systemic Insect Killer, Ortho® Bug-B-Gon® Multi-Purpose Insect Killer Ready-Spray®, or the bacterial insecticide *Bacillus thuringiensis* (Bt).

Problem: The youngest needles are curled and twisted, with their lighter underside turned upward. Needles drop from the plant prematurely. Some needles die. Young twigs are twisted, and bark is roughened. Shoots may become saturated with a shiny, sticky secretion and needles adhere to one another. A black, sooty mold may grow on this sticky substance. Clustered on the shoots are tiny (⅛-inch), waxy, bluish-gray adult or pale green, immature soft-bodied insects with woolly secretions.

Analysis: The balsam twig aphid (*Mindarus abietinus*) does little damage in small numbers. Aphids are extremely prolific, however, and populations can rapidly build to damaging numbers during the growing season. Damage occurs when the aphid injects its saliva into the plant as it sucks the sap from the fir shoots. The aphid is unable to digest all the sugar in the sap, and it excretes the excess in a fluid called *honeydew*. The honeydew often drops onto the shoots or other plants below. A sooty mold fungus may develop on the honeydew, causing the fir needles to appear black and dirty. Late in the summer, females lay small (⅒-inch) eggs, covered with tiny rods of white wax, in bark crevices. Eggs are conspicuous and a useful index of the amount of injury that may occur during the next year.

Solution: Kill aphids by spraying with Ortho® Systemic Insect Killer or Ortho® Malathion Plus® Insect Spray Concentrate at bud-break in late April or early May. Repeat the spray in two weeks if the tree becomes reinfested.

Douglas fir tussock moths

Tussock moth damage. Inset: Larva (life size).

Problem: Much of the foliage is eaten, starting at the top of the tree. The entire tree may be defoliated in one season. Trees that lose most of their needles a second year usually die. Inch-long, hairy, gray or light brown caterpillars with black heads and tufts of orange hairs on their backs may be feeding on the needles.

Analysis: Douglas fir tussock moth (*Orgyia pseudotsugata*) populations are cyclical. Every 7 to 10 years, forest populations build to epidemic proportions. When this occurs, true firs, Douglas firs, spruce, pine, and larch may be completely defoliated. In cities, damaging numbers may be found every year. In mid- to late summer the hairy, wingless female moths lay their eggs in a frothy substance covered with a layer of hairlike scales. When the eggs hatch the following spring, the caterpillars begin feeding on the new needles at the top of the tree. As the younger foliage is devoured, the caterpillars move downward, feeding on older needles. Large numbers of tan excrement pellets accumulate around the base of the tree. Since conifers don't replace their old needles, defoliated trees often die after two seasons. Less severely damaged trees may be killed later by bark beetles. In August, the caterpillars pupate to emerge as adults.

Solution: When you first notice damage or caterpillars in May or early June, spray with an insecticide containing *acephate* or with the bacterial insecticide *Bacillus thuringiensis* (Bt). Repeat the spray two weeks later if damage continues.

Balsam woolly adelgids

Balsam woolly adelgid damage.

Problem: Ends of twigs swell, forming knobs. Trunk, limbs, and needles may be covered by white, woolly masses or by a dirty white crust. Young needles turn yellow from the tips down and drop off. No new growth is evident. More susceptible species, such as balsam fir or subalpine fir, may be killed before swelling on terminal growth occurs.

Analysis: The balsam woolly adelgid (*Adelges picae*), a small, soft-bodied insect related to the aphid, is a pest only of true firs. The adult is covered by dense, white, woolly material. When this substance is removed, the minute wingless insect appears purplish to black. Adults lay eggs on the bark of fir trees in early spring. Eggs hatch into tiny spiderlike *crawlers* that are blown long distances by the wind. Once the adelgid has found a suitable tree, it sucks the sap from the needles. A growth-promoting substance is injected into the tree at the same time, causing swelling of branch tips. The wood becomes reddish and brittle. As the insect matures, it becomes immobile, legs atrophy, and it secretes white filaments of wax that eventually cover its body.

Solution: Spray with Ortho® Systemic Insect Killer or Ortho® Malathion Plus® Insect Spray Concentrate when woolly tufts first appear in early spring. The insects will be killed, but the woolly material will remain on the tree. Thorough coverage is necessary to achieve adequate control. To penetrate the waxy filaments, use high-pressure equipment. A fall spray may help control overwintering insects on the tree.

Pear thrips

Pear thrips damage on sugar maple.

Problem: Leaves are small, mottled yellow and brown, and distorted. Blisterlike scars may be found on the veins. In moderate infestations, the leaves in the crown are yellow and sparse, a condition resembling the damage caused by late frost. When damage is severe, the tree is defoliated in spring but produces new leaves in June or July.

Analysis: Pear thrips (*Taeniothrips inconsequens*) infest a variety of forest trees but have recently become a serious pest of sugar maples. The insects damage the foliage by piercing the leaves and sucking the plant sap. Pear thrips have slender, brownish bodies less than 1/16 inch long. They emerge from the soil in April or May and migrate to the expanding buds of the trees, where they lay eggs in the buds and feed on the young foliage. Larvae hatch from the eggs within two weeks, feed until early June, and then drop to the soil to pupate. Pear thrips populations are cyclical, building up over several years to damaging numbers, then dropping again.

Solution: No control for this pest is presently available. Researchers are studying the problem. Contact your local county extension office for advice.

ACER (Maple, box elder) *(continued)*

Bladder gall mites and spindle galls

Galls caused by bladder gall mites.

Problem: In early spring, maple leaves develop irregular, spherical, or bladderlike growths, known as galls, on upper surfaces of the leaves. Leaves next to the trunk and on large branches are most affected. The galls are yellowish green at first but later turn pinkish to red and finally black. If the galls are numerous, leaves become deformed, and some turn yellow and drop prematurely.

Analysis: Bladder galls (*Vasates quadripedes*), which grow on silver maples, and spindle galls (*V. aceriscrumena*), which grow on sugar maples, are caused by tiny mites too small to be seen with the naked eye. Each gall contains many mites. The mites congregate on buds just before they open in the spring. As the buds open, each mite punctures and enters a leaf on the underside, injecting a growth-promoting substance that causes abnormal tissue formation. A gall encloses the mite, with an opening remaining on the underside. The mite feeds and the female mite lays eggs inside its gall. The eggs hatch, and as they mature, the young mites crawl out through the opening and infest new leaves. In July, mite activity stops and the mites migrate to the bark to spend the winter.

Solution: Once galls are formed, you can't do anything about them. The galls cause no serious injury, however. If you wish to prevent unsightly leaves the following year, spray buds, branches, and trunk with a dormant oil spray, Ortho® Systemic Insect Killer, or Ortho® Orthenex® Garden Insect & Disease Control before the buds start to open in the spring.

Cottony maple scales and mealybugs

Cottony cushion scales on maple (¼ life size).

Problem: The undersides of leaves, stems, or branch crotches are covered with white, cottony, masses. Leaves turn yellow and drop prematurely. Sometimes a shiny or sticky substance coats the leaves. A black, sooty mold often grows on the sticky substance. Numerous side shoots sometimes grow out of an infested crotch area. Twigs and branches may die back.

Analysis: Cottony maple scales and mealybugs are common on maples throughout North America. Similarities in these insects' appearance make separate identification difficult. Young insects are yellowish brown to green. They feed throughout the summer on the stems and undersides of leaves. Damage is caused by the withdrawal of plant sap from leaves and branches. The insects are unable to digest all the sugar in the sap, and they excrete the excess in a fluid called *honeydew*. Honeydew drops onto leaves or onto plants, cars, and lawn furniture. A sooty mold fungus may develop in the honeydew, causing the maple leaves and other plants to appear black and dirty. If insects are not controlled, heavily infested branches may die after several seasons. A small black ladybird beetle with two red spots is often present with the scales. It is eating the immature scales.

Solution: Apply Ortho® Systemic Insect Killer, Ortho® Malathion Plus® Insect Spray Concentrate, or Ortho® Volck® Oil Spray in midsummer when the young are active. The following spring, when trees are dormant, apply a dormant spray with lime sulfur mixed with spray oil.

Tar spot

Tar spot.

Problem: Tar spots appear on maple leaves in late spring and early summer after full maturation of the leaf. When the spots first appear, they are light green or yellowish. During mid- to late summer, raised black, tarlike spots ⅛ to ½ inch develop within the yellowish spots.

Analysis: Tar spot is caused by a fungus (*Rhytisma acerinum*) that most commonly affects the leaves of silver and Norway maples. The fungus survives through the winter on fallen leaves. In the spring, spores from the diseased leaf debris are transferred by wind to young maple leaves. The disease does little harm to plants, but the black spots disfigure the leaves.

Solution: Tar spot is rarely injurious enough to require fungicide treatment. Rake up and destroy fallen leaves in the autumn to destroy the fungi's overwintering site.

Summer leaf scorch

Leaf scorch.

Problem: During hot weather, usually in July or August, leaves turn brown on the edges between the veins. Sometimes the whole leaf dies. Leaves may drop during late summer. This problem is most severe on the youngest branches. Trees don't generally die from leaf scorch.

Analysis: Summer leaf scorch is caused by excessive loss of moisture from the leaves due to evaporation. In hot weather, water evaporates rapidly from the leaves. If the roots can't absorb and convey water fast enough to replenish this loss, the leaves turn brown and wither. This usually occurs in dry soil, but leaves can also scorch when the soil is moist. Drying winds, severed roots, limited soil area, and low temperatures can also cause scorch. (For more information on scorch, see page 427.)

Solution: To prevent further scorch, deep-water trees during periods of hot weather to wet down the entire root space. (For more information on watering, see pages 407 to 408.) Water newly transplanted trees whenever the rootball is dry 1 inch below the surface. Scorch occurring on trees in moist soil can't be controlled. Plant trees adapted to your climate.

Maple anthracnose

Anthracnose on Norway maple.

Problem: Irregular, light brown spots appear on the leaf from late May to August. They develop during or just following cool, wet, humid weather. Many spots occur along the veins. They may enlarge, causing the death of the entire leaf. Leaves partially killed appear as if sunscorched. This disease is distinguished from sunscorch by the presence of dark dots (spore-producing structures) barely visible on the undersides of the leaves. Spore-producing structures develop while leaves are still on the tree. Sunken reddish oval areas often develop on the infected twigs.

Analysis: Maple anthracnose is caused by one of two related fungi (*Discula* spp. and *Kabatiella apocryta*) that spend the winter on fallen leaves or in sunken cankers on twigs. During cool, rainy weather, spores are blown and splashed onto young leaves. Dead spots develop on the leaf where the fungus enters the tissue. The spots expand, and the fungus can kill the leaves in rainy seasons, causing premature defoliation. The tree will grow new leaves if defoliation takes place in spring or early summer. When the tree is severely affected for successive years, the fungus will enter and kill branches.

Solution: Trees affected by this disease for a single year don't require a chemical control. Rake and burn old leaves, and prune out dead twigs below the canker to reduce the amount of disease the following year. If the following spring is wet and humid, spray valuable specimens with a fungicide containing *mancozeb* when the leaves uncurl. Repeat the treatment twice.

Verticillium wilt

Verticillium wilt. Inset: Infected stem.

Problem: Leaves on a branch turn yellow at the margins, then brown and dry. During hot weather, the leaves may wilt. New leaves may be stunted and yellowish. The infected tree may die slowly, branch by branch, over several seasons—or the whole tree may wilt and die within a few months. Some trees may recover. The tissue under the bark on the dying side shows dark streaks, which may be very apparent or barely visible when exposed. To examine for streaks, peel back the bark at the bottom of the dying branch.

Analysis: Verticillium wilt disease affects many ornamental trees and shrubs. It is caused by a soil-inhabiting fungus (*Verticillium* species) that persists indefinitely on plant debris or in soil. The disease is spread by contaminated seeds, plants, soil, equipment, and groundwater. The fungus enters the tree through roots and spreads up into branches through the water-conducting vessels in the trunk. The vessels become discolored and plugged. This plugging cuts off the flow of water and nutrients to the branches, causing leaf discoloration and wilting. (For more information on verticillium wilt, see page 420.)

Solution: No chemical control is available. Fertilize with Scotts® Evergreen, Flowering Tree & Shrub Slow Release Plant Food to stimulate growth. Remove all deadwood. Don't remove branches on which leaves have recently wilted. These branches may produce new leaves in a few weeks or the following spring. Remove dead trees. If replanting in the same area, plant trees and shrubs that are resistant to verticillium wilt.

AESCULUS (Horsechestnut, buckeye)

Leaf blotch

Leaf blotch.

Summer leaf scorch

Summer leaf scorch.

ALBIZZIA (Mimosa, silk tree)

Mimosa webworms

Mimosa webworm damage.

Problem: Reddish-brown blotches with bright yellow margins appear on the leaf. Spots may be as small as ¼ inch, or they may nearly cover the leaf. When the whole leaf is infected, it becomes dry and brittle. Many leaves may drop from the tree. The first infection occurs in spring, but blotches may not appear until summer. Blotching is most severe in very wet spring weather. This problem is sometimes confused with leaf scorch caused by hot summer weather. It can be distinguished from scorch by the black specks in the center of the blotch and the bright yellow margins around the blotch.

Analysis: Leaf blotch is a plant disease caused by a fungus (*Guignardia aesculi*). In the spring, spores that develop on dead leaves on the ground are blown and splashed by water onto young leaves. Water-soaked blotches appear in early summer but aren't usually noticed until they turn brown. In midsummer, numerous pinpoint, black, spore-producing structures develop in the blotches. The disease is disfiguring but does not severely affect the growth of the plant.

Solution: Leaf blotch can't be controlled once infection has occurred. Rake up and destroy leaves in the fall. If the weather is wet and there is danger of infection, when the first leaves appear the following spring, spray with Ortho® Garden Disease Control. Repeat two times at intervals of 10 days.

Problem: During hot weather, usually in July or August, leaves turn brown around the edges and between the veins. Sometimes the whole leaf dies. Many leaves may drop during late summer. This problem is most severe on the youngest branches. Trees don't generally die.

Analysis: In hot weather, water evaporates rapidly from the leaves. If the roots can't absorb and convey water fast enough to replenish this loss, the leaves turn brown and wither. This usually occurs in dry soil, but leaves can also scorch when the soil is moist. Horsechestnut trees vary in their susceptibility; one tree may be very susceptible, although the tree next to it may show no sign of scorch. Drying winds, severed roots, limited soil area, and low temperatures can also cause scorch. (For more information on scorch, see page 427.)

Solution: To prevent further scorch, deep-water trees during periods of hot weather to wet down the entire root space. Add mulch over the root system. (For more information on watering, see pages 407 to 408.) Water newly transplanted trees whenever the rootball is dry 1 inch below the surface. Scorch on trees in moist soil can't be controlled. Plant trees adapted to your climatic zone.

Problem: Clumps of leaves tied together with silk threads are scattered over the tree. Upper surfaces of leaves are skeletonized. Leaves turn brown and die, causing the trees to appear scorched. Small (up to 1-inch) gray or brown caterpillars with five white stripes feed inside silken nests. Damage appears from June to September. Small trees may be completely defoliated in late summer. Trees aren't killed, but repeated defoliation can seriously weaken them.

Analysis: The mimosa webworm (*Homadaula anisocentra*) is the larval stage of a small gray moth that feeds only on mimosa and honeylocust trees. The webworm winters as a pupa in a white silken cocoon. The moth emerges in spring and lays eggs on leaf stems or on old silk from previous infestations. The eggs hatch, and the larvae feed on the leaflets for several weeks, webbing the leaflets together for protection against predators and weather. In August, a second generation of webworms appears. The larvae of this second generation are the most damaging because they are usually quite numerous. In cooler areas of the country, two generations occur each year between June and August. In warmer areas, a third generation occurs in September.

Solution: Spray with Ortho® Systemic Insect Killer before webbing first appears, at about the time philadelphus and catalpas are in bloom. Repeat in August. Use high-pressure equipment to penetrate the webs and thoroughly cover the tree. In the fall rake and destroy debris under infested trees, or turn over the soil and bury the leaves.

ARAUCARIA
(Norfolk Island pine)

Spider mites

Spider mite damage.

Problem: Needles turn light green, then yellow, and finally brown. Damage generally appears on the inside of the tree, next to the trunk, and then spreads upward and outward along the branches. Lower portions of the tree are usually affected first, and damage is most severe during periods of hot, dry weather. To check for pests, examine the bottoms of leaves with a hand lens. Or hold a piece of white paper beneath a dying area and tap the needles sharply. Minute red or yellow specks the size of pepper grains will drop to the paper and begin to crawl. They are easily seen against the white background.

Analysis: Spider mites (*Oligonychus* species), related to spiders, damage plants by sucking the juices from the leaves and stems. This feeding results in the discoloration and sometimes death of the needles. Damage is often severe enough to kill small trees. Mite levels increase rapidly in hot, dry weather (70°F and higher). Spider mites are most active during late spring and early summer, but some mite activity occurs throughout the year in warm regions.

Solution: Apply Ortho® Systemic Insect Killer or Ortho® Rose & Flower Insect Killer when browning needles are first noticed. Repeat sprays at intervals of 7 to 10 days according to label directions until the mites are controlled. Mites in missed areas continue to reproduce and rapidly reinfest treated areas.

ARBUTUS
(Madrone)

Canker and dieback

Twig dieback on madrone. Inset: Canker.

Problem: Leaves on infected trees are stunted and lighter green than normal. Some leaves turn brown and drop. Twigs may die back. Sunken, brownish to purplish, water-soaked areas appear on branches or near the base of the trunk. Sometimes a black liquid is exuded from the canker. The tree may die.

Analysis: Several different fungi cause canker and dieback on madrone. They enter the tree at a wound, killing the surrounding healthy tissue. A sunken canker develops and expands through the wood in all directions. Tree sap containing the fungus may ooze from the wound. The canker cuts off the flow of nutrients and water to the branch. The tree may stop the spreading disease by producing callus tissue, a rapid growth of barklike cells, to wall off the fungus. If the expanding canker is stopped before it covers half the diameter of the trunk, the tree usually survives. The fungus may grow faster than the callus, however, or the tree may not produce a callus, resulting in the death of the branch or the tree.

Solution: Prune dead twigs and small cankered branches, cutting at least 4 inches below the canker. Cankers on larger branches can be excised with a knife and chisel. Remove all discolored bark and wood, as well as a 1-inch border of apparently healthy bark around the wound. After each cut, disinfect the knife and chisel. Clean the wound with alcohol. Destroy all removed plant parts. Avoid wounding trees. Water trees occasionally during dry periods.

ARCTOSTAPHYLOS
(Manzanita)

Manzanita leaf gall aphids

Leaf gall.

Problem: Green or reddish galls appear at the edges or tips of the newest leaves. The leaves are twisted and distorted. When the gall is torn open, a small (⅛-inch), dark green to black insect or insect excrement is seen. On kinnikinnick (*Arctostaphylos uva-ursi*), the entire leaf may be thickened and reddish. Leaf galls appear in early summer.

Analysis: This manzanita leaf gall aphid (*Tamalia coweni*) is only a pest of *Arctostaphylos* species. Damage occurs when the aphid sucks the juices from the leaf and rolls a third of the leaf around itself. A growth-promoting substance is injected into the leaf at the same time, causing the leaf to thicken. The aphid begins feeding in spring, but the gall does not form until early summer. On most species of *Arctostaphylos*, the galls are more disfiguring than damaging. On kinnikinnick, however, all new leaves may be disfigured, preventing growth and spread of the ground cover.

Solution: Once the gall has formed around the aphid, this insect is difficult to control. Pick off and destroy disfigured leaves. The following spring, spray with Ortho® Malathion Plus® Insect Spray Concentrate to protect new foliage.

AUCUBA

Sunburn

Sunburn.

Problem: Dark brown or black patches develop on leaves exposed to direct sunlight. The entire leaf or shoot may turn black.

Analysis: Aucuba plants love shade; they can't tolerate direct sun, especially intense afternoon sun. The sunlight burns the leaves, causing them to turn brown or black. Sunburn is most severe when the soil is dry. Some pests and diseases may cause symptoms similar to those of sunburn.

Solution: You can't save foliage that has been damaged. Prune dead leaves and shoots. Prevent further sunburn by transplanting plants to a shady location or providing shade around the plants. Keep plants well watered.

BAMBOO

Bamboo flowering

Bamboo flowers.

Problem: Groves of bamboo flower heavily, then die, perhaps over a period of several years. They don't respond to watering and fertilizing, and no insects or diseases are obvious. Bamboo flowers have no petals and are usually messy and unattractive.

Analysis: Some types of bamboo flower heavily at periods of 10 to more than 100 years, then die or almost die. The time of flowering seems to be genetically—rather than environmentally—controlled. Plants of the same species sometimes flower at the same time all over the world. Giant timber bamboo (*Phyllostachys bambusoides*) and other large bamboos seem most prone to this type of flowering. Other bamboos flower less vigorously, then recover their strength after flowering. Flowering and dying might occur in a single year or might take several years.

Solution: Flowering can't be cured, and nothing can stop it, including removing the stalks as they flower. Removing the flowering stalks may make the plants more attractive, however. If you can wait until the flowering runs its course, the plants may recover slowly, or new plants may grow from suckers or seeds. This may take several years. Water and fertilize plants well during this period to hasten recovery. If you can't wait to see if the plants will recover, dig them up and replace them with another bamboo species.

BETULA (Birch)

Aphids

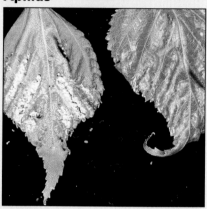

Aphids (½ life size).

Problem: Young leaves are puckered, twisted, and yellowing. A shiny or sticky substance may drip from the trees and coat the leaves. Sometimes twigs or branches die back. Tiny (⅛-inch) yellow, green, or blackish soft-bodied insects cluster on the undersides of leaves or on stems.

Analysis: Aphids do little damage in small numbers. They are extremely prolific, however, and populations can rapidly build to damaging numbers during the growing season. Damage occurs when the aphid sucks the sap from birch leaves or stems. Some aphid species attacking birch are unable to digest all the sugar in the sap and excrete the excess in a fluid called *honeydew*. The honeydew often drops onto the leaves below. Plants or objects beneath the tree may also be coated with honeydew. Ants feed on honeydew and are often present where there is an aphid infestation.

Solution: Control with Ortho® Systemic Insect Killer, Ortho® Bug-B-Gon® Multi-Purpose Insect Killer Concentrate, or an insecticidal soap when aphids first appear. Direct the spray to the undersides of leaves or at the bark, depending on where the aphids are feeding. Repeat the spray in summer if the tree becomes reinfested.

Oystershell scales

Oystershell scale.

Problem: Small, immobile brown structures that look like oyster shells appear in clusters on a few branches. The structures spread all over the tree during a period of several years. Heavily infested sections suffer dieback or are killed outright. The brown structures are most abundant on older branches of the tree.

Analysis: The insect pest oystershell scale (*Lepidosaphes ulmi*) is found throughout the world, in just about every environment, although it is most frequent in cool climates. Because the body of the insect is hidden under its shell, oystershell scale does not look like an insect. Adults are immobile, with no eyes, antennae, or legs. Females lay eggs under their shells and overwinter there. Barely visible nymphs, called *crawlers*, are highly mobile, but they soon attach themselves to a stem surface and form their shells. One generation is produced per year in cold climates; two generations are produced annually in warm areas.

Solution: Spray plants with Ortho® Volck® Oil Spray in late winter prior to bud-break to smother eggs. In the spring, when crawlers are present, spray with Ortho® Systemic Insect Killer. Even when treatment has been effective, scales may still be visible. Their shells can cling to branches for several years unless forcibly removed by scrubbing.

Birch leafminers

Leafminer damage.

Problem: Brown blisters appear on the new leaves. Eventually the blisters run together, forming a large blotch. The upper portion of the tree is generally most severely affected, but in some areas the entire tree is infested and brown. A small (up to ¼-inch), whitish larva may be found inside the blister.

Analysis: Birch leafminer (*Fenusa pusilla*), a sawfly, is a common pest of gray birch (*Betula populifolia*), paper birch (*B. papyrifera*), white birch (*B. alba*), and cut leaf birch (*B. pendula* 'Dalecarlica'). It rarely attacks black (*B. lenta*), yellow (*B. alleghaniensis*), European white (*B. pendula*), or river birch (*B. nigra*). When the first birch leaves are half grown in spring, the sawfly hovers around the trees and lays eggs on leaves. When eggs hatch, larvae feed between the upper and lower surfaces of leaves, causing blisters. Mature larvae chew their way out of the leaves and drop to the ground to pupate. Adult sawflies emerge, and the cycle repeats itself three or more times during the growing season. Adults lay eggs only on young leaves, so later in the season only terminal growth is affected.

Solution: Larvae are difficult to control once they are inside the leaf. If blotches are noticed in spring, spray with Ortho® Systemic Insect Killer or Ortho® Bug-B-Gon® Multi-Purpose Insect Killer Ready-Spray® in early July to control young larvae of the second generation. Repeat in mid-July. The following spring, spray about one week after bud-break, as the leaves are unfolding, to prevent leafminer damage. Repeat two times, 10 days apart.

Bronze birch borers

Dieback. Inset: Adult borer (½ life size).

Problem: Leaves are yellowing, and foliage is sparse at the top of the tree. Side growth on the lower branches is increased. Twigs and branches may die. The leaves on these branches turn brown but don't drop. D-shape holes and ridges are on the trunk and branches. Swollen ridges are packed with sawdust. Weak, young, or newly transplanted trees usually die.

Analysis: The bronze birch borer (*Agrilus anxius*) is the larva of an iridescent olive-brown beetle about ½ inch long. For about 6 weeks in summer, adult beetles lay eggs in bark crevices, usually around a wound. The larvae that hatch from these eggs are white and have flat heads. They bore into the wood just beneath the bark. The feeding and tunneling of the larvae stop the flow of water by cutting the conducting vessels; branch and twig dieback result. If the tree is healthy, sap flow helps defend against borers; the insect burrows into the wood, and tree sap fills the hole and drowns the insect. Weakened trees—from poor growing conditions, transplanting, or mechanical injuries—are more susceptible to attack by female beetles.

Solution: Cut out and destroy all dead and dying branches. Severely infested young trees should be removed. In spring, have an arborist spray the tree with an insecticide containing *bendiocarb* or *permethrin*, to kill young larvae before they burrow into the wood. Repeat two times at intervals of two weeks. Maintain tree vigor by watering and fertilizing regularly. Plant resistant varieties.

BUXUS (Boxwood)

Boxwood leafminers

Boxwood leafminer larvae (5x life size).

Problem: The leaves are puckered or blistered. The lower surfaces of the leaves are spotted yellow; the upper surfaces are green at first and then flecked brown and yellow. Leaves may drop prematurely. Growth is poor and the plant is rangy. Twigs may die back if the plant is infested more than one year. When a leaf is torn, two or more small (⅛-inch) yellowish maggots or brownish pupae may be found between the upper and lower surfaces.

Analysis: The boxwood leafminer (*Monarthropalpus buxi*) is one of the most serious pests of boxwood. The larvae spend the winter in the leaf. When the weather warms in spring, they feed on the tissue between the leaf surfaces. In late April or May, a tiny (⅒-inch) gnatlike orange fly emerges from the pupal case inside the leaf. The emerging flies swarm around the plant in early morning, mating and laying eggs in the leaves. New blisters develop in midsummer from feeding by this next generation of larvae. When the weather turns cold, the larvae become inactive until the following spring.

Solution: Leafminer control is most effective when insecticides are applied just before eggs are laid in late spring. Spray with Ortho® Systemic Insect Killer or with an insecticide containing *bifenthrin* in late April or early May. Plant resistant varieties.

Boxwood psyllids

Boxwood psyllid damage.

Problem: Terminal leaves are cupped and yellowing. Buds inside the cupped leaves are often dead. No new growth occurs on branch tips. When cupped leaves are peeled open in early May, a tiny (¹⁄₁₆-inch), grayish-green, immature insect is found inside. It is usually covered with a white, waxy material. Damage begins in early spring when buds first open. Small (⅛-inch) flies with transparent wings are sometimes seen jumping on leaves or flying around the plant from late May until the end of summer. Leaves may be covered with a shiny, sticky substance or with a dark powder.

Analysis: The boxwood psyllid (*Psylla buxi*) is prevalent in temperate regions of the country where boxwood is grown. American boxwood is more severely attacked than English boxwood. The immature psyllid feeds by sucking the juices from growing leaves, resulting in the yellowing and cupping. As it feeds, it secretes a white, waxy material that protects it from parasites and chemical sprays. The insect is unable to digest all the sugar in the juices, and it excretes the excess as *honeydew*, a sticky substance that covers the leaves. A black, sooty mold often grows on the honeydew. The insect matures in early summer, and the female fly lays her eggs in the base of buds in the fall, where they remain until the following spring.

Solution: Control with Ortho® Systemic Insect Killer or an insecticide containing *malathion* when damage is first noticed in early spring. Repeat two weeks later.

Winter injury

Winter injury on Japanese boxwood.

Problem: Leaves are dry and rusty brown to red. Twigs and branches may die back. The shrub is growing in an area where cold, dry, windy days are common or where plants may be exposed to late-fall or early-spring freezes.

Analysis: Boxwood is severely damaged by cold, drying winter winds, especially if temperatures are below freezing and the weather is clear. The leaves lose their moisture more rapidly than it can be replaced by the root system. Cells in the leaves dry out and die. This condition is most pronounced when water is unavailable because the soil is frozen. Leaves, along with twigs and branches, also die during early-fall or late-spring freezes, when the plant is growing. Young succulent growth can't withstand the cold temperatures.

Solution: No cure is available once plants have been injured. Pick off damaged leaves where practical, and prune dead twigs and branches. Provide shelter and windbreaks for plants growing in cold regions. Covering boxwoods with burlap bags helps prevent leaf-drying. To avoid succulent growth in the fall, don't fertilize or prune late in the season. Water in late fall or winter, if necessary, to ensure adequate soil moisture. One or more applications of an antidesiccant spray beginning in late fall may reduce damage. Mulch plants after they become dormant to reduce the depth of frost penetration into the soil.

Phytophthora root rot

Dieback caused by phytophthora root rot.

Problem: The young leaves are yellowish or off-color and wilting. Eventually part or all of the plant wilts and dies, even though the soil is sufficiently moist. Dead leaves remain attached to the plant. Heavy, poorly drained soil encourages disease development. When cut, the tissue under the bark close to ground level shows a dark discoloration. To look for discoloration, peel back the bark at the bottom of the plant. A distinct margin divides white, healthy wood from dark, diseased wood. If the plant is pulled up, examination of young roots reveals browning, decay, and an absence of white rootlets. Healthy roots are firm and white.

Analysis: Phytophthora root rot is a plant disease caused by a soil-inhabiting fungus (*Phytophthora* species) that attacks more than 100 kinds of ornamental plants. The fungus is carried in infected plants, infested soil, or soil water. It enters the roots and works its way up the plant, blocking the upward flow of water and nutrients. Plants in overwatered or poorly drained soils are more susceptible to attack.

Solution: Drench the soil with a fungicide containing *metalaxyl*. Ongoing treatment may be necessary; the fungus may be suppressed but is difficult to eradicate. Remove and destroy diseased plants; don't replant the same area with susceptible plants. If replanting is necessary because the plant is part of a hedge, replace the soil in that area to reduce the chance of root rot. Remove as much soil as possible in the area where roots have penetrated, and replace with uninfected soil. Avoid overwatering.

Volutella canker and blight

Volutella blight.

Problem: In the spring before new growth appears, leaves on the tips of affected branches turn pale green, then bronze, and finally tan or straw-colored. The bark may loosen and peel at the base of infected stems and branches, revealing areas of darkened, discolored wood. The twig or stem eventually dies. Cream-pink pustules appear on the undersides of infected leaves that have survived the winter. Later in the season, new growth may turn yellow or tan and develop pustules, especially if the weather is wet.

Analysis: Volutella canker and blight is a plant disease caused by a fungus (*Volutella buxi*) that attacks both American and English boxwood. Plants are more susceptible to the disease if they have been weakened by winter injury, poor growing conditions, or insect infestation. The fungus survives the winter on infected stems, leaves, and plant debris. Wind and splashing water spread the spores to healthy leaves and twigs. In the early spring, cankers form in twigs and branches, resulting in dieback. The fungus can continue to blight new growth throughout the growing season as long as conditions remain moist.

Solution: Fungicides are not effective in controlling this disease. Remove shrubs that are dying. Prune and destroy infected twigs and branches. Clean up accumulated plant debris. Maintain plants in good health.

Spider mites

Spider mite damage.

Problem: Leaves are stippled yellow or whitish and dirty. A silken webbing may be on the lower surfaces of leaves. New leaves may be distorted. To determine if a plant is infested with mites, examine the bottoms of the leaves with a hand lens. Or hold a sheet of white paper underneath a branch that has stippled leaves and tap the branch sharply. Minute reddish or green specks the size of pepper grains will drop to the paper and crawl around. These pests are easily seen against the white background.

Analysis: Spider mites, related to spiders, are major pests of many garden plants. They cause damage by sucking sap from the undersides of leaves. As a result of their feeding, the plant's chlorophyll disappears, producing the stippled appearance. Spider mite webbing traps cast-off skins and debris, making the plant dirty. Mites that infest boxwood are most prolific in cooler weather. They are most active in the spring and occasionally in the fall. By the onset of hot weather (70°F and higher), the mites have caused their maximum damage.

Solution: Control with Ortho® Systemic Insect Killer or Ortho® Orthenex® Garden Insect & Disease Control when stippling is first noticed. Spray the undersides of leaves thoroughly. Repeat two times at 7- to 10-day intervals to kill young mites as they hatch from eggs. To prevent unsightly injury to foliage, apply control measures early in the season when damage first appears. Injured leaves remain on the plant for more than one growing season. Hose down plants frequently to knock off webs and mites.

213

BUXUS (Boxwood) (continued) CAMELLIA

Nematodes

Nematode damage.

Problem: The leaves are bronze to yellow or straw-colored. They may wilt on hot, dry days but recover at night. The plant lacks vigor. After several years, plants are noticeably stunted and branches may die back. The roots are stunted and often bushy and dark. There may be knots on the roots.

Analysis: Nematodes are microscopic worms that live in the soil. They feed on plant roots, damaging and stunting them. The damaged roots can't supply sufficient water and nutrients to the aboveground plant parts, and the plant is stunted or slowly dies. Nematodes prefer moist, sandy loam soils. They can move only a few inches each year on their own, but they may be carried long distances by soil, water, tools, or infested plants. Testing roots and soil is the only positive method for confirming the presence of nematodes. Contact your local county extension office for sampling instructions and addresses of testing laboratories. Soil and root problems such as poor soil structure, drought stress, nutrient deficiency, and root rots can also produce symptoms similar to those caused by nematodes. These problems should be eliminated as causes before soil and root samples are sent for testing.

Solution: No available chemicals kill nematodes in planted soil. The worms can be controlled before planting, however, by soil fumigation or solarization. Properly watered and fertilized plants can tolerate some nematode feeding. If replanting, consider a shrub that is resistant to nematodes.

Camellia flower blight

Camellia flower blight.

Problem: Tan or brown spots or blotches spread across the flower. Infection takes place anytime after camellia buds begin to show color. The whole flower may turn brown. This disease is distinguished from other problems by a pattern of darkened veins, which give a netted effect in the spots. Dark brown to black resting structures form in the base of the flower.

Analysis: Camellia flower blight is a serious and widespread plant disease caused by a fungus (*Ciborinia camelliae*) that attacks the flowers of camellias. In late winter to early spring, black fungal resting structures in the soil produce spores that are carried by the wind to new flowers. If moisture is present, the spores germinate and cause infection. Flowers may turn brown within 48 hours. The fungus continues to grow in the flowers, eventually producing black resting structures that drop from the shrub with the flowers. These resting structures can persist in the soil for at least five years.

Solution: Remove and destroy spent flowers to eliminate the source of new infections. Rake up and destroy old leaves, flowers, and plant debris. To inhibit spore production, spray the soil under the shrubs with a fungicide containing *captan*, *ferbam*, or *ziram*. Begin spraying in December and repeat every three to four weeks throughout the blooming season. If this disease is a problem in your area, protect the flowers with a fungicide containing *mancozeb* or *triadimefon* as soon as they begin to show color. Repeat every three days to protect new flowers.

Cottony camellia scales and mealybugs

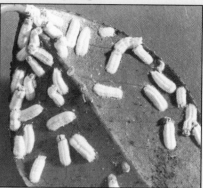

Cottony cushion scales (life size).

Problem: Buds, young branches, and the undersides of leaves are covered with white, cottony masses. The leaves are yellowing, and the plant may be weak and stunted. A shiny, sticky substance may coat the leaves. A black, sooty mold often grows on this sticky substance. Ants may be present.

Analysis: Cottony camellia scales (*Pulvinaria floccifera*) and mealybugs are common on camellias. The visual similarities between these insects make separate identification difficult. Females lay egg masses on leaves or branches. The young insects, called *crawlers*, are pale yellow to yellowish brown and inconspicuous. They feed throughout the summer on the stems and leaves. Damage is caused by the withdrawal of plant sap from the leaves and young branches. Some species of scales and mealybugs that infest camellias are unable to digest all the sugar in the plant sap, and they excrete the excess in a fluid called *honeydew*. A sooty mold fungus may develop on the sticky substance, causing the camellia leaves to appear black and dirty. Plants infested for more than one year are weakened, and their growth may be stunted.

Solution: Control with Ortho® Malathion Plus® Insect Spray Concentrate or Ortho® Systemic Insect Killer in midsummer when the young are active. Consult your county extension office for the best timing. Repeat if plants become reinfested. For control early or late in the season, spray with Ortho® Volck® Oil Spray in spring after blooming or in fall prior to blooming. Cover plants thoroughly.

Camellia yellow mottle leaf virus

Camellia virus.

Problem: Irregular yellow splotches of various sizes and shapes appear on the leaves. Some leaves may be entirely yellow. Uninfected portions remain dark green. Colored flowers may have irregular white blotches. White flowers show no symptoms. Some camellia varieties with extensive leaf yellowing may be weak and stunted, and they are more susceptible to sunburn and frost injury.

Analysis: The camellia yellow mottle leaf virus is transmitted by propagating from an infected plant or by grafting from an infected plant to a healthy one. This generally occurs in the nursery where the plant is grown. Sometimes the virus is intentionally transmitted to form variegated flowers. The disease is usually fairly harmless unless there is extensive leaf yellowing. Yellowing results when chlorophyll development is suppressed by the virus. The leaves produce less food, causing the plant to weaken.

Solution: Once the plant is infected, no chemical will control the virus. There is no danger of the virus spreading to other camellias unless you graft with infected plants. Remove excessively weak camellias. Buy only healthy plants. (For information on selecting healthy plants, see page 415.)

Sooty mold

Sooty mold.

Problem: A black, sooty mold grows on leaves and twigs. It can be wiped off the surfaces.

Analysis: Sooty mold is a common black mold caused by several species of fungi that grow on the sugary material left on plants by aphids, mealybugs, scales, whiteflies, and other insects that suck sap from the plant. The insects are unable to digest all the sugar in the sap, and they excrete the excess in a fluid called *honeydew*, which drops onto the leaves below. The honeydew may also drop out of infested trees and shrubs onto camellias growing beneath them. Sooty mold is unsightly but is fairly harmless, because it does not attack the leaf directly. Extremely heavy amounts prevent light from reaching the leaf, so the leaf produces fewer nutrients and may turn yellow. The presence of sooty mold indicates that the camellia or another plant near it is infested with insects.

Solution: Hose off sooty mold or wipe it from the leaves with a wet rag. Rain also will eventually wash it off. Prevent more sooty mold from growing by controlling the insect that is producing the honeydew. Inspect the leaves and twigs above the sooty mold to find out what type of insect is present. (For control information, see the following pages: aphids, page 443; mealybugs, page 444; scales, pages 444 to 447; whiteflies, page 448.)

Catalpa sphinx

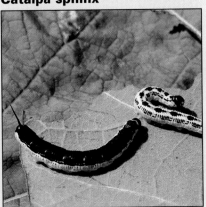

Catalpa sphinx caterpillars (½ life size).

Problem: Small holes are chewed in the upper surfaces of leaves. Large yellow-and-black-striped caterpillars with a sharp "horn" at the tail end feed in groups on young leaves. As the caterpillars develop (1 to 3 inches), they spread throughout the tree and feed singly on leaf edges. The tree may be completely defoliated. Damage occurs from May to August.

Analysis: The catalpa sphinx (*Ceratomia catalpae*) caterpillar is the larval stage of a large night-flying moth that is seldom seen. The moth passes the winter as a pupa in the ground. In spring, the moth emerges and the female lays her eggs on young catalpa leaves. The eggs hatch and the larvae feed for several weeks. If the larvae are left uncontrolled, they develop into moths, producing a second generation of caterpillars that may completely defoliate the tree by mid- to late summer.

Solution: Control with Ortho® Systemic Insect Killer or the bacterial insecticide *Bacillus thuringiensis* (Bt) when damage is first noticed in the spring. Repeat in midsummer if the tree becomes reinfested. In fall, clean up debris beneath the tree to reduce the number of overwintering pupae.

CATALPA (continued)

CEANOTHUS (Wild lilac)

Verticillium wilt

Verticillium wilt.

Leaf spot

Leaf spot.

Root and crown rot

Canker on ceanothus.

Problem: Leaves on a branch turn yellow at the margins, then brown and dry. During hot weather, leaves may wilt. New leaves are stunted and yellow. Leaves on uninfected portions remain green. The infected tree may die slowly over several seasons—or the whole tree may wilt and die within a few months. Some trees may recover. Tissue under bark on the dying side shows brown streaks when cut. To examine for streaks, peel back the bark at the bottom of the dying branch. The brown discoloration may be very apparent or barely visible in the cut.

Analysis: Verticillium wilt disease affects ornamental trees and shrubs. It is caused by a soil-inhabiting fungus (*Verticillium* species). The disease is spread by contaminated seeds, plants, soil, equipment, and groundwater. The fungus enters the tree through the roots and spreads up into the branches through the water-conducting vessels in the trunk. The vessels become discolored and plugged. The plugging cuts off the flow of water and nutrients to the branches, causing leaf discoloration and branch wilting.

Solution: No chemical control is available. Feed with Scotts® Evergreen, Flowering Tree & Shrub Slow Release Plant Food to stimulate growth. Remove all deadwood. Do not remove branches on which leaves have recently wilted. These branches may produce new leaves in three to four weeks or the following spring. Remove dead trees. If replanting in the same area, plant trees and shrubs that are resistant to verticillium wilt. (For a list of plants resistant to verticillium wilt, see page 540.)

Problem: Spots and blotches appear on the leaves. The spots may be yellow, red, tan, gray, or brown. They range in size from barely visible to ¼ inch. Several spots may join to form blotches. Leaves may yellow and die. Some leaves may fall. Leaf spotting is most severe in moist, humid weather.

Analysis: Several fungi cause leaf spots on ceanothus. These spots are unsightly but rarely harmful to the plant. Plants weakened by low temperatures and wind exposure are most susceptible to invasion by leaf spot fungi. The fungi are spread by wind and splashing water. If wet or humid weather persists, the fungi spread through the tissue and blotches form. The fungi survive the winter on the leaves and twigs. Most leaf organisms do their greatest damage in mild weather (50° to 85°F).

Solution: Once the leaves become spotted, they will remain so. Where practical, remove infected leaves from the plant. Collect and destroy any fallen leaves. To reduce unsightly damage, spray with a fungicide containing *zineb* when new growth begins in the spring. Repeat two times at intervals of two weeks or for as long as the weather remains favorable for infection. Add a spreader-sticker to the spray.

Problem: Young leaves are yellowish or off-color. Many of the leaves wilt and fall, and overall plant growth is sparse. Eventually the plant dies. The roots are dark and rotted. A dark, sunken canker may be on the stem near the soil line.

Analysis: Root and crown rot is a disease caused by any of several different fungi, also known as *water molds*, that thrive in waterlogged, heavy soils. (For information on water molds, see page 419.) Some attack the plant stems at the soil level, while others attack the roots. Infection causes roots and stems to decay, resulting in wilting, then yellowing leaves, and death of the plant. These fungi are spread by infested soil and infected transplants.

Solution: Remove dead and dying plants. Allow the soil around the plants to dry out. (For information on this technique, see page 419.) Avoid future root rot problems by planting in well-drained soil. (For information on drainage, see page 406.)

CELASTRUS (Bittersweet) CELTIS (Hackberry)

Euonymus scales

Euonymus scale (4× life size).

Problem: Yellow or whitish spots appear on the upper surfaces of leaves. Leaves may drop, and the plant may become bare by midsummer. In severe cases, stems die back. The stems and undersides of leaves are covered with dark brown, oyster-shell–shape, crusty bumps (females) or with soft, white, ridged, elongated scales (males). The bumps and scales can be scraped off.

Analysis: Euonymus scale (*Unaspis euonymi*), a serious pest of bittersweet and other ornamental shrubs and vines, is found throughout the country. The scales spend the winter on the twigs and branches of bittersweet, laying their eggs in spring. In late spring to early summer the young scales, called *crawlers*, settle on leaves or stems. The small (1/10-inch), soft-bodied young feed by inserting their mouthparts and sucking sap. The legs atrophy, and a crusty or waxy shell develops over the body. The males are white and very noticeable on the leaves and stems. Mature female scales are brown and shaped like an oyster shell. They lay their eggs underneath their shell. The cycle may be repeated up to three times during the growing season. An uncontrolled infestation may kill the plant after two or three years. Other species of scales also infest bittersweet.

Solution: Spray with Ortho® Systemic Insect Killer or Ortho® Malathion Plus® Insect Spray Concentrate in early summer (late spring in the South), when the young are active. The following spring, before new growth begins, spray the trunk and branches with a dormant oil spray to control overwintering insects.

Witches'-broom

Witches'-broom.

Problem: There are broomlike growths of twigs throughout the tree. The clusters of twigs are most noticeable after leaves fall. Affected branches are weakened and break easily during windstorms.

Analysis: Witches'-broom is most severe on common or American hackberry (*Celtis occidentalis*). The cause of this problem is not definitely known. A powdery mildew fungus (*Sphaerotheca phytophila*) and a gall mite (*Eriophyes* species), however, are usually associated with witches'-broom. Gall mites cause proliferation of tissue in many plants. In spring, affected buds are larger and more open than normal. The microscopic mites and black spore-producing bodies from the fungus may be found inside. Branches from the affected buds become dwarfed and clustered, giving the witches'-broom effect. Although the damage is unsightly, trees with this problem are not seriously harmed.

Solution: No chemical effectively controls this problem. If the brooms are unsightly, prune them.

Hackberry leaf gall psyllids

Hackberry nipple galls.

Problem: The lower surfaces of leaves are covered with cylindrical nipple- or crater-shape or blisterlike growths. The upper surface of leaves are spotted and yellowing. If the growth is broken open during the summer, a tiny (1/10-inch), yellowish-orange insect is found inside. In late August or September, houses are invaded, and windows and screens are covered with dark-colored flying insects 1/8 inch long.

Analysis: Hackberry leaf gall psyllid (*Pachypsylla* species) adults are considered more of a nuisance than a destructive tree pest. The insects don't noticeably affect the growth and vigor of the tree. Adult psyllids spend the winter in protected places such as buildings, trash, and bark crevices. In spring, just as the hackberry buds swell, the adults emerge from hibernation and fly or crawl around the ends of twigs. Eggs are deposited on the undersides of unfolded leaves. After the eggs hatch, the immature insects feed by sucking the sap. This feeding stimulates abnormal leaf growth, producing the galls that enclose the insects and protect them from predators. The adults emerge in early fall, invading homes and buildings around hackberry trees.

Solution: Once protective galls have formed around the insects, the insects can't be killed. To control overwintering adults and newly hatched immature psyllids before galls are formed, spray trees with Ortho® Systemic Insect Killer as leaves are unfolding in the spring. If adult psyllids invade the home, vacuum them up and destroy the vacuum-cleaner bag contents.

CERCIS (Redbud)

Cankers

Canker.

Problem: The leaves on a branch wilt and turn brown. Eventually they drop. Twigs or branches are often dead or dying. Sunken oval areas with black centers and cracks along the edges may be at the base of the affected twigs or branches, but the cankers are not always visible on the surface.

Analysis: Cankers, a plant disease caused by a fungus (*Botryosphaeria ribis*), is the most destructive disease of redbud. It also affects more than 50 woody plants in the eastern half of the country. (For a list of susceptible plants, see page 538.) Spores produced in the sunken areas during wet periods in spring and summer are spread to healthy branches by splashing rain and wind. The fungus enters the tree through wounds or dead and dying twigs, and a sunken canker develops. The fungus slowly spreads through the wood in all directions, cutting off the flow of nutrients and water to the affected branch. The leaves wilt and die, and branches above the cankered area are usually killed.

Solution: No effective chemical control is available. Prune and destroy dead twigs and branches, cutting at least 3 inches below the cankered area. Disinfect pruning shears after each cut. Remove dying trees. To help prevent infection, avoid wounding trees.

Verticillium wilt

Verticillium wilt.

Problem: Leaves on a branch turn yellow at the margins, then brown and dry. During hot weather, the leaves may wilt. New leaves may be stunted and yellowish. The infected tree may die slowly, branch by branch, over several seasons—or the whole tree may wilt and die within a few months. Some trees may recover. The tissue under the bark on the dying side shows dark streaks when cut. To examine for streaks, peel back the bark at the bottom of the dying branch. The dark discoloration may be very apparent or barely visible in the area just underneath the bark.

Analysis: Verticillium wilt disease attacks many ornamental trees and shrubs. It is caused by a soil-inhabiting fungus (*Verticillium* species). The disease is spread by contaminated seeds, plants, soil, equipment, and groundwater. The fungus enters the tree through the roots and spreads up into the branches through the water-conducting vessels in the trunk. The vessels become discolored and plugged. The plugging cuts off the flow of water and nutrients to the branches, causing leaf discoloration and wilting.

Solution: No chemical control is available. Feed with Scotts® Evergreen, Flowering Tree & Shrub Slow Release Plant Food to stimulate vigorous growth. Remove all deadwood. Do not remove branches on which leaves have recently wilted. These branches may produce new leaves in three to four weeks or the following spring. Remove dead trees. If replanting in the same area, plant trees that are resistant to verticillium wilt.

CORNUS (Dogwood)

Spot anthracnose

Spot anthracnose.

Problem: Small (up to ⅛-inch), circular, reddish-purple spots with light tan centers appear on the flower petals (bracts) and leaves. If spotting is severe, the flowers and leaves may become malformed or puckered as they enlarge. The centers of the spots eventually dry and may drop out, leaving a small round hole. The leaves are infected after blooming, showing dark purple, circular spots or blotches. Young shoots and berries are also infected. White varieties are most severely affected, but pink varieties are also susceptible. The disease is the worst during extended wet weather.

Analysis: Spot anthracnose is a plant disease caused by a fungus (*Elsinoe corni*). The fungus survives the winter on infected plant tissue. During wet weather in early spring, the fungus is splashed by rain water onto the dogwood blooms. Spots develop where the fungus enters the tissue. If wet weather continues, the disease spreads to the leaves and twigs.

Solution: If spots are noticed on dogwood blooms in spring, spray with a fungicide containing Ortho® Garden Disease Control, *azoxystrobin*, or *mancozeb* at petal fall. Repeat four weeks later and again in late summer after flower buds form. The following spring, begin spraying when flower buds start to open. Prune and destroy infected twigs. Rake up and destroy leaves in the fall.

Dogwood anthracnose

Anthracnose canker.

Problem: Irregular dark brown, streaky lesions appear on the flower bracts in spring. Small purple-rimmed spots or large brown blotches are found on leaves. Spots may enlarge to kill entire leaves, which cling to stems after normal leaf fall. Twigs and branches die back, beginning in the lower parts of the tree. Numerous small shoots may sprout along the trunk and branches. These become infected and die. Cankers may be found at the base of the dead shoots. The tree may be killed in three to five years.

Analysis: Dogwood anthracnose is a plant disease first reported in the United States in the 1980s. The fungus (*Discula destructiva*) is spread by splashing water and infects dogwoods most severely in wet, shaded areas. Native dogwoods *Cornus florida* and *C. nuttallii* are particularly susceptible to the disease. *C. kousa* and *C. kousa* var. *chinensis* appear to be resistant to the canker phase of the disease, but they can display leaf spots.

Solution: To protect leaves as they emerge in the spring, spray with Ortho® Garden Disease Control or Ortho® Lawn Disease Control. Begin spraying when buds open, and continue spraying at weekly intervals until leaves are fully grown. After the leaves are fully grown, spray the tree once a month for the rest of the season. Prune and destroy dead twigs and branches. To avoid spreading the fungus, prune only in dry weather. Remove severely infected trees to prevent spread. When planting new dogwoods, select resistant varieties. Plant in full sun if possible, but remember that dogwoods in full sun need lots of water.

Powdery mildew

Powdery mildew.

Problem: Patches of powdery grayish-white material appear on leaves and branch tips from late spring to early summer. The patches occur primarily on the upper surfaces and are more likely to appear on new leaves. Infected leaves may be distorted and curled.

Analysis: Powdery mildew is a common plant disease caused by several closely related fungi (*Oidium* species) that are active in both humid and dry weather. The powdery patches consist of fungal strands and spores. The spores are spread by wind to healthy dogwoods, where they attack new growth and recently matured leaves. The fungus saps the plant nutrients, causing the leaves to turn yellow and sometimes to die. It has little long-term effect on tree vigor and overall health.

Solution: In most years, powdery mildew doesn't do enough damage to warrant spraying. Keep the trees vigorous with regular feeding and watering. If many leaves are being killed or distorted, spray with a fungicide containing *triadimefon* or *thiophanate-methyl* to arrest the spread of the disease. Repeat the treatment if new leaves become infected. When replanting, select resistant varieties.

Summer leaf scorch

Summer leaf scorch.

Problem: During hot weather, usually in July or August, leaves turn brown at the edges and between the veins. Sometimes the whole leaf dies. Many leaves may drop during late summer. This problem is most severe on the youngest branches. Trees do not generally die. Browning and withering can develop even if the soil around the roots is moist.

Analysis: Summer leaf scorch is caused by excessive evaporation of moisture from the leaves. In hot weather, water evaporates rapidly from the leaves. If the roots can't absorb and convey water fast enough to replenish this loss, the leaves turn brown and wither. For optimum growth, dogwoods require moist soil. Leaf scorch is most severe when water is unavailable because soil is dry. Scorch may also develop when the soil is moist, however, if the weather is extremely hot. Drying winds, severed roots, and limited soil area can also cause scorch. (For more information on scorch, see page 427.)

Solution: To prevent further scorch, deep-water trees during periods of hot weather to wet down the entire root space. (For more information on watering, see pages 407 to 408.) If practical, apply 3 to 4 inches of mulch over the root system. Water newly transplanted trees whenever the rootball is dry 2 inches below the surface. Scorch on trees in moist soil can't be controlled. Plant trees adapted to your climate. In hot summer areas, plant dogwoods in partial shade.

CORNUS (Dogwood) *(continued)*

Flatheaded apple tree borers

Borer damage.

Dogwood borers

Dogwood borer damage. Inset: Adult (life size).

Crown canker

Crown canker.

Problem: Branches or entire trees die during hot weather. Patches of bark may become sunken, discolored, and ooze droplets of moisture. If the tree is not killed, bark patches may die and flake off, leaving bare wood.

Analysis: The flatheaded apple tree borer (*Chrysobothris femorata*) is a destructive beetle that attacks weakened and newly planted trees. Adults emerge in late spring and early summer to lay eggs under loose bark, usually on the sunny side of the tree. These eggs hatch into white, legless larvae with flat heads. The larvae bore into the inner bark and sapwood, disrupting the flow of water to the top of the tree. The bark over their meandering tunnels dies and eventually sloughs off. When enough of the circumference of the trunk is tunneled, the tree dies. Newly planted dogwoods are particularly susceptible, often being killed within two or three years.

Solution: If you discover damaged bark while the larvae are still present, try to kill them with a knife or by probing with a piece of wire. Be careful not to cause more damage than the larvae are causing. If possible, prune out infested branches. Keep trees healthy and growing vigorously. Water during drought. Protect newly planted dogwoods with a trunk wrap for their first couple of years.

Problem: In midsummer, the leaves turn red and drop prematurely; eventually twigs or branches die back. Bark sloughs off around holes in a swollen area on the trunk or at the base of branches. Late in the summer, a fine sawdust may drop from the holes. Young trees are usually killed.

Analysis: The dogwood borer (*Synanthedon scitula*), also known as the *pecan borer*, is the larva of a brownish, ½-inch-long, clear-wing moth. The borer infects flowering dogwood, pecan, and many other ornamental and fruit trees. The moth is active from May until September and lays its eggs on the bark, usually near a wound or old borer injury. After the eggs hatch, the ½-inch-long white larvae with brown heads find an opening in the bark. They feed in the wood just under the bark, girdling the branches and causing the dieback. The larvae spend the winter inside the tree. Several other borers also infest dogwood. (For more information on borers, see page 434.)

Solution: No insecticides that give adequate protection are available to home gardeners. Contact an arborist if you would like to apply protective sprays. Feed the tree regularly with Scotts® Evergreen, Flowering Tree & Shrub Slow Release Plant Food to maintain vigor. To prevent borer entrance, avoid pruning during the summer months when moths are present, and avoid wounding the trunks and branches. You can also reduce damage by inserting a fine wire in entry holes to kill the larvae.

Problem: The leaves on one or more branches at the top of the tree are small and pale green. They turn prematurely red in mid- or late summer. Twigs and branches die back, and sometimes the whole tree dies. The symptoms usually develop over several years. At the base of the tree, dark-colored sap may ooze from one spot. As the disease progresses, a sunken area develops around the oozing sap, and the bark crumbles, leaving wood exposed. The exposed wood in the sunken area is dark and discolored.

Analysis: Crown canker, a plant disease also known as *collar rot*, is caused by a soil-inhabiting fungus (*Phytophthora cactorum*). The fungus is carried in affected plants or in infested soil or soil water. It is often a problem following periods when flooding has resulted in standing water around the base of trees. It enters the root crown through wounds and slowly kills the tissue, causing a sunken canker. The aboveground symptoms are caused by the blockage of water and nutrients through the trunk. When the canker encircles the trunk, the tree dies.

Solution: Small cankers can be removed surgically with some success if all discolored bark and wood, including a 1-inch border area of apparently healthy bark and wood, is cut out. Remove an elliptical piece of wood from the tree with a sharp knife, sterilizing the knife after each cut. Clean the wound with alcohol. If the tree dies, don't plant another dogwood in the same area for three to five years. Avoid wounding and watering the base of the tree.

COTONEASTER

Fire blight

Fire blight.

Problem: New shoots suddenly wilt in the spring and turn black as if scorched by fire. The bark at the base of the blighted shoots becomes water-soaked, then dark, sunken, and dry; cracks may develop at the edge of the sunken area. In warm, moist spring weather, drops of brown ooze appear on the sunken bark. Young plants may die.

Analysis: Fire blight is a plant disease caused by a bacterium (*Erwinia amylovora*) that is very destructive to many trees and shrubs. (For a list of susceptible plants, see page 535.) Bacteria spend the winter in sunken cankers on the branches. In spring, bacteria ooze out of the cankers. Bees, flies, and other insects are attracted to the sweet, sticky ooze and become smeared with it. When insects visit a cotoneaster flower for nectar, they infect it with the bacteria. The bacteria spread rapidly through the plant tissue in warm (65°F or higher), humid weather. Insects visiting these infected blossoms carry bacteria-laden nectar to healthy blossoms. Rain, wind, and tools may also spread the bacteria. Tender or damaged leaves may be infected in midsummer.

Solution: During spring and summer, prune out infected branches 12 to 15 inches beyond any visible discoloration and destroy them. Disinfect pruning shears after each cut. A protective spray of an antibiotic containing *streptomycin* applied before bud-break in the spring will help prevent infection. Repeat at intervals of five to seven days until the end of bloom. In the fall, prune out any remaining infected branches.

Hawthorn lace bugs

Damaged leaves. Inset: Lace bugs (⅓ life size).

Problem: Upper surfaces of leaves are mottled yellow and green. Mottling may be confused with mite or leafhopper damage but can be distinguished from other insect damage by hard, black, shiny droplets found on the undersides of damaged leaves. Small (⅛-inch), spiny wingless insects or brownish insects with clear lace wings may be visible around the droplets and next to the leaf midrib. The plant may be stunted. Damage occurs in spring and summer.

Analysis: The hawthorn lace bug (*Corythucha cydoniae*) is found on hawthorn, pyracantha, and fruiting quince, as well as on cotoneaster. It overwinters as an adult on the shrub in bark crevices, branch crotches, or other protected areas. Both the spiny, wingless, immature insects and the lace-winged adults suck sap from the undersides of leaves throughout the growing season. As a result of their feeding, the chlorophyll disappears, causing the characteristic yellowing. Droplets of black excrement accumulate around the insects while they feed. Damage is unsightly, and food production by leaves is reduced, resulting in a loss of plant vigor.

Solution: When damage first appears in the spring, spray with Ortho® Systemic Insect Killer or Ortho® Malathion Plus® Insect Spray Concentrate. Thoroughly cover the undersides of the leaves, where insects feed. Repeat 7 to 10 days later. A third application may be necessary if the plant becomes reinfested in the summer.

CRATAEGUS (Hawthorn)

Fire blight

Fire blight.

Problem: Blossoms and leaves of infected twigs suddenly wilt and turn black as if scorched by fire. Brown or blackened leaves cling to the branches. The bark at the base of the blighted twig becomes water-soaked, then dark, sunken, and dry. Cracks may develop at the edges of the sunken area. In warm, moist spring weather, drops of brown ooze appear on the sunken bark. Young trees may die.

Analysis: Fire blight is a disease caused by a bacterium (*Erwinia amylovora*) that is very destructive to hawthorn and many other related plants. (For a list of susceptible plants, see page 535.) The bacteria spend the winter in the sunken cankers on the branches. In spring, the bacteria ooze out of the cankers and attract bees and other insects. When the insects visit a hawthorn flower for nectar, they infect it with the bacteria. The bacteria spread rapidly through the plant tissue in warm (65°F or higher), humid weather. Insects visiting these infected blossoms carry bacteria-laden nectar to healthy blossoms. Rain, wind, and tools may also spread the bacteria.

Solution: During spring and summer, prune infected branches 12 to 15 inches beyond any visible discoloration, and destroy them. Disinfect pruning shears after each cut. A protective spray of a bactericide containing basic copper sulfate or *streptomycin* applied before bud-break in the spring will help prevent infection. Repeat at intervals of five to seven days until the end of bloom. In the fall, prune out any remaining infected branches. When planting new trees, use resistant varieties.

CRATAEGUS (Hawthorn) *(continued)*

Hawthorn rust

Hawthorn rust.

Problem: In the summer, orange, red, gray, or brown spots develop on the upper surfaces of leaves. Leaves are often distorted, and many may drop. Infected twigs and fruit are also deformed. Tiny whitish tubes may develop on the fruit and twigs, or brownish, horn-shaped bodies may develop in the fruit and on the undersides of leaves.

Analysis: Hawthorn rust is a plant disease caused by any of several species of fungi (*Gymnosporangium* species) that infect both hawthorn and juniper (including red cedar). The fungi can't spread from hawthorn to hawthorn but must alternate between juniper and hawthorn. In the spring, orange spores from juniper are carried by the wind to hawthorns. With warm, wet weather, the spores germinate and infect the leaves, twigs, and fruit. Depending on the species of rust, leaves become spotted, or the leaves, twigs, and fruit become deformed. Fruiting bodies develop on infected parts, producing spores that are blown back to red cedar. Some species of rust cause little damage, while others may cause severe defoliation.

Solution: If rust is a problem on your hawthorns, spray trees with Ortho® Garden Disease Control, beginning just as the flower buds open. Repeat the spray two more times at intervals of 7 to 10 days. Remove the alternate host, juniper (including red cedar), from nearby areas. Plant resistant varieties of hawthorn, such as Washington and cockspur.

Leaf spot

Entomosporium leaf spot.

Problem: Spots and blotches appear on the leaves. The spots may be red, yellow, brown, black or purple. They range in size from barely visible to ¼ inch in diameter. Several spots may join to form blotches. Infected leaves may die and drop. If spotting is severe, the tree may defoliate prematurely. Leaf spotting is most severe in moist, humid weather.

Analysis: Several different fungi, including *Fabraea theumenii*, cause leaf spots on hawthorn. These spots are unsightly but rarely harmful to the plant. Severe, recurrent infection can cause repeated defoliation that may weaken the tree and reduce its flowering potential, however. The fungi are spread by wind and splashing water. Spots develop where the fungi enter the leaf tissue. The fungi survive the winter on twigs and in fallen leaves and plant debris. Most leaf-spotting fungi do their greatest damage in moist, mild to warm weather (between 50° and 85°F).

Solution: There is no way to get rid of spots once leaves are infected. To help prevent spotting the following year, clean up and destroy fallen leaves and other plant debris. In spring when the leaves emerge, spray trees with Ortho® Garden Disease Control or with a fungicide containing *captan*. Respray when the leaves are half grown and again when they are fully grown. Continue spraying at intervals of 10 to 14 days for as long as wet weather continues.

Hawthorn lace bugs

Lace bug damage.

Problem: The upper surfaces of leaves are mottled yellow and green. The mottling may be confused with mite or leafhopper damage but can be distinguished from other insect damage by hard, black, shiny droplets found on undersides of damaged leaves. Small (⅛-inch), light or dark spiny wingless insects or brownish insects with clear lace wings may be visible around the droplets and next to the leaf midrib. The plant may be stunted. Damage occurs in spring and summer.

Analysis: The hawthorn lace bug (*Corythucha cydoniae*) is found on pyracantha, cotoneaster, and fruiting quince, as well as on hawthorn. It survives the winter as an adult on the plant in bark crevices, branch crotches, or other protected areas. Both the spiny, wingless, immature insects and the lace-wing adults suck sap from the undersides of leaves throughout the growing season. As a result of their feeding, the chlorophyll disappears, causing the characteristic yellowing. Droplets of black excrement accumulate around the insects while they feed. Damage is unsightly, and food production by the leaf is reduced, resulting in a loss of plant vigor.

Solution: Spray with Ortho® Systemic Insect Killer or Ortho® Bug-B-Gon® Multi-Purpose Insect Killer Ready-Spray® when damage first appears in the spring. Thoroughly cover the undersides of the leaves where insects feed. Repeat 7 to 10 days later. A third application may be necessary if the plant becomes reinfested in the summer.

Pear slugs

Pear slug (2× life size).

Problem: Leaves are eaten between the veins so that a pattern of veins is exposed. Slimy, tadpole-shaped insects are on the leaf.

Analysis: The pear slug (*Caliroa cerasi*) is an insect that looks like a slug but is not related to the slug. It is the larva of a sawfly, a relative of wasps and bees. Besides hawthorn, it attacks European mountain ash (*Sorbus aucuparia*) and several fruit trees, including pear, cherry, plum, and quince. Larvae are up to ½ inch long, greenish black, and slimy. Adult sawflies emerge as cherries and pears come into full leaf in late spring. They lay eggs inside the leaf tissue. The pear slugs that hatch from these eggs feed and grow for about a month, then drop to the ground and pupate in the soil. A second generation emerges in midsummer.

Solution: If possible, wash the larvae off the leaves with a strong spray of water. The larvae can't climb back into the tree. Spray with Ortho® Bug-B-Gon® Multi-Purpose Insect Killer Ready-Spray® or with a horticultural oil.

Scales

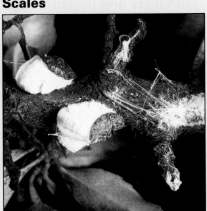

Cottony cushion scales (2× life size).

Problem: White, cottony masses, brown or whitish crusty bumps, or clusters of somewhat flattened brown or white scaly bumps cover the leaves or bark. Bumps can be scraped off. Leaves turn yellow and may drop. Sometimes a sticky substance coats leaves. Black, sooty mold often grows on the substance. Heavy infestations kill branches.

Analysis: Many species of scales infest hawthorn. They lay their eggs on leaves or bark, and in spring to midsummer the young scales, called *crawlers*, settle around them. The small (1/10-inch), soft-bodied young feed by sucking sap from the plant. The legs usually atrophy, and with some types, a shell develops over the body. The types of scales that don't develop shells are conspicuous. The females are covered with a white, cottony egg sac, containing up to 2,500 eggs. Scales covered with a shell are less noticeable. Their shell often blends in with the plant, and the eggs are inconspicuous beneath the coverings. Some species of scales are unable to digest all the sugar in the plant sap, and they excrete the excess in a fluid called *honeydew*. A sooty mold fungus may develop on the honeydew, causing the hawthorn leaves to appear black and dirty.

Solution: Control with Ortho® Malathion Plus® Insect Spray Concentrate or Ortho® Systemic Insect Killer when the young are active. To control scales during the dormant season, spray with Ortho® Volck® Oil Spray.

CYPRESS FAMILY (Arborvitae)

Twig and needle blight

Twig and needle blight damage on western red cedar.

Problem: Needles, twigs, and branches turn brown. In some cases, the upper branches die from the tips back. In other cases, the lower two-thirds of the plant dies. The needles often drop in late summer, starting at the tips and leaving the infected branches bare. Sometimes minute black dots appear on the dead needles and stems. This disease is most serious in wet weather or in shady locations. Plants may be killed.

Analysis: Several different fungi cause twig and needle blight on plants in the cypress family. During wet weather, spores germinate on twigs and spread into the needles and twigs above and below the point of entrance, killing them. Reinfection may continue until the whole plant dies, or the plant may persist for many years in an unsightly condition. With some fungi, black spore-producing bodies develop and spend the winter on dead needles.

Solution: Prune and destroy infected branches below the line between diseased and healthy tissue, making the cut into live tissue. Valuable specimens can be sprayed with a fungicide containing basic copper sulfate at weekly intervals throughout the growing season until new growth stops. Avoid overhead watering. Plant trees in areas with good air circulation and full sun.

CYPRESS FAMILY (Arborvitae) (continued)

Leaf browning and shedding

Leaf browning on cedar.

Problem: The older leaves, on the inside of the tree nearest the trunk, turn brown and drop. This condition may develop in a few days or over several weeks in either spring or fall.

Analysis: Leaf browning and shedding is a natural process similar to the dropping of leaves of deciduous trees. It is usually more pronounced on arborvitae (*Thuja*) than on other plants in the cypress family. Usually it takes place every year; in other cases, it occurs every second or third year. When growing conditions have been favorable the previous season, leaf shedding occurs over several weeks and is less noticeable. If the plant has been exposed to unfavorable conditions during the growing season, leaf drop develops within a few days. Leaf drop is caused also by new growth shading older, interior growth.

Solution: No chemical controls are necessary. Water regularly and feed with Scotts® Evergreen, Flowering Tree & Shrub Slow Release Plant Food according to label directions. Provide full sun. Check plants for insects and mites during the growing season.

Leafminers and tip moths

Leafminer damage to arborvitae.

Problem: Leaf tips turn yellow, then brown and dry, contrasting sharply with the healthy green foliage. Damage is most severe for plants growing in shady areas. When a yellow leaf is torn open, a small (⅓-inch-long), greenish caterpillar with a dark head may be found inside. Gray or brownish moths with a ⅓-inch wingspread may be seen flying around the plant in April, May, or June.

Analysis: Several species of insects known as leafminers (*Argyresthia* species) in the eastern United States and tip moths on the West Coast infest arborvitae, cypress, and juniper. Damage is unsightly, but plants may lose more than half of their foliage and still survive. The larvae spend the winter inside the leaf tips. When the weather warms in late spring, adult moths emerge and lay eggs on the leaves. The eggs hatch, and the larvae tunnel into the leaf tips, devouring the green tissue. The tips above the point of entry yellow and die. The larvae feed until late fall or through the winter until early spring.

Solution: Spray with Ortho® Systemic Insect Killer or Ortho® Bug-B-Gon® Multi-Purpose Insect Killer Ready-Spray® when eggs are hatching in early summer, about the time black locust is in bloom. To kill adults, spray a second time a month later, when mountain laurel and Washington hawthorn are in bloom. Trim and destroy infested leaves in fall and spring.

Winter injury

Winter injury to arborvitae.

Problem: Leaves turn yellow at first, then rusty brown and dry. Twigs and branches may die back. The tree is growing in a climate where cold, dry, windy days are common or where plants may be exposed to late fall or early spring freezes. The soil may be frozen.

Analysis: Arborvitae are damaged by cold, drying winter winds, especially if temperatures are below freezing. These trees are commonly planted as windbreaks and in exposed areas where growing conditions may be unfavorable. Moisture is lost from the leaves more rapidly than it can be replaced by the root system. Cells in the leaves dry out and die. This condition is most pronounced when water is unavailable because the soil is dry or frozen. Leaves, along with twigs and branches, also die during early fall or late spring freezes when the plant is growing. Young tender growth can't withstand freezing temperatures.

Solution: Prune dead twigs and branches. Provide shelter for plants growing in extremely cold areas. To avoid succulent growth in the fall, don't fertilize late in the season. During a dry fall, irrigate plants thoroughly to reduce winter injury. One or more applications of an antidesiccant spray beginning in late fall may reduce damage.

Spider mites

Spider mite webs on Italian cypress.

Problem: The needles are stippled, yellowing, and dirty. A silken webbing is sometimes on the needles and stems. Needles may turn brown and fall off. To determine if a tree is infested with mites, examine the needles with a hand lens. Or hold a sheet of white paper underneath some stippled needles and tap the foliage sharply. Minute dark green, black, or red specks about the size of pepper grains will drop to the paper and begin to crawl around.

Analysis: Spider mites, especially the spruce spider mite (*Oligonychus ununguis*), are among the most destructive pests of evergreen trees. In the cypress family, they attack mainly arborvitae (*Thuja* species) and *Chamaecyparis*. They cause damage by sucking sap from the undersides of needles. As a result of their feeding, the tree's chlorophyll disappears, producing the stippled appearance. Mites are active throughout the growing season but usually become most active in May and September. By midsummer, they have built to tremendous numbers. Young plants may die the first season. If mites are left uncontrolled over a period of years, older trees die progressively from lower branches upward.

Solution: Control with Ortho® Systemic Insect Killer or Ortho® Bug-B-Gon® Multi-Purpose Insect Killer Ready-Spray® in mid- to late May to kill young mites of the first generation. Repeat the spray two more times at intervals of 7 to 10 days. Additional spraying may be needed later in the season if the plant becomes reinfested. In late winter, spray with Ortho® Volck® Oil Spray.

Bagworms

Bagworm cocoon.

Problem: The needles are chewed, and branches may be defoliated. Hanging from the branches are carrot-shape cases, or "bags," from 1 to 3 inches long. The bags are constructed from interwoven bits of dead foliage, twigs, and silk. When a bag is cut open, a tan or blackish caterpillar or a yellowish grublike insect may be found inside, or the bag may be empty. A heavy attack by bagworms may stunt tree growth.

Analysis: The larval stage of the bagworm (*Thyridopteryx ephemeraeformis*) devours foliage of many species of plants in the cypress family. Larvae hatch in spring and begin feeding on the needles. Each larva constructs a bag that covers its entire body. The worm partially emerges from its bag to feed. When leaves on a branch are completely consumed, the bagworm moves to the next branch. By late summer, the full-grown larva spins silken bands to attach the bag permanently and pupate inside. The mature female remains in the bag. The male is a black moth that is sometimes seen in fall around lights at night.

Solution: Spray with Ortho® Systemic Insect Killer, Ortho® Bug-B-Gon® Multi-Purpose Insect Killer Ready-Spray®, or the bacterial insecticide *Bacillus thuringiensis* (Bt) between midspring and midsummer. Spray again 10 days later if new leaf damage occurs. Spray as soon as bagworms are detected in the spring; older bagworms are more difficult to control. Saturate the bags thoroughly to reach the worm inside. Handpicking and destroying bags from fall to spring will reduce the number of overwintering eggs.

Canker and dieback

Stem canker.

Problem: Leaves on a branch, or the entire tree, wilt and turn brown. Eventually they drop. Twigs and branches are often dying or dead. Sunken or swollen brownish or reddish areas appear on branches or trunks.

Analysis: Several fungi cause canker and dieback on Russian olive. The fungi are spread by wind, rain, soil, tools, and equipment. They usually enter the tree at a wound, killing the surrounding healthy tissue. A sunken or swollen canker develops and expands through the wood in all directions. Tree sap containing the fungus may ooze from the wound. As a result of the canker, the flow of nutrients and water to the branch or trunk is cut off, causing the leaves to wilt and die. The tree may stop the spread of the fungus by producing callus tissue, a rapid growth of barklike cells that walls off the fungus. If the expanding canker is stopped before it covers half the diameter of the branch or trunk, the branch or tree usually survives. The fungus may grow faster than the callus, however, or the tree may not produce a callus, resulting in the death of the branch or the entire tree (if the canker is on the main trunk).

Solution: No chemical control is available. Avoid wounding and overwatering trees. Prune and destroy dead branches below the cankered area. Disinfect pruning shears after each cut. Remove dying trees.

EUCALYPTUS

EUONYMUS

Eucalyptus long-horned borers

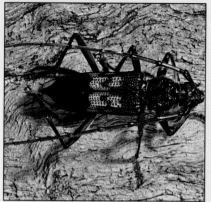

Long-horned borer adult (life size).

Problem: Dying or dead limbs are found on trees. Entire trees can be killed. Copious amounts of sap may ooze from bark. Shiny brown beetles, ¾ to 1¼ inches long with yellow zigzag markings on wing covers and antennae as long as their body, are visible under loose bark. Young larvae leave a dark trail as they feed along the outer tree bark. Broad frass-filled galleries can be found in the growth layer, which is just below the outer bark. Older larvae, off-white and up to 1½ inches long, are found in these galleries.

Analysis: The eucalyptus long-horned borer (*Phoracantha semipunctata*) was first noticed in southern California in 1984. Since then the population has spread across most of southern and central California. Adults are strong fliers. They lay eggs in wounds of diseased or water-stressed trees. Larvae feed on the outer bark for a short time before penetrating the growth region between the bark and the wood. The extensive galleries, or passages, the beetles make interfere with the flow of sap and can girdle branches, killing them. If the trunk is girdled, the whole tree dies.

Solution: Pesticides aren't very effective in fighting these pests. Prevention is the only control. Give eucalyptus trees enough water. Remove and destroy infested trees or branches promptly. Do any pruning in December or January, when the adult beetles aren't flying. Dry eucalyptus firewood quickly to avoid infestation. Several natural predators of this beetle have been imported from Australia and may provide some measure of control.

Powdery mildew

Powdery mildew.

Problem: The surfaces of leaves are covered with a thin layer or irregular patches of a powdery grayish-white mildew. Infected leaves are yellow and may drop prematurely. In late summer, tiny black dots (spore-producing bodies) are scattered over the white patches like ground pepper.

Analysis: Powdery mildew is caused by two species of fungi (*Oidium euonymi japonici* and *Microsphaera alni*) that thrive in both humid and dry weather. Fungal strands and spores make up powdery patches or a thin powdery layer. The spores are spread by wind to healthy plants. The fungi deplete plant nutrients, causing leaf yellowing and sometimes death of the leaf. In late summer and fall, the fungus forms small, black, spore-producing bodies that are dormant during the winter but produce spores to reinfect new plants the following spring. The fungi are especially devastating in low-light situations and are generally most severe in late summer and fall. Because *Microsphaera alni* attacks many kinds of plants, the fungus from a diseased plant may infect other types of plants in the garden.

Solution: Spray with Ortho® RosePride® Rose & Shrub Disease Control or Ortho® Orthenex® Garden Insect & Disease Control when mildew is first noticed. Clean up plant debris in late summer.

Euonymus scales

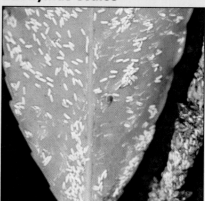

Euonymus scale (2× life size).

Problem: Yellow or whitish spots appear on the leaves. Most of the leaves may drop by midsummer. Branches often die, and heavy infestations may kill the plant. The stems and lower surfaces of leaves are covered with somewhat flattened, white, scaly bumps and dark brown, oyster-shell–shape bumps. In severe cases, the whole plant appears white.

Analysis: Many species of scales infest euonymus, but the most common and destructive is euonymus scale (*Unaspis euonymi*). It is especially damaging to evergreen euonymus. The narrow white scales are males, and larger brown scales are females. Females spend the winter on the plant and lay their eggs in spring. In late spring to early summer young scales, called *crawlers*, settle on the leaves and twigs or are blown by the wind to other susceptible plants. The small (¹⁄₁₀-inch), soft-bodied young suck sap from the plant. The legs atrophy, and a shell develops, brown over the female or white over the male. Females lay their eggs underneath their shells.

Solution: Euonymus scales may be hard to detect until after they have caused serious damage. Check the plant periodically for yellow spotting and scales. During winter, check the base of the plant for hidden overwintering females. Spray with Ortho® Systemic Insect Killer or Ortho® Volck® Oil Spray in early June and mid-July. In the South, a third application may be necessary. To control scales during the dormant season, spray with Ortho® Volck® Oil Spray. For very heavy infestations, cut plants to the ground and spray new growth in June.

Crown gall

Crown gall.

Problem: Large, corky galls up to several inches in diameter appear at the base of the plant and on the stems and roots. The galls are round, with a rough, irregular surface. Plants with numerous galls are weak; growth is slowed and leaves turn yellow. Branches may die back.

Analysis: Crown gall is a plant disease caused by soil-inhabiting bacteria (*Agrobacterium tumefaciens*) that infect many ornamentals, fruits, and vegetables in the garden. The bacteria are often brought to a garden initially on the roots of an infected plant and are spread with the soil and by contaminated pruning tools. The bacteria enter the shrub through wounds in the roots or at the base of the stem (the crown). They produce a substance that stimulates rapid cell growth in the plant, causing gall formation on the roots, crown, and sometimes branches. The galls disrupt the flow of water and nutrients up the roots and stems, weakening and stunting the top of the plant. Galls don't usually cause the plant to die.

Solution: Crown gall can't be eliminated from the shrub. Infected plants may survive many years, however. To improve the appearance of the plant, prune out and destroy affected stems below the galled area. Disinfect pruning shears after each cut. Destroy severely infected shrubs. The bacteria will remain in the soil for two or three years. If you wish to replace the shrub soon, plant only resistant species. (For a list of plants resistant to crown gall, see page 548.)

Scales

Brown scale (4× life size).

Problem: Brown, crusty bumps; thick, white, waxy bumps; or clusters of somewhat flattened yellow or whitish scaly bumps cover the fronds. The bumps can be scraped or picked off. Fronds may turn yellow, and leaflets may drop. In some cases, a shiny, sticky substance coats the fronds. Scales are sometimes mistaken for reproductive spores produced by the fern. The round, flat, sometimes hairy spores are found only on the undersides of fronds, spaced at regular intervals. They are difficult to scrape off.

Analysis: Many different types of scales infest ferns. They lay their eggs on the fronds, and in spring to midsummer the young scales, called *crawlers*, settle down to feed. These small (1/10-inch), soft-bodied young feed by sucking sap from the plant. The legs usually atrophy, and a hard crusty or waxy shell develops over the body. Mature female scales lay their eggs underneath their shells. Some species of scales are unable to digest all the sugar in the sap, and they excrete the excess in a fluid called honeydew, which coats the fronds.

Solution: Spray with Ortho® Rose & Flower Insect Killer when the young are active. Discard severely infested plants.

Cottony cushion scales and mealybugs

Mealybugs (1/3 life size).

Problem: Leaflets or stems are covered with white, cottony, cushionlike masses. Leaflets turn yellow and may drop; fronds may die.

Analysis: Cottony cushion scales and mealybugs infest many plants in the garden. Mealybugs are usually found outdoors only in warmer climates, but they may be found on indoor plants anyplace. The visual similarities between these insects make separate identification difficult. They are conspicuous in late spring and summer because the females are covered with a white, cottony egg sac, containing up to 2,500 eggs. Females lay their egg masses on leaves and stems. The young insects that hatch from these eggs are yellowish brown to green. They feed throughout the summer, causing damage by withdrawing plant sap from the ferns. Some species of scales and mealybugs are unable to digest all the sugar in the plant sap, and they excrete the excess in a sticky fluid called *honeydew*.

Solution: Spray with Ortho® Rose & Flower Insect Killer or Ortho® Systemic Insect Killer when insects are first noticed. Some ferns may be damaged. Test the spray on a small portion of the plant first. Wait a few days to see if the area turns brown. Discard severely infested plants.

FERNS (continued)

Leaf scorch

Scorch.

Problem: The tips and edges of fronds turn brown or black and die. Entire fronds may wilt, turn yellow or brown, and die. The problem usually occurs first on the youngest fronds. This condition usually develops when the soil is dry but may also occur when the soil is moist.

Analysis: Scorch is caused by excessive evaporation of moisture from the fronds. In hot weather, water evaporates rapidly from the fronds. Water loss is especially heavy when the weather is also dry and windy. If the roots can't absorb and convey water fast enough to replenish this loss, the fronds turn brown or black, and they wither. Scorch usually occurs when the soil is allowed to dry out, but ferns can also suffer from scorch when the soil is moist if the weather is exceptionally hot and dry. Winds, severed roots, limited soil area, and low temperatures can also cause scorch. (For more information on scorch, see page 427.)

Solution: To prevent further scorch, water plants thoroughly. Ferns need to be kept moist. They must be watered frequently and deep enough so that the soil doesn't dry out. During periods of exceptionally hot, dry weather, keep ferns wet by gently hosing down or sprinkling the fronds several times a day to reduce scorch. Grow ferns in shady areas that are protected from strong winds. Keep beds mulched.

FORSYTHIA

Four-lined plant bugs

Four-lined plant bug (3× life size).

Problem: Tan to reddish-brown spots, 1/16 inch, each with a small puncture spot in the center, develop on young forsythia leaves. Spots may join together to form a blotch, and leaves may be distorted. Yellowish-green bugs, 1/4 inch long, with four black stripes, may be found feeding on the leaves. Damage occurs May and June.

Analysis: The four-lined plant bug (*Poecilocapsus lineatus*) is a pest on forsythia and many other ornamental and vegetable plants in the northern United States. A small number of bugs can cause many unsightly leaves. Eggs are laid inside the stems in slits cut by the adult females in early summer. The eggs spend the winter there, hatching in spring when the forsythia leaves unfold. The plant bugs feed for about six weeks. Their sharp mouthparts pierce the leaf tissue, injecting a toxic secretion at the same time. As a result of feeding, the plant's chlorophyll disappears. Spots develop where the tissue is killed.

Solution: Spray with Ortho® Malathion Plus® Insect Spray Concentrate or with an insecticide containing *carbaryl* when damage is first noticed in spring. Repeat the spray at intervals of 7 to 10 days if damage continues. Handpicking is not effective against this bug.

FRAXINUS (Ash)

Ash anthracnose

Ash anthracnose.

Problem: During cool, damp weather, irregular light brown spots of dead tissue appear on leaves from late May to August. Sunken reddish areas develop and run together, killing the leaf. Partially killed leaves appear sunscorched. Anthracnose is distinguished from sunscorch by brown dots on the undersides of leaves. Severe defoliation and twig dieback may occur.

Analysis: Ash anthracnose is a plant disease caused by a fungus (*Gloeosporium aridum*). It may be very serious on Modesto ash (*Fraxinus velutina*) or on green ash (*F. pennsylvanica*). Evergreen ash (*F. uhdei*) is resistant. The fungus spends the winter on infected leaves and twigs. During rainy weather, spots develop when spores are blown or splashed onto young leaves. The spots expand and can kill the leaf, causing defoliation of the tree. If defoliation takes place in spring or early summer, the tree will grow new leaves. If the tree is severely affected for two or three successive years, the fungus may enter and kill branches.

Solution: Trees affected by this disease for one year don't need to be treated with a chemical control. Rake and destroy old leaves and, where practical, prune out dead twigs below the sunken reddish canker on the bark. Prune the tree to keep the canopy open. Fertilize with Scotts® Evergreen, Flowering Tree & Shrub Slow Release Plant Food early in the growing season to stimulate growth. If the following spring is wet, spray with Ortho® Garden Disease Control when the leaves uncurl. Repeat the treatment twice more at intervals of 14 days.

Ash yellows

Witches'-broom caused by ash yellows.

Problem: Treetops become thin, with tufts of undersized leaves. Leaves are lighter green than usual. Branches die. Dense clumps of twigs, called witches'-brooms, may appear at the base of the tree or on the lower part of the trunk. Vertical cracks may appear in the bark near the base of the trunk.

Analysis: Because its symptoms are similar to those of trees stressed by environmental problems, the plant disease ash yellows was not discovered until the 1980s. The disease is caused by a bacteria-like organism called a *phytoplasma*. Phytoplasmas are usually transmitted by leafhoppers, but the vector of this disease has not yet been discovered. White ash (*Fraxinus americana*) and green ash (*F. pennsylvanica*) are the most frequently attacked species. Infected trees may live for several years after infection but don't recover or improve. Environmental stress exacerbates the symptoms.

Solution: At present, there's no cure for this disease. If the tree is sufficiently unattractive, remove it and replace it with another species.

Summer leaf scorch

Leaf scorch.

Problem: During hot weather, usually in July or August, leaves turn brown around the edges and between the veins. Sometimes the whole leaf dies. Many leaves may drop during late summer. This problem is most severe on the youngest branches. Trees don't generally die.

Analysis: Summer leaf scorch is caused by excessive evaporation from the leaves, particularly in hot weather. If the roots can't absorb and convey water fast enough to replenish this loss, the leaves turn brown and wither. This usually occurs in dry soil, but leaves can also scorch when the soil is moist. Drying winds, severed roots, and limited soil area can also cause scorch. (For more information on leaf scorch, see page 427.)

Solution: To minimize further scorch, deep-water trees during periods of hot weather to wet down the entire root space. (For information on watering, see pages 407 to 408.) If practical, apply 3 to 4 inches of mulch over the root zone. Water newly transplanted trees whenever the rootball is dry 2 inches below the surface. Leaf scorch on trees in moist soil can't be controlled. To minimize leaf scorch, plant trees adapted to your climate.

Ash flower gall mites

Ash flower galls.

Problem: Irregular galls, from ¼ to ¾ inch in diameter, form on flowers, causing witches'-brooms and deformed flowers. The clusters of brown galls dry out and remain on the tree. They are conspicuous throughout the winter.

Analysis: Ash flower galls are caused by tiny mites (*Aceria fraxinivorus*), too small to be seen with the naked eye. The mites attack the male flowers of white ash (*Fraxinus americana*) and green ash (*F. pennsylvanica*). As the buds open in the spring, the mites puncture the tissue, injecting a growth-promoting substance into it. The flowers develop abnormally and form clusters of galls. The galls are unsightly but rarely harm the tree.

Solution: Once the galls form, you can't do anything about them. Spray valuable specimens with Ortho® Systemic Insect Killer or Ortho® Orthenex® Garden Insect & Disease Control after buds swell and before new growth emerges in the spring.

GLEDITSIA (Honeylocust)

Bagworms

Bagworm (life size).

Problem: Leaves are chewed, and individual branches or the entire tree may be defoliated. Carrot-shape cases, or "bags," from 1 to 3 inches long hang from the branches. The bags are constructed of interwoven bits of dead foliage, twigs, and silk. When a bag is cut open, a tan or blackish caterpillar or a yellowish grublike insect may be found inside.

Analysis: Bagworms (*Thyridopteryx ephemeraeformis*) eat the leaves of many trees and shrubs, including honeylocust. The eggs hatch in late May or early June, and the larvae begin feeding. Each larva constructs a bag that covers its entire body, and the larva adds to the bag as it develops. The worm partially emerges from its bag to feed. By late August, the larva spins silken bands around a twig, attaches a bag permanently, and pupates. In the fall, the winged male moth emerges from his case, flies to a bag containing a female, mates, and dies. After mating, the female lays 500 to 1,000 eggs and dies. The eggs spend the winter in the mother's bag.

Solution: Small numbers of bagworms can be handpicked. Clip the bags with scissors or a small knife. Seal them in a plastic bag, and dispose of them in the garbage. Spray larger numbers with Ortho® Systemic Insect Control or Ortho® Bug-B-Gon® Multi-Purpose Insect Killer. Spray again 10 days later if new leaf damage occurs. You can use the bacterial insecticide *Bacillus thuringiensis* (Bt) on young caterpillars. The following year, inspect closely in early June and spray as soon as tiny bags are seen.

Mimosa webworms

Mimosa webworm damage.

Problem: Small clumps of leaves tied together with silk threads are scattered over the tree. Leaves turn brown and die, causing infested trees to look as if they have been scorched by fire. Small (up to 1-inch), pale gray or brown caterpillars with five white stripes feed inside the silken nests or hang from the trees on threads. Small trees and the 'Sunburst' variety of thornless honeylocust may be defoliated by late summer. Trees are not killed, but repeated defoliation can weaken them.

Analysis: The mimosa webworm (*Homadaula anisocentra*) is the larval stage of a small gray moth. It feeds only on honeylocust and mimosa trees. The webworm passes the winter as a pupa in a white silken cocoon. The cocoon is found in sheltered places such as crevices in the bark of the infested tree, in soil and debris beneath the tree, or under the siding of nearby buildings. The moth emerges in the spring and lays her eggs. When eggs hatch, the larvae feed on the leaflets for several weeks. A second generation of webworms hatches in August. The larvae of this second generation are the most damaging because they are numerous. In warmer areas, a third generation hatches in September.

Solution: When webbing first appears, spray with Ortho® Systemic Insect Killer, Ortho® Bug-B-Gon® Multi-Purpose Insect Killer, or the bacterial insecticide *Bacillus thuringiensis* (Bt). Repeat in August. Use a high-pressure spray to penetrate the webs and cover the tree thoroughly. In the fall, rake up and burn debris under infested trees, or bury the leaves.

Plant bugs and leafhoppers

Plant bug damage.

Problem: In early spring, the new expanding leaves become deformed, curled, and mottled yellow. In severe cases, leaves drop and twigs die back. When the leaves are disturbed, small (¼-inch), green or brownish wedge-shaped or shield-shaped insects hop or fly around the plant.

Analysis: Several plant bugs and a leafhopper may be found on the same tree, feeding on the leaflets. The damage they cause is similar, making it difficult to distinguish the injury caused by each type of insect. Eggs laid the previous summer near the buds and on small twigs hatch as the leaves unfold. The young insects suck the sap from the leaves and may inject toxins, causing the mottling and distortion. Plant bugs and leafhoppers feed until the middle of summer. When infestations are heavy, twigs die back.

Solution: Spray with Ortho® Systemic Insect Killer or Ortho® Rose & Flower Insect Killer when damage is first noticed in the spring. Spray the foliage thoroughly, making sure to cover both the upper and lower surfaces of the leaves. Use a high-pressure spray to adequately cover the bottoms of the leaflets. To prevent damage the following year, spray before the buds open in the spring.

Honeylocust pod gall midges

Pod gall midge damage.

Problem: Green, globular, podlike galls, ⅛ inch in diameter, develop on new leaves

in spring and early summer. The galls turn reddish, then brown, and many of the infested leaflets drop. Twigs or branches sometimes die back after several years of infestation. One to several whitish larvae, ¼ inch long, are feeding inside the gall.

Analysis: The larva of a tiny orange to black fly, called the honeylocust pod gall midge (*Dasineura gleditschiae*), causes unsightly galls on honeylocust trees, especially the thornless varieties. The adult female midge begins laying eggs on new leaflets in the spring. When the eggs hatch, the larvae feed on the tissue, causing the leaflet to fold over them and form a pod gall. As the larvae develop inside, the galls turn brown. The flies emerge to lay more eggs. Honeylocust produces new leaves over a long period, so the cycle may repeat itself up to seven times annually. The galls don't usually damage the tree. The ornamental value of the tree is reduced when the galled leaves dry up and drop prematurely, however. Twigs sometimes die back after repeated attack, but new shoots normally form at the base of the dead twigs.

Solution: Once formed, the galls can't be removed. Prune dead twigs. Spray with an insecticide containing *malathion*. Repeat treatments every 7 to 10 days until no more galls are formed. The following spring, begin spraying as soon as the honeylocust begins to leaf out.

Canker

Canker.

Problem: Leaves on an infected branch or throughout the tree are discolored and wilting.

Eventually the leaves drop and the branch or the entire tree dies. Small (up to ½-inch), slightly sunken, tan to black cankers on the affected area may grow together and enlarge to girdle the trunk or branch. Wood under the bark surrounding the canker is streaked reddish brown. Gummy sap may ooze from the canker.

Analysis: Canker of honeylocust is caused by several fungi. *Thyronectria austroamericana* and *Nectria cinnabarina* are the most prevalent. The fungi are spread by wind and splashing water. The fungus enters the wood through wounds, killing the surrounding healthy tissue. A canker ranging in size from a pinhead to ½ inch in diameter forms. Small raised orange dots may appear in the canker. Cankers often enlarge and grow together, cutting off the flow of nutrients and water through the branch or trunk. Leaves wilt, and the area above the canker dies. If cankers develop on the trunk, the entire tree may die.

Solution: No effective chemical controls are available. Prune dying branches well below the cankered areas. Water plants regularly, and fertilize with Scotts® Evergreen, Flowering Tree & Shrub Slow Release Plant Food to promote vigorous growth. (For more information on watering and fertilizing, see pages 407 to 409.) Avoid wounding the tree. Don't leave branch stubs when pruning.

Failure to bloom

Flowerless plant.

Problem: Hydrangeas fail to produce blooms in the spring.

Analysis: Hydrangeas may fail to bloom for several reasons.
1. Cold injury: Extreme winter temperatures or late spring cold snaps will kill hydrangea flower buds, which form during the late summer or fall.
2. Improper pruning: Some hydrangea species produce flower buds in the late summer or fall. Pruning in the winter or spring will remove these potential flowers.
3. Too much shade: Hydrangeas growing in deep shade may fail to form flower buds.

Solution: The numbered solutions below correspond to the numbered items in the analysis.
1. Plant hydrangeas in a protected spot in the garden. Protect them by placing a wire cylinder around each plant and then either filling the cylinder with loosely packed straw or covering it with burlap. Protect hydrangeas grown in containers by moving them to a cool basement during the winter.
2. Prune hydrangeas after they have finished blooming by cutting back longer branches.
3. Expose the plants to brighter light by pruning some of the surrounding vegetation, or transplant hydrangeas to a location that receives filtered or half-day sun or, in cool-winter areas, full sun.

HYDRANGEA (continued)

Sunburn

Sunburn.

Problem: During warm, sunny weather, leaves on the outside of the plant turn yellowish or brown in the center of the leaf tissue. Some leaves may drop.

Analysis: Hydrangeas are shade plants; their leaves are sensitive to the heat of the sun. Outside leaves facing the light turn yellow or brown when the shrub is planted in full sun. The injury is unsightly but doesn't damage the plant. Plants are more susceptible to sunburn when in dry soil. Hydrangea leaves may also scorch (die and turn brown around the edges) during hot weather. (For more information on sunburn, see page 194.)

Solution: Provide some shade where the plant is growing, or move the plant to a shady location. Keep plants adequately watered. (For information on watering, see pages 407 to 408.)

ILEX (Holly)

Holly leafminers

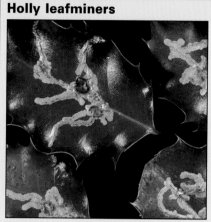

Leafminer damage on holly.

Problem: Yellowish or brown winding trails or blotches appear in the leaves. The leaves may be distorted and have tiny green blisters or multiple pinpricks on the lower surfaces. In severe cases, all the leaves are affected, and most of them may drop from the plant. When the blotch is torn open, a tiny (1/16-inch), yellowish-white maggot is found between the upper and lower surfaces of the leaf.

Analysis: Damage caused by holly leafminers (*Phytomyza* species) is unsightly and ruins the value of those types of holly used in winter holiday decorations. Both the larvae and the adults cause damage. The insect spends the winter as a larva, or pupa, inside a leaf. Adults—tiny black flies—appear in May, when new plant growth is 1/2 to 1 inch long. The female deposits eggs inside the leaf by making a slit in the lower surface. Flies (only the females in some species) feed on the sap by stabbing through the leaf surface. This feeding causes the pinpricks and distortion. Eggs deposited inside leaves hatch into maggots that feed on inner leaf tissue, producing mines, or trails. In a heavy infestation, especially during a dry season, the plant may drop almost all its leaves and will remain bare until the following spring.

Solution: Control with Ortho® Bug-B-Gon® Multi-Purpose Insect Killer Concentrate or Ortho® Systemic Insect Killer when new leaves are swelling in spring. Repeat the spray according to label instructions. Rake up and destroy debris under the tree in fall.

Leaf spot

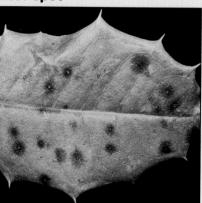

Leaf spot.

Problem: Spots and blotches appear on the leaves. Spots may be yellow, red, tan, gray, or brown. They range in size from barely visible to 1/2 inch. Several spots may join to form blotches. Leaves may turn yellow and die. Some leaves may drop. Leaf spotting is most severe in warm, humid weather.

Analysis: Several fungi cause leaf spot on holly. These spots are unsightly but rarely harmful to the plant. The fungi are spread by wind and splashing water. Spots develop where the fungi enter the tissue. If wet or humid weather persists, the fungi spread through the tissue, and blotches form. The fungi survive the winter on the leaves and twigs. Most leaf spot organisms do their greatest damage in mild to warm weather (50° to 85°F).

Solution: Where practical, remove and destroy infected leaves. On valuable specimens, spray with Ortho® Garden Disease Control or a fungicide containing *ferbam*. Repeat at intervals of two weeks for as long as the weather remains favorable for fungal infection.

Southern red mites

Southern red mite damage on Japanese holly.

Problem: Leaves are stippled yellow or grayish green and dirty and are often smaller than normal. A silken webbing may be on the lower surfaces of the leaves. To determine if the plant is infested with red mites, hold a sheet of white paper underneath a branch that has stippled leaves and tap the branch sharply. Minute reddish specks the size of pepper grains will drop to the paper and begin to crawl. The pests are easily seen against the white background.

Analysis: The southern red mite (*Oligonychus ilicis*), also known as *red spider*, is a major pest of many broadleaf evergreen plants in the eastern half of the United States. Mites cause damage by sucking sap from leaves. As a result of feeding, the chlorophyll disappears, producing the stippled appearance. These mites are most prolific in cooler weather. They feed and reproduce primarily during spring and, in some cases, fall. At the onset of hot weather, the mites have caused their maximum damage.

Solution: At the first sign of stippling in the spring, control with Ortho® Systemic Insect Killer or Ortho® Bug-B-Gon® Multi-Purpose Insect Killer Concentrate. Spray the leaves thoroughly. Repeat the spray two more times at intervals of 7 to 10 days to kill young mites as they hatch from eggs. It's important to apply control measures early in the season, when damage first appears, to prevent unsightly injury to foliage. Injured leaves remain on the plant for more than one growing season. Hose down plants frequently to knock off the webs and mites.

Scales

Cottony cushion scale.

Problem: Brown or black crusty bumps; thick, white, waxy bumps; or clusters of somewhat flattened scaly bumps cover the leaves, stems, or berries. Bumps can be scraped or picked off, and the undersides are usually soft. Leaves may turn yellow and drop, and branches may die. In some cases, a sticky substance coats the leaves. Black, sooty mold grows on the sticky substance.

Analysis: Many different species of scales infest holly. They lay their eggs on the leaves or bark in the spring, and in midsummer the young scales, called *crawlers*, settle on various parts of the tree or shrub. The small (1/10-inch), soft-bodied young feed by sucking sap from the plant. The legs usually atrophy, and a hard crusty or waxy shell develops over the body. Mature female scales lay their eggs underneath their shells. Some species of scales infesting holly are unable to digest all the sugar in the plant sap, and they excrete the excess in a fluid called *honeydew*. A black, sooty mold fungus may develop on the honeydew. An uncontrolled infestation of scales may kill the plant after two or three seasons. (For more information on scales, see pages 444 to 447.)

Solution: Spray with Ortho® Systemic Insect Killer, or an insecticide containing *malathion* when the young are active. The following spring, before new growth begins, spray the trunk and branches with a dormant oil spray.

Phomopsis twig blight

Phomopsis twig blight.

Problem: In the spring, needles, twigs, and smaller branches turn light brown to reddish brown, then gray, gradually dying from the tips back. Plants less than five years old are often killed. Minute black dots may appear on the needles and stems when the needles have dried and turned grayish. The disease is most serious during wet weather or in shady, moist locations. This problem sometimes resembles drought damage. The border between healthy tissue and dead tissue is sharp with this disease but gradual with drought, however. In addition, the disease is found only on isolated branches rather than uniformly throughout the plant, as with drought.

Analysis: Phomopsis twig blight is a plant disease caused by a fungus (*Phomopsis juniperovora*). It is highly destructive to junipers, cryptomeria, chamaecyparis, and arborvitae throughout most of the United States. The spores are spread by splashing rain, overhead watering, insects, and tools. The fungus enters through wounds or healthy tissue, killing the stem and needles above and below the point of entrance. Black spore-producing structures develop and overwinter on dead needles.

Solution: Spray with Ortho® Lawn Disease Control when symptoms first appear in spring. Repeat every 7 to 10 days as long as necessary. Prune and destroy infected branches below the line between diseased and healthy tissue, making the cut into live tissue. Plant trees in areas with good air circulation and full sun. Plant resistant varieties.

JUNIPERUS (Juniper) *(continued)*

Needle browning

Drought damage.

Salt burn damage.

Kabatina twig blight

Kabatina twig blight.

Problem: Needles turn yellow, and then brown and dry. Sometimes only a branch or one side of the plant is affected. In other cases, the whole plant turns brown.

Problem: In warm summer weather, needles and twigs die back from the tips. A small gray canker may be found at the base of the blighted area. Small black dots may be found on the canker or throughout the blighted twigs. In junipers that have a purple winter color, the blighted shoots remain green when the rest of the plant takes on its purple color. This sometimes resembles drought damage. The border between healthy tissue and dead tissue is gradual with drought but distinct with this disease, however. The disease is found only on isolated branches, whereas drought symptoms occur uniformly throughout the plant.

Analysis:

1. Dog urine: When dogs urinate on the plant, the foliage on the outer, lower branches turns yellow, then brown, as if scorched. Salts in the urine burn the foliage.

Solution:

1. Wash the foliage and thoroughly soak the ground around the plant to dilute the salts in the urine if you suspect that a dog has recently urinated on it.

2. Natural leaf browning and shedding: The older needles, on the inside of the plant nearest the trunk, turn brown and drop off in the spring or fall. This is a natural process similar to the dropping of leaves of deciduous plants.

2. No controls are necessary for natural leaf browning and shedding.

3. Drought or winter injury: When the plant is damaged by drought or winter injury, needles gradually turn yellow, then brown or reddish from the top of the plant down and from the tips of the branches back. This may happen when the soil is dry and the plant is not getting enough water or when the soil is frozen in the winter.

3. Prune dead twigs and branches. Provide adequate water during periods of extended drought, and shelter plants growing in windy locations. Water in late fall or early winter, to ensure adequate soil moisture during the winter. Mulch plants after they are dormant to reduce the depth of frost penetration into the soil.

4. Salt burn: Needles turn brown from the tips back. This condition may develop on one side of the plant only or on the whole plant. Salt burn is common in alkaline soils, when water has a high salt content, in soils with poor drainage, in overfertilized soils, or along roadsides where winter runoff contains road salts. The salts in the soil inhibit water and nutrient uptake, causing the needles to turn brown. Similar symptoms can occur in oceanfront plantings from wind-borne salt.

4. Prune badly damaged areas. Avoid new injury by heavily irrigating plants once during the growing season. If you suspect that your water contains salts, have it analyzed through your county extension office or local water department. To keep from overfertilizing plants, follow package directions. Avoid planting in areas where road or sea salt may be a problem. Occasionally hose down oceanfront plantings to remove salt accumulations on the foliage.

Analysis: Kabatina twig blight is a plant disease caused by the fungus *Kabatina juniperi*. It invades the plant through wounds created by insects, injury, winter weather, or abrasion by adjacent branches. A small ash-gray canker is produced at the wound. Within four to six weeks, the canker enlarges to encircle the twig, causing it to dry out and die back. Blighted shoots turn brown by late winter, providing a source of infection for the next season's growth. In wet weather, the fungus produces spores that are washed to other parts of the plant.

Solution: Kabatina twig blight can't be controlled with fungicide sprays. To minimize infection caused by insect wounding, control insect infestations. Prompt removal of blighted shoots will minimize the spread of the disease. Badly diseased plantings should be removed and replaced with resistant varieties.

Root and crown rots

Juniper dieback.

Dieback caused by Phytophthora *root rot*.

Leafminers and tip moths

Tip moth damage. Inset: Moth and cocoon (life size).

Problem: Normal foliage color dulls, and the plant loses vigor. The foliage may wilt, or it may turn yellow or light brown. Major branches or the entire plant may die. The plant sometimes lives for many months in a weakened condition, or it may die quickly. The roots and lower stems are brownish and the roots are often decayed. There may be fine woolly brown strands on the roots and white powdery spores on the soil surface. Or there may be fan-shaped plaques of white strands between the bark and wood of the roots and lower stems. Mushrooms may appear at the base of the plant in the fall.

Analysis: Root and crown rots on junipers are caused by several different fungi. Fungi live in the soil and on living roots.

Solution: The numbered solutions below correspond to the numbered items in the analysis.

1. *Phytophthora* species: These fungi cause browning and decay on the roots and browning of the lower stems. The plants usually die slowly, but young plants may wilt and die rapidly. The disease is most prevalent in heavy, waterlogged soils.

1. Remove dead and dying plants. Drench the soil with a fungicide containing *metalaxyl*. When replanting, use plants that are resistant to *Phytophthora*. (For a list of resistant trees and shrubs, see page 546.) Improve soil drainage (see page 406). Avoid overwatering junipers.

2. *Phymatotrichum omnivorum*: This fungus, also known as *cotton root rot* or *Texas root rot*, is a severe problem on many plants in the Southwest. The plant often wilts and dies suddenly. Older plants may die more slowly, showing general decline and dieback symptoms. Brown strands form on the roots and white powdery spores on the soil. The disease is most severe in heavy, alkaline soils.

2. Remove dead and dying plants. When replanting, buy only resistant varieties. (For a list of resistant trees and shrubs, see page 546.) Before planting, increase the soil acidity by adding 1 pound of ammonium sulfate for every 10 square feet of soil. Make a circular ridge around the planting area and fill the basin with 4 inches of water. Repeat the treatment in 5 to 10 days. Improve drainage.

3. *Armillaria mellea*: This disease, also known as *shoestring root rot, mushroom root rot,* or *oak root fungus,* is identified by the presence of fan-shaped plaques of white fungal strands between the bark and the wood of the roots and lower stems. This fungus grows rapidly under wet conditions.

3. Remove dead plants. The life of a newly infected plant may be prolonged if the disease has not reached the lower stems. Expose the base of the plant to air for several months by removing several inches of soil. Prune diseased roots. When replanting, use only resistant varieties.

Problem: Leaf tips turn yellow at first, then brown and dry. They contrast sharply with the healthy green foliage. Damage is most severe in plants growing in shady areas. When the yellow leaf is torn open, a small (⅕-inch), greenish caterpillar with a dark head may be found inside. Gray or brownish moths with a ⅓-inch wingspread may be seen flying around the plant in April, May, or June.

Analysis: Several species of insects known as leafminers (*Argyresthia* species) in the eastern United States and tip moths on the West Coast infest junipers, arborvitae, and cypress. Damage is unsightly, but plants may lose more than half of their foliage and still survive. The larvae spend the winter inside the leaf tips. When the weather warms in late winter or early spring, the larvae exit from the leaves to pupate in cocoons on the foliage. Adult moths emerge and lay eggs on the leaves. The larvae that hatch from these eggs tunnel into the leaf tips, devouring the green tissue. The tips above the point of entry yellow and die. The larvae feed until late fall or through the winter until early spring.

Solution: Spray with Ortho® Bug-B-Gon® Multi-Purpose Insect Killer Concentrate or Ortho® Systemic Insect Killer as eggs are hatching to control emerging larvae before they enter the leaves. Trim and destroy infested leaves in the fall and spring.

JUNIPERUS (Juniper) (continued)

Spruce spider mite and two-spotted mite

Spider mite damage (on left).

Problem: The needles are stippled yellow and dirty. A fine silken webbing may be on the twigs. Needles may turn brown and fall off. To determine if a plant is infested with mites, hold a sheet of white paper underneath some stippled needles and tap the foliage sharply. Minute specks the size of pepper grains will drop to the paper and begin to crawl. The pests are easily seen against the white background.

Analysis: Spruce spider mites (*Oligonychus ununguis*) and two-spotted spider mites (*Tetranychus urticae*), related to spiders, are among the most important pests of junipers and other evergreen trees and shrubs. They cause damage by sucking sap from the needles. As a result of their feeding, the plant's chlorophyll disappears, producing the stippled appearance. Spruce spider mites are more prolific in cooler weather. They feed and reproduce primarily during spring and, in some cases, fall. By the onset of hot weather (70°F and higher), these mites have caused their maximum damage. Two-spotted mites develop rapidly in hot, dry weather (70°F and higher), so by midsummer they have built to tremendous numbers.

Solution: Spray with Ortho® Systemic Insect Killer or Ortho® Rose & Flower Insect Killer when damage is first noticed. Wet foliage thoroughly, covering tops and bottoms of branches and the plant interior. Repeat the application twice at intervals of seven days. Hose down plants frequently to knock off webs and mites.

Juniper scales

Juniper scale (4× life size).

Problem: The tree looks gray and off-color and has no new growth. Eventually the needles turn yellow. Branches and possibly the whole plant die back. The foliage is covered with clusters of tiny (⅛-inch), somewhat flattened, yellow-and-white scaly bumps. A shiny, sticky substance may coat the needles. A black, sooty mold often grows on the sticky substance.

Analysis: Juniper scale (*Carulaspis juniperi*) is found throughout the United States on many types of juniper and also on cypress (*Cupressus* species) and incense cedar. The female scales spend the winter on the plant. They lay their eggs in the spring, and in midsummer (late spring in the South) the new generation, called *crawlers*, settles on the needles. These small (¹⁄₁₀-inch), soft-bodied young feed by sucking sap from the plant. The legs atrophy, and a crusty shell develops over the body. Mature female scales lay their eggs underneath the shell. Juniper scales are unable to digest all the sugar in the plant sap and excrete the excess in a fluid called *honeydew*. A sooty mold fungus may develop on the honeydew. An uncontrolled infestation of scales may kill the plant in two or three seasons.

Solution: Prune out heavily infested branches. Spray with Ortho® Bug-B-Gon® Multi-Purpose Insect Killer Concentrate or Ortho® Volck® Oil Spray when the young are active in late spring or midsummer. Early the following spring, before new growth begins, spray the trunk and branches with Ortho® Volck® Oil Spray to control overwintering insects.

Bagworms

Bagworm cases (2× life size).

Problem: The needles are chewed, and individual branches or the entire tree or shrub may be defoliated. Hanging from the branches are carrot-shape cases, or "bags," from 1 to 3 inches long. The bags are constructed from interwoven bits of dead foliage, twigs, and silk. When a bag is cut open, a tan or blackish caterpillar or a yellowish grublike insect may be found inside, or the bag may be empty. A heavy attack by this insect may retard or stunt tree growth. Repeated attacks can kill trees.

Analysis: The larvae of the bagworm (*Thyridopteryx ephemeraeformis*) devour the foliage of junipers and many other tree species when populations of the insect are high. The larvae hatch in late May or early June and begin feeding on the juniper needles. Each larva constructs a bag that covers its entire body. The worm partially emerges from its bag to feed. When the leaves are completely eaten off a branch, the bagworm moves to the next branch. In fall, the adult winged male emerges from his case, flies to a bag containing a female, mates, and dies. The female lays 500 to 1,000 eggs and dies.

Solution: Spray with Ortho® Bug-B-Gon® Multi-Purpose Insect Killer Concentrate or Ortho® Systemic Insect Killer, or the bacterial insecticide *Bacillus thuringiensis* (Bt) between late May and mid-July. Older bagworms are more difficult to control. Spray again 10 days later if new leaf damage occurs. Handpicking and destroying bags between October and May will reduce the number of overwintering eggs.

Cedar-apple rust

Cedar-apple rust.

Problem: In spring or early summer, brownish-green swellings appear on the upper surfaces of needles. The galls enlarge until, by fall, they range in size from 1 to 2 inches in diameter. The galls turn chocolate brown and are covered with small circular depressions. The following spring, during warm, rainy weather, the small depressions swell and produce yellow or orange jellylike "horns" up to ¾ inch long. The galls eventually die, but they remain attached to the tree for a year or more. Infected twigs usually die.

Analysis: Cedar-apple rust is a disease caused by one of several fungi (*Gymnosporangium* species) that infect both juniper and apple trees. It can't spread from juniper to juniper, or from apple to apple, but it alternates between the two. Wind-borne spores from apple leaves infect juniper needles in the summer. The fungus grows very little until the following spring, when the galls begin to form. The second spring, spores from the orange "horns" are carried by the wind to infect apple trees. Later, orange spots appear on the apples and upper surfaces of the leaves. In spring or summer, spores are released and carried by the wind back to junipers. The entire cycle takes 18 to 20 months on juniper and an additional four to six months on apple.

Solution: Remove galls and destroy. When possible, don't plant junipers and apple trees within several hundred yards of one another. Spraying junipers with a fungicide containing *ferbam*, *azoxystrobin*, or *mancozeb* may help prevent new infections from apple trees.

LAGERSTROEMIA (Crape myrtle)

Powdery mildew

Powdery mildew.

Problem: Leaves, shoots, and flower buds are covered with a thin layer or irregular patches of a powdery grayish-white material. The leaves and shoots are distorted and stunted, and flower buds usually fail to open. Infected leaves may look reddish beneath the mildew; the leaves often drop prematurely.

Analysis: Powdery mildew is a common plant disease usually caused by a fungus (*Erysiphe lagerstroemiae*) that thrives in both humid and dry weather. The disease is most severe on shaded plants and those in hedges. The fungus spends the winter in buds and develops quickly on shoots from infected buds. The powdery patches consist of fungal strands and spores. The spores are spread by the wind to healthy plants. The fungus depletes plant nutrients, causing leaf and shoot distortion and bud failure. This particular powdery mildew infects only crape myrtle. Several other species of powdery mildew that commonly infect other trees and shrubs occasionally infect this plant as well.

Solution: Spray the upper and lower surfaces of leaves with Ortho® RosePride® Rose & Shrub Disease Control when the plant shows the first signs of mildew. In the spring, before buds open, spray with a lime sulfur fungicide. When replanting, select varieties resistant to powdery mildew.

LIGUSTRUM (Privet)

Privet rust mites and privet mites

Privet rust mite damage.

Problem: The leaves turn bronze, brown, or yellow and cup downward. They may have a silvery stipple. Leaves drop prematurely, sometimes before discoloration occurs. The plant is weak and often stunted.

Analysis: Both privet rust mites (*Aculus ligustri*) and privet mites (*Brevipalpus obovatus*) are extremely small and generally can't be seen without magnification. They cause damage by sucking sap from the leaf tissue. They feed on the undersides of leaves. As a result of their feeding, the leaf cups or curls and often drops from the plant. The privet rust mite may feed only on the cells in the surface of the leaf, causing a bronze russeting or browning. The chlorophyll is unaffected. Or it may feed deeper in the tissue, resulting in leaf yellowing caused by the disappearance of chlorophyll. Some types of privet drop their leaves before discoloration develops. The rust mite is most prolific during cool weather. It feeds and reproduces primarily during spring and fall. The privet mite is usually active throughout the growing season. By midsummer they may build up to tremendous numbers.

Solution: Spray with Ortho® Systemic Insect Killer or with a horticultural oil when damage is first noticed. Spray the foliage thoroughly, being sure to cover both the upper and lower surfaces of the leaves. Repeat the application twice at intervals of 7 to 10 days.

LIGUSTRUM (Privet)
(continued)

Scales

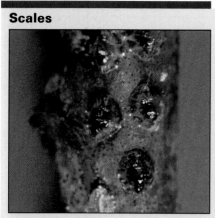

Scales (2× life size).

Problem: Brownish crusty bumps or clusters of flattened yellowish, brown, reddish, gray, or white scaly bumps cover the trunk, the branches, or the undersides of leaves. The bumps can be scraped or picked off. Leaves turn yellow and may drop, and twigs or branches may die back. A sticky substance often coats the leaves. A black, sooty mold may grow on the sticky substance.

Analysis: Many different types of scales infest privet. They lay their eggs on the leaves or bark, and in spring to midsummer the young scales, called *crawlers*, settle on leaves, twigs, or the trunk. These small (1/10-inch), soft-bodied young feed by sucking sap from the plant. The legs usually atrophy, and a hard crusty shell develops over the body. Mature female scales lay their eggs underneath their shell. Some species of scales that infest privet are unable to digest all the sugar in the plant sap, and they excrete the excess in a fluid called *honeydew*. A sooty mold fungus may develop on the honeydew, causing the privet leaves to appear black and dirty. An uncontrolled infestation of scales may kill twigs or branches after two or three seasons. (For more information on scales, see pages 444 to 447.)

Solution: Spray with Ortho® Systemic Insect Killer when the young are active. Early the following spring, before new growth begins, spray the trunk and branches with Ortho® Volck® Oil Spray to control overwintering insects.

LONICERA (Honeysuckle)

Powdery mildew

Powdery mildew.

Problem: The leaves, branch tips, and buds are covered with a thin layer or irregular patches of powdery grayish-white material. Infected leaves may turn yellow and drop. Buds may be deformed or die. In fall, black dots (spore-producing bodies) are scattered over the powdery material and look like ground pepper.

Analysis: Powdery mildew is a common plant disease caused by two fungi (*Microsphaera alni* and *Erysiphe polygoni*) that thrive in both humid and dry weather. The powdery patches consist of fungal strands and spores. The spores are spread by the wind to healthy plants. The fungus depletes plant nutrients, causing leaf yellowing and bud deformation and sometimes the death of the leaf and bud. Since these mildews attack many different kinds of plants, the fungus from a diseased plant may infect other types of plants in the garden.

Solution: Spray both the upper and lower surfaces of leaves with Ortho® Orthenex® Garden Insect & Disease Control or a fungicide containing *chlorothalonil* or *triforine* when the plants show the first sign of mildew. Repeat every two weeks as long as new mildew appears.

Honeysuckle aphids

Witches'-broom. Inset: Infested shoot.

Problem: Young leaves are curled and distorted, and growth is stunted. Affected leaves are curled upward. When these cupped leaves are peeled open, clusters of tiny, green-brown, soft-bodied insects may be found inside. As the growing season progresses, the affected stems die, resulting in a tuft of dead, twiggy branches (a witches'-broom). Witches'-brooms are noticeable throughout the growing season but are especially evident in early spring.

Analysis: Honeysuckle aphids (*Hyadaphis tataricae*), also known as *Russian aphids,* are insects that commonly infest shrub honeysuckle. Damage occurs on new growth when the aphid sucks the juice from the leaves. It's not known whether the characteristic witches'-brooms are caused by the aphids' feeding or whether the aphids transmit a disease organism to the plant that causes the witches'-brooms to develop. Adult aphids are present throughout the growing season. In the fall they lay eggs in the witches'-brooms and around the base of the plant. These eggs hatch early in the spring when the new leaves emerge.

Solution: In winter, remove and destroy witches'-brooms and other infested plant parts. In mid- to late May, or whenever new infestations are noticed, spray with Ortho® Rose & Flower Insect Killer or Ortho® Systemic Insect Killer.

MAGNOLIA

Summer leaf scorch

Leaf scorch.

Problem: During hot weather, usually in July or August, leaves turn brown around the edges and between the veins. Sometimes the whole leaf dies. Many leaves may drop during late summer. This problem is most severe on the youngest branches. Trees don't generally die.

Analysis: Summer leaf scorch is caused by excessive evaporation from the leaves. In hot weather, water evaporates rapidly from the leaves. If the roots can't absorb and convey water fast enough to replenish this loss, the leaves turn brown and wither. For optimum growth, magnolias require moist soil. Leaf scorch is most severe when water is unavailable because the soil is dry. If the weather is extremely hot, scorch may develop even when the soil is moist. Drying winds, severed roots, limited soil area, or low temperatures can also cause scorch. (For more information on scorch, see page 427.)

Solution: To prevent further scorch, deep-water trees during periods of hot weather to wet down the entire root space. (For more information on watering, see pages 407 to 408.) If practical, apply a thick layer of mulch over the root system. Water newly transplanted trees whenever the rootball is dry 2 inches below the surface. If possible, shade trees during very hot weather. Plant trees adapted to your climate.

Magnolia scales

Magnolia scale (2× life size).

Problem: Twigs and stems are covered with powdery white or shiny brown, crusty bumps, ½ inch in diameter, or soft masses of purple insects. Stems that are normally light green may appear enlarged and purple or whitish. The crusty bumps can be scraped or picked off; the undersides are soft. Leaves may be yellowing and smaller than normal. Trees may be weakened or killed. A shiny, sticky substance usually coats the leaves. A black, sooty mold often grows on the sticky substance.

Analysis: Magnolia scale (*Neolecanium cornuparvum*) is the largest scale insect found in the United States. The immature purple insect spends the winter on the twigs and branches of the tree. Starting in spring, it feeds by inserting its mouthparts and sucking the sap and nutrients from the bark tissue. The scale is unable to digest all the sugar in the plant sap, and it excretes the excess in a fluid called *honeydew*. A sooty mold fungus may develop on the honeydew. The scales mature in August, and the female lays her eggs beneath her powdery white or shiny brown shell. In the fall the young scales, called *crawlers*, settle on the twigs to spend the winter. Repeated heavy infestations kill branches and possibly the whole tree. Several other types of scales also infest magnolia.

Solution: Spray with Ortho® Systemic Insect Killer or Ortho® Volck® Oil Spray in early fall when the young are active. The following spring, before new growth begins, spray with a dormant oil spray to control overwintering insects.

Winter injury

Winter injury to Oregon grapeholly.

Problem: The leaves are dry and rusty brown to red. Twigs may die. The shrub is growing in a climate where cold, dry, windy days are common in winter or where plants may be exposed to late-fall or early-spring freezes. The soil may be frozen.

Analysis: Oregon grapeholly is damaged by cold, drying winter wind, especially if temperatures are below freezing and the weather is clear and sunny. The leaves lose their moisture more rapidly than it can be replaced by the root system. Cells in the leaves dry out and die. This condition is most pronounced when water is unavailable because the soil is frozen. Leaves and twigs may also die during early-fall or late-spring freezes when the plant is growing. Young, succulent growth can't withstand the cold temperatures.

Solution: No cure is available once plants have been injured. Where practical, pick off damaged leaves and prune out dead twigs. Provide shelter and windbreaks for plants growing in cold regions. Covering Oregon grapeholly with burlap bags in winter helps prevent leaf drying. To avoid succulent growth in the fall, don't fertilize or prune late in the season. Water in late fall or winter, if necessary, to ensure adequate soil moisture. Mulch plants after they are dormant to reduce the depth of frost penetration into the soil.

MALUS (Crabapple)

Fire blight

Fire blight.

Problem: The blossoms and leaves of infected twigs suddenly wilt and turn black as if scorched by fire. The leaves curl and hang downward. The bark at the base of the blighted twig becomes water-soaked, then dark, sunken, and dry; cracks may develop at the edges of the sunken area. In warm, moist spring weather, drops of brown ooze appear on the sunken bark. Young trees may die.

Analysis: Fire blight is a disease caused by a bacterium (*Erwinia amylovora*) that is very destructive to many trees and shrubs. (For a list of susceptible plants, see page 535.) Bacteria spend the winter in the sunken cankers on the branches. In spring, bacteria ooze out of the cankers. Insects that are attracted to this ooze become smeared with it, and when the insects visit a flower for nectar, they infect it with the bacteria. The bacteria spread rapidly through the plant tissue in warm (65°F or higher), humid weather. Insects visiting these infected blossoms later carry bacteria-laden nectar to healthy blossoms. Rain, wind, and tools may also spread the bacteria. Tender or damaged leaves may be infected in midsummer.

Solution: Prune infected branches 12 to 15 inches beyond any visible discoloration and destroy them. Disinfect pruning shears after each cut. A protective spray of a bactericide containing fixed copper or *streptomycin* applied before bud-break in the spring will help prevent infection. Repeat at intervals of five to seven days until the end of bloom. Avoid overfertilization, which causes lush growth more susceptible to fire blight.

Apple scab

Scab.

Problem: Olive, velvety spots, ¼ inch or more in diameter, appear on the leaves. The tissue around the spots may be puckered. The leaves often turn yellow and drop. In a wet year, the tree may lose all of its leaves by midsummer. The fruit and twigs develop circular, rough-surfaced, olive-green spots that eventually turn corky and black. The fruit is usually deformed.

Analysis: Apple scab is a plant disease caused by a fungus (*Venturia inaequalis*). It is a serious problem on crabapples and apples in areas where spring weather is humid, with temperatures ranging from 60° to 70°F. The fungus spends the winter in infected fallen leaves. In the spring, spore-producing structures in the dead leaves continuously discharge spores into the air. The spores are blown by the wind to new leaves and flower buds. If water is on the tissue surface, the fungus infects the tissue and a spot develops. More spores are produced from these spots and from twig infections from the previous year. The spores are splashed by the rain to infect new leaf and fruit surfaces. As temperatures increase during the summer, the fungus becomes less active.

Solution: To obtain adequate control of scab, apply protective sprays starting as soon as bud growth begins in the spring. Spray with Ortho® Garden Disease Control or Ortho® Lawn Disease Control. Repeat five to eight times at intervals of 7 to 10 days. Rake up and destroy infected leaves and fruit in the fall. Plant resistant varieties.

Cedar-apple rust

Cedar-apple rust.

Problem: Pale yellow spots appear on leaves and fruit in mid- to late spring. Spots gradually enlarge, turn orange, and develop minute black dots. Small (¹⁄₁₆-inch) cups with fringed edges form on the lower surfaces of leaves. Infected leaves and fruit may drop prematurely; the fruit is often deformed.

Analysis: Cedar-apple rust is caused by a fungus called *Gymnosporangium juniperivirginianae* that affects both crabapples and certain species of juniper and red cedar. This disease can't spread from crabapple to crabapple or from juniper to juniper, but, instead, must alternate between the two. In the spring, spores from brown and orange galls on juniper or cedar are blown up to 3 miles to crabapple trees. During mild, wet weather, the spores germinate and infect the leaves and fruit, causing spotting and premature leaf and fruit drop. During the summer, spores are produced in small cups on the undersides of leaves. These spores are blown back to junipers and cedars, causing new infections. (For more information on cedar-apple rust on juniper, see page 237.)

Solution: Cedar-apple rust can't be controlled on the current season's foliage and fruit. The following spring, spray trees with Ortho® Garden Disease Control or Ortho® Lawn Disease Control when the flower buds turn pink, again when 75 percent of the petals have fallen from the blossoms, and once more 10 days later. If possible, don't plant crabapples within several hundred yards of junipers or red cedar. Infestation can take place from junipers as far away as 3 miles.

Scales

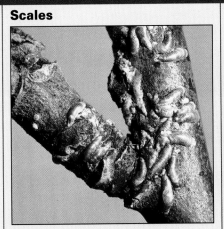

Oyster-shell scale (2× life size).

Problem: Brownish crusty bumps; thick, white, waxy bumps; or clusters of somewhat flattened, yellowish scaly bumps cover the stems or leaves. The bumps can be scraped or picked off; the undersides are usually soft. Leaves turn yellow and may drop. In some cases, a shiny or sticky substance coats the leaves. A black, sooty mold often grows on the sticky substance.

Analysis: Several types of scales infest crabapples. They lay their eggs on leaves or bark, and in spring to midsummer the young scales, called *crawlers*, settle on leaves and twigs. The small (¹⁄₁₀-inch), soft-bodied young feed by inserting their mouthparts and sucking sap from the plant. The legs usually atrophy, and a hard crusty or waxy shell develops over the body. Mature female scales lay their eggs underneath their shell. Some species of scales that infest crabapples are unable to digest all the sugar in the plant sap, and they excrete the excess in a fluid called *honeydew*, which often drops onto the leaves below. A sooty mold fungus may develop on the honeydew, causing the crabapple leaves to appear black and dirty. An uncontrolled infestation of scales may kill the plant after two or three seasons. (For more information on scales, see pages 444 to 447.)

Solution: Spray with Ortho® Systemic Insect Killer in late spring when the young are active. Early the following spring, before new growth begins, spray the trunk and branches with a dormant oil spray to control overwintering insects.

Tent caterpillars

Tent caterpillars.

Problem: In spring, silk webs appear in the crotches of trees or on the ends of branches. The leaves are chewed and the tree may be completely defoliated. Groups of bluish or black hairy caterpillars with yellow or white stripes and blue or white spots are feeding in or around the webs.

Analysis: Tent caterpillars (*Malacosoma* species) feed on many ornamental and fruit trees in the garden. The insects are found in nearly all parts of the United States. In summer, tent caterpillars lay masses of 150 to 300 eggs in bands around twigs. The eggs hatch in early spring when leaves are beginning to unfold; the young caterpillars immediately begin to construct the webs. On warm, sunny days, they devour the surrounding foliage and may strip trees in just a few days. The caterpillars feed for four to six weeks and then pupate. In mid- to late summer, brownish or reddish moths emerge and lay the overwintering eggs.

Solution: Cut out and destroy large webs. Spray smaller webs with Ortho® Systemic Insect Killer, Ortho® Bug-B-Gon® Multi-Purpose Insect Killer Concentrate, or with the bacterial insecticide *Bacillus thuringiensis* (Bt) when webs are first noticed. A bacterial insecticide is most effective against small caterpillars, so it is best to spray before webs are large. Use high-pressure spray equipment to penetrate the webbing. To prevent damage the following year, destroy the brown egg masses that encircle the twigs during the winter.

NANDINA (Heavenly bamboo)

Iron deficiency

Iron deficiency.

Problem: Some of the leaves are pale green (or pale red) to yellow. The newest leaves may be completely yellow, with only the veins remaining green. On older leaves, only the leaf edges may be yellowing. The plant may be stunted.

Analysis: Iron deficiency is a common problem in plants such as heavenly bamboo, which don't tolerate alkaline soil. The plant grows best in soil with a pH between 5.5 and 6.5. (For information on soil pH, see page 407.) The yellowing is due to a deficiency of iron in the plant. The soil is seldom deficient in iron, but iron is often found in an insoluble form that is not available to the plant, especially in soil with a pH above 7.0. A high soil pH can result from overliming or from lime leached from cement or brick. Regions where soil is derived from limestone or where rainfall is low also have high-pH soils.

Solution: Spray the foliage with a chelated iron fertilizer, and apply the fertilizer to the soil around the plant to correct the iron deficiency. Correct the pH of the soil by treating it with ferrous sulfate and watering it in well. Maintain an acid pH by fertilizing with Osmocote® Azalea, Camellia, Rhododendron Slow Release Plant Food.

PALMS

Lethal yellowing

Lethal yellowing.

Problem: Many palm fronds turn yellow and die, beginning with the lower fronds and progressing upward. On coconut palm (*Cocos nucifera*), all the nuts usually drop. The nuts are black where they were attached to the flower stalk. New flower stalks are blackened and don't set any fruit. Dead fronds cling to the tree instead of falling off, and after three to six months, all the fronds and the buds have been killed. Shortly thereafter, the entire palm top falls off, leaving only the bare trunk. No insects are seen on the dying fronds.

Analysis: Lethal yellowing is a serious palm disease caused by bacteria-like organisms called *phytoplasmas*, which are carried from palm to palm by a planthopper (*Myndus crudus*), a tiny sucking insect related to leafhoppers. Planthoppers feed on fronds, especially the newly emerging ones, and are difficult to detect and control. Coconut palms and many other palms are susceptible. The disease was discovered in Key West in the 1950s and has since spread north, killing many of the susceptible palms in the infected areas.

Solution: Lethal yellowing can't be cured. To suppress the disease and prolong the life of palms in the early stages of the disease, inject the palms every four months with the antibiotic *oxytetracycline*. If injections are stopped, the disease will return. Avoid planting susceptible palms. Remove infected palms to avoid spreading the disease.

Bud rot

Bud rot. Inset: Close-up.

Problem: The palm stops producing new fronds. The last new frond to appear turns yellow and then brown, and then it dies. The entire bud can be pulled out; it appears rotten and may have a foul odor. One by one the fronds next to the bud turn yellow, then brown and then die. Eventually the entire top of the palm falls away, leaving the bare trunk standing. Although bud rot is most common on young trees, palms of all ages and sizes are affected. Most damage follows periods of cold, wet weather.

Analysis: Bud rot is an often fatal palm disease caused by a fungus (*Phytophthora palmivora*) that enters the palm through wounds or other openings. The spores can also be washed down into the palm bud by heavy rains. Once infected, palms may die within a short time. Most severe bud rot occurs from spring to fall.

Solution: Spray the entire top of the palm with a fungicide containing basic copper sulfate, soaking the fibers thoroughly. Be sure the bud area is thoroughly covered with the fungicide. Use a spreader-sticker with the fungicide to enable it to coat plant parts more effectively. Also spray nearby palms to keep the disease from spreading to them. Fertilize with Miracle Gro® All Purpose 15-30-15 to speed the palm's recovery. Remove palms that die from bud rot as soon as possible to prevent infection of nearby healthy palms.

PICEA (Spruce)

Spruce budworms

Spruce budworm larva (2× life size).

Problem: Needles on the ends of branches are chewed and webbed together. Brownish caterpillars up to 1 inch long with yellow raised spots are feeding on the needles. Initial damage occurs on new foliage, often near the top of the tree. With severe infestations, older foliage may also be attacked. The whole tree may be defoliated. By midsummer, branch ends may turn reddish brown, becoming gray in the fall. Branches or the entire tree may die after five or more years of defoliation.

Analysis: Spruce budworms (*Choristoneura* species) are very destructive to ornamental spruce, fir, and Douglas fir and may infest pine, larch, and hemlock. The budworm is cyclical. It comes and goes in epidemics 10 or more years apart. Moths are small (½ inch long) and grayish, with bands and spots of brown. Females lay pale green eggs in clusters on the needles in late July and August. Larvae that hatch from eggs crawl to hiding places in the bark or in lichen mats, or they are blown by the wind to other trees, where they hide. The tiny larvae spin a silken case and hibernate there until spring. In May, when the weather warms, the caterpillars tunnel into needles. As they grow, they feed on opening buds; later they chew off needles and web them together. Larvae feed for about five weeks, pupate on twigs, and emerge as adults.

Solution: The following spring, when new needles appear and caterpillars are about ½ inch long, spray with Ortho® Systemic Insect Killer or the bacterial insecticide *Bacillus thuringiensis* (Bt).

Eastern spruce gall adelgids

Galls.

Problem: The ends of branches develop greenish-purple, pineapple-shaped galls, ½ to 1 inch long, in the spring; in late summer, they turn brown and dry. Affected branches may become twisted or stunted, or needles may turn yellow and drop off. Galled stems are weak and may break during storms. When large numbers of galls are formed, the tree may be less vigorous.

Analysis: Eastern spruce gall adelgids (*Adelges abietis*) are closely related to aphids and are often called aphids. This adelgid is most damaging to Norway spruce but may occasionally infest white, black, and red spruce. The insect spends the winter at the base of a terminal bud. When buds begin to grow in the spring, the adelgids lay clusters of several hundred eggs that are covered with white, waxy threads. The young that hatch from these eggs feed on developing needles. They suck the sap from the needles, inducing the formation of galls that enclose them. The adelgids live and feed in chambers inside the galls. In mid- to late summer, the galls turn brown and crack open. Adelgids emerge and lay eggs near the tips of the needles. The young that hatch from these eggs spend the winter at the base of the buds.

Solution: If possible, prune and destroy the greenish purple galls before midsummer. Spray with Ortho® Systemic Insect Killer in the spring just before growth begins. It is usually impractical to spray large trees.

Spruce needle miners

Damaged needles. Inset: Larva (life size).

Problem: Groups of brown needles are webbed together, near the inside of the lower branches. A sawdustlike material surrounds the webbing. The entire tree may be infested, giving it an unsightly appearance. If a partially brown needle is broken open, a small (up to ¼-inch), greenish-brown larva may be seen feeding inside.

Analysis: The spruce needle miner (*Endothenia albolineana*) is the larva of a small (½-inch), dark brown moth. The moth lays eggs in late spring to early summer on the undersides of old needles. The larvae that hatch from these eggs bore into the base of the needles, feeding on the interior. When the interior is consumed, the caterpillars cut off the needles at their base and web them together, forming a nest. The needle miners feed until the first frost and then enter a hollow needle, where they spend the winter. When the weather warms in spring, the larvae continue feeding until April or May. They pupate inside the webbed nest of needles and emerge as adults to lay more eggs. Several other types of needle miners may cause similar damage to spruce trees.

Solution: The following spring, before buds break, wash out infested needles with a strong stream of water from a garden hose. Gather the debris and destroy it. When moths and young larvae appear, usually in late May or early June, spray with Ortho® Systemic Insect Killer. Repeat the treatment in 7 to 10 days.

Pine needle scales

Pine needle scale (4× life size).

Problem: Needles are covered with clusters of flattened, white, scaly bumps. Foliage may appear completely white. The bumps can be scraped or picked off; the undersides are usually soft. Needles turn brown and drop. Repeated severe infestations may kill young trees or weaken older trees.

Analysis: Pine needle scale insects (*Chionaspis pinifoliae*) may seriously damage spruce and pine trees and may infest fir, hemlock, and cedar. The scales survive the winter on the spruce needles as eggs beneath the mother scales. The eggs hatch in late spring, and the young scales, called *crawlers*, move to new green needles. The small (¹⁄₁₀-inch), soft-bodied young feed by inserting their mouthparts and sucking sap from the plant. The legs atrophy, and a crusty white shell develops over the body. Mature female scales lay their eggs underneath their shell in June or July. This next generation feeds throughout late summer and matures in fall. Females of this generation lay the overwintering eggs.

Solution: Spray young trees with Ortho® Systemic Insect Killer or Ortho® Bug-B-Gon® Multi-Purpose Insect Killer Ready-Spray® in late spring when the crawlers are active, at about the time lilacs begin to bloom. Early the following spring, before new growth begins and when the danger of frost is past, spray with a pesticide containing lime sulfur to kill overwintering eggs. Inspect ornamental spruce twice a year for evidence of infestation. Older trees seldom require controls.

PICEA (Spruce) (continued)

Spruce aphids and green spruce aphids

Spruce aphid damage to blue spruce.

Problem: Many of the older needles turn brown and drop. Only the newest needles remain green. The tree looks bare and sickly. Tiny (⅛-inch), green, soft-bodied insects may be seen feeding on the needles.

Analysis: Spruce aphids (*Elatobium abietinum*) and green spruce aphids (*Cinara fornacula*) may be very destructive to spruce. The aphids appear in early spring, around February. They are extremely prolific, and populations can rapidly build to damaging numbers during March and April. Damage occurs when the aphids suck the sap from the spruce needles. They usually remain on a single needle until it is almost ready to drop. By the time the needles turn brown and the damage is noticeable, the insect population has declined. A heavily damaged tree may require several years to recover and replace its lost foliage.

Solution: By the time the damage is noticed, it is too late to treat the tree during the current year. Spray with Ortho® Bug-B-Gon® Multi-Purpose Insect Killer Ready-Spray®, Ortho® Systemic Insect Killer, or an insecticidal soap the following February or March. Repeat the spray 10 days later.

Spruce spider mites

Spruce spider mite damage.

Problem: Needles are stippled yellow and dirty. A silken webbing may be on the twigs and needles. Needles usually turn brown and fall off. To determine if a tree is infested with mites, hold a sheet of white paper under stippled needles and tap the foliage sharply. Minute dark green to black specks about the size of pepper grains will drop to the paper and begin to crawl around.

Analysis: The spruce spider mite (*Oligonychus ununguis*) is one of the most damaging pests of spruces and many other conifers. As a result of their feeding, chlorophyll disappears, causing the stippled appearance. Spider mites first appear between April and June. Spruce spider mites are most active in the cool temperatures of spring and fall, becoming dormant in hot weather (90°F and higher). A complete generation may be produced in only 17 days, so mites can rapidly build up to tremendous numbers during the growing season. Young spruce trees may die the first season. If left uncontrolled for several years, older trees may die, with symptoms progressing from the lower branches upward. Several other kinds of mites may infest spruce trees.

Solution: Spray with Ortho® Malathion Plus® Insect Spray Concentrate or Ortho® Systemic Insect Killer, covering the foliage thoroughly. Repeat the spray two more times, 7 to 10 days apart. Additional sprays may be needed in early fall or spring if the tree becomes reinfested. To control dormant mites and eggs, spray with Ortho® Volck® Oil Spray in late fall or early spring.

Canker and dieback

Dieback. Inset: White pitch on bark.

Problem: The needles on the branches nearest the ground turn brown and dry. Occasionally this condition develops first in the upper branches. Needles may drop immediately, or they may remain attached for a year. Eventually the entire branch dies back. Amber-color pitch usually oozes from the infected area, becoming white as it dries. Infection may spread to the higher branches. To determine if the tree is infected, slice off the bark on a dead branch in the area where the diseased tissue and healthy tissue meet. Small, black spore-producing bodies are found beneath the bark.

Analysis: Canker and dieback is a plant disease caused by fungus (*Cytospora kunzei*) that is very destructive to Norway and Colorado blue spruce. The fungus enters the tree at a wound, killing the surrounding healthy tissue. A canker develops and expands through the wood in all directions. When the canker encircles a branch, the branch dies and the needles turn brown. Sap oozes from the dying branch. Eventually small, black spore-producing bodies develop in the bark. Older (more than 15 years), weak, and injured trees are most susceptible to the disease.

Solution: Prune and destroy dead or dying branches where the branch meets the trunk. Disinfect the pruning shears after each cut. Don't prune during wet weather. Avoid wounding trees with lawn mowers, nails, tools, and other equipment. Keep trees vigorous by watering during dry spells and fertilizing every few years.

PINUS (Pine)

Sphaeropsis tip blight

Blighted pine. Inset: Close-up of needles.

Problem: New growth is stunted and brown. Dead buds and needles remain on the tree for several years, glued in place by resin (sap). Often, very stunted dead needles are found in the same cluster as longer dead needles. Black, pimplelike fruiting bodies appear on the dead needles. With repeated infections, limbs die back and become deformed, and tree growth is stunted.

Analysis: *Sphaeropsis* tip blight, also known as *diplodia tip blight*, is a plant disease caused by a fungus (*Sphaeropsis sapinea*) that may severely damage or kill Austrian pine. Several other types of pines, especially the two- and three-needled pines, may also be infected. Trees 20 to 30 years old are most susceptible. The fungus is commonly found on the decaying tissue of most pine trees that have died from other problems. The fungus from infected trees spreads to living tissue when growing conditions are poor and trees are weakened. During moist weather in spring, spores ooze from black spore-producing bodies on dead tissue. Spores are carried by wind and rain to young needles and buds. The fungus enters and kills the tissue.

Solution: Spray the entire tree with a fungicide containing fixed copper or *azoxystrobin* just as the buds begin to grow, as the needles are emerging from their sheaths. Repeat when the needles are half their full size. When the weather is dry, prune dead branch tips. Keep trees vigorous by watering during dry periods and fertilizing every three to five years.

Needle cast

Needle cast. Inset: Fruiting structures.

Problem: Tips of the needles on the previous year's growth turn brown in winter. By spring, the infected needles are completely discolored, giving the tree a scorched appearance. Many needles may drop from the tree, leaving only new green growth. Tiny, black, elongated structures develop on the midrib of dead needles. The structures may be swollen, with cracks down the middle. In severe cases, branch tips die back. Shaded parts of the tree are more frequently infected.

Analysis: Needle cast is a plant disease caused by either of two fungi (*Hypoderma lethale* or *Lophodermium pinastri*). It is most severe on young pine trees, but older trees may be infected on the lower branches. In summer, during wet weather, spores are released from elongated black fruiting structures on infected needles. Wind and splashing rain may carry the spores several hundred feet. The fungus enters the tissue, but symptoms don't appear until early the following spring. Brown spots with yellow margins develop on needles in March or April. The fungus grows through the tissue, and by late April or May the needles are completely brown. Needles drop, and spores from these infections continue the cycle.

Solution: Remove and destroy fallen needles that collect in branch crotches and on the ground. If needle cast was serious in the spring, spray valuable specimens with Ortho® Garden Disease Control, starting in late July. Repeat the spray at intervals of 10 to 14 days through September. If trees are shaded, remove any shade-producing structures or plants where practical.

Ips engraver beetles

Monterey pines killed by ips engraver beetles.

Problem: The newest growth at the top of the tree turns yellow, then reddish brown. Within four to six weeks the whole tree may turn completely brown. Many tiny (⅛-inch) holes are in the main trunk. A sawdustlike material usually surrounds them. If the bark is peeled back around these holes, Y-shape or H-shape engravings may be seen on the wood. Shiny reddish-brown to black beetles, ³⁄₁₆ inch long, with scooped-out rear portions, may be feeding in the wood.

Analysis: In some areas, ips engraver beetles (*Ips* species) are serious pests of pines. Engraver beetles usually infest only weakened trees. Healthy pines growing near stressed trees, however, are also susceptible to attack. In the spring, adults tunnel into the bark on either the upper or the lower part of the tree, depending on the species of ips beetle. A chemical substance is produced and attracts more beetles, which mate and lay their eggs in the tunnels. After the eggs hatch, the C-shape white grubs burrow under the bark, girdling the wood and cutting off the flow of nutrients and water through the trunk. Several other bark beetles may also infest pines.

Solution: Cut down dead trees and those trees on which more than 50 percent of the foliage is yellowed. Burn the wood, strip off the bark, or remove the wood from the area to eliminate beetle habitat. No insecticides that give adequate protection are available to home gardeners. Contact an arborist to protect your trees. Keep trees vigorous and free from injury. Water trees during droughts. Thin crowded stands.

PINUS (Pine) (continued)

Bark beetles

Pitch tubes from turpentine beetle.

Problem: Needles in the crown of the tree turn yellow at first, then reddish brown. Small holes appear in the trunk. Tubelike masses of pitch, accompanied by sawdust, may also be present. When the bark near the holes or pitch tubes is cut away, legless grubs with brown heads may be found in tunnels under the bark.

Analysis: Bark beetles (*Dendroctonus* species), about the size of rice grains, feed primarily on pine and occasionally on spruce and larch. Injured, weak, and dying trees are most susceptible to attack. Turpentine beetles create tubes of pitch on the lower bark of trees. The pine bark beetle attacks the middle and upper trunk and does not create pitch tubes. Adult beetles of all species burrow under the bark, where they lay eggs. Larvae hatch and tunnel through the bark. They pupate in their tunnels and emerge as adults. A few beetles in a tree won't kill it; however, many pitch tubes indicate that enough beetles are present to kill or weaken the tree.

Solution: Severely infested trees should be removed and destroyed as soon as possible. Prune infested limbs. If pitch tubes are present, smash them with a heavy rubber mallet to close the tunnels and squash the insects in the area beneath. Contact an arborist if you would like to apply protective sprays. Keep the tree in good health by watering it thoroughly every four to six weeks during dry months. Fertilize weakened trees with Scotts® Evergreen, Flowering Tree & Shrub Slow Release Plant Food. Avoid injuring tree roots and trunk.

Root nematodes

Nematode damage.

Problem: The tree is yellowing and growing poorly. Branches die, or the entire tree turns brown and dies.

Analysis: Many different types of root nematodes infect pines. Nematodes are microscopic worms that live in the soil. They are not related to earthworms. Root nematodes feed on plant roots, damaging and stunting them. The damaged roots can't supply sufficient water and nutrients to the aboveground parts, and the plant is stunted or slowly dies. Root nematodes prefer moist, sandy loam soils. They can move only a few inches per year on their own, but they may be carried long distances by soil, water, tools, or infested plants. Testing roots and soil is the only positive method for confirming the presence of nematodes. Contact your local county extension office for sampling instructions and addresses of testing laboratories. Soil and root problems—such as poor soil structure, drought stress, nutrient deficiency, and root rots—can also produce symptoms of decline similar to those caused by nematodes. Eliminate these problems as causes before sending soil and root samples for testing. (For information on soil problems and root rots, see pages 406 and 419.) Another type of nematode that lives inside the conducting vessels causes similar aboveground symptoms.

Solution: No chemicals available to homeowners kill nematodes in planted soil. Nematodes can be controlled before planting, however, by soil fumigation or solarization.

Pine wilt nematodes

Pine wilt nematode damage. Inset: Dying shoot.

Problem: Needles wilt and turn yellow, then brown, in late summer or fall. Dead needles remain on the branches. Some of the branches die, and in severe cases, the entire tree dies. Trees often die suddenly, sometimes within a few weeks. Reddish-brown beetles mottled with white may be seen on the bark. Beetles are 1 inch long and have antennae longer than their bodies.

Analysis: Pine wilt is caused by microscopic nematodes (*Bursaphelenchus xylophilus*). These nematodes damage only certain species of pine, but they may also infest firs, spruces, and other conifers. Pine wilt is endemic to American forests. Pine wilt nematodes are spread by certain species of long-horned beetles, including the sawyer beetle (*Monochamus titillator*). The beetles usually attack weak and dying trees and transfer the nematodes from tree to tree while feeding. The nematodes damage the water-conducting vessels in the trunk and branches; this reduces or cuts off the flow of water through the tree. A diagnostic test is necessary to confirm the presence of pine wilt nematodes.

Solution: If you suspect pine wilt, contact your local county extension office. Remove and destroy all parts of infested trees down to ground level. Clean up tree branches and other debris. Maintain trees in good health to reduce the chances of beetle infestation. Protect valuable specimens by spraying in late spring with an insecticide containing *bifenthrin*. Choose species resistant to pine wilt.

Spruce spider mites

Spruce spider mite damage.

Problem: Needles are stippled yellow and dirty. A silken webbing is sometimes on the twigs and needles. Older needles at the base of the tree are usually attacked first. To determine if a tree is infested with mites, hold a sheet of white paper underneath some stippled needles, and tap the foliage sharply. Tiny specks the size of pepper grains will drop to the paper and begin to crawl.

Analysis: The spruce spider mite (*Oligonychus ununguis*) is one of the most damaging pests of evergreen trees. These mites suck sap from the undersides of needles. As a result of their feeding, the tree's chlorophyll disappears, producing the stippled appearance. This symptom may be mistaken for certain types of damage caused by air pollution (see pages 424 to 425). Spider mites first appear between April and June, hatching from eggs laid at the base of pine needles the previous fall. Mites can rapidly build up to tremendous numbers during the growing season. Young pine trees may die the first season. If left uncontrolled for several years, older trees sometimes die, with symptoms progressing from the lower branches upward.

Solution: Wash webbing and mites from the tree with a strong spray of water. In spring or early fall, treat with Ortho® Systemic Insect Killer or Ortho® Bug-B-Gon® Multi-Purpose Insect Killer Ready-Spray®. Repeat the application two more times at intervals of 7 to 10 days. Additional sprays may be needed if the tree becomes reinfested with mites.

White pine blister rust

White pine blister rust.

Problem: Branches or the main stem develop rough, elongated, slightly swollen areas. Infected areas are usually yellowish orange. Pitch may flow from the swollen areas. Branches or the entire tree often die. Dead foliage appears reddish brown and may be very apparent if surrounded by green trees.

Analysis: White pine blister rust is a plant disease caused by a fungus (*Cronartium ribicola*) that alternately infects pines and either currants or gooseberries (*Ribes* species). Windblown spores from *Ribes* leaves infect pine needles in later summer. The fungus grows into nearby branches. Small yellow to brownish spots develop. In one or two seasons, the bark develops swollen yellowish orange cankers. The canker grows, and the following season, white blisters containing orange-yellow spores push through the bark. Wind carries the spores back to currants and gooseberries. The pine bark in the cankered area dries out and cracks, resulting in the death of the underlying wood. The branches and foliage above this area die and turn reddish brown.

Solution: Spray gooseberry and currant bushes within 400 feet of white pines with Ortho® Brush-B-Gon® Poison Ivy, Poison Oak & Brush Killer Concentrate or Roundup® Brush Killer Concentrate. Cut off and destroy infected pine branches. Cankers on the trunk can be removed surgically with some success if all discolored bark and wood is destroyed, including a border of healthy bark and wood. Disinfect the knife after each cut. Spray the wound with a fungicide containing *cycloheximide*.

Pine adelgids

Pine bark adelgids (life size).

Problem: The needles or trunk are covered with white, woolly masses. If the infestation is heavy, the tree appears to be covered with snow. Infested shoots may droop; the needles turn yellow and may die. Trees heavily infested for several years are usually stunted.

Analysis: Pine adelgids (*Pineus* species), small (⅛-inch), soft-bodied insects, are closely related to aphids and used to be called "woolly aphids." The adults are always covered with dense white filaments of wax. When this substance is removed, the insects appear purplish or green. Some species spend part of their lives on other types of evergreens, usually spruce, often producing galls on the branches. In early summer, the insects migrate to pines and suck sap from the needles. Other species spend their entire lives on pines, feeding and reproducing on the trunks. Species that spend the winter on other types of plants produce a generation in the fall that flies to the winter host.

Solution: Control with Ortho® Systemic Insect Killer or Ortho® Malathion Plus® Insect Spray Concentrate. Spray pines with infested trunks in April; spray pines with infested needles in late June. Cover the tree thoroughly. Repeat the spray if the plant becomes reinfested. In late winter, before spring growth begins, spray with dormant oil. Also spray other pines and spruces in the vicinity. Spray only when the temperature is expected to remain higher than 40°F for 24 hours after spraying.

PINUS (Pine) *(continued)*

Pine needle scales

Pine needle scales (life size).

Problem: Needles are covered with clusters of somewhat flattened, white scaly bumps. When heavily infested, the foliage may appear completely white. The bumps can be scraped or picked off; the undersides are usually soft. Needles develop yellow mottling, turn brown, and eventually drop. Repeated severe infestations may kill young trees or weaken older trees.

Analysis: Pine needle scale insects (*Chionaspis pinifoliae*) may seriously damage pine and spruce trees and may infest fir, hemlock, and cedar. The scales survive the winter on pine needles as eggs beneath the mother scales. The eggs hatch in late spring, and the young scales, called *crawlers*, move to new green needles. The small (1/10-inch), soft-bodied young feed by inserting their mouthparts and sucking sap from the plant. The legs atrophy, and a crusty white shell develops over the body. Mature female scales lay their eggs underneath their shell in July. This next generation feeds throughout late summer and matures in fall. Females of this generation lay the overwintering eggs.

Solution: In late spring when the crawlers are active, spray young trees with Ortho® Systemic Insect Killer or Ortho® Bug-B-Gon® Multi-Purpose Insect Killer Ready-Spray®. Early the following spring, before new growth begins and when the danger of frost is past, spray with Ortho® Volck® Oil Spray or a pesticide containing lime sulfur to kill the overwintering eggs. Inspect ornamental pines twice a year for evidence of infestation. Older trees seldom require controls.

Aphids

Aphids on white pine (life size).

Problem: Needles are discolored and may be deformed; many may drop from the tree. New growth is often slowed, and twigs may die. A shiny, sticky substance often coats the needles and branches. A black, sooty mold may grow on the sticky substance. Small (up to 1/16-inch) green, brown, or black soft-bodied insects cluster on needles, twigs, or main stems of small trees. An uncontrolled infestation may kill young trees.

Analysis: Several types of aphids (*Cinara* and *Eulachnus* species) infest the needles or bark of pines. Aphids do little damage in small numbers. They are extremely prolific, however, and populations can rapidly build to damaging numbers during the growing season. Damage occurs when the aphids suck the sap from the pine needles, growing tips, or bark. The aphids are unable to digest all the sugar in the sap, and they excrete the excess in a fluid called *honeydew*, which often drops onto the needles and bark below. A sooty mold fungus may develop on the honeydew, causing the pine needles, bark, or other coated plants to appear black and dirty. (For more information on aphids, see page 444.)

Solution: Control with Ortho® Bug-B-Gon® Multi-Purpose Insect Killer Ready-Spray®, Ortho® Systemic Insect Killer, or an insecticidal soap when aphids first appear. Repeat the spray if the tree becomes reinfested in mid- or late summer. Be sure to check the tree in the fall as well.

Pine spittlebugs and Saratoga spittlebugs

Pine spittlebug (3× life size).

Problem: A frothy mass of bubbles appears on the twigs at the base of the needles. A small (1/4-inch), tan or green, wingless insect may be found inside the mass. Needles may turn yellow and drop; black, sooty mold may grow on surrounding branches. Continuous heavy infestations of insects kill branches or cause the death of young or weak trees.

Analysis: The pine spittlebug (*Aphrophora parallela*) may cause serious injury to Scotch and white pines. The Saratoga spittlebug (*A. saratogensis*) kills branches of jack and red pines. Pine spittlebug adults are grayish brown, wedge-shape insects, 1/2 inch long. The females lay their eggs at the base of buds in late summer. The eggs hatch the following May, and the young insects suck the sap from twigs and the main trunk. The bug excretes drops of undigested sap mixed with air, producing the frothy "spittle" that surrounds its body. Some of the excreted sap drops onto lower branches, which may be colonized by a black, sooty mold fungus. The life cycle of the Saratoga spittlebug is similar, but the tan females lay their eggs on plants beneath the tree, especially on sweet fern. The adults migrate to trees in late June, feed until late fall, and then return to the low-growing plants to lay their eggs.

Solution: Spray with Ortho® Systemic Insect Killer when insects are first noticed—in late May and again in July for the pine spittlebug, and in late June or early July for the Saratoga spittlebug. Use high pressure.

Pine webworms

Pine webworms.

Problem: Brown, globular nests made of silk, brown needles, and a sawdustlike material appear on the ends of branches in early or midsummer. The branches are often stripped of most of their foliage, and tree growth is slowed. Yellowish-brown caterpillars up to ¾ inch long, with two dark brown stripes down each side, may be feeding inside the nests.

Analysis: The pine webworm (*Tetralopha robustella*) is found throughout the eastern United States on many different pines. The nests are unsightly, but rarely are trees seriously injured. The gray moths lay their eggs on pine needles between May and September. When the eggs hatch, the larvae feed within the needles until they are too large. Then they construct nests made of silk, dead needles, and brown excrement, which they wrap around twigs. Each nest may contain up to 75 worms. When mature, the insects drop to the ground and pupate below the soil surface. In the South, moths may emerge to repeat the cycle one more time. Webworms spend the winter in the soil.

Solution: Cut out and destroy the nests. Or spray with Ortho® Bug-B-Gon® Multi-Purpose Insect Killer or the bacterial insecticide *Bacillus thuringiensis* (Bt) when the larvae are small and before the needles are webbed in mid-June. Repeat the spray in early August if the tree becomes reinfested.

Sawflies

Sawfly larvae (life size).

Problem: The needles are partially chewed, or the entire branch is defoliated. In some cases, only the younger needles are eaten. Usually, however, the older needles are preferred. Gray-green, tan, or black caterpillar-like larvae, up to an inch long, are found on the needles. Larvae may live as single individuals or in conspicuous colonies of more than 100.

Analysis: Many species of sawflies (*Neodiprion* species and *Diprion* species) infest pines. The dark, clear-winged adults are nonstinging wasps. The females insert rows of eggs in the needles with sawlike egg-laying organs. The larvae that hatch from these eggs feed singly or in groups on the needles. Eventually, entire needles are devoured. Small trees may be completely defoliated. Larvae then move to adjacent trees to feed. Some species of sawflies feed only in spring or summer. Others are present throughout the growing season, producing five or six generations per year. When larvae mature, they drop to the ground and spin cocoons. Most sawflies spend the winter in the soil, although several species overwinter as eggs on needles.

Solution: Spray the needles with Ortho® Systemic Insect Killer or Ortho® Bug-B-Gon® Multi-Purpose Insect Killer when damage or the insects are first noticed. Inspect the trees periodically during the growing season to detect infestations before severe defoliation occurs.

Pine tip or shoot moths

European pine shoot moth damage.

Problem: Branch tips turn yellow, then brown and dry. Dead branches contrast sharply with healthy green foliage. In the summer, pitch accumulates around the dead needles. Trees may appear bushier than normal, or they may be crooked and distorted. At the base of the needles or inside a brown, resin-coated tip, cream-colored to reddish-brown worms, up to ¾ inch long, may be found feeding on the tissue. Young trees may die.

Analysis: Seven species of pine tip and shoot moths (*Rhyacionia* species) infest various pines. The adult is a reddish-brown and gray moth, up to 1 inch long. Moths fly at night but may be seen during the day if a branch is disturbed. They lay their eggs in mid- to late spring at the ends of branches. Larvae that hatch from these eggs bore into needles and buds, where they feed and mature. Depending on species, pupation occurs in the mined-out area or in the soil around the base of the tree. Most species produce one generation per year. The Nantucket pine tip moth, *Rhyacionia frustrana*, has as many as five generations yearly in warm climates.

Solution: Spray with Ortho® Systemic Insect Killer or Ortho® Rose & Flower Insect Killer in mid-April to early May. Repeat the spray in mid-May. If reinfestation occurs the same year, the Nantucket pine tip moth is probably involved. Repeated sprayings every four weeks from early May to August may be necessary. If practical, prune out and destroy infested tips from October through January. Avoid pruning when moths are active.

PINUS (Pine) *(continued)*

Pine shoot beetles

Pine shoot beetle damage.

Adult beetle (10× life size).

Zimmerman pine moths

Pitch mass.

Problem: New shoots, primarily near the top of the tree, wilt, turn yellow to red, and break off. Many shoots may break out of the top of the tree, leaving only the top shoot and a few tufts. Infested shoots have a hole in the side about 1/10 inch. Near the broken end, the pith in the center of the shoot has been hollowed out.

Analysis: First discovered in North America in Ohio in 1992, the pine shoot bark beetle (*Tomicus piniperda*) has been spreading ever since. In Europe, it is one of the most serious shoot-feeding insect problems. It breeds only on pine, preferring Scotch pine (*Pinus sylvestris*), but occasionally it feeds on spruce and related trees. The adult is about the size of a match head, cylindrical, and a shiny reddish brown to black. It emerges from hibernation when the temperature reaches 54°F in the spring. Females bore into the bark of pine trees and lay eggs there. Like many borers, they prefer weakened or recently killed trees. The legless white grubs that hatch from these eggs tunnel under the bark. They mature and emerge as adults from early summer through September, when they fly to shoots in the tops of nearby pine trees. They tunnel into the shoots and feed there until the first hard frost, then move into hibernation. One beetle may tunnel several shoots, exiting each through a small hole in the side of the shoot. Damage is caused by feeding in the shoot and also by tunneling under the bark, which interferes with nutrient transport to the roots and can kill the tree if galleries girdle it.

Solution: A few flagging shoots cause little damage but indicate that pine shoot beetles are active. If possible, prune and destroy shoots as soon as they flag. To protect shoots, spray them with an insecticide containing *acephate* (Orthene®) or *chlorpyrifos* as soon as damage is discovered. Repeat every two to four weeks until October. To eliminate breeding sites, remove dying pine trees, remove or cover with soil any stumps of recently cut pines, clean up recently cut shoots, and remove dying pine branches within 1/4 mile of the trees being protected. The following year, begin pesticide spraying in June to protect shoots. Keep trees healthy with regular fertilizing and watering during dry periods.

Problem: Masses of pitch (sap) accumulate on the trunk near a whorl of branches. The trunk may be swollen above the masses and shrunken below them. Tops and branch tips may wilt and droop to resemble a shepherd's crook, then turn brown and die. Trees are stunted and deformed.

Analysis: The Zimmerman pine moth (*Dioryctria zimmermani*) is a serious pest of pines in the North-Central states. It attacks most pine trees and Douglas fir. Adults lay eggs in midsummer close to wounds on pine trees. Worms that hatch from these eggs immediately crawl under loose bark and hibernate until spring. As the new growth begins to expand the following spring, the larvae feed inside the tops of small trees and the branch tips of larger trees, causing the characteristic "shepherd's crook." In late spring, they leave these shoots and crawl to the trunk, where they tunnel into the trunk to feed on the inner bark. Their tunneling causes the swelling and pitch masses where they feed. In midsummer, they pupate and emerge as adult moths.

Solution: Prune and destroy shepherd's crooks as soon as they are discovered to destroy the worms inside them. In midsummer, spray with an insecticide containing *chlorpyrifos*. Wet the bark thoroughly to reach the newly hatched worms hiding under loose bark. In the spring, about the time saucer magnolia (*Magnolia soulangiana*) is beginning to bloom, spray again to kill the worms as they crawl across the bark to enter shoots.

Pitch moths

Pitch moth damage.

Problem: One or more masses of sticky cream, yellow, or pinkish pitch (dried sap) appear on the trunk. These masses may be 2 or 3 inches wide and protrude 1 to 2 inches from the side of the trunk. The pitch masses are usually found in wounds or in branch crotches. When the pitch mass is scraped away, a larva up to 1 inch long may be found underneath.

Analysis: Pitch moths (*Vespamima* species) attack pine, spruce, and Douglas fir. The adults are clear-winged moths that resemble yellowjackets. They lay eggs during the spring and summer in the trunks and larger limbs, particularly at sites of recent trunk injury or where old pitch masses exist. The larvae that hatch feeds on the inner bark for 1 to 2 years, pupate, and finally emerge as adult moths during the summer. Usually there is one larva per pitch mass. Although pitch masses are unsightly, pitch moths do not usually threaten the life of a tree. Tree limbs may be weakened enough to break under the weight of snow.

Solution: Scrape away fresh pitch masses and kill the larvae. The larva can be found in the bark under a pitch mass or in the pitch mass itself. Avoid mechanical injury to trees. Confine pruning of larger limbs to fall and early winter months so injuries dry up before moths appear in the spring.

Western and eastern gall rust

Western gall rust on Monterey pine.

Problem: Rough, spherical swellings develop on branches or on the main trunk. In the spring, the swellings (galls) appear orange or yellow. Growth beyond the galls is often stunted, distorted, and off-color.

Analysis: Western and eastern gall rust are plant diseases caused by two species of fungi (*Endocronartium harknessii* and *E. quercuum*). Western gall rust requires only one host to complete its life cycle; spores from one pine can infect another. Eastern gall rust requires both pine and oak to complete its life cycle. In early spring, orange or yellow spores are produced over the ruptured surfaces of the galls. The spores are blown and carried by insects to susceptible trees. When moisture and temperatures are optimum, western gall rust spores infect pine tissue, causing an increase in the number and size of plant cells. Within six months to one year, swellings develop. The galls enlarge and produce spores after one to two years. Eastern gall rust spores infect only oak. Spores produced on the oak trees reinfect pines. The galls caused by both fungi interrupt the sap movement in the tree. They also stimulate witches'-broom, dense stunted growth beyond the galls. If many of these develop, the tree becomes unsightly and weak, and limbs break during storms.

Solution: Prune galled branches before the galls produce spores in early spring.

White pine weevils

White pine weevil damage.

Problem: The main shoot at the top of a healthy tree stops growing and turns yellow in midsummer. The shoot tip usually droops, producing a "shepherd's crook." Several new shoots may develop from below the dying shoot so that the top of the tree is forked. In fall and winter the drooping shoot appears brown and dry. A white resin is on the bark, and small holes are in the dead shoot. Trees are disfigured but not killed.

Analysis: The white pine weevil (*Pissodes strobi*) attacks the top shoots (leaders) of all pines, most spruces, and some firs. This small (⅕-inch), brown, snouted beetle with white patches spends the winter in dead plant material at the base of the tree. In spring, just before new growth begins, it moves to the top of the tree to feed on the inner bark. Eggs are then laid in small punctures in the bark. Resin droplets that ooze from the punctures dry and turn white. The ¼-inch larvae that hatch from these eggs bore into the wood. The feeding cuts off the flow of water and nutrients through the stem, causing the shoot to droop and die. New shoots often develop from below the dead shoot, destroying the natural shape of the tree. In late summer, larvae mature and return to the ground for the winter.

Solution: Prune and destroy infested twigs in early summer before the beetles emerge. Train a side branch to replace the dead leader by pruning all but one of the new shoots to half the length of the newly selected leader. The following spring, spray the leader with an insecticide containing *methoxychlor* as soon as buds begin to swell.

251

PLATANUS (Sycamore)

Sycamore lace bugs

Sycamore lace bug damage.

Problem: The upper surfaces of leaves are mottled or speckled white and green. The mottling may be confused with mite or leafhopper damage. It can be distinguished from damage caused by other insects, however, by the shiny, hard, brown droplets found on the undersides of damaged leaves. Small (⅛-inch), spiny, wingless insects or brownish insects with clear, lacy wings may be visible around the droplets. Foliage on severely infested trees may be completely white, then turn brown by mid-August.

Analysis: Two species of lace bugs (*Corythucha* species) infest sycamores and London plane trees. They survive winter as adults in bark crevices or in other protected areas on the tree. When the buds begin to open in the spring, the adults attach their eggs to the undersides of leaves with a brown, sticky substance. The eggs hatch, and the spiny, wingless, immature insects—and later the brown, lacy-winged adults—suck sap from the undersides of leaves. The chlorophyll disappears, resulting in the characteristic white-and-green mottling. As the lace bugs feed, droplets of brown excrement accumulate around them.

Solution: Spray young trees with Ortho® Orthenex® Garden Insect & Disease Control or Ortho® Systemic Insect Killer when damage first appears in spring. Cover the undersurfaces of the leaves thoroughly. Repeat 7 to 10 days later. It is important to spray early, preventing as much damage as possible. Inspect trees every two weeks during the growing season to catch infestations before severe damage is done.

Sycamore anthracnose

Anthracnose. Inset: Spore-producing bodies.

Problem: In spring, buds or expanding shoots turn brown and die. Dead areas appear along veins of young leaves. As leaves mature, spots may expand and cover them entirely. Most infected leaves drop from the tree. Later, twigs and older leaves may be infected. Infected twigs hang on the tree or drop to the ground with the leaves. Larger limbs may die. Dark brown spore-producing bodies appear on the bark and dead leaves. The tree is often stunted and bushy.

Analysis: Sycamore anthracnose is a plant disease caused by a fungus (*Apiognomonia veneta*) that is the most serious problem of sycamore and causes minor damage to the London plane tree. The fungus survives the winter on fallen leaves and twigs and in swollen cankers in the tree. During cool (55°F and lower), wet weather, spores are blown and splashed onto tender plant tissue. The fungus enters the tissue and kills it, causing dieback. The fungus moves down onto the twigs, and spores develop. The spores may infect mature leaves or any new growth on the tree, causing a sun-scorched appearance. Swollen, cracked cankers develop on infected twigs and branches. When the cankers encircle the wood, the limbs die.

Solution: Prune and destroy infected twigs and dead branches. Destroy fallen leaves and twigs. Feed and water regularly to keep the tree vigorous. In areas where spring is cool and moist, spray with Ortho® Garden Disease Control when buds begin to grow in the spring. Repeat when leaves reach full size and again two weeks later.

Summer leaf scorch

Summer leaf scorch.

Problem: During hot weather, usually in July or August, leaves turn brown around the edges and between the veins. Sometimes the whole leaf dies. Many leaves may drop during late summer. This problem is most severe on the youngest branches. Trees do not usually die. This problem may be mistaken for damage caused by anthracnose or lace bugs. The brown areas caused by anthracnose cross over the veins and often cover the entire leaf. Lace bugs leave brown droplets of excrement on the lower surfaces of the leaves.

Analysis: Summer leaf scorch is caused by excessive evaporation of moisture from the leaves. In hot weather, water evaporates rapidly from the leaves. If the roots can't absorb and convey water fast enough to replenish this loss, the leaves turn brown and wither. This usually occurs in dry soil, but leaves can also scorch when the soil is moist. Drying winds, severed roots, limited soil area, or salts in the soil also cause scorch. (For more information on scorch, see page 427.)

Solution: To prevent further scorch, deep-water trees during periods of hot weather to wet the entire root space. (For information on watering, see pages 407 to 408.) If practical, apply 3 to 4 inches of mulch over the root system. Water newly transplanted trees whenever the rootball is dry 2 inches below the surface. Scorch occurring on trees in moist soil can't be controlled. Plant trees adapted to your climate.

POPULUS (Poplar, aspen)

Slime flux

Slime flux.

Problem: Sour-smelling sap oozes from wounds, cracks, and branch crotches, mainly during the growing season. The sap drips down the bark and dries, causing unsightly gray streaks. Some wilting may occur on affected branches. Insects are attracted to the sour-smelling ooze.

Analysis: Slime flux, also called *wetwood*, is caused by a bacterium (*Erwinia nimipressuralis*) on poplars. The bacteria affect the heartwood, producing abnormally high sap pressure. The pressure, caused by bacterial fermentation, forces the fermented sap, or *flux*, out of the wounds, cracks, or crotches in the tree. Flux is especially copious when the tree is growing rapidly. Large areas of the bark may be coated with the smelly, bacteria-laden sap, which dries to a grayish-white color. In addition, wounds don't heal, and the bark is unsightly. A tree with this problem is often under water stress, which may cause drought damage to the branches. The problem may persist for many years.

Solution: There are no controls for this condition. To avoid the unsightly stained bark, bore a slightly upward-slanting drainage hole into the water-soaked wood below each oozing wound. Insert a ½-inch-diameter plastic tube just until it stays firmly in place. (If the tube penetrates the water-soaked wood inside the tree, it will interfere with drainage.) The tube will carry the dripping sap away from the trunk, but it will not cure the disease. Disinfect tools after pruning infected trees.

Leaf-feeding caterpillars

Satin moth caterpillars (life size).

Problem: The surface of the leaf is eaten, giving the remaining tissue a lacy appearance, or the whole leaf is chewed. Sometimes leaves or branches are webbed. The tree may be completely defoliated. Damage appears anytime between spring and fall. Caterpillars are feeding on the leaves. Repeated heavy infestations may weaken or kill trees.

Analysis: Many different species of caterpillars feed on poplar leaves wherever the trees are grown. Depending on the species, the moths lay their eggs from early spring to midsummer. The larvae that hatch from these eggs feed singly or in groups on buds, on one leaf surface (these are called *skeletonizers*), or on the entire leaf. Certain caterpillars web leaves together or web a branch as they feed. In some years, damage is minimal because of unfavorable environmental conditions or control by predators and parasites. When conditions are favorable, however, entire trees may be defoliated by late summer. Defoliation weakens trees because no leaves are left to produce food. When heavy infestations occur several years in a row, branches or entire trees may be killed.

Solution: Spray with Ortho® Systemic Insect Killer, Ortho® Bug-B-Gon® Multi-Purpose Insect Killer Concentrate, or with the bacterial insecticide *Bacillus thuringiensis* (Bt) when damage is first noticed. Cover the leaves thoroughly. Repeat the spray if the tree becomes reinfested.

Scales

Oystershell scales (¼ life size).

Problem: Brown, black, or red-orange crusty bumps or somewhat flattened brownish, white, or grayish scaly bumps cover trunks, stems, or the undersides of leaves. The bumps can be scraped or picked off; the undersides are usually soft. Leaves turn yellow and may drop. In some cases, a shiny, sticky substance coats the leaves. A black, sooty mold often grows on the sticky substance. Large portions of the tree may be killed if infestations are heavy.

Analysis: Many different types of scales infest poplar. They lay their eggs on leaves or bark, and in spring to midsummer the young scales, called *crawlers*, settle on the leaves, twigs, and trunk. The small (¹⁄₁₀-inch), soft-bodied young feed by sucking sap from the plant. The legs usually atrophy, and a hard crusty shell develops over the body. Some species of scales that infest poplar are unable to digest all the sugar in the plant sap, and they excrete the excess in a fluid called *honeydew*. A sooty mold fungus may develop on the honeydew, causing the poplar leaves to appear black and dirty. An uncontrolled infestation of scales may kill the tree after two or three seasons. (For more information on scales, see pages 444 to 447.)

Solution: Spray with Ortho® Systemic Insect Killer, Ortho® Rose & Flower Insect Killer, or an insecticide containing *malathion* when the young crawlers are active. To control overwintering insects, spray with Ortho® Volck® Oil Spray before growth begins in the spring.

POPULUS (Poplar, aspen) *(continued)*

Leaf beetles	Poplar-and-willow borers	Poplar borers

Damaged leaves. Inset: Leaf beetles (½ life size).

Poplar-and-willow borer (½ life size).

Damaged tree. Inset: Adult borer (½ life size).

Problem: The leaf tissue is eaten between the veins, giving the leaves a lacy appearance. Sometimes only the major veins remain. The bark of young trees may be chewed. Small blackish larvae or ¼-inch-long yellow beetles with round or oblong black spots are feeding on the leaves. Clusters of yellow eggs may be found on the lower surfaces of leaves. With repeated infestations, young trees may die.

Analysis: Several species of leaf beetles (*Chrysomela* species) may seriously damage poplars, especially in urban plantings. They spend the winter as adults in homes or under the bark in plant debris on the ground. When new growth begins in the spring, the beetles fly to trees to feed on the leaves and twigs. The females lay groups of yellow eggs on the undersides of leaves. The clusters of larvae that hatch from these eggs feed on the leaf tissue between the veins, skeletonizing the leaves. Four or more generations of leaf beetles occur each year, so larvae and adults may be present throughout the growing season.

Solution: Spray with Ortho® Systemic Insect Killer or Ortho® Bug-B-Gon® Multi-Purpose Insect Killer Concentrate when damage is first noticed in spring. If necessary, repeat the spray in mid-July.

Problem: Leaves turn yellow and twigs have holes in them. Large quantities of sawdustlike material cling to the bark just below the holes. Sap often oozes from the holes. Young trees may be killed, and older trees may lose their natural form from the growth of numerous side shoots. Small (⅜-inch), black or dark brown weevils with pale yellow spots and long snouts may be seen around the tree from midsummer until fall.

Analysis: Most species of poplar and all willow trees may be attacked by a weevil named the poplar-and-willow borer (*Cryptorhynchus lapathi*). Adult weevils cause minor injury by chewing holes in the bark of twigs. The major damage is caused by the white, C-shape larvae. During mid- to late summer, the larvae hatch from eggs laid in holes chewed by the female weevils. The larvae burrow into and feed on the inner bark. In the spring, large quantities of frass (sawdust and excrement) are expelled from the holes as the larvae tunnel into the center of the twigs to pupate. The feeding and tunneling cause branches to break easily and disrupt nutrient and water movement through the tree. The leaves yellow, and the tree often becomes bushy from the growth of numerous side shoots. The larvae pupate in June and emerge as adults in midsummer. Several other types of borers may also infest the trunk and branches of poplars.

Solution: Remove and destroy severely infested trees or branches before early summer arrives.

Problem: Liquid oozes from holes in the bark. Swollen areas with holes in their centers develop on twigs, branches, or the trunk. Wood is honeycombed with irregular tunnels. Leaves may discolor and wilt, and branches die. A sawdustlike material and many broken twigs are usually beneath the tree.

Analysis: At least five species of beetles named poplar borers (*Saperda* species) feed on poplars, causing galls to form. The inch-long, striped and spotted, brownish or gray beetles with long antennae appear in late spring or early summer. The females lay eggs in small holes gnawed in the bark of twigs and branches that are more than ½ inch in diameter. As the legless, whitish grubs hatch from these eggs, they tunnel into the wood. Excess tissue grows around the wound, resulting in a swollen area, or gall. When infestations are severe, nearly all twigs and branches more than ½ inch in diameter have one or more galls. The galls weaken the twigs and branches, causing them to break and litter the ground after stormy weather. The grubs remain in the wood for one or two years. Borers select damaged or dying trees; healthy plants are seldom attacked.

Solution: Remove and destroy severely damaged trees. Do not store newly cut wood near other trees; borers may emerge and attack the trees. Spray the bark of less severely damaged trees with an insecticide containing *bifenthrin* in late May or early June. Repeat the treatment two weeks later.

Canker and dieback

Dieback. Inset: Canker.

Problem: Dark sunken areas appear on the twigs, branches, or trunk. Leaves may be spotted, or they may be stunted and lighter green than normal. Twigs and branches are often killed. Young or weakened trees are most susceptible.

Analysis: Several different fungi cause canker and dieback on poplars. Lombardy poplars are especially vulnerable. The fungi enter the tree through a wound or, in some cases, through the leaves, killing the surrounding healthy tissue. A dark, sunken canker develops in the wood and expands through it in all directions. If the fungus infects the leaves first, it grows down through the leaf stems and forms cankers on the twigs. The canker cuts off the flow of nutrients and water to the twigs or branch, causing the leaves to turn yellow. Twig or branch dieback follow if the canker girdles the wood. The tree may wall off the spreading fungus by producing callus tissue, a rapid growth of barklike cells. If the expanding canker is stopped before it covers half the diameter of the trunk, the tree usually survives. The fungus may grow faster than the callus, however, or the tree may not produce a callus, resulting in the death of the branch or the whole tree.

Solution: Prune dead twigs and small affected branches, cutting well below the canker. Remove and destroy severely infected trees. To prevent the development of new cankers, avoid wounding trees. Keep trees vigorous by fertilizing and watering. (For more information on watering and fertilizing, see pages 407 to 409.)

PSEUDOTSUGA
(Douglas fir)

Douglas fir tussock moths

Douglas fir tussock moth larvae (3× life size).

Problem: Starting at the top of the tree, much of the foliage turns brown and is eaten. The entire tree may be defoliated in one season. Trees that lose most of their needles the second year are usually killed. Inch-long, hairy, gray or light brown caterpillars with tufts of orange hairs on their backs may be found feeding on the needles.

Analysis: Douglas fir tussock moth (*Orgyia pseudotsugata*) populations are cyclical. Every 7 to 10 years, forest populations build to epidemic proportions. When this occurs, Douglas firs, true firs, spruce, pine, and larch may be completely defoliated. In cities, damaging numbers may be found every year. In mid- to late summer, hairy, wingless female moths lay eggs in a frothy substance covered with a layer of hairlike scales on the cocoon from which they emerged. The eggs hatch the following spring, and the caterpillars begin feeding on the new needles at the top of the tree. As the younger foliage is devoured, the caterpillars move downward, feeding on older needles. Defoliated trees are often killed after two seasons. Less severely damaged trees may be killed later by bark beetles. In August, the caterpillars pupate, and they later emerge as adults.

Solution: Spray with Ortho® Bug-B-Gon® Multi-Purpose Insect Killer Ready-Spray® or with the bacterial insecticide *Bacillus thuringiensis* (Bt) when caterpillars or damage are first noticed, usually in May or early June. Repeat the spray two weeks later if damage continues.

PYRACANTHA

Fire blight

Fire blight.

Problem: Blossoms and leaves of infected twigs suddenly wilt and turn black as if scorched by fire. The leaves curl and hang downward. The bark at the base of the blighted twigs becomes water-soaked, then dark, sunken, and dry; cracks may develop at the edge of the sunken area. In warm, moist spring weather, drops of brown ooze appear on the sunken bark. Young plants may die.

Analysis: Fire blight is a disease caused by a bacterium (*Erwinia amylovora*) that is very destructive to many trees and shrubs. (For a list of susceptible plants, see page 535.) The bacteria spend the winter in the sunken areas (cankers) on the branches. In the spring, the bacteria ooze out of the canker. Bees, flies, and other insects are attracted to the sweet, sticky ooze and become smeared with it. When the insects visit a flower for nectar, they infect it with the bacteria. The bacteria spread rapidly through the plant tissue in warm (65°F or higher), humid weather. Insects visiting these infected blossoms carry bacteria-laden nectar to healthy blossoms. Tender or damaged leaves may be infected in midsummer.

Solution: During spring and mid- to late summer, prune infected branches 12 to 15 inches beyond any visible discoloration and destroy them. Disinfect pruning shears after each cut. A protective spray of a bactericide containing basic copper sulfate or *streptomycin* applied before bud-break in the spring will help prevent infection. Repeat at intervals of 5 to 7 days until the end of bloom. In the fall, prune any remaining infected branches.

PYRACANTHA (continued)

QUERCUS (Oak)

Hawthorn lace bugs

Damage. Inset: Hawthorn lace bugs (½ life size).

Problem: The upper surfaces of leaves are mottled or speckled gray and green. Mottling may be confused with mite or leafhopper damage. It can be distinguished from other insect damage by the black, shiny, hard droplets found on the undersides of damaged leaves. Small (⅛-inch), spiny, wingless insects or brownish insects with clear, lacy wings may be visible around the droplets and next to the midrib. The plant is usually stunted. Damage occurs in spring and summer.

Analysis: The hawthorn lace bug (*Corythucha cydoniae*) is found on hawthorn, cotoneaster, and fruiting quince as well as pyracantha. It spends the winter as an adult on the host plant in bark crevices, branch crotches, or other protected areas. When growth begins in spring, the adults attach their eggs to the undersides of leaves with a brown, sticky substance. The eggs hatch, and the brown, lace-winged insects suck sap from the undersides of leaves. The chlorophyll disappears, resulting in the characteristic gray and green mottling. As lace bugs feed, droplets of brown excrement accumulate around them. Damage is unsightly, and food production by the leaf is reduced, resulting in a loss of plant vigor.

Solution: Spray with Ortho® Orthenex® Garden Insect & Disease Control or Ortho® Systemic Insect Killer when damage first appears in the spring. Thoroughly cover the undersides of the leaves where insects feed. Repeat 7 to 10 days later. A third application may be necessary if the plant becomes reinfested in the summer.

Oak anthracnose

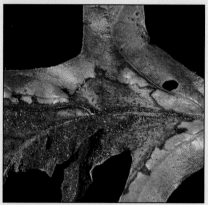

Oak anthracnose.

Problem: Brown, dead spots appear along the veins in the spring and expand outward to the leaf edges. Leaves become curled, puckered, and twisted. In wet seasons, many leaves may fall. Leaves on the lower branches are generally more severely infected. Small sunken areas may form on twigs; the twigs may die.

Analysis: Oak anthracnose, a plant disease also called *twig blight* in California, is caused by a fungus (*Apiognomonia quercina*) that infects the leaves of white oaks and, in California, live oak. The fungus spends the winter on fallen leaves or in sunken cankers on twigs in the tree. During rainy weather, spores are blown and splashed onto young leaves. Dead spots develop where the fungus enters the tissue. The spots enlarge, and the leaves become puckered and twisted. When moist weather continues into summer, the fungus may kill the leaves, causing severe defoliation. The fungus may also enter twigs, causing canker and twig dieback.

Solution: Rake and destroy fallen leaves and twigs. Prune diseased and dead branches. If the following spring is wet, spray young trees and valuable specimens with Ortho® Garden Disease Control when the leaf buds are opening.

Oak leaf blister

Oak leaf blister.

Problem: Puckered, circular areas, up to ½ inch in diameter, appear on the leaves in the spring. The blisterlike spots are yellowish green at first and later die and turn brown. Leaves usually remain attached to the tree.

Analysis: Oak leaf blister is caused by a fungus (*Taphrina caerulescens*) that is unsightly but rarely harms the tree. It is a problem on various species of oak, particularly red, black, scarlet, and live oaks. The fungus spends the winter in the bud scales on the tree. During cool, wet spring weather, it enters the developing leaves. Green blisters form where the fungus enters the tissue. The infected tissue eventually dies and turns brown. In the fall, the fungus produces overwintering spores. If the following spring is cool and wet, the cycle begins again.

Solution: If leaf blister was a problem the previous year and if this year the spring is cool and wet, spray the tree with Ortho® Garden Disease Control when the buds begin to swell, about one or two weeks before the leaves appear. Cover the entire tree thoroughly with the spray.

Borers

Borer larva and holes.

Problem: Foliage on a branch or at the top of the tree is sparse; eventually the twigs and branches die. Holes or tunnels are apparent in the trunk or branches. The bark may die over the tunnels and slough off, revealing trails. Sap or a sawdustlike material sometimes surrounds the holes. Weakened branches may break during storms. Weak, young, or newly transplanted trees are more susceptible to injury and may be killed.

Analysis: Borers are the larvae of beetles or moths. Several kinds of borers attack oaks. Throughout the summer, females lay their eggs in bark crevices. The larvae feed on the bark, sapwood, and heartwood. This stops the flow of nutrients and water in that area by severing the water-conducting vessels; branch and twig dieback results. Sap flow acts as a defense against borers if the tree is healthy; the borer burrows into the wood, and tree sap fills the hole and kills the insect. Factors that weaken the tree—such as mechanical injuries, transplanting, damage by leaf-feeding insects, and poor growing conditions—make it more attractive to egg-laying females.

Solution: Borers are difficult to control once they have burrowed into the wood. Cut out and destroy all dead and dying branches, and remove severely infected young trees. Spray the trunk and branches with an insecticide containing *carbaryl* or *permethrin* in May. Repeat the spray two weeks later and again in July and August. Maintain plant vigor by watering during periods of drought and fertilizing regularly.

Twig pruners and twig girdlers

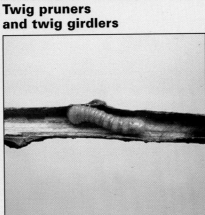

Oak twig pruner (2× life size).

Problem: Small, cleanly cut twigs, ¼ to 2 inches in diameter, lie under the tree in the fall. The tree is often abnormally bushy. Small (up to 1-inch) whitish larvae may be inside the fallen twigs.

Analysis: Several species of wood-boring beetles cause unsightly damage to oaks by altering the natural form of the tree. In midsummer to fall, these wood-boring beetles lay their eggs inside of small twigs. The twig pruner larvae tunnel toward the base of the twigs, eating all but the outer bark. In the fall, they back into the hollowed-out twig. High winds cause the nearly severed twigs containing the larvae to break and drop to the ground. With twig girdlers, adults damage the twigs. After laying their eggs, the adults chew a circle around the outside of the twigs. Girdled twigs die and break off. The eggs in the fallen twig are then able to develop without being hindered by the flow of tree sap through the twig. Both twig pruner and twig girdler larvae mature in the twigs on the ground. The damage to the tree is the result of excessive pruning on the branch tips. Several new side shoots develop where the twigs break off, causing abnormal bushiness and an unnatural shape.

Solution: Gather and destroy all severed twigs in late fall when the insects are inside. This method is quite effective where it is possible to gather all twigs from under the affected trees. Chemical sprays are not effective for control.

Leaf-feeding caterpillars

Gypsy moth caterpillar (2× life size).

Problem: The surface of the leaf is eaten, giving the remaining tissue a lacy appearance, or the whole leaf is chewed. Sometimes the leaves are webbed together. The tree may be completely defoliated. Damage appears anytime between spring and fall. Caterpillars are feeding on the leaves. Repeated heavy infestations may weaken or kill trees.

Analysis: Many species of caterpillars feed on oak leaves wherever the trees are grown. Depending on the species, the moths lay their eggs from early spring to midsummer. Larvae that hatch from these eggs feed singly or in groups on buds, on one leaf surface (these are called *skeletonizers*), or on the entire leaf. Certain caterpillars web the leaves together as they feed. In some years, damage is minimal because of unfavorable environmental conditions or control by predators and parasites. When conditions are favorable, however, entire trees may be defoliated by late summer, which weakens trees because no leaves are left to produce food. When heavy infestations occur several years in a row, branches or entire trees may be killed.

Solution: Spray with Ortho® Systemic Insect Killer, Ortho® Bug-B-Gon® Multi-Purpose Insect Killer Concentrate, or the bacterial insecticide *Bacillus thuringiensis* (Bt). Repeat the spray if the tree becomes reinfested with caterpillars.

QUERCUS (Oak) *(continued)*

Pit scales

Oak pit scales (3× life size).

Problem: During the summer or early fall, leaves turn brown and twigs or branches die back. Dead leaves usually remain attached to the branches throughout the winter. In the spring, new leaves may appear three weeks late on infested deciduous oaks. Repeated heavy infestations often kill young trees. Small (1/12-inch), somewhat flattened, green, golden, or brown scaly bumps cluster on the twigs and branches. The bark is pitted where these insects cluster.

Analysis: Several species of pit scales (*Asterolecanium* species) may seriously damage oaks. The scales lay their eggs in spring and summer. The young scales, called *crawlers*, hatch from these eggs and settle on new growth and the previous year's branches, not far from the parent. The small (1/16-inch), soft-bodied young feed by inserting their mouthparts and sucking sap from the plant. Pits develop where the scales feed. The legs atrophy, and a hard, crusty shell develops over the body. Mature female scales lay eggs underneath their shells. Several other types of scales also infest oak. (For more information on scales, see pages 444 to 447.)

Solution: Spray with Ortho® Systemic Insect Killer in mid-May to June when the young are active. To control overwintering insects, spray with Ortho® Volck® Oil Spray in winter or spring.

Oak wilt

Oak wilt.

Damaged tree.

Problem: The leaves on one or more branches wilt, turn bronze, and then fall prematurely. Infected trees of the red or live oak group may die within a few weeks. Infected trees of the white oak group may die within a few weeks or may die slowly over a period of two to three years. If an affected branch is cut off, a brown discoloration or ring is sometimes seen in the wood just beneath the bark. In the spring, the bark of an infected tree may rupture, exposing mats of fungus.

Analysis: Oak wilt is a plant disease caused by a fungus (*Ceratocystis fagacearum*) that is spread from tree to tree by insects, grafted (intertwined) roots, and tools. Sap-feeding beetles and other insects become coated with the sticky spores formed under ruptured bark and carry them to fresh wounds on healthy trees in the spring. The fungus spreads through the water-conducting vessels in the wood, causing discoloration and plugging. The leaves wilt, and the branches—or the entire tree—dies. Bark-feeding beetles, which feed on dying trees, may spread the disease long distances in some areas. This is a serious and spreading problem in the central and plains states in the United States, killing many valuable forest and landscape oak trees.

Solution: Remove infected trees, being careful not to damage nearby healthy ones. It is best to destroy the wood by burning or burying if possible. If the wood is to be saved, peel off and destroy the bark and split the wood immediately. To prevent the spread of the disease through root grafts of closely planted infected and healthy trees, cut a trench midway between the trees 3 feet deep and extending beyond the spread of the branches. Arborists can inject infected trees with a fungicide that prevents symptoms, but it does not keep the tree from infecting others. Prune trees in winter when the fungus is less active, sterilizing tools after each cut.

Armillaria root rot

Cankers.

Fungal mats.

Leaf galls

Leaf gall on azalea.

Problem: Leaves are stunted and yellow, and the foliage throughout the tree may be sparse. Branches eventually die. Weakened trees are most severely infected. Occasionally trees die suddenly without showing symptoms, but in most cases they die slowly over a period of several years. Honey-colored mushrooms, 2 to 5 inches in diameter, may grow singly or in clusters during the fall or winter on the lower trunk or on the ground near infected roots. If the soil is removed from around the base of the tree, black rootlike strands about the diameter of pencil lead are attached to the larger roots. A white fan-shaped growth occurs between the bark and wood of these larger roots and on the trunk just below the soil surface. The infected tissue has a mushroom odor.

Analysis: Armillaria root rot, a plant disease also called *oak root fungus* or *shoestring root rot*, is caused by a fungus (*Armillaria mellea*) that rots the roots of many woody and nonwoody plants. Oaks are often lightly infected with this fungus for years with no damage. When the trees are under stress from drought, overwatering, physical injury, insects, or disease, however, they often succumb to *Armillaria*. The fungus is spread short distances (under a foot) through the soil by the rootlike fungal strands. When they contact susceptible plant roots, the strands penetrate the host if conditions are favorable. Once the fungus enters the bark tissue, it produces a white fan-shaped mat of fungal strands that invade and decay the tissue of the roots and lower trunk. The fungus spreads rapidly if the oak tree is in a weakened state. Water and nutrient uptake by the roots is inhibited, causing the foliage and branches to die. In the fall, mushrooms—the reproductive bodies of the fungus—often appear around infected trees. A closely related fungus (*Clitocybe tabescens*) found in the Southeast produces symptoms on oak similar to armillaria root rot.

Solution: Remove and destroy infected trees, including the stump and the root system. The fungus can live on the stump and roots for many years, infecting susceptible plants nearby. Healthy-appearing plants growing adjacent to diseased trees may already be infected. Check around the roots and lower stems for signs of the fungus. The life of a tree may be prolonged if it is not severely infected. Remove the soil from around the rotted parts of the roots and trunk. Cut out the diseased tissue down to healthy wood and allow the healthy wood to air-dry through the summer. Deep-watering is recommended if the tree needs water. Avoid surface watering, especially wetting of the crown and trunk root area. Cover the exposed parts before temperatures drop below freezing. When replacing trees that have been infected with *Armillaria*, use resistant plants. Avoid planting susceptible species in recently cleared forests where armillaria root rot is common. To inhibit disease development in an established oak tree, provide optimum growing conditions, avoid injuring the tree, and control pests and diseases.

Problem: Developing leaves and flowers are thickened, fleshy, and distorted. Initially the thickenings are light green. As the thickenings enlarge, they become white or pink and develop a powdery appearance as the light green tissue splits away. Later in the growing season, the distorted leaves turn dark and hard. This problem is most severe in spring, during cool, moist weather, and where plants are growing in areas of poor air circulation or full shade.

Analysis: Leaf gall is a plant disease caused by a fungus (*Exobasidium vaccinii*). It is most common on azaleas but sometimes occurs on rhododendrons. As the buds open in spring, fungal spores blown by wind to the plant or washed by rain from the bark enter the tissue. The spores need moisture to germinate. Plants grown in areas of poor air movement or in deep shade, where moisture levels are high, usually have more galls than other plants. After infection takes place, a growth-promoting substance is triggered in the plant, causing the thickening and distortion. By midsummer the white, powdery fungal spores cover the distorted leaves.

Solution: Fungicides are seldom needed in home plantings. Remove galls by hand before they become white and powdery. This prevents new infections. If the galls aren't removed and destroyed, the disease will be more severe the following year. Provide air circulation, and avoid planting azaleas in deep shade.

RHODODENDRON (Azalea) *(continued)*

Lace bugs

Lace bug damage on rhododendron.

Problem: The upper sides of leaves are mottled or speckled yellow and green. The mottling may be confused with mite or leafhopper damage. It can be distinguished from other insect damage by hard, black, shiny droplets found on the undersides of damaged leaves. Small (⅛-inch), spiny, wingless insects or brownish insects with clear lacy wings may be seen around the droplets. Plant growth is usually stunted. Damage occurs in spring and summer.

Analysis: Populations of lace bugs (*Stephanitis* species) are highest when rhododendrons and azaleas are grown in sunny rather than shady locations. The wingless, immature insects and the lacy-winged adults suck sap from undersides of leaves. As they feed, droplets of black excrement accumulate. Damage is unsightly, and food production by the leaf is reduced, making the plant less vigorous.

Solution: Spray with Ortho® Orthenex® Garden Insect & Disease Control, Ortho® Systemic Insect Killer, or Ortho® Rose & Flower Insect Killer when damage first appears. Cover the undersurfaces of leaves thoroughly. Repeat 7 to 10 days later. A third application may be necessary if plants become reinfested. It is important to spray early to prevent as much damage as possible.

Spider mites

Spider mite (20× life size).

Problem: Leaves are stippled yellow or bronze and are dirty. A silken webbing may be on the lower surfaces of the leaves. Leaves may be distorted. Injured leaves may remain on the plant for more than one growing season. To determine if a plant is infested with spider mites, examine the bottoms of the leaves with a hand lens. Or hold a sheet of white paper underneath an affected leaf or branch and tap sharply. Minute specks the size of pepper grains will drop to the paper and begin to crawl.

Analysis: Spider mites are major pests of many garden plants. They cause damage by sucking sap from buds and the undersides of leaves. As a result of their feeding, the plant's chlorophyll disappears, producing the stippled appearance. Spider mite webbing traps cast-off skins and debris, making the plant dirty. The southern red mite (*Oligonychus ilicis*) is most prolific in cooler weather. It feeds and reproduces primarily during spring and fall. Other spider mites found on rhododendron develop rapidly in dry weather with temperatures of 70°F and higher; by midsummer, they have built to tremendous numbers.

Solution: Spray with Ortho® Systemic Insect Killer or Ortho® Rose & Flower Insect Killer when damage first appears. Spray the undersides of leaves. Repeat application if plant becomes reinfested. It is important to apply control measures early in the season when damage first appears. Hose down plants frequently to knock off webs and mites.

Leaf spot

Leaf spots on rhododendron.

Problem: Spots and blotches appear on the leaves. The spots may be yellow, red, tan, gray, or brown. They range in size from barely visible to ¾ inch in diameter. Several spots may join to form blotches. Leaves may be yellow and dying. Some leaves may drop. Leaf spotting is most severe during warm, humid weather conditions.

Analysis: Several fungi cause leaf spot on rhododendron. The spotting is unsightly but rarely harms the plant. Plants weakened by low temperatures, drought, and wind exposure are most susceptible to invasion by leaf spot fungi. The fungi are spread by wind and splashing water. Spots develop where the fungi enter the tissue. If wet or humid weather persists, the fungi spread through the tissue and blotches form. They survive the winter on the leaves and twigs. Most leaf spot organisms do their greatest damage in mild weather (50° to 85°F).

Solution: Once leaves become spotted, they will remain so. Where practical, remove infected leaves from the plant. Collect and destroy any fallen leaves. Spray with a fungicide containing a spreader-sticker and *chlorothalonil* or *mancozeb* when new growth begins in the spring. Repeat twice at intervals of two weeks, or for as long as the weather remains favorable for infection. To reduce plant susceptibility, provide windbreaks and protection from low temperatures. Water during dry periods, but avoid getting the leaves wet. Avoid wounding the plants.

Iron deficiency

Iron deficiency on rhododendron.

Problem: Leaves are pale green to yellow. Newest leaves may be completely yellow, with only veins and the tissue right next to the veins remaining green. With progressively older leaves, only the leaf edges may be yellowing. The plant may be stunted.

Analysis: Iron deficiency is a common problem in acid-loving plants such as azalea and rhododendron. These plants prefer soil with a pH between 5.0 and 6.0. (For more information on soil acidity, see page 406.) The soil is seldom deficient in iron, but iron is often found in an insoluble form that is not available to the plant, especially in soil with a pH above 7.0. A high soil pH can result from overliming or from lime leached from concrete or brick. Regions where soil is derived from limestone or where rainfall is low also have high-pH soils. Plants use iron in the formation of chlorophyll in leaves. When iron is lacking, new leaves are yellow.

Solution: Spray the foliage with a chelated iron fertilizer, and apply the fertilizer to the soil around the plant to correct the iron deficiency. Correct the pH of the soil by treating it with aluminum sulfate and watering it well. Maintain an acid pH by fertilizing with Osmocote® Azalea, Camellia, Rhododendron Slow Release Plant Food. When planting azalea or rhododendron, add enough peat moss to make up at least 50 percent of the amended soil. This is especially important if you live in an area where the soil is alkaline. Never lime the soil around azalea or rhododendron.

Salt burn

Salt burn.

Problem: Leaf edges are brown and dead. Browning usually occurs on older leaves first. This distinguishes the problem from wind burn, which develops on young, exposed leaves first. Leaves may be lighter green than normal. In severe cases, leaves drop.

Analysis: Salt burn is most common in areas of low rainfall. It also occurs in soils with poor drainage and where too much fertilizer has been applied. Excess salts dissolved in the soil water accumulate in leaf edges, where salts kill the tissue. These salts also interfere with water uptake by the plant. This problem is rare in areas of high rainfall, where the soluble salts are leached from most soils. Poorly drained soils don't leach well; much of the applied water runs off the surface instead of washing through the soil. Fertilizers, which are soluble salts, also cause salt burn if too much is applied or if they aren't diluted with a thorough watering after application.

Solution: Salt burn damage doesn't disappear from the leaves, but injury can be avoided in the future. In areas of low rainfall, leach accumulated salts from the soil with an occasional heavy irrigation (about once a month). If possible, improve drainage around the plants by removing them and adding soil amendments. If plants are severely damaged, replace them with healthy plants. Follow package directions when using commercial fertilizers; water thoroughly after application. Avoid the use of bagged cow manure, which may contain large amounts of salt, on azalea and rhododendron.

Sunburn

Sunburn on azalea.

Problem: During warm, sunny weather, the center portion of the leaf bleaches to a tan or off-white color. Once the initial damage has occurred, the spot rarely increases in size. Injury is generally more severe on plants with light-colored flowers.

Analysis: Rhododendrons and azaleas are generally classified as shade plants. Their leaves are sensitive to the heat of direct sun, which kills leaf tissue. Scalding occurs when the shrub is planted in full sun. The intense reflection from a light-colored, south-facing wall can also scald leaves. Damage appears in only one hot summer day. Injury is unsightly but doesn't kill the plant. Weakened leaves are more susceptible to invasion by fungi and bacteria, however. Plants that don't receive enough water are more susceptible to sunscald.

Solution: Provide some shade where the plant is growing, or move the injured plant to a shady location. Scalded leaves will not recover. Where practical, remove affected leaves. Don't let plants dry out during hot weather.

RHODODENDRON (Azalea) *(continued)*

Windburn and winter injury

Winter injury on rhododendron.

Problem: Young and exposed leaves are brown and dry, especially around the leaf margins and near the tips. The shrub is planted in a windy location or is growing in a climate where cold, dry, windy days are common. The soil may be frozen or dry.

Analysis: Windburn and winter injury on rhododendron and azalea leaves are common on plants growing in windswept locations. In cold climates, where temperatures commonly fall below freezing, strong winds cause leaves to lose their moisture more rapidly than it can be replaced by the root system. The leaf edges dry out and die. This is most pronounced when water is unavailable because the soil is frozen. Leaf burning also occurs on exceptionally windy, dry days in summer.

Solution: Once leaf edges have been damaged, the injury remains. Where practical, pick off damaged leaves. To prevent winter injury and windburn, plant shrubs in locations protected from wind, or provide windbreaks. Fertilize plants regularly with Osmocote® Azalea, Camellia, Rhododendron Slow Release Plant Food to maintain health and vigor. Water in late fall or winter, if necessary, to ensure adequate soil moisture. One or more applications of an antidesiccant spray beginning in late fall may reduce damage. Mulch plants after they are dormant to reduce the depth of frost penetration into the soil.

Dieback

Dieback on rhododendron.

Problem: The leaves and terminal portion of a branch are permanently wilted and dying. Leaves may turn reddish brown and remain attached to the plant, or they may be rolled and have spots that look water-soaked. Sunken, brownish, dead areas are often at the base of the wilted branch. Older branches are generally affected. In hot weather, the entire plant may die.

Analysis: Dieback is caused by several different fungi. Splashing water and rain, infected soil, and tools spread the fungi. They enter the plant through wounds, through dead and dying twigs, and through the leaves. A sunken dead area, or canker, usually develops on the twigs or branches, cutting off the flow of nutrients and water on that side of the plant. Leaves and stems above the canker wilt and die. With some fungi, no canker develops. Instead, the fungus is carried through water-conducting tissue, producing toxins and plugging the tissue, which causes the leaves and branch tips to wilt and die. Plants under stress from hot weather die more rapidly.

Solution: Once the branch is wilted and dying, no chemical can control the disease. Prune out and destroy all wilted or cankered branches by cutting into healthy tissue a few inches below the canker. Those plants in which infection started at the leaves with water-soaked spots can be protected with a spray the following year. Spray with a basic copper sulfate fungicide after blooming. Repeat twice more at intervals of 14 days.

Wilt and root rot

Phytophthora root rot.

Problem: The young leaves are yellowish and wilting. Eventually the whole plant wilts and dies. Dead leaves remain attached to the plant and are rolled along the midrib. The symptoms may develop over a few weeks or may take many months. Heavy, poorly drained soil favors disease development. The tissue under the bark close to ground level reveals a dark discoloration when cut. To check for discoloration, peel back the bark at the bottom of the plant. A distinct margin separates white, healthy wood from dark, diseased wood.

Analysis: Wilt and root rot are plant diseases caused by several different soil-inhabiting fungi. These fungi (*Phytophthora* and *Pythium* species) attack a wide variety of ornamental plants. The fungi destroy the roots and may work their way up the stem. If they girdle the stem, the plant wilts and dies. Very wet conditions promote the fungi, which are most common in heavy, poorly drained soils. Although azaleas and rhododendrons need constant moisture, they must also have good drainage.

Solution: Stop the spread of the disease by drenching the soil with a fungicide containing *metalaxyl, fosetyl aluminum,* or *etridiazole*. Alternatively, dry the plant out. (For information on this technique, see page 419.) Improve the drainage of the soil before replanting azaleas or rhododendrons in the same location. If drainage can't be improved, plant in beds raised a foot or more above grade. Or plant shrubs that are resistant to wilt and root rot. (For a list, see page 536.)

Root weevils

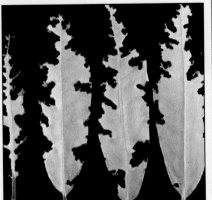

Notching caused by root weevils.

Problem: The leaf margins are scalloped or notched. The leaves may be green and healthy, or they may be yellowing and curled. To determine if a plant is infested with this insect, inspect the foliage after dark, using a flashlight. Black or grayish insects, ⅕ to ⅖ inches long, with elephant-like snouts and with rows of tiny round depressions on their backs, are feeding on leaf edges. These insects are present from May or June to as late as September.

Analysis: Root weevils are common pests of many garden plants. The adult weevils feed at night, notching leaf margins. This feeding detracts from the appearance of the plant but rarely causes serious injury. Severe damage and death of the plant may result from larvae feeding on roots if the weevils are left uncontrolled. The grubs feed unseen on the roots in the spring and from mid- or late summer into fall.

Solution: To control adults, spray the foliage and the ground under the plant with Ortho® Systemic Insect Killer when notching first appears in May or June. Check your plants periodically for notched leaves. Repeat the spray twice more at intervals of three weeks.

Scales

Azalea bark scale (life size).

Problem: Clusters of somewhat flattened white, yellowish, brown, reddish, or gray scaly bumps cover the undersides of leaves, the young branches, or the branch crotches. The bumps can be scraped or picked off; the undersides are usually soft. Leaves may turn yellow and drop off, and branches may die back. The plant is killed when infestations are heavy.

Analysis: Many species of scales infest rhododendrons and azaleas throughout the United States. Scales spend the winter on the trunk and twigs of the plant. They lay eggs in spring and in midsummer; the young scales, called *crawlers*, settle on various parts of the shrub. The small (1/10-inch), soft-bodied young feed by inserting their mouthparts and sucking sap from the plant. The legs usually atrophy, and a scaly or crusty shell develops over the body. Mature female scales lay their eggs underneath their shell. Leaf drop and twig dieback occur when scales completely cover the leaves and branches. An uncontrolled infestation may kill a plant after two or three seasons. (For information on scales, see pages 444 to 447.)

Solution: Spray with Ortho® Systemic Insect Killer or Ortho® Rose & Flower Insect Killer in midsummer (late spring in the South) when the young are active. Early the following spring, before new growth begins, spray the branches and trunk with a dormant oil spray to control overwintering insects.

Flower thrips

Flower thrips damage.

Problem: Young leaves are distorted, and foliage may be flecked with yellow. Flower buds are deformed and usually fail to open. The petals of open blossoms, especially those of white or light-colored varieties, are often covered with brown streaks and red spots. If a deformed or streaked flower is pulled apart and shaken over white paper, tiny yellow or brown insects fall out and are easily seen against a white background.

Analysis: Flower thrips (*Frankliniella tritici*) are the most abundant and widely distributed thrips in the country. They live inside the buds and flowers of many garden plants. Both the immature and the adult thrips feed on plant sap by rasping the tissue. The injured petal tissue turns brown, and the young expanding leaves become deformed. Injured flower buds usually fail to open. Thrips initially breed on grasses and weeds. When these plants begin to dry up or are harvested, the insects migrate to succulent, green ornamental plants. The adults lay their eggs by inserting them into the plant tissue. A complete life cycle may occur in two weeks, so populations can build up rapidly. Most damage to roses occurs in early summer.

Solution: Thrips are difficult to control because they continuously migrate to roses from other plants. Immediately remove and destroy infested buds and blooms. Spray with Ortho® Systemic Insect Killer or Ortho® Bug-B-Gon® Multi-Purpose Insect Killer Ready-Spray® three times at intervals of 7 to 10 days.

ROSA (Rose) (continued)

Few or no blooms

Lack of flowers caused by poor pruning.

Failure to bloom.

Black spot

Black spot.

Problem: Plants fail to bloom or bloom only sparsely.

Problem: Circular black spots with fringed margins appear on the upper surfaces of the leaves in the spring. The tissue around the spots or the entire leaf may turn yellow, and the infected leaves may drop prematurely. Severely infected plants may lose all of their leaves by midsummer. Flower production is often reduced, and quality is poor.

Analysis:

1. Too much shade: Roses grow best in full sun. They need at least four to five hours of direct sunlight for normal blooming.

2. Improper dormant pruning: Most rose varieties are grafted onto a rootstock. Tree roses and some climbing roses are grafted onto an intermediate trunkstock. If the hybrid canes are pruned below the bud union, the rootstock or trunkstock will produce suckers that are flowerless or that produce flowers very different from the desired variety. Some climbing roses and many old-fashioned roses bloom from flower buds formed the previous season. Heavy pruning will remove all the buds.

3. Excessive or improper pruning during the growing season: If roses are excessively trimmed and pruned during the growing season, many developing flower buds may be inadvertently removed.

4. Old flowers left on plant: Roses do not produce as many new flowers when old blooms are allowed to fade and form seeds.

5. Flushes of bloom: Many roses bloom in flushes. The first flush usually occurs in late spring, and the second flush occurs in late summer or early fall.

6. Diseased or infested plants: Roses that have been attacked by diseases or insects don't flower well.

Solution:

1. Thin out shading trees and shrubs, or transplant roses to a sunnier location. Replace them with shade-loving plants.

2. Don't prune roses below the bud union. Take special care when pruning climbing roses and standard tree roses since the bud union between the trunkstock and the grafted variety may be several feet from the ground. Prune old-fashioned roses lightly during the dormant season. If heavy pruning is needed, wait until after the plants have bloomed in spring.

3. During the growing season, prune roses only to shape them or to remove suckers and dead or dying growth. When cutting flowers, leave at least two 5-leaflet leaves on the cane to ensure continued flowering.

4. Remove flowers as they begin to fade.

5. You can't do anything to alter flushes; this is a natural plant cycle.

6. Look up the symptoms beginning on page 263 to determine the cause. Treat accordingly.

Analysis: Black spot is caused by a fungus (*Diplocarpon rosae*) that is a severe problem in areas where high humidity or rain is common in spring and summer. The fungus spends the winter on infected leaves and canes. The spores are spread from plant to plant by splashing water and rain. The fungus enters the tissue, forming spots the size of a pinhead. The black spots enlarge, up to ¾ inch, as the fungus spreads; spots may join to form blotches. Twigs may also be infected. Plants are often killed by repeated infection.

Solution: Spray with Ortho® RosePride® Rose & Shrub Disease Control or Ortho® Orthenex® Garden Insect & Disease Control. Repeat the treatment at intervals of 7 to 10 days for as long as the weather remains wet. Spraying may be omitted during hot, dry spells in summer. Prune infected canes. Avoid overhead watering. In the fall, rake up and destroy the fallen leaves. After pruning plants during the dormant season, spray with a lime-sulfur solution. The following spring, when new growth starts, begin the spray program again. Plant resistant varieties. (For a list, see page 541.)

Powdery mildew

Powdery mildew.

Problem: Young leaves, young twigs, and flower buds are covered with a thin layer of powdery grayish-white material. Infected leaves may be distorted and curled, and many may turn yellow or purplish and drop off. New growth is often stunted, and young canes may be killed. Badly infected flower buds don't open properly. In late summer, tiny black dots (spore-producing bodies) may be scattered over the powdery covering like ground pepper.

Analysis: Powdery mildew is a common plant disease caused by a fungus (*Sphaerotheca pannosa* var. *rosae*). It is one of the most widespread and serious diseases of roses. The powdery covering consists of fungal strands and spores. The spores are spread by the wind to healthy plants. The fungus depletes plant nutrients, causing distortion, discoloration, and often death of the leaves and canes. Powdery mildew may occur on roses any time during the growing season when rainfall is low or absent, temperatures are 70° to 80°F, nighttime relative humidity is high, and daytime relative humidity is low. In areas where there is high rainfall in spring and summer, control may not be needed until the drier months of late summer. Rose varieties differ in their susceptibility to powdery mildew.

Solution: Apply Ortho® RosePride® Rose & Shrub Disease Control or Ortho® Orthenex® Garden Insect & Disease Control at the first sign of mildew. Repeat sprays at intervals of 7 to 10 days if mildew reappears. Rake up and destroy leaves in the fall.

Rust

Rust.

Problem: Yellow to brown spots, up to ¼ inch in diameter, appear on the upper surfaces of leaves, starting in the spring or late fall. The lower leaves are affected first. On the undersides of leaves are spots or blotches containing a red, orange, or black powdery material that can be scraped off. Infected leaves may become twisted and dry and drop off the plant, or they may remain attached. Twigs may also be infected. Severely infected plants lack vigor.

Analysis: Rose rust is caused by any of several species of fungi (*Phragmidium* species) that infest only rose plants. Rose varieties differ in their susceptibility to rust. Wind spreads the orange fungal spores to rose leaves. With moisture (rain, dew, or fog) and moderate temperatures (55° to 75°F), the spores enter the tissue on the undersides of leaves. Spots develop directly above, on the upper surfaces. In the fall, black spores develop in the spots. These spores can survive the winter on dead leaves. In spring, the fungus produces the spores that cause new infections. Rust may also infect and damage young twigs.

Solution: At the first sign of rust, pick off and destroy the infected leaves and spray with Ortho® RosePride® Rose & Shrub Disease Control or Ortho® Orthenex® Garden Insect & Disease Control. Repeat at intervals of 7 to 14 days for as long as conditions remain favorable for infection. Rake up and destroy infected leaves in the fall. Prune and destroy infected twigs. Apply a lime-sulfur solution during the dormant season. Plant resistant varieties.

Spider mites

Spider mite damage and webbing.

Problem: Leaves are stippled, bronzed, and dirty. A silken webbing may be on the lower surfaces of the leaves or on new growth. Infested leaves often turn brown, curl, and drop off. New leaves may be distorted. Plants are usually weak and of poor quality. To determine if a plant is infested with mites, examine the bottoms of the leaves with a hand lens. Or hold a sheet of white paper underneath an affected leaf and tap the leaf sharply. Minute specks the size of pepper grains will drop to the paper and begin to crawl. The pests are easily seen against the white background.

Analysis: Spider mites, related to spiders, are major pests of many garden and greenhouse plants. They cause damage by sucking sap from the undersides of leaves. As a result of their feeding, the plant's chlorophyll disappears, producing the stippled appearance. Spider mite webbing traps cast-off skins and debris, making the plant look dirty. Many leaves may drop off. Severely infested plants produce few flowers. Mites are active throughout the growing season but are favored by hot, dry weather (70°F and higher). By midsummer, they have built up to tremendous numbers. (For more information on spider mites, see page 457.)

Solution: Spray with Ortho® Orthenex® Garden Insect & Disease Control or Ortho® Systemic Insect Killer when damage is first noticed. Cover the undersides of the leaves thoroughly. Repeat the application twice more at intervals of 7 to 10 days.

ROSA (Rose) *(continued)*

Viruses

Virus disease.

Problem: Yellow or brown rings, or yellow splotches of various sizes, appear on the leaves. The uninfected portions remain dark green. New leaves may be puckered and curling; flower buds may be malformed. Sometimes there are brown rings on the canes. The plants are usually stunted.

Analysis: Several viruses infect roses. The viruses are transmitted when an infected plant is grafted or budded to a healthy one. This generally occurs in the nursery where the plant is grown. Some plants may show symptoms only on a few leaves. The virus is throughout the plant, however, and further symptoms may appear later. Most rose viruses are fairly harmless unless there is extensive yellowing or browning. The virus suppresses the development of chlorophyll, causing the splotches or rings. Food production is reduced, which may result in stunted plant growth.

Solution: No cure is available for virus-infected plants. Rose viruses rarely spread naturally; remove only weak plants. When purchasing rose bushes, buy healthy plants from a reputable dealer. (For information on selecting plants, see page 415.)

Rose aphids

Rose aphids (8× life size).

Problem: Tiny (⅛-inch), green or pink, soft-bodied insects cluster on leaves, stems, and developing buds. When insects are numerous, flower buds are usually deformed and may fail to open properly. A shiny, sticky substance often coats the leaves. A black, sooty mold may grow on the sticky substance. Ants may be present.

Analysis: Rose aphids (*Macrosiphum rosae*) do little damage in small numbers. Plants can tolerate fairly high populations without much effect. The aphids are extremely prolific, however, and populations can rapidly build to damaging numbers during the growing season. Damage occurs when the aphid sucks the sap from the rose stems and buds. The aphid is unable to digest all the sugar in the plant sap and excretes the excess in a fluid called *honeydew*, which often drops onto the leaves below. A sooty mold fungus may develop on the honeydew, causing the rose plants to appear black and dirty. Ants feed on the sticky substance and are often present where there is an aphid infestation. When aphid populations are high, flower quality and quantity are reduced.

Solution: Spray with Ortho® Systemic Insect Killer, Ortho® Bug-B-Gon® Multi-Purpose Insect Killer Ready-To-Use, or an insecticidal soap when clusters of aphids are noticed. Repeat the treatment if the plant becomes reinfested.

Leafcutter bees

Leafcutter bee damage.

Problem: Small, precise ovals or circles are cut from the leaves. Rose twigs with broken or cut ends may die back for several inches. Hairy, black or metallic-blue, green, or purple bees are sometimes seen flying around the plant.

Analysis: Leafcutter bees (*Megachile* species) are important pollinators of plants such as alfalfa, clover, and forage crops. The females cut circular pieces of leaf tissue from rose plants to line their nests and cap their egg cells. They usually make their nests in dead rose twigs or other plant twigs that accumulate in the garden. Sometimes they nest in the ends of dying or dead rose stems still attached to the plant. Damage to rose plants is minor.

Solution: Cut out dead and dying stems. Remove dead twigs and plant debris. Leafcutter bees are pollinators, so no chemical controls should be used.

Roseslugs

Roseslug (life size).

Problem: The upper or lower surfaces of leaves are eaten between the veins; the lacy, translucent layer of tissue that remains turns brown. Later, large holes or the entire leaf, except the main vein, may be chewed. Pale green to metallic green sluglike worms, up to ¾ inch long, with large brown heads, may be found feeding on the leaves. Some have hairs covering their bodies, and others appear wet and slimy.

Analysis: Roseslugs are the larvae of black-and-yellow wasps called *sawflies*. The adult wasps appear in spring. They lay their eggs between the upper and lower surfaces of leaves along the leaf edges, with a sawlike egg-laying organ. Depending on the species of sawfly, some of the larvae that emerge exude a slimy substance, giving them a sluglike appearance. Others are hairy. The roseslugs begin feeding on one surface of the leaf tissue, skeletonizing it. Later, several species of these slugs chew holes in the leaf or devour it entirely. When they are mature, the larvae drop to the ground, burrow into the soil, and construct cells in which to pass the winter. Some roseslugs pupate, emerge as sawflies, and repeat the cycle two to six times during the growing season. Severely infested roses may be greatly weakened and produce fewer blooms.

Solution: A small number of roseslugs can be picked off by hand. For larger numbers, spray with an insecticide containing *acephate* or *carbaryl* when damage is first noticed. Repeat sprays as necessary if the rose becomes reinfested.

Scales

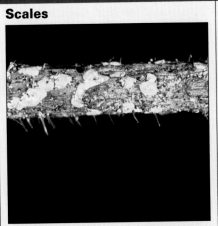

Rose scale (life size).

Problem: White, cottony masses; brown or black crusty bumps; or clusters of somewhat flattened white, yellowish, or brown scaly bumps cover the stems and leaves. The bumps can be scraped or picked off. Leaves turn yellow and may drop. In some cases, a shiny, sticky substance coats the leaves. A black, sooty mold often grows on the sticky substance. Heavy infestations kill the stems.

Analysis: Many types of scales infest roses. They lay their eggs on the leaves or canes, and in spring to midsummer the young scales, called *crawlers*, settle on the leaves and twigs. The small (¹⁄₁₀-inch), soft-bodied young feed by sucking sap from the plant. The legs usually atrophy, and with some types, a shell develops over the body. The types of scales that don't develop shells are conspicuous. Females of the cottony cushion scale are covered with a white, cottony egg sac containing up to 2,500 eggs. Scales covered with a shell are less noticeable. Their shells often blend in with the plant, and the eggs are inconspicuous beneath their coverings. Some species of scales are unable to digest all the sugar in the plant sap, and they excrete the excess in a fluid called *honeydew*. (For more information on scales, see pages 444 to 447.)

Solution: Control with Ortho® Systemic Insect Killer or Ortho® Bug-B-Gon® Multi-Purpose Insect Killer Concentrate when the young are active. To control overwintering insects, treat with Ortho® Volck® Oil Spray in the spring.

Beetles

Fuller rose beetle (4× life size).

Problem: Holes appear in the flowers and flower buds; open flowers may be entirely eaten. Affected buds often fail to open, or they open deformed. Stem tips may be chewed, or the leaves may be notched or riddled with holes. Red, green-spotted, brownish, or metallic-green beetles, up to ½ inch long, are sometimes seen on the flowers or foliage.

Analysis: Several beetles infest roses. They may destroy the ornamental value of the plant by seriously damaging the flowers and foliage. The insects usually spend the winter as larvae in the soil or as adults in plant debris on the ground. In late spring or summer, mature beetles fly to roses and feed on the flowers, buds, and sometimes leaves. Punctured flower buds usually fail to open, and flowers that do open are often devoured. Many beetles feed at night, so their damage may be all that is noticed. Female beetles lay their eggs in the soil or in flowers in late summer or fall. The emerging larvae crawl into the soil to spend the winter, or they mature and pass the winter as adults. The larvae of some beetles feed on plant roots before maturing in the fall or spring.

Solution: Spray with Ortho® Systemic Insect Killer or Ortho® Rose & Flower Insect Killer when damage is first noticed. Repeat the spray if the rose becomes reinfested.

ROSA (Rose) *(continued)*

Crown gall

Crown gall.

Problem: Large, corky galls up to several inches in diameter appear at the base of the plant and on the stems and roots. Galls are rounded, with rough, irregular surfaces, and may be dark and cracked. Plants with numerous galls are weak; growth is slowed and leaves turn yellow. Branches or the entire plant may die back. Plants with only a few galls often show no other symptoms, however.

Analysis: Crown gall is a plant disease caused by a soil-inhabiting bacterium (*Agrobacterium tumefaciens*) that infects many ornamentals and fruit trees in the garden. The bacteria are often brought to a garden initially on the stems or roots of an infected plant and are spread through soil and contaminated pruning tools. The bacteria enter the plant through wounds in the roots or the stem. They produce a compound that stimulates rapid cell growth in the plant, causing gall formation on the roots, crown, and sometimes branches. The galls may disrupt the flow of water and nutrients up the roots and stems, weakening and stunting the top of the plant. Galls do not usually cause the death of the plant.

Solution: Crown gall can't be eliminated from a plant. An infected plant may survive for many years, however. To improve its appearance, prune out and destroy galled stems. Disinfect pruning shears after each cut. Destroy severely infected plants. The bacteria will remain in the soil for two or three years. If you wish to replace the infected roses soon, select other plants that are resistant to crown gall.

Stem canker and dieback

Stem cankers.

Problem: Yellowish, reddish, or brown sunken areas develop on the canes. The sunken areas may have a purple margin, or they may be cracked. The leaves on affected canes are sometimes spotted, yellow, or wilting. Stems may die back.

Analysis: Several different fungi cause stem cankers on roses, with the *Coniothyrium* species being most common. During wet or humid weather, the fungi enter the plant at a wound caused by the thorns or at a cut stem. A canker develops and expands through the tissue in all directions. The fungus may cut off the flow of nutrients and water through the stem, causing the leaves to wilt or yellow and the twigs to die back. Rose plants that are infected with black spot (see page 264) or in a weakened condition are more susceptible to invasion by stem canker fungi.

Solution: Cut out and destroy cankered canes at least 5 inches below the infected area. Disinfect pruning tools after each cut. After pruning, spray the canes with a fungicide containing lime sulfur. Sprays aimed at controlling black spot will help control canker. Or spray with Ortho® Garden Disease Control starting in the spring. Repeat every 7 to 10 days for as long as the weather is wet or humid. Keep the plants vigorous by feeding, watering, and pruning properly.

Borers

Carpenter bee larvae (3× life size).

Problem: Several or all of the larger canes and stems wilt and die. If the bark is peeled back, or if dying stems are sliced open, white to yellowish worms or legless grubs up to ¾ inch long may be revealed. Affected stems may be swollen at the base.

Analysis: Many kinds of insects bore into rose stems, including certain sawflies, beetles, horntail wasps, and solitary bees. Some of these attack old, weakened plants or plants that are under stress from recent transplant or improper care. Borers often attack at the base of plants. Other borers attack healthy rose plants, either traveling in a spiral pattern just under the bark or burrowing down through the center of the rose stems. Most rose borers produce one generation per year.

Solution: Prune and destroy infested rose stems. Make the cut several inches below the point where the stem is wilted or swollen. If an insect has tunneled a hole through the center of the stem, keep cutting the stem lower to the ground until you find and destroy the insect or see the end of the tunnel. If this is a problem year after year, seal rose canes immediately after pruning with a thumbtack to prevent borers from penetrating the soft tissue in the center of the stem. Keep rose plants in good health.

SALIX (Willow)

Willow borers

Damaged stem. Inset: Adult (2× life size).

Problem: Swollen areas with holes in their centers develop on twigs, branches, or the trunk. Many side shoots may grow from below the swellings, destroying the tree's natural form. Leaves on infested twigs and branches turn yellow and may have chewed edges. Sawdust and many broken twigs are often found beneath the tree.

Analysis: At least five species of beetles called willow borers (*Saperda* species) feed on willows, causing galls, or swollen areas, to form. The 1-inch striped and spotted, brownish or gray beetles with long antennae appear in late spring or early summer. Females lay their eggs in small holes that they gnaw into the bark of twigs and branches that are more than ½ inch in diameter. The emerging legless, whitish grubs tunnel into the wood. Excess tissue accumulates around the wound, resulting in a gall. When infestations are severe, nearly all twigs and branches more than ½ inch in diameter have one or more galls. The galls weaken the twigs, causing them to break and litter the ground during stormy weather. The grubs remain in the wood one to two years before maturing into adults.

Solution: Remove and destroy severely damaged trees. Spray the bark of less severely damaged trees with an insecticide containing *bifenthrin* in late May or early June. Repeat the spray two weeks later.

Poplar-and-willow borers

Poplar-and-willow borer (life size).

Problem: Leaves turn yellow and holes appear in the twigs. Large quantities of sawdust cling to the bark just below the holes. Sap oozes from the holes. Young trees may be killed; older trees may lose their natural form from the growth of numerous side shoots. Small (⅜-inch), black or dark brown weevils with pale yellow spots and long snouts may be seen around the tree from midsummer until fall.

Analysis: All willows and most poplars may be attacked by the poplar-and-willow borer (*Cryptorhynchus lapathi*), also called the *mottled willow borer*. Adult weevils cause minor injury by chewing holes in the bark of twigs. The major damage is caused by the C-shape larvae, which are white with brown heads. During mid- to late summer, larvae hatch from eggs laid in holes chewed by female weevils. Larvae burrow into and feed on the inner bark. In spring, large quantities of frass (sawdust and excrement) are expelled from the holes as larvae tunnel into the center of the twigs to pupate. The feeding and tunneling cause branches to break easily and disrupt nutrient and water movement through the tree. The leaves turn yellow, and the tree often becomes bushy from the growth of numerous side shoots. Larvae pupate in June and emerge as adults in midsummer. Several other borers may also infest the trunk and branches of willows.

Solution: Remove and destroy severely infested trees or branches before early summer arrives. Spray the bark with an insecticide containing *bifenthrin* in late July or early August.

Canker and dieback

Dieback.

Problem: Dark sunken cankers appear on the twigs, branches, or trunk. Leaves on infected branches may be spotted or stunted and lighter green than normal. Twigs and branches are often killed. Young or less-vigorous trees are most susceptible.

Analysis: Several fungi cause canker and dieback on willows. A fungus enters a tree through a wound or the leaves, killing the surrounding healthy tissue. A dark sunken canker develops in the wood. If the fungus infects leaves first, it grows down through the leaf stems and forms cankers on twigs. The canker cuts off the flow of nutrients and water to the twigs or branch, causing the leaves to turn yellowish. Twig or branch dieback follows if the canker girdles the wood. The tree may stop the spreading canker by producing callus tissue, a rapid growth of barklike cells, to wall off the fungus. If the expanding canker is stopped before it covers half the diameter of the branch or trunk, the tree usually survives. The fungus may grow faster than the callus, however, or the tree may not produce a callus, resulting in the death of the branch.

Solution: When the weather is dry, prune twigs and small cankered branches, cutting at least 4 inches below the canker. Cankers on larger branches can be excised with a knife and chisel. Remove all discolored bark and wood, as well as a 1-inch border of apparently healthy bark around the wound. Disinfect the tools after each cut. Remove and destroy severely infected trees. To prevent the development of new cankers, avoid wounding trees.

SORBUS (Mountain ash)

Fire blight

Fire blight.

Problem: The blossoms and leaves of infected twigs suddenly wilt and turn black as if scorched by fire. The leaves curl and hang downward. The bark at the base of the blighted twigs becomes water-soaked, then dark, sunken, and dry; cracks may develop at the edge of the sunken area. In warm, moist spring weather drops of brown ooze appear on the sunken bark. Young trees may die.

Analysis: Fire blight is a plant disease caused by a bacterium (*Erwinia amylovora*) that is destructive to many trees and shrubs. (For a list of susceptible plants, see page 535.) Bacteria spend the winter in the sunken cankers on branches. In spring, the bacteria ooze out of the cankers. Bees, flies, and other insects are attracted to the sticky ooze. When insects visit a mountain ash flower for nectar, they infect it with the bacteria. Bacteria spread rapidly through the plant tissue in warm (65°F or higher), humid weather. Insects visiting infected blossoms later carry bacteria-laden nectar to healthy blossoms. Rain, wind, and tools may also spread the bacteria. Tender or damaged leaves may be infected in midsummer.

Solution: Prune infected branches 12 to 15 inches beyond any visible discoloration and destroy them. Disinfect pruning shears after each cut. A protective spray of a bactericide containing basic copper sulfate applied before bud-break in the spring will help prevent infection. Spray with a bactericide containing *streptomycin* during bloom. Repeat at intervals of five to seven days until the end of bloom.

Woolly aphids

Woolly apple aphid (¼ life size).

Problem: Twigs, branches, and possibly the trunk are covered with unsightly white, cottony masses. They often accumulate around wounds and pruning scars. Underneath the white masses are clusters of small (⅛-inch) purplish-brown, soft-bodied insects. Leaves and twigs are yellowing, and the tree may be stunted. A sticky substance, called *honeydew*, may coat the leaves, stems, and trunk. A black, sooty mold may develop on the sticky substance.

Analysis: Several species of woolly aphids (*Eriosoma* species) attack mountain ash. They do little damage in small numbers. They are extremely prolific, however, and populations can rapidly build to damaging numbers during the growing season. Damage occurs when the woolly aphid sucks the sap from twigs, branches, or the trunk. It is unable to digest all the sugar in the plant sap, and it excretes the excess in a fluid called *honeydew*, which often drops onto the leaves below. A sooty mold fungus may develop on the sticky substance, causing the mountain ash leaves to appear black and dirty. The woolly apple aphid (*E. lanigerum*) may also cause damage by burrowing into the soil and feeding on roots. This feeding causes marblelike knots to form and results in stunted roots. The tree is weakened, and growth is poor.

Solution: Control with Ortho® Systemic Insect Killer when damage is first noticed. Aphids protected with the white, woolly material are more difficult to control. Spray the tree thoroughly. Repeat the spray if the tree becomes reinfested.

SPIRAEA (Spirea)

Spirea aphids

Spirea aphids (2× life size).

Problem: Tiny (⅛-inch), dark green, soft-bodied insects cluster on flowers, undersides of leaves, and young shoots. Leaves are curled, yellowing, and stunted, and growth of the plant is slowed. A shiny or sticky substance may coat the leaves. A black, sooty mold often grows on the sticky substance.

Analysis: Spirea aphids (*Aphis spiraecola*) do little damage in small numbers. They are extremely prolific in the early summer, however, and populations can rapidly build to damaging numbers by late June. Damage occurs when the aphids suck the sap from the spirea leaves. The aphid is unable to digest all the sugar in the plant sap, and it excretes the excess in a fluid called *honeydew*, which often drops onto the leaves below. A sooty mold fungus may develop on the honeydew, causing the spirea leaves to appear black and dirty.

Solution: Control with Ortho® Bug-B-Gon® Multi-Purpose Insect Killer Ready-To-Use, Ortho® Systemic Insect Killer, or insecticidal soap when damage is first noticed. Spray the plant thoroughly. Repeat the spray if the plant becomes reinfested. If this aphid is an annual problem, treat with a horticultural oil spray just after the leaves fall or just before buds open in the spring.

SYRINGA (Lilac)

Powdery mildew

Powdery mildew.

Problem: The leaves are covered with a thin layer or irregular patches of a powdery grayish-white material. Infected leaves may turn yellow and drop off. New growth is often stunted. In late summer, tiny black dots (spore-producing bodies) are scattered over the white patches and resemble ground pepper.

Analysis: Powdery mildew is a common plant disease caused by a fungus (*Microsphaera alni*) that thrives in both humid and dry weather. The powdery patches consist of fungal strands and spores. The fungus depletes plant nutrients, causing yellowing and sometimes the death of the leaf. Since this mildew attacks many different kinds of trees and shrubs, the fungus from a diseased plant may infect other plants in the garden.

Solution: Spray plants with Ortho® RosePride® Rose & Shrub Disease Control when the plant shows the first sign of powdery mildew. Cover the upper and lower surfaces of leaves thoroughly. Repeat the treatment at intervals of 7 to 10 days until the mildew disappears.

Bacterial blight

Bacterial blight.

Problem: Brown spots surrounded by large areas of yellow appear on the leaves in early spring. On older leaves, spots slowly increase in size during rainy periods. The leaves are usually distorted. Immature leaves turn black and die. Infected young stems bend over at the lesion, wither, and die. Occasionally, mature stems develop spots that enlarge along the length of the stem. The leaves die within the infected area. Buds may turn dark brown and die without opening. Parts of the flower, or entire flower clusters, may become limp, turn dark brown, and die.

Analysis: Bacterial blight is caused by a bacterium (*Pseudomonas syringae*) that may seriously damage lilacs during cool, wet weather. The bacteria overwinter in lilac buds, infected twigs, and plant debris. They are spread by wind, rain, and splashing water. If there is frost while buds are swelling or shoots are just beginning growth, disease may develop. Bacteria cause spots on leaves that are olive-green at first and later turn brown surrounded by yellow. If wet weather persists, the bacteria spread through the tissue, forming blotches. Young plant parts are more severely affected. Leaves and young shoots blacken rapidly and die. Leaves die on older stems within the infected area.

Solution: Prune out and destroy blighted shoots immediately, cutting below infected tissue. If the disease has been serious, spray with a fungicide containing basic copper sulfate during dormancy and again when buds are swelling. Locate lilacs in places sheltered from frost. Plant resistant varieties.

Lilac borers

Borer damage.

Problem: Branch tips wilt in late summer, during warm, dry periods. Affected branches may die or break off. Stems near the ground are swollen and cracked. Sawdust is often found around holes in stems and on the ground below stems.

Analysis: The lilac borer (*Podosesia syringae*), also called the *ash borer*, is the larva of a brownish, clear-winged moth that resembles a wasp. Moths may be seen flying around the plant in late spring. The moths lay their eggs in cracks or bark wounds at the base of the stems. The cream-colored larvae bore into the wood and feed on the sapwood and heartwood. The stems become swollen and may break where the larvae are feeding. Their feeding also cuts off the flow of nutrients and water through the stems, causing the shoots to wilt and die. The larvae spend the winter in the stems. In the spring, they feed for a few weeks before maturing into moths. Several other borers may infest lilac.

Solution: Before the moths emerge in the spring (April to May), cut out infested stems to ground level and destroy them. In late April, spray or paint the trunks and stems with an insecticide containing *permethrin*. Repeat the treatment two more times at intervals of 7 to 10 days. For more precise spray timing, use pheromone traps to lure pests. Spray 10 days after the first male is trapped. Kill borers by inserting a flexible wire into the borer hole in early summer. Avoid pruning during the spring when moths are present. Avoid wounding the shrubs with lawn mowers.

TAXUS (Yew)

Poor soil

Yew in poorly drained soil.

Problem: Young leaves turn yellow. Eventually the entire plant may turn yellow, wilt, and die. The plant is growing in heavy, poorly drained, acidic or alkaline soil.

Analysis: Yews are particularly sensitive to improper growing conditions. When planted in soil that is heavy, poorly drained, very acidic (between pH 4.5 and 5.5), or very alkaline (above pH 7.5), the plants don't usually survive. The bark on the roots decays and sloughs off, and the roots die. The roots can no longer supply sufficient amounts of nutrients and water to the leaves, resulting in leaf yellowing and wilting. The plant usually dies within several months.

Solution: Improve the soil drainage (see page 406), or if the plant is small, move it to an area with better drainage. Check the acidity of your soil. If the pH is below 6.0, add ground limestone around the base of the plant. Add aluminum sulfate to the soil if the pH is above 7.0. The optimum pH for yews is between 6.0 and 6.5. Avoid watering yews heavily.

Root rot

Root rot.

Problem: Young leaves are yellowish or off-color and wilting. Eventually the whole plant wilts and dies, even though the soil is sufficiently moist. Dead, brown leaves remain attached to the plant. Symptoms may develop over a few weeks or may take many months. Heavy, poorly drained soil favors disease development. When cut, the tissue under the bark close to ground level shows a dark discoloration. To look for discoloration, peel back the bark at the bottom of the plant. A distinct margin usually separates white, healthy wood from dark, diseased wood. If the plant is pulled up, examination of young roots reveals decay and an absence of white rootlets. Healthy roots are firm and white.

Analysis: Root rot is caused by a soil-inhabiting fungus (*Phytophthora cinnamomi*) that attacks more than 100 kinds of ornamental plants. Plants, soil, and soil water carry the fungus. It enters the roots and works its way up the plant, blocking the upward flow of water and nutrients. Plants in overwatered or poorly drained soils are more susceptible to attack.

Solution: Remove badly diseased plants. Drench the soil with a fungicide containing *metalaxyl*. Don't replant the same area with susceptible plants. (For a list of resistant trees and shrubs, see page 536.) If replacement is necessary because the shrub is part of a hedge, remove as much soil as possible in the area where the old roots have penetrated and replace with light, clean soil before planting. Avoid overwatering.

TILIA (Linden)

Leaf-feeding caterpillars

Gypsy moth caterpillars (½ life size).

Problem: The surface of the leaf is eaten, giving the remaining tissue a lacy appearance, or the whole leaf is chewed. Sometimes the leaves and branches are webbed. The tree may be defoliated. Damage appears anytime between spring and fall. Caterpillars are clustered or feeding singly on the leaves. Repeated heavy infestations may weaken or kill trees.

Analysis: Many species of caterpillars feed on linden leaves wherever the trees are grown. Depending on the species, the moths lay their eggs in early spring to midsummer. Larvae that hatch from these eggs feed singly or in groups on buds, on one leaf surface (these are called *skeletonizers*), or on the entire leaf. Certain caterpillars web the branches or leaves as they feed. In some years, damage is minimal because of unfavorable environmental conditions or control by predators and parasites. When conditions are favorable, however, entire trees may be defoliated. Defoliation weakens trees because no leaves are left to produce food. When heavy infestations occur several years in a row, branches or entire trees may be killed.

Solution: Spray with Ortho® Systemic Insect Killer or Ortho® Bug-B-Gon® Multi-Purpose Insect Killer Concentrate when damage is first noticed. Treat trees when caterpillars are young with the bacterial insecticide *Bacillus thuringiensis* (Bt). Spray the leaves thoroughly. Repeat the spray if the tree becomes reinfested.

TSUGA (Hemlock)

Hemlock woolly adelgids

Hemlock woolly adelgids (life size).

Problem: Masses of white, cottony material appear on the undersides of twigs. Affected needles turn yellow and drop off. If uncontrolled, the tree may die.

Analysis: The hemlock woolly adelgid (*Adelges tsugae*), an aphid relative, was first discovered in America in 1956 in Virginia. It feeds only on Canada hemlock (*Tsuga canadensis*) and Carolina hemlock (*T. caroliniana*). The cottony wax is produced by females in September and October. Early the following spring, the females lay eggs under the wax. The eggs hatch from early April through early June into tiny, reddish-brown, mobile young, called *crawlers*, that feed on the sap of young twigs. They mature into gray, soft-bodied adults in a few weeks. Some of the adults are winged and fly to nearby trees to feed. Others remain where they are to cover themselves with wax and lay eggs to produce a second generation. This generation hatches in July, becomes dormant in late summer, and resumes feeding in the fall. Heavily infested branches drop their needles and die. Entire trees may die within a few years.

Solution: This adelgid is protected by its waxy coating much of the time but is susceptible to insecticides when crawlers are active in spring and early fall. Spray with insecticidal soap, horticultural oil, or an insecticide containing *imidacloprid*, *malathion*, or *acephate*. If the hemlock woolly adelgid is present in your area, inspect hemlock trees regularly so you can treat at the first sign of infestation, before serious damage is done.

ULMUS (Elm)

Dutch elm disease

Dutch elm disease.

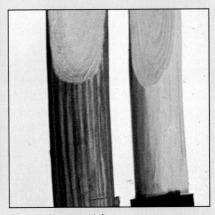

Diseased stem on left.

Problem: Leaves wilt, curl, and turn yellow on branches in the top of the tree; many leaves drop. Trees may die slowly. Or trees wilt and die within a few weeks, in spring soon after they have leafed out. Sections of infected branches may show a ring of brown dots or brown streaks in the wood just underneath the bark. Small holes may be found in the bark of infected branches.

Analysis: Dutch elm disease is caused by a fungus (*Ophiostoma ulmi*) that invades and plugs the water-conducting vessels in the tree. The fungus enters the wood through feeding wounds made by elm bark beetles. In spring, adult beetles emerge from holes in the bark of elm trees where they have spent the winter. If trees are infected with the Dutch elm fungus, beetles have sticky fungal spores on and inside their bodies. The beetles fly to healthy elm trees, where they feed in crotches of small twigs, depositing fungus spores in the wounds. The fungus then spreads downward through the tree. The infected elm usually develops the disease that summer. The fungus produces a toxin that interferes with the water-conducting vessels in the wood, reducing the amount of water available to the leaves. The foliage on the infected branch wilts, turns yellow, and drops. Surrounding branches, and eventually the entire tree, become infected, and the tree dies. When elms are closely planted (50 feet or less between trees), the fungus may spread through natural root grafts between trees.

Solution: Curing a tree of Dutch elm disease is usually not possible. Severely infected trees should be removed promptly to prevent the spread of the disease. Disease development may be delayed on lightly infected trees (less than 5 percent of the foliage and branches show evidence of the disease) that were initially infected by bark beetles rather than by root grafts. Removal of early infections by tree surgery may save a tree for a number of years. Remove yellowing branches at least 10 feet below the point where brown streaks are visible in the wood. Spray the wound with an insecticide containing *methoxychlor*. Systemic fungicides (fungicides that are carried throughout the tree) injected into the tree by a trained arborist may increase the life span of a lightly infected tree. Contact an arborist when yellowing is first noticed. Prevention involves four different measures that should be carried out on a community-wide basis. **1.** A good sanitation program will slow the spread of the fungus. Because bark beetles carrying the fungus breed in dead or dying elm wood, all dead or dying trees, damaged limbs, and prunings should be removed and burned or buried. The bark of all stumps should be peeled to just below ground level. **2.** Controlling bark beetles with insecticides is practical only on valuable specimens and must be used in conjunction with a sanitation program. Spray with an insecticide containing *methoxychlor* in early spring before leaves come out. Use high-pressure spray equipment and cover the entire tree thoroughly. **3.** To prevent transmission of the fungus through the roots of closely planted trees, grafted roots should be severed either by mechanical trenching or by soil injection of a chemical. This is important if a diseased tree is nearby. Contact a professional arborist. **4.** An annual scouting program should be established to detect and deal with infected trees. When replanting, select resistant elms. (For a list of resistant elms, see page 550.)

ULMUS (Elm) *(continued)*

Elm bark beetles

Galleries of elm bark beetles (¼ life size).

Problem: Small (⅛-inch), shiny, dark reddish-brown beetles or dull brown beetles with a rough body surface may be found feeding in the crotches of twigs around the middle of May. The bark is chewed and appears rough. Small holes may be found in the bark of weak or dying trees.

Analysis: Elm bark beetles by themselves cause little injury to elm trees. They can be extremely damaging, however, because they often carry the destructive Dutch elm fungus. The fungus is carried on the bodies of the beetles as they move from infected breeding sites. The shiny, reddish-brown European elm bark beetle is a more important carrier than the dull brown native species because it usually outnumbers the native beetles. Spore-bearing beetles infect a healthy tree with the fungus as they feed on small twigs. Beetles then seek breeding sites under the bark of weakened, dead, or recently cut elm trees up to several miles away. Female beetles tunnel galleries in the wood under the bark, where they lay their eggs. White larvae tunnel through the wood at right angles to the gallery, producing many radiating tunnels. If dead or dying trees are infected with the Dutch elm fungus, the larvae become covered with fungal spores. They emerge as adults in the spring and fly to healthy trees. These trees then become infected with Dutch elm fungus, which spreads through the whole tree.

Solution: For information on controlling bark beetles and preventive and control measures for Dutch elm disease, see page 273.

Elm leaf beetles

Larva (life size). Inset: Adult and eggs (3× life size).

Problem: The lower surfaces of the leaves are eaten between the veins, giving the leaves a lacy appearance. Small holes may be in the leaves. Severely infested leaves turn brown; the entire tree may appear scorched. Many leaves drop by midsummer. Small (½-inch), yellow-and-black larvae or ¼-inch, yellowish green-and-black striped beetles may be found on the undersides of leaves.

Analysis: All species of elm are attacked by the elm leaf beetle (*Pyrrhalta luteola*), but the beetles may have local preferences. The beetles spend the winter as adults in buildings or in protected places outside. In the fall, when the beetles are looking for shelter, they often become a nuisance inside homes. The adults fly back to elm trees in the spring. They eat small holes in the developing leaves, mate, and lay clusters of yellow eggs. The emerging black larvae feed on the lower surfaces of the leaves between the veins. As the larvae mature, they turn a dull yellow with black stripes. After feeding for several weeks, the larvae pupate. Bright yellow pupae may be seen around the base of trees in late June or early July. Adults emerge, and one or two more generations may follow. Trees that lose many of their leaves early in the season may grow new ones, which also may be eaten.

Solution: Spray with Ortho® Systemic Insect Killer when damage is first noticed. To prevent severe leaf damage, apply sprays just as the leaves grow to full size. Repeat the spray if the tree becomes reinfested.

Slime flux

Slime flux.

Problem: Sour-smelling sap oozes from wounds, cracks, and branch crotches, mainly during the growing season. The sap drips down the bark and dries, causing unsightly gray streaks. Some wilting may occur on affected branches. Insects are attracted to the sour-smelling ooze.

Analysis: Slime flux, also called *wetwood*, is caused by a bacterium (*Erwinia nimipressuralis*) on elms. The bacteria infect the heartwood, producing abnormally high sap pressure. This pressure, caused by bacterial fermentation, forces the fermented sap, or *flux*, out of wounds, cracks, or crotches in the tree. Flux is especially copious when the tree is growing rapidly. Large areas of the bark may be coated with the smelly, bacteria-laden sap, which dries to a grayish white color. In addition, wounds don't heal, and the bark is unsightly. A tree with this problem is often under water stress, which may cause drought damage (wilting and scorched leaves) to the branches. The problem may persist for several years.

Solution: There are no controls for this condition. To avoid the unsightly stained bark, bore a slightly upward-slanting drainage hole into the water-soaked wood below each oozing wound. Insert a ½-inch-diameter plastic tube just until it stays firmly in place. (If the tube penetrates the water-soaked wood inside the tree, it will interfere with drainage.) The tube will carry the dripping sap away from the trunk, but it will not cure the disease. Disinfect tools after pruning infected trees.

Powdery mildew

Powdery mildew.

Problem: Leaves are covered with a thin layer or irregular patches of a grayish-white powdery material. Infected leaves may turn yellow and drop. In late fall, tiny black dots (spore-producing bodies) are scattered over the white patches, resembling ground pepper.

Analysis: Powdery mildew is a common plant disease caused by a fungus (*Microsphaera alni*) that thrives in both humid and dry weather. Plants growing in shady areas are often severely infected in the fall. The powdery patches consist of fungal strands and spores. The spores are spread by the wind to healthy plants. The fungus depletes plant nutrients, causing yellowing and sometimes death of the leaf. Since this powdery mildew attacks many different kinds of woody plants, the fungus from a diseased plant may infect other woody plants in the garden.

Solution: Spray the surfaces of the leaves with Ortho® Garden Disease Control when the plant shows the first sign of mildew. Repeat the spray at intervals of 7 to 10 days until mildew disappears.

Aphids

Aphids (life size).

Problem: Tiny (⅛-inch) ash-gray, reddish-brown, or dark green soft-bodied insects cluster on leaves and stem tips. Leaves are discolored and may be extremely curled and distorted. Leaves sometimes drop. A shiny or sticky substance may coat the leaves. A black, sooty mold often grows on the sticky substance.

Analysis: Several different kinds of aphids infest viburnum. They do little damage in small numbers, but they are extremely prolific, and populations can rapidly build to damaging numbers during the growing season. Damage occurs when the aphids suck the sap from the viburnum leaves. The aphids are unable to digest all the sugar in the plant sap, and it excretes the excess in a fluid called *honeydew*, which often drops onto the leaves below. A sooty mold fungus may develop on the honeydew, causing the viburnum leaves to appear black and dirty. The snowball aphid (*Neoceruraphis viburnicola*) causes severe curling and distortion of the leaves and leaf stems of the snowball viburnum (*Viburnum opulus*). Other species of viburnum are usually immune. The other species of aphids that infest viburnum don't cause leaf curling.

Solution: Spray with Ortho® Systemic Insect Killer, Ortho® Rose & Flower Insect Killer, or an insecticidal soap when aphids first appear. Spray the undersides of leaves thoroughly. Repeat the spray if the plant becomes reinfested.

Failure to bloom

Failure to bloom.

Problem: No flowers appear in the spring, but the vine is healthy and growing vigorously.

Analysis: Most wisterias purchased from nurseries bloom after two or three years. These plants are usually asexually propagated (started from cuttings or by some method other than from seed). Vines started from seed often don't bloom for 10 or more years. Wisterias may also fail to bloom because of improper growing conditions, poor pruning practices, or freeze damage. Young plants should be well fed and watered. Plants old enough to bloom will flower best with less food and water. Too much nitrogen during the growing season causes lush, overly vigorous, green growth and poor flower bud production (flower buds for the following season's bloom are produced in early summer). Heavy pruning also may produce lush, overly vigorous growth, but flower buds may be mistakenly removed.

Solution: Don't grow wisteria from seed. Buy nursery-grown vines. If your old wisteria didn't bloom in spring and is lush and growing vigorously, don't use nitrogen fertilizer for an entire season. Fertilize in early summer with 0–10–10 fertilizer to promote flower bud formation for the following season. Prune vigorous shoots in summer. In winter, cut back or thin out side shoots from the main stems. Spurs (short, fat stems bearing flower buds) develop on these side shoots. Cut back spurs to two or three buds. Don't drastically prune side shoots. Drastic pruning will eliminate spurs so no flowers are produced.

Apple 'Summer Red'

The desire to taste old-fashioned fruit flavor has led rural gardeners to experiment with antique varieties and suburban gardeners to plant their first dwarf apple or apricot trees. The savor of a handful of homegrown walnuts has inspired many gardeners to raise their own nut crops. A fresh ripe peach, plum, or pear is one of the delights of summer. Growing healthy trees and a satisfying crop requires thoughtful consideration throughout the plants' life cycle and in all seasons.

PRODUCING A CROP

To tend your fruit and nut trees well, you must be aware of natural production cycles, take an interest in the mysteries of pollination, learn the practical art of thinning, and, as always, remain alert for problems. Most gardeners agree unhesitatingly that the reward of a bumper harvest is worth the trouble.

Pollination: If your fruit tree is festooned with blossoms but yields pea-size fruit that drops instead of grows, poor pollination may be the cause. Some fruit trees, including apricots, nectarines, peaches, pomegranates, persimmons, sour cherries, and most citrus, are self-fruitful. They can be successfully fertilized by their own pollen. But most sweet cherries, plums, apples, papayas, pears, and nut trees must be grown within 100 feet of a different variety of the same fruit or nut tree that flowers at the same time.

An early-blooming tree can't cross-pollinate a late-blooming one. If your garden lacks space for cross-pollinating trees and there are none in the immediate vicinity, talk to your local nursery or a friend with fruit trees. Sometimes setting a bucket of compatible blossom-filled branches under your target tree will do the trick.

You may see labels declaring plums to be self-fruitful. Some are, to a limited extent. But fruiting will be markedly better if pollen comes from another plum tree. Plums are fussy about which plum tree variety provides this pollen, so read specifics when you purchase a tree to prevent disappointment.

Apples and pears have some of the same fussiness about their mates. If the nearby variety blossoms irregularly or has the same genetic base, fruit may not set. If trees were present when you moved onto the property, or the label has been misplaced, you may have to do some investigating to find out which varieties you have in order to improve fruiting. Your local nursery, county extension service, or old-time apple association can usually help.

Insect pollination: Insect pollinators are necessary to transfer pollen within a tree, or from one fruit or nut tree to another. Though birds, animals, and breezes transfer some pollen, insects move most of the pollen within a tree or from one tree to another. In its search for food, an insect may land on the male part of a flower, or anther. The anther contains pollen, which sticks to the insect's body. Later, if the insect visits the female part of a flower, the stigma, pollen may brush off. If it does, pollination occurs. Pollination is the necessary first step to producing a crop.

But bad weather limits insect movements. If there is continued heavy rain, unseasonal cold, or heavy wind during prime flowering season, not only are some of the blossoms knocked off, but pollinators also don't get out to do their jobs.

Honeybees perform most fruit and nut tree pollination. Experts have estimated that they are crucial to more than $20 billion in food crops each year. Honeybees move from flower to flower, collecting both nectar and pollen. Nectar is the sweet juice from inside a flower; bees transform it into honey.

Bees need both nectar and pollen to survive.

In today's world of rapid construction and decreasing open space, the honeybee population seems to be declining. If you want bees for fruit and nut tree pollination, you should take steps to encourage their presence. Provide them with a continuous supply of clean water. A water supply for bees must be shallow, as they may drown when trying to drink from a deeper container. Place some gravel in a bucket, then fill the bucket with just enough water to cover the stones. The gravel provides a place for the bees to settle as they refresh themselves.

Bees are extremely sensitive to controls for other insects. The best course is not to use pesticides on any plant in an area where bees are feeding. If you must use a pesticide, do so in the late afternoon, when fewer bees are visiting flowers.

Insects known as syrphids, hover flies, or flower flies are second only to bees as pollinators. These ¼- to ½-inch-long insects are often confused with honeybees or yellow jacket wasps. Unlike bees and wasps, however, syrphids don't sting. They hover in the air, seemingly motionless, over blossoms, occasionally dipping down to feed on both nectar and pollen. In addition to their work as pollinators, syrphids help control pests.

Young syrphids, ⅛- to ½-inch-long, green or brown worms, eat an average of one aphid

Growing a fruit tree as an espalier is a good way to enjoy a crop in a limited space.

Overgrown with a dense jumble of branches, this 'Mutsu' apple is ready for pruning.

Proper thinning lets in light and air. Branching is reduced by about one-half, while the productive spurs are preserved.

Thinning reduces the number of fruits, but because the remaining fruits receive more nutrients, they are bigger and healthier.

per minute and also feed on mealybugs, leafhoppers, and the like.

Wasps do a share of pollination and pest control. Wasps destroy flies, beetle larvae, and caterpillars. Treat wasps as beneficial insects unless their presence is potentially harmful to people. Some wasp species, most notably the yellow jacket, can be irritated by swatting and other disturbances. The result could be a series of painful stings.

Hand pollination: What do you do if rain, wind, cold, or other environmental factors keep insect pollinators from doing their job? You must literally put your hand to the task. The best time to pollinate by hand is when the weather has been warm and dry for at least two days. Shaking blossoms of one variety over those of another is a reasonably effective means of cross-pollination. To be more precise, move your fingertip over an anther. If yellow grains come off onto your finger, pollen is available. Use a small natural-hair artist's brush or a cotton swab to transfer pollen from anthers of one variety to stigmas of another. Whichever method you use, transfer pollen every day until the trees are finished flowering. In the absence of insect pollinators, hand-pollination is the only alternative if you want fruit or nuts.

UNDERSTANDING CROP PROBLEMS

Fruit and nut yields are subject to natural cycles as well as weather conditions and the unpredictability of pollination.

Failure to bear: Before worrying about a tree that is not bearing fruit or nuts, make

sure it is mature enough to produce a crop. Peaches bear after three years, dwarf apples at two, three or more years, and plum trees at about four years. Sweet-cherry trees bear at five to seven years.

If your tree is mature yet produces little or no fruit despite adequate pollinators, again you may have no cause for concern. Some tree varieties, particularly apple, pear and citrus, tend toward light crops in alternate years, even when they are healthy. Heavy fruiting takes energy away from flower production for the following year. If the number of flowers is low, the yield is small. Thorough thinning helps trees produce consistent yields from year to year.

Poor weather: Poor fruiting and premature fruit drop occur if temperatures are too low or if hot and cold weather alternate in late fall and early spring. In either case the tree is fooled into thinking spring has arrived. It sets new leaves and blossoms, which are particularly susceptible to damage from temperature extremes.

Alternate freezing and thawing can cause soil movement that damages roots. If the damage is severe, the nutrient flow to the trunk is disrupted.

To protect fruit and nut trees from extreme weather, mulch them with a 6-inch layer of straw, evergreen branches, chopped leaves, wood chips, or pine needles. If you expect the temperature to drop below freezing during the night, temporarily cover trees with fabric or plastic sheets. Make sure the covers are loose. Remove them in the morning; left in place they block sunlight and impede air circulation. For prized fruit or nut trees, consider installing a heat

source. Sometimes the heat from a simple 60-watt bulb turned on and set under a tree draped with clear plastic is enough to prevent freezing. Ask local nursery professionals or the county extension agent what heat source works best in your region.

Thinning: By natural dieback and leaf drop, trees normally do some of their own thinning so that the remaining fruit will receive the nutrients to reach proper size. It takes 30 healthy leaves to ripen one full-size orange or apple. If all the fruit a tree set stayed on the branches, each fruit would probably be undersized because of nutrient shortage.

Even so, in most cases you must take an active role in ensuring larger fruit or nuts by removing some immature crop yourself. This process is known as thinning. In addition to providing each remaining fruit or nut with a bigger share of nutrients, thinning opens each fruit to more sun and air, making it less susceptible to disease.

Each type of fruit or nut tree has its own thinning requirements. For example, thin apples and pears by cutting the stems with sharp scissors or pinching the stems between thumb and forefinger. Leave the stem behind when you cut. Thin pears after natural spring fruit drop, when the fruits turn downward. Leave two pears per cluster. With apples, leave one per cluster. When thinning, you may notice that the "crown" apple (the fruit in the middle of a cluster) is malformed. If so, be certain to remove it. But if not, leave it, as it can be larger and quite good. The clusters should be about 6 inches apart.

CORRECTING GENERAL PROBLEMS

In addition to solving problems relative to crops, gardeners must often solve problems such as drought, wind stress, and sucker and seedling growth.

Drought: A lack of water can be caused by a lack of rainfall, of course, but it can also result from inadequate saturation.

Make the most of rain and irrigation by digging a shallow basin around your fruit or nut tree. Extend the basin about a foot beyond the branch tips, and keep enlarging it as the tree grows. Construct an earthen barrier about a foot from the trunk; it should be high enough to keep the water in the basin from touching the trunk.

Lawn watering doesn't suit fruit or nut trees. In most cases, lawn watering only soaks the top few inches of soil. Sprinkler systems keep trunk and top roots wet, encouraging plant diseases. Trees that are watered only along with the lawn may grow slowly and have small yellowing leaves that drop early.

To lessen the problems of lawn watering, aim sprinklers so they don't reach the trunk or base of the tree. If possible, leave a 2-foot space between tree trunk and grass. To ensure soil saturation, irrigate deeply to deliver water 2 to 3 feet below the surface.

Wind stress: Constant wind causes rapid water evaporation. If the roots can't take in and move as much water as the leaves are losing, the result is wilted leaves. Wilting is most common in young trees, which may not have root systems substantial enough to counter the evaporation. Constant wind stress slows growth.

Keeping the stressed plant well watered at all times can mitigate wind damage. Another solution is a windbreak, wall, or shrub that blocks the wind. If you plant a living windbreak, make certain it doesn't compete with the stressed tree for water or sun. In serious cases of wind stress, consider moving the plant to another location.

Suckers: A sucker is a shoot that grows from the roots or the lower part of the trunk. Sucker leaves may look different from those on higher branches. If suckers appear at the base of a new tree and there is no tree top growth, the cause may be root injury during planting or cultivation near the trunk. Cut suckers at the base as soon as they emerge from the ground. Suckers weaken a tree by using nutrients that should go into tree growth. Provide sufficient water and wind protection to prevent stress while roots recover.

Seedlings: Fruits and nuts often fall from the trees that bore them; seedlings often sprout from the fallen crop. Though the seedlings may bear edible fruit, this second generation is usually inferior. In many cases, the seedlings don't develop true to type. If you want to experiment, move a seedling to another site. Otherwise, it may grow larger than the parent tree and shade it out.

PURCHASING A NEW TREE

A tree buyer has two goals: acquiring a healthy tree at the right time of year.

The part of a tree just under the bark is called the cambium. This is the area in which the tree creates new cells; therefore, an assessment of the health of the cambium provides a test of whether the tree you are thinking about buying has the potential to grow in the right conditions. The cambium should be bright green. The bark that covers it should not be shriveled.

Check container-grown trees for girdling, or roots that circle around inside or outside the container. As girdling roots grow, they wrap ever more tightly around each other, cutting off nutrient flow. The result can be the death of the tree. To check for girdling roots inside the container, poke your finger 2 to 3 inches into the soil near the trunk. Brush away a bit of topsoil. If you see or feel a root that is damaged or constricted by another root, select a different tree.

To ease transplant shock, purchase your tree as soon as the weather is warm enough to permit safe planting. In early spring the tree is still dormant; it has no leaves or buds to support. After you plant it, the tree can devote its energy to repairing the damage that even the most careful transplanting causes. By the time the tree is ready to produce spring growth, it has recovered from the trauma of planting.

PLANTING THE TREE

To get a new tree off to the best possible start, provide trunk support, and take care to minimize transplant shock.

Trunk support: Too much trunk movement prevents roots from getting a good grip into the soil. If not anchored solidly by roots, the tree trunk may snap in a strong wind. To prevent this, install support posts before transplanting the tree. A standard-sized tree requires 8-foot posts; semidwarfs, 6-foot posts; and dwarf trees,

A regular spray program ensures the highest quality home-grown fruit.

Cylindrical wire cages that reach 2 feet above the normal snow line protect vulnerable bark from rabbits and mice.

'Eureka' lemon

Clockwise from left: *English walnuts, black walnuts, and Persian walnuts.*

4-foot posts. Oak stakes stand up well to all types of weather. To avoid damage to the roots of the new tree, place the post into the hole before transplanting the tree. Place the post on the side of incoming winds. Use rubber ties, plastic tape, or wire shielded with lengths of garden hose to connect the tree to the post. Provide enough slack to allow the trunk to sway slightly. There must be some leeway, for this encourages a strong trunk. Check the ties regularly, and loosen or replace them as necessary to prevent constriction and damage to the trunk.

Transplant shock: In a nursery, a bare-root, burlapped, or container tree is carefully watered, shaded, and nurtured. Newly arrived in the garden, the same tree may be propped against a heat-reflecting wall, causing it to bake. If the tree is unwrapped or removed from its container, the plant is even more susceptible to hot sun and drying wind. Left unprotected for even a few hours, a fruit or nut tree can be in shock and dying even before being placed in the planting hole. If possible, plant the tree immediately and water it well. When transplanting a tree from a container to the ground, soak the rootball in water while it is still in the container, then place the tree into the planting hole.

If you must wait a few days before planting the tree, place it in a shallow holding trench you have dug in a shady location. Lean the trunk and rootball against one side of the trench. Thoroughly cover the roots with soil and water. Place the tree into the planting hole as soon as possible.

Growing in containers: If you want a fruit crop but have limited space or poor drainage, a dwarf tree in a container may be a solution. A dwarf tree also tends to bear fruit earlier in its life than a standard-size tree, so a dwarf may also be the answer if you want a quick crop. Unfortunately, container-grown dwarf trees are quickly affected by poor care. The results are yellowing, drooping, curling leaves, and poor fruit production.

Purchase only healthy plants. Leaves should be large and green. Choose a tree with few flowers or fruit rather than one full of blossoms or fruit. The less ornamented tree may not be as appealing now, but it will put more energy into valuable first-year root development. Avoid root-bound plants. Circling or matted roots must be cut back to encourage them to grow outward, and cutting roots encourages transplant shock.

The container for a dwarf tree should be about 3 inches wider than the roots when they are spread out. Don't use soil directly from the garden unless you have good loam. Avoid clay, because it holds water and fruit trees don't like soggy soil.

Fruit trees in containers can't expand roots into surrounding soil to obtain moisture or nutrients. What you provide in the container is what they attempt to live on. Lack of water is a major problem.

Water when the top of the soil feels dry to the touch. Don't allow the leaves to dry to the point of wilting; repeated wilting can cause death. Don't overwater. Soil that stays soggy in a container invites crown and root rot.

Apply fruit-tree fertilizer once a month to correct or prevent iron chlorosis or zinc deficiencies. If leaf edges turn brown and dry, excess fertilizer may be accumulating in the container. To leach out the fertilizer, put a garden hose into the container and turn the water on low. Let water run through the container for about 20 minutes.

HARVESTING

Picking fruit at just the right time ensures peak flavor. But it's often difficult to tell exactly when a fruit is ready to be taken off the tree. Color is a good indicator on trees such as pears. Citrus fruit, however, can look ripe for several months before they are actually edible. Your only course is to learn the harvest time for each type of fruit. The list that follows presents guidelines for how to tell when to harvest fruit from a few common trees.

■ Taste citrus fruit to determine picking time. Leaving them on too long will do no harm; ripe citrus can remain on a tree for more than two months.

■ Pears are ready when they reach full size and start to lose their green color. Don't allow them to soften or turn yellow on the tree. Overripe pears are mealy, mushy, or gritty.

■ Pick plums, astringent persimmons, figs, and apricots when they are fully colored and slightly soft.

■ Remove cherries when they are fully colored and soft or firm. Soft cherries tend to be sweeter, but the birds may get to them first.

DISEASES OF FRUIT AND NUT TREES

Anthracnose	Serious fungal diseases affecting mango, papaya, and walnut trees. Brown spots appear on leaves and fruit. Infected areas decay rapidly. Fruit or nuts drop prematurely. Clear and destroy debris regularly. At two-week intervals, spray with fungicide containing dodine.
Bacterial canker	Affects mainly cherry, fig, nectarine, peach, plum, and almond trees. Fruit is not usually infected, but entire branches may die back. Difficult to control; spraying in fall with basic copper sulfate may help. Plant resistant varieties. See page 302.
Bacterial leaf spot	One of the more destructive diseases of stone-fruit trees, infecting apricot, nectarine, peach, and plum. Fruit may be ruined. Spraying with basic copper sulfate when buds open may help combat disease, but no total control exists. Plant resistant varieties. See pages 299, 308, and 316.
Black rot	Infects mainly apple and pear trees. Fruit may be ruined. Remove all rotted fruit from tree and ground. Prune as advised (see page 296). Spray with captan as soon as disease is noticed; respray the following spring when growth begins.
Brown rot	Fungal disease destructive to stone-fruit trees—mainly apricot, cherry, nectarine, peach, and plum. Sometimes infects citrus. Fruit is often ruined. Spray uninfected blossoms and maturing fruit with Ortho® Garden Disease Control. Plant resistant varieties. See pages 302, 309, and 316.
Crown and root rot	May infect nearly any fruit or nut tree. The whole tree generally loses vigor and appears ill. Only the upper branches may bloom and fruit. No controls are available. Infected trees usually die; replace them with resistant varieties. See page 292.
Fire blight	Severe on pear trees; can also infect apple. Fruit may be ruined. Spraying with streptomycin at intervals before and throughout blooming helps combat the disease. Plant resistant varieties. See pages 297 and 311.
Leaf curl	Infects peach and nectarine trees. Fruit crop is decreased, but fruit is edible. Leaf curl can't be treated once it appears, but spraying in fall and spring with lime sulfur or Ortho® Garden Disease Control may prevent recurrence. See page 308.
Powdery mildew	Affects apple, cherry, papaya, and almond trees. Infected apples and papaya may be edible if peeled, but infected cherries are generally ruined. Spray at two-week intervals with myclobutanil or sulfur. See page 289.
Scab	Serious problem on apple trees but can also affect apricot, avocado, citrus, mango, nectarine, peach, pear, and pecan. Infected fruit is edible if peeled. Scab can't be treated once it appears, but spraying with captan or Ortho® Garden Disease Control in spring, after blossoms drop, may prevent recurrence. Plant resistant varieties. See pages 296, 298, and 307.
Shothole fungus	Infects apple, apricot, nectarine, peach, and almond trees. Yield is reduced, but fruit is edible if peeled. Shothole fungus can't be treated once it appears, but spraying in fall with lime sulfur or Ortho® Garden Disease Control should help prevent recurrence. See page 308.

POOR FRUITING

Premature fruit drop

Premature drop of cherries.

Little or no fruit

Poor fruiting on almond.

Failure to fruit on peach.

Problem: Fruit drops
prematurely. The tree
appears to be healthy; no
signs of insect pests or
plant diseases are present.

Analysis: Premature fruit drop may
have several causes.
1. Natural thinning: Most fruit trees
initially produce more fruit than they can
mature. Premature fruit drop is a natural
means of thinning the excess fruit.
2. Stress: Large quantities of fruit may drop
when the tree is under stress. Stress may be
caused by conditions such as excessive heat,
drought, cold, or overwatering or by rapid
changes in soil moisture or air temperature.
3. Freeze damage: Unseasonable spring
frosts often freeze and kill developing young
fruit, causing it to drop.
4. Lack of pollination: If flowers aren't
pollinated, they may not develop or may
develop into pea-size fruit that falls off.

Solution: Solutions below correspond
to the numbered items in the analysis.
1. As long as your tree appears healthy,
you need not worry about it.
2. Help reduce stress to the tree by watering
and fertilizing it properly.
3. Once fruit is damaged by frost, you can't
do anything about it. (To protect trees from
frost damage, see page 413.) Plant late-
blooming trees that are hardy in your area.
(For a list of hardy fruit and nut trees, see
the section beginning on page 552.)
4. Check the lists beginning on page 552 to
determine if your tree requires a pollinator.

Problem: A tree produces little or no fruit. The tree appears
healthy and is growing vigorously. No signs of insect pests or plant
diseases are present.

Analysis:
1. Lack of pollination: In order to
produce fruit, many varieties of fruit trees
must be cross-pollinated (pollinated by a
different variety). If a cross-pollinating
variety is not present in the garden or
nearby neighborhood, the tree may bloom
profusely but produce little or no fruit.

2. Lack of pollinators: Most fruit trees
are pollinated by bees. If bees aren't present
when the tree is flowering because of rain
or cold weather, or if the bees are killed
by tree spraying, pollination and fruit set
won't occur.

3. Cold damage: Flowers or parts of
flowers may be killed when temperatures
drop below freezing. Some fruit tree flowers
can tolerate temperatures in the 20°F range,
but flower hardiness varies considerably with
the species and variety.

4. Biennial bearing: Certain types of fruit
trees, especially apples, pears, and some
citrus varieties, tend to bear a heavy crop
of fruit one year and little or no fruit the
following year. The production of large
quantities of fruit inhibits the formation of
the following year's flowers. Lack of fruit
that year stimulates the production of many
flowers the next year.

5. Improper pruning: If fruit-bearing
wood is pruned during the dormant season,
the tree will fail to flower and fruit.

Solution:
1. Check the lists of common fruit tree
varieties beginning on page 552 to determine
whether your tree requires a pollinator.

2. You can't do anything about lack of bee
activity from rain or cold weather. If your
trees bloom early in the season, when
inclement weather is more likely, plant late-
blooming varieties. Don't spray when your
fruit tree is in bloom.

3. Once flowers have been killed or
damaged by an unseasonable cold spell,
you can't do anything about it. If you expect
temperatures to drop during the night,
protect your trees from the cold. Plant late-
blooming varieties to avoid cold damage.

4. To help even out fruit production from
year to year, thin fruit about four to six
weeks after the trees have bloomed.

5. Avoid pruning large amounts of fruit-
bearing wood.

Fruit too small

Small cherries.

Problem: The tree is healthy and produces many small fruits. No signs of pests or diseases are evident.

Analysis: Certain fruit trees, including peaches, nectarines, Japanese plums, and apples, tend to produce large quantities of small fruits when the trees are not pruned or thinned adequately. If the fruit-bearing wood is not pruned during the dormant season, the tree will set much more fruit than can grow to full size. Even when properly pruned, certain fruit trees have a tendency to overbear. A tree has only a limited amount of nutrients that can be supplied to the fruit. When a tree overbears, it distributes smaller quantities of nutrients to each maturing fruit, resulting in large numbers of small fruits.

Solution: Prune your tree properly during the dormant season, and thin the young fruits when they are thumbnail-size (four to eight weeks after bloom). (For information on pruning and thinning, look up the specific fruit tree in the alphabetical section beginning on page 293.)

Poor-tasting fruit and nuts

Poor-quality pear.

Poor-quality apples.

Problem: Fruit and nuts are not flavorful. Fruits may be dry, watery, pulpy, or grainy and may taste sour or tart.

Analysis: Fruits and nuts may be poor in flavor for several reasons.

1. Lack of nutrients: Trees planted in infertile soil grow poorly and often produce small crops of inferior-tasting fruits and nuts.

2. Environmental stress: Trees may be stressed by too much or too little soil moisture, excessively high or low temperatures or rapid, unseasonable weather changes. Under environmental stress, many types of trees may fail to ripen fruits or nuts properly, producing dry, pulpy, or otherwise poor-tasting fruits and nuts.

3. Disease or insect damage: Diseases and pests often slow root, shoot, and leaf growth and prevent fruits and nuts from ripening properly. Fruits and nuts may also be infected or infested, resulting in poor flavor.

4. Untimely harvest: When fruits are prematurely harvested, they may taste tart, flavorless, dry, or starchy. Pears allowed to ripen on the tree taste gritty or mealy.

5. Fruit naturally unflavorful: Tree varieties vary considerably in the quality of their fruits and nuts. No matter how healthy and vigorous your tree is, the variety may naturally produce a flavorless crop. Seedling trees often produce insipid fruits.

Solution: Solutions below correspond to the numbered items in the analysis.

1. Fertilize trees regularly according to label directions with Scotts® Evergreen, Shrub and Tree Food.

2. To reduce stress caused by too much or too little soil moisture, avoid overwatering or underwatering your tree. (For information on watering, see pages 407 to 408.) Minimize tree stress from weather and temperature fluctuations by maintaining the tree in good health.

3. To help ensure high-quality fruit and nut crops, keep your trees as free of insect pests and diseases as possible.

4. Fruits are usually ripe when fully colored, slightly soft and easy to separate from the branch when gently lifted. (For information on harvesting, look up a specific tree in the alphabetical section starting on page 293.)

5. If your tree appears to be healthy but has continued to produce poor-quality fruit over several years, plant a variety that bears more flavorful fruit or graft the tree with a good variety. Check with your local county extension office for a list of flavorful fruit and nut trees adapted to your area.

ANIMAL DAMAGE

Bark-feeding animals

Ground squirrel damage to almond trees.

Problem: Leaves and buds or shoots are chewed from the trees. Bark may be chewed or gnawed from the trunk or lower branches. In some cases, the trunk is entirely girdled. Deer, rabbits, or mice may be seen in the yard, or their tracks may be seen on the ground or snow. Damage is usually most severe during winter months.

Analysis: Several animals chew on tree bark.
1. Deer damage trees by feeding on the leaves, shoots, buds, and bark. They feed by pulling or twisting the bark or twigs, leaving ragged or bent twig ends or patches of bark. The males may also damage trees by rubbing their antlers on the trunk or branches.
2. Rabbits damage fruit trees by chewing on the bark at the base of the trunk and clipping off tender shoots. They chew bark and twigs off cleanly, leaving a sharp break. The damaged trunk is often marked with paired gouges where the rabbits have fed. They generally feed no more than 2 feet above the ground or snow level. Rabbits damage young or dwarf trees most severely.
3. Field or meadow mice damage fruit trees by chewing off the bark at the base of the trunk, just at or slightly above or below ground or snow level. They may girdle the trunk, killing the tree. Mice leave tiny scratches in the exposed wood.

Solution: Various methods may be used to control deer, rabbits, and mice. (For more information, see page 499 for deer control, page 497 for rabbit control, and page 494 for mouse control.)

Animals eating fruit and nuts

Bird-damaged apple.

Squirrel eating green cherry.

Problem: Ripened fruit and nuts have holes in them and may be partially eaten. Fruit and nuts may disappear from the tree or may have been knocked to the ground. Birds, tree squirrels, or raccoons may be seen feeding in the trees.

Analysis: Some birds and animals feed on tree fruits and nuts.

1. Birds are notorious pests of many tree fruits, especially cherries, figs, persimmons, and other soft, sweet fruits. They peck at the ripening fruit, leaving holes in the flesh. The wounded fruit may decay, becoming inedible. Some birds also feed on fruit blossoms and tiny developing fruits, greatly reducing the overall fruit yield.

2. Tree squirrels feed on a large variety of foods, including bark, leaves, insects, and eggs. They prefer maturing fruit and nuts, however. They can strip entire trees of nuts, many of which they store for later use. They often leave partially eaten nuts on the ground around the tree. Tree squirrels are especially fond of filberts.

3. Raccoons are usually found in wooded areas near a source of water. They feed on a wide variety of foods, including ripening fruit and nuts. Raccoons may strip off fruit and nuts and carry them away or feed on them in the tree. In the process of feeding, they often knock many fruit and nuts to the ground.

Solution: Solutions below correspond to the numbered items in the analysis.

1. The most effective way to control birds is to throw nets over the trees and secure the nets tightly around the trunk. Birds are most likely to damage ripening fruit. Check the trees every morning, and harvest fruit and nuts that have ripened. Bright, shiny objects hung in trees frighten birds and will repel them for a while.

2. Prevent tree squirrels from climbing fruit and nut trees by wrapping 2-foot-wide bands of metal (made from materials like aluminum roof flashing) snugly around tree trunks at least 6 feet above ground level. Prune trees so that all their branches are at least 6 feet above the ground and 6 feet away from other trees and structures. If necessary, completely enclose dwarf trees or shrubs in a chicken-wire cage. If permissible in your area, you can trap tree squirrels. (For more information on squirrels, see page 497.)

3. Raccoons are intelligent, inquisitive animals that can be difficult to control. To discourage raccoons from climbing between trees or from a building to a tree, keep limbs pruned so that they don't touch and don't make contact with the roof. Wrap metal guards at least 18 inches wide around tree trunks at least 3 feet above the ground. (For more information on raccoons, see page 498.)

BARK OR WOOD PROBLEMS

Limb breakage

Fruit overload on apple branch.

Problem: Branches laden with large quantities of ripening fruit break off.

Analysis: Limbs of trees that produce large fruit, such as peaches, nectarines, apples, and pears, may break as the fruit reaches full size. Branches that haven't been pruned or thinned properly are most likely to break. Branches with narrow crotch angles are subject to breakage at the point of attachment to the tree. Trees that produce fruit on thin, year-old wood—for example, peaches and nectarines—are most susceptible to limb breakage.

Solution: Prune stubs where branches have broken. Prop up any branches that are bent or appear to be ready to break. Cut a notch at one end of a board and place the board about one-third of the way in from the tip of the sagging branch. Set the branch into the notch, and then push the board into the ground. If the soil is not soft, you may need to dig a hole in the ground first. The board should be pushed in at a slight angle (20 degrees), leaning toward the trunk of the tree. During the dormant season, prune the tree properly and thin young fruit. (For information on pruning and thinning, look up the specific fruit tree in the section beginning on page 293.)

Gummosis

Gummosis on peach.

Gummosis on apricot.

Problem: Beads of sticky, amber-colored sap appear on healthy bark, cankers, wounds, or pruning cuts.

Analysis: Oozing sap (gummosis) occurs in all trees to some extent and is caused by one or several of the following factors:

1. Natural tendency: Certain species of fruit trees, especially cherries, apricots, peaches, and plums, have a natural tendency to ooze sap. Small beads of sap often form on the bark of these trees.

2. Environmental stress: Trees under stress because they are growing in wet, poorly drained, or very dry soil may produce large quantities of sap, even though they are not diseased. Also, many fruit trees respond to rapid changes in weather conditions or soil moisture by gumming profusely.

3. Mechanical injury: Most trees ooze sap when the bark or wood is wounded. Wounding results from limb breakage; lawn mower injury; pruning; improper staking, tying, or guying techniques; and other practices that damage the bark and wood.

4. Disease: Fruit trees respond to certain fungal and bacterial infections by forming cankers that gum profusely. Gummosis is often one of the initial signs of infection.

5. Insect damage: Several species of insects bore into tree bark, causing sap to ooze from the damaged areas. The tunnels they form in the wood often become infected with decay organisms.

Solution: Solutions below correspond to the numbered items in the analysis.

1. As long as the bark appears healthy, you don't need to worry.

2. If your tree is growing in wet, poorly drained soil, allow the soil to dry out between waterings. Provide for drainage of water away from tree trunks and roots. To help prevent crown rot, carefully remove enough soil around the base of the trunk to expose the first major roots.

3. Avoid unnecessary mechanical injuries to the tree. Stake, tie, and prune properly.

4. Remove badly infected branches and cut out cankers. Keep the tree healthy.

5. Borers are difficult to control once they have burrowed into the wood. (For information on borers, see page 434.)

BARK OR WOOD PROBLEMS *(continued)*

INSECTS

Cankers

Cytospora canker on peach.

Sunscald

Sunscald.

Borers

Borer holes.

Problem: Sunken, oval, or elongated dark lesions (cankers) develop on the trunk or branches. The bark at the edge of the canker may thicken and roll inward. Sticky, amber-colored sap may ooze from the canker. The foliage on infected branches may be stunted and yellowing; some of the leaves may turn brown and drop. Twigs and branches may die back, and the tree may eventually die.

Analysis: Several species of fungi and bacteria cause cankers on fruit and nut trees. These organisms may be spread by wind, splashing water, or contaminated tools. Infection usually occurs through injured or wounded tissue. Bark that has been damaged by sunscald, cold, pruning wounds, or mechanical injury is especially susceptible. The decay organisms sometimes infect the leaves directly, then spread down into healthy twigs. Cankers form as the decay progresses. Many fruit trees produce a sticky sap that oozes from the cankers. The portion of the branch or stem above the canker may die from decay or from clogging of the water and nutrient-conducting vessels in the branch. Cankers that form on the trunk are the most serious and may kill the tree. The tree may halt the development of a canker by producing callus tissue, a growth of barklike cells, to wall off the infection.

Solution: Remove and destroy badly infected branches, and cut out cankers. Keep trees healthy, and avoid wounding.

Problem: Patches of bark on the trunk or branches darken and die. Patches appear on the sunny side of the tree. Cracks and sunken lesions may eventually develop in the dead bark. Damaged trees have been recently transplanted or heavily pruned.

Analysis: When a tree is shaded by other trees or structures or is covered with dense foliage, bark on the trunk and branches remains thin. If the tree is suddenly exposed to intense sunlight, the newly exposed bark and the wood just beneath the bark may be injured by the sun's heat. This frequently happens when young trees are moved from a shaded nursery to an open area and when trees are heavily pruned during periods of intense sunlight. The problem also occurs on cold, clear days in winter, as cold bark is quickly warmed by the sun. Damaged bark usually splits open, forming long cracks or cankers. Decay fungi may invade exposed wood. Sunscald is most severe when the soil is dry. Young trees may die from sunscald.

Solution: Unless the tree is very young or extremely damaged, it will usually recover with proper care. Water the tree and fertilize it with Miracle-Gro® Tree & Shrub Fertilizer Spikes to stimulate new growth. To prevent further damage, wrap trunks and main branches of recently pruned or newly transplanted trees with tree-wrapping paper. Or paint exposed bark with a white interior latex or whitewash. The tree will eventually adapt to increased exposure by growing more foliage and producing thicker bark.

Problem: Foliage on a branch or at the top of the tree is sparse; eventually the twigs and branches die. Holes or tunnels are apparent in the trunk or branches. Sap or sawdust may be present near the holes. The bark over the tunnels may die or slough off, or knotlike swellings may be on the trunk and limbs. Weakened branches break during wind- or snowstorms. Weak, young, or newly transplanted trees may be killed.

Analysis: Borers are the larvae of beetles or moths. Many kinds of borers attack fruit and nut trees. Females lay their eggs in bark crevices throughout the summer. The larvae feed by tunneling through the bark or wood. Borer tunnels stop the flow of nutrients and water through the area by damaging the conducting vessels; branch and twig dieback result. Sap flow may act as a defense against borers if the tree is healthy. When the borer burrows into wood, tree sap fills the hole and drowns the insect. Trees weakened by mechanical injuries, disease, poor growing conditions, or insect infestation are more susceptible to borer attack.

Solution: Cut out and destroy all dead and dying branches, and remove severely infested young trees. Dust the trunk and branches with Ortho® Bug-B-Gon® Multi-Purpose Garden Dust to kill young larvae before they burrow into wood. Make sure that your tree is listed on the product label. Maintain tree health by watering and fertilizing regularly and controlling insects and disease-producing organisms.

Scales

Cherry scales. Inset: Lecanium scales (life size).

Problem: Dark crusty bumps; thick, white, waxy bumps; or clusters of somewhat flattened, scaly bumps cover the stems or undersides of the leaves. The bumps can be scraped or picked off; the undersides are usually soft. Leaves turn yellow and may drop. In some cases, a shiny or sticky substance coats the leaves. A black, sooty mold often grows on the sticky substance.

Analysis: Several different types of scales infest fruit trees. They lay their eggs on leaves or bark, and in spring to midsummer the young scales, called *crawlers*, settle on leaves and twigs. The small ($\frac{1}{10}$-inch), soft-bodied young feed by sucking sap from the plant. The legs usually atrophy, and a hard crusty or waxy shell develops over the body. Mature female scales lay their eggs underneath their shells. Some species of scales are unable to digest all the sugar in the plant sap, and they excrete the excess in a fluid called *honeydew*. An uncontrolled infestation of scales may kill the plant after two or three seasons. (For more information on scales, see pages 444 to 447.)

Solution: Spray with Ortho® Malathion Plus® Insect Spray Concentrate when the young are active. Make sure that your fruit tree is listed on the product label. Early the following spring, before new growth begins, spray the trunk and branches with Ortho® Volck® Oil Spray to control overwintering insects.

Aphids

Aphids (life size).

Problem: The youngest leaves are curled, twisted, discolored, and stunted. Leaves may drop, and in severe cases the tree may defoliate. Developing fruit may be small and misshapen. A shiny or sticky substance may coat the leaves. A black, sooty mold often grows on the sticky substance. Tiny ($\frac{1}{8}$-inch) yellow, green, purplish, or black soft-bodied insects cluster on the young shoots and on the undersides of leaves.

Analysis: Many species of aphids infest fruit trees. Aphids do little damage in small numbers. They are extremely prolific, however, and populations can rapidly build during the growing season. Damage occurs when the aphid sucks the sap from the leaves and immature fruit. The aphid is unable to digest all the sugar in the sap, and it excretes the excess in a fluid called *honeydew*, which often drops onto the leaves below. A sooty mold fungus may develop on the honeydew, causing the leaves to appear black and dirty. At harvest time, the fruit may be small, misshapen, and pitted from aphid damage earlier in the season. (For more information on aphids, see page 443.)

Solution: Treat with Ortho® Malathion Plus® Insect Spray Concentrate or Ortho® Bug-B-Gon® Multi-Purpose Garden Dust. Make sure that your fruit is listed on the product label. Repeat the spray if the tree becomes reinfested.

Cottony cushion scales, mealybugs, and woolly aphids

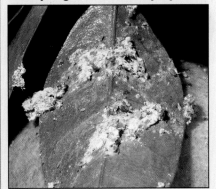

Citrus mealybugs.

Problem: The stems, branch crotches, trunk, or undersides of leaves are covered with white, cottony masses. Leaves may be curled, distorted, and yellowing, and knotlike galls may form on the stems, trunk, or roots. Sometimes a shiny or sticky substance coats the leaves. Twigs and branches may die.

Analysis: Cottony cushion scales, mealybugs, and woolly aphids produce white, waxy secretions that cover their bodies. Their similarity makes separate identification difficult. When the insects are young, they are usually inconspicuous on the host plant. Their bodies range in color from yellowish green to brown, blending in with the leaves or bark. As the insects mature, they exude filaments of white wax, giving them a cottony appearance. Mealybugs and scales generally deposit their eggs in white, fluffy masses. Damage is caused by the withdrawal of plant sap from the leaves, branches, or trunk. The insects are unable to digest all the sugar in the plant sap, and they excrete the excess in a fluid called *honeydew*, which often drops onto the leaves or plants below.

Solution: Spray the branches, trunk, and foliage with Ortho® Malathion Plus® Insect Spray Concentrate or Ortho® Volck® Oil Spray. Make sure that your fruit tree is listed on the product label. During the dormant season, spray the trunk and branches with Ortho® Volck® Oil Spray according to label directions.

INSECTS (continued)

Ants

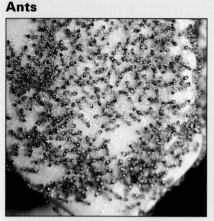

Ants feeding on papaya (½ life size).

Problem: Ants crawl on the trunk, branches, and fruit. In many cases, the trees are also infested with aphids, leafhoppers, mealybugs, scales, and whiteflies.

Analysis: Most ants don't directly damage plants. They may be present for any of several reasons. Many ants feed on *honeydew*, a sweet, sticky substance excreted by several species of insects, including aphids, leafhoppers, mealybugs, scales, and whiteflies. Ants are attracted to plants infested with these pests. Their presence may discourage predators that would otherwise control pests. Ants may also feed on flower nectar, on tree sap, or on fruit that has had its skin broken or is rotting. Ants usually live in underground nests. Some species make colonies in trees and building foundations. (For additional information on ants, see page 459.)

Solution: Control aphids, leafhoppers, mealybugs, scales, and whiteflies by spraying the infested plants with Ortho® Malathion Plus® Insect Spray Concentrate. Make sure that your fruit tree is listed on the product label. To prevent ants from crawling up the trunk, apply a ring of sticky barrier substance to the trunk.

Tent caterpillars and fall webworms

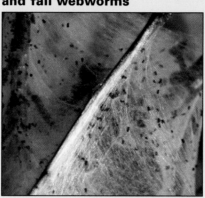

Tent caterpillar nest (life size).

Problem: In the spring or summer, silk nests appear in the branch crotches or on the ends of branches. The leaves are chewed; branches or the entire tree may be defoliated. Groups of bluish, black, tan, or greenish hairy caterpillars with spots or stripes are feeding in or around the nests.

Analysis: Tent caterpillars (*Malacosoma* species) and fall webworm (*Hyphantria cunea*) are insects that feed on many fruit and ornamental trees. The fall webworm and several species of tent caterpillars are distributed throughout the United States. In the summer, adult tent caterpillar moths lay masses of eggs in a cementing substance around twigs. Eggs hatch in early spring as the leaves unfold, and the young caterpillars immediately begin to construct their nests. On warm, sunny days, they devour the surrounding foliage. In mid- to late summer, brownish or reddish adult moths appear. Fall webworm moths lay eggs on undersides of leaves in spring. In early summer, the young caterpillars begin feeding and surrounding themselves with silk nests. Caterpillars drop to the soil to pupate. Up to four generations occur between June and September.

Solution: Spray with Ortho® Malathion Plus® Insect Spray Concentrate or the bacterial insecticide *Bacillus thuringiensis* (Bt). Make sure that your tree is listed on the product label. For the best results, use *Bacillus thuringiensis* (Bt) while the caterpillars are small. Remove egg masses found in the winter. Prune branches with tents and worms.

Honeydew

Yellow jacket feeding on honeydew.

Problem: A shiny or sticky substance coats leaves, fruit, and sometimes twigs. Black, sooty mold often grows on the sticky substance. Insects may be found on leaves, and ants, flies, or bees may be present.

Analysis: Honeydew is a sweet, sticky substance secreted by aphids, mealybugs, psyllids, whiteflies, and some scales. These sucking insects can't digest all the sugar in the plant sap, and they excrete the excess in this sticky fluid. The honeydew drops onto the leaves directly below and onto anything beneath the tree. Ants, flies, and bees feed on honeydew and may be found around the plant. A sooty mold fungus often develops on the sticky substance, causing the leaves, fruit, and twigs to appear black and dirty. The fungus doesn't infect the leaf but grows on the honeydew. Extremely heavy infestations may prevent light from reaching the leaf, reducing food production.

Solution: Honeydew will eventually be washed off by rain, or it may be hosed off. Prevent more honeydew by controlling the insect that is producing it. Inspect the foliage to determine what type of insect is present. (For information on controlling insects, see the following: aphids, page 443; mealybugs, page 444; psyllids, page 449; for scales, pages 444 to 447; whiteflies, page 448.)

POWDERY MATERIAL ON LEAVES

Powdery mildew

Powdery mildew.

Problem: Powdery grayish-white patches appear on the leaves. New growth is often stunted, curled, and distorted. Infected buds may open later than usual, and infected flowers and leaves often turn brittle and die. The fruit is sometimes small and misshapen. It may be russeted in a network pattern or in patches, or it may be covered with white powdery patches.

Analysis: Powdery mildew is a common plant disease caused by a fungus that thrives in both humid and dry weather. The fungus spends the winter in leaf and flower buds. In the spring, spores are blown to the new leaves, which are very susceptible to infection. The fungus depletes plant nutrients, causing distortion and often death of the tender foliage. Powdery mildew is favored by warm days and cool nights, reduced light, and lack of rainfall.

Solution: Spray infected trees with a fungicide containing *myclobutanil* or sulfur. (Don't use sulfur on apricots.) Make sure that your fruit tree is listed on the spray label. Most fruit trees should be sprayed at regular intervals of 10 to 14 days from bud-break until three to four weeks after the petals have fallen from the blossoms. Resume spraying whenever the mildew recurs. (For information on spraying, look for the specific tree in the alphabetical section beginning on page 293.)

DISCOLORED OR MOTTLED LEAVES

Sooty mold

Sooty mold on citrus.

Problem: A black, sooty mold grows on the leaves, fruit, and twigs. It can be wiped off the surfaces of the leaves. Cool, moist weather hastens the growth of this substance.

Analysis: Sooty mold is a common black mold found on a wide variety of plants in the garden. It is caused by any of several species of fungi that grow on the sugary material left on plants by aphids, mealybugs, scales, whiteflies, and other insects that suck sap from the plant. The insects are unable to digest all the sugar in the sap, and they excrete the excess in a fluid called *honeydew*, which drops onto the leaves and fruit below. The sooty mold fungus develops on the honeydew, causing the leaves to appear black and dirty. Sooty mold is unsightly but is fairly harmless because it doesn't attack the leaf directly. Heavy infestations prevent light from reaching the leaf, so the leaf produces fewer nutrients and may turn yellow. The presence of sooty mold indicates that the tree is infested with insects.

Solution: Rain will eventually wash off sooty mold. Prevent more sooty mold from growing by controlling the insect that is producing the honeydew. Inspect the foliage to determine what type of insect is present. (For information on controlling insects, see the following pages: aphids, page 443; mealybugs, page 444; scales, pages 444 to 447; whiteflies, page 448.)

Leaf scorch

Leaf scorch on hickory.

Problem: During hot weather, leaves turn brown around the edges and between the veins. Sometimes the leaves die. Many leaves may drop during late summer. This problem is most severe on the youngest branches. Trees rarely die, but growth is impaired.

Analysis: Leaf scorch occurs when water evaporates from the leaves faster than it can be replenished. In hot weather, water evaporates rapidly from the leaves. If the roots can't absorb and convey water fast enough to replenish this loss, the leaves turn brown and wither. This usually occurs in dry soil, but leaves can also become scorched when the soil is moist and temperatures are very high for extended periods. Drying winds, severed roots, limited soil area, salt buildup, low temperatures, and weed killers can also cause scorch. (For more information on leaf scorch, see page 427.)

Solution: To prevent further scorch, water trees during periods of hot weather to wet the entire root space. (For more information on watering, see pages 407 to 408.) Newly transplanted trees should be watered whenever the rootball is dry 2 inches below the surface. Reduce scorch by providing shade or windbreaks for sensitive plants. Plant trees adapted to your climate.

DISCOLORED OR MOTTLED LEAVES *(continued)*

Iron deficiency

Iron-deficient apple leaves.

Nitrogen deficiency

Nitrogen-deficient citrus.

Nitrogen-deficient peach.

Problem: Leaves turn pale green or yellow. The newest leaves (those at the tips of the branches) are most severely affected. Except in extreme cases, the veins of affected leaves remain green. Older leaves may remain green. Fruit production may be reduced, and fruit flavor may be poor.

Analysis: Plants frequently suffer from deficiencies of iron and other minor nutrients such as manganese and zinc, elements essential to normal tree growth and development. Deficiencies can occur when one or more of these elements are depleted in the soil. Often these minor nutrients are present in the soil, but alkaline soil with a pH of 7.5 or higher or wet soil conditions cause them to form compounds that can't be used by the tree. An alkaline condition can result from overliming, from lime leached from cement or brick, or from calcium occurring naturally in the soil. Regions where soil is derived from underlying limestone or where rainfall is low usually have alkaline soils.

Solution: To correct the iron deficiency, spray a chelated iron fertilizer on the foliage, then apply Miracid® ProSelect® Water Soluble Plant Food, which supplies needed iron and also has an acidic reaction on the soil. Check the soil pH. (For information on pH, see page 406.) Correct the pH of the soil by treating it with ferrous sulfate and watering it well or by adding organic matter to the soil.

Problem: Older leaves turn yellow. Eventually the rest of the leaves turn yellow green and then yellow. Yellow leaves usually die and drop off. New leaves are small, and growth is slow. Fruit production is poor.

Analysis: Nitrogen is deficient or unavailable in most soils. Nitrogen is essential in the formation of plant tissue, chlorophyll, and many other compounds necessary for plant growth. When a tree can't obtain enough nitrogen from the soil, it utilizes nitrogen from its older leaves for new growth. The older leaves become deficient in nitrogen and turn yellow. A continuing shortage of nitrogen causes overall yellowing, stunting, death of the older leaves, and a reduced fruit yield. Fast-growing, young fruit trees usually require large amounts of nitrogen. Nitrogen naturally present in the soil is made available to trees as organic matter decomposes. Soils that are low in organic matter, such as sandy and readily leached soils, are often infertile. Also, nitrogen is leached from the soil more quickly when rainfall or irrigation is heavy. Poorly drained, overwatered, and compacted soils lack oxygen, which is necessary for the utilization of nitrogen. Trees growing in these soils often exhibit symptoms of nitrogen deficiency. In addition, trees growing in cold (50°F and lower), hot (90°F and higher), acid (pH of 5.5 or lower), or alkaline (pH of 7.8 or higher) soils are often low in nitrogen.

Solution: Fertilize trees regularly with a balanced fertilizer, such as Scotts® Evergreen, Shrub and Tree Food. (For information on fertilizing, see page 409.) Add organic matter to compacted soils and soils low in organic substances. Improve drainage in poorly drained soils. (For information on drainage, see page 406.) Do not keep the soil constantly wet. (For information on watering, see pages 407 to 408.) Raise or lower soil pH in soils that are acid or alkaline. (For information on pH, see page 406.)

Mites

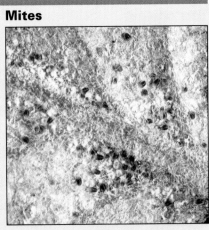

Spider mites (2× life size).

Problem: Leaves are stippled, yellowing, silver, or bronze. There may be webbing over flower buds, between leaves, or on the lower surfaces of leaves. The fruit may be roughened or russet colored. To check for certain species of mites, examine the bottoms of the leaves with a hand lens. Or hold a sheet of white paper underneath an affected leaf and tap the leaf sharply. Minute specks the size of pepper grains will drop to the paper and begin to crawl around.

Analysis: Mites, related to spiders, commonly attack fruit trees and other garden plants. Certain mites, such as the two-spotted spider mite, are large enough to be detected on white paper. Smaller mites, such as plum and pear rust mites, are microscopic and can't be seen without the aid of a strong hand lens or microscope. Mites cause damage by sucking sap from the fruit surface and the undersides of leaves. As a result of their feeding, the plant's chlorophyll disappears, producing the stippled or silver appearance. Mites are active throughout the growing season but thrive in hot, dry weather (70°F and higher). By midsummer, they can build to tremendous numbers. (For more information on mites, see page 457.)

Solution: Spray infested trees with Ortho® Malathion Plus® Insect Spray Concentrate or Ortho® Volck® Oil Spray. Repeat the spray at least two more times at intervals of 7 to 10 days. Make sure that your tree is listed on the spray label. Predatory mites, which feed on other mites, may be available for control.

Nematodes

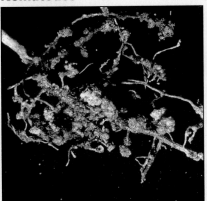

Root knot nematode damage.

Problem: Leaves are bronzed and yellowing. They may wilt on hot, dry days but recover at night. The tree is generally weak. After several years, the tree is stunted, and branches may die. Some nematodes produce galls; others produce lesions on roots.

Analysis: Most nematodes are microscopic worms that live in the soil. Nematodes feed on tree roots, damaging and stunting them. The damaged roots can't supply sufficient water and nutrients to the branches and leaves, and the tree is stunted or slowly dies. Nematodes are found throughout the United States but are most severe in the Southeast. They prefer moist, sandy loam soils. Nematodes can move only a few inches each year on their own, but they may be carried long distances by soil, water, tools, or infested plants. Testing roots and soil is the only positive method for confirming the presence of nematodes. Contact your local county extension office (see page 104) for sampling instructions and addresses of testing laboratories. Soil and root problems such as poor soil structure, drought stress, nutrient deficiency, and root rots also can produce symptoms of decline similar to those caused by nematodes. These problems should be eliminated as causes before soil and root samples are sent for testing. (For information on soil problems and root rots, see pages 404 and 419.)

Solution: No available chemicals kill nematodes in planted soil. The worms can be controlled before planting, however, by soil fumigation or solarization.

Crown gall

Crown gall on roots.

Problem: Large corky galls, up to several inches in diameter, appear at the base of the tree and on the roots. The galls are rounded, with a rough, irregular surface. Trees with numerous galls are weak; growth may be slowed, and the foliage may turn yellow.

Analysis: Crown gall is a plant disease caused by a soil-inhabiting bacterium (*Agrobacterium tumefaciens*) that infects many ornamentals, fruits, and vegetables in the garden. The bacteria are often brought to a garden initially on the roots of an infected plant and are spread in the soil. The bacteria enter the tree through wounds in the roots or the base of the trunk (the crown). They produce a substance that stimulates rapid cell growth in the tree, causing gall formation. The galls disrupt the flow of water and nutrients through the trunk, weakening and stunting the top growth. They don't usually cause the tree to die. (For more information on crown gall, see page 422.)

Solution: Infected trees can't be cured; however, they often survive for many years. Although the disease can't be eliminated from the tree, individual galls can be removed by professionals. If you wish to remove galls from valued trees, consult a professional horticulturist or landscape contractor. The bacteria will remain in the soil for as long as three years after an infected tree has been removed. Replant with a resistant tree.

TREE STUNTED OR DECLINING *(continued)*

Root and crown rot

Crown rot on cherry.

Phytophthora rot on apple.

Tree neglect

Neglected fruit tree.

Problem: Normal leaf color dulls, and the plant loses vigor. Leaves may wilt or turn yellow or light brown. Major branches or the entire tree may die. The tree sometimes lives for many months in a weakened condition, or it may die quickly. Fruit growing only on the upper branches is a common sign of a tree's decline. The roots and cambium (thin layer of tissue just beneath the bark) of the lower trunk are brownish, and the roots may be decayed. In the Southwest only, fine, woolly, brown strands may form on the roots and white, powdery spores on the soil surface. Or fan-shape plaques of white strands may appear between the bark and wood of roots and lower stems. Mushrooms may appear at the base of the plant in the fall.

Problem: Overall growth is slow. Foliage may be sparse, discolored, or stunted. Branches are dense and intertwined. Twigs and branches may be dying or dead, and fruit is small and of poor quality. Twigs and branches may be covered with moss or lichens. The tree may be diseased or infested with insects.

Analysis: Root rot and crown rot are caused by fungi that live in soil and on roots. They spread by water, soil, and transplants.

1. *Phytophthora* species: These fungi cause browning and decay of the roots and browning of the cambium and wood of the lower trunk. The tree usually dies slowly, but young trees may wilt and die rapidly. The disease is most prevalent in heavy, waterlogged soil.

2. *Phymatotrichum omnivorum:* This fungus, commonly known as *cotton root rot* or *Texas root rot*, is a serious problem on many plants in the Southwest. Young trees may suddenly wilt and die. Brown strands form on the roots, and white powdery spores on the soil. The disease is most severe in heavy, alkaline soils.

3. *Armillaria mellea:* This disease is commonly known as *shoestring root rot*, *mushroom root rot*, or *oak root fungus*. It is identified by the presence of fan-shape plaques of white fungal strands between the bark and the wood of the roots and lower trunk. Honey-colored mushrooms may appear at the base of the plant.

Solution: Solutions below correspond to the numbered items in the analysis.

1. Remove dead and dying trees. When replanting, use plants that are resistant to phytophthora. (For a list, see page 536.) Improve drainage. (For information on drainage, see page 406.) Avoid overwatering plants. (For information on watering, see pages 407 to 408.)

2. Remove dead and dying trees. When replanting, use only resistant varieties. (For a list, see page 538.) Before planting, increase the soil acidity by adding 1 pound of ammonium sulfate for every 10 square feet of soil. Make a circular ridge around the planting area, and fill the resulting depression with 4 inches of water. Repeat the treatment in 5 to 10 days. Improve soil drainage.

3. Remove dead trees and as much of the root system as possible. If the plant is newly infected, expose its base for several months by removing 3 or 4 inches of soil. Prune diseased roots. Fertilize with Scotts® Evergreen, Flowering Tree & Shrub Slow Release Plant Food. When replanting, use only resistant plants (see page 539).

Analysis: Most fruit trees decline in vigor and fruitfulness if neglected for several years. Fruit trees are susceptible to several fungal and bacterial diseases that can affect the roots, crown (where the trunk meets the roots), branches, foliage, and fruit. Many insect pests also weaken fruit trees by feeding, boring into, or otherwise damaging them. Most fruit trees need to be pruned annually in order to stimulate the production of new fruiting wood or to eliminate excess or old fruiting wood. In addition, proper watering and fertilizing is important for maintaining tree health, vigor and fruitfulness.

Solution: Control pests and plant diseases. To determine what types of insects and diseases are affecting your tree and how to control them, look up your tree in the section beginning at right. Thin out weak, diseased, intertwined, and dying twigs and branches. If the tree needs to be heavily pruned or restructured, gradually prune it into proper shape over a period of three years. Remove all invasive growth, such as grass or ground cover, from around the base of the tree. Water and fertilize the tree properly.

ALMOND

Shothole fungus

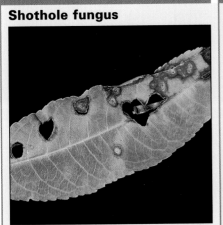

Shothole fungus.

Problem: Small purplish spots appear on the leaves in early spring. The spots turn brown and enlarge to ¼ inch in diameter. The centers of the spots die and drop out, leaving small round holes. Lesions also may appear on young shoots. The blossoms may turn brown and have a gummy sap at the base. Almond yield may be reduced, and corky spots may appear on hulls. In severe cases, the tree may drop all of its leaves.

Analysis: Shothole fungus, also called *coryneum blight* or *peach blight*, is a disease caused by a fungus (*Wilsonomyces carpophilus*) that attacks almonds and other stone fruits. The fungus spends the winter in lesions on the twigs and buds. The spores are spread by spring rains and infect new leaves. Infection causes the leaf tissue to produce a layer of cells that walls off the damaged area. The center of the spot then drops out. Severe infection may defoliate the tree, produce smaller almonds, and cause some almonds to drop. The disease thrives in wet spring weather.

Solution: Nothing adequately controls shothole fungus during the growing season. The following spring, spray the tree with a lime-sulfur spray or a fungicide containing *azoxystrobin* or *chlorothalonil* when the petals have emerged from the bud but before they have fully opened. Spray again when the petals have fallen from the flowers.

APPLE

Codling moths

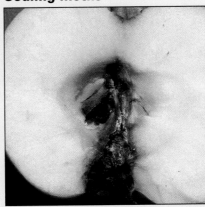

Codling moth damage.

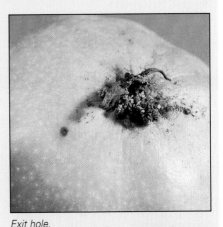

Exit hole.

Problem: The fruit is blemished by small holes surrounded by dead tissue. A brown, crumbly material resembling sawdust may surround the holes. Brown-headed, pinkish-white worms up to 1 inch long may be found in the fruit. The interior of the fruit is often dark and rotted. Affected apples drop prematurely.

Analysis: The codling moth (*Cydia pomonella*) is a small (½-inch-wide), gray-brown moth that is one of the most serious apple pests in the United States. The moths appear in the spring when the apple trees are blooming, usually flying at twilight. They lay their eggs on the leaves, twigs, and developing fruit. When the eggs hatch, the larvae tunnel into the fruit. They feed for several weeks then emerge, often leaving a mass of dark excrement on the skin and inside the fruit. After pupating in sheltered locations on or around the tree, another generation of moths emerges in midsummer. Apples may be damaged by worms throughout the summer. In the fall, mature larvae spin cocoons in protected places, such as under loose bark or in tree crevices. They spend the winter in these cocoons, emerging as moths in the spring. They may also overwinter on other plants under the trees.

Solution: Once worms have penetrated the apples, it is impossible to kill them. To protect uninfested apples, treat with Ortho® Bug-B-Gon® Multi-Purpose Garden Dust or an insecticide containing *carbaryl* every 10 days. Remove and destroy all fallen apples, and clean up debris. The following spring, begin the treatment two to three weeks after petal fall. For more precise spray timing, use pheromone traps to monitor moth flights. After the initial two sprayings, hang traps. Spray one week after moth catches reach five moths per week. Pheromone traps can also be used to control codling moths. Hang at least two per tree.

APPLE (continued)

Apple maggots

Apple maggots (4× life size). Inset: Adult.

Problem: Fruit may be dimpled and pitted, with brown trails winding through the flesh. White, legless maggots about ⅜ inch long may be present in the fruit. Severely infested apples are brown and pulpy inside. Frequently, many apples drop prematurely.

Analysis: Apple maggots (*Rhagoletis pomonella*) are the larvae of flies that resemble the common housefly. Apple maggots infest plums, cherries, and pears in addition to apples. Adult flies emerge from pupae between late June and the beginning of September. They lay eggs in the fruit through holes they puncture in the skin. The maggots that emerge from the eggs make brown trails through the flesh as they feed. Infested apples usually drop to the ground. Mature maggots emerge from the apples and burrow in the soil to pupate. They remain in the soil throughout the winter and emerge as adult flies the following June.

Solution: Maggots can't be killed after apples are infested. Protect healthy apples from adult flies by spraying at intervals of 7 to 10 days from the end of June until the beginning of September with Ortho® Bug-B-Gon® Multi-Purpose Insect Killer Ready-To-Use or an insecticide containing *permethrin*. Pick up and destroy fallen apples every week throughout the summer. For more precise spray timing, use apple maggot traps. These red balls look like ripe apples but are coated with a sticky material that traps adult flies. Spray as soon as adult flies appear. The red ball traps can also be used to control apple maggots without spraying. Hang at least two in each tree.

Plum cucurlios

Plum curculio damage. Inset: (3× life size).

Problem: The ripening fruit is misshapen and rotten, and it drops prematurely. Holes about ⅛ inch in diameter and deep, crescent-shape scars appear on the fruit. When cut open, fruit may contain curved, yellow-gray grubs with brown heads and about ⅓ inch long.

Analysis: Plum curculio (*Conotrachelus nenuphar*), insects found east of the Rocky Mountains, attack stone fruits and pears, as well as apples. The adult insects are brown beetles about ¼ inch long with long, curved snouts. They hibernate in debris and other protected places during the winter. The beetles emerge in the spring when new growth starts and begin feeding on young leaves, blossoms, and developing fruit. After five to six weeks, the female beetles start to lay eggs in the young fruit. The grubs that hatch from the eggs feed for several weeks in the fruit. Infested apples usually drop to the ground. The grubs eventually leave the apples and bore into the soil, where they pupate. The emerging beetles feed on fruit for a few weeks, then go into hibernation. In the South, they lay eggs, producing a second generation of grubs in late summer.

Solution: Once the fruit is infested, you can't kill the grubs inside. Treat with Ortho® Malathion Plus® Insect Spray Concentrate or Ortho® Bug-B-Gon® Multi-Purpose Garden Dust to kill beetles that may be feeding on fruit or laying eggs. Pick up and destroy all fallen fruit. The following spring, spray trees when petals are falling from the blossoms; repeat sprays according to directions on the label.

Sooty blotch and fly speck

Sooty blotch and fly speck.

Problem: Clusters of a few to 100 sharply defined, shiny black spots appear on the fruit. Sooty or cloudy blotches may also appear. Both appear only on the skin of the fruit without affecting the flesh.

Analysis: Although sooty blotch and fly speck are not caused by the same fungus, they are plant diseases so commonly found in association that they are usually described together. Sooty blotch can be caused by any of several related fungi. Fly speck is caused by the fungus *Zygophiala jamaicensis*. These fungi spend the winter on the twigs of apples and many other woody plants. During mild, wet weather, the fungi produce spores that are blown to and infect the developing apples. Infection can occur anytime after petal-fall but is most prevalent in mid- to late summer. About a month after the initial infection, specks and blotches appear on the maturing fruit. Although these diseases are unsightly, they are external and don't generally affect the taste of the apples.

Solution: You can't clear infected apples, but the fruit is edible. To prevent the diseases the following year, improve air circulation by pruning to open dense trees and by thinning apple clusters. Remove wild brambles around the trees to eliminate sources of infection. The following spring, spray with a fungicide containing *captan* every 10 to 14 days, from one or two weeks after petal-fall until three weeks before harvest. Trees in the Southeast need annual spraying.

Bitter rot

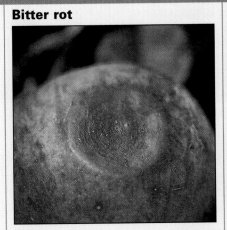

Bitter rot.

Problem: Sunken, light brown, circular spots appear on half-grown to mature fruit. These spots gradually enlarge to 1 inch in diameter. Concentric rings and sticky pink masses of spores may appear on the spotted areas during moist weather. The rotted apple flesh tastes bitter. Sunken lesions may form on the branches.

Analysis: Bitter rot, a plant disease that also affects pears, is caused by two closely related fungi *Glomerella cingulata* and *Colletotrichum gloeosporioides*. The fungi spend the winter in rotted apples left on the tree and on the ground, and in sunken lesions on the branches. Spores are spread by splashing rain to healthy apples in the spring. Infection can occur throughout the fruiting season. In areas where hot, humid conditions last for long periods of time, bitter rot can quickly destroy an entire apple crop. This disease primarily attacks the fruit and does not severely damage the health of the tree.

Solution: Spray infested trees with a fungicide containing *captan*. To prevent recurrence the following year, prune out and destroy deadwood and branches with lesions, and remove and destroy rotted apples. The following spring, spray the trees every 10 to 14 days from petal fall until 7 days before harvest. Trees in the darker zone on the accompanying map need annual treatment. Plant resistant varieties.

San Jose scales

San Jose scales (½ life size).

Problem: Leaves are pale green to yellow and may drop prematurely from weakened limbs. The bark is encrusted with small (1/16-inch), hard, circular, slightly raised bumps with dull yellow centers. If the hard cover is scraped off, the insect underneath is yellow or olive. Limbs may die back, and entire branches may be killed. Red spots with white centers mar the apple skins.

Analysis: San Jose scales (*Quadraspidiotus perniciosus*) are insects that infest the bark, leaves, and fruit of many fruit trees. The scales bear live young in the spring. In late spring to midsummer the young scales, called *crawlers*, settle on leaves and twigs. The soft-bodied young feed by inserting their mouthparts and sucking sap from the plant. The legs atrophy, and a hard, crusty shell develops over the body. An uncontrolled infestation of San Jose scales may kill large branches after two or three seasons. (For more information on scales, see pages 444 to 447.)

Solution: During the dormant season, just prior to growth in early spring, spray the trunk and branches with Ortho® Volck® Oil Spray. Begin checking for crawlers about a month after full bloom. Continue monitoring through the summer to catch later generations. Crawlers may be killed with Ortho® Malathion Plus® Insect Spray Concentrate.

Woolly apple aphids

Woolly apple aphids (2× life size).

Problem: White, cottony masses appear on twigs, branches, and possibly trunks, often near pruning wounds. Beneath the white masses are clusters of small (1/8-inch), reddish-purple, soft-bodied insects. Lumpy galls may be on smaller branches. The roots of the trees have large swellings. Leaves may be yellowing. Young trees are often stunted and may be easily uprooted.

Analysis: Woolly apple aphids (*Eriosoma lanigerum*) are insects that may be found wherever apples are grown. Woolly apple aphids usually suck sap from the twigs and branches, but the most serious damage occurs when some of the aphids burrow into the soil and feed on the roots. This feeding causes root galls to form, inhibiting the flow of water and nutrients up into the tree. In addition to forming galls and nodules, the roots become fibrous and stunted. Young trees sometimes die from root infestations of woolly apple aphids.

Solution: Spray the trunk, branches, and foliage with Ortho® Malathion Plus® Insect Spray Concentrate as soon as the pests are noticed. Repeat as directed on the label. Although sprays cannot rid the roots of aphids, you can usually prevent them from invading the roots by keeping the trunk, branches, and foliage free of aphids. In addition to spraying, use a garden hose to hose off clusters of aphids on the tree between sprays. A band of sticky material applied to the trunk will prevent aphids from migrating to the roots. Remove dying trees. Use rootstocks resistant to woolly apple aphids when replacing trees.

APPLE (continued)

Fruit tree leafroller

Fruit tree leafrollers (life size).

Problem: Irregular holes appear in the leaves and fruit. Some of the leaves are rolled and held together with a web. Inside these rolled leaves are pale green worms with black heads, up to ¾ inch long. The maturing apples are scarred and misshapen.

Analysis: Fruit tree leafrollers (*Archips argyrospilus*), the larvae of brown moths, are common pests of many fruit and ornamental trees. The moths lay their eggs on branches or twigs in June or July. The eggs hatch the following spring, and the emerging larvae feed on the blossoms and developing fruit and foliage. Leafrollers often wrap leaves around ripening fruit, then feed on the fruit inside. After about a month, the mature larvae pupate within rolled leaves, to emerge as moths in June or July.

Solution: If practical, pick off and destroy rolled leaves to reduce the numbers of moths that will emerge later in the season. The following spring, spray the tree with Ortho® Malathion Plus® Insect Spray Concentrate when 75 percent of the petals have fallen from the blossoms. Repeat the spray according to the directions on the label. For more precise timing, use pheromone traps. Begin spraying when moth catches peak and begin to decline. Eggs are hatching at that time.

Scab

Scab.

Problem: Olive brown, velvety spots, ¼ inch or more, appear on the leaves and fruit. Spots develop first on the undersides of leaves, then on top sides. As the infected apples mature, the spots become light to dark brown corky lesions. The fruit is often cracked and malformed and may drop prematurely. Severely infected trees may completely defoliate.

Analysis: Scab is a plant disease caused by a fungus (*Venturia inaequalis*). It is one of the most serious diseases of apples in areas where spring weather is mild (60° to 70°F) and wet. The fungus spends the winter in infected leaf debris on the ground. Beginning at bud-break, spores are ejected into the air when the leaf debris becomes wet. Air currents carry them to emerging leaves. If a film of water is present on a leaf, the spores germinate and infect the leaf. The infected tissues produce more spores, which in turn infect other leaf and fruit surfaces. If the fruit stays wet for two or three days at a time in late summer or early fall, spores can infect the fruit, but symptoms don't develop until the fruit has been stored, sometimes for several months.

Solution: Unless severely infected, the apples are edible. To prevent recurrence of the disease the following year, remove and destroy leaf debris and infected fruit in the fall. The following spring, spray with a fungicide containing *captan* or *myclobutanil*.

Black rot

Black rot.

Problem: A firm spot composed of concentric light and dark brown rings appears on the apple. This spot gradually turns dark brown or black and enlarges, rotting part or all of the fruit. Spots on the leaves, first appearing from one to three weeks after petal fall, are also formed of light and dark concentric rings. Reddish-brown, slightly sunken lesions up to several feet in length often appear on the branches or trunk of the tree.

Analysis: Black rot is caused by a fungus (*Botryosphaeria* species) that also attacks pears. The fungus spends the winter in rotted apples, deadwood, and old fire blight cankers. When temperatures reach 60°F and higher in the spring, spores are produced on infected tissues and splashed by water to the foliage and fruit. Branches and trunks may be infected with black rot, especially when the bark has been infected by fire blight or weakened by sunscald, cold, or heavy shading. As the fungus decays the wood, cankers form, weakening the branches and reducing the overall vigor of the tree. Fruit infection is generally more severe in warm, moist areas, and canker formation is more prevalent in cooler climates.

Solution: Spray with a fungicide containing *captan* as soon as infestation is noticed. Remove all rotted apples from the tree and ground, and destroy them. Prune out deadwood and branches infected with fire blight. Destroy the prunings. Thin densely branched trees to provide adequate light and air circulation. The following spring, begin spraying when buds break. Spray every 10 to 14 days.

Cedar-apple rust

Cedar-apple rust.

Problem: Pale yellow spots appear on the upper surfaces of leaves and on fruit in mid- to late spring. These spots gradually enlarge, turn orange, and develop minute black dots. Small (⅙-inch) cups with fringed edges form on the lower surfaces of leaves. Infected leaves and fruit may drop prematurely; the fruit is often small and deformed.

Analysis: Cedar-apple rust is a plant disease caused by a fungus (*Gymnosporangium juniperi-virginianae*) that affects both apples and certain species of juniper and red cedar. This fungus can't spread from apple to apple, or from juniper to juniper, but, instead, must alternate between the two. In the spring, spores from brown and orange galls on juniper or cedar are blown up to 3 miles to apple trees. During mild, wet weather, the spores germinate and infect the leaves and fruit, causing spotting and, eventually, premature leaf and apple drop. During the summer, spores are produced in the small cups on the undersides of leaves. These spores are blown back to junipers and cedars, causing new infections and starting the cycle again.

Solution: Cedar-apple rust can't be controlled on the current season's apples and leaves. The following spring, spray apple trees with a fungicide when the flower buds turn pink, again when 75 percent of the petals have fallen from the blossoms, and once more 10 days later. When practical, don't plant apples within several hundred yards of junipers or red cedar.

Fire blight

Twig dieback. Inset: Bacterial ooze.

Problem: Blossoms turn brown and die. Shoots turn brown or black from the tips and a bend often develops at the tips. Spurs and branches wilt from the tips down, turn brown, and die. Leaves remain attached. On the branches, the bark becomes water-soaked, then dark, sunken, and dry, forming a canker. In warm, moist spring weather, drops of milky to reddish-brown sticky liquid appear on the surface of infected regions. During the summer, shoots, branches, or entire trees may wilt and turn black.

Analysis: Fire blight is a plant disease caused by a bacterium (*Erwinia amylovora*) that commonly affects apples, pears, and several ornamental trees. The bacteria spend the winter in cankers on the branches and twigs. Just before blooming, the bacteria ooze out of the cankers and are carried by splashing rain and insects to the apple blossoms. Honey bees and other insects continue to spread the bacteria to healthy blossoms. Summer storms can spread bacteria, leading to sudden and severe fire blight outbreaks. Cankers develop on the twigs and branches, often resulting in conspicuous branch and twig dieback.

Solution: Prune infected twigs and branches at least 12 inches below visible decay and destroy debris. During the growing season, disinfect pruning shears after each cut. The following spring, spray with basic copper sulfate before the blossoms open. When 25 percent of the flowers have opened, spray with a bactericide containing *streptomycin*. Repeat every three to five days until the end of the blooming period.

Flat-headed borers

Pacific flat-headed borer (2× life size).

Problem: Leaves wilt and turn brown. Patches of bark on the trunk are sunken and discolored and may be soaked with sap. Holes about ⅜ inch in diameter may appear in the affected bark. Sawdust-filled tunnels in the wood may contain yellowish white, flat-headed grubs about ¾ inch long. In late spring to midsummer, bronze or copper-colored beetles ½ to ¾ inch long may be seen feeding on the foliage. Newly planted or weak trees are most severely affected.

Analysis: In addition to damaging apples, flat-headed borers (*Chrysobothris* species) are insects that attack many other trees and shrubs. In late spring to midsummer, the females begin to lay eggs in crevices in the bark. The emerging larvae bore through the bark into the outer layer of wood, creating winding tunnels. These tunnels damage the nutrient- and water-conducting vessels in the tree, causing twig and branch dieback and sometimes killing the tree. The mature larvae bore deep into the heartwood to pupate; adult beetles emerge the following spring. Newly transplanted, weakened, and diseased trees are most susceptible to borer infestation. Borers often invade sunburned areas on the trunk of newly planted trees.

Solution: Treat with an insecticide containing *carbaryl* to kill borers before they burrow into the wood. Keep trees healthy and vigorous by watering, fertilizing, and pruning properly. (For more cultural information, see pages 402 to 415.) Discourage borer infestation by wrapping the trunk soon after bloom with tree-wrapping paper or burlap.

APRICOT

Brown rot

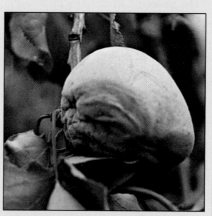

Brown rot.

Brown rot on stems, leaves, and fruit.

Scab

Scab.

Problem: Blossoms and young leaves wilt, decay, and turn brown during the first two weeks of the bloom period. Often the decayed blossoms and leaves fail to drop, and they may hang on the tree throughout the growing season. In humid conditions, masses of gray spores may appear on the infected flower parts. Extensive twig dieback often occurs. (Twig dieback is more common in the West than the East.) Sunken lesions (cankers) may develop on the twigs and branches as the season progresses; a thick, gummy material often oozes from these cankers.

On the fruit: Small circular brown spots appear on the young apricots. Later in the season, as the apricots start to mature, these spots may enlarge to rot part or all of the fruit. During moist weather, the rotted apricots are covered with tufts of gray spores. When the infected fruit is sliced open, the flesh inside is brown, firm, and fairly dry. Infected apricots either drop prematurely or dry out, turn dark brown, and remain on the tree past the normal harvest period.

Analysis: Brown rot, a plant disease caused by either of two closely related fungi, (*Monilinia laxa* or *M. fructicola*), is very destructive to apricots and stone fruits. The fungi spend the winter in twig cankers or in rotted apricots (mummies) on the tree or on the ground. In the spring, spores are blown or splashed from cankers or mummies to healthy flower buds. After penetrating and decaying the flowers, the fungus grows down into the twigs, producing brown, sunken cankers. During moist weather a thick, gummy sap sometimes oozes from the cankers, and tufts of gray spores may form on the infected areas. Spores from cankers and infected blossoms or mummies are splashed and blown to maturing fruit. Young apricots are fairly resistant to infection, but maturing apricots are vulnerable. Brown rot develops most rapidly in mild, moist conditions.

Solution: If uninfected blossoms remain on your tree, spray with Ortho® Garden Disease Control to protect them from infection. Repeat the spray 10 days later. The following spring, spray trees when the first flowers begin to open and continue to spray according to label directions. Remove and destroy all infected apricots and mummies. Prune cankers and blighted twigs. Clean up and destroy all debris around the tree. Plant resistant varieties.

Problem: Small olive-green spots appear on the half-grown fruit. These spots are usually centered around the stem end of the apricot. The spots eventually turn brown and velvety. The fruit is often dwarfed, deformed, or cracked. The leaves may have small brown spots and holes in them, and many twigs die back.

Analysis: Scab is a plant disease caused by a fungus (*Cladosporium carpophilum*) that attacks peaches, nectarines, cherries, and plums as well as apricots. The fungus spends the winter on twig lesions. In the spring, spores are splashed and blown to the developing foliage and fruit. The young fruit doesn't show scab lesions for at least a month after it is infected. Spores produced on the infected leaves, twigs, and fruit continue to infect healthy apricots throughout the fruiting season. The disease resembles shothole fungus and is often confused with it.

Solution: You can't do anything about the spots on the current year's fruit, but it is edible if peeled. The following year, spray Ortho® Garden Disease Control when the buds begin to show color and again at full bloom. If the weather is cool and moist, make a third application at petal-fall. Apply once more when the fruit begins to form.

Plum curculios

Plum curculio (5× life size).

Problem: The ripening fruit is misshapen and rotten and often drops prematurely. Holes about ⅛ inch in diameter and deep, crescent-shape scars appear on the fruit. When cut open, the damaged fruit may contain crescent-shape grayish-white grubs about ⅓ inch long.

Analysis: Plum curculio (*Conotrachelus nenuphar*), an insect found east of the Rocky Mountains, attack stone fruits, apples, pears, and apricots. The adult insects are mottled brown beetles, about ¼ inch long, with long, curved snouts. They hibernate in debris and other protected places during the winter. The beetles emerge in the spring when new growth starts and begin feeding on young leaves, blossoms, and developing fruit. After five to six weeks, the female beetles start to lay eggs in the young fruit. The grubs that hatch from the eggs feed for several weeks in the fruit. Usually the infested apricots drop to the ground. The grubs eventually leave the fruit and bore into the soil, where they pupate. The emerging beetles feed on fruit for a few weeks, then go into hibernation. In the South, they lay eggs, producing a second generation of grubs in the late summer.

Solution: Once the fruit is infested, you can't kill the grubs inside. Spray with Ortho® Malathion Plus® Insect Spray Concentrate to kill beetles that may be feeding on fruit or laying eggs. Pick up and destroy all fallen fruit. The following spring, spray the trees when the petals are falling from blossoms; repeat applications according to directions on the label.

Bacterial leafspot

Bacterial leafspot.

Problem: Water-soaked spots on the undersides of leaves turn brown or black; often the centers of the spots fall out. The tips of the leaves may die, and eventually the leaves drop. When the fruit sets, the surfaces may be dotted with spots that later turn into deep, sunken brown pits, often surrounded by yellow rings. Sunken lesions can often be seen at the joints of the twigs.

Analysis: Bacterial leaf spot is a disease caused by a bacterium (*Xanthomonas arboricola* pv. *pruni*) that also attacks peaches, nectarines, and plums. The disease is common east of the Rocky Mountains and is one of the more destructive stone-fruit diseases. The bacteria spend the winter in the lesions on the twigs, oozing out in the spring to be carried by splashing rain to the young leaves and shoots, which they infect and decay. Periods of frequent rainfall promote the infection.

Solution: This disease is difficult to control adequately. Remove and destroy infected twigs in the fall. Spray with basic copper sulfate as soon as the leaves shed in the fall and again in the spring as buds begin to fatten.

Cytospora canker

Cytospora canker.

Problem: Oval or oblong sunken lesions on the bark enlarge gradually. A sticky gum may ooze from the lesions and is sometimes followed by the emergence of curly orange threads. Later, small black freckles appear on the bark along the edges of the lesions. Leaves on affected branches may turn brown and die, or the entire branch may die.

Analysis: Cytospora canker, a plant disease also known as *perennial canker*, is caused by two related fungi (*Cytospora cincta* and *C. leucostoma*) that also attack peach, plum, and cherry. The fungi spend the winter in cankers or on deadwood. In the spring, black fungal bodies develop in the bark, and curly orange fungal chains form. These chains release spores that are spread by wind and splashing rain to healthy trees. Infection usually occurs through injured tissues. Bark that is damaged by sunscald, cold, pruning wounds, or mechanical injury is especially susceptible. Depressed cankers form and may ooze a sticky gum. The branch or stem above the canker may die, because the water-conducting tissue of the branch decays or clogs. Mild, wet weather (70° to 85°F) enhances disease development.

Solution: No fully adequate control is available; a combination of procedures must be used. Remove badly infected branches and cut out cankers. Avoid mechanical injuries to trees, and paint the trunks with white latex paint to protect against cold injury and sunburn. Avoid fertilizing in late summer or fall.

APRICOT *(continued)*

Peach twig borers

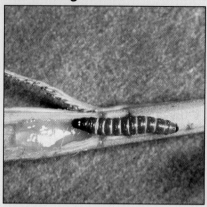

Peach twig borer (2× life size).

Problem: New growth at the tips of the twigs wilts and dies. When the affected twigs are sliced open lengthwise, worms about ½ inch long are found inside. The reddish-brown color of these worms distinguishes them from oriental fruit moth worms, which cause similar damage. Later in the season, these worms may be found in some cut-open maturing fruit. During summer, cocoons may be attached to the branches or tree crotches.

Analysis: Peach twig borer (*Anarsia lineatella*) attacks all of the stone fruits and is particularly damaging along the Pacific coast. The young larvae hibernate during the winter in burrows under loose bark or in other protected places on the tree. When the tree blooms in the spring, the larvae emerge and bore into the young buds, shoots, and tender twigs, causing twig and leaf death. When mature, they leave the twigs and pupate in cocoons attached to branches. After several weeks, gray moths emerge and lay eggs on the twigs, leaves, and fruit. Egg laying and larval damage can occur all through the growing season. Later in the summer, larvae feed primarily on the maturing fruit. In addition to ruining the fruit, these pests may cause abnormal branching on young trees.

Solution: Once borers have infested twigs, they can't be killed. Destroy hibernating larvae by spraying during the dormant season with horticultural oil. In the spring, spray with an insecticide containing *carbaryl* or the biological insecticide *Bacillus thuringiensis* (Bt) as flower buds begin to open. Repeat 7 to 10 days later.

CHERRY

Cherry fruit fly maggots

Cherry fruit fly maggots (3× life size).

Problem: The fruit is malformed, shrunken, or shriveled. Often the cherries are rotten and pulpy, with one side turning red before maturity. Holes may appear in the fruit. Tapered, yellow-white, legless worms up to ¼ inch long may be found in the cherries.

Analysis: Cherry fruit fly maggots are the larvae of several closely related flies. The adult flies (*Rhagoletis* species), about half the size of the common housefly, are black with dark bands on the clear wings. Adults appear in the late spring for a period of about a month. They lay eggs in the cherries through holes they puncture in the skin, beginning when the fruit has turned yellow. After several days, eggs hatch into maggots that tunnel through the cherry flesh. Mature maggots exit fruit and drop to the ground, where they burrow into the soil to pupate. They remain in the soil throughout the winter and emerge as adults the following spring. Damaged cherries have an exit hole. They may fall or remain on the tree.

Solution: You can't control the worms in the current year's fruit, but you can try to prevent the problem from happening the following year. Look for the adult flies in late spring as the fruit is coloring. Monitor their presence with yellow sticky traps. As soon as fruit flies appear, treat with Ortho® Bug-B-Gon® Multi-Purpose Insect Killer Ready-To-Use or Ortho® Bug-B-Gon® Multi-Purpose Garden Dust. Repeat the application twice more at intervals of 7 to 10 days. Prevent maggots from burrowing into the ground to pupate by spreading black plastic under the tree.

Pear slugs

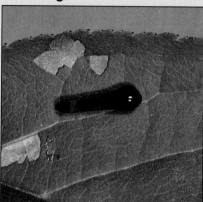

Pear slug larva (2× life size).

Problem: The upper surfaces of leaves are chewed between the veins, leaving a lacy, translucent layer of tissue that turns brown. Olive-green to blackish, slimy, sluglike worms with heads wider than the bodies, up to ½ inch long, may be feeding on the leaves. Severely infested trees may be defoliated.

Analysis: Although pear slugs (*Caliroa cerasi*), also called *cherry slugs*, closely resemble slugs, they are actually the larvae of black-and-yellow flies that infest pears, plums, and some ornamental trees in addition to cherries. Adult flies, which appear in the late spring, lay their eggs in the leaves. The larvae that hatch from these eggs exude a slimy, olive-green substance, giving them a sluglike appearance. They feed on the foliage for about a month, then drop to the ground, burrow into the soil, and pupate. Young trees severely infested by pear slugs may be greatly weakened and will produce fewer, poor-quality cherries.

Solution: Wash off minor infestations with a strong spray of water from a garden hose. For problem infestations, spray with Ortho® Bug-B-Gon® Multi-Purpose Insect Killer Ready-To-Use. Repeat if reinfestation occurs.

Oriental fruit moths

Oriental fruit moth damage.

Problem: New growth at the tips of the twigs wilts and dies. When the affected twigs are sliced open lengthwise, pinkish-white worms with brown heads, up to ½ inch long, are found inside. Later in the season, some of the maturing fruit may also be found to contain these worms.

Analysis: The larvae of the night-flying oriental fruit moth (*Grapholitha molesta*) damage stone fruits, apples, and pears. The larvae hibernate in cocoons on tree bark or in branch crotches. In the spring they pupate, emerge as brown adult moths, and lay eggs on the young cherry twigs and leaves. The larvae bore into the young buds, shoots, and tender twigs, causing twig and leaf death. When mature they leave the twigs, spin cocoons, and pupate in the tree or in debris on the ground. After several weeks, moths emerge to lay their eggs. Egg laying and larval damage can occur all through the growing season. Later in the summer, larvae feed primarily on the maturing cherries. They leave gum-filled holes in the cherries when they exit to pupate. In addition to ruining the fruit, these pests may cause abnormal branching patterns on young trees when large numbers of twigs are infested.

Solution: Worms in the twigs and fruit can't be killed with pesticides. Kill the moths by treating infested trees with Ortho® Bug-B-Gon® Multi-Purpose Garden Dust or an insecticide containing *carbaryl*. Apply as directed on the label.

Peachtree borers

Peachtree borer larva (life size).

Problem: Holes appear in the lower part of the trunk or in the upper trunk and lower crotches. Gummy sap oozes from these holes. Sawdust may surround the holes. In mid- to late summer, empty pupa skins may protrude from these holes. During spring and summer, some leaves and branches may wilt. Severely affected trees may die. One or two borers may be enough to kill young trees.

Analysis: The larvae of peachtree borers (*Synanthedon* species) damage stone fruits and some ornamental trees. The blue to black, clear-winged moths (which resemble wasps) lay their eggs in mid- to late summer. The larvae bore into the bark either at or just below the ground level or in the upper trunk and main crotches. Their tunnels interfere with the circulation of water and nutrients, causing twig and branch wilting and dieback. The borers feed throughout the winter and into the spring in their tunnels. A gummy sap may ooze from the borer tunnels. This sap is often mixed with sawdustlike particles, the product of larval feeding. The borers pupate in early to midsummer; their cocoons are located at the base of the tree or just inside their tunnels. The moths emerge several weeks later.

Solution: In early summer, apply Ortho® Bug-B-Gon® Multi-Purpose Garden Dust or an insecticide containing *carbaryl* to the trunk and lower branches. Consult your local county extension office for the best time to spray in your area. Don't spray the fruit or foliage. Make a second application two weeks later and a third after harvest. Avoid wounding trees.

Shothole borers

Shothole borer beetle.

Problem: Many small holes (1/16 to 1/8 inch in diameter) are bored into twigs, branches, and sometimes the trunk of the tree. Sticky gum oozes from the holes. Holes may be plugged with bodies of dead insects. When sliced open, branches reveal sawdust-filled tunnels in the wood. Pinkish-white grubs may be found in the tunnels. Brownish-black beetles 1/10 inch long are often present on the bark. The foliage on damaged branches sometimes wilts and turns brown. Twigs and buds may be killed, and entire branches may die.

Analysis: The shothole borer (*Scolytus rugulosus*) also attacks other stone fruits and many ornamental trees. The adult beetles that emerge in the late spring or early summer feed at the base of buds and small twigs, often killing them. Female beetles bore into the wood, creating tunnels, in which they lay their eggs. The grubs that hatch from the eggs bore into the inner wood, creating sawdust-filled burrows 2 to 4 inches long. The grubs pupate just under the bark, then emerge as adult beetles. The last generation of grubs spends the winter in the tunnels, emerging the following spring. Weakened, diseased, and dying trees are most susceptible to borer infestation.

Solution: Keep trees healthy by watering and fertilizing properly. Healthy trees exude resin, drowning the larvae. Weakened trees cannot produce enough resin to defend themselves. Protect sour cherries from borer damage by spraying the trunk and larger branches with an insecticide containing *carbaryl*. Chemical treatment is not recommended on sweet cherries.

CHERRY (continued)

Bacterial canker

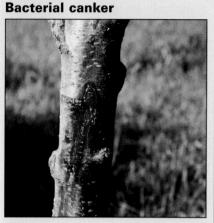

Bacterial canker.

Brown rot

Blossom and shoot blight.

Fruit rot.

Problem: Sunken, elliptical lesions appear on the trunk or branches. Thick, amber, sour-smelling gum oozes from lesions throughout fall, winter, and spring. In spring, especially when the weather is very wet and cold, blossoms may die or fail to open, or they may open, then turn brown and wither. Individual branches may die back. Angular holes may appear in the leaves.

Analysis: Bacterial canker, a plant disease also known as *bacterial gummosis* or *bacterial blast*, is found on various fruit and nut trees but is most severe on cherries. This disease is caused by bacteria (*Pseudomonas syringae*). Splashing rain spreads the bacteria to dormant buds, twigs, and branches. Infection occurs through wounds in the twigs and branches, and bacterial decay causes cankers to form. Bacterial activity decreases in the summer. Slowly developing cankers may encircle a branch, however, and by midsummer, affected branches and limbs start to die back. With the onset of cool, wet, fall weather, bacterial activity increases again. This disease is most serious on young trees.

Solution: Bacterial canker is difficult to control. Prune diseased branches. Disinfect pruning shears after each cut. In the fall, spray with a fungicide containing basic copper sulfate. Prune in late winter or early spring rather than early in the dormant season. Keep the tree healthy.

Problem: Blossoms and young leaves wilt, decay, and turn brown during the first two weeks of the bloom period. The decayed blossoms may fail to drop and may hang on the tree through the growing season. In humid conditions, masses of gray spores may appear on the infected flower parts. Extensive twig dieback often occurs. Cankers sometimes develop on the twigs and branches as the season progresses. These cankers may exude a sticky ooze. Blossom blight is most likely to occur west of the Rocky Mountains.

On the fruit: Small, circular brown spots appear on the young cherries. Later in the season, as the fruit begins to mature, these spots may enlarge to rot part or all of the cherries. During moist weather, the rotten fruit is covered with tufts of gray spores. Infected cherries either drop prematurely or dry out, turn dark brown, and remain on the tree past the normal harvest period.

Analysis: Brown rot, a plant disease caused by either of two closely related fungi, (*Monilinia laxa* or M. *fructicola*), is very destructive to all of the stone fruits. The fungus spends the winter in twig cankers or in rotted cherries (mummies) in the tree or on the ground. In the spring, spores are blown or splashed from cankers or mummies to healthy flower buds. After penetrating and decaying the flowers, the fungus grows down into the twigs, producing brown, sunken cankers. During moist weather, a thick, gummy sap oozes from the lesions, and tufts of gray spores may form on the infected areas. Spores from cankers and infected blossoms or mummies are splashed and blown to the maturing cherries. Young cherries are fairly resistant to infection, but maturing cherries are vulnerable. Brown rot develops most rapidly in mild, moist conditions.

Solution: If uninfected blossoms remain on the tree, spray with Ortho® Garden Disease Control to protect them from infection. Repeat the spray 10 days later. To protect maturing cherries from infection, spray again about three weeks before they are to be harvested. Remove and destroy all infected fruit and mummies. Prune cankers and blighted twigs. Clean up and destroy all debris around the tree. The following spring, spray with Ortho® Garden Disease Control when most flowers show white color and the first flowers are beginning to open and again when the tree is in full bloom.

San Jose scales

San Jose scales.

Problem: Some of the leaves are pale green to yellow and may drop prematurely from weakened limbs. Or they may turn brown and wither but remain attached to the tree into the winter. The bark is encrusted with small (¹⁄₁₀-inch), gray, hard, circular, slightly raised bumps with dull yellow centers. If the hard cover is scraped off, the insect found underneath is yellow or olive. Limbs may die back severely, and entire branches may be killed. The fruit may be marred by specks.

Analysis: San Jose scales (*Quadraspidiotus perniciosus*) are insects that infest the bark, leaves, and fruit of many fruit trees. The scales bear young in the spring. In late spring to midsummer, the young scales, called *crawlers*, move about and settle on leaves and twigs. The small (¹⁄₁₆-inch), bright yellow, soft-bodied young feed by inserting their mouthparts and sucking sap from the plant. The legs atrophy, and a hard, crusty shell develops over the body. An uncontrolled infestation of San Jose scales may kill large branches after two or three seasons. (For further information on scales, see pages 444 to 447.)

Solution: During the dormant season, just prior to growth in early spring, spray the trunk and branches with Ortho® Volck® Oil Spray. Begin checking for crawlers about a month after full bloom. Continue monitoring through the summer to catch later generations. Crawlers may be controlled with Ortho® Malathion Plus® Insect Spray Concentrate.

Cherry leaf spot

Cherry leaf spot.

Problem: Purple spots appear on the upper surfaces of leaves. The centers of the spots may fall out, leaving holes. Many of the spotted leaves are yellow and dying. Undersides of leaves may be dotted with cream-colored masses of spores. In severe cases, the fruit is also spotted. The tree defoliates prematurely, and cherry yield is reduced and of poor quality. The fruit is often soft and watery.

Analysis: Cherry leaf spot, also known as *yellow leaf spot*, is caused by a fungus (*Coccomyces hiemalis*). The fungus spends the winter in fallen leaves. About the time the cherry trees are finished blooming, large numbers of spores are splashed and blown from leaves on the ground to the emerging leaves. Infection and premature death of the leaves greatly reduces the amount of food the tree can make and store. This results in weakened trees and reduced fruit yields. Infested trees are much more susceptible to cold injury during the following winter. Cherry leaf spot is most severe during mild (60° to 70°F), wet weather.

Solution: Spray with Ortho® Garden Disease Control. In the fall, remove and destroy all leaf debris around the trees. The following spring, spray when the petals fall from the tree; repeat the spray at least two more times at intervals of 10 to 14 days. If the problem is severe, continue spraying until seven days before harvest.

Citrus thrips

Citrus thrips damage.

Problem: Leaf buds shrivel and turn brown. Some of the leaves are silvery gray, leathery, curled, and distorted. The fruit may be silvery, scabbed, or streaked, often in a distinct ring around the stem.

Analysis: Citrus thrips (*Scirtothrips citri*), minute pale yellow or orange insects, are pests of citrus and various ornamental trees. Thrips cause their damage by rasping the tissue of young leaves and immature fruits. They feed on the plant sap that exudes from the injured tissue. Adult thrips lay their eggs in leaves and stems in the fall. The following spring, the young thrips that emerge from these eggs begin feeding on the new growth. These pests are often found in protected areas such as the insides of leaf buds. Thrips damage occurs throughout the growing season and is especially severe during hot, dry weather.

Solution: Damage to the fruit is only cosmetic; fruit may be eaten. Spray infested plants with Ortho® Malathion Plus® Insect Spray Concentrate. Follow directions carefully, and repeat at regular intervals of 7 to 10 days as long as new damage is seen. Keep plants well irrigated and vigorous. Vigorous plants often outgrow thrips damage.

CITRUS *(continued)*

Scales

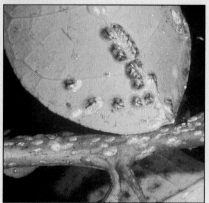

Brown soft scales (2× life size).

Problem: Crusty, waxy, or smooth bumps up to ¼ inch in diameter are found on the trunk, stems, foliage, and sometimes fruit. Often leaves turn yellow and drop. Fruit may also drop. In some cases, a sticky substance coats the leaves. A black, sooty mold may grown on the sticky substance.

Analysis: Many species of this insect attack citrus. Some of the most damaging are California red scale, Florida red scale, brown soft scale, black scale, and citrus snow scale. Scales spend the winter on the trunk and twigs of the tree. They lay eggs or bear young in late spring to midsummer. The young scales, called *crawlers*, move about and settle on the leaves, on twigs, and sometimes on developing fruit. The tiny (¹⁄₁₀-inch), soft-bodied young resemble small aphids. They feed by sucking sap from plants. As they mature, the legs usually atrophy, and a hard crusty or waxy shell develops over the body. Some species of scales are unable to digest all the sugar in the plant sap, and they excrete the excess in a fluid called *honeydew*. An uncontrolled infestation of scales may seriously damage or even kill limbs after two or three seasons. (For more information on scales, see pages 444 to 447.)

Solution: Spray with Ortho® Malathion Plus® Insect Spray Concentrate according to label directions in the spring after the bloom period. The spray is most effective when crawlers are active. In late summer or fall, spray with Ortho® Volck® Oil Spray.

Mealybugs and cottony cushion scales

Cottony cushion scales (2× life size).

Problem: White, cottony masses cluster on the leaves, the stems, the branches, and possibly the trunk. Some of the foliage may wither and turn yellow; leaves and fruit may drop. A shiny or sticky substance often coats the leaves. A sooty mold may grow on the sticky substance.

Analysis: Mealybugs (*Planococcus citri*) and cottony cushion scale (*Icerya purchasi*), insects frequently found together on citrus plants, look so much alike that separate identification is difficult. In late spring and summer, females are covered with white, cottony masses containing up to 800 eggs. Females lay their conspicuous egg masses on leaves, twigs, and branches. The inconspicuous young insects that hatch from these eggs are yellow to red. They feed by sucking sap from the plant tissues. They are unable to digest all the sugar in the plant sap, and they excrete the excess in a fluid called *honeydew*. A sooty mold fungus may develop on the honeydew, causing the citrus leaves to appear black and dirty. Mealybugs and scales can be spread in several ways. The wind can blow egg masses and insects from plant to plant, or active young insects can crawl to new locations.

Solution: Natural enemies usually control these pests. Don't spray unless leaves begin to turn yellow. Then spray infested trees with Ortho® Malathion Plus® Insect Spray Concentrate, covering both surfaces of the leaves. Repeat the spray five to seven days later. Don't spray when the plant is in full bloom. Don't apply within seven days of harvest.

Mites

Damaged leaves. Inset: Citrus red mite (10× life size).

Problem: Leaves are stippled, yellowing, or scratched in appearance. Webbing may form on flower buds, between leaves, or on the lower surfaces of leaves. The fruit is often brown or russet colored, leathery, or silvery and may drop prematurely. To determine if a plant is infested with mites, examine the bottoms of the leaves with a hand lens. Or hold a sheet of white paper underneath an affected branch and tap sharply. Minute green, red, or yellow specks will drop to the paper and begin to crawl around.

Analysis: Mites, related to spiders, are very damaging to all types of citrus. Several species of mites attack citrus, including citrus red mites, citrus bud mites, purple mites, and citrus rust mites. Mites cause damage by sucking sap from the leaves and young fruit. As a result of their feeding, the plant's chlorophyll disappears, producing a yellow, stippled appearance. Mite webbing traps cast-off skins and debris, making the plant dirty. Feeding damage also causes tissue death, resulting in browning and silvering of the fruit and foliage. Mites are active throughout the growing season but thrive in hot, dry weather (70°F and higher). By midsummer, they have built to tremendous numbers. A severe mite infestation weakens the plant and can seriously reduce the size and quality of the fruit.

Solution: Spray infested trees with Ortho® Malathion Plus® Insect Spray Concentrate or Ortho® Volck® Oil Spray. Cover both the upper and lower surfaces of the leaves. Repeat the spray at least twice more at intervals of seven days.

Lack of nitrogen

Nitrogen-deficient citrus leaves.

Problem: Foliage turns pale green, and the older leaves gradually turn yellow and often fall off. Overall growth is stunted. The tree may flower profusely but usually fails to set much fruit.

Analysis: Nitrogen is deficient in most soils. Nitrogen is essential in the formation of plant protein, fiber, enzymes, chlorophyll (green leaf pigment), and many other compounds. When a plant becomes deficient in nitrogen, it breaks down chlorophyll and other compounds in its older leaves to recover nitrogen, which it reuses for new growth. This loss of chlorophyll causes the older leaves to turn yellow. Soils that are low in organic matter or that are sandy and readily leached are frequently deficient in nitrogen. These kinds of soils in particular need to be supplemented with fertilizers. Poor drainage, cold (50°F and below), and acidity or alkalinity can also cause soil nitrogen to become less available for plant use.

Solution: Fertilize plants with Scotts® Citrus Food as directed on the label.

Iron deficiency

Iron deficiency on orange leaves.

Problem: Some of the leaves turn pale green or yellow. Newest leaves (those at the tips of the branches) are most severely affected. Except in extreme cases, the veins of affected leaves remain green. In extreme cases, the newest leaves are small and all-white or yellow. Older leaves may remain green.

Analysis: Citrus trees frequently suffer from deficiencies of iron and other minor nutrients such as manganese and zinc, elements essential to normal plant growth and development. Deficiencies can occur when one or more of these elements are depleted in the soil. Often these minor nutrients are present in the soil, but alkaline soil with a pH of 7.5 or higher or wet soil conditions cause them to form compounds that can't be used by the tree. An alkaline condition can result from overliming or from lime leached from cement or brick. Regions where soil is derived from limestone or where rainfall is low usually have alkaline soil. Some citrus trees turn yellow naturally in cold weather, but if iron is available, the foliage will turn green again when the weather warms.

Solution: For a quick response, apply a chelated iron fertilizer to the foliage. Then use Miracle-Gro® Fruit & Citrus Fertilizer Spikes to keep the problem from recurring. Improve soil drainage. (For information on drainage, see page 406.)

Tristeza

Tristeza.

Problem: Leaves are ash colored, bronze, or yellowing and often curl upward around the midrib. New growth is sparse. Growth has been slow, and some twigs and branches die. Or the tree may suddenly die within several weeks or months, leaving the foliage attached. The upper portion of the bud union often bulges over the lower rootstock portion. With the aid of a hand lens, when small patches of bark along the rootstock area of the bud union are removed, tiny pinholes can frequently be seen dotting the inner surface of the patches.

Analysis: Tristeza, also known as *quick decline*, is caused by a virus that affects the rootstocks of citrus plants. Aphids spread the virus to trees grafted onto susceptible rootstocks. Orange and grapefruit trees grafted onto *sour orange* rootstocks are especially susceptible to this virus. The virus attacks food-conducting vessels in the rootstock bark, impeding the flow of nutrients and causing starvation and death of the root system. Trees often live for several years after they have been infected but continue to decline in vigor and yield. Sometimes trees die rapidly after infection, especially during periods of drought.

Solution: This disease has no cure. Remove infected trees. Replace with citrus trees on rootstocks tolerant of tristeza. Gardeners with citrus trees on sour orange rootstock in Florida should consider planting replacement trees on tristeza-resistant rootstock. The prognosis for all citrus on sour orange rootstock is poor in areas that have brown citrus aphid.

CITRUS *(continued)*

Cold damage

Cold-damaged Valencia oranges.

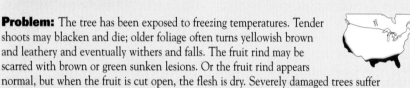

Cold damage.

Problem: The tree has been exposed to freezing temperatures. Tender shoots may blacken and die; older foliage often turns yellowish brown and leathery and eventually withers and falls. The fruit rind may be scarred with brown or green sunken lesions. Or the fruit rind appears normal, but when the fruit is cut open, the flesh is dry. Severely damaged trees suffer twig and branch dieback. The bark along the branches or trunk may split.

Analysis: Citrus plants are frost tender and are easily damaged by temperatures below 32°F. Although many citrus plants can recover from a light frost, they can't tolerate long periods of freezing weather. Damage to fruit occurs when the juice-filled cells freeze and rupture. The released fluid evaporates through the rind, leaving the flesh dry and pulpy. In addition to causing leaf and twig dieback, temperatures of 20°F and lower promote bark splitting, which may not become apparent for several weeks or months.

Solution: Avoid pruning damaged branches immediately. If danger of frost continues, drive four stakes into the ground around the tree and cover the tree with fabric, cardboard, or plastic. If possible, place a lamp under the cover. Turn the light on during cold nights. Remove this cover when the weather warms up. To protect the trunks and main limbs of young trees, wrap them with cornstalks, palm fronds, or fiberglass building insulation. Don't shade the foliage. Keep the soil moist during a freeze, but be careful not to overwater. Limit fertilizer to a minimum. Damaged fruit can be removed immediately following the freeze. Always wait for new growth to appear before pruning. As soon as the danger of frost is past, you can prune blackened shoots and withered foliage. If the tree has suffered serious injury, you may not be able to determine the extent of the damage to the trunk and main limbs for up to six months. You can then prune the deadwood.

Brown rot gummosis

Brown rot gummosis.

Problem: Firm brownish patches of bark appear at the base of the trunk. Often a thick, amber gum oozes from the infected area. The bark eventually dries, cracks, and withers away, leaving a dark sunken canker. Some of the maturing fruit may be brown and decaying. The foliage may turn yellow and die.

Analysis: Brown rot gummosis, a plant disease also known as *root rot* or *collar rot*, is caused by a soil-inhabiting fungus (*Phytophthora* species). The fungus thrives in heavy, wet soils. Infection occurs when spores are splashed to the trunk, penetrating the bark directly or through wounds. As the canker develops, the branches above the infected trunk may start to die. Fruit infection can occur when spores are splashed to the developing fruit. Sometimes cankers heal over by themselves, but often they continue to spread, causing a loss in vigor and fruit production and eventually killing the tree.

Solution: Gently remove the soil from around the trunk until the main lateral roots are just barely covered. Remove small trunk lesions by cutting away the diseased bark and an additional surrounding ½ inch of the healthy bark. Spray the diseased portion and the bottom 2 feet of the trunk with a fungicide containing *fosetyl-aluminum* or *metalaxyl*. Don't let water settle around the base of the tree. When planting new trees, purchase plants that are grafted onto phytophthora-resistant rootstocks, such as Trifoliate orange and Troyer citrange.

FIG

PEACH AND NECTARINE

Bird damage

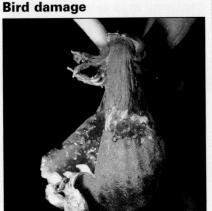

Bird damage to Mission fig.

Problem: Ripened figs have holes in them and may be partially eaten. They may have been knocked to the ground.

Analysis: Some birds feed heavily on ripening figs. When the fruit is fully ripe, birds peck at the soft flesh, leaving holes in the fruit. The wounded figs may decay, becoming inedible.

Solution: You can save many of your figs by harvesting daily. Check the tree every morning and harvest those figs that have ripened. Nets thrown over the tree are also effective in reducing bird damage. Purchase nets at your local nursery or hardware store.

Plum curculios

Plum curculio larva (4× life size).

Problem: The ripening fruit is misshapen and rotten and often drops prematurely. Holes about ⅛ inch in diameter and deep, crescent-shape scars appear on the fruit. When cut open, damaged fruit may contain crescent-shape yellow-gray grubs with brown heads.

Analysis: Plum curculio (*Conotrachelus nenuphar*) are insects that attack figs, stone fruits, apples, and pears. The adults are mottled gray-and-brown beetles with long, curved snouts. They hibernate in debris and other protected places during the winter. The beetles emerge in the spring when new growth starts and begin feeding on young leaves, blossoms, and developing fruit. After five to six weeks, the female beetles start to lay their eggs inside the young fruit, cutting distinctive, crescent-shaped slits into the peaches and nectarines. The grubs that hatch from the eggs feed for several weeks inside the fruit. Infested fruits usually drop to the ground. The grubs eventually leave the fruit and bore into the soil, where they pupate. The emerging beetles feed on fruit for a few weeks and then go into hibernation. In the South, they lay eggs, producing a second generation of grubs in late summer.

Solution: You can't kill the grubs inside the fruit. Spray with Ortho® Malathion Plus® Insect Spray Concentrate to kill beetles that are feeding on fruit or laying eggs. Pick up and destroy all fallen fruit. The following spring, spray the trees when the petals are dropping from the blossoms. Repeat applications according to directions on the label.

Scab

Scab.

Problem: Small olive-green spots appear on the half-grown fruit. These spots are generally centered around the stem end of the peach or nectarine. The spots eventually turn brown and velvety. The fruit is often dwarfed, deformed, or cracked. Leaves may have small brown spots and holes in them. Oval lesions with raised purple margins occasionally appear on shoots and twigs.

Analysis: Scab is a plant disease caused by a fungus (*Cladosporium carpophilum*) that attacks all the stone fruits. In the spring, spores are splashed and blown from lesions on the twigs to the developing foliage and fruit. The young fruit doesn't show scab lesions for at least a month after it is initially infected. Spores that are produced on the infected leaves, twigs, and fruit continue to infect healthy peaches and nectarines throughout the growing season.

Solution: You can't do anything about the spots on the current year's fruit, but it is edible if peeled. The following year, spray with Ortho® Garden Disease Control when the petals are dropping from the blossoms. If scab is a serious problem in your area, continue to spray at intervals of 10 to 14 days until about a month before the fruit is harvested.

PEACH AND NECTARINE *(continued)*

Shothole fungus

Shothole fungus. Inset: Infected fruit.

Problem: Small purplish spots appear on the young twigs, leaves, and developing fruit in early spring and eventually turn brown. These leaf spots often drop out, leaving shot holes in the leaves. Infected buds, shoots, and leaves may die. The spots on the maturing peaches and nectarines turn scablike, drop off, and leave rough, corky lesions.

Analysis: Shothole fungus, a plant disease also called *coryneum blight* or *peach blight,* is caused by a fungus (*Wilsonomyces carpophilus*) that attacks peaches, nectarines, apricots, plums, and almonds. The fungus spends the winter in lesions on the twigs and buds. In spring, the spores are splashed by rain onto the developing buds, leaves, and fruit, causing spotting and tissue death. Infection causes the leaf tissue to produce a layer of cells that walls off the damaged area. The center of the spot then drops out. Severe infection may cause twig and bud blighting and premature defoliation, reducing peach and nectarine yield. The disease thrives in wet, spring weather.

Solution: To prevent twig and leaf bud infection, prune infected twigs and branches immediately when they are discovered. Spray the tree with a lime-sulfur solution or Ortho® Garden Disease Control in the fall immediately after the leaves have dropped. To reduce or prevent fruit infection, apply Ortho® Garden Disease Control one to two weeks after petals have fallen.

Leaf curl

Leaf curl on peach.

Problem: Leaves are puckered, thickened, and curled from the time they first appear in the spring. Emerging shoots are swollen and stunted. Initially the infected foliage may be pink or red, but frequently it is pale green to yellow. As the season progresses, a powdery grayish-white material develops on the leaves. Eventually these leaves shrivel and drop. Fruiting is poor, and the fruit that is present may be covered with raised, wrinkled, irregular lesions.

Analysis: Leaf curl is a plant disease caused by a fungus (*Taphrina deformans*) that attacks peaches and nectarines wherever they are grown. Infection occurs as soon as the buds begin to swell in the very early spring. Fungal spores are splashed from the bark to the buds by spring rains. Later in the season, the infected leaves develop a grayish-white covering of spores that are blown onto the bark. Infected trees are greatly weakened by the premature loss of foliage in early summer. Leaf curl is most severe when spring weather is cool and wet.

Solution: Infected leaves cannot be cured. To prevent recurrence of the disease the following year, spray trees with a lime-sulfur solution or Ortho® Garden Disease Control in the fall immediately after the leaves have dropped or in the spring before the buds begin to swell. If the disease has been severe in past years, spray in both fall and spring.

Bacterial leaf spot

Bacterial leaf spot on nectarine.

Problem: Brown or black angular spots appear on the leaves. The centers of the spots often fall out. The tips of the leaves may die, and eventually the leaves turn yellow and drop. The surface of the fruit may be dotted with brown to black spots and become pitted and cracked. Sunken lesions may form on the twigs. Severely infected trees may drop all their leaves by harvest time.

Analysis: Bacterial leaf spot is a plant disease caused by a bacterium (*Xanthomonas campestris* pv. *pruni*) that also attacks apricots and plums. This is one of the more destructive diseases of stone fruits east of the Rocky Mountains. In the spring, bacteria ooze from lesions on the twigs to be carried by splashing rain to the young leaves, shoots, and developing fruits. Frequent rainfall favors the infection. Trees that defoliate early in the summer are weakened and produce small crops of poor-quality peaches and nectarines.

Solution: This disease can't be adequately controlled. Spraying with basic copper sulfate when the flower buds open in the spring may help suppress the disease but will not eliminate it. When planting new trees, use resistant varieties.

Peach twig borers

Peach twig borer (life size).

Brown rot

Blighted shoots.

Fruit rot.

Problem: New growth at the tips of the twigs wilts and dies. When affected twigs are sliced open lengthwise, worms about ½ inch long are discovered inside. The reddish-brown color and alternating light and dark bands and dark head of these worms distinguishes them from oriental fruit moth worms, which cause similar damage. Maturing fruit also contain these worms. During the summer, cocoons may be attached to the branches or tree crotches.

Analysis: Peach twig borers (*Anarsia lineatella*) attack all of the stone fruits, particularly along the Pacific coast. Young larvae hibernate during winter in silk-lined burrows under loose bark or in other protected places on the tree. When the tree starts to bloom in the spring, larvae bore into young buds and shoots. They feed on tender twigs, killing twigs and leaves. When mature, they leave the twigs and pupate in cocoons attached to branches. After several weeks, gray moths emerge and lay eggs on twigs, leaves, and fruit. Egg laying and larval damage can occur all through the growing season. Later in summer, larvae feed primarily on maturing fruit. In addition to ruining fruit, peach twig borers may cause abnormal branching patterns on young trees.

Solution: Worms in the twigs and fruit can't be killed with pesticides. To prevent future worm damage, kill the moths by treating infested trees with Ortho® Bug-B-Gon® Multi-Purpose Garden Dust. The following spring, treat again just before blossoms open. Repeat the treatment according to label directions.

Problem: Blossoms and young leaves wilt, decay, and turn brown during the first two weeks of the bloom period. The decayed blossoms may fail to drop and may hang on the tree throughout the growing season. In humid conditions, masses of gray spores may appear on infected flower parts. Extensive twig dieback often occurs. Sunken lesions (cankers) develop on the twigs and branches as the season progresses. A second wave of twig dieback may develop around harvest time as the fungus grows from the infected fruit into spurs and small branches.

On the fruit: Small circular brown spots appear on the young fruit. Later in the season, as the peaches or nectarines start to mature, these spots may enlarge to rot part or all of the fruit. During moist weather, the rotted fruit is covered with tufts of gray spores. When the infected peaches or nectarines are sliced open, the flesh inside is found to be brown, firm, and fairly dry. Infected fruit either drops prematurely or dries out, turns dark brown, and remains on the tree past the normal harvest period. Healthy fruit may rot when it contacts infected fruit in storage.

Analysis: Brown rot, a plant disease caused by either of two closely related fungi, (*Monilinia laxa* or *M. fructicola*), is very destructive to all of the stone fruits. The fungi spend the winter in twig cankers or in rotted fruit (mummies) on the tree or on the ground. In the spring, spores are blown or splashed from cankers or mummies to healthy flower buds. After penetrating and decaying the flowers, the fungus grows down into the twigs, producing brown, sunken cankers. During moist weather, a thick, gummy sap oozes from the lesions, and tufts of gray spores may form on the infected areas. Spores from cankers and infected blossoms or mummies are splashed and blown onto the maturing fruit. Young peaches and nectarines are fairly resistant to infection, but maturing fruit is vulnerable. Brown rot develops most rapidly in mild, moist conditions.

Solution: If uninfected blossoms remain on your tree, spray with Ortho® Garden Disease Control to protect them from further infection. Repeat the spray 10 days later. To protect maturing peaches and nectarines from infection, spray them with a fungicide containing *captan* about three weeks before they are to be harvested. Remove and destroy all infected fruit and mummies. Prune cankers and blighted twigs. Clean up and destroy all debris around the tree. The following spring, spray trees when most flowers show pink color and the first flowers are beginning to open. Continue to spray according to label directions.

PEACH AND NECTARINE *(continued)*

Catfacing

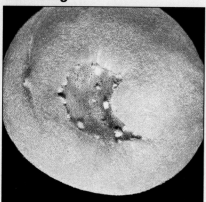

Catfacing on peach.

Problem: Sunken, corky areas mar the fruit surface. Blossoms may drop without setting fruit. Many of the young fruits drop prematurely. Some of the developing leaves and twigs are deformed. Brown, green, or rust-colored bugs ¼ to ½ inch long may be feeding on the buds and fruit.

Analysis: The sunken, corky "catface" disfigurations that appear on the fruit are usually caused by the tarnished plant bug (*Lygus lineolaris*) and various species of stinkbugs. The insects hibernate in vetch or other broadleaf weeds during the winter. When the trees start to bloom in the spring, these bugs feed on the young buds, blooms, and fruits, causing bud and fruit drop, twig malformation, and catfacing. Most of the damage occurs early in the season, although the bugs may occasionally feed on the fruit up until harvest. Hail or cold weather may also damage the tender blooms and fruit surfaces, causing catface injuries.

Solution: To control plant bugs, treat with Ortho® Malathion Plus® Insect Spray Concentrate or Ortho® Bug-B-Gon® Multi-Purpose Garden Dust when the buds turn pink. Repeat the spray when the petals have dropped from most of the blossoms and whenever bugs are seen on trees. The following fall, clean up weeds and plant debris to eliminate hibernating locations for the overwintering bugs.

Aphids

Aphid damage.

Problem: New leaves are curled and twisted. Leaves may turn yellow and drop. Developing fruit may be small and misshapen. A shiny or sticky substance may coat the leaves. A black, sooty mold often grows on the sticky substance. Tiny (⅛-inch) yellow, light green, or black soft-bodied insects cluster on the young shoots and on the undersides of leaves. Ants may be present.

Analysis: Several species of aphids, including the green peach aphid (*Myzus persicae*), infest peaches and nectarines. Aphids do little damage in small numbers. They are extremely prolific, however, and populations can rapidly build to damaging numbers during the growing season. Damage occurs when aphids suck the sap from the young peach and nectarine leaves. The aphids are unable to digest all the sugar in the sap, and they excrete the excess in a fluid called *honeydew*, which often drops onto the leaves below. A sooty mold fungus may develop on the honeydew, causing the leaves to appear black and dirty. Ants feed on this sticky substance and are often present where there is an aphid infestation.

Solution: Spray with Ortho® Malathion Plus® Insect Spray Concentrate or Ortho® Volck® Oil Spray as soon as the insects appear. Repeat the spray if the tree becomes reinfested. To avoid killing bees, don't spray during bloom.

Peachtree borers

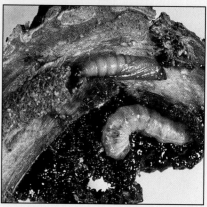

Peachtree borer larva and pupa (life size).

Problem: Holes appear in the lower part of the trunk or in the upper trunk and lower crotches. A thick, gummy substance often oozes from these holes. Sawdust may surround the holes or collect at the base of the tree under the holes. In mid- to late summer, empty pupa skins may protrude from the holes. During the spring and summer, some of the leaves and branches may wilt. Severely affected trees may die.

Analysis: Peachtree borers (*Synanthedon* species) are moth larvae that are very damaging to peaches and nectarines. The adults are blue to black, clear-winged moths that resemble wasps. The females lay their eggs near the base of trees in mid- to late summer. The larvae that emerge bore into the bark near the soil surface. Their tunnels interfere with the circulation of water and nutrients, causing twigs and branches to wilt and die. These borers feed throughout the winter and into the spring. A gummy sap—often mixed with sawdustlike particles—may ooze from the tunnels. Borers pupate in early to midsummer in cocoons located at the base of the tree or just inside their tunnels. Moths emerge several weeks later.

Solution: Spray the trunk and lower branches with an insecticide containing *carbaryl*. The following year, kill the egg-laying moths by spraying the trunk and crotches in early summer. Contact your local county extension office for peachtree borer emergence dates in your area. Locate the holes and kill the larvae inside by inserting a wire into each hole or by making vertical cuts with a knife.

Bacterial canker

Bacterial canker on peach.

Fire blight

Infected blossoms.

Blighted twig.

Problem: Sunken elliptical lesions appear on the trunk or branches. A thick, sour- smelling, amber gum oozes from these lesions throughout the fall, winter, and spring. In the spring, especially when the weather is excessively wet and cold, blossoms may turn brown and wither, and some of the leaf and flower buds die and become covered with gum. Individual branches may fail to produce foliage, or entire branches may die back. Angular holes may appear in the leaves. Often, many shoots sprout from the rootstock.

Analysis: Bacterial canker, a plant disease also known as *bacterial gummosis* or *bacterial blast*, is caused by either of two varieties of a bacterium (*Pseudomonas syringae*). Splashing rain spreads the bacteria to dormant buds, twigs, and branches. Infection occurs through wounds in the twigs and branches, and bacterial decay causes cankers to form. Slowly developing cankers may encircle a branch, and by midsummer the affected branches and limbs die back. With the onset of cool fall weather, bacterial activity increases. This disease is most serious on young trees.

Solution: Prune out diseased branches. Disinfect the pruning shears after each cut. In the fall, spray with a fungicide containing basic copper sulfate to obtain partial control. Keep the tree healthy by fertilizing and watering properly.

Problem: Blossoms turn black and die. Young leafy twigs wilt from the tips down, turn black, and die. Leaves remain attached. A bend often develops at the tips of the infected shoots. On the branches, and at the base of the blighted twigs, the bark becomes water-soaked in appearance, then dark, sunken, and dry. Cracks may develop at the edges of the sunken area. In warm, moist spring weather, drops of brown ooze appear on the surfaces of these lesions. During the summer, shoots or branches may wilt and turn dark brown to black. Infected fruit shrivels, turns black, and remains on the tree.

Analysis: Fire blight is a plant disease caused by a bacterium (*Erwinia amylovora*) that is very severe on pears and also affects apples and several ornamental plants in the rose family. (For a list of susceptible plants, see page 535.) The bacteria spend the winter in cankers on the branches and twigs. In the spring, the bacteria ooze out of the cankers and are carried by insects to the pear blossoms. Once a few of the blossoms have been contaminated, splashing rain, honeybees, and other insects continue to spread the bacteria to healthy blossoms. The bacteria spread down through the flowers into the twigs and branches, where cankers develop. Often, developing cankers encircle a shoot or branch by midsummer, causing conspicuous branch and twig dieback. Although fire blight is spread primarily through flower infection, leaves and twigs damaged by hail or wounded in some other manner are also susceptible to infection, as are tender, succulent shoots and sprouts. Severely diseased trees may be killed, but more commonly only the fruiting stems (spurs) die, resulting in greatly reduced fruit yields. Fire blight is most severe during warm (65° to 85°F), wet weather.

Solution: After the infection has stopped spreading in the summer or fall, prune and destroy infected twigs and branches at least 12 inches beyond visible decay. Disinfect pruning shears after each cut. The following spring, apply a protective spray of basic copper sulfate soon after bud-break, when about ¼ inch of green tip is showing. To prevent blossom infections, apply a bactericide containing *streptomycin* when about 20 percent of the blossoms have opened, and repeat at intervals of three to five days until the end of the blooming period. To prevent excess growth of shoots and suckers, avoid fertilizing with high-nitrogen fertilizers. Plant tree varieties that are less susceptible to fire blight.

PEAR *(continued)*

Scab

Scab.

Codling moths

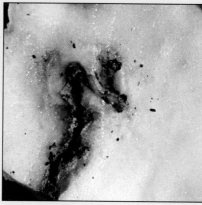

Codling moth larva (¾ life size).

Adult (3× life size).

Problem: Olive-brown velvety spots, ¼ inch or more in diameter, appear on the leaves and young fruit. As the infected pears mature, the spots develop into light to dark brown corky lesions. The fruit is often cracked and malformed and may drop prematurely. Many of the green twigs have small, blisterlike pustules on them.

Analysis: Scab is a plant disease caused by a fungus *(Venturia pirina)* that commonly infects pears. The fungus spends the winter in infected plant debris and twig lesions. In the spring, spores are produced and discharged into the air. They are blown to the developing leaves, flowers, twigs, and young pears. If the leaves and fruit are wet, the fungus infects them and spots develop. The infected tissues produce more spores, which further spread the fungus. As temperatures increase in the summer, the fungus becomes less active.

Solution: Unless they are severely infected, the pears are edible if the scabby areas are removed. To prevent recurrence of the disease the following year, remove and destroy leaf debris and infected fruit in the fall. The following spring, spray with a fungicide containing *mancozeb* when buds are just opening and green tips are about ¼ inch long. Repeat every 10 days until three or four weeks after petal-fall.

Problem: Fruit is blemished by small holes surrounded by dead tissue. A brown, crumbly material that resembles sawdust may surround the holes. Brown-headed, pinkish worms up to 1 inch long may be found in the fruit. The interior of the fruit may be dark and rotted. Many pears drop prematurely.

Analysis: The codling moth *(Cydia pomonella)* larvae come from small (½-inch) gray brown moths and attack apples, quinces, and several other fruit and nut trees in addition to pears. The moths appear in the spring and lay their eggs on the leaves, twigs, and developing fruit, flying at sunset when temperatures are above 65°F. The eggs hatch in about a week, and the larvae that emerge tunnel into the fruit. They feed for several weeks, then emerge from the pears, often leaving a mass of dark excrement on the skin and inside the fruit. After pupating in sheltered locations on or around the tree, another generation of moths emerges in midsummer. Pears may be damaged by worms continuously throughout the summer. In fall, the mature larvae spin cocoons in protected places, such as under loose bark or in tree crevices. They spend the winter in these cocoons and, with the warming temperatures of spring, pupate and emerge as moths.

Solution: Once worms have penetrated the pears, it is impossible to kill them. To protect uninfested pears, treat with Ortho® Malathion Plus® Insect Spray Concentrate or Ortho® Bug-B-Gon® Multi-Purpose Garden Dust at intervals of 10 to 14 days as directed on the label. Remove and destroy all fallen pears, and clean up debris around the trees. The following spring, begin spraying 10 to 14 days after petal-fall. This may control moths for the rest of the summer. If codling moths have been a serious problem in the past, continue spraying according to label directions. To more accurately predict when to make the first treatment, record temperatures at sunset each day. Spray one week after sunset temperatures have been above 65°F for two or more days.

Fruit harvested too late

Overripe pear.

Problem: The fruit tastes mealy, mushy, or gritty. The flavor is poor, and the inner flesh may be soft and discolored. The fruit was picked when it had softened or turned yellow on the tree.

Analysis: Unlike most other fruits, pears must be harvested before they are fully ripe. When left to ripen on the tree, they turn mealy, develop clusters of hard cells (stone cells), and lose their flavor and succulence.

Solution: Most pear varieties should be picked when they have reached their mature size and are starting to lose their green color. Don't allow them to soften or turn entirely yellow before harvesting. As a general rule, most pears may be safely picked during September. Pears are ready to pick when they have just begun to soften and turn yellow and when they release easily from the stem when lifted and twisted slightly. Contact your local county extension office for specific harvest dates for your location and pear varieties. After harvesting, place the pears in a closed plastic bag and refrigerate them for at least two weeks. To soften them, remove them from the bag and keep them at room temperature. After 5 to 10 days, they should be fully ripe.

Mites

Spider mite damage.

Problem: Leaves are stippled, yellowing, or bronzed. There may be webbing around flower buds, between leaves, or on the lower surfaces of leaves. Fruit may be russeted. To determine if a tree is infested with mites, examine the bottoms of the leaves with a hand lens. Or hold a sheet of white paper underneath an affected leaf and tap the leaf sharply. Minute specks the size of pepper grains will drop to the paper and begin to crawl around.

Analysis: Several species of mites, including the two-spotted spider mite (*Tetranychus urticae*) and the pear rust mite (*Epitrimerus pyri*), attack pears. Two-spotted spider mites, which cause leaf stippling and webbing, may be detected on white paper. Pear rust mites, which cause fruit russeting and leaf stippling and bronzing, can't be seen without the aid of a microscope or strong hand lens. These pests cause damage by sucking plant sap. As a result of their feeding, the tree's chlorophyll disappears, producing the stippled or bronze appearance. Mites are active throughout the growing season but thrive in hot, dry weather (70°F and higher).

Solution: Spray infested trees with Ortho® Malathion Plus® Insect Spray Concentrate. Repeat the spray twice more at intervals of 7 to 10 days. After the leaves have dropped the following fall, spray the tree with a mix of a lime-sulfur solution and Ortho® Volck® Oil Spray. If you're not sure whether your trees are infested with pear rust mites, bring an infested fruit spur to your local county extension office for confirmation.

San Jose scales

San Jose scales (life size).

Problem: Some of the leaves are pale green to yellow and may drop prematurely on weakened limbs. The bark is encrusted with small (1⁄16-inch), gray, hard, circular, slightly raised bumps with dull yellow centers. If the hard cover is scraped off, the insect underneath is yellow or olive. Entire branches may be killed. Red-purple spots mar some of the infested fruit and shoots. An uncontrolled infestation of San Jose scales may kill large branches or entire trees after two or three seasons.

Analysis: San Jose scales (*Quadraspidiotus perniciosus*) are insects that infest the bark, leaves, and fruit of many fruit trees. The scales bear young in the spring. In late spring to midsummer, the young, bright yellow scales, called *crawlers*, move about and then settle on leaves, twigs, and fruit. The small (1⁄16-inch), soft-bodied young feed by inserting their mouthparts and sucking sap from the plant. The legs atrophy, and a hard, crusty shell develops over the body. (For further information on scales, see pages 444 to 447.)

Solution: During the dormant season, just prior to growth in early spring, spray the trunk and branches with Ortho® Volck® Oil Spray. Begin checking for crawlers a month after full bloom. Continue monitoring through the summer to catch later generations. When crawlers are present, spray with Ortho® Malathion Plus® Insect Spray Concentrate.

PECAN

Pecan weevils

Pecan weevil (2× life size).

Problem: Immature pecans that drop to the ground during August are marked with dark patches. Later in the season, some of the ripe nuts have ⅛-inch holes in them. When cut open, the kernels are found to be destroyed and may contain creamy-white curved grubs up to ½ inch long. Reddish-brown to gray, long-beaked beetles ½ inch long may be seen in the tree. If the limbs are shaken, these beetles drop to the ground.

Analysis: Immature and adult stages of pecan weevils (*Curculio caryae*) are very damaging to pecans and hickories. Adult weevils emerge from the soil in late summer and feed on immature pecans. Affected nuts drop from the tree. As soon as the kernels harden, female weevils drill holes through shucks and shells and lay eggs in the kernels. Grubs that hatch from these eggs feed on the kernels for several weeks, then chew a hole in the shell about ⅛ inch in diameter, leave the nut, drop to the ground, and burrow into the soil. They emerge as adult weevils after two to three years.

Solution: Spray severely infested trees with an insecticide containing *carbaryl*. If nut drop is excessive, spray prior to shell hardening. Otherwise, beginning at shell hardening, spray at intervals of 7 to 10 days until the shucks split from the shells. Weevils may also be partially controlled by shaking them from lightly infested trees. Place sheets under the tree, then lightly jar the limbs. Collect and kill the dislodged weevils that fall onto the sheet. Repeat every three or four days until the weevils are no longer present.

Hickory shuckworms

Hickory shuckworm (2× life size).

Problem: Cream- colored worms up to ½ inch long, with reddish brown heads and black spots, are feeding in the immature nuts, many of which fall to the ground prematurely. Later in the season, after the shells have hardened, the worms may be found in the green shucks.

Analysis: Hickory shuckworms (*Laspeyresia caryana*), the larvae of small, dark gray moths, are also known as *pecan shuckworms*. They are pests of pecan and hickory trees wherever they are grown. The larvae spend the winter in shucks on the ground or in the tree. The shuckworms pupate and emerge as adult moths in the spring to lay their eggs on pecan leaves and nuts. The young larvae that hatch from these eggs tunnel into the soft green pecan shells and feed on the developing kernels. Infested nuts usually drop. Later in the season, after the nutshells have hardened, the larvae tunnel into the shucks. Their feeding damage interferes with the development of the kernels. Shuckworm damage may occur throughout the spring and summer.

Solution: Chemical controls are not practical for the home gardener. Clean up and destroy all dropped nuts and shucks to eliminate many of the overwintering larvae.

Pecan nut casebearers

Pecan nut casebearer damage.

Problem: Olive-green worms up to ½ inch long with yellow-brown heads are feeding on the twigs, foliage, and developing nuts. Some of the young shoots are wilting. Nut clusters may be webbed together. Some nuts may have holes in them, and many kernels have been destroyed. Many nuts drop prematurely. Some may contain worms or pupae, either in the kernel or in the shuck.

Analysis: Pecan nut casebearer (*Acrobasis nuxvorella*), the larvae of small, dark gray moths, are very damaging to pecans. The larvae come out of hibernation when buds open in the spring. They feed on developing buds for a short time, and then tunnel into the new shoots to pupate. Adult moths emerge just as the nuts start to form and lay their eggs on the young pecans. This second generation of worms webs clusters of nuts together, then bores into and feeds on them. This generation usually damages many pecans, because each worm eats three or four of the immature nuts during its larval stage. After reaching mature size, the larvae pupate inside nuts and become moths. Damage by larvae continues throughout the summer but lessens in severity as the nuts enlarge to full size.

Solution: Spray with an insecticide containing *malathion* or *carbaryl*. The following spring, contact your local county extension office to determine when moths are laying eggs in your area. Spray during this period and again six weeks later. Destroy all infested nuts that fall to the ground.

PERSIMMON

Sunburn

Sunburn.

Problem: During hot weather, usually in August or September, dark brown or black patches appear on the developing fruit. Leaves may turn brown around the edges and between the veins.

Analysis: Sunburn is caused by excessive evaporation of moisture from the leaves and fruit. In hot weather, water evaporates rapidly from the fruit and foliage. If the roots can't absorb and convey water fast enough to replenish this loss, fruit surfaces exposed to the sun overheat and burn; in severe cases, the leaves turn brown and wither. This usually occurs in dry soil, but fruit and leaves can also burn when the soil is moist and temperatures are around 100°F. Drying winds, severed roots, and a limited soil area can also cause sunburn. (For more information on leaf scorch, see page 427.)

Solution: You can't do anything about damaged fruit, but it is still edible. To help prevent further sunburn, deep-water plants during periods of hot weather to wet down the entire root space. (For information on watering, see pages 407 to 408.) Water newly transplanted trees whenever the rootball is dry 2 inches below the surface.

Fruit drop

Fruit drop.

Problem: Fruit drops prematurely. The tree appears to be healthy; no signs of insects, pests, or diseases exist.

Analysis: Persimmons have a natural tendency to drop their fruit prematurely. Large quantities of fruit may drop when the tree is under stress. Stress may be caused by conditions such as excessive heat, drought, cold, or overwatering. Excessive fruit drop may also occur on trees that are growing vigorously because of heavy nitrogen fertilization.

Solution: Although fruit drop can't be eliminated, it can be reduced. Avoid overfertilizing and overwatering or under watering the tree.

PLUM

Plum curculios

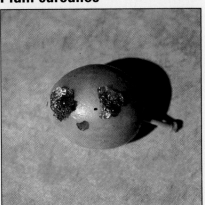

Plum curculio damage.

Problem: Ripening fruit is misshapen and rotten and often drops prematurely. Holes about ⅛ inch in diameter and deep, crescent-shape scars appear on the fruit. When cut open, such fruit may be found to contain crescent-shape, yellow-gray, legless grubs with brown heads.

Analysis: Plum curculio (*Conotrachelus nenuphar*), commonly attack stone fruits, apples, and pears. Adult insects are brown beetles with long, curved snouts. They hibernate in debris and other protected places during the winter. The beetles emerge in the spring when new growth starts and begin feeding on young leaves, blossoms, and developing fruit. After five to six weeks, the female beetles start to lay eggs inside the young fruit. During this process they cut distinctive, crescent-shape slits into the plums. The grubs that hatch from the eggs feed for several weeks inside the fruit. The infested plums usually drop to the ground. The grubs eventually leave the fruit and bore into the soil, where they pupate. The emerging beetles feed on fruit for a few weeks, then go into hibernation. In the South, they lay eggs, producing a second generation of grubs in the late summer.

Solution: Once the fruit is infested, you can't kill the grubs inside the fruit. Spray with an insecticide containing *malathion* or *phosmet* to kill beetles that may be feeding on fruit or laying eggs. Pick up and destroy all fallen fruit. The following spring, spray the trees when the petals are dropping from the blossoms; repeat applications according to directions on the label.

PLUM *(continued)*

Brown rot

Blossom blight.

Fruit rot.

Problem: Blossoms and young leaves wilt, decay, and turn brown during the first two weeks of the bloom period. Often the decayed blossoms fail to drop, and they may hang on the tree through the growing season. In humid conditions, masses of gray spores may appear on infected flower parts and twigs. Extensive twig dieback often occurs. Cankers sometimes develop on the twigs and branches as the season progresses. These cankers usually exude a sticky ooze.

On the fruit: Small circular brown spots appear on the young fruit. Later in the season, as the plums start to mature, these spots may enlarge to rot part or all of the fruit. During moist weather the rotted fruit is covered with tufts of gray spores. When the infected plums are sliced open, the flesh inside is brown, usually firm, and fairly dry. Infected plums either drop prematurely or dry out, turn dark brown, and remain on the tree past the normal harvest period.

Analysis: Brown rot, a plant disease caused by either of two closely related fungi, (*Monilinia laxa* or *M. fructicola*), is very destructive to stone fruit. The fungus spends the winter in twig cankers or in rotted fruit (mummies) in the tree or on the ground. In spring, spores are blown or splashed from cankers or mummies to healthy flower buds. After penetrating and decaying the flowers, the fungus grows down into the twigs, producing brown, sunken cankers. During moist weather a thick, gummy sap oozes from the lesions, and tufts of gray spores may form on the infected areas. Spores from cankers and infected blossoms or mummies are splashed and blown to maturing fruit. Young fruit is fairly resistant to infection, but maturing fruit is vulnerable. Brown rot develops most rapidly in mild, moist conditions.

Solution: If uninfected blossoms remain on the tree, protect them from further infection by spraying with Ortho® Garden Disease Control or a fungicide containing *captan*. Repeat the spray 10 days later. To protect maturing plums from infection, spray them with a fungicide containing *captan* about three weeks before they are to be harvested. Remove and destroy all infected fruit and mummies. Prune cankers and blighted twigs. Clean up and destroy all debris around the tree. The following spring, spray trees when the first flowers begin to bloom. Continue to spray according to label directions.

Bacterial leafspot

Bacterial leafspot on Stanley plums.

Problem: Brown or black angular spots develop on the leaves. The centers of the spots often fall out. The tips of the leaves may die, and severely infected leaves turn yellow and drop. When the fruit sets, the surface may be dotted with brown to black spots. The surface of the fruit becomes pitted and cracked. Sunken lesions may form on the twigs. Severely infected trees may defoliate.

Analysis: Bacterial leaf spot, a plant disease caused by bacteria (*Xanthomonas campestris* pv. *pruni*), also attacks apricots and peaches. The disease is common east of the Rocky Mountains. The bacteria spend the winter in lesions on the twigs and in buds, oozing out in the spring to be carried by splashing rain to young leaves, shoots, and developing fruit. Periods of frequent rainfall promote the infection. Trees that defoliate early in summer become weakened and produce few, poor-quality plums.

Solution: This disease can't be adequately controlled. Spraying when the flower buds open in the spring with basic copper sulfate may help suppress the disease but won't eliminate it.

Aphids

Aphids (2× life size).

Problem: The youngest leaves are curled, twisted, discolored, and stunted. Leaves may drop. In severe cases, the tree may defoliate. Developing plums may be small and misshapen. A shiny or sticky substance may coat the leaves. A black, sooty mold often grows on the sticky substance. Tiny (⅛-inch) green, yellow, purplish, or black soft-bodied insects cluster on the young shoots and on the undersides of leaves.

Analysis: Several species of aphids infest plums. These insects do little damage in small numbers, but they are extremely prolific, and populations can rapidly build to damaging numbers during the growing season. Damage occurs when aphids suck the sap from plum leaves. The aphids are unable to digest all the sugar in the plant sap and excrete the excess in a fluid called *honeydew*, which often drops onto the leaves and fruit below. A sooty mold fungus may develop on the honeydew, causing the plum leaves to appear black and dirty. (For more information on aphids, see page 444.)

Solution: Spray with Ortho® Bug-B-Gon® Multi-Purpose Insect Killer as soon as the insects appear. Repeat if the tree becomes reinfested. To kill overwintering insects or eggs, spray with Ortho® Volck® Oil Spray just prior to bud-break in the spring while the tree is still dormant.

Oriental fruit moths

Oriental fruit moth damage.

Problem: New growth at the tips of the twigs wilts and dies. When the affected twigs are sliced open lengthwise, worms about ½ inch long with brown heads are found inside. The pinkish-white color of these worms distinguishes them from peach twig borers, which cause similar damage. Later in the season, some of the maturing fruit also contain these worms. Often the plums have holes in them filled with a sticky gum.

Analysis: The larvae of the night-flying oriental fruit moth (*Grapholitha molesta*) damage stone fruit, apples, and pears. The larvae hibernate in cocoons on the tree bark or buried in branch crotches. In the spring they pupate, emerge as brown adult moths, and lay eggs on the young plum twigs and leaves. The larvae bore into the young buds, shoots, and tender twigs, causing twig and leaf death. When mature, they leave the twigs, spin cocoons, and pupate in the tree or in debris on the ground. After several weeks, moths emerge to lay eggs. Egg laying and larval damage continue throughout the growing season. Later in the summer, the larvae feed mainly on the maturing fruit. They leave gum-filled holes in the plums when they exit to pupate. In addition to ruining the fruit, these pests may cause abnormal branching on young trees.

Solution: Worms in the twigs and fruit can't be killed with pesticides. To prevent additional worm damage, kill the moths by spraying infested trees with a pesticide containing *malathion*. The following spring, spray again when the petals have fallen from the blossoms.

Scales

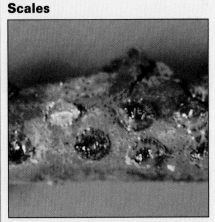

Terrapin scale (3× life size).

Problem: Brownish crusty bumps; thick, white, waxy bumps; or clusters of flattened yellowish, gray, or brownish scaly bumps cover the stems, small branches, or undersides of leaves. The bumps can be scraped or picked off; the undersides are usually soft. Leaves turn yellow and may drop. In some cases, a shiny or sticky substance coats the leaves. A black, sooty mold often grows on the sticky substance.

Analysis: Several different types of scales infest plum trees. They lay their eggs on leaves or bark, and in spring to midsummer the young scales, called *crawlers*, move around and then settle on leaves and twigs. The small (⅒-inch), soft-bodied young feed by inserting their mouthparts and sucking sap from the plant. The legs usually atrophy, and a hard crusty or waxy shell develops over the body. Mature female scales bear young or lay their eggs underneath their shells. Some species of scales are unable to digest fully all the sugar in the plant sap, and they excrete the excess in a fluid called *honeydew*, which often drops onto the leaves below. A sooty mold fungus may develop on the honeydew, causing the plum leaves to appear black and dirty. (For more information on scales, see pages 444 to 447.)

Solution: Spray with Ortho® Volck® Oil Spray in midsummer when the crawlers are active. Early the following spring, while the tree is still dormant, spray the trunk and branches with Ortho® Volck® Oil Spray to control overwintering insects.

PLUM *(continued)*

WALNUT

Black knot

Black knot.

Walnut husk flies

Walnut husk fly damage.

Walnut blight

Walnut blight.

Problem: Soft greenish knots or elongated swellings form on twigs and branches. These knots develop into black, corky, cylindrical galls that range from ½ to 1½ inches in diameter and may be more than 12 inches in length. Twigs and branches beyond the galls are usually stunted and eventually die.

Analysis: Black knot is a plant disease caused by a fungus (*Apiosporina morbosa*) that is severe on plums and occasionally attacks cherries. Fungal spores form during wet weather in the spring. Galls appear six months to one year after infection. The galls slowly enlarge and elongate. They eventually cut off the flow of water and nutrients to the branches, causing stunting, wilting, and dieback. Black knot spreads most rapidly during warm (55° to 75°F), wet, spring weather.

Solution: Prune and destroy infected twigs and branches during the fall and winter. When pruning, cut at least 4 inches below visible signs of infection. Cut out knots on the trunk or large limbs down to the wood and at least ½ inch outward past the diseased tissue. The following spring, spray the tree with a fungicide containing *thiophanate-methyl* or *captan* just before the buds open. Repeat the spray twice more at intervals of 7 to 10 days. Plant resistant varieties of plums.

Problem: Soft, blackened, decayed areas cover part or all of the walnut husk. Cream- to yellow-colored maggots up to ⅜ inch long are feeding inside the husk. The walnut shells are stained dirty black; sometimes the husks stick to the shells. Kernels are often stained and may be shriveled.

Analysis: Walnut husk fly (*Rhagoletis* species) maggots are the larvae of several closely related flies. The adult flies, slightly smaller than a housefly, are yellow-brown with banded wings. The flies begin laying their eggs in developing walnut husks in late July and early August. The maggots that hatch from these eggs feed in the husks for about a month, then drop to the ground and pupate in the soil until the following summer. As a result of maggot feeding, the husks become black and decayed, and the shells and kernels are stained. The maggots never feed on the kernels, and although the walnut meats may be shriveled or discolored, they usually taste normal.

Solution: Walnut husk flies are very difficult to control. Partial control may be obtained by killing the adult flies before they lay their eggs. Spray with an insecticide containing *malathion*, covering all of the foliage thoroughly. Respray according to label directions. Don't apply after the husks split. Contact your local county extension office for information regarding husk fly emergence dates in your area. To decrease infestation, keep the area under the tree clear of fallen walnuts. Dispose of husks in a tightly sealed container.

Problem: Buds turn dark brown to black and die. Brown spots are on the leaves, and dead, sunken lesions are on the shoots. A shiny black fluid may exude from these lesions. Some of the leaves may be deformed. Black, sunken, hard areas develop on the nuts. Infected nuts have stained shells or shriveled kernels. Nut yield may be reduced.

Analysis: Walnut blight is a plant disease caused by a bacterium (*Xanthomonas campestris* pv. *juglandis*) that is common on walnuts. The bacteria spend the winter in diseased buds, twig lesions, and old infected nuts attached to the tree. A thick, shiny fluid containing millions of bacteria exudes from the infected plant parts in the spring. Spring rains splash the bacteria to the buds, shoots, flowers, and developing nuts, starting new infections. Bacterial infection reduces nut set and can continue to spread to healthy nuts and foliage throughout the summer during periods of wet weather. If the nuts are infected before their shells harden (when the nuts are three-quarters grown), the bacteria may spread into and decay the kernels. Because the wet, rainy conditions of spring promote the rapid spread of walnut blight, early blooming walnut varieties are most susceptible to this disease.

Solution: The following spring, spray with basic copper sulfate when *catkins* (flower spikes resembling cats' tails) start to shed pollen; spray again when the small nutlets start to appear. If the weather remains wet, spray once more after two weeks. Plant late-blooming varieties.

Walnut caterpillars

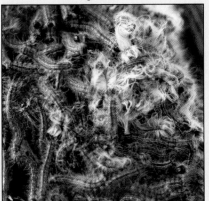

Walnut caterpillars (½ life size).

Problem: Reddish-brown to black hairy caterpillars with pale yellow to gray stripes running lengthwise along their bodies are feeding on walnut leaves. These caterpillars, which range in size up to 2 inches, feed in clusters. Leaves are chewed, and severely infested trees may be completely defoliated.

Analysis: The walnut caterpillar (*Datana integerrima*), the larva of a brown moth, is a common pest of walnut, pecan, and several other nut trees. Adult moths emerge in the spring to lay their eggs on the young leaves. The larvae that hatch from these eggs feed on the foliage, often clustered together. When disturbed, the caterpillars arch their heads and tails. Caterpillars group together on the trunk and molt (shed their skins) several times during their life cycle, leaving behind an unsightly patch of hairy cast-off skins each time. When mature, they drop to the ground and pupate in the soil, emerging as adult moths either later in the season or the following spring. Caterpillar damage may occur throughout the growing season. These pests can be very destructive. Severely infested trees may be defoliated within 24 hours.

Solution: Spray infested trees with an insecticide containing *malathion*. Repeat as directed on the label. If practical, pick off and kill caterpillars when they are clustered on the trunk while molting.

Walnut anthracnose

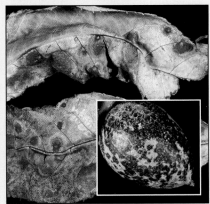

Anthracnose. Inset: Infected nut.

Problem: Circular reddish-brown to grayish-brown spots up to ¾ inch appear on the  leaves from May to the end of summer. Oval or irregular brown sunken lesions may develop on the green shoots. Tiny, dark sunken spots may appear on the walnut husks. Infected nuts often drop prematurely. The kernels of harvested nuts may be dark and shriveled. Infected leaves usually drop, and the tree may defoliate by midsummer.

Analysis: Walnut anthracnose is a plant disease caused by a fungus (*Gnomonia leptostyla*) that attacks walnuts and butternuts. The fungus spends the winter in twig lesions and on plant debris on the ground. In the spring, spores are discharged during rainy weather and blown to the new growth. If the surfaces of the leaves are wet, the spores can infect the leaves and shoots. The fungus can continue to infect healthy leaf, nut, and shoot tissue throughout the growing season, especially during periods of wet and humid weather. Trees that defoliate prematurely become weakened and frequently suffer a large reduction in nut yield and size.

Solution: If you notice the problem early in the summer, spray the infected tree with a fungicide containing *dodine*. Repeat the spray twice more at intervals of two weeks. Remove and destroy all plant debris. The following spring, spray the tree when the leaves are half their mature size. Spray again twice more at intervals of two weeks.

Crown rot

Crown rot.

Problem: The bark on part or all of the trunk just above or below the soil line is darkened. Sap may ooze from the affected bark. When the diseased bark is scraped away, the underlying sapwood is found to be discolored tan to black. Foliage may be sparse and yellowing. Little new growth occurs, and the tree may be stunted.

Analysis: Crown rot is a plant disease caused by soil-inhabiting fungi (*Phytophthora* species) that infect many trees and shrubs. The fungi penetrate the bark of the lower trunk or upper roots, forming lesions. As the fungi progress inward, they decay the nutrient-conducting tissue under the bark, interfering with the flow of nutrients to the roots. If left unchecked, the fungi will encircle the entire trunk, eventually causing the death of the tree. Crown rot thrives in wet soil. Trees planted in lawns, flower beds, or other moist areas are susceptible.

Solution: If the fungus hasn't completely encircled the tree, the tree might be saved. To let the crown dry out, remove the soil within 4 feet of the base of the tree, exposing the major roots. Keep this area dry. During the rainy season, slope the remaining soil away from the hole to keep it from filling with water. After the tree shows signs of recovering (look for healthy new growth), replace the soil around the base of the tree. Or, if possible, fill the hole with stones instead of soil to help keep the roots dry. Avoid planting flowers, shrubs, or other vegetation immediately around the tree.

A bountiful vegetable harvest is the reward of careful planning and good gardening techniques.

Raising your own vegetables can be a source of enormous satisfaction. It can also be an extremely frustrating enterprise if your crop is attacked by insects, overrun by weeds, eaten by birds and other animals, or it just simply dies. Planning and regular maintenance, however, should ensure a bumper crop.

MINIMIZING TRAFFIC DAMAGE

Pathways between vegetable rows are a way to reach produce without trampling on anything tasty. A narrow, uncomfortable path or a muddy one takes much of the pleasure out of picking, however.

Gardeners usually make paths wide enough to allow easy foot traffic, but problems occur when the access is too narrow for wheelbarrows, carts, or other large equipment. What looks like a sufficient path in spring can become annoyingly tight by summer, when vegetable foliage spreads over furrows and into the passageways. In gardens in which space is at a premium, plan 12- to 18-inch-wide pathways—the minimum width for comfort. If possible, make pathways 2 feet wide.

Some gardeners like to establish grass pathways, which are appealing to the eye and comfortable to walk on. These pathways require mowing, however, and grass may escape into the vegetable beds if path edges aren't trimmed faithfully.

Permanent pathways can be created from brick, concrete, or stone. They absorb sunlight during the day, then warm the surrounding soil at night.

Mulches make effective pathways, too, and many varieties of mulch are available. Path mulches include leaves, sawdust, wood chips, grass clippings, and aged hay. Unfortunately, these materials provide shelter for pests such as snails, slugs, sowbugs, rodents, and earwigs. And, since organic mulches decompose, you will have to renew them regularly. Keep path mulches at least 3 inches thick—a thin layer of organic mulch can permit weeds to emerge. The disadvantages of mulch pathways are balanced by the benefits the soil receives from mulch decomposition.

The list of path mulches includes newspapers. Being lightweight, they must be held down by stones or other material. Try putting a layer of organic mulch over a layer of newspaper to create a solid, renewable walkway. Black plastic or weed block rolled out along pathways does the job, too. Though not the most attractive path material, plastic coverings don't need to be constantly removed. In addition, black plastic prevents almost all weeds in the covered area. Clear plastic can be used as a covering, but it doesn't control weeds as well.

After two to three years, plastic becomes brittle and may crack. Though still usable as a walkway, cracked plastic allows weeds to emerge. Weeds that spread into vegetable beds can prove an enormous problem because applying an herbicide in already planted areas requires much care. Check plastic mulches at the beginning of each planting season, and replace them when they begin to show signs of wear.

CONTROLLING WEEDS

Weeds in the vegetable garden compete for water, nutrients, and sunlight. If prolific, weeds, when dry, post a fire hazard, give shelter to furry as well as insect pests, and make harvesting difficult.

Some crops—onions, carrots, strawberries, lettuce, spinach, and celery—need intensive weeding because their tops don't grow large enough to shade sunlight-reaching weeds. Brussels sprouts, pole tomatoes, and corn require comparatively minimal weeding once past the seedling stage. They provide enough shade to reduce weed competition.

Methods of weed control in the vegetable garden include hand-weeding, cultivation, mulching, solarization, and herbicide use. These methods are often used in combination, depending on the garden crop and soil needs.

Annual weeds germinate, flower, and die back in one season. Their seeds are extremely plentiful, however, and are spread by gardeners, mulches, manure, compost, birds, animals, wind, and rain.

Common annual vegetable-garden weeds are annual bluegrass, barnyardgrass, bristly oxtongue, bur clover, cheeseweed, chickweed, crabgrass, fleabane, groundsel, horseweed, lambsquarters, milk thistle, mustards, nettle, nightshade, prickly lettuce, purslane, shepherd's purse, sow thistle, sweet clovers, wild barley, and wild oats. A single barnyardgrass weed can produce over one million seeds in its short life.

Perennial weeds live on through winter, although they may die back. They reproduce from underground bulbs, rhizomes, or crowns on taproots. Common perennial weeds interfering with crop growth include bermudagrass, dallisgrass, field bindweed, johnsongrass, milkweed, nutsedge, oxalis, and witchgrass. If some of these names seem familiar, it is because what's considered a weed in the vegetable garden may be considered grass in the front yard.

Unfortunately, grass seeds germinate as well in a strawberry bed or tomato patch as they do in a lawn; sometimes better, if you keep garden soil in top condition. All that open space provides much less competition than that in a crowded front yard.

The cardinal precept of weed control is to eliminate them. Hand-pull all weeds as soon as they appear. Never let them go to seed in the vegetable garden or in a surrounding area. Keeping a thriving berry patch weed-free is difficult but necessary; consider the size of the weed crop of tomorrow if berry-eating birds spread the weed seeds through your garden today.

Make certain all commercially purchased soil additives, manures, or mulches are certified as weed-free. Even then, be vigilant—weed seeds may survive sterilization. Fresh manure is loaded with weed seeds, because most animals feed outdoors. Compost fresh manure, and make certain the compost pile is hot enough to kill weed seeds.

Another weed source is seed set out for birds. Keep it in containers and away from planting areas. Weeds may also be spread by dumping leftover food of caged birds, guinea pigs, and hamsters, as well as the animals' waste products, outdoors.

Living sunlight blockers: Some vegetable plants can be a definite help in weed control. For example, tall corn shades out weeds. It is also easy to cultivate between the rows. Other weed shaders include cauliflower, broccoli, and tomato plants. Potato plants also shade the ground, but don't use them in any area infested with nutsedge—this particular weed encourages potato rot by piercing tubers. After two successive years of weed-shading vegetables, plant garlic, lettuce, carrots, strawberries, and other minimal-shade plants to reinvigorate the soil.

Mulching with translucent polyethylene film discourages weeds, reduces water loss caused by evaporation, and helps to warm the soil in the spring.

Raised beds make it easier to reach weeds and require less stooping.

Soil solarization: An increasingly popular way to decrease weeds as well as insect pests that overwinter or pupate in the ground is through soil solarization. Solarization involves using the rays of the sun to bake out problems. You need steady sun to accomplish this, because the temperature of the treated soil should stay at 80°F or higher. Therefore, solarization works best in the hottest months of summer or fall.

Before beginning solarization, level and smooth the soil to be treated. Then wet the soil to encourage maximal heat penetration. Cover the entire area with a sheet of clear polyethylene plastic. Plastic that is 1 mil thick will do for most areas. If your garden receives a lot of wind, however, 2-mil-thick plastic has greater resistance to tearing. Smooth out the plastic as you place it; close contact with the wet soil encourages transmission of sunlight into the earth. Leave the plastic in place for four to six weeks. After that, unless you are using plastic that contains an ultraviolet inhibitor, you will have to remove the solarization covering. Left on too long, it may shred and be difficult to remove completely.

Not all weeds and weed seeds are destroyed by soil solarization. Nutsedge, sweet clover, purslane, crabgrass, and field bindweed are particularly resistant.

Hand-weeding: Pulling weeds manually may not be effective, because leaving behind even a portion of some weeds, such as dandelion, results in the regrowth of the plant. Various implements are available to make weeding more effective, including hand tines, weeding hoes, chopping hoes, and push-pull hoes. You must remove all tuber and rhizome segments, and this may mean digging deep. Some gardeners use rotary tilling as a means of weed control. Although it benefits soil with aeration, tilling may make a weed problem worse by chopping and spreading the still-viable weed roots and by lifting weed seeds to the surface.

Don't leave chopped or dug-out weed parts in the garden; put them in the compost heap or in a closed container. Weed seeds can spread from your gleanings, and weeds such as purslane can actually reroot where thrown if water is available.

Mulches: Weeds tend to be opportunists. They come up earlier than vegetables and grow much faster, crowding out desirable crops. By applying weed-blocking mulch early, you can give vegetable seedlings a head start on the weeds. Mulch keeps soil cool and may deter weed sprouting as well as early growth. Remove all weed parts before applying the covering. If weeds sprout through the mulch, dig them out immediately by hand. Be careful not to damage adjacent vegetable roots when hand-pulling or hoeing.

New synthetic weed-blocking fabrics avoid many of the disadvantages of organic mulches, such as pest shelter and insufficient coverage. Your local garden center may offer photodegradable plastic film, nonwoven polypropylene fabric, or heavy pressed fibrous paper. Each has advantages you may want to investigate.

Herbicides: Using herbicides is an option if weeds can't be satisfactorily controlled by other means. Preemergent herbicides eliminate annual weeds as they sprout. They may be used among perennial crops such as cane berries and asparagus. Preemergent herbicides aren't always selective about which annual seeds they eliminate, however. Check container instructions for a list of seeds that won't be killed by the herbicide. Be sure the seeds you intend to sow are included in that list, or don't use the herbicide.

Herbicide use in the vegetable garden always requires caution. Some weeds have susceptible crop cousins, so read the list of herbicide-resistant vegetables and berries carefully. Follow label instructions about when to apply the control, and learn what weeds are present, so you can select a postemergent herbicide with the appropriate ingredients. Avoid long-life herbicides. They might protect your summer crop, but they'll remain in soil past harvest and harm future plantings in the same area.

Weeder geese: Some gardeners use Chinese geese to control weeds in the vegetable and berry garden. The birds eat slugs, also. If you wish to try this option, read books on goose management before beginning. Geese must be kept in a fenced area away from domestic and wild animals. Use 3-foot-high stakes and chicken wire of similar height to create a movable fence line. Like any other animal, geese will need clean water and protection from rain, heat, and cold. In the vegetable garden, some supplemental food will be necessary.

Geese eat young tender weeds. If there is not a sufficient supply of weeds, they also eat crop seedlings. Move the fence to varying sites to provide an ongoing food supply. All geese feed primarily in the early morning and late evening. If you must set them out in the garden at specific times, work according to their natural habits. Never use pesticides or herbicides in any area immediately before introducing weeder geese or when they are present. The herbicide label will cite the length of time that must pass before you can reintroduce animals in the treated area; follow the label instructions exactly.

A sturdy weeding hoe is an essential gardening tool. When mechanically pulling weeds, be sure to remove all plant parts.

Growing vegetables in containers reduces the need for weeding. These potatoes enjoy quickly warmed soil in black plastic trash

bags that make harvesting a snap. A short length of PVC pipe facilitates deep watering.

323

CONTROLLING EROSION

If your vegetable garden is on a hillside, erosion may present a problem. With water and wind action, soil tends to move from high areas to low ones. If the topsoil is depleted, bolster the soil with fresh topsoil and fertilizer before attempting to plant anything.

Also, develop some type of erosion control. You may find examples of terracing and retaining structures in pictures of hillside gardening in Peru, Bolivia, Japan, India, China, Switzerland, and Italy, among many other countries where agricultural space is at a premium.

The basic concept of terracing is to provide a retaining structure that prevents soil loss. Heavy rain can wash soil past even the most effective retainers, however, so a sturdy wall of some type must be at the bottom of the terraced garden to hold the topsoil that makes it down the hill.

Construct retaining walls from railroad ties, concrete blocks, tires held with concrete and wire mesh, logs, brick, or stone. You can terrace the entire area or separate sections, depending on need. Always follow the land contour, rather than altering it, and plant across it rather than down it.

PROVIDING FERTILIZER

Lack of available soil nutrients can ruin a vegetable or berry crop. Plants may grow but be stunted or distorted, or produce a limited yield. Plants in poor health tend to suffer more from insect and disease attack than healthy plants, and other problems may follow nutrient deficiency.

If symptoms of nutrient deficiency continue after the correct fertilizer is applied, pH imbalance may be the cause. A soil pH higher than 8.0 may make certain nutrients, such as manganese and iron, unavailable to plants.

Treatments for deficiencies:

Nutrients required in soil for plant growth include boron, iron, magnesium, manganese, molybdenum, potassium, phosphorus, nitrogen (see page 410), calcium, and zinc. The sections that follow describe how various deficiencies affect specific plants.

■ **Boron deficiency:** Most common in dry weather and in alkaline sandy soil, boron deficiency in beets causes a condition known as heart rot. Black areas appear on the skin of the beet and inside the root. The root may be wrinkled and cracked. Most leaves die, leaving only a few deformed leaves. Plant growth slows markedly. Boron deficiency in celery causes brown horizontal cracks to appear across stalks. Leaves turn yellow and may die. Growth slows.

As soon as you identify boron deficiency in your garden soil, add borax, which is available in several forms. Before sowing, rake sodium tetraborate into the soil at the rate of 1 ounce for every 20 square yards of soil; mix in enough light sand to provide even distribution. Or, if plants are already growing, use 1 tablespoon of household borax dissolved in 12 quarts of water. This solution is sufficient for a 100-foot row. Repeat the treatment in two to three weeks. If necessary, correct soil pH to bring it between 6.0 and 7.0.

Water as needed to prevent the soil from drying out.

■ **Iron deficiency:** Also called lime-induced chlorosis, iron deficiency causes leaves to turn pale green or yellow. New leaves are most severely affected, and they may be undersized. Leaf edges and leaftips may scorch. In severe cases, new leaves are all-yellow or all-white, though leaf veins may remain green. Iron deficiency almost always occurs when soil pH is above 7.5. (The condition affects raspberries at pH 8.0.) Reduce soil pH by adding acidic materials such as peat, or use an elemental sulfur or ferrous sulfate additive. After treatment, wait until the pH reaches at least 7.0 before planting.

■ **Magnesium deficiency:** A shortage of magnesium shows up as yellowing (chlorosis) of older leaves and upward curling of leaf edges. The edges may yellow, leaving a green area in the center of the leaf. Symptoms begin in the lower plant and proceed upward. Magnesium deficiency is common in all types of berries and vegetables, because magnesium is easily washed out of soil during heavy rains. In addition, magnesium becomes unavailable to plants in the presence of potassium.

Vegetable plants are notoriously heavy feeders; adequate soil fertility is essential throughout the growing season for plants such as this Swiss chard to produce maximum yields.

Magnesium deficiency of potatoes appears as yellowing of leaf areas between veins. The leaf then browns and becomes brittle. Plant growth slows. Magnesium deficiency of beets causes older leaves to turn pale between veins, then brown. Some beet varieties may develop bright red leaf tints. Magnesium deficiency of tomato plants is common in plants receiving high-potassium fertilizers. Yellow-orange bands appear between leaves. A similar coloring may appear on raspberry leaves. Lower leaves are affected first. Symptoms spread upward, turning older leaves brown. In grapevines, magnesium deficiency may appear as purple blotches rather than the typical yellow-orange discoloration between veins.

To treat magnesium deficiency, spray with a product containing magnesium sulfate at 7- to 10-day intervals throughout the growing season. Some leaf yellowing may persist on tomato plants, but the crop will be unaffected.

■ **Manganese deficiency:** The symptoms of manganese deficiency resemble those of magnesium deficiency and often in conjunction with iron deficiency. In general, leaf yellowing occurs. In beet and spinach plants, leaves also roll inward. Beet leaves may assume a triangular appearance. Yellow blotches appear between leaf veins. In severe cases, entire leaves may turn pale yellow.

Manganese deficiency in peas, which is called marsh spot, causes a dark rust-red spot or cavity in pea centers. Pods appear normal, but leaves may be slightly yellow between veins. Manganese deficiency usually occurs in sand, alluvial silt, and clay soils. It is more common where pH is higher than 7.5. Symptoms may appear suddenly after a heavy rainfall, because soggy soil may impede manganese release to plants. Prevention includes adding manganese to soil before planting, or spraying with a solution of 2 ounces of manganese sulfate in 3 gallons of water. Add an agent to help the solution stick to the plants. Repeat two or three times at two-week intervals.

■ **Molybdenum deficiency:** Called whiptail, molybdenum deficiency is a problem on brassicas such as broccoli and cauliflower. Heads of affected plants fail to develop. Leaf blades become thin, straplike, and rippled. Molybdenum deficiency occurs only in acidic soils. Add lime before sowing or planting.

■ **Potassium deficiency:** Also known as potash deficiency, a lack of potassium causes small brown spots to appear along leaf edges. Leaf edges turn yellow, then gradually turn brown, curl downward, and die. Vegetable and berry yields are small. The crops that do appear may be distorted and ripen poorly. Vegetables and berries with potassium deficiency are susceptible to fungus and viral diseases.

Potassium aids in moving food supplies from leaves to roots and stems. Without it, crops can't grow properly. Light, sandy soil and peat and chalk soil are often low in potassium, as are soils in high-rainfall areas. Some crops, notably tomatoes, beans, and raspberries, demand more potassium than others. To remedy potassium deficiency, spray plant foliage with a liquid plant food, or water with a liquid plant-food additive. Apply a general-purpose fertilizer formulated for tomatoes—such fertilizers are usually high in potassium. For raspberries, apply a fertilizer that contains sulfate of potash.

Fertilizer burn: The condition called fertilizer burn may occur when gardeners use too much fertilizer or too strong a concentration, don't water fertilizer in properly, or allow undissolved granules to remain on leaves. In these cases, the accumulation of salts from both spray and granular fertilizers interferes with water use by the plant. Salts may accumulate in leaf edges, causing a burned or scorched appearance. In strawberries, leaf edges and areas between veins turn dark brown and die. After fertilizer burn occurs in any plant, no amount of watering will restore the green to browned edges. The burned leaves may drop. Plant growth may slow or stop. In severe cases of fertilizer burn, plants die.

To prevent fertilizer burn, follow application instructions carefully. In areas with poor drainage, be especially careful, because fertilizer will remain in the standing water. If possible, improve drainage before applying the treatment. Add fertilizer to moist soil only. Water fertilizer well; don't permit it to rest on leaves or on the soil surface. If you apply excess fertilizer by

Trenching next to rows is a good way to deliver water and fertilizer to roots, as these healthy beans show.

mistake, water the area thoroughly to leach salts out.

If you plan to add a dry fertilizer at seeding time, make furrows for fertilizer 3 inches from the empty seed rows and 2 inches deeper than seed depth. Put fertilizer in the furrows, and refill them with soil, then plant the seeds.

Seedlings are especially sensitive to fertilizer burn. Excess fertilizer can cause seedling root damage or prevent seedlings from emerging. The key to correct application is following label directions.

Like commercial fertilizers, fresh manure from cattle and poultry can cause fertilizer burn because the manure is high in salts. Avoid using fresh manure of any kind. In addition to causing fertilizer burn, fresh manure may contain large numbers of weed seeds, depending on what the animal ingested. Fresh manure may also contain insect eggs and larvae, if these were on the grasses eaten by the animals. Though fresh manure is often touted for its high nitrogen content, the amount varies considerably—again, according to the producer's diet. Before applying fresh manure to the soil or using manure as a mulch, thoroughly compost it. Add just a bit at a time to the compost heap or the pile may overheat, destroying beneficial microorganisms and earthworms.

PREVENTING COMPETITION

Competition from trees can prove fatal to many vegetables. Feeder roots, which may reach out underneath the soil three times as far as the branches reach overhead, can divert nutrients and water from crops. If possible, establish your garden far from shallow-root trees such as elms, maples, poplars, and willows. If limited space makes proximity to shallow-root trees unavoidable, dig a 3-foot-deep trench around the garden. If feeder roots are visible, cut them; limited root pruning will not harm the trees. Line the dividing trench with heavy-duty plastic or sheet metal, then refill with soil. The feeder roots will take a while to penetrate this barrier.

Black walnut trees present special problems for tomato plants. Black walnut roots give off a substance that causes wilting and dwarfing of many tomato varieties. (Falling walnut leaves won't cause problems.) Digging a dividing trench may not be sufficient to save the plants. If you have no other growing space, plant tomatoes in containers.

WATERING

Without water to soften and break seed coats, seeds will not germinate. Once germinated, seedlings are especially sensitive to water stress. Their delicate roots may reach only into the top inch of soil. If this dries out, the seedling may die despite diligent rescue efforts. In hot weather, if soil becomes dry to the touch, seedlings may need water once a day. Even mature plants may not have a root system deep enough to allow them to survive temporary dry periods.

Effects of drought: Plant wilting, followed by recovery after watering, is usually the first sign of water stress. Repeated wilting results in poor plant growth. Fruit on stressed plants may not mature properly. It may crack open and have poor flavor. Cucumbers without sufficient water grow in odd shapes and have a bitter taste. Overcompensating for water stress by overwatering can also be harmful. Under these conditions, sweet-potato tubers may develop cracks and black spots within roots.

Berry bushes can tolerate water stress better than other garden plants. Once berry bushes are established, they have an extensive root system. Unfortunately, their outstretched feeder roots are also pathways for fungi. The natural susceptibility of berry bushes to fungus diseases is enhanced by overwatering and high humidity.

Irrigation schedules and methods: When establishing a watering schedule for your garden, include one thorough soaking per week during the growing season. Remember that most common vegetables are almost 90 percent water and must retain this amount to mature into tasty table food.

The amount of watering you need to do depends greatly on what type of soil you have. Sandy soil retains less water than clay and requires more frequent irrigation. Use water effectively by adding organic materials, such as compost, to the soil. Compost greatly improves the moisture retention and water distribution in any soil.

■ **Drip irrigation:** When watering vegetables, avoid overhead sprinkling if possible. Leaves that don't dry quickly support fungi and water-transmitted viruses. Some form of drip irrigation—whether a drip, trickle, or soaker system—provides water without encouraging runoff. Drip systems are becoming increasingly popular because they are economical as well as effective. They provide water at a slow rate, allowing it to seep to where it is most needed, at the root zone. If you want to give your tomato seedlings an even bigger boost than a drip system alone can provide, make shallow watering depressions, or basins, around each plant and fill them at each watering.

■ **Water conservation through mulching:** Using mulch helps slow water evaporation, cutting watering needs by as much as one-third. Mulching may be a necessity for gardeners in warm climates where water is scarce. Put mulch down early for weed control, but don't apply it around crops until late spring, giving soil a chance to warm up. Use mulch around transplants and any seedling that has grown to a height of at least 6 inches.

Effective organic mulches include peat moss, seaweed, sawdust, dry composted manure, wood chips, bark chips, and straw. Don't use fresh hay as a mulch. If you have an ample hay supply, let it rot outdoors for a

Regular watering is essential for vegetable and fruit plants grown in containers.

year before applying in the garden to reduce problems from germinating weed seeds.

Mulch depth should be about 3 inches; piling too high may encourage rot.

Black plastic mulch discourages weed growth and lessens evaporation caused by wind. However, black plastic allows water to reach the ground only through whatever holes you make in it. During and after rain, puddles may form and stay on top of the covering. A new product, weed-blocking fabric, avoids this disadvantage. This fabric effectively prevents weeds but allows sunlight and water to pass through to the soil.

Application instructions vary slightly with each product. Basically, however, installation involves covering the vegetable garden with the plastic or fabric, then cutting holes for areas to be seeded or for transplanted seedlings. Seed holes will be slightly larger than seedling holes but, to prevent weed infiltration, make openings only as large as necessary. Hold the material in place with soil, wood chips, or rocks at the edges. Black plastic or woven plastic mulch is valuable for vine crops, such as squash and melon. The vines are free to spread without competition from weeds, and the crop is kept off of damp soil.

Clear plastic is not effective for water conservation or weed prevention. Sunlight penetrates clear plastic, warming soil. This added warmth can encourage heat-loving seeds, but it can also aid weed germination or produce too much heat and kill the plants.

WEATHERPROOFING

The two most common weather problems for home gardeners are wind and extremes in temperature.

Windbreaks: If wind is a constant or intermittent problem, create a windbreak for the vegetable garden. Windbreaks serve multiple purposes. Not only do they cut the effect of drying summer winds and destructive winter winds, but they also help retain heat—of special importance to spring seedlings. Also, windbreaks encourage bees to visit and pollinate—bees don't like strong winds any more than plants do.

Placing the garden where natural features or buildings shield it from the wind is the first step toward solving a wind problem. Building a tall fence around the garden is another solution.

Young transplants need protection from hot sun and wind; a few shingles will do.

They also need protection from late frosts; these are getting an early start.

Hedges that don't block sunlight work well as living windbreaks. Protective hedges that also attract birds include barberry, yew, euonymus, and arborvitae. Trees can also be effective windbreaks if their branches aren't allowed to grow dense and shade the garden. Trees or large shrubs may be inappropriate, however, if space is limited, because in a small area they compete with garden plants for nutrients, water, and light. Plan living windbreaks carefully, with growth patterns in mind, and prune hedge or tree foliage as necessary.

Since it takes time and labor to establish a fence or hedge windbreak, consider planting a flower windbreak. Some annuals grow high enough in a season to block a light breeze, although they are ineffective against strong winds. To protect garden seedlings against strong winds, shield the plants by placing cans with the ends removed around the stems.

Protection from heat and cold: If you have access to old tires and don't mind their appearance, they make fine windbreaks for warmth-loving vegetables such as tomatoes and eggplant. Tires hold heat, particularly if you put stones in the space for the inner tube. Some gardeners create raised beds throughout their gardens from tires of various sizes that are filled with fertile soil. The elevation of the plants in the tires alleviates drainage problems. Just as a tire holds heat during cold spells, however, it can produce a warmer environment

during hot weather. Plants inside tires may need extra watering.

During extremely hot weather, drape newspaper tents or floating row cover over susceptible crops. Anchor the coverings with stones or soil.

Frost is a continuing concern in some areas and an intermittent concern in others. Among the possible solutions is covering the garden with plastic, blankets, or sheets on nights when frost is expected. Another emergency measure is covering plants with temporary terrariums made from clear plastic, milk jugs or plastic bottles, bottoms removed. If frost threatens frequently, you may want to place heat-absorbing objects in the garden such as large, dark-colored rocks—objects that, after sunset, release absorbed heat and protect the vegetables from frost.

If you must plant warmth-loving vegetables in frost pockets, keep in mind that cold air tends to collect in low places. Block cold air with a hedge, stone fence, or embankment. Cold air, however, like water collecting behind a dam, can overflow and needs an outlet. Make a pathway through the embankment, allowing the air to flow harmlessly away from susceptible plants.

Since cold air, and the frost that accompanies it, settles in ditches and ground hollows, you might want to go one step further and dig out a low-lying catch basin at a site of your choosing, away from your vegetable garden. Raising the vegetable beds is another means of frost protection.

Trellises can be an attractive part of the garden.

PROVIDING SUPPORT

Staking vegetable and berry plants can be a nuisance. The alternative, however—leaving plants to trail on the ground—can produce as much rot as food. Some plants, such as cane berries, grow into impenetrable thickets unless controlled by staking.

Always use rot-resistant wood when staking vegetables. A metal stake or uninsulated wire will heat up in summer, possibly burning any plant that touches it.

Gardeners sometimes underestimate the growth potential of plants. If you decide to stake them, provide 8-foot-high stakes at planting time rather than trying to lash

This A-frame trellis is ideal for supporting cucumbers.

stakes together to rig a higher support late in the season. Lashed stakes don't balance properly and are prone to toppling. Dig stakes 1 foot into the soil to anchor them against plant weight and wind. Keep stakes about 4 inches away from plants.

To stake red and yellow raspberries, use sturdy 3-foot-high posts that are 3 inches thick. Anchor the posts well into the ground; superficially anchored posts will topple in the wind or fall over from the weight of the canes or shifting wet soil. String two smooth 10- or 11-gauge wires between the posts, one wire near the tops and the other halfway up from the ground.

Climbing vegetables, such as beans and peas, do best off the ground, away from insects. One type of support structure for climbers consists of wood supports tilted into an A-frame shape. To create this structure, place 8-foot-high supports in two rows. Place the rows 24 inches apart, and set the stakes within each row 12 inches apart. Tilt the tops inward and secure them. Make certain that supports are extremely well anchored. If they fall over while supporting a heavy crop, they will be difficult to replace without damaging plants.

Mesh netting with large openings is a space-effective support alternative for pea and bean vines. Attach the netting to any vertical support. To avoid wind damage to the support system, encourage the vines to grow through the netting.

Cucumbers left to lie on the ground can take up quite a bit of space in a garden. An easy way to let them climb is to provide nylon netting, which can be hooked over a sunny fence. Garden-supply stores and catalogs offer green nylon netting, which is easily camouflaged by growing foliage.

For tomato plants, staking continues to be controversial. Some gardeners prefer to let them sprawl, keeping foliage open and fruit exposed to the sun. You will need at least 15 square feet per plant if you choose this option. Slugs and hornworms go after lower tomatoes first, and ground rot may occur. Watch low-lying plants carefully, and take corrective action if necessary.

One compromise between staking tomato plants and letting them sprawl is placing them on a 6-inch-thick mulch. Setting plants through slits in protective black plastic is another alternative. Tomatoes also receive ground protection from multiple layers of newspaper.

Cages to support tomato plants are available at most garden-supply stores. Place a cage around a plant when it is small. Placing a cage over a maturing bush or vine often damages foliage. Anchor the cage securely into the ground.

Tomato vines damage easily. Tie them to stakes or supports with soft cloth strips, bits of old nylon stocking, or commercially available tomato ties. Never bend vines at a sharp angle when handling. If you do accidentally angle a stem and it partially breaks, you may be able to do some garden doctoring. Join, then tape, the edges together. If the leaves don't wilt in a few days, the vine will survive.

HARVESTING

■ Asparagus should not be harvested the first year. The second year, take no more than two spears from each plant, and remove them from mid-April to mid-June only. After this, the spears become spindly. Allow them to form feathery foliage to help build plant strength for the following season.
■ Harvest all beets before severe frost. Beets are especially delicious when small, about the 1-inch in diameter. They become less tender as they get larger.
■ Pick broad beans when the seeds are about fingernail size. Left on the vine too long, the pods develop black streaks, which indicate that the seeds have ripened and their skins have become tough.
■ Harvest brussels sprouts from the bottom of the plant upward. Snap or cut them off

cleanly and as close to the stem as possible.

■ Dig up carrots when they reach baby length, about 3 inches. Although they can remain in soil for quite a while when mature, carrots longer than 3 inches tend toward woodiness. Remove all carrots before winter. Left in damp ground they are easy targets for wireworms and slugs, and heavy rains may cause split roots.

■ Inspect corn carefully to determine picking time. Turn back the corn sheath until just a few kernels are visible. Pierce a kernel with your fingernail. If the juice is watery, the corn is still forming. Test again a few days later. If the juice is milky white, the corn is ready. Remove the ear by giving it a quick twist. Cook corn as soon as possible after harvesting it.

■ Harvest the cucumber crop regularly, and don't allow the cucumbers to get too large. Pickling size is 2 inches long; slicing cucumbers range from 6 to 8 inches long. If the vine is overburdened, production will be limited.

■ Butterhead lettuce is ready for the table when a loose head forms. Tight-growing crisp lettuce varieties are best when heads are firm.

■ Pick melons when they pass the smell test—that is, when the stem end exudes a strong, pleasant aroma. The exception is cantaloupe, which is ready when fruit comes off the stem easily.

■ Harvest onions when leaftips turn yellow and start bending over. Be sure that these are indeed signs of maturity, not of damage by thrips. Don't jerk the onions from the ground; ease them out with a hand spade. Let bulbs dry in the sun. If you have many onions and limited drying space, make an onion rope from heavy twine. Attach onions to the dangling cord, beginning at the bottom of the twine.

■ Harvest summer squash when the skin is not yet firm. The converse is true of winter squash, which should have firm skin, not easily punctured, when harvested.

■ Pick tomatoes at their peak, which comes about six days after first color appears. At their ripest, they are brightly colored, full-flesh, and shiny. Three days after ripening, they begin to lose flavor. Even refrigerator storage doesn't maintain prime taste. If you must pick full-size tomatoes while they are still green, ripen them indoors between 60° to 70°F. Shield them from direct sunlight. Keep fruit from touching in the ripening container.

ANIMAL-PROOFING

As housing moves into former forests and fields, many native animals become garden pests. Rabbits, gophers, moles, raccoons, and others can cause damage. So can birds, both exotic species and common city and suburban residents.

Birds: Starlings, cowbirds, grackles, blackbirds, and crows are particularly voracious feeders. They and other species are as fond of berries as are people and insects. Birds are attracted to the high sugar level in ripe fruit and often get to a juicy berry right before you're ready to pick it. Many gardeners like birds so much that they place a few extra berry plants in the yard to provide enough fruit for all. But if birds are eating into the family food supply, several remedies are available.

For raspberry protection, create a wood or metal frame around plants. Over this, drape netting with ¾-inch mesh. This size lets in air, water, and sunlight. Secure netting at the bottom so berry predators can't slip underneath it.

To protect blueberries, set 8-foot posts around the growing area to form a frame; keep the frame at least a foot away from the blueberry bushes. Nail netting with ¾-inch mesh around sides and tops of posts. In small growing areas, cover individual bushes with netting gathered at the base to prevent birds from getting under the netting.

For strawberry protection, cover plants with wire cages or netting with ¾-inch mesh stretched over a frame.

To protect grapes, loosely tie paper bags over ripening fruit clusters. Allow just enough space around the vine to permit air circulation. Cut off the bottom corners of bags for additional necessary circulation. Provide bagged clusters with some afternoon shade, or grapes within may cook.

To protect vegetable seedlings from bird feeding, use floating row covers. Sold in rolls at most local garden centers, these sheets of breathable white fabric were created especially for the vegetable garden. They are lightweight and permit sun, water, and air to pass through.

Cover the seedling rows with the fabric. Secure the edges by weighting them down or burying them so animal pests can't crawl underneath. Hefty rocks are effective weights, as are 2×4's. If you bury the edges, add weights at corners and at intervals along the sides. The drawback to row covers is that they can create temperatures underneath

The best way to protect blueberries from birds is to cover the bushes with bird netting. Be sure to gather it at the base of the plants to keep birds out.

that are up to 30°F higher than the air temperature. Remove row covers in summer to avoid baked plants.

In some areas, crows are a particular problem. With great skill, these large noisy birds pick up coverings, shred material, and find their way around obstacles. Ordinary row covers or nylon netting may not keep them away. Try using removable chicken wire cages over vegetable seedlings. Anchor the cages.

Scarecrows seldom work. Birds become accustomed to them quickly and learn that they are harmless. Shiny aluminum foil streamers fluttering from rope placed across the garden may discourage bird feeding. However, birds soon get accustomed to this, too. If netting or row covering is not an option, an active cat may do the job. A cat may be too effective, however, in that birds will flee the garden entirely, leaving insect pests unchecked.

Rabbits: In small numbers, rabbits just nibble on row ends; large populations go after the greenery as it comes from the ground. Dogs can sometimes keep them away. Some rabbits, however, just seem to run circles around canine protectors.

The first thing to do if you see signs of rabbit feeding is get rid of potential hiding places. These might include a woodpile, tall grass, and weeds.

One method to deter rabbit feeding is to create a 24-inch fence. Around the garden periphery, pound in green plastic stakes of the appropriate height. Use metal clips to attach green plastic-coated wire fencing

with 1×2-inch mesh to the stakes. The green mesh will blend with garden foliage, and the clips will allow you to adjust the fence when necessary.

Since rabbits can bury underneath fences, you may want to extend the wire mesh at least 6 inches under ground. Determined rabbits will eventually tunnel underneath, but the belowground shield may delay them long enough to allow crops to mature and be harvested. An alternative, particularly if you want mobile fencing, is to buy 36-inch-wide wire mesh and fold out the bottom 12 inches around the periphery. Securely staked or weighted down, this horizontal portion will make it more difficult for rabbits to dig under the fence edge.

If fencing your garden is impractical, try protecting seedlings from rabbits by shielding the plants with large tin cans from which the tops and bottoms have been removed. In early spring, when the temperature needs a boost anyway, leave on the plastic top that comes with many cans. It allows sunlight to come through and provides protection from wind and cold. Make certain that sufficient water condenses inside the containers to provide moisture. If necessary, remove the top to water the seedlings, then replace the lid. Using cans as protection becomes ineffective once the plant tops peek over the metal edges.

Gophers and moles: Signs of gopher or mole invasion include wilted plants that have no roots and mounds of fresh pulverized earth. Gophers eat underground vegetable parts, often eliminating them

altogether in just one evening. They also pull entire plants down into their burrows. While moles don't eat vegetables, their tunneling disrupts roots and provides entry for mice which may feed on the roots.

Although gophers and moles aren't communal animals, there can be as many as 20 per acre, each with a separate series of tunnels. If your garden is severely infested, you may have to dig the entire vegetable bed to a depth of 2 feet, line it with ½-inch mesh chicken wire, and replace the soil.

If you can't line the entire bed, consider making or purchasing individual wire-mesh baskets for each plant. Again, mesh must be ½ inch or less and protect all belowground portions of the plant.

Trapping is the most thorough method of gopher and mole control. Using just one trap works if there is only one hole. Gophers and moles make many exit and entry holes, so they have many escape routes. Purchase at least two traps. Box traps are easier to use than Maccabee traps, but both are effective when used according to directions.

Dig down to the main horizontal runway that connects with the surface hole. The runway can be as deep as 18 inches. Place traps on each side of your digging hole. Since commercial traps vary, read and follow instructions. For gophers, bait the area with carrot tops or other fresh greens. Cover your hole with a board to block all light. Check the traps frequently.

Many gardeners don't consider poison an option because of the potential danger to cats, dogs, and even curious youngsters. If you do choose to use poison, place bait

Grapes protected in paper bags.

Strawberries protected under bird netting.

Blueberries protected by bird netting.

in the deep tunnels close to living quarters rather than in surface tunnel runways, which may be used intermittently. Make certain to close your digging hole with boards or earth after placing the bait.

Gopher and mole elimination may require persistence as well as multiple control methods.

Raccoons: Raccoons are becoming much more common in urban and suburban vegetable gardens as home construction cuts a swath into their natural habitats. Raccoons are adaptable creatures, handy at removing garbage-can lids in search of food and curious enough to crawl down the chimney. Cute as they may be, raccoons are wild animals and may bite. Never handle a raccoon under any circumstances. If a raccoon is trapped under the house or by a dog, call animal control for help.

Because raccoons feed on pest insects as well as fruit and seeds, many homeowners tolerate their presence. Once raccoons have discovered a food source, however, they keep returning. In the process, they may discover your vegetable garden and berry patch. Therefore, protecting your garden means keeping the whole area free of raccoon-attracting food. Secure garbage-can lids thoroughly; locking devices are available. A spotlight on the garbage-can area is another raccoon deterrent. Bring pet food inside at night. Keep your compost pile turned and hot enough to decompose fruit and other kitchen remainders.

Traps are most effective before your crop ripens. A ripe crop provides foods that compete successfully with baits. Raccoons like sweets, so marshmallows or bread with honey are effective attractants. Raccoons may be protected by law in your vicinity. Ask at the county extension service or local animal control agency about regulations.

Deer: Like raccoons, deer are becoming increasingly problematic as suburbia intrudes into forested areas. Deer can easily jump 5-foot fences to get at vegetable greens. They tend to feed in the early morning or late evening, when few gardeners are around to chase them off. A large watchdog may scare them away, although barking can annoy neighbors.

Fencing is perhaps the best deerproofing. To exclude deer, a traditional fence must be at least 8 feet high. In some areas a fence of this height is prohibited by building codes or isn't feasible. Since deer jump high or wide, but usually not both ways at the same time, a deer fence may be the answer. This is 6 feet high with a 3-foot-wide section across the top, parallel to the ground.

Some gardeners in deer areas have tried electric fencing. The strands of such a fence should be 10 inches apart and the bottom one not more than 8 inches from the ground. Consult the county extension service for rules concerning electrified fencing in your area.

Rats and mice: Rodents take up residence where the food pickings are easy, such as in a garden with a lot of debris or in an inefficient compost heap. Organic mulches provide hiding places for rats and mice. To make sure they don't take up winter residence near your food supply, thin out strawberry plants in early fall and wait until the first frost to mulch.

In all seasons, keep your yard clear of debris. This includes trash piles, leaves, firewood, newspapers, boxes, pipes, logs, and tree cuttings. Clean out and close off the area under steps. If you must store construction materials outdoors, put them on platforms 12 to 18 inches off the ground.

Rats and mice may enter your garden from a neighboring property. If the problem is severe, you may have to press local officials to enforce trash abatement rules. This procedure can take a while. In the meantime, a pair of feisty cats may persuade rodents that living elsewhere is an easier solution.

Ground squirrels: Vegetable gardens that abut fields or open space are often plagued by ground squirrels. They feed on roots and tubers as well as aboveground plants. These squirrels store excess food in burrows, which may be as deep as 4 feet below the surface.

In some areas, regulations protect ground squirrels, so consult the county extension service before using traps or poison. Place baited box traps outside burrows. Don't use any type of poison bait if pets or children are present. Peanut butter is an effective bait for a live trap. Be sure to release squirrels in more appropriate surroundings, where they will not do more damage.

Wooden frames covered with netting protect vegetables from rabbits.

High fences protect plants from deer.

Wire over a frame protects lettuce from rabbits.

POOR PRODUCE AND SLOW GROWTH

Poor produce and slow growth

Poor-quality tomatoes.

Slow growth

Phosphorus deficiency on corn.

Slow growth from soil too acidic.

Problem: Fruit has poor or strong flavor and is smaller than normal. Fruit yield is low.

Analysis: Vegetables and berries may yield poor-quality produce for many reasons.
1. Hot weather affects the flavor of some fruits, especially cool-season crops such as lettuce and members of the cabbage family. Their taste becomes strong and bitter.
2. Fluctuations in soil moisture affect the flavor of many fruits, especially cucumbers. Sweet and white potato tubers crack and appear unappetizing. Alternating wet and dry soil results in erratic growth with poor-quality fruit.
3. Low soil fertility causes plants to grow poorly and yield little if any fruit. Any fruit produced is frequently off-flavor and may not develop fully.
4. Overmature fruit deteriorates rapidly and loses its flavor. Allowing fruit to overripen on the plant reduces future yields by taking energy the plant could have used to produce more fruit.

Solution: Follow these guidelines for better-quality produce. (For more information, look for the plant in the alphabetical section beginning on page 343.) Numbered solutions below correspond to the numbered items in the analysis.
1. Plant vegetables and small fruits at the times of year suggested on page 555.
2. Follow irrigation guidelines for your vegetable.
3. Fertilize your plants as instructed.
4. Pick fruit as it matures so more fruit will be produced. Follow the harvesting guidelines specific to your plant.

Problem: Plants grow slowly. Leaves are pale green to yellow, or darker than normal, and dull. Few flowers and fruit are produced. Fruit that is produced matures slowly. Plants pulled from the soil may have small, black, rotted root systems. Plants may die.

Analysis:
1. Excess water: If the soil is constantly wet, either from frequent watering or poor drainage, lack of oxygen causes the roots to become shallow, stunting and sometimes killing the plant. Wet soil also encourages fungi that destroy the root system and kill the plant.

2. Phosphorus deficiency: Phosphorus is a major nutrient needed by plants for root formation, flower and fruit production, and overall cell growth. Phosphorus-deficient plants grow slowly and have dark leaves that may be tinted with purple or have purple veins. This nutrient may be lacking either because it is not present in the soil in sufficient quantities or because it is in a form that is unavailable to plants.

3. Incorrect pH: The soil pH limits the amounts and kinds of nutrients available to plants. Vegetables grow best with a pH of 6.0 to 7.0. Required nutrients are usually available in adequate amounts within this range. (For more information on pH, see pages 406 and 407.)

4. Cool weather: Warm-season vegetables, such as tomatoes, beans, and okra, require temperatures higher than 70°F for best growth and fruit production. If they are planted too early, the cool weather slows their growth. Affected plants may take several months to recover from this setback and still may not produce abundantly.

Solution:
1. Allow the soil around plants to dry out. Remove and destroy any plants with rotting roots. Avoid future root rot problems by planting in well-drained soil. (For information on drainage, see page 406.)

2. Spray the leaves with a liquid or soluble fertilizer for a quick response. Fertilize with a balanced fertilizer. Follow the rates on the label or those given for each vegetable in the section beginning on page 343.

3. Test the soil pH and correct to 6.0 to 7.0.

4. Plant vegetables at the correct time of year. (For planting times in your area, see page 555.) Discard warm-season vegetable plants that have been set back by cool temperatures. Replace with healthy new transplants or seedlings.

Insufficient light

Slow growth due to insufficient light.

Problem: Plants grow slowly or not at all. Leaves are light green, and few or no flowers or fruit are produced. Plants are shaded for much of the day. Lower leaves may turn yellow and drop.

Analysis: Plants need sunlight to manufacture food and produce fruit. Without adequate sunlight, they grow slowly. Vegetable and berry plants that yield fruit such as tomatoes, raspberries, strawberries, beans, and peppers require at least six hours of sunlight per day. Some leafy and root vegetables, however, will tolerate light shade.

Solution: Prune any surrounding trees to allow more sunlight. Plant vegetables that require less sunlight in somewhat shady areas of the garden. If possible, move your garden site, or grow vegetables in containers on a sunny patio or porch.

Seedlings eaten

Pea seedlings eaten by rabbits.

Bean seedlings eaten by slugs.

Problem: Seedling leaves are chewed ragged. Seedlings may completely disappear, or short stubs of stems may remain.

Analysis:

1. Birds: Many kinds of birds, especially grackles, blackbirds, and crows, eat entire seedlings. The plants are most susceptible to bird attack when they have just emerged.

2. Snails and slugs: These pests feed at night and on cloudy days, chewing holes in leaves or devouring entire seedlings. Silvery winding trails are evidence of their presence. During the day they hide in damp places, such as under rocks or in debris.

3. Earwigs: These dark brown insects with pincers projecting from the rear of their bodies feed at night, chewing holes in leaves and stems.

4. Rabbits: These animals may eat entire seedlings or may leave only short stubs of the stems standing in the soil.

5. Grasshoppers: These insects are present throughout the growing season and migrate from area to area as their food source is depleted. They eat entire seedlings. Grasshoppers are most prevalent during hot, dry weather.

Solution:

1. Cover seedlings with a tent made of row cover or netting stretched over a frame. Scarecrows and dangling aluminum pie plates may temporarily deter birds.

2. Control snails and slugs with Ortho® Bug-Geta® Snail & Slug Killer. Lightly wet the area before application to activate the pellets. The moisture will also attract snails and slugs. Treat along the seeded rows and in hiding places, such as under rocks, boards, and flower pots and around compost piles.

3. To control earwigs, treat with Ortho® Bug-Geta® Plus Snail, Slug & Insect Killer or Ortho® Bug-B-Gon® Multi-Purpose Insect Killer Granules along the seeded rows and in hiding places, such as under rocks and in garden debris.

4. Keep rabbits out of the garden by erecting a 2-foot-high fence of small-gauge fencing wire around the garden. Anchor the bottom of the fence with boards 6 inches deep in the soil to prevent rabbits from digging underneath it.

5. Control grasshoppers and protect uneaten seedlings with Ortho® Bug-Geta® Plus Snail, Slug & Insect Killer or Ortho® Bug-B-Gon® Multi-Purpose Insect Killer Granules. Repeat at weekly intervals as long as grasshoppers are present.

SEEDLING PROBLEMS *(continued)*

Damping-off

Damping-off of radish seedlings.

Cutworms

Climbing cutworm.

Cutworms on celery (life size).

Problem: Seeds rot. Seedlings fail to emerge or fall over soon after they emerge. Areas on the stem at the soil line are water-soaked and discolored. The base of the stem is soft and thin.

Analysis: Damping-off is a common problem caused by several fungi and aggravated by wet soil with a high nitrogen level. Wet, rich soil promotes damping-off because the fungi that cause it are more active under these conditions. Damping-off is often a problem when the weather remains cloudy and wet and when seedlings are heavily shaded or crowded. Seedlings started indoors in a wet, unsterilized medium are also susceptible.

Solution: To prevent fungi from attacking seedlings, take the following precautions.
1. Allow the surface of the soil to dry slightly between waterings.
2. Don't start seeds in soil that has a high nitrogen level. Add nitrogen fertilizer only after the seedlings have produced their first true leaves.
3. Purchase seeds that have been treated with fungicide to protect them from damping-off.
4. Start seeds indoors, in a sterilized medium, such as a pasteurized potting soil, seed-starting mix, or a mixture of peat moss, perlite, and vermiculite.
5. Thin seedlings to allow good air circulation.

Problem: Stems of young plants are chewed or cut off near the ground. Gray, brown, or black worms, up to 2 inches long, may be found in the top 2 inches of the soil near the base of the damaged plants. The worms coil when disturbed.

Analysis: Several species of cutworm attack plants in the vegetable garden. Surface-feeding cutworms are common pests of young vegetables planted early in the season. A single surface-feeding cutworm can sever the stems of many young plants in one night. Cutworms eat through the stems just above ground level. Tomatoes, peppers, peas, beans, and members of the cabbage family are particularly susceptible. Some cutworms can climb up the stem or trunk of grapes, blueberries, raspberries, blackberries, tomatoes, and other garden crops to feed on young leaves, buds, and fruit. Cutworms hide in the soil during the day and feed only at night. Adult cutworms are dark, night-flying moths with bands or stripes on their forewings. (For more information on cutworms, see page 440.)

Solution: Apply Ortho® Bug-Geta® Plus Snail, Slug & Insect Killer or Ortho® Bug-B-Gon® Multi-Purpose Insect Killer Granules around the base of undamaged plants. Make sure that your plant is listed on the product label. Cutworms are difficult to control, so applications may need to be repeated at weekly intervals. Cultivate the soil thoroughly in late summer and fall to expose and destroy eggs, larvae, and pupae. Work Ortho® Bug-B-Gon® Multi-Purpose Insect Killer Granules into the soil before planting. Further reduce damage with a cutworm collar (see page 414) around the stem of each plant. To reduce injury from climbing cutworms, inspect your plants at night with a flashlight and pick off and destroy any cutworms you find.

WILTING

Wilt diseases

Fusarium wilt on tomato.

Problem: Leaves wilt, turn yellow, and may turn brown. Little or no fruit is produced. Growth slows and plants may be stunted. When the stem is sliced open lengthwise, the tissue just under the bark is usually found to be brown.

Analysis: Wilt diseases infect many vegetables and berries. They may be caused by any of several fungi that live in the soil. The fungi are spread by contaminated plants, soil, and equipment. They enter the plant through the roots and spread through water-conducting vessels in the stems. The vessels become discolored and plugged. This plugging cuts off the flow of water and nutrients to the leaves, resulting in leaf yellowing and wilting. The plugging also results in a reduced yield and poor-quality fruit. Severely infected plants die. (For more information on wilt diseases, see page 420.)

Solution: No available chemicals will cure infected plants. Wilt fungi can be removed from the soil only by fumigation or solarization techniques. The best solution is usually to avoid plants that are susceptible to wilt diseases. The same kind of plant is unlikely to thrive where a wilt-infected plant grew. (For a list of vegetables and berries susceptible to wilt diseases, see page 556.)

Root and stem rot

Root rot on broccoli.

Problem: Leaves wilt and turn yellow. Lower leaves are affected first, then the upper ones. Little or no fruit is produced. Plants don't recover when watered, and they usually die.

Analysis: Root and stem rot are caused by any of several different fungi known as water molds. These fungi thrive in waterlogged, heavy soils. The fungi attack the plant roots or the stems at the soil level. Infection causes the roots and stems to decay, resulting in wilting, then yellowing leaves, and eventually the death of the plant. Many of these fungi also cause *damping-off* of seedlings. (For more information on damping-off, see page 420.)

Solution: Allow the soil around the plants to dry out. (For information on this technique, see page 419.) Remove and discard severely infected plants. Avoid future root rot problems by planting in well-drained soil. (For information on drainage, see page 406.) Follow the watering guidelines for your plant found in the alphabetical section beginning on page 343.

Nematodes

Nematode damage on bean leaves.

Problem: Plants wilt in hot, dry weather and recover at night. They are stunted and yellow. Round and elongated nodules may occur on the roots. Plants may die.

Analysis: Nematodes are microscopic worms that live in the soil. They are not related to earthworms. Nematodes feed on plant roots, damaging and stunting them. The damaged roots can't supply sufficient water and nutrients to the aboveground plant parts, and the plant is stunted or slowly dies. Nematodes may also transmit certain viruses. Nematodes are found throughout the United States but are most severe in southeastern areas. They prefer moist, sandy loam soil. Nematodes can move only a few inches each year on their own, but they may be carried long distances by soil, water, tools, or infested plants. Testing roots and soil is the only positive method for confirming the presence of nematodes. Contact your local county extension office for sampling instructions and addresses of testing laboratories. Soil and root problems, such as poor soil structure, drought stress, nutrient deficiency, and root rots, can also produce symptoms of decline similar to those caused by nematodes. These problems should be eliminated as causes before soil and root samples are sent for testing. (For information on soil problems and root rots, see pages 406 and 419.)

Solution: No chemicals available to homeowners kill nematodes in planted soil. The worms can be controlled before planting, however, by soil solarization.

DISCOLORED OR MOTTLED LEAVES

Root rot

Root rot on bush bean.

Problem: Leaves turn yellow, starting with the older, lower leaves and progressing to the younger ones. Plants grow very little. Flowers yellow and drop. Fruit shrivels and does not ripen. When the plant is pulled up, the roots appear black, soft, and rotted. The soil has frequently been very moist.

Analysis: Root rot is a plant disease caused by any of several different fungi present in most soils. (For information on water molds, see page 419.) Some of these fungi normally do little damage but can cause root rot in wet or waterlogged soil. Waterlogged soil may result from overwatering or from poor soil drainage. Infection causes the roots to decay, resulting in wilting, yellowing leaves, flower and fruit drop, reduced fruit yield, and eventually the death of the plant.

Solution: To avoid root rot problems, don't overwater. Follow the watering guidelines under the entry for your plant in the alphabetical section beginning on page 343. Remove and destroy severely infected plants. Avoid future root rot problems by planting in well-drained soil. (For information on drainage, see page 406.) Don't plant the same crop in a part of the garden where root rot was a problem in the past three to five years. (For more information on root rot, see page 419.)

Nitrogen deficiency

Nitrogen-deficient tomato.

Problem: The bottom leaves, including the veins, turn light green to pale yellow and may die or drop. Growth slows, and new leaves are small. Flowers turn yellow and drop. Fruit is small and may be distorted and discolored.

Analysis: Plants need nitrogen to make chlorophyll, the essential green pigment in their leaves, and for overall healthy growth and high-quality fruit production. When plants lack nitrogen, growth slows, blossoms drop, and fruit yield is reduced. Nitrogen may either be lacking in the soil or be present in a form that is not available to the plant. In cool, rainy, early-spring weather, little or no nitrogen is available. Later in the season, as vegetables grow rapidly and mature, plants may deplete the supply of nitrogen in the soil. During a drought, nitrogen is carried to the soil surface as the water it is dissolved in evaporates. Once the nitrogen is above the plant's root zone, the roots are unable to absorb it. Rain or irrigation water carries nitrogen back to the root zone, where it is available to the plant.

Solution: For a quick response, spray the foliage with a liquid or soluble fertilizer. Water the plant with the same solution. Remove any fruit from severely affected plants to allow the plants time to resume normal growth. Fertilize according to instructions for your plant in the alphabetical section beginning on page 343.

Spider mites

Spider mite damage on string bean.

Problem: Leaves are stippled, yellowing, and dirty. Leaves may dry out and drop. There may be webbing on flower buds, between leaves, or on the lower surfaces of leaves. To determine if a plant is infested with mites, examine the bottoms of the leaves with a hand lens. Or hold a sheet of white paper underneath an affected leaf or stem and tap the leaf or stem sharply. Minute specks the size of pepper grains will drop to the paper and move about. The pests are easily seen against the white background.

Analysis: Spider mites are major pests of many garden and greenhouse plants. They cause damage by sucking sap from the undersides of leaves. As a result of their feeding, the plant's chlorophyll disappears, producing the stippled appearance. Spider mite webbing traps cast-off skins and debris. Although mites don't attack the fruit directly, they do cause leaf drop, which weakens the plant and reduces fruit yield. If plants are severely infected, flowers don't form or don't bloom and don't produce fruit. Mites are active throughout the growing season but thrive in dry weather with temperatures of 70°F and higher. By midsummer they may have built to tremendous numbers.

Solution: Treat infested plants with Ortho® Malathion Plus® Insect Spray Concentrate or an insecticidal soap at the first sign of damage. Repeat weekly until no further damage occurs. Make sure that your vegetable or berry is listed on the label. Hose plants frequently with a strong stream of water to wash off mites and webs.

Salt damage

Salt damage on radishes.

Problem: Leaf edges and areas between the veins turn dark brown and die. Burned leaves may drop. Growth slows or stops. A white or dark crust may be on the soil.

Analysis: Salt damage occurs when salt accumulates in the soil to damaging levels. This can happen in one of two ways: (1) the garden does not receive enough water from rainfall or irrigation to wash the salts from the soil; or (2) the drainage is so poor that water does not pass through the soil. In either case, as water evaporates from the soil and plant leaves, the salts that were dissolved in the water accumulate near the soil surface. Sometimes a white or dark brown crust of salts forms on the surface. Salts can originate in the soil, in irrigation water, or in applied fertilizers.

Solution: The only way to eliminate salt problems is to wash the salts through the soil with water. If the damage is only at a low spot in the garden, fill in the spot to level the area. If the entire garden drains poorly, improve the drainage according to the directions on page 406. If the soil drains well, increase the amount of water applied at each watering by 50 percent or more so that excess water will leach salts below the root zone of the plants. Fertilize according to instructions for your plant in the alphabetical section beginning on page 343.

Pesticide burn

Grape with spray injury.

Problem: Irregular spots occur on leaves. Young leaves and blossoms may be distorted and brown. Plants may have recently been sprayed with a pesticide.

Analysis: Insecticides, fungicides, and herbicides damage plants when used improperly. Damage usually occurs within 24 hours of the time the plants were sprayed. In some crops, such as grapes, however, damage may not be apparent for several days after spraying. Pesticides may drift from other areas on windy days and damage plants. Pesticides may burn plants when the temperature is higher than 90°F at the time of spraying or within a few hours after spraying. Damage is also common during damp, humid weather when spray is slow to dry on the plant. Pesticides not mixed and applied according to label directions also burn plants. Because traces of herbicides are difficult to remove from sprayers, other pesticides used in tanks once used for herbicides may be contaminated.

Solution: Once plants are damaged, you can't do anything except try to keep the plants healthy with regular watering and fertilizing. Don't spray when temperatures are higher than 90°F. Avoid spraying on windy days, when sprays may drift. Mix according to label directions. Don't increase the dosage. When mixing two or more chemicals, be sure they are compatible. Always keep the solution well mixed by shaking the tank periodically while spraying. Purchase fresh pesticides each year. Keep a separate sprayer for herbicides.

Leaf spot

Leaf spot on strawberry.

Problem: Spots and blotches appear on the leaves. The spots may be yellow, red, tan, gray, or brown. They range in size from barely visible to ¼ inch. Several spots may join to form blotches. Leaves may be yellow and dying. Leaf spotting is most severe in warm, humid weather. Fruit may be spotted like the leaves or be discolored brown or yellow. A fine gray or white mold sometimes covers the infected leaf or fruit tissue in damp conditions.

Analysis: Several different fungi cause leaf spots. Some of these may eventually kill the plant or weaken it so that it becomes susceptible to attack by other organisms. Others merely cause spotting that is unsightly but not harmful. Infected fruit is less appetizing, some is inedible, and the yield is reduced. Fruit infected only slightly is still edible if the discolored tissue is cut away. Leaf-spotting fungi are spread by splashing water or wind. They generally survive the winter in diseased plant debris. Most of the fungi do their greatest damage in mild weather (50° to 85°F).

Solution: Treat infected plants with a fungicide containing *chlorothalonil* at the first sign of the disease. Repeat the treatment at intervals of 7 to 10 days until weather conditions favorable to the spread of the disease no longer occur. Make sure that your plant is listed on the product label. Remove all plant debris from the garden after harvest to reduce the overwintering spores capable of infecting plants the following growing season.

DISCOLORED OR MOTTLED LEAVES *(continued)*

PLANTS CHEWED

Powdery mildew

Powdery mildew on cucumber.

Problem: A white powdery growth covers the upper surfaces of the leaves and sometimes the stems. Areas of the leaves turn brown and dry. Older leaves are affected first, with the disease progressing to younger leaves. Leaves may become cupped, showing a silvery underside. Fruit may also be covered with the white powdery growth.

Analysis: Powdery mildew is a common plant disease caused by fungi that thrive in both humid and dry weather. The powdery patches consist of fungal strands and spores. The spores are spread by the wind to healthy plants. The fungus saps plant nutrients, causing yellowing and sometimes death of the leaf. Fruit yield may also be reduced. A severe infection may kill the plant. Since powdery mildews attack many different kinds of plants, the fungus from a diseased plant may infect other types of plants in the garden. (For a list of powdery mildews and the plants they attack, see page 537.) Under favorable conditions, powdery mildew can spread rapidly through a closely spaced planting.

Solution: Control powdery mildew on vegetable and berry plants with Ortho® Garden Disease Control or with a sulfur dust at the first sign of the disease. Continue spraying at intervals of seven days as long as the disease is a problem. Make sure that your plant is listed on the label. Clean up and destroy plant debris after harvest. When available, grow varieties that are resistant to powdery mildews.

Leafminers

Leafminer trails on tomato.

Problem: Light-colored, irregular blotches, blisters, or tunnels appear on the leaves. The tan areas peel apart easily like facial tissue. Tiny black specks are found inside the tunnels.

Analysis: The tiny black or yellow adult fly lays its white eggs on the undersides of leaves or in the leaves. The maggots that hatch from these eggs tunnel between the upper and lower surfaces of the leaves, feeding on the inner tissue. The tunnels and blotches are called *mines*. The black specks inside are the maggots' droppings. Damaged portions of leaves are no longer edible. The yield is usually not affected on fruit-producing vegetables and berries unless many leaves are damaged. Several overlapping generations occur during the growing season, so larvae are present continually from spring until fall.

Solution: Control leafminers with Ortho® Bug-B-Gon® Multi-Purpose Insect Killer or Ortho® Malathion Plus® Insect Spray Concentrate when the egg clusters are first seen under the leaves. Repeat two times at weekly intervals to control succeeding generations. Once leafminers enter the leaves, sprays are ineffective. Spraying after the mines first appear will control only those leafminers that attack after the application. Make sure that your plant is listed on the insecticide label. Clean all plant debris from the garden after harvest to reduce overwintering spots for the pupae. Adult flies can be kept from laying eggs by protecting plants with floating row covers.

Snails and slugs

Slug damage.

Problem: Irregular holes with smooth edges are chewed in the leaves. Some leaves may be sheared entirely. Silvery trails wind around the plant and soil nearby. At night, check with a flashlight for slimy creatures—with or without brown shells—feeding on the leaves.

Analysis: Snails and slugs are mollusks and are related to clams, oysters, and other shellfish. They feed on the leaves of a wide variety of garden plants and may devour seedlings. Snails and slugs may attack ripe and unripe fruit lying on the ground, especially if the fruit is shaded by the foliage, as with strawberries and unstaked tomatoes. Like other mollusks, snails and slugs need to be moist all the time. For this reason, they avoid direct sun and dry places and hide during the day in damp places, such as under flowerpots or in thick ground covers. They emerge at night or on cloudy days to feed. Slugs lay white eggs encased in a slimy mass in protected places. Snails bury their eggs in the soil, also in a slimy mass. The young look like miniature versions of their parents.

Solution: Apply Ortho® Bug-Geta® Snail & Slug Killer in the areas you wish to protect. Also apply in areas where snails and slugs might be hiding, such as in dense ground covers, weedy areas, compost piles, or flowerpot-storage areas. Wet down the treated areas to encourage snail and slug activity that night. Repeat every two weeks as needed.

INSECTS ON THE PLANT

Nocturnal pests

Cabbage plants damaged by nocturnal pests.

Problem: Young plants are chewed or cut off near the ground. Some of the leaves, stems, flowers, and fruit are chewed. When affected plants are inspected at night, insects may be seen feeding on them.

Analysis: Several kinds of insects, including some beetles, weevils, and caterpillars as well as all earwigs and cutworms, feed on plants only at night. Beetles are hard-bodied insects with tough, leathery wing covers. Weevils are a type of beetle with a long snout. Earwigs are reddish-brown, flat, elongated insects up to 1 inch long with pincers projecting from the rear of the body. Caterpillars and cutworms are smooth or hairy, soft-bodied worms. All of these nocturnal pests usually hide in the soil, in debris, or in other protected locations during the day.

Solution: Control nocturnal pests by treating with Ortho® Bug-Geta® Plus Snail, Slug & Insect Killer or Ortho® Bug-B-Gon® Multi-Purpose Insect Killer Granules. (For more information on these pests, see the following pages: beetles, page 434; weevils, page 435; earwigs, page 460; caterpillars, page 439; and cutworms, page 440.)

Caterpillars

Cabbage looper (2× life size).

Problem: Irregular or round holes appear in the leaves and buds. Leaves, buds, and flowers may be entirely chewed off. Worms or caterpillars are feeding on the plants.

Analysis: Several species of caterpillars, which are moth or butterfly larvae, feed on many vegetable and berry plants. Some common caterpillars are budworms, hornworms, and loopers. Most moths or butterflies start to lay their eggs on garden plants with the onset of warm weather in the spring. The larvae that emerge from these eggs feed on the leaves, flowers, and buds for two to six weeks, depending on weather conditions and species. Mature caterpillars pupate in cocoons attached to leaves or structures or buried in the soil. There may be one or more overlapping generations during the growing season. The last generation of caterpillars in the fall survives the winter as pupae. Moths and butterflies emerge from the pupae the following spring.

Solution: Spray infested plants with Ortho® Malathion Plus® Insect Spray Concentrate, Ortho® Bug-B-Gon® Multi-Purpose Insect Killer Ready-To-Use, or Ortho® Bug-B-Gon® Multi-Purpose Garden Dust. The bacterial insecticide *Bacillus thuringiensis* (Bt) is effective against the early stages of caterpillars. Make sure that your plant is listed on the product label. Repeat the treatment if reinfestation occurs, allowing at least seven days between applications of spray or dust.

Japanese beetle

Japanese beetles on grape (⅓ life size).

Problem: Leaf tissue has been chewed between the veins, giving the leaf a lacy appearance. Metallic-green-and-bronze beetles, ½ inch long, feed in clusters on the foliage, especially on the tender new leaves.

Analysis: As its name suggests, the Japanese beetle (*Popillia japonica*) is native to Japan. It was first seen in New Jersey in 1916 and has since become a major pest in the eastern United States. It feeds on hundreds of different plant species. The adult beetles are present from the beginning of summer to early fall. They feed only in the daytime, rapidly defoliating plants. Leaves exposed to direct sun are the most severely attacked. Badly damaged leaves drop. Any reduction in leaf tissue ultimately affects the overall vigor and production of fruit. The larva of the Japanese beetle, a white grub, feeds on grass roots, frequently killing entire lawns. (For more information on Japanese beetles, see page 435.)

Solution: Treat infested plants with Ortho® Malathion Plus®. Japanese beetles can fly up to 5 miles and travel from garden to garden. Consequently, repeated sprayings are necessary to control them. Make sure that your plants are listed on the product label. Treat for grubs in the lawn as outlined on page 67. Use resistant plants.

INSECTS ON THE PLANT *(continued)*

| Cucumber beetles | Flea beetles | Grasshoppers |

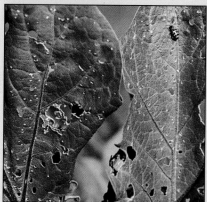

Spotted cucumber beetle (½ life size).

Flea beetles on turnip leaf (2× life size).

Grasshopper on blueberry (2× life size).

Cucumber beetles

Problem: Holes are chewed in the leaves, leafstalks, and stems by yellow-green beetles with black spots or stripes.

Analysis: Both striped cucumber beetles (*Acalymma* species) and spotted cucumber beetles (*Diabrotica* species) are common pests of vegetable plants. It is important to control these beetles, because they may infect plants with two serious diseases that damage and may kill cucurbits (such plants as squash, melons, and cucumbers): squash mosaic virus (see page 370) and bacterial wilt (see page 369). Adult beetles survive the winter in plant debris and weeds. As soon as vegetable plants are set in the garden in the spring, the beetles attack the leaves and stems and may totally destroy the plants. Adults lay their yellow-orange eggs in the soil at the base of the plants. The grubs that hatch from these eggs eat the roots and the stems below the soil line, causing the plants to be stunted or to die prematurely. Severely infested plants produce little fruit. The slender white grubs feed for several weeks, pupate in the soil, and emerge as adults to repeat the cycle. One generation occurs per year in northern parts of the United States and two or more in southern areas.

Solution: Treat plants with Ortho® Bug-B-Gon® Multi-Purpose Insect Killer Ready-To-Use, Ortho® Bug-B-Gon® Multi-Purpose Garden Dust, or Ortho® Malathion Plus® Insect Spray Concentrate at the first sign of the beetles. Make sure that your plant is listed on the product label.

Flea beetles

Problem: Leaves are riddled with shot holes about ⅛ inch in diameter. Tiny (1/16 inch) black beetles jump like fleas when disturbed. Leaves of seedlings and eventually whole plants may wilt and die.

Analysis: Flea beetles jump like fleas but are not related to fleas. Both adult and immature flea beetles mostly feed on a wide variety of garden vegetables and berries. The immature beetle, a legless gray grub, injures plants by feeding on the roots and the lower surfaces of leaves. Adults chew holes in leaves. Flea beetles damage seedlings and young plants most. Leaves of seedlings riddled with holes dry out quickly and die. Adult beetles survive the winter in soil and garden debris. They emerge in early spring to feed on weeds until vegetables sprout or plants are set in the garden. Grubs hatch from eggs laid in the soil and feed for two to three weeks. After pupating in the soil, they emerge as adults to repeat the cycle. There are one to four generations per year. Adults may feed for up to two months.

Solution: Control flea beetles on vegetable and berry plants with Ortho® Malathion Plus® Insect Spray Concentrate or Ortho® Bug-B-Gon® Multi-Purpose Insect Killer when the leaves first show damage. Watch new growth for evidence of further damage, and repeat the treatment at weekly intervals as needed. Make sure that your plant is listed on the product label. Clean up and destroy plant debris after harvest to reduce overwintering habitat for adult beetles.

Grasshoppers

Problem: Large holes are chewed in the margins of leaves. Greenish-yellow to brown jumping insects, ½ to 1½ inches long, with long hind legs, are eating the plants. Some fruit and corn ears may be chewed.

Analysis: Grasshoppers attack a wide variety of plants. They eat leaves and occasionally fruit, migrating as they deplete their food sources. In vegetable gardens, they are most numerous in the rows near weedy areas. In late summer, adult grasshoppers lay their eggs in pods in the soil. The adults continue to feed until cold weather kills them. The eggs hatch the following spring. Grasshopper problems are most severe during hot, dry weather. Grasshoppers migrate into green gardens and yards as surrounding areas dry up in the summer heat. Periods of cool, wet weather help keep their numbers under control.

Solution: Treat soil around plants with Ortho® Bug-Geta® Plus Snail, Slug & Insect Killer or spray plants with Ortho® Bug-B-Gon® Multi-Purpose Insect Killer as soon as grasshoppers appear. Repeat at weekly intervals if plants become reinfested. Make certain that your plant is listed on the product label.

Leafhoppers

Leafhopper (3× life size).

Problem: Spotted, pale green insects up to ⅛ inch long hop, move sideways, or fly away quickly when a plant is touched. The leaves are stippled. Cast-off skins may be found on the undersides of leaves.

Analysis: Leafhoppers feed on many vegetables and small fruits. They generally feed on the undersides of leaves, sucking the sap, which causes stippling. Severely infested vegetable and berry plants may become weak and produce little edible fruit. One leafhopper, the aster leafhopper (*Macrosteles fascifrons*), transmits aster yellows, a plant disease that can be quite damaging. (For information on aster yellows, see page 423.) Leafhoppers at all stages of maturity are active during the growing season. They hatch in the spring from eggs laid on perennial weeds and ornamental plants. Even areas where the winters are so cold that the eggs can't survive aren't free from infestation, because leafhoppers migrate in the spring from warmer regions. (For more information on leafhoppers, see page 448.)

Solution: Spray infested plants with Ortho® Malathion Plus® Insect Spray Concentrate, Ortho® Bug-B-Gon® Multi-Purpose Insect Killer Concentrate, or an insecticidal soap. Be sure to cover the lower surfaces of the leaves. Repeat the spray as often as necessary to keep the insects under control. Allow at least 10 days between applications. Make sure that your plants are listed on the product label. Eradicate nearby weeds that may harbor leafhopper eggs.

Whiteflies

Whiteflies (life size).

Problem: Tiny white-winged insects feed mainly on the undersides of leaves. Nonflying, scalelike larvae covered with white, waxy powder may also be present on the undersides of leaves. When the plant is touched, insects flutter rapidly around it. Leaves may be mottled and yellowing.

Analysis: Whiteflies are a common insect pest of many garden and greenhouse plants. The four-winged adult lays eggs on the undersides of leaves. The larvae are the size of a pinhead, flat, oval-shape, and semitransparent. Both immature and adult forms suck sap from the leaves. The nymphs are more damaging because they feed more heavily. Adults and nymphs can't digest all the sugar in the plant sap. They excrete the excess in a fluid called *honeydew*, which often drops onto the leaves or plants below. A sooty mold fungus may develop on the honeydew, causing the leaves to appear black and dirty. Whiteflies are unable to live through extended periods of freezing weather. The silverleaf whitefly (*Bemisia argentifolii*) began causing serious damage to vegetable crops in the Southwest in 1990.

Solution: There is no completely effective remedy for whiteflies on vegetables. You can gain some control by spraying with Ortho® Bug-B-Gon® Multi-Purpose Insect Killer every 7 to 10 days as necessary. Spray the foliage thoroughly, covering the upper and lower surfaces of the leaves. Be sure your plant is listed on the label. Whiteflies may also be partially controlled with yellow sticky traps.

Aphids

Bean aphids (4× life size).

Problem: Pale green, yellow, purple, or black soft-bodied insects cluster on the undersides of leaves. Leaves turn yellow and may be curled, distorted, and puckered. Plants may be stunted and produce little fruit.

Analysis: Aphids are one of the most common pests in the garden. They do little damage in small numbers, but they are extremely prolific, and populations can rapidly build to damaging numbers during the growing season. Damage occurs when the aphids suck the sap from vegetable or berry leaves and flower buds. Aphids usually prefer young, tender leaves. Severely infested plants may be stunted and weak, producing little fruit. Fruit yield is also reduced when the aphids spread plant viruses. Aphids feed on nearly every plant in the garden and are spread from plant to plant by wind, water, and people. Aphids are unable to digest all the sugar in the plant sap, and they excrete the excess in a fluid called *honeydew*, which often drops onto lower leaves. Ants feed on this sticky substance and are often present where there is an aphid infestation. (For more information on aphid control, see page 443.)

Solution: Control aphids on vegetable and berry plants with Ortho® Malathion Plus® Insect Spray Concentrate, Ortho® Bug-B-Gon® Multi-Purpose Garden Dust, Ortho® Bug-B-Gon® Multi-Purpose Insect Killer, or an insecticidal soap as soon as the insects appear. Repeat the spray if plants become reinfested. Make sure that your plant is listed on the product label.

INSECTS IN THE SOIL

Earwigs

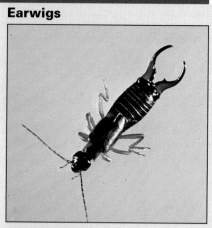

Earwig (2× life size).

Problem: Dark, reddish-brown insects up to ¾ inch long with pincers projecting from the rear of the body are found under objects in the garden. They scurry for cover when disturbed. Holes may be chewed in leaves and blossoms.

Analysis: Although seen in most gardens, earwigs are only minor pests of vegetables and berries. When populations are high, they can become major pests. They feed predominantly on decaying plant material and other insects. Earwigs feed at night and hide under stones, debris, and bark chips in the daytime. They have wings but seldom fly, preferring to run instead. Adult earwigs lay eggs in the soil in late winter to early spring. The young that hatch from these eggs may feed on green shoots and eat holes in leaves. As the earwigs mature, they feed occasionally on blossoms and ripening fruit. Earwigs are beneficial when they feed on other insects larvae and on snails. They sometimes invade homes.

Solution: Because earwigs typically cause only minor damage, insecticide control is seldom needed in the vegetable garden. If they are numerous and troublesome, however, treat the soil with Ortho® Bug-Geta® Plus Snail, Slug & Insect Killer. Because earwigs are most active at night, treat in the late afternoon or evening. Make sure that your plant is listed on the product label. Pick fruit as it ripens. (For more information on earwigs, see page 508.)

ANIMAL PESTS

Wildlife

Snap beans eaten by rabbits.

Raccoon.

Problem: Plants are chewed or eaten. Ripening fruit, pods, and ears are partially or completely eaten. Deer, raccoons, squirrels, rabbits, woodchucks, or mice may be seen in the garden.

Analysis:

1. Deer feed on leaves and fruit. They are most active at dawn and dusk.

2. Raccoons knock over cornstalks to feed on maturing ears. They may also feed on other ripening fruit. Raccoons feed at night.

3. Squirrels feed on ripening fruit and climb cornstalks to feed on maturing ears.

4. Rabbits feed on young bean, pea, lettuce, and cabbage plants, eating the leaves and frequently leaving short stubs of the stems standing in the soil.

5. Woodchucks, also called *groundhogs,* feed in the afternoons but avoid tomatoes, eggplants, peppers, chives, and onions.

6. Mice may bite into ripening tomatoes, cucumbers, and beans that are close to the ground to eat seeds inside. Mice frequently travel underground in mole tunnels.

Solution:

1. The only sure way to exclude deer is with a woven-wire fence 8 feet high. Deer are sometimes repelled by cotton drawstring bags filled with bloodmeal fertilizer or human hair. (For more information on deer, see page 499.)

2. Exclude raccoons with a 4-foot-high fence. Electric fencing above the fence also may be needed. Protect corn by interplanting with members of the cucurbit family. Raccoons will not walk on the prickly vines. Sprinkle ripening corn with cayenne pepper. (For more information on raccoons, see page 498.)

3. Protect ears of corn from squirrels by sprinkling corn silks with cayenne pepper. (For more information on squirrels, see page 496.)

4. To exclude rabbits, erect a fence 18 to 24 inches high and anchor it by burying the edges 3 to 4 inches deep into the soil. (For more information on rabbits, see page 497.)

5. Deter woodchucks with a wire fence about 3 feet high and buried horizontally underground. (For more information on woodchucks, see page 498.)

6. Stake, trellis, or cage plants to keep fruit off the ground and away from mice. (For more information on mice, see page 494.)

ASPARAGUS

Small spears

Small spears.

Problem: Spears are small and skinny.

Analysis: Asparagus spears may be small for any of several reasons:
1. **Poor fertility:** Underfertilized plants can't produce adequate fern growth and food for the following year's crop.
2. **Immature plants:** Asparagus crowns produce small spears for the first two or three years following planting.
3. **Poor drainage:** Asparagus plants don't produce well in poorly drained soil.
4. **Overharvested plants:** When harvest continues late in the season, the plants are unable to produce enough foliage and don't store enough food for the following year's crop.

Solution: Improve soil drainage and aeration as outlined on page 406.

Crooked spears

Crooked spears.

Problem: Spears are crooked or misshapen.

Analysis: Asparagus spears grow crooked when the growing shoot is damaged by insects (especially the asparagus beetle—see page 344), cultivation wounds are on the crown, or the tender shoots have been pelted by windblown soil and sand. The injured areas grow more slowly than the uninjured side, causing the stem to curve. Although the spears are misshapen, they are still edible.

Solution: Control asparagus beetles. To avoid wounding the crown, don't cultivate closer or deeper than 2 inches. Tall plants or fencing can be used as windbreaks to prevent wounds.

Freeze injury

Damaged spear.

Problem: Spears turn brown and soft, or they may dry and wither.

Analysis: Asparagus is one of the earliest vegetables in the spring garden and is sometimes damaged by spring frosts. The damage may not be noticed in the early morning following the frost, but as the temperature warms through the day, the tissue discolors and softens. Damaged spears then dry rapidly as temperatures rise and humidity drops. A slight freeze injury may result in a crooked spear or slightly damaged tip of the spear.

Solution: Harvest and discard frost-damaged spears. When night temperatures lower than 32°F are predicted, protect the spears with a mulch of straw, newspaper, or leaves. Remove the mulch in the morning.

ASPARAGUS *(continued)*

| Fusarium wilt | Asparagus beetles and spotted asparagus beetles | Rust |

Fusarium wilt

Fusarium wilt.

Problem: The growing shoot turns yellow to dingy brown and wilts. During wet weather, white or pink cottonlike strands often appear under the leaf scales. Wilting is most severe among full-grown plants during the months of July and August. When the infected plant is dug up, all or part of the root system is a reddish color. The plant eventually dies.

Analysis: Fusarium wilt disease is caused by a fungus (*Fusarium* species). Asparagus plants under stress from poor growing conditions (drought, poor drainage, insect or disease injury) are more severely affected. The fungus lives on organic matter in the soil. The disease is spread by contaminated seeds, transplants, soil, and equipment. The fungus enters the plant through the roots and spreads up into the stems and leaves through water-conducting vessels in the stems. The vessels become discolored and plugged, cutting off the flow of nutrients and water to the leaves. Because *Fusarium* is favored by wet weather and warm temperatures (70° to 85°F), the fungi build up in warm soils. (For more information on fusarium wilt, see page 420.)

Solution: No chemical control is available. It is best to destroy infected plants. The following year, plant healthy crowns where asparagus has not been planted for two to four years. The fungi can be eradicated from the soil by fumigation or solarization techniques. (For more information on solarization, see page 322.)

Asparagus beetles and spotted asparagus beetles

Larvae (4× life size). Inset: Adults (life size).

Problem: The tips of young asparagus spears are chewed and scarred. Later, when the spears develop into asparagus ferns, the ferns are also chewed. Small (¼-inch), metallic-blue-black or black beetles with yellow markings and a narrow red head may feed on the tips of the spears and later on the ferns and stems. Reddish-orange beetles with black spots may be present. Shiny black specks are found on the spear tips. Humpback orange or slate-gray grubs also may be seen.

Analysis: Asparagus beetle (*Crioceris asparagi*) and spotted asparagus beetle (*C. duodecimpunctata*) injure asparagus plants throughout the growing season. The blue-black asparagus beetle is found throughout the United States. The orange-and-black spotted asparagus beetle is found east of the Mississippi River. The beetles are particularly a problem when young asparagus shoots emerge in the spring. Both adults and grubs injure the plants by feeding on shoots, ferns, and stems. This feeding robs the root system of food manufactured in the foliage and necessary for healthy growth the following year.

Solution: Apply Ortho® Bug-B-Gon® Multi-Purpose Garden Dust or an insecticide containing *rotenone* or *pyrethrins* when the beetles are first noticed. Repeat the applications as long as the beetles or grubs are feeding. Also treat leaf growth in late summer or early fall to prevent adults from overwintering on the leaves and reinfesting the following year's crop. Handpick adults where practical.

Rust

Rust.

Problem: Leaves turn yellow, then brown, and die back in early to midsummer. Reddish-brown, orange, or black blisters appear on the fernlike foliage and stems but not on newly emerged spears. Spears mature earlier than usual.

Analysis: Rust is a plant disease caused by a fungus (*Puccinia asparagi*). The current year's rust weakens the plant by reducing the amount of food manufactured in the leaves to be stored in the roots. Because this stored food supplies the energy for the following year's crop, fewer shoots are produced the next year. Damage is worse when the tops are attacked several years in a row. In severe cases, the plants die. Warm temperatures and high humidity from fog, heavy dew, or overhead watering promote rust infection. Rust spores from diseased tops that have been left in the garden infect new shoots as they emerge in the spring. Wind spreads the spores from plant to plant.

Solution: After the harvest, spray the leaves and stems with a fungicide containing *mancozeb*. Repeat the treatment at intervals of 10 days when weather conditions favor rust infection. Don't spray while spears are still being harvested. Cut the tops close to the ground after they die in the fall, and destroy them. Don't add them to the compost pile or leave the tops lying in the garden. If you plant more asparagus, select rust-resistant varieties.

BEANS

Mexican bean beetles

Mexican bean beetle (2× life size).

Problem: The tissue between the leaf veins is eaten, giving the leaves a lacelike appearance. Copper-colored beetles about ¼ inch long feed on the undersides of the skeletonized leaves. Each beetle has 16 black spots on its back. Orange to yellow soft-bodied grubs about ⅓ inch long with black-tipped spines on their backs may also be present. Leaves dry up, and the plant may die.

Analysis: The Mexican bean beetle (*Epilachna varivestis*) is found throughout the United States. It prefers lima beans but also feeds on pole and bush beans and black-eyed peas. Feeding damage by both adults and larvae can reduce pod production. Adult beetles spend the winter in plant debris in the garden and emerge in late spring and early summer. They lay yellow eggs on the undersides of leaves. Larvae that hatch from these eggs, in early to midsummer, are green at first and gradually turn yellow. One to four generations occur per year. Frequently, all stages of beetles appear at the same time during the season. Hot, dry summers and cold winters reduce the beetle population.

Solution: Apply Ortho® Bug-B-Gon® Multi-Purpose Insect Killer Ready-To-Use or Ortho® Malathion Plus® Insect Spray Concentrate when the adults first appear. Be sure to spray the undersides of leaves, where the insects feed. Early treatments to control the adults may save extra applications later to control the larvae, which are more damaging and harder to control. Remove and destroy all plant debris after the harvest to reduce habitat for overwintering adults.

Bean leaf beetles

Bean leaf beetle (life size).

Problem: Round holes are chewed in the leaves. Yellow to red beetles with black spots and a black band around the outer edge of the body are feeding on the undersides of leaves. The plant may later turn yellow and wilt. If you pull the plant up, you may see slender white grubs up to ⅓ inch long feeding on the roots.

Analysis: The bean leaf beetle (*Cerotoma trifurcata*) is a widely distributed insect that attacks all beans, as well as peas. Adult beetles feed on the undersides of leaves, blossoms, and pods throughout the growing season. Grubs feed on the roots and stems below the soil line. Females lay clusters of orange eggs on the soil at the base of plants. The grubs that hatch from these eggs attack the plant below the soil, feeding on the roots and sometimes girdling the stem at soil level. This feeding can kill the plant. Both adults and grubs cause serious damage to young plants. One to three generations occur per year.

Solution: Apply Ortho® Malathion Plus® Insect Spray Concentrate at the first sign of damage. Be sure to spray the undersides of the leaves, where the beetles feed. Repeat at intervals of 7 to 10 days whenever damage occurs. Clean all debris from the garden at the end of the season to eliminate habitat for overwintering adult beetles.

Two-spotted spider mites

Two-spotted spider mite damage.

Problem: Leaves are wilted, stippled, dirty, and yellowing. Leaves may dry out and drop. There may be a fine webbing may covering flower buds, between leaves, or on the lower surfaces of leaves. Plants lose vigor. To determine infestation, hold a sheet of white paper underneath an affected leaf and tap the leaf sharply. Minute specks the size of pepper grains will drop to the paper and begin to crawl. Mites are easily seen against the white background and can also be seen with a 10× hand lens.

Analysis: Two-spotted spider mites (*Tetranychus urticae*), related to spiders, are major pests of many garden and greenhouse plants. They cause damage by sucking sap from the undersides of leaves. As a result of their feeding, the plant's chlorophyll disappears, producing the stippled appearance. Spider mite webbing traps cast-off skins and debris, making the plant dirty. Mites are active throughout the growing season but are favored by hot, dry weather (70°F and higher). By midsummer, they have built to tremendous numbers. (For more information on spider mites, see page 457.)

Solution: Apply Ortho® Malathion Plus® Insect Spray Concentrate or a horticultural oil when damage is first seen. Spray thoroughly, being sure to cover both upper and lower surfaces of the leaves. Mites are difficult to control because they reproduce so rapidly. Repeated applications are necessary, especially during hot, dry weather, at intervals of 7 to 10 days. Hose down plants with a high-pressure spray every few days to knock off webs and mites.

BEANS *(continued)*

Failure to set pods

Failure to set pods.

Problem: The plants look healthy, but only a few fully formed pods are on them.

Analysis: Failure to set pods may result from any of several factors.

1. High temperatures: Maturing bean plants prefer temperatures between 70° and 80°F. If the maximum temperature is consistently above 85°F, as it often is in the summer, flowers often drop without setting pods—a condition known as *blossom drop*. Heat can also cause the blossoms to deteriorate on the plant without actually dropping off. This condition is known as *blossom blast*. Hot, dry winds also contribute to both blossom drop and blossom blast.

2. Extremes in soil moisture: Plants growing in soil that is either too wet or too dry are stressed by a lack of oxygen and water. Irregular watering contributes to stress. Weakened plants produce few pods.

3. Overmature pods: Leaving mature pods on the vine forces the plant to put its energy into seed formation in the pod, rather than into forming new pods.

Solution: Solutions below correspond to the numbered items in the analysis.
1. In areas where very hot summers or hot, dry winds are common, plant beans for late spring harvest and again for fall harvest.
2. Water regularly, allowing the soil surface to dry out between waterings. To conserve moisture during hot, dry weather, apply a 3- or 4-inch mulch of straw or chopped leaves.
3. Pick pods regularly when they are young and tender and before large seeds develop inside. Don't allow pods to mature.

Bean anthracnose

Anthracnose spots.

Problem: Small brown specks on pods enlarge to black, circular, sunken spots. In wet weather, a salmon-colored ooze appears in the infected spots. Elongated dark reddish-brown spots appear on the stems and veins on the undersides of leaves. If seedlings are attacked, the stems may rot, or the first young leaves may be spotted. In either case, the seedlings die.

Analysis: Bean anthracnose is a bean disease caused by a fungus (*Colletotrichum lindemuthianum*) that affects all kinds of beans, but it is most destructive on lima beans. It occurs in the eastern and central states, rarely west of the Rocky Mountains. The fungus thrives in warm, wet weather. The salmon-colored ooze that often appears in the infected spots during wet weather are masses of spores. The spores are carried by splashing water, animals, people, or tools to healthy plants. The fungus survives from one season to the next on diseased bean seeds and on plant debris that has been left in the garden.

Solution: Remove and destroy any diseased plants. The disease spreads rapidly on moist foliage, so don't work in the garden when the plants are wet. To avoid reintroducing this fungus into your garden, purchase seeds produced in western United States. Don't plant beans in the infected area for two or three years. Rotate your bean planting site every year.

Bacterial blight

Halo blight.

Problem: Small, water-soaked spots appear on the leaves. These spots enlarge, turn brown, and may kill the leaf. In cool weather, narrow greenish-yellow halos may border the infected spots. Leaves either turn yellow and die slowly or turn brown rapidly and drop off. Long reddish lesions may girdle the stem. In moist conditions, a tan or yellow ooze is produced in spots on pods.

Analysis: Two widespread bacterial blights on beans are *common blight* (*Xanthomonas phaseoli*) and *halo blight* (*Pseudomonas phaseolicola*). These bacteria attack all kinds of beans. Common blight is more severe in warm, moist weather; halo blight thrives in cool temperatures. The bacteria are usually introduced into a garden on infected seed and can live on infected plant debris in the soil for as long as two years. They are spread by rain, splashing water, and contaminated tools. The bacteria multiply rapidly in humid weather. If water-conducting tissue is invaded, bacteria and dead cells eventually clog the veins, causing leaf discoloration. Often bacteria ooze from infected spots in a cream-colored mass.

Solution: No chemical controls bacterial blights. Avoid overhead watering. Don't work with beans when the plants are wet. Don't plant beans in the same area more often than every third year. Purchase new seed each year from a reputable company.

Bean rust

Rust.

Problem: Rust-
colored spots form,
mostly on the undersides
of leaves. Angular
yellow spots develop above each rust spot on
the top sides of the leaves. Severely infected
leaves turn yellow, wilt, dry, and fall off.
Stems and pods also may have spots.

Analysis: Bean rust is caused by a fungus
(*Uromyces phaseoli*) that affects only bean
plants. It is most common on mature plants
and most damaging to pole beans and lima
beans. Scarlet runner beans are mildly
affected. Each rust spot develops thousands
of spores that are spread by wind and
splashing water. The disease develops rapidly
during periods of cool nights and warm days.
High humidity from rain, dew, or watering
encourages rust. Heavy vine growth that
shades the ground and prevents air
circulation produces ideal conditions for the
disease. At the end of the summer, the
fungus produces another type of spore. This
thick-walled black spore spends the winter
in infected bean plant debris.

Solution: Apply Ortho® Garden Disease
Control to beans at the first sign of the
disease. Weekly applications may be
necessary if conditions favorable to the
disease continue. Avoid overhead irrigation.
Water in the morning rather than evening
to allow wet foliage to dry quickly. Thin
seedlings, and space plants far enough apart
to allow air to circulate freely. In the fall,
remove and destroy all infected plants to
prevent the fungus from surviving and
reinfecting in the spring. Don't plant beans
in the same area more often than every third
year unless you plant resistant varieties.

Mold

White mold. Inset: Gray mold.

Problem: Soft, watery
spots appear on the
stems, leaves, or pods.
Under moist conditions,
these spots enlarge rapidly. A fuzzy gray,
gray-brown, or white mold forms on the
infected tissue. Small, hard, black, seedlike
structures may be embedded in the white
mold. Bean plants may yellow, wilt, and die.
Rotted pods are soft and mushy.

Analysis: Mold on beans is caused by
two related fungi. One fungus, (*Sclerotinia
sclerotiorum*), is responsible for white mold,
also known as *watery soft rot*. The white
mold fungus forms dark, seedlike structures
that can drop to the soil and survive
through adverse conditions to infect bean
crops for the next few years. The other
fungus (*Botrytis cinerea*) is responsible for
gray mold. This fungus produces tan to gray-
brown fungal strands. Both fungi often
attack weak or dead plant parts, such as old
blossoms. Once established on a plant, these
diseases can be spread to healthy plants by
wind or splashing water or when infected
plant parts touch healthy ones. Mold spreads
quickly in cool, wet weather.

Solution: Remove and destroy all diseased
plants as soon as symptoms appear. Spray
the beans with Ortho® Garden Disease
Control. Water plants early in the day so
they have time to dry. Avoid wetting plant
foliage. Don't plant beans in the affected
area for three to four years. Until then, plant
other resistant vegetables, such as corn,
beets, Swiss chard, or spinach. Always plant
beans in well-drained soil, and to improve
air flow, avoid overcrowding.

Hopperburn

Hopperburn. Inset: Leafhopper (3× life size).

Problem: Leaves are
stippled. Some are
scorched, with a green
midrib and brown edges
curled under. Spotted, pale green, winged
insects up to ⅛ inch long hop, run, or fly
away quickly when the plant is touched.

Analysis: Hopperburn is caused by the
potato leafhopper (*Empoasca fabae*), which
injects a toxin into the leaves as it feeds.
Bean yields may be drastically reduced from
hopperburn. Leafhoppers are active
throughout the growing season. They hatch
in the spring from eggs laid on perennial
weeds and ornamental plants. Even areas
that have winters so cold that the eggs can't
survive are not free from infestation, because
leafhoppers migrate in the spring from
warmer regions.

Solution: Treat infested plants with
Ortho® Malathion Plus® Insect Spray
Concentrate, Ortho® Bug-B-Gon® Multi-
Purpose Insect Killer Ready-To-Use, or an
insecticidal soap at the first sign of damage.
Be sure to cover the lower surfaces of leaves,
where the leafhoppers feed. Repeat the spray
as often as necessary to keep the insects
under control. Allow at least 10 days
between applications.

BEANS (continued)

Root rot

Fusarium root rot.

Problem: Leaves turn yellow and fall prematurely. Overall growth is slow, and the plant may be dwarfed. In hot, dry weather, the plant suddenly wilts and sometimes dies. Few pods are produced. Red spots or streaks may be seen on stems and roots. Underground stems may be streaked dark brown or black.

Analysis: Root rot is a plant disease caused by several soil-inhabiting fungi (*Fusarium* species, *Pythium* species, and *Rhizoctonia solani*) that attack beans and many other vegetables. The fungi live in the soil, invading the plant through the roots and underground stem. Plants are usually attacked when they are in a weakened state. As the disease progresses, the roots decay and shrivel. The leaves turn yellow, and growth slows. The plant becomes dwarfed, wilts, and sometimes dies. Under favorable growing conditions, bean plants may grow new side roots to replace the rotted ones. These plants will survive, but the yield will be reduced. Root rots develop most rapidly at soil temperatures of 60° to 85°F.

Solution: No chemical completely and effectively controls this problem. Pull out and discard wilted plants. Rotate your bean planting site yearly. Plant in well-drained soil, and let the soil surface dry out between waterings. Keep plants growing vigorously.

Bean mosaic

Bean yellow mosaic.

Problem: Leaves are mottled yellow and green and may be longer and narrower than usual and puckered. Raised dark areas develop along the central vein, and the leaf margins curl downward. The whole plant is stunted. Pods on affected plants may be faded, rough, and few in number. The seeds inside are shriveled and small.

Analysis: Bean common mosaic and bean yellow mosaic are widespread virus diseases that are difficult to distinguish from one another. Common mosaic virus affects only French and snap beans; yellow mosaic virus affects lima beans, peas, summer squash, clover, gladiolus, and other perennial flowers. Both diseases are spread by aphids, which transmit the virus as they feed. (For more information on aphids, see page 443.) In warmer parts of the country with large aphid populations, the disease spreads rapidly. Bean common mosaic is also spread in infected seed. If the infection occurs early in the season when the plants are young, the plants may not bear pods. Infection later in the season doesn't affect pod production as severely. (For more information on viruses, see page 423.)

Solution: No chemical controls plant viruses. Remove all infected plants and all clover plants in the vicinity of the garden. Plant virus-resistant varieties.

Seedcorn maggots

Weak seedlings. Inset: Seedcorn maggot (life size).

Problem: Seeds may not sprout. If they do, the weak plants wilt and collapse shortly after emerging. Cream-colored, legless maggots about ¼ inch long are feeding on the seeds.

Analysis: The seedcorn maggot (*Hylemya platura*) feeds on many vegetables, including beans, beets, cabbage cucumbers, onions, and peas. It damages seeds and germinating seedlings by tunneling into them and feeding on the tissue. If the seed is only partially destroyed, the plants that sprout are weak and sickly and soon die. The seedcorn maggot thrives in cold, wet soil with a high manure content. The larva or a pupa spends the winter in soil, plant debris, or manure and becomes active in the early spring. Adults—flies slightly smaller than house-flies—emerge from May to July and lay eggs in the rich soil or on seeds or seedlings. The overwintering maggots cause the most damage. Those of later generations are of less importance. Three to five generations occur per year.

Solution: Remove any damaged seeds and sickly plants. Replant with insecticide-treated seeds. Plant seeds when the soil has warmed above 55°F in the spring so they germinate quickly. Shallow-planted seeds germinate more quickly. Use only moderate amounts of manure, and till it in thoroughly.

BEETS

Flea beetles

Flea beetle (5× life size).

Problem: Leaves are riddled with shot holes about ⅛ inch in diameter. Tiny (1/16-inch) black beetles jump like fleas when disturbed. Leaves of seedlings and eventually whole plants may wilt and die.

Analysis: Flea beetles jump like fleas but are not related to fleas. Both adult and immature flea beetles feed on a wide variety of garden vegetables. The immature beetle, a legless gray grub, injures plants by feeding on the roots and the lower surface of leaves. Adults chew holes in leaves. Flea beetles damage seedlings and young plants most. Leaves of seedlings riddled with holes dry out quickly and die. Adult beetles spend the winter in soil and garden debris. They emerge in early spring to feed on weeds until vegetables sprout or plants are set in the garden. (Damage is often worse in weedy areas.) Grubs hatch from eggs laid in the soil and feed for two to three weeks. After pupating in the soil, they emerge as adults to repeat the cycle. One to four generations occur per year. Adults may feed for up to two months.

Solution: Control flea beetles with an insecticide containing *carbaryl* or *rotenone* or with an insecticidal soap when the leaves first show damage. Watch new growth for further evidence of feeding, and repeat treatments at weekly intervals as needed. Remove all plant debris from the garden after the harvest to eliminate habitat for the overwintering adult beetle. Remove weeds in and around the garden.

Beet leafminers

Leafminer damage.

Problem: Light-colored, irregular blotches, blisters, or tunnels appear in the leaves. Brown areas peel apart easily like facial tissue. Tiny black specks are found inside the tunnels.

Analysis: The beet leafminer (*Pegomya hyoscyami*) is an insect pest that belongs to a family of leafmining flies. The tiny black or yellow adult fly lays its white eggs on the undersides of leaves. When the eggs hatch, the cream-colored maggots bore into the leaf. They tunnel between the upper and lower surfaces of the leaf, feeding on the inner tissue. The tunnels and blotches are called *mines*. The black specks inside are the maggot's droppings. The beet leaves are no longer edible, but the root is. Several overlapping generations occur during the growing season, so larvae are present from spring until fall.

Solution: Spray with Ortho® Malathion Plus® Insect Spray Concentrate when the white egg clusters are first seen under the leaves. Repeat two more times at weekly intervals to control succeeding generations. Once the miners enter the leaves, sprays are ineffective. Spraying after the mines first appear will control only those leafminers that attack after the application. If practical, destroy infested leaves. Adult flies can be kept from laying eggs by covering plants with floating row covers.

Leaf spot

Cercospora leaf spot.

Problem: The leaves have small, circular, distinct spots with dark borders. These spots may run together to form blotches or dead areas. The leaves often turn yellow and die. Leaf spotting is most severe in warm, humid weather, when a fine gray mold may cover the infected tissue. Older leaves are more severely affected than younger ones.

Analysis: Leaf spot is a common, destructive fungus (*Cercospora beticola*) that attacks beets, spinach, and Swiss chard. The fungus invades the leaves but not the beet root. Severe infection damages many leaves and hinders the development of the root, however. The spotting makes the leaves unappetizing. The fungus is spread by wind, contaminated tools, and splashing water and is favored by moist conditions and high temperatures. Leaf spot is most common during the summer months and in warm areas. This fungus survives the winter on plant debris left in the garden.

Solution: Picking off and destroying the first spotted leaves retards the spread of leaf spot. Leaf spot on beets seldom causes enough damage to warrant fungicide sprays. If possible, avoid overhead watering; use drip or furrow irrigation instead. Use a mulch to reduce the need for watering. Clean all plant debris from the garden after the harvest to reduce the number of overwintering spores.

BEETS *(continued)*

Curly top

Curly top.

Misshapen roots

Misshapen roots.

BLUEBERRIES

Cherry fruitworms or cranberry fruitworms

Cranberry fruitworms (¾ life size).

Problem: The leaf margins roll upward and feel brittle. Undersides of leaves are rough, with puckering along the veins. The leaves and roots are stunted; the plant may die.

Analysis: Curly top is a virus that affects many vegetables and fruit, including beans, beets, melons, squash, and tomatoes. The virus is transmitted from plant to plant by the beet leafhopper (*Circulifer tenellus*) and is common only in the West, where this insect lives. The beet leafhopper is a pale greenish-yellow insect about ⅛ inch long that feeds from early May through June. It sucks the sap and virus from the infested leaves and then injects the virus into healthy plants at its next feeding stop. (For more information on leafhoppers, see page 448.) Curly top symptoms vary in severity, depending on the variety and age of the plant. Young infected plants usually die. Older plants may turn yellow and die.

Solution: Nothing directly controls curly top. To reduce the chance of infection, control the beet leafhopper with Ortho® Malathion Plus® Insect Spray Concentrate, beginning when the insect swarms first appear. (For information on disease-carrying insects, see page 449.) Destroy infected plants.

Problem: Beet roots are distorted, elongated, knobby, and crooked. They are not smooth and round.

Analysis: Beet roots may be misshapen for any of several reasons:
1. Overcrowding: The beet "seed" is actually a dried fruit containing two or more seeds. As it germinates, seedlings emerge through the soil in clusters instead of individually as do beans and corn. When the seedlings are too crowded, the root doesn't have room to develop properly.
2. Lumpy soil: Beet roots may be distorted because rocks, clods of soil, or clumps of manure don't allow the root to expand evenly in all directions.
3. Variety: Some beet varieties don't produce smooth, round roots. Some are roughly cylindrical and others are elongated and smooth.

Solution: Follow these suggestions for round, smooth beets. The numbered solutions below correspond to the numbered items in the analysis.
1. Plant beet seeds ½ inch deep and 1 inch apart. When seedlings have their first set of leaves, thin them so they are two or three inches apart.
2. Rake out and discard rocks ½ inch in diameter and larger. Break up clods of soil and manure.
3. Plant varieties that grow smooth, round roots (see page 556).

Problem: Clusters of berries are webbed together with silk. Berries may be shriveled and full of sawdustlike material. Inside the berries are smooth, pink-red or pale yellow-green caterpillars about ⅜ to 1 inch long.

Analysis: Cherry fruitworm (*Grapholitha packardii*) and cranberry fruitworm (*Acrobasis vaccinii*) are serious pests of blueberries and cranberries. They also attack cherries and apples. Each caterpillar destroys two to six berries. The caterpillars don't damage the leaves. In midspring, adult moths lay eggs on developing berries and leaves. The caterpillars that hatch from these eggs bore into the berries at the junction of the stem and berry. When they are about half grown, the fruitworms move to another berry, usually one touching the infested berry. This way the fruitworm can move to a new food source without exposing itself. About mid-June, when the caterpillar is grown, it crawls to the soil, garden debris, or a pruning stub, where it remains through the rest of the growing season and the winter. Adult moths emerge in midspring to start the cycle again.

Solution: Once the fruit is infested, the worms inside can't be killed. Handpick and destroy all infested fruit. If your planting is large, or if the fruitworm infestation the current year was severe, spray the plants immediately after bloom with the biological insecticide *Bacillus thuringiensis* (Bt). Repeat the spray every three days.

Blueberry maggots

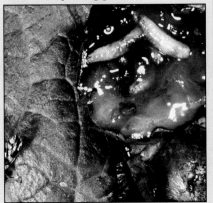

Blueberry maggots and adult (2× life size).

Problem: Ripening blueberries leak juice and are soft and mushy. White, tapered maggots about 3/8 inch long feed inside the berries.

Analysis: Blueberry maggot (*Rhagoletis mendax*), an insect also called the *blueberry fruit fly*, is the most threatening pest of blueberries in the Midwest and on the East Coast. Maggots attack both green and ripe fruit and often ruin an entire crop. They are most severe after unusually cold winters and when the weather is very wet at harvest time and frequent pickings aren't possible. The maggots spend the winter as pupae in the soil. From late June through August, the adult flies lay eggs just under the skin of the fruit. Maggots that hatch from the eggs feed in the berry for about 20 days, then drop to the soil, where they pupate for one to two years. Only one generation occurs per year.

Solution: Harvest frequently, destroying any infested berries. Strip all remaining berries from the bushes at the end of the harvest period. The following year, beginning in early July, treat the plants with an insecticide containing *malathion*. Repeat the treatment at intervals of 10 days throughout the harvest. Treatments the following year may be necessary to control any pupae that mature after two years.

Ripe rot

Ripe rot.

Problem: The tips of ripe berries soften, become puckered, and mushy. This condition may develop on the plant or while the berries are in storage. In wet or humid weather, the soft tips may be covered with a salmon-colored slime. Shoot tips may turn black and die. Brown to black spots may appear on the leaves.

Analysis: Ripe rot, a plant disease also called *anthracnose fruit rot*, is caused by a fungus (*Colletotrichum gloeosporioides*) that infects apples, grapes, strawberries, and several other fruits and vegetables, as well as blueberries. The fungus spends the winter in infected twigs, releasing spores during rainy periods throughout the growing season. The spores can infect blossoms, growing tips, leaves, and developing fruit. The fruit doesn't show any symptoms until it ripens. The disease spoils berries and kills twigs but doesn't kill the plants.

Solution: If ripe rot is discovered in berries, harvest fruit frequently and either eat it or cool it immediately. The disease doesn't develop in the refrigerator. Avoid overhead irrigation. In late winter or early spring, prune and destroy dead twig tips and branches. The following spring, spray with a fungicide containing *captan* during bloom and weekly until two weeks prior to harvest. When replanting, select disease-resistant varieties.

Mummy berry

Mummy berry.

Problem: Infected flowers turn brown and wither. New shoots are blackened in the center and eventually wither and die. As infected berries ripen, they become cream to salmon pink, then tan or whitish gray. Initially soft, they shrivel and harden. Mummified berries usually drop to the soil before harvest.

Analysis: Mummy berry is a plant disease caused by a fungus (*Monilinia vaccinii-corymbosi*) that occurs irregularly and may be severe some years and nonexistent other years. This is due primarily to the spring weather. Wet weather promotes the fungus. The disease spends the winter in infected fruit mummies on the ground. The spores produced from these mummies infect leaves, shoots, and flower clusters shortly after they begin growing in the spring. Spores formed on blighted shoots and blossom clusters infect fruit first by infecting flowers. In order for the disease to develop, spores must land on very young tissue before a natural waxy layer covers the plant surfaces.

Solution: This disease is difficult to control. Once the berries have mummied, it is too late to do anything. No currently listed fungicides control this disease. To prevent the disease the following year, destroy all mummies found on the twigs and the ground. Cultivate around the plants in early spring to bury any remaining mummies. Add 2 inches of mulch to keep the spores from reaching the new growth.

BRAMBLES

Red berry mites

Red berry mite damage.

Problem: Some individual sections of blackberries don't ripen, remaining hard and green or bright red.

Analysis: The red berry mite (*Acalitus essigi*) belongs to a class of mites called *Eriophyid* mites. They are microscopic, causing symptoms that look more like those of plant diseases than of pest problems. Red berry mites live within ripening fruit. They feed at the base of the individual sections (*drupelets*), preventing them from ripening. This condition is sometimes called *red berry*. The mites spend the winter in cracks on the canes or deep within buds. As the plants grow, the mites move to remain near the growing tip. As soon as fruit is set, the mites move into it. They breed rapidly, building to enormous numbers as the season progresses. For this reason, the problem is more severe in late-maturing blackberries, which ripen when more mites are present. Uncontrolled mites can infest entire plantings in a couple of seasons.

Solution: Once symptoms appear, it is too late to help the current year's crop. Control the mite in the following year's crop with two applications of a lime-sulfer solution—one after leaf drop in the fall and the other after growth begins in the spring, when new growth is 2 to 6 inches long. Use high pressures to force the spray into cracks where the mites hide. Annual treatments are rarely necessary; monitor for red berry symptoms at harvest and treat only when they appear. When selecting blackberry varieties in an area where red berry occurs, select early-maturing varieties.

Viruses

Raspberry bushy dwarf virus.

Problem: Leaves have pale green or yellow rings, bright yellow margins, or green blisters surrounded by yellow tissue. In some cases the leaves are crinkled. The plant may be stunted and may bear few berries. Fruit may be small or crumbly.

Analysis: Several viruses infect brambles (blackberries and raspberries). Some can be very serious, but others seem to cause little harm to the plant and fruit. Viruses may be spread by aphids, soil-borne nematodes, or pollen. If diseased plants are touched or pruned, viruses can be transferred to healthy plants on hands and equipment contaminated by plant sap or pollen. Viruses persist in the plant indefinitely. Once a plant is infected with a virus, it can't be cured.

Solution: No chemicals control or eliminate plant viruses. Remove and destroy infected plants before bloom to reduce the spread of pollen-borne viruses. Wash your hands thoroughly and disinfect pruning shears after working on infected plants. Purchase only certified disease-free plants. Wild raspberries and blackberries can be a source of infection; remove them from areas close to cultivated plantings. Keep the aphid population under control. Some raspberry varieties are resistant to viruses.

Fruit rot

Fruit rot on blackberry.

Problem: Ripening berries are covered with tufts of gray, green, white, or black cottony growth. A smelly, watery liquid may ooze from the berries.

Analysis: Several fungi (*Botrytis cinerea*, *Rhizopus nigricans*, *Penicillium* species, *Cladosporium* species, and *Alternaria* species) cause fruit rot on raspberries and blackberries. These diseases are widespread and develop fastest on overripe and bruised raspberries and blackberries. Warm, wet weather, especially during bloom and harvest, favors these fungi. They can infect the fruit before or after harvest.

Solution: Fungicide sprays help reduce fruit rot, but good cultural and harvest practices are a must. Pick ripening berries frequently to avoid an accumulation of overripe fruit. Harvest in the cool early morning, and handle the fruit carefully to avoid bruising. Store the picked berries in the refrigerator immediately. Avoid overhead irrigation. Keep the plant rows narrow and the canes far enough apart to allow good air circulation. To reduce fruit rot, spray the plants with a fungicide containing *captan*. Repeat at intervals of 7 to 10 days from bloom through harvest.

Leaf spot and cane spot

Leaf spot and cane spot.

Problem: Tiny (1/12-inch) spots appear on leaves. The spots have whitish centers and brown to purplish borders. Spots also appear on canes but are longer. The plant grows slowly and may drop its leaves early.

Analysis: Leaf spot and cane spot, also called *septoria leaf spot*, is a plant disease caused by a fungus (*Septoria rubi*) that infects only blackberries. The fungus spends the winter on canes and old leaves. In the spring, spores are produced during wet weather and spread by splashing rain.

Solution: Remove infected canes immediately after harvest, and destroy them. In trailing blackberries, train new canes in August to get them off the ground. Spray new canes with a fungicide containing *captan* or fixed copper three times, when they are 6 inches, 12 inches, and 2 feet long. After harvest and training of new canes, spray with a fixed copper fungicide mixed with horticultural oil, or apply a lime-sulfur spray. Spray once more with a fixed copper fungicide before heavy fall rains begin. The following spring, before new growth is 3/4 inch long, spray again with fixed copper or lime sulfur.

Cane and leaf rust

Cane and leaf rust.

Problem: In late spring, lemon-yellow powder appears in cracks in the bark of the previous year's blackberry and raspberry canes. As leaves develop, the same rust may be found on their undersides. Sometimes the rust also appears on the fruit. Canes may defoliate prematurely. Canes may die.

Analysis: Cane and leaf rust, also called *yellow rust*, is a plant disease caused by a fungus (*Kuehneola uredinis*) that spends the winter in cracks in the canes and on dead leaves caught in the canes. The yellow powder consists of spores splashed by rain onto nearby canes and leaves. In the fall, infected leaves produce the spores that invade newly developing canes. The fungus is favored by wet weather. Infected fruit is inedible. Don't confuse this disease, which has lemon-yellow spores, with orange rust, which has orange spores. The diseases are quite different and require different treatments. (For information on orange rust, see page 356.)

Solution: If the infestation is so severe that you aren't able to harvest, cut the planting to the ground. Trellis the new growth to harvest the following year. If a harvest is possible, remove the infected canes after fruiting. Train and tie up the canes after leaf fall so dead leaves are not caught in the canopy. As soon as canes are trellised, spray them with a fixed copper fungicide. Spray again just as the buds are beginning to turn green and once more just before bloom. Avoid overhead irrigation.

Raspberry crown borers

Raspberry crown borers (life size).

Problem: In early summer, canes wilt and begin dying. Some canes are spindly, lack vigor, and grow very little. Canes often break off easily at ground level. White grubs, 1/4 to 1 1/4 inches long, may be inside canes.

Analysis: Raspberry crown borer (*Pennisetia marginata*), an insect pest also called the *raspberry root borer*, attacks brambles in the northern United States. The borer damages plants by feeding on the roots and crown (base) of the plant. Root feeding weakens all cane fruits but often kills raspberries. The crown borer has a 2-year life cycle. In late summer, the adult moth lays a total of about 100 eggs on the undersides of several leaves. The eggs hatch in early fall, and the larvae move to the soil near the plant crown, where they spend the winter. As the weather warms in the spring, the larvae enter the plant and begin hollowing out the crown. This feeding causes the canes to swell and eventually die. The larvae continue feeding throughout the year, spend the winter in the canes, and feed again the following spring. They mature and emerge from the canes as adults in late summer. There may be one- and two-year-old larvae present at the same time.

Solution: In early spring, drench the crown and lower 2 feet of the canes with an insecticide containing *permethrin*. Repeat controls annually for at least two years because of this insect's two-year life cycle. Cut out and destroy damaged canes when pruning.

BRAMBLES *(continued)*

Raspberry cane borers and red-necked cane borers

Borer damage.

Problem: Shoot tips wilt. Some canes die. Two rows of small holes, 1 inch apart, may encircle the cane below the wilted tips. Cigar-shaped swellings ¼ to 3 inches long may occur on the cane. The cane breaks off easily at the swelling. Some leaves may be chewed and ragged.

Analysis: Raspberry cane borers (*Oberea maculata*) and red-necked cane borers (*Agrilus ruficollis*) attack blackberries, raspberries, and dewberries. The adult beetles are black with copper or yellow just behind the head and are ½ inch long. On sunny summer days, adult red-necked cane borers may be seen feeding on the leaves. Females lay their eggs in the bark of new, tender growth. The white grublike larvae then tunnel around and inside the cane, feeding on the inner tissue. This feeding often causes cane swellings; it also interferes with the flow of water and nutrients through the cane, resulting in shoot wilting and cane death. The borers spend the winter in tunnels in the canes.

Solution: Cut off infested canes 6 inches below the swelling or wilted tip and destroy them. The following year, apply an insecticide containing *rotenone* or *malathion* immediately before bloom and again two weeks later.

Cane blight

Cane blight on raspberry.

Problem: Branches wilt and die in mid-summer. Brownish-purple areas occur on pruned ends or wounded areas of canes and extend downward, sometimes encircling the stem. Infected canes turn gray in late summer. Symptoms are associated with wounds and are usually not visible on first-year canes.

Analysis: Cane blight is a plant disease caused by a fungus (*Leptosphaeria coniothyrium*). It is more prevalent on black raspberries than on red and purple raspberries and blackberries. The fungus spends the winter on diseased canes. The spores are spread from plant to plant by the wind. In wet weather in late spring and early summer, the spores enter canes through cracks in the bark, broken fruit stems, and wounds from pruning and insects. Canes weakened from cane blight are more subject to winter injury.

Solution: Apply a lime-sulfur solution in late fall and early spring. Follow with two applications of a fungicide containing *ferbam*: one just before bloom, when the new canes are 1½ to 2 feet tall, and the other just after harvest. Remove infected canes before growth starts in the spring. Prune just above a bud in dry weather at least three days before rain so the wounds have time to dry. Follow the summer topping of black raspberries with an application of a fungicide containing *captan*. Avoid overhead irrigation. Also avoid unnecessary wounding of canes.

Cane and crown gall

Crown gall on blackberry.

Problem: Plants are stunted, break, and fall over easily, and they produce dry, seedy berries. Irregular, wartlike growths (galls) may appear on canes, especially near soil level. The canes may dry out and crack. Galls also occur just below soil level on roots and crowns. They range from pinhead-size to several inches in diameter, and they are white or grayish brown.

Analysis: Cane and crown gall are diseases caused by bacteria (*Agrobacterium rubi* and *A. tumefaciens*) that occur on blackberries, raspberries, boysenberries, loganberries, and youngberries throughout the United States. The plants become weak and produce fewer berries. The bacteria are often brought to a garden on the roots of an infected plant and are spread with the soil and by contaminated pruning tools. The bacteria enter the plant through wounds in the roots or the base of the stem (the crown). They produce a substance that stimulates rapid cell growth in the plant, causing gall formation on the roots, crown, and canes. The galls disrupt the flow of water and nutrients up the roots and stems, weakening and stunting the top of the plant. Galls don't usually cause the plant to die.

Solution: Crown gall can't be eliminated from the plant. Although infected plants may survive for many years, they produce few berries. Dig up and discard diseased plants and the soil within 6 inches of a gall. Wait at least three years before replanting gall-free plants in clean soil. Prune and cultivate carefully to avoid wounding plants. Select resistant varieties.

Spur blight

Spur blight on raspberry.

Problem: In summer, leaves near the bottom of new canes develop V-shaped brown lesions with yellow margins. The infection spreads down the leaf to the stem, where it causes a brown to purple lesion on the cane around the leaf node. Cane lesions from adjacent nodes often merge. Infected leaves often drop prematurely.

Analysis: Spur blight is a plant disease that is most severe on red raspberries, but may also affect black raspberries and blackberries. It is caused by a fungus (*Didymella applantata*) that infects only leaves and the very outer layer of tissue on the cane. If the cane lesions are scraped, healthy green tissue is found underneath. Buds on infected canes may not develop or may develop into weak shoots that yield few berries. The fungus overwinters on canes. During wet weather from May to August, spores are produced and splashed onto leaves of new canes.

Solution: Remove and destroy fruiting canes immediately after harvest. Grow fall-bearing varieties for a fall crop only by cutting all canes to the ground in late winter. To avoid crowding canes, keep plant rows narrow. Keep the area free of weeds. At bud-break in the spring, before new growth is ¾ inch long, spray with a lime-sulfur solution. When new canes are 8 to 10 inches long, spray with a fungicide containing *captan*. Select resistant varieties.

Anthracnose

Anthracnose spots on raspberry.

Problem: Stem tips die. Oval spots with purple edges and light gray centers appear on the canes. Spots enlarge, sometimes circling the entire stem. Canes may dry and crack. Most of the spots occur on the inside of the canes toward the center of the plant and from 6 to 30 inches up from the ground. The leaves may have small yellow spots with purple margins. The centers of the spots often drop out, leaving a hole. Spots may also occur on other parts of the plant. Individual berry sections may become brown and scabby.

Analysis: Anthracnose, a disease caused by a fungus (*Elsinoe veneta*), is one of the most destructive diseases of black and purple raspberries. Overgrown, unpruned bushes are very susceptible to anthracnose. The disease is most serious when heavy rains continue late in the spring and into the summer. The fungus survives the winter in infected canes and infects new growth in the early spring. Canes weakened by anthracnose are more susceptible to winter injury.

Solution: Apply a fungicide containing lime sulfur in early spring when the leaf buds swell and expose from ½ to ¾ inch of the new leaves. This is the most effective time to spray. Follow with three applications of a fungicide containing *ferbam* or *captan*: (1) when the new canes are 6 to 8 inches tall; (2) when they are 12 to 15 inches tall; and (3) just before bloom. Avoid overhead watering. After harvest, prune and destroy old infected canes. Keep the area around the planting free of wild blackberries and raspberries.

Powdery mildew

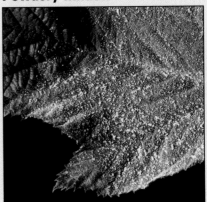

Powdery mildew on raspberry.

Problem: A whitish-gray powder covers the leaves, fruit, and young growing tips of canes. Canes may be dwarfed or distorted. Fruit may be covered with white powder.

Analysis: Powdery mildew is a common plant disease that seriously affects red raspberries and occasionally attacks purple and black raspberries and blackberries. It is caused by a fungus (*Sphaerotheca macularis*) that thrives in both humid and dry weather. The powdery patches consist of fungal strands and spores. The spores are spread by the wind to healthy plants. The fungus saps plant nutrients, causing yellowing and sometimes the death of the leaf. A severe infection may kill the plant. Because this powdery mildew attacks many different kinds of plants, the fungus from a diseased plant may infect other types of plants in the garden. (For a list of susceptible plants, see page 537.) Under favorable conditions, powdery mildew can spread through a closely spaced planting of berries in a matter of days or weeks.

Solution: Spray the plants with flowable sulfur when the blossoms first open. Repeat at weekly intervals if the plants become reinfected. The following fall, and again in the spring as the buds begin to swell, spray the plants with a lime-sulfur solution. Keep the row width narrow or the canes far enough apart to allow good air circulation so they can dry rapidly after rain or watering.

BRAMBLES *(continued)*

Orange rust

Orange rust on blackberry.

Problem: Leaves are dwarfed, misshapen, and yellowish. Young shoots are spindly and clustered. Blisterlike pustules and bright orange dust cover the undersides of leaves. Plants remain infected throughout their lives and produce no blossoms.

Analysis: Orange rust is a plant disease caused by the fungi *Arthuriomyces peckianus* and *Gymnoconia nitens*. It is severe on wild and cultivated blackberries. It sometimes attacks black raspberries but doesn't affect red and purple raspberries. The disease spreads throughout the plant. Infected plants never recover and never bloom. Spores are produced on the plant each year after it is infected. The fungus spreads from plant to plant on the wind. In the spring, orange spores land on leaves. After infecting them, the fungus spreads throughout the plant into the canes, crown, and roots. The disease spreads into new shoots as the plant continues to grow.

Solution: Fungicide sprays and pruning are not effective. Remove and destroy infected plants as soon as they are noticed. Remove any wild blackberries growing nearby. Thin the plants for good air circulation. Pull out all weeds. Grow rust-resistant varieties.

CABBAGE

Growth cracks

Growth cracks.

Problem: The head of the cabbage plant cracks open soon after it reaches picking size.

Analysis: A cabbage head may crack if not harvested soon after it matures. Splitting results from the pressure of water taken up into the head after the head is solid and mature. Tomatoes, carrots, potatoes, and sweet potatoes are also prone to growth cracking. Cracked vegetables are still edible if harvested immediately.

Solution: Harvest cabbage heads as soon as they feel firm. Stagger planting times so that heads mature at different times. Or select several varieties that will ripen at different times. To delay harvest, reduce the water supply to mature heads in any of the following ways:
1. When the heads are firm, give the plants less water at each watering.
2. Break off some of the roots by lifting and twisting the cabbage plant.
3. Cut the roots on two sides of the plant by pushing a spade into the soil 6 to 8 inches deep. Surplus cabbage heads can be stored in the crisper section of a refrigerator.

Bolting

Bolting broccoli.

Problem: In hot weather, an elongated stalk with flowers grows from the main stem of broccoli, cauliflower, and brussels sprouts plants. On cabbage, the head splits open, and the stalk emerges from within.

Analysis: Bolting, or seed stalk formation, results from exposure of the plants to cold temperatures early in their lives. Once a plant has matured to the point where its leaves are about 2 inches wide, exposure to cold (40° to 50°F) temperatures for several days in a row causes flower buds to form within the growing point. These buds remain dormant until warm weather arrives. With arrival of warm weather, buds develop into tall flower stalks. As the plant bolts, its flavor deteriorates and becomes bitter.

Solution: Discard plants that have bolted. Avoid setting out plants too early in the winter or spring. If cabbage plants are set out in the fall or winter, harvest them before warm weather causes them to bolt. Cutting the flower stalk will not prevent poor flavor from developing.

Discolored heads

Discolored cauliflower head.

Problem: Yellow, green, or purple discoloration mars cauliflower heads. The leaves are healthy and green.

Analysis: Developing cauliflower heads need to be protected from sunlight to remain white. Exposure to light causes yellow, green, or purple pigment to form. The resulting discoloration not only affects the appearance, but also causes a stronger flavor. A similar symptom, brown or black spots up to 1 inch on the head may be caused by the disease downy mildew.

Solution: Prevent further discoloration by tying the lower leaves up over the developing heads. To avoid possible head rotting, wait until the head is 2½ inches in diameter. Be sure the heads are dry, and then tie the leaves loosely, giving the head room to grow. Secure the leaves with soft twine or a wide elastic band. This "blanching" or whitening process takes one to two weeks, depending on the weather and the variety of cauliflower. Check occasionally under the protective canopy for pests. The head is ready for harvest when it is firm.

Diamondback moth

Diamondback moth larva (life size).

Problem: Small holes and transparent holes appear in the leaves. Small (¼-inch) green worms feed on the undersides of leaves. When disturbed, worms wriggle rapidly and often drop from the plant on a silk thread.

Analysis: Diamondback moth (*Plutella xylostella*) worms are the larvae of gray or brown moths that fly in the evening. The adults don't damage plants. The pale green larvae feed on the undersides of leaves of members of the cabbage family, chewing holes and eating the lower surfaces of leaves. The feeding damage often allows soft rots to enter the leaves. After feeding for about two weeks, the larvae pupate in transparent silken cocoons attached to the undersides of leaves. Adult moths spend the winter hidden under plant debris. Two to seven generations per year damage both spring and fall plantings.

Solution: Apply Ortho® Bug-B-Gon® Multi-Purpose Insect Killer Ready-To-Use, Ortho® Bug-B-Gon® Multi-Purpose Garden Dust, or the bacterial insecticide *Bacillus thuringiensis* (Bt) to the foliage when the young worms first appear or when the leaves show feeding damage. The insecticide must reach the undersides of the leaves to be most effective. Repeat the treatment each week as long as the caterpillars are found. Adults can be kept from laying eggs with row covers. Clean up plant debris in the fall and cultivate the soil thoroughly to expose and destroy overwintering moths. Kill wild mustard and other weeds of the cabbage family in the vicinity of the garden several weeks before planting in the spring.

Cabbageworms

Imported cabbageworm. Inset: Adult (life size).

Problem: Round or irregular holes appear in leaves. Green worms with light stripes down their backs, up to 1½ inches long, feed on the leaves or heads. Masses of green or brown pellets may be found between the leaves. Cabbage and cauliflower heads may be tunneled.

Analysis: Cabbageworms are destructive worms that are either the *cabbage looper* (*Trichoplusia ni*) or the *imported cabbageworm* (*Pieris rapae*). Both worms attack all members of the cabbage family, as well as lettuce. Adults lay eggs throughout the growing season. Adults of the imported cabbageworm attach yellow, bullet-shape eggs to the undersides of leaves. These white butterflies are frequently seen around cabbage plants in the daytime. The brownish cabbage looper moth lays pale green eggs on the upper surfaces of leaves in the evening. Worms may be present from early spring until late fall. In the South, they may be present year-round. Worms spend the winter as pupae attached to a plant or nearby object.

Solution: Control cabbageworms with Ortho® Bug-B-Gon® Multi-Purpose Insect Killer Ready-To-Use, Ortho® Malathion Plus® Insect Spray Concentrate, or an insecticidal soap. Spray as soon as damage is seen. Cabbageworms can also be killed with the bacterial insecticide *Bacillus thuringiensis* (Bt) while they are small. Repeat treatments weekly as long as worms are found, but stop three days before harvest. Adults can be kept from laying eggs on plants by covering plants with row covers. Remove plant debris after harvest to destroy the pupae.

CABBAGE *(continued)*

Cutworms

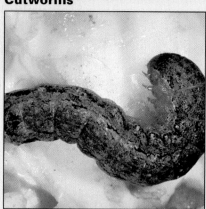

Cutworm (2× life size).

Problem: Seedlings and young transplants are chewed or cut off near the ground. About 2 inches down into the soil are dull gray, brown, or black worms. They have spots or stripes on their smooth bodies, are about 1½ or 2 inches long, and coil when disturbed.

Analysis: Several species of moth larvae are pests in the vegetable garden. The most likely pests of young cabbage plants set out early in the season are surface-feeding cutworms. They spend the days hidden in the soil and feed at night. A single cutworm can sever the stems of several young plants in a single night. Adults are dark, night-flying moths with stripes on their forewings. (For more information on cutworms, see page 440.)

Solution: Apply Ortho® Bug-Geta® Plus Snail, Slug & Insect Killer around the base of plants when stem cutting is observed. Treat in late evening just before cutworms become active. Applications may need to be repeated at weekly intervals. Clean up any weedy growth in the vicinity of the garden. Work Ortho® Bug-B-Gon® Multi-Purpose Insect Killer Granules into the soil before planting. Further reduce damage with a cutworm collar around the stem of each plant. Cultivate the soil in late summer and fall to expose and destroy eggs, pupae, and larvae of the pest.

Cabbage maggots

Cabbage maggots (6× life size).

Problem: Young plants wilt in the heat of the day. They may later turn yellow and die. Soft-bodied, white maggots about ⅓ inch long are feeding in the roots. The roots are honeycombed with slimy channels and scarred by brown grooves. Damage is particularly severe during cool, moist weather in spring, early summer, and fall.

Analysis: The cabbage maggot (*Hylemya brassicae*) is a major pest in the northern United States. Early maggots also attack the roots and stems of broccoli, cauliflower, radishes, and turnips in the spring and early summer. Later insects injure cabbage, radishes, and turnips in the fall. The adult is a gray fly, somewhat smaller than a housefly, with black stripes and bristles down its back. It lays eggs on stems and nearby soil. The maggots hatch in two or three days and tunnel into the stems and roots of plants, sometimes to a depth of 6 inches. The cabbage maggot causes feeding damage and also spreads black rot bacteria. (For information on black rot, see page 359.)

Solution: Once the growing plant wilts and turns yellow, nothing can be done. Adult flies can be kept from laying eggs on cabbages by protecting them with floating row covers. Place the row covers as soon as plants are set out or seedlings emerge. Make sure they are completely closed and tight to the ground.

Flea beetles

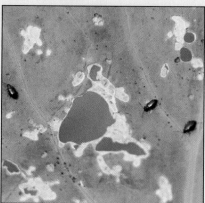

Flea beetles (2× life size).

Problem: Leaves are riddled with shot holes, about ⅛ inch in diameter. Tiny (1/16 inch) black or striped beetles jump like fleas when disturbed. Seedlings may wilt and die.

Analysis: Flea beetles jump like fleas but aren't related to fleas. Both adult and immature flea beetles feed on a wide variety of garden vegetables. The immature beetle, a legless gray grub, injures plants by feeding on the roots. Adults chew holes in leaves. Flea beetles damage seedlings and young plants most. Adult beetles spend the winter in soil and garden debris. They emerge in early spring to feed on weeds until vegetables sprout or plants are set in the garden. Grubs hatch from eggs laid in the soil and feed for two to three weeks. After pupating in the soil, they emerge as adults to repeat the cycle. One to four generations occur per year. Adults may feed for up to two months during the growing season.

Solution: Control flea beetles with Ortho® Bug-B-Gon® Multi-Purpose Garden Dust, Ortho® Bug-B-Gon® Multi-Purpose Insect Killer Ready-To-Use, or an insecticidal soap when the leaves first show damage. Watch new growth for evidence of further damage, and repeat the treatment at weekly intervals as needed. Clean all debris from the garden after harvest to eliminate habitat for overwintering adult beetles. Remove weedy growth in the vicinity of the garden to eliminate alternate hosts of the beetles. Use row covers to exclude beetles.

Aphids

Aphids on cabbage (2× life size).

Problem: Some leaves are yellowed and cupped downward. Tiny (⅛-inch) pale green or gray soft-bodied insects cluster under leaves, on stems, and on heads. A sticky substance may coat the leaves. Ants may be present.

Analysis: Aphids do little damage in small numbers. They are extremely prolific, however, and populations can rapidly build to damaging numbers during the growing season. Damage occurs when the aphids suck the sap from the plant. The aphid is unable to digest all the sugar in the plant sap, and it excretes the excess in a fluid called *honeydew*. The honeydew often drops onto the leaves below. Ants feed on the sticky substance and are often present where there is an aphid infestation. The most common aphid attacking the cabbage family is the cabbage aphid (*Brevicoryne brassicae*). Cabbage aphids spend the winter as eggs on plant debris in the garden. In the South, they are active year-round. (For more information on aphids, see page 443.)

Solution: Treat with Ortho® Bug-B-Gon® Multi-Purpose Insect Killer, Ortho® Malathion Plus® Insect Spray Concentrate, or an insecticidal soap as soon as the insects appear. Repeat at intervals of one week if the plant is reinfested. Clean all plant debris from the garden after harvest to reduce the number of overwintering eggs.

Black rot

Black rot.

Problem: Young plants turn yellow, then brown, and die. On older plants, yellow areas develop along the leaf margins, then progress into the leaf in a V-shape. These areas later turn brown and die. Lower (older) leaves wilt and drop off. The veins running from the infected leaf margins to the center stem are black. When the stem is cut across, a black ring and sometimes yellow ooze are seen in the cross section.

Analysis: Black rot is a plant disease caused by a bacterium (*Xanthomonas campestris*) that affects all members of the cabbage family at any stage in their growth. The bacteria live in or on seed or in infected plant debris for as long as 2 years. Insects, splashing water, and garden tools carry bacteria to other leaves and plants. The bacteria enter the plant through natural openings or wounds and spread in the water- and nutrient-conducting vessels of the plant. The infected tissue may form pockets where dead cells and bacteria accumulate as a yellow ooze. Warm, humid weather promotes the spread and development of the bacteria. Black rot can kill seedlings rapidly. The diseased heads are edible but unappetizing.

Solution: No chemical controls black rot. Discard infected plants. To avoid further infection, plant only disease-free seed and healthy plants. Place plants far enough apart to allow good air circulation. Avoid overhead watering. Plant in soil that has not grown cabbage for at least two years.

Clubroot

Clubroot on kohlrabi.

Problem: The plant wilts on hot, sunny days and recovers at night. The older, outer leaves turn yellow and drop. The roots are swollen and misshapen. The largest swellings are just below the soil surface. Growth slows, and the plant eventually dies.

Analysis: Clubroot is a plant disease caused by a soil-inhabiting fungus (*Plasmodiophora brassicae*) that persists in the soil for many years. Warm, moist weather together with an acid soil promotes the infection. The fungus causes cells to grow and divide within the root tissue. This causes swelling and a general weakening of the plant, allowing other fungi and bacteria to invade the roots and cause root rot. As the roots decompose, they release millions of spores into the soil, which spread by shoes, tools, and in water runoff. Most members of the cabbage family are susceptible to clubroot, but most rutabaga varieties and many turnip varieties are resistant. Weeds in this family, such as mustard, pennycress, and shepherd's purse, can also harbor the fungus.

Solution: Once a plant is infected, it can't be cured. To reduce the severity of the disease the following year, don't grow susceptible plants where any member of the cabbage family has grown for the past seven years. To discourage infection, lime the soil with garden lime to a pH of 7.2.

CARROTS

Green root tops

Green root top.

Problem: Carrot root tops are green and have a strong flavor. Leaves are healthy.

Analysis: Tops of carrot roots turn green when exposed to sunlight. The root tops may become exposed when heavy rain or irrigation water washes away the soil. Soil may also be moved away during cultivation. The green portions of the root have a strong flavor. The orange part of the root is edible.

Solution: Cut away the green portion of the carrot before eating. Protect the carrot root tops in the ground by covering with 1 to 2 inches of soil whenever exposed. Or mulch the plants with a 4- to 6-inch layer of straw or several sheets of newspaper to prevent water from washing away the soil. Don't cultivate closer than 6 to 8 inches to the plants.

Misshapen roots

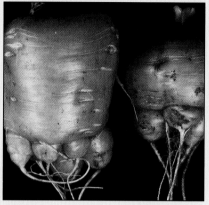

Carrots stunted from growing in heavy soil.

Problem: Roots are forked, twisted, or abnormally shaped.

Analysis: Carrot roots may be misshapen for any of several reasons:
1. Overcrowding: Crowded seedlings don't have room to develop properly.
2. Soil debris: Stones or clods of soil prevent even expansion of the root.
3. Fresh manure: Fresh, uncomposted manure stimulates root branching.
4. Heavy soil: Carrot roots have difficulty expanding in heavy, tight soil. Soil-inhabiting rot fungi that may cause forking are also prevalent in wet soils.
5. Nematodes: These microscopic worms live in the soil and feed on plant roots.

Solution: The numbered solutions below correspond to the numbered items in the analysis. Follow these suggestions:
1. Plant carrot seeds ¼ to ½ inch deep and ½ inch apart. When the seedlings are 1 inch tall, thin them to ½ to 2 inches apart, depending on the variety planted.
2. Before planting, rake out and discard stones ½ inch and larger. Break up soil clods.
3. If you add manure, use only composted manure, or fertilize with a balanced fertilizer.
4. Incorporate organic matter such as peat moss or humus into heavy soil. Provide good drainage to discourage molds. Short, blunt varieties of carrots that do well in heavy soil include 'Short 'n Sweet,' 'Oxhart,' and the Nantes and Chantenay types.
5. For information on nematodes, see details at right.

Nematodes

Misshapen carrots.

Problem: Plants are stunted and yellow. The main root may be forked, and numerous side roots are produced, or tiny beads or knots are attached to the roots.

Analysis: Nematodes are microscopic worms that live in the soil. They aren't related to earthworms. Nematodes feed on plant roots, damaging and stunting them. The damaged roots can't supply sufficient water and nutrients to the aboveground plant parts, and the plant is stunted or slowly dies. Nematodes are found throughout the United States but are most severe in southeastern areas. They prefer moist, sandy loam soil. Nematodes can move only a few inches each year on their own, but they may be carried long distances by soil, water, tools, or infested plants. Testing roots and soil is the only positive method for confirming the presence of nematodes. Contact your local county extension office for sampling instructions and addresses of testing laboratories. Soil and root problems, such as poor soil structure, drought stress, nutrient deficiency, and root rots, also can produce symptoms similar to those caused by nematodes. These problems should be eliminated as causes before soil and root samples are sent for testing.

Solution: No chemicals available to homeowners kill nematodes in planted soil. The worms can be controlled before planting, however, by soil fumigation or solarization. (For more information on solarization, see page 322.) Mulching will help to discourage nematodes.

Carrot weevils

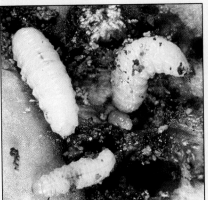

Carrot weevil larvae (3× life size).

Problem: The upper part of the root is scarred with zigzag tunnels. White, curved, legless grubs, about 1/3 inch long, may be found in the root and soil.

Analysis: The carrot weevil (*Listronotus oregonensis*) is an insect that feeds on carrots, celery, dill, parsley, parsnips, and Queen Anne's lace. The adult is a dark brown, nonflying beetle that lays eggs in the carrot tops. In May and June the eggs hatch into white grubs, which travel down to the developing root. There the grub tunnels into and feeds on the upper tissue, scarring the root. After a short resting period in the soil, the pest emerges as an adult and lays eggs that hatch into a second generation in August. The adults of this second generation spend the winter in debris in and around the garden. The following spring, the cycle repeats itself.

Solution: No insecticides are currently registered for home use on this insect pest. Some control may be obtained when spraying for leafhoppers. Keep adults from laying eggs by protecting plants with row covers, especially when the young carrots have five or six leaves. Remove Queen Anne's lace from the garden area. Clean up garden debris in the fall to eliminate overwintering habitat for adults. Don't add infested debris to the compost pile. The following year, rotate carrots to an area previously planted with a nonsusceptible crop.

Wireworms

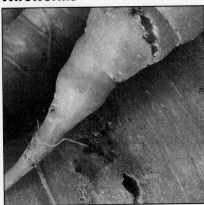

Wireworm damage.

Problem: Plants are stunted and grow slowly. Roots are poorly formed. Tunnels wind through the roots. Shiny, hard, jointed, creamy-yellow, dark brown, orange, or gray worms up 5/8 inch long are found in roots and soil.

Analysis: Wireworms attack beans, beets, carrots, corn, lettuce, peas, potatoes, and many other plants. They feed only on underground plant parts, devouring seeds, underground stems, tubers, and roots. Infestations are most extensive in soil where lawn grass has previously grown. The adult is known as a *click beetle* because it makes a clicking sound when turning from its back to its feet. The adult lays eggs in the spring. After the eggs hatch, the wireworms feed for two to six years before maturing into adult beetles. All sizes and ages of wireworms may be found in soil at the same time.

Solution: Wireworms may be difficult to control. Avoid planting carrots in areas that have held clover, grass, pasture, or grassy weeds.

Aster yellows

Aster yellows. Inset: Infected root.

Problem: Inner leaves are yellow, stunted, and grow in tight bunches. Outer leaves turn rusty red to reddish purple. The roots are stunted and deformed and have a bitter taste. Tiny hairlike roots grow in great profusion out of the main root. Numerous tiny leaves grow from the top of the root.

Analysis: Aster yellows is a plant disease caused by phytoplasmas, microscopic organisms similar to bacteria. The phytoplasmas are transmitted from plant to plant primarily by leafhoppers. (For information on leafhoppers, see page 423.) The symptoms of aster yellows are more severe and appear more quickly in warm weather. Even when the disease is present in the plant, aster yellows may not manifest its symptoms in temperatures of 55°F or lower. The disease infects many other vegetables, ornamental plants, and weeds. (For a list of plants susceptible to aster yellows, see page 546.)

Solution: Aster yellows can't be eliminated entirely, but it can be controlled. Move and destroy infected plants. Eradicate nearby weeds that may harbor aster yellows and leafhopper eggs. Treat leafhopper-infested plants with Ortho® Bug-B-Gon® Multi-Purpose Insect Killer Concentrate or Ortho® Bug-B-Gon® Multi-Purpose Insect Killer Ready-To-Use. Repeat the treatment whenever leafhoppers are seen. (For more information on disease-carrying insects, see page 449.) Keep leafhoppers from the plants with floating row covers.

CORN

Armyworms

Armyworm (½ life size).

Problem: Leaf edges are chewed, and some leaves may be completely eaten. Light tan to dark brown caterpillars 1½ to 2 inches long with yellow, orange, or dark brown stripes are feeding on the leaves and may be boring into the ears.

Analysis: Armyworms attack corn, grains, grasses, and other garden crops. These pests don't overwinter in cold-winter areas, but the moths migrate in the spring in search of places to lay their eggs. The tan to gray adult moths lay eggs on blades of grasses and grains. Caterpillars that hatch from these eggs feed on corn leaves, ears, and ear stalks. After they have eaten everything in one area, they crawl in droves to another area in search of more food. After several weeks of feeding, they pupate in the soil, then emerge as adult moths to repeat the cycle. Several generations occur each year. These pests are most numerous after cold, wet spring weather that slows the development of the natural parasites and diseases that help keep the population in check.

Solution: When the worms are first seen, treat with Ortho® Bug-B-Gon® Multi-Purpose Garden Dust or Ortho® Bug-B-Gon® Multi-Purpose Insect Killer Concentrate. Results may not be seen for four or five days. Repeat at weekly intervals if the plants become reinfested. To control worms that bore into the ears, spray when 10 percent of the ears show silk. Repeat three or four more times at intervals of three days. Because armyworms are most active in the evening and early in the morning, the best time to spray is evening.

Corn earworms

Corn earworms (¾ life size).

Adult (2× life size).

Problem: Striped yellow, brown, or green worms are feeding on the tip of the ear inside the husk. The worms range in size from ¾ to 2 inches long. Leaves may be chewed and ragged.

Analysis: Corn earworm (*Helicoverpa zea*, formerly *Heliothis zea*) is the most serious pest of corn. It attacks many other garden vegetables and flowers as well, and it is also known as the *tomato fruitworm* and the *cotton bollworm*. The worm is the larva of a light gray-brown moth with dark lines on its wings. In the spring, the moth lays yellow eggs singly on corn silks and on the undersides of leaves. The worms that hatch from these eggs feed on the new leaves in the whorls. This feeding doesn't reduce the corn yield, but the leaves that develop are ragged and plant growth may be stunted. More serious damage is caused when worms feed on the silks, causing poor pollination, and when they feed on the developing kernels. Worms enter the ear at the silk end, or they may bore through the husk. Several generations occur per year. In the South, where these pests survive the winter, early and late plantings suffer the most damage. Adult moths migrate into northern areas, where late plantings are severely damaged. Uneaten parts of infested ears are still edible.

Solution: Once the worms are in the ears, insecticides are ineffective. In the future, spray or dust plants with an insecticide containing *pyrethrins, endosulfan,* or *permethrin* when 10 percent of the ears show silk. Repeat the treatment three or four times at intervals of three days. If infestation continues, repeat as necessary until harvest. To avoid unnecessary spraying, monitor for adult moths with pheromone traps (see page 414). Put out traps when the ears begin to silk. Begin spraying when moths are trapped. Steps taken to make it difficult for the young worm to enter the ear are somewhat effective: Select varieties with long, tight husks, or pinch the husks closed with clothespins where the silks exit the husks.

Poor pollination

Poor pollination.

Problem: Corn ears are not completely filled with kernels, but plants are healthy.

Analysis: Poorly filled ears result from ineffective or incomplete pollination. Pollen grains produced on the tassels must fall on the sticky silks for complete pollination. Each strand of silk is attached to a kernel, so for each silk that is pollinated, one kernel develops on the ear. Corn pollen is spread by the wind; if the wind blows across a single row of corn, the pollen on the tassels is carried away from the silks, resulting in poorly filled ears. Poor pollination can also result from dry soil during pollination and from hot, dry winds. Prolonged periods of rain reduce the amount of pollen shed from the tassels. Damage to the silks from corn earworms (see page 362), rootworm adults (see page 365), armyworms (see page 362), and grasshoppers (see page 364) may also result in incomplete ears.

Solution: To help ensure pollination, grow corn in blocks of at least three short rows rather than in one long row. Plant seeds 12 to 16 inches apart in rows 30 to 36 inches apart. Keep the soil moist, letting the surface dry slightly between waterings. Control corn insect pests. Corn can be hand-pollinated by shaking the tassels onto the silks.

Corn smut

Corn smut.

Problem: Puffballs or galls appear on the stalk, leaves, ears, or tassels. Galls are white and may be smooth, or they may be covered with a black, greasy, or powdery material. They range from pea-size to 5 inches in diameter.

Analysis: Corn smut is a plant disease caused by a fungus (*Ustilago maydis*) that attacks any aboveground part of corn. Germinating seedlings are not affected. Galls are full of black powdery spores that survive the winter in soil and corn debris. They are spread from plant to plant by wind and water. A gall forms only where a spore lands. The disease doesn't spread throughout the plant. Younger plants are more susceptible; most plants are infected when they are 1 to 3 feet tall. Corn is less susceptible after the ears have formed. Corn smut is most prevalent in warm temperatures (80° to 95°F) and when dry weather early in the season is followed by moderate rainfall as the corn matures. Smut doesn't reduce yield directly but saps the plant's energy, reducing ear development.

Solution: No chemical controls this disease. Cut off smuts before they break open and release the black powdery spores. Grow varieties tolerant of corn smut (see page 556). Clear all plant debris from the garden after harvest.

Flea beetles

Flea beetle (12× life size).

Problem: Leaves are riddled with shot holes about ⅛ inch in diameter. Tiny (1/16-inch) black beetles jump like fleas when disturbed. Leaves of seedlings and eventually whole plants may wilt and die.

Analysis: Flea beetles jump like fleas but are not related to fleas. Both adult and immature flea beetles feed on a wide variety of garden vegetables. Some flea beetles are responsible for spreading the bacterial wilts that kill corn plants. (For more information on these wilts, see page 422.) The immature beetle, a legless gray grub, injures plants by feeding on the roots and the lower surfaces of leaves. Adults chew holes in leaves. Flea beetles damage seedlings and young plants most. Leaves of seedlings riddled with holes dry out quickly and die. Adult beetles survive the winter in soil and garden debris. They emerge in early spring to feed on weeds until vegetables sprout or plants are set in the garden. Grubs hatch from eggs laid in the soil and feed for two or three weeks. After pupating in the soil, they emerge as adults to repeat the cycle. One to four generations occur per year. Adults may feed for up to two months.

Solution: Control flea beetles on corn with Ortho® Bug-B-Gon® Multi-Purpose Insect Killer Concentrate or Ortho® Bug-B-Gon® Multi-Purpose Garden Dust when the leaves first show damage. Watch new growth for evidence of further damage, and repeat the treatment at weekly intervals as needed. Remove all plant debris from the garden after harvest to eliminate habitat for overwintering adult beetles.

CORN *(continued)*

Corn rootworms	Grasshoppers	European corn borers

Rootworm damage. Inset: Adult (35× life size).

Grasshopper (½ life size).

European corn borer (2× life size).

Corn rootworms

Problem: Yellow, pale green, or brownish-red beetles with very long antennae crawl on the plants. Some may have black spots or stripes. The ears are malformed, with undeveloped or partially developed kernels; leaves may be chewed.

Analysis: Both the beetles and worms of the corn rootworm (*Diabrotica* species) attack corn. (For information on the larva, see page 365.) The adult beetles feed on the pollen, silks, and tassels, resulting in malformed ears and undeveloped kernels from improper or incomplete pollination. Some beetles may also feed on the leaves. Adults lay yellow-orange eggs in the soil at the base of the corn plants. Worms that hatch from eggs feed on the corn roots for several weeks, then pupate in the soil to emerge as beetles in late July and August. These pests are most common where corn has grown consecutively for two or more years. Late-planted corn and corn under drought stress are the most susceptible.

Solution: Treat with Ortho® Bug-B-Gon® Multi-Purpose Insect Killer Concentrate, Ortho® Bug-B-Gon® Multi-Purpose Insect Killer Ready-To-Use, or Ortho® Bug-B-Gon® Multi-Purpose Garden Dust when the beetles first appear on the plants. (For information on the rootworm larvae, see page 365.)

Grasshoppers

Problem: Large holes are chewed in margins of leaves. Greenish-yellow to brown jumping insects, ½ to 1½ inches long with long hind legs, infest corn plants. Kernels on ears may be chewed or undeveloped.

Analysis: Grasshoppers attack a wide variety of plants, including corn, grains, and grasses. They eat corn leaves and silk, migrating as they mature and as they deplete their food sources. They are most numerous in the rows adjacent to weedy areas. In the late summer, adult grasshoppers lay eggs in pods in the soil. The adults continue to feed until cold weather kills them. The eggs hatch the following spring. Grasshopper populations are most severe during hot, dry weather. The insects migrate into green gardens and yards as surrounding areas dry up in the summer heat. Periods of cool, wet weather help keep their numbers under control. The loss of a small amount of leaf tissue to a small population of grasshoppers doesn't reduce the corn yield significantly.

Solution: Apply Ortho® Bug-Geta® Plus Snail, Slug & Insect Killer or Ortho® Bug-B-Gon® Multi-Purpose Insect Killer Ready-To-Use as soon as grasshoppers appear. Repeat at weekly intervals if the plants become reinfested. Clean up weedy areas near the garden, and destroy plant debris after harvest.

European corn borers

Problem: Leaves are riddled with tiny shot holes. Tassels may be broken and ear stalks bent. Holes filled with sawdust are bored into main stalks. Pinkish caterpillars with dark brown heads are found inside the stalks or within the ears.

Analysis: The European corn borer (*Ostrinia nubilalis*) is one of the most destructive pests of corn. It also feeds on tomatoes, potatoes, and peppers. Early plantings are most affected, although late plantings can also be severely damaged in areas where more than one generation occurs in a season. The borer survives the winter in corn plants, pupates in the spring, and emerges as an adult moth in early summer. The moth, which is tan with dark wavy lines on the wings, lays clusters of eggs on undersides of the lower corn leaves. The borers that hatch from these eggs feed first in the whorl of leaves, riddling the leaves with shot holes. Later they bore into stalks and the bases of ears. This feeding results in broken stalks and tassels, poor ear development, and dropped ears. The borers continue feeding for a month, pupate, and emerge as moths to repeat the cycle.

Solution: At the first sign of borers or when 10 percent of the ears show silk, treat ear shoots and centers of leaf whorls with Ortho® Bug-B-Gon® Multi-Purpose Insect Killer Concentrate, Ortho® Bug-B-Gon® Multi-Purpose Garden Dust, or with the bacterial insecticide *Bacillus thuringiensis* (Bt). Repeat at weekly intervals until borers are no longer seen. Destroy the plants at the end of the season. Avoid early planting.

Common stalk borers

Stalk borer damage. Inset: Larva (life size).

Problem: Young plants are stunted and may die. Leaves are chewed and ragged. Stalks don't produce ears and may be distorted and curled. Dark brown to purple caterpillars, 1 inch long with white stripes and bands, may be found inside the stalks.

Analysis: The common stalk borer (*Papaipema nebris*) is a serious pest of corn east of the Rocky Mountains. These borers feed on a variety of plants but prefer corn. They spend the winter as eggs on grasses and weeds, especially on giant ragweed. After hatching in the early spring, the worms feed in the leaf whorls and then bore into the sides of the stalks and burrow upward. After pupating in the soil, the adult moths emerge in late summer and early fall. These grayish-brown moths lay eggs on grasses for the following year's generation. Only one generation occurs per year.

Solution: Once the damage is noticed, it is too late for any controls. Destroy all infested plants. Clean all plant debris from the garden after harvest. Eliminate nearby grasses and weeds, especially giant ragweed. If stalk borers are a serious problem, treat the plants the following year with an insecticide containing *carbaryl* in early to midspring.

Corn rootworm larvae

Corn rootworm larvae (life size).

Problem: Corn plants are dwarfed and yellow, and they fall over easily. The base of the stalks may have a crook-necked shape. The remaining roots have a stubby appearance. In the soil, white worms, from ½ to ¾ inch long with brown heads, are eating the roots.

Analysis: Several species of the corn rootworm larvae (*Diabrotica* species) attack corn. The worm feeds on corn roots, devouring small ones and tunneling into larger ones. Worms hatch from eggs in early summer to midsummer and migrate through the soil, feeding on corn roots. Feeding damage can be so serious to young plants that some gardens may need to be replanted. When populations are large, all the roots may be destroyed. Worms pupate in soil and emerge as greenish-yellow or light brown beetles, some with black spots or stripes, to repeat the cycle. One to three generations occur per year. Adult beetles feed on leaves and silks. Corn plants are affected most severely when they're growing in dry soil, where root regrowth is minimal. Rot diseases may enter damaged roots, injuring them further. Several parasitic insects and diseases help keep beetle populations under control most years.

Solution: Discard damaged plants and clean up weedy areas where insects lay eggs and spend the winter. Apply an insecticide containing *bifenthrin* to the soil at planting time. To control adults, dust the leaves with Ortho® Bug-B-Gon® Multi-Purpose Garden Dust or Ortho® Bug-B-Gon® Multi-Purpose Insect Killer Ready-To-Use.

Cutworms

Black cutworm (⅓ life size).

Problem: Young plants are chewed or cut off near the ground. Gray, brown, or black worms, 1½ to 2 inches long, may be found about 2 inches deep in the soil near the base of the damaged plants. The worms coil when disturbed.

Analysis: Several species of cutworms attack plants in the vegetable garden. The most likely pests of corn seedlings are surface-feeding cutworms. The two most common on corn are the black cutworm (*Agrotis ipsilon*) and the dingy cutworm (*Feltia ducens*). A single surface-feeding cutworm can sever the stems of many young plants in one night. Cutworms hide in the soil during the day and feed only at night. All adult cutworms are dark, night-flying moths with bands or stripes on their forewings. (For more information on cutworm control, see page 440.)

Solution: Apply Ortho® Bug-Geta® Plus Snail, Slug & Insect Killer around the base of undamaged plants when stem cutting is observed. Because cutworms are difficult to control, applications may need to be repeated at weekly intervals. Protect plants with Ortho® Bug-B-Gon® Multi-Purpose Insect Killer Ready-To-Use or Ortho® Bug-B-Gon® Multi-Purpose Garden Dust. Work Ortho® Bug-B-Gon® Multi-Purpose Insect Killer Granules into the soil before planting. Cultivate the soil thoroughly in late summer and fall to expose and destroy eggs, larvae, and pupae.

CORN (continued)

CUCURBITS

Seedcorn maggots

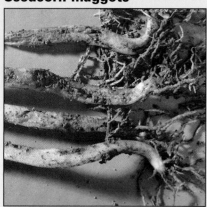

Seedcorn maggot damage.

Few fruit

Healthy plants with no fruit.

Bitterness

Bitter cucumbers.

Problem: Seeds don't sprout, or the seedlings are weak and don't develop leaves. Pearly-white worms, ¼ inch long, are feeding in the seeds. The seeds are hollow.

Analysis: Seedcorn maggots (*Hylemya platura*) feed on seeds and seedlings. They are attracted to large-seeded vegetables such as beans, corn, cucumbers, peas, and watermelon. The maggots are most numerous in cool periods in the spring and fall and in cold soil that is high in organic matter. The black, hairy adult flies are attracted to the organic matter and lay eggs in the soil. The maggots that hatch from these eggs burrow into the seeds and eat the inner tissue, leaving a hollow shell. Rot fungi may enter a damaged seed and further destroy it. After one to two weeks, the maggots burrow deep into the soil and pupate. The adult flies that emerge feed on nectar and plant juices before laying more eggs. Several generations occur per year. In warm-winter areas, these pests are active year-round. In cold-winter areas, they survive the winter as pupae and emerge as adults in the early spring.

Solution: Treat seed with an insecticide that contains *permethrin* or *imidacloprid*. Shake off the excess insecticide and plant the seeds 1 to 2 inches deep. To speed germination, plant seeds when the soil has reached a temperature of 55°F or higher. Since adult flies are attracted to organic matter, don't add manure to the soil in the spring when planting beans, corn, cucumbers, peas, or watermelon.

Problem: Little or no fruit is produced on melon, squash, or cucumber plants. Plants are healthy, with no signs of insect or disease problems.

Analysis: Little or no fruit is produced on cucurbit plants because of poor pollination. Members of this family produce two kinds of flowers: male and female. For fruit production, pollen produced on male flowers must be carried by insects, especially honeybees, to female flowers. The male flower, on the end of a long stalk, is the first to bloom. The female flower blooms shortly thereafter, not on a stalk but attached to a swelling resembling a miniature fruit. Once pollination is complete, the small swelling at the base of the female flower grows into a full-size edible fruit. Anything that interferes with pollination reduces fruit set and yield. Cold, rainy weather reduces bee activity. Improper use of insecticides may kill bees, which are primary pollinators. Sometimes the male flower is through blooming before the female opens.

Solution: Male and female flowers are produced all season, so fruit may develop in time. To aid pollination, transfer pollen from male to female flowers with a small brush. Spray insecticides in the late afternoon when bees are not flying.

Problem: Cucumbers taste bitter.

Analysis: Bitter cucumbers are usually produced on unhealthy plants late in the season. A bitter taste results from adverse growing conditions that stress the plant. These conditions include hot temperatures, dry soil, and low fertility. Plants with diseased foliage may also produce bitter fruit. Usually only the stem end is affected, but sometimes the entire fruit is bitter. Some older varieties produce fruit that is more bitter than newer varieties. Bitter fruit doesn't result from cross-pollination between cucumbers and squash or melons. Different varieties of cucumbers cross-pollinate with one another, but not with melons or squash.

Solution: As long as hot weather continues or the plant is stressed, it will continue to produce bitter fruit. This is especially true late in the season.

Misshapen and tough fruit

Misshapen and tough cucumbers.

Problem: Fruit is misshapen or tough, and contains large seeds. Plants may be wilted or growing slowly.

Analysis: Cucumbers are misshapen when the flowers are improperly pollinated. This can result from reduced bee activity or from hot temperatures that kill the pollen. Squash and cucumber plants growing in dry soil with low fertility frequently produce misshapen fruit. Overmature fruit is tough, with large seeds. They lack a sweet flavor.

Solution: Discard all misshapen fruit. Keep your plants healthy and productive by following the cultural and harvesting guidelines for cucurbits.

Blossom-end rot

Blossom-end rot on squash.

Problem: A water-soaked, sunken spot develops on the blossom end (opposite the stem end) of squash and watermelon. The spot enlarges and turns brown to black. Mold may grow on the spot.

Analysis: Blossom-end rot is a disorder of squash, watermelon, tomatoes, and peppers caused by a lack of calcium in the developing fruit. This lack of calcium is the result of slowed growth and damaged roots caused by any of the following factors:
1. Extreme fluctuations in soil moisture, either very wet or very dry.
2. Rapid plant growth early in the season, followed by extended dry weather.
3. Excessive rain that smothers root hairs.
4. Excess soil salts.
The first fruits of the season are the most severely affected. As the name implies, the disorder always starts at the blossom end, and it may enlarge to affect half of the fruit. Moldy growths on the rotted area are caused by fungi or bacteria.

Solution: Solutions below correspond to the numbered items in the analysis.
1. Maintain uniform soil moisture by mulching and by following the proper watering guidelines.
2. Avoid high-ammonia fertilizers and large quantities of fresh manure. Water regularly during dry periods.
3. Plant in well-drained soil.
4. Provide more water at each watering to help leach salts through the soil. Avoid using high-ammonia fertilizers and fresh manure.

Beet leafhoppers

Beet leafhopper damage to zucchini.

Problem: Spotted, pale green, winged insects up to ⅛ inch long hop and fly away quickly when a plant is touched. The leaves are stippled and may be curled, puckered, and brittle.

Analysis: The beet leafhopper (*Circulifer tenellus*) is a western insect found only as far east as Missouri and Illinois. It attacks all members of the cucurbit family and frequently infects them with the virus that causes curly top. Plants infected with curly top are stunted and brittle, and they sometimes die. The beet leafhopper feeds from early May through June. It sucks the sap and the virus from infected leaves and then injects the virus into healthy plants at its next feeding stop.

Solution: Treat infested plants with Ortho® Malathion Plus® Insect Spray Concentrate, Ortho® Bug-B-Gon® Multi-Purpose Insect Killer Ready-To-Use, or an insecticidal soap. Be sure to cover the lower surfaces of the leaves. Repeat the treatment at intervals of 7 to 10 days if the plants become reinfested. (For more information on disease-carrying insects, see page 449.)

CUCURBITS *(continued)*

Cucumber beetles	Squash bugs	Squash vine borers

Striped cucumber beetle (4× life size).

Squash bugs (⅓ life size).

Borer damage.

Cucumber beetles

Problem: Holes are chewed in the leaves, leafstalks, and stems by yellow-green beetles with black stripes or spots. Plants may wilt and die.

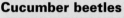

Analysis: Cucumber beetles, both striped (*Acalymma* species) and spotted (*Diabrotica* species), are common pests of cucumbers, melons, pumpkins, and squash. It is important to control these beetles, because they carry two serious diseases that damage and may kill cucurbits: mosaic (see page 370) and bacterial wilt (see page 369). The adults survive the winter in plant debris and weeds. They emerge in the early spring and feed on a variety of plants. As soon as cucurbits are planted in the garden, the beetles attack the leaves and stems and may destroy the plant. They lay their yellow-orange eggs in the soil at the base of the plants. The grubs that hatch from these eggs eat the roots and the stems below the soil line, causing the plant to be stunted or to wilt. The slender white grubs feed for several weeks, pupate in the soil, and emerge as adults to repeat the cycle. One generation occurs per year in northern parts of the United States and two or more in southern areas.

Solution: Treat plants with Ortho® Bug-B-Gon® Multi-Purpose Insect Killer Ready-To-Use or Ortho® Bug-B-Gon® Multi-Purpose Garden Dust at the first sign of the beetles. Repeat at weekly intervals as the plants become reinfested. Control early in the season helps prevent susceptible seedlings and plants from becoming infected with bacterial wilt and mosaic virus.

Squash bugs

Problem: Squash and pumpkin leaves wilt and may become black and brittle. Bright green to dark gray or brown, flat-backed bugs, about ½ inch long, cluster on the plants.

Analysis: Both the young (nymphs) and adult squash bugs (*Anasa tristis*) attack cucurbits and are most serious on squash and pumpkins. They injure and kill the plants by sucking sap from leaves and stems. Seedlings are especially susceptible. Dark brown adults, which are sometimes incorrectly called *stinkbugs*, emit a disagreeable odor when crushed. They lay brick-red egg clusters on leaves in the spring. Although only one generation occurs per year, all stages are found throughout the summer.

Solution: Squash bugs are elusive and difficult to control. Handpick the bugs and crush egg masses. Trap adults by laying boards on the ground and destroying bugs that congregate under them during the day. Treat the plants with Ortho® Bug-B-Gon® Multi-Purpose Insect Killer Concentrate or Ortho® Bug-B-Gon® Multi-Purpose Garden Dust when the bugs first appear. Repeat the treatment every seven days until the bugs are controlled. Plant varieties that are resistant to squash bugs.

Squash vine borers

Problem: Squash vines suddenly wilt. Holes in the stems are filled with a green or tan sawdustlike material that spills out of the holes. Fat, white worms, up to 1 inch long, are found in the affected vines when the stems are slit open lengthwise.

Analysis: The squash vine borer (*Melittia satyriniformis*) primarily attacks squash, pumpkins, and gourds and only rarely attacks cucumbers and melons. Hubbard squash is especially susceptible. The larvae damage and kill the plants by tunneling into the stems, preventing the rest of the vine from receiving the water and nutrients it needs. The metallic-green moth lays eggs on the vines in early summer. Egg laying occurs in April and May in the South and in June and July in the North. When the eggs hatch, the white larvae bore into the stems and feed for four to five weeks. They then crawl out of the stem and into the soil to pupate.

Solution: Applying insecticides after the borer is inside the stem is not effective. Instead, slit the affected stems with a knife and destroy the borer. If the plant has not died, cover the damaged portion of the stem with soil. Keep the soil moist to encourage new roots to grow. The vine may recover. Destroy plant residues in the fall. The following year, treat the plant with Ortho® Malathion Plus® Insect Spray Concentrate or Ortho® Bug-B-Gon® Multi-Purpose Insect Killer Ready-To-Use during the egg-laying period, at about the time the vines start to run. Adults can be kept from laying eggs on plants by protecting squash with row covers.

Bacterial wilt

Bacterial wilt. Inset: Bacterial ooze.

Problem: A few leaves wilt and dry and may be chewed. Wilted leaves often recover at night but then wilt again on sunny days and finally die. Fruit shrivels. To test for bacteria, cut a wilted stem near the base of the plant and squeeze out the sap, looking for a milky white substance. Touch a knife to the sap and withdraw it slowly. Look for a white ooze that strings out in a fine thread as you withdraw the knife.

Analysis: Bacterial wilt, a plant disease caused by a bacterium (*Erwinia tracheiphila*), is more prevalent on cucumbers and muskmelons than on pumpkins and squash. Watermelons are not affected. The bacteria are carried by striped or spotted cucumber beetles and are spread to plants when the beetles feed in early spring. (For more information on cucumber beetles, see page 368.) An entire plant may become infected within 15 days. The disease is most prevalent in cool weather in areas with moderate rainfall.

Solution: No chemicals control bacterial wilt. Remove and discard all infected plants promptly. Control cucumber beetles with Ortho® Bug-B-Gon® Multi-Purpose Insect Killer. Repeat the treatments every seven days if the plants become reinfected. (For more information on disease-carrying insects, see page 449.) Grow varieties resistant to this disease.

Alternaria leaf spot

Alternaria leaf spot on muskmelon.

Problem: Circular water-soaked spots up to ½ inch in diameter appear on the leaves. Dark concentric circles appear in the spots. Spots eventually enlarge into dry blotches, and the leaves drop. Center or older leaves are affected first, with the disease progressing to leaves at the tips of the vines.

Analysis: Alternaria leaf spot, a plant disease caused by a fungus (*Alternaria cucumerina*), is severe on muskmelons and also occurs on cucumbers and other cucurbits. The fungus defoliates the vines, reducing fruit yields. Weak plants, especially those bearing heavily and those suffering from poor fertility, are most susceptible to attack. Vigorous, healthy vines are rarely attacked. The disease is its worst in humid climates. Fungal spores survive the winter in plant debris left in the garden, and in and on seeds. They infect plants at temperatures from 60° to 90°F, causing the most damage above 80°F.

Solution: Treat plants at the first sign of the disease with a fungicide containing *chlorothalonil*. Repeat every 7 to 10 days. Keep the plants healthy with adequate water and fertilizer and the correct soil pH (6.0 to 7.0). (For more information on soil pH, see page 406.) Avoid overhead watering during dry periods. Clean up or turn under crop residues at the end of the growing season.

Anthracnose

Anthracnose on melon.

Problem: Yellow, water-soaked areas spot melon and cucumber leaves, enlarge rapidly, and turn brown and dry. These spots then drop out, leaving a ragged hole in the spot. On watermelon leaves, the spots turn black. Elongated dark spots with light centers may appear on the stems. Whole leaves and vines die. Large fruit is spotted with sunken, dark brown, circular spots. Pinkish ooze may emerge from the spots. Young fruit darkens, shrivels, and dies.

Analysis: Anthracnose is a plant disease caused by a fungus (*Colletotrichum lagenarium*) and is the most destructive disease of melons and cucumbers in the East. It rarely attacks squash and pumpkins. The disease affects all aboveground parts of the plant and is most prevalent in humid weather with frequent rain and a temperature range of 70° to 80°F. The spores overwinter in seeds and plant debris left in the garden. They are spread by splashing water, cucumber beetles, and contaminated tools.

Solution: Treat plants with Ortho® Garden Disease Control at the first appearance of the disease. Repeat every seven days or more frequently if warm, humid weather occurs. Grow varieties resistant to this disease (see page 557). Avoid overhead watering. Clean up crop residue or turn it under at the end of the season.

CUCURBITS *(continued)*

Angular leaf spot

Angular leaf spot.

Mosaic virus

Mosaic on squash. Inset: Mosaic on cucumbers.

Powdery mildew

Powdery mildew on cucumber.

Problem: Water-soaked, angular spots appear on the leaves. Tearlike droplets may ooze from the spots and dry into a white residue. Spots turn gray or tan, then drop out, leaving ragged holes. Fruit may be covered with cracked white spots.

Analysis: Angular leaf spot is a plant disease caused by a bacterium (*Pseudomonas lachrymans*) that attacks the leaves, stems, and fruits of cucurbits. The bacteria survive the winter on seed and plant debris not removed from the garden. The bacteria are spread from the soil to the plants by splashing rain, cucumber beetles, and hands and clothing and infect the leaves and stems when they are wet with dew, rain, or irrigation water. The disease is most active between 75° and 80°F.

Solution: Treat the plants with a pesticide containing basic copper sulfate at the first sign of the disease. Repeat every 7 to 10 days as long as the disease is a problem. To reduce the spread of the bacteria, don't work among wet plants. Avoid overhead watering by using drip or furrow irrigation. Clean all plant debris from the garden after harvest to reduce the amount of overwintering bacteria. Purchase seeds and plants from a reputable company. Grow varieties resistant to this disease.

Problem: Leaves are mottled yellow and green and are distorted, stunted, and curled. Cucumber fruits are mottled with dark green and pale green to white blotches and covered with warts. Sometimes the skin is smooth and completely white. Summer squash fruit may also be covered with warts.

Analysis: Mosaic virus is a plant disease caused by several viruses that attack cucumbers, muskmelons, and summer squash. Viruses overwinter in perennial plants and in weeds, including catnip, pokeweed, wild cucumber, motherwort, and milkweed. Viruses are spread from plant to plant by aphids and cucumber beetles and can infect plants at any time from seedling stage to maturity. Infection early in the season is more damaging. Affected fruit tastes bitter. Fruit that is more than half grown at the time of infection is immune to attack from the virus.

Solution: No chemical controls viruses. Remove and destroy all infected plants immediately. Control aphids and cucumber beetles with Ortho® Bug-B-Gon® Multi-Purpose Insect Killer Ready-To-Use or Ortho® Bug-B-Gon® Multi-Purpose Garden Dust. Repeat at intervals of 7 to 10 days if the plants become reinfested. (For more information on controlling disease-carrying insects, see page 449.) Remove weeds in and near the garden. Grow resistant cucumber varieties. No summer squash or muskmelon varieties are resistant.

Problem: A white powdery growth covers the upper surfaces of the leaves. Areas of the leaves and stems turn brown, wither, and die. Fruit may be covered with white powdery growth.

Analysis: Powdery mildew is a common plant disease caused by either of two fungi (*Erysiphe cichoracearum* or *Sphaerotheca fuliginea*) that thrive in both humid and dry weather. The powdery patches consist of fungal strands and spores. The spores are spread by the wind to healthy plants. The fungus depletes plant nutrients, causing yellowing and sometimes death of the leaf. A severe infection may kill the plant. Since these powdery mildews attack several different kinds of plants, the fungus from a diseased plant may infect other types of plants in the garden. (For a list of powdery mildews and the plants they attack, see page 537.) Under favorable conditions, powdery mildew can spread rapidly through a closely spaced planting.

Solution: Treat the plants with Ortho® Garden Disease Control at the first sign of the disease. Continue treatment at intervals of seven days as long as the disease is a problem. Grow varieties resistant to powdery mildew (see page 557).

EGGPLANT

Flea beetles

Flea beetle (2× life size).

Problem: Leaves are riddled with shot holes about ⅛ inch in diameter. Tiny (1/16-inch) black beetles jump like fleas when disturbed. Leaves of seedlings and eventually whole plants may wilt and die.

Analysis: Flea beetles jump like fleas but are not related to fleas. Both adult and immature flea beetles feed on a wide variety of garden vegetables, including eggplants. The immature beetle, a legless gray grub, injures plants by feeding on the roots and the lower surfaces of leaves. Adults chew holes in leaves. Flea beetles damage seedlings and young plants most. Leaves of seedlings riddled with holes dry out quickly and die. Adult beetles survive the winter in soil and garden debris. They emerge in early spring to feed on weeds until vegetable seeds sprout or plants are set in the garden. Grubs hatch from eggs laid in the soil and feed for two to three weeks. After pupating in the soil, they emerge as adults to repeat the cycle. One to four generations occur per year. Adults may feed for up to two months.

Solution: Control flea beetles on eggplants with Ortho® Bug-B-Gon® Multi-Purpose Insect Killer Concentrate, Ortho® Bug-B-Gon® Multi-Purpose Insect Killer Ready-To-Use, or an insecticidal soap when the leaves first show damage. Watch new growth for evidence of further damage, and repeat the treatment at weekly intervals as needed. Clean all plant debris from the garden after harvest to eliminate habitat for overwintering adult beetles.

Greenhouse whiteflies

Whiteflies (½ life size).

Problem: Tiny, white, winged insects feed on the undersides of leaves. Nonflying larvae covered with white waxy powder may also be present. When the plant is touched, insects flutter rapidly around it. Leaves may be mottled and yellow. The plant may grow poorly.

Analysis: The greenhouse whitefly (*Trialeurodes vaporariorum*) is a common insect pest of many garden and greenhouse plants. The four-winged adult lays eggs on the undersides of leaves. The larvae are the size of a pinhead, flat, oval-shaped, and semitransparent, with white waxy filaments radiating from the body. Both larval and adult forms suck sap from the leaves. The larvae are more damaging because they feed more heavily. Adults and larvae can't digest all the sugar in the plant sap, and they excrete the excess in a fluid called *honeydew*. A sooty mold fungus may develop on the honeydew, causing the eggplant leaves to appear black and dirty. In warm-winter areas, the insect can be active year-round, with eggs, larvae, and adults present at the same time. The whitefly is unable to live through freezing winters. Spring reinfestations come from migrating whiteflies and from infested greenhouse-grown plants placed in the garden.

Solution: Control whiteflies by spraying with Ortho® Bug-B-Gon® Multi-Purpose Insect Killer Concentrate, Ortho® Malathion Plus® Insect Spray Concentrate, or an insecticidal soap every 7 to 10 days as necessary. Spray the foliage thoroughly, being sure to cover both surfaces of the leaves.

Tomato hornworms and tobacco hornworms

Tomato hornworm (½ life size).

Problem: Fat green or brown worms, up to 5 inches long with wide white diagonal stripes, chew on the leaves. A red or black "horn" projects from the rear end. Black droppings are found on the leaves.

Analysis: Tomato hornworms (*Manduca quinquemaculata*) and tobacco hornworms (*M. sexta*) feed on the fruit and foliage of eggplants, peppers, and tomatoes. Although only a few worms may be present, each consumes large quantities of foliage and causes extensive damage. The large gray or brown adult moth with yellow-and-white markings emerges from hibernation in late spring and drinks nectar from petunias and other garden flowers. Worms hatch from eggs laid on the undersides of leaves and feed for three to four weeks. Then they crawl into the soil and pupate, later emerging as adults to repeat the cycle. One generation occurs per year in the North, but two to four cycles per year are common in the South.

Solution: Handpicking works well with hornworms. If handpicking is not practical, treat the plants with Ortho® Bug-B-Gon® Multi-Purpose Garden Dust, Ortho® Bug-B-Gon® Multi-Purpose Insect Killer Ready-To-Use, or the bacterial insecticide *Bacillus thuringiensis* (Bt).

GRAPES

Black rot

Black rot.

Grape berry moths

Damage caused by grape berry moth larvae.

Grape leaf skeletonizers

Grape leaf skeletonizers (life size).

Problem: Light brown spots surrounded by a dark brown line appear on the grapes. The grapes turn black, shrivel, and dry up like raisins. They remain attached to the stems. Reddish-brown spots appear on the leaves. Leaves may wilt. Sunken purple to black elongated lesions dot the canes, leaf stems, and tendrils.

Analysis: Black rot is caused by a fungus (*Guignardia bidwellii*). It is the most destructive disease that attacks grapes, often destroying all the fruit. The fungus spends the winter in infected dormant canes, tendrils, and mummified fruit. In warm, moist spring weather, spores infect new shoots, leaves, tendrils, and the developing fruit. The fruit is affected in all stages of development but most severely when it is one-half to two-thirds grown. Spores for future infections are produced on infected leaves, canes, and fruit. The severity of the disease depends on the amount of diseased material that survives the winter and on the spring and early summer weather.

Solution: Destroy all infected fruit and prune infected canes and tendrils. Once the fruit has begun to shrivel, fungicide sprays are ineffective. The following year, spray plants with a fungicide containing *captan*. Spray early in the growing season to keep spread of the disease to a minimum. Treat when new shoots are 6 to 10 inches long. Spray just before and immediately after bloom, and continue at intervals of 10 to 14 days until grapes are full-size. Treat more frequently if leaf symptoms develop or if the weather is wet.

Problem: Grapes are webbed together and to leaves. Dark green to purple worms, up to ⅜ inch long with dark brown heads, are inside the grapes. White cocoons cling to the leaves between flaps of leaf tissue.

Analysis: The grape berry moth (*Endopiza viteana*) is the most serious insect pest of grapes in the East. Worms damage green and ripening fruit by feeding on inner pulp and seeds. They web grapes together and to leaves with silken threads. Worms spend the winter as pupae on leaves and on the ground. Moths emerge in late spring and lay eggs on blossom stems and small fruit. Larvae that hatch from these eggs feed on the buds, blossoms, and fruit. After three or four weeks of feeding, they cut a small bit of leaf, fold it over, and make a cocoon inside, where they pupate. Within a few weeks, adult moths emerge to repeat the cycle, this time laying eggs on ripening fruit. This second generation feeds for three or four weeks, then pupates for the winter.

Solution: Destroy infested grapes. Avoid cultivation in late summer so that the cocoons remain on top of the ground to be cleaned up with fallen grape leaves at the end of the season. This will reduce the number of overwintering pupae. The following year, treat the plants immediately after bloom with Ortho® Bug-B-Gon® Multi-Purpose Insect Killer. Repeat the application 7 to 10 days later. To control the second generation, spray again in midsummer. For more precise spray timing, use pheromone traps. Spray when the first moth is captured. Hang traps again in July to monitor the second generation.

Problem: Yellow caterpillars with purple or black stripes feed in rows on the leaves. The caterpillars may be covered with black spines. They chew on the upper and lower surfaces of leaves, eventually eating everything but the leaf veins.

Analysis: Grape leaf skeletonizers (*Harrisina* species) frequently attack grapes in home gardens and abandoned vineyards. The caterpillars characteristically feed side by side in a row on the leaves. They feed heartily and may defoliate a vine in several days. The loss of leaf tissue slows the growth of the vine and fruit and reduces production. These pests survive the winter as pupae in cocoons on leaves and in debris on the ground. In late spring the metallic-green or smoky-black moths emerge and lay their eggs on the lower surfaces of leaves. The yellow caterpillars that hatch from those eggs feed on the leaves, usually chewing on the upper or lower surfaces; sometimes, as they mature, they eat all the tissue between the veins. Two to three generations occur per year, so damage continues from mid-May to August.

Solution: Treat infested plants with an insecticide containing *carbaryl* or with the bacterial insecticide *Bacillus thuringiensis* (Bt) as soon as caterpillars appear. Thoroughly spray both the upper and lower surfaces of leaves. Repeat the treatment if the plants become reinfested.

Grape leafhoppers

Grape leafhopper (15× life size).

Problem: Areas on the leaves are stippled and turn pale yellow, white, and then brown. Leaves may cup or roll under at the margins. Some of the leaves may fall. Black spots may be evident on berries. On the undersides of leaves are pale yellow or white, ⅛-inch, flying or jumping insects with red or yellow marks.

Analysis: Both the young and adult grape leafhoppers (*Erythroneura* species) suck the sap from grape leaves, causing white spots that later turn brown. This damage reduces normal vine growth, resulting in delayed maturity of fruit and poor vine growth the following year. The insects' black droppings may also mar the fruit, making it unappetizing. Leafhoppers survive the winter as adults in protected places. When new growth begins in spring, adults emerge and begin feeding. Adults lay eggs in leaves, causing blisterlike swellings. Two or three overlapping generations occur each year, so leafhoppers of all stages of maturity may be found feeding from the time of new growth in the spring until the leaves drop in the fall. Leafhoppers may also transmit plant diseases.

Solution: Treat infested grape vines with Ortho® Malathion Plus® Insect Spray Concentrate as soon as leafhoppers are noticed. For more precise spray timing, set out yellow sticky traps and spray when catches exceed five per day. Spray both the upper and lower surfaces of leaves. Repeat the treatment at intervals of 10 to 14 days if the plants become reinfested. Clean up and destroy plant debris after harvest to reduce the number of overwintering leafhoppers.

Eutypa dieback

Eutypa dieback.

Problem: Dark, irregular spots develop on the young leaves. These spots may drop out, leaving holes in the leaves. Elongated, sunken spots develop on the current season's canes. Shoot growth may be weak and stunted, and the leaves are small, yellowish, and cupped, with crinkled margins. Later in the season, the leaves may become scorched and tattered. Sunken lesions (cankers) may develop on the woody canes and trunk. Entire branches may die back.

Analysis: Eutypa dieback is a plant disease caused by a fungus (*Eutypa armeniacae*). The fungus survives the winter in trunk and branch cankers. Fungal spores that form in the cankers are carried by splashing water to pruning wounds, where they infect the plant. Infection causes the formation of cankers that reduce the flow of water and nutrients through the trunk and branches. The portion of the plant above the canker weakens and may eventually die.

Solution: Prune and destroy infected branches and canes. Late-winter pruning reduces the probability of infection. Make the pruning cut at least 6 inches below the canker and any discolored wood. If cankers are present on the trunk, remove and destroy the entire plant, cutting the trunk below the lowest canker but above the bud union. Maintain two to four suckers on the trunk. The plant will not produce grapes the current year but will yield a normal crop the following year.

Anthracnose

Anthracnose.

Problem: Circular, sunken spots with light gray centers and dark borders appear on shoots, fruit, tendrils, and leafstalks. The fruit remains firm. The leaves may curl downward, and the brown areas drop out.

Analysis: Anthracnose is a plant disease caused by a fungus (*Elsinoe ampelina*) that may do considerable damage a few years in a row and then disappear. It is often called *bird's-eye rot*. It is seldom severe on Concord or muscadine grape vines. The disease first attacks the new growth. The spots on the stems often merge, girdling the stem and killing the vine tips. Anthracnose is prevalent during wet periods in the spring and in poorly maintained vineyards. The fungus survives the winter on old lesions on the canes. Although this disease doesn't kill the grape vines, the infected fruit is often misshapen and unappetizing. Several years of attack from anthracnose sufficiently weaken vines to make them more susceptible to other disease or insect problems.

Solution: Discard infected fruit, and prune diseased canes. Sprays applied after spotting occurs are ineffective. The following spring, before the buds open, spray the vines with a fungicide containing lime sulfur. Treat plants with a fungicide containing *ferbam* when shoots are 1 to 2 inches long, when they are 6 to 10 inches long, just before bloom, just after blossoms fall, and twice more at intervals of two weeks. Spray canes and leaves thoroughly.

GRAPES (continued)

Botrytis bunch rot

Botrytis bunch rot.

Problem: In white grape varieties, the fruit is brown and shriveled. In purple grape varieties, the fruit has a reddish tinge. As the disease progresses, a fuzzy brown or grayish mold forms on the fruit. The leaves may have dull, green spots that rapidly turn brown.

Analysis: Botrytis bunch rot is a plant disease caused by a fungus (*Botrytis cinerea*) that is found on most dead plant tissue. Grapes that have been damaged by hail, wind, birds, or insects are susceptible to the disease. Fruit that has split from internal pressure or that was damaged by powdery mildew infection earlier in the season is particularly susceptible. The fungus needs moist conditions. Varieties that have tight clusters of grapes are more susceptible than varieties with loose clusters, because the fruit doesn't dry out as quickly after rain, dew, or watering.

Solution: Spray the plants with a fungicide containing *captan* at the first sign of the disease. Grape vines should be well trained and pruned to expose the clusters to the sun so that they will dry quickly. Also remove the leaves directly below and above clusters to improve the circulation of air around the fruit. Harvest the clusters as soon as they ripen. Protect the vines from birds. Try to avoid wetting the foliage and fruit when watering.

Birds

Bird damage.

Problem: Ripening grapes disappear. Some may be broken, with holes pecked in them. Birds are active in the area where the grapes are grown.

Analysis: Starlings, robins, finches, grackles, mockingbirds, and blackbirds like the sweetness of ripe grapes. Entire bunches of grapes may disappear within a few hours. Birds are hearty eaters and, if not discouraged from the vineyard, may devour all the grapes in a planting. The sugar level in grapes increases during ripening. As the grapes approach maturity, birds keep a watchful eye on their progress. Birds seem to be more attracted to wine grapes than to American bunch grapes. Early-ripening varieties and those with red or black fruit are most often attacked. When hungry, however, birds are not choosy.

Solution: To protect ripening grapes, loosely tie a paper bag or piece of cheesecloth over each cluster as it begins to ripen. Don't use plastic bags, because moisture will build inside. Pick grapes promptly as they ripen. Bird netting placed over the plants and secured at the base with rocks or logs also protects the bunches. Netting is available at garden centers.

Phylloxeras

Galls. Inset: Grape phylloxeras (3× life size).

Problem: Vines grow slowly and produce few clusters of grapes. Very often plants die. Tubers or swellings are found on the roots. Pea-shaped galls that are open on the underside may appear on the leaves.

Analysis: The grape phylloxera (*Phylloxera vitifoliae*) is a serious pest of grape vines in California and Europe. In the late 1800s, it killed almost one-third of the vineyards in France. It was discovered that American varieties were resistant and that European varieties could be grafted onto these rootstocks and then planted in phylloxera-infested soil. This orange to yellow aphidlike pest is native to the eastern United States, where cultivated grapes have become resistant to its attack and only wild grapes are affected. This pest occurs in two forms. One, found only in the East, attacks the leaves and roots. The other, found only on the West Coast, attacks only the roots. The grape phylloxera sucks the sap from the roots and injects saliva, causing galls to form. These galls interrupt the nutrient flow in the roots, and the vines become stunted and unproductive and often die. American varieties commonly grown in the East are resistant to this pest, but the European or wine varieties grown in California, Oregon, and Washington are very susceptible. French hybrid types are only mildly affected.

Solution: No chemical controls the grape phylloxera for home gardeners. Select resistant American grape varieties, or plant European varieties grafted onto phylloxera-resistant rootstocks.

Downy mildew

Downy mildew.

Problem: Small yellow spots appear on the upper surfaces of leaves. The lower surfaces are covered with a white, cottony growth. Older leaves are affected first. Leaves, shoots, and tendrils turn brown and brittle and are often distorted. Grapes may be covered with the white growth, or they may be shriveled and brown, yellow, or red.

Analysis: Downy mildew is a plant disease caused by a fungus (*Plasmopara viticola*) that attacks grape foliage and fruit from before bloom to the end of harvest. Downy mildew causes leaf defoliation and prevents proper ripening. When the disease is severe, entire grape clusters may be killed. Reduced vine vigor results in poor growth the following season. This disease is more prevalent in cool, moist weather and is always more serious in rainy growing seasons. The fungus survives the winter in diseased leaves on the ground.

Solution: Destroy severely infected leaves and fruit. At the first sign of the disease, spray the vines with a fungicide containing *captan*. Repeat every 10 days until 7 days before harvest. Remove and destroy plant debris at the end of the season to reduce the number of overwintering spores. The following year, spray immediately before bloom, just after petals fall, when the grapes are about the size of peas, and every 10 days thereafter until 7 days before harvest.

Bolting

Bibb lettuce bolting.

Problem: A seed stalk emerges from the center of the lettuce plant. The lettuce tastes bitter.

Analysis: Lettuce is a cool-weather crop and grows best from 55° to 60°F. When temperatures rise above 60°F for several days in a row, the plants form a flower stalk if they are mature enough. As the stalk grows, sugars and nutrients are withdrawn from the leaves for the growth of the stalk, making the leaves bitter and tough. The formation of a flower stalk in vegetables grown for their leaves is called *bolting*. Once bolting begins, it can't be stopped; cutting off the stalk doesn't help.

Solution: If harvested as soon as bolting begins, the lettuce may still be edible, but quality deteriorates rapidly as the stalk forms. In the future, plant lettuce so that it matures during cool weather, or grow varieties that are slow to bolt.

Cabbage loopers

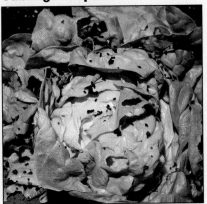

Cabbage looper damage and droppings.

Problem: Leaves have round or irregular holes. Green worms up to 1½ inches long, with light stripes down their backs, feed on the leaves or heads. Masses of green or brown pellets may be found between the leaves.

Analysis: Several worms attack lettuce; the most damaging is the cabbage looper worm (*Trichoplusia ni*). The looper attacks all varieties of lettuce, as well as members of the cabbage family. Adults lay eggs throughout the growing season. The brownish cabbage looper moth lays pale green eggs on the upper sides of leaves in the evening. The worms eat lettuce leaves and heads. Their greenish-brown excrement makes the plants unappetizing. Worms may be present from early spring until late fall. In the South, they may be present year-round. Worms spend the winter as pupae attached to a plant or nearby object.

Solution: Control cabbage loopers with Ortho® Bug-B-Gon® Multi-Purpose Garden Dust, Ortho® Malathion Plus® Insect Spray Concentrate, or the bacterial insecticide *Bacillus thuringiensis* (Bt). Bt is effective only while the caterpillars are small. Repeat treatments at weekly intervals if the plants become reinfested. Use row covers to keep adults from laying eggs on the plants. Clear all plant debris from the garden to reduce the number of overwintering pupae.

LETTUCE *(continued)*

Cutworms

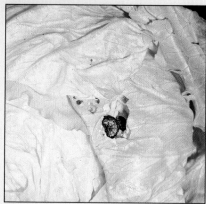

Cutworm (⅓ life size).

Problem: Young plants are chewed or cut off near the ground. Gray, brown, or black worms, 1½ to 2 inches long, may be found about 2 inches deep in the soil near the base of the damaged plants. The worms coil when disturbed.

Analysis: Several species of cutworms attack plants in the vegetable garden. The most likely pests of lettuce plants in the spring are surface-feeding cutworms. A single surface-feeding cutworm can sever the stems of many young plants in one night. Cutworms hide in the soil during the day and feed only at night. Adult cutworms are dark, night-flying moths with bands or stripes on their forewings. In southern parts of the United States, cutworms may also attack fall-planted lettuce. (For more information on cutworms, see page 440.)

Solution: Apply Ortho® Bug-Geta® Plus Snail, Slug & Insect Killer around the base of undamaged plants when cut stems are observed. Protect plants with Ortho® Bug-B-Gon® Multi-Purpose Garden Dust. Because cutworms are difficult to control, applications may need to be repeated at weekly intervals. Cultivate the soil thoroughly in late summer and fall to expose and destroy eggs, larvae, and pupae. Work Ortho® Bug-B-Gon® Multi-Purpose Insect Killer Granules into the soil before planting.

ONION

Seed stalk formation

Onion seed stalk.

Problem: A tall seed stalk emerges from the onion bulb. Purple or white flowers bloom on top of the stalk.

Analysis: Onions prefer cool temperatures in their early growth and warm temperatures near maturity. When temperatures fluctuate between cool and warm, the plants may become dormant. Dormancy then initiates seed stalk formation. Plants from larger bulbs or sets form seed stalks more readily than do those from smaller bulbs. As the seed stalk grows, sugars and nutrients are withdrawn from the bulb for the growth of the stalk, inhibiting bulb enlargement. Once the seed stalk begins growing, it can't be stopped; cutting off the stalk doesn't help.

Solution: Onion bulbs with seed stalks are edible but shouldn't be stored. Harvest and use bulbs as soon as possible. In the future, plant onions recommended for your area at the proper time. See page 558 for a list of regional onion recommendations and planting times.

Onion maggots

Onion maggot damage.

Problem: Plants grow slowly, turn yellow, wilt, and die. Bulbs may rot in storage. White legless maggots burrow inside the bulb.

Analysis: Onion maggot (*Hylemya antiqua*), a fly larva, is the most serious pest of onions. The larvae burrow into the onion bulb, causing the plant to wilt and die. Once the bulb is damaged by the maggot's feeding, it is susceptible to attack by bacterial soft rot. Early plantings are the most severely injured. When the onions are young and growing close together, the maggots move easily from one bulb to another, destroying several plants. Cool, wet weather promotes serious infestations. Maggots spend the winter as pupae in plant debris or in the soil. The brownish-gray fly emerges in the spring to lay clusters of white eggs at the base of plants. The maggots that hatch from these eggs burrow into the soil and bulbs. After feeding, they pupate in the soil and later emerge as flies to repeat the cycle. Two or three generations occur per year, the last one attacking onions shortly before they are harvested. When maggot-infested bulbs are placed in storage, maggots continue to feed and damage the bulbs.

Solution: Discard and destroy maggot-infested onions. Clean all debris from the garden at the end of the season to reduce the number of overwintering pupae. Keep flies from laying eggs by protecting onions with row covers. Rotate the onions to a new place in the garden, then put the covers in place at the time the onions are set out or seeded. Be sure they are tight to the ground, without spaces the flies can enter.

Fusarium basal rot

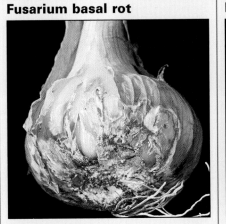

Fusarium basal rot.

Problem: Leaf tips wilt and die back. The neck of the bulb is soft. A white fungal growth may appear on the outside of the base of the bulb. The bulb is soft and brown inside. Bulbs may also be affected in storage.

Analysis: Fusarium basal rot is a plant disease caused by a soil-inhabiting fungus (*Fusarium* species) that attacks onions, shallots, garlic, leeks, and chives. It persists indefinitely in the soil. The disease is spread by contaminated bulbs, soil, and equipment. The fungus enters the bulb through wounds from maggots and old root scars and spreads up into the leaves, resulting in leaf yellowing and dieback. Bulbs approaching maturity are the most susceptible to attack. If infection occurs during or after harvest, the rot may not show until the bulbs are in storage. Fusarium basal rot is most serious when bulbs are stored in a moist area at temperatures above 70°F.

Solution: No chemical controls are available. Destroy infected plants and bulbs. Harvest healthy bulbs promptly at maturity. *Fusarium* can be removed from the soil only by fumigation or solarization techniques. Control onion maggots to reduce chances of infection. Store bulbs in a cool (35° to 40°F), dry place. Rotate the planting site if possible.

Pink root

Pink root.

Problem: Plants grow slowly, and their tops may be stunted. Roots turn light pink and shrivel, then a darker pink, and then die. Leaves may turn yellow or white and die.

Analysis: Pink root is a plant disease caused by a fungus (*Pyrenochaeta terrestris*) that attacks onions, garlic, shallots, leeks, and chives. It persists indefinitely in the soil and infects plants at all stages of growth. Mature and weakened bulbs are the most susceptible to attack. Plants infected early in their lives seldom produce large bulbs. Pink root thrives in warm weather (60° to 85°F).

Solution: No chemical control is available. Discard all infected plants. Pink root fungus can be removed from the soil only by fumigation and solarization techniques. Weak plants are the most susceptible to attack, so keep the plants healthy with adequate water and nutrition. Grow varieties that are resistant to the pink root fungus.

Onion thrips

Onion thrips damage.

Problem: White streaks or blotches appear on onion leaves. Tips may be distorted. Plants may wilt, wither, turn brown, and die. Bulbs may be distorted and small. Small pale green to white insects are observed at the base of the leaves.

Analysis: Onion thrips (*Thrips tabaci*) attack many vegetables, including onions, peas, and cabbages. Thrips are barely visible insects, less than $\frac{1}{25}$ inch long and dark brown to black. They reduce the quality and yield of onion bulbs by rasping holes in the leaves and sucking out the plant sap. This rasping causes the white streaks. Plants often die when thrips populations are high. Damage is most severe in the leaf sheath at the base of the plant. Thrips favor this protected area where the elements and pesticides have difficulty reaching them. Onion thrips survive winter in grass stems, plant debris, and bulbs in storage. Thrips are active throughout the growing season; in warm climates they are active all year.

Solution: Treat infested onion plants with Ortho® Bug-B-Gon® Multi-Purpose Garden Dust or Ortho® Malathion Plus® Insect Spray Concentrate at the first sign of thrips damage. Repeat at weekly intervals until there's no damage on the new growth.

PARSLEY

Parsleyworms

Parsleyworm (life size).

Problem: Parsley leaves are eaten. Green worms, 2 inches long with a black band on each body segment, feed on the leaves. When disturbed, these worms emit a sickly sweet odor, and two orange "horns" project behind the head.

Analysis: Parsleyworm (*Papilio polyxenes asterius*) is the larva of the black swallowtail butterfly. It is also called the *celeryworm*. As its names suggest, it feeds on parsley and celery, as well as on dill and parsnips. Although seldom a serious pest, these worms may strip plants of foliage. In the North, they spend the winter in tan cocoons hanging from host plants. The adult butterfly overwinters in the South. The butterfly has black wings spotted with yellow, orange, and blue dots and a wingspan of 3 to 4 inches. The worms that hatch from eggs laid on the leaves feed on the foliage for several weeks, pupate in suspended cocoons, and emerge as adults to repeat the cycle. Two to four generations occur per year.

Solution: Handpick as the worms appear. They are seldom serious enough to warrant sprays. If they are numerous, however, spray with an insecticide containing *malathion* or with the bacterial insecticide *Bacillus thuringiensis* (Bt). Bt is effective only while the worms are small. Protect plants with row covers.

PEAS

Hot weather

Hot weather damage.

Problem: Pea plants stop producing pods. Leaves turn yellow and then brown, and die.

Analysis: The garden pea is a cool-season vegetable. It grows best with daytime temperatures below 80°F and nighttime temperatures below 65°F. When temperatures are hotter than this, the plants stop producing and gradually die. In the South, garden peas grow best in the fall, winter, and spring. In the North, grow them as spring and fall crops.

Solution: Plant peas early enough in the season that they mature in cool weather. Grow varieties that tolerate hot weather.

Powdery mildew

Powdery mildew.

Problem: A white powdery coating develops first on the upper surfaces of the lower leaves. Stems, pods, and other leaves may then become infected. Leaves may turn yellow and be malformed. Pods may be distorted, with dark streaks or spots.

Analysis: Powdery mildew is a common plant disease caused by a fungus (*Erysiphe polygoni*) that thrives in both humid and dry weather. The powdery coating consists of fungal strands and spores. The spores are spread by the wind to healthy plants. The fungus depletes plant nutrients, causing yellowing and sometimes death of the leaf. A severe infection reduces pea yield considerably and may kill the plant. Fall crops are most susceptible to serious damage; spring crops are infected late in the season. Since this powdery mildew forms on many vegetables, the fungus from a diseased plant may infect other plants in the garden. Under conditions favorable to the fungus, powdery mildew can spread rapidly through a planting.

Solution: Treat plants with garden sulfur. Repeat at intervals of 7 to 10 days as needed. This fungicide doesn't cure infected leaves, but it does protect healthy leaves from infection.

Pea aphids

Pea aphids (2× life size).

Problem: Plants turn yellow and wilt. Pods may not be completely filled with peas. Clustered on the leaves—especially the young, tender ones—are tiny, soft-bodied, light to deep green insects with red eyes. Leaves may be covered with a sticky material or black mold.

Analysis: Several species of aphids attack peas, but the most common and damaging is the pea aphid (*Acyrthosiphon pisum*). Aphids generally do little damage in small numbers. They are extremely prolific, however, and populations can build to damaging numbers during the growing season. Damage occurs when the aphids suck the sap from the pea leaves, stems, blossoms, and pods. This feeding results in stunted plants and fewer and smaller pods that may be only partially filled with peas. The aphids are unable to digest all the sugar in the plant sap, and they excrete the excess in a fluid called *honeydew*. The honeydew often drops onto the leaves below. Ants feed on this sticky substance and are often present where there is an aphid infestation. Some aphids also transmit viruses. Infected pea plants and pods are distorted, and plants sometimes die. (For more information on viral diseases, see page 423.)

Solution: Spray infested plants with an insecticidal soap or Ortho® Malathion Plus® Insect Spray Concentrate as soon as the aphids appear. Repeat the spray if the plants become reinfested. Use yellow sticky traps (see page 414) to monitor aphid arrival.

Pea weevils

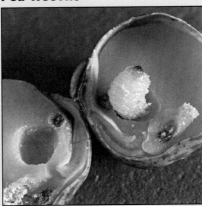

Pea weevil (5× life size).

Problem: Peas have small round holes. The peas are partially or completely hollow. Fat, white legless grubs with brown heads may be found inside. When the pea plants are blooming, 1/5-inch-long dark brown beetles with light markings may be seen crawling or flying around the plants.

Analysis: The pea weevil (*Bruchus pisorum*) is an insect pest that attacks all varieties of edible peas. Weevils emerge from hibernation as peas are beginning to bloom. The adults feed on pea nectar and pollen. This feeding doesn't harm the plant. Adults can migrate up to three miles in search of food. They lay orange to white eggs on the developing pods. The white grubs that hatch from these eggs eat through the pod and into the pea. They continue feeding for six to eight weeks, then pupate inside the hollow pea. The adult weevils emerge in one to three weeks and the following year hibernate to repeat the cycle. Only one generation occurs per year. Infested peas are inedible.

Solution: Insecticides must be applied to kill the adults before they lay eggs. Once the eggs are laid on the pods, it is too late to prevent injury. Treat the plants with Ortho® Bug-B-Gon® Multi-Purpose Insect Killer Ready-To-Use soon after the first blooms appear and before pods start to form. Additional sprays may be needed to control migrating weevils. Destroy infested peas.

Blossom drop

Blossom drop.

Problem: Little or no fruit develops. Fruit that does develop may have rough skin or be misshapen. Plants remain vigorous, with lush foliage.

Analysis: Pepper blossoms are sensitive to temperature fluctuations during pollination. Normal pollination and fruit set don't occur when night temperatures fall below 58°F and daytime temperatures rise above 85°F. Under these temperature conditions, the blossoms fall off, often before pollination. If pollination has occurred and the fruit has begun to set but isn't completely fertilized at the time the blossoms drop, rough and misshapen fruit result.

Solution: Blossom drop causes only a delay in fruit production. When the temperatures are less extreme, a full crop of fruit will set, and the plants will be productive the rest of the season. Discard rough or misshapen fruit; it won't develop fully. Irrigation for cooling during hot periods can help to reduce losses.

PEPPERS *(continued)*

Sunscald

Sunscald.

Blossom-end rot

Blossom-end rot.

Corn earworms

Corn earworm larva (life size).

Problem: An area on the pepper fruit becomes soft, wrinkled, and light in color. Later, this area dries and becomes slightly sunken, with a white, paperlike appearance. An entire side of the fruit may be affected. Black mold may grow in the affected areas.

Analysis: Pepper fruit exposed directly to sunlight may be burned by the heat of the sun. The fruit may be exposed to the sun as a result of leaf diseases that cause leaf drop. Early fruit on small plants without enough protective foliage may be burned. Also, some varieties don't produce enough foliage to shade the fruit. Rot organisms sometimes enter fruit through the damaged area, making the fruit unappetizing or inedible. Sunscalded fruit without these molds is still edible if the discolored tissue is removed prior to consumption.

Solution: Control leaf diseases that may defoliate the plants. Fertilize to keep plants healthy with lush foliage. Select pepper varieties that form a protective canopy of leaves.

Problem: A round, sunken, water-soaked spot develops on the bottom of fruit. The spot enlarges, turns brown or black, and feels leathery. Mold may grow on the surface.

Analysis: Blossom-end rot occurs on peppers, squash, tomatoes, and watermelons from a lack of calcium in the developing fruit. This lack of nutrient results from slowed growth and damaged roots caused by the following factors:
1. Extreme fluctuations in soil moisture, either very wet or very dry.
2. Rapid plant growth early in the season, followed by extended dry periods.
3. Excessive rains that smother root hairs.
4. Excess soil salts.
5. Cultivation too close to the plant. The first fruits are the most severely affected. The disorder always starts at the blossom end (the end farthest from the stem), and it may enlarge to affect up to half of the fruit. Moldy growths on the rotted area are from fungi or bacteria that frequently invade the damaged tissue. The unrotted part of the fruit is edible.

Solution: Blossom-end rot is difficult to eliminate, but it can be controlled by following these guidelines.
1. Water regularly.
2. Avoid overuse of high-nitrogen fertilizers and large quantities of fresh manure.
3. Plant in well-drained soil.
4. Provide more water at each watering to help leach salts through the soil.
5. Don't cultivate deeper than 1 inch within 1 foot of the plant.

Problem: Holes are chewed in the fruit. Inside the fruit are striped yellow, green, or brown worms from ½ to 2 inches long. Worms may also be feeding on the leaves.

Analysis: Corn earworm (*Helicoverpa zea*), also known as the *tomato fruitworm* or *cotton bollworm*, attacks many vegetables and flowers. Worms feed on foliage and chew holes in the fruit, making it inedible. The worm is the larva of a light gray-brown moth. In spring, the moth lays yellow eggs on the leaves and stems. The worms that hatch from these eggs feed on the new leaves. When they are about ½ inch long, the worms move to the fruit and bore inside. After feeding for two to four weeks, they drop to the ground and pupate 2 to 6 inches deep in the soil. After several weeks they emerge as adults to repeat the cycle. Several generations occur per year. In the South, where earworms survive the winter, early and late plantings suffer the most damage. Adult moths migrate into northern areas, where they don't survive the winter.

Solution: Once worms are inside the fruit, sprays are ineffective. Pick and destroy infested fruit. Clear plant debris after harvest to reduce the number of overwintering adults. The following year, treat plants with Ortho® Bug-B-Gon® Multi-Purpose Insect Killer Concentrate or Ortho® Bug-B-Gon® Multi-Purpose Garden Dust when worms are feeding on foliage or when fruit is 1 to 2 inches in diameter. Repeat treatment every 10 to 14 days if the plants become reinfested. Protect peppers with row covers to keep adults from laying eggs on the plants.

European corn borers

European corn borers (½ life size).

Problem: Pink or tan worms, up to 1 inch long with dark brown heads and two rows of brown dots, feed in the seed cavity of the pepper. The fruit is decayed inside.

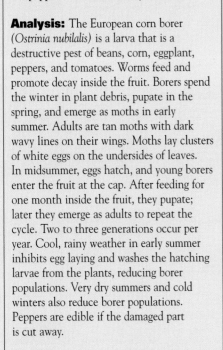

Analysis: The European corn borer (*Ostrinia nubilalis*) is a larva that is a destructive pest of beans, corn, eggplant, peppers, and tomatoes. Worms feed and promote decay inside the fruit. Borers spend the winter in plant debris, pupate in the spring, and emerge as moths in early summer. Adults are tan moths with dark wavy lines on their wings. Moths lay clusters of white eggs on the undersides of leaves. In midsummer, eggs hatch, and young borers enter the fruit at the cap. After feeding for one month inside the fruit, they pupate; later they emerge as adults to repeat the cycle. Two to three generations occur per year. Cool, rainy weather in early summer inhibits egg laying and washes the hatching larvae from the plants, reducing borer populations. Very dry summers and cold winters also reduce borer populations. Peppers are edible if the damaged part is cut away.

Solution: Remove infested fruit. Treat the plants with Ortho® Bug-B-Gon® Multi-Purpose Garden Dust when fruit is 1 to 1½ inches in diameter. Repeat twice more, seven days apart. For more precise timing, monitor adult moths with pheromone traps. Spray when numbers trapped exceed 25 in five days. Keep adults from laying eggs by protecting plants with row covers. Clear all debris from the garden after harvest to reduce overwintering habitat for larvae.

Tomato hornworms or tobacco hornworms

Tomato hornworm (⅓ life size).

Problem: Fat green or brown worms, up to 5 inches long with white diagonal side stripes, chew on the leaves. A red or black "horn" projects from the rear end. Black droppings are found on the leaves and the soil surface beneath the damaged foliage.

Analysis: Tomato hornworms (*Manduca quinquemaculata*) and tobacco hornworms (*M. sexta*) feed on the fruit and foliage of eggplant, peppers, and tomatoes. Although only a few worms may be present, each worm consumes large quantities of foliage and causes extensive damage. The large gray or brown moth with yellow-and-white markings emerges from hibernation in late spring and drinks nectar from petunias and other garden flowers. The worms hatch from eggs laid on the undersides of leaves and feed for three to four weeks. Then they crawl into the soil and pupate; later they emerge as moths to repeat the cycle. One generation occurs per year in northern parts of the United States; two to four in southern areas.

Solution: Hornworms can be handpicked effectively. If that is not practical, treat the plants with Ortho® Bug-B-Gon® Multi-Purpose Insect Killer Concentrate, Ortho® Bug-B-Gon® Multi-Purpose Garden Dust, or the bacterial insecticide *Bacillus thuringiensis* (Bt).

Green tubers

Green potato tuber.

Problem: Potato tubers turn green while growing in the ground or in storage.

Analysis: Potato tubers turn green when exposed to light. Tubers are modified stems and produce chlorophyll when they receive light. Tubers may be exposed to light when the plants aren't properly hilled or when they are stored in a light place. Excessively green tubers are bitter and inedible. If slightly green, the tubers are still edible if the green tissue is peeled.

Solution: Discard tubers, or peel them before eating. Protect tubers in the ground from sunlight by mounding loose soil around the plants to completely cover developing tubers when the plants are 5 to 6 inches tall. Replace the soil if it is washed away by rain or irrigation water. Store potatoes in a dark, humid place at temperatures between 35° and 45°F.

POTATOES (continued)

Common scab

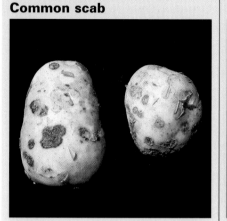

Scab.

Wireworms

Damaged potato. Inset: Wireworms (life size).

Ring rot

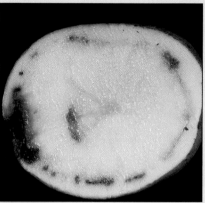

Bacterial ring rot.

Problem: Brown corky scabs or pits occur on potato tubers. Spots enlarge and merge, sometimes covering most of the tuber. Leaves and stems aren't affected.

Analysis: Common scab is a plant disease caused by a bacterium (*Streptomyces scabies*) that persists in the soil for long periods of time. Besides potatoes, scab also infects beets, carrots, and parsnips. Scab affects only the tubers, not the leaves or stems. The bacteria spend the winter in the soil and in infected tubers left in the garden. Infection occurs through wounds and through the breathing pores in the tuber skins when the tubers are young and growing rapidly. Scab is most severe in warm (75° to 85°F), dry soil with a pH of 5.7 to 8.0. The severity of scab often increases when the pH is raised with lime or wood ashes. Scab is not a problem in acidic soil with a pH of 5.5 or less. Poorly fertilized soil also encourages scab. Bacteria withstand temperature and moisture extremes. Because they pass intact through the digestive tracts of animals, bacteria can be present in manure and can spread the disease. Tubers infected with scab are edible, but much may be wasted as the blemishes are removed.

Solution: No chemical control is available. Test your soil pH, and if necessary correct it to 5.0 to 5.5 with aluminum sulfate. Keep the soil moist for one to two months after tuber set. Avoid alkaline materials such as wood ashes and lime. Do not use manure on potatoes. Plant potatoes in the same area only once every three to four years. Use certified seed pieces that are resistant to scab.

Problem: Plants are stunted and grow slowly. Tunnels wind through stems, roots, and in and on the surfaces of tubers. Shiny, hard, jointed, yellow to reddish-brown worms up to 2 inches long are found in the tuber and in the soil.

Analysis: Wireworms feed on beans, beets, carrots, corn, lettuce, peas, potatoes, and many other plants. Wireworms feed entirely on underground plant parts, devouring seed potatoes, underground stems, tubers, and roots. Infestations are most extensive in soil where grass or grassy weeds have grown during the preceding two years. Adults, about ½ inch long, are brown, gray, or blackish beetles with a body that tapers at both ends. They are known as *click beetles* because they make a clicking sound when turning upright. Wireworm larvae feed for two to six years before maturing into adult beetles, so all sizes and ages of wireworms may be found in the soil at the same time. Undamaged portions of the tubers are edible.

Solution: Wireworms may be difficult to control. Avoid planting potatoes in areas that were covered by clover, grass, pasture, or grassy weeds. Don't store damaged tubers.

Problem: Shoot tips are stunted, forming rosettes. Leaves turn yellow, then brown between the veins. Leaf margins curl upward, and stems may wilt. Stems cut at the ground level exude a creamy-white odorless ooze. Only a few stems on a plant may show symptoms. Tubers may be cracked and, when cut near the stem end, reveal a yellow to light brown ring of crumbly decay.

Analysis: Ring rot is a plant disease caused by a bacterium (*Clavibacter michiganense sepedonicus*) that attacks both tubers and stems. Infected tubers are inedible. Tuber decay may be evident at harvest, or it may not develop until after several months in storage. Other rot organisms frequently invade and completely rot the tubers. Ring rot bacteria enter plants through wounds, especially those caused by cutting seed pieces before planting. They don't spread from plant to plant in the field. The bacteria survive between seasons in infected tubers and storage containers.

Solution: Discard all infected tubers and plants at the first sign of the disease. Don't plant potatoes in the location where ring rot occurred for the following two years. Use only certified potato seed pieces for plants. Plant whole tubers, or if you cut seed pieces, disinfect the knife between cuts. Disinfect storage containers with a chlorine bleach solution. Wash storage bags in hot water.

Hollow heart

Hollow heart.

Problem: Tubers develop irregular white to brown cavities and are generally very large.

Analysis: Discolored cavities result when potato tubers develop too rapidly during the growing season. This rapid growth may be encouraged by excessive soil fertility and moisture. Plants spaced too far apart may also develop hollow heart. These cavities occur mainly on very large or oversized tubers. Tubers are still edible if the discolored cavities are cut away. The cavities don't decay unless bacterial or fungal rot organisms enter the tubers from the outside.

Solution: Follow proper planting and maintenance guidelines for potatoes.

Colorado potato beetles

Colorado potato beetle (½ life size).
Inset: Larva (life size).

Problem: Yellow-orange beetles with black stripes, about ⅜ inch long, are eating the leaves. Fat, red, humpback larvae with two rows of black dots may also be present.

Analysis: The Colorado potato beetle (*Leptinotarsa decemlineata*) is an insect that often devastates eggplant, pepper, potato, and tomato plantings. Both adults and larvae damage plants by devouring leaves and stems. Small plants are most severely damaged. The beetle was native to the Rocky Mountains and spread eastward in the late 1800s. Now it is found in all states except California and Nevada. In some areas of the country, the beetle population may reach epidemic proportions. The beetles lay their yellow-orange eggs on the undersides of leaves as the first potato leaves emerge from the ground in the spring. The larvae that hatch from these eggs feed for two to three weeks, pupate in the soil, and emerge one to two weeks later as beetles, which lay more eggs. One generation is completed in a month. One to three generations occur per year.

Solution: Potato beetles are developing resistance to insecticides, so control may be difficult. Treat with Ortho® Bug-B-Gon® Multi-Purpose Insect Killer Concentrate or Ortho® Bug-B-Gon® Multi-Purpose Garden Dust. Treat when the insects are first noticed, and repeat every seven days for as long as infestation continues. Floating row covers will also keep beetles away from potatoes. Varieties resistant to potato beetles are being developed.

Flea beetles

Flea beetle damage.

Problem: Leaves are riddled with shot holes about ⅛ inch in diameter. Tiny (1/16-inch) black beetles jump like fleas when disturbed. Leaves of seedlings and eventually whole plants may wilt and die.

Analysis: Flea beetles jump like fleas but are not related to fleas. Both adult and immature flea beetles feed on a wide variety of garden vegetables, including potatoes. The immature beetle, a legless gray grub, injures plants by feeding on the roots and lower surfaces of leaves. Adults chew holes in leaves. Flea beetles damage young plants most. The beetles survive the winter in soil and garden debris. They emerge in early spring to feed on weeds until potatoes sprout. Grubs hatch from eggs laid in the soil and feed for two to three weeks, damaging the tubers. After pupating in the soil, they emerge as beetles to repeat the cycle. One to four generations occur per year. Adults may feed for up to two months.

Solution: Control flea beetles on potatoes with Ortho® Bug-B-Gon® Multi-Purpose Insect Killer Ready-To-Use or Ortho® Bug-B-Gon® Multi-Purpose Garden Dust when the leaves first show damage. Spray carefully at the base of stems. Watch new growth for evidence of further damage, and repeat the treatment at weekly intervals as needed. Clean all plant debris from the garden after harvesting to eliminate overwintering habitat for adult beetles.

POTATOES *(continued)*

Potato leafhoppers	Early blight	Late blight

Potato leafhoppers

Potato leafhopper damage. Inset: Potato leafhopper (4× life size).

Problem: Spotted, pale green insects up to ⅛ inch long hop, run sideways, or fly away quickly when a plant is touched. The leaves are stippled or appear scorched, with a green midrib and brown edges curled under.

Analysis: The potato leafhopper (*Empoasca fabae*) is an insect pest that feeds on beans, potatoes, and some fruit and ornamental trees. It sucks plant sap from the undersides of leaves, causing leaf stippling. This leafhopper is responsible for hopperburn and the browning and curling of the edges of potato leaves. The leafhopper injects toxic saliva into the nutrient-conducting tissue, interrupting the flow of water and food within the plant. Potato yields may be reduced drastically by hopperburn. Leafhoppers at all stages of maturity are active during the growing season. Both early and late varieties of potatoes are affected. Leafhoppers live year-round in the Gulf states and migrate northward on warm spring winds, so even areas that have winters so cold that the eggs can't survive may be infested.

Solution: Spray infested plants with Ortho® Malathion Plus® Insect Spray Concentrate or Ortho® Bug-B-Gon® Multi-Purpose Insect Killer. Be sure to cover the lower surfaces of leaves. Repeat the spray as often as necessary to keep the insects under control. Allow at least 10 days between applications. Eradicate nearby weeds that may harbor leafhopper eggs.

Early blight

Early blight.

Problem: Irregular dark brown to black spots, ⅛ to ½ inch in diameter, appear on the lower leaves. Concentric rings develop in the spots, which may enlarge, causing the leaves to die and fall off. Tubers may develop dark, sunken spots, often with a purplish raised border.

Analysis: Early blight is caused by a fungus (*Alternaria solani*) that attacks both vines and tubers. The same fungus causes early blight of tomatoes. It is most severe toward the end of the growing season when the vines approach maturity and the tubers are formed. Many leaves may be killed. The potato yield is reduced, but the plant seldom dies. Tubers are frequently infected through wounds inflicted during harvest. Early blight is favored by alternating periods of wet and dry weather and by temperatures from 65° to 85°F. The fungal spores spend winter in plant debris left in the garden. Infected tubers are inedible.

Solution: Spray plants with Ortho® Garden Disease Control as soon as leaf spotting occurs. Repeat the treatment every 7 to 10 days until leaves die back naturally. Clean up and destroy plant debris after harvest. Don't store infected tubers. Avoid overhead watering by using drip or furrow irrigation. Maintain adequate fertility. Use seed potatoes certified by states' Department of Agriculture to be free of diseases.

Late blight

Late blight.

Problem: Brownish, water-soaked spots appear on the leaves. Spots enlarge rapidly, turn black, and kill leaves, and then leafstalks and main stems. In moist weather, a gray mildew grows on the lower surfaces of leaves. Tuber skins are infected in the ground or in storage with brownish-purple spots that become a wet or dry rot.

Analysis: Late blight is caused by a fungus (*Phytophthora infestans*) that seriously injures potatoes and tomatoes. The disease was responsible for the potato famine in Ireland and is the most damaging disease of potatoes worldwide. Tubers are infected when spores wash off the leaves, into the soil. The fungus spreads rapidly, killing an entire planting in a few days. Infected tubers are inedible. Tubers can be infected during harvest and rot in storage. A soft rot often invades the damaged tubers. Foggy, misty weather and heavy dew provide enough moisture for infection. Spores survive the winter in infected tubers in the garden or on plant debris in the compost pile.

Solution: If late blight is an annual problem in your area, spray plants with Ortho® Garden Disease Control when the plants are 6 inches tall. Continue at intervals of 7 to 10 days until the plants naturally turn yellow and die. Avoid overhead watering; use drip or furrow irrigation. Wait at least a week after plants die naturally before digging the tubers. This allows time for the spores to die. Handle the tubers gently to avoid wounding them. Clean up and destroy plant debris. Plant certified disease-free seed pieces.

Bacterial soft rot

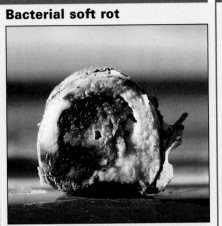

Bacterial soft rot.

Problem: A slimy, smelly decay develops on potatoes in the ground or in storage. Small, soft, circular, discolored spots may occur on tubers.

Analysis: Bacterial soft rot is a plant disease caused by a bacterium (*Erwinia carotovora* var. *carotovora*) that attacks carrots, parsnips, peppers, potatoes, tomatoes, and many other vegetables. The bacteria rarely attack potato leaves but do severely infect the tubers, rendering them inedible. The tubers may be infected either in the ground or in storage. Bacteria can rot tubers completely in 3 to 10 days. Tubers bruised during harvest are likely to become infected and rot in storage. The bacteria that cause soft rot are usually present in the soil, but they infect only potatoes that have been wounded or are growing in wet soil.

Solution: No chemical controls are available. Keep potato plants healthy, and control insect and disease problems. Wait until vines turn yellow and die before digging potatoes. Dig carefully to avoid bruising them. If you want to store the tubers, cure them in the dark for one week at 70°F to heal any bruises and to condition them. Then store them in a humid area between 35° and 45°F. Consume blemished tubers immediately, or destroy them. The following year, plant in well-drained soil, on hills or mounds to encourage good drainage.

Flea beetles

Flea beetle damage.

Problem: Leaves are riddled with shot holes ⅛ inch in diameter. Tiny (¹⁄₁₆-inch) black beetles jump like fleas when disturbed.

Analysis: Flea beetles jump like fleas but aren't related to fleas. Both adult and immature flea beetles feed on a wide variety of garden vegetables. The immature beetle, a legless gray grub, injures plants by feeding on the roots and the lower surfaces of leaves. Adults chew holes in leaves. Beetles survive the winter in soil and garden debris. They emerge in early spring to feed on weeds until vegetable seeds sprout. Grubs hatch from eggs laid in the soil and feed for two to three weeks. After pupating in the soil, they emerge as adults to repeat the cycle. One to four generations occur per year. Beetles may feed for up to two months.

Solution: Control flea beetles on radishes with Ortho® Bug-B-Gon® Multi-Purpose Garden Dust or Ortho® Bug-B-Gon® Multi-Purpose Insect Killer when the plants first emerge through the soil or at the first sign of damage. Watch new growth for evidence of further damage, and repeat the treatment at weekly intervals as needed. Clean up and destroy plant debris to eliminate overwintering habitat for adult beetles.

Root maggots

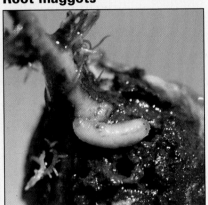

Root maggot (life size).

Problem: Young plants wilt in the heat of the day. They may later turn yellow and die. Soft-bodied, yellow-white maggots about ¼ inch long are feeding in the roots. The roots are honeycombed with slimy channels and scarred by brown grooves. Decay often accompanies feeding damage. Infested roots may break off when plants are pulled up. Younger plants are more severely affected than older ones.

Analysis: Root maggots (*Delia* species) are most numerous during cool, wet weather in spring, early summer, and fall. Early maggots attack the roots, stems, and seeds of broccoli, cabbage, radishes, and turnips in the spring and early summer. Later insects damage fall crops. The adult is a gray fly slightly smaller than a housefly, with black stripes and bristles down its back. It lays eggs on stems and nearby soil. The maggots hatch in two to five days and tunnel into radish roots, making them inedible.

Solution: Once the growing plant wilts and turns yellow, nothing can be done. Next spring, keep adult flies from laying eggs on plants by protecting radishes with row covers. Put them in place when you plant the radishes, and make sure they are tight to the ground all around.

RADISHES (continued)

Poor root development

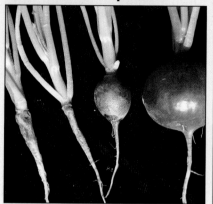

Poorly developed roots.

Problem: Radish plants are all leaves with no plump roots. Roots that do develop are thin.

Analysis: Radishes fail to develop bulbous roots for any of several reasons.
1. Seedlings that aren't thinned and that grow too close together compete with one another for water and nutrients and never fully develop plump roots.
2. Plants may be growing at temperatures above 85°F. Radishes prefer the cooler temperatures of the spring and fall.
3. Plants may not be receiving enough sunlight to make the food they need to develop plump roots.
4. High-nitrogen fertilizers or soils high in organic material promote bushy top growth at the expense of root development.

Solution: The numbered solutions below correspond to the numbered items in the analysis. Follow these guidelines for good radish root development.
1. Plant seeds in rows 9 to 18 inches apart. When seedlings are 1 to 2 inches tall, thin to ½ to 1 inch apart.
2. Plant radish seeds in the spring and fall so that they mature when temperatures are lower than 85°F.
3. Plant radishes in an area that receives at least six hours of sunlight per day.
4. Use a balanced fertilizer and moderate amounts of organic matter.

RHUBARB

Crown rot

Crown rot.

Problem: Leaves wilt. Brown, sunken, water-soaked spots appear on the base of the leafstalks. Leaves yellow, and stalks collapse and die. The plant eventually dies.

Analysis: Crown rot, a plant disease also called *stem rot, foot rot,* or *root rot,* is caused by a fungus (*Phytophthora* species) that lives in the soil. It thrives in waterlogged, heavy soils and invades the crown and base of the stems. The stems and eventually the roots rot, resulting in wilting and finally the death of the plant. The fungus is most active in warm (60° to 75°F), moist soils in the late spring and early summer. The spores are spread to healthy plants in running or splashing water or by contaminated soil or infected plants brought into the garden.

Solution: Remove and destroy dying leaves and plants. Apply a drench of fungicide containing *captan* or basic copper sulfate to the crown or base of the plant and to the surrounding soil. When replanting, purchase disease-free plants from a reputable company, and plant in well-drained soil. (For information on drainage, see page 406.) Avoid overwatering.

Small stalks

Small stalks.

Problem: Rhubarb stalks are thin and small.

Analysis: Rhubarb stalks may be small for several reasons.
1. End of the harvest season: Rhubarb stalks are produced from food stored in the roots. Toward the end of the harvest season, the food is used up and the stalks become smaller and smaller.
2. Lack of fertilization: Rhubarb plants are heavy feeders, requiring large amounts of fertilizer to encourage healthy growth so that an adequate food supply will be stored for the following year's harvest.
3. Young plants: Rhubarb stalks are small until the plants establish their roots and are able to store an adequate amount of food. This may take two years after planting.
4. Overcrowding: Rhubarb plants are vigorous growers with deep roots and may compete with one another if not divided every five to seven years.
5. Crown rot: This disease reduces plant vigor and kills the roots. (For more information, see left.)
6. Poor soil drainage: Rhubarb does not tolerate wet soil. The roots rot and the plants eventually die.

Solution: To improve your harvest, follow proper growing and harvesting guidelines for rhubarb. Control crown rot and improve the soil drainage. (For information on drainage, see page 406.)

Seed stalk formation

Seed stalks.

Problem: Large yellow seed stalks grow from the center of rhubarb plants.

Analysis: Rhubarb forms seed stalks when the days become long and warm enough to trigger this response in the plant, usually about the time the harvest is ending. Sugars manufactured in the leaves move to the rapidly growing seed stalk at the expense of the roots. As a result, less sugar is stored in the roots to produce the following year's crop, so the yield is reduced.

Solution: Cut off seed stalks as soon as they begin to grow.

Bolting

Bolting spinach.

Problem: Flower stalks grow from the center of spinach plants in spring and summer.

Analysis: Spinach makes seed stalks (bolts) in late spring and summer as temperatures rise and the length of the day increases. Some varieties bolt more easily than others. Once the flower stalk forms, leaves may become bitter, and edible foliage is no longer produced. Fall-planted spinach seldom bolts.

Solution: Plant spinach as soon as possible in the late winter or early spring. Plant approximately four to six weeks before the last spring frost and no later than six to eight weeks before the daytime temperatures remain above 75°F. Use bolt-resistant or long-standing varieties for spring planting. For a summer crop, plant New Zealand spinach, a spinach substitute that thrives in summer heat. Although it's not a true spinach, the taste is similar.

Leafminers

Leafminers (life size).

Problem: Irregular tan blotches, blisters, or tunnels appear in the leaves. The tan areas peel apart like facial tissue. Tiny black specks and white or yellow maggots are found inside the tunnels.

Analysis: Leafminers belong to a family of leafmining flies. The tiny black or yellow fly lays her white eggs on the undersides of leaves. The maggots that hatch from these eggs bore into the leaf and tunnel between the upper and lower surfaces, feeding on the inner tissue. The tunnels and blotches are called *mines*. The black specks inside are the maggots' droppings. Several overlapping generations occur during the growing season, so larvae are present continuously from spring until fall. Infested leaves aren't edible.

Solution: Control leafminers on spinach with Ortho® Malathion Plus® Insect Spray Concentrate when the white egg clusters are first seen under the leaves. Repeat twice more at weekly intervals to control succeeding generations. Once leafminers enter the leaves, sprays are ineffective. Spraying after the mines first appear will control only those leafminers that attack after the application. Clean all plant debris from the garden after harvest to reduce overwintering habitat for the pupae. Flies can be kept from laying eggs on the plants by protecting spinach with row covers.

STRAWBERRIES

Snails and slugs

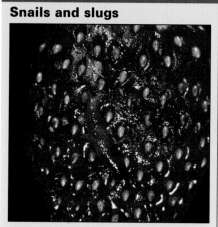

Slug (3x life size).

Problem: Stems and leaves may be sheared and eaten. Holes are often found in ripening berries, especially under the berry cap. Silvery trails wind around on the plants and soil nearby. Snails or slugs may be seen moving around or feeding on the plants, especially at night. Inspect the garden for them at night by flashlight.

Analysis: Snails and slugs are mollusks and are related to clams, oysters, and other shellfish. They feed on a wide variety of garden plants. Like other mollusks, snails and slugs need to be moist all the time. For this reason, they avoid direct sun and dry places, and they hide during the day in damp places, such as under flowerpots or in thick ground covers. They emerge at night or on cloudy days to feed. Snails and slugs are similar except that the snail has a hard shell into which it withdraws when disturbed. Slugs lay white eggs encased in a slimy mass in protected places. Snails bury their eggs in the soil, also in a slimy mass. The young look like miniature versions of their parents.

Solution: Apply Ortho® Bug-Geta® Snail & Slug Killer in areas you wish to protect. Also apply in areas where snails or slugs might be hiding, such as in dense ground covers, weedy areas, compost piles, or flowerpot-storage areas. Before applying, wet down the areas to be treated to encourage snail and slug activity that night. Repeat the application every two weeks for as long as snails and slugs are active. Don't apply directly to leaves.

Meadow spittlebugs

Meadow spittlebug (½ life size).

Problem: White, frothy masses of bubbles, ½ inch long, appear on leaves, stems, and flowers. Hidden in this froth is a small, smooth, tan to green insect.

Analysis: Meadow spittlebugs (*Philaenus spumarius*) are related to leafhoppers (see page 448). Both the adults and the nymphs damage plants by sucking the sap from the leaves and stems. When populations are high, this results in stunted plants and smaller berries. Leafstalks and leaf blades may be distorted and killed. Small numbers of spittlebugs do little damage to strawberry plants. Spittlebug eggs overwinter in plant parts and debris, hatching in the early spring. The nymphs produce the frothy spittle, which protects them from the sun and from other insects. The nymphs remain in the spittle until they emerge in early summer as hopping, tan to black adults. The adults feed until frost, laying eggs in late summer. Spittlebugs are most numerous in areas with high humidity. One generation occurs per year.

Solution: Once the nymphs are protected inside the froth, insecticides are ineffective. Hose off the frothy masses with a strong stream of water. If spittlebugs are numerous and plants are suffering, control the adults in the summer and fall with Ortho® Malathion Plus® Insect Spray Concentrate. Clean up and destroy plant debris at the end of the season to reduce the number of overwintering eggs.

Botrytis blight

Botrytis blight.

Problem: Light tan spots appear on berries. Some berries are soft, mushy, and rotting. A fluffy, gray mold may cover rotting berries.

Analysis: Gray mold is caused by a fungus (*Botrytis cinerea*). It is the most damaging rot of strawberries, attacking both flowers and berries, and greatly reduces the amount of edible fruit. The flowers are infected when in bloom and may not produce berries. Berries are attacked at all stages of development. They are infected directly when a healthy berry touches a decaying one, the ground, or a dead leaf. The fuzzy gray mold on the berries is composed of fungal strands and millions of microscopic spores. The fungus is most active in cool, humid weather and is spread by splashing water, tools, hands, or infected fruit. Crowded plantings, rain, and overhead watering enhance its spread.

Solution: Destroy infected fruit. To reduce spread to uncontaminated fruit, treat with Ortho® Home Orchard Spray or with a fungicide containing *captan* at the first sign of disease. Continue treating every 8 to 10 days. Pick berries as they ripen. Avoid overhead watering by using soaker or drip hoses. Mulch with straw, pine needles, or other material to keep fruit off the ground. To help prevent infection the following year, remove and destroy plant debris in the fall and treat the plants when in bloom. Repeat treatment every 8 to 10 days. When setting out new plants, provide enough space between plants to allow for good air circulation and rapid drying after wetting periods from rain and watering.

Strawberry bud weevils

Weevil-damaged buds. Inset: Adult (5x life size).

Problem: Flower buds droop, turn brown and dry, and hang from the plant or fall to the ground. Small holes appear in sides of the buds. Dark reddish-brown, ⅛-inch weevils with curved snouts crawl on the plants.

Analysis: Strawberry bud weevils (*Anthonomus signatus*), insect pests of blueberries, dewberries, strawberries, and wild blackberries, are also known as clippers because they clip the flower bud stems, causing buds to droop and fall to the ground. By destroying the flower buds, they reduce the berry crop. Adult weevils survive the winter in debris in and near the garden. In the spring, they puncture holes in the sides of unopened flower buds and lay an egg in each hole. Then the adult cuts a notch in the flower stem ⅛ to ¼ inch below the bud. The buds droop for a few days and then fall to the ground. Within a week the eggs hatch and fat, white grubs feed on the pollen inside the buds. After feeding for about four weeks, the grubs pupate and emerge as adults in early to midsummer. These adults feed on blackberry and dewberry pollen, hibernate, and emerge in the spring to repeat the cycle. One generation occurs per year.

Solution: Treat plants with an insecticide containing *carbaryl* when drooping buds first appear. Repeat through the closed-bud stage as long as damage occurs. Clean up and destroy plant debris in and near the garden at the end of the season to reduce habitat for overwintering weevils.

Spider mites

Spider mite webbing.

Problem: Leaves are stippled, yellowing, and dirty. Leaves may dry out and drop. There may be webbing between leaves or on the lower surfaces of leaves. Few berries are produced. To determine if a plant is infested with mites, examine the bottoms of the leaves with a hand lens. Or hold a sheet of white paper underneath an affected leaf and tap the leaf sharply. Minute specks the size of pepper grains will drop to the paper and begin to crawl. These pests are easily seen against the white background.

Analysis: Spider mites, related to spiders, are major pests of many garden and greenhouse plants. Spider mites are larger than cyclamen mites, which also attack strawberries. Spider mites attack the older leaves, while cyclamen mites attack the younger leaves. Spider mites cause damage by sucking sap from the undersides of leaves. As a result of their feeding, chlorophyll disappears, producing the stippled appearance. Spider mite webbing traps cast-off skins and debris, making the plant dirty. Mites are active throughout the growing season but thrive in hot, dry weather (70°F and higher). By midsummer, they have built to tremendous numbers.

Solution: Treat infested strawberry plants with Ortho® Malathion Plus® Insect Spray Concentrate when damage first appears. Repeat the treatment at intervals of 7 to 10 days until harvest or until damage no longer occurs. Be sure the pesticide contacts the undersides of the leaves where the mites live.

Viruses

Viral disease.

Problem: Strawberry leaves are crinkled, yellow, or distorted. Plants may be stunted, have cupped leaves, or grow in a tight rosette. Small, dull fruit or no fruit is produced. Plants produce few runners.

Analysis: Two types of viruses attack strawberries: killer viruses and latent viruses. Killer viruses have obvious symptoms and kill individual mature plants and those attached to the ends of runners. Latent viruses show few or no symptoms. A single latent virus may merely reduce the number of runners and fruit produced. Plants infected with more than one kind of latent virus, however, are weakened and frequently attacked and killed by other diseases. Viruses are transmitted by aphids and nematodes through runners from the mature plants to the new plants. Aphids are most numerous in cool spring and fall weather.

Solution: Remove and destroy all infected plants. If aphids are present, control them with Ortho® Malathion Plus® Insect Spray Concentrate. (For more information on disease-carrying insects, see page 449.) When replanting, buy certified plants from a reputable company. Certified plants are grown under special isolated conditions and are essentially virus-free. Or choose virus-tolerant varieties. (For information on disease-resistant strawberries, see page 560.)

STRAWBERRIES *(continued)*

Leaf spots

Fungal leaf spot.

Problem: Purple spots, ⅛ to ¼ inch in diameter with tan to white centers, occur on young leaves, fruit stalks, runners, and berry caps. Small, dark, sunken spots may appear on unripe berries.

Analysis: Several fungi cause leaf spots on strawberries. One of the most prevalent (*Mycosphaerella fragariae*) may kill many leaves. The most serious injury, however, occurs from spotting on fruit stalks and caps, which reduces the size of the fruit or kills the entire cluster. Berries attacked before they ripen never fully ripen and are inedible. Infected caps are discolored and killed, making the fruit unappetizing. New plants growing at the ends of infected runners are weak and produce poorly. Leaf spot is most prevalent in cool, damp weather in spring and fall, but it occurs through the summer in moist weather.

Solution: Fungicides aren't practical for this disease. Clean up and destroy plant debris during and at the end of the season. Grow disease-free strawberry transplants of resistant varieties. (For information on disease-resistant varieties, see page 560.)

Anthracnose

Infected crown.

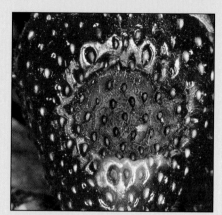

Infected fruit.

Problem: Dark brown, sunken lesions appear on leaf stems and runners. Leaves and new runner plants may die. Mature plants may wilt and die. The crowns of dead plants are a distinctive reddish brown color on the inside, sometimes in streaks. Cut the crown with a knife to expose this tissue. Sunken spots that remain dry and firm may develop on fruit.

Analysis: Anthracnose is a plant disease caused by one of several related fungi (*Colletotrichum* species) that can attack the stems, crowns, or fruit of strawberry plants. The disease usually begins with stem infections, either of the leaf stems or of runners. If the infection girdles the stem, the leaf or runner plant beyond the girdled point dies. Sometimes leaf stems are only partially infected, causing the leaf to droop but remain green. If the fungus invades the crown of the plant, it kills the plant, causing a characteristic darkening of the crown tissue. It may invade fruit in any stage of development, including after harvest. Anthracnose thrives in wet weather and moderate temperatures (from 60° to 85°F). Spores are extruded during these conditions in a pinkish mass. Spores are spread by splashing water to adjacent plants. Strawberry plants are usually infected in the nursery. Once infected plants are placed in the home garden, the disease can travel quickly to other plants. The fungus lives for only a limited period of time in the soil and rarely survives from one year to the next.

Solution: Remove and destroy plants that wilt suddenly. Remove and destroy infected fruit. To protect the rest of the fruit, spray weekly with a fungicide containing *captan*. Purchase only strawberry plants that are free of symptoms. Inspect the stems and runners carefully for lesions. Irrigate with drip or furrow systems, avoiding overhead watering. Although some strawberry varieties are resistant, resistance varies with the species of fungus and even with the location. Ask your county extension agent to recommend resistant varieties for your area. (For information on disease-resistant varieties, see page 560.)

Verticillium wilt

Verticillium wilt.

Problem: Outer leaves wilt and turn dark brown along the margins and between the veins. Younger leaves are stunted but tend to remain green without wilting until the plant eventually dies. Few new leaves are formed. Plants are flattened, and few berries are produced. Brown spots or streaking may appear on leafstalks and runners and in crown tissue.

Analysis: Verticillium wilt disease affects many ornamental plants. It is caused by soil-inhabiting fungi (*Verticillium dahliae* and *V. albo-atrum*) that persist indefinitely on plant debris or in the soil. The disease is spread by contaminated seeds, plants, soil, and equipment. The fungus enters the plant through the roots and spreads up into the crown and leaves through water-conducting vessels that become discolored and plugged. This plugging cuts off the flow of water and nutrients to the leaves, causing leaf yellowing and wilting. Affected plants may or may not recover and yield fruit the following year. Sometimes the disease appears in mature plants but not in the rooted runner plants. (For more information on verticillium wilt, see page 420.)

Solution: No chemical control is available. It is best to destroy infected plants. *Verticillium* can be removed from the soil only by fumigation or solarization (see page 322). Plant varieties that are tolerant of verticillium wilt. (For information on disease-resistant varieties, see page 560.)

Red stele

Red stele.

Problem: Plants grow poorly, are stunted, and frequently wilt. The young leaves turn bluish-green. Older leaves turn yellow and red. In the spring, the center of the root is discolored reddish brown instead of the normal pale yellow color. Black tips or patches may appear on feeder roots. Few berries are produced, and the plants eventually die.

Analysis: Red stele is a root rot disease of strawberries caused by a fungus (*Phytophthora fragariae*) that persists in the soil for many years. It is one of the most damaging diseases that attacks strawberries. The small feeder roots are attacked first. Then the fungus invades the center core—the stele—of the roots. The reddish-brown discoloration is most visible in the spring. In the summer the rotted roots are replaced by new healthy roots, so the symptoms often disappear. Red stele is most destructive in cool spring and fall weather in poorly drained, heavy soil or low spots in the garden. Plants growing in well-drained soil are less frequently attacked.

Solution: No chemical control is available for red stele. The most practical method of control is to plant tolerant varieties in well-drained soil. (For information on disease-resistant varieties, see page 560.)

Growth cracks

Growth cracks.

Problem: Sweet potato roots are cracked when harvested. Some may also develop cracks in storage.

Analysis: Cracking of sweet potato roots results from prolonged dry periods followed by excessive moisture. In some varieties, it seems to be an inherited characteristic. The cracks heal over by harvest time, with no loss in eating or storage quality. Roots may also crack in storage if the temperature and humidity fluctuate greatly.

Solution: Avoid excessively wet or dry soil. For best yields, sweet potatoes require adequate water throughout the growing season, especially when they are older and growing vigorously in hot weather in sandy soil. Store roots in a cool place (55° to 60°F) with high humidity (85 percent).

SWEET POTATOES *(continued)*

Black rot

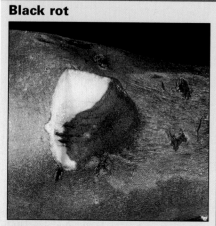

Black rot.

Problem: Black spots appear on roots in the ground and in storage. Tiny black specks appear in the centers of blackened areas. Black lesions develop on stems at the soil line. Leaves are yellow and dwarfed.

Analysis: Black rot is a plant disease caused by a fungus (*Ceratocystis fimbriata*) that attacks all underground parts of sweet potato plants. The fungus usually enters plants through injuries, but healthy tissue may also be attacked under favorable conditions. Infections can occur between 50° and 93°F during periods of high soil moisture. Infected roots may not show symptoms when dug up, but once in storage they develop sunken, blackened areas. Both discolored tissue and the surrounding healthy tissue taste bitter. The fungus survives in sweet potato debris, manure, and weeds for at least two years. Spores are spread by wind, water, and insects, including the sweet potato weevil.

Solution: This disease can be prevented but not cured. Remove and discard all infected plants and roots. Disinfect the storage area thoroughly. Purchase certified slips or seed potatoes. Don't plant sweet potatoes in the same soil more than once in three years.

Scurf

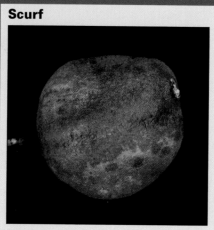

Scurf.

Problem: Dark brown to black spots or irregular patches stain sweet potato skins. Discoloration affects only the skin, not the flesh of the root.

Analysis: Scurf, also called *soil stain*, is caused by a fungus (*Monilochaetes infuscans*) that attacks only the roots. Although the appearance of scurf is unappetizing, the roots are still edible and the flavor is not affected. Scurf is most severe in wet, poorly drained soils and in soils high in organic matter. The disease develops most rapidly at temperatures around 75°F. Spots may enlarge in storage. Injury to the root surface allows rapid water loss, causing roots to shrivel. The fungus is introduced into the garden on infected roots and slips. Spores survive for one or two years in infected vines rotting in the garden and in humus or partially decomposed organic matter.

Solution: Eat scurf-infected roots promptly, without storing them. Use sweet potatoes free of the disease as seed. Cut transplants at least ½ inch above the soil line. Avoid planting in heavy soil. Improve soil drainage as instructed on page 406. If you add organic matter, till it into the soil a year before planting so it will decompose. Plant sweet potatoes in the same place only once in every three or four years.

Sweet potato flea beetles

Flea beetle larva (½ life size).

Problem: Yellow irregular channels are chewed in the surfaces of leaves. Tiny (¹⁄₁₆- inch), black beetles jump like fleas when disturbed. Shallow, dark tunnels scar the root.

Analysis: Sweet potato flea beetles (*Chaetocnema confinis*) jump like fleas but are not related to them. Both adults and immature flea beetles feed on sweet potatoes. The immature beetle, a legless white grub, feeds on the surface tissue of the roots, making them unattractive, although they are still edible. Adults chew channels in leaves. Flea beetles are present nearly everywhere sweet potatoes are grown. They are most damaging to young plants. The beetles survive the winter in soil and garden debris. They emerge in early spring to feed on weeds until slips are set in the garden. Grubs hatch from eggs laid in the soil and feed for two or three weeks. After pupating in the soil, they emerge as beetles to repeat the cycle. Several generations occur per year.

Solution: Control flea beetles on sweet potatoes with Ortho® Malathion Plus® Insect Spray Concentrate when the leaves first show damage. Watch new growth for evidence of further damage, and repeat the treatment at weekly intervals as needed. Clean all plant debris from the garden after harvest to eliminate overwintering spots for the adult beetles.

TOMATOES

Poor fruit set

Poor fruit set.

Problem: Little or no fruit develops. Plants are healthy and may even be extremely vigorous.

Analysis: Poor fruit set occurs on tomatoes for any of several reasons.

1. Extreme temperatures: Blossoms drop off without setting fruit when night temperatures fall below 55°F or day temperatures rise above 90°F for extended periods of time.

2. Dry soil: Blossoms dry and fall when the plants don't receive enough water.

3. Shading: Few blossoms are produced when the plants receive less than six hours of sunlight per day.

4. Excessive nitrogen: High levels of nitrogen in the soil promote leaf growth at the expense of blossom and fruit formation.

Solution: Solutions below correspond to the numbered items in the analysis.

1. Plant early-, mid-, and late-season varieties at the appropriate time of year. (For a list of these varieties, see page 559.)

2. Water tomatoes regularly, never allowing the soil to dry out. Mulch with straw, black plastic, or other material to reduce the need for watering.

3. Plant tomatoes in an area that receives at least six hours of sunlight per day. If your yard is shady, grow tomatoes in containers on your porch or patio.

4. Correct the nitrogen imbalance with superphosphate or 0–10–10 fertilizer.

Sunscald

Sunscald on tomatoes.

Problem: On green and ripening fruit, a light patch develops on the side facing the sun. This area blisters and finally becomes slightly sunken and grayish white, with a paperlike surface. A black mold may grow on the affected area, causing the fruit to rot.

Analysis: Sunscald occurs on tomatoes when they are exposed to the direct rays of the sun during hot weather. It is most common on green fruit, but ripening fruit is also susceptible. It is most prevalent on varieties with sparse foliage and on staked plants that have lost their foliage because of leaf diseases, such as early blight, late blight, or fusarium wilt (see page 397), verticillium wilt (see page 398), leaf roll (see page 399), or septoria leaf spot (see page 399). Fruit on plants that have been pruned to hasten ripening is also subject to sunscald. Tomatoes are still edible if the sunscalded area is removed. Rot fungi frequently invade the damaged tissue, resulting in moldy, inedible fruit.

Solution: Cover exposed fruit with straw or other light material to protect it from the sun's rays. Don't prune leaves to hasten ripening. Control leaf diseases. Grow wilt-resistant varieties.

Growth cracks

Growth cracks.

Problem: Circular or radial cracks mar the stem end (top) of ripening fruit. Cracks may extend deep into the fruit, causing rots to develop.

Analysis: Tomatoes crack when certain environmental conditions encourage rapid growth during ripening. The rapid growth is frequently promoted by a drought followed by heavy rain or watering. Tomatoes are most susceptible to cracking after they have reached full size and begin to change color. Some varieties crack more easily than others. Cracking is more severe in hot weather. Some cracks may be deep, allowing decay organisms to enter the fruit and rot it. Shallow cracks frequently heal over but may rupture if the fruit is roughly handled when picked. Cracked tomatoes are still edible.

Solution: Maintain even soil moisture with regular watering. Grow crack-tolerant varieties of tomatoes.

TOMATOES (continued)

Blossom-end rot

Blossom-end rot.

Problem: A round, sunken, water-soaked spot develops on the bottom of fruit. The spot enlarges, turns brown to black, and feels leathery. Mold may grow on the surface.

Analysis: Blossom-end rot occurs on tomatoes, peppers, squash, and watermelons from a lack of calcium in developing fruit. This results from slowed growth and damaged roots caused by several factors.
1. Extreme fluctuations in soil moisture, from very wet to very dry.
2. Rapid plant growth early in the season, followed by extended dry weather.
3. Excessive rains that smother root hairs.
4. Excess soil salts.
5. Cultivation too close to the plant.
The first fruits are the most severely affected. The disorder always starts at the blossom end, and it may enlarge to affect up to half of the fruit. Moldy growths on the rotted area are from fungi or bacteria that invade the damaged tissue. The unaffected part of the fruit is edible.

Solution: To prevent future blossom-end rot, follow these guidelines.
1. Maintain uniform soil moisture.
2. Avoid using high-nitrogen fertilizers or large quantities of fresh manure.
3. Plant in well-drained soil.
4. Provide more water at each watering to help leach salts through the soil.
5. Don't cultivate deeper than 1 inch within 1 foot of the plant.

Anthracnose

Anthracnose.

Problem: Sunken spots up to ½ inch in diameter occur on ripe tomatoes. The centers of the spots darken and form concentric rings. Spots may merge, covering a large part of the tomato.

Analysis: Anthracnose is caused by a fungus (*Colletotrichum coccodes*) that rots ripe tomatoes. Green tomatoes are also attacked, but the spots don't appear until the fruit ripens. Infected fruit is inedible. Anthracnose is most common on overripe fruit close to the ground. Fruit on plants partially defoliated by leaf spot disease is also prone to infection. Leaves may be infected but are usually not severely damaged. The fungus is most active in wet weather with a temperature range of 60° to 90°F. When infection is severe, fruit is damaged in a short period of time. Infections frequently become epidemic during hot, rainy weather. Water from heavy dew, overhead watering, and frequent abundant rain provides the moisture necessary for infection.

Solution: Spray tomato plants at the first sign of the disease with Ortho® Garden Disease Control. Repeat at intervals of 7 to 10 days until harvest. Destroy all infected fruit. Pick tomatoes as they mature, and use them promptly. To reduce the spread of the disease, don't work around wet plants. Avoid overhead watering by using ditch or drip irrigation. Clean up and destroy plant debris after harvest.

Bacterial spot

Bacterial spot.

Problem: Dark, raised, scablike spots, ⅛ to ¼ inch in diameter, appear on green fruit. The centers of the spots are slightly sunken. Dark, greasy, ⅛-inch spots develop on the older leaves, causing them to drop.

Analysis: Bacterial spot is a plant disease caused by a bacterium (*Xanthomonas vesicatoria*) that attacks green but not red tomatoes. Peppers are also attacked. The bacteria infect all aboveground parts of the plant at any stage of growth. Infected blossoms drop, reducing the fruit yield. Fruit is infected through skin wounds caused by insects, blowing sand, and mechanical injuries. Infected fruit doesn't ripen properly and is frequently invaded by rot organisms. The bacteria are most active after heavy rains and in temperatures of 75° to 85°F. They spread rapidly in the rain, often resulting in severe defoliation that weakens the plant and exposes the fruit to sunscald. The bacteria spend the winter in the soil and are carried on tomato seeds.

Solution: Pick and destroy all infected green fruit. If infection is severe, spray with a fungicide containing basic copper sulfate at the first sign of the disease. Repeat at intervals of 7 to 10 days as long as weather conditions favorable to the spread of bacterial spot continue. To reduce the spread of the disease, don't work around wet plants. Avoid overhead watering by using drip or furrow irrigation. Purchase disease-free plants or seeds from a reputable dealer. Don't save seeds from infected fruit.

Catface

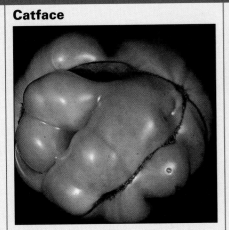

Catface.

Problem: Green and red tomatoes are malformed, scarred, and puckered. Greenish tan streaks and bands of scar tissue mar the blossom end (bottom) of the fruit.

Analysis: Certain conditions that occur during bloom disturb the normal growth of the tomato flower, resulting in catface fruit. These conditions include extreme heat (higher than 85°F) or cold (lower than 55°F), drought, and 2,4–D herbicide sprays. Usually only the first fruit to form is affected. This fruit is of poor quality and ripens unevenly. Although some varieties seem to be more susceptible to this disorder, many modern varieties are seldom affected.

Solution: Water tomatoes regularly. Avoid exposing tomato plants to herbicides by washing sprayers thoroughly after herbicide use or by keeping separate sprayers for herbicides and other sprays. Select varieties that seldom catface.

Tomato fruitworms

Tomato fruitworm damage.

Problem: Deep holes are chewed in the fruit. Striped yellow, green, or brown worms from ¼ to 2 inches long are feeding in them. Worms may also be feeding on the leaves.

Analysis: Tomato fruitworms (*Helicoverpa zea*), also known as *corn earworms* or *cotton bollworms*, attack many plants, including tomatoes, corn, and cotton. The worms feed on the foliage and also chew deep holes in the fruit and feed inside. Damaged fruit is inedible. The adult tomato fruitworm is a light grayish-brown moth with dark lines on the wings. In the spring, the moths lay white eggs on the leaves and stems. The worms that hatch from these eggs feed on the leaves until they are about ½ inch long. Then they move to the fruit and bore inside. After feeding for two to four weeks, they drop to the ground, burrow 2 to 6 inches deep, and pupate; they emerge in several weeks as adults. Several generations of worms occur per year, so damage may continue until fall.

Solution: Once fruitworms are inside the tomatoes, you can't do anything about them. Destroy infested fruit. Clean all plant debris from the garden after harvest to reduce the number of overwintering adults. If fruitworms were numerous in the current year, treat your plants the following year. Use an insecticide containing *methoxychlor* or *carbaryl* or with the bacterial insecticide *Bacillus thuringiensis* (Bt) when the worms are feeding on the foliage and fruit is about ½ inch in diameter. Repeat in two and four weeks if the plants become reinfested.

Tomato hornworms and tobacco hornworms

Tomato (top) and tobacco hornworms.

Problem: Fat green or brown worms up to 5 inches long with white diagonal stripes chew on leaves. A red or black "horn" projects from the rear end. Black droppings from the worm soil the leaves.

Analysis: Tomato hornworms (*Manduca quinquemaculata*) and tobacco hornworms (*M. sexta*) feed on the fruit and foliage of tomatoes, peppers, and eggplants. Although only a few worms may be present, each worm consumes large quantities of foliage and causes extensive damage. The large gray or brown moth with yellow-and-white markings emerges from hibernation in late spring and drinks nectar from petunias and other garden flowers. Worms that hatch from eggs laid by the moth on undersides of leaves feed for three to four weeks. Then they crawl into the soil and pupate, later emerging as moths to repeat the cycle. One generation occurs per year in the North, although two to four are common in the South.

Solution: Handpicking is usually effective against hornworms. If not, spray with Ortho® Bug-B-Gon® Multi-Purpose Insect Killer Concentrate or with the bacterial insecticide *Bacillus thuringiensis* (Bt).

TOMATOES (continued)

Stinkbugs

Stinkbug (2× life size).

Problem: Light yellow to white cloudy spots occur on the tomato fruit. The tissue under these spots is pithy and corky. Young fruit is deformed and may drop. Bright green, gray, blue, or red insects, ⅝ inch long and shaped like a shield, are present on the plants.

Analysis: Stinkbugs attack a wide variety of vegetables, including beans, okra, peppers, squash, and tomatoes. They emit a strong odor when crushed. Both the adults and nymphs damage tomato plants by sucking sap from buds, blossoms, and fruit even when the fruit is green. This feeding causes the fruit to become distorted and dimpled, with corky inner tissue as it ripens. Calluses form around the spots where the stinkbugs feed. Damaged tomatoes are edible but unappetizing. Young, tender growth is the most susceptible to attack. Stinkbugs spend the winter as adults in sheltered areas. In the spring, they lay clusters of eggs on the undersides of leaves. The young that hatch from these eggs mature into adults in six weeks. Several generations occur each year, so damage is throughout the season.

Solution: Treat infested tomato plants with an insecticide containing *carbaryl* as soon as stinkbugs are noticed. Repeat the treatment at intervals of 7 to 10 days if the plants become reinfested.

Flea beetles

Flea beetle damage.

Problem: Leaves are riddled with shot holes ⅛ inch in diameter. Tiny (1/16-inch) black beetles jump like fleas when disturbed. Leaves of seedlings may wilt and die.

Analysis: Flea beetles jump like fleas but are not related to fleas. Both adult and immature flea beetles feed on a wide variety of garden vegetables, including tomatoes. The immature beetle, a legless gray grub, injures plants by feeding on the roots and the lower surfaces of leaves. Adults chew holes in leaves. Flea beetles damage seedlings and young plants most. Leaves of seedlings riddled with holes dry out quickly and die. Adult beetles survive the winter in soil and garden debris. They emerge in early spring to feed on weeds until vegetables sprout or plants are set in the garden. Grubs hatch from eggs laid in the soil and feed for two to three weeks. After pupating in the soil, they emerge as adults to repeat the cycle. One to four generations occur per year. Adults may feed for up to two months.

Solution: Control flea beetles on tomatoes with Ortho® Bug-B-Gon® Multi-Purpose Insect Killer Concentrate or an insecticidal soap. Treat when the leaves first show damage. Watch new growth for evidence of further damage, and repeat the treatment at weekly intervals as needed. Clean all plant debris from the garden after harvest to eliminate overwintering habitat for adult beetles.

Aphids

Aphids (life size).

Problem: Leaves turn yellow and may be curled, distorted, and puckered. Pale green, yellow, or purple soft-bodied insects cluster on stems and on the undersides of leaves.

Analysis: Aphids do little damage in small numbers. They are extremely prolific, however, and populations can rapidly build to damaging numbers during the growing season. Damage occurs when the aphid sucks sap from tomato leaves. Aphids feed on nearly every plant in the garden and are spread from plant to plant by wind, water, and people. Aphids can also spread diseases.

Solution: Control aphids on tomatoes with Ortho® Bug-B-Gon® Multi-Purpose Garden Dust, Ortho® Bug-B-Gon® Multi-Purpose Insect Killer Concentrate, or an insecticidal soap. Treat at the first sign of infestation, and repeat at intervals of 7 to 10 days if plants become reinfested.

Greenhouse whiteflies

Greenhouse whiteflies (life size).

Problem: Tiny, white, winged insects $\frac{1}{16}$ inch long feed mainly on the undersides of leaves.

Nonflying, scalelike larvae covered with white waxy powder may also be present on the undersides of leaves. When the plant is touched, insects flutter rapidly around it. Leaves may be mottled and yellow. In warm-winter areas, black mold may cover the leaves. The plant may grow poorly.

Analysis: The greenhouse whitefly (*Trialeurodes vaporariorum*) is a common insect pest of many garden and greenhouse plants. The adult lays eggs on the undersides of leaves. The larva is the size of a pinhead and semitransparent, with white waxy filaments radiating from the body. Both larval and adult forms suck sap from the leaves. The larvae are more damaging because they feed more heavily. Adults and larvae can't digest all the sugar in the plant sap, and they excrete the excess in a fluid called *honeydew*, which often drops onto the leaves of plants below. In warm-winter areas, these insects can be active year-round. Whiteflies are unable to live through freezing winters. Spring infestations in freezing-winter areas come from migrating whiteflies and from infested greenhouse-grown transplants placed into the garden.

Solution: Control whiteflies with Ortho® Bug-B-Gon® Multi-Purpose Insect Killer, Ortho® Malathion Plus® Insect Spray Concentrate, or an insecticidal soap every 7 to 10 days as necessary. Spray the upper and lower surfaces of the leaves. Whiteflies may also be partially controlled with yellow sticky traps (see page 414).

Fusarium wilt

Fusarium wilt.

Problem: Lower leaves turn yellow, wilt, and die. Then upper shoots wilt, and

eventually the plant dies. Wilting usually occurs first on one side of the leaf or plant, then on the other. When the stem is sliced lengthwise near the soil line, the tissue $\frac{1}{8}$ inch under the bark is found to be dark brown.

Analysis: Fusarium wilt disease is caused by a soil-inhabiting fungus (*Fusarium oxysporum lycopersici*) that infects only tomatoes. The fungus persists indefinitely on plant debris or in the soil. *Fusarium* is most prevalent in warm-weather areas. The disease is spread by contaminated soil, seeds, plants, and equipment. The fungus enters the plant through the roots and spreads up into the stems and leaves through water-conducting vessels in the stems. These vessels become discolored and plugged. This plugging cuts off the flow of water and nutrients to the leaves, causing leaf yellowing and wilting. Affected plants may or may not produce fruit. Fruit that is produced is usually deformed and tasteless. Many plants die. (For more information on fusarium wilt, see page 420.)

Solution: No chemical control is available. Destroy infected plants promptly. *Fusarium* can be removed from the soil only by fumigation and solarization techniques. The best solution is to use plants that are resistant to fusarium wilt. This is denoted by the letter *F* after the tomato variety name. (For a list of wilt-resistant varieties, see page 559.)

Walnut wilt

Wilting caused by nearby walnut tree.

Problem: Tomato plants suddenly wilt and die. Inner stem tissue is dark brown. A black walnut tree is growing nearby.

Analysis: Some plants growing within 50 feet of black walnut trees are killed by a toxic substance called *juglone* that is released from the tree roots. Tomato plants are very sensitive to juglone, which is emitted from both living and dead tree roots. Juglone remains active in the soil and root debris for at least three years after a black walnut tree is removed. The substance kills the tomato roots, causing the inner tissue to darken and the plant to suddenly die.

Solution: Place tomato plants at least 50 feet from black walnut trees. Wait at least three years before planting tomatoes in an area where black walnut trees once grew.

TOMATOES *(continued)*

| Verticillium wilt | Nematodes | Early blight |

Verticillium wilt.

Nematode damage to roots.

Early blight.

Verticillium wilt

Problem: Older, lower leaves turn yellow, dry, and fall. Leaves at stem tips curl upward at the margins but remain green. When the stem is sliced lengthwise near the soil line, the tissue ⅛ inch below the bark is seen to be tan in color.

Analysis: Verticillium wilt disease affects many plants in the garden, including eggplants, peppers, potatoes, raspberries, strawberries, and tomatoes. It is caused by a soil-inhabiting fungus (*Verticillium* species) that persists indefinitely on plant debris or in the soil. It is more prevalent in cool-weather areas. The disease is spread by contaminated seeds, soil, plants, and equipment. The fungus enters the plant through the roots and spreads into the stems and leaves through the water-conducting vessels in the stems. The vessels become discolored and plugged. This plugging cuts off the flow of water and nutrients to the leaves, causing leaf yellowing and death. Affected plants may or may not produce fruit. Fruit that is produced is usually small, deformed, and tasteless. The plant is not usually killed. (For more information on verticillium wilt, see page 420.)

Solution: No chemical control is available. Destroy infected plants promptly. *Verticillium* can be removed from the soil only by fumigation or solarization techniques. The best solution is to use plants that are resistant to this wilt disease. This is denoted by the letter V after the tomato variety name. (For a list of wilt-resistant varieties, see page 559.)

Nematodes

Problem: Plants are stunted, are yellow, and wilt in hot, dry weather. Round and elongated nodules occur on roots.

Analysis: Nematodes are microscopic worms that live in the soil. Some of the various types are highly beneficial, some highly destructive. They aren't related to earthworms. Destructive nematodes feed on plant roots. The damaged roots can't supply sufficient water and nutrients to the aboveground plant parts, and the plant is stunted or slowly dies. Nematodes are found throughout the country but are most severe in the Southeast. They prefer moist, sandy loam soils. Nematodes can move only a few inches each year on their own, but they may be carried long distances by soil, water, tools, or infested plants. Testing roots and soil is the only method for confirming the presence of nematodes. Contact your local county extension office for sampling instructions and addresses of testing laboratories. Soil and root problems—such as poor soil structure, drought stress, nutrient deficiency, and root rots—can produce symptoms of decline similar to those caused by nematodes. Eliminate these problems as causes before sending soil and root samples for testing.

Solution: No chemicals available to homeowners kill nematodes in planted soil. The worms can be controlled before planting, however, by soil fumigation or solarization. Some varieties are resistant to nematodes. (For a list of disease-resistant varieties, see page 559.)

Early blight

Problem: Irregular brown spots, ¼ to ½ inch with concentric rings in their centers, appear on the lower leaves. A yellow margin may outline the spot. When many spots appear, the entire leaf turns yellow and drops. Dark spots with light centers and concentric rings may occur on stems. Dark, leathery, sunken spots with concentric rings mar the fruit where it joins the stem. Discoloration extends from the stem into the fruit.

Analysis: Early blight is a plant disease caused by a fungus (*Alternaria solani*) that attacks tomatoes at any stage of growth. Some leaf spotting appears early in the season, but most occurs as the fruit matures. Plants heavily loaded with fruit and those that are poorly fertilized are the most susceptible to attack. Severe early blight causes partial to complete defoliation that weakens the plant, reduces the size and quality of fruit, and exposes the fruit to sunscald. Infected fruit shouldn't be canned, but it can be eaten fresh if the diseased portion is removed. The spores survive in plant debris in the soil for at least a year. The fungus is most active in humid weather with a temperature range of 75° to 85°F.

Solution: Treat infected plants with Ortho® Garden Disease Control or a fungicide containing *captan* at the first sign of the disease. Repeat at intervals of 7 to 10 days as long as weather conditions favorable to the spread of the disease continue. Clean up and destroy plant debris after harvest to reduce the number of overwintering spores. Fertilize for optimum growth.

Late blight

Late blight. Inset: Close-up.

Problem: Bluish-gray water-soaked patches appear on the leaves. During humid weather, a white, downy mold grows on the lower surfaces of leaves. Leaves dry, shrivel, and turn brown. Water-soaked spots also occur on the stems. Grayish-green water-soaked spots appear on the fruit. The spots turn dark brown, become wrinkled and corklike, and may enlarge to cover the entire fruit. Such fruit remains firm. Dying plants have an offensive odor.

Analysis: Late blight is a plant disease caused by a fungus (*Phytophthora infestans*) that attacks both tomatoes and potatoes. Late blight doesn't attack tomatoes every year but is very destructive when it does occur. The fungus attacks leaves, stems, and fruit, causing severe defoliation and rotted fruit. Infected fruit is inedible. Plants can be infected at all stages of growth. Late blight frequently enters the garden on infected transplants or on infected potato seed pieces. The fungus is most active in wet weather with cool nights (45° to 60°F) and warm days (70° to 85°F). Spores spend the winter in infected potato tubers in the garden or compost pile.

Solution: Treat infected plants with Ortho® Garden Disease Control at the first sign of the disease. Repeat the treatment at intervals of 7 to 10 days as long as weather conditions favorable to the spread of the disease continue. Avoid overhead watering. Clean up and destroy potato and tomato plant debris after harvest. Don't compost infected tubers.

Septoria leaf spot

Septoria leaf spot.

Problem: Numerous brown spots, $\frac{1}{8}$ inch in diameter with dark borders, appear on the older, lower leaves. A few tiny black specks appear in the centers of the spots. Severely spotted leaves turn yellow, dry, and then fall. In warm, wet weather, all the leaves may become spotted and drop except for a few at the top of the plant.

Analysis: Septoria leaf spot is caused by a fungus (*Septoria lycopersici*) that is most severe in wet weather with a temperature range of 60° to 80°F. Tomato plants are attacked at any stage of growth but most commonly after the first fruit is set. Fruit is rarely infected. Severe infection causes extensive leaf yellowing and defoliation. This weakens the plant, reduces the size and quality of the fruit, and exposes the fruit to sunscald. Spores are formed in the tiny black specks in the spots and are spread by splashing water and by people and animals brushing against wet foliage. Foggy, misty weather and heavy dew provide enough moisture for infection. The fungus survives on tomato plant debris for at least three years.

Solution: Treat infected plants with Ortho® Garden Disease Control or a fungicide containing *captan* at the first sign of the disease. Repeat treatment at intervals of 7 to 10 days as long as weather conditions favorable to the spread of the disease continue. To help prevent spread of the disease, don't work around wet plants. Clean up and destroy plant debris after harvest to reduce the number of overwintering spores. Avoid overhead watering by using drip or furrow irrigation.

Leaf roll

Tomato leaf roll.

Problem: Older, lower leaves roll upward until the margins touch or overlap. Eventually most of the leaves may be rolled. Leaves feel leathery and remain green. No other symptoms develop.

Analysis: Leaf roll on tomatoes is a temporary disorder resulting from excessively wet soil, especially after heavy rains. It occurs most commonly during wet growing seasons on staked tomatoes, although unstaked tomatoes may also be affected. Leaf roll does not slow the plant's growth, and a normal crop of fruit is produced. Within a few days, as the soil dries, the symptoms disappear and the plants return to normal. The varieties 'Big Boy', 'Floramerica', and 'Beefsteak' are affected more often than are other varieties.

Solution: Plant tomatoes in well-drained soil, where this problem is least likely to occur. Water regularly so that the soil is neither excessively wet nor dry.

TOMATOES *(continued)*

Mosaic virus

Mosaic virus.

Problem: Leaves are mottled light and dark green, curled, and deformed. Plants are stunted. Fruit is mottled and deformed, with a rough texture and poor flavor. Some young leaves may look like shoestrings.

Analysis: Mosaic is caused by a plant virus. The two most common virus diseases that infect tomatoes are tobacco mosaic virus and cucumber mosaic virus. Viruses weaken the plants, reducing fruit quality and yield. Plants that are infected when young don't produce fruit. Viruses may be introduced into the garden on infected transplants, but most viruses live in weeds, including catnip, horsenettle, jimsonweed, motherwort, plantain, and pokeweed. Once the viruses are present in or near the garden, aphids spread them from plant to plant while feeding. Viruses are also transmitted when diseased and healthy leaves rub together, especially during weeding and transplanting. Tobacco mosaic virus is sometimes present in cigar, pipe, and cigarette tobacco, and smokers may carry the virus on their hands.

Solution: No chemical controls viruses. Destroy infected plants promptly. Control aphids with Ortho® Bug-B-Gon® Multi-Purpose Insect Killer, an insecticidal soap, or Ortho® Malathion Plus® Insect Spray Concentrate. Repeat at intervals of 7 to 10 days if the plants become reinfested. (For more information on disease-carrying insects, see page 449.) Wash your hands thoroughly with soap and water after smoking and before working in the garden. Remove host weeds around the garden.

Cutworms

Cutworm damage.

Problem: Young plants are chewed or cut off near the ground. Gray, brown, or black worms, 1½ to 2 inches long, may be found about 2 inches deep in the soil near the base of the damaged plants. The worms coil when disturbed.

Analysis: Several species of cutworms attack plants in the vegetable garden. The most likely pests of young tomato plants set out early in the season are surface-feeding cutworms. A single surface-feeding cutworm can sever the stems of many young plants in one night. Cutworms hide in the soil during the day and feed only at night. Adult cutworms are dark, night-flying moths with bands or stripes on their forewings. (For more information on cutworms, see page 440.)

Solution: Apply Ortho® Bug-Geta® Plus Snail, Slug & Insect Killer around the base of undamaged plants when cut stems are observed. Because cutworms are difficult to control, applications may need to be repeated at weekly intervals. Cultivate the soil thoroughly in late summer and fall to expose and destroy eggs, larvae, and pupae. Work Ortho® Bug-B-Gon® Multi-Purpose Insect Killer Granules into the soil before planting. Further reduce damage by placing a cutworm collar (see page 414) around each plant stem.

Damping-off

Damping-off.

Problem: Seeds don't sprout, or seedlings fall over soon after they emerge. The stem at the soil line is water-soaked and discolored. The base of the stem is soft and thin.

Analysis: Damping-off is a common problem in wet soil with a high nitrogen level. Wet, rich soil promotes damping-off in two ways: the fungi are more active under these conditions, and the seedlings are more succulent and susceptible to attack. Damping-off is often a problem with crops that are planted too early in the spring, before the soil has had a chance to dry and warm sufficiently for quick seed germination. Damping-off can also be a problem when the weather remains cloudy and wet while seeds are germinating or if seedlings are too heavily shaded.

Solution: To prevent damping-off, take the following precautions.
1. Allow the surface of the soil to dry slightly between waterings.
2. Don't start seeds in soil that has a high nitrogen level. Add nitrogen fertilizers to the soil after the seedlings have produced their first true leaves.
3. Plant seeds after the soil has reached at least 70°F, or start seeds indoors in sterilized potting mix.
4. Protect seeds during germination by coating them with a fungicide containing *captan* or *thiram*. Add a pinch of fungicide to a packet of seeds and shake well to coat the seeds with the fungicide.

TURNIPS

Root maggots

Root maggots (½ life size).

Problem: Young plants wilt in the heat of the day. They may later turn yellow and die. Soft-bodied, yellow-white maggots, ¼ to ⅓ inch long, are feeding in the roots and on seeds. Roots are honeycombed with slimy channels and scarred by brown grooves.

Analysis: Root maggots (*Hylemya* species) are damaging pests of turnips in the northern United States. They are most numerous during cool, wet weather in the spring, early summer, and fall. Early maggots attack the roots, stems, and seeds of turnips, cabbage, broccoli, and radishes in the spring and early summer. Later insects damage crops in the fall. The adult is a gray fly somewhat smaller than a housefly, with black stripes and bristles down its back, that can often be seen clinging to plants. It lays eggs on stems and in nearby soil. Maggots hatch in two to five days to feed and tunnel into the roots, rendering them inedible.

Solution: Once the maggots are in the roots, nothing can be done. To prevent egg laying, screen adult flies from the seedbed with a row cover.

Wireworms

Wireworm (2× life size).

Problem: Plants are stunted and grow slowly. Holes are drilled into the base of the plants. In the soil and among the roots are hard, jointed, shiny, cream-colored to yellow worms up to ⅝ inch long.

Analysis: Wireworms feed on turnips, corn, carrots, beets, peas, and many other plants. They feed on the roots and seeds of turnips. Infestations are most extensive in soil where lawn grass has previously grown, in poorly drained soil, and in soil that is high in organic matter. The adult is known as the *click beetle* because it makes a clicking sound when turning from its back over. Adults lay their eggs in the spring. Wireworms feed for two to six years before maturing into adult beetles, so all sizes and ages may be present in the soil at the same time. Infestations are often spotty.

Solution: Wireworms may be difficult to control. Avoid planting turnips in areas that have held clover, grass, pasture, or grassy weeds.

Cabbage caterpillars

Cabbage looper (life size).

Problem: Leaves have ragged, irregular, or round holes. Green caterpillars, up to 1½ inches long, are feeding on the leaves. Masses of greenish-brown pellets may be found when the outer leaves are parted.

Analysis: Destructive cabbage caterpillars are either the cabbage looper (*Trichoplusia ni*), native to the United States, or the imported cabbageworm (*Pieris rapae*), introduced into North America from Europe around 1860. Both species attack all members of the cabbage family, including turnips. Adults lay eggs singly on leaves in the spring. The white cabbage butterfly attaches its tiny, yellow, bullet-shaped eggs to the undersides of leaves; the brownish cabbage looper moth lays its pale green eggs at night on the upper surfaces of leaves. The larvae from these eggs feed on leaves. The cabbageworm contaminates plants with its greenish-brown excrement. As many as five generations exist per season, so caterpillar damage can occur from early spring through late fall. Caterpillars spend the winter as pupae attached to a plant or nearby object. Cabbage loopers migrate from the South in early summer.

Solution: When the caterpillars first appear, treat the turnip leaves with Ortho® Malathion Plus® Insect Spray Concentrate or the bacterial insecticide *Bacillus thuringiensis* (Bt). Or, if practical, handpick caterpillars from the leaves and destroy them. Keep adults from laying eggs by protecting plants with row covers. Clear all plant debris from the garden to reduce the number of overwintering pupae.

Turning organic amendments into the soil can improve almost any soil. See page 404.

This section contains garden problems that aren't related to a particular plant or even to a particular part of the garden. It also contains general cultural guidelines applicable to many types of plants.

Most of the soil problems a gardener might experience are described in this section. Some soils are more difficult to work with than others, but any garden soil that will grow weeds will grow garden plants, too. The difference between good garden soil and difficult garden soil is the amount of latitude gardeners have in their cultural practices. If your soil drains well, you don't have to worry about overwatering. If it holds ample water, you are less likely to under water. But if you have a heavy clay or a droughty sand, proper watering takes skill and attention. Good garden plants can still be raised in these soils; they just take more careful handling. Another option is to improve the undesireable soil in your garden by adding organic matter. Organic matter improves drainage of heavy soils by loosening tightly packed clay particles, creating channels for moisture and oxygen to penetrate deeply into the soil. In sandy soils, organic matter helps bind the loose soil particles into aggregates that retain more moisture. At either extreme of soil type, addition of organic matter improves growing conditions for plants. Avoid the temptation to add sand to claylike soils with the thought that sand will loosen the clay. While it is true that if enough sand is added to clay, soil texture will be improved, it usually takes at least 50 percent sand by volume to make a difference. If less than optimal amounts of sand are added, the sand may combine with the clay to form soil the density of adobe brick.

There are two basic approaches to both soil and climate problems. One—by far the simplest—is to grow plants adapted to the soil and climate of your garden. This requires no extra work on your part and little skill or garden knowledge beyond that needed to select the right plants. The limitation of this system is that you may not like the plants available to you or you may want plants other than those common in your area. For instance, lawns are not adapted to much of the arid West. In some areas, it takes almost heroic measures to keep a lawn healthy. But gardeners are so fond of lawns that the majority of homes in these areas have them. Turf grasses vary considerably in their adaptability to drought.

Deep-watering of pumpkin seedlings. The slow flow from this punctured can allows water to penetrate deep into the soil. See page 408 for other methods of irrigation.

Selecting those that are better suited to dry climate conditions will lessen the number of problems likely to develop on the lawn. For trees, shrubs, and flowers, carefully examine the yard to discover *microclimates*, small pockets that differ significantly from the surrounding conditions, in which to grow plants otherwise unsuited to the region. For example, the shaded north side of the house may provide enough protection from heat, drying sun and wind to allow you to grow a Japanese maple that would develop leaf scorch in full sun. The second method is to adapt your garden to the plants. This may involve installing irrigation systems, building structures to shelter garden plants from the sun, wind, or cold, or amending soils with organic matter to improve drainage or increase moisture-holding capacity. In effect, you create a microclimate in the garden by building the structure or supplying extra irrigation.

You will also find some garden practices in this section. These practices solve garden problems in general, but not any one problem. In many cases, when diseases or insects are observed on garden plants, the disease or insect may merely be a symptom of an underlying cultural problem or environmental condition that makes the plant more susceptible to the pest. If this is true, treating for the pest will not solve the problem. It will temporarily rid the plant of its infection or infestation, but until the underlying condition or cultural problem is corrected, the pest is almost certain to return.

403

SOIL PROBLEMS

Heavy soil

Heavy soil.

Sandy soil

Sandy soil.

Shallow soil

Shallow soil.

When used to describe soil, the word *heavy* refers not to weight but to the sensation of working the soil. Heavy soils can be difficult to work. Heaviness comes from a high proportion of clay in the soil. If the soil does not have a crumbly texture, the pores in the clay soil are very small. These pores let air and water into the soil.

Difficulties with heavy soil: Heavy soil may be sticky when wet and hard when dry, and it may transform rapidly from one to the other. Water passes through its small pores very slowly. It is easy to overwater, keeping the soil pores full of water but lacking air.

Advantages of heavy soil: When heavy soil has a crumbly structure, it drains well yet still retains much water. Heavy soils also hold onto nutrients well and are fertile. Because they need feeding and watering less often than other soils, they are usually easier to manage.

Managing heavy soil: Be careful not to overwater. Water slowly and deeply but infrequently. The heavier your soil, the more important it is to work it when the water content is just right. There is a point between too wet and too dry when the soil works easily. Gypsum sometimes improves the structure of clay soils. Work a cup of gypsum into the soil in a watering basin (see page 408) to see if drainage is improved. Organic matter, such as manure, compost, or ammoniated sawdust, always improves heavy soil. Spread from 1 to 4 inches of organic matter on the surface and turn it in every time you work the soil. In two or three years, the soil will be greatly improved.

Sandy soil contains a high proportion of sand. It can be identified by a characteristic grittiness when the soil is rubbed between the thumb and fingers. Sandy soil has large pore spaces, so water and air enter it easily; the soil dries out rapidly, however, and doesn't retain nutrients well. Sandy soil is easily cultivated either dry or wet. It seldom puddles or becomes muddy or sticky and seldom is erosion a problem, because water enters it immediately, so there is nothing to run off on the surface.

Managing sandy soil: Sandy soil must have both water and fertilizer applied lightly and frequently. Because it retains little water, plants wilt quickly. This type of soil is often called *droughty*. A simple way to feed the garden is to use liquid fertilizers or a water-soluble fertilizer. Apply these with a hose-end sprayer or a siphoning fertilizer injector. Fertilize once per month during the growing season. Improve sandy soil by adding organic matter, such as peat moss, compost, or manure, each year. Spread from 1 to 4 inches of organic material on the surface and turn it under every time you till the soil. The organic matter acts like a sponge, retaining water and nutrients. Drip irrigation systems are especially effective and useful in sandy soils. Use plants that are adapted to a sandy soil (For information on sandy soil, see page 532).

Depth of soil matters in the growth of plants. Shallow soil doesn't provide as much root space as deep soil and has less water-storage capacity. It dries out rapidly. On flat land, it is also easy to overwater, because the water has no place to drain. Soil depth can be determined by digging a hole and examining the layers. A lawn can be grown in 6 inches of soil, but trees need from $1\frac{1}{2}$ to 4 feet. Sometimes the underlayer isn't bedrock but a rocklike layer called *hardpan*, which can be penetrated only with difficulty. (For more information on hardpan, see page 405.)

Living with shallow soil: If your garden is already planted, watch the amount of water you apply. You may need to water more frequently than if the soil were deeper but apply less at each watering. Guy trees to keep them from blowing over.

Improving shallow soil: In areas that are not yet planted, you have two options. One is to choose shallow-rooted plants, such as lawns and annuals. A second option is to deepen the soil by creating raised planting beds. But avoid planting large trees, even in raised beds. Resist the temptation to deepen the soil by digging into the underlayer. Drainage would be nonexistent in these holes, so plants would struggle and maintenance would be very difficult.

Erosion

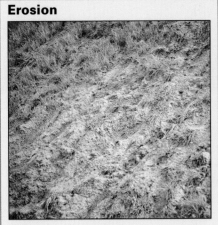

Erosion.

Erosion occurs on bare ground when soil is worn away by wind and water. Eroding winds can carry away dry soil, but water erosion is more common and more severe. When raindrops fall on bare soil, their impact loosens soil particles. On a slope, water starts to flow over the surface as soon as the ground stops absorbing it. The force of the moving water and the scouring action of the soil particles carried in the water erode the bare ground farther down the slope. Erosion is most severe on long, steep slopes. Stop erosion by covering the soil. If the slope is not too steep, cover it with a heavy mulch, such as gravel or bark. Cover steep slopes with burlap or coarse netting sold for this purpose. Plant a ground cover through holes in the fabric. By the time the fabric rots, the ground cover will be established. The most effective plantings for erosion control are low, dense ground covers or turfgrasses. The roots help to hold soil particles in place, and the leaves and stems break the impact of water drops and reduce the momentum of runoff. If slopes are already deeply eroded, it may be necessary to construct retaining walls or check dams to prevent further erosion.

Compaction

Compacted soil.

The pressure of foot or vehicle traffic can pack soil tightly, squeezing the pores closed. Compacted soil contains little air, restricting root growth to the surface levels. Also, roots have difficulty penetrating the dense soil. Water penetrates the soil slowly, making irrigation difficult. Some soils, especially clay soils and some loamy sands, are more susceptible to compaction than others, and dry soil resists compaction more than wet soil. Correct soil compaction before planting. Different techniques are needed in planted and unplanted areas.

Before planting: Till the soil to loosen the compaction. Large areas that are badly compacted require the use of a rotary tiller. Organic matter should be mixed in as the soil is tilled. If heavy construction equipment caused the compaction, the soil may need to be loosened to a depth of 2 feet with a chisel plow. Foot traffic compacts only a couple of inches of surface soil.

In planted areas: Relieve compaction in planted areas by aerating the soil, using the type of aerator that removes cores of soil. Aerate when the soil is moist but not muddy. Make passes over the compacted ground in alternate directions until holes are within 3 inches of each other. Leave the cores on the soil, or drag a heavy board over them to break them up.

Preventing compaction: The most effective way to prevent compaction is to keep traffic off the soil. Make paths, or place fences or shrubs to act as barriers. If heavy equipment must be driven across the soil, make sure the soil is as dry as possible at the time. If foot traffic can't be kept off, mulch the area with 4 inches of gravel or rocks.

Hardpan

Turf over hardpan killed by drought.

Hardpan is a cementlike layer of soil that impedes the downward flow of water and restricts root growth. Soil particles in the hardpan layer are cemented together by minerals, usually iron compounds, that have accumulated there. Hardpan is usually within a foot or so of the surface and is only a few inches thick. It may be very close to the soil surface if erosion has washed away the topsoil. The hardpan has two effects on plants growing above it. Since roots can't grow through hardpan, they are restricted to the shallow soil layer above it. Trees grow slowly and may be blown over in a windstorm. Also, since water does not penetrate it, the hardpan impedes drainage. To determine if your soil has a hardpan layer, dig a hole 2 or 3 feet deep. The rocklike layer can, with persistence, be penetrated. It is not necessary to remove hardpan but only to provide a hole or channel through it for water flow and root growth. Around established plants, break holes in the hardpan with a crowbar or jackhammer. Depending on the depth of the soil, the holes should be 4 to 6 feet apart. When establishing a new planting area, break up hardpan with a chisel plow or backhoe. Hardpan reforms very slowly, so any holes made in it will last for many years. Or install drain pipes on top of the hardpan to drain water away from the plant roots. Another possibility is to grow vegetables and flowers in raised beds.

DRAINAGE PROBLEMS

SOIL ACIDITY

Soil types

Drainage problems from heavy soil.

Soil structure

Poor drainage from layered soil.

pH

Soil pH test kit.

Certain soil types have drainage problems.
Soils that crust: Some types of soil form a thin (⅛- to ¼-inch) crust on the soil surface. The crust can be broken with the fingers, and it flakes when handled. Even though the soil below the crust drains well, water doesn't penetrate quickly and tends to puddle or run off. Prevent crusting by cultivating organic matter into the soil or by mulching. (For more information on mulching, see page 415.)
Sodic soils: Sodic soils are high in certain forms of sodium. They are impermeable to water; puddling and runoff are common. Sodium hydroxide (caustic soda) in sodic soils dissolves organic matter, which becomes suspended in puddled water, turning it brown or black. (For more information on sodic soils, see page 410.)
Heavy soils: Heavy soils are those with a large proportion of clay. They crack and are very hard when dry and are sticky and difficult to mix or turn over when wet. To determine if your soil is heavy, dig a hole 2 feet deep in a poorly drained area. Fill the hole with water. If the water level drops more slowly than 1/10 inch per hour, heavy soil is probably causing your problem. To reduce runoff and puddling on heavy soils (and other poorly drained soils), apply water more slowly. Use sprinkler heads with a lower water output, or cycle sprinklers by pausing for half an hour when runoff begins. (For more information on heavy soil, see page 404.)

The soil structure may be altered by natural processes or by human activities, causing poor drainage.
Compacted soils: Compacted soils are hard, dense, and impermeable to water. Compacted areas are usually on the surface and only 2 to 4 inches deep. Compaction is usually caused by foot traffic, but motor vehicles and construction equipment can compact the soil 2 feet deep. Dig a hole through the compacted layer in the poorly drained area when the soil is moist but not wet. Fill the hole with water. If the water level drops slower than 1/10 inch per hour, compaction is the problem. (For more information on compacted soil, see page 405.)
Layered soils: Layered soils are those in which soils of different textures are layered like a cake. If the layers are very different in texture, drainage problems may result. This kind of problem is most often caused when soil of a different texture than the native soil is added as fill material. Even a thin layer of added soil can slow drainage. Dig a hole to see if your soil has distinctly different layers. If layered soils are causing your drainage problem, stir the layers together by tilling or, if the layers are deep, by chisel plowing. If the area is planted, dig holes or a trench through the layers. Fill the holes to the surface with gravel or wood chips. Water will drain quickly through these holes.
Hardpan: Hardpan is a cementlike layer of soil that sometimes forms a foot or two below the surface. Water doesn't drain through this layer. When struck with a shovel or pick, hardpan feels like rock. (For more information on hardpan, see page 405.)

Soil pH is a measure of acidity and alkalinity, on a scale from 0 to 14. The lower the number, the more acid the soil. A pH of 7.0 is neutral, neither acid nor alkaline. Many of the chemical reactions that occur in all soils depend on the pH. The soil pH often determines what nutrients are available for plant use. Soils are rarely more acidic than 4.0 or more alkaline than 9.0. Most plants will grow in soils with a pH of 5.5 to 7.5. Some plants need acidic soil (4.0 to 5.5). Others tolerate alkaline conditions (7.5 to 9.0). (For a list, see page 531.) To determine your soil pH, have your soil tested.

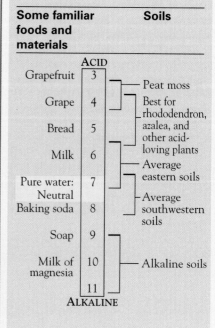

THE pH SCALE

Some familiar foods and materials	ACID	Soils
Grapefruit	3	Peat moss
Grape	4	Best for rhododendron, azalea, and other acid-loving plants
Bread	5	
Milk	6	
Pure water: Neutral	7	Average eastern soils
Baking soda	8	Average southwestern soils
Soap	9	
Milk of magnesia	10	Alkaline soils
	11	
ALKALINE		

Alkaline soil

Pin oak in alkaline soil.

Alkaline soils are those with a pH of more than 7.0, the neutral point. The soil is usually alkaline in regions that receive less than 20 inches of rain per year and in regions where the soil is derived from underlying limestone.

Effect on plants: Most plants grow well in slightly alkaline soil (pH of 7.0 to 8.0). In soils that are more alkaline than 8.0, however, some plant nutrients, including iron and manganese, become insoluble and are not available to plants even though they are present in the soil. Plants growing in soil that is too alkaline for them develop yellow areas between the veins on their newest leaves. Older leaves usually remain green, unless the plant has been growing for some time in soil that is too alkaline.

Acid-loving plants: Plants adapted to acidic soil, such as azaleas and rhododendrons, may show symptoms of iron deficiency in alkaline soils.

Overlimed soils: If soil that is naturally acidic has so much lime added to it that the pH rises above 7.2, plants may show symptoms of iron deficiency.

Decreasing soil alkalinity: Make soils more acidic by adding ferrous sulfate or soil sulfur. Add 2 pounds per 100 square feet, wait two weeks, and then test the soil pH. Reapply these acidifying amendments until the desired pH has been attained. Maintain acidity by using a fertilizer that has an acidic formulation, such as ammonium sulfate. Alternately, select plants that are tolerant of alkaline soil.

Acid soil

Magnesium deficiency caused by acidic soil.

Strictly speaking, any soil with a pH below 7.0—the neutral point—is acid. The term *acid soil* usually refers to a soil that is too acidic for good plant growth, however—one with a pH below about 5.5. As the pH decreases, the soil becomes increasingly acidic. Acidity develops naturally in a soil that is heavily leached by rainfall. Most plants grow well in slightly acidic soil (pH of 6.0 to 7.0).

Effect on plant nutrients: As acidity increases, chemical changes occur in the soil that reduce the overall growth and health of most plants, except for acid-loving plants such as rhododendrons, azaleas, and blueberries. Many plant nutrients—especially phosphorus, calcium, and magnesium—become less available for plant use in acidic soils. Other elements, such as aluminum and manganese, become available in quantities toxic to plants. The beneficial soil organisms that decompose organic matter are less active in acidic soils, so the nitrogen obtained from the breakdown of organic matter is reduced.

Effect on plants: Plants growing in acidic soil are often stunted and off-color. Their roots are sparse and small.

Decreasing soil acidity: To decrease soil acidity, add a ground dolomitic limestone material according to the chart on page 531. In addition to raising the soil pH, dolomitic limestone supplies magnesium and calcium, nutrients usually deficient in acidic soil. Don't overlime acid soil, because availability of some nutrients may be decreased when the soil pH is too high.

How much water to apply

Measuring sprinkler output.

Each time you water, apply enough water to wet the soil to the bottom of the root zone. Water is measured in inches. If a tin can is placed on a lawn when the sprinklers are running, the soil has received an inch of water when the water in the container is an inch deep. If a watering basin is 3 inches deep, 3 inches of water is applied to the soil when the basin is filled with water. Because sandy soils don't hold as much water as clay soils, it takes less water to wet them to the same depth. To wet 1 foot of a sandy loam soil that has dried out to the point when average plants need water (just barely moist), apply about 1 inch of water.

To wet 1 foot of a loam or clay loam that is just barely moist, apply about 1½ inches of water. Soils vary greatly in their ability to hold water, so these figures are only guidelines. To see how much water your soil needs to wet it a foot deep, measure the amount of water you apply during watering. The next day, after the water has moved down as far as it will go (clay soils may take two or three days), dig a hole to see where the extent of wet soil is. You will be able to calculate from this how much water you need to apply to wet the soil to the bottom of the root zone. Then, by measuring the time it takes your sprinkler system to apply an inch of water, you can calculate how long you need to leave the system on to apply enough water.

WATERING *(continued)*

About watering

Sprinkler irrigation.

Drip irrigation.

When to water

Watering annual bed.

Plants suffer more from improper watering than from any other cause. Watering is more difficult to master than other gardening techniques because it depends on many variables. The amount of water a plant needs varies with the kind of plant, the soil, the location, and all of the continually changing components of the weather, including temperature, humidity, and wind—so it is easy to overwater or underwater. Several methods are commonly used to irrigate plants. Some methods, including hand-watering and some sprinklers, make water puddle or run off long before the soil receives as much water as it needs. Many gardeners stop watering when the soil surface becomes soggy or when water starts to puddle or run off. This practice wets only the top few inches of the soil. Because the rate of water absorption into the soil is slow, it may take several hours to several days to wet some types of soil to 3 or 4 feet deep. To water deeply and prevent runoff, apply water at the same rate at which it enters the soil.

Hand-watering: This method involves watering the garden with a handheld hose, usually with a spray head on the end. Hand-watering is the simplest method of irrigation. It involves no previous soil preparation or equipment installation. But it is time-consuming and leads to under watering because most gardeners don't have the patience to water for many hours at a time or to wait for water to soak into the root zone.

Furrow irrigation: Furrow irrigation works best when you are watering rows of plants; it is often used in vegetable gardens. Furrows are dug beside plant rows and filled with water. The water is left in the furrows for several hours. Plant foliage stays dry when furrow irrigation is used; only the roots receive water.

Basin irrigation: Watering basins are used mainly around shrubs and trees. A circular ridge of soil is built around the plant to contain the water, and then the basin formed by this ridge is filled with water, either from a handheld hose or a bubbler head on a permanent sprinkler system. A few basins can be filled quickly with water, but if many plants are irrigated by hand in this manner, watering may be time-consuming.

Sprinklers: Both hose-end sprinklers and underground installed sprinklers water a large area at once. They are most effective when used to water heavily planted areas. Sprinklers are wasteful if they are used to irrigate sparsely planted areas. They are also hard to control in windy areas, and they get plant leaves wet, which may lead to disease problems. But they are effective for delivering water evenly over a large area and require less time than most other systems.

Drip irrigation: Drip-irrigation systems apply water very slowly, allowing it to seep into the soil. They are left on for many hours at a time, often for 4 to 16 hours per day. Many types of delivery systems are available. If they are properly operated, drip systems do the best watering job because they keep the soil at a relatively constant state of moisture, without the wet-to-dry fluctuations of other methods. Drip systems work best in light soils and are a perfect solution to watering plants on steep slopes. They don't wet the leaves.

There are two primary skills involved in watering plants: knowing how much water to apply at each irrigation (see page 407) and knowing when to water. There are many methods for knowing when to water, some of them very sophisticated. The method described here is one of the simplest and easiest to learn, and it always works. The first step is to dig a hole into the root zone of the plant, from 2 to 6 inches deep. In loose soil, you can dig a hole with a finger. Otherwise, use a trowel or a shovel. Then feel the soil in the hole. Dig a new hole each time you check. Below, the plants are divided into three watering categories: those that can't tolerate drought, average plants, and those that can't tolerate wet soil. When the soil reaches a certain level of dryness, it is time to water again.

Plants that can't tolerate drought: The soil in the root zone is moist but not wet. When you touch it, it makes your finger damp but not muddy. If you squeeze a ball of this soil, water won't run out.

Average plants: The soil in the root zone is barely moist. When you touch it, it feels cool and moist but doesn't dampen your finger. Most soils are crumbly at this stage but not dusty.

Plants that can't tolerate wet soil: When it is time to water, the soil in the root zone feels completely dry. It is not cool to the touch, and it may be dusty. It is important to water these plants as soon as the soil reaches this state. Although they can usually withstand periods of drought, they grow much better if watered regularly.

FERTILIZING

About fertilizing

Fertilizer.

Controlled-release fertilizers.

Fertilizer is often called *plant food*, but that term is misleading. Plants get their energy from light through photosynthesis. Fertilizers are more like food supplements than food. The soil they grow in is a reservoir of mineral nutrients. The gardener's job is not to feed the plant, but to keep the reservoir from becoming depleted. When selecting a fertilizer, the two primary considerations are the nutrients it contains and its convenience.

Nutrients: The nutrients that plants use in large quantities and that might be deficient are nitrogen (chemical symbol N), phosphorus (P), and potassium (K). Plants also need sulfur, calcium, and magnesium in large quantities, but these are seldom deficient, or they are added as lime. Plants need another group of minerals in minute amounts. Of these, iron and manganese are the most commonly deficient. (For more information on nitrogen, see page 410, and for minor nutrients, see at right.) Nitrogen should be added regularly in just about all situations. Phosphorus and potassium are usually needed in areas that receive lots of summer rainfall.

Convenience: Fertilizers come in many forms, each of which reacts in its own way. The right form for you depends on how you prefer to manage your soil. The most commonly available are *water-soluble fertilizers*. They may be applied as a granule and dissolved with irrigation water, or they may be dissolved in water and applied as a liquid. This type persists in the soil for the least amount of time. It is easy to apply and inexpensive, but it must be applied more frequently than other types. *Organic fertilizers* are derived from plant or animal parts, such as leaf mold or bone meal, which decompose in the soil to release mineral nutrients. Because decomposition takes some time, the nutrients are released over a long period of time. The nonmineral portion of organic fertilizers decomposes to humus, an excellent soil amendment. Organic fertilizers are more expensive and bulky than soluble fertilizers but only need to be added infrequently. *Controlled-release fertilizers* are chemically constituted to release their nutrients slowly, sometimes over a period of years.

Formulations: Many fertilizers are formulated for a specific crop, such as African violets, lawns, and citrus trees. These fertilizers contain the correct balance of nutrients for one crop and often adjust other factors, such as the soil acidity. (For more information on soil acidity, see page 407.)

Minor nutrients

Iron-deficient piggyback plant.

Minor nutrients, also called *trace elements* or *micronutrients*, are nutrients that plants need in small amounts. They include boron, iron, manganese, copper, zinc, molybdenum, and chlorine. Yearly applications of minor nutrients are not necessary; they need to be added only when deficiency symptoms appear in the plant. (For more information on nutrient deficiencies, see pages 428 to 429.)

Minor nutrient deficiencies in the soil: When deficiencies develop in soils, they are usually in localized areas. The most commonly deficient minor nutrient is iron, which is tied up in insoluble forms in alkaline or poorly aerated soils and, in some cases, very sandy soils. Alkaline soils may also be deficient in manganese and zinc. Zinc deficiency is much more common than manganese deficiency, especially in citrus and other tree and vegetable crops.

Correcting minor nutrient deficiencies: Minor nutrient deficiencies in the plant are corrected by applying fertilizers to the soil or spraying the foliage. Minor nutrients may be contained in complete fertilizers and are often contained in specialty fertilizers. For immediate results, minor nutrients can be applied in a spray using a chelated iron fertilizer on the foliage of the plant.

FERTILIZING *(continued)*

Nitrogen

Nitrogen-deficient euonymus.

Nitrogen-deficient tomato.

Sodic soil

Leaf scorch on oleander caused by salty soil.

Nitrogen is one of the three primary nutrients necessary for plant growth. Plants use it to form proteins required for the development of new shoots and leaves and to make chlorophyll. Most soils require additional nitrogen to produce healthy plants. (For information about nitrogen deficiency in plants, see page 428.) There are three major forms of nitrogen: ammoniacal, nitrate, and organic.

Ammoniacal nitrogen: Ammoniacal nitrogen includes ammonium, ammonia, and urea, all of which quickly become ammonium in the soil. Ammonium is not readily leached from the soil. It binds to the surfaces of soil particles, which keeps it from washing away. Although many plants use ammonium, the availability of ammoniacal nitrogen is low to most plants, because soil microorganisms must change it to nitrate before it can be washed to the plant roots. The activity of these microbes depends on soil moisture, aeration, and temperature. In warm, well-aerated soils, the nitrogen is changed to nitrate and is available to plants for a couple of weeks. The process is much slower in cold, wet soils and will not take place at all when the soil temperature is below 30° to 40°F. If a plant growing in cold soil is in immediate need of nitrogen, a fertilizer should be applied that also contains nitrate nitrogen (see following information). Ammoniacal nitrogen fertilizers have an acidifying effect on the soil. In areas of high rainfall, where soils are already acidic, it may be necessary to add lime.

Nitrate nitrogen: Fertilizers containing nitrate nitrogen are fast acting. They are useful for plants in immediate need of nitrogen. The nitrogen is in a form that is readily available to plants. Microorganisms are not needed to break down the nitrogen, so the fertilizers are effective in cold or warm soils. Nitrate nitrogen doesn't become attached to soil particles but floats freely in the soil water. With heavy rains or deep watering, the nitrogen may be washed below the root zone. Nitrate fertilizers are most effective if applied in frequent, light feedings or in combination with a long-lasting ammoniacal or organic form of nitrogen.

Organic nitrogen: Organic nitrogen is in the form of protein or other insoluble compounds. It is found in plant and animal derivatives such as bloodmeal, manure, and sewage sludge. In organic material that has not been composted, the nitrogen is not available to plants. The protein must be decomposed by soil microorganisms to ammonium and then to nitrate before the plant can use it. As with ammoniacal nitrogen, the rate of decomposition depends on soil temperature and moisture. Organic nitrogen usually lasts for a few months in the soil.

Soil salts are soluble minerals. They include table salt (sodium chloride) as well as salts of calcium, magnesium, and potassium. Salty soil, also called sodic soil, occurs mainly in arid regions where there is not enough rainfall to wash the salts from the soil. Soil salts originate from several sources. As soil minerals weather, they slowly break down into salts that dissolve in the soil water. Irrigation water that contains dissolved salts contributes to soil salinity, and so do fertilizers. As water evaporates from the surface, it moves up through the soil, bringing dissolved salts up into the topsoil. Salts may accumulate in poorly drained soils because rainfall and irrigation water can't drain through and leach the soil. Roadside soil may become saline in areas where deicing salts are used to melt ice and snow in the winter. Salty soil may develop a white crust of salt deposits on the surface. Most garden plants don't tolerate much salt in the soil. (For more information on salt damage, see page 426.)

Removing salts: Leach salty soils periodically by watering them deeply. About 12 inches of water are needed to remove most of the salts in a foot of soil. If soil salinity is a result of poor drainage, improve the soil drainage. (For information on drainage, see page 406.) The use of mulches in arid regions destroys the soil structure and causes clay particles to become lodged in soil pores, making the soil impermeable to

Salt damage to white pine.

Tree and shrub removal

Stump grinding.

Tree stump to be removed.

water. Water puddles on sodic soils and usually evaporates before it enters the soil. Some of the sodium forms caustic soda (sodium hydroxide), which dissolves organic matter. The dissolved organic matter is dark brown or black. A black crust often forms on sodic soils. Sodic soils are often very alkaline and rarely support plant growth. To improve sodic soils, add gypsum at a rate of 5 pounds to every 100 square feet. Cultivate the gypsum into the soil and then water well to leach the sodium from the soil. If drainage is only slightly improved, add more gypsum.

Small trees and shrubs can be dug out of the ground if their root systems are small and shallow. To remove large trees and shrubs, follow these guidelines.

Cutting the plant to a stump: Saw larger, established plants to a stump. Contact a professional arborist to do this job if the tree or shrub is very large or in an area where the falling branches and trunk might damage nearby structures or property, injure people, or fall on power lines. Kill the remaining stump before removing it; stumps that are alive are much more difficult to remove. If you choose to keep the stump as a decorative element in your landscape, it may continue to sprout unless it is dead.

Killing freshly cut stumps: Remove any sprouts growing from the trunk, and then paint or daub undiluted brush-killer herbicide over the entire surface of the stump within 30 minutes after the tree or shrub has been cut. If runoff from rain could affect adjacent desirable plants, cover the stump with a plastic bag secured around the base of the stump.

Killing old, sprouting stumps: With a hatchet, make a continuous horizontal cut or an overlapping ring of notches around the base of the stump, angling downward into the bark. Cut through but don't remove any of the bark. Pour as much brush-killer herbicide into the cut as it will hold. Reapply the treatment if the stump resprouts. Cover the stump with a plastic bag secured around the base of the stump if runoff may be a problem.

Removing small stumps: Large brush or small trees (with trunk diameters less than 2 inches) can often be pulled from the ground. Remove the top, leaving the stump long enough to give a good purchase—3 to 5 feet if possible. Using a tractor or four-wheel-drive utility vehicle, tie a chain to the top of the stump and to the hitch of the tractor, and pull the stump from the ground. If no vehicle is available, or if vehicle access is not possible, stumps may be pulled with a lever. Cut a section of log from 1 or 2 feet in diameter and 1 foot long. Drill a hole in the side to accommodate a crowbar. With the hole facing up, place the log against the stump to be pulled. Insert a crowbar into the hole. Wrap a length of chain tightly around the base of the stump and around the crowbar. When the crowbar is pulled back, the stump will be pulled up and out of the ground.

Removing large stumps: A stump is dead if it fails to sprout during the next growing season. Dig it out, or contact a professional landscape contractor or arborist who can quickly remove a living or dead stump with a stump grinder.

REPAIRING TREES

Making pruning cuts

Pruning cut just outside the branch collar.

Bark wounds

Bark wounds.

Protecting trees in lawns

Tree wrap.

Pruning trees and shrubs causes wounds. Make clean wounds that the tree can heal as quickly as possible. Woody plants heal wounds by growing a roll of callus over them, beginning from the bark at the edge of the wound. A good pruning cut leaves a smooth, clean-cut surface for this callus to grow on and does not tear the bark at the edge of the wound.

Removing small branches: Small branches—those you can prune with a single cut of handheld shears or loppers—should be cut from the bottom up, with the cutting blade on the underside of the branch. Cut close to the trunk or parent branch, but don't cut into the trunk itself.

Removing medium-size branches: Branches that are large enough to need a saw but small enough that you can support them as you make the cut are pruned with two cuts. Cutting just outside the branch collar, the roll or swelling of trunk bark at the base of the branch, saw one-third of the way through the branch from the bottom. Then finish the cut from the top, supporting the branch as it separates.

Removing large branches: If you have any question about your ability to control a large branch, have an arborist remove it. Remove large branches with three cuts. Make the first a foot or so from the trunk, one-third of the way through the branch from the bottom. Make the second cut from the top, an inch or so farther from the trunk than the first cut. These cuts remove the weight of the branch without endangering the bark of the trunk. Make the third cut just outside the branch collar to remove the stub. Don't cut into the branch collar.

Bark protects trees in the same way skin protects you. When this layer is breached, disease organisms and insects may invade the plant through the break. Directly under the bark is the conductive tissue of the plant—the circulatory system that carries water and minerals to the leaves and the sugar and protein to the roots. If the break in the bark doesn't heal quickly, this tissue dries out and dies, stopping circulation through that part of the trunk or branch. Bark wounds that encircle more than one-quarter of the circumference of a trunk or branch slow the growth of the plant past that point. Small breaks in a healthy tree—those less than ½ inch wide—usually heal within a couple of weeks during the growing season. Larger breaks heal more slowly as the tree grows a layer of tissue across them. If the break remains open for too long, heart-rot fungi often invade the wound, rotting the wood and beginning the process that leads to hollow trees. If the edges of a wound are ragged, trim the bark with a sharp knife to make a clean edge, but don't remove any more bark than is necessary. Smooth the underlying wood with a chisel, and allow the area to dry. If the wound has begun to heal, a roll of new tissue can be seen at the edge of the wound. Don't cut into this developing tissue.

Most trees don't grow very well in lawns. Turfgrass is an aggressive competitor, taking up most of the nutrients and water, leaving the tree undernourished. Also, lawn mowers and string trimmers bump and damage the bark of the base. Slight repeated damage often causes the bark to die and slough off a portion of the trunk. Water can't move up the trunk through this damaged area, further depleting the tree of water and nutrients. A tree growing in a lawn can be protected from competition and damage in several ways.

Keep a bare area around the trunk: Commercial lawn-care firms often use weed killer to maintain a bare area for a few inches around the tree trunk. The bare area eliminates the necessity of mowing close to the trunk and the danger of damaging it.

Make a bed around the trunk: A planting bed around the tree trunk protects it from lawn mowers and string trimmers. In addition, if the bed is large enough, it protects the tree roots from turfgrass competition. The bed can be filled with flowers or a ground cover or a mulch of organic material or stones.

Apply tree wraps: Commercial tree wraps are flexible plastic sheaths that protect the base of the trunk until the tree bark itself has grown thick enough to protect the tree. Besides protecting against lawn mowers, tree wraps prevent animals from chewing the bark in the winter.

TEMPERATURE PROBLEMS

Heat protection

Protection from the sun.

Plants cool their leaves through evaporation. If the soil dries out during hot weather, leaf temperatures rise rapidly to killing levels. To prevent heat injury to plants, keep the plants well watered during hot weather, never letting the soil around them dry out. For small plants such as annuals and vegetables, and for plants growing in containers, this may mean watering as often as twice per day during heat waves. The lawn grasses that are used in the northern states are especially susceptible to heat. Keep the soil moist during hot weather. The lawn—and most other plants in the garden—benefits from being wet down during the hottest part of the day. Irrigation that aims at the roots of plants, such as drip methods, is advisable because it avoids having water droplets sit on leaves or grass blades, where they can act as miniature lenses, focusing the sun's rays and causing the plant to burn. To protect sensitive plants further, erect temporary shade structures. Shade larger plants with burlap or row covers stretched on a wooden frame. Shade small plants with shingles or pieces of cardboard set at an angle in the soil beside the plant.

Protecting plants from the cold

Fir branches used as protective mulch.

Low temperatures can cause severe damage in the home garden. Take these precautions against winter cold.

1. Protect tender plants from light frost with newspapers or sheets of fabric or plastic. When night temperatures lower than 32°F are predicted, cover the plants loosely. The heat generated under the cover by a single lightbulb can raise the temperature to help protect the plants. Remove the covers in the morning. In the South, protect tender or half-hardy plants during especially cold weather by covering them or by providing heat sources throughout the garden. Many small heat sources are more effective than a few large ones. Use electric lights, piles of charcoal, cans of jellied alcohol, or other slow-burning material.

2. In the North, continue watering the garden until the ground freezes in the winter. Plants need water in the soil to replace any lost through their leaves to the winter winds.

3. After the ground freezes, mulch perennials, trees, and shrubs with chopped leaves, wood chips, straw, evergreen boughs, or pine needles. A 4- to 6-inch layer will help maintain even soil temperatures and prevent alternate freezing and thawing, which can heave plants out of the soil, tearing their roots. If plants are heaved, replant them as soon as the soil can be worked. Mulch the disrupted roots.

4. Wrap the trunks of newly planted trees with burlap or tree-wrap paper to prevent sunscald or cracks in the trunk caused by fluctuating day and night temperatures.

5. Shield evergreens from drying winds and sun with burlap stretched over wooden frames or with snow fencing.

Chilling injury

Chilling injury.

Plants that have been grown in a house or greenhouse may be damaged if they are planted in the garden while night temperatures are still lower than 55°F. The growth of damaged plants may be temporarily halted, or parts of the leaves may die and turn black. To prevent this damage, accustom your plants to cool weather by a technique called hardening off. A week or two before planting them outdoors, place them outside in a sunny spot for one to three hours. Each day, increase the amount of time they are outside until it reaches a full day by the end of the 1- or 2-week period. If frost is predicted, bring them indoors. Water wilted plants promptly. Plants can also be hardened off in a cold frame. Gradually open the top more each day to expose the plants to cooler temperatures. Remove any shading gradually to allow in more sunlight.

CULTURAL PRACTICES

Preventing houseplant problems

Plants in quarantine.

Relatively few pests and diseases attack houseplants, but some of these can be difficult to control once they are established. By following these preventative measures, you can avoid many problems:

Quarantine: Before bringing any plants into the house, inspect them carefully for insects or signs of disease. Then place them in quarantine in a separate room from the other plants for a couple of weeks to give any hidden problems time to develop to the visible stage. This procedure should also be followed for houseplants that have been outdoors.

Prevention: Avoid bringing pests into the house on your person. After working in the garden or being around outdoor plants, wash your hands and change your clothes before working with houseplants. Mites, scale crawlers, and other pests can hitch rides into the home on your clothes or skin.

Cleanliness: Keep houseplants clean. Pick off dying leaves and blossoms, keep the soil surface clean of plant parts, and wash off leaves occasionally. Take the plants outdoors or into the shower, and wash dust off their leaves with a strong stream of water. Clean off the pot at the same time, and water the soil several times to leach out excess salts.

Observation: Pay close attention to your houseplants to catch problems while they are small and easy to control. Periodically inspect leaves and soil for anything unusual. Look especially at the undersides of leaves and protected crevices for insects or mites that might be hiding there.

Pheromone traps

Pheromone trap.

Insect traps can be used to determine when insects are present. By knowing when insect pests arrive, it is possible to time spraying precisely for maximum effectiveness. There are many types of traps, but those used most commonly attract insects either to a color (usually yellow) or a scent. The scents used are called *pheromones*. Pheromones are chemicals released by insects that send signals to other insects of the same species. Some of the most common pheromones are sex attractants, usually emitted by female insects to attract males. Males are extremely sensitive to these chemicals, following minute traces upwind for hundreds of yards to find the source of the scent. Pheromones are used as bait to attract male insects to traps. These traps are usually paperboard structures with a sticky lining that holds the insects. Pheromone traps can be purchased through the mail or from local garden centers. One or two traps, hung in a home garden or orchard, will tell you when the insects are mating. Monitor the traps at least once a week, more often as insects become active, removing the insects with a pointed stick or piece of wire and wiping them on a rag. Record the numbers trapped each time. If the spray is meant to kill the adult, apply it either when the first adult is caught or when the numbers peak (when a week's count is the same or less than the previous week's). If the spray is meant to kill the larvae hatching from eggs, delay spraying for a week or more to allow for egg laying and hatching. Pheromone traps come with instructions.

Barriers to pests

Row cover.

Sometimes the most effective way to protect plants from pests is to keep the pests completely away from the plants. Barriers such as fences are frequently used with animal pests, and many are described under the sections on controlling each animal. Barriers are often effective against smaller pests, too, however. Following are a few examples of pest barriers.

Row covers: These covers allow light, water, and air to pass freely but exclude insects, protecting vegetable gardens from many types of flying insect pests. The most useful cover is a floating row cover, a nonwoven fabric that is so light it doesn't need to be supported over the plants. Spread the cover over the plants, leaving enough slack for the plants to push it up as they grow. Hold down the edges with boards or soil. To make the plants more accessible, staple one edge to a light board. Throw the board back over the row to expose the plants for easy access.

Cutworm collars: Cutworms (see page 440) live in the soil during the day and feed on aboveground parts of the plants at night. Fence them out with collars around each plant. These collars should be at least 2 inches high, surround the plant stem fairly closely, and be pressed into the soil. Make collars out of stiff paper or aluminum foil bent into a cylinder or out of tin cans or paper cups with the bottoms removed.

Sticky bands: Nonflying insects, such as ants, can be kept out of trees and shrubs with bands of sticky material around the trunk. Purchase a commercial product sold for this purpose, or use heavy oil or grease.

Copper strip protecting tree.

Choosing plants

Checking roots.

Mulching

Wood chip mulch in a perennial bed.

Refresh the stickiness by stirring the product on the trunk or applying more every couple of weeks. These materials can damage smooth green bark by excluding air. Wrap green bark with paper or plastic film first and apply the sticky material to that.

Copper slug and snail guards: Slugs and snails won't cross copper because it causes a galvanic shock similar to that experienced when you bite a piece of aluminum foil with a metal filling. Surround planting beds, tree trunks, and containers with a strip of copper foil, screen, or tape from 2 to 4 inches wide. Purchase copper strips made for this purpose, or get thin sheet copper or copper window screen and cut it into strips. Surround the container with the strip, and don't allow any part of the plants inside to touch the ground outside the barrier. The copper will turn green with exposure but will remain effective for years.

Plants can be purchased in several different forms. Inspect all plants for visible insects and diseases. Here are some standards for choosing plants.

Balled-and-burlapped (B&B): The leaves are large, of good color, and free from spots or dead areas. The stems don't show signs of recent heavy pruning. Stem diameter is in proportion to the size of the plant. The roots don't encircle the base of the trunk, and the rootball inside the burlap is not broken or very dry.

Bare-root: The trunk is a good diameter for the size of the plant. The stem is flexible, and the bark is not broken or dried. The roots are symmetrical and flexible. The buds and roots are still dormant, with no new growth evident.

Container-grown: The leaves are large, of good color, and free from spots or dead areas. The stems don't show signs of recent heavy pruning. The stem diameter is in proportion to the size of the plant. The roots don't encircle the base of the trunk, and the plant is firmly rooted. When the plant is removed from the container, many roots are visible on the outside of the rootball, but they are not thick or woody.

Flats or small pots: Plants are young and stocky, without dead or discolored leaves. No plants are missing from the flat.

Sod: The grass is a good green color, without yellow blades. The soil is about 3/4 inch thick and moist. The sod holds together when handled.

Bulbs: The bulbs are firm, without wounds or blemishes. They aren't moldy or dried, and the basal plate is firm and not cracked. The skins may be loose.

Mulch is an insulating layer of material spread over the ground to hinder weed growth, slow evaporation from the soil, and moderate soil temperatures. The most important mulches are the following:

Organic material: A wide variety of organic materials are used as mulch. Some of the most common are straw, leaves, lawn clippings, wood chips, shredded bark, and ground corncobs. Organic mulches conserve soil moisture and modify the soil temperature near the surface. As these materials decompose, they improve the tilth of the soil. Choose a mulching material that is free of weed seeds and that hasn't been recently sprayed with an herbicide. Apply organic mulch 3 to 6 inches thick. A thick mulch also controls weeds.

Inorganic material: These materials don't decompose, so they are more permanent than organic mulches. Inorganic mulches include rocks, gravel, and coarse sand. These materials cost more but last longer than organic mulches. There is also less danger of bringing weed seeds or diseases into your garden.

Impervious films: The most popular impervious film mulch is black polyethylene. Clear plastic and builder's paper are also used. Black plastic provides an excellent control for weeds. It can even be placed over existing weeds to kill them. Films also control water loss and warm the soil slightly. Clear plastic doesn't control weeds, but it warms the soil quickly and can even be used to pasteurize the soil with heat. Because plastic films reduce the amount of oxygen that penetrates the soil, don't use them over large areas around trees and shrubs.

Disease-free impatiens and begonias brighten a garden corner.

416

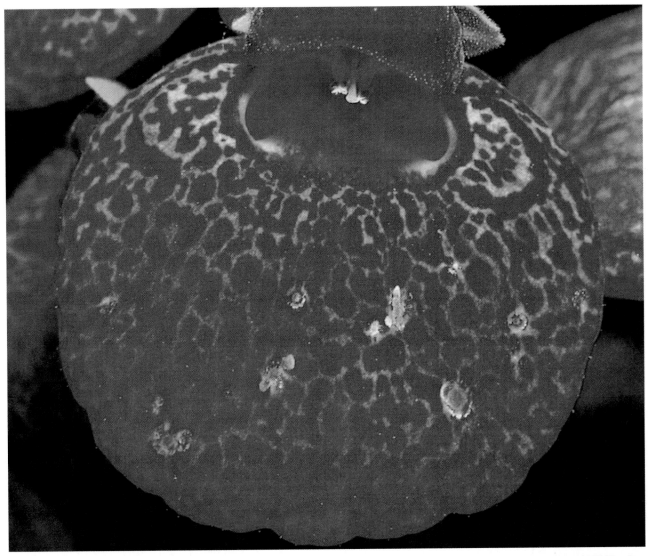

Botrytis blight on a calceolaria blossom. See page 418.

Most plant diseases are caused by fungi or bacteria. A key to understanding plant diseases and their prevention lies in the fact that both fungi and bacteria need moist conditions.

Plant diseases can be divided into two broad categories: (1) those that are spread by wind or splashing water, and (2) those that live in the soil.

Most diseases in the first category are spread as spores by wind or splashing raindrops to plant leaves or flowers. The spores germinate—usually within a drop of water on the leaf surface—and enter the leaf. Infection from this type of disease can usually be prevented by protecting the leaf with a fungicide and by keeping the leaf as dry as possible. Most fungicides provide a protective barrier on the leaf surface,

preventing the spore from germinating or killing it before it enters the leaf. To be effective, the protective barrier must be in place before the spore lands on the leaf, so timing is important with fungicidal sprays. The fungicide must also be renewed periodically as it wears off or as new unprotected growth appears.

If you live in an area where summer rainfall is frequent, relative humidity is high, and dew forms on the foliage most nights, you can't do much to keep the leaves dry. But if you must water during the summer, choose methods that don't wet the leaves. Or water in the morning so the leaves will dry as rapidly as possible.

The second category of plant diseases consists of those living in the soil. These diseases usually attack plants through their

roots or the base of their stem or trunk. Some of these organisms—such as the water molds—are present in most soils but aren't a problem if the soil is allowed to dry out periodically. This can be accomplished by improving the drainage so that water can escape from the soil, and by watering thoroughly but less frequently so that the soil has a chance to dry out between watering cycles.

Other disease organisms are present only in some soils. They are usually transferred to a garden on the roots of infected plants. Buy plants only from reputable nurseries, most of which pasteurize their planting mixes or use soilless mixes. Or quarantine new plants for a few weeks to make sure they are healthy before planting them in your garden.

FUNGAL DISEASES

Powdery mildew

Powdery mildew on lilac.

Different strains of powdery mildew, probably the most familiar plant disease, infect all types of plants in the garden and in the house. Unlike most other fungal plant diseases, powdery mildew grows on the outside of leaves, forming a white or gray "powder" composed of fungal strands and spores. Also unlike other fungal diseases, which infect only wet leaves, powdery mildew invades dry as well as wet leaves. This trait makes it the only fungal leaf disease that is active during dry weather. Spores are spread by the wind. The fungus causes leaves to yellow and dry and can kill whole branches or entire plants.

Control: Spray with Ortho® Garden Disease Control or Ortho® RosePride® Rose & Shrub Disease Control, or a fungicide containing sulfur, lime, or copper. Spraying with an antitranspirant may also help prevent infection. Repeat treatments every 10 to 14 days. Provide good air circulation by pruning branches to make the plant more open or by thinning to avoid crowding. Plant mildew-resistant varieties if available.

Rust

Rust on geranium.

These fungi are aptly named: Most rusts produce rust-colored or brown powdery pustules on the undersides of leaves and on the stems of their host plants. Rusts infect all kinds of plants, but most rust fungi infect only one or two plant species or only certain varieties of a species. Some rusts, such as cedar-apple rust (see page 297), must alternate between two specific host plants. Diseased plants are usually weak and stunted, and severely infected plants may die. Spores may be blown hundreds of miles to infect healthy plants. Some rust fungi can't infect their host unless the foliage remains wet for at least six hours. Most rusts require a living host to survive the winter; others can survive on plant debris.

Control: Many methods can be used to control or prevent rust infection. Spray infected plants with Ortho® RosePride® Rose & Shrub Disease Control or Ortho® Garden Disease Control. Make sure that your plant is listed on the product label. Space plants far enough apart for good air circulation, clean up fallen debris, and pick off and destroy badly infected leaves. Keep the foliage as dry as possible. One way to do this is to water in the morning, which allows the plant to dry quickly, reducing the chance of infection. The best way to avoid rust infection is to plant resistant varieties.

Botrytis blight

Botrytis blight on strawberry.

Botrytis blight, a plant disease also known as *gray mold, blossom blight,* or *bud and flower blight,* is caused by any of several closely related species of fungi (*Botrytis* species) that infect many vegetables, flowers, trees, and shrubs. The fungus usually begins to grow on plant debris or weak or inactive plant tissue, such as old leaves, flowers, and overripe fruit. After the fungus becomes established it invades healthy, growing plant tissue. *Botrytis* causes spotting and decay of flowers and foliage and of fruits and berries, both before and after harvest. In some plants, it causes cankers or rots stems, corms, and bulbs. *Botrytis* spores are present in most garden soils. The fungus thrives in cool, moist conditions.

Control: The key to avoiding problems is good sanitation. Remove and destroy dead leaves and flowers, especially those in contact with damp soil, so the fungus will not produce the thousands of spores necessary to infect healthy plants. Keep the foliage as dry as possible. Water the plants at soil level (instead of from overhead), and space them far enough apart so that air can circulate among them. Fungicides can also be helpful. Spray with Ortho® Garden Disease Control every 10 to 14 days as long as the mold is visible. Make sure that your plant is listed on the product label.

Water molds

Phytophthora rot of rhododendron.

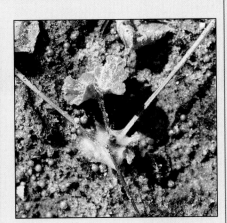

Pythium stem and root rot of geranium.

Leaf spot

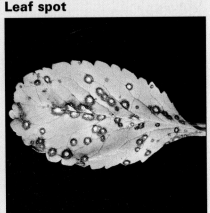

Septoria leaf spot.

Water molds are fungi (*Pythium* and *Phytophthora* species) that thrive in wet, poorly drained soils. They produce motile spores that swim through soil water to attack the roots of susceptible plants. Water molds are most active in warm (55° to 80°F) soils, but they survive as spores when the soil is cold or dry. Water molds are especially troublesome in frequently watered areas such as lawns or flower beds. They cause *damping-off* of seedlings and young plants (see page 420). Both fungi cause root rots of many plants. In addition, *Phytophthora* causes crown rots and collar rots of many herbaceous and woody plants. The fungus attacks stems or trunks just at or below the soil surface. Reddish to brown lesions usually form on the infected tissue, and sunken, girdling cankers may develop. In some cases, *Phytophthora* attacks the roots and then spreads to the trunk. The foliage of infected plants dulls, and individual branches or the entire plant wilts, turns yellow, and eventually dies. Gardeners frequently mistake this wilting for drought stress and water more heavily, speeding the demise of the plant. If the plant is so severely infected that most or all of the branches are dying, remove it. You may be able to save plants that are mildly infected by water molds by letting the soil dry out.

Control: If the plant is a tree or large shrub, remove the soil from around the rotted parts of the trunk and roots. Exposure to air will slow down or stop further decay.
The drying-out technique: This process involves careful observation in order to let the soil dry out as much as possible without placing plants under too much drought stress. Stop watering infected plants. To dry the soil as quickly as possible, place container plants in a well-ventilated, even breezy location. If they can tolerate direct sun, put them in a sunny spot. But if the roots are damaged badly enough that plants wilt or drop leaves, don't put them in the sun. Eventually the soil will dry out to the point where the plants would normally need another watering. Allow the soil to become drier yet to stop the fungi from continuing their decay. Take steps to minimize the water needs of the plants. Place container plants in a shaded location to reduce evaporation from the foliage. Provide shade for plants in the ground. Spray trees and shrubs that are growing in the shade with an antitranspirant, which reduces the amount of water that evaporates from the leaves. (Antitranspirants are available in many nurseries.) Further relieve drought stress by placing clear plastic tents over the plants. The tents maintain high humidity, reducing the water loss. Use tents only in the shade; if used in the sun, they can heat up enough to kill plants. Begin watering again when the plants show signs of drought stress, such as heavy wilting or yellowing and dropping of leaves.
Prevention: To help prevent future root rot problems, allow the soil to dry slightly between waterings, and provide good drainage. (For information on watering and drainage, see pages 406 to 408.) *Phytophthora*-resistant plants may be used in wet areas that are hard to drain. (For a list, see page 536.)

Most plants are occasionally blemished by leaf spot. Thousands of leaf-spotting fungi and bacteria exist; most cause only cosmetic damage. Many of these organisms infect only one narrow group of plant species. Spotting is sometimes accompanied by oozing, leaf yellowing, wilting, and decay. Fungal spores are blown or splashed on healthy leaves, and a spot forms wherever spores infect a leaf. Leaf-spotting bacteria are usually spread by splashing water or contaminated hands or tools. Leaf spot is most severe in mild, wet weather.

Control: If your plant is only lightly spotted, pick off and destroy infected leaves. If spotting is severe in your garden, try additional control methods. Control fungal leaf spot by spraying infected plants with Ortho® Garden Disease Control. Bacterial leaf spot organisms cannot be as easily controlled. Bactericides such as basic copper sulfate or *streptomycin* will help control bacterial leaf spot if used in combination with good sanitation practices. Badly infected plants should be destroyed. After working with infected plants, wash your hands and disinfect your tools. Keep foliage as dry as possible to reduce spotting. Avoid overhead watering, and water in the morning to give the foliage a chance to dry quickly. When using fungicides, make sure that your plant is listed on the product label. Use resistant plant varieties whenever possible.

FUNGAL DISEASES (continued)

Damping-off

Damping-off of beet seedlings.

Damping-off is a plant disease caused by any of several species of fungi (including *Pythium, Rhizoctonia, Fusarium, Phytophthora,* and *Sclerotium* species). These fungi, common in soils throughout the world, are among the major causes of poor germination. They infect seeds and seedlings at several stages. Seeds are often attacked before they germinate. Or seeds germinate, but the growing tips are infected and killed before they emerge from the soil. Seedlings are susceptible even after they emerge. The fungi can attack the stems and roots just at or below the soil level, causing the seedlings to fall over. Although older seedlings are more resistant, damping-off fungi may still infect them, producing dark lesions on the lower stems and roots that stunt and weaken their growth. Damping-off is most severe in soil rich in nitrogen and in soil that is constantly wet. Seedlings growing in soil that is too warm or cold for rapid germination and growth are also more susceptible to infection.

Control: Incorporate sand or perlite into the soil mix to increase drainage. Don't add fertilizers that are high in nitrogen until seedlings have produced at least one pair of true leaves. Encourage rapid growth by planting seeds in soil that is the proper temperature for rapid germination (see page 555). Provide germinating seedlings with bright light and good air circulation. Coating seeds with a fungicide containing *captan* will help discourage damping-off. Cover seeds started indoors with a thin (⅙- to ¼-inch) layer of peat moss.

Verticillium wilt or fusarium wilt

Fusarium wilt on cabbage.

These fungi (*Verticillium* and *Fusarium* species) cause wilting, stem and leaf discoloration, and the death of many plants. Both types of fungi live in the soil for years, even after the host plants have died. *Fusarium* thrives in warm soils and is most severe in the southern states. *Verticillium* is more of a problem in the cooler soils of the northern states. Both fungi infect annual vegetables, flowers, and herbaceous perennials. *Verticillium* also infects many woody shrubs and ornamental, fruit, and nut trees. Infection begins when fungal strands penetrate the roots of a susceptible plant. The fungus spreads up into the water-conducting vessels in the stems and leaves and breaks down some of the plant cells, producing gels and gums. The accumulation of gels, gums, cell debris, and fungal strands and spores in the vessels reduces nutrient and water flow up into the leaves. The clogging results in wilting, leaf and stem discoloration, and eventually death of the plant. The fungus also produces toxins that move up into uninfected leaves. These toxins interfere with photosynthesis and the production of chlorophyll, which is necessary for plant health and growth.

Control: Once plants have been infected, they usually die, but diseased flowers and vegetables often last through the season if they are cared for properly. Replace infected plants with varieties resistant to these wilt diseases. If you want to use susceptible plants, eliminate the fungus from the soil by fumigation or solarization.

Armillaria root rot

Armillaria root rot on sour cherry.

Armillaria root rot, a plant disease also known as *mushroom root rot, honey mushroom, oak root fungus,* and *shoestring fungus,* is caused by a soil-borne fungus (*Armillaria mellea*) that rots the roots of a wide range of plants. Many diseased ornamental and fruit trees die slowly over a period of years. These plants may die suddenly, however, especially if they are under stress. The fungus spreads short distances (less than a foot) through the soil by thick fungal strands (rhizomorphs) that penetrate the roots of nearby susceptible plants. Infection is most severe in heavy, poorly drained soil. Once the fungus enters the plant, it produces a white, fan-shaped mat between the bark and the wood that decays the roots and lower trunk. As the roots die, the top of the plant slowly starves. If the crown is girdled by the fungus, the top wilts and dies quickly. In the fall, mushrooms—the spore-producing fruiting bodies of the fungus—often appear around the base of the infected plant. A different fungus (*Clitocybe tabescens*), also known as *mushroom root rot,* causes similar and often identical damage to woody trees and shrubs in the Southeast.

Control: Remove badly infected trees, including the stumps and, if possible, the roots. You can usually save mildly infected plants, or at least prolong their lives. Remove the soil from around the rotted parts of the roots and trunk. Cut out the diseased tissue and allow the healthy wood to air through the summer. When temperatures drop toward freezing, cover the exposed roots with loose soil. Replace dying plants with *Armillaria*-resistant plants.

Sclerotium root rot

Sclerotium root rot on carrot.

Sclerotium root rot, a plant disease also known as *southern wilt*, *southern blight*, and *crown rot*, is caused by a soil-borne fungus (*Sclerotium rolfsii*) that occurs primarily in the southern states. The fungus infects many flowers and vegetables—especially carrots and bulbous flowers such as iris and tulip—and a few woody shrubs. *Sclerotium* causes root and crown rots, stem cankers, and bulb and tuber rots. It usually attacks plant stems at or just below the soil level. Infected plants wilt, turn yellow, and decay as the fungus spreads throughout the roots and stems. White fungal threads that surround or cover infected plants produce oxalic acid, which kills healthy plant cells, allowing the fungus to gain entrance. Sclerotium rot forms yellow or tan pellets called sclerotia that resemble mustard seeds. Under adverse conditions, these sclerotia pellets and fungal strands survive in the soil and plant debris to reinfect healthy plants when conditions become favorable. This disease is most severe in warm (80°F and higher), moist, sandy soil that is low in nitrogen.

Control: Once plants become infected, they can't be saved. It's best to pull out and destroy infected plants and remove the soil in the diseased area and 6 inches beyond. You can discourage reinfection by making the soil unfavorable for fungal growth. Add a fertilizer and liberal quantities of compost, leaf mold, or other organic matter. Clean up and destroy plant debris to eliminate fungal pellets.

Cotton root rot

Cotton root rot.

Cotton root rot, a plant disease also known as *Texas root rot*, is caused by a fungus (*Phymatotrichopsis omnivora*) that lives in soils throughout much of the Southwest. This fungus infects more than 1,700 species of plants, eventually killing them by rotting their roots. Infected plants wilt and may die within a few days if they are suffering from drought or heat stress. When pulled out of the ground, the roots are covered with yellow or tan fungal growth. The fungus thrives in warm, poorly aerated, alkaline (pH of 8.0 and higher) soils that are low in organic matter. In many areas, the fungal strands and spores are concentrated 1 to 3 feet below the soil surface. Cotton root rot can survive in the soil for five years after plants have died. It is spread from plant to plant by brown fungal strands that grow through the soil and by the movement of contaminated soil and transplants. Cotton root rot is most destructive from midsummer to frost.

Control: Creating a soil environment unfavorable to the development of cotton root rot can reduce its severity. Improve soil aeration by digging or tilling your soil. To improve the drainage and increase the number of competing beneficial microorganisms, incorporate lots of mulch, compost, or other organic matter into the soil. Reducing the alkalinity of the soil also helps. (For information on soil pH, see page 407.) Fumigating the soil will kill the fungus. (For a list of plants resistant to cotton root rot, see page 538.)

Fire blight

Fire blight on apple. Inset: Close-up of damage.

The bacterium that causes the disease fire blight (*Erwinia amylovora*) infects only members of the rose family. Apples, cotoneaster, firethorn, hawthorn, mountain ash, and pears are very susceptible. Bacteria spend the winter in infected bark and ooze out in the spring to attract insects. Although humans, splashing raindrops, and several insects may spread the bacteria, the primary vector is honeybees, which transfer bacteria to blossoms. In warm (65°F or higher), humid weather, the disease spreads rapidly from the blossom into the twig and adjoining leaves. Infected parts suddenly wilt and turn dark brown or black, looking as if they have been scorched by fire. The infection slows its spread as it reaches older, more mature wood. Severe cases can girdle and kill major branches or whole trees.

Control: Prune fire blight "strikes" 12 to 15 inches below any visible discoloration and destroy the debris. Disinfect shears between cuts. A protective spray of a bactericide containing basic copper sulfate or *streptomycin* applied before bud-break in the spring will help prevent infection. Repeat at intervals of five to seven days until the end of bloom. In the winter, prune any infected branches. (For lists of plants susceptible and resistant to fire blight, see page 535; resistant crabapples, see page 549; resistant apples, see page 552; resistant pears, see page 553.)

BACTERIAL DISEASES (continued)

Bacterial wilt

Bacterial wilt on cucumber.

Several kinds of bacteria can cause bacterial wilt in vegetables, flowers, tropical plants, and other herbaceous plants. Infection begins when bacteria in the soil or on contaminated tools and hands penetrate wounds in the roots, leaves, or stems or when infected seed is planted. In some cases, infection begins when insects transmit the bacteria to healthy plants. The bacteria enter the water-conducting vessels of the plant, where they break down plant cells, producing gums and gels. The bacteria also move out of these vessels to attack and dissolve the walls of adjacent cells. Sometimes bacterial ooze emerges from cracks in the leaf and stem tissue. The accumulation of gels, gums, cell debris, and bacteria in the vessels clogs the water flow throughout the plant. This clogging and the destruction of cell walls cause the plant to discolor, wilt, and finally die.

Control: Bacteria can't be stopped once they infect a plant. It's best to throw out the plant to avoid spreading the infection. Keep the garden clean; destroy infected plant debris. Some bacterial wilt diseases are spread by insects, so insect control is important. Some wilt diseases are spread on transplants, so be sure transplants are healthy. If you want to replant in infested soil, use resistant varieties. Because bacteria may remain in the seed, destroy seed obtained from infected plants. If infection is widespread and severe, you can kill the bacteria in the soil by using fumigation or solarization techniques.

Bacterial soft rot

Bacterial soft rot of cabbage.

Bacterial soft rot occurs on succulent fruits, vegetables, bulbs, and tubers. Any diseased, weak, or overripe fruit, vegetable, or flower is susceptible. A few kinds of bacteria can infect and decay actively growing plants, however. These bacteria penetrate the plant through wounds made by insect feeding or by damage from tools or handling. The bacteria produce enzymes that break down plant cells, causing the infected tissue to turn soft, mushy, and watery. Masses of bacteria and cell debris may ooze through growth cracks in the plant tissue. This sticky ooze dries and turns tan, gray, or brown. Bacterial soft rot is most severe in warm (80° to 85°F), moist conditions. The bacteria survive from season to season in infected plant debris and soil. Infection is spread by diseased plants or plant parts, water, and contaminated tools, soil, and plant debris.

Control: Chemicals aren't effective in controlling this disease; once plants are infected, you can't help them. The key to control is good sanitation. Help prevent bacterial soft rot by cleaning up plant debris around the garden. When working in the yard, be careful not to injure plants with hoes, cultivators, or other garden tools. You can further reduce infection by leaving enough space between plants so they get a chance to dry out after they are watered. Plant in well-drained soil.

Crown gall

Crown gall on euonymus.

Crown gall is caused by bacteria (*Agrobacterium tumefaciens*) that infect the plant through wounds in the roots, crown, or stems. After infection, the bacteria produce a substance that stimulates plant cells to enlarge and divide rapidly, independent of the normal hormonal control of the host plant, similar to tumors in animals and humans. As galls enlarge, they become woody and hard, turning brown and corky. Galls resemble natural burls, which don't harm the plant, except burls are solid healthy wood throughout, and galls are corky inside. The galls interfere with the plant's circulation, slowing the flow of water and nutrients through the galled area. Infected plants are often weak, stunted, and more susceptible to other sources of plant stress, such as drought and winter injury. The bacteria are spread by infested soil, transplants, and contaminated tools and soil water.

Control: Infected plants can't be cured; however, they usually survive for many years. The plants look better if stems with galls are pruned. Properly removing galls from tree roots and trunks is much more difficult, but professional horticulturists or landscape contractors can remove large galls. Galls on fruit and nut trees can be painted with the bactericide Gallex®, which often cures the gall. Follow label instructions. Cuttings and bare-root plants can be treated with the bacterial dip Galltrol®, which prevents crown gall. Avoid any unnecessary wounding of trunk or roots. Inspect new plants for galls. When you replant in infested soil, choose plants that are resistant to crown gall or dip the new plants in Galltrol®.

VIRAL DISEASES

Viruses

Rose mosaic.

Viral infection of mint.

Viruses are complex, submicroscopic particles composed of proteins and nucleic acids. They are much smaller than fungi or bacteria and don't have cell walls. A few viral diseases of plants are serious or fatal. These are usually transmitted by insects or spread by hands or equipment. Most viruses only slightly impair the growth of the plant and manifest symptoms only under certain conditions. They are usually transmitted when diseased stock is propagated by cuttings or grafting. Viruses may spread slowly from cell to cell, eventually infecting all of the plant tissue. Or they may spread quickly through the nutrient-conducting vessels to specific parts of the plant. Infection usually decreases the plant's ability to manufacture food. Less chlorophyll is produced, and the amounts of nitrogen and stored foods in the plant are reduced. Some common types of viruses, such as mosaics, ring spots, and stunts, produce specific symptoms. Mosaic viruses cause the foliage to become mottled or streaked. Ring-spot viruses cause pale rings to form on the leaves. Stunt viruses cause stunting of plant foliage. Often the symptoms overlap. In some hosts, these viruses cause leaf thickening, curling, and distortion; slow growth; and reduced yields of fruit, flowers, and vegetables. The severity of viral infections varies, depending on the host plant and the strain of virus. Sometimes viruses infect certain host plants without symptoms of disease showing. In other cases, symptoms appear with changes in the environment, such as a rise or drop in temperature.

Control: No chemical cures viral infections. Aphids, leafhoppers, certain other insects, and nematodes transmit viruses while feeding, so you can control infection by keeping down the populations of these organisms. (For more information on disease-carrying insects, see page 449.) Pulling out infected plants will also help reduce the spread of viral diseases. Seeds, bulbs, corms, and cuttings taken from infected plants are likely to be infected. It's best to purchase healthy plants and seeds from a reputable nursery and to discard seeds and cuttings from diseased plants. Some virus diseases are readily transmitted by hands and equipment. When handling plants, thoroughly wash hands and equipment between plants to reduce the possibility of spreading diseases. Discard obviously virus-infected plants. Wash the container and your hands in hot, soapy water.

PHYTOPLASMA DISEASES

Aster yellows

Aster yellows. Infected marigold bud on left.

Aster yellows is a plant disease caused by phytoplasmas, microscopic organisms similar to bacteria. Many vegetables, ornamentals, and weeds are susceptible to this disease. Infected plants are usually stunted and yellowing. They produce many spindly stems and flower stalks. The flowers are often green and don't produce seeds or fruit. Phytoplasmas are spread from plant to plant by leafhoppers. (For more information on leafhoppers, see page 448.) When a leafhopper feeds on a diseased plant, phytoplasmas are transferred into its body along with the plant sap. The phytoplasmas multiply in the insect's body. After an incubation period of 10 days, the leafhopper infects healthy plants when it feeds. (For a list of plants susceptible to aster yellows, see page 546.)

Control: Once the plant is infected, there is no way to cure it. Control aster yellows by destroying infected plants and keeping the garden free of weeds, especially those that are likely to be infected. Spray leafhoppers early in the season to keep populations from soaring later. Spray leafhopper-infested plants with Ortho® Bug-B-Gon® Multi-Purpose Insect Killer Concentrate or Ortho® Systemic Insect Killer according to label directions. Make sure that your plant is listed on the product label.

NEMATODES

Nematodes

Root knot nematode damage to snap bean.

Root knot nematode damage to carrot.

Nematodes are also known as *eelworms, nemas,* and *roundworms.* They include some well-known parasites of humans, such as pinworms. Nematodes are found throughout the world in soil, fresh and salt water, and plants and animals. The several hundred species of nematodes that parasitize plants are microscopic. Most live in the soil and feed on plant roots; a few (foliar nematodes) feed on aboveground plant parts. Nematodes are found throughout the United States, but they are most severe in the Southeast. They prefer moist, sandy loam soils.

Root nematodes: Root-feeding nematodes are attracted to substances exuded by plant roots. Some remain on the outside of the root while feeding; others penetrate the root tissue and live inside it. Roots may be damaged from the punctures made during feeding, but the most significant damage occurs when nematodes inject "saliva" into the roots. This saliva contains a toxin that causes cells to collapse or disintegrate, resulting in dark lesions and dead areas along the roots. In some cases, the toxin stimulates rapid cell growth or enlargement, resulting in numerous dark, bushy roots or in galls, or swellings, on roots. Nematode damage limits the ability of the root system to supply the aboveground plant parts with water and nutrients, causing plant wilting, discoloration, stunting, and in severe cases, death. Some nematodes indirectly injure plants by rendering them more susceptible to root rot fungi. Although nematodes don't directly transmit fungi, they can transmit certain virus diseases while feeding. Nematodes can move through the soil by themselves, but they move slowly, traveling, at most, 3 feet during a season. They are spread more rapidly by infested soil and transplants, contaminated equipment, and irrigation water.

Foliar nematodes: Foliar nematodes live and feed mainly inside plant stems and leaves. They spread through the plant by swimming through moisture on wet leaves. The foliage of infested plants is stunted and distorted, and brownish-black blotches develop on the leaves.

Control: Nematode damage is difficult to distinguish from other soil and root problems. Test the plants and a soil sample to confirm nematode damage. No chemicals can be used to kill nematodes in planted soil. Remove and destroy infested plants, and fumigate or solarize the soil to control nematodes before replanting. Many varieties of plants are resistant to nematodes. If you have a serious problem with nematodes, plant resistant varieties. For a list of nematode-resistant plants adapted to your area, check with your local county extension office. Avoid moving infested soil and transplants to clean soil.

AIR POLLUTION

Ozone

Ozone damage to bean.

Ozone forms when gases produced by combustion engines and other industrial processes interact in the presence of sunlight with materials given off by automobiles, solvents, and vegetation. Ozone is common throughout the United States and is the primary air pollutant on the East Coast. All types of plants are affected. Ozone causes small white to tan flecks to appear on the upper surfaces of leaves. On some plants, the flecks are visible on both the upper and lower surfaces. Conifers display mottled needles, or the needle tips of the current season's growth suddenly turn reddish brown to gray. Repeated exposure to ozone reduces growth; causes blossom, fruit, and needle drop; and may eventually kill the plant. Ozone injury usually occurs when the air is still. Concentrations are highest in the early afternoon from mid- to late summer. Ozone is absorbed through leaf pores. Once inside the leaf, it disrupts the cell membranes. This causes the cells to collapse, resulting in the white flecks. Environmental factors influence the susceptibility of plants to injury. Plants growing in light, moist soil with optimum nutrient levels are more sensitive to injury, as are those growing in warm temperatures (80° to 90°F) and high light levels at the time of exposure.

Control: Regular watering and fertilizing will speed the recovery of damaged plants. In smoggy areas, select plants that are tolerant of ozone (For a list of plants, see page 534).

Sulfur dioxide and nitrogen dioxide

Sulfur dioxide damage to azalea.

Sulfur dioxide is an industrial pollutant resulting from burning sulfur-containing fuels such as coal and refining oil and from smelting ores. Full-grown and nearly grown leaves are the most susceptible to injury. All types of plants are affected. Injured areas first become water-soaked and then turn yellowish; or they dry up, turning ivory or brown. Injured areas may appear along the margins and between the veins on both surfaces of the leaves. On conifers, the young needles turn orange-red. Severely injured plants drop their leaves or needles and eventually die. Plants are most sensitive to sulfur dioxide from late spring to late summer. Sensitive plants are more likely to be injured at midday than in the early morning or evening. Plants are more sensitive at temperatures above 60°F and when they are growing in moist soil.

Nitrogen dioxide causes symptoms similar to those of sulfur dioxide. It can be a problem in areas near factories that manufacture munitions or nitric acid or that do electroplating, engraving, or welding. The greatest concentrations of this pollutant occur in midsummer. Nitrogen dioxide damage occurs mainly during the night. Plants growing in moist soil are especially sensitive to injury. Nitrogen dioxide frequently interacts with other pollutants, causing extensive injury.

Control: Help injured plants to recover by watering and fertilizing them regularly. In industrial areas, select plants tolerant of sulfur dioxide and nitrogen dioxide from the list on page 534.

Dwarf mistletoe

Dwarf mistletoe on digger pine.

Dwarf mistletoe (*Arceuthobium* species) is a parasitic plant that grows only on conifers. The grayish-green to brownish-green scaly shoots of this parasite rarely grow longer than 8 inches; they are usually 4 inches or shorter. Unlike leafy mistletoe, dwarf mistletoe is a true parasite, obtaining all its food from the host plant. The rootlike attachment organs (*haustoria*) penetrate the host's food-conducting vessels. As the haustoria continue to spread through a limb, they form buds that sprout tufts of dwarf mistletoe along the infected branch. This parasite disrupts the normal functioning and hormonal balance of infected branches, often starving the branch growth beyond the point of infection. Limbs usually swell around the infected area, and cankers and witches'-brooms (many small tufted branches) may form. Infected trees are stunted, weakened, and sometimes killed by this parasite.

Control: The only effective way to get rid of dwarf mistletoe is to prune the limbs on which it is growing. The haustoria spread several feet inside the branch from the site of the mistletoe tufts, so cut the branch off at the trunk to make sure that you've eliminated all of the haustoria. Prune additional mistletoe; prune it out as soon as you see it. If a tree is severely infected (more than half of the branches are parasitized), consider removing the tree. The tree is bound to decline in health if it hasn't already and will be a source of infection for other trees.

Leafy mistletoe

Leafy mistletoe.

Leafy mistletoe (*Phoradendron* species) is a plant that grows on broadleaf trees throughout the United States; it rarely attack conifers. Leafy mistletoe has chlorophyll and can manufacture its own food. To obtain water and minerals, the rootlike attachments (*haustoria*) penetrate the host plant's water-conducting vessels. Haustoria can grow through the branch, sending up more leafy tufts several feet from the original site. Branches usually swell around the infected area, and branch growth is sometimes sparse beyond the mistletoe site. Leafy mistletoe spreads to other areas of the tree when its sticky seeds drop to branches below. Also, the seeds may be eaten or carried by birds and other tree-dwelling animals and deposited on other trees. Trees infested with leafy mistletoe usually survive for many years, but their overall growth and vigor may be reduced.

Control: The most effective way to get rid of leafy mistletoe is to prune the branch on which it is growing. To be sure that the haustoria have been removed, prune the branch at its point of origin or at least 18 inches below the point of mistletoe attachment. Haustoria are visible as green streaks or dots in the wood. If it is not possible to remove the branch, cut off the mistletoe and wrap the branch in several layers of black plastic. Mistletoe needs light to survive and will eventually die without it. Check the wrapping every few months to be sure that the binding is not damaging the branch and that the plastic is still intact. Replace it if the mistletoe is still alive.

WEATHER AND CULTURAL DISEASES

Drought

Drought.

Salt damage

Salt damage.

Overwatering

Overwatered primrose.

Plants suffer from drought stress anytime they receive less water than they need. Water is essential to the normal maintenance and growth of all plants. It moves into plant roots from the soil and is transported up through the water-conducting vessels in the branches, stems, and foliage to all the plant cells. The pressure exerted by water in the cells keeps them turgid. Eventually the water evaporates from the plant through microscopic breathing pores in the leaves. When plants don't receive enough water, the water pressure in the cells drops, the cells lose their turgidity, and the plant wilts. If drought continues, normal metabolic functions are disrupted. Plants grown in mild drought conditions are usually stunted and slow growing. They are also hardier and better able to withstand stress. Plants grown in more severe drought conditions stop growing, discolor, drop their leaves and fruit, and eventually starve and die. Plants wilt permanently when deprived of water for long periods or when grown in soil so dry that the roots can't extract water at all.

Control: Growth will be more rapid and luxuriant if you give plants enough water. (For information on watering techniques, see pages 407 to 408.) If drought is a common problem in your area because of low rainfall, plant drought-tolerant plants.

Salts in the soil come from naturally occurring minerals in the soil or in irrigation water. They also come from improperly applied manure, lime, or fertilizer or from salts used to melt winter snow and ice. If the concentration of salts dissolved in the soil water is too high, plants can't get enough water for healthy growth. As a result, growth slows and the leaves turn yellow. As the water in which salt is dissolved evaporates, salt also enters the plant where it is deposited in the tips or edges of leaves. When enough salt accumulates, the tissues at the edges of the leaves turns yellow and then dies. As water evaporates from the soil, the salts become more concentrated and more damaging. Salt damage and drought damage often occur together, compounding the problem. Salt accumulation in the soil is often caused by poor drainage, which keeps the salts from being leached through the soil.

Control: Leach salts from the soil with periodic heavy irrigation. Enough water should be applied to wash the salts below the plant roots. If the soil doesn't drain well, improve drainage according to the instructions on page 406. Keep the soil moist enough so that plants are never under stress. Follow label instructions when using fertilizer. Apply the fertilizer to moist soil, and water it in thoroughly. If you apply lime to soil already high in salts, use ground limestone rather than agricultural lime or quicklime; it is less soluble and less likely to cause problems. If you have a salt problem, don't use bagged cow or poultry manure, both of which contain high levels of salts.

Overwatering is one of the most common plant problems, especially in areas where the soil is heavy and poorly drained. Plant roots require oxygen to function normally. They obtain oxygen from tiny air spaces (*pores*) in the soil. When the soil is irrigated, air is pushed out of the soil pores and replaced with water. Pores refill with air after water drains through the soil, plant roots absorb water, and water evaporates through the soil surface. If water is constantly reapplied, the soil pores remain filled with water. Roots rot and die because they can't absorb the oxygen they need. The dying roots decay and then are unable to supply the plant with water and nutrients. This results in plant stunting, weakening, and eventual death. Sometimes plants respond to wet soil conditions by growing roots just under (in some cases just above) the soil surface where the soil dries out more rapidly and oxygen is more available. These plants are often stunted and grow slowly. They may wilt and die quickly if the soil is allowed to dry out past their shallow root zone. Overwatering frequently causes root rot diseases. (For more information on root rot, see page 419.)

Control: Allow the soil to dry out somewhat between waterings. (For information on watering, see pages 407 to 408.) If your soil is heavy and poorly drained, improve the soil drainage. (For information on drainage, see page 406.) Some plants can tolerate wet soil. (For a list, see page 533.)

Leaf burn and leaf scorch

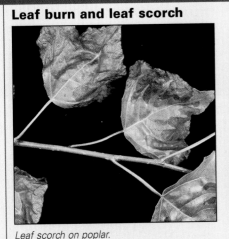

Leaf scorch on poplar.

Leaf burn on fuchsia.

Sunscald

Sunscald on maple.

Leaf burn and leaf scorch occur when leaf cells overheat. Although the two terms are sometimes used interchangeably, leaf scorch usually refers to browning and tissue death around leaf margins and between veins, while leaf burn usually refers to dead patches in the middle of the leaf. Normally, leaves are cooled by the evaporation of water from their surfaces. When leaves dry out, the amount of water that evaporates is reduced and the leaves overheat, then burn or scorch. Sometimes entire leaves or shoots are damaged. Several conditions may cause leaf burn or leaf scorch. Many of these factors are interrelated; when they occur in combination, damage may be severe.

Lack of water: Leaf burn and leaf scorch often occur when plant roots can't get enough water. Many soil conditions may cause dehydration. Plants growing in dry, salty, frozen soils or areas with limited rooting may not get as much water as they need.

Too much water: Overwatered or heavy, poorly drained soils can cause burn or scorch. Roots require oxygen to function properly. Wet soils are often low in oxygen, causing root death. As the roots start to die, they absorb less water.

Wind and heat: Hot, windy conditions cause burn and scorch in some plants, even when the soil is moist. Wind and heat cause water to evaporate more quickly from the leaves than it can be replaced.

Freeze damage: Leaf burn or leaf scorch may result when foliage freezes. Frozen leaf cells rupture or dry out and die.

Other factors: Roots that are diseased or mechanically damaged often can't supply as much water as the plant needs, resulting in leaf burn or leaf scorch. Burn and scorch can also be caused by an accumulation of salt in the leaf tissue.

Control: Leaves damaged by leaf scorch or leaf burn won't recover. Keep plants properly watered to help reduce further damage. (For information on watering, see pages 407 to 408.) If possible, shade plants during very hot weather, and hose down foliage a couple of times a day. Protect shade-loving plants by providing adequate shade. (For information on heat protection, see page 413.) Make sure the soil is moist when it freezes, and reduce chances of dehydration resulting from frozen soils by applying a mulch around the base of the plant. (For information on mulching, see page 415.) Inspect damaged plants for root rot or mechanical damage. (For information on root rot, see page 419.)

Sunscald occurs when bark is killed by overexposure to the sun. Trees that have been recently transplanted or pruned and young trees with thin bark are most susceptible to sunscald. When a tree is shaded by other trees, buildings, or dense foliage, the bark on the trunk and branches remains thin and tender. If exposed to intense sunlight, the bark cells heat up rapidly. Because they are not adapted to such high temperatures, the cells are easily injured or killed. Dark brown or black bark is particularly susceptible to sunscald because it absorbs more heat than lighter bark. Sunscald may also occur during cold, sunny winter days. The injured or dead bark turns dark and splits open, forming long cracks or cankers, usually on the southwest side of the tree. Decay organisms may invade the damaged bark and wood. Sunscald is most severe when the tree is suffering from drought stress.

Control: Unless the tree is very young or extremely damaged, it will usually recover with proper care. Water and fertilize the tree to stimulate new growth. As the tree adapts to its sunnier location, its bark will thicken; new growth will also shade the bark, protecting it from sunscald. To prevent damage, wrap the trunk and main branches of recently pruned or newly transplanted trees with burlap or tree-wrapping paper. Or paint the exposed bark with whitewash or white interior latex paint. If possible, transplant in overcast, cool weather, and water trees as soon as they've been transplanted. (For information on watering, see pages 407 to 408.)

TEMPERATURE-RELATED DISEASES *(continued)*

Cold damage

Upper flower buds killed by winter cold.

Frost cracks.

Low temperatures damage plants in several ways.

Freezing: Leaves, stems, and sometimes the entire plant may be killed by freezing. Foliage damaged by freezing temperatures looks water-soaked and wilts. In a few hours or days, it darkens and turns black.

Tender plants: Tender plants are most likely to suffer from freezing temperatures in the fall and spring. Seedlings or plants that have been raised in the house or greenhouse are very susceptible to freeze damage if they are planted outdoors too early in the spring or left out too late in the fall.

Early or late cold snaps: Plants that are hardened off (adjusted to outdoor conditions) and adapted to the area in which they are growing don't usually sustain freeze damage unless the temperature drops much lower than normal. During mild fall weather, however, hardening off is delayed, and unexpected cold snaps in early fall may freeze tender leaves and stems. When premature warm spells during the spring stimulate the production of new growth, cold snaps can be very damaging to this tender foliage.

Chilling injury: Cold-sensitive, tender plants growing in warm-winter areas and greenhouse-grown or house-raised plants may be susceptible to chilling temperatures (50°F and lower). Chilling injury usually occurs when these plants are set outdoors and night temperatures drop below 50°F. Even though the leaf tissue doesn't freeze, these tender plants can't tolerate cool conditions. Their foliage may discolor and die.

Winter sunscald and frost cracks: For information on cold damage to woody plants, see page 413.

Control: If you anticipate temperatures low enough to cause damage, cover plants with burlap, cardboard, or heavy paper during the night. Irrigation can also be used to modify temperatures. Wait until spring before pruning dead twigs and branches. Often the full amount of dieback caused by cold damage isn't obvious until the tree or shrub begins to grow again in the spring. Prune or pinch off frozen leaves, flowers, and stems of herbaceous flowers and vegetables, however, as soon as damage is noticed. Use only plants adapted to your area, or be prepared to shelter or protect tender plants when temperatures drop lower than 50°F. Harden off house-raised plants before setting them outside by gradually exposing them to cool temperatures over a period of a week. (For information on hardening off, see page 413.)

NUTRIENT DEFICIENCIES

Nitrogen deficiency

Nitrogen-deficient corn.

Nitrogen is the nutrient plants most commonly lack. Nitrogen-starved plants grow slowly. New leaves are small and pale green. Older leaves turn yellow and fall off or die and remain hanging on the plant.

Nitrogen in the plant: Nitrogen is taken up by plant roots from the soil and is used in the formation of many plant tissues and compounds, such as proteins, chlorophyll, enzymes, and nucleic acids. Because plants use nitrogen to form new tissues, they use this nutrient in large quantities whenever growth is rapid; plants that are dormant or slowly growing use less nitrogen.

Soil deficient in nitrogen: If the soil is deficient in nitrogen, plants break down the compounds in older leaves to recycle the nitrogen for new growth. This is why the older leaves of plants suffer from nitrogen deficiency, turn yellow, and die.

High nitrogen levels: High nitrogen levels stimulate leaf growth, often at the expense of root growth, flower and fruit production, and tuber development.

Control: Most plants need to be fertilized regularly with nitrogen fertilizers. While plants need nitrogen whenever they aren't dormant, they need the greatest amounts when leaves are growing most rapidly. For most plants, this is from spring through early summer. (For more information on nitrogen fertilizing, see page 410.)

Phosphorus deficiency

Phosphorus-deficient chrysanthemum.

Plants that are starved for phosphorus are stunted and darker than usual. The leaves are dull and gray-green and may be tinged with magenta. Some plants develop magenta coloring under the leaves, especially on the veins or around the edges of leaves. Flowering and fruiting are usually poor. Plants that are only slightly deficient in phosphorus grow more slowly than normal and produce fewer flowers and fruit, but often they have no specific symptoms.

Phosphorus in the plant: Phosphorus is used in the enzyme systems that produce new cells and supply energy to the plant tissues. It promotes healthy root growth and the production of flowers and fruit.

Seedlings: Seedlings and other plants with limited root systems need more phosphorus than plants with more developed root systems. Even in areas where phosphorus seldom needs to be applied to growing plants, seedlings may be deficient. If this is the case, their growth is slowed for a few weeks until the root system develops enough to supply the plant with phosphorus. Trees seldom need additional phosphorus.

Control: For a quick response, spray the leaves with Miracle-Gro® Bloom Booster, which contains 52 percent phosphorus. Water the soil with the same fertilizer. Add Scotts® Bulb Food to the soil, placing it within the root zone either by cultivating or by dropping it into holes dug into the root zone. In the future, use a fertilizer that contains at least 5 percent phosphorus.

Potassium deficiency

Potassium-deficient leaf.

Plants that are deficient in potassium grow slowly. The older leaves are mottled with yellow or pale green smudges. The edges of the leaves scorch and die. The dead area may extend inward between the leaf veins. Badly scorched leaves usually drop. Slightly deficient plants grow more slowly and have low yields of flowers and fruit. They are especially susceptible to disease.

Potassium in the plant: Potassium is essential to the normal functioning of many plant enzymes and facilitates the production of chlorophyll, proteins, carbohydrates, and other plant tissues. Potassium is used in the production of new cells and is necessary for the proper opening and closing of the microscopic breathing pores (stomata) in leaves. This nutrient is used most heavily in rapidly growing plant parts.

Lack of potassium: When potassium is in short supply, plants break down potassium-containing compounds in their older leaves and recycle the potassium to new growth. This is why symptoms develop first and are most pronounced on older leaves.

Control: Fertilize the plant with Scotts® All Purpose Plant Food, which contains 18 percent postassium. After the first treatment, use a fertilizer that contains at least 5 percent potassium.

Minor nutrient deficiency

Iron-deficient blackberry leaves.

The leaves of plants deficient in minor nutrients are pale green or yellow between the veins; the veins remain bright green. In extreme cases, the entire leaf is bright yellow or almost white and small, so that the new growth looks like a flower. Older leaves usually remain green.

Minor nutrients in the plant: Iron and several other elements (including manganese and zinc) are essential plant nutrients. They are called *minor* only because they are needed by the plant in small quantities. Minor nutrients are required for the production of chlorophyll and are essential to the proper functioning of many plant enzymes.

Minor nutrients in the soil: These nutrients are present in most soils. Alkaline soil or wet soil, however, often causes them to form compounds that can't be used by the plant. Minor nutrients aren't mobile throughout the plant. Once they have been incorporated into leaf tissue, the plant can't reuse them for new growth. Deficiencies of minor nutrients therefore show up in the newest growth first.

Control: Spray the foliage with Miracid® Plant Food and apply it to the soil around the plants to correct the deficiency of minor nutrients. Check the soil pH. (For information on pH, see page 406.) If your soil is too alkaline, correct the pH by treating with soil sulfur or aluminum sulfate. Maintain an acid pH by using Miracid® Plant Food.

SPOTS AND GROWTHS

Edema

Edema on cabbage.

Edema affects houseplants and some outdoor herbaceous plants. This condition is caused not by an insect or a disease but by a buildup of water in the plant. Edema usually develops in plants that are overwatered and growing in a cool, humid atmosphere. Under these conditions, water is absorbed rapidly from the soil and lost slowly through the leaves. The excess water that builds up in the plant causes cells to burst. Water-soaked spots or pale green blisters or bumps form on the leaves and stems. Eventually these bumps and spots develop into reddish-brown corky ridges and spots. Some of the badly affected leaves may turn yellow and drop off.

Control: Edema is not a serious condition in itself but often indicates an overwatering problem. Eliminate edema by planting in well-drained soil and watering properly. (For information on watering, see pages 407 to 408; for information on improving drainage, see page 406.)

Galls

Oak gall.

Galls are growths on plants. They may be simple lumps, or they may have a complicated structure. Some galls are brightly colored. Galls form on leaves, twigs, and branches. In most cases they are unsightly but not damaging to the plant, although small plants may be stunted. The water and nutrient circulatory system of a small plant may be disrupted by the galls. Some galls form when insects (certain wasps, midges, and aphids) or mites feed on or lay eggs in leaves, stems, and twigs. While feeding or laying eggs, these insects inject a toxin that stimulates rapid and abnormal cell growth. Galls may also develop as a response to infection by any of several kinds of fungi, bacteria, and viruses. Galls caused by fungi and bacteria are usually most numerous during unusually wet seasons. A soil-inhabiting bacterium (*Agrobacterium tumefaciens*) causes a common plant disease called *crown gall*. (For more information on crown gall, see page 422.)

Control: Pruning gall-infested growth usually takes care of the problem. If galls are especially unsightly and numerous, you can control the insects or diseases that are causing them. Look up your plant in the index to determine which pests may be causing the galls.

Witches'-broom

Witches'-broom on hackberry.

Witches'-broom is a dense tuft of weak, twiggy growth that develops on the branches of woody trees and shrubs. The foliage that grows on a witches'-broom is usually smaller and paler than normal. Witches'-broom is not a disease in itself; it grows when a hormonal imbalance develops in the plant, usually as the result of disease. Some mites or an infestation of dwarf mistletoe can also cause witches'-broom. (For more information on dwarf mistletoe, see page 425.) Sometimes environmental factors or chemicals such as herbicides stimulate the growth of witches'-brooms. Certain kinds of plants are more likely to develop these growths. Although a witches'-broom weakens the affected branch, it does not seriously damage the plant. The disease or mite that caused the witches'-broom, however, may kill the plant.

Control: If a plant has many growths of witches'-broom, it is probably diseased or infested. You can improve the appearance of the tree or shrub by pruning off the witches'-broom, but unless you can control the disease or mite that is causing these growths, witches'-brooms will continue to develop. Look up your plant in the index to determine what may be causing these growths. Contact a professional horticulturist or your local county extension office for additional help.

Cankers

Cankers on chestnut.

Most cankers are dark, sunken areas on trunks or branches. The bark over these areas cracks, then usually dies and falls off, revealing the wood beneath. Many trees produce a sticky sap that oozes from cankers. Cankers are caused by fungi and bacteria that infect the soft tissue just under the bark. Bark that has been damaged by sunscald, cold injury, pruning or insect wounds, or mechanical injury is especially susceptible. As infection spreads, the infected bark and wood tissues darken and die. The water- and nutrient-conducting vessels that pass through the cankered area are cut off. If the canker girdles a branch, the branch dies; if the trunk is girdled, the whole tree dies. Sometimes the plant walls off and stops canker growth by surrounding the canker with corky, barklike cells. Trees and shrubs aren't usually killed by cankers but are weakened and become more vulnerable to insects, diseases, and winter injury.

Control: During dry weather, remove badly infected branches and cut out cankers. Keep tree wounds to a minimum to cut down on canker formation. When pruning or working around plants, use the proper equipment. Steer carefully around trunks when mowing the lawn. Maintain edging around trees so that the area immediately surrounding a tree does not have to be mowed. Infected trees will heal more quickly if they are watered and fertilized properly. (For information on fertilizing and watering, see pages 407 to 409.)

Conks

Conk on an oak.   *Conk on a palm.*

Conks are mushrooms that grow from the trunk of a tree, often near the base. Most begin as hemispheres, then develop slowly into shelflike plates. They are frequently tough and woody after maturation, and range in color from cream to dark brown. Some conks are perennial, producing spores for several years. Others die after producing spores, but may persist on the trunk for years. Most of the fungi that make conks cause serious diseases called *heart rot*, *butt rot*, and *root rot*. The conks are produced only after the disease has progressed to the point where it is difficult to save the tree. (For information on heart rot, see page 193.)

Mushrooms and conks are the reproductive bodies of fungi. When fresh, they produce microscopic spores. Most fungi live on decaying matter, but some infect the roots or heartwood of trees, rotting them. Most of these grow only in older wood, which they enter through wounds. Others invade the roots, spreading until they rot the base of the tree. These fungi produce enzymes that break down the structure of the wood, weakening and rotting it. Following are some common heart and root rot fungi:

Fomes fomentarius causes heart rot. The conks are hoof shaped and hard, with gray tops and white bottoms. They grow larger each year, up to 8 inches across.

Ganoderma species cause root rots. The conks are shelflike and have a shiny reddish-brown top with a whitish margin, up to 14 inches across. They may appear on roots or at the base of the trunk.

Inonotus dryadeus is a root rot that eventually works its way up into the trunk. The conks are formed just above the soil line. They are tough, large, irregularly shaped, and brown. With time, they become rough and dark brown.

Laetiporus sulfureus causes root rot. Its conks are bright yellow to orange. New conks are formed during the summer, and they fall off during the winter.

Armillaria mellea, although not a heart rot, causes similar symptoms. It produces honey-colored mushrooms around the base of the tree. For more information, see page 420. (For information about heart rot, see page 193.)

Control: Heart or butt rot can weaken large limbs so that they break during storms. Root rot can weaken the entire root system, causing the tree to blow over during a storm. Once conks are produced, the disease has progressed to an advanced stage, and the tree should be considered dangerous. Trees can become dangerous even before conks are produced. If conks or any heart rot is visible on a large tree, it should be inspected by an arborist and pruned or removed if necessary. To prevent heart rot, avoid wounding trees. Keep pruning wounds small, and make pruning cuts properly. (For information on pruning, see page 412.)

This tobacco hornworm is feeding on a pepper plant. The horn on the backend is harmless (see page 395).

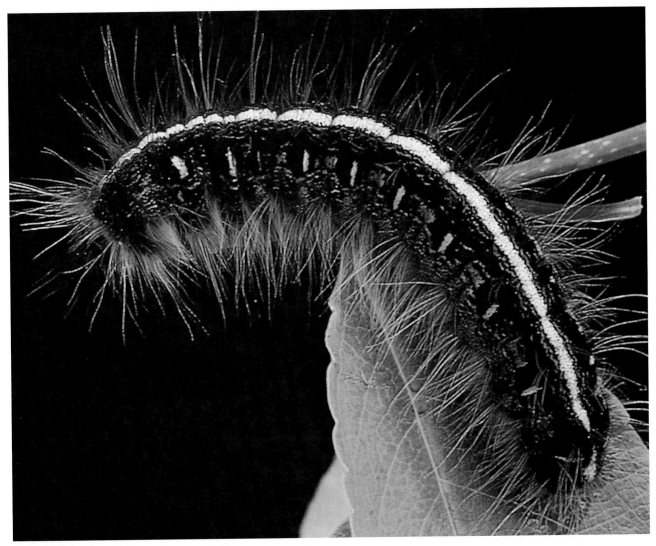

Tent caterpillar. See page 241.

Insects and plants have evolved together. Insects exist in vast numbers; they will always be present in our gardens. Our goal should be not to eradicate all insects, or even the harmful ones, but to control their numbers and hold in check the damage they do to plants.

Entomologists—scientists who study insects—place a great deal of importance on developing life histories of insects they study. A life history tells when the eggs hatch, what the larvae eat, how they survive the winter, where they lay eggs, and other information about an insect's growth and development cycles.

Life histories help us to locate weaknesses—times of year or stages of growth when the insect is most susceptible to control measures. Scale insects, for instance, are covered with a waxy shell for most of their lives. This shell protects them from predators and insecticides. But when they first hatch, they are soft-bodied and easily killed by insecticides. A well-timed spray or two can control a whole generation of scales.

Timing is particularly important with insects that have a single generation each year. All the eggs of single-generation insects hatch at once, and they go through the life stages simultaneously. Other insects, such as aphids, have multiple generations per year. All life stages of these insects are apt to be present at once. Control of multigenerational insects usually depends on a series of treatments over a period of time to kill new generations as they hatch from eggs.

Winter is a particularly vulnerable time for many insects. Being cold-blooded, insects must spend the winter in an inactive state, often as eggs or pupae. Sanitation measures—such as removing dead plants from the garden, picking up trash, and tilling—remove, kill, or expose to the cold many insect pests. Dormant oil sprays suffocate eggs and insects on trees. Winter may be the best time to reduce the following summer's insect population.

Also, many plants now being bred are resistant to their most damaging pests. Ask your county extension agent or local nursery and garden center professionals about insect-resistant varieties that are adapted to your area.

BEETLE ORDER

Beetles

Elm leaf beetles (4× life size).

Bark beetles and borers

Eastern ash bark beetle (8× life size).

Flat-headed borer (2× life size).

Beetles are members of the order *Coleoptera*, the largest insect order, containing 40 percent of all insects. The shiny or dull insects are easily recognized by their tough, leathery wing covers, called *elytra*. The wing covers meet in the middle of the back, forming a straight line down the insect's body. Some beetles, distinguished by their long snouts, are also called *weevils* or *curculios*. When beetles are at rest, the elytra hide a pair of clear, membranous wings. Some beetles don't have functional wings and can't fly. The larvae of beetles are sometimes called *grubs*. Those grubs that have legs usually have three pairs. The larvae of weevils and curculios are legless. Both larvae and adults may be harmful to plants. They have chewing mouthparts and feed on plant tissue, on other insects, or as scavengers. Plant feeders may devour any part of the plant. Some beetles feed inside the leaf tissue as leafminers (see page 455), borers (see at right), or bark beetles (see at right and page 200). Others feed outside the plant or on the roots.

Control: Which of the many methods for controlling beetles you use depends on the part of the plant infested. Control measures are often aimed at the adults, because grubs may be hidden or protected from chemicals inside plants or in the ground. Several insecticides, including Ortho® Systemic Insect Killer, Ortho® Bug-B-Gon® Multi-Purpose Insect Killer Concentrate, and Ortho® Malathion Plus® Insect Spray Concentrate are used to control adult beetles. Look in the index for your specific plant.

Most borers that tunnel into wood or soft stems are the larvae of beetles or moths. Their presence is usually indicated by the sap or sawdust that surrounds holes in the tissue and by wilting and dying foliage on the affected stems or branches. Hundreds of different kinds of borers infest trees, shrubs, and herbaceous plants. Borers that infest trees and shrubs usually favor weak, wounded, or newly planted specimens. Borers, however, commonly attack healthy flowers and vegetables as well. Vigorous trees and shrubs are often able to resist borer infestations. When the larvae try to burrow into such plants, they are overcome by oozing plant sap. Weak plants, such as those that have damaged roots or are suffering from drought, have reduced sap flow, making it easier for borers to enter them and develop inside. Beetle borers fall into two general categories: bark beetles and flat-headed and round-headed borers.

Bark beetles: These beetles mainly attack and kill weak conifer trees but are also capable of attacking and killing a healthy tree when present in large numbers. The larvae are white or cream-color and from ¹⁄₁₆ to ¼ inch long. Adult bark beetles are the same size and are usually black, brown, or dark red. The adults tunnel into and under the bark and lay eggs along the tunnels. Larvae hatch and generally bore away from the parent tunnel, creating characteristic patterns that experts can use to identify the specific kind of bark beetle.

Flat-headed and round-headed borers: These larger insects attack severely weakened trees or freshly killed trees. The larvae, usually white or cream-color, are approximately ¾ inch in length at maturity. Some have heads that are flattened and triangular; others have rounder heads. Adults are from ¼ to 1½ inches long and are often metallic or brightly colored. The larvae bore tunnels that travel in meandering, random paths, mostly in the wood but also just underneath the bark.

Control: The best control for borers in many herbaceous plants is to cut out and destroy infested stems and remove and destroy dying plants. To control borers with chemicals, sprays must be applied before the insects burrow into the plant. The time varies with different species. For timing of sprays, look up your plant in the index, or contact your local county extension office. Spray plants with an insecticide containing *carbaryl*. Make sure that your plant is listed on the product label. Keep plants vigorous by fertilizing and watering regularly and by controlling diseases and other insects. Avoid wounding plants. Prune woody plants carefully, avoiding stubs that can attract or harbor borers. Avoid injuries to roots, major shoots, and trunks.

Eucalyptus long-horned beetles

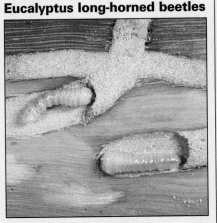

Long-horned borer larvae (life size).

The eucalyptus long-horned borer (*Phoracantha semipunctata*) is a new pest of  eucalyptus trees, imported to California from Australia. The female beetle lays eggs under loose bark. In 10 to 14 days, the larvae hatch and, after feeding briefly on the surface of the bark, bore into the tree to feed beneath the bark. The larvae tunnel through the wood as they feed, leaving galleries filled with their sawdustlike frass. The tunnels block the flow of nutrients in the branch, causing it to wilt and die back. In severe cases, the trunk is girdled and the whole tree dies. The mature larvae bore deep into the tree to pupate; adult beetles emerge through oval holes in the bark. In warm conditions, the entire cycle from egg to adult can be completed in two months. In cool areas, the cycle may take up to nine months. The larvae can only infest weak or dead trees. Healthy trees exude copious amounts of gum, drowning the penetrating larvae. Trees stressed by drought or other problems don't produce enough gum to stop the borers.

Control: No chemical effectively treats for this pest. Remove infested branches and burn them or bury them at least 8 inches deep. Arrange eucalyptus logs kept for firewood in uniform piles wrapped tightly with a thick plastic tarp to prevent infestation by the borers. Keep trees healthy by watering them in times of drought and fertilizing them if necessary. Several natural predators of this beetle have been imported from Australia and may provide some measure of control.

Japanese beetles

Japanese beetle (life size).

The Japanese beetle is a metallic-green insect with bronze wing covers. It was first noticed in New Jersey in 1916 and since then has been a problem throughout the eastern half of the country. Adults feed during the day on a variety of plants. They devour flowers, ripening fruit, and tender leaves, but they eat only the tissue between the veins on tree leaves. Beetles are often seen in clusters of 20 or more hanging from fruit or flowers. When beetles emerge in June, they begin feeding on low-growing plants and then fly to tree leaves. Adults live for 30 to 45 days and are most abundant in July. Just before they die, females lay their eggs under the soil surface in lawns or other grassy areas. Grubs that hatch from eggs are grayish white with brown heads and have a characteristic C-shape. They feed on grass roots until cold weather drives them below the frost line. When the soil warms, the grubs move back up and resume feeding on grass roots. The grubs pupate in the soil and then emerge as adults to feed above ground.

Control: Adult beetles can be controlled on ornamentals with Ortho® Rose & Flower Insect Killer, Ortho® Bug-B-Gon® Multi-Purpose Insect Killer Concentrate, or Ortho® Systemic Insect Killer. Spray food crops with Ortho® Malathion Plus® Insect Spray Concentrate. Controls may have to be repeated, because new beetles continue to emerge for about six weeks. To better time insecticide applications, use Ortho® Bug-B-Gon® Full-Season Japanese Beetle Traps to monitor the emergence of adult beetles. Before spraying, make sure your plant is listed on the label.

Weevils

Weevil-damaged rose. Inset: Rose curculio (life size).

Weevils, also known as *snout beetles*, are beetles that have long snouts with chewing mouthparts at the end. Some weevils, called *curculios*, usually have snouts that are longer and more curved than those of other weevils. Weevil adults are hard-bodied, usually dark-colored insects that play dead when disturbed. They feed on many different types of plants, often chewing holes in leaves, buds, and flowers. The larvae are white, fleshy, legless grubs that usually live inside plant tissue. Grubs may feed inside seeds, fruit, buds, leaves, and stems. Some weevil grubs live in the soil and feed on plant roots. These *root weevils* are very damaging to their host plants. (For more information on root weevils, see page 436.)

Control: Control is most often aimed at adults, since the larvae are usually protected inside plant tissue. Several different insecticides, including some containing *carbaryl*, are used to control weevils on fruit and vegetables. Treat ornamentals with Ortho® Systemic Insect Killer or Ortho® Rose & Flower Insect Killer.

BEETLE ORDER (continued)

Root weevils

Black vine weevil larvae (life size).

Root weevils are serious pests of berries, ornamentals, and grasses. Both adults and larvae cause damage. The adults are snout beetles, with chewing mouthparts at the ends of their long snouts. They have light brown to black hard-shelled bodies and rows of tiny round depressions on their backs. The adults of most species can't fly because their elytra (wing covers) are fused down the middle of their backs. Adult weevils feed at night, notching the edges of leaves. In the summer, each female lays hundreds of eggs on the soil at the base of plants. Emerging larvae are white, C-shape, legless grubs with brown heads. The grubs sometimes feed on the base of plant stems before burrowing into the soil to feed on roots. They spend the winter in the soil and resume feeding in the spring. Larval feeding is most severe in spring and often results in weakening or death of the plant.

Control: Because the grubs are protected by soil, there is no effective control for them. Control of root weevils must be aimed at the adults. The best time to spray is when the adults emerge from the soil. Check your plants periodically for notched leaves (make sure the damage is not confused with that caused by cutter bees). On ornamentals, spray the foliage and the ground under the plant thoroughly with Ortho® Systemic Insect Killer. Make sure that your plant is listed on the product label. Repeat the spray two more times at intervals of three weeks.

Darkling beetles

Darkling beetle.

Darkling beetles are a large group of slow-moving beetles that range from 1/16 to more than 1 inch in length. They are mostly black or brown; a few have white or red markings. The head is broad and short. Some darkling beetles have a peculiar habit of raising their abdomens in the air at about 45 degrees from the ground and running in this position. When disturbed, they emit a black, foul-smelling fluid. Darkling beetle adults and larvae both live under stones and leaf debris. They are commonly seen at dusk. Both adults and larvae of most species eat decaying plant material or fungi and are harmless. The larvae of some, known as *false wireworms*, feed on the roots and seedlings of grasses and other plants, but these are not common. A few species eat stored grain products; these are known as *mealworms* as larvae, or *flour beetles* as adults (see 523). Beetles occasionally wander indoors.

Control: Collect and remove darkling beetles that wander indoors. (For information on mealworms and flour beetles, see page 523.)

Ground beetles

Ground beetle.

Ground beetles, also known as *predaceous ground beetles*, are a large group of common insects. They vary from 1/8 to more than 1 inch in length. Many are a shiny black color; others are brown or an iridescent green, blue, or purple. Characteristic of these beetles is that their rather thin heads are narrower than their thorax (the middle body segment). Most ground beetles and their larvae feed on other insects or slugs. They have strong jaws, and some are capable of eating large caterpillars. Ground beetles rarely fly but move quickly. They are active at night and hide during the day under stones, loose bark, or other debris. Most ground beetles are beneficial predators; though one in California, the tule beetle (*Agonum maculicolle*), can become a pest when it invades homes in large numbers at dusk following fall rains. These beetles also have an offensive odor. Tule beetles breed in the marshlands along rivers or in moist, weedy areas. They invade homes from the direction of their breeding grounds.

Control: Most ground beetles are beneficial. If the tule beetle becomes a problem by invading homes in large numbers, collect and destroy the beetles indoors. Outdoors spray along foundations and beneath and around porches and doorsills with an insecticide containing *carbaryl*. Also spray the property along the edge in the direction the beetles invaded. Seal cracks and crevices in the walls and foundation, and make sure screens fit tightly.

Fireflies

Firefly.

Butterflies and moths

Gulf fritillary butterfly.

Imported cabbageworm (4× life size).

Fireflies, or *lightning bugs*, are actually beetles. These insects are well-known for their ability to produce light by means of a luminescent organ near the abdomen. Both male and female fireflies east of the Rockies can fly and blink their light organs. In the West, the adult female glows but can't fly, and the male flies but doesn't produce light. Larvae of some fireflies also produce light and are called *glowworms*. Adult fireflies are soft-bodied beetles ¼ to ¾ inch in length. Their heads are concealed from above by a hard covering. All larvae and some adults are beneficial, predaceous insects that feed at night on other insects and small slugs and snails. The larvae live in moist places among debris on the ground or on low-growing herbs and grasses. Adult fireflies use their flashing lights as signals in courting. They become active at dusk, with the number of flashes increasing as the night falls.

Control: Controls aren't necessary.

Insects in the butterfly and moth family (*Lepidoptera*) include some of the most admired insects in the world. The adults have two pairs of wings covered with tiny overlapping scales. The scales, which rub off easily, give the wings their striking colors. A few moths are wingless. Female cankerworms (see page 440), female bagworms (see page 442), and some tussock moths (see page 205) are examples. Butterflies can be distinguished from moths by their slender bodies and antennae with small clubs on the ends. Moths have stout bodies and antennae without clubs. Moths usually fly at night and have wings with dull colors, while butterflies fly during the day and are usually brightly colored. Butterflies and moths are not harmful in the adult stage, and many are beneficial. They feed on flower nectar with a long, coiled tongue and are a minor aid in pollinating some flowers. A few butterflies and moths lap up tree sap or juices from rotting fruit, carrion, and animal droppings.

Butterfly and moth development: The caterpillar is the immature stage and has chewing mouthparts. Some caterpillars are serious pests of plants, stored food, and fabrics. (For information on caterpillars, see pages 438 to 443.) Butterflies and moths lay their tiny eggs singly or in groups, usually on the plant or other food that the caterpillar eats. The eggs usually hatch in just a few days, although some are laid in the fall and don't hatch until warm spring weather arrives. The caterpillars emerge and immediately begin to eat and grow. They reach maturity after several weeks to several months, depending on the species, the abundance of food, and the temperature. Development is fastest in warm temperatures.

Pupation: At maturity, the caterpillars look for a place to pupate. The moth pupa is either enclosed in a silken cocoon or formed in some protected place such as within a plant, in debris on the soil surface, or buried in soil. The butterfly pupa, also called a chrysalis, is attached to a stem or some other support and usually is much more exposed than a moth pupa. At this stage, a dramatic transformation takes place. Many of the internal organs, muscles, and nerves dissolve, and the resulting fluids form new structures, producing a creature whose appearance and functions are entirely different. Some of the butterflies and moths emerge from their pupae in as few as 10 days; others spend the winter as pupae. The adult butterfly or moth emerges by splitting the pupal shell, spends several hours pumping fluid into its wings and hardening them, and then flies off. Male and female mate, and the female then lays eggs. Butterflies and moths live a few days to several months. Some gardeners attract butterflies to their gardens by providing plants the caterpillars feed on, as well as plants that produce flowers particularly attractive to the adults. Good flowers to attract butterflies are butterfly bush (*Buddleia*), butterfly weed, lantana, thistles, tithonia, zinnia, and many herbs. Plants eaten by the caterpillars of particularly pretty butterflies include milkweed, nettles, parsley, fennel, spicebush, and willow.

Control: Most butterflies and moths are harmless and don't require control. If you have a problem with caterpillars, look up your plant in the index to determine what kind of caterpillars may be damaging it, and follow the control method described.

BUTTERFLY ORDER (continued)

Monarch butterflies

Monarch butterfly larva (life size).
Inset: Monarch butterfly.

The monarch is perhaps the best-known butterfly. Its wings are orange with black veins and black margins. The margins are sprinkled with white and orange spots. This large butterfly has a wingspan of up to 4 inches. It is often seen flying from plant to plant, sipping nectar from a wide variety of flowers. Monarchs lay pale green eggs on the leaves of milkweed, a plant that has a white, milky sap. The eggs hatch in about four days. The caterpillar is banded with white, black, and yellow stripes and has a pair of soft spines at both its front and rear ends. It feeds on the leaves of milkweed for about 10 days and, when fully mature, reaches a length of about 2 inches. It then attaches itself to a leaf or stem and forms a cocoon (chrysalis). The chrysalis is jade-green with gold trimmings. It slowly darkens. After about 12 days, the butterfly emerges from the chrysalis. Up to four generations may occur per year. The monarch is the only butterfly species that migrates yearly both north and south. In the spring, monarchs migrate in a northerly direction, laying eggs and sipping nectar in the process. In the fall they migrate in a southerly direction. Monarchs that emerge in late summer and fall in the East or Midwest spend the winter in fir forests in northern Mexico; monarchs in the West spend the winter on the coast of central and southern California in groups of pine, cypress, and eucalyptus. Monarchs are also seen yearly in certain stands of trees along the Atlantic and Gulf coasts and the Great Lakes.

Control: Controls aren't necessary.

Mourning cloak butterflies

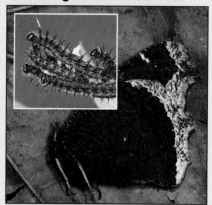

Mourning cloak butterfly. Inset: Spiny elm caterpillar.

The mourning cloak butterfly (Nymphalis antiopa) is a common butterfly with dark purplish-brown wings with blue spots along the back edge next to a band of yellowish gold. The wingspread is about 3 inches. The mourning cloak caterpillar is sometimes called the *spiny elm caterpillar* because of the large spinelike projections on its body that are harmless to touch. The caterpillar is black with tiny white dots, red legs, and a row of red spots along its back. A full-grown caterpillar is about 2 inches long. It feeds on the foliage of many hardwood trees, particularly elm, willow, and poplar. Caterpillars feed in groups, devouring the leaves one branch at a time. When mature, each caterpillar suspends itself from a twig and hangs downward, then forms a brown-and-gray pupa (chrysalis). Within one week, a mourning cloak butterfly emerges. The butterfly mates, and the female lays eggs in masses of 300 to 450 on twigs. Butterflies emerging in the late summer spend the winter in protected spots. One generation occurs yearly in northern climates and two generations yearly in southern climates.

Control: Prune the branches containing caterpillars, or spray with an insecticide containing *carbaryl* or *acephate* when the caterpillars are first seen. Make sure that your plant is listed on the product label.

Gypsy moths

Gypsy moth larvae (½ life size).

Gypsy moth (Lymantria dispar) larvae are large (up to 2½ inches long), hairy, blackish caterpillars with two longitudinal rows of red and blue spots on their backs. They are the most serious shade-tree pest in the United States. Caterpillars prefer to feed on oak leaves, but as population levels increase, the insects spread to other types of trees and shrubs. The gypsy moth was introduced into the United States in the mid-1800s from Europe, where it is a native pest. The East Coast has large forests of oak, the insects' preferred food, that can support huge populations of gypsy moths. This allowed the moths to increase in numbers rapidly. Besides defoliating and weakening plants, the insects are a nuisance. In mid- to late summer, the female moths attach masses of eggs covered with yellow hairs to almost any outdoor object. The larvae that hatch from these eggs from April to June may completely cover the sides of houses or other objects during the day when they're not feeding. Some people are allergic to the hairs of the larvae, which blow about in the wind. Where insects are feeding, large amounts of excrement accumulate beneath the plant. Only one generation of gypsy moths occurs per year. If you live in an area not infested with gypsy moths but think you have found them, contact your county extension office.

Control: It may not be necessary to spray your tree if it is healthy and vigorous. Hardwood trees can generally withstand two to five successive years of defoliation before dying (although a single season's defoliation can stress a tree so badly that it may take many years to recover). Evergreen trees may die after one complete defoliation because

Gypsy moth adult and pupae (½ life size).

Caterpillars

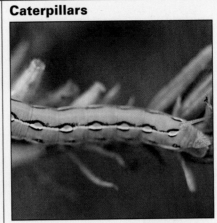

White-lined sphinx caterpillar (life size).

Red-humped caterpillar

Red-humped caterpillar.

they can't totally replace their foliage. If the insects are bothersome, or if a tree is weak or unhealthy either from the previous year's gypsy moth feeding or from drought, mechanical damage, or other insects and diseases, consider treatment with an insecticide. Apply the insecticide in the spring or early summer before the larvae are 1 inch long. Cover the tree thoroughly. It is best to contact a professional arborist for spraying large trees. Spray smaller trees with Ortho® Systemic Insect Killer or the bacterial insecticide *Bacillus thuringiensis* (Bt). Bt is most effective against young caterpillars. Repeat the sprays at intervals of 7 to 10 days if damage continues. Homeowners can reduce infestations by destroying egg masses found on walls, woodpiles, buildings, trees, and other objects when they are noticed during the winter months. During the spring, when larvae are feeding, place burlap bands on trees, leaving the bottom edge unattached. Caterpillars will crawl under these flaps to hide during the daylight hours. Collect and destroy them. This is most effective when infestations are light to moderate. Keep trees in a healthy growing condition; avoid damaging the roots or injuring trees. Fertilize and water trees during periods of drought. When planting trees in the yard, choose species that are less favored by the gypsy moth. (For a list of these plants, see page 551.) Trees less favored by the insects are damaged only slightly by larval feeding. In addition, when interplanted with more favored hosts, they may reduce the mortality of the favored trees by preventing a large buildup of insects in the area.

Caterpillars, the larvae of moths and butterflies, are serious pests of garden plants. Moths and butterflies don't feed on tissue or harm plants, but drink nectar from flowers. They may also help to pollinate flowers. Caterpillars are smooth, hairy, or spiny wormlike creatures with three pairs of legs near their heads and several pairs of prolegs (false legs) in the middle and rear of the abdomens. Their mouthparts are adapted for chewing plant tissue. They generally confine themselves to tissue that is soft and succulent. After hatching, caterpillars go through as many as 11 stages of development (instars). At the end of each instar, caterpillars must molt (shed their skin) to make room for their larger body size. During the first instars, caterpillars may feed as leafminers (between the upper and lower surfaces of leaves) or as skeletonizers (eating only one leaf surface). As the caterpillars increase in size in later stages, they require more food, devouring entire leaves. Caterpillar populations fluctuate greatly from year to year because of environmental conditions and natural enemies such as birds, rodents, diseases, and other insects.

Control: Inspect garden plants periodically for signs of caterpillar infestation. Control caterpillars on ornamentals with Ortho® Rose & Flower Insect Killer or Ortho® Systemic Insect Killer. Spray food crops with Ortho® Malathion Plus® Insect Spray Concentrate or the bacterial insecticide *Bacillus thuringiensis* (Bt). Make sure that your plant is listed on the product label.

The red-humped caterpillar (*Schizura concinna*) is so named because of the brick-red hump on its back. This caterpillar also has a red head and red stripes along its body. It is up to 1½ inches long when fully grown, and it has the unusual characteristic of resting with its hind end elevated. The red-humped caterpillar feeds on a wide variety of deciduous fruit, nut, and ornamental trees. Sweet gum, walnut, and plum are favorite hosts. Caterpillars feed in groups on the undersides of leaves when young. As they grow, they tend to disperse and eat entirely through leaves, leaving only the largest leaf veins. Often, just one section of a tree will be defoliated, but occasionally a large population will defoliate the entire tree. This slows growth and may reduce fruit quality, but the tree will usually recover from the defoliation. When mature, the caterpillars form cocoons in plant litter on the ground. Emerging adults are grayish-brown moths with a wingspan of 1 to 1⅜ inches. They lay eggs in groups on the undersides of leaves. As many as five generations occur per year.

Control: Spray infested areas of trees with Ortho® Rose & Flower Insect Killer or *Bacillus thuringiensis* (Bt). Bt is most effective against young caterpillars. To preserve predator insects, spray only the caterpillars, not the whole tree. If caterpillars are no longer present, delay spraying until the next generation of caterpillars is seen. Branches containing caterpillars can be cut off and destroyed while the caterpillars are young and grouped together. Search for and destroy leaves with egg masses.

BUTTERFLY ORDER *(continued)*

Cutworms

Surface cutworm (2× life size).

Climbing cutworms (½ life size).

Cankerworms

Cankerworm (2× life size).

Cutworms are large (up to 2 inches long), fleshy, hairless caterpillars that curl up when disturbed. They are serious pests of vegetables and flowers and sometimes infest vines and trees. Many species of cutworms exist in the United States. They are grouped according to their feeding habits.

Surface cutworms: These pests of early-season vegetables and flowers feed on the succulent tissue of newly transplanted or emerging plants. A single surface-feeding cutworm may destroy many plants in one night. These cutworms chew or cut off the plant at or below the soil surface and then hide under dirt clods or in the soil during the day. They don't eat much of the plant but take only a few bites from the stem, often causing the plant to topple at the point of feeding injury.

Climbing cutworms: These feed above ground on any part of the plant. Their favorite foods are the tender young leaves, buds, and flowers of vegetables and herbaceous plants. Sometimes they infest vines or climb up into the tops of fruit trees to feed on leaves or buds. In one night, climbing cutworms may devour all but the stem of a young plant and then move to another plant to feed.

Subterranean cutworms: These spend their lives in the soil. They feed day and night on the roots and underground stems of vegetables, sod, and grains, causing plants to wilt and die. Many other insects and diseases cause similar symptoms. Dig in the soil around the dying plant for cutworms to confirm that they are the cause of the problem.

The adults of all cutworms are dark, night-flying moths with bands or stripes on their forewings and lighter-color hindwings. They feed at dusk on the nectar from flowers, and they may be seen fluttering around lights at night. Cutworm damage is often severe when it occurs, but may not occur again for years.

Control: Because cutworms feed in the soil or hide there during the day, insecticides are most effective if they are applied around the base of plants. Use Ortho® Bug-Geta® Plus Snail, Slug & Insect Killer on vegetables and lawns when cut stems or chewed leaves are observed. To control subterranean cutworms, water the soil lightly after applying the insecticide. Make sure that your plant is listed on the product label. Because cutworms are difficult to control, dusting or spraying may need to be repeated at weekly intervals. To reduce injury from climbing cutworms, inspect your plants at night with a flashlight and pick off and destroy any cutworms you find. Cultivate the soil thoroughly in late summer and fall to expose and destroy larvae and pupae. Work Ortho® Bug-B-Gon® Multi-Purpose Insect Killer Granules into the soil before planting.

The spring cankerworm (*Paleacrita vernata*) and fall cankerworm (*Alsophila pometaria*) belong to the group of insects known as *inchworms* or *loopers*. Cankerworms have legs only at the front and the rear of their bodies. Spring cankerworms spend the winter as pupae in the soil and emerge as adults in early spring. The adult male is an ash-gray moth with a wingspread of about 1 inch. The female is entirely wingless. She climbs the tree to lay eggs on the branches; they hatch when the foliage begins to appear in the spring. The young cankerworms eat the leaves for three to five weeks before dropping to the ground and forming pupae. Fall cankerworms lay their eggs in November and early December. The eggs hatch the following spring, and the young worms feed, pupate, and emerge as adults in the fall. Trees defoliated two or three years in succession are weakened and may die. Favored host trees include elm, apple, oak, hickory, and maple.

Control: As soon as worms are noticed, spray with Ortho® Systemic Insect Killer on ornamentals. The bacterial insecticide *Bacillus thuringiensis* (Bt) is effective against young cankerworms. During the dormant season, kill eggs of fall cankerworms with Ortho® Volck® Oil Spray. The following spring, prevent spring cankerworm females from climbing trunks with a barrier of sticky material around the trunk. As soon as leaves have expanded and cankerworms are active, apply one of the previously mentioned sprays. A spray applied too early, when the leaves are still rapidly expanding, is not effective.

Uglynest caterpillar

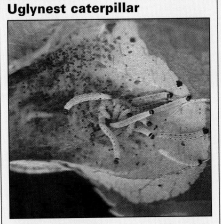

Uglynest caterpillars.

The uglynest caterpillar (*Archips cerasivorana*) gets its name from the unsightly silken nests it forms on the ends of branches. The nests are built around several small stems and are filled with pieces of dead leaves and black droppings from the caterpillars. Inside the webbing are dozens of yellowish-green caterpillars with shiny black heads. Uglynest caterpillars feed on the foliage of a variety of trees and shrubs, including cherry, hawthorn, and rose, but they are seldom abundant enough to cause lasting damage to their hosts. The caterpillars feed from late spring through the summer, when they form pupae within their nests. The adult moths emerge from July to September. They are dull orange with a wingspread of just under 1 inch.

Control: Prune and destroy the webbed portions of branches, or spray with Ortho® Rose & Flower Insect Killer when the webs are first seen. Use Ortho® Systemic Insect Killer on the oak webworm, a similar species that feeds on oak trees. Make sure that your plant is listed on the product label. Apply the spray at a high pressure to force it into the webs and improve control.

Woolly bear caterpillar

Woolly bear caterpillar.

These hairy caterpillars, sometimes called *saltmarsh caterpillars*, are commonly seen crawling across roads and pathways. Woolly bears are large caterpillars that can grow to more than 2 inches long. They are covered with dense, stiff, reddish-brown to black hairs that give them a woolly or furry appearance. The hairs break off easily when the caterpillar is picked up. One common woolly bear, the banded woolly bear (*Isia isabella*), has black hairs at each end and reddish-brown hairs around its middle. In the fall, woolly bears become very active and crawl about in search of a protected place to spend the winter, such as under loose bark or dry leaves. There they either form a cocoon and emerge as an adult moth in the spring or simply curl up for the winter and continue feeding in the spring. The adult is a pretty moth with a wingspan of up to 2½ inches. Depending on the species of woolly bear, the wings may be white with black spots or may have bold patterns of orange or yellow. The moths mate and lay eggs on low vegetation. The caterpillars eat the leaves of a wide variety of plants, including many weeds.

Control: If caterpillars are feeding on garden plants, handpick them or spray them with Ortho® Rose & Flower Insect Killer. Make sure that your plant is listed on the product label. A few caterpillars crawling about the garden can be safely ignored.

Leafrollers and leaftiers

Leafroller.

Leafrollers and leaftiers are small caterpillars that feed inside leaves, which they roll or tie around themselves. They are similar in their habits, but leafrollers roll up the leaves around their bodies and leaftiers bind the leaves around them with silk threads. This feeding habit gives the insects some protection from unfavorable weather, predators, and chemical sprays. Leafrollers and leaftiers may be serious pests in the garden, feeding on many fruits, vegetables, and ornamentals. Their feeding habits vary, depending on their age. Only part of their life may be spent feeding inside the rolled or tied leaves. At other times they may feed inside buds, flowers, and fruit. They often drop from their protected location when disturbed. The species of leafrollers and leaftiers that feed on flowers and fruit are usually much more damaging than the species that feed exclusively on leaves.

Control: Insecticides are most effective if they are applied before the larvae are protected inside the leaves. Check your plants periodically in the spring for the first sign of infestation. Spray ornamentals with Ortho® Systemic Insect Killer. Spray fruits with Ortho® Malathion Plus® Insect Spray Concentrate. Make sure that your plant is listed on the product label.

BUTTERFLY ORDER (cont.)

Bagworms

Bagworm cases.

Bagworms are the larvae of moths. The characteristic brown bags are often seen attached to twigs. The bags are up to 2 inches long and composed of interwoven bits of dead foliage, twigs, and silk. During the summer, a dark brown to black caterpillar can be found inside the bag. At first it drags the bag around as it feeds on leaves, enlarging the bag as it grows. By late August, the caterpillar finishes feeding and attaches the bag to a twig. Inside the bag it forms a pupa. Several days later, an adult moth emerges from the pupa. The female is wingless and stays within her bag. The male flies to the bag containing the female, and mating may take place. She then lays a mass of eggs within the bag and dies. The eggs hatch in May or June. Newly hatched caterpillars crawl out of the old bag and immediately begin feeding on leaves. With severe infestations, the entire plant is defoliated and bags hang on many of the twigs. This type of infestation often kills evergreens such as arborvitae and cedar but may only slow the growth of a deciduous plant.

Control: Spray with Ortho® Systemic Insect Killer or the bacterial insecticide *Bacillus thuringiensis* (Bt) between early May and mid-July. If possible, treat as soon as larvae hatch, before they construct bags. Make sure that your plant is listed on the product label. Repeat the spray after 10 days if leaf damage is still occurring. When possible, handpick and destroy bags in the winter to reduce the number of eggs the following year.

BUG ORDER

Plant bugs

Harlequin bugs (life size).

Plant bugs are a large group of insects that infest many plants in the garden. This group includes many species of plant bugs, leaf bugs, lygus bugs, predaceous bugs, and stinkbugs. These insects are true bugs, of the order *Hemiptera*. They have long legs and antennae and large eyes, and the adults hold their wings flat over their bodies. Immature plant bugs often have clearly visible wing pads. Both the immature and mature bugs feed on succulent plant tissue. They pierce the tissue and remove the cell contents, resulting in tan or bleached spots and distortion. Infested fruits and flowers often drop off the plant. The mature females may also damage plants by laying eggs inside the leaves or stems. Many plant bugs have two or more generations per year, so late-season populations can be large and damaging.

Control: It is important to control plant bugs before they build up to damaging numbers. Watch for signs of infestation during the growing season. If damage is noticed, spray plants with Ortho® Malathion Plus® Insect Spray Concentrate. Make sure that your plant is listed on the product label. If migrating plant bugs reinfest the plant, repeat the spray as necessary.

Stinkbugs

Green stinkbug (4× life size).

Stinkbugs are medium to large insects, usually ¼ to ¾ inch long. They are usually dull green, gray, or brown, but one common stinkbug, the harlequin bug, is black with bright orange marks. Stinkbugs get their name from the foul smell they produce when disturbed. This smell comes from a fluid they discharge from special glands. The great majority of stinkbugs suck the sap from tender young foliage and fruit. They can be destructive when numerous. Infested fruit develops hard calluses around feeding punctures, and the fruit may be deformed if punctured early in its development. Leaves that are heavily infested may become distorted and scorched. A few species are predators on other insects, however.

Control: Treat infested plants with Ortho® Bug-B-Gon® Multi-Purpose Insect Killer Concentrate. Repeat the treatment at intervals of 7 to 10 days if the plants become reinfested. Make sure that your plant is listed on the product label. Handpick egg masses. Clean up weeds in orchards and gardens to eliminate stinkbug breeding places.

Lace bugs

Lace bug (10× life size).

Aphids

Oleander aphids (3× life size).

Green peach aphid

Green peach aphids (6× life size).

Lace bugs are small (⅛-inch) insects of the family *Tingidae*, which means *ornamented*. The adults have delicate clear wings that they hold flat over their bodies. The wings have many veins, giving them a lacy appearance. Immature lace bugs are dark and wingless, with spines radiating from the edges of their bodies. Lace bugs are pests primarily of ornamental trees and shrubs, although several species infest a few vegetables. Most lace bugs feed only on one type of plant. They damage plants by sucking the sap and cell contents from the undersides of leaves, producing a mottling or speckling on the upper surfaces. Lace bug damage often resembles leafhopper or spider mite damage. Lace bugs excrete shiny, varnishlike drops, which accumulate around them as they feed. Several generations of lace bugs occur each year. Certain lace bugs may build to such tremendous numbers on their host plant that very little chlorophyll remains to produce food for the plant.

Control: Lace bugs should be controlled early, before they cause much damage. This is especially important on broadleaf evergreen plants because they retain the unproductive leaves for several years. Spray ornamentals with Ortho® Systemic Insect Killer. Control lace bugs on food crops with Ortho® Malathion Plus® Insect Spray Concentrate. Make sure that your plant is listed on the product label. Reinfestations may come from infested plants in nearby gardens. Check your plant periodically for insects. Repeat the spray if the plant becomes reinfested.

Aphids, also called *plant lice*, are small (up to ¼-inch) soft-bodied insects that infest most garden plants. Some aphids spend their lives on one type of plant; others infest several plant species. Aphids have a complicated life history. Aphids that hatch from overwintering eggs are wingless females, called *stem mothers*. They give birth without fertilization by a male. Many generations of only females may be produced throughout the summer. Some of these aphids develop wings so they can fly to less densely populated plants or to another species of plant. In the fall, female aphids give birth to males and females that mate and produce the fertilized eggs that survive the winter. In warm climates, production of young may continue without the development of sexual males and females. Large numbers of aphids may cause little damage to a plant, or just a few aphids on a plant may cause severe distortion and stunting. Certain aphids are also carriers of plant diseases (see page 449).

Control: Aphids are usually easy to control if they aren't protected by tightly curled leaves, galls, or cottony material. Use Ortho® Malathion Plus® Insect Spray Concentrate to quickly knock out existing aphids on food crops. Use Ortho® Systemic Insect Killer or Ortho® Bug-B-Gon® Multi-Purpose Insect Killer Concentrate on ornamentals to protect them for a couple of weeks from new infestations. Make sure that your plant is listed on the product label. Aphids may continually reinfest the garden from other plants nearby. Inspect your plants regularly for aphids.

The green peach aphid (*Myzus persicae*) is one of the most common aphids in North America. It is present in every state and is often seen on vegetables, fruit, and ornamental plants. It is yellowish-green with tiny red eyes. In most areas the green peach aphid lays black shiny eggs that survive the winter on cherry, peach, plum, and related trees. In spring, the eggs hatch, and two or three generations of aphids develop on the trees. The aphids then migrate to other, usually herbaceous, plants such as weeds, flowers, and vegetables. In the vegetable garden, green peach aphids are especially attracted to spinach and potatoes, but they also feed on many other vegetables and flowers. They complete many generations on these plants during the summer. In the autumn, winged females fly back to fruit trees, complete one or more generations, mate, and produce females, which lay the overwintering eggs. Green peach aphids rarely damage fruit trees, but at times they seriously injure vegetables and flowers because they remove plant sap and can transmit plant viruses. Many insects feed on aphids but don't always keep the population under control.

Control: Apply control measures as for other aphids (see left). Apply Ortho® Volck® Oil Spray to cherry, peach, plum, and related trees to kill overwintering eggs.

443

HOMOPTERA ORDER (continued)

Woolly aphids and adelgids	Mealybugs	Armored scales

Woolly hemlock adelgids (2× life size).

Mealybugs and ants.

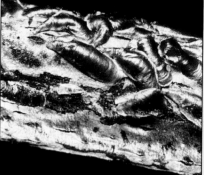

Oyster-shell scales (3× life size).

Woolly aphids and adelgids

Aphids covered with white or gray waxy threads that look like wool or cotton are called *woolly aphids.* (Some woolly aphids that infest conifers have been reclassified as *adelgids.*) If the threads are removed, small (⅛-inch), dark, soft-bodied insects are found clustered beneath. Woolly aphids and adelgids infest only woody plants. Woolly adelgids infest only conifers, but some woolly aphids also infest conifers. Some species infest leaves, often causing them to curl inward. The damage is unsightly but rarely fatal to the plant. Other types of woolly aphids and adelgids cover the trunk, branches, and roots. Galls may develop where they feed. Severely infested young plants are often stunted and may die. Older plants with galls on the roots may be weak and produce less fruit. Most of these insects spend the summer on one type of plant and then, in the fall, produce a generation that migrates to another plant species. Sometimes, especially in warmer climates, they spend the entire year on the summer host.

Control: Woolly aphids protected inside curled leaves are best controlled with a systemic insecticide such as Ortho® Systemic Insect Killer. Use Ortho® Bug-B-Gon® Multi-Purpose Insect Killer Concentrate or Ortho® Systemic Insect Killer on woolly aphids and adelgids infesting branches or trunks. Make sure that your plant is listed on the product label. Repeat the spray if the plant becomes reinfested. To destroy overwintering eggs, spray trees with Ortho® Volck® Oil Spray during the dormant season.

Mealybugs

Mealybugs are soft-bodied insects that are close relatives of scales. Their name derives from the white or gray threads of wax with which they cover themselves. Plant parts heavily infested with mealybugs often appear to be covered with cotton. Mealybugs may damage any part of the plant by sucking out the sap, which may cause leaf distortion, yellowing, stunting, galls, and death of the plant. Mealybugs also coat the plant with large quantities of undigested sap, called *honeydew.* Most mealybugs are garden pests only in the subtropical areas of the country, infesting houseplants and greenhouse plants in the colder northern states. Several species that infest woody plants can survive the extreme cold of northern winters. Mealybugs are very active when young, crawling all over the plant until they find a suitable place to settle. As the young mealybugs mature, they become sluggish. Mature females move around very little, but males develop into winged insects that look like minute flies. Adult males don't feed but die after mating.

Control: Mealybugs are often difficult to control because they are protected by their waxy threads. Spray ornamentals thoroughly with Ortho® Systemic Insect Killer. Spray food crops with Ortho® Volck® Oil Spray or Ortho® Malathion Plus® Insect Spray Concentrate. Check to make sure that your plant is listed on the product label. Repeat the spray if the plant becomes reinfested.

Armored scales

Armored scales appear as somewhat flattened bumps, either round or very elongated, and are often clustered together on leaves, stems, or bark. Small, immobile, soft-bodied insects live beneath these shells, which are made of wax and cast skins. The shells are not attached to the insect; if the shells are picked off, the insects remain attached to the plant. Females lay their eggs underneath the shells. The scales that hatch, called *crawlers,* are active, usually moving from beneath their mothers' shells to find suitable feeding sites. The crawlers eventually settle down in one spot, where they remain for the rest of their lives, feeding on plant sap. Some armored scales produce a toxin that causes discolored or dead spots on leaves or fruit. Armored scales don't produce honeydew as other scales do.

Control: Mature scales are difficult to control because they are protected by their shells. Control is usually aimed at the crawlers, whose seasonal appearance varies with species. Spray crawlers with Ortho® Systemic Insect Killer. Treat indoor plants with Ortho® Rose & Flower Insect Killer. Ortho® Volck® Oil Spray may be used very effectively to smother scales during the dormant season and during the growing season. Some plants are sensitive to oil sprays, so make sure that your plant is listed on the product label before spraying.

Tea scale

Adults and crawlers (16× life size).

One of the armored scales, tea scale (*Fiorinia theae*), is a serious pest of camellias in California and in the South. It also attacks Chinese holly (*Ilex cornuta*), ferns, palms, orchids, and many other plants. In the North, it is a pest of greenhouse plants and houseplants. The adult female is dark brown to black, boat-shape, and tiny (¹⁄₂₅ inch). The male is slightly smaller and white. Both are covered by a thin tangle of cottony fibers. Females lay eggs, which hatch into tiny yellow insects called *crawlers*. The crawlers move about for a while, then settle down.
Tea scales feed on the undersides of leaves. Infested leaves develop yellow blotches and drop prematurely. In warm weather, a complete life cycle of egg to adult can occur in only 40 days. All life stages are usually present at once.

Control: Control tea scale with Ortho® Volck® Oil Spray, Ortho® Malathion Plus® Insect Spray Concentrate, or Ortho® Systemic Insect Killer beginning in early spring. Repeat the spray whenever crawlers are discovered.

Scurfy scale

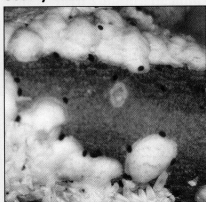

Scurfy scales (8× life size).

The armored scurfy scale (*Chionaspis furfura*) prefers members of the rose family, such as apple, pear, hawthorn, and pyracantha. It also feeds on other trees, such as ash, aspen, elm, hickory, maple, and willow. Adults are white or dirty gray, about ¹⁄₁₀ inch long. They are usually found on the bark but may also be found on leaves and fruit. On yellow fruit, such as 'Yellow Delicious' apples, a red spot appears around the white scale. About the time the tree leafs out in the spring, eggs hatch into young called *crawlers*. Crawlers move about for a time, then settle down and develop waxy shells. In the South, they mature in June and lay eggs that become a second generation. The second generation lays overwintering eggs in September and October. In the North, a single generation is produced.

Control: Chemical control is most effective against the crawlers. Spray when crawlers are present with Ortho® Volck® Oil Spray, Ortho® Malathion Plus® Insect Spray Concentrate, or Ortho® Systemic Insect Killer. Early the following spring, before the tree leafs out, treat with Ortho® Volck® Oil Spray to smother overwintering eggs.

San Jose scale

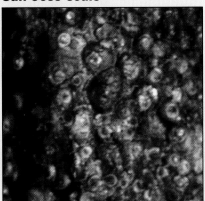

San Jose scales (4× life size).

The armored San Jose scale (*Quadraspidiotus perniciosus*) was accidentally imported from Asia into the San Jose Valley in California in 1870. San Jose scale infests a wide variety of trees and shrubs. The adults cover twigs and branches with a gray crust as they multiply and can kill branches and entire trees if uncontrolled. Individual insects are less than ¹⁄₁₆ inch across and look like miniature volcanoes. Females are round, with a nipple in the center; males are oblong, with an offset nipple. Females give birth to young, minute yellow *crawlers* that wander around for a while, then settle down to feed in one spot and secrete a waxy shell, under which they spend the rest of their lives. Two to five generations may be produced per year, depending on the length of the growing season, so all life stages may be present most of the summer.

Control: If not controlled, San Jose scale can do severe damage to trees. As with most scales, control is aimed at the overwintering immature scales and at the crawlers. Spray the tree with Ortho® Volck® Oil Spray before buds swell in the spring. Watch for crawlers to emerge in late summer. Spray with an insecticide containing *diazinon* or *chlorpyrifos* when crawlers appear. If more crawlers appear later, repeat the treatment.

HOMOPTERA ORDER (continued)

Obscure scale

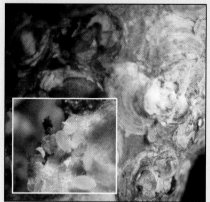

Adults. (4× life size) Inset: Crawlers (10× life size).

The armored obscure scale (*Melanaspis obscura*) is common on oak (especially pin oak), hickory, chestnut, walnut, pecan, and several ornamental trees. Adult scales are about ⅛ inch across and dark gray with a dark spot slightly offset in the raised center. When rubbed, the spot turns orange. Armored scales often cluster together, sometimes several insects deep. Because their color is often the same as that of the bark, they are difficult to detect. Infestations generally begin on the lower and inner branches of a tree. Eggs are laid under the mothers' shells and hatch out from summer through early fall. Newly hatched young (*crawlers*) frequently crawl under the shell of nearby scales, contributing to the crowded appearance of insects and making them difficult to kill with insecticides.

Control: This scale is difficult to control because many of the crawlers aren't exposed. Prune and dispose of heavily infested branches. With a stiff brush, remove all the remaining scales possible. When crawlers are active, spray with Ortho® Volck® Oil Spray, Ortho® Systemic Insect Killer, or Ortho® Bug-B-Gon® Multi-Purpose Insect Killer. During the dormant season, apply Ortho® Volck® Oil Spray to smother overwintering insects.

Soft scales

Hemispherical scales (3× life size).

Soft scales are serious pests of hundreds of woody plants, appearing as crusty bumps on bark and leaves. This scale group contains some of the largest species of scales found in the United States. Soft scales (see also page 447) are related to both mealybugs (see page 444) and armored scales (see page 444). Many soft scales look like mealybugs; they are covered with a white, powdery wax during part of their lives. Like mealybugs, soft scales excrete large quantities of undigested sap, called *honeydew*, as they feed on plant tissue. Soft scales develop an external skeleton that looks like the armored scales' shell-like covering. Removal of this skeleton kills the insect. Depending on the species, female scales lay eggs or give birth to young beneath their bodies. The egg-laying females die and shrivel, and the skeletons protect the eggs until they hatch. The young scales, called *crawlers*, move away from their protected sites to find a suitable spot to feed. This stage of the insect, when it is not protected by a skeleton, is most susceptible to insecticides.

Control: Control is often aimed at the susceptible crawler, whose seasonal appearance varies with each species. Spray crawlers on ornamentals with Ortho® Systemic Insect Killer. Control scales on fruit trees with Ortho® Malathion Plus® Insect Spray Concentrate. Treat indoor plants with Ortho® Rose & Flower Insect Killer. Ortho® Volck® Oil Spray is very effective against the eggs during the dormant season and often against the crawlers.

Hemispherical scale

Adult and crawlers (10× life size).

Hemispherical scale (*Saissetia coffeae*) is a soft scale. (For information on soft scales, see at left.) It infests ferns, palms, and woody trees and shrubs in warm climates. It may also be found indoors and in greenhouses—where it is a serious problem—throughout the country. Scales are glossy brown bumps in clusters and look like little inverted walnut halves. Female scales lay eggs beneath their bodies from May until February of the following year. After an incubation period of a few weeks, the immature scales, called *crawlers*, leave the bodies of their now-dead mothers and wander around the plant for a while until they find a suitable spot to feed. If uncontrolled, hemispherical scales can cause leaves to turn yellow and drop prematurely. Twigs and branches may die.

Control: To control small infestations of scales in the home or greenhouse, scrape off the scales with fingernails or a knife. Its waxy shell makes the adult hemispherical scale difficult to wet or control with insecticides. The most effective control is aimed at the crawlers. For control indoors, when crawlers are active spray the plant with insecticidal soap or take the plant outdoors and spray with Ortho® Systemic Insect Killer or Ortho® Bug-B-Gon® Multi-Purpose Insect Killer. (For information on spraying houseplants, see page 810.) For control outdoors, spray when crawlers are active with Ortho® Systemic Insect Killer or Ortho® Bug-B-Gon® Multi-Purpose Insect Killer. Hemispherical scale crawlers may be present from July through February, so inspect for crawlers every two weeks during this period and spray if any are present.

Lecanium scales

Adults and crawlers (6× life size).

A dozen species of soft scales in four genera make up the lecanium scale group. Most are brown, turtle-shape, and ¹⁄₁₆ to ⅛ inch long. The calico scale, however, has a black-and-white marbled-color pattern, thorn scale has a white cross-hatched pattern, and kuno adults are mottled red, yellow, and black. In general, after lecanium scale females produce eggs, they die and dry out, becoming dull brown and brittle. Lecanium scales afflict fruit, nut, and shade trees and deciduous woody ornamentals, as well as some ground covers, such as Boston ivy. Female scales produce up to 3,000 eggs each. Scale crawlers emerge from under their mothers' shells in spring or summer, crawl to leaves, and feed there through the summer months. In the fall, before leaves drop, the scales migrate to adjacent twigs and branches, where they overwinter. One generation occurs per year.

Control: If possible, wash and scrub off scales with a stiff brush. In early spring, before bud-break, treat with Ortho® Volck® Oil Spray to smother overwintering scales. The following spring or summer, when crawlers are active, spray with Ortho® Bug-B-Gon® Multi-Purpose Insect Killer or Ortho® Systemic Insect Killer.

Cottony cushion scales

Cottony cushion scales (2× life size).

Cottony cushion scales are a type of soft scale (see page 446). Like other soft scales, they have a crusty skeleton on the outside of their bodies. The skeleton is rarely seen, however, because mature female scales lay hundreds of eggs in white, waxy egg sacs attached to their bodies, giving them a cottony appearance. The females die and shrivel after they lay their eggs. The young scales, called *crawlers*, emerge from the egg sacs and migrate to leaves and young twigs. They insert their mouthparts into the plant and suck sap throughout the summer. Trees and shrubs infested with cottony cushion scales may be coated with large quantities of a sticky substance called *honeydew*, undigested sap excreted by the insects. Male cottony cushion scales are tiny-winged insects that mature earlier than the females. They mate with immature females and die. Before the leaves drop, scales migrate to bark to spend the winter.

Control: Cottony cushion scales may be difficult to control because they are protected by the waxy egg sacs. Control is often aimed at the crawlers, whose emergence varies with the species. Spray crawlers on ornamentals with Ortho® Systemic Insect Killer. Crawlers on fruit trees can be controlled with Ortho® Malathion Plus® Insect Spray Concentrate. Ortho® Volck® Oil Spray is very effective against the eggs and often against the crawlers.

Wax scales

Japanese wax scales on holly (2× life size).

Wax scales are a type of soft scale (see page 446) that are serious pests of hundreds of ornamental plants and fruit trees, mostly in the warmer parts of the country. Their reddish or brown bodies are covered with a hard, thick, white wax, often tinged pink or gray. Females lay hundreds of eggs underneath their bodies, which shrink as the eggs accumulate. The young scales, called *crawlers*, leave the waxy covering and settle down to feed on leaves and stems. As the young scales mature, they begin excreting cones of wax on top of their bodies. The wax gives the scales a different appearance in various stages of development (*instars*). When the immature insects have reached their second instar, they have a "cameo" appearance. The wax is secreted rapidly during the third instar, producing a cone—the "dunce cap" stage. By the time the insects mature, the wax is very thick and convex or globular.

Control: Mature female wax scales are difficult to control, because they are protected by the thick wax covering. Control is often aimed at the crawler, whose emergence varies with each species. Spray crawlers on ornamentals with Ortho® Systemic Insect Killer. Ortho® Volck® Oil Spray is very effective against the eggs and often against the crawlers.

HOMOPTERA ORDER (continued)

Whiteflies

Whiteflies (life size).

Leafhoppers

Blue sharpshooter leafhopper (10× life size).

Treehoppers

Treehopper.

Whiteflies are tiny (1/16 inch) winged insects found mainly on the undersides of leaves. When the plant is touched, insects flutter rapidly around it. Wings of the adults are covered with a white powdery substance. Larvae are the size of a pinhead, and look like tiny flakes of plastic. They are usually found on the undersides of leaves. Because they feed more heavily than the adults do, they cause more damage. Whiteflies survive winter outdoors only in the South. Their population may build to tremendous numbers during the growing season. They may also infest outdoor plants in colder climates. Infestations come from migrating whiteflies and from infested greenhouse-grown plants placed in the garden. Some whiteflies serve as disease vectors (see page 449), and many produce copious amounts of honeydew.

Control: Whiteflies have several stages of development, and each stage has a different tolerance to insecticides. Crawlers that hatch from the eggs can be controlled by contact insecticides, such as Ortho® Malathion Plus® Insect Spray Concentrate, Ortho® Rose & Flower Insect Killer, or Ortho® Systemic Insect Killer. Crawlers feed by inserting their mouthparts into plant tissue. This stage is resistant to contact insecticides but can be controlled on ornamentals by insecticides—such as Ortho® Systemic Insect Killer—that act systemically. All life stages may be present at the same time, but a single application of insecticide affects only susceptible stages. Sprays must be applied at least three times at intervals of four to six days to achieve control. Whiteflies may be partially controlled with yellow sticky traps.

Leafhoppers are small (less than 1/2 inch), wedge-shape insects that hop or fly away quickly when disturbed. Some can travel backward and sideways as rapidly as they move forward. The adults have wings that are held over their bodies in a rooflike position. Immature leafhoppers are wingless. All stages have large eyes on the sides of their heads and piercing and sucking mouthparts for feeding on plant sap. Leafhoppers feed on many garden plants, causing leaf stippling, stunting, and distortion of the leaves and stems. As they feed, most leafhoppers excrete large quantities of a sticky substance called *honeydew*, undigested sap that coats the plants. Many of these pests also carry plant diseases that can damage plants severely (see page 449). In addition, certain leafhoppers cause a condition called *hopperburn*. Infested leaves turn brown on the edges and curl upward. Leafhopper saliva kills leaf tissue as it is injected into the vessels that carry water and nutrients through the plant.

Control: Leaves that are severely damaged by leafhoppers are unsightly and lose much of their ability to produce food. Insects should be controlled early before damage is serious. Spray ornamentals with Ortho® Systemic Insect Killer. Spray food crops with Ortho® Malathion Plus® Insect Spray Concentrate. Cover the undersides of the leaves thoroughly. Make sure that your plant is listed on the product label.

Treehoppers are small to medium-size insects, 1/4 to 5/8 inch long. They may be dull colored or brightly colored. These insects are distinctive for the hard covering that protrudes up and back from the head. The covering makes some appear humpbacked; on others, it takes the form of a sharp point that makes the insect look like a thorn. Treehoppers suck plant sap, but this seldom causes significant injury. More severe damage is caused when they lay eggs. The female cuts slits in the stems of trees, shrubs, and herbaceous plants and inserts her eggs underneath the bark at the wound. A canker forms at the injury site, and the stem may die. Sometimes disease-causing fungi enter through the wounds. Most treehoppers never become abundant enough to be serious pests.

Control: Treehoppers can be safely ignored unless abundant. When numerous, spray infested plants with an insecticide containing *malathion* or *carbaryl*. Spray with a horticultural oil to kill overwintering eggs on trees and shrubs.

Psyllids

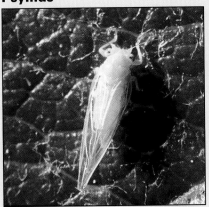

Apple sucker psyllid (4× life size).

Psyllids are related to aphids and are often called *jumping plant lice*. The winged adults are small (up to ⅙ inch), brownish or green insects that can spring from leaves into flight with their large hind legs. The wingless immature psyllids are often covered with white, waxy threads or with drops of honeydew. Psyllids damage plants by sucking the plant sap. They feed on shoots and leaves, causing distortion, stunted growth, and sometimes tip dieback. They may also cover the plant with *honeydew*, undigested plant sap that is excreted as they feed. Some psyllids transmit plant diseases; others cause leaf galls to form. Infested leaves curl around one or more insects and enlarge to form a gall that completely surrounds them; or blisterlike galls develop in the center of leaves. The insects feed and mature inside the galls, and the galls split open to release the adult psyllids. When plants are heavily infested, thousands of adults may swarm and invade homes.

Control: Psyllids should be controlled early before they are protected inside curled leaves and galls. In mid-May, spray ornamentals with Ortho® Systemic Insect Killer; spray fruits and vegetables with Ortho® Malathion Plus® Insect Spray Concentrate. Make sure that your plant is listed on the product label. Repeat the spray in 10 to 14 days.

Spittlebugs

Spittlebugs on rosemary.

Immature spittlebugs (*nymphs*) are small, green, soft-bodied insects. The nymphs, clustered between leaves and stems, surround themselves with a frothy, white mass that looks like spit, which protects them from sun and preying insects. Adult spittlebugs are small (¼-inch), winged insects that hop or fly away quickly when disturbed. They feed on plant sap and lay their eggs inside stems or between the leaf blades and stems of many garden plants and forage crops. The greenish nymphs that hatch from the eggs suck sap from the plant. The insect excretes drops of undigested sap mixed with air. Its tail moves up and down as if working a bellows, forcing out bubbles of sap. The bug then reaches back and covers itself with the frothy spittle. Spittlebugs are most noticeable in the spring when the nymphs are feeding, but adults may be found on plants throughout summer.

Control: A few spittlebugs do little harm, and can be washed off the plant with a hose. If the insects appear to be weakening the plant, however, control them on ornamentals with Ortho® Systemic Insect Killer and on food crops with Ortho® Malathion Plus® Insect Spray Concentrate. Make sure that your plant is listed on the product label.

Vectors of plant disease

Grape leafhoppers (3× life size).

Many different insects transmit plant diseases, but the most common and widespread carriers are aphids and leafhoppers. Aphids transmit most plant diseases, especially those caused by viruses. A single species of aphid may transmit up to 50 different plant viruses. Aphids and leafhoppers are small insects with sucking mouthparts. Their needlelike mouths pierce plant tissue and suck out the sap. Aphids and leafhoppers may acquire disease organisms as they feed on an infected plant. Disease organisms may also be transmitted to offspring through the eggs laid by the infectious mother. When the infectious insects feed on healthy, susceptible plants, they inject the disease organisms into the tissue, infecting the plant. Less-common plant disease vectors are treehoppers, whiteflies, mealybugs, grasshoppers, beetles, earwigs, and mites.

Control: Controlling insect vectors is especially difficult because it takes only one insect to infect a plant. Reduce future damage by taking the following precautions:
1. Begin a spray program before the insect is expected in the spring. To determine when the insect becomes active, contact your local county extension office. Spray the plants you wish to protect and any nearby plants.
2. Destroy any diseased plants and weeds that may harbor the disease. Don't use diseased materials for mulch, and don't put them in a compost pile or turn under in planting beds.
3. If possible, use row covers to keep insects away from plants. These fabric tents provide a physical barrier to the pests. Be sure the row covers are secured at ground level.

BEE AND WASP ORDER

Leafcutting bees

Leafcutting bee (3× life size).

Leafcutting bees
(*Megachile* species) are
hairy black or metallic-
blue, green, or purple
insects related to honeybees. The females
cut circular pieces of leaf tissue from rose
plants to line their nests and plug their egg
cells. They usually make their nests in the
dead twigs of roses and other plants in the
garden. Sometimes they nest in the ends of
dying or dead rose stems still attached to
the plant. Leafcutting bees are important
pollinators of agricultural plants such as
alfalfa, clover, and forage crops. The damage
they do to ornamentals is negligible.

Control: Prune dead or dying stems.
Remove dead twigs and plant debris from
around the garden. Because leafcutting
bees are pollinators, chemical controls
should be avoided.

Honeybees

Honeybee.

Honeybees are members
of the insect order
Hymenoptera. Other
insects in this group
include wasps, ants, and sawflies. Although
some of these insects are plant and
household pests, a great many prey on other
insects or are important pollinators (well
over 100 food crops depend on or benefit
from insect pollination). Of all these insects,
bees—and particularly honeybees—are by
far the most important pollinators of flowers.
They can be recognized by the furry body,
two pairs of wings, and bands of black or
brown alternating with lighter brown or tan
on the abdomen. The queen is ¾ inch long.
Other bees are slightly shorter. One reason
the honeybee is such an effective pollinator
is that its body and legs are covered with
special branched hairs to which pollen
clings. The bee is attracted to flowers for
their sweet nectar, which it sucks up
through its hollow tongue. Once the bee is
on the flower, pollen rubs off onto the hairy
body. Some of the pollen falls off when the
bee visits other flowers, thus completing the
pollination process. Honeybees also collect
pollen as food for their young. It is collected
on a special "pollen basket" on the hind
legs. Honeybees usually visit flowers within
¼ mile of their colony, but they have been
known to forage as far away as 8½ miles.
They use a "bee dance" to communicate the
direction, distance, and quantity of pollen
to other bees in the colony. (For more
information on honeybees, see page 518.)

Control: See page 518 for information
on controlling honeybees.

Bumblebees

Bumblebee.

Bumblebees are
recognized by their
robust shape, hairy
bodies, and large size
(⅜ to 1 inch long). They are usually
black with a yellow or orange patch on
the abdomen. Bumblebees are closely related
to honeybees and are excellent pollinators.
Bumblebees nest in the ground, often in
abandoned rodent nests or among dry grass
and other debris on the ground. The
colonies are small in comparison to those of
honeybees, usually containing no more than
several hundred adults. The individual cells
that make up bumblebee nests are roundish
and shaped like pots. The cells may contain
honey, pollen, or immature bumblebees.
Bumblebee colonies die out in the fall; only
younger queens survive the winter. Queens
start new colonies in the spring. The colony
is small at first and attains its largest size in
the late summer or early fall. Bumblebees
visit many kinds of flowers. Because they
have longer tongues than honeybees, they
feed on the nectar of some flowers from
which honeybees can't feed. Bumblebees
are not aggressive insects unless they are
defending their nest. Most stings result
when the nest is accidentally stepped on.

Control: Control of a bumblebee colony is
seldom necessary unless children or pets may
disturb the nest. Contact a professional pest
control operator to spray the nest. If you are
stung, apply a cold compress or ice pack to
the swollen area. If a severe reaction
develops, call a doctor.

Solitary wasps

Digger wasp.

Solitary wasps include mud daubers, spider wasps, tarantula hawks, and cicada killers. These wasps live alone. Some build mud nests under eaves, against walls, or under twigs or rocks; others dig tunnels in the ground and use these as nests. Although nests of several solitary wasps may be built close to each other, the wasps don't cooperate in building nests or feeding their young. Most solitary wasps resemble yellowjackets and other social wasps. Some, though, are metallic blue or black. Many have a long, thin waist and are sometimes called *thread-waisted wasps*. Solitary wasps stock their nests with insects or spiders that they either kill or paralyze with their sting. The wasp larvae in nests feed on the paralyzed prey and later form a cocoon and then emerge as adults. Solitary wasps rarely defend their nests and don't sting unless they are handled, stepped on, or highly provoked.

Control: Control is often not necessary, but if mud nests are a problem, eliminate them by hosing or knocking them down. Kill wasps by spraying them with Ortho® Hornet & Wasp Killer or Ortho® Outdoor Insect Fogger according to label directions. Control solitary wasps nesting in the ground (sometimes known as digger wasps) in lawns and other areas where they may be a nuisance by applying an insecticide containing *carbaryl* in and around the nest openings. Apply it at dusk when the wasps are not active. If you are stung, apply a cold compress or ice pack to the swollen area. If a severe reaction develops, call a doctor.

Social wasps

Social wasp nest.

Social wasps are so named because they live in colonies. Some common social wasps include yellowjackets, hornets, and umbrella or paper wasps. These insects all live in paper nests they build either in abandoned rodent burrows or hanging from eaves or branches. The paper nest material is a combination of plant fibers and wasp saliva. A mature colony contains from 200 to 15,000 individuals, depending on the kind of wasp. In fall, most of the wasps die, and the colony is abandoned. The old nests are rarely used again. Only recently mated females (queens) live until the next year. They establish new colonies in the spring, and by late summer the number of individuals in the colony is at a peak. At this time social wasps become pests around picnic tables, ripe fruit, and garbage cans as they search for sweets and bits of meat. Normally, however, social wasps prey on other insects. They feed partially digested bits of the prey to their young. Adults also feed on sweet substances such as nectar and honeydew. Some social wasps aggressively defend their nests and may attack en masse if disturbed. Unlike the honeybee, the social wasp can easily withdraw its stinger and escape or sting again.

Control: Keep food and garbage covered to discourage wasps from becoming pests. (For information on controlling yellowjackets and paper wasps, see pages 518 to 519.)

Sawflies

Sawfly larvae. Inset: Sawfly. (life size).

Sawflies are among the few insects in the bee and wasp family that feed on plants. They are a diverse group of insects. The immature sawfly resembles either a slug, having a soft, glistening body and tiny legs, or a caterpillar, having three pairs of larger legs and seven pairs of smaller legs. When feeding, most sawflies eat most of the leaf, leaving only the larger leaf veins. Some sawflies eat just one leaf surface (upper or lower), leaving translucent tan spots (windows) where they have fed. Others are leafminers that live and feed entirely between the upper and lower surfaces of the leaves. Adult sawflies are wasplike in general body shape but don't have the constricted threadlike waist characteristic of wasps. Some adults are colored like wasps, with yellow and black markings; others are entirely black. The adults don't eat and can't sting. They lay eggs on or in leaves. The hatching larvae feed and spin a cocoon when fully grown. Most sawflies go through one generation per year; some go through two or three. If enough sawflies are feeding, they may weaken a plant, stunting its growth and causing fewer blooms and less fruit. Sawflies feeding on conifers can kill the plant if they defoliate it once or several years in a row.

Control: Spray sawflies feeding on ornamental plants with Ortho® Systemic Insect Killer. Spray sawflies on fruit trees with an insecticide containing *malathion*. Make sure that your plant is listed on the product label. Repeat the spray if reinfestation occurs.

GRASSHOPPER ORDER

Grasshoppers

Grasshopper (life size).

Grasshoppers are large (up to 2½ inches long), light green or brown, dark-mottled insects with large hind legs for jumping. Hundreds of different species exist throughout the United States, but only a few damage garden plants. Grasshoppers are not a serious pest every year. They are found primarily in areas that receive only 10 to 30 inches of rain annually. When winter temperatures are mild and other conditions are optimum, grasshopper populations increase to tremendous numbers. Under these conditions, many types of grasshoppers become nonselective in their food preference. Millions of migratory grasshoppers have been known to form swarms hundreds of miles across, devouring every green plant in their path. When swarming like this, they are often called *locusts*. When infestations build up to such tremendous numbers, these grasshoppers pollute water, invade homes, destroy fabrics, and become a hazard to motorists.

Control: Handpicking eliminates small populations of grasshoppers. In order to minimize damage, apply controls while the grasshoppers are young. As grasshoppers mature, they require larger quantities of food. They will migrate to find food, usually from drying crops and weeds to tender garden plants. Treat vegetable gardens with Ortho® Bug-Geta® Plus Snail, Slug & Insect Killer, or spray with an insecticide containing *malathion*. Treat lawns with Ortho® Lawn Insect Killer Granules and ornamental plants with Multi-Purpose Insect Killer or Ortho® Rose & Flower Insect Killer.

Cicadas

Cicada (2× life size).

Cicadas are large (up to 1½ inches long), dark-bodied insects with transparent wings. Males have special organs that vibrate to produce loud, strident sounds. Immature cicadas suck sap from roots, and adults may suck sap from young twigs. The main damage to plants is from egg laying, however. Females use their sawlike egg-laying organ to cut the bark and sapwood of twigs. Rows of 24 to 48 eggs are deposited in the sapwood, up to 20 times per female, causing the leaves on damaged twigs to turn brown. Damaged twigs may eventually break and fall to the ground. The young insects that hatch from the eggs enter the soil, where they burrow to the roots. Many species of cicadas live in the United States. The periodical cicada (*Magicicada septendecim*), found only in the eastern United States, is the longest-lived insect in North America. The southern race has a 13-year life cycle; the northern race is called the *17-year locust* because of the length of its cycle. The various broods (populations) are tracked, and their appearance can be accurately predicted. On the 13th or 17th spring, as many as 40,000 cicadas appear from beneath a single tree.

Control: Control mature cicadas by spraying with an insecticide containing *carbaryl* when their singing is first heard and then repeating the spray after six or seven days. Cut off and destroy injured twigs as soon as possible. Protect young trees with mosquito netting. Don't plant new trees in the spring of years when periodical cicada emergence is predicted.

Walkingsticks

Walkingstick.

Walkingsticks are slow-moving insects that resemble twigs. They have long slender legs, a thin twiglike body, and long slender antennae. They are usually green when immature and turn brown as adults. Some walkingsticks grow to a length of 5 or 6 inches. At night they feed on a wide variety of plants; oak is favored by the insect. Walkingsticks have been known to become numerous enough to defoliate trees, but such occurrences are rare. Females lay eggs while in trees. The eggs fall to the ground, lie among the leaf litter during the winter, and hatch in the spring. Only one generation is produced each year. Dark pelletlike spots on leaves may indicate a heavy population before the insects themselves are seen.

Control: Walkingsticks are seldom numerous enough to cause plant damage and are usually more of a curiosity than anything else. No insecticides are registered for their control; handpick them if they are numerous and causing damage.

Crickets

Field cricket.

Crickets are black, brown, or green insects, up to 1½ inches long, that are closely related to grasshoppers (see page 452). Outdoors they feed on many plants; indoors they feed on clothes or other materials that have food or perspiration on them. Some crickets are beneficial, feeding on aphids and other small pests. Crickets fly or jump with their large legs and have long antennae that reach down their backs. The males produce a loud chirping sound by rubbing together parts of their front wings. Females have long, spear-shaped ovipositors (egg-laying organs). Depending on the species, females insert eggs either in the soil or in plant tissue, which may kill the tissue. Crickets have chewing mouthparts and feed at night on foliage, flowers, seeds, and seedlings or on other insects. They hide during the day in trash, around plants, along walkways, at the foot of walls or fences, and in the ground. The ground species are called *mole crickets*. (For more information on mole crickets, see page 71.) Crickets also invade homes, especially in the fall when their natural food supply disappears. (For more information on crickets as household pests, see page 507.)

Control: If crickets become a problem outdoors, treat with Ortho® Lawn Insect Killer Granules or spray according to label directions with Ortho® Home Defense® Perimeter & Indoor Insect Killer Pull 'N Spray.

Tree crickets

Tree cricket.

Tree crickets are slender, whitish to pale green or brown insects up to ¾ inch long, with long slender antennae. They live in trees and shrubs, where they feed on aphids and other insects and, to a lesser extent, on fruits, flowers, and foliage. The main damage they cause occurs when the female makes a place to lay her eggs by cutting a row of deep punctures in berry canes or twigs of trees and shrubs. The twigs or canes may later break or die at the puncture sites. Tree crickets lay their eggs in the fall, and the young crickets emerge in the spring. Only one generation occurs per year. Tree crickets produce a high-pitched, sustained chirping or trilling sound. They emit the sound in unison; if one cricket stops, it restarts in time with the others. The snowy tree cricket (*Oecanthus fultoni*) is common throughout the country except in southeastern states. This famous species alters its rate of chirping in relation to the temperature; add 40 to the number of chirps made in 15 seconds to get a good approximation of the temperature in degrees Fahrenheit.

Control: Prune out and destroy infested canes and twigs during the winter. No insecticides are registered for control of this insect pest.

Jerusalem crickets

Jerusalem cricket (¾ life size).

Jerusalem crickets (*Stenopelmatus fuscus*), also known as *potato bugs*, are large (up to 2 inches), brown insects. Their big heads and legs and long antennae give them a somewhat bizarre appearance. Jerusalem crickets are often found under rocks or other debris or when spading up garden soil. Sometimes they wander indoors, where they may become trapped. Jerusalem crickets are not poisonous. Handle them with care, however; their powerful jaws can deliver a forceful pinch, and the spines on their legs can pierce skin. They are called potato bugs because they occasionally damage potatoes grown on land that has not previously been in crop production. Although they feed on roots, they prefer other small insects. They find their food by burrowing into the soil and are most commonly found in freshly cultivated or light loamy or sandy soil.

Control: Scoop the insect into a jar or box or onto a newspaper and throw it outdoors or dispose of it. No insecticides are registered for control of this insect.

GRASSHOPPER ORDER
(continued)

Katydids

Katydid nymph.

Katydids belong to the same order (*Orthoptera*) as grasshoppers, crickets, walkingsticks, praying mantids, cicadas, and cockroaches. The immature katydid, called a *nymph*, looks like the adult, except that its wings are shorter or not visible. Nymphs gradually develop into the adult form. Katydids are usually green but are sometimes brown. The adults are from ¾ to more than 2 inches long. Wings of many katydids look very similar to leaves; even the veins in the wings look like leaf veins. Katydids have large hind legs for jumping and slender antennae that are usually longer than the body. The female has a flattened swordlike egg-laying device, called an ovipositor, which protrudes from the tail end of the body. She lays eggs in overlapping rows, usually on stems or leaves. The eggs are about the shape of pumpkin seeds but a little smaller. Only one generation occurs per year. Katydids chew holes in the margins of leaves. They seldom occur in large enough numbers to do much damage, but occasionally they defoliate citrus trees or ornamental plants. Katydids are well-known for their chirping sounds, which are an important part of courtship.

Control: The presence of a few katydids is not enough to harm plants. If katydids are numerous, handpick and destroy the insects, or spray with an insecticide containing *carbaryl*. Make sure that your plant is listed on the product label.

FLY ORDER

Flies and maggots

Housefly adult, pupa, and maggot.

All flies are two-winged insects belonging to the insect order *Diptera*. Some familiar members of this group are crane flies, fruit flies, bluebottle flies, houseflies, hover flies, mosquitoes, and gnats. Depending on the species, adult flies feed on other insects, blood, nectar, or liquids from decaying organic matter. Some adult flies don't eat at all. Immature flies, called *maggots*, are legless creatures that lead a life quite different from the adults. Many live in and feed on moist, decaying organic material, such as compost, animal manure, and garbage. Others are beneficial parasites or predators of other insects. Some feed on living plants. When the maggots have completed their development, they change into brownish pupae and finally emerge as adults. Some flies complete their life cycle in days, while others may take a full year. Flies can transmit diseases to humans through their bites or as they crawl over food. Some flies are important pollinators, help to decompose decaying matter, help control other insects, and are used as food by small animals.

Control: Kill household flies indoors with Ortho® Flying Insect Killer, or treat entire rooms with Ortho® Indoor Insect Fogger. Kill flies outdoors with Ortho® Outdoor Insect Fogger or Ortho® Home Defense® Perimeter & Indoor Insect Killer Pull 'N Spray, or trap them with an Ortho® Bug-B-Gon® Full-Season Fly Trap. (For more information on controlling household flies and biting flies, see the section beginning on page 506.) For information on flies infesting plants, look under the listing for your plant.

Crane flies

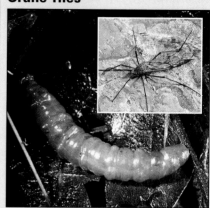

Larva (2× life size). Inset: Adult (½ life size).

Crane flies, also called *mosquito eaters*, resemble huge, overgrown mosquitoes. They range from ⅜ to 2½ inches long, with the wings spanning as many as 3 inches. They have long, slender legs that break off easily. Crane flies often find their way into homes and garages, where they can cause alarm because of their large size. They can't bite, however, and are completely harmless. The adult flies don't eat. Most crane fly larvae (or maggots) feed on decaying plant material in damp soil or shallow water. One type, the European crane fly, is a lawn pest. Crane fly larvae range from ½ to 1½ inches long when fully grown. One or two generations occur per year.

Control: Usually only one or two crane flies are seen indoors. Spray them with an insecticide containing *pyrethrins*, or capture them and release them outdoors.

Fruit flies

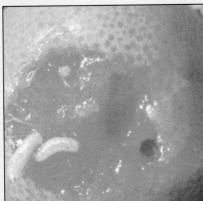
Mediterranean fruit fly larvae (¾ life size).

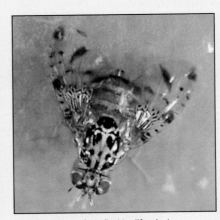
Mediterranean fruit fly (4× life size).

Leafminers

Leafminer trails.

Fruit flies are insects that lay their eggs in the developing fruit of a number of species of fruits, vegetables, and nuts. When the eggs hatch, the larvae feed on and spoil the flesh of the fruit, usually causing the fruit to drop from the tree. When mature, the larvae leave the fruit and burrow into the ground, where they pupate. Adult fruit flies resemble common houseflies but may be smaller or larger, depending on the species.

Various species: Several species of fruit flies are damaging pests in the United States. These include the apple maggot (*Rhagoletis pomonella*), Caribbean fruit fly (*Anastrepha suspensa*), Mexican fruit fly (*Anastrepha ludens*), walnut husk fly (*Rhagoletis completa*), and Mediterranean fruit fly (*Ceratitis capitata*). The apple maggot (see page 294) is a pest of apples, plums, cherries, and pears. The Caribbean fruit fly and the Mexican fruit fly spoil the fruit of citrus. The walnut husk fly tunnels into the flesh of walnuts and peaches. The Mediterranean fruit fly, commonly known as the *medfly*, is potentially one of the most damaging fruit flies, infesting more than 250 species of plants, including fruits, vegetables, and nuts.

The medfly: The Mediterranean fruit fly is a native of tropical West Africa. Since the mid-1800s, it has been spreading to many of the warmer parts of the world, including Hawaii, southern Europe, and Central and South America. It has been found in the United States off and on since 1929, when it was first discovered in central Florida. Since that time, many outbreaks in Florida, Texas, and southern California have been eradicated. Like other fruit flies, the medfly is usually transported as a larva in infested fruit. Many new infestations are the result of travelers bringing home infested fruits and vegetables.

Control: Because it is not possible to eradicate the larvae of fruit flies once they have infested the fruit, most control measures involve prevention. To avoid infestations, harvest fruit as soon as it matures, and pick up and dispose of fruit that falls from the tree.

Quarantine laws: The spread of most fruit flies is controlled by quarantine laws. State and federal departments of agriculture operate detection traps and constantly monitor fruit flies. Fruit shipped from areas with fruit fly infestations must be fumigated or otherwise treated. Travelers are prohibited from bringing fruits and vegetables into the United States; many states also have restrictions. Despite these precautions, the insects sometimes gain entry to new areas. Because of the medfly's wide range of host plants, it is especially threatening. Late spring to fall is the most likely time to detect the medfly. If you live in an infested area or an area where infestations have occurred, you should learn to identify the medfly and notify the local county extension office if you suspect an outbreak in your area.

Leafminers are insect larvae that feed inside a leaf, between the upper and lower surfaces. They may be the larvae of flies, moths, sawflies, or beetles. Females lay their eggs on or in the leaves, and the larvae that hatch from these eggs burrow into the leaves. Leafminers must be able to survive in a small living space, so they are tiny and somewhat flat. The thinner the leaf, the flatter and smaller the leafminer. As the larvae mine the leaf tissue, they have more room to expand, but their heads always remain somewhat flat. Leafminer feeding produces blisters, blotches, or tunnels in the leaf, which turns yellow or brown as the tissue dies. If more than one larva is mining the tissue, the tunnels often run together, forming large blotches that cover much of the leaf. Infested plants may have a scorched appearance. Many adult leafminers continue to feed on leaves, using their ovipositor to puncture the leaf and suck out the plant sap.

Control: Leafminers are protected inside leaves for most of their lives, which makes control difficult. Unless the spray used for control is a systemic insecticide, sprays must be applied when the adults emerge to lay their eggs. Most ornamentals can be sprayed with Ortho® Rose & Flower Insect Killer or Ortho® Systemic Insect Killer. Protect vegetables from egg-laying flies with row covers. Put the covers in place when plants are set out or seeds are planted. Be sure they are secured to the ground and have no gaps through which flies can enter.

THRIPS ORDER (continued)

Thrips

Leaf thrips damage to viburnum.

Flower thrips

Flower thrips damage to pansy.

Greenhouse thrips

Greenhouse thrips (20× life size).

Thrips are tiny (less than ¹⁄₁₆ inch), slender insects of the order *Thysanoptera*, which means *bristle wings* or *fringe wings*. Adults are tan to dark brown or black with two pairs of featherlike wings. The immature insects (*nymphs*) are wingless and are usually lighter in color. Thrips are serious pests of hundreds of plants in the garden. Nymphs and adults feed by scraping or rasping the plant tissue and then sucking out the released plant sap. Blossoms, fruit, foliage, and shoots become flecked, streaked, or distorted. Females lay fertilized or unfertilized eggs in plant tissue. The unfertilized eggs develop only into males. Most species of thrips complete a life cycle in two or three weeks, so populations can rapidly build to tremendous numbers. In warm-winter areas, reproduction may continue throughout the year. Thrips spread tomato spotted wilt disease and often discolor flowers, especially roses.

Control: Exposed thrips (those that feed unprotected on foliage) are easier to control than flower thrips, which are protected from chemicals inside the flowers or growing points of the plant. Remove infested buds and blooms. Spray ornamentals for exposed thrips with Ortho® Systemic Insect Killer or Ortho® Rose & Flower Insect Killer. Control thrips on food crops with Ortho® Malathion Plus® Insect Spray Concentrate. Apply sprays twice more at intervals of 7 to 10 days to control thrips as they hatch.

Flower thrips (*Frankliniella* species) are tiny (¹⁄₂₀ inch) insects that infest the flowers, flower buds, and growing points of many plants. They are able to distinguish different colors of flowers and usually prefer those that are yellow or light colored. The amber-colored adults and lemon-yellow nymphs (immature thrips) feed by rasping the plant tissue and then sucking the released plant sap. The injured tissue dies, producing dead spots, distorted blossoms and new leaves, and balled flowers (flower buds that turn brown and never open). The larvae drop to the ground to pupate. Flower thrips are most abundant between late spring and midsummer. They reproduce mainly on the flowers of trees, grasses, and weeds and then migrate to gardens nearby. In the western states, thrips are most damaging when uncultivated plants dry up in summer, forcing the insects to migrate to gardens where plants are still green. Thrips spread tomato spotted wilt disease and often discolor flowers, especially roses.

Control: Flower thrips are difficult to control because they are usually protected in plant tissue, and they constantly reinfest garden flowers from nearby plants. Spraying ornamentals with a systemic insecticide (one that moves through the plant) will protect flowers for up to 10 days. Use Ortho® Systemic Insect Killer at the first sign of damage. Control thrips on food crops with Ortho® Malathion Plus® Insect Spray Concentrate. Make sure that your plant is listed on the label. Repeat the spray two more times at intervals of 7 to 10 days to control thrips as they hatch.

Greenhouse thrips (*Heliothrips haemorrhoidalis*) are serious pests of many greenhouse plants and also damage many garden ornamentals and fruits in the southern states. They feed openly in dense colonies on leaves and fruit. Greenhouse thrips don't survive well in hot, dry conditions, so they are usually found in shady areas or on the inner parts or the north side of a plant. As the thrips remove sap from the plant tissue, leaves become silvery or bleached. Damaged leaves wilt, become papery, and usually drop prematurely. The thrips also leave large quantities of black, varnishlike spots of excrement around the areas where they feed, giving the plant an unsightly appearance. Adult greenhouse thrips are black with silvery-black wings. They aren't strong fliers like other types of thrips, so infestations spread slowly. Females insert their eggs inside leaves or fruit, producing blisters. The young thrips that hatch from these eggs are translucent white and wingless. They feed for several weeks and then develop into adults. Seven or more generations may occur per year.

Control: Greenhouse thrips are easier to control than other types of thrips that are protected in buds and flowers (see previous column). Spray infested plants with Ortho® Systemic Insect Killer, Ortho® Rose & Flower Insect Killer, or Ortho® Malathion Plus® Insect Spray Concentrate. Cover the leaf surfaces thoroughly. Before spraying, make sure that your plant is listed on the product label. Do not use Ortho® Systemic Insect Killer on food crops.

SPIDERS

Spiders

Spider and prey.

Spiders are not insects but belong to the class *Arachnida*, along with mites, ticks, scorpions, and harvestmen. All *Arachnida* have four pairs of legs and two main body segments; insects have three pairs of legs and three main body segments. There are many different kinds of spiders. Many spin intricate webs to trap their prey; others do not spin webs. Spiders that don't build webs either actively hunt their prey or wait motionless and grab their victims as the victims approach. Most spiders in homes and gardens build neat, organized webs or sheets of webbing that lead into a funnel. The poisonous black widow and the brown recluse spiders (see page 521) both spin an irregular, tangled web in a dark, quiet location or among debris on the ground. Many nonpoisonous species also build tangled webs. Most spiders lay eggs in silken sacs. The young spiderlings resemble adults and are cannibalistic. Some spiderlings leave the egg sac by sending out a long silken thread that catches the wind and pulls the spider into the air. This process is called *ballooning*. In the fall, the air is sometimes filled with masses of these threads, called *gossamer*. Spiders feed mostly on insects, but they play only a minor role in controlling insect pests.

Control: Spiders rarely need to be controlled unless they become a nuisance in or around the home. (For information, see page 507 for control of household spiders and page 521 for control of specific poisonous spiders.)

MITES

Mites

Mite damage on hollyhock.

Mites are minute pests that infest many garden plants. Some are commonly called *spider mites*. Some mites may injure humans or animals; others are beneficial predators of plant pests. Mites are not insects but belong to the animal class *Arachnida*, along with spiders, ticks, and several other groups. They have four pairs of legs instead of three and lack antennae and true jaws. Each mite has a pair of needlelike stylets that pierce plant tissue. The sap and cell contents are sucked from the plant, resulting in leaf stippling. Most mites have many generations each year, often completing a life cycle in 7 to 10 days. Mites, cast-off skins, eggshells, and webbing may cover the surfaces of leaves or other plant parts. Mites are more numerous on dusty plants. Heavy rains usually limit spider mite populations by washing them and the dust off the plants. Mites also cause more damage to water-stressed plants because the plants are unable to quickly replenish the sap sucked out by the mites.

Control: Mites can be difficult to control because the egg stage has resistance to most chemical sprays. Chemicals are effective against other stages, however. They must be applied at least three times at intervals of 7 to 10 days for effective control. Spray ornamentals with Ortho® Rose & Flower Insect Killer or Ortho® Systemic Insect Killer. Control mites on fruits and vegetables with Ortho® Malathion Plus® Insect Spray Concentrate or Ortho® Volck® Oil Spray. Be sure your plant is on the label. Rinse dust off plants with a water spray. Reduce mite damage by keeping plants watered. Use a spray of water to knock mites off plants.

SILVERFISH

Silverfish

Bristletail (4× life size).

Silverfish belong to the order *Thysanura*. Some members of this group are called *bristletails*. These insects are less than ½ inch long and are covered with silvery scales that rub off easily. Immature silverfish resemble the adults except for their smaller size. After hatching, they periodically shed their skin (*molt*) as they grow. They may molt as many as fifty times during their lifetime. In very warm climates, silverfish take as little as three months to become adults; in cooler climates, they mature in about two years. Under optimum conditions, silverfish can live for three or four years. Silverfish are commonly found indoors, where they feed on materials with a high starch content, such as paper, wallpaper, book bindings, and starched clothing. The species that live outdoors, usually called bristletails, live under stones, beneath bark, in leaf litter, and in other dark, protected spots. They mainly feed on lichens, molds, and dead insects. Silverfish and bristletails are most active at night. (For more information on silverfish occurring in homes, see page 509.)

Control: Spray with Ortho® Home Defense® Perimeter & Indoor Insect Killer Pull 'N Spray or Ortho® Roach, Ant & Spider Killer in areas such as cracks along baseboards and door and window frames, in closets, behind drawers and shelves, and around bookcases. Store valued papers and clothes in tightly sealed plastic bags. Dispose of unwanted books, papers, and magazines. Seal holes in walls around pipes, and seal other cracks and crevices. Eliminate sources of excess moisture such as leaking plumbing.

TERMITES

Termites

Damaged wood.

Termites and larvae (2× life size).

Termites cause great economic damage in this country. These insects have special protozoa in their stomachs that help them digest wood. Termites may be winged or wingless. The winged forms emerge from the nests in the spring and fall, often on a warm day following a rain. After mating in the air, the winged termites drop their wings and search for a suitable place to start a new colony. Only a small percentage survive and are successful. Colonies consist of eggs, nymphs, workers, soldiers, one or more egg-laying queens, and winged termites that will one day leave the colony. There are three kinds of termites. Subterranean termites are the most common (see page 514). They maintain their colonies within the ground and build their characteristic mud tubes over rocks and concrete foundations to bridge the gap between soil and wood. Their nests or galleries in wood always contain soil. Drywood termites (see page 514) don't require such contact with the ground and don't build mud tubes. Their galleries are free of soil. Dampwood termites (see page 513) don't require contact with the ground but do require wood or soil with a high moisture content. Their galleries are free of soil. Although termites are beneficial in nature because they help decompose the wood of fallen trees and shrubs, they sometimes weaken or kill living trees and shrubs. They usually enter the plant through wounds, dead branches, or roots. Drywood termites confine their feeding primarily to dried heartwood. They seldom kill the plant, but they weaken it structurally if they continue feeding over a long period. In warm climates, subterranean termites sometimes eat the bark and living tissues underneath, killing the plant.

Control: If termites are in the structure of a building, identify the kind of termite, determine the extent of damage, and apply the control measures given for that termite. (For more information on subterranean and drywood termites, see page 514, and for dampwood termites, see page 513.) Accurate diagnosis and effective control of termites usually require the aid of a professional termite or pest control operator. Prevent termites from damaging your home with Ortho® Termite & Carpenter Ant Killer used according to label directions. Prevent termite occurrences in the garden by pruning dead branches, burning or digging out stumps, removing wood debris, and painting or treating garden stakes and fence posts with a wood preservative. Remove debris from around termite-infested plants and prune infested plant parts if possible. No insecticides are registered for control of termites in plants.

DRAGONFLIES AND DAMSELFLIES

Dragonflies and damselflies

Dragonfly (⅔ life size).

Dragonflies and damselflies are both in the order *Odonata*, a name referring to their toothed jaws. They are common around lakes and streams. Dragonflies, which have wider bodies and stiffer wings than damselflies, are strong fliers and may be seen well away from water. Dragonflies hold their wings perpendicular to their bodies when at rest, while damselfies hold their wings parallel to their bodies and behind them. Both may have clear wings or wings with black or colored bands. Colorful, sometimes iridescent markings cover their bodies. The largest dragonflies in the United States are more than 4 inches long and have a wingspan of nearly 6 inches. The adult insects feed on other flying insects while in flight. Dragonflies and damselflies deposit their eggs in water or in boggy areas close to water. The immature insects, called *naiads*, live at the bottoms of streams and ponds, where they feed on insects, tadpoles, and small fish. Larger fish eat the naiads in turn. Naiads bear little resemblance to the adults; they are broad-bodied, wingless, and have three pairs of legs that are as long as or longer than their bodies. They are up to 2½ inches long. When naiads are fully grown, they crawl out of the water on a plant stem, post, or other nearby object, shed their skins, and emerge as adults. Their outgrown skins may be seen along the water's edge.

Control: Controls aren't necessary.

MAYFLIES

Mayflies

Mayfly.

Mayflies are in the order
Ephemeroptera, a name
referring to the
extremely short life of
the adults. Mayflies are soft-bodied, delicate
creatures, from ⅛ to 1 inch long, with
triangular wings that they hold upright over
their bodies when at rest. They have two or
three long antennae-like filaments at their
tail end. Mayfly adults can't feed. They live
only one to three days. Large numbers of
them often emerge at the same time.
On certain spring and summer nights, swarms
of mayflies may be seen flying around lights
near lakes and streams. Their dead bodies
may pile up in enormous numbers. The dried-
out bodies and skins of mayflies cause allergy
problems in some people when large flights
of adults occur. Mayflies swarm and mate
at twilight and lay eggs within an hour in
nearby water. The immature mayflies, known
as *naiads*, live at the bottom of streams,
ponds, and lakes, feeding on tiny aquatic
plants and animals. Naiads are wingless and
have three tail-end filaments that are shorter
than their bodies and about as long as the
antennae. Most naiads live from one to four
years before emerging as adults. Both naiads
and adult mayflies are important food sources
for fish, frogs, and other creatures in and
around water.

Control: Controls aren't necessary.

ANTLIONS

Antlions

Antlion larva (3.5× life size).

The adult antlion
closely resembles a
damselfly except for its
antennae, which have
tiny clubs on the tips. The immature
antlion, also known as a *doodlebug*, makes
cone-shaped pits in dry, sandy, or dusty soil.
The pits are often located at the base of
trees and near or beneath buildings. The
largest pits are up to 2 inches in diameter.
The antlion lies concealed at the bottom of
the pit, ready to grab any ant or other small
insect that tumbles in. The antlion has
large, sickle-shaped jaws that it uses to
hold the prey as it sucks out the body fluids.
It lives from one to three years and makes
many pits during its lifetime. It makes a
cocoon at the base of the pit and emerges
as an adult antlion during the summer.
Antlions are very weak fliers and are easily
blown by the wind. They are sometimes
attracted to lights. Although antlions are
beneficial predators, their role in controlling
garden pests is minor.

Control: Controls aren't necessary.

SOIL PESTS

Ants

Ants (2× life size).

Ants are social insects
that live in colonies or
nests. Each colony has
large egg-laying queens,
larvae, pupae, and wingless sterile workers,
all females. In spring or early summer, the
queen produces winged males and females
that may leave the nest to start new
colonies. After mating, the males die,
and the queens shed their wings and begin
laying eggs. Many different types of ants
are found throughout the United States.
All ants have a constricted abdomen, and
they range in color from yellow to black.
Some ants invade homes looking for food
(see page 510). Others find their food
outdoors, where they feed on insects, seeds,
vegetable roots, flower nectar, or *honeydew*,
a sweet, sticky excretion of sucking insects
such as aphids, soft scales, mealybugs,
leafhoppers, and whiteflies. Certain ants
caress aphids to increase their production of
honeydew or carry them to uninfested plants
to supply them with ample food. Some types
of leaf-cutting ants bring the leaves back to
the nest to grow a fungus garden. Ant
colonies, or mounds located in a garden,
lawn, or cultivated field disturb plant roots
and interfere with the use of equipment.
The mounds are often more of a nuisance
than the ants themselves.

Control: Treat ant mounds in the garden
with Ortho® Lawn Insect Killer Granules or
Ortho® Bug-B-Gon® Multi-Purpose Insect
Killer Concentrate. Control aphids, scales,
mealybugs, leafhoppers, and whiteflies to
eliminate the production of honeydew, which
attracts ants. Ants can be kept off individual
trees and plants with sticky barriers.

459

SOIL PESTS (continued)

Fire ants

Fire ant mound.

Earwigs

Earwig (2× life size).

Centipedes

Centipede (life size).

Fire ants (*Solenopsis* species) are small (up to ¼ inch long) red or black ants that build

large, hard nests in the ground, 1 to 2 feet high. Mounds or nests are found in lawns and gardens or in houses when ants are driven inside by rain or drought. They are especially numerous in pasturelands, where there may be up to 60 mounds per acre. Damage from fire ants is caused mainly by their mounds, which interfere with mowing or cultivating in the garden and with harvest operations in commercial vegetable production. The large mounds break garden equipment and machinery. Fire ants may also damage plants. Some species feed on young succulent vegetables, bark, and insects, while others eat almost anything, including seeds, plants, insects, nesting birds, household foods, and clothes. The ants may attack and kill young animals and ground birds, such as quail; they also sting people who disturb their nests. Depending on the degree of allergy, people react differently to the sting, which is usually on the feet or legs and may be very painful and serious. The ant first bites the skin, raising it slightly, and then inserts its stinger, leaving it there for up to 25 seconds. It may repeat this procedure two or three more times, causing a cluster of stings. Within 24 hours, pustules up to ⅛ inch in diameter develop.

Control: Control fire ants by treating their mounds as they appear with Ortho® Orthene® Fire Ant Killer or Ortho® Fire Ant Killer Broadcast Granules. If you have a severe reaction to a fire ant sting, call a doctor.

Earwigs are hard, reddish-brown insects up to 1 inch long with pincers that extend from

the back end. The pincers on the females are almost straight, with a sharp inward curve on the end. On the males, the pincers are longer and have a wide curve. Earwigs use their pincers as offensive and defensive weapons and sometimes to catch the insects on which they feed. Their main sources of food, however, are plants, ripe fruit, and decaying organic matter. Young earwigs eat ragged holes in the leaves of many vegetables and flowers in spring or early summer. Older earwigs feed on blossoms and corn silk, causing poor kernel development on the cobs. The insects may even climb into large fruit trees, such as apricot and peach trees, and feed on ripening fruit. Earwigs are nocturnal insects, feeding at night and hiding during the day. In daylight hours they hide in damp, dark places, such as under flowerpots or in woodpiles, plant refuse, inside garden hoses, and homes, where they become household pests.

Control: If you think earwigs are eating your plants, inspect the plants at night with a flashlight. Spray Ortho® Home Defense® Perimeter & Indoor Insect Killer Pull 'N Spray around plants, flowerpots, house and porch foundations, woodpiles, or anywhere else you think earwigs may be hiding. Do not use on food crops. To keep earwigs out of fruit trees in lawn areas, sprinkle Ortho® Bug-Geta® Plus Snail, Slug & Insect Killer pellets around the base of the trees a month before fruit ripens, or use a sticky band to keep earwigs from climbing the tree.

Centipedes, often called *hundred-legged worms,* are not true insects, but they are closely related.

They have no wings, only two main body parts instead of three, and one pair of legs on each segment of their bodies instead of three pairs as true insects have. Most centipedes have at least 15 pairs of legs. Their bodies are long in relation to width and somewhat flat, which makes it possible for them to squeeze into cracks and crevices of foundations and around windows. Most centipedes are about 1 inch long, but some of the tropical species reach 18 inches in length. Centipedes look like millipedes (see page 461) but are more active. Centipedes scurry rapidly away when disturbed; millipedes usually curl into a tight spiral. Centipedes don't injure plants. They are beneficial, preying on snails, insects, and earthworms. Centipedes hide in damp areas under logs and stones, and in plant debris. They can move swiftly to catch their prey, which they paralyze by injecting poison from claws located behind the head. Some of the larger species of centipedes may inflict a painful bite if handled by humans.

Control: It is usually unnecessary to control centipedes unless they start infesting your home. Sealing cracks in the foundation or holes in window frames will help prevent centipedes from entering the house. Clear wood, stones, and dead vegetation away from the base of the house. Spray outdoors using Ortho® Home Defense® Perimeter & Indoor Insect Killer Pull 'N Spray around areas where centipedes hide. Do not use on food crops. Inside the home, use Ortho® Roach, Ant & Spider Killer.

Millipedes

Millipede (4× life size).

Millipedes, also called *thousand-legged worms,* are distant relatives of centipedes (see page 460). Millipedes are 1 to several inches long, hard-bodied, cylindrical, and wormlike, usually brown, pinkish brown, or grayish. They have two very short legs on each body segment and a total of 30 to 400 legs (but not 1,000 legs, as their name suggests). Young millipedes look like the adults but initially have only three pairs of legs. Millipedes curl up in a coil when they are touched or picked up. They hide in damp, dark places, such as under stones or boards or in plant debris. Large numbers of them may crawl into houses during heavy rains or during dry periods in summer and fall. Millipedes normally feed on decaying matter. When they become numerous, however, they may feed on small roots, seedlings, or vegetable seeds. Root crops, decaying flower bulbs, and overripe fruit that touches damp ground—especially muskmelons, tomatoes, and strawberries—may attract millipedes.

Control: If millipedes are numerous in your garden, spray Ortho® Home Defense® Perimeter & Indoor Insect Killer Pull 'N Spray around plants and other areas where millipedes hide. Don't use the spray around food crops. Protect ripening fruit on the ground with straw or other mulch. Millipedes move slowly, which makes them simple to remove from inside the house. Pick them up by hand or with a vacuum cleaner, or sweep them up with a broom.

Snails and slugs

Slug (life size).

Snails and slugs are mollusks and belong to the same phylum as oysters and clams. Snails and slugs are quite similar to each other except that snails have an external shell. Both secrete mucus, which helps them glide along. The mucus dries to become the familiar shiny slime trail, a good clue to the presence of snails and/or slugs. These land mollusks require moisture to survive and are therefore most troublesome in wet areas. When conditions are dry, they go dormant, becoming active again only when moisture is available. Slugs lay white eggs encased in a slimy mass in protected places. Snails bury their eggs in the soil, also in a slimy mass. Snails and slugs take from two months to two years to become adults. Dense ground covers, such as ivy, are ideal hiding and breeding places for them. They feed on either living or decaying plant material or on both. Some species are more troublesome than others, and size alone is not a good indicator of how serious the pest is.

Control: Scatter Ortho® Bug-Geta® Snail & Slug Killer in bands around the areas you wish to protect. Also scatter the bait in areas where snails or slugs might be hiding, such as in dense ground cover, weedy areas, compost piles, or flowerpot-storage areas. Before spreading the bait, wet down the areas to be treated to encourage snail and slug activity that night. Repeat the application every two weeks for as long as snails and slugs are active. Handpicking and disposing of snails and slugs consistently over a long period will greatly reduce populations.

Sowbugs and pillbugs

Sowbugs (6× life size).

Sowbugs and pillbugs are crustaceans related to lobsters and shrimp. They are dark gray, with hard, flat, segmented bodies about ½ inch long, and they have legs. Pillbugs roll up into a ball when disturbed. Sowbugs and pillbugs are nocturnal insects. They feed at night on decaying vegetable matter and are destructive to plants only when their populations build to very large numbers. When this happens, they feed on the fine roots of seedlings in the garden or greenhouse. They also feed on fruit and leaves in contact with the ground. During the day, sowbugs and pillbugs hide in damp, dark places, such as under boards, rocks, and flowerpots or in plant debris. Sometimes they invade homes through cracks or windows, and they hide in dark places such as basements. They cause no damage inside but can be a nuisance.

Control: If you notice large numbers of sowbugs or pillbugs under your flowerpots or in the garden, scatter Ortho® Bug-Geta® Plus Snail, Slug & Insect Killer lightly in a 2- to 4-foot band around plants, flowerpots, boards, plant debris, and other areas where sowbugs and pillbugs congregate. Don't use around food crops. Where possible, eliminate moist, dark breeding sites such as rocks, boards, and leaf litter. Spread Ortho® Bug-B-Gon® Multi-Purpose Insect Killer Granules around the foundation of the house.

BENEFICIAL INSECTS

Ladybugs

Ladybugs (2× life size).

Lady beetles, also called *ladybugs* or *ladybird beetles*, are beneficial insects that prey mostly on aphids but also eat scales, mealybugs, and mites. The many different species range in color from gray and black to bright orange. The larvae are flat, orange or gray, alligator-shaped insects with legs on the front half of the body. Unlike the adults, they have no wings or wing covers. The cigar-shaped eggs are usually orange and stand upright in clusters of a dozen or more. A single lady beetle may lay up to 1,500 eggs during her lifetime. The larvae that hatch from the eggs feed on aphids or other insects, devouring up to 25 aphids per day. Because lady beetles are such voracious eaters, they require high populations of aphids to maintain themselves. Adults may eat 50 or more aphids per day. If the prey population is reduced to such low numbers that there are not enough aphids on which to feed, the lady beetles will migrate or starve to death. The aphid population will gradually rebuild, possibly followed by a return of the lady beetle population. These population fluctuations are common between predators and their prey. Lady beetles can be purchased at garden stores or through mail-order houses. These insects have been collected from masses in areas where they hibernate. When they are placed in the garden, there is no guarantee that they'll stay. Even when food is available, lady beetles often have an urge to migrate.

Control: Controls aren't necessary.

Praying mantids

Praying mantid (¾ life size).

Praying mantids are considered beneficial insects because they eat many insect pests. They are just as likely to eat a harmless insect or even another beneficial insect, however, such as a honeybee or another praying mantid. Their name is derived because they look like they are praying as they wait for an insect victim. They are large (up to 5 inches), slender, green or straw-colored insects with wings and long legs. The front legs are larger than the hind legs and have spines that grasp and hold their prey. The immature mantids look just like the adults but are smaller and don't have wings. In the fall, the females lay 100 or more eggs in foamlike, straw-colored masses attached to any type of plant in the garden. After mating, the female often devours the male mantid. The following May or June, the emerging young begin feeding on aphids or other small, slow-moving prey. They may also feed on one another. As they increase in size, they feed on larger insects. The mantids kill their prey by biting the back of the neck, which severs the main nerves and renders the insect helpless. Praying mantid eggs can be purchased or can be gathered from roadside borders, from around fields, or from shrubs. Leave them attached to a section of the plant and place them in your garden off the ground where they won't be soaked by rain. Because they are not heavy feeders, mantids are relatively ineffective as insect controls. But they are interesting.

Control: Controls aren't necessary.

Hover flies

Hover fly.

Hover flies, also called *syrphids* and *flower flies*, resemble bees and wasps. They are about the same size as these other insects (¼ to ¾ inch long) and have similar color patterns—black with bands of yellow or orange. Some are fuzzy like bees and wasps. Unlike bees and wasps, however, they can remain stationary, or hover, in the air. They have one pair of wings rather than two, as bees and wasps do. They can't sting. Hover flies sip nectar from flowers. Immature hover flies are maggots with feeding patterns that vary, depending on the species. One, the narcissus bulb fly, feeds on bulbs. Others feed on decaying plant material. Most hover fly larvae prey on plant-feeding insects, however, particularly on aphids, young mealybugs, and scale insects. They grasp and puncture these insects with tiny hooks in their mouths, suck out the body fluids, and then abandon the empty carcass. Predaceous hover fly larvae are common in gardens and are often seen feeding on aphids. They have voracious appetites and are highly beneficial. When abundant, they can completely control a colony of aphids within a few days.

Control: Controls aren't necessary.

Lacewings

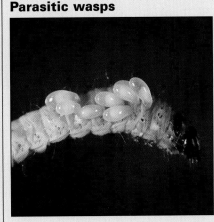

Lacewing larva (6× life size). Inset: Adult (2× life size).

Lacewings are beneficial insects that belong to a group called *nerve-winged* insects. The adults are up to ¾ inch long with long antennae and transparent green or brown lacy wings held over the body in a rooflike position. The green species has iridescent red-gold eyes. The adult is considered to be one of the most beautiful insects. The larvae are small (up to ½ inch), flat, and spindle-shaped, resembling miniature alligators. They are yellow to gray with reddish-brown markings and sickle-shaped jaws for capturing their prey. The larvae suck the body fluids from aphids, mealybugs, scales, and other small insects. Some species carry the remains of their victims on their backs. The larvae are such voracious eaters that they are commonly called *aphid lions*. The female green lacewing lays her eggs singly on top of a delicate, hairlike stalk that she constructs on the surface of a leaf or twig. This prevents the hatching larvae from devouring other unhatched eggs. At night, adult lacewings are attracted to bright lights and may cling to screen doors. Green lacewings can be purchased from insectaries, companies that raise insect predators and parasites. Because they don't survive the winter well, they should be reintroduced each spring.

Control: Controls aren't necessary.

Parasitic wasps

Parasitic wasp larvae on navel orangeworm.

Parasite of pine tip moth (3× life size).

Many wasps are insect parasites. They lay eggs in or on living insects or eggs, and the emerging immature wasp, which is white and grublike in appearance, feeds on tissues inside the host insect, eventually killing it. Many of these parasitic wasps are far more effective in controlling a certain pest than are predators such as lady beetles, praying mantids, and lacewings.

Aphid parasites: One parasitic wasp that attacks aphids (*Aphidius testaceipes*) is present throughout the country. It is responsible for creating the aphid "mummies" so commonly seen. The mummy is the brown shell of an aphid that has been killed by this tiny wasp parasite. The wasp larva develops in the aphid's body. After the larva pupates, it emerges as an adult wasp through a hole it cuts in the mummy's back. This wasp reproduces throughout the warmer months of the year and effectively controls many aphid colonies.

Whitefly parasites: The whitefly parasite (*Encarsia formosa*) is a wasp that is particularly useful for control of whiteflies in greenhouses. The adult wasp lays eggs in whitefly pupae and larvae. As the immature wasp develops inside, the whitefly host turns black and dies. Several days later an adult wasp emerges. The entire life cycle takes as little as 20 days in warm weather. The whitefly parasite is effective only when temperatures average 75°F or warmer. In cooler temperatures, the development of this parasite is delayed too much to control the whitefly population.

Caterpillar parasites: *Trichogramma*, a minute wasp, is so small it can lay its egg inside another insect's egg. The adult is about 1/64 of an inch long. The host egg dies and turns black as the wasp larva develops. *Trichogramma* primarily attacks eggs of butterflies and moths. It is an important parasite of codling moth eggs. Attempts to control codling moths, however, by releasing large numbers of wasps haven't been very successful. For maximum effectiveness, thousands of wasps must be released weekly during the time the pests are laying their eggs. The common wasp parasite of tomato and tobacco hornworms is *Apanteles congregatus*. This wasp lays eggs on the skin of the caterpillar. The wasp larvae hatch and burrow into the host. Many immature wasps feed and develop within the body of the caterpillar. They then move to the surface of the host and form small white cocoons that protrude from the back of the insect. Adult wasps emerge from the cocoons. The hornworm usually dies before adult parasites hatch.

Control: Controls aren't necessary.

Dandelions in a lawn. These common weeds are a nuisance in many lawns. See page 483.

Horsetail. See page 471.

Most gardeners would agree that weeds are the most time-consuming and persistent garden problem. Yet efforts made now will pay off later. Spending one or two growing seasons diligently removing every weed before it makes seeds can reduce the need for future weed control to a minimum. This year or two of extra effort will pay off with many years of reduced work in the garden. Weeds should still be removed before going to seed, but fewer of them will appear.

Weeds can be divided into two categories. Some produce a copious amount of seeds and begin producing it early in life. These weeds are often easy to kill, either with herbicides or with a hoe, but new ones keep appearing. Weeds in the second category are hard to kill, often because they have persistent underground parts that can sprout into new plants. A few weeds, such as dandelions, have both of these characteristics.

The first category of weeds is most easily controlled by keeping the seeds from sprouting. Begin the battle in the spring, or whenever seeds germinate, by applying a preemergent herbicide—an herbicide that kills seeds as they germinate—or a mulch wherever the weed has been a problem. Then, once a week throughout the growing season, remove every weed that appears in your yard, either with a hoe or by spot-treating with an herbicide.

The second category of weeds is best controlled with a systemic herbicide—one that is carried to every part of the plant.

Glyphosate, the active ingredient in the herbicide brand Roundup®, has been a real help to gardeners (but it can't be used in the vegetable garden or applied to leaves of desirable plants). It controls most of the difficult weeds, then breaks down in the soil, so it has no lasting effect on garden plants. Or cover the area with a black plastic mulch for a growing season. This treatment kills all plants under the mulch by excluding light. Then, as with weeds in the first category, inspect the entire garden once a week, and kill every weed. If you follow this routine carefully for a year, almost all the weeds in your garden will be eliminated, and only those few that blow in will bother you in future years. Weed control will have been reduced to a routine maintenance chore.

465

GRASSLIKE WEEDS

Annual bluegrass

Annual bluegrass.

Annual bluegrass (*Poa annua*), also called *annual speargrass, dwarf speargrass*, and *walkgrass*, is a troublesome weed in all areas of the yard. In lawns it is not easily noticed because it resembles Kentucky bluegrass. Annual bluegrass prefers areas with moist, rich, or compacted soil. This pale green grass reproduces by seeds and lives for only one year, although in some areas there are perennial strains. Annual bluegrass grows most rapidly in cool spring weather. In mid- to late spring, white seed heads appear on the plants. The seeds fall to the soil and germinate in the cooler weather of late summer to midfall. Annual bluegrass is not heat or drought tolerant and dies in the summer in most areas.

Control: For information on controlling annual bluegrass in lawns, see page 78. Around trees and shrubs and in flower and vegetable gardens, use Scotts® Halts® Crabgrass Preventer. Apply to the soil in late summer to midfall. While the weeds are actively growing, use Ortho® Grass-B-Gon® Grass Killer for Landscapes. Around trees and shrubs and in flower beds and unplanted areas, use Roundup® Weed & Grass Killer. Correct compacted soil. (For information, see page 405.) Reduce the chances of invasion by allowing the soil to become moderately dry between waterings when the seeds are germinating in the fall. This will also provide a measure of control if the plants become stressed because of high temperatures and drought in the spring.

Quackgrass

Quackgrass.

Quackgrass (*Agropyron repens*), also called *couchgrass*, is one of the most troublesome perennial grasses in the northern United States. Its extensive fibrous root system consists of long, yellow-white roots that may grow 5 feet or more in a single growing season. The narrow, bluish-green blades grow on stalks 1 to 3 feet tall. Wheatlike spikes produce seeds from May to September. These seeds may survive in the soil for up to four years, but most germinate in the spring within two years. The underground creeping rhizomes also send up new shoots, increasing the infestation. Quackgrass tolerates any type of soil. Its roots are very competitive and crowd out desirable plants.

Control: Hand-digging is impractical, because any rhizome pieces left behind will generate new plants. Kill existing weeds in lawns, around trees and shrubs, and in unplanted areas with Roundup® herbicides. Selectively kill quackgrass in flower beds and around ornamentals with Ortho® Grass-B-Gon® Grass Killer for Landscapes. Use an herbicide containing *eptam, oryzalin*, or *trifluralin* to prevent quackgrass seedlings from becoming established in flower beds and landscaped areas. Apply in early spring two weeks before the last expected frost (about the time forsythia blooms). Patches of quackgrass can be killed by covering them with black plastic sheeting for one year.

German velvetgrass

Velvetgrass.

German velvetgrass (*Holcus mollis*) is a perennial grassy weed. In unmowed areas, the stems grow 2 to 4 feet tall. In mowed areas, they grow flat and root wherever their joints touch the soil. The 4- to 8-inch leaves are velvety and bright green. Seeds are produced from July to August on seed heads 2 to 4 inches long. They lie dormant in the soil over the winter and germinate in the spring. Plants grow from vigorous, slender underground rhizomes. Velvetgrass thrives in damp areas with rich soil. Although mostly a problem in fields and along roadways and walkways, it can become established and unsightly in lawns, forming large patches of hairy, velvety growth.

Control: Kill existing velvetgrass in walkways and lawns and around trees, shrubs, and flower beds with Roundup® Weed & Grass Killer. Treat any time the plants are actively growing but preferably before the seeds appear.

Bermudagrass

Bermudagrass.

Bermudagrass (*Cynodon dactylon*) is a perennial grass also called *devilgrass*, *wiregrass*, and *dog's tooth grass*. It is adapted to areas where the ground doesn't freeze. Its vigorous creeping habit makes it a weed that invades lawns, unplanted areas, and flower and other landscaped beds, where it crowds out desirable plants. The leaf blades are ⅛ inch wide and attached to slightly hairy, gray-green stems. The leaves aren't cold tolerant and turn brown when the temperature falls lower than 50°F. Seeds are formed on three to seven short, fingerlike segments that are about 3 inches across and grow taller than the stems. The vigorous roots may grow several feet deep, making the plants drought and heat tolerant and also difficult to eliminate. Bermudagrass reproduces by seeds, aboveground stems, and underground stems. It prefers sandy soil and won't grow in dense shade.

Control: To control bermudagrass in lawns where it is not wanted, see page 79. To control bermudagrass around trees and shrubs, flower beds, and unplanted areas, use Roundup® Weed & Grass Killer or Ortho® Grass-B-Gon® Grass Killer for Landscapes. (Grass-B-Gon® Grass Killer can be applied over broadleaf ornamentals without injury.) Apply anytime the plants are actively growing. A treatment in the early fall, about two to three weeks before the first killing frost, is very effective. Treat again in the spring as soon as plants are noticed. Repeated treatments are usually necessary because of the tough, extensive rhizomes. Hand-digging is not effective; any pieces left behind will sprout into new plants.

Crabgrass

Smooth crabgrass.

Crabgrass (*Digitaria* species) is one of the most troublesome weeds in yards throughout the United States. Although most gardeners know it as a lawn weed, it is also frequently found in flower and vegetable gardens and in cracks in sidewalks and driveways. In some areas, crabgrass is called *fingergrass* or *crowfootgrass*. This annual grassy weed grows in most soils but prefers light, sandy areas. Crabgrass is most troublesome in hot, dry weather. The pale, bluish-green blades are 2 to 5 inches long and ⅓ inch wide. They may be slightly hairy. Stems root at the lower joints. Seed heads that are 1 to 3 inches across (smooth crabgrass) or 4 to 5 inches across (large crabgrass) grow from the center of the plant from July to October. The seeds remain dormant over the winter and then sprout in the spring. The plants are killed by the first fall frost. Plants grow in broad, flat clumps that crowd out desirable plants.

Control: Around trees and shrubs and in flower beds and unplanted areas, kill existing weeds with Ortho® Grass-B-Gon® Grass Killer for Landscapes or with Roundup® Weed & Grass Killer. Prevent crabgrass from sprouting in lawns, flower beds, and around trees and shrubs with Scotts® Halts® Crabgrass Preventer. Apply in the early spring about two weeks before the last expected frost (about the time forsythia and crabapple bloom). The many fibrous roots make this weed difficult to remove by digging. (For more information about controlling crabgrass in lawns, see page 79.)

Nimblewill

Nimblewill.

The leaves of the perennial grass nimblewill (*Muhlenbergia schreberi*), also known as *muhly*, are flat, smooth, bluish green, and ½ to 2 inches long. The wiry stems grow up to 10 inches tall, first outward and then upward from the central crown (where the stem meets the roots). The stems root at the lower nodes, increasing the size of the plant. Seeds are produced on inconspicuous spikes from August to October. The seeds lie dormant in the soil for the winter and sprout in late spring. Plants develop a shallow root system. Plant tops turn whitish tan and become dormant with the first killing frost in the fall. They begin growth again late the following spring. This warm-season grass invades moist lawns, gardens, and unplanted areas that have gravelly soil.

Control: Kill existing weeds with Ortho® Grass-B-Gon® Grass Killer for Landscapes or Roundup® herbicides. Nimblewill is easiest to kill when it is a seedling, from late spring to early summer. In vegetable gardens, remove the weeds by hand-digging them.

GRASSLIKE WEEDS *(continued)*

Dallisgrass

Dallisgrass.

The coarse leaves of dallisgrass (*Paspalum dilatatum*), a perennial grass, are ½ inch wide and 4 to 10 inches long. Stems 2 to 6 inches long radiate from the center of the plant in a star pattern. Plants grow in spreading clumps with deep roots. Seeds are produced on three to five fingerlike segments that grow from the top of the stems from May to October. Silken hairs cover the seeds, which lie dormant over the winter and sprout very early in the spring. Dallisgrass also reproduces by underground stems. Dallisgrass grows across the southern states in lawns, gardens, and fields. It prefers moist soil but will tolerate any type of soil. It grows most vigorously in warm summer weather but remains green in the winter.

Control: Treat actively growing clumps of dallisgrass in lawns with Ortho® Weed-B-Gon® Crabgrass Killer for Lawns in spring or summer. Repeated treatments are often necessary, since dallisgrass has deep roots. In landscaped beds and unplanted areas, treat with Ortho® Grass-B-Gon® Grass Killer for Landscapes or Roundup® Weed & Grass Killer. Patches of dallisgrass can also be killed by covering them with black plastic sheeting for one year.

Goosegrass

Goosegrass.

Goosegrass (*Eleusine indica*) is an annual grassy weed also called *silver crabgrass* and *yardgrass*. Goosegrass is frequently confused with crabgrass, but it is darker green, doesn't root at the stem joints, and germinates later in the spring. (For more information on crabgrass, see page 467.) Goosegrass stems are smooth and flat, forming a rosette that resembles the spokes of a wheel. The leaf blades are ¼ inch wide and 2 to 10 inches long. Seeds are produced on stalks 2 to 6 inches tall from July to October. The seeds fall to the soil, remain dormant over the winter, and sprout in the spring. The first fall frost kills the plants. Goosegrass has an extensive root system and grows in lawns and gardens, as well as in cracks in walkways where soil is compacted and low in fertility.

Control: Eliminate existing goosegrass in lawns by spot-treating with Ortho® Weed-B-Gon® Crabgrass Killer for Lawns. Around trees and shrubs and in unplanted areas, kill existing weeds with Roundup herbicides. Prevent goosegrass in vegetable and flower gardens, in lawns, and around trees and shrubs with a preemergent herbicide containing *trifluralin* or *pendimethalin*. Apply to the soil before the plants sprout in early spring. Where appropriate, reduce soil compaction as outlined on page 405. Improve soil fertility with regular fertilizing. In turf, improve turfgrass growth to compete with the goosegrass. Decrease wear to the turf.

Johnsongrass

Johnsongrass.

Johnsongrass (*Sorghum halepense*), also called *Egyptiangrass*, is a persistent perennial plant that is a serious problem in the South and Southwest. The roots may penetrate 3 to 6 feet into loose, rich soil. The stems grow 1 to 6 feet tall and frequently root at their lower nodes, forming dense clusters that crowd out desirable plants. The leaves grow 1 to 2 feet long and up to 1 inch wide, with a conspicuous greenish-white midvein. Hairy purple seed heads, from 4 to 16 inches long, appear on the ends of the stems from June to October. The reddish-brown seeds germinate in the spring. New plants also sprout from creeping rhizomes. Johnsongrass is commonly found in areas with rich, moist soil. It also grows along roadways and in fields, lawns, landscaped beds, and unplanted areas.

Control: Johnsongrass is difficult to control because of its extensive rhizomes. To eliminate the weeds in landscaped beds and unplanted areas, and to spot-treat in lawns, use Ortho® Grass-B-Gon® Grass Killer for Landscapes. Repeated treatments may be necessary if new growth appears. To prevent seeds from sprouting, use a preemergent herbicide containing *trifluralin*. Apply to the soil in the spring about the time of the last frost (two weeks after forsythia blooms). Hand-pulling is not a practical control, because new plants will sprout from any rhizomes left in the soil. Digging small clumps will often work, so watch for seedlings and control them before they enlarge.

Barnyardgrass

Barnyardgrass.

Barnyardgrass (*Echinochloa crus-galli*), also called *cockspurgrass* and *watergrass*, is an annual that has upright, reddish-purple stems that grow 1 to 4 feet tall. When mowed in lawns, the stems grow close to the ground. The large, smooth leaves are ¼ to ½ inch wide with a prominent midvein. Plants develop deep, fibrous root systems. Seeds are produced on six to eight segments on the stems from July to September. One plant may produce as many as 1 million seeds. The seeds fall to the soil, remain dormant over the winter, and sprout the following year in early summer. Barnyardgrass is a troublesome weed from midsummer to midfall. It thrives in lawns, gardens, and unplanted areas with rich, moist soil. Barnyardgrass is sometimes confused with jungle rice, a low-growing grass with a similar seed head. Jungle rice has a distinguishing purple stripe across the leaf.

Control: Barnyardgrass is not usually a problem in lawns unless turf is weak with open patches. To control in cool-season turf, use a preemergent herbicide containing *DCPA* or *pendimethalin*; in warm-season turf, use an herbicide containing *oryzalin*. Kill existing weeds around trees and shrubs and in unplanted areas with Ortho® Grass-B-Gon® Grass Killer for Landscapes or Roundup® Weed & Grass Killer. Plants can also be hand-pulled. To prevent barnyardgrass from becoming established, treat the soil with Scotts® Halts® Crabgrass Preventer. Apply in early spring before the plants sprout.

Sandbur

Sandbur.

Sandbur (*Cenchrus* species), also called *burgrass* and *sandbur grass*, is an annual grass that grows 6 inches to 2 feet tall. The narrow, yellow-green leaf blades are ¼ inch wide and 2 to 5 inches long. They may be rough on the upper surface. The blades are attached to flattened stems that may grow upright or spread along the soil. Plants have shallow, fibrous roots, and when growing in mowed lawns, they form low mats. From July to September, seeds are produced inside the spiny, ½-inch, straw-colored burs that are formed on the stems. Each bur contains only two seeds, but one plant may produce as many as one thousand seeds. Seeds are spread to new areas when the burs cling to clothing and animals. The seeds germinate in the spring. Sandbur is most troublesome in orchards, vineyards, fields, and lawns with light, sandy, well-drained soils.

Control: In lawns, control selectively with Ortho® Weed-B-Gon® Crabgrass Killer for Lawns. To kill all grasses use Ortho® Grass-B-Gon® Grass Killer for Landscapes or an herbicide containing *glyphosate*. Use Roundup® herbicide around trees and shrubs and in flower beds and unplanted areas. For best results, treat in early to midsummer before burs and seeds are produced. Prevent sandbur from returning to these areas by applying a preemergent herbicide containing *trifluralin* or *eptam* in early spring. Plants can be removed by hand if handled carefully with gloves.

Foxtails

Foxtails.

Foxtails (*Setaria* species), sometimes called *bristlegrass* or *pigeongrass*, are summer annual grasses that grow 1 to 2 feet tall. In a mowed lawn, they will form low mats. The leaves are flat, sometimes twisted, ¼ to ½ inch wide and 2 to 6 inches long. Spikelets consisting of five to twenty bristles, 2 to 4 inches long, appear from July to September. The bristle resembles a fox's tail, hence the name. The bristles contain seeds that sprout from midspring to early summer. Foxtails grow in clumps and are often mistaken for crabgrass, but they form smaller clumps than crabgrass. (For information on crabgrass, see page 467.) Foxtails are found in yards with rich soil bordering fields, roadways, and other unmaintained areas.

Control: Spot-treat existing weeds in lawns, around trees and shrubs, and in flower beds and unplanted areas with Ortho® Weed-B-Gon® Crabgrass Killer for Lawns. In ground covers and flower beds, kill foxtails with Ortho® Grass-B-Gon® Grass Killer for Landscapes. Around trees and shrubs you can also use an herbicide containing *oryzalin* or *pendimethalin*. To prevent foxtails in lawns, in flower and vegetable gardens, and around trees and shrubs, apply Scotts® Halts® Crabgrass Preventer in early spring, two weeks before the last expected frost (about the time forsythia blooms). Plants can also be successfully removed by hand.

GRASSLIKE WEEDS *(cont.)* RUSHES

Wild garlic and wild onion

Wild garlic.

Wild garlic (*Allium vineale*) and wild onion (*A. canadense*) are perennial weeds that

grow from underground bulbs. They are easily recognized by the garlic or onion odor of their crushed leaves. The slender, hollow leaves grow 10 to 15 inches tall. Greenish-purple or white flowers bloom from May to July. Although they produce seeds in the spring that germinate in the fall, they reproduce mostly by bulbs and bulblets formed in the summer. In addition to the bulbs that are formed underground, tiny bulblets that look like leaves are formed at the tips of the flower stalks. Some of the new bulbs germinate in the fall; others can remain dormant in the soil for a year or two before germination. Wild garlic and onion thrive in heavy soil and tolerate wet soil, cold, and drought. They spread rapidly and are difficult to control.

Control: In the lawn, control these weeds with Ortho® Weed-B-Gon® Weed Killer for Lawns. Around trees and shrubs and in flower beds, spot-treat with Roundup® Weed & Grass Killer. Treat as soon as the leaves emerge in the spring or anytime the plants are actively growing. Because dormant bulbs sprout at different times, treatments will probably need to be repeated for the next two or three years. Hand-digging is impractical, because any bulbs left behind will sprout into new plants.

Nutsedge

Nutsedge invading roses.

The two most common troublesome nutsedges are yellow nutsedge (*Cyperus esculentus*) and

purple nutsedge (*C. rotundus*). Purple nutsedge is primarily a problem in the southeastern United States and in coastal California. Yellow nutsedge is found throughout the United States. These perennials are also called *nutgrass, cocosedge,* or *cocograss.* Some annual nutsedges are also troublesome in the Southeast. Nutsedges prefer poorly drained, rich soil. They thrive in frequently watered garden areas. Nutsedges are particularly noticeable in lawns in the summer, when they grow more quickly than the mowed grass and stand above it. The grasslike, yellow-green leaves grow on erect triangular stems. Seed heads are purple or yellow, appearing from July to October. Nutsedges reproduce by seeds, underground stems, and nutlike tubers. The tubers store food and are drought tolerant.

Control: To control nutsedges in lawns, see page 80. To control existing weeds around trees and shrubs and in flower beds and unplanted areas, use Ortho® Weed-B-Gon® Crabgrass Killer for Lawns or Roundup® Weed & Grass Killer. Treat as soon as the plants are noticed, preferably before seed heads appear. Nutsedges are difficult to control, so repeated treatments may be necessary. To control nutsedge seeds as they germinate around trees and shrubs and in flower beds, use an herbicide containing *eptam* or *metolachlor* in the mid- to late spring. Hand-pulling is not practical, because any tubers left behind will sprout into new plants.

Bamboo

Invasive bamboo.

Many species of bamboo are aggressive weeds. Creeping types of bamboo in particular can

become very invasive. Unlike the slower-spreading clumping bamboos, creeping bamboos form underground rhizomes that spread quickly. The rhizomes grow through the soil and send up shoots every couple of feet. The large types of creeping bamboo are especially vigorous and difficult to control. Removal of the shoot is ineffective because the rhizomes resprout.

Control: Locate the rhizome where it leaves the original planting, usually 2 to 4 inches below the soil surface in a direct line between the invasive shoot and the parent planting. Cut the rhizome and pull it up, with all the shoots attached to it. Prevent reinvasion by surrounding the bamboo planting with an underground barrier. Sink lengths of 40-mil high-density polyethylene sheets 24 inches deep into the soil. Slant the top of the barrier outward so it doesn't force the rhizome deeper into the soil. Or dig a trench to the same depth and fill it with concrete. To kill the entire clump, spray two or more applications of Roundup® Weed & Grass Killer on actively growing bamboo. If you want to save some of the clump, sever any rhizome connecting it to the parts being sprayed; Roundup will travel along the rhizome and kill all the plants in the clump. Do not prune bamboo before spraying.

Horsetail

Horsetail.

Common cattail

Cattails.

Mosses, liverworts and algae

Moss.

Horsetail (*Equisetum* species) is a perennial that grows in wooded areas, along roadsides, and on stream banks with wet, sandy, or gravelly soil. Two types of stalks—branched and unbranched—grow from the deep, thick rhizomes. The unbranched stalks, topped by cones, appear in April and May. The cones, 1 to 4 inches long, are filled with pale green to yellowish spores. Horsetail reproduces from these spores, as well as from the rhizomes. After the spores mature, these stalks die. From late spring until fall, jointed hollow stalks grow 1 to 3 feet tall. Branches 4 to 6 inches long grow in whorls at the joints on the stalks. These stems are killed by the first frost in the fall. Food is stored in the thick roots to enable the plant to survive adverse growing conditions.

Control: Control horsetail with Ortho® Brush-B-Gon® Poison Ivy, Poison Oak, and Brush Killer.

Common cattails (*Typha latifolia*) grow from perennial, creeping rootstocks in swamps, marshes, shallow water, and frequently wet areas. The flat swordlike leaves are pale to grayish green and 1 inch wide. Plants grow 3 to 8 feet tall. Two types of flowers bloom from May to July. Female flowers are borne on the brown, 8-inch cattails for which the plants are known. Above these are produced the light yellow spikes of male flowers.

Control: Cattails are difficult to control because of their vigorous creeping roots. Hand-pulling is not practical, because any pieces of root left behind will sprout into new plants. Treat cattails with an herbicide containing *glyphosate* that is formulated for aquatic use. Repeated treatments may be necessary if the plants are firmly established and regrowth occurs. If large numbers of cattails are killed at once, the rotting material may cause an oxygen depletion in the water, killing fish. To avoid this problem, kill small sections of cattails at a time. It will also be helpful to aerate the pond, especially at night.

Most moss grows only ¼ to 2 inches tall. A mat of moss consists of thousands of tiny plants with stems and leaves. They attach themselves to the soil and absorb nutrients through threadlike *rhizoids*, or rootlike structures. Liverworts grow in thin, lobed sheets along the ground. Algae are simple, primitive, freshwater plants that thrive in constantly or frequently wet conditions. Algae may be found growing on wet, compacted soil that is high in nitrogen and organic matter. Both mosses and liverworts grow best in moist, shady areas with acid soil. In cultivated gardens and lawns, they indicate excess acidity, poor fertility, overwatering, or poor drainage or aeration. Moss, liverworts, and algae sometimes grow on pavement and structures.

Control: Kill moss in lawns with Ortho® Moss-B-Gon® Granules for Lawns. You may also remove moss and liverworts from lawns and gardens by hand-raking. Reduce shade by pruning nearby trees. Improve soil fertility with regular fertilization, and improve soil drainage. Correct pH if necessary (see page 406). Spray patches of algae with a fungicide containing *mancozeb* or wettable sulfur two times, one month apart, in early spring. Prevent algae from returning by reducing soil compaction (see page 405) and pruning nearby vegetation to reduce shade. Remove moss, liverworts, and algae from structures by treating with a soap or compound containing potassium salts.

BROADLEAF WEEDS

Virginia peppergrass

Virginia peppergrass.

St. Johnswort

St. Johnswort.

Wild mustard

Wild mustard.

Virginia Peppergrass (*Lepidium virginicum*), an annual broadleaf also known as *bird's pepper* or *tonguegrass*, grows 1 to 2 feet tall with slightly hairy, branched stems. The blades are toothed and 1 to 3 inches long. Very small, white flowers with greenish petals bloom from May to November. They produce seeds in ½-inch reddish-yellow pods. Seedpods and flowers are generally present on the plant at the same time. Peppergrass usually grows along roadsides and in waste places and fields. It grows in most types of soil but is more troublesome in dry areas. In home gardens, it frequently sprouts in landscaped beds, lawns, and cracks in walkways.

Control: Eliminate peppergrass from lawns with Ortho® Weed-B-Gon® Weed Killer for Lawns or spot-treat with Ortho® Weed-B-Gon® Ready-To-Use Weed Killer. Treat when the plants are actively growing in the spring or early summer, preferably before the flowers and seedpods appear. To prevent peppergrass seeds from germinating in landscaped beds, use a preemergent herbicide containing *napropamide*. Apply to the soil in early spring about the time of the last expected frost (when forsythia blooms). In unplanted areas, kill existing weeds with Roundup® Weed & Grass Killer. Treat in the spring when the plants are growing. Peppergrass plants have shallow roots and can be hand-pulled.

St. Johnswort (*Hypericum perforatum*), also known as *Klamath weed*, is a perennial that reproduces by seeds and short runners. These horizontal stems grow from the crown of the plant out along the soil or just below it. The roots grow deep in the soil. The main upright stems are branched and grow 1 to 2 feet tall. The ½- to 1-inch-long, oblong leaves are marked with clear dots. From June to September, flowers ¾ inch in diameter bloom and produce seeds. The flowers are orange-yellow with black dots along the edges of the petals. Black fruit capsules are evident from late summer into the fall. Each contains several seeds that lie dormant over the winter and sprout in the spring. The tops of the plants die back to the ground in cold weather. St. Johnswort is poisonous to livestock that graze on it. It prefers dry, sandy, or gravelly soil in fields and pastures and along roadways. In home gardens, it may become established in landscaped beds and unmaintained areas.

Control: Around trees and shrubs and in flower beds, unplanted areas, and lawns, kill existing weeds with Roundup® Weed & Grass Killer. Repeated applications are often necessary to kill St. Johnswort because of this plant's deep root system.

Wild mustard (*Brassica kaber*) is an annual also known as *field mustard* and *charlock*. The erect stems grow 1 to 3 feet tall and have bristly hairs at their bases. The upper portion is branched. The lower leaves are irregularly lobed or toothed, and the upper leaves are oval. From May to August, yellow clusters of flowers bloom and produce seeds. Severely infested fields appear completely yellow. Seeds lie dormant in the soil for 1 or more years, germinating in the spring or fall. Although primarily troublesome in grain fields in the Midwest, wild mustard also sometimes occurs in home gardens.

Control: In lawns, frequent mowing usually controls mustard, or control with Ortho® Weed-B-Gon® Weed Killer for Lawns. Around trees and shrubs, and in unplanted areas, prevent the seeds from sprouting with a preemergent herbicide containing *oxyfluorfen*. Apply in early fall or in early spring before the seeds germinate. Kill existing weeds with Roundup® Weed & Grass Killer. Treat anytime the plants are actively growing but preferably before they bloom and produce seeds. Wild mustard has a shallow root system and can be removed by hand-pulling or hoeing.

Russian thistle

Russian thistle.

Russian thistle (*Salsola kali* var. *tenuifolia*), a native of eastern Europe, is an annual also known as *tumbleweed*. The plants grow ½ to 3 feet tall, with reddish, spreading, or erect stems. The leaves on seedlings and younger plants are fleshy and cylindrical. As the leaves mature, they drop, and stiff, narrow leaves ending in a spike appear. From July to October, greenish flowers bloom and produce seeds throughout the plant. Each plant produces thousands of seeds. When the plants mature in early fall, they break off at the soil line and tumble about, distributing the seeds. Russian thistle prefers areas with dry soil along roadways and in fields and unmaintained areas. It is a host to the beet leafhopper, which spreads *curly top*, a plant disease.

Control: Eliminate Russian thistle from lawns with Ortho® Weed-B-Gon® Weed Killer for Lawns. To prevent seeds from germinating around trees and shrubs and in flower beds, use a preemergent weed killer containing *trifluralin* or *pendimethalin*. Apply to the soil in the spring about the time of the last frost (approximately two weeks after forsythia blooms).

Puncturevine

Puncturevine.

Puncturevine (*Tribulus terrestris*), also called *caltrop* and *ground burnut*, is an annual weed found in dry, sandy areas. The prostrate stems branch from the base of the plant, forming dense mats that crowd out desirable plants. The stems grow 6 to 8 feet long and may twine up buildings and fences. Oblong leaves, 1 to 2 inches long, consist of five to eight pairs of oval leaflets. Both the stems and the leaves are covered with silken hairs, giving the plants a silvery appearance. Small yellow flowers bloom in the leaf axils from June to September. They open only in the morning on clear days. They are followed by pods consisting of five spiny burs, ¼-inch in diameter. When the burs mature, they separate and fall to the soil, where they may lie for several years before germinating. The plant develops from a short taproot that branches into many fine roots, enabling it to survive periods of drought.

Control: Treat puncturevine around trees, shrubs, and buildings and in unplanted areas with Roundup® Weed & Grass Killer. For best results, treat before burs are produced. To prevent seedlings from becoming established, apply a preemergent herbicide containing *trifluralin* to the soil before seedlings emerge. Puncturevine weevils may be an effective control in sites that aren't disturbed.

Common yarrow

Common yarrow.

Common yarrow (*Achillea millefolium*), also called *milfoil*, is a perennial that grows 1 to 3 feet tall. If it occurs in mowed lawns, it forms a rosette. The fernlike leaves are covered with fine gray hairs and are aromatic when crushed. The flat flower heads are white or whitish-yellow and bloom and produce seeds from June to November. Common yarrow reproduces by creeping underground rhizomes as well as by seeds. Its flowers are sometimes dried and used in flower arrangements. Some other species of *Achillea* are valued as ornamental perennials. Yarrow is most common in gardens bordering roadways, fields, and vacant lots and thrives in poor, dry soil where few plants can survive.

Control: In flower beds and vegetable gardens, and around trees and shrubs, dig the plants while still young, before flowers bloom and seeds form. In noncrop areas, use Roundup herbicide. Eliminate yarrow in lawns with Ortho® Weed-B-Gon® Weed Killer for Lawns or Scotts® GreenSweep® Weed & Feed. Treat anytime the plants are actively growing, from spring to fall.

BROADLEAF WEEDS (continued)

Cudweed

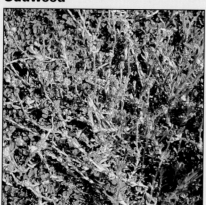

Cudweed.

Pineappleweed

Pineappleweed.

Mayweed

Mayweed.

Cudweed (*Gnaphalium* species), also called *fragrant everlasting* and *cotton batting plant*, is an annual or biennial. The stems branch at their base and grow ½ to 2 feet tall. They are woolly white and fragrant when rubbed. The lance-shape leaves are also fragrant and woolly on the underside. The top is smooth and dark green. Tubular white, tan, or purple flowers bloom and produce seeds in August and September. They appear at the ends of the branches and in the axils of the upper leaves. Seeds lie dormant in the soil over the winter, sprouting in cool, moist spring weather. Plants grow slowly in the summer heat, resuming normal growth in late summer until the first killing frost in the fall. Cudweed grows in moist or dry soil. It is most commonly found along roadways and in fields and wooded lots but may appear in lawns and landscaped beds.

Control: For overall lawn treatment, use an herbicide containing *2,4–D* and *dicamba*. Treat in the spring when the plants are growing most rapidly. Use Roundup® Weed & Grass Killer as a spot-treatment to control existing cudweed in lawns and around trees and shrubs in flower beds and unplanted areas. Treat anytime the plants are actively growing but preferably in the spring before they bloom and produce seeds.

The stems and leaves of the annual pineappleweed (*Matricaria matricarioides*) have a pleasant pineapple fragrance when crushed. Many stems, 6 to 18 inches tall, grow from the base of the plant. The finely dissected leaves grow 1 to 4 inches long. Greenish-yellow, ¼-inch flowers shaped like pineapples bloom at the ends of the branches from May to September. The seeds they produce don't sprout until early the following spring. Pineappleweed grows along roadsides, in fields, in waste places, and sometimes in landscaped beds. It tolerates many types of soil and frequently grows where other plants don't survive.

Control: Healthy, thriving lawns will crowd out pineappleweed, so good fertilization and regular mowing will greatly reduce or eliminate this weed. To kill established plants around trees and shrubs, in flower beds, and unplanted areas, use Roundup® Weed & Grass Killer. Use Ortho® Weed-B-Gon® Weed Killer for Lawns to kill weeds in lawns. The plants have shallow roots and can be hand-pulled or hoed, especially when young and when the soil is moist.

Mayweed (*Anthemis cotula*) is an annual weed also called *dog fennel* and *stinkweed*. The erect stems grow ½ to 2 feet tall, and the plant has short, thick taproot. The 1- to 3-inch-long, fernlike leaves have a pungent odor when crushed. Daisylike flowers, ¼ to ½ inch in diameter, have yellow centers with white petals. They bloom and produce seeds from May to October. The seeds lie dormant in the soil over the winter and sprout in the spring. The plants die with the first killing frost in the fall. In warm-weather areas, seeds germinate in both the spring and fall. Those that germinate in the fall grow through the winter and flower in the spring. Mayweed grows in fields and gardens with rich, gravelly soil. A closely related plant, corn chamomile (*A. arvensis*) looks similar and is controlled much the same way.

Control: Eliminate mayweed by spot-treating around trees and shrubs in lawns, around trees and flower beds, and in unplanted areas with Roundup® weed killers. Treat anytime the plants are actively growing but preferably before they flower and produce seeds. Plants can be hoed or hand-pulled.

Prostrate knotweed

Prostrate knotweed.

Prostrate knotweed (*Polygonum aviculare*) is an annual weed also called *knotgrass* or

doorweed. It grows in areas with compacted, infertile soil, such as driveways, dirt walkways, and recreation areas where the soil and grass are trampled. Oval, bluish-green leaves, 1 inch long and ¼ inch wide, are attached to the stems at swollen joints. Very tiny greenish-white flowers bloom and produce seeds at the leaf and stem joints from June to November. The seeds produced by these flowers remain dormant over the winter and germinate in the spring as the soil warms. Prostrate knotweed grows low to the ground, forming dense wiry mats up to 3 feet in diameter that crowd out desirable plants.

Control: For overall treatment in lawns, use Ortho® Weed-B-Gon® Weed Killer for Lawns or Scotts® GreenSweep® Weed & Feed. To help prevent knotweed in the lawn, maintain a vigorous turf. Around trees and shrubs, and in unplanted areas, kill existing weeds with Roundup® Weed & Grass Killer. Cultivating is also helpful. In flower and vegetable gardens, hand-pulling or hoeing is the best control.

Creeping veronica

Creeping veronica.

Creeping veronica (*Veronica filiformis*), also called *speedwell*, is a weed that prefers acidic

soil in moist, shady garden areas. There are both perennial and annual varieties. It is found in sunny areas if the soil remains moist. It doesn't invade areas that are well-fertilized, are well-drained, and get lots of sunlight. Oval, bright green leaves with scalloped edges are paired opposite each other on low-growing creeping stems. Tiny white flowers with blue or lavender edges bloom from May to July. Seeds are produced in heart-shaped pods. The seeds seldom mature, so the plant doesn't reproduce from them. The creeping stems, however, root easily wherever the stem joints touch the soil. Pieces of stem cut and distributed by lawn mowers also root to start new plants. If uncontrolled, veronica can cover an entire lawn or flower bed within a few years. It doesn't completely crowd out other plants, however.

Control: Creeping veronica is difficult to control. In lawns, treat with Ortho® Weed-B-Gon® Weed Killer for Lawns. Veronica dies slowly, so repeated applications may be necessary. In landscaped beds and flower beds, prevent veronica from sprouting by treating in the spring or early fall with an herbicide containing *DCPA* (Dacthal®). Veronica can also be hand-pulled; remove all parts of the plant so new plants don't emerge from remaining plant segments.

Common chickweed

Common chickweed.

Common chickweed (*Stellaria media*), also called *starwort*, *satin flower*, and *starweed*,

prefers damp, shady areas with rich, cultivated soil. Common chickweed is a winter annual that grows from seeds that sprout in the fall. It grows vigorously in cool, wet weather, forming a dense mat that crowds out desirable plants. The ½- to 2-inch heart-shape leaves are attached to the stems by a slightly hairy stalk. Fine white hairs grow in a single line on one side of the stem. The creeping stems root at their joints wherever they touch the soil. Small, white, starlike flowers bloom in clusters on the ends of the stems from March to December. In mild-winter areas, they bloom and produce seeds throughout the winter. Seeds are carried by birds and by the wind.

Control: In lawns, control chickweed with Ortho® Weed-B-Gon® Weed Killer for Lawns or Scotts® GreenSweep® Weed & Feed. Around trees and shrubs and in unplanted areas, kill existing weeds with Roundup® Weed & Grass Killer. Apply Roundup® to actively growing plants in the early spring or late fall just after they have sprouted. Cultivating is also helpful. Prevent weeds from returning around trees, shrubs, and in flower gardens with a preemergence herbicide containing *trifluralin* or *pendimethalin*. Apply in the fall before the seeds sprout.

BROADLEAF WEEDS *(continued)*

Florida pusley

Florida pusley.

Florida pusley (*Richardia scabra*) is an annual also known as *Florida purslane* or *Mexican clover*. The hairy stems grow 4 to 12 inches tall and are tinged with red. The leaves are oblong, 1 to 3 inches in length, and hairy. Starlike white flowers bloom in the leaf axils near the ends of the branches from May to September. The seeds produced by these flowers don't germinate until the following spring. Florida pusley thrives in sandy soils in the warm southern states. This weed hugs the ground, forming dense patches that crowd out desirable plants, especially lawn grasses. It also grows in landscaped beds and in cracks in walkways.

Control: In lawns, eliminate Florida pusley with Ortho® Weed-B-Gon® Weed Killer for Lawns. Don't use this product on St. Augustine grass or centipedegrass lawns. Use Roundup® Weed & Grass Killer to kill existing weeds around trees and shrubs and in unplanted areas. Treat when the weeds are actively growing. For best results, apply before the plants flower and produce seeds for the following year. To prevent Florida pusley seeds from germinating throughout the yard, apply a preemergence herbicide containing *trifluralin* or *pendimethalin* to the soil in early spring, two weeks before the last expected frost (when forsythia blooms). Florida pusley has shallow roots and can be hand-pulled or hoed.

Purslane

Purslane.

Purslane (*Portulaca oleracea*), also called *wild portulaca* or *pusley*, is a particularly troublesome weed in vegetable and flower gardens. This summer annual thrives in hot, dry weather and is seldom found in the spring when gardeners are controlling other weeds. Leaves are ½ to 1½ inches long, rubbery, and wedge-shape. Small yellow flowers open only in full sunlight from midsummer to frost. The seeds may remain viable in the soil for many years and will sprout in warm weather when brought to the surface during plowing or cultivating. The thick, reddish-brown stems grow vigorously, forming a thick mat and rooting wherever they touch the soil. The stems and leaves store water that enables purslane to survive drought periods and to grow in cracks in sidewalks and driveways. Plants pulled and allowed to lie on the soil will reroot. Plants are killed by the first fall frost.

Control: In lawns, control purslane with Ortho® Weed-B-Gon® Weed Killer for Lawns or spot-treat with Roundup® Weed & Grass Killer. To help prevent purslane in the lawn, maintain vigorous turf. Kill existing weeds around trees and shrubs and in driveways and flower beds with Roundup® herbicides. Keep weeds from returning around trees and shrubs with a preemergent herbicide containing *DCPA*, *oryzalin*, or *pendimethalin*. Purslane may also be hand-pulled. Remove the plants from the garden.

Spotted spurge

Spotted spurge.

Spotted spurge (*Euphorbia maculata*) an annual weed also called *prostrate spurge* or *milk purslane*, thrives in open turf and in most soils. It is often found in lawns and shrub beds and in cracks in walkways and driveways. Spurge is a low-growing plant that may form dense mats up to 2 feet in diameter. Leaves are oval, ¼ to ¾ inch long, and pale to dark green with a purple smudge. The slender reddish stems ooze a milky-white sap when broken. The sap may irritate the skin. Small pinkish-white flowers bloom and produce seeds from May to October. Many of the seeds remain dormant over the winter and sprout the following spring. Some sprout immediately. They die with the first fall frost.

Control: For overall lawn treatment, use Ortho® Weed-B-Gon® Weed Killer for Lawns or Scotts® GreenSweep® Weed & Feed. To spot-treat weeds in lawns, use Ortho® Weed-B-Gon® Weed Killer for Lawns Ready to Use. Kill existing weeds around trees and shrubs and in walkways and driveways with Roundup® Weed & Grass Killer. Treat spurge anytime the plants are actively growing in the spring and summer. Don't treat in the fall, because the first frost will kill the plants anyway. Prevent spurge seeds from germinating in lawns with Scotts® Halts® Crabgrass Preventer. These shallow-rooted plants can be hand-pulled or hoed. Because spotted spurge forms seeds after only two weeks, it is especially important to follow a regular control program.

Mouse-ear chickweed

Mouse-ear chickweed.

Mouse-ear chickweed (*Cerastium vulgatum*) is a perennial weed that is troublesome throughout the United States in lawns, in vegetable and flower gardens, around trees and shrubs, and in unplanted areas. It thrives in full sunlight on wet, infertile soil. The hairy leaves are ½ inch long and lance-shape. Starlike white flowers bloom and produce seeds from April to October. These low-growing plants root easily wherever their stem joints touch the soil, starting new plants. Seeds germinate throughout the growing season, rapidly increasing the number of plants. Dense mats of mouse-ear chickweed crowd out desirable plants.

Control: For overall lawn treatment, use Ortho® Weed-B-Gon® Weed Killer for Lawns when plants are actively growing in the early spring and fall. Or spot-treat with Ortho® Weed-B-Gon® Weed Killer for Lawns Ready to Use. Around trees and shrubs, and in flower beds, kill existing weeds with Roundup® herbicides. Mouse-ear chickweed is difficult to control, so repeated treatments may be necessary. These shallow-root plants can also be hand-pulled or hoed, but be sure to remove all parts of the plants so they don't resprout.

Lippia

Lippia.

Lippia (*Phyla nodiflora*), a perennial also known as *matchweed* or *matgrass*, is used in hot, dry areas as a ground cover or lawn substitute. The creeping stems grow 1 to 3 feet long and root wherever their nodes touch the soil, forming dense mats that crowd out desirable plants. Lippia has wedge-shaped, slightly hairy leaves up to 1¾ inches long. The edges are toothed. Bees are attracted to the white or pink flowers that bloom on oblong heads from late spring through early summer. In the sun, lippia grows 1 to 2 inches tall; in the shade, it grows up to 6 inches tall. Lippia grows vigorously, creeping from its planted areas into surrounding areas.

Control: In lawns, eliminate lippia with Ortho® Weed-B-Gon® Weed Killer for Lawns. In landscaped beds and noncrop areas, treat with Roundup® Weed & Grass Killer. Apply in the spring or fall. The plants have shallow roots and can also be hand-pulled or cultivated for control.

Oxalis

Oxalis.

Some oxalis (*Oxalis* species) are grown for ornamental purposes, but two, *Oxalis stricta* (an annual) and *O. corniculata* (a perennial), are common weeds throughout the yard and in greenhouses. Also called *yellow woodsorrel* and *sourgrass*, these perennials grow most commonly in well-maintained areas. The pale green or purple leaves are divided into three heart-shape leaflets, like clover leaves. The leaflets usually close up at night. Small, bright, ½-inch yellow flowers with five petals bloom from May to September. Cucumber-shape light green seedpods develop from the fading flowers. The seeds germinate throughout the growing season. Plants grow 4 to 12 inches tall. Although the stems root wherever they touch the soil, new plants don't form at these spots. Oxalis leaves contain oxalic acid, which gives them a sour, lemony taste.

Control: In lawns, treat oxalis with Scotts® GreenSweep® Weed & Feed, Ortho® Weed-B-Gon® Weed Killer for Lawns, or Ortho® Weed-B-Gon® Chickweed, Clover and Oxalis Killer for Lawns. Around trees and shrubs, flower beds, driveways, and other unplanted areas, kill the weeds with Roundup weed killers. Treat weeds when they are actively growing in the spring or late summer to fall. This late application is the most effective. Oxalis is not easy to kill, so several treatments may be necessary. Oxalis can also be hand-pulled or hoed if it is done before rooting occurs on stems.

BROADLEAF WEEDS (continued)

Dichondra

Dichondra.

Ground ivy

Ground ivy.

Wild violets

Violet.

Dichondra (*Dichondra repens*) is a popular grass substitute in the South and West that sometimes becomes a weed when it creeps into other types of lawns and landscaped beds. Dichondra is a broadleaf perennial, a member of the morning glory family, with heart-shape, rounded leaves ¼ to ½ inch in diameter. The leaves are attached to the stems opposite each other. The creeping stems root wherever the nodes touch the soil. Inconspicuous flowers produce seeds that may remain in the soil for many years before sprouting. Dichondra will not grow where temperatures fall lower than 25°F. It grows in both sun and shade but prefers fertile soil in areas that are watered frequently. Dichondra seldom grows in areas that are not maintained.

Control: Eliminate dichondra from nondichondra lawns with Ortho® Weed-B-Gon® Weed Killer for Lawns. In unplanted areas and around trees and shrubs, use Roundup® Weed & Grass Killer. Treat anytime the plants are actively growing. Or use a preemergent herbicide containing *DCPA* or *pendimethalin* to keep dichondra seeds from germinating. Several applications of this preemergent may be necessary. Dichondra has shallow roots and can be removed by hand from landscaped beds and other areas. Regrowth may occur from underground stems; cultivation can control such regrowth.

Ground ivy (*Glechoma hederacea*), a perennial, is also called *creeping ivy*, *creeping Charlie*, and *gill-over-the-ground*. It was originally planted in many areas as a shade-tolerant ground cover but has since become a nuisance, invading lawns and landscaped areas. Rounded, scalloped leaves about the size of a nickel or quarter grow opposite each other on creeping stems. Light blue to purple flowers, ½ to ¾ inch long, bloom and produce seeds from April to July. These seeds germinate as soon as they ripen. Ground ivy also reproduces by creeping stems that root wherever they touch the soil. It has shallow roots and forms a dense mat, crowding out desirable plants. Ground ivy prefers damp, shady areas with rich soil but may also grow in the sun.

Control: Control ground ivy in the lawn with Ortho® Weed-B-Gon® Weed Killer for Lawns, Scotts® GreenSweep® Weed & Feed, or spot-treat with Ortho® Weed-B-Gon® Weed Killer for Lawns Ready to Use. Around trees, shrubs, and unplanted areas, use Roundup® Weed & Grass Killer. Treat anytime the plants are actively growing but preferably in the spring when the leaves are still tender. If ground ivy has grown into a dense mat, annual treatments may be necessary for the following two to three years. Although ground ivy has shallow roots, hand-pulling is not a practical control method because any pieces of stem left in the soil will sprout into new plants.

Wild violet (*Viola* species), also called *violet*, *field pansy*, and *hearts-ease*, is an annual or short-lived perennial with dense, fibrous roots. The leaves emerge from the crown of the plant on long, angular leafstalks, forming a rosette from 6 to 24 inches tall. The leaves are dark green, heart-shape or almost round, and 1 to 2½ inches long with slightly saw-toothed edges. Small flowers resembling florist's violets are individually borne on slender flower stalks. The flowers may be pale yellow, purple, white, or a combination of these colors. The plants bloom from April to June and produce seeds from May to July. The seeds sprout in spring or, in mild-winter areas, in fall and spring. The plants often produce small bulblets in the fall that resprout the following spring. Wild violets thrive in moist shaded or semishaded conditions. They are a persistent weed in partially shaded lawns and planting beds.

Control: In lawns, control wild violets with Ortho® Weed-B-Gon® Weed Killer for Lawns. In nonlawn areas, spot-treat with Ortho® Weed-B-Gon® Weed Killer for Lawns Ready to Use. Violets are persistent, so retreatment will probably be necessary. Apply a preemergent herbicide containing *DCPA* (Dacthal®) in early spring to prevent seeds from sprouting. In warm-winter areas, apply a preemergent herbicide containing *DCPA* (Dacthal®) in late fall and early spring.

Black medic

Black medic.

Black medic, (*Medicago lupulina*) sometimes called *black clover*, is frequently confused with clover. The low-growing, hairy, trailing stems of this summer or winter annual form dense mats that crowd out desirable plants. Cloverlike leaves grow in threes on the stems. Small, bright yellow flowers bloom and produce seeds in black, kidney-shape pods from May to September. In warm-weather areas, blooming may last until December. Seeds lie dormant in the soil, sprouting in the spring and also in the fall in warm-weather areas. Black medic grows in lawns and gardens with low nitrogen fertility and in cracks in sidewalks and driveways.

Control: Eliminate black medic from lawns with Ortho® Weed-B-Gon® Weed Killer for Lawns or Scotts® GreenSweep® Weed & Feed. Treat from late spring to early summer or midfall, when the weeds are actively growing and preferably before seeds form. In landscaped beds and unplanted areas, kill existing weeds with Roundup® Weed & Grass Killer. Prevent black medic from becoming established by mulching landscaped beds as discussed on page 415. Where appropriate, improve nitrogen fertility with regular fertilizing to reduce black medic invasion. Black medic can also be hand-pulled.

Lawn pennywort

Lawn pennywort.

Lawn pennywort (*Hydrocotyle sibthorpioides*) is a member of the parsley family. It is a perennial that has bright green, ½-inch, rounded leaves with wavy margins. Small white flowers bloom from July to August. The creeping stems root wherever their nodes touch the soil, increasing the number of plants. If not controlled, pennywort can form dense mats that crowd out desirable plants. Pennywort grows in moist, shady lawns, gardens, and unplanted areas. It is frequently mistaken for ground ivy (see page 478). Some gardeners prefer to allow pennywort to grow as a shade-tolerant ground cover rather than try to eliminate it.

Control: In lawns, control pennywort with Ortho® Weed-B-Gon® Weed Killer for Lawns or spot-treat with Ortho® Weed-B-Gon® Weed Killer for Lawns Ready to Use. Around trees and shrubs and in flower beds and unplanted areas, kill existing weeds with Roundup® herbicides. Treat weeds anytime they are actively growing, from late spring to fall. In vegetable gardens, remove weeds by hand-digging. Be careful to remove all the stem pieces to prevent resprouting. Where possible, dry out the soil and cultivate to control pennywort.

Prickly lettuce

Prickly lettuce.

Prickly lettuce (*Lactuca serriola*), also known as *wild lettuce*, is an annual or biennial. Pale green or straw-colored stems grow 1½ to 6 feet tall. The lower part is covered with prickly spines. The lower leaves are 2 to 12 inches long and lobed, with prickly edges. The upper leaves are short, elongated, and lobed or prickly toothed. Both kinds of leaves are bluish green with prickles on the midrib. A milky sap oozes from the leaves and taproot when they are broken. Prickly lettuce reproduces by seeds that are formed on flowers that bloom from July to September. These yellow flowers are ⅓ inch in diameter and bloom at the ends of the lateral stems. When the seeds are mature, they fall to the soil and sprout in either the fall or, in colder areas, the following spring. Prickly lettuce prefers areas with dry or light soil and is troublesome along roadways and in fields and unmaintained areas.

Control: Keep lawns healthy and thick through proper fertilizing and mowing, and they will crowd out many of the weeds. Seeds blow in from areas outside the lawn, so maintain the periphery of the property. Control this weed in lawns with Ortho® Weed-B-Gon® Weed Killer for Lawns. Around trees and shrubs, in flower beds and unplanted areas, and to spot-treat in lawns, use Roundup® Weed & Grass Killer. Apply the weed killer when the plants are actively growing, preferably before they bloom and produce seeds.

BROADLEAF WEEDS (continued)

Mallow

Mallow.

Mallows (*Malva* species), weeds that are also called *cheeseweed*, *cheeses*, and *musk plant*, are found in lawns, fields, vacant lots, and landscaped beds throughout the country. They are annuals or—in warmer climates—biennials. Although mallow tolerates all types of soil, it prefers infertile, poorly maintained areas. The hairy stems grow from several inches to a foot or more in length. They may grow from close to the soil to 6 feet tall. The taproot is straight and deep. The hairy, round, heart-shape leaves are ½ to 5 inches wide. The edges are slightly lobed. From April to October, flowers with five white to lavender petals bloom at the leaf and stem joints. Mallow reproduces by seeds that remain dormant in the soil over the winter and germinate in the spring. Seeds may remain in the soil for many years. The first fall frost kills the plants. In warmer climates, the plant survives the winter and grows and flowers a second year.

Control: In lawns, eliminate mallow with Ortho® Weed-B-Gon® Weed Killer for Lawns. Around trees and shrubs and in flower beds and unplanted areas, treat existing weeds with Roundup® Weed & Grass Killer. Treat with these herbicides from midspring to early summer when the plants are still young and before they produce flowers and seeds for the following year's generation. Follow the lawn maintenance guidelines beginning on page 49 to help prevent mallow from becoming established in the lawn.

Curly dock

Curly dock.

Curly dock (*Rumex crispus*), a persistent perennial, is also called *sour dock* or *yellow dock*. Plants may be found anywhere in the yard except in the shade. Curly dock prefers wet, low areas with heavy soil. The curly leaves, which form a rosette, are 6 to 12 inches long and reddish green. A 2- to 3-foot stalk with green to brown flowers grows from June to September. The flowers turn dark brown and dry and cling to the stalk. Seeds produced by these flowers fall to the soil and remain dormant over the winter, sprouting in the spring and summer. The first fall frost kills the plant tops. The thick, yellow taproot is drought resistant and very difficult to dig from the soil. It remains dormant over the winter and resprouts in the spring. Once curly dock is established, it is very difficult to eliminate.

Control: To control curly dock in the lawn, use Ortho® Weed-B-Gon® Weed Killer for Lawns. Or spot-treat individual plants with Roundup® Weed & Grass Killer. Around trees and shrubs and in flower gardens and unplanted areas, kill existing weeds with Roundup® Weed & Grass Killer. Hand-digging is not practical, because any root pieces left behind will resprout into new plants.

Lady's thumb

Lady's thumb.

Lady's thumb (*Polygonum persicaria*), also known as *spotted smartweed*, prefers moist soil. It is usually found growing in waste places and fields and along roadways. It may occur in lawns, as well as in landscaped beds and cracks in walkways. The smooth stems grow 6 inches to 3 feet tall. The narrow leaves are pointed at both ends and have a peppery taste. They are marked in the middle with a triangular purple spot. Tiny pink flowers bloom on 1-inch spikes from July to October. The seeds they produce lie dormant in the soil over the winter and sprout in the spring.

Control: Eliminate lady's thumb in lawns with Ortho® Weed-B-Gon® Weed Killer for Lawns. Around trees and shrubs and in flower beds and unplanted areas, use Roundup® Weed & Grass Killer. Treat anytime the plants are actively growing but preferably before they flower and produce seeds for the following year. To prevent seeds from germinating around trees and shrubs, apply an herbicide containing *oryzalin* to the soil just after the last expected frost in the spring (two weeks after forsythia blooms). This weed has shallow roots and can be hand-pulled or hoed.

Plantain

Broadleaf plantain.

The two most common plantains (*Plantago* species) that invade landscaped areas are buckhorn plantain (*P. lanceolata*) and broadleaf plantain (*P. major*). These are perennial weeds that grow in all kinds of soils but prefer rich, moderately moist areas. The lance-shaped leaves of buckhorn plantain are 4 to 12 inches long, with three to five prominent veins in each leaf. White flower spikes 4 to 12 inches tall appear from May to October. Broadleaf plantain has oval leaves, 2 to 10 inches long, with five to seven veins per leaf. Greenish-white flower spikes, 2 to 10 inches tall, appear from May to September. The plantains reproduce from seeds formed on the flower spikes through the summer and fall. Seeds remain dormant over the winter and germinate the following spring. New plants also sprout from the perennial roots throughout the growing season. These ground-hugging, rosette-shaped plants suffocate desirable plants as they increase in size.

Control: Plantain has fairly shallow roots and can be dug out of landscaped areas. Control plantains in lawns with Ortho® Weed-B-Gon® Weed Killer for Lawns. Spot-treat lawns with Ortho® Weed-B-Gon® Weed Killer for Lawns Pull-N-Spray or Ready-to-Use. Around trees and shrubs and in flower beds, driveways, and unplanted areas, use Roundup herbicides. Treat in the spring or fall when the plants are actively growing. Repeated applications are often necessary.

Ragweed

Ragweed.

Ragweeds (*Ambrosia* species) are part of a group of annual and perennial plants that may also be called *wild tansy* or *hogweed*. The hairy stems grow 1 to 6 feet tall and has shallow roots. The fernlike smooth leaves are 2 to 4 inches long. Two kinds of flowers bloom from August to September. The greenish male flowers appear at the tips of the stems and produce vast quantities of pollen. The female flowers are less noticeable, blooming in the axils of the leaves. The seeds produced by the female flowers lie dormant in the winter and sprout in the spring. Ragweed tolerates many types of soil and is found most commonly in fields and vacant lots and along roadways.

Control: The best defense against ragweed is maintenance of a healthy, thriving lawn through good fertilization and mowing practices. Eliminate ragweed in lawns with Ortho® Weed-B-Gon® Weed Killer for Lawns. Around trees and shrubs and in flower beds and unplanted areas, kill existing weeds with Roundup® herbicide. Treat ragweed anytime it is actively growing. For best results, treat by midsummer, before the flowers open and produce seeds. Plants have shallow roots and can be hand-pulled.

Canada thistle

Canada thistle.

Canada thistle (*Cirsium arvense*), also known as *creeping thistle*, is a perennial adapted only to cool climates. The slender, prickly stems grow 1 to 4 feet tall. The prickly leaves have smooth upper surfaces, with woolly undersides. They are lobed and 4 to 8 inches long. Small purple, rose, or white flowers bloom from June to October. The seeds they produce are attached to a tuft of hairs that makes them readily wind-borne. Seeds germinate throughout the growing season, usually within two weeks of the time they mature and fall from the flower. The first frost kills the tops of the plants. The rhizomes grow horizontally through the soil, often up to 15 feet from the plant. New plants that sprout from the rhizomes grow rapidly, blooming in seven to eight weeks. Food stored in the roots enables the plants to survive extended periods of drought and other adverse growing conditions for several years. Canada thistle tolerates many types of soil but is most troublesome in moist areas with rich, heavy soil. It is very competitive in fields and pastures.

Control: Treat Canada thistle in lawns with Ortho® Weed-B-Gon® Weed Killer for Lawns or an herbicide containing *triclopyr* in the spring and fall. Around trees and shrubs and in flower beds and unplanted areas, use Roundup weed killers. For best results, treat plants when they are growing vigorously and approaching the flowering stage. Use Ortho® Weed-B-Gon® Weed Killer for Lawns in the spring when food reserves in the roots are low. Before beginning spot-treatment in lawns, forgo mowing one or two times in the late spring to allow the thistle to grow.

BROADLEAF WEEDS (continued)

Yellow star thistle

Yellow star thistle.

Yellow star thistle (*Centaurea solstitialis*), also known as *Barnaby's thistle*, is an annual or sometimes a biennial. The stems grow 1 to 3 feet tall and branch at the base. Both the stems and the leaves are covered with a white cottony fleece. The deeply lobed basal leaves are 2 or 3 inches long and form a rosette. The upper leaves are narrow and ½ to 1 inch long. Small yellow tubular flowers grow at the ends of the branches. They bloom and produce seeds from May to the first killing frost in the fall. The seeds germinate readily throughout the growing season and are spread by the wind. The sharp ¼- to 1-inch spines at the base of the flowers make this plant injurious to livestock and people. Yellow star thistle is found in fields and vacant lots and in roadside ditches.

Control: In lawns, treat young plants with Ortho® Weed-B-Gon® Weed Killer for Lawns before spines form. Around trees or shrubs or in flower beds, apply Ortho® Weed-B-Gon® Weed Killer for Lawns Ready to Use, or hand-pull or hoe the plants when small, before they develop a long taproot. In nonfood crop areas, apply Roundup® Weed & Grass Killer before the weed bolts, forming upright, elongated stems.

Common groundsel

Common groundsel.

Common groundsel (*Senecio vulgaris*), an annual also known as *grimsel*, grows ½ to 1½ feet tall, with hollow stems that may root at the lower nodes. The toothed leaves are 4 inches long. The lower leaves are attached to the stems by a short leafstalk, and the upper leaves cling directly to the stems. From April to October, yellow flowers up to 1 inch in diameter bloom on the ends of the branches. The seeds they produce germinate in cool, moist weather. Common groundsel is most troublesome in the fall and spring. It prefers areas with moist, rich soil and is found in fields, along roadways, and throughout home gardens.

Control: Hand-pull or hoe groundsel plants before they produce seeds. Mulching in landscaped areas reduces germination of groundsel seed blown in from neighboring areas. To control this weed around trees and shrubs and in flower beds and unplanted areas, use Roundup® Weed & Grass Killer. Treat anytime the plants are actively growing but preferably soon after they germinate. To prevent the seeds from sprouting around trees and shrubs, apply a preemergence herbicide containing *trifluralin* or *pendimethalin* to the soil in early fall and again in early spring.

Chicory

Chicory.

Chicory (*Cichorium intybus*), also called *succory* and *blue daisy*, is a perennial weed along roadways, in fields, and occasionally in lawns. Although it tolerates most types of soil, it is most troublesome in areas with neutral or alkaline soil. Chicory reproduces by seeds and by a deep, fleshy taproot. Hollow stems grow 1 to 3 feet tall. Stems and roots ooze a white milky juice when broken. The 3- to 8-inch basal leaves spread outward into a rosette. The oval upper leaves have toothed or smooth edges. Flowers bloom and produce seeds on the ends of the branches or in the axils of the upper leaves. Flowers appear from March to August and are usually sky blue but are sometimes white or, rarely, pink. They open in the early morning and close by midday.

Control: In lawns, control chicory with Ortho® Weed-B-Gon® Weed Killer for Lawns. Treat in the spring or early fall. Repeated treatments may be necessary because of the deep taproot. In shrub and flower beds, treat chicory with Roundup® Weed & Grass Killer. Be careful not to spray desirable plants.

Sheep sorrel

Sheep Sorrel.

Sheep sorrel (*Rumex acetosella*) is a perennial weed also called *red sorrel* or *field sorrel*.
It prefers cool, moist weather but thrives in dry, sandy soil in lawns and landscaped beds. It frequently indicates low nitrogen fertility and acidic soil but will survive in neutral or slightly alkaline soil. (For information on soil acidity, see page 407.) The stems on this rosette-shaped plant grow 4 to 14 inches tall. The leaves are 1 to 4 inches long and arrow shaped, with two lobes at the base of each leaf. Flowers bloom from May to September. The yellow male flowers are on separate plants from the red female flowers. The first fall frost kills plant tops. The rootstocks and seeds remain dormant until spring. Red sorrel has a shallow but extensive root system. The plants reproduce by seeds and red underground root stalks.

Control: In lawns, treat sheep sorrel with Ortho® Weed-B-Gon® Weed Killer for Lawns in the spring or fall. To help prevent it from growing in lawns, maintain a vigorous turf. Kill sheep sorrel around trees, shrubs, and in flower beds with Roundup® Weed & Grass Killer. Sheep sorrel can also be removed by cultivating or hand-pulling. Remove all the rootstocks, because any left behind will resprout. Test the soil pH, and correct if necessary.

Dandelion

Dandelion.

Dandelions (*Taraxacum officinale*) are the most common and easily identified weed in the
United States. They grow anywhere there is bare soil and full sunlight. They do, however, prefer wet soil and may indicate overwatering or poor drainage. These rosette-shaped perennial plants have thick, fleshy taproots that may grow 2 to 3 feet deep in the soil. A white milky sap oozes from broken flower stems and leaves. The yellow flowers bloom from midspring until frost. In warm-weather areas, they bloom all year. As the flowers mature and ripen, they form white "puff balls" containing seeds. The wind carries the seeds for miles to other lawns and bare spots of soil. The seeds sprout the following spring. The first frost kills the tops of the plants, but the taproot survives even the severest winters to resprout in the spring.

Control: In lawns, control dandelions with Ortho® Weed-B-Gon® Weed Killer for Lawns or Scotts Green Sweep Weed & Feed, or spot-treat with Ortho® Weed-B-Gon® Weed Killer for Lawns Ready to Use. To help prevent dandelions in the lawn, maintain a vigorous turf. Around trees and shrubs and in flower beds and unplanted areas, treat with Roundup® Weed & Grass Killer. Apply to actively growing plants, preferably before the seeds ripen. Hand-digging is impractical, because pieces of root that are broken off and left in the soil will sprout new plants.

Sow thistle

Sow thistle.

Sow thistles (*Sonchus* species) are annual weeds that are found throughout the United
States but are most common in the South and along the West Coast. The reddish stems arise from a short taproot and grow upright 1 to 6 feet. In mowed lawns they form tight rosettes. A milky sap oozes from the stems when the stems are broken. The upper branches may be covered with hairs. From July to September, yellow flowers, ½ to 1 inch in diameter, bloom on branches at the top of the plants. In Florida, Texas, and California, the plants may germinate or bloom year-round. The seeds these flowers produce are contained in brownish seed heads. They germinate either that fall or the following spring. Sow thistles prefer rich soil along roadways and in fields, lawns, and landscaped beds.

Control: A vigorous, healthy lawn will prevent most sow thistle, so good fertilizing and mowing practices are very important. Spray with Ortho® Weed-B-Gon® Weed Killer for Lawns. Or frequently mow off the flower stalks before they produce seeds. The fall frost will then kill the plants. Around trees and shrubs and in unplanted areas, use Roundup® Weed & Grass Killer. Prevent sow thistle seedlings from becoming established in landscaped beds by applying a preemergent herbicide containing *pendimethalin, oryzalin* or *DCPA* to the soil in early fall or early spring. Sow thistle can be hand-pulled, but wear gloves. The fine hairs can irritate the skin.

BROADLEAF WEEDS (continued)

Horseweed

Horseweed.

Horseweed (*Conyza canadensis*) is an annual plant that grows in dry soil in fields, along roadways, in lawns and landscaped beds, and in unplanted areas. It is also known as *mare's tail* and *bitterweed*. Horseweed has erect, bristly stems that grow 1 to 4 feet tall, branching in the upper portion. In lawns, the stems form a rosette. The narrow, dark green leaves are covered with white bristles. Clusters of small yellow to white flowers bloom on the upper stems from July to October. The seeds they produce may blow long distances in the wind. They lie dormant in the soil over the winter, germinating in the early spring. The first fall frost kills the plants. Horseweed grows from a short taproot that can be hand-pulled or hoed.

Control: Maintaining a healthy lawn through good fertilizing and mowing practices will keep horseweed from establishing. Any plants that do develop can be controlled by hand-pulling or with Ortho® Weed-B-Gon® Weed Killer for Lawns. Hand-pull horseweed in flower beds and around trees and shrubs, or treat with Roundup® Weed & Grass Killer. Apply in the spring and early summer. For best results, treat before the plants bloom and produce seed for the following year.

Shepherd's purse

Shepherd's purse.

Shepherd's purse (*Capsella bursa-pastoris*), also called *lady's purse* and *shepherd's bag*, is a common summer or winter annual. It grows in lawns, landscaped beds, unplanted areas, and fields throughout the United States. It tolerates most types of soil but will not grow in the shade. Lobed or toothed leaves form a rosette at the base of the plant. Arrow-shaped leaves and tiny white flowers grow on stems 3 to 18 inches tall. Flowers bloom and produce seeds in triangular pods from March to December. The seeds fall to the soil and may remain dormant for several years before germinating in the spring. Fall frost kills the plants. In warm-winter areas, seeds may germinate in the fall. The plants then grow through the winter until the fall.

Control: Eliminate shepherd's purse from lawns with Ortho® Weed-B-Gon® Weed Killer for Lawns. Treat when the weeds are actively growing. Around trees and shrubs, flower beds, and unplanted areas, kill existing weeds with Roundup® herbicides. Prevent this weed from growing around trees and shrubs with an herbicide containing *bensulide* or *dithiopyr*. Apply in the early spring or, in warm-winter areas, in the early fall, before the weeds sprout. Shepherd's purse can also be hand-pulled or hoed.

Tansy ragwort

Tansy ragwort.

Tansy ragwort (*Senecio jacobaea*) is a prolific biennial or perennial that grows 1 to 4 feet tall and is most noticeable when the golden flowers bloom in late summer. The leaves are 5 to 9 inches long and lobed, with a full blade at the tip. Seeds produced by the flowers germinate in the fall into rosette-shaped plants. The first year, the plants remain rosettes. The second year, most plants blossom, produce seeds, and die. Sometimes the plants survive a third year, blossom again, and produce more seeds. Each plant may produce as many as 150,000 seeds that remain viable in the soil for three or four years. Tansy ragwort survives most soil conditions. It is troublesome in fields and pastures, along roadways, and in unmaintained areas. It may be introduced into home gardens by windblown seeds or when straw contaminated by tansy ragwort is used as mulch.

Control: Hand-pull tansy ragwort before it blooms. If it is in bloom, cover it with a plastic bag before you pull to keep the seeds from spreading. Or spray with Roundup® weed killers. Treat in early spring or midfall when the plants are rosettes. Plants in bloom are much more difficult to control, and repeated treatments are often necessary.

Milkweed

Milkweed.

Milkweed (*Asclepias syriaca*) is a perennial also known as *silkweed* and *cottonweed*. The hairy, erect stems grow 2 to 5 feet tall. A milky sap oozes from the stems when they are broken. The 4- to 8-inch elliptical leaves are smooth on the upper surface; the lower surface is covered with white hairs. Young milkweed shoots resemble asparagus spears. Plants reproduce from their thick creeping rhizomes, as well as from seeds. Clusters of fragrant, pinkish-white flowers bloom from June to August. The milkweed plant is best known for its gray pods, 2 to 4 inches long, covered with soft spines. Evident in late summer and fall, the pods contain brown seeds with white silken hairs attached. When mature, they split open, releasing the seeds. The seeds lie dormant over the winter, sprouting in the spring. Milkweed usually grows in patches in rich, sandy, or gravelly loam soils in fields and along roadways. Because seeds are wind-borne, milkweed may be found in flower and vegetable gardens.

Control: Spot-treat milkweed plants with Roundup® Weed & Grass Killer. Or pull plants while young before they develop extensive rhizomes. Plants will sprout from pieces of rhizome left behind.

Pigweed

Pigweed.

Members of the pigweed group (*Amaranthus* species) are annuals that grow upright, except in mowed lawns, where they form mats. Leaves are oval or egg shaped and may be hairy. Flower spikes bloom and produce seeds from July to October. In one season, each plant may produce thousands of seeds, which sprout in the spring. Pigweed prefers hot, dry weather and dry soil. It grows in fields and vacant lots, along roadways, and in lawns and gardens.

Control: Good turf management will keep out many varieties of pigweed. Different grass types will crowd out different varieties of the weed. Control pigweed in lawns with Ortho® Weed-B-Gon® Weed Killer for Lawns anytime it is actively growing. In other areas, use Roundup® weed killers. For best results, and to reduce the number of plants the following year, treat before flowers and seeds are produced. Prevent pigweed from growing around trees and shrubs, in flower and vegetable gardens, and in lawns with an herbicide containing *trifluralin* or *pendimethalin*. Apply to the soil two weeks before the last expected frost (about the time forsythia blooms). Pigweed has shallow roots and can be removed by hand-pruning.

Mugwort

Mugwort.

Mugwort (*Artemisia vulgaris*), also called *chrysanthemum weed* and *wormwood*, is a perennial with underground creeping rhizomes and upright stems 3 to 6 feet high. The segmented leaves, green on the upper surface and woolly white on the lower surface, are 2 to 6 inches long and aromatic when crushed. From July to September, greenish yellow flower spikes bloom and produce seeds. Mugwort reproduces from seeds, which germinate in the spring, and from the extensive rhizomes. It prefers limy soil and grows primarily in moist areas near streams, highways, and fields. In yards, mugwort often creeps from lawns into landscaped beds and sprouts in cracks in walkways.

Control: Mugwort is difficult to control. Spot-treat with Roundup® Weed & Grass Killer. To prevent seeds from germinating around trees and shrubs and in flower beds, use a preemergent herbicide containing *eptam*. Apply to the soil in the spring, two weeks before the last expected frost (about the time forsythia blooms). In lawns, use Ortho® Weed-B-Gon® Weed Killer for Lawns. Hand-pulling is not effective, because any rhizome pieces left behind will sprout into new plants.

485

BROADLEAF WEEDS (continued)

Common lamb's-quarter

Common lamb's-quarter.

Common lamb's-quarter (*Chenopodium album*) is an annual also known as *white pigweed* and *white goosefoot*. The ridged stems are frequently lined with red or light green stripes. Common lamb's-quarter grows 1 to 4 feet tall from a short, branched taproot. The wedge-shaped leaves are 1 to 3 inches long with toothed edges. The undersides of the leaves are covered with a white, mealy coating. At the ends of the branches and in the leaf axils, small green flowers bloom and produce seeds from June to October. The pollen from these flowers irritates hay fever sufferers. The seeds remain dormant over the winter and sprout in the spring. The first frost kills the entire plant. Common lamb's-quarter is a troublesome weed in cultivated fields and gardens. It is a major host for the beet leafhopper, which transmits *curly top*, a viral disease of beets.

Control: Good fertilizing and mowing practices to maintain a thick, vigorous lawn will crowd out most weeds. In lawns, eliminate lamb's-quarter with Ortho® Weed-B-Gon® Weed Killer for Lawns. Treat in the spring when the plants are young. Kill existing weeds around trees and shrubs and in flower beds and unplanted areas with Roundup® Weed & Grass Killer. Treat anytime the plants are actively growing but preferably before they bloom and produce seeds. Prevent the seeds from germinating in these areas as well as in vegetable gardens with a a preemergence herbicide containing *trifluralin* or *pendimethalin*. Apply in the spring two weeks before the last expected frost Lamb's-quarter can also be hand-pulled or removed by hoeing.

Horsenettle

Horsenettle.

Horsenettle (*Solanum carolinense*), also called *bull nettle* and *Carolina nettle*, is a perennial that grows 1 to 3 feet tall. The stems, petioles, midribs, and veins of the leaves are prickled with yellow spines. Oval, 2- to 6-inch leaves with lobed or wavy margins are covered with fine hairs. Clusters of white to purple flowers that look like tomato flowers bloom from the sides of the stems from May to October. They are followed by ½-inch yellow-orange berries that are first smooth and later become wrinkled. New plants sprout from the seeds contained in these berries, as well as from the rhizomes. Horsenettle thrives in areas with sandy, well-drained soil. It spreads 5 or more feet across, crowding out desirable plants.

Control: Horsenettle has deep roots and is difficult to control. To kill existing weeds around trees and shrubs and in flower beds and unplanted areas, and to spot-treat lawns, use a Roundup® herbicide containing *glyphosate*. Regular mowing will also control horsenettle in lawns. Hand-pulling is not practical, because any root pieces left behind will sprout into new plants.

Stinging nettle

Stinging nettle.

Tiny hairs on stinging nettle (*Urtica dioica*), when touched, cause welts or inflammation on the skin. The 3- to 8-foot-tall stems and the leaves are covered with these stinging hairs. Irritation caused by contact with nettles usually heals in a day or so. The egg-shape leaves are 5 inches long and 3 inches wide, with saw-toothed margins. Small, greenish flowers bloom on clusters of spikes in leaf axils from June to September. Stinging nettle grows in damp, rich soil. It is found along creeks, in waste places, on edges of wooded lots, and occasionally in lawns, unplanted areas, and landscaped beds. It reproduces by seeds and underground rhizomes. A greenish-yellow dye can be made from the upper part of the plant.

Control: Stinging nettle can be hoed or hand-pulled, but be sure to wear gloves and a long-sleeved shirt. Spray unplanted areas with Roundup® Weed & Grass Killer. Repeated applications may be necessary to kill all the roots. Treat the plants anytime they are growing actively but preferably before they bloom. Prevent seeds from germinating in vegetable gardens with a preemergent herbicide containing *trifluralin*. Check the label for vegetables that can be safely treated. Apply to the soil in the early spring, about two weeks before the last expected frost (when forsythia blooms).

Morning glory

Morning glory.

Morning glory (*Ipomoea* species) is an annual weed with twining, hairy stems that grow 2 to 20 feet long. The heart-shaped, hairy leaves may be lobed and 2 to 6 inches long. Trumpet-shape white, purple, red, or blue flowers bloom in the leaf axils from July to October. Seeds are formed within bristly, brown, egg-shape pods that adhere to clothing or animal fur and are carried to other areas. The seeds lie dormant in the soil over the winter and germinate in the spring. Seeds can remain in the soil for many years. The first fall frost kills the plants. Morning glory is found in fields and along roadsides. The plants may sprout anywhere in the yard and frequently creep into yards from neighboring areas. They tolerate any type of soil but are most troublesome in areas with sandy soil.

Control: In a frequently mowed lawn, morning glory should not be a problem, but if control is necessary, use Ortho® Weed-B-Gon® Weed Killer for Lawns. Treat in the spring and early summer when the plants are growing most actively. Kill existing weeds around trees and shrubs and in noncrop areas with Roundup herbicides. To prevent morning glory seeds from sprouting around trees and shrubs, use a preemergent herbicide containing *simazine* or *oryzalin*. Apply to the soil in the spring about the time of the last expected frost. Young plants can be hand-pulled, hoed, or controlled with a deep mulch.

Field dodder

Dodder.

Field dodder (*Cuscuta* species), leafless, parasitic annuals, are also known as *lovevine*, *strangleweed*, and *devil's hair*. The threadlike, golden-yellow stems twine and coil on other plants. Short suction-cup–like suckers then sprout along the undersides of the dodder stems, penetrating the stems of the host plant. Dodder obtains its nourishment through these suckers. The stems branch repeatedly, attacking additional host plants. White or creamy flowers, ¼ inch in diameter, bloom and produce seeds from April to October. The seeds may germinate that year or lie dormant in the soil for many years before sprouting in the spring. The seeds germinate in the soil, but the roots die as soon as the dodder is attached to a host plant. Once attached, the dodder lives completely off its host plant. Dodder is killed by the first fall frost. It is found most commonly in pastures and fields where alfalfa has been grown. Occasionally it may be found on herbaceous and woody plants in the home garden.

Control: Once dodder has attached itself to another plant, you can't remove it. Destroy infested host plants. Don't pull dodder off the plants, because any stem pieces left behind will continue to grow. Prevent the seeds from germinating with a preemergent herbicide containing *DCPA*, *trifluralin*, or *pendimethalin*. For best results, apply in early spring, about the time of the last expected frost, when the majority of dodder seeds sprout. Repeat the application in six to eight weeks.

Field bindweed

Field bindweed.

Field bindweed (*Convolvulus arvensis*), a troublesome perennial, is also called *wild morning glory*, *perennial morning glory*, and *cornbind*. It grows in lawns, in flower and vegetable gardens, and around trees and shrubs. The creeping, twining stems frequently invade yards from nearby roadways, fields, and vacant lots. Field bindweed thrives in rich, heavy soil. The stems may be 3 to 9 feet long with arrow-shaped leaves 1 to 2 inches long. White to pink funnel-shape flowers the size of a quarter bloom and produce seed from May to September. Field bindweed is difficult to control. It reproduces by seeds and pieces of the rhizome. The seeds may remain dormant in the soil for many years before sprouting. Any rhizome pieces left behind after hand-pulling will sprout into new plants.

Control: In lawns, control field bindweed with Ortho® Weed-B-Gon® Weed Killer for Lawns. Apply from late spring through early summer or from early to late fall. Around trees and shrubs and in flower beds and unplanted areas, kill existing weeds with Roundup® Weed & Grass Killer. Repeat the treatments as new growth emerges. Hand-pulling or hoeing can't control bindweed.

BROADLEAF WEEDS (continued)

Nightshades

Nightshade.

Nightshades (*Solanum* species) are members of a group of annual and perennial weeds that includes bitter nightshade (*S. dulcamara*), black nightshade (*S. nigrum*), and hairy nightshade (*S. sarachoides*). Nightshades belong to the same family as eggplant, peppers, potatoes, and tomatoes. They grow in rich, moist soil and frequently creep into home gardens from surrounding fields, hedgerows, and unmaintained areas. The stems may grow up to 9 feet, creeping along the ground or twining on fences and plants. The stems frequently root where they touch the soil. Dark green to purple leaves 1 to 4 inches long may be mitten-shape, heart-shape, or lobed at the base. Blue, violet, or white flowers with yellow centers resemble tomato flowers. They bloom from May to November. The flowers are followed by green berries that, in some species, turn red or black when ripe. Birds often spread the yellow seeds from inside the berries, which sprout into new plants in the spring.

Control: In vegetable gardens, hand-pull weeds before they form seeds. Spot-treat around trees and shrubs and in other noncrop areas with Roundup® Weed & Grass Killer. Repeated treatments are often necessary because of the long, woody stems. Or hand-pull the vines, being careful not to drop any berries. Any pieces of stem left behind will sprout into new plants.

Carpetweed

Carpetweed.

Carpetweed (*Mollugo verticillata*), an annual weed also known as *Indian chickweed* and *whorled chickweed*, has smooth, prostrate stems that form circular mats up to 20 inches in diameter, crowding out desirable plants. Whorls of five to six leaves grow at each stem joint. Small white flowers bloom in the leaf axils from June to November. They produce orange-red, kidney-shape seeds that lie dormant in the soil over the winter and sprout slowly in the spring. The plants develop a short taproot and grow rapidly in the summer heat. Carpetweed prefers fertile, dry, sandy, or gravelly soil in lawns and gardens and along walkways.

Control: In lawns, treat with Ortho® Weed-B-Gon® Weed Killer for Lawns or Scotts® GreenSweep® Weed & Feed. Apply in early to midsummer when the plants are actively growing. If the lawn is kept vigorous through good fertilizing and mowing practices, carpetweed should not be a problem. Prevent seeds from germinating throughout the yard with a preemergence herbicide containing *trifluralin* or *pendimethalin*. Apply to the soil in midspring about the time of the last expected frost (two weeks after forsythia blooms). Carpetweed can be hand-pulled or hoed.

Henbit

Henbit.

Henbit (*Lamium amplexicaule*) is a winter annual or biennial also called *dead nettle* and *bee nettle*. It grows rapidly in early spring, fall, and winter in lawns and landscaped beds with rich soil. Rounded, toothed leaves up to ¾ inch wide grow on creeping square (four-sided) stems. Lavender flowers, ½ inch in diameter, bloom and produce seeds from April to June and again in September. Seeds sprout in the fall. Henbit also reproduces by the creeping stems that root wherever they touch the soil.

Control: In lawns, eliminate henbit with Ortho® Weed-B-Gon® Weed Killer for Lawns or Scotts® GreenSweep® Weed & Feed. Or spot-treat individual plants with Ortho® Weed-B-Gon® Weed Killer for Lawns Ready to Use. Treat in the spring when henbit is actively growing. Around trees and shrubs and in flower beds, kill existing weeds with Roundup® herbicides, or prevent henbit by mulching. Apply the treatment in the fall before the plants sprout.

MUSHROOMS

WOODY WEEDS

Mushroom

Mushrooms.

The folklore surrounding mushrooms has given them the additional name of *toadstool*. Some types are also known as *puffballs*. The mushroom is the aboveground fruiting or reproducing structure, the "flower," of a fungus that lives on and helps to decay organic matter in the soil. In wooded areas, some mushrooms live on the leaves that accumulate on the ground. Others may grow on the roots of trees and benefit both the trees and the mushrooms. Mushrooms thrive in warm, damp areas. They are seldom found in cool, dry spots. In cold-winter areas, they disappear with the first frost and return with wet spring weather. Spores are produced on the undersides of mushroom caps and are spread by the wind. Some mushrooms are poisonous; identify them carefully before eating. Mushrooms growing in circles in lawns are called *fairy rings*. (For more information on fairy rings, see page 76.)

Control: There is no practical way to eliminate mushrooms. When the buried organic matter is completely decayed, the mushrooms will disappear. For temporary control, break the mushrooms with a rake, or mow the lawn. (For information on suppressing mushroom growth in lawns, see page 85.)

Japanese honeysuckle

Japanese honeysuckle.

Japanese honeysuckle (*Lonicera japonica*), a perennial woody vine, is best known for its fragrant flowers, which are used to scent soaps, perfumes, and bath oils. They are white tinged with pink or yellow and bloom in pairs in the upper leaf axils from April to November. The twining, climbing stems grow on valuable plants, strangling them. As the stems creep along the ground, they root wherever the nodes touch the soil. The oval leaves, 1 to 3 inches long, smooth on the upper surface and hairy underneath, frequently remain on the plant through the winter. Honeysuckle fruit, evident from September to November, are ¼-inch black berries that contain two or three seeds. The seeds sprout the following spring. New plants also sprout from underground rootstocks.

Control: In lawns, kill honeysuckle with Ortho® Weed-B-Gon® Weed Killer for Lawns. Japanese honeysuckle is hard to kill; repeated applications will probably be necessary. In landscaped beds and unplanted areas, spot-treat with Roundup® Weed & Grass Killer. Apply in mid- to late summer when the plants will readily absorb the herbicide. Hand-pulling is not practical, because any roots left behind will sprout into new plants.

English ivy

Ivy climbing a tree.

English ivy (*Hedera helix*) is a popular evergreen woody vine that is often used as a ground cover. Some varieties of English ivy are bicolored with unusually shaped leaves, but most commonly the leaves are 1 to 4 inches long, dark green, and glossy. They usually have three to five lobes. The plant trails and roots as it spreads, creating a dense mat of foliage. The vines can climb onto and smother nearby shrubs, flowers, and lawns. The small rootlike projections (holdfasts) produced along the stems enable vigorous ivy plants to cling to walls, fences, tree trunks, and other vertical surfaces.

Control: English ivy is a persistent weed. Remove as much of it as possible by pruning the runners and digging out major roots. Dig out small plants that regrow. If necessary, treat with Ortho® Brush-B-Gon® Poison Ivy, Poison Oak, and Brush Killer. Repeated applications may be necessary.

WOODY WEEDS (continued)

Kudzu vine

Kudzu. Inset: Kudzu flowers.

Wild blackberry

Wild blackberry.

Poison ivy

Poison ivy and flower buds.

Kudzu vine (*Pueraria lobata*) is a woody perennial vine with heavy, brown hairy stems. The leaves have three leaflets, 3 to 6 inches long, with margins that may be smooth or slightly lobed. Tiny, reddish-purple, fragrant flowers produced in July and August are followed by small, long, hairy seedpods. In the past, kudzu vine was widely planted in the Southeast for erosion control and for use as a forage crop. In many areas, kudzu has become an aggressive weed. This twining vine spreads rapidly, growing up to 60 feet per year. It invades roadsides, vacant lots, fence lines, and neglected yards. Kudzu can twine over trees, shrubs, limbs, and branches. Plants completely covered may be killed by the shade.

Control: Treat kudzu vine with Ortho® Brush-B-Gon® Poison Ivy, Poison Oak, and Brush Killer or with Roundup® Weed & Grass Killer Super Concentrate. Control is most effective during mid- to late summer when the weed is in full leaf and growing actively. Spot-treat if resprouting occurs. If kudzu vine has climbed up or over trees and shrubs, cut the runners and remove them before treatment. Retreatment will likely be required to maintain control.

Wild blackberries (*Rubus* species) are perennial shrubs with thorny, arching stems that grow 3 to 8 feet tall and live for only two years. The first year only leaves are produced. They have three to five leaflets that are hairy with toothed edges, green on the upper surface and silver on the lower surface. Spines grow on the midrib on the underside of the leaflets. The second year, clusters of 12 to 30 white or pink flowers bloom in May and June. Red to black edible fruit then appears in July. New plants may sprout from underground runners or from seeds spread by birds that eat the fruit. Wild blackberry plants have deep roots, making them difficult to control. They prefer dry gravelly or sandy soil along roadways, fences, and unmaintained areas.

Control: Treat existing plants with Roundup® Brush Killer Concentrate or with Ortho® Brush-B-Gon® Poison Ivy, Poison Oak, and Brush Killer anytime the plants are actively growing. Repeated treatments are often necessary to kill the deep roots. Hand-pulling is not effective against blackberries; any roots left behind will sprout into new plants.

Poison ivy (*Rhus radicans*) is a woody perennial that may grow as a small shrub in full sunlight. The stems often reach 8 feet long and may be 5 inches in diameter. The leaves have three leaflets, 2 to 4 inches long, with margins that may be toothed, smooth, or lobed. All three forms may occur on the same plant. The terminal leaflet is attached by an elongated leafstalk. In the spring, the small new leaves are red, turning a glossy or dull green as they enlarge. In the fall, they turn bright red or reddish yellow. Poison ivy is sometimes confused with Virginia creeper (*Parthenocissus quinquefolia*), which has five leaflets and blue berries. Clusters of greenish white flowers bloom on poison ivy from late spring to early summer. They produce ¼-inch white waxy berries with seeds. The fruit first appears in the late summer and remains on the plant through the winter. The plant can be identified by the fruit in the winter, when there are no leaves. Some plants produce only male flowers, so fruit won't be present on all poison ivy plants. Poison ivy reproduces by seeds, which birds distribute, and by underground creeping stems and roots. It is frequently found climbing buildings, trees, and fences or along the ground. An oil present in all parts of poison ivy plants causes skin irritations, which can occur throughout the year and from live or dead plants. These irritations develop after contact with the plant or with contaminated clothing, tools, pet hair, or smoke from burning plants.

Poison oak and Pacific poison oak

Poison ivy.

Poison oak.

Fall color.

Control: Hand-pulling and burning are not practical controls. Any roots left behind will sprout into new plants. The irritating oil in poison ivy vaporizes when burned, and the smoke causes lung, eye, and skin irritations. Control poison ivy around trees, on fences and buildings, and in noncrop areas with Ortho® Brush-B-Gon® Poison Ivy, Poison Oak, and Brush Killer or with Roundup® Brush Killer Concentrate. Treat anytime the plants are actively growing but at least two weeks before the first killing frost in the fall. Spray the leaves thoroughly. Plants turn white or brown in 10 to 14 days. The vigorous roots are difficult to kill, so repeated treatments may be necessary if new growth appears. Handle dead plants with rubber gloves, because they may still contain oils. Dispose of plants and rubber gloves in sealed garbage bags. If you come in contact with poison ivy, wash as soon as possible with a drying agent, such as rubbing alcohol, or a solution of baking soda and water.

Poison oak (*Rhus toxicodendron*) and Pacific poison oak (*R. diversiloba*) are perennials that grow as upright shrubs and as twining vines. The leaves, 1½ to 4 inches long with three to seven shallow lobes, are composed of three elliptical or oval leaflets. The terminal leaflet is attached with an elongated petiole. The lower surface of the leaves and the petiole are velvety; the upper surface is hairy. The leaflets resemble white-oak leaves, except that oak leaves are smooth. Poison oak leaves turn a brilliant orange to red color in the fall. In May and June, clusters of greenish flowers bloom from the centers of the leaves. They are followed by round, green to tan fruit containing seeds. New plants sprout from these seeds, and from the creeping underground stems. Poison oak prefers dry areas with poor, sandy soil. It is frequently found in wooded lots, along roadways, and in yards and noncrop areas. It is well-known for the irritating rash caused by its oily sap. The oil is found in all parts of the plant. The greatest irritations occur in the spring and summer when the sap is flowing freely. Rashes can develop any time of the year, however, if the plant is contacted. Irritations develop after contact with the plant directly or with contaminated clothing, tools, pet hair, or smoke from burning plants.

Control: Do not hand-pull or burn poison oak plants. Any pieces of root left behind will sprout into new plants. Also, the oil remains potent on clothing for up to two years. When burned, the oil vaporizes, and the smoke causes skin, eye, and lung irritations. Use of herbicides is the safest way to rid an area of this weed that is found around homes, buildings, fences, noncrop areas, and trees. Treat the plants with Ortho® Brush-B-Gon® Poison Ivy, Poison Oak, and Brush Killer or with Roundup® Brush Killer Concentrate. Treat anytime the plants are actively growing but at least two weeks before the first killing frost in the fall. Spray the leaves thoroughly. Plants begin to turn white or brown in 10 to 14 days. The vigorous roots are difficult to kill, so repeated treatments may be necessary if new growth appears. In lawns, kill poison oak with Ortho® Weed-B-Gon® Weed Killer for Lawns. Handle dead plants with rubber gloves, because they may still contain oils. Place dead plants in plastic bags and tie securely. Discard bags and rubber gloves. If you come in contact with poison oak, wash as soon as possible with a drying agent, such as rubbing alcohol, or a solution of baking soda and water.

Woodchucks often knock down large plants to reach the flower buds and succulent tips they prefer. See page 498.

Tree squirrel. See page 496.

Animals in the garden can be the worst problem the gardener faces. Their presence influences the gardener's way of working and often the plants selected. Control of animals in the garden is difficult. For one, animals, unlike insects or plant diseases, are intelligent and can overcome the obstacles we place in their paths. Also, we can't simply eliminate them as we can insects or disease-causing organisms. The sight of a deer browsing in our backyard may give us as much pleasure as the roses they are eating. The removal of foraging rabbits may simply mean neighboring rabbits will move to our yard.

The pest may be our neighbor's cat—or even our own!

Over the centuries, gardeners have developed a multitude of ways to repel animals. These methods may work for some animals but not for others, or they work one year and fail the next. Repellents aren't very reliable, because animals and birds learn from experience. A radio in the orchard may frighten off deer one year or for a few months, but eventually the deer learn that the radio is harmless and they will browse next to it. Deer in populated areas even learn which dogs to fear and which are harmless nuisances.

Usually the most effective way to control animal pests is to erect barriers—anything from a fence around the garden to a sheet of hardware cloth laid over a flower bed to keep mice from digging up bulbs.

When animal pests need to be removed, traps are usually more effective than poisons, although in some cases poison baits work well. Traps let you see that you have caught the animal, for one thing. If you don't want to kill the animal, you can catch it in a live trap and release it in a nearby wilderness area. Local regulations may govern this. Ask your county agricultural commissioner about the rules in your area.

ANIMAL PESTS

Mice

Damaged bark. Inset: Field mouse.

House mice

House mouse.

House mouse.

Several kinds of field mice (*Microtus* species), or voles, invade gardens throughout the United States. Mice live in grassy or brushy areas, nesting underground in shallow burrows or above ground in densely vegetated, protected spots. Mice usually move along narrow runways from their nesting areas to their food sources. They also feed on bulbs, tender vegetables, and flowers and may severely damage young trees by gnawing on bark and roots. Mice do most of their damage at night.

Control: Keep mice out of the garden by putting up a fence. Surround the area you wish to protect with a woven wire fence (¼-inch mesh) at least 12 inches high. To prevent mice from tunneling underneath, extend the fence 12 inches below the soil surface. Or dig a ditch 12 inches wide and 2 inches deep just outside the fence. Lay the bottom foot of wire mesh in this ditch, bend it upright at the fence posts, and fasten to the fence posts. Cover the horizontal portion of the wire with soil. Protect young tree trunks by placing hardware cloth cylinders 12 inches high around the tree. The cloth cylinders should extend an additional 12 inches above the average snow level. You may also protect the trunk with tree-wrapping plastic, starting at the bottom. Remove weeds from around the tree trunks. Keep your garden free of grassy areas and hay or leaf mulches to reduce possible hiding and breeding areas for mice. Protect bulbs by covering the planted areas with hardware mesh, burying the edges in the ground. Traps or poisoned baits may be placed along runways.

Problem: Mice are seen in the shed, garage, or home, or signs of mouse infestation—including droppings, tracks, or gnawed doors, baseboards, or kitchen cabinets—are found. Books, fabrics, furniture, and other objects may be chewed or shredded, and packages of food may be gnawed open and the contents eaten.

Analysis: House mice (*Mus musculus*) are familiar pests that often go unnoticed if only a few are present but may cause significant damage when their numbers are large. In addition to gnawing on clothing, furniture, and other items, mice contaminate food with their urine and droppings and may spread parasites and diseases. Mice are generally active at night. Under ideal conditions, the females produce up to 50 young in a year. Mice are very agile and can jump as high as 12 inches off the ground, run up almost any rough vertical surface, swim, and squeeze through openings slightly larger than ¼ inch. House mice feed primarily on cereal grains but will eat many other kinds of foods, including butter, fat, meat, sweets, and nuts.

Solution: Apply anticoagulant bait or a bait consisting of cereal grains treated with *cholecalciferol* (vitamin D-3), a new generation rodenticide. This cereal bait is safer to use around pets and other domestic animals than anticoagulant baits. The bait is contained in packets that should be placed in the same areas in which traps would be placed. Be sure to put them out of the reach of children and pets. Another way to eliminate mice in the home is to trap them. Mice are more likely to seek bait in traps if their normal source of food is scarce. Remove food from areas where mice can get to it, and store grains in sealed metal, glass, or heavy plastic containers. Place traps where mouse droppings, gnawings, and damage indicate the presence of mice. These include such areas as behind refrigerators and other protective objects, in dark corners, along baseboards, and in cupboards. Bait the traps with pieces of bacon, nut meats, raisins, or peanut butter. Tie the bait to the trigger so the mouse can't remove the bait without springing the trap. Check the traps daily to dispose of trapped mice. Wear gloves when handling dead mice, or use tongs to pick them up to avoid bites from mouse parasites. If you are unable to eliminate all the mice, contact a professional pest control operator. After mice have been eliminated, prevent them from returning by sealing holes or cracks larger than ¼ inch in walls, floors, windows, doors, and areas of the foundation open to the outside. For details on mouse-proofing your home, contact your local county extension office.

Rats

Roof rat.

Norway rat.

Pocket gophers

Gopher mound. Inset: Gopher.

Problem: Rats are seen or heard in the attic, garage, basement, wall spaces, or other areas of the home. Signs of rat infestation include droppings, tracks, and loosely constructed nests made of rags, paper, and other scraps. Pipes, beams, and wiring may be gnawed. Books, fabrics, furniture, and other objects may be chewed or shredded, and packages of food may be gnawed open and the contents eaten.

Analysis: Rats (*Rattus* species) are distributed worldwide and infest well-maintained suburban residences as well as run-down urban houses and apartments. The species that most frequently infest houses are the Norway rat (also known as the brown, house, wharf, or sewer rat) and the roof rat. Rats enter buildings through any opening, including toilets, pipes, chimneys, and garbage chutes. They are excellent climbers and can gain access to homes from nearby trees. Young rats can squeeze through openings as small as ½ inch wide. These animals make their nests and breed in wall spaces, attics, crawl spaces, basements, and other secluded locations. They also breed in heavy vegetation, such as ivy or juniper ground covers, near the home. Their long front teeth grow constantly. To keep them worn down, rats gnaw on almost anything, including clothing, furniture, and electrical wires. They can also gnaw through gas lines, causing gas leaks. Rats are notorious for contaminating food with their urine, droppings, and hair, spreading parasites and diseases. They occasionally bite people, especially sleeping infants. The bites are dangerous and must be treated by a doctor.

Solution: Apply anticoagulant bait or a bait consisting of cereal grains treated with *cholecalciferol* (vitamin D-3), a new generation rodenticide. This cereal bait is safer to use around pets and other domestic animals than anticoagulant baits. The bait is contained in packets that should be placed in the same areas as traps would be placed. Be sure to put them out of the reach of children and pets. Another way to control rats in the home is by trapping them. Use rat traps; the smaller mouse traps are ineffective. Rats are more likely to seek bait in traps if their normal source of food is scarce. Remove food from areas where rats can get to it easily. Store food in glass or tin containers with screw-on or tightly sealed lids. Place traps along rat runways, anchoring the trap securely to a nearby object so the animal won't drag it away. Bait traps with pieces of beef, bacon, fish, nut meats, or carrots. Tie the bait to the trigger so the rat can't remove the bait without springing the trap. Check the traps daily to dispose of captured rats. Rats are very wary creatures. Unlike mice, they will not accept strange objects in their territory, even if baited. Be patient: It may take several days to a few weeks before a rat moves into a live trap or takes bait from a snap trap. Wear gloves or use tongs to pick up rats to avoid bites from rat parasites such as fleas and mites. If you are unable to eliminate the rats, contact a professional pest control operator. Rat-proof the building. Clear landscape plantings to at least 18 inches from the structure. Identify ground burrows, place bait inside, and cover the hole. Seal all openings larger than ¼ inch leading into the building from the outside. Sealing such small openings also keeps out mice.

Pocket gophers are burrowing rodents that live and feed primarily underground. Pocket gophers eat roots, bulbs, and plants that they pull into their burrows. They can kill shrubs, vines, and trees by eating most of the roots and girdling the underground part of the trunk or stems. Damaged plants wilt, sometimes only on one side. Pocket gophers are solitary and fiercely territorial, so only one gopher inhabits a tunnel system at a time. They are also quite active and seem to be constantly digging new tunnels. The crescent-shape mounds of soil they leave on the surface are excavated from new runs. Their tunnels sometimes drain off irrigation ditches or basins so the water doesn't get to the intended area.

Control: Gophers are best controlled by trapping. Find the main runway by probing with a sharp rod about 1 foot deep near a fresh mound or an eaten plant. Dig a hole to intersect the tunnel, and insert two wire traps or box traps in the run, one facing each direction. Tie the traps together or to a stake above ground. To keep soil from falling on the traps, cover the hole with sod or a board, and sprinkle with soil to block out all light. Check and move the traps daily. Although only one gopher occupies a burrow system at a time, a migrating gopher will move into an abandoned burrow. Level all the mounds, and watch for new mounds, evidence that the burrow has been reoccupied.

ANIMAL PESTS (continued)

Moles

Mole tunnels.

Tree squirrels

Tree squirrel.

Gray squirrel.

Moles are small (up to 6 inches long), gray to black mammals with fine velvety fur. They have slender, hairless snouts and inconspicuous eyes and ears. Their eyesight is poor, but they have superior senses of smell, touch, and hearing. The front feet are much larger than the hind feet and have long, trowel-like claws used for tunneling in the ground. Moles live in burrows made up of many interconnecting runways, usually about 6 to 8 inches underground. Some species also dig many shallow feeding runways only a few inches below ground, which produces ridges on the soil surface. These ridges are especially noticeable in lawns. Moles dig lateral tunnels to the surface, where they deposit surplus soil in volcano-shaped mounds. Moles seldom feed on plants. They eat slugs, earthworms, grubs, and other small insects. They damage plants by their tunneling, which uproots plants or loosens the soil around roots and causes them to dry out and die.

Control: The best way to rid your lawn of moles is to eliminate the insects that they feed on. (For information, see page 77.) Traps are generally used for the rest of the garden and can also be used in lawns. Before placing traps in shallow tunnels, you must determine which tunnels are still active. Roll or tamp down the ridges. Those that are raised the following day are still active. Trapping in main runways is usually more productive. To detect these deeper runways, probe between mounds with a rod. Poison baits and repellents are generally ineffective. Fumigants are effective in some areas.

In the garden: Tree squirrels are mainly a problem in forested or lightly wooded rural or suburban areas. These animals establish nests in tree hollows or build nests of leaves, twigs, and bark in trees. They are omnivorous, feeding on fruits, seeds, nuts, insects, and bark. Tree squirrels are agile climbers and jumpers; they can easily leap 6 feet from the ground to a branch or structure or between branches. These animals damage gardens by digging up newly planted seeds and bulbs and sometimes entire plants. They may strip the bark or leaves from trees and shrubs and feed on fruit and nuts.

Control: Keep tree squirrels out of newly planted seed and bulb beds by placing chicken-wire mesh over the planted area. Bury the edges of the mesh in the soil, or weight them down with bricks. Remove the wire before the plants are too large to fit through the mesh. Prevent tree squirrels from climbing up fruit and nut trees by placing 2-foot-wide bands of metal (made from material such as aluminum roof flashing) snugly around tree trunks at least 6 feet above the ground. Prune branches so that they are at least 6 feet above the ground and 6 feet away from structures or the branches of other trees. If permissible in your area, you can also trap tree squirrels. Contact your state's Department of Fish and Game to determine local regulations. Place or tie traps near tree squirrel trails or nests. Bait the traps with nuts, sunflower seeds, peanut butter, or raisins.

In the home: Squirrels are seen or heard in the building. Nuts or other food remnants, droppings, gnawed holes, and nesting materials in the attic, garage, wall spaces, and other areas indicate the presence of squirrels.

Several species of tree squirrels invade houses, including the fox squirrel (*Sciurus niger*), the eastern gray squirrel (*S. carolinensis*), and flying squirrel (*Glaucomys* species). Squirrels enter buildings through vents, broken windows, construction gaps under eaves and gables, and occasionally chimneys and fireplaces. They may build nests or store food in attics, wall spaces, garages, and similar locations, and they may damage items stored in attics or garages.

Control: Contact your state's Department of Fish and Game for regulations governing the control of tree squirrels in your area. Eliminate the animals inside buildings by placing traps in the areas they are inhabiting. Bait the traps with nut meats, peanut butter, sunflower seeds, or raisins. If tree squirrels are entering a building by climbing trees or power lines, secure traps to tree limbs or the rooftop to intercept them. Once squirrels have been eliminated from the building, seal entry routes into the home with sheet metal or hardware cloth. Prune tree limbs at least 6 feet from the roof or any other part of the building.

Ground squirrels

Ground squirrel.

Several types of ground squirrels are found throughout the United States, but these animals are mainly a problem west of the Rocky Mountains. Ground squirrels live in underground burrows located in open, sunny areas. Many species are social, forming large underground colonies that may extend over an acre. Sometimes ground squirrels excavate burrows under buildings, causing stress cracking of the foundations. In certain areas, ground squirrels and some of their parasites may transmit serious diseases to humans. These animals can cause severe damage to gardens. In the late winter and spring, they emerge from hibernation to invade gardens, feeding on tender green growth. Later in the season they feed on seeds, grains, vegetables, fruit, and nuts.

Control: Ground squirrels are agile climbers; they can climb over most fences. If only a few ground squirrels are causing damage, trap them. Set the traps near burrow entrances or along routes used by the animals. Use baits such as peanut butter, nuts, raisins, or cereals. Because ground squirrels may carry diseases, always wear gloves and protective clothing when handling them. Contact the local humane society or county extension service for information on how to get rid of the trapped animals. If large colonies (more than a dozen ground squirrels) are present, contact a pest control operator, who will eliminate the colony using fumigants or poisoned baits.

Skunks

Skunk.

Skunks are mainly a problem in rural and outlying suburban areas. They are omnivorous and nocturnal, feeding on insects, small rodents, fruits, berries, corn, other garden vegetables, and garbage, primarily at night. They rarely cause much damage in the garden but are unacceptable to many people because of the strong scent they spray when threatened or provoked. In addition, skunks may carry rabies. Rabid skunks often show abnormal behavior such as listlessness, unprovoked aggressiveness, or a tendency to wander around during the day. Such animals bite when handled.

Control: The best way to keep skunks out of the garden is with a fence. Enclose the area you want to protect with a 3-foot-high fence of chicken wire. Bend the bottom 12 inches of the wire mesh under in a trench a few inches deep and bury it to discourage animals from digging beneath it. In some areas, you may also trap skunks, placing the traps near their dens or trails. Bait traps with sardines or cat food. Before attempting to trap or kill skunks, contact your agricultural commissioner or state's Department of Fish and Game to find out if these animals are protected in your area. If you or your pets are sprayed, neutralize the scent with tomato juice or *neutroleum alpha*, a compound available through pest control operators or hospital supply outlets. Pet supply stores also carry products to neutralize skunk odors on pets. Immediately contact a physician if you are bitten by a skunk; contact a veterinarian if a pet is bitten by a skunk.

Rabbits

Rabbit damage to dwarf apples.

Rabbits are often considered cute little animals, but they may be very annoying and damaging pests in the garden. Their reproductive rate is high. They produce several litters per year, with four to seven babies in each litter. Rabbits are active all year long, mainly during the day. In the summer, they feed on any tender young plants, especially garden vegetables. During the winter, they gnaw on bark, twigs, and buds. They are especially destructive to young fruit trees in the winter. Much of the bark on small trees may be eaten. Young branches are often clipped off cleanly, without ragged edges. Rabbits can also clip off twigs on older trees up to 2 feet above snow or ground level.

Control: The best way to keep rabbits out of a vegetable garden or small orchard is to enclose it with a 1½-inch mesh chicken-wire fence. The fence should be 2 feet high in areas with little snow or 2 feet above snow level in areas where snow accumulates. The bottom should be buried 3 or 4 inches under the soil, with the wire lying away from the garden. Or build portable cages to place over small garden plots. To protect single trees, build a cylindrical chicken-wire fence 2 feet high around the trunk. Dried bloodmeal sprinkled near plants may repel rabbits, and it is also beneficial to the soil. It must be reapplied every few days during wet weather. Chemical repellents, cats, dogs, or live traps may also be used to protect the garden from rabbits.

ANIMAL PESTS (continued)

Raccoons

Raccoon.

Woodchucks

Woodchuck.

Porcupines

Porcupine.

Raccoons are a nuisance mainly in wooded rural or suburban areas, but in some cities they have become urban pests. They usually establish their dens in hollow logs, trees, or other natural shelters near a source of water. Raccoons are omnivorous, feeding on insects, small mammals, fish, fruit, nuts, grains, and vegetables; they are especially fond of corn. Raccoons are nocturnal, foraging at night and returning to their dens during the day. They are agile climbers and scale trees to feed on fruit or nuts, often knocking many to the ground. Sometimes they invade attics and basements.

Control: Raccoons are intelligent, inquisitive animals that can be very difficult to deter. You can discourage raccoons from invading your vegetable garden by erecting a 4-foot-high chicken-wire fence, with its top extending 18 inches above the fence post. As the raccoon climbs up onto the unattached portion of the fence, his weight will pull him backward toward the ground. Low-voltage electric fences also are effective in excluding raccoons from the garden. To keep raccoons from climbing between trees or from a building to a tree, keep the limbs pruned so that they don't touch or make contact with the roof. Prevent raccoons from climbing trees by wrapping metal guards at least 18 inches wide around the trunk. Place the guards at least 3 feet above the ground.

Woodchucks, also known as *groundhogs*, are a problem in rural and suburban areas throughout much of the United States. They live in underground burrows, from which they emerge in the early morning and late afternoon to feed. Woodchucks prefer tender vegetables, flowers, and other succulent greenery, but they occasionally gnaw on tree bark. These animals seldom invade gardens in large numbers. They don't tunnel to their food source but feed above ground. Woodchucks occasionally contract diseases such as rabies that may transmit to humans.

Control: The best way to eliminate damage is to fence out the woodchucks. Surround the area you wish to protect with a woven-wire fence about 3 feet high. To prevent woodchucks from burrowing under the fence, bend the bottom 12 inches of the wire mesh under before burying it a few inches deep in the soil. To prevent woodchucks from climbing over the top, leave the upper 18 inches of mesh unattached to the supporting stakes. Bend this upper portion outward. As the animal climbs the fence, the weight of its body will pull the upper portion backward toward the ground. Traps may also be used. In some states, these animals are protected by law. Before attempting to trap or kill woodchucks, contact your state's agricultural commissioner or Department of Fish and Game for proper regulations in your area. Always wear gloves and protective clothing when handling woodchucks; they may be diseased.

Porcupines are only problems in rural areas. During the summer, they eat a varied diet of leaves, fruit, and nuts. In winter, however, their diet consists mostly of the inner bark of trees, and they can do a great deal of damage to individual trees. Porcupines often feed high in a tree, girdling it and killing the top above their feeding spot. Like all rodents, their front teeth grow constantly, and they gnaw on hard and rubbery material to wear them down. Porcupines may chew on tool handles, rubber hoses and belts, leather, plastic pipes, plywood, and a variety of other items. They do most of their feeding at night. They remain active all winter. They prefer coniferous forests but are also found in mixed and deciduous forests and among riverside trees. They are abundant in most parts of their range.

Control: Porcupines can be excluded from gardens and orchards with a low fence. Use chicken-wire mesh 18 inches high, with an electric wire placed just above the top strand or with a "floppy top"— an unattached portion 18 inches high that is bent backward at a 45-degree angle from the vertical. The electric wire or floppy top prevents the porcupine from climbing over the fence. Protect individual trees with a band of aluminum flashing, 30 inches wide, around the trunk. Small trees can be completely enclosed in a chicken-wire basket. Porcupines can also be shot or poisoned. For help with a persistent porcupine problem, contact an animal control office of the U.S. Fish and Wildlife Service.

Deer

Deer.

Hosta damaged by deer.

Deer can cause severe damage to gardens in rural and suburban areas. They feed on many vegetables and flowers, stripping new growth and often eating the entire plant. Deer may also browse on the tender bark, leaves, and twigs of shrubs and trees. Usually they feed on tree buds and bark during the winter or when other sources of food are scarce. Males may damage trees by rubbing their antlers on trunks and branches. While feeding, they may trample other plants.

Control: The best way to prevent deer damage is to fence the animals out. Deer are strong and agile jumpers; to be effective, a vertical fence must be at least 8 feet high. Enclose all areas of the garden that are accessible to deer. The fencing material should be a woven wire mesh. Stretch it between wooden or steel posts placed 10 to 12 feet apart. The wire mesh should fit tightly along the ground to prevent deer from forcing their way under the fence. A strand of barbed wire stretched along the ground will discourage deer from attempting to go under the fence. If the ground is uneven, secure the mesh to depressions in the ground, or fill in the depressions with soil, rocks, or other material.

Mesh fences: A fence made of plastic mesh is not only effective, but also less visible than other fences, especially in wooded or brushy country. Most mesh is about 2×2 inches. The mesh is lightweight, inexpensive, and easier to install than metal fencing. It can be attached to trees in wooded areas.

Slanted fences: A slanted fence is also effective. Although deer are good, high jumpers, they will not jump a barricade that is both high and wide. You can keep deer out with a fence that is only 4 feet high if it is also 4 feet wide. Anchor 6-foot steel posts into the ground 30 to 40 feet apart, burying the bottom third of the post. Attach a heavy guy wire along the top. Stretch 6-foot-wide wire-mesh fencing at a 45-degree angle along the posts, securing the mesh with stakes at the bottom and attaching it to the guy wires at the top. Build the fence so that the deer will approach it from the same side as the posts are anchored. If you live in an area where snowfall is heavy, wire mesh is likely to be crushed by settling snowpack. Instead, use smooth wire stretched horizontally 4 inches apart.

Other methods: Electric fences are sometimes effective. Individual trees or small areas can be protected with wire-mesh cages (1- or 2-inch mesh). You can also spray a repellent containing *tetramethylthiuram disulfide* on trees to prevent browsing damage. Check the label for your tree, and don't use repellents on fruit trees except during the dormant season. Deer may also be repelled by nylon stockings filled with human hair or small sacks of bloodmeal hung on the trees you want to protect. Kerosene- or creosote-soaked rags or perforated cans of mothballs hung from trees may also repel deer. Sometimes all deer-control measures fail, and killing certain problem deer may be the only solution. Because deer are protected by law, contact your agricultural commissioner or your state Department of Fish and Game regional office for regulations.

Dogs

Dog digging in garden.

Dogs can devastate a garden, especially when allowed to play or romp freely in a small yard. They cause damage by trampling or lying on plants, digging up the soil, and depositing feces and urine around the yard.

Control: Discourage dogs from digging around or urinating on plants by spraying the affected area with a repellent containing *methyl nonyl ketone* according to label directions. Further dog-proof these spots by putting up a fence. The type and sturdiness of the fence will be dictated by the size, strength, and determination of your pet. A flimsy fence made of wire strung between stakes may be adequate for a small, well-behaved animal. Larger, more rambunctious dogs require sturdier fences. Eventually the animal will adjust to the new boundaries and will be less likely to damage planted areas when the fence is removed. Proper discipline and the provision of an alternate location in which the animal can play will reduce its damage to garden plants.

ANIMAL PESTS (continued)

Cats

Cat in vegetable garden.

Birds

Starling.

Pigeon.

Cats are usually beneficial to a home garden; they help keep mice, rats, and other rodents under control, and they chase away nuisance birds. But cats can be damaging in newly planted areas. They dig up soft, loose soil to bury their feces and urine. They unearth seeds and transplants while digging and may continue to damage these areas until the soil becomes compacted or until plants fill in the area.

Control: You can discourage cats from digging in newly planted areas by spraying the soil with a repellent containing *methyl nonyl ketone* according to label directions. Protect seedbeds by laying chicken wire on the soil; remove the wire before the plants are too large to slip through the mesh. If plants are already present, set up cages made of 1-inch chicken wire over newly planted spots. You can take away protective devices after the soil packs down or when vegetation covers bare areas.

In the garden: Many types of birds feed on seeds, seedlings, fruit, and berries in the garden. Birds scratch away at soft soil to unearth newly planted seeds. They peck at seedlings and young leaves. Birds are especially damaging to berries, grapes, and ripening fruit.

Control: Once birds develop the habit of feeding in your garden, you will probably have to keep them out with wire or fabric cages. Make wire cages out of 1-inch chicken wire. Cages that are about 10×10×24 inches are self-supporting. Larger cages may need to be reinforced with heavy wire. You can also make cages or protective coverings with row covers or plastic bird netting supported by stakes or a wooden frame. If birds have not yet developed the habit of feeding in your garden, you may be able to repel them without having to construct cages. Set up stakes around the plantings you wish to protect and tie crisscrossing strings between the stakes. Attach strips of aluminum foil to the strings. Birds will not readily fly through the crossed strings and will avoid the shiny aluminum. Scarecrows aren't usually effective for very long. You can remove protective devices once plants have produced several sets of mature leaves or, in the case of berries, after you've harvested all of the fruit. To prevent birds from digging up seeds, lay hardware cloth (¼-inch mesh) over the seedbed. It must be removed before the plants are too large to grow through the mesh.

In the home: Birds are roosting or nesting in wall spaces, under eaves, and in other areas around the home. Most birds are harmless and pleasant, but a few species, especially pigeons, starlings, and sparrows, may become a nuisance around the home. These birds are adapted to urban and suburban environments. They roost and build nests on chimneys, ledges, rafters, eaves, drainpipes, and similar locations, and they often return to the same nesting site year after year. In addition to their messy droppings and irritating chirping, birds may transmit diseases to humans, such as pigeon psittacosis, aspergillosis, encephalitis, and histoplasmosis.

Control: Where possible, exclude birds by installing screens. Apply a bird repellent adhesive or jelly to roosting and nesting areas. Clean up potential nest-building materials (such as dried weeds or vegetation) to discourage bird activity in the vicinity. Place flashings of hard slippery plastic or metal at a 45-degree angle on nesting or roosting areas. Hang protective netting from roof eaves. Birds may also be trapped or poisoned. If you are considering poison, contact a licensed pest control operator or your county agricultural commissioner for regulations pertaining to your area.

Cliff swallows

Swallow nests.

Mud nests are found beneath eaves of the building. The nests are about 6 inches in diameter, are shaped like gourds, and have necklike entrances with round holes in them. Nests are usually grouped together. Bird droppings and mud are scattered beneath the mud structures. In spring, birds fly in and out of the nests.

Cliff swallows (*Hirundo pyrrhonota*), birds also known as *mud swallows*, spend their winters in South America and annually migrate northward to the United States. From March through June they build their mud nests, usually against a vertical wall just beneath an overhang such as an eave. The same nesting sites are used year after year, and many of the birds return to the same area they nested in the previous year. The birds abandon the nests by the end of June.

Control: Swallows are protected by state and federal regulations, so obtain a permit from the U.S. Fish and Wildlife Service before removing swallow nests. Wash nests from under eaves with a strong stream of water. This must be done consistently over an extended period, otherwise the birds will rebuild the mud colony. Or, after washing nests away, string a wire across the area along the junction of the wall and the roof overhang and drape a 12-inch curtain of aluminum foil or polyethylene sheeting over it. This prevents cliff swallows from attaching their nests to the wall—the new surface is too smooth. If the problem continues, contact a licensed pest control operator.

Sapsuckers

Sapsucker damage.

Sapsuckers are members of the woodpecker family that feed on tree bark and sap. The red-breasted sapsucker (*Sphyrapicus varius ruber*) is found in the Pacific Northwest and British Columbia. The yellow-bellied sapsucker (*S. varius varius*) is common throughout much of the United States. Sapsuckers peck into many trees before finding a suitable one that has sap with a high sugar content. Once the birds find a favorite tree, they visit it many times per day and feed on it year after year. Sapsucker damage to the tree is very distinctive. The bird drills uniform round or rectangular holes in the bark, ¼ inch in diameter, arranged in horizontal rings around the trunk. Sap often oozes from the holes, and portions of the tree bark may fall off after sapsuckers have drilled many holes. The tree trunk may eventually be girdled by sapsucker drilling, causing the tree above the damaged area to die. Sometimes birds' beaks are contaminated with fungus spores, or the spores are blown or splashed into the holes. Once inside the tree, the disease organisms may damage or kill the tree.

Control: It is difficult to stop sapsucker damage to trees. Wrapping the damaged trunk with burlap or smearing a sticky material (such as the latex used for ant control) above and below the holes may inhibit new pecking damage. (For a list of trees commonly attacked by sapsuckers, see page 547.)

Earthworms

Earthworm (life size).

Earthworms are beneficial soil-dwelling animals. They surface in large numbers during a heavy rain or at other times when the soil is saturated with water. As they tunnel through the ground, earthworms ingest soil, digesting any organic matter in it. They may deposit the soil that passes through their bodies into crumbly mounds (castings) on the soil surface. A large population of earthworms can sometimes be a nuisance in a lawn when many castings accumulate. Earthworm tunnels help to aerate and loosen the soil, however, improving soil drainage and tilth and facilitating root growth. Although earthworms are most numerous in the top 6 inches of soil, they may tunnel 6 feet into the ground, bringing up deep layers of soil to the surface. Sometimes earthworms enter the drainage holes of containers sitting on the soil or sunken into the ground. As their castings accumulate in the container, the drainage becomes clogged.

Control: For the most part, earthworm activity in the ground is beneficial and should be encouraged. If you have trouble with castings on your lawn, see page 78 for information on how to treat this problem. To prevent earthworms from getting into containers in or on the ground, place a piece of screen over the drainage hole, elevate the container slightly, or set the container on a layer of gravel or cinders; earthworms will not move through such a coarse layer.

A Gallery of Household Pests

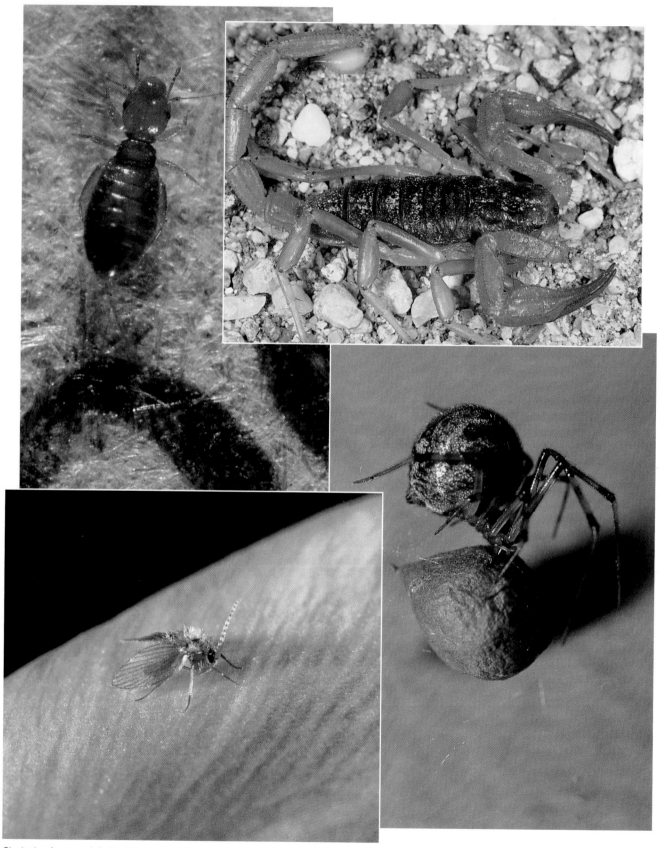

Clockwise from top left: booklouse, scorpion, house spider, and drain fly.

Improved living standards have markedly diminished parasite and fly problems. Yet the same buildings that shelter people also shelter household pests, which are often attracted to homes by conditions in the yard and garden.

INSPECTING THE OUTDOORS

Piles of grass clippings or other damp trash, along with weather conditions, can encourage sowbugs and pillbugs. Dampness can lead them into your home. Caterpillars of all sorts may wander indoors, looking for warmth and shelter. Larvae may even be blown in by the wind. Spiders and termites can inhabit your woodpile or wainscoting. Because indoor pest problems usually start outdoors, take your pest-control efforts out there. Is landscaping overgrown with weeds or plants that badly need thinning or trimming? Insects find such areas prime nesting habitat. If there is outdoor pet food or an open garbage can, you may be providing food and water, too. If you feed pets outdoors, remove food at night. Cover garbage cans tightly so raccoons and stray dogs can't invade and scatter contents. Sometimes the food you leave out for the birds becomes a pest attractant; remove leftovers from the ground.

Wear protective gloves at all times when cleaning yard trash. If you live in an area where brown recluse spiders, black widow spiders, poisonous snakes, biting ants, ground wasps, or scorpions are common, work with long-sleeved clothing and a long stick or pry bar when turning over logs or construction remnants.

Put leaves and lawn clippings in a container with a secure lid or in a properly constructed compost pile. Be aware that a compost pile must be functioning properly to reach temperatures high enough to destroy pests living in the clippings and debris. If your compost pile is not decaying adequately, destroy debris or haul it away promptly. Moving trash from one section of the yard to another merely moves the problem to another site.

Standing water in fishponds, decorative ponds, or unused aboveground or belowground swimming pools attracts all kinds of water-loving insects, from water beetles to mosquitoes. Bees and wasps like standing water, too—they are attracted by both reflected light and moisture.

When inspecting the building exterior, pay particular attention to the area where building meets earth. This is a favorite pest entrance. Wood piles invite termites, carpenter beetles, carpenter ants, and other cellulose chewers.

Discard excess construction materials or move them away from the house. If you are saving wood to burn in a fireplace, stack it well away from the house, on an elevated platform. If firewood won't be used for some time, spray it with Ortho® Termite & Carpenter Ant Killer to hold down pest populations. Follow label directions regarding time to allow between spraying and burning the wood.

Keep shrubs that are close to the house trimmed back so they do not touch the walls. Use mulch sparingly on any plants near the foundation of the home. Consider treating areas around the foundation with Ortho® Termite & Carpenter Ant Killer or Ortho® Home Defense® Perimeter & Indoor Insect Killer Pull 'N Spray to prevent pest entry; heed warnings regarding pets and beneficial wildlife such as birds.

Are there cracks or holes around doors or windows where insect pests can gain entry? Check all exterior doors, including garage doors and side entry doors. Check any areas where utility lines, such as power or phone lines, make entry. Use a good-quality caulk and a caulking gun to seal every crack you find. Weather-strip around doors and windows. This won't only help keep pests out, it will help insulate your home, thereby reducing your heating and cooling bills.

Inspect screens on doors, windows, and vents. Patch or replace them as necessary with screening small enough to keep tiny insects out. Buy or build a spark-arrester screen for your chimney, preferably of 1-inch mesh hardware cloth. Be sure your clothes dryer vent has a flap closure in proper working order.

How you eliminate indoor pests depends on many factors. These include the pest type, its life cycle, how it entered the home, how it moves about, and whether pets or children limit treatment options. A thorough inspection indoors will help keep potential entries closed to pests and ensure that you spot problems before they become severe.

Once pests enter your home, they need food, water, and appropriate hiding places. Eliminating these necessities will go a long way toward eliminating the pests.

Caulk cracks along baseboards and cabinets to destroy potential insect homes. Be aware that items stored for recycling can be attractive havens for pests. Piles of newspapers and bins of empty soft-drink cans offer both hiding places and food. If your community offers weekly curbside recycling, put out whatever materials you have collected each week. If you must take your efforts to a recycling center, add a trip there to your list of weekly chores.

Leaky pipes anywhere in the home provide the damp environment many insects seek. These pipes can become highly populated breeding grounds. Repair or replace faulty plumbing as soon as possible.

Drop ceilings, often used in converted basements or garages, may be inviting homes for rodents. Push one of the sections aside and flash a light around the space above the ceiling. You may find that it is littered with mouse and/or rat droppings and chewed insulation. Since neither children nor pets can reach this area, it is a fairly safe place for setting out traps or bait. Handle either with care.

Specific rooms in the house present particular pest-proofing problems. The sections that follow constitute a room-by-room tour and will alert you to problem areas that may attract pests.

Firewood can be a source of indoor pests. It is best to stack it well away from the house.

Top: Keep pantry food sealed in lock-tight plastic containers. Right: Before using any control spray in cabinets, remove all food, dishes, and other articles.

The kitchen: A seemingly immaculate kitchen may still be host to a daunting number of ants, cockroaches, grain moths, and beetles. Pests can gain entrance in packages of food or even in the bags from the grocery store.

Cockroaches and silverfish hide within the seams of cardboard cartons. If bringing cartons into the house is unnecessary or if you suspect the cleanliness, leave them outdoors.

Grains are particularly prone to insect pests. Check all flours, cake mixes, and cereals for infestation when you bring them into the home. Destroy contaminated foods immediately. Or, if you intend to return them to the store, keep them in an animal-proof container outdoors. If foods seem pest-free, seal each product in a separate lock-tight plastic container. Sealing these foods keeps insects out or, if the products are infested, keeps insects from spreading to other packages. Don't store grain products for long periods. Check them often so that if an infestation does occur it can be stopped as quickly as possible. Store large bags of pet food in a metal or plastic garbage can with a tight-fitting lid. Plastic is usually effective, but desperate rodents may actually chew through it and force you to turn to metal.

Of course, crumbs littering the counter, fruit ripening in a bowl, vegetable trimmings in the sink, and cake or bread protected only by plastic wrap offer a banquet to pests. Vigorous cleaning and a constant eye toward food protection will help starve invaders out of your home.

Pests need water as well as food. Repair leaky pipes. The kitchen offers other water

Use caulk and weather stripping to seal cracks around exterior doors.

sources. Water in the dish rack or the soggy sponge at the sink can provide plenty of liquid refreshment. Water may be collecting in the drain pan of your frost-free refrigerator. If you have pets, the water you put out for them can be used by less desirable animals.

Make a thorough stove check, both back and sides. Foods tend to drop or spill here and may attract household pests. If possible without disturbing gas or other connections, pull the stove away from the wall. Clean walls and all stove parts thoroughly and regularly.

Areas under the sink often contain sweaty or leaky pipes, paper bags, and other items among which pests hide. Use a flashlight to inspect pipe and utility-line entryways. Home centers sell caulk and other products that can be used to fill or cover the area between pipe and wall so

insects can't enter from outdoors. Clean trash containers daily. Clean areas under the sink thoroughly on a regular basis.

Every so often, clean behind kitchen drawers. Caulk around cupboards where they meet the wall. Purchase caulk that can be painted to match the surroundings.

Keeping a clean kitchen isn't always enough to prevent pests. You must also eliminate pest access, make regular sweeps through their hiding places, remove sources of food and water, and react quickly to pest infestations.

The bathroom and laundry room:
Although these rooms don't usually contain food for pests, they do provide an array of possible water sources. Repair leaky faucets and leaky or damaged toilet backs and bowls. A leak provides continual dampness for destructive insects and fungi that require water, and even a tiny long-term drip can cause severe damage to your home. Caulk cracks where pipes enter walls, and seal any open areas between toilet bowls and floor. Empty and clean bathtub and sink drain traps every week. Hair and other organic matter trapped there can provide a breeding ground for small flies of all kinds.

Check water connections to washing machines. Drips can occur anywhere along the lines. Clean filters in both washer and dryer regularly.

An often-overlooked infestation source is laundry brought home from a vacation or by youngsters returning from camp or college. Wash it immediately. Moths are the most common pest cargo in dirty clothing, though it may harbor other insects too.

The living room and bedrooms:
Garage-sale finds, thrift-store treasures, antiques, and donations from friends or relatives can be alive with pests. Inspect all used furniture carefully. Consider spraying newly acquired pieces with insecticide before bringing them indoors.

Vacuuming regularly is a good front-line pest preventive. Use a corner attachment to clean hard-to-reach areas, where carpet insects and fleas tend to hide. Move heavy furniture occasionally so you can vacuum behind and underneath it, including where furniture legs meet carpet. Vacuum under furniture cushions and into furniture folds. After each vacuuming, empty the vacuum-cleaner bag outdoors, and place the contents in a sealed bag for disposal. Many insects find the vacuum-cleaner bag a perfect place to breed.

Regular dusting is also important. Scientists are determining the dust mite is a source of human allergy.

In sensitive individuals, dust mites may cause asthmatic symptoms. Wash bedclothes frequently to keep dust mites from accumulating in mattresses and pillows.

The attic: Even if it is only a storage place, clean your attic regularly. Pest bugs frequently move into attics because they are dark, unoccupied, and often somewhat damp. Discard attic debris, and use a broom to sweep spiderwebs out of the corners. Consider using a high-powered indoor insect fogger on a regular basis to discourage problems. Seal all cracks, and put small-mesh screen on vents.

In addition to damaging items in your home and encouraging rot and other structural problems, roof and plumbing leaks can provide water for many unwanted attic residents. Trace a leak to its source—water tends to run along rafters or framing before it seeks an exit—and correct the problem as soon as possible.

One potential inhabitant of the attic should be encouraged to stay outside, but not driven away. Bats devour an immense number of insect pests, and can be highly beneficial. If one or more has taken up residence in your attic, wait until they have left on their nightly feeding flight and install screening to prevent reentry. Purchase a bat house and hang it in an appropriate site. Your insect-control program will get a welcome boost.

The basement: Like attics, basements are dark, damp, unoccupied, and often full of stored materials. These conditions provide ideal hiding and breeding places for pests. Use an indoor fogger in your basement if it appears to be harboring large numbers of insects.

Regularly inspect basement floors for damp areas and cracks. These can indicate overhead leaks from plumbing. Correct leaks and patch cracked areas so that insects don't crawl up from the soil underneath the floor. Check all exposed wood, particularly in areas close to the ground. Decay organisms often enter a home at low points and move to the rest of the house.

CONTROLLING PESTS SAFELY

The improper use and disposal of insect and rodent control materials may cause more problems than the pest.

Control preparation: Before using any control, read all the instructions thoroughly. If the instructions are unclear, ask a knowledgeable clerk or an agent from your county extension service to explain them to you. Follow instructions exactly. If you are physically unable to use the material as stated, call a licensed pest control contractor for assistance.

To avoid having to store spray mixtures, try to use all the fluid on the day it's made. Store mixed and unmixed controls where children can't reach them by any means, including by climbing on something. Don't transfer control materials from one container to another—children and pets can easily spill pesticides or rodenticides in cups, glasses, or open bottles. Immediately return any undiluted excess to the original labeled container. Never leave control materials in an unlabeled container.

Safe use: To avoid inhaling chemical vapors, have good air movement available when using controls. Open windows and doors for cross-ventilation. Make certain, before using an aerosol, that the spray is pointed away from you. Don't use a spray near an open flame and don't smoke while spraying—some controls are flammable. Don't throw aerosol cans into a fire, because

heat may make them explode. If any chemical control gets on your body, wash it off immediately. After handling chemicals, wash your hands before touching food.

Safe disposal: Pest control presents two disposal problems: getting rid of chemicals and their containers and getting rid of dead pests.

■ **Disposal of chemicals:** In some communities throwing chemicals or their containers in the trash or pouring them down the drain is illegal. Most of these communities have set aside special days for the collection of hazardous wastes. On these days you can dispose of your pest controls and pest-control containers along with used motor oil, empty paint cans, and the like. If such a service is unavailable in your area, take your controls and containers to a local collection site as soon as possible.

If pest-control containers can go into the regular trash, rinse them out thoroughly. Then wrap them in newspaper before putting them out for pickup with the rest of the garbage.

■ **Disposal of dead pests:** Don't forget that the end product of your efforts is chemically destroyed insects or rodents. Sweep or vacuum up dead insects, and seal the remnants in a plastic bag. Keep dead rodents away from children and pets by sealing carcasses in bags and discarding them in a garbage can with a tight-fitting lid. If this isn't possible, or if trash pickup is infrequent, bury rodents deep in the soil so animals can't dig them up.

When storing clothing in plastic bags, wrap mothballs in paper before inserting them into clothing, making sure that they don't touch the fabric or plastic.

PESTS AROUND THE HOME

Houseflies

Housefly (7× life size).

Problem: Flies are present in the home and outdoor living areas.

Analysis: The housefly (*Musca domestica*) is a common insect pest throughout the world. In addition to being annoying, it can spread parasites and several diseases serious to humans. Several other closely related fly species, including face flies (*M. autumnalis*) and little houseflies (*Fannia canicularis*), may also infest the home. Flies feed on and lay their eggs in decaying organic materials. The eggs hatch within several days or even 12 hours, if conditions are ideal. The creamy-white maggots (up to ⅓ inch long) burrow into and feed on the decaying material for several days, pupate, and then emerge as adult flies. Under warm conditions, the entire life cycle may be completed within 14 days. Cooler conditions will greatly extend this period. The flies usually live for 15 to 25 days.

Solution: To reduce the fly population, maintain sanitary conditions in the home and garden. Keep garbage tightly covered, and dispose of it regularly. Keep the undersides of lawn mower decks clean of grass clippings. Maintain mulch piles well away from the living area. Keep door and window screens in good condition. Kill flies indoors with Ortho® Flying Insect Killer or Ortho® Home Defense® Perimeter & Indoor Insect Killer Pull 'N Spray. Treat entire rooms with Ortho® Indoor Insect Fogger. Kill flies outdoors with Ortho® Home Defense® Perimeter & Indoor Insect Killer Pull 'N Spray. Catch flies outdoors with Ortho® Bug-B-Gon® Full-Season Fly Traps.

Drain flies

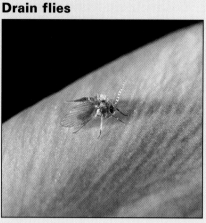

Drain fly (6× life size).

Problem: Small mothlike flies with hairy wings and tan bodies emerge from drains of sinks and bathtubs, particularly in spring. Flies may also appear from under floors, in crawl spaces, or, rarely, from air conditioners or dehumidifiers. Once present, flies travel throughout the indoor living space.

Analysis: Several species of insects in the *Psychodidae* family lay their eggs in drainpipes, leaky pipes, or faulty air-conditioning or dehumidifying equipment. Larvae live in films that develop above the permanent water level in pipes. Exact size and color vary according to species, but all drain flies are mothlike. Life cycles also vary with species and conditions. Check for larvae in drains using a screwdriver or knife to scrape the film off the inside of the drainpipe. If present, larvae are clearly visible to the eye.

Solution: Use a stiff brush to clean all drains, and then apply drain cleaner. Spraying affected areas with an insecticide containing *malathion* can control adult drain flies. To avoid recurrence, keep drains clean. Flies coming from crawl spaces, from under floors, or from air conditioners or similar equipment indicate leaking pipes or other problems that should be repaired. After repairs are made, allow the affected area to dry, and apply an appropriate insecticide to kill adult flies.

Vinegar flies

Vinegar fly (20× life size).

Problem: Tiny (up to ⅙ inch), yellowish-brown, clear-winged insects fly around rotting fruit and vegetables, garbage cans, and other wet, fermenting, or rotting materials. These insects fly in a slow, hovering manner.

Analysis: Vinegar flies (*Drosophila* species), insects also known as fruit flies, don't constitute a serious health menace but can be annoying in locations where garbage, fruit, or vegetables are allowed to rot and ferment. The adult female flies lay their eggs in the decaying fruit or vegetables. The eggs hatch in a few days, and the tiny maggots feed on yeasts growing in the decaying food. The maggots pupate and become adults; the entire life cycle takes only 10 to 20 days.

Solution: To control the fly population, maintain sanitary conditions. Keep garbage tightly covered, and dispose of it regularly. Wash garbage cans on a regular basis. Kill flies with a spray or fogger containing *allethrin*, *chlorpyrifos*, or *pyrethrins*.

Household spiders

House spider with web case.

Problem: Spiderwebs and spiders are in secluded, rarely disturbed areas in and around the home.

Analysis: Many kinds of spiders wander into the home. With only a few exceptions, these familiar creatures are harmless and can't reproduce in the home. Spiders are often beneficial, feeding on other spiders and insects, including such household pests as flies and moths. The more insects there are inside the home, the more likely spiders will live there. Most spiders spin silken webs. Some, such as tarantulas, are active hunting spiders that don't produce webs. When spiders bite humans, it is usually because they were threatened, or somehow provoked. Only a few spiders, particularly the black widow and brown recluse, are dangerous to people, but their bites are rarely fatal. (For information on black widow and brown recluse spiders, see page 521.)

Solution: Knock down webs with a broom or dust mop. Kill spiders and the insects they feed on by spraying infested areas with Ortho® Home Defense® Perimeter & Indoor Insect Killer Pull 'N Spray, or treat entire rooms with Ortho® Indoor Insect Fogger. To reduce the number of spiders entering the home, seal cracks, inspect and repair window screens, and clean up debris outdoors that may harbor spiders or their prey. Spray with Ortho® Home Defense® Perimeter & Indoor Insect Killer Pull 'N Spray around doors, windows, and foundations, where spiders may enter.

Crickets

House cricket (life size).

Problem: Crickets are chirping in the home. These insects are light to dark brown, ½ to ¾ inch long, and have long antennae that curve back along the sides of the body.

Analysis: The two types of crickets that may invade the home are field crickets (*Gryllus*) and house crickets (*Acheta domesticus*). Field crickets usually live outdoors, feeding on vegetation and plant debris. In the fall, when their natural food supply fails, or during periods of heavy rainfall, they may invade buildings in search of food. Field crickets can't reproduce in the home and usually die by winter. House crickets, however, can survive and reproduce indoors. During the day, both types of crickets hide in dark, warm locations. Male crickets make a chirping sound by rubbing the file and scraper on their forewings together. Crickets may chew on fabric and paper items, and large numbers of them may cause serious problems.

Solution: To control crickets outdoors, apply Ortho® Home Defense® Perimeter & Indoor Insect Killer Pull 'N Spray along the foundation of the house. To control crickets indoors, spray with Ortho® HomeDefense Hi-Power Brand Roach, Ant & Spider Killer or Ortho® Home Defense® Perimeter & Indoor Insect Killer Pull 'N Spray, or treat entire rooms with Ortho® Indoor Insect Fogger. Remove dense vegetation and debris from around the building foundation where crickets may hide. Seal openings around doors and windows. Apply a barrier spray of Ortho® Bug-B-Gon® Multi-Purpose Insect Killer around the house.

Night-flying insects

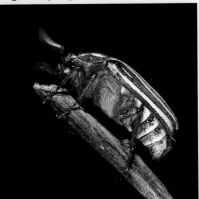

June beetle.

Problem: Numerous insects are flying around indoor or outdoor lights at night. Their physical presence as well as their buzzing or droning is bothersome. Dead insects may accumulate below lights, attracting ants and other insects to the site.

Analysis: Many night-flying insects use the moon and stars as points of orientation to help them discern direction. When they see a brighter source of light, such as a lightbulb, they mistake it for one of these objects and orient to it, eventually colliding with the light. Lights attract a wide variety of night-flying insects, including most moths, certain beetles, mosquitoes, flies, gnats, and leafhoppers. When many insects become adults during a short period, large numbers may be attracted to lights.

Solution: Spray Ortho® Home Defense® Perimeter & Indoor Insect Killer Pull 'N Spray or burn citronella candles to temporarily eliminate outdoor flying insects. Spray Ortho® Home Defense® Perimeter & Indoor Insect Killer Pull 'N Spray to control flying insects indoors. Replace white lightbulbs with yellow ones; yellow light is less visible to insects and therefore less attractive to them. Use lightbulbs of lower wattage, and turn off lights when not needed. Locate outdoor lights at least 25 feet from doors and windows. Install or repair screens to prevent insects from moving indoors. If entertaining outdoors, consider using candles for light. Their lower light intensity is less attractive to insects.

PESTS AROUND THE HOME (continued)

Swimming pool pests

Water boatman (8× life size).

Earwigs

Earwig (2× life size).

Outdoor-originating cockroaches

American cockroach (life size).

Problem: Insects are in the swimming pool. The insects may be actively swimming in the pool, or they may be floundering or dead. Even well-maintained pools can have this problem. Some of these insects may inflict painful bites.

Analysis: Many insects and related organisms become pests in swimming pools. They may either fall in the pool and drown or live in the pool. Sowbugs, millipedes, springtails, and other insects living in nearby vegetation may crawl into the pool and drown. They are particularly common if there is an abundance of organic matter under shrubbery near the pool. Bees and wasps may fall into the pool as they search for water. Insects that can live in clean pools include back swimmers, giant water bugs, the water boatman, and water striders. Back swimmers and giant water bugs can inflict painful bites similar to bee stings. These insects, as well as many moths, are attracted to pool lights. If a swimming pool is not kept chlorinated and clean, mosquitoes and midges may breed in the water.

Solution: Skim insects off the surface with a dip net. Use lights sparingly near pools, and switch to yellow lights (which are less attractive to insects) if you have a continual problem. Or place a very bright light source a couple of hundred feet away to attract night fliers away from the pool. Keep the pool chlorinated and reasonably clean. Keep grass and shrubbery trimmed near the pool. Control insects in nearby shrubbery. Don't spray the pool directly.

Problem: Reddish-brown, elongated insects up to 1 inch long with straight or curved

pincers projecting from the rear of the body are present in the home. They are often found in dark, secluded places such as in pantries, closets, and drawers and even in bedclothes. They may be seen scurrying along baseboards or moving from room to room.

Analysis: Several species of earwigs may infest the home, including the European earwig (*Forficula auricularia*), the ringlegged earwig (*Euborellia annulipes*), and the striped earwig (*Labidura riparia*). Earwigs are usually found in the garden, where they feed on moss, decaying organic matter, vegetation, and other insects. Earwigs may invade homes, however, through cracks or openings in the foundation, doors, and window screens, especially during hot, dry spells. Although they don't damage household furnishings, their presence is annoying, and they may feed on stored food items or hide in areas where food is kept. They may inflict painful pinches when provoked.

Solution: Store food in sealed containers. Repair cracks and openings in window screens, doors, and the building foundation. Use a barrier treatment of Ortho® Home Defense® Perimeter & Indoor Insect Killer Pull 'N Spray to prevent entrance to the house. Control earwigs indoors by spraying with Ortho® Home Defense® Perimeter & Indoor Insect Killer Pull 'N Spray or spray with Ortho® Roach, Ant & Spider Killer. To prevent reinfestations, control earwigs outdoors.

Problem: Cockroaches are found outdoors in woodpiles, ground covers, leaf litter,

and other protected areas. Occasionally they wander indoors.

Analysis: Outdoor-originating cockroaches, often called *wood roaches*, live mainly outdoors; they occasionally wander inside but cannot reproduce there. The American cockroach (*Periplaneta americana*) and the smoky-brown cockroach (*P. fuliginosa*) are two species that can live equally well indoors and outdoors in warm climates. The smoky-brown cockroach, in particular, is a pest in many southern states. It moves indoors when weather conditions outside become adverse. Cockroaches that live outdoors are more likely to wander indoors if there are suitable places for them to live and breed next to the house. Favorite habitats include plantings of ground covers and piles of wood, compost, and other debris. Cockroaches are scavengers, eating decaying plant and animal material.

Solution: To keep cockroaches from coming indoors, move compost and woodpiles away from the house. Clean up litter and debris near the home. Apply Ortho® Home Defense® Perimeter & Indoor Insect Killer Pull 'N Spray as a 2- to 5-foot barrier around the foundation and in nearby ground covers. Repair windows, screens, cracks, and crevices in the walls and foundation. Inspect firewood before bringing it indoors.

House centipedes

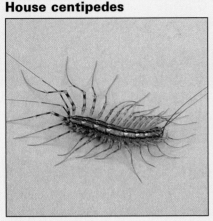

House centipede (life size).

Problem: A thin wormlike creature with long legs is crawling on the floor or wall. It is up to 1½ inches long, with very long antennae and legs in comparison with its body size. The antennae and rear set of legs can be more than twice the length of the body. The creature runs quickly, with sudden stops.

Analysis: House centipedes (*Scutigera coleoptrata*) are found both indoors and outdoors in warm regions of the United States but only indoors where winters are colder. Unlike other centipedes, which wander indoors but can't reproduce there, house centipedes live and reproduce indoors. House centipedes prey on other insects and become most numerous where there is an abundance of insects to eat. They prefer dampness and thrive in typically moist areas such as cellars, closets, and bathrooms. Outdoors they are common in moist piles of compost and other debris. House centipedes are most active at night. They seldom bite humans, but when they do, the bite is no more severe than a bee sting.

Solution: To control house centipedes and the insects they feed on, spray indoor areas with Ortho® Home Defense® Perimeter & Indoor Insect Killer Pull 'N Spray or Ortho® Roach, Ant & Spider Killer. Eliminate moist areas in and around the home. Air out damp places. Outdoors, remove piles of compost and other materials that provide hiding places near the house. Treat the perimeter of the house with Ortho® Home Defense® Perimeter & Indoor Insect Killer Pull 'N Spray.

Silverfish and firebrats

Silverfish (3× life size).

Problem: Paper and fabric products are stained yellow, chewed, or notched and may be covered with excrement and silver or gray scales. Flat, slender, wingless insects up to ½ inch long may scurry away when infested products are moved. These insects have long, thin antennae and are either silvery and shiny or dull and mottled gray.

Analysis: Silverfish (*Lepisma* species) and firebrats (*Thermobia* species) are common household pests that are similar in size, shape, and feeding habits except for their coloration and hiding places. Silverfish are silvery and prefer damp, cool to warm locations (70° to 80°F) such as basements. Firebrats are mottled gray and prefer damp, hot locations (90° to 105°F) such as hot-water pipes and areas near the oven or furnace. These pests are active at night and hide during the day. They feed on a wide range of foods, especially products high in starches, including human food, paper, paste, and linen and other fabrics. Silverfish damage books by feeding on the bindings. These pests crawl throughout the house, along pipes and through holes and crevices in the walls and floor. The adult females lay eggs in cracks and openings behind baseboards and in other protected areas.

Solution: Treat with Ortho® Indoor Insect Fogger according to label directions. Where practical, seal cracks and crevices in the infested areas. Outdoors, treat the perimeter of the house with Ortho® Bug-B-Gon® Multi-Purpose Insect Killer Granules. Store valued papers and clothes in tightly sealed plastic bags.

Booklice

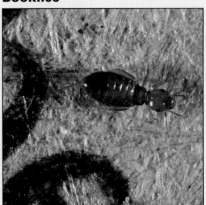

Booklouse (15× life size).

Problem: Numerous tiny insects the size of a pinhead are crawling in stored food products or around books. These insects may emerge from behind walls for several months after construction of a building. They move quickly along surfaces in a hesitating, jerky manner.

Analysis: Booklice thrive in warm, damp, undisturbed places. They feed mainly on microscopic molds that may develop on certain kinds of adhesives used in book binding and wallpaper. Booklice sometimes infest damp Spanish moss, straw, or other vegetable matter used in making upholstered furniture. They feed directly on cereals and other starchy materials and on dead insects. Although booklice contaminate stored food with their body parts, they don't cause other damage. Insect damage seen on books is caused by other insects, such as silverfish or cockroaches. Booklice don't bite or carry disease organisms.

Solution: Dry out infested areas of the home. If booklice are in the food pantry, search for and throw out any infested food. Ventilation and artificial heat can aid in drying out cupboards. Booklice will disappear from new homes as the structure dries. Control infested furniture by thoroughly drying the item in sunlight for several days, having it fumigated by a pest control operator, or, if practical, discarding the infested stuffing. Infested areas can also be treated with an insecticide containing *pyrethrins*. Make sure the site you spray is listed on the product label.

PESTS AROUND THE HOME (continued)

Carpet beetles

Carpet beetles and larvae (4× life size).

Ants

Black ants (2× life size).

Clothes moths

Clothes moths (life size).

Problem: Irregular holes are chewed in carpets, blankets, clothing, and other articles made of animal fur, hair, feathers, or hides. Light brown to black grubs up to ¼ inch long may be seen crawling on both damaged and undamaged items. The grubs are distinctly segmented and covered with circular rows of stiff, dark hairs.

Analysis: The larvae of carpet beetles (*Attagenus megatoma* and *Anthrenus* species) damage carpets, clothes, upholstery, and other products of animal origin. Some species also feed on stored foods. The adult beetles are about ⅛ inch long and may be black or mottled gray, brown, and white. They usually live outdoors, feeding on pollen and nectar. The beetles fly into homes during the late spring or early summer and lay their eggs in cracks and crevices and on clothes, carpets, or other materials. The emerging larvae seek out dark, undisturbed locations in which to feed. They shed their skins several times during their development. Most of the larvae hibernate during the winter and pupate in the spring.

Solution: Shake out, brush, and air infested clothes and blankets. To kill remaining grubs, dry-clean infested items. Vacuum infested rooms, particularly under furniture and in corners. Destroy the sweepings immediately. Kill remaining insects with Ortho® Home Defense® Perimeter & Indoor Insect Killer Pull 'N Spray.

Problem: Ants are present in the house. Trails of ants may crawl on floors, walls, base boards, and counters and in cupboards. Ants are generally most troublesome in the kitchen or pantry.

Analysis: Several species of ants invade households. Most ants are strongly attracted to sweets, starches, fats, and grains and invade households in order to carry these foods back to their nests. Adverse outdoor conditions, such as flooding or drought, may cause ants to move their nests or colonies into buildings. Ant colonies are often built underground in the garden but may also be found under flooring and in building foundations, wall partitions, attics, and other protected locations. Ant colonies may contain from several hundred to several thousand individuals. Colonies may be located by following the established ant trails to their source. (For more information on ants, see page 459.)

Solution: Destroy ant colonies by dusting with Ortho® Ant-B-Gon® Dust or by spraying the nests and ant trails with Ortho® Home Defense® Perimeter & Indoor Insect Killer Pull 'N Spray. Eliminate ant colonies by treating anthills with Ortho® Orthene® Fire Ant Killer. Store food in sealed containers, and keep kitchens and pantries free of exposed foods. Place Ortho® Ant-B-Gon® Baits in areas where ants have been observed.

Problem: Holes are chewed in clothing, blankets, carpets, pillows, and upholstery. Infested articles may be covered with a webbing of silken tubes, cases, or strands. Shiny white caterpillars up to ½ inch long may be seen crawling on damaged items.

Analysis: The larvae of the small, yellowish to tan clothes moth (*Tineola bisselliella* and *Tinea pellionella*) damage clothes and other items made of fur, wool, feathers, and leather. Female moths attach their eggs to the fabric. Soon after the larvae emerge they spin silken tubes, strands, or cases. The larvae usually feed from within these protective casings but may crawl out to feed while unprotected. The larvae pupate in cocoons attached by silken threads to the infested item and emerge as moths. New infestations occur when moths lay eggs on clothing, carpets, and other articles and when moth-, larva-, and egg-ridden items are stored with uninfested articles. Clothes moths aren't attracted to light.

Solution: Shake out, brush, and air infested clothes and blankets in a sunny location. To kill remaining moths, dry-clean infested items. Place in airtight containers with mothballs or flakes. Vacuum or sweep infested rooms, and destroy the sweepings immediately. Seek professional help to protect carpets and furs.

Clover mites

Clover mite (30× life size).

Problem: Reddish-brown mites smaller than a pinhead, with long front legs, are present in the home in the fall. They may be found on walls, windowsills, floors, and furniture and even in bedclothes and clothing. When crushed, these mites leave a blood red stain. They are often so numerous that they give infested surfaces a reddish appearance.

Analysis: Clover mites (*Bryobia praetiosa*) are found throughout the United States. Clover mites feed and reproduce on clover, grasses, and other plants. They are most active in spring and fall and on warm winter days. The mites lay eggs during the summer and fall. The young, which hatch from these eggs, feed on vegetation and then migrate into homes and other protected areas during the early fall. Mites enter homes through cracks or openings in the foundation and around doors and windows. Mite activity usually decreases when temperatures are higher than 85°F or lower than 40°F.

Solution: Remove mites from household furnishings by vacuuming them from infested surfaces. Don't crush the mites, because they will leave a red stain. Kill mites indoors by spraying them directly with Ortho® Home Defense® Perimeter & Indoor Insect Killer Pull 'N Spray. Treat outdoor areas with Ortho® Home Defense® Perimeter & Indoor Insect Killer Pull 'N Spray as a barrier treatment around the foundation. Keep a strip of soil 18 to 24 inches wide around the foundation of the building free of vegetation and debris to reduce mite movement into homes.

Box elder bugs

Box elder bug (4× life size).

Problem: During the fall, hordes of brownish-black bugs ½ inch long with red stripes on their wings swarm into the home and outdoor living areas. They congregate on walls, walks, furniture, drapes, and other objects. When crushed, they emit a strong, unpleasant odor.

Analysis: Box elder bugs (*Leptocoris* species) are insects that are common in all parts of the country. They are most numerous in areas where box elder trees (*Acer negundo*) grow. In the spring, the females lay their eggs in the bark of box elders or sometimes of maples, ash, and fruit trees. The young feed on tender twigs, foliage, and seeds through the spring and summer. During the fall, especially on bright, sunny days, the bugs migrate in large numbers into tree trunks, homes, buildings, or other dry, protected locations to hibernate for the winter. Box elder bugs don't feed on fabric or furniture, but they may stain household items with their excrement. Box elder bugs occasionally bite, and they may feed on houseplants.

Solution: Vacuum box elder bugs with a tank-type vacuum cleaner, and then destroy the bag, or spray the bugs with an insecticide containing *pyrethrins*. Spray outdoor areas with Ortho® Home Defense® Perimeter & Indoor Insect Killer Pull 'N Spray or Ortho® Termite & Carpenter Ant Killer. Keep the door and window screens repaired and the cracks around them well sealed.

Chiggers

Chigger-infested field.

Problem: Welts and hard, raised bumps (papules) appear on the skin, particularly on parts of the body where clothing is binding or where body parts come in contact, such as at the belt line, the armpits, or the backs of the knees and under cuffs and collars. Itching is severe and may last as long as two weeks. Welts and itching often develop within several hours to a day after the affected person has been in a scrubby, thicket-covered, or otherwise heavily vegetated area.

Analysis: Chiggers (*Trombicula* species), parasites also known as red bugs, are the larval forms of several closely related microscopic mites. Only the larvae are harmful. They hatch from eggs laid in the soil of uncultivated, scrubby woodland or marshy areas and attach themselves to people and other hosts as they pass by. Chiggers insert their mouthparts into the skin and feed on blood for several days until they become engorged and drop off.

Solution: To remove chiggers from your skin, bathe thoroughly in hot, soapy water. Contact your pharmacist for compounds to relieve the itching. When walking through chigger-infested areas, wear protective clothing, and tightly button or tape sleeves, pant cuffs, and collars. Apply a repellent containing *diethyl toluamide* (DEET) to the skin and clothing, especially around the ankles, underarms, waist, sleeves, and cuffs. Treat infested lawns around your home with Ortho® Bug-B-Gon® Multi-Purpose Insect Killer Granules.

PET AND BODY PESTS (continued)

Fleas

Fleas.

Flea larvae (6× life size).

Bedbugs

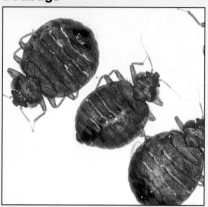

Bedbugs (6× life size).

Problem: Fleas infest pets, pet quarters, rooms, carpets, upholstered furniture, and the garden.

Analysis: Fleas, pests of humans, dogs, cats, and many other warm-blooded animals, are found throughout the world. In addition to causing annoying bites, they can transmit several serious diseases such as bubonic plague, murine typhus, and tapeworms. The cat flea (*Ctenocephalides felis*), the dog flea (*C. canis*), and the human flea (*Pulex irritans*) are the most common species found around the home. These fleas have a wide host range, attacking humans, dogs, cats, and several other animals. The female fleas lay eggs shortly after feeding on animal blood. The eggs are usually laid on the host's body or in the host's bedding. The eggs often fall off the host's body into floor crevices, dog and cat boxes, carpets, and other areas where the infested animals spend time. Within 10 days, the eggs hatch into tiny, wormlike larvae that feed on dried blood and excrement. Pupation occurs after one week to several months. The adult fleas may emerge after only one week if conditions are favorable, or emergence may be delayed up to one year. The adults often remain in their pupal cocoons until a host is present. A flea's life cycle may vary from two weeks up to two years. Because fleas have the ability to survive for many months in their cocoons, they can remain in vacated residences for long periods of time, waiting to emerge and bite returning pets and humans. Fleas are mainly spread by infested animals. Uninfested animals can easily pick up fleas when visiting flea-ridden areas. Fleas may also be spread by infested articles of clothing or furniture.

Solution: First, treat infested pets. Spray, dust, or shampoo them with a product made for killing fleas. Alternatively, add a product containing *lufenuron* to their food or place spots of a product containing *fipronil* or *imidacloprid* on their skin according to label directions. Next, spray infested animal quarters with Ortho® Home Defense® Perimeter & Indoor Insect Killer Pull 'N Spray. Destroy infested pet bedding, or wash it in hot, soapy water. Vacuum carpeting, chairs, sofas, and other areas or objects that may contain eggs and larvae-ridden lint or debris, and then dispose of the vacuum bag. Kill remaining indoor fleas with Ortho® Indoor Insect Fogger. Kill fleas in the yard with Ortho® Bug-B-Gon® Multi-Purpose Insect Killer Granules. To prevent reinfestation, keep infested animals out of the house and yard, and keep pets away from infested areas. Flea collars treated with *methoprene* or *pyriproxyfen* render flea eggs sterile, preventing fleas from multiplying.

Problem: Painful swellings develop on the body. Dark brown to black spotted stains appear on pillows, sheets, and other bedclothes. When the lights are turned on at night, reddish-brown, oval-shape bugs about ¼ inch long may be seen crawling on the skin and bedding.

Analysis: Distasteful bedbugs (*Cimex lectularius*) infest homes where living conditions are unsanitary, and they may be transported to well-maintained residences on infested clothing and furniture. Bedbugs hide during the day behind baseboards and in mattresses and upholstered furniture, cracks and crevices in the floor, bed frames, ceilings, and similar locations. These pests are nocturnal and become very active at night. They crawl onto a sleeping person, pierce the skin, and suck the blood for several minutes. Bedbugs usually deposit telltale masses of dark excrement on bedding or resting sites after they feed. They are very mobile and may crawl from room to room during the night.

Solution: Spray baseboards, wall crevices, and floor cracks with an insecticide containing 2 percent *malathion* or *pyrethrin*. Spray bed frames and springs with an insecticide containing 1 percent *malathion* or *pyrethrin*. Mist mattresses with an insecticide containing 1 percent *malathion*, but don't soak them. Be sure to spray mattress seams and tufts. Let mattresses dry completely before reusing. Don't spray infant cribs and bedclothes. Treat again in 10 days to kill newly hatched bedbugs. Launder all bedding thoroughly. Keep the house clean.

Ticks

Pajaroello tick (2× life size).

Deer tick larva, nymph, and adult.

Dampwood termites

Dampwood termites.

Problem: Leathery, oval-shaped reddish-brown to dark brown pests are walking over or burrowed into the skin of a person or pet. Ticks range in size from 1/16 to 1/8 inch before feeding. On humans, they are usually found where skin is exposed; on pets, they are most often on the ears or neck. Ticks are most likely to be discovered after the host has walked through tall grass or vegetation, especially at the end of summer or in fall. In some instances a rash may break out at the site of the bite. The bite itself forms a strawberry-colored bull's-eye in the midst of the rash. The rash may also appear with no sign of a tick bite. Typical cold symptoms (fever, aches, pains, runny nose, cough) may follow and then disappear after a few days. Months to years later, pains in joints or periodic muscle pains can develop. For susceptible individuals, effects can be severely debilitating.

Analysis: Ticks, blood-sucking pests that are members of the *Ixodidae* family, are related to spiders. Ticks feed on humans, dogs, cats, and other animals by sinking their mouthparts and heads into the flesh of their hosts. If left undisturbed, they may continue to suck blood for as many as 15 days before dropping off. Severely infested dogs may become weak and even die if ticks aren't removed. Ticks can live for up to 18 months without food or water. Lyme disease is spread mainly by the deer tick (*Ixodes dammini*), although other tick species have also been found to be vectors for the disease. The bacterium that causes the disease, *Borrelia burgdorferi*, is a spirochete that affects large warm-blooded animals, causing joint stiffness, neurological problems, or both. In many cases, tick bites and the rash that accompanies them go unnoticed. Only when serious health problems appear, months to years later, is Lyme disease diagnosed. Even then, it is often mistaken for arthritis or a cold.

Solution: Reduce the danger of tick infestation by clearing yards of tall grass and weeds. Avoid setting out food for animal hosts, especially deer. Treat pets with tick repellents during tick season. If walking in fields, wear protective clothing and apply tick repellent. Tuck trousers into socks and shirts into trousers to avoid exposing skin. After spending time in tick habitat, inspect your body and clothing for ticks. Remove ticks by pulling them straight out with tweezers. Attempting to remove ticks by using a lighted cigarette, flame, or alcohol could induce the tick to regurgitate infection into the host. Save the removed tick in a jar in a refrigerator to show to a doctor if problems develop. If a rash appears within a month after a tick bite, see a physician. Early treatment with an antibiotic can destroy the Lyme disease. If animals are severely infested, consult a veterinarian. Control ticks around the home with Ortho® Bug-B-Gon® Multi-Purpose Insect Killer. Kill ticks in lawns with Ortho® Bug-B-Gon® Multi-Purpose Insect Killer Granules. A vaccine is now available for Lyme disease.

Problem: Yellowish-brown, winged insects, 1 inch long, swarm in or around buildings at dusk and tend to fly toward lights. They usually appear in the late summer or early fall but may be seen throughout the year. These insects resemble large flying ants but have thick rather than constricted waists. Their wings, which are shed after the reproductive stage, may be found around the building. Tiny, round or elongated, brown fecal pellets may be piled below cracks in infested wood.

Analysis: Dampwood termites are wood-feeding insects that cause structural damage to buildings with moist or wet, poorly ventilated timbers. Dampwood termites can't tolerate desiccation and can establish themselves only in moist wood. Except for the dark, winged swarmers, termites are white and wingless. Infestations start when a pair of winged reproductive termites leaves the main colony and burrows into a moist wood structure. As the colony grows, the wood is hollowed out. Infestations develop slowly and are usually small. Damage is most severe when many colonies are present.

Solution: If many swarmers emerge from the floorboards or from the perimeter of the building, contact a professional pest control operator. If the soil around the foundation and the foundation itself remain moist from faulty plumbing or improper grade, repair the plumbing or alter the grade. Prevent reinfestations by following the same procedures used to prevent subterranean termite infestations.

STRUCTURAL PESTS *(continued)*

Subterranean termites

Termites.

Termite-damaged book.

Drywood termites

Drywood termites.

Problem: On warm, sunny spring or fall days, brown to brownish-black winged insects, about ⅜ inch long, swarm in and around the house. These insects resemble flying ants but have thick rather than constricted waists and beaded rather than elbowed antennae. Their discarded wings may be found around the building. Earthen tubes extend from the soil up along the foundation and any other termite-proof surface to the infested wooden structures. Tubes are commonly found in basements and crawl spaces under buildings. When broken off, they are rebuilt within several days. Dark or blistered areas may develop in the flooring.

Analysis: Subterranean termites are wood-feeding insects that cause more structural damage to buildings than any other insect. Subterranean termites live in colonies as deep as 5 feet in the ground and infest wooden structures through tubes of soil they build over masonry or metal to bridge the gap from soil to wood. Except for dark, winged swarmers, these termites are white, wingless, and sensitive to moisture loss. They always remain within the nest, soil tubes, or infested wood, protected from desiccation and predators. Within their colony, termites maintain a complicated caste system that includes sterile workers and soldiers, winged reproducers, and an egg-laying queen. Colonies are formed when a pair of winged reproducers leaves the parent colony and excavates a nest in a piece of wood. As the new colony develops, galleries are formed deep in the soil. Termite colonies develop slowly—three or four years usually pass before the reproductive swarmers develop, and structural damage may not be noticed for several more years. When buildings are erected over established termite colonies, however, serious damage may occur within a year. Termites hollow out the inside of a wooden structure, leaving only an outer shell. Damage is most severe when they infest main supporting wooden beams and girders. One species of subterranean termite, the Formosan termite (*Coptotermes formosanus*), is not native to the United States but is present in areas of the Southeast and Southwest. This termite is more vigorous and aggressive than native North American species and is more difficult to control.

Solution: Termite infestations can be treated most effectively only after a thorough and accurate diagnosis of the damage is made. Accurate diagnosis is usually difficult and requires the aid of a professional termite or pest control operator. Once the termite colony has been located and the damage revealed, a physical or chemical barrier is placed between the soil and the building to prevent the termites from reaching the building. Apply Ortho® Termite & Carpenter Ant Killer to the soil around the building according to label instructions. Severe infestations should be treated by professional pest control operators. Prevent termite damage with Ortho® Termite & Carpenter Ant Killer used according to label directions. Discourage additional infestations by keeping the area under and around the house free of wood debris above and below the ground. If the soil around the foundation remains moist due to faulty plumbing or improper grade, repair the plumbing and alter the grade; termites prefer moist soil. For details on termite-resistant construction methods, contact a reliable building contractor or your local county extension office.

Problem: On warm, sunny days, ½-inch winged insects with reddish-brown heads may be seen flying in and around a building. These insects resemble flying ants but have thick rather than constricted waists. Their discarded wings may be found around the building. Tiny brown fecal pellets are piled below cracks in infested wooden structures.

Analysis: Drywood termites are wood-feeding insects that cause structural damage to buildings in warmer areas of the country. They live in colonies within wooden structures, including furniture. Except for dark, winged swarmers, drywood termites are white and wingless. They can withstand dry conditions for long periods of time. Infestations start when a pair of winged reproductive termites leaves the main colony and burrows into a wooden structure. As the colony grows, the wood is slowly hollowed out. Piles of termite pellets are pushed out through cracks in the weakened wood. Drywood termite infestations develop slowly and are usually small.

Solution: Drywood termites are most effectively controlled by fumigation, which must be done by a professional pest control operator. Several measures should be followed when building new structures to prevent future infestation. For details on termite-resistant construction methods, contact a reliable building contractor. Prevent infestations by following the same procedures used to prevent subterranean termite infestations (see at left).

Powderpost beetles

Powderpost beetle and larva (3× life size).

Emergence holes.

Problem: Wood flooring, structural timbers, cabinets, furniture, and other items are riddled with round holes that range in size from $\frac{1}{16}$ to $\frac{3}{8}$ inch. Wood powder or tiny pellets may be piled around the holes or on the floor below. When the infested item is tapped, wood powder or additional pellets are expelled from the holes. Tiny red, brown, or black beetles ranging in size from $\frac{1}{12}$ to $\frac{1}{3}$ inch may be seen crawling around the infested wood or, in the evening, flying around windows and electric lights. When the damaged wood is cut open, the inside is found to be riddled with sawdust-filled tunnels; or it may be pulverized into a mass of wood powder or pellets.

Analysis: Powderpost beetles, wood-feeding beetles that include the powderpost, false powderpost, and deathwatch beetles, damage wooden houses and household furnishings throughout the country. Powderpost beetles feed only on dead wood. They are brought into the home in infested timber or furnishings, or they may fly from infested lumber or woodpiles in the yard. The female beetles deposit their eggs in unfinished wood. The grubs that hatch from the eggs tunnel through the wood, leaving masses of wood powder or pellets behind them. They pupate just under the surface of the wood and emerge as adult beetles through the round holes they chew in the wood. Beetle eggs or larvae apparent in wood before it has been coated with paint, varnish, shellac, or other finishings can chew through the finished surface when they have matured, leaving behind round emergence holes. They don't lay eggs in coated wood surfaces, however, and reinfestation can't occur.

Solution: If the infestation is localized, remove and destroy badly infested timbers. Replace them with kiln-dried or insecticide-treated wood. Or treat unfinished exterior wood by painting it or spraying it with Ortho® Termite & Carpenter Ant Killer. Wherever possible, apply paint, shellac, varnish, paraffin wax, or other wood coatings to unfinished wood around the home to prevent further infestation. Inspect woodpiles periodically for signs of powderpost beetle infestation. Infested wood may also be treated with Ortho® Termite & Carpenter Ant Killer. If infestation is widespread, contact a professional pest control operator to fumigate the building. Individual pieces of furniture may also be fumigated to kill beetle eggs and larvae. Many pest control operators maintain fumigation chambers for movable items. Eggs and larvae in small wooden items may be killed by placing the items in the freezer for four days. When purchasing furniture, get assurances from the dealer that all woodwork is made from kiln-dried stock.

Carpenter ants

Slitlike holes. Inset: Carpenter ant (2× life size).

Problem: Black or reddish-black, winged or wingless ants up to $\frac{1}{2}$ inch long are seen around the home. Piles of sawdust may be found in the basement or attic, under porches, or near supporting girders or joists. Slitlike holes are often present in woodwork. On warm spring days, swarms of winged ants may cluster around windows. Unlike termites, these pests have constricted waists.

Analysis: Many closely related species of wood-damaging carpenter ants (*Camponotus* species) are found throughout the United States. Carpenter ants bore into moist, decaying wood, forming extensive galleries in which they make nests. They don't eat their sawdustlike wood borings but feed on other insects, plant sap, pollen, and seeds. When ant colonies grow too large, part of the colony migrates, often invading nearby homes. They either colonize undisturbed hollow spaces, such as walls, or bore into structural timbers, ceilings, and floors. They require damp and rotted wood. In addition to weakening wood, carpenter ants may infest pantries. They can inflict painful bites.

Solution: Dust baseboards, windowsills, door frames, and other places where ants crawl with Ortho® Ant-B-Gon® Dust. Sprinkle into nests if possible. Remove nearby logs, stumps, and woodpiles. Seal openings in the foundation, windows, and other access areas into the home. Spray along the foundation and around the outside of door and window frames and sills with Ortho® Home Defense® Perimeter & Indoor Insect Killer Pull 'N Spray or Ortho® Termite & Carpenter Ant Killer.

STRUCTURAL PESTS (continued)

Roundheaded borers

Old house borer (4× life size).

Old house borer damage.

Problem: Oval holes ¼ to ⅓ inch wide appear in walls and flooring. Or holes appear in wallpaper, plaster, linoleum, or other types of wood coverings. Sawdustlike borings may be piled around the holes. In some cases, rasping or ticking sounds may be heard before the holes appear, and the wood may be blistered or rippled. Grayish brown to black beetles, 1 inch long, with antennae, may be seen around the house.

Analysis: The larvae of roundheaded borer beetles, including the new house borer (*Arhopalus productus*) and the old house borer (*Hylotrupes bajulus*), cause damage to fir, pine, and other softwood structural timbers. The adults lay their eggs in the bark of weak and dying forest trees and, in the case of old house borers, in seasoned lumber. The yellow grubs tunnel into wood that is later incorporated into a building before the adult beetles emerge. Sometimes the grubs make rasping or clicking noises while they feed. If they are tunneling close to the surface, wood blistering or rippling may result. New house borers continue to emerge through holes in wood and wood coverings for up to a year after construction. New house borers generally don't cause structural damage. The holes they make in wood or covered wood surfaces are of cosmetic concern only, and the borers can't reinfest the building. Old house borer beetles generally don't emerge from timbers until three to five years after the building has been constructed. They are the only species of roundheaded borer that reinfests wood, and they may cause serious structural damage.

Solution: If damage occurs within a year after construction, new house borers are the problem. To repair new house borer damage, seal or fill emergence holes. Localized areas may be painted with Ortho® Termite & Carpenter Ant Killer, but because damage is only cosmetic and will stop within a year, this procedure is seldom necessary. If damage occurs three or more years after construction, old house borers are the problem. Buildings infested with old house borers must be fumigated. Contact a professional pest control operator to fumigate the building. To prevent future infestations of old house borers when building new structures, purchase pressure-treated wood.

Carpenter bees

Galleries. Inset: Adult carpenter bee (life size).

Problem: Metallic-blue or black buzzing bees fly around the home and yard. They may be seen entering and leaving holes about 1 inch wide in decks, posts, beams, rafters, and other wooden structures. When damaged wood is sliced open, partitioned galleries may be seen. The partitions may contain immature bees.

Analysis: Carpenter bees (*Xylocopa* species) are insects that don't usually cause serious damage; continued burrowing and gallery formation year after year will eventually weaken wooden structures, however. These insects burrow into wood to make their nests. The female bees partition the galleries into small cells in which the carpenter bee larvae mature. When bee nests are approached, the males hover around the head of the intruder. Although they are frightening because of their loud buzzing and large size, male bees do not sting, and females sting only when handled.

Solution: Paint wood surfaces once a year to discourage bee tunneling. Flood galleries in exposed wood with Ortho® Termite & Carpenter Ant Killer. Close the holes with putty, caulking compound, dowel pins, or plastic wood to prevent bees from returning to the nest.

Woodwasps

Woodwasp (life size).

Problem: Round holes about ¼ inch in diameter appear in wood floors, walls, doors, and other surfaces. Or holes appear in wallpaper, linoleum, carpeting, and other types of coverings over wood. Metallic blue, black, or multicolored wasplike insects may be seen flying around the home. These buzzing insects are 1 to 2 inches long and may have hornlike "tails."

Analysis: Woodwasps, insects also known as *horntails*, don't cause structural damage; the holes they make in wood or covered wood surfaces are only of cosmetic concern. Woodwasps lay their eggs in weak and dying forest trees. The adult insects emerge from the wood two to five years later, often long after the tree has been used for construction. Most woodwasp holes occur within the first two years after the cut wood has been used. These insects lay their eggs only in forest trees; they don't reinfest buildings.

Solution: Seal or fill emergence holes. You can't do anything to prevent the woodwasps from emerging. For future construction, purchase lumber that has been kiln dried or vacuum fumigated. These processes kill woodwasp larvae embedded in the wood.

Dry rot

Dry rot.

Problem: Foundation timbers, paneling, flooring, and other wooden structures are damp and soft, or they are dry, cracked, brown, and crumbling. Often the wood is broken into small, cubical pieces. Thin mats of white fungal strands may be seen on the rotted wood. Thick white, brown, or black fungal cords up to 2 inches wide may extend across the rotted area. Cords often extend over impenetrable surfaces such as brick and concrete to reach wood surfaces beyond.

Analysis: Dry rot is caused by fungi that live in the soil and grow into wood that is in direct contact with damp soil. The white fungal strands penetrate and decay the wood fibers, causing a soft rot. In some cases, the fungus draws water from the soil up through the thick fungal cords that extend across the rotted area. The water is used to moisten dry wood, providing the damp condition in which the fungus thrives. After the fungus dies, badly rotted wood cracks and crumbles into chunks when handled.

Solution: Remove any water-conducting fungal cords from the wood. Eliminate moist soil conditions around wood structures as much as possible by improving ventilation, changing soil grade and drainage, or fixing leaky plumbing. As soon as the soil and wood dry out, the fungus will become dormant. Replace badly rotted wood with wood that has been pressure-treated with preservatives. Remove all wood scraps around the foundation. When building new structures, use pressure-treated wood in all areas where wood and soil make contact.

Firewood insects

Beetle grub on firewood.

Problem: Firewood is riddled with holes. Small piles of sawdust accumulate around the holes or on the ground around the firewood. If the wood has been stored indoors, insects may be crawling around the firewood pile or flying around lights or windows.

Analysis: Many insects develop in and emerge from cut firewood. If infested wood is stored either indoors or outdoors so that it rests against the house, insects may invade the wooden structure of the house. Insects capable of moving from firewood into the structure include carpenter ants and powderpost beetles (see page 515) and termites (see pages 513 to 514). Some insects, such as bark beetles, most flat-headed borers, and round-headed borers (see page 434), and woodwasps (see at left), emerge from firewood but invade only living or recently killed trees; these insects won't damage structural wood or household articles.

Solution: Spray infested firewood outdoors with Ortho® Termite & Carpenter Ant Killer. Sprayed firewood may be burned one month following treatment. Store all firewood outdoors unless you plan to burn it within a couple of days. Don't lean an outdoor woodpile against the house; stack it so that there is an inch or more between the wood and the structure. If practical, choose a location for the woodpile at least 10 feet from the house.

BITING AND STINGING PESTS

Yellow jackets

Yellow jackets (2× life size).

Yellow jacket (2× life size).

Honeybees

Honeybee.

Problem: Yellow jackets are present around the home. They hover around patios, picnic areas, garbage cans, and other areas where food or garbage is exposed. Yellow jackets may be seen flying into underground nests. They will also nest in wall spaces or heating ducts if access is available. Yellow jackets inflict painful stings when threatened or harmed or when their nests are approached.

Analysis: Unlike most other species of wasps, yellow jackets (*Vespa* and *Vespula* species) live in large colonies, often numbering in the thousands. Some species of yellow jackets feed their offspring insects and spiders, while others scavenge scraps of meat from recreational areas or dump sites. These pests may also feed on nectar, sap, and other sugary fluids and may be seen hovering around soft drinks and cut fruit. Yellow jackets can inflict painful stings and are capable of repeated stings. The venom injected along with the sting causes reddening, swelling, and itching of the affected area. Some people who are very sensitive to the stings experience extreme swelling, dizziness, difficulty in breathing, and even death. yellow jackets are very protective of their nests, and large numbers may emerge to sting intruders. Some species of yellow jackets build their nests underground; the only evidence of the nest is a raised mound of dirt surrounding a depression several inches deep. Other species build football-shaped nests in trees or shrubs or under eaves. Most yellow jackets die in the late fall, and overwintering queens start new nests the following spring in a different location.

Solution: Keep food and garbage covered, and empty garbage cans frequently. To kill yellow jackets before picnicking, place an Ortho® Bug-B-Gon® Full-Season Yellow Jacket Trap downwind from the picnic or barbecue area (yellow jackets will be attracted to the bait and die within minutes after entering the trap). To remove yellow jackets from the vicinity, you must eliminate the nests. After locating the nests, spray them at dusk or during the night with Ortho® Hornet & Wasp Killer. Stay 8 feet away from the nest, and spray directly into the entrance hole. If you need to illuminate the area, use a flashlight covered with red cellophane. Use it for only short periods of time. Stop spraying when the yellow jackets begin to emerge; leave the nest area quickly by walking, not running, away. Repeat the spraying every evening until the insects fail to emerge, then quickly cover the hole with moistened soil. Contact a professional pest control operator to remove yellow jacket nests from difficult locations or from inside the home. If you are stung, apply a cold compress or ice pack to the affected area. If a severe reaction develops, call a doctor.

Problem: Bees hover around flowering plants in the garden or yard and may inflict stings when threatened or harmed. Large numbers of bees may cluster on shrubs or trees or other landscape plants. Hives may be located in attics, chimneys, and wall spaces.

Analysis: Honeybees (*Apis mellifera*) are familiar and often feared insects that provide honey and wax and are very important as pollinators. On warm, sunny days, bees forage for nectar among flowering garden plants, then return to their hives in the evening. When an established hive gets too crowded, thousands of bees leave in a swarm. Swarms fly for a mile or so before settling in a new location. En route, bees often rest in a tight cluster on a tree branch or other object. Some people are allergic to bee stings and experience extreme swelling, dizziness, difficulty in breathing, and possibly death. A bee doesn't sting more than once, because the stinger and venom sac rip out of its body when it flies away. The injured bee subsequently dies.

Solution: When stung, scrape the stinger off the skin with a knife or fingernail. Avoid squeezing it; this forces more venom into the wound. Apply cold compresses or ice packs to the swollen area. If a severe reaction develops, call a doctor immediately. Avoid using plants that are attractive to bees, especially around pools, patios, and other recreational areas. Rather than remove hives or swarms yourself, contact a professional beekeeper or pest control operator if you find a swarm or if bees are nesting in your home or garden.

Paper wasps

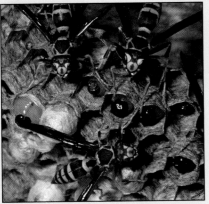

Paper wasps (life size).

Problem: Paper nests are suspended from eaves, ceilings, or branches. These nests are composed of exposed, open cells and have a honeycomb appearance. They are often umbrella-shape. Black or brown wasps with yellow or red stripes may be seen hovering around or crawling on the nests.

Analysis: Paper wasps (*Polistes* species), also known as *umbrella wasps*, usually live in small colonies consisting of 20 to 30 wasps. They build paper nests in which they raise their young. Paper wasps feed on insects, nectar, and pollen. They are not as aggressive and protective of their nests as are yellow jackets. (For information on yellow jackets, see page 518.) They will sting if threatened, however, causing swelling, itching, and more generalized symptoms in sensitive individuals.

Solution: To remove paper wasps from the vicinity, you must eliminate their nests. Spray the nests at dusk or during the night with Ortho® Hornet & Wasp Killer. Spray the nest from a distance of 8 feet. Stop spraying when wasps begin to emerge; leave the nest area quickly by walking, not running, away. Repeat the spraying every evening until the insects fail to emerge. Remove the nest and dispose of it. If you are stung, apply a cold compress or ice pack to the swollen area. If a severe reaction develops, call a doctor.

Solitary wasps

Mud dauber nest.

Problem: Wasps are flying around the garden. Some of these insects are black with yellow, red, or white markings. Others are black, brown, blue, red, or yellow. Many wasps have very thin, elongated waists. Their mud nests may be found under eaves or on plants or rocks.

Analysis: Unlike the social yellow jackets, many species of wasps, including the potter and mason wasps, mud daubers, and spider wasps, live alone. Most of them build nests of mud and sand in which they raise their young. Many of these wasps feed on insects; a few feed on pollen and nectar. These wasps aren't as aggressive and protective of their nests as are yellow jackets and don't sting as readily. (For information on yellow jackets, see page 518.) If highly provoked, however, they can sting, causing swelling, itching, and more generalized symptoms in sensitive individuals.

Solution: Eliminate mud nests by hosing or knocking them down. Kill wasps by spraying them with Ortho® Hornet & Wasp Killer according to label directions. Even though many solitary wasps are docile, they may be confused with yellow jackets; it is best to avoid threatening or provoking them. If you are stung, apply a cold compress or ice pack to the swollen area. If a severe reaction develops, call a doctor.

Stinging caterpillars

Saddleback caterpillar.

Problem: A rash forms where a hairy or spiny caterpillar has touched the skin. Reactions vary depending on the caterpillar and the individual, and they include mild itching, rash, swelling, severe local pain, local lesions, and fever.

Analysis: There are about 25 species of stinging caterpillars. These insects have hollow hairs that contain a mild poison. The hairs release the irritating substance when people handle the caterpillars or accidentally brush against them. Most of these caterpillars are capable of causing only a mild itching or skin rash. The puss caterpillar (*Megalopyge opercularis*), however, causes a severe reaction. It can cause intense itching, swelling, local numbness, nausea, and fever (especially in children). This caterpillar is widely distributed in the southeastern and south-central states and feeds on a wide variety of deciduous trees and shrubs. During some years it increases to unusually large numbers. The saddleback caterpillar (*Sibine stimulea*), the io moth caterpillar (*Automeris io*), and the flannel moth caterpillar (*Norape ovina*) are other caterpillars known for their stinging hairs.

Solution: Avoid handling hairy and spiny caterpillars. Spray shrubs and trees on which these caterpillars are found with an insecticide containing *carbaryl*. Make sure that your plant is listed on the product label. Contact a physician if a severe reaction begins to develop.

BITING AND STINGING PESTS *(continued)*

Biting flies

Horsefly (3× life size).

Problem: Black, brown, or black-and-white biting flies about ½ to 1 inch long are present around the home. They are especially bothersome in areas where horses and domestic animals are common.

Analysis: Biting flies, including several species of horseflies and deerflies, are most common in rural and suburban areas. They attack humans and domestic animals. The female flies deposit their eggs in still pools of water, in moist soil, or on vegetation. Larvae feed on other insects or decaying vegetation and pupate in damp plant debris. The adult flies inflict painful bites that often bleed. Some people bitten by horseflies may suffer from fever and general illness.

Solution: Keep screens repaired on doors and windows. Treat outdoor living areas with Ortho® Home Defense® Perimeter & Indoor Insect Killer Pull 'N Spray. Kill biting flies indoors by spraying with Ortho® Roach, Ant & Spider Killer or Ortho® Home Defense® Perimeter & Indoor Insect Killer Pull 'N Spray. Apply insect repellent to the skin. Repellent may be purchased at drugstores. Remove fly breeding areas by cleaning up stagnant pools of water and wet, decaying vegetation around the yard.

Biting midges

Biting midge (15× life size).

Problem: During the spring and summer, tiny, black, biting midges ½₅ to ⅛ inch long infest the yard. They are most common in coastal areas and near lakes, streams, marshlands, and swamps.

Analysis: Biting midges are annoying insects that are also known as *no-see-ums*, *sand flies*, and *black gnats*. They feed on warm-blooded animals, including humans and birds. Biting midges breed in wet sand or mud, damp rotting vegetation, very shallow stagnant or brackish water, and similar locations. They rarely infest the home but are bothersome outdoors, inflicting bites around the feet, legs, ears, eyes, and around cuff, collar, and belt areas where clothing binds. The bites are rarely painful but produce tiny swellings or blisters that itch for several days.

Solution: Spray infested areas of the yard with Ortho® Home Defense® Perimeter & Indoor Insect Killer Pull 'N Spray according to label directions. Apply insect repellents to the skin. Such repellents may be purchased at drugstores.

Black flies

Black flies (3× life size).

Problem: During the late spring and summer, many black or gray humpback flies ½₅ to ⅓ inch long are present around the home. They inflict painful bites.

Analysis: Annoying black flies, also known as *buffalo gnats* and *turkey gnats*, attack humans and domestic animals in rural and suburban areas throughout the United States. The female flies deposit their eggs in swiftly running water, including streams and irrigation ditches. The larvae develop in the water and emerge as adult flies during the spring and summer. Black flies may be blown many miles from their breeding areas. They bite any exposed part of the body and may also bite where clothes are binding, such as around belts and collars. These irritating bites often swell and itch for several days. The victim may suffer headaches, fever, and nausea.

Solution: Keep window and door screens repaired. Spray outdoor living areas with Ortho® Home Defense® Perimeter & Indoor Insect Killer Pull 'N Spray. Kill black flies indoors by spraying with Ortho® Home Defense® Perimeter & Indoor Insect Killer Pull 'N Spray. Treat entire rooms with Ortho® Indoor Insect Fogger. Apply insect repellents to the skin. Repellents may be purchased at drugstores.

Mosquitoes

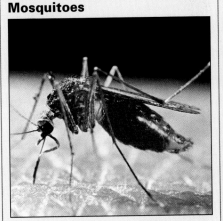

Mosquito (8× life size).

Problem: Biting mosquitoes are present in the home and yard. They are most bothersome at dusk and during the night.

Analysis: Many species of mosquitoes occur throughout the world. In addition to having an annoying bite, this insect pest transmits encephalitis, within the United States, and other serious diseases, such as yellow fever and malaria, in other parts of the world. Adults emerge from hibernation with warm spring weather. The males feed on nectar, honeydew, and plant sap; the females require a blood meal in order to produce their eggs. Larval development takes place exclusively in water. Typically, eggs are laid in shallow accumulations of fresh, stagnant, and salty water. The larvae may mature within five days or may take months to mature.

Solution: Maintain door and window screens in good repair. Kill mosquitoes indoors by fogging with Ortho® Indoor Insect Fogger or spraying with Ortho® Home Defense® Perimeter & Indoor Insect Killer Pull 'N Spray. Kill mosquitoes outdoors by spraying with Ortho® Malathion Plus® Insect Spray Concentrate around the lawn and foundation of the house. Spray resting areas under house eaves with Ortho® Home Defense® Perimeter & Indoor Insect Killer Pull 'N Spray. Apply insect repellents to the skin. Drain standing water. Stock ornamental ponds with mosquito fish (*Gambusia affinis*), which eat mosquito larvae. Goldfish also eat mosquito larvae but are not as effective as mosquito fish.

Black widow spiders

Black widow spider (life size).

Problem: Black widow spiders are shiny, black, about the size of a quarter, and have a red hourglass marking on the underside of the abdomen. Outdoors, they live under rocks or clods of dirt and in wood and rubbish piles. Indoors, they are found in garages, attics, cellars, and other dark secluded places, such as under boards or cluttered debris, in old clothing, or in crevices. Black widow webs are coarse and irregular, about 1 foot wide. The strands break with a snap when the web is torn.

Analysis: Several species of poisonous black widow spiders (*Latrodectus* species) are found throughout the United States. Black widows live in secluded locations and feed on insects trapped in their webs. If the spiders are touched, or if their webs are disturbed, they will bite the intruder. The venom may cause serious illness and, on rare occasions, death. The females produce egg sacs that contain hundreds of eggs. The tiny spiderlings that emerge are also capable of inflicting poisonous bites. They may be carried long distances by the wind.

Solution: Kill spiders by spraying webs and infested areas with Ortho® Roach, Ant & Spider Killer or Ortho® Home Defense® Perimeter & Indoor Insect Killer Pull 'N Spray. Remove loose wood and trash from areas where spiders might hide. Wear gloves and protective clothing when cleaning up infested areas. Vacuum infested areas to remove egg sacs and destroy the contents of the vacuum cleaner bag. Put ice on a spider bite and call a doctor immediately.

Brown recluse spiders

![Brown recluse spider]

Brown recluse spider (2× life size).

Problem: Brown recluse spiders are light to dark brown, 1/3 to 1/2 inch in length, with a violin-shape marking behind the head. Outdoors, they are found under rocks. Indoors, they are found in secluded places. Grayish, irregular, sticky webs and round white egg sacs 3/4 inch wide may be found in infested areas.

Analysis: Poisonous brown recluse spiders (*Loxosceles reclusa*) are found in the Midwest and Southeast. Other related but less poisonous spiders (*Loxosceles* species) are found throughout most of the United States. Brown recluse spiders live in secluded places and are very shy, moving away quickly when disturbed. If they are touched or trapped in shoes, clothing, or bedclothes, they may bite. Their venom is rarely fatal, but it causes a severe sore that is slow to heal and sometimes causes illness.

Solution: Kill spiders by spraying webs and infested areas with Ortho® Home Defense® Perimeter & Indoor Insect Killer Pull 'N Spray or Ortho® Roach, Ant & Spider Killer. Or spray outdoor areas where spiders may hide with Ortho® Home Defense® Perimeter & Indoor Insect Killer Pull 'N Spray. Remove loose wood, trash, or clutter from areas where spiders might hide. Wear gloves and protective clothing when cleaning up infested areas. Spray outdoor living areas and clean up debris around the house that may harbor spiders. Vacuum infested areas to remove egg sacs and destroy the contents of the vacuum bag. Put ice on a spider bite and call a doctor immediately.

BITING AND STINGING PESTS (continued)

Fire ants

Mound. Inset: Fire ant (4× life size).

Problem: Small (¼-inch) reddish to black ants crawl to and from large mounds of soil in the lawn and garden. These ants inflict painful stings on people or animals disturbing the mounds.

Analysis: Fire ants (*Solenopsis* species) are notorious for the large mounds they create and for the painful stings they inflict. The mounds, which are their nests, are usually found in lawns and gardens. Occasionally the ants move into or underneath homes during periods of rain or drought. They feed mainly on other insects but will also feed on young succulent plants, seeds, fruit, household foods, and even small, weak animals, such as newly hatched birds. Because fire ants feed on other insects, they are of some benefit in the yard. Their presence, however, can greatly limit use of the garden because of the threat of painful stings. A sting results in a pustule that develops within 24 hours and heals within several weeks.

Solution: Control fire ants in the lawn by treating the mound with Ortho® Orthene® Fire Ant Killer or Ortho® Fire Ant Killer Broad Granules. Also treat the area surrounding mounds out to a distance of 4 feet. Spray ants indoors with Ortho® Home Defense® Perimeter & Indoor Insect Killer Pull 'N Spray. If a severe reaction to fire ant stings develops, call a doctor immediately.

Harvester ants

Harvester ant mound.

Problem: Large ants up to ½ inch long are crawling on cleared areas on the ground. Ants are seen entering holes or large craters in the ground. The holes are surrounded by a large cleared area from 3 to 35 feet in diameter. The cleared area may be strewn with small pebbles and seed husks. Ant trails radiate from the nest in all directions. If there is a mound, it is usually low. If disturbed, the ants will inflict a painful sting.

Analysis: Harvester ants (*Pogonomyrmex* species) don't invade the home but may be a problem in lawns and gardens. These ants eat all tender vegetation surrounding their nests, resulting in a large cleared area where they dump small pebbles removed from their nests as well as husks and other inedible portions of seeds. They are primarily seed eaters. The holes in the center of the cleared areas lead to their underground nests. Harvester ants aggressively sting and bite anyone who disturbs their nests. They have been known to kill very small animals that accidentally wander over their nests.

Solution: Treat the entrances to the ant nests and the cleared area around them with Ortho® Home Defense® Perimeter & Indoor Insect Killer Pull 'N Spray or Ortho® Ant-B-Gon® Dust. If you are stung, apply a cold compress or ice pack to the swollen area. If a severe reaction develops, call your doctor.

Scorpions

Scorpion (1½× life size).

Problem: Scorpions are found in the garden under rocks, boards, and protective debris. Indoors, they may be found in attics or crawl spaces under the home. They may move down into living areas such as kitchens and bathrooms when attic temperatures are higher than 100°F.

Analysis: All scorpions are capable of inflicting stings, but a few species found only in the Southwest are dangerous. Scorpions are nocturnal creatures, feeding at night on insects and small animals. During the day, they hide in dark, protected locations. They are shy and sting only when touched, trapped, or otherwise provoked. Except for a few fatally poisonous scorpions (*Centruroides* species), most scorpions deliver stings that are no more serious than a bee sting. The venom varies in potency from season to season, however, and like many insect stings may cause severe illness in a sensitive individual. Although scorpions live mostly in the garden, they may crawl into the home through open or loose doors and windows.

Solution: Remove loose boards, rocks, and other debris around the yard and in the home to eliminate scorpion hiding places. Wear gloves and protective clothing when cleaning up infested areas. Spray locations where scorpions might hide with Ortho® Home Defense® Perimeter & Indoor Insect Killer Pull 'N Spray or Ortho® Roach, Ant & Spider Killer. Maintain window and door screens and weather stripping in good repair. Call a doctor if you are stung by a scorpion.

Tarantulas

Black Mexican tarantula.

Problem: A large, hairy spider, up to 5 inches across, is crawling around in the house or outside in the garden.

Analysis: Tarantulas are spiders that are often feared because of their large size and hairy bodies. Although a few South American species can give a very painful bite, all tarantulas occurring in the United States inflict a bite that is like a bee sting. Their hairs, which easily rub off their bodies, can irritate the skin. When cornered, tarantulas may make a purring sound or rear up on their back legs. Tarantulas are sluggish, bite rarely, and can be handled with ease. Female tarantulas may live 20 years or more in captivity. Males are shorter lived. Tarantulas are nocturnal, living in dark cavities or burrows during the day and hunting at night.

Solution: Capture the spider in a large jar or box and release it in a secluded area. Chances of being bitten while catching it are minimal, but it is wise to wear protective clothing, such as long rubber gloves, and to avoid sudden, quick movement. If a severe reaction to a tarantula bite develops, call your doctor. To control spiders, treat a 2-foot band around the foundation with Ortho® Home Defense® Perimeter & Indoor Insect Killer Pull 'N Spray.

Flour moths

Angoumois grain moth (6× life size).

Problem: Pinkish or greenish caterpillars up to ⅝ inch long are feeding inside silken webbing in stored grain, flour, cereals, and other grain products. Beige-, gray-, and coppery-winged moths, ⅓ inch long, may be seen flying in the home.

Analysis: The larvae of Indian meal moths (*Plodia interpunctella*) and Mediterranean flour moths (*Anagasta kuehniella*) damage ground or broken grain products, dried cereals, dried fruits, powdered milk, and other pantry items. The larvae of angoumois grain moths (*Sitotroga cerealella*) infest whole wheat and corn kernels. Adult moths lay eggs in stored grain products. Larvae that emerge spin silken webs, under which they feed. When mature, they usually leave the infested food to pupate in a corner or crack in the cupboard.

Solution: Discard all infested food. Clean out cupboards thoroughly before restocking. If infestation is widespread, remove all food and utensils and fog the infested area with Ortho® Indoor Insect Fogger; or treat cracks and crevices along shelves in the pantry with Ortho® Home Defense® Perimeter & Indoor Insect Killer Pull 'N Spray or Ortho® Roach, Ant & Spider Killer. Don't treat countertops or other food work areas. Reline shelves with paper and replace food after the spray has dried. Kill the eggs, larvae, and pupae by deep-freezing food for four days or heating it in a shallow pan at 150°F for half an hour. Store foods in airtight glass, plastic, and metal containers. Keep the pantry clean, and avoid buying damaged packages; they are more likely to be infested.

Mealworms

Mealworms (life size).

Problem: Shiny yellow to brown grubs up to 1¼ inches long are feeding in damp or moldy flour, grain, or cereal products. Flat, shiny, brown to black beetles ¼ to ¾ inch long may also be found.

Analysis: Mealworms (*Tenebrio* and *Alphitobius* species) are insects that prefer to feed on damp or moldy grain products stored in dark, rarely disturbed, dusty locations. If infested food items are brought into the pantry, the mealworms and beetles may migrate to infest and reproduce in poorly sealed bags of flour, bran, crackers, and other grain products.

Solution: Chemical control is not necessary. Discard infested food items. Clean out cupboards thoroughly. Keep grain products in dry, tightly sealed glass, plastic, and metal containers.

PANTRY PESTS *(continued)*

Cockroaches

German cockroaches (life size).

Oriental cockroach (1¾× life size).

Flour beetles

Red flour beetle (6× life size).

Problem: Cockroaches infest the kitchen, bathroom, and other areas of the home. These flat, shiny insects range in size from ½ to 1¾ inches long. They may be light brown, golden tan, reddish brown, or black. In large numbers, they emit a fetid odor.

Analysis: Cockroaches are insect pests that thrive in human habitations throughout the world. The most significant household species in the United States are the German cockroach (*Blattella germanica*), the brown-banded cockroach (*Supella longipalpa*), the Oriental cockroach (*Blatta orientalis*), the American cockroach (*Periplaneta americana*), and the Asian cockroach (*Blattella asahinai*), a recent arrival in North America and similar in appearance to the German cockroach. In addition to their annoying presence, cockroaches spread diseases, such as salmonella and parasitic toxoplasmosis, by contaminating food with their infected droppings. These pests proliferate in areas where food and water are available. Cockroaches prefer starchy foods but will feed on any human and pet food scraps, garbage, paper, and fabrics soiled with food. Unless infestations are heavy or their hiding places are disturbed, they are rarely seen in exposed locations during the day. These nocturnal insects seek out dark, protected areas in which to live and breed. Usually they congregate in kitchens and bathrooms. They may be found behind or under sinks, refrigerators, and water heaters, within the walls of household appliances, behind baseboards and molding, in wall spaces, around pipes, in garbage cans, and in piles of cluttered paper or grocery bags. They may be present in cracks or crevices in cupboards, cabinets, desks, dressers, and closets. They may infest basements, crawl spaces, and sewers. Cockroaches move from one room to another through wall spaces, cracks in walls, floors, and ceilings, and along pipes and conduits. If their living conditions become too crowded, they may migrate. Infestations usually begin when stray insects or egg cases are brought into the home with shipped items, secondhand furniture and appliances, grocery bags, and debris. They may also move into homes from sewers.

Solution: Eliminate cockroach food sources by keeping the kitchen and other areas of the home free of food scraps. Clean up the kitchen after each meal and store food in tightly sealed metal, glass, and heavy-plastic containers. Empty household garbage and pet litter regularly. Don't leave pet food out overnight. Fix leaking faucets and pipes. Clean up puddles and moist areas around the kitchen, basement, and other infested areas. Plug cracks around baseboards, shelves, cupboards, sinks, and pipes with a filling material, such as putty or caulk. Remove food and utensils, then apply Ortho® Home Defense® Perimeter & Indoor Insect Killer Pull 'N Spray or Ortho® Roach, Ant & Spider Killer in cracks in cupboards, on surfaces underneath sinks, along molding, behind appliances, and in other areas where insects are likely to congregate. Allow the spray to dry and then reline the shelves with fresh paper before replacing food and utensils.

Problem: Reddish to dark brown elongated beetles, ⅒ to ⅐ inch long, and yellowish-white wiry grubs, ⅕ inch long, are feeding in flour, cereals, cake mixes, macaroni, and other flour and grain products.

Analysis: Several species of flour beetles (*Tribolium* and *Oryzaephilus* species), including the sawtoothed grain beetle, the red flour beetle, and the confused flour beetle, infest grain products in the pantry, grocery store, and packing plant. These pests feed on and reproduce in stored flour products. They can migrate to and infest nearby broken or poorly sealed containers and can also chew through and infest flimsy paper and cellophane packages. Even when infested packages are removed, the beetles can live on flour and cereals that sift into cracks in the cupboard.

Solution: Discard all infested food. Clean out cupboards thoroughly before restocking. If infestation is widespread, remove all food items from the pantry and treat cracks and areas behind shelves with Ortho® Home Defense® Perimeter & Indoor Insect Killer Pull 'N Spray or Ortho® Roach, Ant & Spider Killer. Let the treatment dry before replacing food. Keep food in airtight glass, plastic, and metal containers. If you suspect food is contaminated, kill the beetles, grubs, and eggs by deep-freezing food for four days or heating it in a shallow pan at 150°F for half an hour. Keep the pantry clean and avoid buying damaged packages; they are more likely to be infested.

Larder beetles

Larder beetle larva (4× life size).

Problem: Larvae or adult insects are discovered in the home. The larvae are about ⅝ inch long, brown, and hairy, with a pair of curved spines on the last segment. Adults are ⅜ inch long and black with a yellow band across the middle, dotted with a few black spots.

Analysis: The larder beetle (*Dermestes lardarius*), a relative of the carpet beetle, eats animal products of all types. It is most commonly found in dry pet food or where animals have died in remote places in the house. Mice in walls, dead birds in nests, and bunches of flies in hidden areas, such as lighting fixtures, often attract larder beetles. Larvae are often discovered in the home in late spring after they have consumed the last of the cluster flies inside the walls and are wandering in search of more food or a place to pupate. Adults spend the winter outdoors, entering the home in May and June to lay eggs near a food source. Larvae feed for a time, then bore into wood or other material to pupate. Their strong jaws can chew through all but the hardest material. Unless their numbers are very large, however, the boring does little damage.

Solution: Adults and larvae are easily picked up by hand for disposal. Search for the food source if larvae are discovered wandering about the house. Insects in the kitchen are probably infesting stored food. In other parts of the house, they may have found a dead animal or insects. Clean up the area and treat cracks and hidden areas with Ortho® Home Defense® Hi-Power Brand Roach, Ant & Spider Killer.

Grain weevils

Rice weevils (6× life size).

Problem: Reddish-brown to black beetles, ⅛ to ⅙ inch long with elongated snouts, are feeding in stored whole-grain rice, corn, wheat, and beans. The beetles may be seen crawling around the pantry. Yellow-white grubs may be found inside infested kernels.

Analysis: Grain weevils (*Sitophilus* species) are pantry pests that include the granary weevil and the rice weevil. They usually damage whole grains but occasionally infest flour and other broken or processed grain products. The adult weevils lay eggs inside grain kernels. Larvae that hatch from the eggs mature inside the kernels, pupate, and emerge as adult weevils. The adults wander about and are often seen far from the site of infestation.

Solution: Discard all infested food. Clean out cupboards thoroughly before restocking. If the infestation is widespread, remove all food items and fog the kitchen with Ortho® Indoor Insect Fogger; or spray shelves and cracks in pantry cupboards with Ortho® Home Defense® Perimeter & Indoor Insect Killer Pull 'N Spray or Ortho® Roach, Ant & Spider Killer. Don't spray countertops or other food preparation areas. Reline shelves with paper and replace food after the spray has dried. Keep food in airtight glass, plastic, and metal containers. Avoid buying damaged packages, which are more likely to be infested.

Cigarette beetles and drugstore beetles

Cigarette beetle, larva, and pupa (4× life size).

Problem: Reddish or reddish-brown oval-shaped beetles, ⅛ inch long, or yellowish-white curved grubs are feeding in stored tobacco, cigars, or cigarettes. They may also be found in red pepper and paprika, coffee beans, and other stored foods derived from plants.

Analysis: Cigarette beetles (*Lasioderma serricorne*) and drugstore beetles (*Stegobium paniceum*) are native to tropical parts of the world and can survive in the United States only in warm buildings (65°F and higher). These pests feed on and reproduce in foods and spices. They may also feed on wool, leather, paper, drugs, and other household items. When infested products are brought into the home, the beetles can invade nearby uncontaminated foods kept in unsealed or flimsy containers. They may also chew through sealed paper containers.

Solution: Remove and destroy all infested foods. Clean out cupboards thoroughly before restocking. Set traps made for these pests in cupboards and drawers. If the infestation is widespread, remove all food items and spray shelves and cracks with Ortho® Roach, Ant & Spider Killer. Let the spray dry before replacing food. Kill insects in packaged products by freezing for a day. Keep foods and spices in airtight glass, metal, and plastic containers. Refrigerate food kept in paper packages. Don't purchase items in damaged or unsealed packages; they are more likely to be infested.

Appendix

TABLE OF CONTENTS

In this appendix you will find a wealth of information packed into more than 100 lists, charts, and maps.

For More Information

ABOUT PLANT PROBLEMS

Animal and Plant Health Inspection Service (APHIS)
This U.S.D.A. site describes problem pests, diseases, and weeds, and the steps being taken to combat them.
www.aphis.usda.gov

Factsheet Database
Searches universities, government agencies, and extension factsheets in all states. From Ohio State.
plantfacts.osu.edu/web/

National IPM Network
Links to pest-control sites.
www.reeusda.gov/agsys/nipmn/index.htm

INSECTS

Insects on WWW
Virginia Tech
A vast and well-organized collection of links to insect sites.
atum.isis.vt.edu/~fanjun/text

Insect Notes
North Carolina State University
www.ces.ncsu.edu/depts/ent/notes/index.html

PLANT DISEASES

American Phytopathological Society Plant Pathology Online
Information and links about plant diseases.
www.apsnet.org

New and Emerging Plant Diseases Project
North Carolina State University
Information about new plant diseases from all over the country.
www.ces.ncsu.edu/depts/ent/clinic/emerging/index.htm

WEEDS

Weed Science Society of America
www.wssa.net

USDA Noxious Weeds Home Page
www.aphis.usda.gov/ppq/weeds/

Weed Photo Gallery
University of California, Davis
www.ipm.ucdavis.edu/PMG/weeds_common.html

ANIMAL PESTS

Controlling Nuisance Birds & Wildlife
University of Wisconsin
cf.uwex.edu/ics/infosource/birds.cfm

PESTICIDES

EXTOXNET Pesticide Information Profiles
Information about the toxicity of pesticides.
ace.orst.edu/info/extoxnet/pips/ghindex.html

CDMS Label and Material Safety Data Sheets
Full text of labels and material safety data Sheets for most pesticides, provided by the manufacturers.
www.cdms.net/manuf/manuf.asp

Pesticide Management Education Program
Cornell University
pmep.cce.cornell.edu/

HOUSEPLANTS

Horticulture Solutions: Houseplants
University of Illinois Extension
www.ag.uiuc.edu/~robsond/solutions/horticulture/house.html

Diagnosing Problems of Indoor Plants
Ohio State University
ohioline.osu.edu/hyg-fact/3000/3068.html

LAWNS

Lawn Challenge
University of Illinois
www.urbanext.uiuc.edu/lawnchallenge/index.html

Lawn Diseases
North Dakota State University
www.ext.nodak.edu/extpubs/plantsci/landscap/pp950w.htm

Managing Lawn and Turf Insects
University of Minnesota
www.extension.umn.edu/distribution/horticulture/DG1008.html

Control Lawn Insects
Mississippi State University
msucares.com/pubs/publications/pub401.htm

ANNUALS, PERENNIALS, AND BULBS

Ohioline: Flowers
Ohio State University
ohioline.osu.edu/lines/flwrs.html

Flowers Outdoors
University of Wisconsin
cf.uwex.edu/ics/infosource/flowers.cfm

TREE AND SHRUB PROBLEMS

Tree Injuries—Prevention and Care
University of Nebraska, Lincoln
www.ianr.unl.edu/pubs/forestry/g1035.htm

Insect Pests of Shrubs (Southeastern U.S.)
North Carolina State University
ipm.ncsu.edu/ag189/html/

FRUIT TREE PROBLEMS

Home Fruit Production—Citrus
Texas Agricultural Extension Service
aggie-horticulture.tamu.edu/extension/homefruit/citrus/citrus.html

Common Tree Fruit Insects
Michigan State University Extension
www.canr.msu.edu/vanburen/fruitbug.htm

Tree Fruit Research & Extension Center
Washington State University
www.tfrec.wsu.edu/

VEGETABLE PROBLEMS

Vegetable Growing
Oregon State University
eesc.orst.edu/agcomwebfile/garden/vegetable/

Small Fruit in the Home Garden
Virginia Tech
www.ext.vt.edu/pubs/envirohort/426-840/426-840.html#L4

Insect Pest Management in the Home Vegetable Garden
Auburn University
www.acesag.auburn.edu/department/ipm/HMEVEG1.htm

Weeds in the Home Vegetable Garden
Virginia Tech
www.ext.vt.edu/pubs/envirohort/426-364/426-364.html

GENERIC AND TRADE NAMES OF COMMON CHEMICALS

This is a partial list of trade names to assist in locating pesticides. It contains only a few of the most widely available products. Ortho cannot guarantee the quality of any products except those sold by Ortho or Scotts, our parent company.

Generic Name	Action	Trade Names
2,4–D	Herbicide, selective for broadleaf weeds	Ortho® Weed-B-Gon® Lawn Weed Killer
Acephate	Insecticide, systemic	Ortho® Orthene® Systemic Insect Control
Acifluorfen	Herbicide	Ortho® Kleeraway Grass & Weed Killer
Allethrin	Insecticide	Ortho® Home Defense® Flying & Crawling Insect Killer
Atrazine	Herbicide, selective for broadleaf weeds	Atrazine
Benomyl	Fungicide, broad-spectrum	Benlate
Bensulide	Herbicide, preemergence	Betasan® Pre-San®
Captan	Fungicide, broad-spectrum	Ortho® Home Orchard Spray
Carbaryl	Insecticide	Sevin®
Chloroneb	Fungicide, seed-treatment	Terraneb®
Chlorothalonil	Fungicide	Ortho® Multi-Purpose Fungicide Daconil 2787® Plant Disease Control
Chlorpyrifos	Insecticide	Ortho® Borer & Leaf Miner Spray Ortho® Dursban® Lawn & Garden Insect Control
Cycloheximide	Fungicide	Acti-dione
DCPA	Herbicide, preemergence	Dacthal®
Diazinon	Insecticide	Ortho® Bug-B-Gon® Insect Killer Ortho® Diazinon® Granules Ortho® Diazinon® Ultra Insect Spray
Dicamba	Herbicide	Banvel D
Dichlobenil	Herbicide, preemergence	Ortho® Casoron Granules
Dicofol	Acaricide	Kelthane®
Dimethoate	Insecticide	Cygon
Disulfoton	Insecticide, systemic	Ortho® RosePride® Systemic Rose & Flower Care
Dithiopyr	Herbicide	Dimension®
DSMA	Herbicide, selective for broadleaf weeds	DSMA
Endosulfan	Insecticide	Thiodan
Eptam	Herbicide	Eptam®
Ethazole	Fungicide, soil	Terrazole® Truban®
Fenarimol	Fungicide	Dodine® Rubigan®
Ferbam	Fungicide	Ferbam®
Ferrous sulfate monohydrate	Moss killer	Scotts Moss Control Granules
Fluazifop-P-butyl	Herbicide, selective for grassy weeds	Ortho® Grass-B-Gon Grass Killer
Fosetyl-aluminum	Bactericide, fungicide	Aliette®
Glyphosate	Herbicide, systemic	Roundup®
Halofenozide	Insecticide, soil	Ortho® Grub-B-Gon®
Hexakis	Acaricide	Vendex®
Imazapyr	Herbicide	Ortho® GroundClear® Triox Total Vegetation Killer
Imidacloprid	Insecticide	Scotts Grubex®
Lime-sulfur	Fungicide, insecticide, miticide	Ortho® Dormant Disease Control Lime-Sulfur Spray
Linuron	Herbicide	Lorox®
Malathion	Insecticide	Malathion

Generic Name	Action	Trade Names
Mancozeb	Fungicide	Dithane® M–45 Manzate®
Maneb	Fungicide	Maneb
MCPP	Herbicide	Mecoprop
Metaldehyde	Molluscicide	Ortho® Bug-Geta® Snail & Slug Killer
Methanearsonate, calcium acid	Herbicide	Ortho® Crabgrass & Nutgrass Killer
Methoprene	Insecticide (insect growth regulator)	Ortho® Flea-B-Gon® Total Flea Killer Indoor Fogger Precor®
Methoxychlor	Insecticide	Ortho® Home Orchard Spray
Myclobutanil	Fungicide	Eagle® Nova® Rally®
Napropamide	Herbicide	Devrinol®
Oryzalin	Herbicide, preemergence	Surflan®
Oxyfluorfen	Herbicide	Ortho® GroundClear® Triox Total Vegetation Killer
PCNB	Fungicide, soil	Terraclor®
Pendimethalin	Herbicide, preemergence	Scotts Halts® Crabgrass Preventer Scotts Turf Weedgrass Control
Permethrin	Insecticide	Ambush® Ortho® Flea-B-Gon® Total Flea Killer Indoor Spray
Phosmet	Insecticide	Imidan®
Prometon	Herbicide, preemergence and postemergence	Ortho® GroundClear® Triox Total Vegetation Killer
Propiconazole	Fungicide	Alamo® Banner®
Pyrethrins	Insecticide	Ortho® RosePride® Rose & Flower Insect Killer Ortho® Tomato & Vegetable Insect Killer
Resmethrin	Insecticide	Ortho® Orthenex® Garden Insect & Disease Control
Rotenone	Insecticide	Rotenone
Siduron	Herbicide, preemergence	Siduron
Simazine	Herbicide	Princep®
Streptomycin	Bactericide	Streptomycin
Sumithrin	Insecticide	Ortho® Home Defense® Home & Garden Insect Killer
Tetramethrin	Insecticide	Ortho® Home Defense® Home & Garden Insect Killer
Thiophanate-methyl	Fungicide, systemic	Cleary 3336® Topsin®
Thiram	Fungicide	Thiram
Triadimefon	Fungicide	Bayleton® Scotts ProTurf® Fungicide
Triclopyr	Herbicide	Ortho® Brush-B-Gon® Poison Ivy , Poison Oak & Brush Killer
Trifluralin	Herbicide	Treflan®
Triforine	Fungicide	Ortho® RosePride® Funginex Rose & Shrub Disease Control
Zineb	Fungicide	Cuprothex®
Ziram	Fungicide	Ziram

THE USDA PLANT HARDINESS ZONE MAP

Plants are classified according to the amount of cold weather they can handle. For example, a plant listed as hardy to Zone 6 will survive a winter in which the temperature drops to –10° F.

Warm weather also influences whether a plant will survive in your region. Although this map does not address heat hardiness, in general, if a range of hardiness zones is listed for a plant, the plant will survive winter in the coldest zone as well as tolerate the heat of the warmest zone.

To use this map, find the location of your community, then match the color band marking that area to the zone key at left.

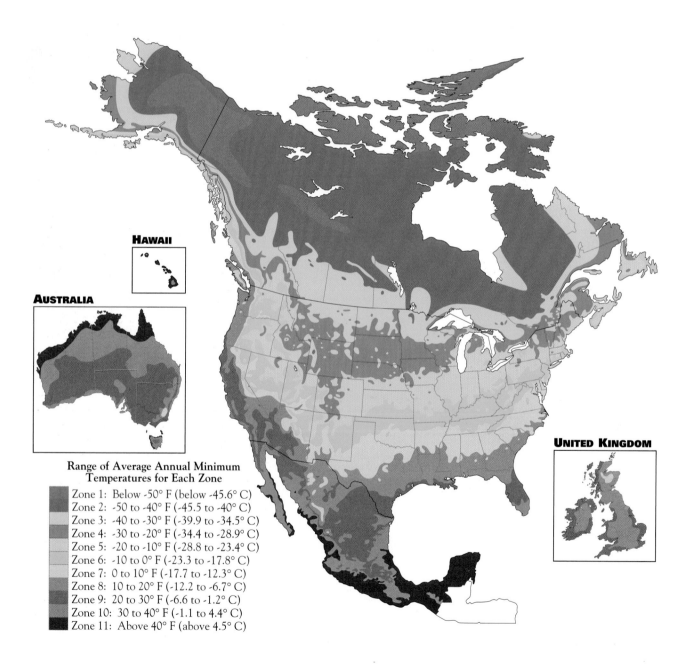

HAWAII

AUSTRALIA

UNITED KINGDOM

Range of Average Annual Minimum Temperatures for Each Zone

Zone 1: Below -50° F (below -45.6° C)
Zone 2: -50 to -40° F (-45.5 to -40° C)
Zone 3: -40 to -30° F (-39.9 to -34.5° C)
Zone 4: -30 to -20° F (-34.4 to -28.9° C)
Zone 5: -20 to -10° F (-28.8 to -23.4° C)
Zone 6: -10 to 0° F (-23.3 to -17.8° C)
Zone 7: 0 to 10° F (-17.7 to -12.3° C)
Zone 8: 10 to 20° F (-12.2 to -6.7° C)
Zone 9: 20 to 30° F (-6.6 to -1.2° C)
Zone 10: 30 to 40° F (-1.1 to 4.4° C)
Zone 11: Above 40° F (above 4.5° C)

METRIC CONVERSIONS

U.S. Units to Metric Equivalents			Metric Units to U.S. Equivalents		
To Convert From	Multiply By	To Get	To Convert From	Multiply By	To Get
Inches	25.4	Millimeters	Millimeters	0.0394	Inches
Inches	2.54	Centimeters	Centimeters	0.3937	Inches
Feet	30.48	Centimeters	Centimeters	0.0328	Feet
Feet	0.3048	Meters	Meters	3.2808	Feet
Yards	0.9144	Meters	Meters	1.0936	Yards
Square inches	6.4516	Square centimeters	Square centimeters	0.1550	Square inches
Square feet	0.0929	Square meters	Square meters	10.764	Square feet
Square yards	0.8361	Square meters	Square meters	1.1960	Square yards
Acres	0.4047	Hectares	Hectares	2.4711	Acres
Cubic inches	16.387	Cubic centimeters	Cubic centimeters	0.0610	Cubic inches
Cubic feet	0.0283	Cubic meters	Cubic meters	35.315	Cubic feet
Cubic feet	28.316	Liters	Liters	0.0353	Cubic feet
Cubic yards	0.7646	Cubic meters	Cubic meters	1.308	Cubic yards
Cubic yards	764.55	Liters	Liters	0.0013	Cubic yards

To convert from degrees Fahrenheit (F) to degrees Celsius (C), first subtract 32, then multiply by ⅝.

To convert from degrees Celsius to degrees Fahrenheit, multiply by ⅗, then add 32.

QUANTITIES OF GROUND LIMESTONE NEEDED TO RAISE pH TO 6.5

Present pH of soil	Pounds needed per 100 sq ft of sandy loam	Pounds needed per 100 sq ft of loam	Pounds needed per 100 sq ft of clay loam
4.0	11.5	16	23
4.5	9.5	13.5	19.5
5.0	8	10.5	15
5.5	6	8	10.5
6.0	3	4	5.5

Dolomitic limestone is recommended because it adds magnesium as well as calcium to the soil. The limestone should be cultivated into the soil. Adapted from Soil Acidity Needs of Plants, New York County Extension Service, publication D-2-25.

THE pH SCALE

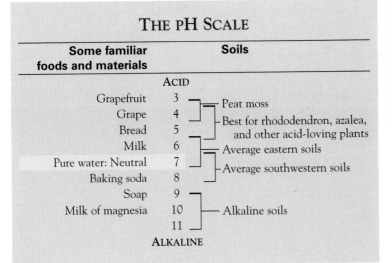

Some familiar foods and materials		Soils
	ACID	
Grapefruit	3	Peat moss
Grape	4	
Bread	5	Best for rhododendron, azalea, and other acid-loving plants
Milk	6	Average eastern soils
Pure water: Neutral	7	
Baking soda	8	Average southwestern soils
Soap	9	
Milk of magnesia	10	Alkaline soils
	11	
	ALKALINE	

PLANTS THAT WILL GROW IN ACID SOIL (pH OF 4.5 TO 5.5)

Common Name	Botanical Name
TREES AND SHRUBS	
Andromeda	Pieris
Broom	Cytisus
Camellia	Camellia
Crape myrtle	Lagerstroemia indica
Gardenia	Gardenia
Heath	Erica
Heather	Calluna
Hemlock	Tsuga
Holly	Ilex
Hydrangea	Hydrangea
Leucothoe	Leucothoe
Magnolia	Magnolia
Manzanita	Arctostaphylos
Mountain ash	Sorbus
Mountain laurel	Kalmia
Pin oak	Quercus palustris
Pine	Pinus
Quaking aspen	Populus tremuloides
Rhododendron, azalea	Rhododendron
Serviceberry	Amelanchier
Spruce	Picea
Weeping willow	Salix babylonica
FLOWERS	
Baby's breath	Gypsophila
Coreopsis	Coreopsis
Lily-of-the-valley	Convallaria
Lupine	Lupinus

PLANTS FOR SANDY SOIL

Common Name	Botanical Name
TREES	
American holly	Ilex opaca
Black gum	Nyssa sylvatica
Crabapple	Malus
Eastern red cedar	Juniperus virginiana
Eastern white pine	Pinus strobus
Jack pine	P. banksiana
Japanese black pine	P. thunbergii
Japanese pagoda tree	Sophora japonica
Jerusalem thorn	Parkinsonia aculeata
London plane tree	Platanus × acerifolia
Longleaf pine	Pinus palustris
Pin oak	Quercus palustris
Post oak	Quercus stellata
Red pine	Pinus resinosa
Russian olive	Elaeagnus angustifolia
Short-leaf pine	Pinus echinata
Slash pine	Pinus elliottii
Washington hawthorn	Crataegus phaenopyrum
White oak	Quercus alba
White poplar	Populus alba
White spruce	Picea glauca
SHRUBS	
Amur privet	Ligustrum amurense
Bayberry	Myrica pensylvanica
Beach plum	Prunus maritima
Bush clover	Lespedeza thunbergii
Butterfly bush	Buddleia davidii
Common buckthorn	Rhamnus catharticus
Firethorn	Pyracantha coccinea
Flowering quince	Chaenomeles speciosa
Highbush blueberry	Vaccinium corymbosum
Japanese barberry	Berberis thunbergii
Japanese kerria	Kerria japonica
Japanese spirea	Spiraea japonica

Common Name	Botanical Name
Mockorange	Philadelphus coronarius
Mountain laurel	Kalmia latifolia
Pfitzer juniper	Juniperus × media 'Pfitzeriana'
Red chokeberry	Aronia arbutifolia
Rugosa rose	Rosa rugosa
Sheep laurel	Kalmia angustifolia
Shrubby cinquefoil	Potentilla fruticosa
Smooth sumac	Rhus glabra
Tamarisk	Tamarix parviflora
Tatarian honeysuckle	Lonicera tatarica
Wax myrtle	Myrica cerifera
Weigela	Weigela florida
VINES AND GROUND COVERS	
American bittersweet	Celastrus scandens
Bearberry	Arctostaphylos uva-ursi
Bracken	Pteridium aquilinum
Common thyme	Thymus vulgaris
Creeping juniper	Juniperus horizontalis
Fragrant sumac	Rhus aromatica
Grape	Vitis
Hall's Japanese honeysuckle	Lonicera japonica 'Halliana'
Hardy kiwi	Actinidia arguta
Japanese garden juniper	Juniperus procumbens
Lilyturf	Liriope spicata
Lippia	Phyla nodiflora
Memorial rose	Rosa wichuraiana
Shore juniper	Juniperus conferta
Stonecrop	Sedum acre
Trailing lantana	Lantana montevidensis
Trumpet creeper	Campsis radicans
Virginia creeper	Parthenocissus quinquefolia
Wedelia	Wedelia trilobata

PLANTS TOLERANT OF SALINE (SODIC) SOIL

Common Name	Botanical Name
Aleppo pine	Pinus halepensis
Blue dracaena	Cordyline indivisa
Bougainvillea	Bougainvillea
Brush cherry	Syzygium paniculatum
Capeweed	Arctotheca calendula
Coyote brush	Baccharis pilularis
European fan palm	Chamaerops humilis
Firethorn	Pyracantha
Gazania	Gazania
Japanese euonymus	Euonymus japonica
Karo	Pittosporum crassifolium
Lippia	Phyla nodiflora
Mirror plant	Coprosma repens
Natal plum	Carissa grandiflora
Norfolk Island pine	Araucaria heterophylla
Oleander	Nerium oleander
Pampas grass	Cortaderia selloana
Rosea ice plant	Drosanthemum
Rosemary	Rosmarinus officinalis 'Lockwood de Forest'
Trailing ice plant	Lampranthus
Weeping bottlebrush	Callistemon viminalis
White ice plant	Delosperma 'Alba'

PLANTS FOR GROWING IN AREAS WITH RESTRICTED ROOT SPACE

Common Name	Botanical Name
Amur maple	Acer tataricum ginnala
Black haw	Viburnum prunifolium
Chinese pistachio	Pistacia chinensis
Cinquefoil	Potentilla fruticosa
Cotoneaster	Cotoneaster
Crabapple	Malus
Dogwood	Cornus
Dwarf mugo pine	Pinus mugo var. mugo
Flowering cherry	Prunus
Golden rain tree	Koelreuteria paniculata
Hawthorn	Crataegus
Hedge maple	Acer campestre
Holly	Ilex
Hornbeam	Carpinus
Japanese maple	Acer palmatum
Juniper	Juniperus
Maidenhair tree	Ginkgo
Mountain mahogany	Cercocarpus
Peach	Prunus
Pinyon pine	Pinus edulis
Plum	Prunus
Redbud	Cercis
Rosemary	Rosmarinus
Russian olive	Elaeagnus angustifolia
Saucer magnolia	Magnolia × soulangiana
Siebold viburnum	Viburnum sieboldii
Silk tree	Albizia julibrissin
Snowbell	Styrax
Southern black haw	Viburnum rufidulum
Star magnolia	Magnolia stellata
Strawberry tree	Arbutus unedo

PLANTS FOR WET SOIL

Common Name	Botanical Name
TREES	
Alder	Alnus
American holly	Ilex opaca
American larch	Larix laricina
Bald cypress	Taxodium distichum
Black gum	Nyssa sylvatica
Dahoon	Ilex cassine
Horsetail tree	Casuarina equisetifolia
Kanooka tristania	Tristaniopsis laurina
Pin oak	Quercus palustris
Plane tree, sycamore	Platanus
Poplar	Populus
Red maple	Acer rubrum
River birch	Betula nigra
Serviceberry	Amelanchier arborea
Silver maple	Acer saccharinum
Swamp white oak	Quercus bicolor
Sweet bay magnolia	Magnolia virginiana
Sweet gum	Liquidambar styraciflua
Willow	Salix
SHRUBS	
Arborvitae	Thuja
Bayberry	Myrica pensylvanica
Buttonbush	Cephalanthus occidentalis
Carolina allspice	Calycanthus
Cranberry bush	Viburnum trilobum
Fern-leaf bamboo	Bambusa disticha
Inkberry	Ilex glabra
Pink-shell azalea	Rhododendron vaseyi
Red chokeberry	Aronia arbutifolia
Red osier dogwood	Cornus stolonifera
Spicebush	Lindera benzoin
Swamp rose	Rosa palustris
Sweet azalea	Rhododendron arborescens
Water birch	Betula occidentalis
Willow	Salix
Winterberry	Ilex verticillata
PERENNIALS	
Astilbe	Astilbe
Bloodroot	Sanguinaria canadensis
Bugbane	Cimicifuga racemosa
Calla	Zantedeschia
Canada lily	Lilium canadense
Cardinal flower	Lobelia cardinalis
Common cattail	Typha latifolia
Elephant's ear	Colocasia esculenta
Fern family	Polypodiaceae
Forget-me-not	Myosotis scorpioides
Globe flower	Trollius
Golden-eyed grass	Sisyrinchium californicum
Great blue lobelia	Lobelia siphilitica
Japanese iris	Iris ensata
Japanese primrose	Primula japonica
Joe Pye weed	Eupatorium maculatum
Lance-leaved violet	Viola lanceolata
Marsh mallow	Althaea officinalis
Marsh marigold	Caltha palustris
Mint	Mentha
Moneywort	Lysimachia nummularia
Monkey flower	Mimulus
Monkshood	Aconitum
New England aster	Aster novae-angliae
Piggyback plant	Tolmiea menziesii
Ranunculus	Ranunculus
Ribbon grass	Phalaris arundinacea 'Picta'
Sedge	Carex
Siberian iris	Iris sibirica
Sweet flag	Acorus calamus
Sweet white violet	Viola blanda
Virginia waterleaf	Hydrophyllum virginianum

PLANTS TOLERANT OF INDUSTRIAL POLLUTION (SO₂)

Common Name	Botanical Name
TREES AND SHRUBS	
American arborvitae	*Thuja occidentalis*
American holly	*Ilex opaca*
Black locust	*Robinia pseudoacacia*
Black gum	*Nyssa sylvatica*
Cottonwood	*Populus deltoides*
Dwarf mugo pine	*Pinus mugo* var. *mugo*
Eastern sycamore	*Platanus occidentalis*
English holly	*Ilex aquifolium*
English oak	*Quercus robur*
European hornbeam	*Carpinus betulus*
Grapefruit	*Citrus × paradisi*
Green ash	*Fraxinus pennsylvanica*
Hedge maple	*Acer campestre*
Juniper	*Juniperus*
Lemon	*Citrus limon*
Lime	*Citrus aurantiifolia*
Linden	*Tilia*
London plane tree	*Platanus × acerifolia*
Maidenhair tree	*Ginkgo biloba*
Mountain maple	*Acer spicatum*
Privet	*Ligustrum*
Red oak	*Quercus rubra*
Sourwood	*Oxydendrum aboreum*
Sweet orange	*Citrus sinensis*
Western red cedar	*Thuja plicata*
VEGETABLES AND FRUITS	
Cabbage	*Brassica oleracea* var. *capitata*
Celery	*Apium graveolens* var. *dulce*
Corn	*Zea mays*
Muskmelon	*Cucumis melo*
Onion	*Allium cepa*

PLANTS TOLERANT OF SMOG (OZONE AND PAN)

Common Name	Botanical Name
TREES AND SHRUBS	
American arborvitae	*Thuja occidentalis*
Balsam fir	*Abies balsamea*
Burning bush	*Euonymus alatus*
Chinese azalea	*Rhododendron molle*
English oak	*Quercus robur*
European white birch	*Betula pendula*
Gray dogwood	*Cornus racemosa*
Norway maple	*Acer platanoides*
Red pine	*Pinus resinosa*
Sugar maple	*Acer saccharum*
White fir	*Abies concolor*
FLOWERS	
California poppy	*Eschscholzia californica*
Columbine	*Aquilegia*
Coral bells	*Heuchera sanguinea*
Daffodil	*Narcissus*
Iris	*Iris*
Lily	*Lilium*
Lily-of-the-Nile	*Agapanthus*
Snapdragon	*Antirrhinum*
GROUND COVERS	
English ivy	*Hedera helix*
Periwinkle	*Vinca minor*
VEGETABLES AND FRUITS	
Strawberry	*Fragaria xananassa*
Sweet potato	*Ipomoea batatas*

PLANTS ATTRACTIVE TO BEES

Common Name	Botanical Name
TREES AND SHRUBS	
Abelia	*Abelia*
Acacia	*Acacia*
Barberry	*Berberis*
Bottlebrush	*Callistemon*
Broom	*Cytisus*
California lilac	*Ceanothus*
Cotoneaster	*Cotoneaster*
Escallonia	*Escallonia*
Firethorn	*Pyracantha*
Heath	*Erica*
Heather	*Calluna*
Honeylocust	*Gleditsia*
Honeysuckle	*Lonicera*
Indian hawthorn	*Rhaphiolepis*
Lantana	*Lantana*
Loquat	*Eriobotrya*
Manzanita	*Arctostaphylos*
Myrtle	*Myrtus*
Oleander	*Nerium*
Pittosporum	*Pittosporum*
Privet	*Ligustrum*
Rosemary	*Rosmarinus*
Star jasmine	*Trachelospermum*
Thyme	*Thymus*
Wisteria	*Wisteria*
FLOWERS	
Bellflower	*Campanula*
Flowering tobacco	*Nicotiana*
Forget-me-not	*Myosotis*
Lavender	*Lavandula*
Sage	*Salvia*
Sunflower	*Helianthus*
Sweet alyssum	*Lobularia*
Yarrow	*Achillea*

PLANTS RELATIVELY FREE OF INSECTS AND DISEASES

Common Name	Botanical Name	Common Name	Botanical Name
Anise magnolia	Magnolia salicifolia	Japanese pagoda tree	Sophora japonica
Bald cypress	Taxodium	Japanese kerria	Kerria
Bayberry	Myrica	Katsura tree	Cercidiphyllum japonicum
Black gum	Nyssa	Kentucky coffee tree	Gymnocladus dioica
Bottletree	Brachychiton		
Broom	Cytisus	Kobus magnolia	Magnolia kobus
Buckthorn	Rhamnus	Maidenhair tree	Ginkgo
Carob	Ceratonia siliqua	Mediterranean hackberry	Celtis australis
Castor-aralia	Kalopanax pictus		
Cedar	Cedrus	Myrtle	Myrtus
Chinese pistachio	Pistacia chinensis	Persian parrotia	Parrotia persica
Cinquefoil	Potentilla	Podocarpus	Podocarpus
Cork tree	Phellodendron	Shiny xylosma	Xylosma congestum
Cornelian cherry	Cornus mas		
Cucumber tree	Magnolia acuminata	Siebold viburnum	Viburnum sieboldii
Dawn redwood	Metasequoia	Silk oak	Grevillea robusta
Fig	Ficus	Smoke tree	Cotinus
Franklin tree	Franklinia	Snowbell	Styrax
Golden rain tree	Koelreuteria paniculata	Star magnolia	Magnolia stellata
		Stewartia	Stewartia
Goldenchain tree	Laburnum	Tamarisk	Tamarix
Hardy rubber tree	Eucommia ulmoides	Tree of heaven	Ailanthus
		Turkish filbert	Corylus colurna
Hop hornbeam	Ostrya	Umbrella pine	Sciadopitys verticillata
Hornbeam	Carpinus		
Incense cedar	Calocedrus decurrens	Wax-leaf privet	Ligustrum lucidum
Japanese cornelian cherry	Cornus officinalis		

PLANTS RESISTANT AND SUSCEPTIBLE TO CEDAR-APPLE RUST (GYMNOSPORANGIUM JUNIPERI-VIRGINIANAE)

Common Name	Botanical Name
RESISTANT	
Chinese juniper 'Foemina' 'Keteleeri'	Juniperus chinensis
Common juniper 'Aureospica' 'Saxatilis' 'Suecica'	J. communis
Dwarf juniper	J. communis var. depressa
Eastern red cedar 'Tripartita'	J. virginiana
Sargent's juniper	J. sargentii
Savin juniper 'Broadmoor' 'Knap Hill' 'Skandia'	J. sabina
Singleseed juniper	J. squamata
SUSCEPTIBLE	
Apple, crabapple	Malus
Eastern red cedar	Juniperus virginiana
Rocky Mountain juniper	J. scopulorum
PARTICULARLY SUSCEPTIBLE APPLE VARIETIES	
Bechtel (crabapple)	
Imperial	
Jonathan	
Parkman (crabapple)	
Rome	
Wealthy	
York	

PLANTS SUSCEPTIBLE TO FIRE BLIGHT

Common Name	Botanical Name	Common Name	Botanical Name
TREES AND SHRUBS		Photinia	Photinia
Apple, crabapple	Malus	Rose	Rosa
Cotoneaster	Cotoneaster	Serviceberry	Amelanchier
Flowering almond, plum, and cherry	Prunus	Spirea	Spiraea
		FRUIT TREES AND BERRIES	
Flowering quince	Chaenomeles	Apple	Malus
Hawthorn	Crataegus	Pear	Pyrus
Loquat	Eriobotrya	Quince	Cydonia
Mountain ash	Sorbus	Raspberry	Rubus

PLANTS SUSCEPTIBLE AND RESISTANT TO PHYTOPHTHORA CINNAMOMI AND P. LATERALIS

Common Name	Botanical Name	Common Name	Botanical Name	Common Name	Botanical Name
SUSCEPTIBLE TREES AND SHRUBS		Juniper	Juniperus	Meyer juniper	Juniperus squamata 'Meyeri'
Abelia	Abelia	Larch	Larix		
Acacia	Acacia	Manzanita	Arctostaphylos	Pfitzer juniper	Juniperus × media 'Pfitzeriana'
Andromeda	Pieris	Myrtle	Myrtus		
Aralia	Fatsia	Oak	Quercus	Rose daphne	Daphne cneorum
Arborvitae	Thuja	Olive	Olea	Sasanqua camellia	Camellia sasanqua
Bald cypress	Taxodium	Pine	Pinus		
Beefwood	Casuarina	Pittosporum	Pittosporum	Savin juniper	Juniperus sabina
California lilac	Ceanothus	Plane tree, sycamore	Platanus	Sawara cypress	Chamaecyparis pisifera
Camphor tree	Cinnamomum	Rhododendron, azalea	Rhododendron		
Cedar	Cedrus	St. Johnswort	Hypericum	White cedar	Chamaecypario thyoides
Chestnut	Castanea	Spruce	Picea		
Coast redwood	Sequoia sempervirens	Sweet bay	Laurus	**SUSCEPTIBLE FRUITS AND BERRIES**	
		Viburnum	Viburnum	Apricot	Prunus armeniaca
Common camellia	Camellia japonica	Walnut	Juglans	Avocado	Persea
Cypress	Cupressus	Willow	Salix	Blueberry (highbush)	Vaccinium corymbosum
Daphne	Daphne	Yew	Taxus		
Dogwood	Cornus	**RESISTANT TREES AND SHRUBS**		Cherry	Prunus
Douglas fir	Pseudotsuga	Alaska cedar	Chamaecyparis nootkatensis	Citrus	Citrus
Eucalyptus	Eucalyptus			Peach	Prunus persica
Fir	Abies	American arborvitae	Thuja occidentalis	Pear	Pyrus
Heath	Erica	Dwarf mugo pine	Pinus mugo var. mugo	**RESISTANT BERRY**	
Heather	Calluna			Blueberry (rabbiteye)	Vaccinium ashei
Hibiscus	Hibiscus	Hiryu azalea	Rhododendron obtusum		
Incense cedar	Calocedrus				

PLANTS SUSCEPTIBLE TO SOUTHERN BLIGHT* (SCLEROTIUM ROLFSII)

Common Name	Botanical Name	Common Name	Botanical Name	Common Name	Botanical Name
SHRUBS		Gladiolus	Gladiolus	Tulip	Tulipa
Daphne	Daphne	Hollyhock	Alcea	Viola	Viola
Hydrangea	Hydrangea	Iris	Iris	Violet	Viola
Pittosporum	Pittosporum	Lily	Lilium	Zinnia	Zinnia
Rose	Rosa	Lupine	Lupinus	**VEGETABLES AND FRUITS**	
FLOWERS		Marguerite	Chrysanthemum	Apple	Onion
Anemone	Anemone	Marigold	Tagetes	Artichoke	Pea
Bellflower	Campanula	Mum	Chrysanthemum	Avocado	Peanut
Black-eyed Susan	Rudbeckia	Pansy	Viola	Bean	Pepper
Canna	Canna	Phlox	Phlox	Beet	Potato
Carnation	Dianthus	Pincushion flower	Scabiosa	Cabbage	Rhubarb
China aster	Callistephus	Pink	Dianthus	Cantaloupe	Squash
Cosmos	Cosmos	Pot marigold	Calendula	Carrot	Strawberry
Daffodil	Narcissus	Stonecrop	Sedum	Cucumber	Tomato
Dahlia	Dahlia	Sweet pea	Lathyrus	Eggplant	Turnip
Delphinium	Delphinium	Sweet William	Dianthus	Lettuce	Watermelon
				Okra	

* Southern blight has been reported on hundreds of plants. This is a partial list of plants that are frequently infected by this disease.

POWDERY MILDEWS AND SOME OF THE PLANTS THEY INFECT

Common Name	Botanical Name
ERYSIPHE CICHORACEARUM	
Aster	Aster
Bachelor's button	Centaurea
Begonia	Begonia
Black-eyed Susan	Rudbeckia
Carpet bugle	Ajuga
Cineraria	Senecio
Cosmos	Cosmos
Coyote brush	Baccharis
Dahlia	Dahlia
Daisy	Chrysanthemum
Eucalyptus	Eucalyptus
Forget-me-not	Myosotis
Hebe	Hebe
Hollyhock	Alcea
Lettuce	Lactuca
Marguerite	Chrysanthemum
Mum	Chrysanthemum
Painted tongue	Salpiglossis
Poppy	Papaver
Pot marigold	Calendula
Ranunculus	Ranunculus
Sage	Salvia
Smoke tree	Cotinus
Snapdragon	Antirrhinum
Spirea	Spiraea
Sumac	Rhus
Sunflower	Helianthus
Transvaal daisy	Gerbera
Verbena	Verbena
Watermelon	Citrullus
Yarrow	Achillea
Zinnia	Zinnia
ERYSIPHE POLYGONI	
Amaranth	Amaranthus
Bean	Phaseolus
Beet	Beta
Begonia	Begonia
Cabbage family	Brassica
California poppy	Eschscholzia

Common Name	Botanical Name
Candytuft	Iberis
Carnation	Dianthus
Cherry	Prunus
Cherry laurel	Prunus
Columbine	Aquilegia
Delphinium	Delphinium
Pansy	Viola
Pea	Pisum
Periwinkle	Vinca
Pink	Dianthus
Radish	Raphanus
Sweet alyssum	Lobularia
Sweet pea	Lathyrus
Sweet William	Dianthus
Viola	Viola
Violet	Viola
MICROSPHAERA ALNI	
Alder	Alnus
Hazelnut	Corylus
Honeysuckle	Lonicera
Lilac	Syringa
Oak	Quercus
Plane tree, sycamore	Platanus
Snowberry	Symphoricarpos
OTHER MICROSPHAERA SPECIES	
Acacia	Acacia
Blueberry	Vaccinium
Catalpa	Catalpa
Crape myrtle	Lagerstroemia
Euonymus	Euonymus
Heath	Erica
Honeysuckle	Lonicera
Hydrangea	Hydrangea
Indian hawthorn	Rhaphiolepis
Locust	Robinia
Magnolia	Magnolia
Passion flower	Passiflora
Plane tree, sycamore	Platanus
Poplar	Populus
Privet	Ligustrum

Common Name	Botanical Name
Rhododendron, azalea	Rhododendron
Tulip tree	Liriodendron
Viburnum	Viburnum
Walnut	Juglans
California lilac	Ceanothus
PHYLLACTINIA CORYLEA	
Blackberry	Rubus
Dogwood	Cornus
Horsechestnut	Aesculus
Mockorange	Philadelphus
Oak	Quercus
PODOSPHAERA SPECIES	
Apple, crabapple	Malus
Ash	Fraxinus
Firethorn	Pyracantha
Maple	Acer
Pear	Pyrus
Photinia	Photinia
Plum, peach, apricot	Prunus
Spirea	Spiraea
SPHAEROTHECA FULIGINEA	
Cantaloupe	Cucumis
Cucumber	Cucumis
Squash	Cucurbita
SPHAEROTHECA SPECIES	
Blanket flower	Gaillardia
Cinquefoil	Potentilla
Coral bells	Heuchera
Cotoneaster	Cotoneaster
Currant, gooseberry	Ribes
Flowering tobacco	Nicotiana
Hawthorn	Crataegus
Heath	Erica
Kalanchoe	Kalanchoe
Petunia	Petunia
Phlox	Phlox
Piggyback plant	Tolmiea
Rose	Rosa
Strawberry	Fragaria

PLANTS SUSCEPTIBLE TO QUINCE RUST (GYMNOSPORANGIUM CLAVIPES OR G. LIBOCEDRI)

Common Name	Botanical Name
Chokeberry	Aronia
Common juniper	Juniperus communis
Eastern red cedar	J. virginiana
Hawthorn	Crataegus
Incense cedar	Calocedrus decurrens
Mountain ash	Sorbus
Serviceberry	Amelanchier

PLANTS THAT MAY BE INFESTED BY THE MEDITERRANEAN FRUIT FLY

Apple	Peach
Apricot	Pear
Avocado	Pepper
Cantaloupe	Persimmon
Cherry	Plum
Citrus	Pumpkin
Cucumber	Pyracantha
Fig	Quince
Grape	Squash (Hubbard)
Guava	Strawberry
Loquat	Tomato
Olive	Walnut

Adapted from California Agriculture, *March–April 1981.*

PLANTS SUSCEPTIBLE TO BOTRYOSPHAERIA RIBIS

Common Name	Botanical Name
TREES AND SHRUBS	
Black gum	Nyssa
Chestnut	Castanea
Dogwood	Cornus
Firethorn	Pyracantha
Forsythia	Forsythia
Holly	Ilex
Maple	Acer
Poplar	Populus
Redbud	Cercis
Rhododendron, azalea	Rhododendron
Rose	Rosa
Sweet gum	Liquidambar
Willow	Salix
FRUITS, NUTS AND BERRIES	
Apple	Malus
Avocado	Persea
Citrus	Citrus
Currant	Ribes
Fig	Ficus
Hickory	Carya
Pear	Pyrus
Pecan	Carya

PLANTS SUSCEPTIBLE TO BACTERIAL BLIGHT (PSEUDOMONAS SYRINGAE)

Almond	Oleander
Apple	Pea
Avocado	Peach
Bean	Pear
Cherry	Plum
Citrus	Rose
Lilac	Stock

PLANTS RESISTANT TO COTTON ROOT ROT (PHYMATOTRICHUM OMNIVORUM)

Common Name	Botanical Name
TREES AND SHRUBS	
Deutzia	Deutzia
Ferns	
Hackberry	Celtis
Oak	Quercus
Palms	
Pomegranate	Punica
Weeping mulberry	Morus alba 'Pendula'
FLOWERS	
Amaranth	Amaranthus
Baby's breath	Gypsophila
California poppy	Eschscholzia
Calla	Zantedeschia
Candytuft	Iberis
Cyclamen	Cyclamen
Daffodil	Narcissus
Foxglove	Digitalis
Freesia	Freesia
Hyacinth	Hyacinthus
Iris	Iris
Moss rose	Portulaca
Nasturtium	Tropaeolum
Petunia	Petunia
Phlox	Phlox
Poppy	Papaver
Primrose	Primula
Slipper flower	Calceolaria
Snapdragon	Antirrhinum
Stock	Matthiola
Sweet alyssum	Lobularia
Zinnia	Zinnia
VEGETABLES AND FRUITS	
Asparagus	Grape
Cabbage family	Leek
Cantaloupe	Onion
Celery	Pumpkin
Cranberry	Spinach
Cucumber	Squash
Currant	Strawberry
Dewberry	Watermelon
Garlic	

PLANTS RESISTANT TO ARMILLARIA ROOT ROT

Common Name	Botanical Name	Common Name	Botanical Name	Common Name	Botanical Name
TREES AND SHRUBS		Japanese flowering crabapple	Malus floribunda	Southern catalpa	Catalpa bignonioides
American elder	Sambucus canadensis	Japanese maple	Acer palmatum	Southern magnolia	Magnolia grandiflora
Austrian pine	Pinus nigra	Japanese pagoda tree	Sophora japonica	Star acacia	Acacia verticillata
Bald cypress	Taxodium distichum	Judas tree	Cercis siliquastrum	Swamp birch	Betula pumila
Barberry	Berberis polyantha	Lawson's cypress	Chamaecyparis lawsoniana 'Ellwoodii'	Sweet gum	Liquidambar styraciflua
Bigleaf maple	Acer macrophyllum			Ternstroemia	Ternstroemia
Boxleaf honeysuckle	Lonicera nitida	Leyland cypress	Cupressocyparis leylandii	Torrey pine	Pinus torreyana
Boxwood	Buxus sempervirens	Madrone	Arbutus menziesii	Tree heath	Erica arborea
		Maidenhair tree	Ginkgo biloba	Tree of heaven	Ailanthus altissima
Bush acacia	Acacia longifolia	Mayten tree	Maytenus boaria		
Canary Island pine	Pinus canariensis	Modesto ash	Fraxinus velutina 'Modesto'	Tulip tree	Liriodendron tulipifera
Carob	Ceratonia siliqua			Valley oak	Quercus lobata
Carrotwood	Cupaniopsis anacardioides	Monterey pine	Pinus radiata	Western redbud	Cercis occidentalis
		Mulberry	Morus		
Catalina cherry	Prunus lyonii	Northern bayberry	Myrica pensylvanica	White fir	Abies concolor
Chaste tree	Vitex agnus-castus			Yedda hawthorn	Rhaphiolepis umbellata
Cherry laurel	Prunus laurocerasus	Oregon grapeholly	Mahonia aquifolium		
Chinese elm	Ulmus parvifolia			**FRUITS, NUTS, AND BERRIES**	
Chinese pistachio	Pistacia chinensis	Oriental sweet gum	Liquidambar orientalis	American chestnut	Castanea dentata
Chinese wisteria	Wisteria sinensis			Apple	Malus
Coast redwood	Sequoia sempervirens	Palms	Palmae	Avocado	Persea americana
		Plane tree, sycamore	Platanus	Black cherry	Prunus serotina
Dawn redwood	Metasequoia glyptostroboides	Queensland pittosporum	Pittosporum rhombifolium	Black walnut	Juglans nigra
				Callery pear	Pyrus calleryana
English holly	Ilex aquifolium	Red gum	Eucalyptus camaldulensis	Cherry plum	Prunus cerasifera
Eugenia	Eugenia			American persimmon	Diospyros virginiana
Evergreen ash	Fraxinus uhdei	Rose of Sharon	Hibiscus syriacus		
Flowering quince	Chaenomeles speciosa	Russian olive	Elaeagnus angustifolia	Japanese persimmon	Diospyros kaki
				Kadota fig	Ficus carica 'Kadota'
Fragrant sumac	Rhus aromatica	St. Johnswort	Hypericum patulum		
Hackberry	Celtis			Loganberry	Rubus ursinus
Heavenly bamboo	Nandina domestica	Scotch pine	Pinus sylvestris	Mission fig	Ficus carica 'Mission'
Holly-leaved cherry	Prunus ilicifolia	Shademaster locust	Gleditsia triacanthos 'Shademaster'		
Holly-leaved oak	Quercus ilex			Pear	Pyrus
Incense cedar	Calocedrus decurrens	Silver-dollar gum	Eucalyptus polyanthemos	Pecan	Carya illinoinensis
Jacaranda	Jacaranda mimosifolia	Smoke tree	Cotinus coggygria		
Japanese cedar	Cryptomeria japonica	Smooth Arizona cypress	Cupressus arizonica var. glabra		

PLANTS RESISTANT TO VERTICILLIUM WILT

Common Name	Botanical Name	Common Name	Botanical Name
TREES AND SHRUBS		Anemone	*Anemone*
American yellowwood	*Cladrastis lutea*	Baby blue-eyes	*Nemophila*
Apple	*Malus*	Baby's breath	*Gypsophila*
Ash	*Fraxinus*	Balloon flower	*Platycodon*
Bamboo		Begonia	*Begonia*
Barberry	*Berberis*	Blanket flower	*Gaillardia*
Beech	*Fagus*	Bulbs	
Birch	*Betula*	Cacti	
Black locust	*Robinia pseudoacacia*	Candytuft	*Iberis*
		Carnation	*Dianthus*
Box elder	*Acer negundo*	Christmas rose	*Helleborus*
Boxwood	*Buxus*	Cinquefoil	*Potentilla*
California lilac	*Ceanothus*	Columbine	*Aquilegia*
Conifers (cypress, fir, juniper, larch, pine, sequoia, spruce, and others)		Coral bells	*Heuchera*
		Ferns	
Crabapple	*Malus*	Gladiolus	*Gladiolus*
Currant	*Ribes*	Hollyhock	*Alcea*
Dogwood	*Cornus*	Impatiens	*Impatiens*
Eucalyptus	*Eucalyptus*	Iris	*Iris*
Firethorn	*Pyracantha*	Lantana	*Lantana*
Ginkgo	*Ginkgo biloba*	Monkey flower	*Mimulus*
Hawthorn	*Crataegus*	Moss rose	*Portulaca*
Holly	*Ilex*	Nasturtium	*Tropaeolum*
Honeylocust	*Gleditsia*	Nemesia	*Nemesia*
Hornbeam	*Carpinus*	Orchids	
Juniper	*Juniperus*	Ornamental grasses	
Katsura tree	*Cercidiphyllum japonicum*	Pansy	*Viola*
		Penstemon	*Penstemon*
Larch	*Larix*	Periwinkle	*Vinca*
Linden	*Tilia*	Pincushion flower	*Scabiosa*
Manzanita	*Arctostaphylos*	Pink	*Dianthus*
Maple	*Acer*	Pot marigold	*Calendula*
Mulberry	*Morus*	Primrose	*Primula*
Oak	*Quercus*	Ranunculus	*Ranunculus*
Oleander	*Nerium*	Sun rose	*Helianthemum*
Palms		Sweet William	*Dianthus*
Pear	*Pyrus*	Verbena	*Verbena*
Plane tree	*Platanus*	Viola	*Viola*
Redbud	*Cercis canadensis*	Violet	*Viola*
Russian olive	*Elaeagnus*	Zinnia	*Zinnia*
Sweet gum	*Liquidambar*	**VEGETABLES**	
Sycamore	*Platanus*	Asparagus	*Asparagus*
Viburnum	*Viburnum*	Bean	*Phaseolus*
Walnut	*Juglans*	Carrot	*Daucus*
Willow	*Salix*	Celery	*Apium*
Yew	*Taxus*	Corn	*Zea*
FLOWERS		Lettuce	*Lactuca*
Ageratum	*Ageratum*	Pea	*Pisum*
Alyssum	*Alyssum*	Sweet potato	*Ipomoea*

Houseplants

HOUSEPLANTS THAT TOLERATE FULL LIGHT

Common Name	Botanical Name
Amaryllis	Hippeastrum
Asparagus fern	Asparagus
Cactus family	Cactaceae
Caladium	Caladium
Chrysanthemum	Chrysanthemum
Citrus	Citrus
Coffee plant	Coffea
Coleus	Coleus
Column flower	Columnea
Croton	Codiaeum
False aralia	Dizygotheca
Geranium	Pelargonium
Ivy	Hedera
Japanese aralia	Fatsia
Lipstick plant	Aeschynanthus
Miniature rose	Rosa
Ornamental fig, rubber plant	Ficus
Ornamental pepper	Capsicum
Parlor ivy, string-of-beads	Senecio
Passion flower	Passiflora
Poinsettia	Euphorbia
Sago palm	Cycas
Schefflera	Brassaia
Velvet plant	Gynura
Wax begonia	Begonia
Wax plant	Hoya

HOUSEPLANTS THAT TOLERATE LOW LIGHT

Common Name	Botanical Name
Arrowhead vine	Syngonium
Cast-iron plant	Aspidistra
Chinese evergreen	Aglaonema
Dracaena	Dracaena
Dumb cane	Dieffenbachia
Grape ivy	Cissus
Mother-in-law's tongue/snake plant	Sansevieria
Palms	Palmae
Kentia palm	Howea
Lady palm	Rhapis
Parlor palm	Chamaedorea
Peace lily	Spathiphyllum
Philodendron	Philodendron
Pothos	Scindapsus and Epipremnum

HOUSEPLANTS THAT ROOT EASILY

Common Name	Botanical Name
African violet	Saintpaulia
Aluminum plant	Pilea
Arrowhead vine	Syngonium
Begonia	Begonia
Chinese evergreen	Aglaonema
Chrysanthemum	Chrysanthemum
Coleus	Coleus
Geranium	Pelargonium
Grape ivy	Cissus
Impatiens	Impatiens
Ivy	Hedera
Jade plant	Crassula
Nerve plant	Fittonia
Philodendron	Philodendron
Piggyback plant	Tolmiea
Pothos	Scindapsus
Prayer plant	Maranta
Spider plant	Chlorophytum
Swedish ivy	Plectranthus
Velvet plant	Gynura
Wandering Jew	Tradescantia

HOUSEPLANTS SENSITIVE TO SALTS IN THE SOIL

Common Name	Botanical Name
Avocado	Persea
Cast-iron plant	Aspidistra
Citrus	Citrus
Coffee plant	Coffea
Fern family	Polypodiaceae
Grape ivy	Cissus
Haworthia	Haworthia
Ivy	Hedera
Japanese aralia	Fatsia
Kentia palm	Howea
Ornamental fig, rubber plant	Ficus
Parlor palm	Chamaedorea
Peace lily	Spathiphyllum
Philodendron	Philodendron
Piggyback plant	Tolmiea
Prayer plant	Maranta
Sago palm	Cycas
Screw pine	Pandanus
Spider plant	Chlorophytum
Split-leaf philodendron	Monstera
Strawberry geranium	Saxifraga
Ti plant	Cordyline
Zebra plant	Aphelandra and Calathea

TURFGRASS CLIMATE ZONES

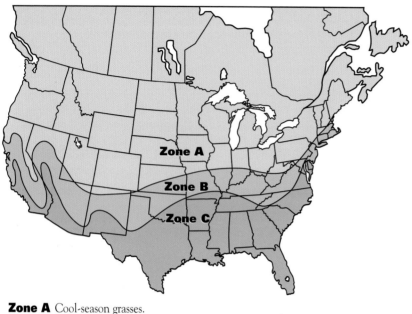

Zone A Cool-season grasses.
Zone C Warm-season grasses.
Zone B This is a transition zone in which both warm-season and cool-season grasses are grown. Because warm-season grasses have long dormant periods in this zone, cool-season grasses are usually preferred. Tall fescue does particularly well in this zone.

From *Turf Managers Handbook,* W. H. Daniel and R. P. Freeborg.

CHARACTERISTICS OF SOME TURFGRASSES

Grass	Zone[1]	Drought Resistant	Shade Tolerant	Days to Germinate	Low Maintenance[1,2]
Bahiagrass	C			21–28	
Bentgrass	A		•	5–12	
Bermudagrass, common	C	•		14–20	•
Bermudagrass, improved	C	•		Sprigs[3]	•
Carpetgrass	C			21	
Centipedegrass	C			14–20	
Fescue, red	A	•	•	5–12	•
Fescue, tall	A	•	•	5–12	•
Kentucky bluegrass	A			20–30	
St. Augustinegrass	C		•	Sprigs[3]	
Zoysiagrass	C	•	•	Sprigs[3]	•

[1] For information on Zones, see map above.
[2] Low-maintenance turfgrasses tolerate irregular fertilizing, watering, and mowing.
[3] Usually planted as sprigs or plugs, rather than as seed.

TURFGRASSES RESISTANT TO DOLLAR SPOT

BLUEGRASS

A–20	Midnight
Adelphi	Parade
Ascot	Park
Bonnieblue	Preakness
Bristol	Princeton
Columbia	Rita
Eagleton	SR 2000
Eclipse	Touchdown
Kenblue	Unique
Liberty	Vantage
Majestic	Victa

FINE FESCUE

Chewings	Creeping
Brittany	Aruba
Jamestown	Dawson
Molina	Florentine
Sandpiper	Flyer II
Tiffany	Jasper
Treazure	Pennlawn
Victory	Shademaster II
Victory II	Silverlawn

Hard
Defiant
Ecostar
SR 3100

BENTGRASS

Allure	Egmont
Arlington	Pennpar
Bardot	Tracenta

BLUEGRASS RESISTANT TO RUST

A–20	Glade
A–34	Haga
Alpine	Majestic
Baron	Miracle
Bartitia	Park
Bonnieblue	Pennstar
Classic	Rugby
Fylking	Suffolk
Georgetown	Washington

Bluegrass Resistant and Susceptible to Fusarium Blight

Resistant

A–20	Parade
Adelphi	Rugby
Bonnieblue	Sydsport
Columbia	Trenton
Enmundi	Vantage
Glade	Windsor

Susceptible

Arboretum	Modena
Belturf	Newport
Brunswick	Nugget
Campus	Park
Cougar	Pennstar
Delft	Pio-Cebaco
Enita	Plush
Fylking	Ram 1
Geronimo	South Dakota
Merion	

Bluegrass Resistant to Fusarium Patch

Adelphi	Cynthia
Barcelona	Gnome
Bartitia	Liberty
Barzan	Merit
Birka	Miracle
Bonnieblue	Nublue
Bronco	Ram 1
Crest	Touchdown

Bluegrass Resistant and Susceptible to Helminthosporium Leaf Spot

Resistant

A–20	Eclipse
Able I	Limousine
Adelphi	Majestic
Alpine	Merion
Apex	Minstrel
Ascot	Noblesse
Barblue	Nugget
Barcelona	Parade
Birka	Pennstar
Blacksburg	Rita
Bonnieblue	Rugby
Bristol	SR 2000
Brunswick	Sydsport
Caliber	Touchdown
Cardiff	Vantage
Cobalt	Victa

Susceptible

Allure	Greenley
Barzan	Kenblue
Chelsea	Miracle
Cynthia	Nottingham
Delta	Park
Eagleton	Ram I
Fairfax	Raven
Geary	Ronde
Ginger	South Dakota
Glade	

Bluegrass Resistant to Red Thread

A–34	Eclipse
Able I	Fortuna
Adelphi	Gnome
Ampella	Indigo
Apex	Kelly
Ascot	Marquis
Aspen	Merion
Baron	Minstrel
Baronie	Miranda
Belmont	Nassau
Birka	Nublue
Blacksburg	Nustar
Bonnieblue	Princeton
Broadway	Rita
Cannon	SR 2000
Challenger	Touchdown
Conni	Trenton
Destiny	Viva

Bluegrass Resistant to Stripe Smut

A–20	Cobalt
A–34	Conni
Adelphi	Dawn
Alpine	Destiny
Apex	Eclipse
Aquila	Enmundi
Aspen	Eva
Banff	Freedom
Barcelona	Georgetown
Baronie	Glade
Barzan	Indigo
Belmont	Julia
Birka	Newport
Blacksburg	Plush
Bonnieblue	Ram I
Brunswick	Sydsport
Caliber	Touchdown
Cardiff	Vantage
Classic	

Ground Covers

GROUND COVERS FOR SUNNY AREAS

Common Name	Botanical Name
Bearberry	Arctostaphylos uva-ursi
Bearberry cotoneaster	Cotoneaster dammeri
California lilac	Ceanothus griseus var. horizontalis
Chadwick yew	Taxus × media 'Chadwicki'
Creeping cotoneaster	Cotoneaster adpressus
Creeping thyme	Thymus
Dwarf coyote brush	Baccharis pilularis
Dwarf rosemary	Rosmarinus officinalis 'Prostratus'
Ice plant	Carpobrotus, Lampranthus, and other genera
Juniper	Juniperus
Lantana	Lantana
Lavender cotton	Santolina
Lippia	Phyla nodiflora
Low-bush blueberry	Vaccinium angustifolium
Moss phlox	Phlox subulata
Rockspray cotoneaster	Cotoneaster horizontalis
Rockcress	Arabis
St. Johnswort	Hypericum
Santa Cruz firethorn	Pyracantha koidzumii 'Santa Cruz'
Snow-in-summer	Cerastium tomentosum
Star jasmine	Trachelospermum jasminoides
Stonecrop	Sedum
Sun rose	Helianthemum nummularium
Woolly yarrow	Achillea tomentosa
Wormwood	Artemisia

GROUND COVERS FOR SHADY AREAS

Common Name	Botanical Name
Asparagus fern	Asparagus densiflorus
Baby's tears	Soleirolia soleirolii
Barrenwort	Epimedium
Carpet bugle	Ajuga
Dwarf Himalayan sweet box	Sarcococca hookeriana var. humilis
Ivy	Hedera
Japanese holly fern	Cyrtomium falcatum
Japanese painted fern	Athyrium nipponicum 'Pictum'
Japanese spurge	Pachysandra terminalis
Lily turf	Liriope
Maidenhair fern	Adiantum pedatum
Mock strawberry	Duchesnea indica
Mondo grass	Ophiopogon japonicus
Periwinkle	Vinca
St. Johnswort	Hypericum
Sweet violet	Viola odorata
Sweet woodruff	Galium odoratum
Wild ginger	Asarum
Winter creeper	Euonymus fortunei
Wood fern	Dryopteris

DROUGHT-RESISTANT GROUND COVERS

Common Name	Botanical Name
Bearberry cotoneaster	Cotoneaster dammeri
Blue fescue	Festuca glauca
Creeping cotoneaster	Cotoneaster adpressus
Crown vetch	Coronilla varia
Dwarf coyote bush	Baccharis pilularis
Dwarf rosemary	Rosmarinus officinalis 'Prostratus'
Goutweed	Aegopodium podagraria
Ice plant	Carpobrotus, Lampranthus, and other genera
Juniper	Juniperus
Lavender cotton	Santolina
Lippia	Phyla nodiflora
Manzanita	Arctostaphylos manzanita
Peruvian verbena	Verbena peruviana
Ribbon grass	Phalaris arundinacea var. picta
Rockspray cotoneaster	Cotoneaster horizontalis
Rock rose	Cistus
St. Johnswort	Hypericum
Stonecrop	Sedum
Sun rose	Helianthemum nummularium
Thyme	Thymus
Wormwood	Artemisia

PLANTING AND BLOOMING TIMES OF FLOWERS

Flower	Plant	Planting Season	Blooming Season	Ideal Soil Temperature for Germination (°F)	Days to Germination
Ageratum	A	Sp*	Sp–Su	60–65	10
Amaranth	A	Sp	Sp–Su	60–70	12
Anemone	Tu	F or Sp	Sp	**	**
Aster	P	Sp	Sp–Su–F	70	12–14
Astilbe	P	Sp	Sp–Su	60–70	14–21
Begonia	Tp	Sp	Sp–Su	70–75	15–20
Bellflower	P	Sp	Sp–Su–F	68–86	10–14
Black-eyed Susan	A, P	Sp	Su–F	70–75	5–10
Blanket flower	A, P	Sp*	Su–F	70	15–20
Candytuft	A, P	Sp*	Sp–Su	70–85	7–15
Canna	Rh	Sp	Su–F	**	**
Cape marigold	A	Sp	Su	70–85	15–20
Chrysanthemum	A, P	Sp	Su–F	70	7–10
Cineraria	A	Sp*	W–Sp	45–60	20
Cockscomb	A	Sp	Su	70–85	7–14
Columbine	P	F or Sp	Sp–Su	70–85	21–28
Coral bells	P	F or Sp	Sp–Su	70–85	5–20
Coreopsis	A, P	F or Sp	Su–F	70	15–20
Cosmos	A	Sp	Su–F	70–85	10–15
Crocus	Corm	F	Sp	**	**
Dahlia	Tu	Sp	Su–F	70–85 (seed)	15–20
Daylily	Tu	Sp*	Su	**	**
Delphinium	A, P	Sp*	Su	55–60	15–30
Flowering onion	Bu	F or Sp	Sp–Su	**	**
Foxglove	Bi, P	Sp	Sp–Su	70–85	15–20
Freesia	Corm	Sp*	Sp	**	**
Geranium	P	Sp	Sp–Su–F	68–85	15–65
Gladiolus	Corm	Sp	Su–F	**	**
Hollyhock	Bi	Sp–Su	Sp–Su	68	7–21
Hyacinth	Bu	F	Sp	**	**
Impatiens	A, Tp	Sp	Su	70	15–20
Iris	Rh, Bu	F	Sp–Su	**	**
Lantana	Tp	Sp	Sp–F	70	40–50
Lily	Bu	Sp	Su	**	**
Lily-of-the-valley	P	F (from pips)	Sp	**	**
Lobelia	A	Sp*	Su–F	70–85	15–20
Marigold	A	Sp	Su–F	70–75	5–7
Ornamental pepper	A	Sp	Su	70	15–20
Painted tongue	A	Sp	Su	70–75	15–20
Phlox	A, P	Sp*	Su–F	55–65	8–20
Pink	A, P	Sp*	Sp–Su	70	15–30
Pot marigold	A	Sp*	W–Sp	70–85	7–14
Primrose	A, P	Sp*	W–Sp	55–65	20
Ranunculus	Tu	F or Sp	Sp–Su	**	**
Sage	A, P	Sp	Su	70	12–15
Snapdragon	A	Sp*	Sp–Su	70	15
Solanum	A, P	Sp	Su–F	70	15–30
Spider flower	A	Sp*	Su	55–85	10–14
Stock	A	Sp	Sp–Su	55–90	15
Sunflower	A, P	Sp	Su–F	70–85	15–20
Sun rose	P	F or Sp	Su	70	15–20
Sweet alyssum	A, P	Sp	Sp–Su–F	70	7–15
Sweet pea	A	W–Sp	Sp	70	15
Transvaal daisy	Tp	Sp	Su	70	15
Yarrow	P	Sp	Su–F	70	5–15

PLANT KEY

A	Annual
Bi	Biennial
Bu	Bulb
P	Perennial
Rh	Rhizome
Tp	Tender Perennial, grown as annual in all but Zones 9 and 10
Tu	Tuber

PLANTING SEASON KEY

Sp	Spring
Su	Summer
F	Fall
W	Winter

Florida gardeners may find differences in planting times and soil temperatures. Check with your local county extension service.

* *Planted in the fall in Zones 9 and 10. See USDA Plant Hardiness Zone Map, page 530.*

** *Not usually planted from seed.*

FLOWERS TOLERANT OF PHYTOPHTHORA

Common Name	Botanical Name
RESISTANT OR VERY TOLERANT	
Begonia	*Begonia*
Cockscomb	*Celosia*
Flossflower	*Ageratum*
Flowering tobacco	*Nicotiana*
Geranium	*Pelargonium*
Marigold	*Tagetes*
Pincushion flower	*Scabiosa*
SOMEWHAT TOLERANT	
Black-eyed Susan	*Rudbeckia*
Impatiens	*Impatiens*
Petunia	*Petunia*
Zinnia	*Zinnia*

CHRYSANTHEMUM VARIETIES RESISTANT TO CHRYSANTHEMUM RUST

Achievement
Copper Bowl
Escapade
Helen Castle
Mandalay
Matador
Miss Atlanta
Orange Bowl
Powder Puff

Adapted from Chrysanthemum Cultivars Resistant to Verticillium Wilt and Rust, *University of California County Extension leaflet 21057.*

PLANTS SUSCEPTIBLE TO ASTER YELLOWS

Common Name	Botanical Name
FLOWERS	
Anemone	*Anemone*
Aster	*Aster*
Bachelor's button	*Centaurea*
Blanket flower	*Gaillardia*
Cape marigold	*Dimorphotheca*
Carnation, pink, sweet William	*Dianthus*
China aster	*Callistephus*
Cockscomb	*Celosia*
Coreopsis	*Coreopsis*
Cosmos	*Cosmos*
Delphinium	*Delphinium*
Gladiolus	*Gladiolus*
Lobelia	*Lobelia*
Marigold	*Tagetes*
Mum, Daisy, Marguerite	*Chrysanthemum*
Petunia	*Petunia*
Phlox	*Phlox*
Pincushion flower	*Scabiosa*
Pot marigold	*Calendula*
Snapdragon	*Antirrhinum*
Strawflower	*Helichrysum*
VEGETABLES	
Broccoli	Parsley
Cabbage	Parsnip
Carrot	Potato
Cauliflower	Pumpkin
Celery	Radish
Endive	Spinach
Lettuce	Squash
New Zealand spinach	Tomato
Onion	
WEEDS	
Dandelion	*Taraxacum*
Fleabane	*Erigeron*
Horseweed	*Conyza*
Plantain	*Plantago*
Ragweed	*Ambrosia*
Plume thistle	*Cirsium*
Wild carrot	*Daucus*

LILIES TOLERANT OF AND SUSCEPTIBLE TO VIRUSES

TOLERANT OR MODERATELY TOLERANT

SPECIES

Lilium amabile
L. bulbiferum
L. callosum
L. candidum
L. cernuum
L. concolor
L. dauricum
L. davidii
L. hansonii
L. henryi
L. humboldtii
L. leichtlinii var. *maximowiczii*
L. leucanthum var. *centifolium*
L. longiflorum
L. maculatum
L. martagon
L. monadelphum
L. pardalinum
L. parryi
L. pumilum
L. pyrenaicum
L. regale
L. speciosum
L. taliense

L. tsingtauense
L. wardii
L. wilsonii

HYBRIDS

Asiatics (1a)[1]
Connecticut King
Pollyanna
Yellow Blaze
Impact
Gran Paradiso
Redsong
Montreaux
Nepal
White Ballerina

Asiatics (1b, 1c)[1]
Ariadne
Aloft
Discovery
Citronella
George Slate
Iowa Rose
Red Velvet

Pixies
Buff Pixie
Butter Pixie
Lemon Pixie

Aurelians (5c)[1]
Gold Eagle
White Henryi

Orientals (7)[1]
Allegra
Casablanca
Journey's End

Orienpets (8)
Black Beauty
Leslie Woodriff
Scheherazade
Silk Road
Starburst Sensation

SUSCEPTIBLE

Lilium auratum
L. brownii var. *australe*
L. canadense
L. duchartrei
L. formosanum
L. lancifolium[2] (*L. tigrinum*)
L. lankongense
L. mackliniae
L. nepalense
L. philippinense
L. rubellum
L. sulphureum
L. superbum
L. wallichianum var. *neilgherrense*

[1] Horticultural classification.

[2] Easily infected, but not apparently injured; can become a carrier to other susceptible species.

Trees, Shrubs, and Vines

TREES AND SHRUBS THAT WILL GROW IN ALKALINE SOIL (pH OF 7.5 TO 8.4)

Common Name	Botanical Name
Arizona ash	Fraxinus velutina
Arrowwood	Viburnum dentatum
Beefwood	Casuarina
Box elder	Acer negundo
Bridalwreath	Spiraea × prunifolia
Bush cinquefoil	Potentilla fruticosa
Common jujube	Ziziphus jujuba
Date palm	Phoenix dactylifera
Deutzia	Deutzia
Forsythia	Forsythia
Fragrant honeysuckle	Lonicera fragrantissima
Fremont cottonwood	Populus fremontii
Hackberry	Celtis
Japanese barberry	Berberis thunbergii
Japanese pagoda tree	Sophora japonica
Japanese kerria	Kerria japonica
Linden viburnum	Viburnum dilatatum
Locust	Robinia
Mockorange	Philadelphus
Mountain mahogany	Cercocarpus
Rose of Sharon	Hibiscus syriacus
Russian olive	Elaeagnus angustifolia
Sargent crabapple	Malus sargentii
Silk tree	Albizia
Washington palm	Washingtonia

TREES SUSCEPTIBLE TO LIGHTNING INJURY

Common Name	Botanical Name
SUSCEPTIBLE	
Ash	Fraxinus
Elm	Ulmus
Oak	Quercus
Pine	Pinus
Poplar	Populus
Spruce	Picea
Tulip tree	Liriodendron
LESS SUSCEPTIBLE*	
Beech	Fagus
Birch	Betula
Horsechestnut	Aesculus

* No species is totally immune, and location and size of the tree also influence susceptibility.

Adapted from Tree Maintenance, P. P. Pirone. Copyright 1978 Oxford University Press. Reprinted by permission.

TREES SUSCEPTIBLE TO LANDFILL DAMAGE

Common Name	Botanical Name
MOST SUSCEPTIBLE	
Beech	Fagus
Dogwood	Cornus
Oak	Quercus
Pine	Pinus
Spruce	Picea
Sugar maple	Acer saccharum
Tulip tree	Liriodendron
MODERATELY SUSCEPTIBLE	
Birch	Betula
Hemlock	Tsuga
Hickory	Carya
LEAST SUSCEPTIBLE	
Elm	Ulmus
Locust	Robinia
Pin oak	Quercus palustris
Plane tree	Platanus
Poplar	Populus
Sycamore	Platanus
Willow	Salix

Adapted from Tree Maintenance, P. P. Pirone. Copyright 1978 Oxford University Press. Reprinted by permission.

TREES COMMONLY DAMAGED BY SAPSUCKERS

Common Name	Botanical Name
Acacia	Acacia
Apple, crabapple	Malus
Beech	Fagus
Beefwood	Casuarina
Birch	Betula
Douglas fir	Pseudotsuga menziesii
Fir	Abies
Hemlock	Tsuga
Larch	Larix
Loquat	Eriobotrya
Magnolia	Magnolia
Palms	Palmae
Pine	Pinus
Quaking aspen	Populus tremuloides
Red maple	Acer rubrum
Red spruce	Picea rubens
Silk oak	Grevillea
Sugar maple	Acer saccharum
Willow	Salix

TREES WITH WEAK FORKS AND BRITTLE WOOD

Common Name	Botanical Name
Acacia	Acacia
Bottlebrush	Callistemon citrinus
Chestnut oak	Quercus prinus
Chinaberry	Melia azedarach
Coast redwood	Sequoia sempervirens
Eucalyptus	Eucalyptus
Horsechestnut	Aesculus
Locust	Robinia
Melaleuca	Melaleuca
Modesto ash	Fraxinus velutina 'Modesto'
Poplar	Populus
Sassafras	Sassafras
She oak	Casuarina stricta
Siberian elm	Ulmus pumila
Silver maple	Acer saccharinum
Southern magnolia	Magnolia grandiflora
Tree of heaven	Ailanthus
Tulip tree	Liriodendron
White mulberry	Morus alba
Willow	Salix

TREES AND SHRUBS RESISTANT TO CROWN GALL

Common Name	Botanical Name
Abelia	Abelia
Andromeda	Pieris
Barberry	Berberis
Beech	Fagus
Birch	Betula
Black gum	Nyssa
Boxwood	Buxus
Catalpa	Catalpa
Cedar	Cedrus
Cryptomeria	Cryptomeria
Deutzia	Deutzia
Elderberry	Sambucus
Firethorn	Pyracantha
Goldenchain tree	Laburnum
Golden rain tree	Koelreuteria
Heather	Calluna
Hemlock	Tsuga
Holly	Ilex
Hornbeam	Carpinus
Kentucky coffee tree	Gymnocladus
Larch	Larix
Leucothoe	Leucothoe
Magnolia	Magnolia
Maidenhair tree	Ginkgo
Mountain laurel	Kalmia
Oregon grapeholly	Mahonia aquifolium
Redbud	Cercis
Sassafras	Sassafras
Serviceberry	Amelanchier
Silk tree	Albizia
Smoke tree	Cotinus
Spruce	Picea
Sumac	Rhus
Sweet gum	Liquidambar
Tree of heaven	Ailanthus
Tulip tree	Liriodendron
Yellowwood	Cladrastis
Zelkova	Zelkova

Adapted from Crown Gall, W. A. Sinclair and W. T. Johnson. Cornell University Tree Pest leaflet A-5.

TREES AND SHRUBS WITH SHALLOW ROOT SYSTEMS

Common Name	Botanical Name
Acacia	Acacia
Alder	Alnus
Black locust	Robinia
Elm	Ulmus
Eucalyptus	Eucalyptus
Evergreen ash	Fraxinus uhdei
Fig	Ficus
Honeylocust	Gleditsia
Mulberry	Morus
Pacific dogwood	Cornus nuttallii
Plane tree, sycamore	Platanus
Poplar	Populus
Silver maple	Acer saccharinum
Sumac	Rhus
Tree of heaven	Ailanthus altissima
Willow	Salix

TREES THAT TOLERATE COMPETITION FROM LAWN GRASS

Common Name	Botanical Name
Amur maple	Acer tataricum ginnala
Crape myrtle	Lagerstroemia
Dogwood	Cornus
Flowering cherry, peach, plum	Prunus
Golden rain tree	Koelreuteria
Hawthorn	Crataegus
Hedge maple	Acer campestre
Japanese maple	Acer palmatum
Modesto ash	Fraxinus velutina 'Modesto'
Saucer magnolia	Magnolia × soulangiana
Silk tree	Albizia julibrissin
Smoke tree	Cotinus
Star magnolia	Magnolia stellata

LOW-GROWING TREES SUITABLE FOR PLANTING UNDER OVERHEAD WIRES

Common Name	Botanical Name
Amur maple	Acer tataricum ginnala
Crabapple	Malus
Crape myrtle	Lagerstroemia indica
Flowering cherry, peach, plum	Prunus
Golden rain tree	Koelreuteria paniculata
Hedge maple	Acer campestre
Japanese maple	Acer palmatum
Mountain maple	Acer spicatum
Redbud	Cercis
Smoke tree	Cotinus
Snowbell	Styrax japonicus
Tatarian maple	Acer tataricum

SMALL TREES FOR AREAS WITH RESTRICTED ROOT SPACE

Common Name	Botanical Name
Amur maple	Acer tataricum ginnala
Black haw	Viburnum prunifolium
Chinese pistache	Pistacia chinensis
Crabapple	Malus
Dogwood	Cornus
Flowering cherry	Prunus
Golden rain tree	Koelreuteria
Hawthorn	Crataegus
Hedge maple	Acer campestre
Holly	Ilex
Hornbeam	Carpinus
Japanese maple	Acer palmatum
Peach	Prunus
Plum	Prunus
Redbud	Cercis
Russian olive	Elaeagnus angustifolia
Saucer magnolia	Magnolia × soulangiana
Siebold viburnum	Viburnum sieboldii
Silk tree	Albizia julibrissin
Snowbell	Styrax
Southern black haw	Viburnum rufidulum
Star magnolia	Magnolia stellata

Adapted from Trees for American Gardens, Donald Wyman. Copyright 1951, 1965, MacMillan Publishing Co. Reprinted by permission.

TREES AND SHRUBS FOR SHADY AREAS

Common Name	Botanical Name
Andromeda	*Pieris*
Arborvitae	*Thuja*
Azalea	*Rhododendron*
Boxwood	*Buxus*
Camellia	*Camellia*
Carolina allspice	*Calycanthus*
Daphne	*Daphne*
David viburnum	*Viburnum davidii*
Dogwood	*Cornus*
False cypress	*Chamaecyparis*
Heavenly bamboo	*Nandina*
Hemlock	*Tsuga*
Holly	*Ilex*
Hydrangea	*Hydrangea*
Japanese aucuba	*Aucuba japonica*
Japanese maple	*Acer palmatum*
Laurel	*Laurus nobilis*
Laurustinus	*Viburnum tinus*
Leucothoe	*Leucothoe*
Mountain laurel	*Kalmia*
Oregon grapeholly	*Mahonia aquifolium*
Pittosporum	*Pittosporum*
Privet	*Ligustrum*
Redbud	*Cercis*
Rhododendron	*Rhododendron*
Serviceberry	*Amelanchier*
Silverbell	*Halesia*
Sweet box	*Sarcococca*
Vine maple	*Acer circinatum*
Witch hazel	*Hamamelis*
Yew	*Taxus*

CRAPE MYRTLE VARIETIES IMMUNE TO POWDERY MILDEW

Acoma	Muskogee
Apalachee	Osage
Choctaw	Tonto
Fantasy	

RESISTANT VARIETIES

Basham's Party Pink	Pecos
Comanche	Regal Red
Glendora White	Sioux
Hopi	Tuscarora
Lipan	Tuskegee
Miami	Wichita
Near East	Yuma

DISEASE-RESISTANT CRABAPPLES

Species or Variety	Scab	Fire Blight	Powdery Mildew	Description
Adams	VR	VR	VR	Flowers opening to pink; fruit vivid red, ¾" across.
Beverly	VR	SR	—	Flowers opening to white; fruit red, ½" to ¾" across.
Centurion	R	—	—	Flowers rose red; fruit glossy cherry red, ⅝" across.
Christmas Holly	VR	—	—	Flowers opening to white; fruit bright red and lasting, ⅛" across.
David	VR	R	—	Flowers opening to white; fruit scarlet, ½" across.
Dolgo	VR	VR	—	Flowers white; fruit red, 1¼" across.
Donald Wyman	VR	SR	VR	Flowers opening to white; fruit glossy red, ¾" across.
Harvest Gold	SR	—	—	Flowers white; fruit gold and lasting, ⅜" across.
Henning	VR	—	—	Flowers white; fruit orange-red, ⅝" across.
Jewelberry	VR	VR	—	Flowers pink and white; fruit glossy red, ½" across; dwarf, shrubby tree.
Liset	VR	VR	R	Flowers rose red to light crimson; fruit glossy dark red, ⅝" across.
Malus baccata var. *jackii*	VR	SR	VR	Flowers white, fragrant; fruit glossy red, ½" across.
M. floribunda	VR	R	VR	Flowers opening to pink and white; fruit yellow and red, ⅜" across.
M. sargentii	VR	R	—	Flowers white, fragrant; fruit dark red, ¼" across; broad habit.
Mary Potter	R	R	R	Flowers opening to white; fruit red, ½" across.
Ormiston Roy	VR	VR	—	Flowers pink; fruit yellow, ⅝" across.
Red Baron	R	VR	—	Flowers very dark red; fruit glossy dark red, medium-sized; columnar habit.
Red Jewel	R	SR	VR	Flowers white; fruit cherry red, ⅜" across; broad habit.
Selkirk	R	VR	R	Flowers purplish pink; fruit glossy bright red.
Sentinel	R	VR	—	Flowers pale pink; fruit red, small.
Silver Moon	VR	—	—	Flowers white; fruit tiny, red, persistent.
Sugartyme	VR	—	—	Flowers white; fruit bright red, persistent, ¼" across.
White Angel	VR	R	—	Flowers opening to white; fruit red, ½" across.
White Cascade	VR	VR	VR	Flowers opening to white; fruit lime-yellow; weeping habit.

VR: Very resistant
R: Resistant
SR: Somewhat resistant

ELM VARIETIES RESISTANT TO DUTCH ELM DISEASE

Accolade	Pathfinder
Autumn Gold	Patriot
Cathedral	Pioneer
Dynasty	Princeton
Frontier	Prospector
Homestead	Regal
Independence	Sapporo
New Harmony	Urban
New Horizon	Valley Forge
Ohio	

FUCHSIAS RESISTANT TO GALL MITE

Baby Chang	Liebesfraud
Berg NIMF	Machu Picchu
Cara Mia	Mary
Chance Encounter	Mendocino
Chang	Mini
Chickadee	Miniature
Cinnabarina	Jewels
Curly Q	Ocean Mist
Encliandra hybrids	Perky
Fabian Franck	San Francisco
Fanfare	Scarlet Ribbons
First Success	Space Shuttle
Isis	Tangerine
Jamboree	Texas Longhorn
Lena	Wave of Life

OAKS THAT NEED ADDED WATER DURING DROUGHTS

Common Name	Botanical Name
Bur oak	Quercus macrocarpa
English oak	Q. robur
Pin oak*	Q. palustris
Red oak	Q. rubra
Scarlet oak	Q. coccinea
Swamp white oak*	Q. bicolor
White oak	Q. alba
Willow oak	Q. phellos

Will tolerate wet soil.

SUSCEPTIBILITY OF JUNIPERS TO KABATINA TWIG BLIGHT

Common Name	Botanical Name
HIGHLY SUSCEPTIBLE JUNIPERS	
Chinese juniper 'Spartan' 'Torulosa'	Juniperus chinensis
Creeping juniper 'Bar Harbor' 'Blue Rug' 'Plumosa Compacta' 'Wiltonii'	J. horizontalis
Rocky Mountain juniper 'Skyrocket'	J. scopularum
RESISTANT JUNIPERS	
Chinese juniper 'Hetzii Glauca' 'Parsonii'	J. chinensis
Common juniper 'Hornibrookii'	J. communis
Creeping juniper 'Marcellus'	J. horizontalis
Hybrid juniper 'Gold Coast' 'Pfitzeriana Aurea'	J. × media
Sargent's juniper 'Glauca' 'Viridis'	J. sargentii
Savin juniper 'Tamariscifolia'	J. sabina
Single-seed juniper 'Prostrata'	J. squamata

OAKS THAT NEED NO WATER AFTER THE FIRST TWO YEARS

Common Name	Botanical Name
Blue oak	Quercus douglasii
California black oak	Q. kelloggii
California scrub oak	Q. dumosa
Canyon oak	Q. chrysolepis
Coast live oak	Q. agrifolia
Cork oak	Q. suber
Holly oak	Q. ilex
Interior live oak	Q. wislizenii
Mesa oak	Q. engelmannii
Oregon white oak	Q. garryana
Valley oak	Q. lobata

JUNIPERS RESISTANT TO PHOMOPSIS TWIG BLIGHT

Common Name	Botanical Name
Chinese juniper 'Foemina' 'Keteleeri'	Juniperus chinensis
Common juniper 'Repanda' 'Suecica'	J. communis
Single-seed juniper 'Prostrata'	J. squamata
Creeping juniper	J. horizontalis
Dwarf juniper	J. communis spp. depressa
Hybrid juniper 'Pfitzerana Aurea'	J. × media
Savin juniper 'Broadmoor' 'Fargesii' 'Pumila' 'Skandia'	J. sabina

SUSCEPTIBILITY OF PINES TO PINE WILT

Common Name	Botanical Name
SUSCEPTIBLE PINES	
Austrian pine	Pinus nigra
Japanese black pine	P. thunbergii
Japanese red pine	P. densiflora
Loblolly pine	P. taeda
Lodgepole pine	P. contorta ssp. latifolia
Maritime pine	P. pinaster
Monterey pine	P. radiata
Mugo pine	P. mugo
Scotch pine	P. sylvestris
Scrub pine	P. virginiana
Sugar pine	P. lambertiana
Western white pine	P. monticola
RESISTANT PINES	
Cuban pine	Pinus caribaea
Jack pine	P. banksiana
Jeffrey pine	P. jeffreyi
Longleaf pine	P. palustris
Pitch pine	P. rigida
Short-leaf pine	P. echinata
Slash pine	P. elliottii
Table mountain pine	P. pungens
White pine	P. strobus

PALMS FREQUENTLY ATTACKED BY PALM LEAF SKELETONIZER

Common Name	Botanical Name
Cabbage palm	*Livistona australis*
Chinese fan palm	*Livistona chinensis*
Coconut palm	*Cocos nucifera*
Date palm	*Phoenix*
Paurotis palm	*Acoelorrhaphe wrightii*
Pindo palm	*Butia capitata*
Washington palm	*Washingtonia*

PYRACANTHA AND HAWTHORN TOLERANT OF FIRE BLIGHT

Common Name	Botanical Name
PYRACANTHA	
Laland's firethorn	*Pyracantha coccinea* var. *lalandei* P. *fortuneana*
Pyracantha	*Pyracantha crenatoserrata*
HAWTHORN	
Washington hawthorn	*Crataegus phaenopyrum*

These species are not immune to fire blight but are not damaged by it as severely as are other species.

PYRACANTHA RESISTANT TO SCAB

Mohave	Shawnee
Orange Glow	Watereri
Rogersiana	

GYPSY MOTH FOOD PREFERENCES

Common Name	Botanical Name
MOST PREFERRED	
Apple, crabapple	*Malus*
Gray birch	*Betula alleghaniensis*
Hawthorn	*Crataegus*
Linden	*Tilia*
Mountain ash	*Sorbus*
Oak	*Quercus*
Paper birch	*Betula papyrifera*
Quaking aspen	*Populus tremuloides*
Rose	*Rosa*
Serviceberry	*Amelanchier*
Tamarisk	*Tamarix*
Willow	*Salix*
Witch hazel	*Hamamelis*
SOMEWHAT PREFERRED	
Beech	*Fagus*
Black gum	*Nyssa*
Cottonwood	*Populus deltoides*
Elm	*Ulmus*
Hackberry	*Celtis*
Hemlock	*Tsuga*
Hickory	*Carya*
Magnolia	*Magnolia*
Maple	*Acer*
Pine	*Pinus*
Redbud	*Cercis*
Sassafras	*Sassafras*
Sweet cherry	*Prunus avium*
Sweet gum	*Liquidambar*
LEAST PREFERRED	
Ash	*Fraxinus*
Black walnut	*Juglans nigra*
Catalpa	*Catalpa*
Dogwood	*Cornus*
Fir	*Abies*
Holly	*Ilex*
Horsechestnut	*Aesculus*
Locust	*Robinia*
Mountain laurel	*Kalmia*
Mulberry	*Morus*
Plane tree	*Platanus*
Sycamore	*Platanus*
Tulip tree	*Liriodendron*

ROSE VARIETIES RESISTANT TO BLACK SPOT, POWDERY MILDEW, AND RUST

HYBRID TEAS	
Audie Murphy	R
Aztec	PM, R
Carousel	PM
Charlotte Armstrong	BS
Chrysler Imperial	BS
Command Performance	BS, R
Coronado	BS
Ernest H. Morse	BS
Forty-niner	BS
Fred Howard	R
Garden Party	BS, R
Golden Rapture	PM
Grand Opera	BS
Jamaica	PM
John F. Kennedy	BS, R
Lowell Thomas	PM
Lucy Cramphorn	BS
Matterhorn	PM
Miss All-American Beauty	PM
Pascali	PM
Pink Favorite	R
Queen Charlotte	PM
Radiant	BS
Sante Fe	PM
Sierra Dawn	PM, R
Simon Bolivar	PM, R
Sphinx	BS
Sutter's Gold	BS, PM
Tiffany	BS

Trade Winds	R
Tropicana	BS
White Bouquet	R
FLORIBUNDAS	
Alain	R
Burma	R
Donald Prior	R
Etiole de Hollande	R
Fashionette	R
Garden Party	R
Gold Cup	R
Red Gold	BS, R
Red Radiance	R
Sarabande	BS, PM, R
Simplicity	BS
Summer Snow	R
Tiara	BS
Wildfire	PM
CLIMBERS	
Blaze	BS, PM
Bonfire	PM
Cecile Brunner	PM
Paul's Scarlet	BS, PM

DISEASE KEY	
BS	Black Spot
PM	Powdery Mildew
R	Rust

APPLE DISEASE RESISTANCE AND ADAPTATION

Variety	Pollination	AS	BR	CAR	FB	PM	2	3	4	5	6	7	8	9	10
		Disease Resistance[1]					Zone Adaptation[2]								[3]
Anna	D	S											•	•	•
Baldwin	A	S		VR	S	HS	•	•	•	•					
Braeburn	B	S	S	HS	HS	R									
Cortland	B	HS		S	S	HS		•	•	•	•				
Dorsett Golden	D	S										•	•	•	•
Ein Shemer	D	S											•	•	•
Empire	B	S		R	MR	S		•	•	•	•	•			
Enterprise	B	VR		VR	R	MR				•	•	•	•		
Freedom	B	VR		VR	R	R			•	•	•				
Fuji	B	S	HS	HS	HS	R					•	•	•	•	
Gala	B	S	S	HS	HS	R				•	•	•	•	•	
Golden Delicious	A	S	HS	HS	S	S				•	•	•	•	•	
Goldrush	B	VR		R	MR	R				•	•	•	•		
Granny Smith	B	S	HS	R	HS	HS							•	•	
Gravenstein	E	S		VR		HS					•	•	•	•	
Honeycrisp	B	R		S	HS				•	•	•	•	•		
Idared	E	S	HS	S	HS	HS			•	•	•	•			
Jonagold	E	HS	S	S	HS	S				•	•	•	•		
Jonathan	B	S	S	HS	HS	HS				•	•	•	•		
Liberty	B	VR		VR	MR	S			•	•	•				
McIntosh	B	HS		VR	S	S			•	•	•	•			
Northern Spy	B	S	S	S	S	S		•	•	•	•	•			
Prima	C	VR		HS	MR	R				•	•	•	•		
Priscilla	C	VR		R	MR	R				•	•	•	•		
Pristine	B	VR		R	MR	R				•	•	•	•		
Red Delicious	B	S	R	VR	R	R				•	•	•	•		
Rhode Island Greening	E	S		S	HS	S			•	•	•				
Rome Beauty	A	HS	MR	HS	HS	HS				•	•	•	•		
Sir Prize	C	VR		HS	MR	R				•	•	•	•		
Stayman Winesap	E	HS	S	S	S	HS				•	•	•	•		
Winesap	E	HS	MR	R	S	R				•	•	•	•		
Winter Banana	B	S		HS	S					•	•	•	•		
Yellow Transparent	B	R		R	HS	R			•	•	•	•	•		

[1] Adapted from www.caf.wvu.edu/kearneysville/wvufarm8.html.
[2] Based on USDA Plant Hardiness Zone Map (see page 530).
[3] Florida only.

POLLINATION KEY

A Self-fruitful, but crop is improved with a pollinator
B Pollinate with any A or B
C Prima and Priscilla cross-pollinate well; Sir Prize needs either Prima or Priscilla for pollination but will not pollinate them
D Pollinate with another D
E Not a pollinator; pollinate with an A or a B

DISEASE KEY

AS	Apple Scab	HS	Highly Susceptible
BR	Bitter Rot	S	Susceptible
CAR	Cedar-Apple Rust	MR	Moderately Resistant
FB	Fire Blight	R	Resistant
PM	Powdery Mildew	VR	Very Resistant

RESISTANCE KEY

(see Disease Key table above)

CITRUS COLD HARDINESS

Varieties are listed from most hardy to least hardy.

Kumquat
Orangequat
Sour orange
Meyer lemon
Rangpur lime
Mandarin orange (tangerine)
Sweet orange
Bearss lime
Tangelo
Lemon
Grapefruit
Limequat
Mexican lime

Home gardeners in Florida and California can grow a wide variety of citrus in the milder areas of their states. In the warmest areas, you will have success with the more tender citrus, such as grapefruit, lemons, and limes. South Texas gardeners can plant Meyer lemon, Satsuma mandarin, and 'Marrs Early' orange.

AVOCADO HARDINESS

Varieties are listed from most hardy to least hardy.

For California	For Florida
Bacon	Brogdon
Zutano	Tonnage
Fuerte	Choquette
Hass	Pollock

APRICOT DISEASE RESISTANCE AND ADAPTATION

Variety	Pollination	Brown Rot Resistance	Zone Adaptation[1] 4	5	6	7	8	9[2]	10
Blenheim	A	S				•	•	•	•
Goldcot	A				•	•	•	•	
Perfection	B					•	•	•	
Royal	A	S				•	•	•	
Stella	A				•	•	•	•	
Tilton	A	R				•	•	•	•

[1] Based on USDA Plant Hardiness Zone Map (see page 530).
[2] California only.

CHERRY DISEASE RESISTANCE AND ADAPTATION

Variety	Pollination	Disease Resistance BC	CLS	Zone Adaptation[1] 2	3	4	5	6	7	8	9[2]	10
SWEET CHERRIES												
Bing	A	S					•	•	•	•	•	
Black Tartarian	B						•	•	•	•	•	•
Corum	C	R					•	•	•			
Early Burlat	C	VR					•	•	•	•	•	
Lambert	A	S					•	•	•			
Lapins	D						•	•	•			
Royal Ann	A	S					•	•	•			
Sam	C	R					•	•	•	•		
Stella	D						•	•	•	•		
Sue	C	R					•	•	•			
Van	B	S					•	•	•	•	•	•
SOUR CHERRIES												
Balaton	D						•	•	•	•		
Meteor	D		R			•	•	•	•			
Montmorency	D						•	•	•			
North Star	D		R			•	•	•	•	•		

[1] Based on USDA Plant Hardiness Zone Map (see page 530).
[2] California only.

PEAR DISEASE RESISTANCE AND ADAPTATION

Variety	Pollination	Fire Blight Resistance	Zone Adaptation[1] 4	5	6	7	8	9[2]	10
Bartlett	B	HS		•	•	•		•	
Bosc	B	HS		•	•	•		•	
Clapp	B	HS		•	•	•			
Comice	B	S		•	•	•		•	
D'Anjou	B	HS		•	•	•			
Kieffer[3]	A	R	•	•	•	•	•	•	
Moonglow	A	VR		•	•	•	•		
Orient[3]	A	VR		•	•	•	•	•	•
Seckel	C	R		•	•	•	•		

[1] Based on USDA Plant Hardiness Zone Map (see page 530).
[2] California only, except Orient variety.
[3] Grown in Florida.

PEACH DISEASE RESISTANCE AND ADAPTATION

Variety	Pollination	Resistance to Bacterial Leaf Spot	2	3	4	5	6	7	8	9	10[2]
Belle of Georgia	A	VR				•	•	•	•		
Desert Gold	A								•	•	•
Early Red Free	A	VR				•	•	•	•		
Elberta	A	S					•	•	•	•	
Flordasun	A					•	•	•	•		
J. H. Hale	B					•	•	•	•		
Harbrite	A	R				•	•	•	•		
Loring	A								•	•	•
Madison[3]	A	R				•	•	•	•		
Newhaven	A	S					•	•	•	•	
Redhaven	A	R				•	•	•	•		
Redskin	A	R				•	•	•	•		
Reliance[3]	A				•	•	•	•			
Rio-Oso-Gem	A	S				•	•	•	•		
Sunhaven	A	R				•	•	•	•		

Zone Adaptation[1]

[1] Based on USDA Plant Hardiness Zone Map (see page 530).
[2] Florida only.
[3] Does well in colder areas of Zone 5.

POLLINATION KEY
A   Self-fruitful; requires no pollinator
B   Requires pollinator; use an A

RESISTANCE KEY
VR Very Resistant
R   Resistant
S   Susceptible

PLUM DISEASE RESISTANCE AND ADAPTATION

Variety	Type	Pollination	Resistance to Black Knot	4	5	6	7	8	9[2]
Blue Damson	E	B	S		•	•	•		
Burbank	J	D			•	•	•	•	•
Ember	J	E		•	•	•	•	•	
Greengage	E	B					•	•	•
Italian Prune (Fellenberg)	EPP	F	R		•	•	•	•	
Methley	J	C	R		•	•	•	•	•
Ozark Premier	J	D			•	•	•	•	•
President	E	A	VR		•	•	•	•	•
Santa Rosa	J	C	R		•	•	•	•	•
Shiro	J	D	R	•	•	•	•	•	
Stanley	EPP	F	S		•	•	•	•	•
Underwood	J	E			•	•	•	•	•

Zone Adaptation[1]

[1] Based on USDA Plant Hardiness Zone Map (see page 530).
[2] California only.

TYPE KEY
E   European plum
EPP   European prune plum
J   Japanese red plum

RESISTANCE KEY
VR Very Resistant
R   Resistant
S   Susceptible

POLLINATION KEY
A Not self-fruitful; pollinate with a B
B Self-fruitful; no pollinator necessary
C Self-fruitful, but crop is improved by a pollinator; use a D
D Not self-fruitful; pollinate with another D
E Cross-pollinates well with another E
F Self-fruitful, but crop is improved by a pollinator; use another F

VEGETABLE SEED INFORMATION

Vegetable	Optimum Germination Temperatures(°F)	Days to Germination
Asparagus	70–75	14–21
Bean, lima	70	7–10
Bean, snap	70	6–10
Beet	50–85	10–14
Broccoli	70–75	10–14
Brussels sprouts	70–75	10–14
Cabbage	70–75	10–14
Carrot	50–85	14–21
Cauliflower	70–75	8–10
Cucumber	70	7–10
Eggplant	70	10–15
Lettuce	65–70	7–10
Melon	75	5–7
Onion	70–75	10–14
Parsley	70–75	14–21
Pea	40–75	7–10
Pepper	75–80	10
Radish	45–85	4–6
Spinach	70	8–10
Squash	70–75	7–10
Sweet corn	70	5–7
Tomato	70–75	5–8
Turnip	60–85	7–10

EARLIEST DATES FOR SAFE SPRING PLANTING OF VEGETABLES

Crop	Average Date of Last Spring Freeze								
	Feb. 1	Feb. 15	Mar. 1	Mar. 15	Apr. 1	Apr. 15	May 1	May 15	June 1
Asparagus	—	—	—	2/1	2/15	3/15	3/15	4/15	5/1
Bean, lima	2/1	3/1	3/15	4/1	4/15	5/1	5/15	6/1	—
Bean, snap	2/1	3/1	3/15	3/15	4/1	4/15	5/1	5/15	6/1
Beet	1/1	1/15	2/15	2/15	3/1	3/15	4/1	4/15	5/1
Broccoli[1]	1/1	1/15	2/1	2/15	3/1	3/15	4/1	4/15	5/15
Brussels sprouts[1]	1/1	1/15	2/1	2/15	3/1	3/15	4/1	4/15	5/15
Cabbage[1]	1/1	1/1	1/15	2/1	2/15	3/1	3/15	4/15	5/15
Carrot	1/1	1/15	2/1	2/15	3/1	3/15	4/1	5/1	5/15
Cauliflower[1]	1/1	1/15	1/15	2/1	2/15	3/1	4/1	4/15	5/15
Cucumber	2/15	2/15	3/1	4/1	4/15	5/1	5/15	6/1	—
Eggplant[1]	2/1	2/15	3/15	4/1	4/15	5/1	5/15	6/1	—
Lettuce	1/1	1/1	1/1	2/1	2/15	3/15	4/1	4/15	5/15
Muskmelon	2/15	2/15	3/1	4/1	4/15	5/1	6/1	—	—
Onion	1/1	1/1	1/1	2/1	2/15	3/1	3/15	4/15	5/1
Parsley	1/1	1/1	1/15	2/1	2/15	3/1	3/15	4/15	5/1
Pea	1/1	1/1	1/15	2/1	2/15	3/1	3/15	4/15	5/1
Pepper[1]	2/1	3/1	3/15	4/1	4/15	5/1	5/15	6/1	6/1
Potato	1/1	1/15	1/15	2/1	3/1	3/15	4/1	4/15	5/1
Radish	1/1	2/2	1/1	1/15	2/15	3/1	3/15	4/1	5/1
Spinach	1/1	1/1	1/1	1/15	2/1	2/15	3/15	4/1	4/15
Squash	2/1	3/1	3/15	4/1	4/15	5/1	5/1	5/15	6/1
Tomato[1]	2/1	3/1	3/15	4/1	4/15	5/1	5/15	5/15	6/1
Turnip	1/1	1/15	2/1	2/1	2/15	3/1	3/15	4/1	5/1
Watermelon	2/15	2/15	3/1	3/15	4/15	5/1	5/15	6/1	—

[1] Seeds may be started indoors 4 to 6 weeks before planting date.
To find the average date of the last freeze, ask at your local nursery or call your county extension service.

VEGETABLE VARIETIES RESISTANT TO SOUTHERN ROOT KNOT NEMATODE

Bean	Corn	Pea	Pepper	Sweet Potato	Tomato
Bountiful	Carmel Cross	Burpeeana Early	All Big	Apache	All Round
Brittle Wax	Golden Beauty Hybrid	Wando	Bontoc Sweet Long	Carver	Anahu
Tender Pod	Golden Cross Bantam		World Beater	Hopi	Anahu-R
Wingard Wonder	Span Cross			Jasper	Atkinson
				Jewel	Auburn 76
				Nemagold	Beefeater
				Nugget	Beefmaster
				Ruby	Big Seven
				Sunnyside	Calmart
				White Bunch	Chicogrande
				White Triumph	Coldset
				Whitestar	Eurocross
					Extase
					Monte Carlo
					Nemared
					Nematex
					Patriot
					Peto 662 VFN
					Ponderosa
					VFN–8

VEGETABLES SUSCEPTIBLE TO FUSARIUM

Asparagus	Onion
Bean	Pea
Brussels sprouts	Pepper
Cabbage	Radish
Cauliflower	Spinach
Celery	Sweet potato
Cucumber	Tomato
Melon	Turnip
Okra	

BEAN VARIETIES RESISTANT TO RUST

Cape
Dade
Kentucky Wonder
Resisto

BEAN VARIETIES RESISTANT TO MOSAIC VIRUS

Aristocrop	Green Arrow
Astro	Harvester
Bonanza Wax	Improved
Bush Blue Lake	Tendergreen
Bush Blue Lake 47	M.R.
and 274	Peak
Cape	Provider
Cherokee	Resistant
Contender	Cherokee
Romano	Resisto
Dade (pole)	Roma II PVP
Del Rey	Spartan
Eagle	Spurt
Early Gallatin	Strike
Early Harvest	Stringless Blue
Flo	Lake
FM–IK	Sungold
Gallatin 50	Tendercrop
Gator Green 15	Tenderlake
Goldcrop	Topcrop
Golden Rod	Win

VEGETABLES SUSCEPTIBLE TO VERTICILLIUM WILT

Artichoke	Pepper
Beet	Potato
Brussels sprouts	Pumpkin
Cabbage	Radish
Eggplant	Rhubarb
Melon[1]	Spinach
New Zealand spinach	Strawberry[2]
Okra	Tomato
Peanut	

[1] *Watermelon, cantaloupe, and honeydew become infected but aren't seriously damaged. Persian, casaba, and crenshaw melons are very susceptible.*
[2] *See page 560 for strawberry varieties resistant to verticillium.*
Adapted from Plants Resistant or Susceptible to Verticillium Wilt, University of California County Extension leaflet 2703.

CORN VARIETIES TOLERANT OF DISEASES

Apache	S, B, Bl, M
Atlantic	Bl
Aztec	S, B
Bellringer	S, B
BiQueen	Bl
Calico	S, B
Calumet	S, B, M
Capitan	Bl
Cherokee	B, Bl, M
Comanche	S, B
Comet	S, B, Bl
Florida Staysweet	Bl
Gold Cup	S, B
Guardian	Bl
Merit	S, B, M
Mevak	S, B
Quicksilver	S, B, M
Seneca Sentry	B, M
Silver Queen	B
Sweet Sue	S
Wintergreen	S, B, Bl, M

DISEASE KEY

S Smut
B Bacterial Wilt
Bl Southern and Northern Leaf
   Blights
M Maize Dwarf Mosaic

BEET VARIETIES THAT PRODUCE SMOOTH, ROUND ROOTS

Albino White Beet
Detroit Dark Red
Earlisweet Hybrid
Early Wonder, Green Top
Early Wonder, Tall Top
Garnet
Golden Beet
Perfected Detroit
Red Ace Hybrid
Red Ball
Ruby Queen

BLUEBERRY REGIONAL ADAPTATION

FOR THE SOUTH AND SOUTHERN CALIFORNIA

Rabbiteye *(Vaccinium ashei)*
Bluebelle
Bluegem
Climax
Tifblue
Woodward
Highbush *(Vaccinium corymbosum)*
Avonblue
Flordablue
Sharpblue

FOR THE VERY COLDEST REGIONS

Meader
Northland

WIDELY ADAPTED

Berkeley
Bluecrop
Blueray
Bluetta
Collins
Jersey
Patriot

DISEASE-RESISTANT CUCUMBERS

SLICING CUCUMBERS

A & C Hybrid Imp	L+, S+, A+, P+, D+, C+
A & C Hybrid 1810	L+, S+, A+, P+, D+, C+
Cherokee 7	L+, S+, A+, P, D, C+
Dasher	L, S, A, P, D, C
Dasher II	L, S+, A+, P+, D+, C+
Early Triumph	L, S, A, P, D, C
Gemini 7	L, S, A, P, D, C
Medalist	S+, P, D, C+
Poinsett	L+, A+, P+, D+
Poinsett 76	L+, S+, P+, D+
Roadside Fancy	L, S, A, P, D, C
Setter	L, S+, A, P+, D+
Shamrock	L, S, P, D, C
Slicemaster	L, S+, A, P, D, C
Slice-Mor	S+, A+, P, D+, C
Southernsett	L, S+, P, D, C+
Sprint 440	L, S, A, P, D
Sweet-Slice	L, S+, A, P, D, C
Sweet Success	S, P, D, C

PICKLING CUCUMBERS

Addis	L, A, P, D, C
Bounty	L, S, A, P, D, C
Calypso	L, S, A, P, D, C
Carolina	L, S, A, P, D, C
Chipper	L, A, P, D, C
County Fair	S, A, P, D, C
Explorer	L, P, D
Flurry	L, S, A, P, D, C
Liberty	L, S, D, C
Lucky Strike	S, A, P, C
Multipik	L, S, A, D, C
Panorama	L, S, A, P, D, C
Picarow	L, S, A, P, D, C
Premier	L, S, A, P, D, C
Salty	S, P, D, C
Sampson	L, A, P, D, C
Score	L, S, A, D, C
Spear-It	L, S, A, P, D, C
Sumter	L, S, A, P, D, C
Tamor	L, S, A, P, D, C
Triple Crown	L, S, A, P, C
Triplemech	L, S, A, P, D, C
V.I.P.	L, S, A, P, D, C

DISEASE KEY

A variety's tolerance of a disease is indicated by the codes below. If a variety is resistant to the disease, the code is followed by a plus (+).

L Angular Leaf Spot
S Scab
A Anthracnose
P Powdery Mildew
D Downy Mildew
C Cucumber Mosaic Virus

DISEASE RESISTANCE OF BRAMBLES

	Disease Resistance	Widely Adapted	North	South	Pacific Northwest	California
ERECT BLACKBERRIES						
Black Satin	A, LS	•		•	•	•
Brazos				•		
Cherokee	A, OR	•				
Chester Thornless	C	•				
Darrow		•				
Ebony King	OR	•				
Eldorado	OR			•		
Flordagrand[1]	LS			•		
Hull Thornless		•				
Lawton	OR, V			•		
Navaho	A	•				
Shawnee	A, OR	•				
Triple Crown		•				
TRAILING BLACKBERRIES						
Black Butte					•	•
Boysenberry	OR, V				•	•
Loganberry					•	•
Marionberry					•	
Olallieberry	M, V				•	•
Youngberry	OR					
RED RASPBERRIES, SUMMER-BEARING						
Canby		•				
Chilliwack		•				
Latham		•				
Meeker	PM				•	
Sumner	PM	•			•	
Titan	M		•			
Willamette	PM				•	•
RED RASPBERRIES, EVERBEARING						
Amity		•				
August Red			•			
Autumn Bliss		•				
Heritage		•				
Redwing			•			
Southland	A, LS, PM			•		
Summit						•
BLACK RASPBERRIES						
Bristol	PM	•				
Cumberland			•			
Munger	PM				•	

[1]Needs cross-pollination.

DISEASE KEY

A   Anthracnose
C   Cane Blight
LS Leaf Spot
M   Mosaic
OR Orange Rust
PM Powdery Mildew
V   Verticillium Wilt

DISEASE RESISTANCE AND ADAPTATION OF GRAPES

Variety	Disease Resistance			Adaptation				
	Black Rot	Downy Mildew	Powdery Mildew	Northeast	Midwest	Pacific Northwest	Southeast	California, Arizona
Aurora		R	R	•		•		
Beta	R			•	•	•		
Buffalo		R	R	•	•	•		
Campbell's Early	R	R		•		•		
Canadice				•	•	•		
Concord		R		•	•	•		
Delaware	R			•	•	•		
Flame Seedless						•		•
Fredonia	R			•				
Glenora		R	R	•	•	•		
Himrod			R	•	•	•		
Interlaken			R	•	•	•		
Magnolia							•	
Niagara			R	•	•	•		•
Reliance		R	R	•	•	•		
Scuppernong[1]							•	
Suffolk Red			R	•	•	•		
Thompson Seedless								•
Tokay								•
Worden	R		R	•	•	•		

[1]*Muscadine grape; use Magnolia as pollinator.*

RESISTANCE KEY

R Resistant

REGIONAL ADAPTATION OF ONION VARIETIES

FOR THE SOUTH
Excel
Granex
Texas Grano
Tropicana Red
White Granex

FOR THE WEST
California Early Red
Early Yellow Globe
Southport Yellow Globe
Yellow Bermuda

FOR THE NORTH
Downing Yellow Globe
Early Yellow Globe
Empire
Nutmeg
Spartan Lines

LETTUCE VARIETIES TOLERANT OF TIP BURN

Calmar
Climax
Empire
Empress
Fairton
Great Lakes 118, 366, 659, 659–700, and 6238
Green Lake
Ithaca
Merit
Mesa 659
Minetto
Montello
Montemar
New York 515 Improved
Oswego
Parris Island Cos
Pennlake
Salinas
Super 59
Vanguard
Vanguard 75
Vanmax

ONION VARIETIES TOLERANT OF PINK ROOT

Autumn Spice
Beltsville Bunching
Brown Beauty
Buccaneer
Colossal
Copper Coast
Danvers
Early Supreme
El Capitan
Evergreen White Bunch
Fiesta
Granada
Granex Yellow
Henry's Special
Majesty
Red Commander
Rialto
Ringer
Spanish Main
White Granex
White Robust
Yellow Globe
Yellow Grano-New Mexico

WATERMELON VARIETIES TOLERANT OF ANTHRACNOSE

Blackstone
Calhoun
Charleston Gray
Crimson Sweet
Dixielee
Family Fun
Graybelle
Imperial
Madera
Smokylee
Sweet Favorite Hybrid
Verona
You Sweet Thing Hybrid

PEPPERS TOLERANT OF TOBACCO MOSAIC VIRUS

Ace
Allbig
Annabelle
Argo
Beater
Bell Boy
Big Bertha
Burlington
Early Canada Bell
Early Niagara Giant
Early Wonder
Emerald Giant
Gatorbelle
Gypsy
Hybelle
Lady Bell
Liberty Bell
Ma Belle
Merced
Mercury
Midway
Miss Belle
New Ace
Pennwonder
Pimientol
Puerto Rico
  Perfection
Puerto Rico
  Wonder
Resistant
  Florida Giant
Rutgers World
  Beater
Shamrock
Skipper
Staddon's Select
Thick Walled
  World Beater
Titan
Valley Giant
Yolo Wonder

POTATO VARIETIES TOLERANT OF SCAB

Alamo
Cascade
Cherokee
La Rouge
Lemhi
Nooksack
Norchip
Norgold Russet
Norland
Ona
Onaway
Ontario
Plymouth
Pungo
Russet Burbank
Shurchip
Sioux
Superior
Targhee

SPINACH VARIETIES RESISTANT TO DOWNY MILDEW

Aden
Badger Savoy
Basra
Bismark
Bouquet
Califlay
Chesapeake
Chinook
Dixie Market
Duet
Early Smooth
Grandstand
High Pack
Long Standing
  Savoy
Marathon
Melody
Nares
Salma
Savoy Supreme
Skookum
Vienna
Winter
  Bloomsdale

REGIONAL ADAPTATION AND DISEASE RESISTANCE OF TOMATO VARIETIES

	Disease Resistance	Widely Adapted	South	North	West
EARLY SEASON					
Early Cascade	V, F	•			
Jetfire	V, F				•
New Yorker	V			•	
Porter Improved					•
Small Fry	V, F, N	•			
Spring Set	V, F	•			
MIDSEASON					
Ace 55	V, F				•
Atkinson	F, N		•		
Better Boy	V, F, N	•			
Big Girl Hybrid	V, F	•			
Big Set	V, F, N	•			
Bonus	V, F, N	•			
Burpees VF	V, F	•			
Columbia	V, F, CT	•			
Floradel	F		•		
Floramerica	V, F	•			
Heinz 1350	V, F	•			
Jet Star	V, F			•	
Marglobe	F	•			
Parks Whopper	V, F, N, T	•			
Roma VF	V, F	•			
Rowpac	V, F, CT				•
Roza	V, F, CT				•
Salad Master	V, F, CT				•
Supersonic	V, F			•	•
Terrific	V, F, N	•			
Tripi-Red	V, F		•		
LATE SEASON					
Beefeater	V, F, N	•			
Beefmaster	V, F, N	•			
Manalucie	F		•		
Ramapo	V, F			•	
Tropic	V, F, T		•		
Vineripe	V, F, N	•			
Wonder Boy	V, F	•			

DISEASE KEY

V   Verticillium Wilt
F   Fusarium Wilt
N   Nematodes
T   Tobacco Mosaic Virus
CT Curly Top

DISEASE RESISTANCE OF STRAWBERRIES

Variety	Leaf Spot	Powdery Mildew	Red Stele	Scorch	Verticillium Wilt	Virus	South	North	California	Pacific Northwest
Allstar		VR	VR	VR	VR			•		
Badgerbelle	VR							•		
Badgerglo	R							•		
Benton			R			R				•
Blakemore	R			VR	VR		•	•		
Cardinal	VR	VR		VR			•	•		
Catskill				VR	VR			•		
Cyclone	VR							•		
Darrow	R	R	VR	R	R			•		
Delite	VR		VR	VR	VR		•	•		
Earlibelle	VR			VR			•			
Earliglow		R	VR	VR	VR			•		
Florida 90						R	•			
Fort Laramie								•		
Guardian		VR	VR	VR	VR			•		
Honeoye	R			R				•		
Hood	R	VR	VR		VR					•
Jewel	VR			VR				•		
Lateglow		R	VR	R	VR			•		
Midway			R		VR			•		
Ogallala	VR						•	•		
Ozark Beauty	VR			VR			•	•		
Pocahontas	R			VR			•			
Redchief		VR	VR	VR	R			•		
Scarlet	VR			VR				•		
Seascape									•	•
Selva									•	
Sequoia									•	
Shuksan			VR			R				•
Sparkle	VR		VR					•		
Stoplight	R			R				•		
Surecrop	VR		VR	VR	VR			•		
Tilikum										•
Tioga	R					R	•		•	
Totem	R	R	R	R						•
Tribute	VR	VR	VR				•			•
Tristar			VR	R	VR		•		•	•
Trumpeter					VR			•		

RESISTANCE KEY

VR Very Resistant

R   Resistant

Photographers

In order to make *Ortho's Home Gardener's Problem Solver* as useful as possible, we have published a color photograph of every problem in the book. Gathering this many photographs was a massive task. We relied extensively on college professors and County Extension agents for photographic contributions. Many of the photographs were taken originally to help teach students or the public about plant problems. We wish to thank the following photographers for their invaluable assistance in supplying these photographs. After each photographer's name, we list the pages on which his or her photographs appear. The letter that follows the page number shows the position of the photograph on the page, from left to right. A lowercase letter i refers to an inset photograph.

William D. Adams: 311L, 421C

Ralph J. Adkins: 180, 192R, 212L, 215R, 226R, 228C, 239L, 256L, 261L, 268L, 272L, 274L, 289L, 358R, 363L, 367C, 392C, 394C, 400L, 447R, 469R, 480R, 487L

Scott T. Adkins: 200C, 357Ri, 476R

Roger D. Akre: 442R, 451C

W. Allen: 317C

American Phytopathological Society: 36C, 283R, 296R, 370L

William C. Aplin: 54, 89

J. E. Appleby, Univ. of Illinois: 250R, 258R

Max E. Badgley: 25L, 71L, 75R, 116R, 226L, 266C, 274C, 274Ci, 287R, 310C, 334C, 334R, 364C, 373L, 380R, 396R, 414C, 435L, 441C, 443C, 447C, 448C, 452L, 459L, 459R, 460R, 461L, 461R, 463C, 463R, 467C, 506R, 509L, 512L, 518L, 521C, 524C

D. R. Bienz: 427R, 428L, 428C

Ray R. Bingham: 293L, 372R

Allen Boger: 65R, 70L, 71C, 91L, 92L, 114C, 114R, 174L, 185L, 187L, 188R, 194C, 197R, 198, 199L, 200L, 200R, 202L, 207L, 218C, 219R, 220R, 221C, 221Ci, 228R, 229C, 230C, 241C, 246R, 262C, 272C, 285L, 286C, 289C, 333L, 333C, 335C, 337, 346L, 348R, 366C, 372L, 373L, 375C, 379R, 387L, 390L, 393C, 393R, 399C, 404L, 405C, 406C, 413R, 422C, 422R, 494L, 499R

R. Harper Brame: 237C, 260L, 275C, 315R, 338C, 347Ri, 365L, 395C, 397L, 490L

Bartow H. Bridges Jr.: 174C, 187L, 195C, 198, 202R, 212C, 213L, 233L, 239C, 246L, 426L

Gay Bumgarner: 492

Jackie D. Butler: 28R, 65C, 68L, 75L, 79L, 96C, 209C, 223C, 232R, 247C, 256C, 263L, 268L, 271C, 295R, 299C, 319C, 347C, 347Ci, 351C, 351R, 352R, 355L, 355C, 360L, 360R, 391L, 391R, 395L, 418R, 427L, 427C, 428R, 447L, 501L, 518R

Ralph S. Byther: 112R, 115L, 151L, 162L, 162C, 179C, 201C, 201R, 204R, 215C, 223R, 231L, 232C, 244L, 244C, 247L, 252C, 252Ci, 265L, 296C, 302L, 308L, 308C, 316L, 338L, 354R, 355R, 370R, 378R, 379L, 384R, 388R, 389R

D. Caldwell, Davey Tree Expert Co.: 70R, 93R, 124R, 147C, 156C, 205R, 206L, 211L, 219C, 231C, 250L

Kristie Callan: 29R, 32C, 32R, 34R, 38R, 41R, 44C, 99L, 108L, 109C, 110C, 110R, 111L, 113L, 113C, 113R, 114L, 116L, 116C, 119L, 119C, 119R, 120C, 121L, 121C, 122L, 122R, 123L, 124L, 124C, 125L, 126L, 126C, 127C, 127R, 128C, 129R, 131L, 131R, 132L, 132C, 133L, 134L, 134C, 134R, 135L, 135C, 136L, 136C, 137L, 137R, 138C, 139C 139R, 140L, 140C, 142, 144C, 145, 147L, 147R, 148L, 149C, 150L, 150C, 150R, 154L, 155C, 155R, 156R, 157C, 157R, 158L, 159C, 160L, 160R, 161L, 161C, 161R, 163C, 164, 165R, 216C, 225C, 292R, 360L, 375R, 376L

T. D. Canerday: 460L

Rob Cardillo: 87, 88

Clyde Childress: 173

Jack K. Clark: 93C, 125C, 289C, 304Ri, 369L, 374Ri, 455L, 455C, 463L, 493, 494R, 496C, 500C, 513L, 520C, 521L, 522R

Clemson University: 364R, 384Li, 511C

James S. Coartney: 24L, 262L

Josephine Coatsworth: 277, 279L

Sharon J. Collman: 79C, 121R, 140R, 159L, 178R, 177C, 181, 182L, 185L, 186C, 186R, 189C, 191L, 191C, 193L, 195R, 201L, 224L, 224R, 226C, 239L, 249C, 251C, 253C, 254L, 254Li, 254R, 260R, 263C, 264R, 267L, 267R, 284C, 378C, 393L, 396L, 425C, 466C

Rollin E. Colville: 458L, 458C

Coop. Ext. Assoc. of Nassau County, NY: 227L, 251R

Alan Copeland: 31C

David M. Coppert: 336L

Cornell Univ. Dept. of Plant Pathology: 229L

Wendy W. Cortesi: 498C

Samuel Cotner: 123R, 356C, 357L, 359L, 361R, 362L, 368C, 368R, 371R, 383Ci, 387C, 398R

Whitney Cranshaw, Colorado SU: 254Ri, 269L, 269Li, 445C

David J. Cross: 40R, 519C

J. A. Crozier: 27C, 78L, 78Ri, 81C, 94R, 94Ri, 95C, 109R, 123C, 155L, 179L, 225L, 232L, 233C, 264L, 264C, 265C, 266R, 283C, 341C, 357C, 357R, 367L, 385R, 399R, 401L, 421L, 443R, 468L, 473L, 476L, 479C

Maynard W. Cummings: 77C, 284L, 284R, 307L, 494C, 495, 496L, 497C, 500R

Margery Daughtrey: 131C. 136L, 154C, 233R

Davey Tree Expert Co.: 191R, 210R, 255L, 270C, 425R

Spencer H. Davis, Jr.: 22L, 30R, 73L, 98L, 139L, 141L, 162R, 190R, 204L, 208L, 217C, 224C, 237L, 245Li, 245Ci, 259R

A. A. De Hertogh: 149R

Jim DeFilippis: 176R, 288L, 304C, 438R, 439L, 448R

James F. Dill: 66R, 72L, 133R, 165L, 176L, 176C, 196L, 204C, 217L, 223L, 236C, 242R, 243R, 248L, 248R, 286L, 297L, 333R, 340R, 342L, 344C, 344Ci, 345L, 345R, 354L, 354R, 356R, 361C, 363C, 365Li, 368L, 383R, 385C, 386R, 395R, 396C, 401C, 436L, 441L, 444L, 449L, 451R, 457L, 462C, 462R, 474R, 501L, 501R, 509L, 514L, 514C, 515R, 517C, 518C, 519L, 525L, 525C

Michael A. Dirr: 90C, 143L, 143C, 158R, 175L, 222R, 229R, 252L, 261C, 275L, 275R, 412C, 430R, 431L, 487C

E. Dutky, University of Maryland: 129L

Walter Ebelingr: 510L, 512R, 514R, 515Ri, 516R, 521R, 523C

C. L. Elmore: 57T, 57B, 58L, 80C, 81L, 467L, 468C, 477R, 478L, 478C, 479R, 481L, 481R, 482L, 482R, 484C, 485C

Thomas E. Eltzroth: 466L

Barbara H. Emerson: 82C, 83R, 467R, 473R, 475L, 477L, 477C, 485R, 487R, 488R, 489C

Arthur W. Engelhard: 419L, 419C

Entomological Soc. of America: 443L, 452C

FDACS/DPI: 27L, 445L, 446R

James Feucht: 73C, 76L, 148C, 152L, 152C, 180, 181L, 193L, 196L, 205L, 247L, 253L, 253R, 269R, 273C, 290L, 297C, 405R, 429R

Charles M. Fitch: 24C, 146L, 257R, 342R, 433

W. E. Fletcher: 212R

Lee Foster: 497L

Randolph Foulds: 102B, 105

Paul F. Frese: 151R

Malcomb Furniss: 246L, 434C, 434R

Raymond J. Gill: 25C, 32L, 39R

David Goldberg: 103, 104T, 106, 166, 170

Nelson Groffman: 498L, 500L

John E. Hafernik, Jr.: 438C, 453C, 454L, 454R, 457R, 459C, 508R

Frank A. Hale: 67C, 220L, 227C, 301C, 391R, 446L

Dennis H. Hall: 344L, 350L, 370C, 392L, 397C

Mary Ann Hansen: 64R, 256R, 421R, 421Ri

M. Ali Harivandi: 66C, 70C, 74L, 77R, 80L, 405L, 412L, 474L, 476C, 479L, 480L, 480C, 483C

Jessie M. Harris: 470L

Raymond F. Hasek: 26L

Duane L. Hatch: 332R, 338R, 353R, 359R, 376C

George R. Hawkes: 282C, 282R, 290C, 290R, 305L, 332C, 429C

Richard W. Henley: 42R

Larry Hodgson, HortiCom Inc.: 24R

G. J. Holmes: 390C, 390R, 398C, 415L

Saxon Holt: 56, 59, 171 (Orchard Nursery, Lafayette, CA), 491C, 503, 504TL, 504TR, 504B, 505

R. K. Horst: 42L, 43C, 46L, 128L, 148R, 154R, 302C, 302R, 334L

Tony Howarth: 436C, 452R, 513R

Angus J. Howitt: 294L, 294Li, 299L, 300C

E. E. Janne: 68C, 68R, 430C, 472L, 511

Dr. Russell Johnson: 386C, 506C, 513C

Alan L. Jones: 292L, 292C, 295L, 298R, 303C, 307R, 308R, 308R, 309C, 309R, 312L, 316C, 316R, 318L, 420R

Deborah Jones: 320

R. K. Jones: 37L, 153L, 153R, 194L, 214L, 219L

Gene Joyner: 71R, 71Ri, 74R, 85C, 209L, 234L, 242L, 306C, 373R, 469C, 473C

M. Keith Kennedy: 26Li, 43L, 67L, 73R, 93L, 97L, 115R, 122C, 132R, 178L, 195L, 211R, 222R, 227R, 241L, 243L, 243C, 300R, 313C, 319L, 339C, 446C

Marvin G. Kinsey: 507R

C. S. Koehler: 258L, 389C

Balthazar Korab: 100, 107

R. R. Kriner: 69L, 249C, 291L, 294Ci, 294R, 295C, 296L, 307C, 309L, 310L, 310R, 345C, 350R, 351L, 358L, 361L, 372C, 388L, 388C, 392R, 440R, 475L, 488C, 510R, 522L, 522Li

F. Laemmlen: 120R, 199C, 199R, 367R, 380C

Susan M. Lammers: 144R

Michael Landis: 48, 51, 52, 55, 60, 276, 278, 315L, 322L, 323BL, 323BR, 402, 408R

David Liebman: 84C, 152R, 458R, 461C, 468R, 486C, 490R, 491L, 502BR, 506L, 507L, 519R

Peter Lindtner: 118R, 271L, 285C, 286R, 299R, 411C, 485L

Susanne Lucas, Amer. Bamboo Soc.: 210C, 470R

Robert E. Lyons: 25R

J. D. MacDonald: 97R, 97Ri

John Marriott: 498R

Steven L. Mayer: 374C

Phil Mayor: 496R

Arthur H. McCain: 96R

Bryan McCay: 50, 104B, 167

Charles A. McClurg: 365R

Dennis McFarland: 522C

Jim McGraw/NCSU: 205C

J. R. McGrew: 374R, 375L

Michael McKinley: 33R, 40L, 40C, 90L, 90R, 91C, 92L, 92R, 102T, 159R, 174R, 184R, 185L, 186L, 189R, 193R, 194L, 404R, 411R, 456L

J. A. Menge: 306R

Richard W. Meritt: 520L, 520R

Jeffery C. Miller: 437C, 437R

R. H. Miller: 255C, 515C

Richard L. Miller: 267C, 381L, 387R, 389L, 497L, 511L, 517L

Wayne S. Moore: 36R, 39C, 97C, 99R, 163L, 175C, 228L, 293C, 293R, 451L, 456R, 489R

N. C. Cooperative Ext. Service: 268R

Steve Nameth: 120L, 206R

Nassau County NY Coop. Ext. Assoc.: 47R, 66L, 66Li, 82L

Jean R. Natter: 23R, 85L, 95L, 203L, 423R, 424L, 424C, 442C, 483R, 489L, 508C

Lester P. Nichols: 26C, 41L, 218L, 238C, 274R

R. A. Norton: 282L, 283L, 287C, 313L, 317L

NY State Turfgrass Assoc.: 78R, 80R, 80Ri, 81R

NYS Ag. Exper. Station, Harvo Tashiko: 389Li

Howard D. Ohr: 75C

Ortho Photo Library: 53, 84L, 279R, 280, 322R, 323T, 324, 325, 326, 327, 328, 329, 330, 331, 341L, 404C, 408L, 408C, 413L

OSU, Ken Gray Collection: 67Li, 69Li, 71Li, 151R, 175R, 214R, 251L, 270R, 312C, 318C, 364L, 364Li, 366L. 376R, 379C, 434L

J. Parker: 432

John W. Parrish: 76C

Jerry M. Parsons: 343L, 343C, 366R, 377R, 400C

John Pehrson: 303R, 305R

Pamela K. Peirce: 47C, 85R, 386L, 471R, 475R, 484L

Sandra Perry: 35L, 126R, 240C, 344R

Plant Photo Library: 179R, 306L

Mary Pindar: 101

D. K. Pollet: 238L, 314, 317R

Daniel A. Potter: 220C

C. C. Powell: 27R, 44R, 45R, 91C, 94C, 95R, 98L, 127L, 130L, 130R, 137C, 138R, 149L, 153C, 207L, 207R, 208L, 225R, 240L, 240R, 245C, 246Ri, 262R

Cecil B. Quirino: 29C, 31L, 37R, 118L, 365C, 453L, 453R, 454C, 454Ri, 460C, 472R, 507C, 510C, 523R, 524L, 524R

Robert D. Raabe: 23L, 26R, 28L, 28C, 29L, 33C, 34L, 35C, 35R, 36L, 38L, 38C, 39L, 41C, 42L, 43R, 44L, 45L, 46C, 47L, 112C, 115C, 130C, 133C, 135R, 138L, 146R, 157L, 165C, 189L, 214C, 215L, 235L, 235C, 255R, 260C, 263R, 265R, 291R, 318R, 332L, 394R, 398L, 417

Roscoe Randell: 238R

Ann F. Rhoads: 211C, 378L, 424R

Ken Rice: 19

Paul A. Rogers: 242C, 259L, 407R

Barbara Rothenberger: 34C, 111R, 118C, 129C, 164C, 230R, 271R, 406R, 426R

Ray Rothenberger: 163R

Alvin D. Rutledge: 356L

Anita Sabarese: 67Ri, 84R, 112L, 117L, 177R, 183L, 183R, 184L, 184C, 188L, 231R, 236R, 287L, 335R, 336R, 339L, 371C, 383C, 414R, 435C, 437L, 438L, 448L, 455R, 462L, 466R, 469L, 470C, 471C, 472L, 481C, 482C, 483L, 488L, 490C, 516Ri

Eric Salmon: 169

Doug Sanders: 343R

Joseph Savage: 208R

D. F. Schoeneweiss: 99C, 128R, 192C, 216L, 222L, 270L, 273R, 407L

Donald L. Schuder: 217R, 220Ci, 249L, 254C, 257C, 269C, 301L, 303L, 444R, 445R

Carl H. Shanks: 484R

A. F. Sherf: 141C, 258R, 311R, 319R, 335L, 339R, 342C, 346C, 346R, 347L, 347R, 348L, 349R, 358R, 359C, 363R, 369C, 369R, 377L, 377C, 380L, 382L, 382C, 382R, 384L, 384C, 397R, 399L, 399Li, 400R, 407C, 420L, 420C, 422L, 430L, 457C, 499L, 499C

James Sikkema: 76R, 78C, 79R, 83L, 108C, 108R, 110L, 143R, 156L, 160R, 178C, 203R, 203L, 248C, 288C, 288R, 341R, 381C, 406L, 412L, 415R, 478R

G. W. Simone: 30L, 30C, 37C, 218R

Robert W. Sites: 450R, 508L

C. Smiley: 65L, 65Li

Richard W. Smiley: 69C, 69R, 77L

John J. Smith: 58R

Michael D. Smith: 23C, 46R, 64L, 64C, 72C, 82R, 109L, 158C, 177L, 182C, 182R, 182Ri, 187R, 188C, 190L, 190C, 192L, 196C, 197L, 197C, 202C, 210L, 216R, 261R, 298L, 298C, 301R, 304R, 305C, 315C, 336C, 340L, 340C, 348C, 371C, 409, 410L, 410C, 414L, 415L, 419R, 423L, 423C, 429L, 431C, 431R, 435R, 436L, 456C, 465, 471L, 474C, 486L, 486R, 517C

Kenneth Sorensen, NCSU: 312R, 362R, 439C

Donald Specker: 273L, 394L, 450C

Leon Stacey: 272R, 349L, 349C, 401R

Arvil R. Stark: 67R, 72R, 74C

Deni Weider Stein: 146C, 266L

Bernadine C. Strik: 352L, 352C, 353L, 353C

Steve Struse: 18, 20B

Studio Central: 20T, 21

Lauren Bonar Swezey: 22C, 22R, 31R, 94L, 96L, 98R, 117C, 209R, 213R, 221L, 221R, 234C, 234R, 241R, 374L

George Taloumis: 410R, 411L, 413C

Sherman V. Thomson: 117R, 207Ri, 244R, 252R, 285R, 311C, 426C

UCB, Coop. Ext.: 206C, 235R, 245R, 449C

UCD, Coop. Ext.: 83C, 304L, 449R

UCR, Statewide Air Pollution Research: 425L

University of California: 125R, 236L, 259C, 291C, 297R, 300L, 313R, 382Ci, 525R

University of Illinois, Champaign-Urbana: 45C, 141R, 162Ci

USDA Forest Service: 362C, 515L, 516L, 516C

Van Waters & Rogers: 439R, 512L, 523L

John A. Weidhaas Jr.: 144L, 237R, 257L

Ron West: 418C, 450L, 502TL, 502TR, 502BL, 509R

Robert L. Wick: 213C

John A. Wott: 111R, 183C, 245L

David F. Young, Jr.: 440L, 440C

Thomas Zitter: 350C, 361Ri, 383L, 385L, 441R, 442L, 444C

Index

569

whiptail, 325
Cabbage looper
  (*Trichoplusia ni*)
  on cabbage, 357
  on *Calendula*, **127**
  on lettuce, 375
  on turnip, **401**
Cabbage maggot (*Delia
  radicum*), **358**
Cabbageworm, imported
  (*Pieris rapae*), **437**
  on cabbage, **357**
  on flowering plants, 107
  on turnip, 401
Cactus, Christmas. *See
  Zygocactus*
Cactus, indoor
  bacterial soft rot, **30**
  Christmas cactus, 21, 47
  Easter cactus, *21*
  light tolerance, 19, 21, 30,
    541
  scab, **30**
Cages. *See also* Fencing and
    screening
  to exclude deer, *331*
  to exclude rabbits and mice,
    279, *331*, *342*
  gopher, 145, 161
  for tomato plants, 328
Caladium, light tolerance, 541
Calathea zebrina (Zebra plant)
  insufficient light, *23*
  salt sensitivity, 541
Calceolaria (Slipper flower)
  cotton root rot resistance,
    538
  gray mold, *417*
Calcium deficiency
  blossom-end rot and, 367,
    380, 394
  fertilizers for, 409
  pH and, 104, 407
Calendula
  aster yellows susceptibility,
    546
  cabbage looper, **127**
  planting and blooming
    times, 545
  powdery mildew, 537
  southern blight
    susceptibility, 536
  verticillium wilt resistance,
    540
California lilac. *See Ceanothus*
Caliroa cerasi. See Pearslug
Calla. *See Zantedeschia*
Callistemon (Bottlebrush)

bees attracted to, 534
  saline-soil tolerance, 532
  weak forks and brittle wood,
    547
Callistephus (China aster)
  aster yellows, **128**
  aster yellows susceptibility,
    546
  southern blight
    susceptibility, 536
Calluna (Heather)
  bees attracted to, 534
  crown gall resistance, 548
  pH tolerance, 531
  phytophthora susceptibility,
    536
Callus cells, defined, 14
Calocedrus decurrens (Incense
    cedar)
  armillaria root rot resistance,
    539
  insect and disease resistance,
    535
  phytophthora susceptibility,
    536
  quince rust susceptibility,
    538
Caltha palustris (Marsh
    marigold), for wet soils,
    533
Caltrop. *See* Puncturevine
Calycanthus (Carolina allspice)
  for shady areas, 549
  for wet soils, 533
Cambium, *12*
  about, 11
  defined, 14, 279
Camellia
  camellia yellow mottle leaf
    virus, **215**
  catalpa sphinx caterpillar,
    215
  cottony camellia scale, **214**
  flower blight, **214**
  leaf gall, 171
  mealybugs, 214
  pH tolerance, 531
  phytophthora susceptibility,
    536
  for shady areas, 549
  sooty mold, **179, 215**
Camellia yellow mottle leaf
    virus, 215
Campanula (Bellflower)
  bees attracted to, 534
  leaf spots, fungal, **128**
  planting and blooming
    times, 545

Camphor tree. *See
    Cinnamomum*
Campsis radicans (Trumpet
    creeper), 532
Candytuft. *See Iberis*
Cane and leaf rust of brambles
  (*Kuehneola uredinis*), **353**
Cane blight of brambles
  (*Leptosphaeria
    coniothyrium*), **354,** 557
Cane gall of brambles
  (*Agrobacterium rubi*), 354
Canker and blight of *Buxus*
  (*Volutella* spp.), **213**
Canker and dieback
  of *Arbutus*, 209
  of *Eleagnus*, **225**
  of *Picea* (*Cytospora kunzei*),
    244
  of *Populus*, **255**
  of *Rosa* (Coniothyrium spp.),
    268
  of *Salix*, 269
  of *Vinca* (*Phomopsis livella*
    and *Phoma exigua*), **99**
Cankers, **431**
  bacterial
    of cherry (*Pseudomonas
      syringae*), **302**
    of fruit and nut trees
      (*Pseudomonas syringae*),
      281, 286
    of peach/nectarine
      (*Pseudomonas syringae*),
      311
  defined, 14
  fungal
    of *Cercis* (*Botryosphaeria
      ribis*), **218**
    crown, of *Cornus*
      (*Phytophthora cactorum*),
      220
    of fruit and nut trees, 286
    of *Gleditsia* (*Thyronectria
      austoamericana* and
      Nectria cinnabarina), **231**
    of woody ornamentals, 169,
      185, 188, 190, 198
Cankerworms (*Alsophila
    pometaria* and *Paleacrita
    vernata*), 173, **440**
Canna
  bud rot, **128**
  planting and blooming
    times, 545
  southern blight
    susceptibility, 536

Capeweed. *See Arctotheca
    calendula*
Capsella bursa-pastoris. See
    Shepherd's purse
Capsicum (Ornamental
    pepper), 541
Carbon dioxide, role in
    photosynthesis, 11
Cardinal flower. *See Lobelia
    cardinalis*
Carex spp. (Sedges), for wet
    soils, 533
Caribbean fruit fly (*Anastrepha
    suspensa*), 455
Carissa grandiflora (Natal
    plum), 532
Carnation. *See Dianthus*
Carob. *See Ceratonia siliqua*
Carolina nettle. *See*
    Horsenettle
Carpenter ants (*Camponotus*
    spp.), 503, **515,** 517
Carpenter bees (*Xylocopa*
    spp.), **516**
Carpet beetles (*Attagenus
    megatoma* and *Anthrenus*
    spp.), **510**
Carpet bugle. *See Ajuga*
Carpetgrass, 542
Carpetweed (*Mollugo
    verticillata*), **488**
Carpinus (Hornbeam)
  crown gall resistance, 548
  industrial pollution
    tolerance, 534
  insect and disease resistance,
    535
  for restricted root space,
    533, 548
  verticillium wilt resistance,
    540
Carrot
  diseases
    aster yellows, **361**
    aster yellows susceptibility,
      546
    sclerotium root
      rot/southern blight,
      421, 536
    verticillium wilt resistance,
      540
  green root tops, **360**
  harvesting, 328–329
  insect pests
    carrot weevil, **361**
    wireworms, 361
  planting times, 555
  roots misshapen, 360

Index (continued)

diseases, fungal
armillaria resistance, 539
black rot, 281
Botryosphaeria ribes
susceptibility, 538
phytophthora
susceptibility, 536
powdery mildew, 537
scab, 281, 312
fruit quality poor, *283*
harvesting, 281, 313
insect pests
codling moth, 312
Mediterranean fruit fly,
538
mites, 313
San Jose scale, 313
pollination, 277, 553
regional adaptation, 553
Pear rust mite (*Epitrimerus
pyri*), 313
Pear slugs (*Caliroa cerasi*), on
cherry, 300
Pear thrips (*Taeniothrips
inconsequens*), on *Acer*,
205
Peas
animal damage, *333*
diseases
bacterial blight
susceptibility, 538
fusarium susceptibility, 556
powdery mildew, 378, 537
southern blight
susceptibility, 536
verticillium wilt resistance,
540
hot weather, 378
insect pests
pea aphid, 379
pea weevil, 379
manganese deficiency, 325
planting times, 555
root knot nematode
resistance, 555
seed germination, 555
Peat moss
to correct pH, 105
defined, 16
for iron deficiency, 324
as soil amendment, 49
Pecan
diseases
armillaria resistance, 539
Botryosphaeria ribes
susceptibility, 538
scab, 281
insect pests
hickory shuckworm, **314**

pecan nut casebearer, **314**
pecan weevil, **314**
Pecan nut casebearer
(*Acrobasis nuxvorella*), **314**
Pecan shuckworm. *See*
Hickory shuckworm
Pecan weevil (*Curculio
caryae*), **314**
Pegomya hyoscyami. See Beet
leafminer
Pelargonium (Geranium)
caterpillars, 155
diseases
alternaria leaf spot, 154
bacterial blight, 154
black stem rot, 154
gray mold, 153
phytophthora tolerance,
546
pythium stem and root rot,
419
rust, *115, 153, 418*
edema, 153
light tolerance, *109*, 541
planting and blooming
times, 545
propagating, 541
Pellicularia filamentosa. See
Root and stem rot: of
Vinca
Penicillium corm rot of
Gladiolus, 142
Pennisetia marginata. See
Raspberry crown or root
borer
Pennywort, lawn (*Hydrocotyl
sibthorpioides*), **479**
Penstemon, verticillium wilt
resistance, 540
Peony. *See Paeonia*
Peperomia
mealybugs, 43
root and stem rot, 43
Pepper
blossom drop, 379
blossom-end rot, 380
diseases
fusarium susceptibility, 556
southern blight
susceptibility, 536
tobacco mosaic virus
tolerance, 559
verticillium wilt
susceptibility, 556
insect pests
aphids, *116*
corn earworm, 380
European corn borer, 381

Mediterranean fruit fly,
538
tobacco hornworm, 381
tomato hornworm,
381, *432*
planting times, 555
root knot nematode
resistance, 555
seed germination, 555
sunscald, 380
Pepper (ornamental), planting
and blooming times, 545
Perennial canker. *See*
Cytospora canker
Perennial plants. *See also*
Flowering plants; *specific
perennial plants*
advantages/disadvantages,
102
defined, 16, 102
dividing, 102
dormancy, 110
information resources, 527
as lawn weeds, 58–59
phytophthora tolerant, 546
planting and blooming
times, 545
planting and growing, 102
treated as annuals, 102, 164
as vegetable garden weeds,
321
wet-soil tolerant, 533
Periplaneta spp. *See*
Cockroaches
Periwinkle. *See Vinca*
Permanent wilting point,
defined, 16
Peroxyacetl nitrate. *See* PAN
Persimmon
fruit drop, 315
harvesting, 281
Mediterranean fruit fly, 538
sunburn, 315
Pest barriers, **414–415**
Pesticide burn
fungicides, 114, 337
herbicides, 114, 337,
395, 430
insecticides, 114, 337
Pesticide resistance, defined,
16
Pesticides. *See also*
Bactericides; Fungicides;
Herbicides; Insecticides;
Miticides; Rodenticides;
Snails and slugs, control
methods
applying, 7, 505
danger to animals, 323

defined, 16
disposal of, 505
formulations, defined, 15
for fruit and nut trees, *279*
generic and trade names, 7,
528–529
information resources, 527
safe use of, 322–323,
330–331, 503, 505
spreader-stickers, defined, 17
surfactants, defined, 17
systemic, defined, 17
wetting agents, defined, 17
Pet and body pests
bedbugs, **512**
chiggers, **511**
fleas, **512**
ticks, **513**
Petunia
diseases
aster yellows susceptibility,
546
cotton root rot resistance,
538
damping-off, *120*
gray mold, 155
phytophthora tolerance,
546
powdery mildew, 537
insect pests
caterpillars, 155
cutworms, *121*, 156
pH. *See also* Soil pH
defined, 16, 406
Phalaris arundinacea 'Picta'
(Ribbon grass)
drought resistance, 544
for wet soils, 533
Phellodendron (Cork tree),
insect and disease
resistance, 535
Pheromone traps, 271, 293,
372, 381, **414**
Philadelphus (Mock orange)
alkaline-soil tolerance, 547
powdery mildew, 537
salt burn, *193*
for sandy soils, 532
wilting problems, *185*
Philaenus spumarius. See
Meadow spittlebug
Philodendron
bacterial leaf spot, 44
heartleaf, *18*
light tolerance, 541
propagating, 541
root rot, 44
salt sensitivity, 44, 541
split-leaf (*Monstera*), 41, 541

sapsucker damage, 547
Psocids. *See* Booklice
Psychodidae. See Drain flies
Psylla buxi. See Boxwood
     psyllid
Psyllids, **449**
  apple sucker, *449*
  boxwood, on Buxus, 212
  hackberry leaf gall, 171, 217
  honeydew and, 212, 449
Pteridium aquilinum (Bracken),
     for sandy soils, 532
Puccinia spp. *See* Rust
Pueraria lobata. See Kudzu vine
Puffballs. *See* Mushrooms
Pulex irritans. See Fleas
Pulvinaria floccifera. See
     Cottony camellia scale
Pumpkins. *See* Cucurbits
Puncturevine (*Tribulus
     terrestris*), **473**
Puncturevine weevils, 473
Punica (Pomegranate), cotton
     root rot resistance, 538
Pupas
  butterfly and moth
     development, 437
  defined, 16
Purslane, Florida. *See* Florida
     pusley
Purslane (*Portulaca oleracea*),
     476
  in lawns, **82**
  in vegetable gardens, 321
Pus caterpillar (*Megalopyge
     opercularis*), 519
Pustules, defined, 16
Pyracantha (Firethorn)
  bees attracted to, 534
  diseases
     Botryosphaeria ribes
        susceptibility, 538
     crown gall resistance, 548
     fire blight, 255, 551
     powdery mildew, 537
     scab, 551
     verticillium wilt resistance,
        540
  insect pests
     hawthorn lace bug, 256
     Mediterranean fruit fly,
        538
  saline-soil tolerance, 532
  for sandy soils, 532
  for sunny areas, 544
Pyrenochaeta terrestris. See Pink
     rot of onions

Pyrrhalta luteola. See Elm leaf
     beetle
Pythium spp. *See also* Damping
     off, of seedlings
  black stem rot of
     Pelargonium, 154
  blight of lawns, 68
  root and bulb rot of *Lilium*,
     148
  root and stem rot
     of geranium, *419*
     of houseplants, 29, 34,
        44, 47
  root rot of beans, 348
  wilt and root rot of
     Rhododendron, 262

Q

Quackgrass (*Elytrigia* or
     Agropyron repens), 79, **466**
Quadraspidiotus perniciosus. See
     San Jose scale
Quarantines
  for fruit flies, 455
  for new houseplants, 19, 414
Queen Anne's lace, as weevil
     host, 361
Quercus (Oak)
  conks, *431*
  diseases
     armillaria root rot, 259
     cotton root rot resistance,
        538
     oak anthracnose, 256
     oak leaf blister, 256
     oak wilt, 258
     phytophthora
        susceptibility, 536
     powdery mildew, 537
     verticillium wilt resistance,
        540
  drought-tolerant species, 550
  insect pests
     borers, 257
     galls, 171, *430*
     gypsy moth susceptibility,
        551
     leaf-feeding caterpillars,
        257
     pit scales, 258
     twig pruners and girdlers,
        257
  landfill damage
     susceptibility, 547
  lawn-mower blight, *198*
  lightning injury
     susceptibility, 547
  Q. alba (White oak), for
     sandy soils, 532

Q. bicolor (Swamp white
     oak), for wet soils, 533
Q. ilex (Holly-leaved oak),
     armillaria root rot
     resistance, 539
Q. lobata (Valley oak),
     armillaria root rot
     resistance, 539
Q. palustris (Pin oak)
     pH tolerance, 531
     for sandy soils, 532
     for wet soils, 533
Q. prinus (Chestnut oak),
     weak forks and brittle
     wood, 547
Q. robur (English oak)
     industrial pollution
        tolerance, 534
     smog tolerance, 534
Q. rubra (Red oak),
     industrial pollution
     tolerance, 534
Q. stellata (Post oak), for
     sandy soils, 532
  species. that need added
     water, 550
Quick decline. *See* Tristeza
     virus
Quince, flowering. *See*
     Chaenomeles speciosa
Quince rust
     (*Gymnosporangium clavipes*
     or *G. libocedri*), plants
     susceptible to, 538

R

Rabbits, **497**
  as bulb pest, 107
  fencing to exclude, *279,
     330, 331, 342*, 497
  as fruit tree pest, *279, 284*
  as lawn pest, 62–63
  as seedling pest, 121, 330
  as vegetable pest, 330, *331,
     333, 342*
  as woody ornamental pest,
     189
Rabies, skunks and, 497
Raccoons, **498**
  fencing to exclude, 342, 498
  as fruit and nut tree pest,
     284
  as seedling pest, 121
  as vegetable pest, 331, 342
Radish
  diseases
     aster yellows susceptibility,
        546
     damping-off, *334*

fusarium susceptibility, 556
  powdery mildew, 537
  verticillium wilt
     susceptibility, 556
  insect pests
     flea beetles, 385
     root maggots, 385
  planting times, 555
  root development poor, 386
  salt damage, *337*
  seed germination, 555
  seed stalk formation, 387
Ragweed (*Ambrosia* spp.),
     481, 546
Railroad worms. *See* Apple
     maggot
Rainwater, for houseplants, 20
Raised beds
  for shallow soils, 404, 405
  in vegetable gardens,
     322, 327
Ranunculus
  bird damage, 156
  mosaic virus, 157
  planting and blooming
     times, 545
  powdery mildew, 537
  verticillium wilt resistance,
     540
  for wet soils, 533
Raspberries. *See* Brambles
Raspberry cane borer (*Oberea
     maculata*), 354
Raspberry crown or root borer
     (*Pennisetia marginata*), 353
Rats (*Rattus* spp.), 331, **495**
Red ball traps, 294
Red berry mite (*Acalitus
     essigi*), 352
Red bugs. *See* Chiggers
Red chokeberry. *See* Aronia
     arbutifolia
Red stele of strawberry
     (*Phytophthora fragariae*),
     391, 560
Red thread of lawn grasses,
     54, 543
Redbud. *See* Cercis
Redhumped caterpillar
     (*Schizura concinna*), **439**
Red-necked cane borer
     (*Agrilus ruficollis*), 354
Redwood, coast. *See* Sequoia
     sempervirens
Redwood, dawn. *See*
     Metasequoia
Repellents
  bird, 500
  biting fly, 520

609

S